Look for this iPod icon throughout the text.

Icons connect textbook content to your iPod or other MP3 device.

Images courtesy of Apple.

What if I Don't Have an iPod?

Content can be downloaded and viewed on any computer, with or without an iPod.
Visit this text's Web site for directions or use the DVD available for purchase with this text.

iPod content includes:

- Lecture presentations
  - *Audio-based*
  - *Video-based*
  - *Slideshow only*
- Demonstration problems+
- Interactive self quizzes
- Videos on various course topics

+Available with some textbooks

iPod® Content Installer DVD for use with

Fundamentals of Financial Accounting, 2/e

PHILLIPS | LIBBY | LIBBY

MEDIA INTEGRATED

This DVD-rom will autostart on most machines. OR, from the start menu, select run, and type: D:\ Autorun.exe where D represents the letter of your DVD-rom drive.

DVD ROM

MADE WITH macromedia®

INCLUDES Adobe Acrobat

ISBN 978-0-07-721776-1
MHID 0-07-721776-4

McGraw-Hill Irwin

FUNDAMENTALS OF **Financial Accounting**

Phillips · Libby · Libby

Want to see iPod in action?

Visit **www.mhhe.com/ipod** to view a demonstration of our iPod® content.

McGraw-Hill's
HOMEWORK MANAGER PLUS™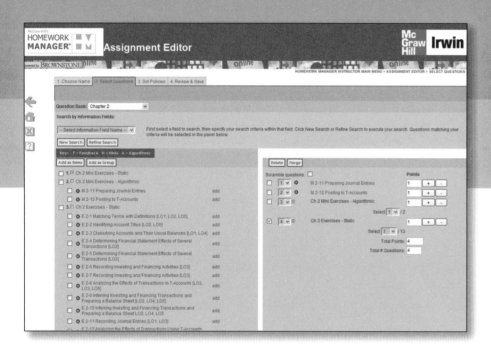

THE COMPLETE SOLUTION

McGraw-Hill's
Homework Manager®

 This online homework management solution contains the textbook's end-of-chapter material. Now you have the option to build assignments from static and algorithmic versions of the text problems and exercises or to build self-graded quizzes from the additional questions provided in the online test bank.

Features:

- Assigns book-specific problems/exercises to students

- Provides integrated test bank questions for quizzes and tests

- Automatically grades assignments and quizzes, storing results in one grade book

- Dispenses immediate feedback to students regarding their work

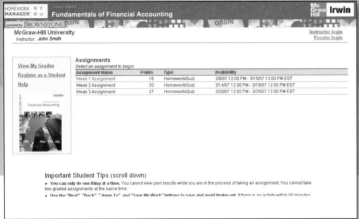

Interactive Online Version
of the Textbook

In addition to the textbook, students can rely on this online version of the text for a convenient way to study. The interactive content is fully integrated with McGraw-Hill's Homework Manager® to give students quick access to relevant content as they work through problems, exercises, and practice quizzes.

Features:

- Online version of the text integrated with McGraw-Hill's Homework Manager

- Students referred to appropriate sections of the online book as they complete an assignment or take a practice quiz

- Direct link to related material that corresponds with the learning objective within the text

McGraw-Hill's Homework Manager Plus™ combines the power of McGraw-Hill's Homework Manager® with the latest interactive learning technology to create a comprehensive, fully integrated online study package. Students working on assignments in McGraw-Hill's Homework Manager can click a simple hotlink and instantly review the appropriate material in the Interactive Online Textbook.

By including McGraw-Hill's Homework Manager Plus with your textbook adoption, you're giving your students a vital edge as they progress through the course and ensuring that the help they need is never more than a click away. Contact your McGraw-Hill representative or visit the book's Web site to learn how to add McGraw-Hill's Homework Manager Plus to your adoption.

Fundamentals of
FINANCIAL ACCOUNTING

Second Edition

FRED PHILLIPS
University of Saskatchewan

ROBERT LIBBY
Cornell University

PATRICIA A. LIBBY
Ithaca College

McGraw-Hill
Irwin

Boston   Burr Ridge, IL   Dubuque, IA   Madison, WI   New York
San Francisco   St. Louis   Bangkok   Bogotá   Caracas   Kuala Lumpur
Lisbon   London   Madrid   Mexico City   Milan   Montreal   New Delhi
Santiago   Seoul   Singapore   Sydney   Taipei   Toronto

 **McGraw-Hill Irwin**

FUNDAMENTALS OF FINANCIAL ACCOUNTING

Published by McGraw-Hill/Irwin, a business unit of The McGraw-Hill Companies, Inc., 1221 Avenue of the Americas, New York, NY, 10020. Copyright © 2008 and 2006 by The McGraw-Hill Companies, Inc. All rights reserved. No part of this publication may be reproduced or distributed in any form or by any means, or stored in a database or retrieval system, without the prior written consent of The McGraw-Hill Companies, Inc., including, but not limited to, in any network or other electronic storage or transmission, or broadcast for distance learning.

Some ancillaries, including electronic and print components, may not be available to customers outside the United States.

This book is printed on acid-free paper.

1 2 3 4 5 6 7 8 9 0 DOW/DOW 0 9 8 7

ISBN   978-0-07-313648-6
MHID   0-07-313648-4

Editorial director: *Stewart Mattson*
Senior sponsoring editor: *Alice Harra*
Senior developmental editor: *Kimberly D. Hooker*
Marketing manager: *Scott Bishop*
Media producer: *Greg Bates*
Lead project manager: *Mary Conzachi*
Senior production supervisor: *Debra R. Sylvester*
Senior designer: *Artemio Ortiz Jr.*
Photo research coordinator: *Lori Kramer*
Photo researcher: *Editorial Image, LLC*
Media project managers: *Matthew Perry and Susan Lombardi*
Cover design: *Asylum Studios*
Typeface: *10.5/12 Goudy*
Compositor: *Aptara, Inc.*
Printer: *R. R. Donnelley*

Library of Congress Cataloging-in-Publication Data

Phillips, Fred.
    Fundamentals of financial accounting / Fred Phillips, Robert Libby,
Patricia A. Libby.—2nd ed.
        p. cm.
    Includes index.
    ISBN-13: 978-0-07-313648-6 (alk. paper)
    ISBN-10: 0-07-313648-4 (alk. paper)
    1. Accounting. I. Libby, Robert. II. Libby, Patricia A. III. Title.
HF5636.P545 2008
657—dc22
                                        2007026479

www.mhhe.com

I dedicate this book to the best teachers I've ever had: my Mom and Dad, Barb, Harrison, and Daniel

FRED PHILLIPS

Jenni, John, and Emma Rose Drago, Herman and Doris Hargenrater, Laura Libby, Oscar and Selma Libby

PATRICIA AND ROBERT LIBBY

A Letter to Instructors

Dear Colleagues,

As we finish the second edition of *Fundamentals of Financial Accounting*, we want to thank each of you who adopted the first edition. As fellow financial accounting instructors, we appreciate the importance of selecting the right book for your students; a book that will give them an engaging, relevant, and understandable introduction to the world of accounting. We set out to write a book that students could understand—a book that would carefully walk them through the fundamentals of financial accounting—and we are pleased that so many of you found that it accomplished this goal and met your needs.

The first edition was highly praised for its lively writing style geared directly to the student, as well as study tools throughout each chapter to carefully guide students through all of the important details of financial accounting. You will find that these strengths remain in the second edition and are enhanced and refined by the insightful suggestions and observations of so many thoughtful colleagues, like you.

In the development of the second edition, we received feedback from over 200 financial accounting instructors. **Over 132 financial accounting colleagues provided us guidance** through text reviews and surveys, and **an additional 79 participated in focus groups and events around the country.** We thank all of you who participated in this process for generously sharing your time, as well as your excellent and astute suggestions.

It is our continuing commitment to provide a financial accounting textbook that is both the best possible learning tool for introductory students and the best teaching tool for instructors. We promise to continue to be diligent in our writing, development, and preparation of the textbook and ancillary materials, so that you can count on a total teaching package that is as reliable and accurate, as it is engaging and readable. We also promise to continue to listen to you, our colleagues, every step along the way.

Sincerely,

Fred Phillips   Bob Libby   Pat Libby

About the Authors

Fred Phillips

Fred Phillips is a professor and the George C. Baxter Chartered Accountants of Saskatchewan Scholar at the University of Saskatchewan, where he teaches introductory financial accounting. He also has taught introductory accounting at the University of Texas at Austin and the University of Manitoba. Fred has an undergraduate accounting degree, a professional accounting designation, and a PhD from the University of Texas at Austin. He previously worked as an audit manager at KPMG.

Fred's main interest is accounting education. He has won 11 teaching awards, including three national case-writing competitions. Recently, Fred won the 2007 Alpha Kappa Psi Outstanding Professor award at The University of Texas at Austin, and in 2006, he was awarded the title Master Teacher at the University of Saskatchewan. He has published instructional cases and numerous articles in journals such as *Issues in Accounting Education, Journal of Accounting Research,* and *Organizational Behavior and Human Decision Processes.* He received the American Accounting Association's Outstanding Research in Accounting Education Award in 2006 and 2007 for one of his articles. Fred is a past associate editor of *Issues in Accounting Education,* and a current member of the Teaching & Curriculum and Two-Year College sections of the American Accounting Association. In his spare time, he likes to work out, play video games, and drink iced cappuccinos.

Robert Libby

Robert Libby is the David A. Thomas Professor of Accounting at Cornell University, where he teaches the introductory financial accounting course. He previously taught at the University of Illinois, Pennsylvania State University, the University of Texas at Austin, the University of Chicago, and the University of Michigan. He received his BS from Pennsylvania State University and his MAS and PhD from the University of Illinois; he also is a CPA.

Bob is a widely published author specializing in behavioral accounting. He was selected as the AAA Outstanding Educator in 2000 and received the AAA Outstanding Service Award in 2006.* His prior text, *Accounting and Human Information Processing* (Prentice Hall, 1981), was awarded the AICPA/AAA Notable Contributions to the Accounting Literature Award. He received this award again in 1996 for a paper. He has published numerous articles in *The Accounting Review, Journal of Accounting Research, Accounting, Organizations, and Society;* and other accounting journals. He has held a variety of offices in the American Accounting Association and is a member of the American Institute of CPAs and the editorial boards of *The Accounting Review, Accounting, Organizations, and Society, Journal of Accounting Literature;* and *Journal of Behavioral Decision Making.*

> *** This award, which has been awarded only five times in the Association's 90-year history, was given "in recognition of visionary stewardship of the publications collection of the AAA." Professor Libby is the only person to have received all three of the association's highest awards for research, teaching and service. He was the AAA Outstanding Accounting Educator in 2000 and received the AAA Notable Contributions to the Literature Award in 1985 and 1996.**

Patricia A. Libby

Patricia Libby is associate professor of accounting and coordinator of the financial accounting course at Ithaca College, as well as faculty advisor to Beta Alpha Psi, Ithaca College Accounting Association, and Ithaca College National Association of Black Accountants. She previously taught graduate and undergraduate financial accounting at Eastern Michigan University and the University of Texas at Austin. Before entering academe, she was an auditor with Price Waterhouse (now PricewaterhouseCoopers) and a financial administrator at the University of Chicago. She received her BS from Pennsylvania State University, her MBA from DePaul University, and her PhD from the University of Michigan; she also is a CPA.

Pat conducts research on using cases in the introductory course and other parts of the accounting curriculum. She has published articles in *The Accounting Review, Issues in Accounting Education,* and *The Michigan CPA.* She has also conducted seminars nationwide on active learning strategies, including cooperative learning methods.

Financial Accounting

Instructors tell us that the number one challenge in teaching financial accounting is helping students to understand the vital role financial accounting plays in business today. They want to know how financial accounting is used by decision makers and why it is important for them to understand accounting concepts. Students become motivated to learn financial accounting concepts that are explained in the context of what real-world companies are doing. That's where *Fundamentals of Financial Accounting* comes in. This text motivates and engages your students by combining the real-world focus company approach, pioneered by Robert and Patricia Libby in their market-leading *Financial Accounting* text, with an engaging writing style and student-friendly pedagogy.

The key to the success of *Fundamentals of Financial Accounting* is its **clear, concise, and conversational language.** Students will understand the important business activities and how to prepare and interpret financial information in an accurate and relevant way because it is explained to them in a unique and engaging manner.

from the Ground Up

Fundamentals of Financial Accounting clearly presents the fundamentals of financial accounting like no other text can. Simply put, Phillips/Libby/Libby is the most student-friendly financial book on the market. Flip to any page and you will see examples of Phillips' innovative student-centered approach using three of the most compelling tools:

- ENGAGING WRITING. While maintaining its rigor, *Fundamentals of Financial Accounting* uses a mix of conversational wording, humor, and everyday examples to introduce students to the world of financial accounting. This is done without sacrificing any of the content important to grasping financial accounting.

- STUDENT-RELEVANT FOCUS COMPANIES. This successful approach was pioneered by coauthors Robert Libby and Patricia Libby. Each chapter of *Fundamentals of Financial Accounting* makes financial accounting come alive by using **a real company whose products and services are popular with students** to illustrate fundamental accounting concepts. These companies include Skechers (shoes), Activision (video games), and Oakley (sunglasses). (See page viii for more on the focus companies.)

- LEARNING THROUGH REINFORCEMENT. *Fundamentals of Financial Accounting* introduces students to several tools that help reinforce the concepts in the text. Coach Tips and You Should Know are innovative and student-friendly pedagogical features appearing in the margins to reinforce concepts in the text as well as provide helpful insight.

The authors avoid the use of complicated words when explaining complex topics. I think this is the real strength in the readability of the text ~ Martha Lou Fowler, Missouri Western State University

The authors of FFA do not presume all students have a lot of experience in business... this is really good ~ Linda Bressler, University of Houston-Downtown

The authors use a very friendly tone to help students to understand important concepts ~ Bea Bih-Horng Chiang, The College of New Jersey

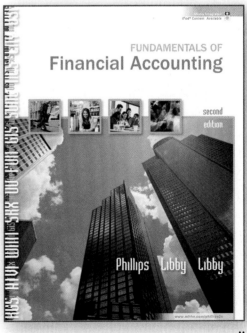

How does *Fundamentals of Financial Accounting* give students a window on the real world of business?

The key idea behind *FFA*'s focus company approach is knowing that the best way for students to learn to prepare and use financial statements is to study accounting in real business contexts. Each chapter's material is integrated around a real company, its decisions, and its financial statements.

We have carefully chosen focus companies that students will recognize. We further heighten student engagement by injecting our discussions with issues and questions that actually matter in the real world.

- How can a slight improvement in gross profit percentage translate into over half a billion dollars of profit for Wal-Mart?

- What decisions does Cedar Fair make when investing in and reporting its roller coasters and other long-lived assets?

- How does Nautilus Group monitor and manage its fluctuating cash flows during the pre- and post-holiday seasons?

Companies and issues like these are discussed throughout this book.

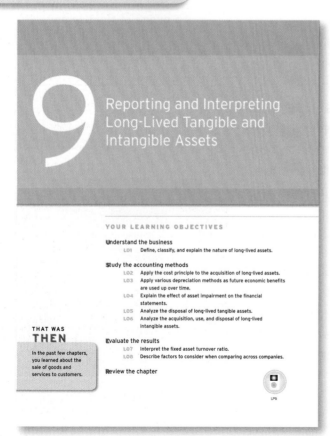

9 Reporting and Interpreting Long-Lived Tangible and Intangible Assets

YOUR LEARNING OBJECTIVES

Understand the business
- LO1   Define, classify, and explain the nature of long-lived assets.

Study the accounting methods
- LO2   Apply the cost principle to the acquisition of long-lived assets.
- LO3   Apply various depreciation methods as future economic benefits are used up over time.
- LO4   Explain the effect of asset impairment on the financial statements.
- LO5   Analyze the disposal of long-lived tangible assets.
- LO6   Analyze the acquisition, use, and disposal of long-lived intangible assets.

Evaluate the results
- LO7   Interpret the fixed asset turnover ratio.
- LO8   Describe factors to consider when comparing across companies.

Review the chapter

THAT WAS THEN
In the past few chapters, you learned about the sale of goods and services to customers.

CedarFair.L.P.

If you're an average American, you gobble about three pounds of peanut butter per year, which equals 1,500 peanut butter sandwiches eaten before your high school graduation.[1] That makes you an expert at knowing how much peanut butter to spread on sandwiches. It also prepares you for learning how to report depreciation on long-lived assets. Really. Reporting depreciation is a lot like spreading peanut butter on sandwiches. The amount of peanut butter to spread on each sandwich is just like the amount of depreciation to spread over each accounting period. It depends on three factors: (1) the amount that you begin with in the jar (or the cost you begin with in the account), (2) the amount you need to leave in the jar (or account), and (3) the number of sandwiches (or accounting periods) that you'll be spreading it over. Just like peanut butter on a sandwich, there'll be a little depreciation if it's spread over many years or lots if it's spread over fewer years.

For the rest of this chapter, we're going to focus on the amusement park business at Cedar Fair. We're not leaving peanuts completely behind, because just as Mickey is Disney's mascot and Bugs Bunny gives character to Six Flags, Snoopy and the whole Charlie Brown gang from the PEANUTS® comic strip are featured at Cedar Fair. With seven amusement parks and six waterparks throughout the United States, Cedar Fair is one of the biggest and best amusement park businesses in the world.[2] As of December 31, 2005, its rides, hotels, and other long-lived assets accounted for over 96 percent of its total assets, so it's the perfect setting for you to learn how these assets are reported and the analyses you can conduct to determine how well they're managed.

THIS IS NOW
This chapter focuses on the assets that enable companies to produce and sell goods and services.

---
[1] Retrieved September 8, 2006, from www.peanutbutter.com/funfacts.asp.
[2] "Cedar Fair, L.P.'s Flagship Park, Cedar Point, again Voted Best Amusement Park in the World," company press release, August 28, 2006.

How does *Fundamentals of Financial Accounting* provide a foundation for comprehension?

Ethical Insights

Fundamentals of Financial Accounting is loaded with innovative pedagogical features. From quick review tools to thought provoking ethical dilemmas, *FFA*'s pedagogy continually reinforces and expands on what the students are learning.

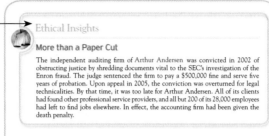

> ### Ethical Insights
>
> #### More than a Paper Cut
>
> The independent auditing firm of Arthur Andersen was convicted in 2002 of obstructing justice by shredding documents vital to the SEC's investigation of the Enron fraud. The judge sentenced the firm to pay a $500,000 fine and serve five years of probation. Upon appeal in 2005, the conviction was overturned for legal technicalities. By that time, it was too late for Arthur Andersen. All of its clients had found other professional service providers, and all but 200 of its 28,000 employees had left to find jobs elsewhere. In effect, the accounting firm had been given the death penalty.
>
> Laurie's advice to Mauricio and to all managers is to strive to create an ethical environment and establish a strong system of checks and controls inside the company. Do not put up with blatant acts of fraud, such as employees making up false expenses for reimbursement, punching in a time card belonging to a fellow employee who will be late for work, or copying someone's ideas and claiming them as his or her own.

Clear and careful explanation of the most detailed points. Coach's tips are particularly effective in this regard
~ R. Eugene Bryson, University of Alabama Huntsville

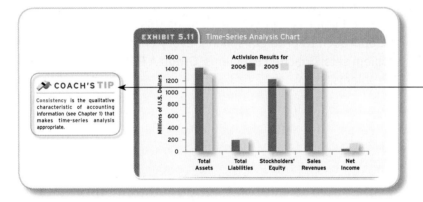

Coach's Tips

Every student needs encouragement and Coach's Tips are just one way *FFA* fulfills that need. *FFA* features tips, advice, and suggestions about how to learn the fundamentals of accounting.

You Should Know

Quick recaps reinforce the important terminology and concepts discussed in the text.

> **YOU SHOULD KNOW**
> A **classified balance sheet** is one that shows a subtotal for current assets and current liabilities. **Current assets** will be used up or converted into cash within 12 months of the balance sheet date. **Current liabilities** are debts and obligations that will be paid, settled, or fulfilled within 12 months of the balance sheet date. **Noncurrent** (or long-term) assets and liabilities are those that do not meet the definition of current.

To prepare a balance sheet for your Supercuts salon after recording transactions (a)–(g), just take the ending balances from each T-account in Exhibit 2.9 and group them as assets, liabilities, and stockholders' equity in balance sheet format. If you do this, you should end up with a balance sheet like the one presented way back in Exhibit 2.1. We realize that the odds of you flipping all the way back to page 45 right now are slim, so we've taken this opportunity to show you a slightly different balance sheet format in Exhibit 2.10 called the **classified balance sheet**. A classified balance sheet contains subcategories for assets and liabilities labeled *current*. **Current assets** are assets your business will use up or turn into cash within 12 months of the balance sheet date. For example, your salon will spend the cash and use the supplies during the next 12 months, so these assets are classified as current. Current assets are listed in order of how fast they will be used up or turned into cash. **Current liabilities** are debts and other obligations that will be paid or fulfilled within 12 months of the balance sheet date. In our example, accounts payable is the only current liability. The other liability—note payable—is expected to be paid in two years, so it is considered **noncurrent**.

How's It Going? Self-Study Quiz

This active learning feature helps students master complex subjects by means of innovative review boxes throughout each chapter. **How's It Going?** boxes pose review questions at key points throughout the chapter for students to test their knowledge of the material. The answer is printed on the same page but positioned sideways so the student doesn't accidentally read it before answering the question.

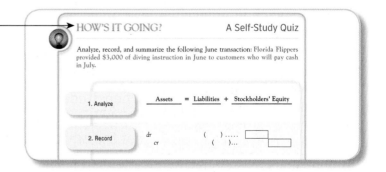

How can you get your students to practice?

The end-of-chapter material is traditionally where students go from reading to doing: answering review questions, solving problems, and wrestling with issues that help them assimilate the material and apply it in a realistic context. *FFA* doesn't see reading as a passive process; the end-of-chapter material offers a wealth of opportunities for students to connect to the chapter material and for you to enliven your class with a variety of assignments and discussion questions.

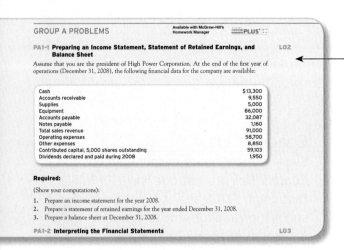

Problems with (and without) the Coach's Help

We know how important decision-making skills are for students entering business and *FFA* recognizes this through an innovative approach to problem solving. Every chapter includes three problem sets: Coached Problems, Group A Problems, and Group B Problems.

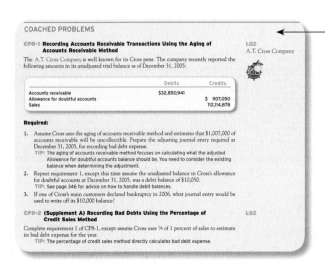

Coached Problems

The Coached Problems go beyond the traditional check figures to advise students on the process of solving a problem rather than just its outcome. Students are given TIPs at each step of the problem-solving process.

When students can solve the Coached Problems, they'll be ready to tackle the Group A or Group B problems, which echo the content without the advice offered by the Coached Problems.

Ethics Cases

Whether your students graduate into the business world as accountants or other majors, a strong ethical grounding is vital. **Every chapter of *FFA* includes two ethics cases.** These ethics cases are unique because they focus on real-life issues at companies that students know or products they are familiar with, such as Aurora Foods, maker of Duncan Hines® and Mrs. Butterworth® products (Chapter 5), Activision (Chapter 11), Famous Footwear (Chapter 6), and Blockbuster (Chapter 4).

LO1, LO2, LO6
Aurora Foods Inc.

S5-4 Ethical Decision Making: A Real-Life Example

On February 18, 2000, the board of directors of Aurora Foods Inc.—the maker of Duncan Hines® and Mrs. Butterworth's® products—issued a press release announcing that a special committee had been formed to conduct an investigation into the company's accounting practices. During the financial statement audit for the year ended December 31, 1999, Aurora's auditors had discovered documents that raised questions about how the company accounted for marketing costs incurred to entice grocery stores to promote Aurora's products. The company's stock price fell by 50 percent in the week following this announcement.

After nearly a year of investigation, Aurora filed revised quarterly reports with the SEC, showing that the company had not accrued adequately for liabilities and expenses that had been incurred during the third and fourth quarter of 1998 and during the first three quarters of 1999. Key financial figures for these quarters as initially reported and as later restated are shown below.

(in millions of U.S. dollars)	1998 Q3 (September 30)		1998 Q4 (December 31)		1999 Q1 (March 31)		1999 Q2 (June 30)		1999 Q3 (September 30)	
	Initial Report	Restated Report	Initial Report	Restated Report	Initial Report	Restated Report	Initial Report	Restated Report	Initial Report	Restated Report
Assets	$1,457	$1,455	$1,434	$1,448	$1,474	$1,463	$1,558	$1,521	$1,614	$1,553
Liabilities	869	879	830	868	862	882	937	944	983	972
Revenues	220	219	280	277	261	254	222	214	238	231
Net income (loss)	1	(12)	16	5	8	0	8	(4)	11	4

Annual Report Cases

FFA comes complete with an annual report for Landry's Restaurants bundled free with every new copy. End-of-chapter cases make extensive use of these data, showing students how to draw information from an annual report and providing them with a valuable perspective on how financial accounting information is used in decision making.

SKILLS DEVELOPMENT CASES

LO1 **S3-1 Finding Financial Information**

Refer to the financial statements of Landry's Restaurants in Appendix A at the end of this book, or download the annual report from the *Cases* section of the text's Web site at www.mhhe.com/phillips2e.

Required:

1. Have Landry's total revenues increased, or decreased, in the most recent year? By how much? Calculate this change as a percentage of the previous year's total revenues by dividing the amount of the change by the previous year's revenues and multiplying by 100.
2. State the amount of the largest expense on the most recent income statement and describe the transaction represented by the expense. Did this expense increase, or decrease, from the previous year and by what percentage?

LO1 **S3-2 Comparing Financial Information**

Refer to the financial statements of Outback Steakhouse, Inc. in Appendix B at the end of this book, or download them from the *Cases* section of the text's Web site at www.mhhe.com/phillips2e.

Required:

1. Has Outback's total revenues increased, or decreased, in the most recent year? By how much? Calculate this change as a percentage of the previous year's total revenues. Is the trend in Outback's revenues more or less favorable than Landry's?
2. State the amount of the largest expense on Outback's income statement and describe the transaction represented by the expense. Did this expense increase, or decrease, and by what percentage, as compared to the previous year? Is the trend in Outback's largest expense more favorable, or less favorable, than the trend for Landry's largest expense?

LO1, LO5 **S3-3 Internet-Based Team Research: Examining the Income Statement**

As a team, select an industry to analyze. Using your Web browser, each team member should access the annual report or 10-K for one publicly traded company in the industry, with each member selecting a different company. (See S1-3 in Chapter 1 for a description of possible resources for these tasks.)

Team Cases

Every chapter also includes a team case that directs groups to search the Internet for companies to analyze, using the tools covered in that chapter. Students not only learn useful research skills but gain valuable practice solving accounting problems in group settings.

LO5, LO6 **S5-3 Internet-Based Team Research: Examining an Annual Report**

As a team, select an industry to analyze. Using your Web browser, each team member should access the annual report or 10-K for one publicly traded company in the industry, with each member selecting a different company (see S1-3 in Chapter 1 for a description of possible resources for these tasks).

Required:

1. On an individual basis, each team member should write a short report that incorporates the following:
   a. Calculate the debt-to-assets ratio at the end of the current and prior year, and explain any change between the two years.
   b. Calculate the asset turnover ratio at the end of the current and prior year and explain any change between the two years. (To calculate average assets for the prior year, you will need the total assets number for the beginning of the prior year. If this isn't reported in the summarized financial data section in the current annual report, you will need to get it from the prior year's annual report or 10-K.)
   c. Calculate the net profit margin ratio at the end of the current and prior year and explain any change between the two years.
2. Then, as a team, write a short report comparing and contrasting your companies using these attributes. Discuss any patterns across the companies that you observe as a team. Provide potential explanations for any differences discovered.

LO1, LO2, LO6
Aurora Foods Inc. **S5-4 Ethical Decision Making: A Real-Life Example**

On February 18, 2000, the board of directors of Aurora Foods Inc.—the maker of Duncan Hines® and Mrs. Butterworth's® products—issued a press release announcing that a special committee had been formed to conduct an investigation into the company's accounting practices. During the financial statement audit for the year ended December 31, 1999, Aurora's auditors had discovered documents that raised questions about how the company accounted for marketing costs incurred to entice grocery stores to promote Aurora's products. The company's stock price fell by 50 percent in the week following this announcement.

After nearly a year of investigation, Aurora filed revised quarterly reports with the SEC, showing that the company had not accrued adequately for liabilities and expenses that had been incurred during the third and fourth quarter of 1998 and during the first three quarters

Multiple-Choice Questions

Students are likely to see these kinds of questions on tests and exams, so give them some practice with these quick checks of basic concepts.

MULTIPLE CHOICE

1. If total assets increase but total liabilities remain the same, what is the impact on the debt-to-assets ratio?
   a. Increases.
   c. Remains the same.
   b. Decreases.
   d. Cannot be determined without additional information.
2. Costco and Sam's Club are two companies that offer low prices for items packaged in bulk. This strategy increases total sales volume but generates less profit for each dollar of sales. Which of the following ratios is improved by this strategy?
   a. Net profit margin.
   c. Debt-to-assets.
   b. Asset turnover.
   d. All of the above.
3. Which of the following would increase the net profit margin ratio in the current year?
   a. Increase the amount of research and development in the last month of the year.
   b. Decrease the amount of sales in the last month of the year.
   c. Postpone routine maintenance work that was to be done this year.
   d. All of the above.
4. The asset turnover ratio is directly affected by which of the following categories of business decisions?
   a. Operating and investing decisions.
   b. Operating and financing decisions.
   c. Investing and financing decisions.
   d. Operating, investing, and financing decisions.
5. Which of the following reports is filed annually with the SEC?
   a. Form 10-Q
   c. Form 8-K
   b. Form 10-K
   d. Press release
6. Which of the following describes a cross-sectional analysis of your academic performance?
   a. Counting the number of A's on your transcript.
   b. Comparing the number of A's you received this year to the number you received last year.
   c. Comparing the number of A's you received this year to the number your friend received.
   d. Counting the total number of A's given out to your class as a whole.
7. Which of the following describes a time-series analysis of your academic performance?
   a. Counting the number of A's on your transcript.
   b. Comparing the number of A's you received this year to the number you received last year.
   c. Comparing the number of A's you received this year to the number your friend received.

Topic Tackler

PLUS

Check out www.mhhe.com/phillips2e for more multiple choice questions.

Quiz 5

Solutions to Multiple Choice Que

1. b   2. b   3. c   4. a   5. b

Carol Yacht and Peachtree® Designated Exercises and Problems

Students entering the accounting profession can never have too much practice working on Peachtree, so *FFA*'s end-of-chapter material includes specially designated problems to be solved with the educational version of Peachtree Complete (see page xviii). These problems are marked with an icon and make ideal homework assignments.

COACHED PROBLEMS

CP4-1 Preparing an Adjusted Trial Balance, Closing Journal Entry, and Post-Closing Trial Balance

LO3, LO5
Dell Inc.

Dell Inc., which originally was named PC's Limited, is the world's largest computer systems company selling directly to customers. The following is a list of accounts and amounts reported for the fiscal year ended February 3, 2006. The accounts have normal debit or credit balances and the dollars are rounded to the nearest million.

Accounts payable	$ 9,840	Long-term debt	$ 504
Accounts receivable	5,452	Other assets	14,635
Accrued liabilities	6,087	Other liabilities	2,549
Accumulated depreciation	749	Property, plant, and equipment	2,005
Cash	9,807	Research and	
Contributed capital	4,129	development expense	463
Cost of goods sold	45,958	Retained earnings	5,045
Income tax expense	1,002	Sales revenue	55,908
Interest revenue	227	Selling, general, and	
Inventories	576	administrative expenses	5,140

Required:

1. Prepare an adjusted trial balance at February 3, 2006. Is the Retained earnings balance of $5,045 the amount that would be reported on the balance sheet as of February 3, 2006?
   TIP: Dell Inc. did not declare a dividend during 2006 but it did earn net income.
2. Prepare the closing entry required at February 3, 2006.
3. Prepare a post-closing trial balance at February 3, 2006.

CP4-2 Analyzing and Recording Adjusting Journal Entries LO1, LO2

Jordan Company's annual accounting year ends on December 31. It is now December 31, 2008, and all of the 2008 entries have been made except for the following:

a. The company owes interest of $400 on a bank loan taken out on October 1, 2008. The interest will be paid when the loan is repaid on September 30, 2009.

What's New in the Second Edition?

Building on the first edition's strength to motivate student interest in accounting, the second edition features:

- Each chapter clearly establishes learning objectives, highlights numerous real-world examples, and introduces new features such as Ethical Insights, Control Spotlight, and Financial Analysis Tools.

- Cartoons, crossword puzzles, and caricature-like illustrations have been replaced with new material that better explains challenging topics and provides abundant opportunity for practice.

- Over 150 new items have been introduced in the end-of-chapter practice material and the remaining practice material has been checked and refined to ensure compatibility with the second edition.

- This edition also retains the engaging explanations with the professional, yet conversational, writing style that was so popular among students using the first edition.

1 Business Decisions and Financial Accounting

- New entrepreneurial focus company—provides a realistic context that all students can relate to for introducing organizational forms, types of accounting, financial statement users, and ethics.

- New material introducing the Sarbanes-Oxley Act.

- New Ethical Insights relating to Arthur Andersen and Enron.

- Simplified statement of cash flow coverage.

- Simplified illustrations of financial statement articulation.

- No cartoons or superfluous illustrations.

- End of chapter: a new demonstration case, 12 new mini-exercises, exercises and problems, including three new problems on interpreting F/S, and revisions to 30 other exercises, problems, and cases.

2 Reporting Investing and Financing Results on the Balance Sheet

- New three-step accounting cycle framework.

- New illustrations and streamlined discussions for transaction analysis.

- Simplified balance sheet presentation with the classified balance sheet moved to the end of the chapter and comparative balance sheets moved to Chapter 5.

- Revised Self-Study Quizzes.

- New Ethical Insights related to conservatism in accounting.

- End of chapter: five new mini-exercises, exercises, and problems, and revisions to 34 other mini-exercises, exercises, problems, and cases.

3 Reporting Operating Results on the Income Statement

- New three-step accounting cycle framework continued from Chapter 2 and replacing former DECIDES framework from previous edition of text.

- New Ethical Insights related to Computer Associates to the time period assumption; new real-world example of revenue recognition policies.

- Revised presentation linking revenues and expenses to changes in stockholders' equity.

- Revised matching principle discussion.

- Simplified income statement presentation illustrating only single-step income statements. (The multistep income statement is explained in Chapters 5 and 6.)

- End of chapter: 29 new questions, mini-exercises, exercises, and problems and revisions to 37 other mini-exercises, exercises, problems, and cases.

4 Adjustments, Financial Statements, and the Quality of Financial Reporting

- New three-step accounting cycle framework continued from Chapter 3.
- New Self-Study Quiz.
- New discussion of accrued payroll.
- Revised Self-Study Quizzes.
- End of chapter: 15 new questions, mini-exercises, exercises, and problems and revisions to 47 other mini-exercises, exercises, problems, and cases.

5 Corporate Financial Reporting and Analysis

- Reorganized chapter topics following the sequence in which Activision prepares and releases financial reports.
- New discussion of accounting fraud and Sarbanes-Oxley Act.
- New Ethical Insights related to Bausch & Lomb.
- Introduction of comparative balance sheets and multi-step income statements (introduced in Chapters 1 and 3 in prior edition).
- New discussion of statement of stockholders' equity.
- Two new Self-Study Quizzes.
- New contrast company in financial analyses.
- End of chapter: 16 new questions, mini-exercises, exercises, and problems and revisions to 25 other mini-exercises, exercises, problems, and cases; also moved problems that illustrate vertical analysis to Chapter 13 (replaced with interpretation problems).

6 Internal Control and Financial Reporting for Cash and Merchandising Operations

- Change of chapter title to Internal Control and Financial Reporting for Cash and Merchandising Operations.
- New discussion of principles and limitations of internal control, tied to Sarbanes-Oxley Act.

- New Ethical Insights related to cash receipts and inventory control weaknesses.
- Application of internal control discussion to a few select companies.
- Simplified discussion of contra-revenue accounts; moved credit card discounts to Chapter 8.
- End of chapter: 15 new questions, mini-exercises, exercises, and problems and revisions to 45 other mini-exercises, exercises, problems, and cases.

7 Reporting and Interpreting Inventories and Cost of Goods Sold

- Change in sequence to have the inventory chapter follow the merchandising chapter to improve coherence.
- No references to Oakley's manufacturing operations.
- New discussion of inventory on consignment and in transit.
- Addition of weighted-average cost to expand illustrations of costing methods.
- New Control Spotlight linking RFID technology to inventory costing.
- New illustration of the first-in, first-out cost flow assumption.
- Revised presentation of computations, showing direct calculation of both cost of goods sold and ending inventory with "force-out" as accuracy check.
- End of chapter: eight new questions, mini-exercises, exercises, and problems, including comprehensive financial statement preparation exercise, and revised 42 other mini-exercises, exercises, problems, and cases.

8 Reporting and Interpreting Receivables, Bad Debt Expense, and Interest Revenue

- Change of chapter sequence (This chapter was Chapter 7 in prior edition.)
- New explanation of challenges of matching bad debts to sales revenue.

- New illustration (Exhibit 8.2) to explain the allowance method.

- Simplified discussion of the allowance method (percentage of sales estimation moved to Chapter Supplement A).

- New Self-Study Quiz.

- New Ethical Insights related to MCI.

- New contrast company in financial analyses.

- End of chapter: 15 new questions, mini-exercises, exercises, and problems, including comprehensive financial statement preparation exercise, and revisions to 35 other mini-exercises, exercises, problems, and cases.

⑨ **Reporting and Interpreting Long-Lived Tangible and Intangible Assets**

- New Chapter Supplement A on natural resource assets.

- New discussion of partial year depreciation in Chapter Supplement B.

- End of chapter: 7 new questions, mini-exercises, exercises, and problems revisions to 40 other mini-exercises, exercises, problems, and cases.

⑩ **Reporting and Interpreting Liabilities**

- New Ethical Insight related to current ratio.

- New Self-Study Quiz.

- Revised note payable illustration that mirrors note receivable illustration in Ch 8.

- No discussion of capital leases.

- Streamlined explanation of bonds payable.

- End of chapter: new demonstration case, 3 new questions, mini-exercises, exercises, problems, and cases, and revisions to 44 other mini-exercises, exercises, problems, and cases.

⑪ **Reporting and Interpreting Stockholders' Equity**

- New Focus Company (Sonic Corporation) and new contrast companies.

- New discussion of P/E ratio.

- New illustration of authorized, issued, and outstanding stock.

- New illustration of differences between stock splits, stock dividends, and cash dividends.

- Simplified discussions of stock dividends and stock options.

- End of chapter: 7 new questions, mini-exercises, exercises, problems, and cases, and revisions to 47 other mini-exercises, exercises, problems, and cases.

⑫ **Reporting and Interpreting the Statement of Cash Flows**

- New introduction explaining the purpose of the statement of cash flows.

- New Ethical Insights relating to W. T. Grant Co.

- New illustration for classifying cash flows by type of business activity.

- New contrast company in financial analyses.

- Simplified explanation of the indirect method.

- End of chapter: 10 new questions, mini-exercises, exercises, problems, and cases, and revisions to 41 other mini-exercises, exercises, problems, and cases.

⑬ **Measuring and Evaluating Financial Performance**

- New explanation of vertical analysis.

- New Self-Study Quiz.

- Simplified review of the conceptual framework.

- New contrast company in financial analyses.

- End of chapter: more-comprehensive demonstration case, 17 new questions, mini-exercises, exercises, problems, and cases, and revisions to 33 other mini-exercises, exercises, problems, and cases.

The Total Teaching Package

Use these additional McGraw-Hill digital and print resources to enhance your classroom, online, or hybrid course

GET YOUR STUDENTS TO PRACTICE AND READ

ONLINE LEARNING CENTER WWW.MHHE.COM/PHILLIPS2E

An innovative, text-specific Web site where students can study and practice before or after class. Chapter-by-chapter Web site full of study resources, with no setup required by you.

- iPod downloadable content
- Tutorial
- Glossary
- Study Guide Sample Chapter
- Working papers sample chapter
- Updates
- Mobile resources link

- PowerWeb link
- Chapter objectives
- Chapter overview
- Focus company links
- PowerPoint presentations
- Excel template assignments

HAVE EASY ACCESS TO ALL YOUR DIGITAL RESOURCES ONLINE

A secured Instructor Resource Center at the Online Learning Center site stores your essential course materials to save you prep time before class. Everything you need to run a lively classroom and an efficient course is included:

- Instructor's Manual
- Sample syllabi
- Additional appendices or chapter material
- Transition notes
- Updates
- PageOut link

- Mobile resources link
- Posting of author's teaching ideas, articles, and research
- Solutions to Excel template assignments
- Solutions Manual
- PowerPoint presentations

- Focus company links
- Chapter objectives
- Chapter overview
- Excel template assignments

HAVE ALL YOUR COURSE ASSETS EASILY ORGANIZED WITH MCGRAW-HILL'S ENHANCED ONLINE COURSE MANAGEMENT SYSTEM

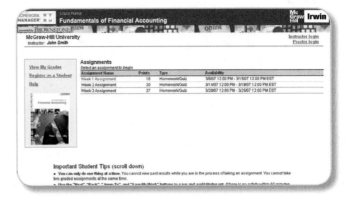

The Enhanced Cartridge will help you get your course up and running with less time and effort. Unlike the standard course cartridge, the enhanced course provides you with more practice and test assignments and more study materials. It is pre-populated into appropriate chapters and content categories, which eliminates the need for you to cut and paste our content into your course—it's already there!

In addition to the standard instructor supplement content, this cartridge also includes:

- Pre-populated course syllabus
- iPod/MP3 content
- Chapter pre- and post-tests
- Mid-term and Final tests
- Discussion boards
- Additional assignments
- Personalized graphics/banners/icons for your school
- Gradebook functionality

SAVE TIME BY ASSIGNING HOMEWORK ONLINE AND HAVING THOSE ASSIGNMENTS AUTOMATICALLY GRADED

McGraw-Hill's Homework Manager is also a useful grading tool. All assignments can be delivered over the Web and are graded automatically, with the results stored in your private grade book. Detailed results let you see at a glance how each student does on an assignment or an individual problem—you can even see how many tries it took to solve it.

End-of-chapter materials are now online and interactive, with algorithmic generation of limitless numbers of self-graded practice problems. Assignments and tests with unique versions of every problem are also available. Say goodbye to cheating in your classroom; say hello to the power and flexibility you've been waiting for in creating assignments.

Students receive full access to McGraw-Hill's Homework Manager when they purchase McGraw-Hill's Homework Manager Plus, or you can have Homework Manager pass codes shrinkwrapped with the textbook.

GIVE YOUR STUDENTS AN ONLINE VERSON OF THIS TEXTBOOK WITH MCGRAW-HILL'S HOMEWORK MANAGER PLUS

Full integration of online content and tools from McGraw-Hill PLUS an online version of *Fundamentals of Financial Management* 2e.

Available for purchase.

www.blackboard.com

ORGANIZE ALL YOUR DIGITAL ASSETS INTO BLACKBOARD OR WEBCT

Fundamentals of Financial Accounting's content is available for complete online courses and works with your institutions' adopted course management system. To make this possible, we have joined forces with the most popular delivery platforms currently available. These platforms are designed for instructors who want complete control over course content and the way it is presented to students. You can customize the *FFA* Online Learning Center content and author your own course materials. It's entirely up to you. If your department or school is already using a platform, we can help. For information on McGraw-Hill/Irwin's course management supplements, contact your McGraw-Hill/Irwin representative.

CREATE A WEB SITE FOR YOUR COURSE WITH PAGEOUT

Simple and efficient. Pick one of our professional designs. Alternatively, we can build a custom Web site to your specifications. Call a McGraw-Hill/Irwin PageOut specialist to start the process.

PageOut is free when you adopt *FFA*! To learn more, please visit www.pageout.net.

GET EVEN MORE DIGITAL ASSETS FOR YOUR FINANCIAL ACCOUNTING COURSE

Video Segments

Combining original location footage, interviews, eye-catching graphics and spoken narration, these vignettes explain how the concepts covered in each chapter make a difference in the world of business.

Animated Crossword Puzzles

These puzzles provide countless variations on the highly popular format for learning key terms. Yet another example of what makes *FFA* so much fun for students. www.mhhe.com/phillips2e.

Carol Yacht's General Ledger and Peachtree Complete 2004 CD-ROM

From one of the most trusted names in computer accounting education, Carol Yacht, comes a general ledger package that's a perfect fit for your course, no matter how you like to teach it.

The CD-ROM includes two full-featured accounting applications on one disk: **Carol Yacht's General Ledger**, a suite developed under Yacht's direction to provide the utmost in flexibility and power, and **Peachtree Complete**, the same software relied upon by thousands of firms throughout the world.

Students using Carol Yacht's General Ledger can move from financial statements to the specific journal entries with just a click of the mouse; **changing an entry updates the financial statement on the fly**, allowing students to see instantly how journal entries impact financial statements.

If you want your students to practice on the same software the professionals use, the educational version of Peachtree Complete 2004 is bundled on the CD with no disabled features to work around!

Carol Yacht's General Ledger and Peachtree CD-ROM is an incredible value—and it's included FREE with your *FFA* adoption!

ORGANIZE ALL YOUR TEXT-SPECIFIC RESOURCES ON ONE CD-ROM

ISBN-13: 978-007-313654-7   ISBN-10: 007-313654-9

This is your all-in-one in-class resource. Create stimulating custom presentations from your own materials or from the many text-specific materials provided in the CD's asset library:

- Instructor's Resource Manual

- Solutions Manual

- Computerized Test Bank (see below)

- Microsoft PowerPoint® slides, a multimedia lecture slide package that illustrates chapter concepts and procedures. It allows revision of lecture slides and includes a viewer, enabling screens to be shown with or without the software.

- Excel template exercises

- Link to PageOut

- Video clips

Instructor's Resource Manual

This manual contains a lecture outline for each chapter, a chart linking all assignment materials to learning objectives, a list of relevant active learning activities, and additional visuals with transparency masters. An electronic version is available on the Web site and on the Instructor's Resource CD-ROM. **Prepared by Jeannie Folk, College of DuPage.**

PowerPoint Slides

This overhead presentation package includes color teaching transparencies selected from the PowerPoint slides, as well as a booklet of black and white masters for every PowerPoint slide. **Prepared by Jon A Booker, Tennessee Technological University, Charles Caldwell, Tennessee Technological University, and Susan Galbreath, David Lipscomb University**

Solutions Manual

The solutions for all in-text problems and exercises are in this manual. **Prepared by Fred Phillips.**

Computerized Test Bank

This electronic test-generating engine is stocked with hundreds of true/false, multiple choice, and short answer questions. Generating quizzes and tests is as easy as clicking a mouse.

Test Bank

ISBN-13: 978-007-313651-6   ISBN-10: 007-313651-4

Thousands of questions in true/false, multiple choice, and short answer format written specifically for *FFA* are contained in this test bank. A Windows-compatible Computerized Test Bank is also available. **Prepared by Robert Braun, Southeastern Louisiana University.**

Check Figures

Available only online, at www.mhhe.com/phillips2e. Check Figures provide key answers for selected end-of-chapter exercises and problems. **Prepared by Angela Sandberg, Jacksonville State University.**

Use these additional McGraw-Hill digital and print resources to get a good grade.

Review and practice online anytime

Online Learning Center

Check out the Web site **www.mhhe.com/phillips2e.**

Practice what you're learning. Lots of free practice problems are online whenever you're ready. Even 1 AM. Practice makes perfect. You want good grades, right?

Listen to chapter outlines in your car, or wherever you are

iPod, Zune, or any MP3 device
content: Downloadable

An iPod Install DVD is available for additional purchase. It will allow you to save valuable time downloading MP3 and MP4 files. Plug in your iPod, Zune, or portable MP3 device. Listen to any chapter's outline before or after class. In your car. On your bike. At the gym. At your job. Look smart when you get to class.

Practice without being plugged in

Study Guide

ISBN-13: 978-007-313658-5   ISBN-10: 007-313658-1

Like a map of the course, every chapter is outlined and summarized for you. It provides more problems to practice, plus their solutions. **Prepared by Cheryl Bartlett Central New Mexico Community College.**

Get a good grade

McGraw-Hill's Homework Manager™

ISBN-13: 978-007-313662-2   ISBN-10: 007-313662-X

See page xvii for details on McGraw-Hill's Homework Manager.

Get experience with resources you'll actually use after college

Landry's Restaurants, Inc., 2005 Annual Report

ISBN-13: 978-007-313652-3   ISBN-10: 007-313652-2

Use this report—containing the very same information distributed to Landry's stockholders and potential investors—to solve problems and exercises. That's how real financial data are prepared and used.

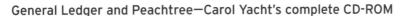

General Ledger and Peachtree—Carol Yacht's complete CD-ROM

ISBN-13: 978-007-313660-8   ISBN-10: 007-313660-3

From one of the most trusted names in computer accounting education, Carol Yacht, comes a general ledger package that's a perfect fit for your course.

The CD-ROM includes two full-featured accounting applications on one disk: Carol Yacht's General Ledger, a suite developed under Yacht's direction to provide the utmost in flexibility and power, and Peachtree Complete, the same software relied upon by thousands of firms throughout the world.

Use Carol Yacht's General Ledger to move from financial statements to the specific journal entries with just a click of the mouse; by changing entry updates of the financial statement on the fly, you can see instantly how journal entries impact financial statements.

If you want to practice on the same software the professionals use, the educational version of Peachtree Complete is bundled on the CD with no disabled features to work around!

Computerized Accounting Practice Sets

Gold Run Snowmobile, Inc. (007-2957883)

Granite Bay Jet Ski, Inc. (007-3080160)

When it comes to financial accounting, there's no such thing as too much practice. Our computerized practice sets give you even more opportunities to work with realistic accounting information and make a great addition to your financial accounting course.

Need help?

Customer Service (1-800-262-4729)

Quick Reference to Codes and Icons

		Topic Tackler PLUS		eXcel
Lecture Presentations available for download to your **iPod, Zune, or MP3 device** (audio and visual depending on your device)	Topical videos available for download to your **iPod, Zune, or MP3** (depending on your device)	Go to www.mhhe.com/phillips2e Topic Tackler Plus offers additional practice quizzes, lecture presentations, and videos specific to the most difficult to master topics in each chapter	Multiple Choice quizzes available for download to your **iPod, Zune, or MP3** (depending on your device)	Go to www.mhhe.com/phillips2e Excel templates allow students to practice accounting like a real professional. Designated demonstration cases, problems, and cases make ideal homework assignments.

Assurance of Learning Ready

Many educational institutions today are focused on the notion of assurance of learning, an important element of some accreditation standards. *Fundamentals of Financial Accounting* is designed specifically to support your assurance of learning initiatives with a simple, yet powerful, solution.

Each test bank question for *Fundamentals of Financial Accounting* maps to a specific chapter learning outcome/objective listed in the text. You can use our test bank software, *EZ Test* to easily query for learning outcomes/objectives that directly relate to the learning objectives for your course. You can then use the reporting features of *EZ Test* to aggregate student results in similar fashion, making the collection and presentation of assurance of learning data simple and easy.

McGraw-Hill Companies is a proud corporate member of AACSB International. Recognizing the importance and value of AACSB accreditation, the authors of *Fundamentals of Financial Accounting,* 2e, have sought to recognize the curricula guidelines detailed in AACSB standards for business accreditation by connecting selected questions in *Fundamentals of Financial Accounting* and its test bank to the general knowledge and skill guidelines found in the AACSB standards. It is important to note that the statements contained in *Fundamentals of Financial Accounting* are provided only as a guide for the users of this text.

The AACSB leaves content coverage and assessment clearly within the realm and control of individual schools, the mission of the school, and the faculty. The AACSB does also charge schools with the obligation of doing assessment against their own content and learning goals. While *Fundamentals of Financial Accounting* and its teaching package make no claim of any specific AACSB qualification or evaluation, we have, within the Instructor's Manual of *Fundamentals of Financial Accounting*, identified selected questions according to the six general knowledge and skills areas. The labels or tags within *Fundamentals of Financial Accounting* Test Bank are as indicated. There are, of course, many more questions within the test bank, the text, and the teaching package that might be used as a "standard" for your course. However, the labeled questions are suggested for your consideration.

Acknowledgments

We are deeply indebted to the following individuals who helped develop, critique, and shape the extensive ancillary package: Jeannie Folk, College of DuPage; Cheryl Bartlett, Central New Mexico Community College; Robert Braun, Southeastern Louisiana University; Jon A. Booker, Tennessee Technological University; Charles W. Caldwell, Tennessee Technological University; Susan C. Galbreath, David Lipscomb University; John Rude, Bloomsburg University; Angela H. Sandberg, Jacksonville State University; Rita Kingery Cook, University of Delaware; Barbara Schnathorst, The Write Solution; Ilene Persoff, Long Island University; Jocelyn Kauffunger, University of Pittsburgh; Debra L. Schmidt, Cerritos College; and Mary E. Harston.

We also received invaluable input and support from present and former colleagues and students, in particular Jocelyn Allard, Anders Bergstrom, Shari Boyd, Kara Chase, Shana M. Clor, Nicole Dewan, Erin Ferguson, Aaron Ferrara, Robin Harrington, Lee Harris, Blair Healy, Carrie Hordichuk, Lorraine Hurst, Jennifer Johnson, Nancy Kirzinger, Paul Knepper, Deborah Loran, Diana Mark, Roger Martin, Jason Matshes, Jennifer Millard, Kimberley Olfert, Ryan Olson, David Pooler, Jessica Pothier, Emery Salahub, Bailey Schergevitch, Marie Tait, and Kory Wickenhauser.

We thank the extraordinary efforts of a talented group of individuals at McGraw-Hill/Irwin, including Stewart Mattson, our editorial director; Alice Harra, our sponsoring editor; Daniel Silverberg, director of marketing; Scott Bishop, our marketing manager; Kimberly Hooker, our developmental editor; Mary Conzachi, our project manager; Artemio Ortiz, our designer; Debra Sylvester, our production supervisor; Matthew Perry and Susan Lombard, our media project managers; Lori Kramer, our photo research coordinator; David Tietz, our photo researcher; and Marcy Lunetta, our permissions researcher, for her patience and persistence;

We also want to recognize the valuable input of all those who helped guide our developmental decisions:

Advice on Using Your Textbook

THE FOLLOWING ADVICE IS GENERATED FROM AN IN-DEPTH STUDY OF 172 UNDERGRADUATE STUDENTS OF VARYING BACKGROUNDS, ALL OF WHOM WERE ENROLLED IN AN INTRODUCTORY FINANCIAL ACCOUNTING COURSE.

think and focus while reading

- **Read the chapters to learn rather than just to get through them.** Learning doesn't miraculously occur just because your eyes have skimmed all the assigned lines of the textbook. You have to think and focus while reading to ensure that you sink the material into your understanding and memory. Use the learning objectives in the text to focus on what's really important in each chapter.

- **Don't get discouraged if you initially find some material challenging to learn.** At various times, both the best and weakest students describe themselves as "confused" and "having a good grasp of the material," "anxious" and "confident," and "overwhelmed" and "comfortable." The simple fact is that learning new material can be challenging and initially confusing. Success does not appear to depend as much on *whether* you become confused as it does on *what you do* when you become confused.

- **Clear up confusion as it arises.** A key difference between the most and least successful students is how they respond to difficulty and confusion. When successful students are confused or anxious, they immediately try to enhance their understanding through rereading, self-testing, and seeking outside help if necessary. In contrast, unsuccessful students try to reduce anxiety by delaying further reading or by resorting to memorizing without understanding. Aim to clear up confusion when it arises because accounting in particular is a subject for which your understanding of later material depends on your understanding of earlier material.

- **Think of reading as the initial stage of studying.** Abandon the idea that "studying" only occurs during the final hours before an exam. By initially reading with the same intensity that occurs when later reviewing for an exam, you can create extra time for practicing exercises and problems. This combination of concentrated reading and extensive practice is likely to contribute to better learning and superior exam scores.

To learn more about the study on which this advice is based, see Phillips, B. J., and F. Phillips (2007) "Sink or Skim: Textbook Reading Behaviors of Introductory Accounting Students," *Issues in Accounting Education* 22 (February), pp. 21–44. Download a copy of the article from http://www.commerce.usask.ca/faculty/phillips/publications.asp.

BRIEF CONTENTS

CONTENTS

Fundamentals of
FINANCIAL ACCOUNTING

Second Edition

1

Business Decisions and Financial Accounting

USER

YOUR LEARNING OBJECTIVES

Understand the business

LO1 Describe various organizational forms and business decision makers.

Study the accounting methods

LO2 Describe the purpose, structure, and content of the four basic financial statements.

Evaluate the results

LO3 Explain how financial statements are relevant to users.

LO4 Describe factors that enhance the reliability of financial reporting.

Review the chapter

LP1

You might be surprised to hear that your personal life experiences are relevant to learning accounting, but they are. For example, in this chapter you'll learn how the reports used in accounting are like your digital pictures and videos that record what's happened so they can be shared with others. In a later chapter, you'll see how your system of taking notes in class is basically the same as the system of recordkeeping used in accounting. So, keep your mind and your eyes open, and you'll discover how your life connects with accounting.

One of our goals for this book is to help you see the role that accounting plays in helping people turn their good ideas into successful businesses. The founder of FedEx first introduced his ideas about a nationwide transportation business in a college essay. With the help of accounting, FedEx has become a multi-billion dollar business. Perhaps the only thing stopping you from doing this is that you don't fully know what's involved in starting and running a business. In this chapter you will hear the story of how one person turned his dream into a real business called Pizza Aroma.

→ reports
→ record
what has happened
so it can be
→ shared
with others

THIS IS
NOW

This chapter focuses on the key financial reports that business people rely on when evaluating a company's performance.

In 1990, Mauricio Rosa brought his young family from El Salvador to America to build a better life. While working in several New York pizza restaurants, he perfected a gourmet pizza concept. Thinking gourmet pizza would be a great addition to the local restaurant scene, Mauricio decided to start his own pizza business. Although eager to get started, Mauricio had several questions and decisions to consider. He contacted Laurie Hensley, a local CPA (certified public accountant) to ask her advice. As you read how Laurie helped Mauricio, use the following as an outline to organize your notes.

ORGANIZATION OF THE CHAPTER

Understand the business	Study the accounting methods	Evaluate the results	Review the chapter
• Organizational forms • Accounting for business decisions	• The basic accounting equation • Financial statements	• Relevance to financial statement users • Reliability of results	• Demonstration case • Chapter summary • Key terms • Practice material

Understand the Business

"Mauricio, we should start by talking about how you want to organize your business."

"Well, I'm opening a gourmet pizza restaurant. What else do I need to know?"

ORGANIZATIONAL FORMS

Learning Objective 1
Describe various organizational forms and business decision makers.

Laurie outlined three primary ways businesses can be organized. While other business forms exist, such as limited liability companies, BizStats.com reports that the following three are the most common: sole proprietorship, partnership, and corporation.

Sole Proprietorship

"one individual" can be a married couple

This is a form of business owned by one individual who often manages the business as well. It is the easiest form of business to start because it doesn't require any special legal maneuvers. Just get a business license and you're basically good to go. A sole proprietorship is considered just another part of the owner's life, with all profits (or losses) becoming part of the taxable income of the owner, and the owner being personally liable for all debts of the business.

Partnership

This form of business is similar to a sole proprietorship, except that profits, taxes, and legal liability are the responsibility of two or more owners instead of just one. It is slightly more expensive to form than a sole proprietorship because a lawyer typically is needed to draw up a partnership agreement, which describes exactly how profits are shared between partners and what happens if new partners are added or existing partners leave. The key advantage of a partnership over a sole proprietorship is that it typically has more resources available to it, which can fuel the business's growth.

Corporation

Unlike proprietorships and partnerships, a corporation is a separate entity from both a legal and accounting perspective. This means that a corporation, not its owners, is legally responsible for its own taxes and debts. Thus, owners cannot lose more than their investment in the corporation, which is a major advantage to the owners. The legal fees for creating a corporation can be high, which is a major disadvantage of incorporation.

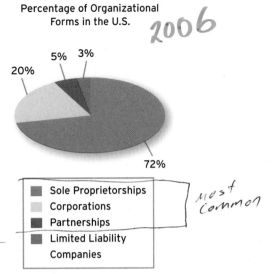

Percentage of Organizational Forms in the U.S.

2006

- 20%
- 5%
- 3%
- 72%

Sole Proprietorships
Corporations
Partnerships
Limited Liability Companies

Source: BizStats.com.

Corporations can raise large amounts of money for growth because they divide ownership of the corporation into shares that can be sold to new owners. A share of the corporation's ownership is indicated on a legal document called a stock certificate. The owners of a company's stock (stockholders) can buy and sell stock privately behind closed doors or publicly on a stock exchange, provided the company has legally registered to do so. Most corporations start out as private companies and will become public companies ("go public") if they need a lot of financing, which they obtain from selling new stock certificates to investors. Some big-name corporations, like Cargill and Chick-Fil-A, haven't gone public because they get enough financing from private sources, but many that you are familiar with (and most examples in this book) are public companies.

"I'm interested in limiting my legal liability and getting some financing by selling ownership shares to investors, so I will incorporate a private company called Pizza Aroma Inc. What's next?"

ACCOUNTING FOR BUSINESS DECISIONS

Most companies exist to earn profits for their stockholders. They earn profits by selling goods or services to customers for more than they cost to produce. Mauricio's company will be successful if it is able to make pizzas at a cost of $2 and sell them for $9. To know just how successful his company is, Mauricio will need to establish and maintain a good system of financial recordkeeping—an accounting system. **Accounting** is a system of analyzing, recording, and summarizing the results of a business's activities. It's such a key part of business that business people typically talk about their companies using accounting terms, which is why they often call it the "language of business."

Every organization needs accountants to help in understanding the financial effects of business decisions. Mauricio can get this help in one of two ways. He can hire an accountant to work as an employee of his business (a "private accountant") or he can contract with someone like Laurie who provides advice to a variety of businesses (a "public accountant"). Because Mauricio's business is small, he doesn't yet need a full-time accountant. Instead, he agrees that Pizza Aroma will pay fees to Laurie for basic services. She'll help him to set up an accounting system and advise him on key business decisions.[1]

> **YOU SHOULD KNOW**
>
> **Accounting** is a system of analyzing, recording, and summarizing the results of a business's activities.

---

[1] The chapter supplement on page 20 describes the wide variety of accounting career choices available.

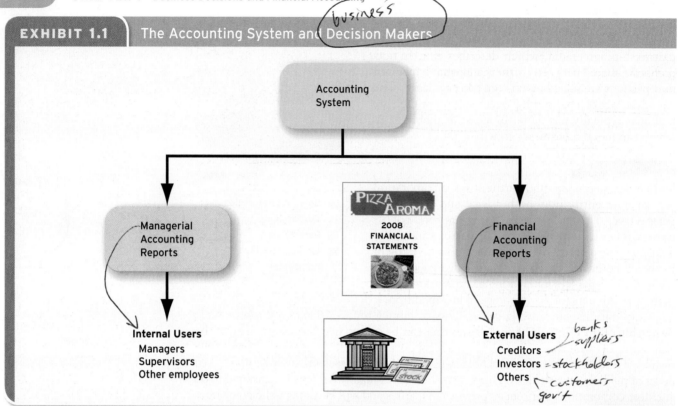

EXHIBIT 1.1   The Accounting System and Decision Makers

business

Accounting System

Managerial Accounting Reports

PIZZA AROMA
2008 FINANCIAL STATEMENTS

Financial Accounting Reports

Internal Users
Managers
Supervisors
Other employees

External Users
Creditors   *banks / suppliers*
Investors   *= stockholders*
Others   *customers / gov't*

"How will an accounting system help me run my business?"

Whether focused on marketing, human resources, finance, or production and operations, all business people need accounting information to understand the financial condition and performance of a business. As Exhibit 1.1 indicates, the accounting system produces two kinds of reports: managerial accounting reports and financial accounting reports. Managerial accounting reports include detailed financial plans and continually updated reports about the financial performance of the company. These reports are made available only to employees of the company so that they can make business decisions such as whether to build, buy, or rent a building, whether to continue or discontinue making particular products, how much to pay employees, and how much to borrow. As manager of the restaurant, Mauricio will regularly need managerial accounting reports to monitor the quantity of supplies on hand, evaluate the various costs associated with making and selling his gourmet pizza, and assess the productivity of his employees.

"Others outside your business will need financial information about your restaurant. For example, where will the money come from to start your business?"

"My wife and I will contribute $30,000 from personal savings. But I'll still need to ask the bank for a $20,000 loan to buy equipment. What will the bank want to know?"

Laurie described financial accounting reports called **financial statements**, which are prepared periodically to provide information to people not employed by the business. These external financial statement users aren't given access to detailed internal records of the company, so they rely extensively on the financial statements. Creditors and investors are the two primary external user groups, but other external users also find the information helpful.

- **Creditors**—anyone to whom money is owed.
  - Banks use financial statements to evaluate the risk that they will not be repaid the money they've loaned out to a company. Because banks are taking a risk, they want periodic financial reports from the company so they can keep an eye on how it is doing and intervene if it looks like the company will have trouble repaying the loan.
  - Suppliers also want to be sure a business can pay them for the goods or services they deliver. They are likely to ask for financial statements before entering into significant business relationships.

- **Investors**
  - Stockholders are a major external user group. Both existing and future stockholders rely on financial statements to evaluate whether the company is financially secure and likely to be a profitable investment.

- **Other external users**
  - Certain customers use financial statements to judge the company's ability to provide future service on its products and honor warranties.
  - Various local, state, and federal governments also collect taxes based on the financial statements.

In Mauricio's case, the bank will be the main external user of Pizza Aroma's financial statements. Mauricio will be expected to prepare financial statements to obtain the loan and then regularly provide updated financial reports until the loan is repaid. If the company's stock is ever sold to other investors, they will rely on financial statements to predict what their shares will be worth in the future and whether to buy, sell, or hold Pizza Aroma stock.

While Mauricio understood everything Laurie had told him up to this point, he had another major concern.

"I want to sound intelligent when I talk to my banker, but I don't know much about accounting."

"This is a common concern for new business owners, so let's start with the most basic thing you need to know about accounting."

Study the Accounting Methods

THE BASIC ACCOUNTING EQUATION

One of the central concepts to understanding financial reports is that what a company owns must equal what a company owes to its creditors and stockholders. In accounting, there are special names for what a company owns and what a company owes to creditors and stockholders, as shown below.

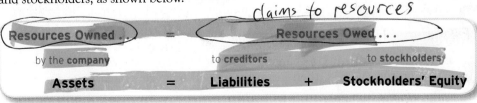

claims to resources

Resources Owned...	=	Resources Owed...
by the **company**	to **creditors**	to **stockholders**
Assets	= **Liabilities**	+ **Stockholders' Equity**

owned — owed — ownership

Video1.1

The relationship between assets (A), liabilities (L), and stockholders' equity (SE) is known as the **basic accounting equation.** The business itself, not the stockholders who own the business, is viewed as owning the assets and owing the liabilities. This is called the **separate entity assumption,** which requires that a business's financial reports include only the activities of the business and not those of its stockholders.

Assets

An **asset** is any resource controlled by the company that has measurable value and is expected to provide future benefits for the company. For Pizza Aroma, assets would include things like cash, supplies and ingredients, tables and chairs, and pizza ovens.

Liabilities

Liabilities are measurable amounts that the company owes to creditors. If Pizza Aroma borrows from a bank, it would owe a liability called a *note payable.* This particular name is used because banks require borrowers to sign a legal document called a *note,* which describes details about the company's promise to repay the bank. The business also would owe payments to suppliers who deliver ingredients and other supplies to Pizza Aroma. When a company buys goods from another company, it usually does so on credit by promising to pay for them at a later date. The amount owed is called an *account payable* because purchases made using credit are said to be "on account." Pizza Aroma could also owe wages to employees (wages payable) and taxes to governments (taxes payable). As you may have noticed, anything with the word *payable* in its name is considered a liability.

Stockholders' Equity

Stockholders' equity represents the owners' claims to the business. These claims arise for two reasons. First, the owners have a claim on amounts they invested in the business by making direct contributions to the company (contributed capital). Second, the owners have a claim on amounts the company has earned through profitable business operations (retained earnings). The goal of most business owners is to generate profits because this increases stockholders' equity and allows owners to get more money back from the company than what they put in (a return on their investment).

Profits are generated when the total amount earned from selling goods and services is greater than all the costs incurred to generate those sales. This means Pizza Aroma will be profitable if it earns more from selling its pizzas (revenues) than what it costs to make its pizzas and run the business (expenses). The difference between total revenues and expenses is sometimes loosely called "profit" or "earnings," but the preferred term in accounting is "net income."

> **Revenues – Expenses = Net Income**   *aka "profit"*
>
> *preferred term in accounting*

Revenues

Revenues are the sales of goods or services to customers. They will be measured at the amount Pizza Aroma charges its customers for the pizza it sells them.

Expenses

Expenses are all of the costs of doing business necessary to earn revenues. For Pizza Aroma, these include advertising, utilities, rent, wages to employees, insurance, repairs, and supplies used in making pizza. Expenses are said to be "incurred" to generate revenues, which means that the activities giving rise to a cost (e.g., running an ad, using electricity) have occurred.

Net Income

If Pizza Aroma is successful in charging more for its pizzas than what it costs to make them and run the business, then Pizza Aroma will have generated a **net income.** (If revenues are less than expenses, Pizza Aroma would have a net loss but for now let's assume that doesn't happen.) **By generating net income, a company increases its stockholders' equity.** Net income (or earnings) can either be left in the company to accumulate (with other retained earnings) or paid out to the company's stockholders for their own personal use (called dividends).

Dividends

Dividends are distributions of a company's earnings paid periodically to stockholders as a return on their investment. The simplest type of dividend, and the most common for a small business like Pizza Aroma, is a dividend paid in cash. Dividends are not an expense of the company because they are determined at the discretion of the company's stockholders. If Mauricio and his wife wanted, they could choose to leave all the profits in Pizza Aroma by never declaring a dividend.

"Okay, I think I get it, but can you tell me how all those items relate to each other and where they are reported in the financial statements?"

FINANCIAL STATEMENTS

Assets, liabilities, stockholders' equity, revenues, expenses, and dividends appear in different reports in the financial statements. The term *financial statements* refers to four accounting reports, typically prepared in the following order:

1. Income Statement
2. Statement of Retained Earnings
3. Balance Sheet
4. Statement of Cash Flows

The basic accounting equation, shown in blue at the top of Exhibit 1.2, provides the structure for the **balance sheet.** The purpose of a balance sheet is to report a company's financial position at a point in time, kind of like a picture or snapshot of the company.

The red box in Exhibit 1.2 shows that net income is equal to revenues minus expenses. Net income is a measure of financial performance over a period of time. This information is reported on an **income statement.** Think of the income statement as a video, accumulating events that occurred over a period of time. The purple box in Exhibit 1.2

Topic Tackler

PLUS

Check out www.mhhe.com/phillips2e for audio, visual, and PowerPoint presentations on this topic.

EXHIBIT 1.2   Financial Statement Equations

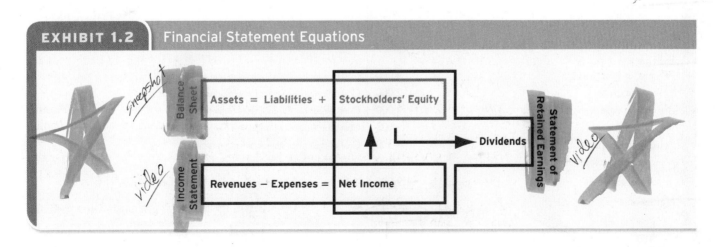

shows that the **statement of retained earnings** links the balance sheet and income statement. Specifically, the arrow from Net Income to Stockholders' Equity indicates that stockholders' equity in the business will increase as Pizza Aroma generates net income. These earnings are retained in the company until paid out as dividends. The **statement of cash flows** reports changes in a specific asset (cash) so it is not illustrated in Exhibit 1.2.

Financial statements can be prepared at any time during the year, although they are most commonly prepared monthly, every three months (quarterly reports), and at the end of the year (annual reports). Companies are allowed to choose any date for the end of their accounting (or fiscal) year. For example, the toy maker Mattel uses a December 31 year-end because this is the start of its slow business period. Fewer toys are sold in January through May than in the first three weeks of December. The only U.S. professional sports team operating as a public company—Green Bay Packers, Inc.—has chosen a fiscal year-end of March 31, the month after the season wraps up with the Pro Bowl. Laurie shows Mauricio what Pizza Aroma's financial statements might look like after September 30, his first month of operations.

The Income Statement = statement of operations

The first financial statement prepared is the income statement (also called the statement of operations). Exhibit 1.3 shows Pizza Aroma's income statement. The heading identifies who, what, and when: the name of the business, the title of the report, and the time period covered by the financial statement. For larger businesses with thousands or millions of dollars in revenues and expenses, a fourth line may be added under the date to indicate if the numbers reported are rounded to the nearest thousand or million. For international companies, this fourth line also reports the currency used in the report. An international company based in the United States, like Papa John's, will translate any foreign currency into U.S. dollars—basically assuming all its business was done in U.S. dollars. This is the **unit of measure assumption.** We see it in the reporting currency used in other countries: Nestlé (Swiss franc), Lego (Danish kronen), and Adidas (euro).

Notice that Pizza Aroma's income statement has three major parts—revenues, expenses, and net income—corresponding to the equation for the income statement (Revenues − Expenses = Net Income). Under the revenues and expenses headings,

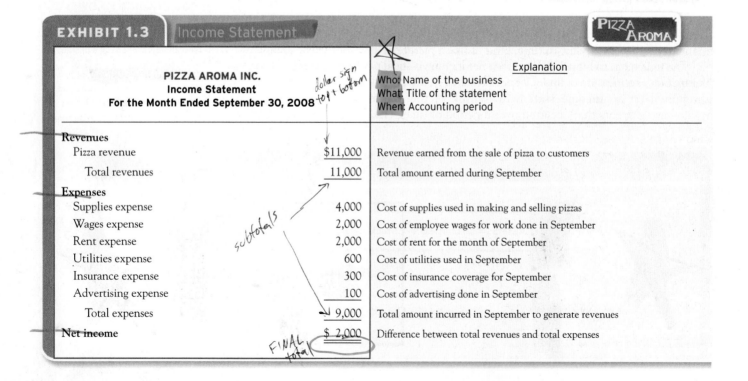

EXHIBIT 1.3   Income Statement   PIZZA AROMA

PIZZA AROMA INC.
Income Statement
For the Month Ended September 30, 2008

dollar sign top + bottom

		Explanation
Who:	Name of the business	
What:	Title of the statement	
When:	Accounting period	

Revenues		
Pizza revenue	$11,000	Revenue earned from the sale of pizza to customers
Total revenues	11,000	Total amount earned during September
Expenses		
Supplies expense	4,000	Cost of supplies used in making and selling pizzas
Wages expense	2,000	Cost of employee wages for work done in September
Rent expense	2,000	Cost of rent for the month of September
Utilities expense	600	Cost of utilities used in September
Insurance expense	300	Cost of insurance coverage for September
Advertising expense	100	Cost of advertising done in September
Total expenses	9,000	Total amount incurred in September to generate revenues
Net income	$ 2,000	Difference between total revenues and total expenses

subtotals

FINAL total

individual types of revenues and expenses are reported. These **accounts,** as they are called, are typical for most businesses, whether small or big. Notice that each major caption has a subtotal, and the bottom line amount for net income has a double underline to highlight it. Finally, a dollar sign appears at the top and bottom of a column of numbers.

When listing the accounts on the income statement, revenues are on top, usually with the largest, most relevant revenue listed first. Then expenses are subtracted, again usually with the largest and most relevant expense listed first.

"So, does the $2,000 of net income mean I'll have that much more cash?"

"No. Net income is a measure of how much better off your business is, not how much cash you made."

Laurie's point is one of the key ideas of the income statement. Revenues are the amounts charged to customers when goods or services are provided, and expenses are the costs of the activities involved in providing those goods or services. It's quite common for a business to provide goods or services to customers in one month, but not collect cash from them until a later month. Similarly, expenses for the current month's activities may actually be paid in a different month. You'll have a chance to learn this in more detail later, but it's worth trying to understand from the beginning that revenues don't necessarily equal cash coming in during the month and expenses don't always equal cash going out during the month.

Mauricio seemed disappointed with a net income of $2,000, so Laurie reassured him that it's typical for new businesses like Pizza Aroma to initially struggle to generate a profit because they have lots of expenses related to advertising and employee training but relatively little revenues because they haven't yet built a loyal customer base. In fact, 50 percent of all new businesses fail or close within the first six years of opening.[2] Not many start out with a positive net income in the first month. And you can probably expect Pizza Aroma's net income to become even bigger in the future after the business becomes established. By selling more pizza, revenues will increase without a major increase in expenses, except for the cost of ingredients and supplies that will be used in making the additional pizzas. Expenses like employee wages and rent will likely not increase all that much.

"I guess that's not so bad. It does make me want to watch my expenses and try to boost my pizza sales quickly. What about the amount Pizza Aroma owes to the bank? Should we talk about the balance sheet?"

"Before we look at that, I want to show you the next statement that connects the income statement to the balance sheet, so you'll understand the relationships between the reports."

[2] For more information on small business failures, see Brian Headd "Redefining Business Success: Distinguishing between Closure and Failures," *Small Business Economics*, 21: 51–61, 2003.

The Statement of Retained Earnings

Pizza Aroma will report a statement of retained earnings, as shown in Exhibit 1.4. A more comprehensive statement of stockholders' equity that explains changes in all stockholders' equity accounts is provided by large corporations. But for Pizza Aroma, most changes in stockholders' equity relate to generating and distributing earnings, so a statement of retained earnings is just as good as a full-blown statement of stockholders' equity. The heading in Exhibit 1.4 identifies the name of the company, the title of the report, and the accounting period. The statement starts with the retained earnings balance at the beginning of the period. Remember that retained earnings are the profits that have accumulated in the company over time. Because this is a new business, there aren't any accumulated profits yet so the beginning balance is $0. Next, the statement adds the net income and subtracts any dividends for the current period, to arrive at retained earnings at the end of the period.[3] Again, a dollar sign is used at the top and bottom of the column of numbers and a double underline at the bottom.

EXHIBIT 1.4	Statement of Retained Earnings	PIZZA AROMA

PIZZA AROMA INC. Statement of Retained Earnings For the Month Ended September 30, 2008		Explanation Who: Name of the business What: Title of the statement When: Accounting period
Retained earnings, Sept. 1, 2008	$ 0	Last period's ending retained earnings balance
Add: Net income	2,000	Reported on the income statement (Exhibit 1.3)
Subtract: Dividends	(1,000)	Distributions to stockholders in the current period
Retained earnings, Sept. 30, 2008	$1,000	This period's ending retained earnings balance

The Balance Sheet = statement of financial position

The next financial report is the balance sheet. It is also known as the statement of financial position. The purpose of the balance sheet is to report the amount of a business's assets, liabilities, and stockholders' equity (collectively called the business's *financial position*) at a particular point in time. The balance sheet for Pizza Aroma is shown in Exhibit 1.5. Notice again that the heading specifically identifies the name of the company and title of the statement. Unlike the other financial reports, the balance sheet is presented for a point in time (at September 30, 2008). The balance sheet provides a snapshot of resources (what the company owns) and claims to those resources at the end of that day. The assets are listed in order of how soon they are to be used or turned into cash. Likewise, liabilities are listed in order of how soon each is to be paid or settled.

The balance sheet first lists the assets of the business, which for Pizza Aroma total $58,000. The second section lists the business's liabilities and stockholders' equity balances, also totaling $58,000. The balance sheet "balances" because the resources

---

[3] For companies that have a net loss (expenses exceed revenues), the statement of retained earnings would subtract the net loss rather than add net income.

EXHIBIT 1.5	Balance Sheet		PIZZA AROMA

PIZZA AROMA INC.
Balance Sheet
At September 30, 2008

Explanation
Who: Name of the business
What: Title of the statement
When: Point in time

					Explanation
Assets					
Cash			$14,000		Amount of cash in the business's bank account
Accounts receivable			1,000		Amount owed to Pizza Aroma for prior credit sales
Supplies			3,000		Amount of food and paper supplies on hand
Equipment			40,000		Cost of ovens, tables, etc.
Total assets		*A*	$58,000		Total amount of the business's resources
Liabilities and Stockholders' Equity					
Liabilities					
Accounts payable	\\		$ 7,000		Amount owed to suppliers for prior purchases on credit
Notes payable			20,000		Amount of loan owed to the bank
Total liabilities		*L*	27,000		Total claims on the resources by creditors
Stockholders' equity					
Contributed capital		+	30,000		Amount contributed to the company by stockholders
Retained earnings			1,000		Amount retained in the business (Exhibit 1.4)
Total stockholders' equity		*S/E*	31,000		Total claims on the resources by stockholders
Total liabilities and stockholders' equity			$58,000		Total claims on the business's resources

[handwritten] listed in order of how soon to be used (or turned into cash)

[handwritten] listed in order of how soon to be paid/settled

equal the claims to the resources. The basic accounting equation (or balance sheet equation) reflects the business's financial position at September 30, 2008:

Accounting Equation	**Assets**	=	**Liabilities**	+	**Stockholders' Equity**
	$58,000	=	$27,000	+	$31,000

Cash is the first asset reported. The $14,000 represents the total amount of cash on hand and in Pizza Aroma's bank account. The $1,000 reported as accounts receivable represents the amount that Pizza Aroma has the right to collect from customers for prior sales made on credit. Pizza Aroma allows the area's colleges to buy pizza for events on account by running a tab that Pizza Aroma sends as a bill after the deliveries are made. The $3,000 reported for supplies indicates the cost of pizza supplies that remain on hand at September 30, 2008. The same is true for the $40,000 of equipment. According to the cost principle of accounting, assets are reported on the balance sheet based on their original cost to the company.

Under liabilities, the $7,000 of accounts payable is the amount Pizza Aroma still owes to suppliers for food and paper supplies purchased on account. The note payable is the written promise to repay the loan from the bank. As with all liabilities, these are financial obligations of the business arising from past business activities.

Finally, within stockholders' equity, contributed capital reflects all contributions made by Mauricio and his wife (the stockholders). Retained earnings includes all earnings still retained in the company as of September 30, 2008. It matches the amount reported for ending retained earnings on the statement of retained earnings (Exhibit 1.4).

COACH'S TIP
Any account name containing *receivable* is an asset and any containing *payable* is a liability.

"Besides monitoring my revenues and expenses, it looks like I need to make sure I have enough assets to pay my liabilities."

"Sharp observation! Your creditors are most interested in your ability to pay cash to them in the future. However, not all assets can be easily turned into cash and not all revenues and expenses are received or paid in cash. So, there is one more important financial statement."

The Statement of Cash Flows

Pizza Aroma's income statement showed positive net income of $2,000, but net income is not necessarily equal to cash because revenues are reported when earned and expenses when incurred regardless of when cash is received or paid. The fourth financial report of interest to external users, then, is the statement of cash flows. It includes only those activities that result in cash changing hands, like a video camera with a telephoto lens focused on activities affecting cash. Exhibit 1.6 shows Pizza Aroma's statement of cash flows for the month ended September 30, 2008.

EXHIBIT 1.6	Statement of Cash Flows		PIZZA AROMA

PIZZA AROMA INC.
Statement of Cash Flows
For the Month Ended September 30, 2008

Explanation
Who: Name of the entity
What: Title of the statement
When: Accounting period

		Explanation
Cash flows from operating activities		Activities directly related to earning income
Cash from customers	$10,000	Amount of cash received from customers
Cash to suppliers and employees	(5,000)	Amount of cash paid to suppliers and employees
Cash provided by operating activities	5,000	Cash inflow minus outflow ($10,000 – $5,000)
Cash flows from investing activities		Activities related to the sale/purchase of productive assets
Cash to buy equipment	(40,000)	Amount of cash spent on equipment
Cash used in investing activities	(40,000)	
Cash flows from financing activities		Activities involving investors and banks
Capital contributed by stockholders	30,000	Amount of cash received from owners
Cash dividends paid to stockholders	(1,000)	Amount of cash paid to owners
Cash borrowed from the bank	20,000	Amount of cash received from bank
Cash provided by financing activities	49,000	Cash inflow minus outflow ($30,000 – $1,000 + $20,000)
Change in cash	14,000	Sum of three categories of cash flows [$5,000 – $40,000 + $49,000]
Beginning cash balance, Sept. 1, 2008	0	Balance at the beginning of the accounting period
Ending cash balance, Sept. 30, 2008	$14,000	Amount reported on the balance sheet (Exhibit 1.5)

> **COACH'S TIP**
>
> Parentheses are used on the statement of cash flows to indicate negative cash flows (outflows rather than inflows).

The statement of cash flows is divided into three categories of business activities:

1. **Operating:** These activities are directly related to running the business to earn profit. They include buying supplies, making pizza, serving food to customers, cleaning the store, advertising, renting a building, repairing ovens, and obtaining insurance coverage.

2. **Investing:** These activities involve buying and selling productive resources with long lives (such as buildings, land, equipment, and tools) and lending to others.

3. **Financing:** Any borrowing from banks, repaying bank loans, receiving contributions from stockholders, or paying dividends to stockholders are considered financing activities.

Pizza Aroma's statement of cash flows is typical of a new start-up business or a business in expansion. The negative number for cash flows from investing activities indicates that the company has spent cash this period to buy equipment. The bank will be interested in watching how the cash flows reported on this statement change in the future to assess Pizza Aroma's ability to make cash payments on the loan.

A summary of the four basic financial statements is presented in Exhibit 1.7.

EXHIBIT 1.7 | Summary of Four Basic Financial Statements

Financial Statement	Purpose: To report ...	Structure	Examples of Content
Income Statement	The financial performance of the business *during the current accounting period*.	Revenues − Expenses = Net income	Sales revenue, wages expense, supplies expense, interest expense
Statement of Retained Earnings	The accumulation of earnings retained in the business *during the current accounting period* with that of prior periods.	Beginning retained earnings + Net income (this period) − Dividends (this period) = Ending retained earnings	Net income is from the income statement. Dividends are amounts distributed this period.
Balance Sheet	The financial position of a business *at a point in time*.	Liabilities Assets = + Stockholders' Equity	Cash, receivables, supplies, equipment, accounts payable, notes payable, contributed capital, retained earnings
Statement of Cash Flows	Inflows (receipts) and outflows (payments) of cash *during the current accounting period*.	+/− Cash flows from operating activities +/− Cash flows from investing activities +/− Cash flows from financing activities = Change in cash + Beginning cash balance = Ending cash balance	Cash collected from customers, cash paid to suppliers, cash paid for equipment, cash borrowed from banks, cash received from selling stock

Notes to the Financial Statements

The four basic financial statements are not complete without notes to help financial statement users understand how the amounts were derived and what other information may affect their decisions. We'll talk about notes later.

"How does the whole picture fit together?"

Relationships among the Financial Statements

Exhibit 1.8 shows how the four basic financial statements connect to one another. The arrows show that net income, from the income statement, is a component in determining ending retained earnings on the statement of retained earnings, which is then reported on the balance sheet. Also, the ending number on the statement of cash flows is equal to the cash reported on the balance sheet at the end of the period.

EXHIBIT 1.8   Relationships among the Financial Statements

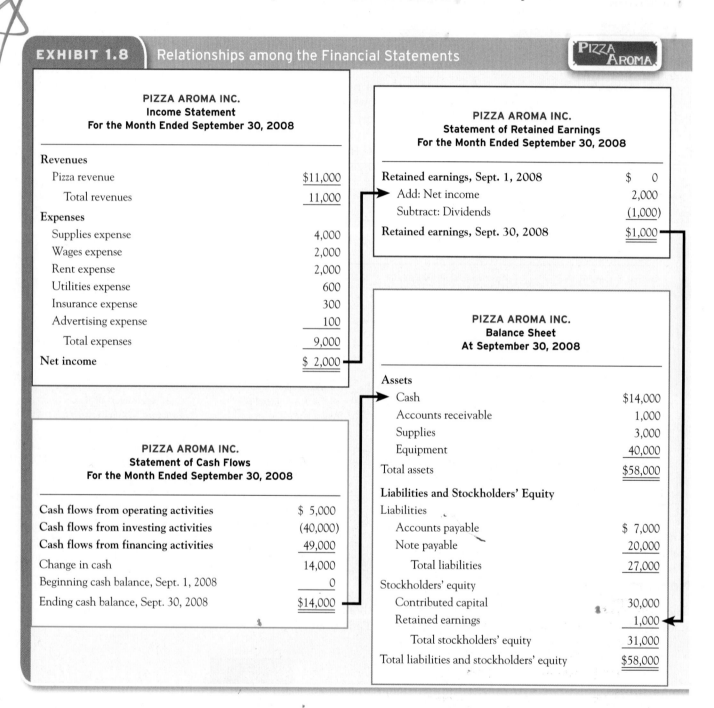

PIZZA AROMA INC.
Income Statement
For the Month Ended September 30, 2008

Revenues	
Pizza revenue	$11,000
Total revenues	11,000
Expenses	
Supplies expense	4,000
Wages expense	2,000
Rent expense	2,000
Utilities expense	600
Insurance expense	300
Advertising expense	100
Total expenses	9,000
Net income	$ 2,000

PIZZA AROMA INC.
Statement of Retained Earnings
For the Month Ended September 30, 2008

Retained earnings, Sept. 1, 2008	$ 0
Add: Net income	2,000
Subtract: Dividends	(1,000)
Retained earnings, Sept. 30, 2008	$1,000

PIZZA AROMA INC.
Statement of Cash Flows
For the Month Ended September 30, 2008

Cash flows from operating activities	$ 5,000
Cash flows from investing activities	(40,000)
Cash flows from financing activities	49,000
Change in cash	14,000
Beginning cash balance, Sept. 1, 2008	0
Ending cash balance, Sept. 30, 2008	$14,000

PIZZA AROMA INC.
Balance Sheet
At September 30, 2008

Assets	
Cash	$14,000
Accounts receivable	1,000
Supplies	3,000
Equipment	40,000
Total assets	$58,000
Liabilities and Stockholders' Equity	
Liabilities	
Accounts payable	$ 7,000
Note payable	20,000
Total liabilities	27,000
Stockholders' equity	
Contributed capital	30,000
Retained earnings	1,000
Total stockholders' equity	31,000
Total liabilities and stockholders' equity	$58,000

You have seen lots of new and important material in this section. Before moving on, take a moment to complete a short quiz. This is the best way to make sure you've paid enough attention when reading about how business activities are reported in financial statements.

HOW'S IT GOING? A Self-Study Quiz

In the space provided, indicate: (1) the type of account (A=asset, L=liability, SE=stockholders' equity, R=revenue, E=expense, D=dividend), and (2) whether it is reported on the income statement (I/S), statement of retained earnings (SRE), balance sheet (B/S), or statement of cash flows (SCF).

Account Title	Type	Statement
1. Land	_____	_____
2. Wages Expense	_____	_____
3. Accounts Receivable	_____	_____
4. Rent Revenue	_____	_____
5. Contributed Capital	_____	_____
6. Note Payable	_____	_____

When you've finished, check your answers with the solutions in the margin.

Quiz Answers	Type	Statement
1.	A	B/S
2.	E	I/S
3.	A	B/S
4.	R	I/S
5.	SE	B/S
6.	L	B/S

"So, you've just seen how your financial statements should look in one month and how they relate. Are you feeling okay with all this?"

"It actually makes me anxious to get started. What will my external users look for?"

Evaluate the Results

RELEVANCE TO FINANCIAL STATEMENT USERS

> **Learning Objective 3**
> Explain how financial statements are relevant to users.

The financial statements are a key source of information when external users, like creditors and investors, make decisions concerning a company. As you will see throughout this course, the amounts reported in the financial statements can be used to calculate percentages and ratios that reveal important insights about a company's performance. For now, however, let's consider how creditors and investors might gain valuable information simply by reading the dollar amounts reported in each financial statement.

- Creditors are mainly interested in assessing two things:
  1. Is the company generating enough cash to make payments on its loan? Answers to this question will come from the statement of cash flows. In particular, creditors would be interested in seeing whether operating activities are producing positive cash flows. Pizza Aroma's net inflow of $5,000 cash from operating activities is very good for a new business.
  2. Does the company have enough assets to cover its liabilities? Answers to this question will come from comparing assets and liabilities reported on the balance sheet. At September 30, Pizza Aroma owns slightly more than twice what it owes to creditors (total assets of $58,000 versus total liabilities of $27,000). With $14,000 in cash, Pizza Aroma could pay all of its accounts payable and part of its notes payable right now if needed.

- Investors look for either an immediate return on their contributions to a company (through dividends) or a long-term return (by selling stock certificates at a price higher than what they were bought for). Dividends and higher stock prices are more likely if a company is profitable. As a result, investors look closely at the income statement (and statement of retained earnings) for information about the company's ability to generate profits (and distribute dividends).

"I've heard a lot about 'cooking the books.' How do users know the information they're getting is reliable and can be trusted?"

RELIABILITY OF FINANCIAL STATEMENTS

Laurie indicated that, to enhance the reliability of financial reporting, business must apply accounting principles in an ethical business environment.

Generally Accepted Accounting Principles

As it turns out, the system of financial statement reporting in use today has a long history—all the way back to a publication in 1494 by an Italian monk and mathematician, Luca Pacioli. Now, the primary responsibility for setting the underlying rules of accounting falls to the Financial Accounting Standards Board (FASB) in the U.S. and to the International Accounting Standards Board (IASB) in most other countries. As a group, these rules are called **generally accepted accounting principles,** or **GAAP** for short (pronounced like the name of the clothing store).

For financial information to be useful, managers, creditors, stockholders, and others need to have confidence that the information is

Topic Tackler

PLUS

- Relevant (that is, it helps in making decisions).
- Reliable (that is, it is unbiased and verifiable).
- Comparable (against other companies).
- Consistent (over time).

Generally accepted accounting principles follow these guidelines to provide useful information to users.

As a summary, Laurie gave Mauricio the information shown in Exhibit 1.9—the key concepts used by FASB for developing new accounting principles. The concepts discussed in this chapter are highlighted in red and the rest will be introduced in later chapters. Mauricio was surprised at how many concepts he had already learned.

Many of the FASB rules that result from following these key concepts are quite complex and apply mostly to large public companies. In future chapters, we will focus on accounting rules that have the greatest impact on financial statements at an appropriate introductory level.

EXHIBIT 1.9	Key Concepts for External Financial Reporting

Objective:	To provide useful financial information to external users for decision making.
Characteristics of Useful Financial Information:	Relevance, reliability, comparability, consistency
Elements:	Assets, liabilities, stockholders' equity, revenues, expenses
Assumptions:	Unit of measure, separate entity, going concern, time period
Principles:	Cost, revenue recognition, matching, full disclosure
Constraints:	Cost-benefit, materiality, industry practices, conservatism

"Who is responsible for ensuring that businesses follow GAAP?"

Laurie told Mauricio that a company's managers have primary responsibility for following GAAP. To provide additional assurance, some private companies and all public companies hire independent auditors to scrutinize their financial records. Following rules approved by the Public Company Accounting Oversight Board (PCAOB) and other accounting bodies, these auditors report whether, beyond reasonable doubt, the financial statements represent what they claim to represent and whether they comply with GAAP. In a sense, GAAP are to auditors and accountants what the criminal code is to lawyers and the public. The Securities and Exchange Commission (SEC) is the government agency that supervises the work of the FASB and PCAOB.

"Overall, users expect information that is truthful, and this assumes that the company is following strong ethical business and accounting practices."

Accounting Ethics

Primary responsibility for the financial statements lies with management, led by the chief executive officer (CEO) and chief financial officer (CFO) of the company. Big problems arise if these individuals fail to act in an ethical manner, as has happened in several high-profile accounting frauds involving Enron, WorldCom (now part of Verizon), Global Crossing, and Xerox. Investigators discovered that their top managers had led financial statement users astray by misrepresenting their companies' financial results. In many cases, the top executives were convicted of fraud and sentenced to long terms in prison.

In response to these frauds, the U. S. Congress stepped in to create the **Sarbanes-Oxley Act of 2002 (SOX)**, which has had a huge impact on managers and auditors of public companies. The act requires that the top managers sign a report certifying their responsibilities for the financial statements, maintain an audited system of internal controls to ensure accuracy in accounting reports, and maintain an independent committee to ensure managers cooperate with auditors. As a result of SOX, corporate executives now face severe consequences—20 years in prison and $5 million in fines—if they are found guilty of committing accounting fraud.

To ensure audits are performed appropriately, the American Institute of Certified Public Accountants (AICPA) requires all of its members to adhere to a professional code of ethics and professional auditing standards. The Sarbanes-Oxley Act also requires that auditors of public companies follow additional rules established by the PCAOB.

Intentional financial misreporting is both unethical and illegal. Initially, some people may appear to benefit from fraudulent reporting. Managers may negotiate bank loans that the business would not otherwise obtain, employees may receive higher bonuses and save their jobs, and stockholders may enjoy temporarily higher stock prices. However, in the long run, most individuals and organizations are harmed. When fraud is uncovered, the company's stock price usually drops dramatically. In a case involving MicroStrategy, the stock price dropped 65 percent in a single day, from $243 on Friday to $86 per share on Monday. Creditors also are harmed by fraud. The most recent statistics show that

WorldCom's creditors recovered only 42 percent of what they were owed. They lost $36 billion. Innocent employees also are harmed by fraud. In the case of Enron, 5,600 employees lost their jobs and many lost all their retirement savings. Finally, customers can be hurt by fraud by having to pay higher prices for the company's goods or services, because the fraud either inappropriately inflated company costs or caused the company to charge higher prices to recover other costs of the fraud.

Ethical Insights

More than a Paper Cut

The independent auditing firm of Arthur Andersen was convicted in 2002 of obstructing justice by shredding documents vital to the SEC's investigation of the Enron fraud. The judge sentenced the firm to pay a $500,000 fine and serve five years of probation. Upon appeal in 2005, the conviction was overturned for legal technicalities. By that time, it was too late for Arthur Andersen. All of its clients had found other professional service providers, and all but 200 of its 28,000 employees had left to find jobs elsewhere. In effect, the accounting firm had been given the death penalty.

Laurie's advice to Mauricio and to all managers is to strive to create an ethical environment and establish a strong system of checks and controls inside the company. Do not put up with blatant acts of fraud, such as employees making up false expenses for reimbursement, punching in a time card belonging to a fellow employee who will be late for work, or copying someone's ideas and claiming them as his or her own. Also, be aware that not all ethical dilemmas are clear-cut. Some situations will require you to weigh one moral principle (e.g., honesty) against another (e.g., loyalty). Advise your employees that, when faced with an ethical dilemma, they should follow a three-step process:

1. Identify who will benefit from the situation (often, the manager or employee) and how others will be harmed (other employees, the company's reputation, owners, creditors, and the public in general).
2. Identify the alternative courses of action.
3. Choose the alternative that is the most ethical—that which you would be proud to have reported in the news. Often, there is no one right answer and hard choices will need to be made. But strong ethical practices are a key part of ensuring good financial reporting by businesses of all sizes.

Epilogue

Mauricio Rosa's dream has become reality. Pizza Aroma has been voted the "Best Pizza" maker by the *Ithaca Times* readers' poll several years in a row. And two of the authors of this text are among Pizza Aroma's most regular customers.

SUPPLEMENT: ACCOUNTING CAREERS

According to the government's labor department, accounting is one of the fastest growing fields, with 49,000 new jobs a year expected to be added through 2014. Exhibit 1S.1 summarizes the career opportunities available in private and public accounting. Accountants employed by a single organization are in private accounting. Accountants,

EXHIBIT 1S.1 Overview of Career Choices in Accounting

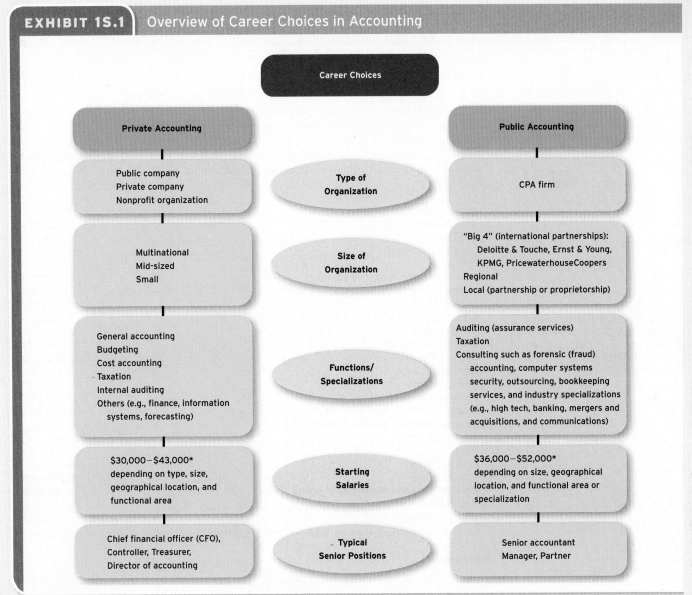

* Amounts have been rounded and were current as of December 2006.
Source: www.collegegrad.com/careers/all.shtml.

like Laurie, who charge fees for services to a variety of organizations, are in public accounting. Accounting graduates often start their careers in public accounting firms and then at some point move into private accounting within business, governmental organizations such as the Internal Revenue Service (IRS) and Federal Bureau of Investigation (FBI), or not-for-profit organizations (NPOs). Many become top managers of large companies. Some even enter academia after earning a graduate degree to teach and conduct research.

Accountants may pursue a variety of certifications, including the CPA (Certified Public Accountant), CFE (Certified Fraud Examiner), CMA (Certified Management Accountant), CIA (Certified Internal Auditor), CFM (Certified Financial Manager), Cr. FA (Certified Forensic Accountant) and CFA (Chartered Financial Analyst), among others. For additional information on accounting careers, certifications, salaries, and opportunities, visit www.aicpa.org, www.collegegrad.com, and www.imanet.org.

REVIEW THE CHAPTER

DEMONSTRATION CASE

www.mhhe.com/phillips2e

The introductory case presented here reviews the items reported on the income statement, statement of retained earnings, and balance sheet, using the financial statements of Under Armour Inc.— a public company founded in 1996 by a former University of Maryland football player to develop, market, and distribute athletic apparel and gear. Following is a list of items and amounts adapted from Under Armour Inc.'s financial statements for the quarter ended March 31, 2006.

Accounts payable	$ 45,650,000
Accounts receivable	63,217,000
Cash	58,292,000
Contributed capital	123,899,000
Dividends	0
General and administrative expenses	30,132,000
Income tax expense	5,944,000
Inventories	53,475,000
Net income	8,734,000
Notes payable	4,605,000
Operating expenses	43,384,000
Other assets	12,588,000
Other liabilities	276,000
Other revenues	498,000
Property and equipment	23,659,000
Retained earnings, March 31, 2006	36,801,000
Retained earnings, January 1, 2006	28,067,000
Sales revenues	87,696,000
Total assets	211,231,000
Total expenses	79,460,000
Total liabilities	50,531,000
Total liabilities and stockholders' equity	211,231,000
Total revenues	88,194,000
Total stockholders' equity	160,700,000

COACH'S TIP

Notes payable are like accounts payable except that they (a) charge interest, (b) can be outstanding for periods longer than one year, and (c) are documented using formal documents called notes.

Required:

1. Prepare an income statement, statement of retained earnings, and a balance sheet for the quarter, following the formats in Exhibits 1.3, 1.4, and 1.5.
2. Describe the content of these three statements.
3. Name the other statement that Under Armour would include in its financial statements.
4. Did financing for Under Armour's assets come primarily from liabilities or stockholders' equity?
5. Explain why Under Armour would subject its statements to an independent audit.

EXHIBIT 1S.1 Overview of Career Choices in Accounting

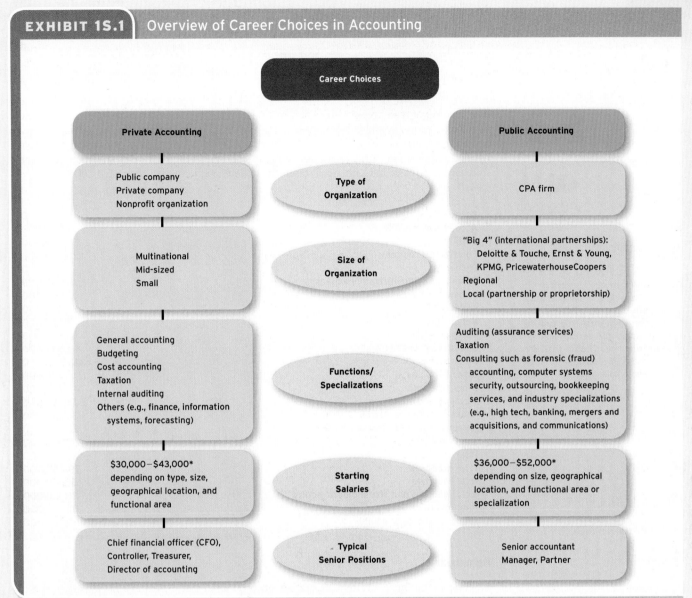

Career Choices

Private Accounting	Type of Organization	Public Accounting
Public company Private company Nonprofit organization	**Type of Organization**	CPA firm
Multinational Mid-sized Small	**Size of Organization**	"Big 4" (international partnerships): Deloitte & Touche, Ernst & Young, KPMG, PricewaterhouseCoopers Regional Local (partnership or proprietorship)
General accounting Budgeting Cost accounting Taxation Internal auditing Others (e.g., finance, information systems, forecasting)	**Functions/ Specializations**	Auditing (assurance services) Taxation Consulting such as forensic (fraud) accounting, computer systems security, outsourcing, bookkeeping services, and industry specializations (e.g., high tech, banking, mergers and acquisitions, and communications)
$30,000–$43,000* depending on type, size, geographical location, and functional area	**Starting Salaries**	$36,000–$52,000* depending on size, geographical location, and functional area or specialization
Chief financial officer (CFO), Controller, Treasurer, Director of accounting	**Typical Senior Positions**	Senior accountant Manager, Partner

* Amounts have been rounded and were current as of December 2006.
Source: www.collegegrad.com/careers/all.shtml.

like Laurie, who charge fees for services to a variety of organizations, are in public accounting. Accounting graduates often start their careers in public accounting firms and then at some point move into private accounting within business, governmental organizations such as the Internal Revenue Service (IRS) and Federal Bureau of Investigation (FBI), or not-for-profit organizations (NPOs). Many become top managers of large companies. Some even enter academia after earning a graduate degree to teach and conduct research.

Accountants may pursue a variety of certifications, including the CPA (Certified Public Accountant), CFE (Certified Fraud Examiner), CMA (Certified Management Accountant), CIA (Certified Internal Auditor), CFM (Certified Financial Manager), Cr. FA (Certified Forensic Accountant) and CFA (Chartered Financial Analyst), among others. For additional information on accounting careers, certifications, salaries, and opportunities, visit www.aicpa.org, www.collegegrad.com, and www.imanet.org.

REVIEW THE CHAPTER

DEMONSTRATION CASE

UNDER ARMOUR®

www.mhhe.com/phillips2e

The introductory case presented here reviews the items reported on the income statement, statement of retained earnings, and balance sheet, using the financial statements of Under Armour Inc.— a public company founded in 1996 by a former University of Maryland football player to develop, market, and distribute athletic apparel and gear. Following is a list of items and amounts adapted from Under Armour Inc.'s financial statements for the quarter ended March 31, 2006.

Accounts payable	$ 45,650,000
Accounts receivable	63,217,000
Cash	58,292,000
Contributed capital	123,899,000
Dividends	0
General and administrative expenses	30,132,000
Income tax expense	5,944,000
Inventories	53,475,000
Net income	8,734,000
Notes payable	4,605,000
Operating expenses	43,384,000
Other assets	12,588,000
Other liabilities	276,000
Other revenues	498,000
Property and equipment	23,659,000
Retained earnings, March 31, 2006	36,801,000
Retained earnings, January 1, 2006	28,067,000
Sales revenues	87,696,000
Total assets	211,231,000
Total expenses	79,460,000
Total liabilities	50,531,000
Total liabilities and stockholders' equity	211,231,000
Total revenues	88,194,000
Total stockholders' equity	160,700,000

COACH'S TIP

Notes payable are like accounts payable except that they (a) charge interest, (b) can be outstanding for periods longer than one year, and (c) are documented using formal documents called notes.

Required:

1. Prepare an income statement, statement of retained earnings, and a balance sheet for the quarter, following the formats in Exhibits 1.3, 1.4, and 1.5.
2. Describe the content of these three statements.
3. Name the other statement that Under Armour would include in its financial statements.
4. Did financing for Under Armour's assets come primarily from liabilities or stockholders' equity?
5. Explain why Under Armour would subject its statements to an independent audit.

Suggested Solution

1.

UNDER ARMOUR INC.
Income Statement
For the Quarter Ended March 31, 2006
(in thousands of dollars)

Revenues	
Sales revenues	$87,696
Other revenues	498
Total revenues	88,194
Expenses	
Operating expenses	43,384
General and administrative expenses	30,132
Income tax expense	5,944
Total expenses	79,460
Net income	$ 8,734

UNDER ARMOUR INC.
Statement of Retained Earnings
For the Quarter Ended March 31, 2006
(in thousands of dollars)

Retained Earnings, January 1, 2006	$28,067
Add: Net income	8,734
Subtract: Dividends	0
Retained Earnings, March 31, 2006	$36,801

UNDER ARMOUR INC.
Balance Sheet
At March 31, 2006
(in thousands of dollars)

Assets	
Cash	$ 58,292
Accounts receivable	63,217
Inventories	53,475
Property and equipment	23,659
Other assets	12,588
Total assets	$211,231
Liabilities	
Accounts payable	$ 45,650
Notes payable	4,605
Other liabilities	276
Total liabilities	50,531
Stockholders' Equity	
Contributed capital	123,899
Retained earnings	36,801
Total stockholders' equity	160,700
Total liabilities and stockholders' equity	$211,231

2. The income statement reports the most common measure of financial performance for a business: net income (revenues minus expenses during the accounting period). The statement of retained earnings links the net income number from the income statement to the end-of-period retained earnings balance on the balance sheet. The income statement reports the amount of assets, liabilities, and stockholders' equity of a business at a point in time.

3. Under Armour would also present a statement of cash flows.

4. Financing for Under Armour's assets is provided primarily from stockholders' equity ($160,700) rather than liabilities ($50,531).

5. Like all public companies, Under Armour will subject its financial statements to an audit because it is required by the SEC to have an independent audit. Also, an audit will give users greater confidence in the accuracy of financial statement information because the people who audited the statements are required to meet professional standards of ethics and competence.

CHAPTER SUMMARY

LO1   Describe various organizational forms and business decision makers. p. 4

-   Sole proprietorships are owned by one individual, are relatively inexpensive to form, and are not treated legally as separate from their owners. Thus, all profits or losses become part of the taxable income to the owner who is also responsible personally for all debts of the business.

-   Partnerships are businesses legally similar to proprietorships, but with two or more owners.

-   Corporations are separate legal entities (thus, corporations pay taxes) that sell shares of stock to investors (stockholders) and are more costly to establish. Stockholders cannot be held liable for more than their investment in the corporation. Private corporations sell stock to a few individuals while public corporations sell stock in the stock market.

-   Business decision makers include creditors (banks, suppliers), investors (stockholders), customers, governments, and other external users.

LO2   Describe the purpose, structure, and content of the four basic financial statements. p. 7

-   The *income statement* reports the net amount that a business earned (net income) over a period of time by subtracting the costs of running the business (expenses) from the total amount earned (revenues).

-   The *statement of retained earnings* explains changes in the retained earnings account over a period of time by considering increases (from net income) and decreases (from dividends to stockholders).

-   The *balance sheet* reports what the business owns (reported as assets) at a particular point in time and how much of the financing for these assets came from creditors (reported as liabilities) and stockholders (reported as stockholders' equity).

-   The *statement of cash flows* explains changes in the cash account over a period of time by reporting inflows and outflows of cash from the business's operating, investing, and financing activities.

LO3   Explain how financial statements are relevant to users. p. 17

-   Creditors are mainly interested in assessing whether the company: (1) is generating enough cash to make payments on its loan, and (2) has enough assets to cover its liabilities. Answers to these questions are indicated by the statement of cash flows and the balance sheet.

-   Investors look closely at the income statement for information about a company's ability to generate profits, and at the statement of retained earnings for information about a company's dividend distributions.

LO4   Describe factors that enhance the reliability of financial reporting. p. 18

-   Reliable financial reporting is enhanced by applying generally accepted accounting principles in an ethical business environment.

-   Reliable financial reporting is further enhanced through the involvement of regulators, like the Public Company Accounting Oversight Board (PCAOB) and the Securities and Exchange Commission (SEC), and regulations like the Sarbanes-Oxley Act of 2002.

KEY TERMS

Accounting p. 5
Accounts p. 11
Balance Sheet p. 9
Basic Accounting Equation p. 8

Financial Statements p. 7
Generally Accepted Accounting
   Principles (GAAP) p. 18
Income Statement p. 9

Sarbanes-Oxley Act of 2002 (SOX) p. 19
Separate Entity Assumption p. 8
Statement of Retained Earnings p. 10
Unit of Measure Assumption p. 10

PRACTICE MATERIAL

answers page II

QUESTIONS

5 1. Define *accounting*.

6 2. Briefly distinguish financial accounting from managerial accounting.

6 3. The accounting process generates financial reports for both internal and external users. Describe some of the specific groups of internal and external users.

8 4. Explain what the separate entity assumption means when it says a business is treated as separate from its owners for accounting purposes.

5. List the three main types of business activities and give an example of each.

10 6. What information should be included in the heading of each of the four primary financial statements?

7. What are the purposes of (*a*) the balance sheet, (*b*) the income statement, (*c*) the statement of retained earnings, and (*d*) the statement of cash flows?

8. Explain why the income statement, statement of retained earnings, and statement of cash flows would be dated "For the Year Ended December 31, 2007," whereas the balance sheet would be dated "At December 31, 2007."

9. Briefly explain the difference between *net income* and *net loss*.

10. Describe the basic accounting equation that provides the structure for the balance sheet. Define the three major components reported on the balance sheet.

11. Describe the equation that provides the structure for the income statement. Explain the three major items reported on the income statement.

12. Describe the equation that provides the structure for the statement of retained earnings. Explain the four major items reported on the statement of retained earnings.

13. Describe the equation that provides the structure for the statement of cash flows. Explain the three major types of activities reported on the statement.

14. Briefly describe the organizations that are responsible for developing accounting measurement rules (generally accepted accounting principles) in the United States.

15. Briefly explain the impact of financial statement fraud and the steps that have been taken to address it.

16. Briefly define what an ethical dilemma is and describe the steps to consider when evaluating ethical dilemmas.

17. In what ways might accounting frauds be similar to cases of academic dishonesty?

MULTIPLE CHOICE

1. Which of the following is *not* one of the four basic financial statements?
   a. The balance sheet
   b. The audit report
   c. The income statement
   d. The statement of cash flows

Topic Tackler

Quiz1

PLUS

Check out www.mhhe.com/phillips2e to practice more multiple choice questions.

2. Which of the following is true regarding the income statement?

   a. The income statement is sometimes called the statement of operations.

   b. The income statement reports revenues, expenses, and liabilities.

   c. The income statement only reports revenue for which cash was received at the point of sale.

   d. The income statement reports the financial position of a business at a particular point in time.

3. Which of the following is false regarding the balance sheet?

   a. The accounts shown on a balance sheet represent the basic accounting equation for a particular business.

   b. The retained earnings balance shown on the balance sheet must agree to the ending retained earnings balance shown on the statement of retained earnings.

   c. The balance sheet summarizes the net changes in specific account balances over a period of time.

   d. The balance sheet reports the amount of assets, liabilities, and stockholders' equity of a business at a point in time.

4. Which of the following regarding retained earnings is false?

   a. Retained earnings is increased by net income.

   b. Retained earnings is a component of stockholders' equity on the balance sheet.

   c. Retained earnings is an asset on the balance sheet.

   d. Retained earnings represents earnings not distributed to stockholders in the form of dividends.

5. Which of the following is not one of the items required to be shown in the heading of a financial statement?

   a. The financial statement preparer's name.

   b. The title of the financial statement.

   c. The financial reporting date or period.

   d. The name of the business entity.

6. Which of the following statements regarding the statement of cash flows is false?

   a. The statement of cash flows separates cash inflows and outflows into three major categories: operating, investing, and financing.

   b. The ending cash balance shown on the statement of cash flows must agree with the amount shown on the balance sheet at the end of the same period.

   c. The total increase or decrease in cash shown on the statement of cash flows must agree with the "bottom line" (net income or net loss) reported on the income statement.

   d. The statement of cash flows covers a period of time.

7. Which of the following regarding GAAP is true?

   a. GAAP is an abbreviation for goodie, another accounting problem.

   b. Changes in GAAP do not affect the amount of income reported by a company.

   c. GAAP is the abbreviation for generally accepted accounting principles.

   d. Changes to GAAP must be approved by the Senate Finance Committee.

8. Which of the following is true?

   a. FASB creates SEC.

   b. GAAP creates FASB.

   c. SEC creates CPA.

   d. FASB creates GAAP.

9. Which of the following would *not* be a goal of external users reading a company's financial statements?

   a. Understanding the current financial state of the company.

   b. Assessing the company's contribution to social and environmental policies.

c. Predicting the company's future financial performance.

d. Evaluating the company's ability to generate cash from sales.

10. Which of the following is not required by the Sarbanes-Oxley Act of 2002?

  a. Top managers of public companies must sign a report certifying their responsibilities for the financial statements.

  b. Public companies must maintain an audited system of internal control to ensure accuracy in accounting reports.

  c. Public companies must maintain an independent committee to meet with the company's independent auditors.

  d. Top managers of public companies must be members of the American Institute of Certified Public Accountants.

MINI-EXERCISES

Available with McGraw-Hill's Homework Manager   HOMEWORK MANAGER **PLUS**

M1-1 Identifying Definitions with Abbreviations   LO3

The following is a list of important abbreviations used in the chapter. These abbreviations also are used widely in business. For each abbreviation, give the full designation. The first one is an example.

Abbreviation	Full Designation
1. CPA	Certified Public Accountant
2. GAAP	_____
3. FASB	_____
4. SEC	_____

M1-2 Matching Definitions with Terms or Abbreviations   LO1, LO2, LO3

Match each definition with its related term or abbreviation by entering the appropriate letter in the space provided.

Term or Abbreviation	Definition
____ 1. SEC	A. A system that collects and processes financial information about an organization and reports that information to decision makers.
____ 2. Investing activities	B. Measurement of information about a business in the monetary unit (dollars or other national currency).
____ 3. Private company	C. An unincorporated business owned by two or more persons.
____ 4. Corporation	D. A company that sells shares of its stock privately and is not required to release its financial statements to the public.
____ 5. Accounting	E. An incorporated business that issues shares of stock as evidence of ownership.
____ 6. Partnership	F. Buying and selling productive resources with long lives.
____ 7. FASB	G. Transactions with lenders (borrowing and repaying cash) and stockholders (selling company stock and paying dividends).
____ 8. Financing activities	H. Activities directly related to running the business to earn profit.
____ 9. Unit of measure	I. Securities and Exchange Commission.
____ 10. GAAP	J. Financial Accounting Standards Board.
____ 11. Public company	K. A company that has its stock bought and sold by investors on established stock exchanges.
____ 12. Operating activities	L. Generally accepted accounting principles.

LO1, LO2, LO3   **M1-3 Matching Definitions with Terms**

Match each definition with its related term by entering the appropriate letter in the space provided.

Term	Definition
___ 1. Relevance	A. The financial reports of a business are assumed to include the results of only that business's activities.
___ 2. Reliability	B. The resources owned by a business.
___ 3. Comparability	C. Financial information that can be compared over time because similar accounting methods have been applied.
___ 4. Consistency	D. The total amounts invested and reinvested in the business by its owners.
___ 5. Assets	E. The costs of business necessary to earn revenues.
___ 6. Liabilities	F. A feature of financial information that allows it to influence a decision.
___ 7. Stockholders' equity	G. Earned by selling goods or services to customers.
___ 8. Revenues	H. The amounts owed by the business.
___ 9. Expenses	I. Financial information that is unbiased and verifiable.
___ 10. Unit of measure	J. The assumption that states that results of business activities should be reported in an appropriate monetary unit.
___ 11. Separate entity	K. Financial information that can be compared across businesses because similar accounting methods have been applied.

LO2   **M1-4 Matching Financial Statement Items to Balance Sheet and Income Statement Categories**

P&G

According to its annual report, "Procter & Gamble markets a broad range of laundry, cleaning, paper, beauty care, health care, food and beverage products in more than 140 countries around the world, with leading brands including Tide, Ariel, Crest, Crisco, Vicks and Max Factor." The following are items taken from its recent balance sheet and income statement. Mark each item in the following list with letters to indicate whether it would be reported as an <u>A</u>sset, <u>L</u>iability, or <u>S</u>tockholders' <u>E</u>quity account on the balance sheet or a <u>R</u>evenue or <u>E</u>xpense account on the income statement.

___ 1. Accounts payable		___ 5. Selling and administrative expenses
___ 2. Accounts receivable		___ 6. Sales revenue
___ 3. Cash		___ 7. Notes payable
___ 4. Income tax expense		___ 8. Retained earnings

LO2   **M1-5 Matching Financial Statement Items to Balance Sheet and Income Statement Categories**

Mark each item in the following list with letters to indicate whether it would be reported as an <u>A</u>sset, <u>L</u>iability, or <u>S</u>tockholders' <u>E</u>quity account on the balance sheet or a <u>R</u>evenue or <u>E</u>xpense account on the income statement.

___ 1. Accounts receivable	___ 5. Cash
___ 2. Sales revenue	___ 6. Advertising expense
___ 3. Equipment	___ 7. Accounts payable
___ 4. Supplies expense	___ 8. Retained earnings

LO2   **M1-6 Matching Financial Statement Items to Balance Sheet and Income Statement Categories**

Tootsie Roll Industries manufactures and sells more than 60 million Tootsie Rolls and 20 million Tootsie Roll Pops each day. The following items were listed on Tootsie Roll's recent income statement and balance sheet. Mark each item from the balance sheet as an <u>A</u>sset, <u>L</u>iability, or <u>S</u>tockholders' <u>E</u>quity and each item from the income statement as a <u>R</u>evenue or <u>E</u>xpense.

___ 1. Accounts receivable	___ 6. Sales revenue
___ 2. Selling and administrative expenses	___ 7. Notes payable to banks
___ 3. Cash	___ 8. Retained earnings
___ 4. Machinery	___ 9. Accounts payable
___ 5. Promotion and advertising expenses	

M1-7 Matching Financial Statement Items to Balance Sheet and Income Statement Categories

General Mills is a manufacturer of food products, such as Lucky Charms cereal, Pillsbury crescent rolls, and Jolly Green Giant vegetables. The following items were presented in the company's financial statements. Mark each item from the balance sheet as an <u>A</u>sset, <u>L</u>iability, or <u>S</u>tockholders' <u>E</u>quity and each item from the income statement as a <u>R</u>evenue or <u>E</u>xpense.

LO2

GENERAL MILLS

____ 1. Accounts payable   ____ 6. Cash

____ 2. Contributed capital   ____ 7. Retained earnings

____ 3. Equipment   ____ 8. Selling and administrative expenses

____ 4. Accounts receivable   ____ 9. Sales revenue

____ 5. Notes payable   ____ 10. Supplies

M1-8 Matching Financial Statement Items to Balance Sheet and Income Statement Categories

Microsoft Corporation manufactures home entertainment devices like Xbox®, creates software like Word®, and operates networks like MSN Hotmail®. The following items were presented in the company's financial statements. Mark each item from the balance sheet as an <u>A</u>sset, <u>L</u>iability, or <u>S</u>tockholders' <u>E</u>quity and each item from the income statement as a <u>R</u>evenue or <u>E</u>xpense.

LO2

Microsoft Corporation

____ 1. Accounts payable   ____ 6. Contributed capital

____ 2. Cash   ____ 7. Accounts receivable

____ 3. Retained earnings   ____ 8. Sales revenue

____ 4. Property and equipment   ____ 9. Selling and administrative expenses

____ 5. Notes payable   ____ 10. Promotion expense

M1-9 Matching Financial Statement Items to the Four Basic Financial Statements

LO2

Match each element with its financial statement by entering the appropriate letter in the space provided.

Element	Financial Statement
____ 1. Cash flows from financing activities	A. Balance sheet
____ 2. Expenses	B. Income statement
____ 3. Cash flow from investing activities	C. Statement of retained earnings
____ 4. Assets	D. Statement of cash flows
____ 5. Dividends	
____ 6. Revenues	
____ 7. Cash flows from operating activities	
____ 8. Liabilities	

M1-10 Matching Financial Statement Items to the Four Basic Financial Statements

LO2

Oakley, Inc., manufactures sunglasses, goggles, shoes, watches, footwear, and clothing. Recently, the company reported the following items in its financial statements. Indicate whether these items appeared on the balance sheet (B/S), income statement (I/S), statement of retained earnings (SRE), or statement of cash flows (SCF).

____ 1. Dividends

____ 2. Total stockholders' equity

____ 3. Sales revenue

____ 4. Total assets

____ 5. Cash flows from operating activities

____ 6. Total liabilities

____ 7. Net income

____ 8. Cash flows from financing activities

LO2

M1-11 Reporting Amounts on the Statement of Cash Flows

Learning which items belong in each cash flow statement category is an important first step in understanding their meaning. Use a letter to mark each item in the following list as a cash flow from Operating, Investing, or Financing activities. **Put parentheses around the letter if it is a cash *outflow* and use no parentheses if it's an *inflow*.**

_____ 1. Cash paid for dividends

_____ 2. Cash collected from customers

_____ 3. Cash received when signing a note

_____ 4. Cash paid to suppliers and employees

_____ 5. Cash paid to purchase equipment

_____ 6. Cash received from issuing stock

LO2

M1-12 Reporting Amounts on the Statement of Cash Flows

Learning which items belong in each category of the statement of cash flows is an important first step in understanding their meaning. Use a letter to mark each item in the following list as a cash flow from Operating, Investing, or Financing activities. **Put parentheses around the letter if it is a cash *outflow* and use no parentheses if it's an *inflow*.**

_____ 1. Cash paid to purchase equipment

_____ 2. Cash collected from customers

_____ 3. Cash received from selling equipment

_____ 4. Cash paid for dividends

_____ 5. Cash paid to suppliers and employees

_____ 6. Cash received from issuing stock

LO2

M1-13 Preparing a Statement of Retained Earnings

Stone Culture Corporation was organized on January 1, 2005. For its first two years of operations, it reported the following:

Net income for 2005	$ 36,000
Net income for 2006	45,000
Dividends for 2005	15,000
Dividends for 2006	20,000
Total assets at the end of 2005	125,000
Total assets at the end of 2006	242,000

On the basis of the data given, prepare a statement of retained earnings for 2005 (its first year of operations) and 2006. Show computations.

LO2

Southwest Airlines, Inc.

M1-14 Preparing an Income Statement, Statement of Retained Earnings, and Balance Sheet

The following accounts are taken from the December 31, 2005, financial statements of Southwest Airlines, Inc.

Cash	$2,280,000,000
Interest expense	83,000,000
Accounts receivable	509,000,000
Salaries expense	2,702,000,000
Supplies	150,000,000
Contributed capital	2,118,000,000
Other revenue	137,000,000
Property and equipment	9,427,000,000
Income tax expense	326,000,000
Landing fees expense	454,000,000
Other assets	1,852,000,000
Other operating expenses	1,836,000,000
Aircraft fuel expense	1,342,000,000
Repairs and maintenance expense	430,000,000
Dividends	14,000,000
Accounts payable	1,774,000,000
Other liabilities	2,074,000,000
Notes payable	3,695,000,000
Retained earnings (as of December 31, 2005)	4,557,000,000
Ticket revenues	7,584,000,000

1. Prepare an income statement for the year ended December 31, 2005.
   TIP: Round the reported amounts to an appropriate unit of measure.
2. Prepare a statement of retained earnings for the period ended December 31, 2005.
   TIP: Assume the balance in retained earnings was $4,023,000,000 at January 1, 2005.
3. Prepare a balance sheet at December 31, 2005.
4. Using the balance sheet, indicate whether the total assets of Southwest Airlines at the end of the year were financed primarily by liabilities or stockholders' equity.

EXERCISES

Available with McGraw-Hill's
Homework Manager

HOMEWORK MANAGER **PLUS**

E1-1 **Reporting Amounts on the Four Basic Financial Statements**

LO2

Using the figures listed in the table below and the equations underlying each of the four basic financial statements, show (*a*) that the balance sheet is in balance, (*b*) that net income is properly calculated, (*c*) what caused changes in the retained earnings account, and (*d*) what caused changes in the cash account.

Assets	$18,200	Beginning retained earnings	$3,500
Liabilities	13,750	Ending retained earnings	4,300
Stockholders' equity	4,450	Cash flows from operating activities	1,600
Revenue	10,500	Cash flows from investing activities	(1,000)
Expenses	9,200	Cash flows from financing activities	(900)
Net income	1,300	Beginning cash	1,000
Dividends	500	Ending cash	700

E1-2 **Reporting Amounts on the Four Basic Financial Statements**

LO2

Using the figures listed in the table below and the equations underlying each of the four basic financial statements, show (*a*) that the balance sheet is in balance, (*b*) that net income is properly calculated, (*c*) what caused changes in the retained earnings account, and (*d*) what caused changes in the cash account.

Assets	$79,500	Beginning retained earnings	$20,500
Liabilities	18,500	Ending retained earnings	28,750
Stockholders' equity	61,000	Cash flows from operating activities	15,700
Revenue	32,100	Cash flows from investing activities	(7,200)
Expenses	18,950	Cash flows from financing activities	(5,300)
Net Income	13,150	Beginning cash	3,200
Dividends	4,900	Ending cash	6,400

E1-3 **Preparing a Balance Sheet**

LO2, LO3
DSW Inc.

DSW is a designer shoe warehouse, selling some of the most luxurious and fashionable shoes at prices that people can actually afford. Its year-end balance sheet, at January 28, 2006, contained the following items (in thousands).

Accounts payable	$ 85,820
Accounts receivable	4,088
Cash	124,759
Contributed capital	278,709
Notes payable	63,410
Other assets	282,947
Other liabilities	53,769
Property, plant, and equipment	95,921
Retained earnings	26,007
Total assets	507,715
Total liabilities and stockholders' equity	?

Required:

1. Prepare the balance sheet as of January 28, solving for the missing amount.
2. As of January 28, did most of the financing for assets come from creditors or stockholders?

LO2, LO3   **E1-4 Completing a Balance Sheet and Inferring Net Income**

Ken Young and Kim Sherwood organized Reader Direct as a corporation; each contributed $49,000 cash to start the business and received 4,000 shares of stock. The store completed its first year of operations on December 31, 2008. On that date, the following financial items for the year were determined: December 31, 2008, cash on hand and in the bank, $47,500; December 31, 2008, amounts due from customers from sales of books, $26,900; property and equipment, $48,000; December 31, 2008, amounts owed to publishers for books purchased, $8,000; one-year note payable to a local bank for $2,850. No dividends were declared or paid to the stockholders during the year.

Required:

1. Complete the following balance sheet as December 31, 2008.

Assets		Liabilities and Stockholders' Equity	
Cash	$____	Liabilities	
Accounts receivable	____	Accounts payable	$____
Property and equipment	____	Note payable	____
		Total liabilities	____
		Stockholders' Equity	
		Contributed capital	____
		Retained earnings	13,550
		Total stockholders' equity	____
Total assets	$____	Total liabilities and stockholders' equity	$____

2. Using the retained earnings equation and an opening balance of $0, compute the amount of net income for the year ended December 31, 2008.
3. As of December 31, 2008, did most of the financing for assets come from creditors or stockholders?
4. Assuming that Reader Direct generates net income of $3,000 and pays dividends of $2,000 in 2009, what would be the ending retained earnings balance at December 31, 2009?

LO2   **E1-5 Labeling and Classifying Business Transactions**

K·Swiss Inc.

The following items relate to business transactions involving K·Swiss Inc.

a. Coins and currency
b. Amounts K·Swiss owes to suppliers of watches
c. Amounts K·Swiss is owed by customers
d. Amounts owed to bank for loan to buy building
e. Property on which buildings will be built
f. Amounts paid from profits to stockholders
g. Earned by K·Swiss by selling watches
h. Unused paper in K·Swiss head office
i. Cost of paper used up during month
j. Amounts given to K·Swiss by stockholders

Required:

1. Identify an appropriate label (account name) for each item as it would be reported in the company's financial statements.
2. Classify each item as an asset (A), liability (L), stockholders' equity (SE), revenue (R), or expense (E).

E1-6 Preparing an Income Statement and Inferring Missing Values

Regal Entertainment Group operates movie theaters and food concession counters throughout the United States. Its income statement for the quarter ended September 28, 2006, reported the following amounts (in thousands):

Admissions revenues	$450,600
Concessions expenses	27,700
Concessions revenues	181,000
Film rental expenses	241,100
General and administrative expenses	65,800
Net Income	?
Other expenses	230,800
Other revenues	44,100
Rent expense	81,000
Total expenses	?

LO2, LO3

Regal Entertainment Group

Required:

1. Solve for the missing amounts and prepare an income statement for the quarter ended September 28, 2006.

   TIP: First put the items in the order they would appear on the income statement and then solve for the missing values

2. What is Regal's main source of revenue and biggest expense?

E1-7 Analyzing Revenues and Expenses and Completing an Income Statement

LO2

Home Realty, Incorporated, has been operating for three years and is owned by three investors. J. Doe owns 60 percent of the total outstanding stock of 9,000 shares and is the managing executive in charge. On December 31, 2007, the following financial items for the entire year were determined: sales revenue, $166,000; selling expenses, $97,000; interest expense, $6,300; promotion and advertising expenses, $9,025; and income tax expense, $18,500. Also during the year, the company declared and paid the owners dividends amounting to $12,000. Complete the following income statement:

_____		
_____		
_____		
Revenues		
Sales revenue		$_____
Expenses		
Selling expenses	$_____	
Interest expense	_____	
Promotion and advertising expenses	_____	
Income tax expense	_____	
Total expenses		_____
Net income		$ 35,175

E1-8 Inferring Values Using the Income Statement and Balance Sheet Equations

LO2

Review the chapter explanations of the income statement and the balance sheet equations. Apply these equations in each of the following independent cases to compute the two missing amounts for each case. Assume that it is the end of 2007, the first full year of operations for the company.

TIP: First identify the numerical relations among the columns using the balance sheet and income statement equations. Then compute the missing amounts.

Independent Cases	Total Revenues	Total Expenses	Net Income (Loss)	Total Assets	Total Liabilities	Stockholders' Equity
A	$100,000	$82,000	$	$150,000	$70,000	$
B		80,000	12,000	112,000		60,000
C	80,000	86,000		104,000	26,000	
D	50,000		13,000		22,000	77,000
E		81,000	(6,000)		73,000	28,000

LO2, LO3 **E1-9 Preparing an Income Statement and Balance Sheet**

Five individuals organized Miami Clay Corporation on January 1, 2009. At the end of January 2009, the following monthly financial data are available:

Total revenues	$131,000
Operating expenses	90,500
Cash balance, January 31, 2009	30,800
Accounts receivable from customers	25,300
Supplies	40,700
Accounts payable (will be paid during February 2009)	25,700
Contributed capital (2,600 shares)	30,600

No dividends were declared or paid during January.

Required:

1. Complete the following income statement and balance sheet for the month of January.

MIAMI CLAY CORPORATION
Income Statement
For the Month of January 2009

Total revenues	$_____
Operating expenses	_____
Net income	$_____

MIAMI CLAY CORPORATION
Balance Sheet
At January 31, 2009

Assets	
Cash	$_____
Accounts receivable	_____
Supplies	_____
Total assets	$_____
Liabilities	
Accounts payable	$_____
Total liabilities	_____
Stockholders' Equity	
Contributed capital	_____
Retained earnings	_____
Total stockholders' equity	_____
Total liabilities and stockholders' equity	$_____

2. Discuss whether Miami Clay Corporation will be able to pay its liabilities. Consider the relationship between total assets and total liabilities.

E1-10 Analyzing and Interpreting an Income Statement

LO3

Three individuals organized Pest Away Corporation on January 1, 2007, to provide insect extermination services. The company paid $10,000 of dividends during the year. At the end of 2007, the following income statement was prepared:

PEST AWAY COROPRATION		
Income Statement		
For the Year Ended December 31, 2007		
Revenues		
Sales revenue (cash)	$192,000	
Sales revenue (credit)	24,000	
Total revenues		$216,000
Expenses		
Supplies expense	$ 76,000	
Salaries and wages expense	33,000	
Advertising expense	22,000	
Other expenses	46,000	
Total expenses		177,000
Net income		$ 39,000

Required:

1. What was the amount of average monthly revenue?
2. What was the average amount of monthly salaries and wages expense?
3. Explain why advertising is reported as an expense.
4. Explain why the dividends are not reported as an expense.
5. Can you determine how much cash the company had on December 31, 2007? Answer yes or no, and explain your reasoning.

E1-11 Matching Cash Flow Statement Items to Business-Activity Categories

LO2
Tech Data Corporation

Tech Data Corporation is a leading distributor of computer peripherals and network solutions and recently was ranked by *Fortune* as the second most admired company in its industry category. The following items were taken from its recent cash flow statement. Mark each item in the following list with a letter to indicate whether it is a cash flow from Operating, Investing, or Financing activities. **Put parentheses around the letter if it is a cash *outflow* and use no parentheses if it's an *inflow*.**

_____ 1. Cash paid to suppliers and employees

_____ 2. Cash received from customers

_____ 3. Cash received from borrowing long-term debt

_____ 4. Cash received from issuing stock

_____ 5. Cash paid to purchase equipment

E1-12 Matching Cash Flow Statement Items to Business-Activity Categories

LO1
Coca-Cola Company

The Coca-Cola Company is one of the world's leading manufacturers, marketers, and distributors of nonalcoholic beverage concentrates and syrups, producing more than 300 beverage brands. Mark each item in the following list with a letter to indicate whether it is a cash flow from Operating, Investing, or Financing activities. **Put parentheses around the letter if it is a cash *outflow* and use no parentheses if it's an *inflow*.**

_____ 1. Purchases of equipment and other productive assets

_____ 2. Cash received from customers

_____ 3. Cash received from issuing stock

_____ 4. Cash paid to suppliers and employees

_____ 5. Cash paid on notes payable

_____ 6. Cash received from selling equipment

COACHED PROBLEMS

LO2

CP1-1 Preparing an Income Statement, Statement of Retained Earnings, and Balance Sheet

Assume that you are the president of Nuclear Company. At the end of the first year of operations (December 31, 2009), the following financial data for the company are available:

Cash	$12,000
Accounts receivable	59,500
Supplies	8,000
Equipment	36,000
Accounts payable	30,297
Notes payable	1,470
Total sales revenue	88,000
Operating expenses	57,200
Other expenses	8,850
Contributed capital, 7,000 shares outstanding	61,983
Dividends declared and paid during 2009	200

Required:

(Show your computations):

1. Prepare an income statement for the year 2009.
   TIP: Begin by classifying each account as asset, liability, stockholders' equity, revenue, or expense. Then use the format shown in the chapter for presenting an income statement.
2. Prepare a statement of retained earnings for the year ended December 31, 2009.
   TIP: Because this is the first year of operations, the beginning balance in retained earnings will be zero.
3. Prepare a balance sheet at December 31, 2009.
   TIP: The balance sheet reports the ending retained earnings balance from the statement of retained earnings.

LO3

CP1-2 Interpreting the Financial Statements

Refer to CP1-1.

Required:

1. Evaluate whether the company was profitable.
2. Evaluate whether the company could have paid a greater amount for dividends.
3. Evaluate whether the company is financed mainly by creditors or stockholders.
4. Determine the amount of cash increase or decrease that would be shown in the statement of cash flows.

GROUP A PROBLEMS

Available with McGraw-Hill's
Homework Manager

MANAGER **PLUS**

PA1-1 **Preparing an Income Statement, Statement of Retained Earnings, and Balance Sheet**

LO2

Assume that you are the president of High Power Corporation. At the end of the first year of operations (December 31, 2008), the following financial data for the company are available:

Cash	$13,300
Accounts receivable	9,550
Supplies	5,000
Equipment	86,000
Accounts payable	32,087
Notes payable	1,160
Total sales revenue	91,000
Operating expenses	58,700
Other expenses	8,850
Contributed capital, 5,000 shares outstanding	59,103
Dividends declared and paid during 2008	1,950

Required:

(Show your computations):

1. Prepare an income statement for the year 2008.
2. Prepare a statement of retained earnings for the year ended December 31, 2008.
3. Prepare a balance sheet at December 31, 2008.

PA1-2 **Interpreting the Financial Statements**

LO3

Refer to PA1-1.

Required:

1. Evaluate whether the company was profitable.
2. Evaluate whether the company could have paid a greater amount for dividends.
3. Evaluate whether the company is financed mainly by creditors or stockholders.
4. Determine the amount of cash increase or decrease that would be shown in the statement of cash flows.

GROUP B PROBLEMS

PB1-1 **Preparing an Income Statement and Balance Sheet**

LO2

Assume that you are the president of APEC Aerospace Corporation. At the end of the first year of operations (December 31, 2009), the following financial data for the company are available:

Cash	$13,900
Accounts receivable	9,500
Supplies	9,000
Equipment	86,000
Accounts payable	30,277
Notes payable	1,220
Total sales revenue	94,000
Operating expenses	60,000
Other expenses	8,850
Contributed capital, 5,000 shares outstanding	62,853
Dividends declared and paid during 2009	1,100

Required:

(Show your computations):

1. Prepare an income statement for the year 2009.
2. Prepare a statement of retained earnings for the year ended December 31, 2009.
3. Prepare a balance sheet at December 31, 2009.

LO3   **PB1-2 Interpreting the Financial Statements**

Refer to PB1-1

Required:

1. Evaluate whether the company was profitable.
2. Evaluate whether the company could have paid a greater amount for dividends.
3. Evaluate whether the company is financed mainly by creditors or stockholders.
4. Determine the amount of cash increase or decrease that would be shown in the statement of cash flows.

SKILLS DEVELOPMENT CASES

LO1, LO3   **S1-1 Finding Financial Information**

Refer to the financial statements of Landry's Restaurants in Appendix A at the end of this book, or download the annual report from the *Cases* section of the text's Web site at www.mhhe.com/phillips2e.

Required:

1. What is the amount of net income for 2005?
2. What amount of revenue was earned in 2005?
3. How much property and equipment does the company have at the end of 2005?
4. How much does Landry's have in cash at the end of 2005?
5. Landry's stock is traded on the New York Stock Exchange under the symbol LNY. What kind of company does this make Landry's?

LO1, LO2, LO3   **S1-2 Comparing Financial Information**

Refer to the financial statements of Outback Steakhouse, Inc. for the year ended December 31, 2005, in Appendix B at the end of this book, or download the 2005 annual report from the *Cases* section of the text's Web site at www.mhhe.com/phillips2e.

Required:

1. Was Outback's net income for 2005 greater or less than Landry's?
2. Was Outback's revenue for 2005 greater or less than Landry's?
3. Did Outback have more or less property, fixtures, and equipment than Landry's at the end of 2005?
4. Did Outback have more or less cash than Landry's at the end of 2005?
5. Is Outback the same type of business organization as Landry's?
6. On an overall basis, was Outback or Landry's more successful in 2005?

LO1, LO2, LO3   **S1-3 Internet-Based Team Research: Examining an Annual Report**

Reuters

As a team, select an industry to analyze. Reuters provides lists of industries and their makeup at www.investor.reuters.com/Industries.aspx. Each group member should access the annual report (or Form 10-K filed with the SEC) for one publicly traded company in the industry, with each member selecting a different company. (In addition to the company's own Web site, a great source is the SEC's Electronic Data Gathering, Analysis, and Retrieval (EDGAR) service. This free source is available by going to the "Filings & Forms" section of www.sec.gov and clicking on "Search for

Company Filings" and then "Companies & Other Filers." Another great site that pulls information from EDGAR is edgarscan.pwcglobal.com.)

Required:

1. On an individual basis, each team member should write a short report that lists the following information:
   a. What type of business organization is it?
   b. What types of products or services does it sell?
   c. On what day of the year does its fiscal year end?
   d. For how many years does it present complete balance sheets? Income statements? Cash flow statements?
   e. Are its financial statements audited by independent CPAs? If so, by whom?
   f. Did its total assets increase or decrease over the last year?
   g. Did its net income increase or decrease over the last year?

2. Then, as a team, write a short report comparing and contrasting your companies using these attributes. Discuss any patterns across the companies that you as a team observe. Provide potential explanations for any differences discovered.

S1-4 Ethical Decision Making: A Real-Life Example

L02, L03, L04
Adelphia Communications

In June 2005, John Rigas, the 80-year-old founder and former chief executive officer (CEO) of Adelphia Communications was sentenced to 15 years in jail for defrauding investors and lenders of over a billion dollars. His son, the former chief financial officer (CFO), was sentenced to 20 years in jail. To understand the charges, you need to first understand a bit about Adelphia's history. Adelphia started as a one-town cable company in 1952 and, at the time the fraud accusations were made public, had grown into the sixth-largest cable television provider in the country. With the company starting as a family-owned business, Adelphia's operations were always a central part of the personal lives of the Rigas family members. However, the extent to which their personal lives were mixed in with the business activities was never clear to stockholders—at least, not nearly as clear as when they were reported in an article in the August 12, 2002, issue of *Fortune*. Below the following questions we present a table from that article, which summarizes how the Rigas family allegedly used over $1.2 billion of Adelphia's money—money that ultimately belonged to Adelphia's stockholders.

1. What is the accounting concept that the Rigas family is accused of violating?

2. Based on the information provided in the following table, can you determine which of the family's dealings are clearly inappropriate and which are clearly appropriate?

3. As a stockholder, how might you attempt to ensure that this kind of behavior does not occur or, at least, does not occur without you knowing about it?

4. Aside from Adelphia's stockholders, who else might be harmed by these actions committed by the Rigas family?

Family Assets, Sort Of		
Some of the notable ways the Rigas family used Adelphia shareholder dollars.		
On the Receiving End	Who's behind the Entity	How Much?
Dobaire Designs	Adelphia paid this company, owned by Doris Rigas (John's wife), for design services.	$371,000
Wending Creek Farms	Adelphia paid John Rigas's farm for lawn care and snowplowing.	$2 million
SongCatcher Films	Adelphia financed the production of a movie by Ellen Rigas (John's daughter).	$3 million
Eleni Interiors	The company made payments to a furniture store run by Doris Rigas and owned by John.	$12 million
The Golf Club at Wending Creek Farms	Adelphia began developing a ritzy golf club.	$13 million
Wending Creek 3656	The company bought timber rights that would eventually revert to a Rigas family partnership.	$26 million
Praxis Capital Ventures	Adelphia funded a venture capital firm run by Ellen Rigas's husband.	$65 million
Niagara Frontier Hockey LP	Adelphia underwrote the Rigases' purchase of the Buffalo Sabres hockey team.	$150 million
Highland 2000	Adelphia guaranteed loans to a Rigas family partnership, which used the funds to buy stock.	$1 billion
Total		$1,271,371,000

LO4   **S1-5 Ethical Decision Making: A Mini-Case**

You are one of three partners who own and operate Mary's Maid Service. The company has been operating for seven years. One of the other partners has always prepared the company's annual financial statements. Recently, you proposed that the statements be audited each year because it would benefit the partners and prevent possible disagreements about the division of profits. The partner who prepares the statements proposed that his uncle, who has a lot of financial experience, can do the job at little cost. Your other partner remained silent.

Required:

1. What position would you take on the proposal? Justify your response in writing.
2. What would you strongly recommend? Give the basis for your recommendation.

LO2, LO3   **S1-6 Critical Thinking: Developing a Balance Sheet and Income Statement**

On September 30, Ashley and Jason started arguing about who is better off. Jason said he was better off because he owned a PlayStation console that he bought last year for $350. Ashley, on the other hand, argued that she was better off because she had $1,000 and a '75 Mustang that she bought two years ago for $800. Jason countered that Ashley still owed $250 on her car and that Jason's dad promised to buy him a Porsche if he does well in his accounting class. Jason said he had $6,000 in his bank account right now because he just received a $4,800 student loan. Ashley knows that Jason still owes an installment of $800 on this term's tuition.

Ashley and Jason met again in early November. They asked how each other was doing. Ashley claimed that she'd become much more successful than Jason. She had a part-time job, where she earned $500 per month. Jason laughed at Ashley because he had won $950 on a lottery ticket he bought in October, and that was merely for the "work" of standing in line for a minute. It was just what he needed because his apartment costs $450 each month. Ashley, on the other hand, pays $120 for her share of the rent. Both Ashley and Jason have other normal living costs that total $300 each month.

1. Prepare a financial report that compares what Ashley and Jason each own and owe on September 30. Make a list of any decisions you had to make when preparing your report.
2. In a written report, identify and justify which of the two characters is better off. If you were a creditor, to whom would you rather lend money?
3. Prepare a report that compares what Ashley and Jason each earned during October. Make a list of any decisions you had to make when preparing your report.
4. In a written report, identify and justify which of the two characters is more successful. If you were a creditor considering a three-year loan to one of these characters, to whom would you rather lend money?

LO2

Electronic Arts Inc.

S1-7 Preparing an Income Statement and Balance Sheet

Electronic Arts is the world's leading developer and publisher of interactive entertainment software for personal computers and advanced entertainment systems made by Sony, Nintendo, and Microsoft. Assume that the company is revising its methods for displaying its financial statements, and the controller in the accounting department has asked you to create electronic worksheets that they can use as their standard format for financial statement reporting. The controller has provided you with an alphabetical list of statement categories and account names (below), with corresponding balances (in millions) as of September 30. She has asked you to use a spreadsheet program to create two worksheets that organize the accounts into a properly formatted balance sheet and income statement, and use formulas to compute amounts marked by a ? below.

Accounts Payable	$ 171	Liabilities		Revenue	
Accounts Receivable	328	Net Income	?	Sales Revenue	675
Assets		Notes Payable	12	Selling Expense	223
Cash	2,412	Other Assets	283	Stockholders' Equity	
Contributed Capital	986	Other Expenses	1	Total Assets	?
Cost of Goods Sold Expense	284	Other Liabilities	587	Total Expenses	?
Expenses		Promotion Expense	107	Total Liabilities	?
Income Tax Expense	9	Property and Equipment	364	Total Liabilities and	
Inventories	367	Retained Earnings	1,998	Stockholders' Equity	?
				Total Stockholders' Equity	?

Not knowing quite where to start, you e-mailed your friend Owen for advice on using a spreadsheet. Owen is an extreme Type A personality, which explains his very detailed reply, as shown below.

Required:

Follow Owen's advice to create a balance sheet and income statement, with each statement saved on a separate worksheet in a file called *me*EA.xls where the *me* part of the filename uniquely identifies you.

From: Owentheaccountant@yahoo.com
To: Helpme@hotmail.com
Cc:
Subject: Excel Help

Hey pal. Long time, no chat. Here's the scoop on creating those worksheets, with a screenshot too. If you need more help, let me know and I'll submit an application for your position there. ☺

1. Start-up Excel to open a new spreadsheet file. You'll need only two worksheets for this assignment, so delete the third worksheet by clicking on the Sheet3 tab at the bottom of the worksheet and selecting Edit/Delete Sheet in the pull-down menu. While you're at it, rename Sheet1 and Sheet2 to Balance Sheet and Income Statement by double-clicking on the worksheet tabs and typing in the new names.

2. Plan the layout for your reports. Use the first column as a blank margin, the second column for account names and their headings, and the third column for the numbers corresponding to each account name or total. If you want to apply the same format to all worksheets, begin by right-clicking on the tab at the bottom of a worksheet and choosing Select All Sheets. Next, resize the first column by clicking on the A at the top of that column, selecting Format/Column/Width . . . from the pull-down menu, and choosing a width of 2. Using this same procedure, resize columns B and C to 50 and 15, respectively.

3. Starting with cell B1, enter the company's name. Enter the report name and date in cells B2 and B3. To merge cells so these headings span more than one column, select the cells to be merged and then click on Format/Cells, select the alignment tab, and use the drop down arrow under Horizontal to select Center Across Selection. Continue with the body of the report in cell B6, entering any necessary amounts in column C. To apply different formats (such as dollar signs, center alignment, single-or double-underlined borders, boldface), select the cell(s), click on Format/Cells . . . in the pull-down menu, and choose the desired options.

4. To use formulas to compute subtotals and totals, the equals sign = is entered first into the cell and is followed immediately by the formula. So, to subtract cell C16 from C13, enter =C16−C13. To add a series of amounts, say C7 through C11, use a formula like =SUM(C7:C11), as shown in the screenshot below.

5. After you get all the data entered and totals calculated, be sure to save the file. To do this, just click on File/Save As . . . and enter the filename.

6. If you need to print the worksheets, it might be best to highlight what you want printed, then click File/Print . . . and choose Selection in the dialog box that pops up.

7. Go to it, you accounting guru!

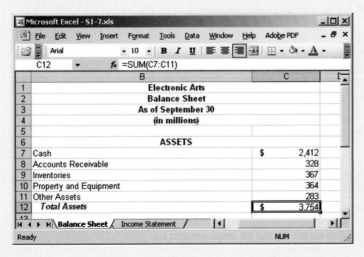

2

Reporting Investing and Financing Results on the Balance Sheet

YOUR LEARNING OBJECTIVES

Understand the business

LO1   Explain and select common balance sheet account titles.

Study the accounting methods

LO2   Apply transaction analysis to business transactions.

LO3   Use journal entries and T-accounts to show how business transactions affect the balance sheet.

LO4   Prepare a classified balance sheet.

Evaluate the results

LO5   Explain the concepts that determine whether an item is reported on the balance sheet and at what amount.

Review the chapter

LP2

SUPERCUTS®

Do you spend hours looking for e-mail messages that you received just a couple of weeks ago? Do your file names contain meaningless labels like "final paper"? If so, you probably could use an organizing system that neatly sorts every e-mail and file into categories. With such a system, you might be able to quickly find that joke about the magician and the parrot, or the marketing assignment due tomorrow.

Businesses also need systems for organizing information. Just think what could happen if FedEx didn't have a system to track the 5 million packages and $88 million in sales revenues that the company handles every day, or to evaluate its use of $10.8 billion to buy airplanes and other equipment. Clearly, big companies need well-organized systems for tracking their business activities and financial results. The same is true for small businesses, like your local Supercuts store. In this chapter, we'll focus on the decisions that business managers make when starting up a single Supercuts salon and how their accounting systems track the financial results of the salon's investing and financing activities. In later chapters, you'll see how things are basically the same, only bigger, at Regis Corporation—a public company that is involved with over 2,000 Supercuts stores and 9,000 other hair salons. With that many stores, Regis is the main player in the U.S. hair business, which generates $53 billion of revenue and 365,000 tons of hair clippings every year.

THIS IS
NOW

This chapter focuses on just the balance sheet and the accounting system used to produce it.

You may remember our earlier promise that, in Chapters 2 through 4, you'd have time to learn the details about specific financial statement accounts. That time has come. We begin this chapter with a look at how business activities map into the balance sheet and its asset, liability, and stockholders' equity accounts. After you become reacquainted with these topics, you'll learn about the accounting cycle that is used to produce accounting reports. We conclude the chapter by looking carefully at what the balance sheet tells you and what it doesn't, and giving lots of review and practice material. The main tasks and chapter topics are summarized below. Notice that the focus of this chapter is on the balance sheet. Income statement reporting is discussed in Chapters 3 and 4.

ORGANIZATION OF THE CHAPTER

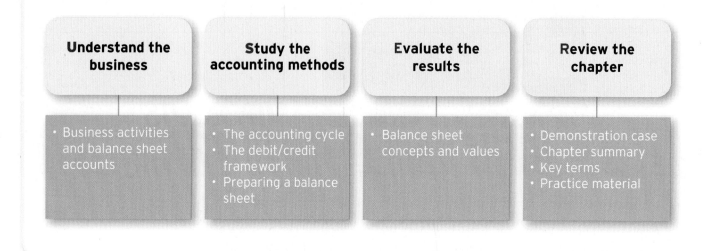

Understand the business	Study the accounting methods	Evaluate the results	Review the chapter
• Business activities and balance sheet accounts	• The accounting cycle • The debit/credit framework • Preparing a balance sheet	• Balance sheet concepts and values	• Demonstration case • Chapter summary • Key terms • Practice material

Understand the Business

Learning Objective 1
Explain and select common balance sheet account titles.

BUSINESS ACTIVITIES AND BALANCE SHEET ACCOUNTS

Let's begin by going over what's needed to get a business, like a Supercuts hair salon, up and running. First, you will need some **financing**, which is money the business obtains through loans or owners' contributions. Most small businesses start with personal funds contributed to the business by the owner and close friends. After lining that up, you will need to decide on a location. Because the idea behind Supercuts is to make hair care convenient for customers, you'll try to find space for your salon in a neighborhood shopping mall, anchored by either a major grocery chain or mass merchandiser. This will ensure your salon attracts what are known as destination shoppers. These are customers who want to go to the grocery store, video store, and hair salon without driving all over the place. Your mall location makes this possible.

Now that you've selected a location, you'll need to start **investing** in some assets that your business will use for many years to come. First, you'll need to install equipment like salon chairs and shampoo stations in your salon space, consistent with the standard Supercuts design. Typically, this takes four to six weeks to complete and costs about $42,000. You'll also need to spend $18,000 on additional equipment for the salon. This might seem like a lot of money, but the next time you get your hair cut, just take a look around at all the different things in a hair salon. You'll need a reception desk, lighting fixtures, styling chairs, shampoo stations, computers, mirrors, scissors, trimmers, razors, and dryers.

But wait! You have been able to scrounge up only $50,000, all of which you will contribute to starting up a company. To finance the cost of all the assets needed for the

EXHIBIT 2.1 Balance Sheet

SUPERCUTS

SUPERCUTS Balance Sheet At August 31, 2008			Who: Company name What: Financial statement name When: Date of report
Assets			
Cash		$10,000	Cash in company's bank account
Supplies		630	Shampoo and other supplies for use
Equipment		60,000	Cost of equipment purchased for use
Total assets		$70,630	= $10,000 + 630 + 60,000
Liabilities and Stockholders' Equity			
Liabilities			
Accounts payable		$ 630	Owed to supplier on account
Note payable		20,000	Owed to bank for loan (formal note)
Stockholders' equity			
Contributed capital		50,000	Contributed by stockholders
Retained earnings		0	No operations yet, so no earnings
Total liabilities and stockholders' equity		$70,630	= $630 + 20,000 + 50,000 + 0

business, your company will need to get a loan from a bank. A $20,000 loan would give the company enough cash to pay for equipment and still leave some money to pay for operating supplies like shampoo and fuzzy pink rollers.

From this description and what you remember from Chapter 1, try to imagine what the balance sheet of your Supercuts store will look like. Really, cover up Exhibit 2.1 and take 10 seconds to picture what should be on the balance sheet of your business. When you're done, compare it to the balance sheet in Exhibit 2.1.

So, how did you do? The most important thing at this stage is that you knew to think about assets, liabilities, and stockholders' equity accounts. One thing to know about balance sheets is that **assets** are listed in order of how fast they will be used up or can be turned into cash. Another thing to notice is that all assets have three features: (1) it is probable that they will generate future economic benefits for the company, (2) the company can obtain these benefits and control others' access to them, and (3) these benefits arise from having acquired the assets in the past. These features obviously exist for the cash in Exhibit 2.1, but they also apply to the other assets shown because (1) both supplies and equipment will allow Supercuts to provide hair care services and charge customers for them, (2) these assets will be used by Supercuts and no one else, and (3) these assets arise from Supercuts having purchased them in the past.

There are three things for you to notice in the bottom half of the balance sheet in Exhibit 2.1. First, **liabilities** are listed in order of how soon they will be paid, satisfied, or fulfilled. Second, all liabilities share the common features that they are unavoidable obligations, requiring a future sacrifice of resources, arising from a past transaction or event. Third, the **stockholders' equity** section contains two accounts. Contributed capital shows the amount of financing contributed to the company by stockholders, and Retained earnings indicates the total earnings of the business that have been retained in the company as of the balance sheet date. In our Supercuts example, this account has a zero balance because the business isn't open to customers yet, so there are no earnings to report as having been retained.

Don't be surprised if you thought of account names that differ from what we used in Exhibit 2.1. It's okay to use different account names as long as they have the same meaning as ours and are properly classified as assets, liabilities, or stockholders' equity. In the real world of financial reporting, even commonly used accounts are given different labels by

YOU SHOULD KNOW

Assets are resources owned by a business that generate future economic benefits.
Liabilities are amounts owed by a business.
Stockholders' equity is the amount invested and reinvested in a company by its stockholders.

EXHIBIT 2.2	Sample Chart of Accounts (Balance Sheet Accounts Only)

Account Name	Description
Assets	
Cash	Includes cash in the bank and in the cash register
Accounts receivable	Amounts owed to your business by customers for sales on credit
Interest receivable	Interest owed to your business by others
Inventories	Goods on hand that are being held for resale
Supplies	Items on hand that will be used to make goods or provide services
Prepaid expenses	Rent, insurance, and other expenses paid for future services
Notes receivable	Amounts loaned to others under a formal agreement ("note")
Land	Cost of land to be used by the business
Buildings	Cost of buildings the business will use for operations
Equipment	Cost of equipment used to produce goods or provide services
Intangible assets	Trademarks, brand names, goodwill, and other assets that lack a physical presence
Liabilities	
Accounts payable	Amounts owed to suppliers for goods or services bought on credit
Wages payable	Amounts owed to employees for salaries, wages, and bonuses
Accrued liabilities	Amounts owed to others for advertising, utilities, interest, etc.
Unearned revenues	Amounts (customer deposits) received in advance of providing goods or services to customers
Notes payable	Amounts borrowed from lenders, involves signing a promissory note
Bonds payable	Amounts borrowed from lenders, involves issuance of bonds
Other liabilities	A variety of liabilities with smaller balances
Stockholders' Equity	
Contributed capital	Amount of cash (or other property) received for stock issued
Retained earnings	Amount of accumulated earnings not distributed as dividends

> **COACH'S TIP**
>
> Read this chart of accounts but don't memorize it. Also, don't try to force this chart of accounts on all problems. Account names vary from company to company.

different companies. Depending on the company, you may see a liability for a bank loan called a *note payable, loan payable,* or simply *long-term debt*. The names you see in the financial statements of most large businesses are actually aggregations (or combinations) of several specific accounts. For example, Regis Corporation—the company that owns most of the Supercuts stores—keeps separate accounts for land, buildings, and equipment, but combines them into one title on the balance sheet called *Property and equipment*.

When choosing account names, companies will attempt to use names that already exist, if appropriate, or come up with one that describes the underlying business activity. Once an account name is selected, it is given a reference number, and this exact name and number are used for all business activities affecting that account. Although companies tend to use similar account names, designated account numbers vary greatly depending on each company's particular accounting system. To ensure consistency in reporting financial results, each company keeps a summary of account names and account numbers called the **chart of accounts.** A simple example from one company (with account numbers removed) is given in Exhibit 2.2. The accounts in blue are used in this chapter and other accounts are used in later chapters.

Now that you reviewed some key parts of the balance sheet, it's time to learn about the systematic accounting process that produces it.

> **YOU SHOULD KNOW**
>
> The **chart of accounts** is a summary of all account names (and corresponding account numbers) used to record financial results in the accounting system.

Study the Accounting Methods

THE ACCOUNTING CYCLE

> **Learning Objective 2**
> Apply transaction analysis to business transactions.

To be sure that financial statements, such as the balance sheet, report all of the financial results of a company's business activities, a systematic process of accounting is used. This process, called the accounting cycle, includes three main steps:

1. Analyze → 2. Record → 3. Summarize

Before we look at each of these steps, we should warn you that learning how the accounting cycle works is a key part of this chapter and is crucial to understanding the rest of this course. So, take your time as you read the following sections.

Step 1: Analyze

Video 2.1

Accounting Transactions   The goal of this first step is to determine the financial effects of your company's business activities on assets, liabilities, or stockholders' equity. If a business activity affects any of these types of accounts and if its effects can be measured in dollars and cents, it is called a **transaction.** Transactions are of special importance because they are the only activities to be recorded (in step 2) and summarized (in step 3). Business activities that do not have direct or measurable financial effects on the company are not recorded in the accounting system. For example, if someone at Supercuts answers the phone or faxes a document to the bank, there is no immediate financial impact so these activities will not be recorded. Activities like cutting hair and buying hair dryers have a direct financial impact, so they are considered transactions and will be recorded.

How do you know if a business activity is considered an accounting transaction? Look for two types of events, both of which are considered accounting transactions:

> **YOU SHOULD KNOW**
>
> A **transaction** has a direct and measurable financial effect on the assets, liabilities, or stockholders' equity of a business.

1. External exchanges: These are exchanges involving assets, liabilities, and/or stockholders' equity that you can see between the company and someone else. When Starbucks sells you a Frappucino®, it is exchanging an icy taste of heaven for your cash, so Starbucks would record this in its accounting system.

2. Internal events: These events do not involve exchanges with others outside the business, but rather occur within the company itself. For example, when the company Red Bull combines sugar, water, taurine, and caffeine, something magical happens: these ingredients turn into Red Bull Energy Drink. This internal event is a transaction because it has a direct financial effect whereby some assets (supplies of sugar, etc.) are used up to create a different asset (an inventory of Red Bull drinks).

One word of warning: not all external exchanges and internal events are considered transactions. If an exchange or event does not have a direct financial impact on the basic accounting equation (A = L + SE) when it occurs, it is not considered a transaction. So, for example, when Supercuts orders supplies to be received in the future, no exchange of assets or services has occurred yet. There has been only the supplier's promise to deliver and Supercuts' promise to pay after the supplies are delivered—an exchange of promises does not qualify as an accounting transaction. Similarly, when Supercuts moves bottles of shampoo from the back of the store to the display case at the front, this internal event has not yet created a financial impact, so it is not considered an accounting transaction.

Transaction Analysis   Once a transaction is identified, you have to analyze it carefully to determine its financial effects. Two simple ideas are used when analyzing transactions:

1. Duality of effects. It's a fancy name, but the idea is simple. Every transaction has at least two effects on the basic accounting equation. To remember this, just think of expressions like "give and receive" or "push and pull" or, if you're a closet scientist, Newton's Third Law of Motion.

2. A = L + SE. You know this already, right? Well, just remember that the dollar amount for assets must always equal the total of liabilities plus stockholders' equity for every accounting transaction. If it doesn't, then you are missing something and you should go back to the first (duality of effects) idea.

Let's do a few examples to show how these ideas are used when analyzing transactions. Suppose Supercuts paid cash to buy a salon chair from a salon supply company called

Etopa. This is a transaction because an exchange exists between Supercuts and Etopa. To apply the duality of effects idea, look for what Supercuts "gives and receives" in this transaction:

Transaction: Pay cash for salon chair.

Give: Cash

Receive: Equipment

The next thing to do is check the effects of this "give and receive" on the accounting equation. In the box below, notice that this transaction involves a decrease in one asset (cash), which is offset by an increase in another asset (equipment). There are no changes in liabilities or stockholders' equity, so the accounting equation remains in balance, as it should.

Accounting Equation	Assets	=	Liabilities	+	Stockholders' Equity
	⇓ Cash				
	⇑ Equipment	=	No change	+	No change

In the example just given, Supercuts paid cash to Etopa immediately upon receiving the chair. Typically, when a company buys goods or services from another company, it will do so on credit with the promise to pay for it later. For the next example, let's assume that Supercuts receives another salon chair from Etopa but promises to pay for this purchase at the end of the month. In this example, Supercuts has entered into two transactions: (1) the purchase of an asset on credit and (2) the eventual payment. The first part of this is considered a transaction because, although Supercuts has given a promise, the exchange involves more than just a promise. Supercuts actually receives equipment (an increase in an asset). The promise to pay that Supercuts has given is called *accounts payable* (an increase in a liability).

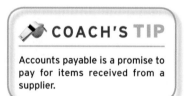

COACH'S TIP

Accounts payable is a promise to pay for items received from a supplier.

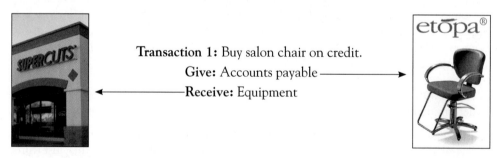

Transaction 1: Buy salon chair on credit.

Give: Accounts payable

Receive: Equipment

Notice that A = L + SE for this transaction, as shown below.

Accounting Equation	Assets	=	Liabilities	+	Stockholders' Equity
	(1) ⇑ Equipment	=	⇑ Accounts payable	+	No change

Let's move on to apply the duality of effects idea to part (2), where Supercuts pays for the purchase in (1). At this point, Supercuts gives up cash (a decrease in an asset) to fulfill its promise to pay Etopa and, as a result, eliminates or receives back its promise (a decrease in the liability called accounts payable). Again, two effects exist:

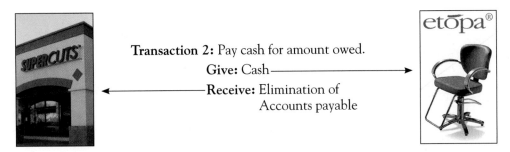

Transaction 2: Pay cash for amount owed.
Give: Cash
Receive: Elimination of Accounts payable

Now, let's make sure that the basic accounting equation is still in balance after we enter these effects:

Accounting Equation	Assets	=	Liabilities	+	Stockholders' Equity
(2)	⇓ Cash	=	⇓ Accounts payable	+	No change

Notice that the accounting equation remained in balance after each of the two transactions. In the first, the increase in an asset was accompanied by a corresponding increase in a liability and, in the second, the decrease in an asset was accompanied by a corresponding decrease in a liability. Although you haven't seen it yet in this chapter, you also will run into transactions where a stockholders' equity account changes and is accompanied by a corresponding change in either an asset or liability account.

We've almost covered everything you need to know about analyzing transactions. The only piece that's missing is the amount of the financial effects. Because transactions are based on the idea of an exchange, their financial effects are based on the company's cost of that exchange. This **cost principle,** as it is called, is one of the main principles of accounting: record transactions at the dollar value of the assets or liabilities involved in the exchange. If Supercuts pays $600 for a salon chair that sells elsewhere for $650, the chair is recorded at what it actually cost Supercuts ($600).

Decide: An Approach to Analyzing Transactions

You've now seen the thought process used in the "Analyze" step of the accounting cycle. At first, you may need some help in remembering this process, so we have created a little memory device to help you DECIDE on the accounting effects of business activities. Train yourself to follow this systematic approach and soon you'll be able to complete the entire analysis step with ease and accuracy:

Detect transactions. Go to the next step only if a transaction exists.

Examine the accounts affected. Put account names on what is given and received.

Classify each account as asset (A), liability (L), or stockholders' equity (SE).

IDentify the financial effects. Do asset, liability, and stockholders' equity accounts increase or decrease, and by how much?

End with the effects on the basic accounting equation. Ensure A = L + SE.

The best way to learn how to account for business activities is to work through examples, so let's use this DECIDE approach to analyze some typical transactions that occur when a business is started. Assume the following events took place in August.

LP2

Topic Tackler
PLUS

Check out www.mhhe.com/phillips2e for audio, visual, and PowerPoint presentations on this topic.

(a) Financing from Stockholders

You incorporate your Supercuts salon on August 1. The company issues stock certificates to you and your parents as co-owners in exchange for $50,000, which is deposited in the company's bank account.

COACH'S TIP

Analyze transactions from the standpoint of the business, not its owners.

Detect transactions.	Supercuts receives cash and gives ownership interests (stock certificates).
Examine accounts.	Cash is cash. Contributions by owners to a company are called Contributed Capital.
Classify accounts.	Cash is an asset (A) and Contributed Capital is a stockholders' equity (SE) account.
IDentify $ effects.	Cash (A) + $50,000 and Contributed Capital (SE) + $50,000.
End with A = L + SE.	

	Assets		=	Liabilities	+	Stockholders' Equity	
(a)	Cash	+50,000	=			Contributed Capital	+50,000

Notice that in the table above, we included a transaction reference (a) so that we can refer back to the original transaction description if needed. You too should use transaction letters (or numbers or dates) as references in your homework problems.

(b) Investing in Equipment

Your salon pays $42,000 cash for equipment.

COACH'S TIP

Although we use the same format for all of our examples, the content in each differs. Don't skip this section with the plan of coming back to it later, because the next part of this chapter builds on this part. Most students say that, of all the topics in this course, transaction analysis is the one they wished they had spent more time on when first learning it.

Detect transactions.	Supercuts receives equipment and gives cash.
Examine accounts.	Equipment typically is called just that: equipment. Cash is cash.
Classify accounts.	Equipment is an asset (A) and Cash is an asset (A).
IDentify $ effects.	Equipment (A) + $42,000 and Cash (A) − $42,000.
End with A = L + SE.	

	Assets		=	Liabilities	+	Stockholders' Equity
(b)	Cash	−42,000	=		No Change	
	Equipment	+42,000				

Notice that even though transaction (b) did not affect liabilities or stockholders' equity, the accounting equation remained in balance because the decrease in one asset (Cash) was offset by the increase in another asset (Equipment).

(c) Financing from Lender

Your company borrows $20,000 from a bank, depositing those funds in its bank account and signing a formal agreement to repay the loan in two years.

Detect transactions.	Supercuts receives cash and gives a formal promise to pay (called a "note").
Examine accounts.	Cash is cash, and the formal promise to pay is called a note payable.
Classify accounts.	Cash is an asset (A), and the Note Payable is a liability (L).
IDentify $ effects.	Cash (A) + $20,000, and Note Payable (L) + 20,000.

End with A = L + SE.

Assets		=	Liabilities		+	Stockholders' Equity
(c) Cash	+ 20,000	=	Note Payable	+ 20,000		

COACH'S TIP

Notes payable are like accounts payable except that they (a) charge interest, (b) can be outstanding for periods longer than one year, and (c) are documented using formal documents called notes.

(d) Investing in Equipment

Your salon installs $18,000 of additional equipment, paying $16,000 in cash and giving an informal promise to pay $2,000 at the end of the month.

Detect transactions.	Supercuts receives equipment and gives both cash and a promise to pay.
Examine accounts.	Equipment is equipment, cash is cash, and the promise to pay is accounts payable.
Classify accounts.	Equipment and Cash are assets (A), and Accounts Payable is a liability (L).
IDentify $ effects.	Equipment (A) + $18,000, Cash (A) − $16,000, and Accounts Payable (L) + 2,000.

End with A = L + SE.

Assets		=	Liabilities		+	Stockholders' Equity
(d) Cash	− 16,000	=	Accounts Payable	+ 2,000		
Equipment	+ 18,000					

If you ever run into a transaction that you have no idea how to analyze, just break it down. Rather than trying to solve it all at once, begin by looking just for what is received. This step is crucial, and you may find that the reason you were having trouble is that there was more than one item received. After you find what is received, look just for what is given. Again, you may find that, as in transaction (d), more than one item is involved. Also, take the time to End with ensuring the accounting equation is in balance, because this may give you a clue about whether you've detected all the accounts affected.

(e) Ordering Supplies

Your salon orders $800 of shampoo and other operating supplies. None have been received yet.

Detect transactions.	This is not a transaction. Supercuts has received nothing and given only a promise.

(f) Paying a Supplier

Your company pays $2,000 to the equipment supplier in (d).

Detect transactions.	Supercuts fulfills its informal promise to pay by giving cash.
Examine accounts.	The informal promise to pay is called accounts payable and cash is cash.
Classify accounts.	Accounts Payable is a liability (L) and Cash is an asset (A).
IDentify $ effects.	Accounts Payable (L) − 2,000 and Cash (A) − 2,000.
End with A = L + SE.	

	Assets		=	Liabilities		+	Stockholders' Equity
(f)	Cash	− 2,000	=	Accounts Payable	− 2,000		

(g) Receiving Supplies

Your company receives $630 of the supplies ordered in (e) and promises to pay for them next month.

Detect transactions.	Supercuts receives supplies and gives a promise to pay.
Examine accounts.	Supplies are called just that: supplies. The promise to pay is accounts payable.
Classify accounts.	Supplies is an asset account (A), and Accounts Payable is a liability (L).
IDentify $ effects.	Supplies (A) + $630 and Accounts Payable (L) + 630.
End with A = L + SE.	

	Assets		=	Liabilities		+	Stockholders' Equity
(g)	Supplies	+ 630	=	Accounts Payable	+ 630		

As we said, the best way to learn accounting is to do examples, so try the following quiz. (Cover the answers in the margin with your thumb until you're done.)

HOW'S IT GOING?   Self-Study Quiz

For the following event, complete the transaction analysis steps by filling in the empty boxes. Then check your answers with the solutions in the margin.

May 1: NIKE, Inc. purchased equipment costing $500,000, paying $200,000 cash and signing a formal promissory note to pay the balance in three years.

Detect transactions.	Nike receives [ ] and gives both [ ] and a promise to pay.
Examine accounts.	Equipment is equipment, cash is cash, and the formal promise to pay is a [ ] payable.
Classify accounts.	Equipment and Cash are [ ], and [ ] Payable is a liability (L).
IDentify $ effects.	Equipment (A) + $500,000, Cash (A) − $200,000, and [ ].
End with A = L + SE.	

		Assets	=	Liabilities	+	Stockholders' Equity
May 1	Cash	*,000*	=	Note Payable *,2,000*		
	Equipment	*+ 5,000.*				

Steps 2 and 3: Record and Summarize

In the previous section, you saw the thought processes that accountants follow when analyzing a company's business activities. This first step of the accounting cycle ended with an understanding of the financial effects of each transaction on assets, liabilities, or stockholders' equity. The next two steps of the accounting cycle will involve recording and summarizing these financial effects so that accounting reports, like the balance sheet, can be prepared and evaluated.

One method for recording and summarizing the financial effects of accounting transactions is to prepare a spreadsheet like the one in Exhibit 2.3 on page 54. The spreadsheet takes the financial effects of each transaction that you determined in the last step of the DECIDE transaction analysis and adds or subtracts these amounts from the balance in each account at the beginning of the month. By summing each spreadsheet column, you could compute new balances at the end of the month and report them on a balance sheet. Although this method would work, you can just imagine how impractical it would be in a company like Regis Corporation, which has to account for transactions with about 8 million customers and 55,000 employees every month. Rather than create a spreadsheet as big as three football fields, a more manageable system is used to record and summarize transactions.

EXHIBIT 2.3 | Using a Spreadsheet to Record and Summarize Transactions

		Assets			=	Liabilities		+	Stockholders' Equity
		Cash	Supplies	Equipment	=	Accounts Payable	Notes Payable	+	Contributed Capital
3	Beginning	0	0	0	=	0	0		0
4	(a)	+50,000			=				+50,000
5	(b)	-42,000		+42,000	=				
6	(c)	+20,000			=		+20,000		
7	(d)	-16,000		+18,000	=	+2,000			
8	(f)	-2,000			=	-$2,000			
9	(g)		+630		=	+630			
10	Ending	10,000	630	60,000	=	630	20,000	+	50,000

The system of recording and summarizing used in business is a lot like what you do as a student when taking notes and preparing for exams. Day after day, you go to class, take notes, go to class, take notes, rinse, repeat. The reason you take notes is to create a record of what happened each day, kind of like an academic diary or journal. Later, when preparing for exams, you copy your notes to summary sheets to study from. The same ideas are used in the accounting cycle. The financial effects of transactions are entered into **journals** each day they occur. Later, these journal entries are summarized in **ledger** accounts that keep track of the financial effects of the transactions on each account (e.g., cash, supplies, and accounts payable). To make this process as efficient as possible, journals and ledger accounts share the same underlying framework discussed in the following section.

THE DEBIT/CREDIT FRAMEWORK

The framework used for journals and ledger accounts was created more than 500 years ago, yet it continues to exist in accounting systems today. Although computers now perform many routine accounting tasks involving journals and ledger accounts, most computerized systems still require you to know how these accounting records work. To understand this framework, think of the accounting equation (A = L + SE) as an old-fashioned weight scale that tips at the equals sign. Assets—like cash and supplies—are put on the left side of the scale and liabilities and stockholders' equity accounts are put on the right. Likewise, each individual account has two sides, with one side used for increases and the other for decreases, similar to what is shown in Exhibit 2.4.

EXHIBIT 2.4 | The Debit/Credit Framework

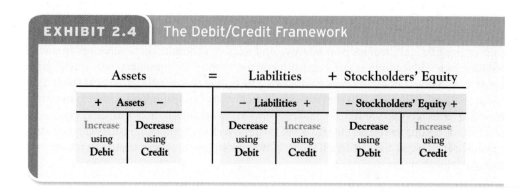

Assets	=	Liabilities	+ Stockholders' Equity
+ Assets −		− Liabilities +	− Stockholders' Equity +
Increase using **Debit**	Decrease using **Credit**	Decrease using **Debit** / Increase using **Credit**	Decrease using **Debit** / Increase using **Credit**

Take special note of two important rules illustrated in Exhibit 2.4:

1. Accounts increase on the same side as they appear in A = L + SE. Accounts on the left side of the accounting equation increase on the left side of the account and accounts on the right side of the equation increase on the right. So
   - Assets increase on the left side of the account.
   - Liabilities increase on the right side of the account.
   - Stockholders' equity accounts increase on the right.
   - Decreases are the opposite, as shown in Exhibit 2.4.

2. Left is debit (*dr*), right is credit (*cr*). The terms (and abbreviations) **debit** (*dr*) and **credit** (*cr*) come from Latin words that had meaning back in the day, but today they just mean *left* and *right*. When combined with how increases and decreases are entered into accounts, the following rules emerge:
   - Use debits for increases in assets (and for decreases in liabilities and stockholders' equity accounts).
   - Use credits for increases in liabilities and stockholders' equity accounts (and for decreases in assets).

Accountants didn't dream up this debit/credit framework just to confuse you. The purpose of this double-entry system is to introduce another check on the accuracy of accounting numbers. In addition to requiring that A = L + SE, the double-entry system also requires that debits = credits. If either of these relationships is not equal, then you know for sure that you've made an error that will need to be corrected.

Step 1: Analyzing Transactions

The debit/credit framework does not change this step. Continue to use the DECIDE approach to determine the financial effects of transactions, which you will enter into the accounting system in step 2.

Step 2: Recording Journal Entries

The financial effects of transactions are entered into a journal using a debits-equal-credits format, as shown in Exhibit 2.5. When looking at these **journal entries,** as they are called, notice the following:

- A date is included for each transaction.
- Debits appear first (on top). Credits are written below the debits and are indented to the right (both the words and the amounts). The order of the debited accounts

EXHIBIT 2.5 | Formal Journal Page

Date	Account Titles and Explanation	Ref.	Debit	Credit
	General Journal			Page G1
2008				
Aug. 1	Cash		50,000	
	Contributed capital			50,000
	(Financing from stockholders.)			
Aug. 2	Equipment		42,000	
	Cash			42,000
	(Bought equipment using cash.)			
Aug. 5	Equipment		18,000	
	Cash			16,000
	Accounts payable			2,000
	(Bought equipment using cash and credit.)			

or credited accounts doesn't matter, as long as for each journal entry debits are on top and credits are on the bottom and indented.

- Total debits equal total credits for each transaction (for example, see the entry on August 5 where $18,000 = $16,000 + $2,000).

- Dollar signs are not used because the journal is understood to be a record of financial effects.

- The reference column (Ref.) will be used later (in step 3) to indicate when the journal entry has been summarized in the ledger accounts.

- A brief explanation of the transaction is written below the debits and credits.

- The line after the explanation is left blank before writing the next journal entry.

When writing journal entries in this course, we'll make a few minor changes to the formal entries, which should make it easier for you to learn the most important aspects of recording journal entries. The way we would show the journal entry for August 5 is:

(d)	*dr* **Equipment** (+A).	18,000	
	cr **Cash** (−A)		16,000
	cr **Accounts Payable** (+L)		2,000

The main differences between our simplified format and a formal journal entry are:

- When a date is not given, use some form of reference for each transaction, such as (*d*), to identify the event.

- Omit the reference column and transaction explanation to simplify the entry.

- Indicate whether you are debiting (*dr*) or crediting (*cr*) each account. This will help to reinforce the debit/credit framework from Exhibit 2.4. Plus, it will make it easier to interpret journal entries when indents aren't clear (sometimes an issue in handwritten homework).

- Include the appropriate account type (A, L, or SE) along with the direction of the effect (+ or −) next to each account title to clarify the effects of the transaction on each account. Again, this will reinforce the debit/credit framework and help you to determine whether the accounting equation has remained in balance.

Step 3: Summarizing in Ledger Accounts

By themselves, journal entries show the effects of transactions, but do not indicate the balance in each account. That's why ledger accounts are needed. After journal entries have been recorded (in step 2), their dollar amounts are copied ("posted") to each ledger account affected by the transaction so that account balances can be computed. In most computerized accounting systems, this happens automatically. In homework assignments, you'll have to do it yourself, so Exhibit 2.6 shows you how this is done using the journal entry for August 5. If account numbers are provided, keep track of the posting of journal entries to general ledger accounts by writing the account number in the Ref. column of the journal and the journal page number in the Ref. column of the ledger.

As we did earlier for journal entries, we will use a simplified format for ledger accounts to make it easier to focus on their main features. The simplified version of a ledger account is called a **T-account.** Compare the T-accounts in Exhibit 2.7 to the Cash and Accounts Payable ledger accounts in Exhibit 2.6. Notice that the T-accounts contain only the debit and credit columns of the ledger account. To remind you of the effects of debits and credits, the title bar for the Cash T-account shows that increases in cash (an asset) appear on the left side and decreases appear on the right side. For Accounts Payable, increases are shown on the right and decreases on the left because it is a liability

EXHIBIT 2.6 Posting from the Journal to the Ledger

General Ledger					Acct. 101
				Cash	
Date	Explanation	Ref.	Debit	Credit	Balance
2008					
Aug. 1		G1	50,000		50,000
Aug. 2		G1		42,000	8,000
Aug. 3		G1	20,000		28,000
Aug. 5		G1		16,000	12,000

General Journal				Page G1
Date	Account Titles and Explanation	Ref.	Debit	Credit
2008				
Aug. 5	Equipment	205	18,000	
	Cash	101		16,000
	Accounts payable	301		2,000
	(Bought equipment using cash and credit.)			

General Ledger					Acct. 205
				Equipment	
Date	Explanation	Ref.	Debit	Credit	Balance
2008					
Aug. 2		G1	42,000		42,000
Aug. 5		G1	18,000		60,000

General Ledger					Acct. 301
				Accounts Payable	
Date	Explanation	Ref.	Debit	Credit	Balance
2008					
Aug. 5		G1		2,000	2,000

account. (If you've forgotten why they work this way, take a quick look back at Exhibit 2.4 on page 54.)

In Exhibit 2.7 below, notice the following:

- Every account starts with a beginning balance, usually on the side where increases are summarized. For balance sheet accounts, the ending balance from the prior period is the beginning balance for the current period. Because our Supercuts salon is a new business, the beginning balance in each account is zero in this example.
- Dollar signs are not needed.
- Each amount is accompanied by a reference to the related journal entry, which makes it easy to trace back to the original transaction should errors occur.

EXHIBIT 2.7 T-Accounts: Simplified Format for Ledger Accounts

dr +	Cash (A)		cr −
Beg.	0		
(a)	50,000	42,000	(b)
(c)	20,000	16,000	(d)
		2,000	(f)
End.	10,000		

dr −	Accounts Payable (L)		cr +
		0	Beg.
		2,000	(d)
(f)	2,000	630	(g)
		630	End.

- To find ending account balances, express the T-accounts as equations:

	Cash	Accounts Payable
Beginning balance	$ 0	$ 0
Add: "+" side	+ 50,000	+ 2,000
	+ 20,000	+ 630
Subtract: "−" side	− 42,000	− 2,000
	− 16,000	
	− 2,000	
Ending balance	$ 10,000	$ 630

Knowing how to use T-accounts in this way will help you answer homework questions that involve solving for missing values in accounts.

- The ending balance is double underlined to distinguish it from transactions and symbolize the final result of a computation. The ending balance is shown on the side that has the greater total dollar amount. Assets normally end with a debit balance (because debits to assets normally exceed credits) and liabilities and stockholders' equity accounts normally end with credit balances (credits exceed debits).

A Review of the Accounting Cycle

Exhibit 2.8 summarizes and illustrates the main tools used in the accounting cycle to analyze, record, and summarize the financial effects of business activities. In the remainder of this section, we will work with you to account for the transactions that were presented earlier in this chapter for the Supercuts salon. Because we show the analyze step in detail on pages 47–53, we do not show it in detail here. Instead, we pick up where step 1 left off—with the effects of each transaction on the accounting equation. By reviewing steps 2 and 3 of the accounting cycle in detail, you will get to practice using the new concepts of debits, credits, journal entries, and T-accounts. Study the following examples carefully. The biggest mistake people make when first learning accounting is they think they understand how it all works without actually going through enough examples. To understand accounting, you have to practice, practice, practice, as if you're learning to play a new sport or musical instrument.

| EXHIBIT 2.8 | Tools Used in the Accounting Cycle |

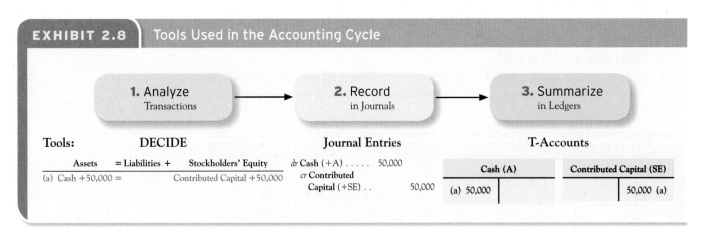

(a) Financing from Stockholders

You incorporate your Supercuts salon on August 1. The company issues stock certificates to you and your parents as co-owners in exchange for $50,000, which is deposited in the company's bank account.

1. Analyze

Assets	= Liabilities +	Stockholders' Equity	
(a) Cash	+50,000 =	Contributed Capital	+50,000

2. Record

(a) dr **Cash** (+A)   50,000
        cr **Contributed Capital** (+SE)   50,000

3. Summarize

dr +	Cash (A)	cr −	dr −	Contributed Capital (SE)	cr +
Beg. Bal.	0			0	Beg. Bal.
(a)	50,000			50,000	(a)

(b) Investing in Equipment

Your salon pays $42,000 cash for equipment.

1. Analyze

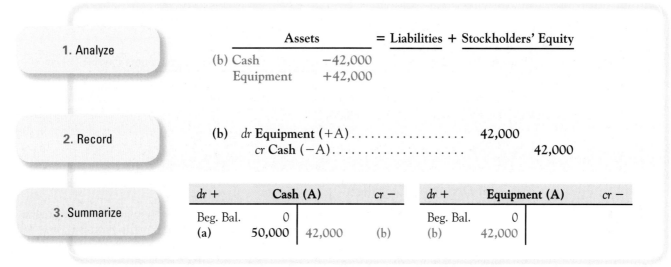

Assets		= Liabilities + Stockholders' Equity
(b) Cash	−42,000	
Equipment	+42,000	

2. Record

(b) dr **Equipment** (+A)   42,000
        cr **Cash** (−A)   42,000

3. Summarize

dr +	Cash (A)	cr −	dr +	Equipment (A)	cr −
Beg. Bal.	0		Beg. Bal.	0	
(a)	50,000	42,000 (b)	(b)	42,000	

(c) Financing from Lender

Your company borrows $20,000 from a bank, depositing those funds in its bank account and signing a formal agreement to repay the loan in two years.

1. Analyze

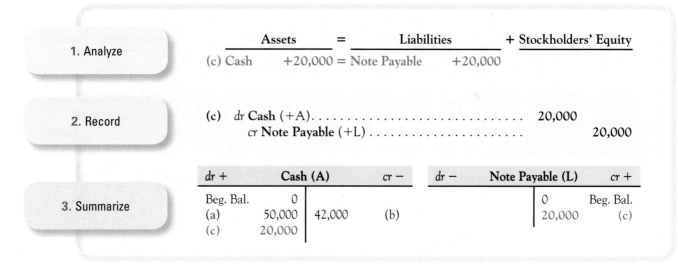

Assets	=	Liabilities	+ Stockholders' Equity
(c) Cash	+20,000 =	Note Payable	+20,000

2. Record

(c) dr **Cash** (+A)   20,000
        cr **Note Payable** (+L)   20,000

3. Summarize

dr +	Cash (A)	cr −	dr −	Note Payable (L)	cr +
Beg. Bal.	0			0	Beg. Bal.
(a)	50,000	42,000 (b)		20,000	(c)
(c)	20,000				

(d) Investing in Equipment

Your salon installs $18,000 of additional equipment, paying $16,000 in cash and giving an informal promise to pay $2,000 at the end of the month.

1. Analyze

Assets	=	Liabilities	+ Stockholders' Equity
(d) Cash −16,000	=	Accounts Payable +2,000	
Equipment +18,000			

2. Record

(d)   dr Equipment (+A)   18,000
      cr Cash (−A)   16,000
      cr Accounts payable (+L).........................   2,000

3. Summarize

dr +	Cash (A)	cr −		dr +	Equipment (A)	cr −		dr −	Accounts Payable (L)	cr +
Beg. Bal.	0			Beg. Bal.	0				0	Beg. Bal.
(a)	50,000	42,000 (b)		(b)	42,000				2,000	(d)
(c)	20,000	16,000 (d)		(d)	18,000					

(e) Ordering Supplies

Your salon orders $800 of shampoo and other operating supplies. None have been received yet. Because this event involves the exchange of only promises, it is not considered a transaction. No journal entry is needed.

(f) Paying a Supplier

Your company pays $2,000 to the equipment supplier in (d).

1. Analyze

Assets	=	Liabilities	+ Stockholders' Equity
(f) Cash −2,000	=	Accounts Payable −2,000	

2. Record

(f)   dr Accounts payable (−L)   2,000
      cr Cash (−A)   2,000

3. Summarize

dr +	Cash (A)	cr −		dr −	Accounts Payable (L)	cr +
Beg. Bal.	0					0 Beg. Bal.
(a)	50,000	42,000 (b)		(f)	2,000	2,000 (d)
(c)	20,000	16,000 (d)				
		2,000 (f)				

(g) Receiving Supplies

Your company receives $630 of the supplies ordered in (e) and promises to pay for them next month.

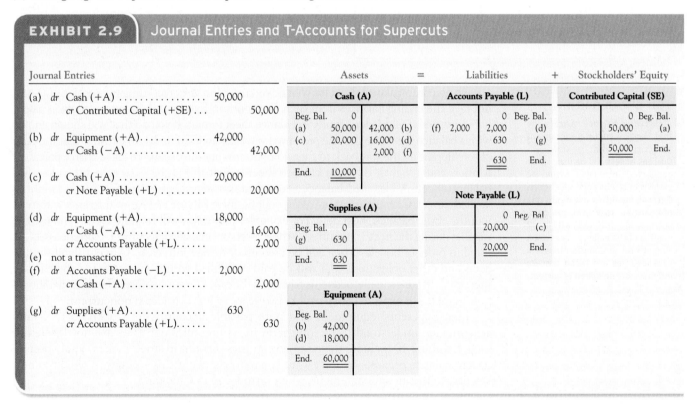

1. Analyze

Assets	=	Liabilities	+ Stockholders' Equity
(g) Supplies +630	=	Accounts Payable	+630

2. Record

(g)   dr Supplies (+A)   630
       cr Accounts payable (+L)   630

3. Summarize

dr +	Supplies (A)	cr −		dr −	Accounts Payable (L)	cr +
Beg. Bal.	0				0	Beg. Bal.
(g)	630		(f)	2,000	2,000	(d)
					630	(g)

Exhibit 2.9 summarizes the journal entries and T-accounts affected by events (a) through (g) for Supercuts. It also reports the ending balances for each account.

EXHIBIT 2.9   Journal Entries and T-Accounts for Supercuts

Journal Entries

(a) dr Cash (+A) 50,000
         cr Contributed Capital (+SE) . . .   50,000

(b) dr Equipment (+A). 42,000
         cr Cash (−A)   42,000

(c) dr Cash (+A) 20,000
         cr Note Payable (+L)   20,000

(d) dr Equipment (+A). 18,000
         cr Cash (−A)   16,000
         cr Accounts Payable (+L).   2,000

(e) not a transaction

(f) dr Accounts Payable (−L)   2,000
         cr Cash (−A)   2,000

(g) dr Supplies (+A).   630
         cr Accounts Payable (+L).   630

Assets = Liabilities + Stockholders' Equity

Cash (A)

Beg. Bal.	0		
(a)	50,000	42,000	(b)
(c)	20,000	16,000	(d)
		2,000	(f)
End.	10,000		

Supplies (A)

Beg. Bal.	0	
(g)	630	
End.	630	

Equipment (A)

Beg. Bal.	0	
(b)	42,000	
(d)	18,000	
End.	60,000	

Accounts Payable (L)

		0	Beg. Bal.
(f)	2,000	2,000	(d)
		630	(g)
		630	End.

Note Payable (L)

	0	Beg. Bal
	20,000	(c)
	20,000	End.

Contributed Capital (SE)

	0	Beg. Bal.
	50,000	(a)
	50,000	End.

PREPARING A BALANCE SHEET

Using the ending amount from each T-account, you could now prepare a balance sheet. Before you do this, however, it's a good idea to check that the accounting records are in balance by determining whether debits = credits. With just six accounts so far, this is easy enough to do ($10,000 + 630 + 60,000 = $70,630 = $630 + 20,000 + 50,000). In Chapter 3, after more accounts have been introduced, we'll show you how to prepare an internal accounting report called the trial balance to check whether debits = credits.

Learning Objective 4
Prepare a classified balance sheet.

EXHIBIT 2.10	Classified Balance Sheet	**SUPER**CUTS®

SUPERCUTS Balance Sheet At August 31, 2008		Explanation of Classification
Assets		
Current assets		
Cash	$10,000	This cash will be used (and replenished) before August 31, 2009.
Supplies	630	These supplies will be used before August 31, 2009.
Total current assets	10,630	
Equipment	60,000	This equipment will be used for many years.
Total assets	$70,630	
Liabilities and Stockholders' Equity		
Current liabilities		
Accounts payable	$ 630	These amounts will be paid before August 31, 2009.
Total current liabilities	630	
Note payable	20,000	Repayment of this note is not required until 2010.
Stockholders' equity		Stockholders' equity accounts are not classified.
Contributed capital	50,000	
Retained earnings	0	
Total liabilities and stockholders' equity	$70,630	

YOU SHOULD KNOW

A **classified balance sheet** is one that shows a subtotal for current assets and current liabilities. **Current assets** will be used up or converted into cash within 12 months of the balance sheet date. **Current liabilities** are debts and obligations that will be paid, settled, or fulfilled within 12 months of the balance sheet date. **Noncurrent** (or long-term) assets and liabilities are those that do not meet the definition of current.

To prepare a balance sheet for your Supercuts salon after recording transactions (a)–(g), just take the ending balances from each T-account in Exhibit 2.9 and group them as assets, liabilities, and stockholders' equity in balance sheet format. If you do this, you should end up with a balance sheet like the one presented way back in Exhibit 2.1. We realize that the odds of you flipping all the way back to page 45 right now are slim, so we've taken this opportunity to show you a slightly different balance sheet format in Exhibit 2.10 called the **classified balance sheet**. A classified balance sheet contains subcategories for assets and liabilities labeled *current*. **Current assets** are assets your business will use up or turn into cash within 12 months of the balance sheet date. For example, your salon will spend the cash and use the supplies during the next 12 months, so these assets are classified as current. Current assets are listed in order of how fast they will be used up or turned into cash. **Current liabilities** are debts and other obligations that will be paid or fulfilled within 12 months of the balance sheet date. In our example, accounts payable is the only current liability. The other liability— note payable—is expected to be paid in two years, so it is considered **noncurrent.**

Like Supercuts' equipment and note payable accounts, its stockholders' equity accounts are understood to be long-term in nature, although they are not labeled as such. Exhibit 2.10 includes the retained earnings account in stockholders' equity despite its zero balance because we don't want you to forget about this account. It will become a key link to the income statement, when introduced in Chapter 3.

Evaluate the Results

Learning Objective 5
Explain the concepts that determine whether an item is reported on the balance sheet and at what amount.

BALANCE SHEET CONCEPTS AND VALUES

Some people mistakenly believe that the balance sheet reports what a business is actually worth. To them, this is not a crazy idea because the balance sheet lists the company's assets and liabilities, so the net difference between the two must be the company's worth.

In fact, *net worth* is a term that many accountants and analysts use when referring to stockholders' equity. So why is it wrong to think that the balance sheet reports what a business is actually worth?

The answer comes from knowing that accounting is based on recording and reporting transactions, as you have seen over and over in this chapter. This focus on transactions does two things to the balance sheet: (1) it affects what is (and is not) recorded, and (2) it affects the amounts assigned to recorded items.

1. **What is (and is not) recorded?** Because accounting is based on transactions, an item will be recorded only if it comes from an identifiable transaction. "Equipment" appears on your Supercuts balance sheet because the company actually bought and received equipment. Had it only been ordered, no equipment would have been recorded. Other events that do not involve identifiable transactions are not entered into the accounting system and, therefore, do not make it to the balance sheet. For example, the value of the name "Regis Salons" is not reported on the balance sheet of Regis Corporation, even though 26 percent of the company's sales come from Regis Salons and only 12 percent come from Supercuts. This doesn't mean that the name isn't valuable in attracting customers or isn't relevant when estimating the value of Regis Corporation's business. It is valuable and relevant. Rather, all it means is that the name Regis Salons wasn't acquired in an identifiable transaction. And, without an identifiable transaction, there is no reporting of it on the balance sheet.

2. **What amounts are assigned to recorded items?** Following the cost principle, assets and liabilities are initially recorded at their original cost to the company. While these amounts are accurate at the time a transaction is entered into, there is no guarantee that these amounts will continue to represent the value of an asset or liability at a later time. It is possible that some assets and liabilities will change in value as time passes. However, the cost principle does not allow increases in asset values (and decreases in liability values) to be recorded unless external exchanges have caused the change in value. So, although real estate values in Chattanooga and the 250,000-square-foot distribution center that Regis Corporation built there in 2001 may have increased in value, this extra value would not be reported in the balance sheet because the dollar amount used to report transactions is based on the original cost to the company.

   Accounting rules do allow decreases in asset values to be recorded. In other words, accountants give up the cost principle to report decreases in value but not increases in value. Why is that? Because there is yet another accounting concept that comes into play—a principle called *conservatism*. **Conservatism** requires that special care be taken to avoid reporting assets at too high an amount or reporting liabilities at too low an amount. Essentially, conservatism requires that, when there is doubt about the amount at which assets and liabilities should be reported, the least optimistic measurement should be used.

Ethical Insights

The Motivation to be Conservative

Why are accountants conservative? It's primarily because they know that the financial statements are going to be used by outsiders such as bankers and investors to make decisions, and accountants don't want to mislead them. This is a very important ethical issue to accountants. If they paint too rosy a picture and lead someone to buy stock in a questionable company, investors may lose their money when things go wrong. So, when faced with uncertainty about the numbers, accountants take a conservative approach.

REVIEW THE CHAPTER

This section provides a chance to solidify your understanding of key points. It's worth your time to work through the following demonstration case, scan the chapter summary, test your understanding of key terms, and then practice, practice, practice.

DEMONSTRATION CASE

COACH'S TIP

For possible account names, see Exhibit 2.2.

www.mhhe.com/phillips2e

On April 1, 2008, three college students started Goodbye Grass Corporation (GGC). A summary of GGC's transactions completed through April 30, 2008 follows:

a. Issued shares of stock to the three investors in exchange for cash totaling $9,000.
b. Acquired rakes and other hand tools (equipment) for $600, paying the hardware store $200 cash and agreeing informally to pay the balance in three months.
c. Ordered lawn mowers and edgers costing $4,000 from XYZ Lawn Supply, Inc.
d. Purchased four acres of land for the future site of a storage garage. Paid cash, $5,000.
e. Received the mowers and edgers that had been ordered and signed a promissory note to pay XYZ Lawn Supply in full in 60 days.
f. Sold for $1,250 one acre of land to the city for a park and accepted a note from the city indicating payment will be received by GGC in six months.
g. One of the owners borrowed $3,000 from a local bank for personal use.

Required:

1. Analyze each event to determine its effects on the accounting equation.
2. Prepare journal entries to record transactions listed above (omit explanations).
3. Set up T-accounts for Cash, Note Receivable (from the city), Equipment (hand tools and mowing equipment), Land, Accounts Payable (to hardware store), Note Payable (to equipment supply company), and Contributed Capital. Indicate the beginning balances of $0 in each T-account, and then summarize the effects of each journal entry in the appropriate T-accounts.
4. Use the amounts in the T-accounts, developed in requirement 3, to prepare a classified balance sheet for Goodbye Grass Corporation at April 30, 2008. Show the balances for all assets, liabilities, and stockholders' equity accounts.
5. As of April 30, 2008, has financing for GGC's assets come primarily from liabilities or stockholders' equity?

Suggested Solution

1. Analyze transactions:

	Assets				=	Liabilities		+	Stockholders' Equity
	Cash	Note Receivable	Equipment	Land	=	Accounts Payable	Note Payable		Contributed Capital
(a)	+9,000				=				+9,000
(b)	−200		+600		=	+400			
(c)		No change*			=		No change		
(d)	−5,000			+5,000	=		No change		
(e)			+4,000		=		+4,000		
(f)		+1,250		−1,250	=		No change		
(g)		No change*			=		No change		

* Event (c) is not a considered a transaction because it involves only the exchange of promises. Event (g) is not considered a transaction of the company because the separate entity assumption (from Chapter 1) states that transactions of the owners are separate from transactions of the business.

2. Record journal entries:

a. *dr* Cash (+A) 9,000
    cr Contributed Capital (+SE) 9,000

b. *dr* Equipment (+A) 600
    cr Cash (−A) 200
    cr Accounts Payable (+L) 400

c. This is not an accounting transaction, so a journal entry is not needed.

d. *dr* Land (+A) 5,000
    cr Cash (−A) 5,000

e. *dr* Equipment (+A) 4,000
    cr Note Payable (+L) 4,000

f. *dr* Note Receivable (+A) 1,250
    cr Land (−A) 1,250

g. This is not a transaction of the business, so a journal entry is not needed.

3. Summarize journal entries in T-accounts:

Assets   =   Liabilities   +   Stockholders' Equity

Cash (A)			
Beg. Bal.	0	200	(b)
(a)	9,000	5,000	(d)
End.	3,800		

Equipment (A)		
Beg. Bal.	0	
(b)	600	
(e)	4,000	
End.	4,600	

Accounts Payable (L)		
	0	Beg. Bal.
	400	(b)
	400	End.

Contributed Capital (SE)		
	0	Beg. Bal.
	9,000	(a)
	9,000	End.

Note Receivable (A)		
Beg. Bal.	0	
(f)	1,250	
End.	1,250	

Land (A)			
Beg. Bal.	0		
(d)	5,000	1,250	(f)
End.	3,750		

Note Payable (L)		
	0	Beg. Bal.
	4,000	(e)
	4,000	End.

4. Prepare a classified balance sheet from the T-accounts:

GOODBYE GRASS CORPORATION
Balance Sheet
At April 30, 2008

Assets		Liabilities	
Current assets		Current liabilities	
Cash	$ 3,800	Accounts payable	$ 400
Note receivable	1,250	Note payable	4,000
Total current assets	5,050	Total current liabilities	4,400
Equipment	4,600		
Land	3,750	**Stockholders' Equity**	
		Contributed capital	9,000
		Retained earnings	0
Total assets	$13,400	Total liabilities and stockholders' equity	$13,400

5. The primary source of financing for GGC's assets (totaling $13,400) has come from stockholders' equity ($9,000) rather than liabilities ($4,400).

CHAPTER SUMMARY

LO1   Explain and select common balance sheet account titles. p. 44

- Typical balance sheet account titles include the following:

    Assets: Cash, Accounts Receivable, Inventories, Supplies, Property and Equipment.

    Liabilities: Accounts Payable, Notes Payable, Bonds Payable.

    Stockholders' Equity: Contributed Capital, Retained Earnings.

LO2   Apply transaction analysis to business transactions. p. 46

- Transactions include external exchanges and internal events.

- Transaction analysis is based on the duality of effects and the basic accounting equation. *Duality of effects* means that every transaction affects at least two accounts.

- Transaction analysis follows a systematic approach of determining whether a transaction exists; examining the transaction for the accounts affected; classifying the accounts as assets, liabilities, or stockholders' equity; identifying the direction and amount of the effects; and ending with the effects on the basic accounting equation.

LO3   Use journal entries and T-accounts to show how business transactions affect the balance sheet. p. 54

- Debit means left and credit means right.

- Debits increase assets and decrease liabilities and stockholders' equity.

- Credits decrease assets and increase liabilities and stockholders' equity.

- Journal entries express, in debits-equal-credits form, the effects of a transaction on various asset, liability, and stockholders' equity accounts. Journal entries are used to record financial information in the accounting system, which is later summarized by accounts in the ledger (T-accounts).

- T-accounts are a simplified version of the ledger, which summarizes transaction effects for each account. T-accounts show increases on the left (debit) side for assets, which are on the left side of the accounting equation. T-accounts show increases on the right (credit) side for liabilities and stockholders' equity, which are on the right side of the accounting equation.

LO4   Prepare a classified balance sheet. p. 61

- A *classified balance sheet* separately classifies assets as current if they will be used up or turned into cash within one year. Liabilities are classified as current if they will be paid, settled, or fulfilled within one year.

LO5   Explain the concepts that determine whether an item is reported on the balance sheet and at what amount. p. 62

- Because accounting is transaction-based, the balance sheet does not necessarily represent the current value of a business.

- Some assets are not recorded because they do not arise from transactions.

- The amounts recorded for assets and liabilities may not represent current values because under the cost principle they generally are recorded at cost, using the exchange amounts established at the time of the initial transaction.

- The concept of conservatism states that when uncertainty exists about the value of an asset or liability, care should be taken to not overstate the reported value of assets or understate the reported value of liabilities.

KEY TERMS

PRACTICE MATERIAL

QUESTIONS

1. Define the following:
   a. Asset   d. Current liability
   b. Current asset   e. Contributed capital
   c. Liability   f. Retained earnings
2. Define a transaction and give an example of each of the two types of events that are considered transactions.
3. For accounting purposes, what is an account? Explain why accounts are used in an accounting system.
4. What is the basic accounting equation?
5. Explain what *debit* and *credit* mean.
6. Briefly explain what is meant by *transaction analysis*. What are the two principles underlying transaction analysis? What are the steps of the DECIDE approach to transaction analysis?
7. What two different accounting equalities must be maintained in transaction analysis?
8. What is a journal entry? What is the typical format of a journal entry?
9. What is a T-account? What is its purpose?
10. What are the key features that all assets possess? What are the key features of all liabilities?
11. Explain what the following accounting terms mean:
    a. *Cost principle*   b. *Conservatism*

MULTIPLE CHOICE

1. Which of the following is not an asset?
   a. Cash   c. Equipment
   b. Land   d. Contributed capital
2. Which of the following statements describe transactions that would be recorded in the accounting system?
   a. An exchange of an asset for a promise to pay.
   b. An exchange of a promise for another promise.
   c. Both of the above.
   d. None of the above.
3. Total assets on a balance sheet prepared on any date must agree with which of the following?
   a. The sum of total liabilities and net income as shown on the income statement.
   b. The sum of total liabilities and contributed capital.
   c. The sum of total liabilities and retained earnings.
   d. The sum of total liabilities and contributed capital and retained earnings.
4. The *duality of effects* can best be described as follows:
   a. When a transaction is recorded in the accounting system, at least two effects on the basic accounting equation will result.
   b. When an exchange takes place between two parties, both parties must record the transaction.
   c. When a transaction is recorded, both the balance sheet and the income statement must be impacted.
   d. When a transaction is recorded, one account will always increase and one account will always decrease.

5. The T-account is used to summarize which of the following?
   a. Increases and decreases to a single account in the accounting system.
   b. Debits and credits to a single account in the accounting system.
   c. Changes in specific account balances over a time period.
   d. All of the above describe how T-accounts are used by accountants.

6. Which of the following describes how assets are listed on the balance sheet?
   a. In alphabetical order.
   b. In order of magnitude, lowest value to highest value.
   c. In the order they will be used up or turned into cash.
   d. From least current to most current.

7. A company was recently formed with $50,000 cash contributed to the company by stock-holders. The company then borrowed $20,000 from a bank and bought $10,000 of supplies on account. The company also purchased $50,000 of equipment by paying $20,000 in cash and issuing a note for the remainder. What is the amount of total assets to be reported on the balance sheet?
   a. $110,000   c. $90,000
   b. $100,000   d. None of the above

8. Which of the following statements are true regarding debits and credits?
   a. In any given transaction, the total dollar amount of the debits and the total dollar amount of the credits must be equal.
   b. Debits decrease certain accounts and credits decrease certain accounts.
   c. Liabilities and stockholders' equity accounts usually end in credit balances, while assets usually end in debit balances.
   d. All of the above.

9. Which of the following statements are true regarding the balance sheet?
   a. One cannot determine the true current value of a company by reviewing just its balance sheet.
   b. Certain assets, which are not acquired through identifiable transactions, are not reported on a company's balance sheet.
   c. A balance sheet shows only the ending balances, in a summarized format, of balance sheet accounts in the accounting system as of a particular date.
   d. All of the above.

10. If a publicly traded company is trying to maximize its perceived value to decision makers external to the corporation, the company is most likely to report too small a value for which of the following on its balance sheet?
    a. Assets
    b. Liabilities
    c. Retained earnings
    d. Contributed capital

Solutions to Multiple Choice Questions
1. d 2. a 3. d 4. a 5. d 6. c 7. a 8. d 9. d 10. b

Topic Tackler

PLUS

Quiz 2

Check out www.mhhe.com/phillips2e to practice more multiple choice questions.

MINI-EXERCISES

LO3   **M2-1 Identifying Increase and Decrease Effects on Balance Sheet Accounts**

Complete the following table by entering either the word *increases* or *decreases* in each column.

	Debit	Credit
Assets		
Liabilities		
Stockholders' Equity		

M2-2 Identifying Debit and Credit Effects on Balance Sheet Accounts LO3

Complete the following table by entering either the word *debit* or *credit* in each column.

	Increase	Decrease
Assets	_____	_____
Liabilities	_____	_____
Stockholders' equity	_____	_____

M2-3 Matching Terms with Definitions LO2, LO3, LO5

Match each term with its related definition by entering the appropriate letter in the space provided. There should be only one definition per term. (That is, there are more definitions than terms.)

Term	Definition
____ 1. Journal entry	A. An exchange or event that has a direct and measurable financial effect.
____ 2. A = L + SE; Debits = Credits	B. Four periodic financial statements.
____ 3. Transaction	C. The two equalities in accounting that aid in providing accuracy.
____ 4. Liabilities	D. The results of transaction analysis in debits-equal-credits format.
____ 5. Assets	E. The account that is debited when money is borrowed from a bank.
____ 6. Income statement, balance sheet, statement of retained earnings, and statement of cash flows	F. A resource owned by a business, with measurable value and expected future benefits.
	G. Cumulative earnings of a company that are not distributed to the owners.
	H. Every transaction has a least two effects.
	I. Debts or obligations to be paid with assets or fulfilled with services.
	J. Assigning dollar amounts to transactions.

M2-4 Classifying Accounts on a Balance Sheet LO1, LO4

The following are a few of the accounts of Aim Delivery Corporation:

____ 1. Wages Payable
____ 2. Accounts Payable
____ 3. Accounts Receivable
____ 4. Buildings
____ 5. Cash
____ 6. Contributed Capital
____ 7. Land
____ 8. Income Taxes Payable
____ 9. Equipment
____ 10. Notes Payable (due in six months)
____ 11. Retained Earnings
____ 12. Supplies
____ 13. Utilities Payable

In the space provided, classify each as it would be reported on a balance sheet. Use the following code:

CA = current asset   CL = current liability   SE = stockholders' equity
NCA = noncurrent asset   NCL = noncurrent liability

M2-5 Identifying Accounts on a Classified Balance Sheet and Their Normal Debit or Credit Balances LO1, LO3, LO4

Hasbro, Inc.

According to a recent report of Hasbro, Inc., the company is "a worldwide leader in children's and family games and toys." Hasbro produces products under several brands including Tonka, Milton

Bradley, Playskool, and Parker Brothers. The following are several of the accounts from a recent balance sheet:

1. Accounts Receivable	6. Property, Plant, and Equipment
2. Short-Term Bank Loan	7. Retained Earnings
3. Contributed Capital	8. Accounts Payable
4. Long-Term Debt	9. Cash
5. Income Taxes Payable	

Required:

1. Indicate how each account normally should be categorized on a classified balance sheet. Use CA for current asset, NCA for noncurrent asset, CL for current liability, NCL for noncurrent liability, and SE for stockholders' equity.
2. Indicate whether the account normally has a debit or credit balance.

LO1, LO3, LO4
Blockbuster, Inc.

M2-6 Identifying Accounts on a Classified Balance Sheet and Their Normal Debit or Credit Balances

Blockbuster, Inc., is the world's leading provider of rentable DVDs and videogames. Blockbuster estimates that 64 percent of the U.S. population lives within a 10-minute drive of a Blockbuster store. The following are several of the accounts included in a recent balance sheet:

1. Income Taxes Payable	5. Long-Term Debt
2. Accounts Receivable	6. Property and Equipment
3. Cash	7. Retained Earnings
4. Contributed Capital	8. Accounts Payable

Required:

1. Indicate how each account normally should be categorized on a classified balance sheet. Use CA for current asset, NCA for noncurrent asset, CL for current liability, NCL for noncurrent liability, and SE for stockholders' equity.
2. Indicate whether the account normally has a debit or credit balance.

LO2
The Toro Company

M2-7 Identifying Events as Accounting Transactions

Do the following events result in a recordable transaction for The Toro Company? Answer yes or no for each.

_____ 1. Toro purchased robotic manufacturing equipment that it paid for by signing a note payable.

_____ 2. Toro's president purchased stock in another company for his own portfolio.

_____ 3. The company lent $550 to an employee.

_____ 4. Toro ordered supplies from Office Max to be delivered next week.

_____ 5. Six investors in Toro sold their stock to another investor.

_____ 6. The company borrowed $2,500,000 from a local bank.

LO2

M2-8 Identifying Events as Accounting Transactions

With 80 locations in 14 states, Half Price Books is the country's favorite new and used bookstore chain. By recycling more than 16 million books, the company estimates it has saved over 65,000 trees. Do the following events result in a recordable transaction for Half Price Books? Answer yes or no for each.

_____ 1. Half Price Books bought an old laundromat in Dallas.

_____ 2. The privately held company issued stock to new investors.

_____ 3. The company signed an agreement to rent store space in Columbia Plaza near Cleveland.

_____ 4. The company paid for renovations to prepare its Seattle store for operations.

_____ 5. The vice president of the company spoke at a literacy luncheon in Indiana, which contributed to building the company's reputation as a responsible company.

M2-9 Determining Financial Statement Effects of Several Transactions   LO2

For each of the following transactions of Spotlighter Inc. for the month of January 2009, indicate the accounts, amounts, and direction of the effects on the accounting equation. A sample is provided.

a. (*Sample*) Borrowed $3,940 from a local bank on a note due in six months.
b. Received $4,630 cash from investors and issued stock to them.
c. Purchased $920 in equipment, paying $190 cash and promising the rest on a note due in one year.
d. Paid $372 cash for supplies.
e. Bought $700 of supplies on account.

Assets	=	Liabilities	+ Stockholders' Equity
a. *Sample*: Cash +3,940		Notes payable +3,940	

M2-10 Preparing Journal Entries   LO3

For each of the transactions in M2-9 (including the sample), write the journal entry using the format shown in this chapter (explanations omitted).

M2-11 Posting to T-Accounts   LO3

For each of the transactions in M2-9 (including the sample), post the effects to the appropriate T-accounts and determine ending account balances.

+ Cash (A) −	+ Supplies (A) −	+ Equipment (A) −

− Accounts Payable (L) +	− Notes Payable (L) +	− Contributed Capital (SE) +

M2-12 Reporting a Classified Balance Sheet   LO4

Given the transactions in M2-9 (including the sample), prepare a classified balance sheet for Spotlighter Inc. as of January 31, 2009.

M2-13 Preparing a Classified Balance Sheet   LO4

Trump Entertainments Resorts

The following accounts are taken from the financial statements of Trump Entertainments Resorts, Inc. at the year-end December 31, 2005.

General expenses	$ 176,763,000
Salaries payable	26,553,000
Interest expense	79,602,000
Accounts payable	38,739,000
Other current liabilities	136,873,000
Food and beverage revenue	77,806,000
Cash	273,559,000
Accounts receivable	45,740,000
Other current assets	25,183,000
Property, equipment, and other assets	1,985,281,000
Long-term note payable	1,700,440,000
Contributed capital	27,000
Retained earnings (as of December 31, 2005)	427,131,000

Required:

1. Prepare a classified balance sheet at December 31, 2005.
   TIP: Some of the above accounts are not reported on the balance sheet.
   TIP: Round the reported amounts to an appropriate unit of measure.
2. Using the balance sheet, indicate whether the total assets of Trump Entertainments Resorts, Inc. at the end of the year were financed primarily by liabilities or stockholders' equity.

EXERCISES

Available with McGraw-Hill's
Homework Manager

HOMEWORK MANAGER PLUS™

LO1, LO2, LO5 **E2-1 Matching Terms with Definitions**

Match each term with its related definition by entering the appropriate letter in the space provided. There should be only one definition per term (that is, there are more definitions than terms).

Term

____ 1. Transaction	____ 6. Current assets
____ 2. Separate entity concept	____ 7. Notes payable
____ 3. Balance sheet	____ 8. Duality of effects
____ 4. Liabilities	____ 9. Retained earnings
____ 5. Assets = Liabilities + Stockholders' Equity	____ 10. Debit

Definition

A. Economic resources to be used or turned into cash within one year.
B. Reports assets, liabilities, and stockholders' equity.
C. Decrease assets; increase liabilities and stockholders' equity.
D. Increase assets; decrease liabilities and stockholders' equity.
E. An exchange or event that has a direct and measurable financial effect.
F. The assumption that businesses will operate into the foreseeable future.
G. Accounts for a business separate from its owners.
H. The principle that assets should be recorded at their original cost to the company.
I. A standardized format used to accumulate data about each item reported on financial statements.
J. The basic accounting equation.
K. The two equalities in accounting that aid in providing accuracy.
L. The account credited when money is borrowed from a bank using a promissory note.
M. Cumulative earnings of a company that are not distributed to the owners.
N. Every transaction has at least two effects.
O. Probable debts or obligations to be paid with assets or services.

LO1, LO2, LO5 **E2-2 Identifying Account Titles**

The following are independent situations.

a. A company orders and receives 10 personal computers for office use for which it signs a note promising to pay $25,000 within three months.
b. A company purchases for $21,000 cash a new delivery truck that has a list ("sticker") price of $24,000.
c. A women's clothing retailer orders 30 new display stands for $300 each for future delivery.
d. A new company is formed and issues 100 shares of stock for $12 per share to investors.
e. A company purchases a piece of land for $50,000 cash. An appraiser for the buyer valued the land at $52,500.
f. The owner of a local company buys a $10,000 car for personal use. Answer from the company's point of view.
g. A company borrows $1,000 from a local bank and signs a six-month note for the loan.
h. A company pays $1,500 owed on its note payable (ignore interest).

Required:

1. Indicate titles of the appropriate accounts, if any, affected in each of the preceding events. Consider what the company gives and receives.

2. At what amount would you record the delivery truck in *b*? The piece of land in *e*? What measurement principle are you applying?

3. What reasoning did you apply in *c*? For *f*, what accounting concept did you apply?

E2-3 Classifying Accounts and Their Usual Balances

LO1, LO3, LO4

As described in a recent annual report, Digital Diversions, Inc. (DDI) designs, develops, and distributes videogames for computers and advanced game systems such as Paystation, Y-Box, Tamecube, and Gamegirl. DDI has been operating for only one full year.

Required:

For each of the following accounts from DDI's recent balance sheet, complete the following table. Indicate whether the account is classified as a current asset (CA), noncurrent asset (NCA), current liability (CL), noncurrent liability (NCL), or stockholders' equity (SE), and whether the account usually has a debit (*dr*) or credit (*cr*) balance.

Account	Balance Sheet Classification	Debit or Credit Balance
1. Land	_____	_____
2. Retained Earnings	_____	_____
3. Notes Payable (due in three years)	_____	_____
4. Accounts Receivable	_____	_____
5. Supplies	_____	_____
6. Contributed Capital	_____	_____
7. Machinery and Equipment	_____	_____
8. Accounts Payable	_____	_____
9. Cash	_____	_____
10. Taxes Payable	_____	_____

E2-4 Determining Financial Statement Effects of Several Transactions

LO1, LO2

The following events occurred for Favata Company:

a. Received $10,000 cash from owners and issued stock to them.
b. Borrowed $7,000 cash from a bank and signed a note.
c. Purchased land for $12,000; paid $1,000 in cash and signed a note for the balance.
d. Bought $800 of equipment on account.
e. Purchased $3,000 of equipment, paying $1,000 in cash and signing a note for the rest.

Required:

For each of the events (*a*) through (*e*), perform transaction analysis and indicate the account, amount, and direction of the effect (+ for increase and − for decrease) on the accounting equation. Check that the accounting equation remains in balance after each transaction. Use the following headings:

Event	Assets	=	Liabilities	+	Stockholders' Equity

E2-5 Determining Financial Statement Effects of Several Transactions

LO1, LO2

Nike, Inc.

Nike, Inc., with headquarters in Beaverton, Oregon, is one of the world's leading manufacturers of athletic shoes and sports apparel. The following activities occurred during a recent year. The amounts are presented in millions of dollars.

a. Purchased $216.3 in equipment; paid by signing a $5 long-term note and fulfilling the rest with cash.
b. Issued $21.1 in additional stock for cash.

c.   Several Nike investors sold their own stock to other investors on the stock exchange for $21 per share of stock.

Required:

1.   For each of these events, perform transaction analysis and indicate the account, amount (in millions), and direction of the effect on the accounting equation. Check that the accounting equation remains in balance after each transaction. Use the following headings:

Event	Assets	=	Liabilities	+	Stockholders' Equity

2.   Explain your response to transaction (c).

LO3   **E2-6 Recording Investing and Financing Activities**

Refer to E2-4.

Required:

For each of the events in E2-4, prepare journal entries, checking that debits equal credits.

LO3, LO5   **E2-7 Recording Investing and Financing Activities**

Refer to E2-5.

Required:

1.   For each of the events in E2-5, prepare journal entries, checking that debits equal credits.
2.   Explain your response to event (c).

LO2, LO3, LO5   **E2-8 Analyzing the Effects of Transactions in T-Accounts**

Mulkeen Service Company, Inc., was incorporated by Conor Mulkeen and five other managers. The following activities occurred during the year:

a.   Received $60,000 cash from the managers; each was issued 1,000 shares of stock.
b.   Purchased equipment for use in the business at a cost of $12,000; one-fourth was paid in cash and the company signed a note for the balance (due in six months).
c.   Signed an agreement with a cleaning service to pay it $120 per week for cleaning the corporate offices, beginning next week.
d.   Conor Mulkeen borrowed $10,000 for personal use from a local bank, signing a one-year note.

Required:

1.   Create T-accounts for the following accounts: Cash, Equipment, Note Payable, and Contributed Capital. Beginning balances are zero. For each of the above transactions, record its effects in the appropriate T-accounts. Include referencing and totals for each T-account.
2.   Using the balances in the T-accounts, fill in the following amounts for the accounting equation:

Assets $_____ = Liabilities $_____ + Stockholders' Equity $_____

3.   Explain your response to events (c) and (d).

LO1, LO2, LO4   **E2-9 Inferring Investing and Financing Transactions and Preparing a Balance Sheet**

During its first week of operations, January 1–7, 2008, Home Comfort Furniture Corporation completed six transactions with the dollar effects indicated in the following schedule:

	Assets			=	Liabilities	+	Stockholders' Equity
	Cash	Equipment	Land	=	Notes Payable		Contributed Capital
Beginning	$ 0	$ 0	$ 0	=	$ 0		$ 0
(1)	+12,000			=			+12,000
(2)	+50,000			=	+50,000		
(3)	−4,000		+12,000	=	+8,000		
(4)	+4,000			=	+4,000		
(5)	−7,000	+7,000		=			
(6)			+3,000	=	+3,000		
Ending	$	$	$	=	$		$

Required:

1. Write a brief explanation of transactions 1 through 6. Explain any assumptions that you made.
2. Compute the ending balance in each account and prepare a classified balance sheet for Home Comfort Furniture Company on January 7, 2008.
3. As of January 7, 2008, has most of the financing for Home Comfort's investments in assets come from liabilities or stockholders' equity?

E2-10 Inferring Investing and Financing Transactions and Preparing a Balance Sheet

LO1, LO2, LO4

During its first month of operations, March 2007, Faye's Fashions, Inc., completed four transactions with the dollar effects indicated in the following schedule:

Accounts	1	2	3	4	Ending Balance
DOLLAR EFFECT OF EACH OF THE FOUR TRANSACTIONS					
Cash	$50,000	$(4,000)	$5,000	$(4,000)	
Computer Equipment				4,000	
Delivery Truck		25,000			
Short-term Bank Loan			5,000		
Long-term Notes Payable		21,000			
Contributed Capital	50,000				

Required:

1. Write a brief explanation of transactions 1 through 4. Explain any assumptions that you made.
2. Compute the ending balance in each account and prepare a classified balance sheet for Faye's Fashions, Inc., at the end of March 2007.
3. As of March 31, 2007, has most of the financing for Faye's investment in assets come from liabilities or stockholders' equity?

E2-11 Recording Journal Entries

LO1, LO3, LO5
Despair.com

Assume Down.com was organized on May 1, 2008 to compete with Despair.com—a company that sells de-motivational posters and office products. The following events occurred during the first month of Down.com's operations.

a. Received $60,000 cash from the investors who organized Down.com Corporation.
b. Borrowed $20,000 cash and signed a note due in two years.
c. Ordered computer equipment costing $16,000.
d. Purchased $10,000 in equipment, paying $1,000 in cash and signing a six-month note for the balance.
e. Received and paid for the computer equipment ordered in (c).

Required:

Prepare journal entries for each transaction. (Remember that debits go on top and credits go on the bottom, indented.) Be sure to use referencing and categorize each account as an asset (A), liability (L), or stockholders' equity (SE). If a transaction does not require a journal entry, explain the reason.

E2-12 Analyzing the Effects of Transactions Using T-Accounts; Preparing and Interpreting a Balance Sheet

LO2, LO3, LO4

Lee Delivery Company, Inc. (LDC), was incorporated in 2008. The following transactions occurred during the year:

a. Received $40,000 cash from organizers in exchange for stock in the new company.
b. Purchased land for $12,000, signing a two-year note (ignore interest).
c. Bought two used delivery trucks at the start of the year at a cost of $10,000 each; paid $2,000 cash and signed a note due in three years for the rest (ignore interest).
d. Paid $2,000 cash to a truck repair shop for a new motor, which increased the cost of one of the trucks.
e. Stockholder Jonah Lee paid $122,000 cash for a house for his personal use.

Required:

1. Analyze each item for its effects on the financial statements of LDC, for the year ended December 31, 2008.

    TIP: Transaction a is presented below as an example.

		Assets	=	Liabilities	+	Stockholder's Equity
(a)	Cash	+40,000	=			Contributed Capital +40,000

    TIP: The new motor in transaction d is treated as an increase to the cost of the truck.

2. Record the effects of each item using a journal entry.

    TIP: Use the simplified journal entry format shown in the demonstration case on pages 64-65.

3. Summarize the effects of the journal entries by account, using the T-account format shown in the chapter.

4. Prepare a classified balance sheet for LDC at the end of 2008.

5. Using the balance sheet, indicate whether LDC's assets at the end of the year were financed primarily by liabilities or stockholders' equity.

LO1, LO2, LO3   **E2-13** **Explaining the Effects of Transactions on Balance Sheet Accounts Using T-Accounts**

Heavey and Lovas Furniture Repair Service, a company with two stockholders, began operations on June 1, 2008. The following T-accounts indicate the activities for the month of June.

	Cash (A)				Supplies (A)				Building (A)	
(a)	17,000	10,000	(b)	(c)	1,500			(b)	50,000	
		1,500	(c)							

	Notes Payable (L)				Contributed Capital (SE)	
		40,000	(b)			17,000	(a)

Required:

Explain events *a* through *c* that resulted in the entries in the T-accounts. That is, for each account what transactions made it increase and/or decrease?

COACHED PROBLEMS

LO2, LO5   **CP2-1** **Determining Financial Statement Effects of Various Transactions**

www.mhhe.com/phillips2e

Lester's Home Healthcare Services (LHHS) was organized on January 1, 2007, by four friends. Each organizer invested $10,000 in the company and, in turn, was issued 8,000 shares of stock. To date, they are the only stockholders. During the first month (January 2007), the company had the following six events:

a. Collected a total of $40,000 from the organizers and, in turn, issued the shares of stock.
b. Purchased a building for $65,000, equipment for $16,000, and three acres of land for $12,000; paid $13,000 in cash and signed a note for the balance, which is due to be paid in 15 years.
c. One stockholder reported to the company that 500 shares of his LHHS stock had been sold and transferred to another stockholder for $5,000 cash.
d. Purchased supplies for $3,000 cash.
e. Sold one acre of land for $4,000 cash to another company.

Required:

1. Was Lester's Home Healthcare Services organized as a partnership or corporation? Explain the basis for your answer.
2. During the first month, the records of the company were inadequate. You were asked to prepare a summary of the preceding transactions. To develop a quick assessment of their

economic effects on Lester's Home Healthcare Services, you have decided to complete the spreadsheet that follows and to use plus (+) for increases and minus (−) for decreases for each account.

TIP: Transaction a is presented below as an example.

		Assets			=	Liabilities	+	Stockholders' Equity	
						Notes		Contributed	Retained
Cash	Supplies	Land	Building	Equipment	=	Payable		Capital	Earnings
(a) +40,000								+40,000	

TIP: In transaction (b), five different accounts are affected.

3. Did you include the transaction between the two stockholders—Event (c)—in the spreadsheet? Why?

TIP: Think about whether this event caused LHHS to receive or give up anything.

4. Based only on the completed spreadsheet, provide the following amounts (show computations):

   a. Total assets at the end of the month.

   b. Total liabilities at the end of the month.

   c. Total stockholders' equity at the end of the month.

   d. Cash balance at the end of the month.

   e. Total current assets at the end of the month.

5. As of January 31, 2007, has the financing for LHHS's investment in assets primarily come from liabilities or stockholders' equity?

CP2-2 Recording Transactions (in a Journal and T-Accounts); Preparing and Interpreting the Balance Sheet

LO2, LO3, LO4, LO5

Athletic Performance Company (APC) was incorporated as a private company on June 1, 2008. The company's accounts included the following at July 1, 2008:

Accounts payable	$ 20,000	Land	$100,000
Factory building	200,000	Notes payable	1,000
Cash	16,000	Retained earnings	238,000
Contributed capital	80,000	Supplies	5,000
Equipment	18,000		

During the month of July, the company had the following activities:

a. Issued 2,000 shares of stock for $200,000 cash.

b. Borrowed $30,000 cash from a local bank, payable June 30, 2010.

c. Bought a factory building for $141,000; paid $41,000 in cash and signed a three-year note for the balance.

d. Paid cash for equipment that cost $100,000.

e. Purchased supplies for $10,000 on account.

Required:

1. Analyze transactions (a)–(e) to determine their effects on the accounting equation. Use the format shown in the demonstration case on page 64.

   TIP: You won't need new accounts to record the transactions described above, so have a quick look at the ones listed before you start this question.

   TIP: In transaction (c), three different accounts are affected.

2. Record the transaction effects determined in requirement 1 using journal entries.

3. Summarize the journal entry effects from requirement 2 using T-accounts.

   TIP: Create a T-account for each account listed above. Enter the July 1, 2008, balances as the month's beginning balances.

4. Prepare a classified balance sheet at July 31, 2008.

5. As of July 31, 2008, has the financing for APC's investment in assets primarily come from liabilities or stockholders' equity?

LO2, LO3, LO4, LO5   **CP2-3** **Recording Transactions (in a Journal and T-Accounts); Preparing and Interpreting the Balance Sheet**

Performance Plastics Company (PPC) has been operating for three years. The December 31, 2007, account balances are:

Cash	$ 35,000	Land	$ 30,000
Accounts receivable	5,000	Other assets	5,000
Inventory	40,000	Accounts payable	37,000
Notes receivable	2,000	Notes payable (due 2009)	80,000
Equipment	80,000	Contributed capital	150,000
Factory building	120,000	Retained earnings	50,000

During the year 2008, the company had the following summarized activities:

a.   Purchased equipment that cost $20,000; paid $5,000 cash and signed a two-year note for the balance.
b.   Issued an additional 2,000 shares of stock for $20,000 cash.
c.   Borrowed $30,000 cash from a local bank, payable June 30, 2010.
d.   Purchased an "other asset" for $4,000 cash.
e.   Built an addition to the factory for $41,000; paid $12,000 in cash and signed a three-year note for the balance.
f.   Hired a new president to start January 1, 2009. The contract was for $95,000 for each full year worked.

Required:

1.   Analyze transactions (a)–(f) to determine their effects on the accounting equation. Use the format shown in the demonstration case on page 64.

   TIP: You won't need new accounts to record the transactions described above, so have a quick look at the ones listed before you start this question.

   TIP: In transaction (e), three different accounts are affected.

   TIP: In transaction (f), consider whether PPC owes anything to its new president for the year ended December 31, 2008.

2.   Record the transaction effects determined in requirement 1 using journal entries.
3.   Summarize the journal entry effects from requirement 2 using T-accounts.

   TIP: Create a T-account for each account listed above. Enter the December 31, 2007, balances as the 2008 beginning balances.

4.   Explain your response to event f.
5.   Prepare a classified balance sheet at December 31, 2008.
6.   As of December 31, 2008, has the financing for PPC's investment in assets primarily come from liabilities or stockholders' equity?

GROUP A PROBLEMS

LO2, LO5   **PA2-1** **Determining Financial Statement Effects of Various Transactions**

www.mhhe.com/phillips2e

Mallard Incorporated (MI) is a small manufacturing company that makes model trains to sell to toy stores. It has a small service department that repairs customers' trains for a fee. The company has been in business for five years. At the end of the most recent year, 2007, the accounting records reflected total assets of $500,000 and total liabilities of $200,000. During the current year, 2008, the following summarized events occurred:

a.   Issued additional shares of stock for $100,000 cash.
b.   Borrowed $120,000 cash from the bank and signed a 10-year note.
c.   Built an addition on the factory for $200,000 and paid cash to the contractor.
d.   Purchased equipment for the new addition for $30,000, paying $3,000 in cash and signing a note due in six months for the balance.
e.   Returned a $3,000 piece of equipment, from (d), because it proved to be defective; received a reduction of the note payable.
f.   Purchased a delivery truck (equipment) for $10,000; paid $5,000 cash and signed a nine-month note for the remainder.
g.   A stockholder sold $5,000 of his capital stock in Mallard Incorporated to his neighbor.

Required:

1. Complete the spreadsheet that follows, using plus (+) for increases and minus (−) for decreases for each account. The first transaction is used as an example.

Assets			=	Liabilities	+	Stockholders' Equity	
Cash	Equipment	Building	=	Notes Payable		Contributed Capital	Retained Earnings
(a) +100,000						+100,000	

2. Did you include event (g) in the spreadsheet? Why or why not?

3. Based on beginning balances plus the completed spreadsheet, provide the following amounts (show computations):

   a. Total assets at the end of the year.

   b. Total liabilities at the end of the year.

   c. Total stockholders' equity at the end of the year.

4. As of December 31, 2008, has the financing for MI's investment in assets primarily come from liabilities or stockholders' equity?

PA2-2 Recording Transactions (in a Journal and T-Accounts); Preparing and Interpreting the Balance Sheet

LO2, LO3, LO4, LO5

Deliberate Speed Corporation (DSC) was incorporated as a private company on June 1, 2008. The company's accounts included the following at June 30, 2008:

Accounts Payable	$ 10,000	Land	$200,000
Factory Building	100,000	Notes Payable	2,000
Cash	26,000	Retained Earnings	259,000
Contributed Capital	180,000	Supplies	7,000
Equipment	118,000		

During the month of July, the company had the following activities:

a. Issued 4,000 shares of stock for $400,000 cash.
b. Borrowed $90,000 cash from a local bank, payable June 30, 2010.
c. Bought a factory building for $182,000; paid $82,000 in cash and signed a three-year note for the balance.
d. Paid cash for equipment that cost $200,000.
e. Purchased supplies for $30,000 on account.

Required:

1. Analyze transactions (a)–(e) to determine their effects on the accounting equation. Use the format shown in the demonstration case on page 64.
2. Record the transaction effects determined in requirement 1 using a journal entry format.
3. Summarize the journal entry effects from requirement 2 using T-accounts.
4. Prepare a classified balance sheet at July 31, 2008.
5. As of July 31, 2008, has the financing for DSC's investment in assets primarily come from liabilities or stockholders' equity?

PA2-3 Recording Transactions (in a Journal and T-Accounts); Preparing and Interpreting the Balance Sheet

LO2, LO3, LO4, LO5
Ethan Allen Interiors, Inc.

Ethan Allen Interiors, Inc., is a leading manufacturer and retailer of home furnishings in 315 retail stores in the United States and abroad. The following is adapted from Ethan Allen's balance sheet as of June 30, 2005. Dollars are in thousands.

Cash	$ 75,688	Other assets	$ 6,665
Accounts receivable	32,845	Accounts payable	80,993
Inventories	174,147	Wages and other expenses payable	48,028
Prepaid expenses and		Long-term debt	9,321
other current assets	36,076	Other long-term liabilities	39,224
Property, plant, and equipment	293,626	Contributed capital	116,719
Intangibles	69,708	Retained earnings	394,470

Assume that the following events occurred in the quarter ended September 30. Dollars are in thousands.

a. Paid $1,400 cash for an additional "other asset."
b. Issued additional shares of stock for $1,050 in cash.
c. Purchased property, plant, and equipment; paid $1,870 in cash and signed a note to pay the remaining $9,300 in two years.
d. Sold, at cost, other assets for $320 cash.
e. Conducted negotiations to purchase a sawmill, which is expected to cost $36,000.

Required:

1. Analyze transactions (*a*)–(*e*) to determine their effects on the accounting equation. Use the format shown in the demonstration case on page 64.
2. Record the transaction effects determined in requirement 1 using journal entries.
3. Summarize the journal entry effects from requirement 2 using T-accounts. Use the June 2005 ending balances (reported above) as the beginning balances for the July–September 2005 quarter.
4. Explain your response to event (*e*).
5. Prepare a classified balance sheet at September 30, 2005.
6. As of September 30, 2005, has the financing for Ethan Allen's investment in assets primarily come from liabilities or stockholders' equity?

GROUP B PROBLEMS

LO2, LO5

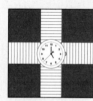

PB2-1 Determining Financial Statement Effects of Various Transactions

Swish Watch Corporation manufactures, sells, and services expensive, ugly watches. The company has been in business for three years. At the end of the most recent year, 2006, the accounting records reported total assets of $2,255,000 and total liabilities of $1,780,000. During the current year, 2007, the following summarized events occurred:

a. Issued additional shares of stock for $109,000 cash.
b. Borrowed $186,000 cash from the bank and signed a 10-year note.
c. A stockholder sold $5,000 of his capital stock in Swish Watch Corporation to another investor.
d. Built an addition on the factory for $200,000 and paid cash to the construction company.
e. Purchased equipment for the new addition for $44,000, paying $12,000 in cash and signing a six-month note for the balance.
f. Returned a $4,000 piece of equipment, from (*e*), because it proved to be defective; received a cash refund.

Required:

1. Complete the spreadsheet that follows, using plus (+) for increases and minus (−) for decreases for each account. The first transaction is used as an example.

Assets			=	Liabilities	+	Stockholders' Equity	
Cash	Equipment	Building	=	Notes Payable		Contributed Capital	Retained Earnings
(*a*) +109,000						+109,000	

2. Did you include event (*c*) in the spreadsheet? Why?
3. Based on beginning balances plus the completed spreadsheet, provide the following amounts (show computations):
   a. Total assets at the end of the year.
   b. Total liabilities at the end of the year.
   c. Total stockholders' equity at the end of the year.
4. As of December 31, 2007, has the financing for Swish Watch Corporation's investment in assets primarily come from liabilities or stockholders' equity?

PB2-2 Recording Transactions (in a Journal and T-Accounts); Preparing and Interpreting the Balance Sheet   LO2, LO3, LO4, LO5

Bearings & Brakes Corporation (B&B) was incorporated as a private company on June 1, 2008. The company's accounts included the following at June 30, 2008:

Accounts Payable	$ 50,000	Land	$444,000
Factory Building	500,000	Notes Payable	5,000
Cash	90,000	Retained Earnings	966,000
Contributed Capital	170,000	Supplies	9,000
Equipment	148,000		

During the month of July, the company had the following activities:

a. Issued 6,000 shares of stock for $600,000 cash.
b. Borrowed $60,000 cash from a local bank, payable June 30, 2010.
c. Bought a factory building for $166,000; paid $66,000 in cash and signed a three-year note for the balance.
d. Paid cash for equipment that cost $90,000.
e. Purchased supplies for $90,000 on account.

Required:

1. Analyze transactions (a)–(e) to determine their effects on the accounting equation. Use the format shown in the demonstration case on page 64.
2. Record the transaction effects determined in requirement 1 using a journal entry format.
3. Summarize the journal entry effects from requirement 2 using T-accounts.
4. Prepare a classified balance sheet at July 31, 2008.
5. As of July 31, 2008, has the financing for B&B's investment in assets primarily come from liabilities or stockholders' equity?

PB2-3 Recording Transactions (in a Journal and T-Accounts); Preparing and Interpreting the Balance Sheet   LO2, LO3, LO4, LO5
Starbucks

Starbucks is a coffee company—a big coffee company. During a 10-year period, the number of Starbucks locations grew from 165 to over 5,800 stores—an average increase of 43 percent every year. The following is adapted from a recent Starbucks annual report. Starbucks' year-end is September 30 and dollars are reported in thousands.

Cash	$ 174,500	Accounts payable	$ 462,600
Accounts receivable	97,500	Short-term bank loans	74,900
Inventories	263,200	Long-term debt	5,100
Other current assets	312,100	Other long-term liabilities	23,500
Property, plant, and equipment	1,265,800	Contributed capital	930,300
Other long-term assets	179,500	Retained earnings	796,200

Assume that the following events occurred in the following quarter, which ended December 31, 2005. Dollars are in thousands.

a. Paid $10,000 cash for additional other long-term assets.
b. Issued additional shares of stock for $5,100 in cash.
c. Purchased property, plant, and equipment; paid $11,200 in cash and signed additional long-term loans for $9,500.
d. Sold, at cost, other long-term assets for $6,000 cash.
e. Conducted negotiations to purchase a coffee farm, which is expected to cost $8,400.

Required:

1. Analyze transactions (a)–(e) to determine their effects on the accounting equation. Use the format shown in the demonstration case on page 64.
2. Record the transaction effects determined in requirement 1 using journal entries.
3. Summarize the journal entry effects from requirement 2 using T-accounts. Use the September 2005 ending balances (reported above) as the beginning balances for the October-December 2005 quarter.

4. Explain your response to event (*e*).
5. Prepare a classified balance sheet at December 31, 2005.
6. As of December 31, 2005, has the financing for the investment in assets made by Starbucks primarily come from liabilities or stockholders' equity?

SKILLS DEVELOPMENT CASES

LO1, LO5   **S2-1 Finding and Analyzing Financial Information**

Refer to the financial statements of Landry's Restaurants in Appendix A at the end of this book, or download the annual report from the *Cases* section of the text's Web site at www.mhhe.com/phillips2e.

Required:

1. What is the company's fiscal year-end? Where did you find the exact date?
2. Use the company's balance sheet to determine the amounts in the accounting equation (A = L + SE).
3. On the balance sheet, the company reports inventories of $59,716,920. Does this amount represent the expected selling price? Why or why not?
4. What is the amount of the company's current liabilities?
5. Has financing for the company's investment in assets primarily come from liabilities or stockholders' equity?

LO1, LO5   **S2-2 Finding and Analyzing Financial Information**

Refer to the financial statements of Outback Steakhouse, Inc. in Appendix B at the end of this book, or download them from the *Cases* section of the text's Web site at www.mhhe.com/phillips2e.

Required:

1. Use the company's balance sheet to determine the amounts in the accounting equation (A = L + SE). (For purposes of this question, treat the "minority interests in consolidated entities" reported by Outback as an additional liability.) Is Outback Steakhouse or Landry's larger in terms of total assets?
2. Does Outback Steakhouse have more or less current assets than Landry's?
3. Does Outback Steakhouse have more or less current liabilities than Landry's?
4. Has financing for the Outback Steakhouse's investment in assets primarily come from liabilities or stockholders' equity?

LO1, LO5   **S2-3 Team Research, Financial Analysis, Technology, and Communication: Examining the Balance Sheet**

As a team, select an industry to analyze. Using your Web browser, each team member should access the annual report or 10-K for one publicly traded company in the industry, with each member selecting a different company. (See S1-3 in Chapter 1 for a description of possible resources for these tasks.)

Required:

1. On an individual basis, each team member should write a short report that lists the following information.
   a. The date of the balance sheet.
   b. The major noncurrent asset accounts and any significant changes in them.
   c. The major noncurrent liability accounts and any significant changes in them.
   d. Any significant changes in total stockholders' equity.
   e. Whether financing for the investment in assets primarily comes from liabilities or stockholders' equity.
2. Then, as a team, write a short report comparing and contrasting your companies using the above dimensions. Discuss any similarities across the companies that you as a team observe, and provide potential explanations for any differences discovered.

S2-4 Ethical Reasoning, Critical Thinking, and Communication: A Real-Life Fraud

In the world of financial fraud, a "Ponzi scheme" is famous. Here is the story behind how the scam got its name. Charles Ponzi started the Security Exchange Company on December 26, 1919. He thought he had discovered a way to purchase American stamps in a foreign country at significantly lower amounts than they were worth in the United States. He claimed his idea was so successful that anyone who gave money to his company would be repaid their original loan plus 50 percent interest within 90 days. Friends and family quickly offered their money to Ponzi and they were handsomely rewarded, being repaid their original loan and the 50 percent interest within just 45 days. Thanks to an article in *The New York Times*, word spread quickly about Ponzi's business, attracting thousands of people seeking a similar payback. He might have had a successful business had his idea actually worked. The problem, however, was that it didn't. The 50 percent interest paid to early investors did not come from the profits of a successful underlying business idea (which didn't even exist) but instead was obtained fraudulently from funds contributed by later lenders. Eventually, the Ponzi scheme collapsed on August 10, 1920, after an auditor examined his accounting records.

Required:

1. Assume that on December 27, 1919, Ponzi's first three lenders provided his company with $5,000 each. Use the basic accounting equation to show the effects of these transactions on December 27, 1919.

2. If the first two lenders are repaid their original loan amounts plus the 50 percent interest promised to them, how much cash is left in Ponzi's business to repay the third lender? Given what you discovered, how was it possible for Ponzi's company to remain in "business" for over eight months?

3. Who was harmed by Ponzi's scheme?

Epilogue: After taking in nearly $15 million from 40,000 people, Ponzi's company failed with just $1.5 million in total assets. Ponzi spent four years in prison before jumping bail, to become involved in fraudulently selling swampland in Florida. We're not kidding.

S2-5 Ethical Reasoning, Critical Thinking, and Communication: A Mini-Case

You work as an accountant for a small land development company that desperately needs additional financing to continue in business. The president of your company is meeting with the manager of a local bank at the end of the month to try to obtain this financing. The president has approached you with two ideas to improve the company's reported financial position. First, he claims that because a big part of the company's value comes from its knowledgeable and dedicated employees, you should report their "Intellectual Abilities" as an asset on the balance sheet. Second, he claims that although the local economy is doing poorly and almost no one is buying land or new houses, he is optimistic that eventually things will turn around. For this reason, he asks you to continue reporting the company's land on the balance sheet at its cost, rather than the much lower amount that real estate appraisers say it's really worth.

Required:

1. Thinking back to Chapter 1, why do you think the president is so concerned with the amount of assets reported on the balance sheet?

2. What accounting concept introduced in Chapter 2 relates to the president's first suggestion to report "Intellectual Abilities" as an asset?

3. What accounting concept introduced in Chapter 2 relates to the president's second suggestion to continue reporting land at its cost?

4. Who might be hurt by the president's suggestions, if you were to do as he asks? What should you do?

S2-6 Financial Analysis and Critical Thinking: Evaluating the Reliability of a Balance Sheet

Betsey Jordan asked a local bank for a $50,000 loan to expand her small company. The bank asked Betsey to submit a financial statement of the business to supplement the loan application. Betsey prepared the following balance sheet.

Balance Sheet
June 30, 2007

Assets

Cash	$ 9,000
Inventory	30,000
Equipment	46,000
Personal residence (monthly payments, $2,800)	300,000
Remaining assets	20,000
Total assets	$405,000

Liabilities

Short-term debt to suppliers	$ 62,000
Long-term debt on equipment	38,000
Total debt	100,000
Stockholders' equity	305,000
Total liabilities and stockholders' equity	$405,000

Required:

The balance sheet has several flaws. However, there is at least one major deficiency. Identify it and explain its significance.

LO2

Elizabeth Arden, Inc.

www.mhhe.com/phillips2e

S2-7 Using Technology with Analyzing Transactions and Preparing a Balance Sheet

Assume you recently obtained a part-time accounting position at the corporate headquarters of Elizabeth Arden, Inc., in Miami Lakes, Florida. Elizabeth Arden is a leading marketer and manufacturer of prestige beauty products, prominently led by the Red Door line of fragrances. The following table summarizes accounts and their balances (in thousands) reported by Elizabeth Arden, Inc., in a recent September 30 balance sheet.

Cash	$ 14,300	Short-Term Notes Payable	$ 125,000
Accounts Receivable	285,400	Accounts Payable	111,800
Inventories	199,700	Other Current Liabilities	75,700
Other Current Assets	31,600	Long-Term Debt	323,600
Property and Equipment	35,800	Other Long-Term Liabilities	10,100
Other Noncurrent Assets	224,100	Contributed Capital	101,800
		Retained Earnings	42,900

Determine how the balance sheet of Elizabeth Arden would change if the company were to enter into the following transactions (amounts in thousands) during October:

Oct. 2   Purchase an additional manufacturing facility at a cost of $15,000 by issuing a promissory note that becomes payable in three years.

Oct. 10   Use $7,000 cash to repay one of the short-term loans.

Oct. 21   Issue additional stock for $20,000 cash.

Oct. 28   Use cash to buy land for $8,000.

Required:

The controller at Elizabeth Arden has asked you to create a spreadsheet in which to display:

a.   The account balances at September 30.

b.   The effects of the four October transactions.

c.   Totals that combine the September 30 balances with the October transactions. You feel like you might be ready to tackle this assignment, but just to be sure, you e-mail your friend Owen for advice. Here's his reply.

From: Owentheaccountant@yahoo.com
To: Helpme@hotmail.com
Cc:
Subject: Excel Help

Wow, I can't believe you gave up that great job at EA. Good thing you landed another one so quickly!

1. My thinking is that you'll really impress your boss if you set up the spreadsheet to look like a bunch of T-accounts, one beside another. Use two columns for each balance sheet account (with the account name spanning the two columns) to make it look just like a T-account. You do remember how to use the cell merge command to make a header span two columns, right? If not, check the last e-mail I sent you. Here's a screenshot of how one part of the left-hand side of your worksheet might look just before you enter the October transactions.

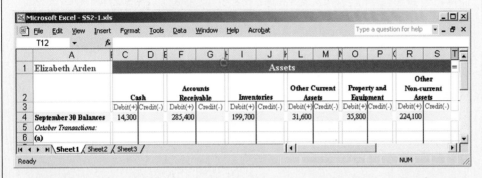

2. See S1-7 for my cell merge advice. For extra spreadsheet skills, you might also try creating a balance sheet with cells that are linked to the corresponding cells in the T-accounts. To do this, open a worksheet in the same file as the T-accounts. Then click on a cell in the balance sheet worksheet where you want to import a number from the T-accounts, then type =, then click on the tab for the T-account worksheet, click on the cell with the total to be transferred, and then press enter. This links the cells so that any changes to the T-accounts automatically update the balance sheet. Also, Excel will let you hide row and column gridlines if you want. Just search Excel's help index for "hide gridlines."

3. I guess the only thing that's left is to remind you that to compute the ending balances in each T-account you have to add the increases to the beginning balance and subtract the decreases. So, to compute the totals for a particular account, your formula might look like =(SUM(C4:C9)-SUM(D5:D9)).

4. Oh yeah, when you're all done, don't forget to save the file using a name that uniquely identifies you.

3

Reporting Operating Results on the Income Statement

YOUR LEARNING OBJECTIVES

Understand the business

LO1   Describe common operating transactions and select appropriate income statement account titles.

Study the accounting methods

LO2   Explain and apply the revenue and matching principles.

LO3   Analyze, record, and summarize the effects of operating transactions, using the accounting equation, journal entries, and T-accounts.

LO4   Prepare an unadjusted trial balance.

Evaluate the results

LO5   Describe limitations of the income statement.

Review the chapter

THAT WAS
THEN

In the previous chapter, you learned how to analyze, record, and summarize the effects of transactions on balance sheet accounts.

LP3

SUPERCUTS®

A side from music, what do Toni Braxton, the San Jose Symphony, and TLC have in common? Here's a hint. They're in the same club as Enron, Kmart, United Airlines, and WorldCom (now called Verizon). That's right, they all have experienced bankruptcy. It may be difficult to believe that these big names could be involved in bankruptcy proceedings, with TLC having enjoyed six top-10 singles in the United States prior to the group's bankruptcy filing and with Kmart celebrating its 100-year anniversary only three years before its bankruptcy filing. But it's true. Despite generating millions and millions of dollars in sales, these celebrities and huge corporations lived beyond their means—a problem that eventually led them to bankruptcy.

Toni Braxton's bankruptcy is an interesting tale that involves love, the law, and an income statement. Well, actually, it doesn't involve an income statement—that was part of the problem. Without an income statement to compare her revenues to her expenses, Toni had no way of seeing that she was headed for financial trouble. As it turns out, her personal revenues were "only" $400,000 a year—hardly enough to cover all the expenses that come from living a lavish celebrity lifestyle. She spent over $10,000 to attend a weekend runway show in New York, $15,000 to buy her Vera Wang wedding dress, and $1,200 to get hair extensions. If only she had known that these and other costs totaled more than her personal revenues—perhaps she could have had her hair done at Supercuts, where the average customer pays a mere $16.[1]

[1] Information for this chapter opener has been obtained from A. M. Dickerson, "Bankruptcy Reform: Does the End Justify the Means?" *American Bankruptcy Law Journal,* April 2001, p. 243; "A Star Is Broke," *Entertainment Weekly,* February 20, 1998; www.bankruptcydata.com/Research/15_Largest.htm; www.chl.ca/JamMusicArtistsB/braxton_toni.html; Regis Corporation's 2006 Form 10-K; and http://people.aol.com/people/news/now/0,10958,123191,00.html

THIS IS
NOW

This chapter focuses on analyzing, recording, and summarizing the effects of operating transactions on balance sheet and income statement accounts.

The first goal of this chapter is to help you to see how an income statement indicates whether a business generated a profit or loss from the day-to-day business activities that occur during an accounting period. Then, we'll show how the transaction analysis approach from Chapter 2 can be used to analyze and record transactions affecting the income statement. Finally, at the end of the chapter, we will highlight some limitations of the income statement. The main tasks and chapter topics are summarized below.

ORGANIZATION OF THE CHAPTER

Understand the business	Study the accounting methods	Evaluate the results	Review the chapter
• Operating transactions and income statement accounts	• Cash basis accounting • Accrual basis accounting • The expanded accounting equation • Unadjusted trial balance • Review of revenues and expenses	• Income statement limitations	• Demonstration case • Chapter summary • Key terms • Practice material

Understand the Business

Video 3.1

OPERATING TRANSACTIONS AND INCOME STATEMENT ACCOUNTS

Just as it was useful in Chapter 2 to understand the balance sheet by thinking about the investing and financing activities needed to start up a Supercuts salon, it's helpful to consider a salon's operating activities before looking at the income statement. Think back to the last time you got your hair cut. How does your salon generate revenues and what expenses does it incur? For hair salons and most other businesses, **revenues** represent the amounts charged to customers. If your salon opens its doors to customers in September, gives 1,560 haircuts, and charges $10 per cut, revenues would total $15,600. The amount of revenues earned during the period is the first thing reported in the body of the income statement.

The costs of operating the business are reported as **expenses** in the body of the income statement just underneath revenues. In general, expenses include any costs incurred to generate revenues in the period covered by the income statement. For hair salons, the big expenses relate to manager salaries and stylist wages, rent, advertising, insurance, and various utilities (telephone, fax, Internet, power, water). Our friends in the business tell us that a salon that gives 1,560 haircuts in a month would typically incur operating expenses of $8,000 for salaries and wages, $2,400 for rent, $600 for utilities, $400 for advertising, and $300 for insurance. Big hair companies have similar expenses, although they are much larger—Regis Corporation

EXHIBIT 3.1 | Income Statement

SUPERCUTS

SUPERCUTS Income Statement For the month ended September 30, 2008			
		Who: Company name **What:** Financial statement name **When:** Accounting period	
Revenues			
Haircut revenues	$15,600	Amount charged to customers in September	
Expenses			
Salaries and wages expense	8,000	Manager salaries and stylists' wages in September	
Rent expense	2,400	Cost of renting store space in September	
Utilities expense	600	Cost of water, power, etc. in September	
Advertising expense	400	Cost of advertising done in September	
Insurance expense	300	Cost of insurance coverage for September	
Total expenses	11,700	Sum of all expenses	
Net Income	$ 3,900	= $15,600 − 11,700	

reports expenses just like those in Exhibit 3.1, except they are about 12,000 times bigger than what we've shown.

By subtracting total expenses from total revenues, it's possible to summarize the overall impact in a single number called **net income** (or net loss if expenses are greater than revenues). Net income indicates how much the owners' value (stockholders' equity) increases as a result of the company's operations. For this reason, net income is a closely watched measure of a company's success.

Exhibit 3.1 shows how revenues, expenses, and net income would be reported in your salon's income statement. Each account title describes the specific type of revenue or expense arising from the business's particular operations. This is true for all companies. Supercuts reports "haircut revenues," but Blockbuster reports "movie rental revenues." Google reports "traffic acquisition expenses" and Southwest Airlines reports "landing fee expenses." You'll become more comfortable with various account titles as this course progresses but to keep things simple right now we'll stick to common types of revenues and expenses. A more complete list of revenue and expense account titles, which will help when doing homework, appears in the chapter supplement on page 106.

The income statement in Exhibit 3.1 is for the month ended September 30, 2008. As it turns out, September 30, 2008, is a Tuesday. You might wonder what's so special about this date. The answer is that there is nothing particularly special about this date—it's just the last day of the month. By dividing the company's long life into meaningful and shorter chunks of time, Supercuts' managers can measure and evaluate the company's financial performance on a timely basis. This is known in accounting as the **time period assumption.** If net income is low in the current month, managers will find out about it quickly and be able to take steps to become more profitable in the following month.

Notice that the Supercuts income statement reports the financial effects of business activities that occurred during just the current period. They relate only to the current period. They do not have a lingering financial impact beyond the end of the current period. This is a key distinction between the income statement and the balance sheet. The revenues and expenses on an income statement report the financial impact of activities in just the current period whereas items on a balance sheet will continue to have a financial impact beyond the end of the current period. Another way people describe this difference is that the balance sheet takes stock of what exists at a point in time whereas the income statement depicts a flow of what happened over a period of time.

YOU SHOULD KNOW

The **time period assumption** assumes that the long life of a company can be divided into shorter time periods, such as months, quarters, and years.

HOW'S IT GOING?   A Self-Study Quiz

For each item listed below, indicate whether the company should report it on the income statement this period (yes/no). If yes, indicate an appropriate account title for the item described.

Description	Yes/No	Account Title
1. Citibank charges customers a monthly service fee.	_____	_____
2. Target buys a new building to use as a retail store.	_____	_____
3. Dell pays to deliver computers to customers.	_____	_____
4. Pizza Hut buys supplies to be used next month.	_____	_____
5. Abercrombie pays weekly wages to employees.	_____	_____

Quiz Answers

Yes/No	Account Title
1. Yes	Service fee revenue
2. No	
3. Yes	Transportation expense
4. No	
5. Yes	Salaries and wages expense

Ethical Insights

35 Days Hath September?

It seems some managers—specifically those at Computer Associates (CA)—haven't learned the time period assumption. CA was charged with financial statement fraud for improperly recording 35 days of sales in September—a month that has only 30 days. To make it look like managers had met their September sales targets, CA included the first five days of sales from October in its September income statement. This accounting fraud led managers to be paid bonuses they hadn't earned and tricked investors into thinking CA was a successful company. When the truth was revealed later, CA's stockholders quickly abandoned the company, causing its stock price to fall 43 percent in a single day. CA ultimately paid stockholders $225 million to make up for its bad accounting and agreed to help the SEC ensure all inappropriate management bonuses were paid back to the company. In addition, several executives, marketing, and accounting personnel are presently serving jail sentences. Proper revenue reporting is obviously a very serious matter.

Study the Accounting Methods

CASH BASIS ACCOUNTING

LP3

What's a good way to determine whether you're doing well financially? Many people simply look at the balance in their bank accounts to gauge their financial performance. If the overall balance increased this month, they take that as a sign that they've done a good job of managing their finances. If it has gone down, that's a clue they need to tame their spending next month. The reason that the change in your bank balance tends to give a decent measure of financial performance is that your cash flows (in and out) occur close in time to the activities that cause those cash flows. For example, if you participate in a psychology experiment, you'll probably get paid on the spot, so the cash inflow is a good measure of how much your participation improved your financial situation. Similarly, if you write a check for groceries, your declining cash balance will provide a timely measure of how much your snacking is costing you. As shown in Exhibit 3.2, when there is little delay between the underlying activities and the reporting of their effects on your bank balance, **cash basis accounting** is good enough.

Generally speaking, cash basis accounting doesn't measure financial performance very well when transactions are conducted using credit rather than cash. The problem is

YOU SHOULD KNOW

Cash basis accounting reports revenues when cash is received and expenses when cash is paid.

EXHIBIT 3.2   Cash Basis Useful Only When No Delays

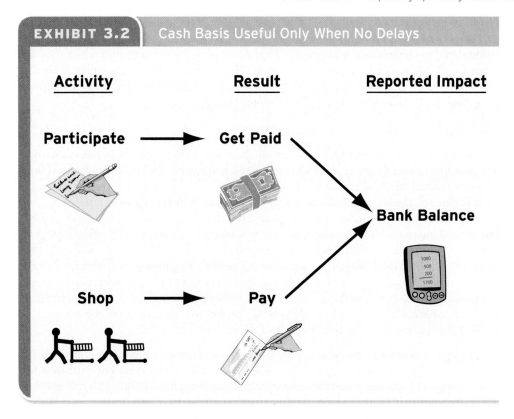

that credit often introduces a significant delay between the time an activity occurs and the time it impacts the bank account balance. If you get a paycheck from your job only once a month, the results of your hard work don't show up until the end of the month. Similarly, if you go crazy with your credit card at the mall, these transactions won't affect your bank balance for at least a month.

The same situation arises in business because most companies use credit for their transactions. DHL, for example, often delivers packages in one month but doesn't get paid for this work until the next month. Under cash basis accounting, DHL would report expenses in Month 1 but wouldn't report revenues until it received payments from its customers in Month 2. This leads to a rather distorted view of the company's financial performance, as shown in Exhibit 3.3. The company reports a net loss in Month 1 and a huge net income in Month 2, when the truth is the business activities generate revenue of $15,000, expenses of $10,000, and net income of $5,000, all of which relate to the activities that occurred in Month 1 when the packages were delivered. A better method of accounting is needed—one that reports the revenues and related expenses during the same period.

ACCRUAL BASIS ACCOUNTING

The method of accounting that reports revenues and related expenses in the same period is called **accrual basis** accounting. According to generally accepted accounting principles, the accrual basis is the only acceptable method for external reporting of income. The cash basis can be used internally by some small companies, but GAAP do not allow it to

> **Learning Objective 2**
> Explain and apply the revenue and matching principles.

> **YOU SHOULD KNOW**
>
> **Accrual basis** accounting reports revenues when they are earned and expenses when they are incurred, regardless of the timing of cash receipts or payments.

EXHIBIT 3.3   Cash Basis Not Useful When Delay Occurs between Activity and Cash Flow

	Month 1 (Activity Occurs)		Month 2 (Cash Exchanged)		Total	
Revenues	$ 0		Revenues	$15,000	Revenues	$15,000
Expenses	10,000		Expenses	0	Expenses	10,000
Net Loss	$(10,000)		Net Income	$15,000	Net Income	$ 5,000

Topic Tackler

PLUS

Check out www.mhhe.com/phillips2e for audio, visual, and PowerPoint presentations on this topic.

> **YOU SHOULD KNOW**
>
> The **revenue principle** is a concept that requires that revenues be recorded when they are earned, not necessarily when cash is received for them.

be used for external reporting. The "rule of accrual" is that the financial effects of business activities are measured and reported when the activities actually occur, not when the cash related to them is received or paid. That is, revenues are recognized when they are earned and expenses when they are incurred. The two basic accounting principles that determine when revenues and expenses are recognized under accrual basis accounting are called the *revenue principle* and the *matching principle*.

Revenue Principle—Revenue Recognition

According to the **revenue principle,** revenues should be recognized when they are earned. The word *recognized* means revenues are measured and recorded in the accounting system. The word *earned* means the company has performed the acts promised to the customer. For most businesses, these conditions are met at the point of delivery of goods or services.

All companies expect to receive cash in exchange for providing goods and services, but the timing of cash receipts does not dictate when revenues are recognized. Instead, the key factor in determining when to recognize revenue is whether the company has done what it promised during the accounting period. Regardless of the length of the period (month, quarter, or year), cash can be received (1) in the same period as the promised acts are performed, (2) in a period before the promised acts are performed, or (3) in a period after the promised acts are performed, as shown on the timeline in Exhibit 3.4. Let's see how to handle each of these cases.

1. **Cash is received in the same period as the promised acts are performed.** This is a common occurrence for Supercuts stores because customers pay within a few minutes of getting a haircut. As with all accounting transactions, this one involves two parts: (a) Supercuts gives the customer a haircut, thus earning revenue, and (b) in exchange, Supercuts receives cash from the customer.

2. **Cash is received in a period before the promised acts are performed.** This situation can occur when your Supercuts salon receives cash for gift cards that customers can use to pay for future haircuts. Supercuts will record the cash received, but the company hasn't provided the promised haircuts, so no revenue is recorded yet. Instead, Supercuts has an obligation to either give a haircut in the future for no additional charge or return the money received for the gift card. Either way, Supercuts has a liability. This liability is called **unearned revenue,** and it is recorded on the balance sheet equal in amount to the cash received. There is no impact on the income statement when the cash is received because Supercuts has given a promise, not a haircut. When Supercuts gives the haircut in the future and fulfills some of the promise represented by the gift card, revenue will be reported on the income statement and the unearned revenue account will be reduced.

3. **Cash is to be received in a period after the promised acts are performed.** This situation typically arises when a company sells to a customer on account. As

> **YOU SHOULD KNOW**
>
> **Unearned revenue** is a liability representing a company's obligation to provide goods or services to customers in the future.

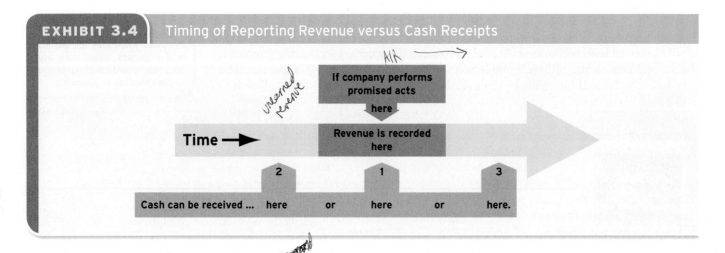

EXHIBIT 3.4 | Timing of Reporting Revenue versus Cash Receipts

dictated by the revenue principle, the company records revenue when the promised act is performed. If Supercuts provides haircuts for a TV station's news reporters on account in September, then the revenue is earned and reported in September, even though Supercuts may not be paid until October. By providing haircuts in September, Supercuts earns revenue as well as the right to collect from the customer. This right to collect is called *accounts receivable*. When Supercuts collects cash from the customer in October, cash will increase and the account receivable will decrease. No additional revenue for this transaction is reported in October because the services were provided in September, not October.

Every company reports its revenue recognition policy in its notes to the financial statements. For example, see how Regis Corporation explains its policy for revenue from its Supercuts stores.

Regis Corporation

Salon revenues are recognized at the time of sale, as this is when the services have been provided. Gift cards issued by the company are recorded as a liability until they are redeemed.

It's worthwhile making sure you understand what sparks the recording of revenues because, in the next section, you'll see that this also triggers the recording of expenses. To ensure that you have a handle on this, spend a couple of minutes on the Self-Study Quiz.

HOW'S IT GOING? A Self-Study Quiz

The following transactions are typical operating activities for Florida Flippers, a scuba diving and instruction company. Indicate the amount of revenue, if any, that should be recognized in June for each activity.

Operating Activity	Amount of Revenue Earned in June
1. In June, Florida Flippers provided $32,000 in diving instruction to customers for cash.	
2. In June, new customers paid $8,200 cash for diving trips to be provided by Florida Flippers; $5,200 in trips were made in June and the rest will be provided in July.	
3. In June, customers paid $3,900 cash for instruction they received in May.	

Expense Recognition

The business activities that generate revenues also create expenses. Under accrual basis accounting, expenses are recognized in the same period as the revenues to which they relate, not necessarily the period in which cash is paid for them. For example, for Supercuts to provide haircuts in September, it must rent mall space and have its stylists work that month. Under accrual basis accounting, Supercuts would report rent expense and wages expense in September, even if the rent were paid in August and the wages were paid in October. This is what accountants call the **matching principle:** record expenses in the same period as the revenues with which they can be reasonably associated. If an expense cannot be directly associated with revenues, it is recorded in the period

> **YOU SHOULD KNOW**
>
> The **matching principle** is a concept that requires that expenses be recorded in the same period as the revenues they generate, not necessarily the period in which cash is paid for them.

EXHIBIT 3.5 | Timing of Reporting Expenses versus Cash Payments

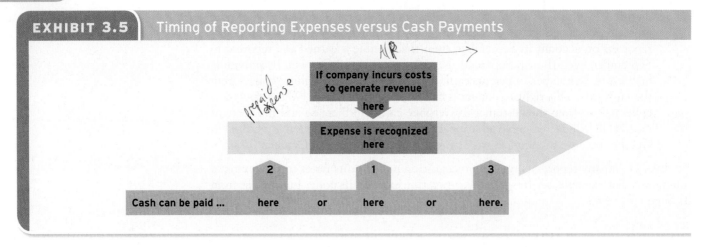

that the underlying business activity occurs. For example, because it's not clear how or when advertising affects revenue, advertising expense is simply reported in the period that ads are run. Notice that it is the timing of the underlying business activities, not the cash payments, that dictates when expenses are recognized. Cash payments may occur (1) at the same time as, (2) before, or (3) after the related expenses are incurred to generate revenue, as shown in Exhibit 3.5.

1. **Cash is paid at the same time as the cost is incurred to generate revenue.** Although this isn't as common in business as in your personal life, expenses are sometimes paid for in the period that they arise. For example, Supercuts could spend $100 cash on muffins on September 1 to celebrate its grand opening that day. This cost would be reported as an expense in the September income statement because the muffins were bought for an activity occurring in September. In other words, the benefits of incurring the cost are entirely used up within the current accounting period. If a cost were to benefit future accounting periods, rather than the current period, it would be reported as an asset (see point 2).

2. **Cash is paid before the cost is incurred to generate revenue.** It's common for companies to pay for something that provides benefits only in future periods. For example, Supercuts might pay for shampoo in August, but not use the shampoo until September. Given the matching principle, the expense for using these supplies should be reported in September when the supplies are used to earn revenue. This is not reported as an expense in August because it does not lead to earning revenues that month. In August, the supplies represent an asset because they will benefit future periods. When they are used in September, the supplies expense will be reported on the September income statement and the asset, Supplies, will decrease. Similar situations arise when a company prepays rent or insurance.

3. **Cash is paid after the cost is incurred to generate revenue.** Because most transactions between businesses are conducted using credit, it is common for a company to incur costs in one period and not pay cash for them until a later period. For example, Supercuts uses electricity to power its hair dryers this month, but doesn't pay for it until next month. Because the cost of the electricity relates to revenues earned this month, it represents an expense that will be reported on this month's income statement. Because the cost has not yet been paid at the end of this month, Supercuts also has incurred a liability to pay for the electricity costs. The expense is called *utilities expense* and the liability is called *accounts payable*. Similar situations arise when employees work in the current period but are not paid their wages until the following period.

It's time for you to practice determining which costs should be reported as expenses on an income statement prepared using accrual basis accounting. As you work through the next Self-Study Quiz, feel free to glance at Exhibit 3.5 for help.

HOW'S IT GOING?   A Self-Study Quiz

The following transactions are typical operating activities for Florida Flippers, a scuba diving and instruction company. Indicate the amount of expense, if any, that should be recognized in June for each activity.

Operating Activity	Amount of Expense Incurred in June
1. At the beginning of June, Florida Flippers paid a total of $6,000 cash for insurance for the months of June, July, and August.	
2. In June, Florida Flippers paid $4,000 in wages to employees who worked in June.	
3. In June, Florida Flippers paid $2,400 for electricity used in May.	

Quiz Answers

Amount
1. $2,000 (the remaining $4,000 will be reported as an asset until used in July and August).
2. $4,000.
3. No expense in June for the $2,400 payment; expense was incurred in May.

THE EXPANDED ACCOUNTING EQUATION

When we introduced the basic accounting equation in Chapter 2, we didn't mention how to account for the income statement effects of operating activities. You already had enough to learn, relating to the effects of investing and financing activities on assets, liabilities, and contributed capital. The time has now come for you to learn how to analyze, record, and summarize the effects of operating activities. To do this, you first need to know how the debit/credit framework works with revenues and expenses.

Let's start with the basic ingredients from Chapter 2. That is, assets equals liabilities plus stockholders' equity, or A = L + SE. For now, we're going to focus on the stockholders' equity category. As you already know from Chapters 1 and 2, stockholders' equity represents the stockholders' investment in the company, which comes from either (1) contributed capital, given to the company by stockholders in exchange for stock or (2) retained earnings, generated by the company itself through profitable operations. Retained earnings is the part that expands to include revenues and expenses, as shown in Exhibit 3.6.

Take a moment to look at how Exhibit 3.6 encourages you to think of revenues and expenses as subcategories within retained earnings. They are shown this way because the effects of revenue and expense transactions eventually flow into retained earnings, but they aren't initially recorded there. Instead, each type of revenue and expense is accumulated in a separate account, making it easier to identify the amount to report for each of these line items on the income statement. At the end of each accounting year, these separate revenue and expense accounts are "closed" into retained earnings through a process we'll demonstrate in Chapter 4. For now, just focus on learning how revenues and expenses are recorded to indicate increases and decreases in the company's earnings, with corresponding effects recorded in the company's asset and/or liability accounts.

Because revenue and expense accounts are subcategories of retained earnings, they are affected by debits and credits in the same way as all stockholders' equity accounts. You already know that increases in stockholders' equity are recorded on the right side. You also know that revenues increase net income, which increases the stockholders' equity account called *Retained Earnings*. So putting these ideas together should lead to the conclusion that revenues are recorded on the right (credit). Here's the logic again: increases in stockholders' equity are on the right, revenues increase stockholders' equity, so revenues are recorded on the right (credit). Decreases in stockholders' equity are recorded on the left side, so to show that expenses decrease net income and retained earnings, expenses are recorded on the left (debit). Exhibit 3.6 summarizes these effects.

Learning Objective 3
Analyze, record, and summarize the effects of operating transactions, using the accounting equation, journal entries, and T-accounts.

Topic Tackler

PLUS

Check out www.mhhe.com/phillips2e for audio, visual, and PowerPoint presentations on this topic.

Video 3.2

EXHIBIT 3.6 The Expanded Debit/Credit Framework

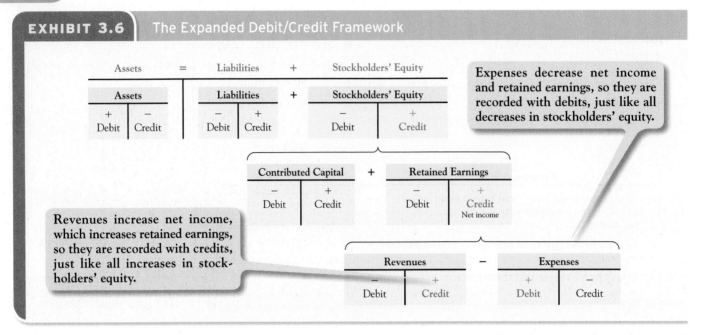

Spend enough time studying Exhibit 3.6 because you'll need to use it often in homework and in the following examples.

Transaction Analysis, Recording, and Summarizing

To learn how to use your new knowledge of the revenue and matching principles, the expanded accounting equation, and the debit/credit framework, you'll need lots of practice. The best place to start is by reading our analysis of the following examples, which involve Supercuts' operating activities during September.

(a) Provide Services for Cash

In September, Supercuts provided services to customers for $15,000 cash. These activities qualify as accounting transactions because your salon receives cash and gives the promised haircut services, which generates revenues. The increase in cash (an asset) must be recorded (with a debit) along with the revenue (which, as a subcategory of stockholders' equity, is recorded with a credit). To indicate that the haircut services increase both revenue and stockholders' equity, we use the notation (+R, +SE) in the journal entry. The increase in cash is summarized in the Cash T-account, which carried a debit balance of $10,000 forward from the end of August (Chapter 2). The revenues earned are recorded in a new account called *Haircut Revenue*, which has a beginning balance of zero because the company began operating only this month.

1. Analyze

	Assets	=	Liabilities	+	Stockholders' Equity	
(a) Cash	+15,000	=			Haircut Revenue (+R)	+15,000

2. Record

(a) *dr* Cash (+A) 15,000
         cr Haircut Revenue (+R, +SE) 15,000

3. Summarize

dr +	Cash (A)	*cr* −
Beg. Bal.	10,000	
(a)	15,000	

dr −	Haircut Revenue (R, SE)	*cr* +
	0	Beg. Bal.
	15,000	(a)

(b) Receive Cash for Future Services

Your salon sold three $100 gift cards at the beginning of September. Supercuts receives cash but gives only gift cards, which represent a promise to provide future services at no additional charge. This promise is recorded as a liability called Unearned Revenue.

COACH'S TIP

The word *unearned* in the Unearned Revenue account means the company hasn't done everything it promised to do. It has a liability to do something in the future.

1. Analyze

Assets	=	Liabilities	+	Stockholders' Equity
(b) Cash +300	=	Unearned Revenue +300		

2. Record

(b)   *dr* **Cash (+A)** 300
        cr **Unearned Revenue (+L)** 300

3. Summarize

dr +	Cash (A)	*cr* −		*dr* −	Unearned Revenue (L)	*cr* +
Beg. Bal.	10,000				0	Beg. Bal.
(a)	15,000				300	(b)
(b)	300					

(c) Provide Services on Credit

Supercuts provided $500 of hairstyling services to employees of a local TV station, which is billed every month. Once again, this is another instance where revenues are recorded based on whether services have been provided, not whether cash has been received. Because services have been provided, your salon has earned revenue and now has the right to collect $500 from the TV station. The right to collect money is an asset called Accounts Receivable.

1. Analyze

Assets	=	Liabilities	+	Stockholders' Equity
(c) Accounts Receivable +500	=			Haircut Revenue (+R) +500

2. Record

(c)   *dr* **Accounts Receivable (+A)** 500
        cr **Haircut Revenue (+R, +SE)** 500

3. Summarize

dr +	Accounts Receivable (A)	*cr* −		*dr* −	Haircut Revenue (R, SE)	*cr* +
Beg. Bal.	0				0	Beg. Bal.
(c)	500				15,000	(a)
					500	(c)

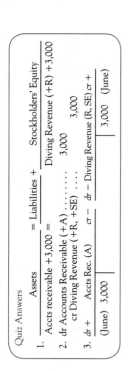

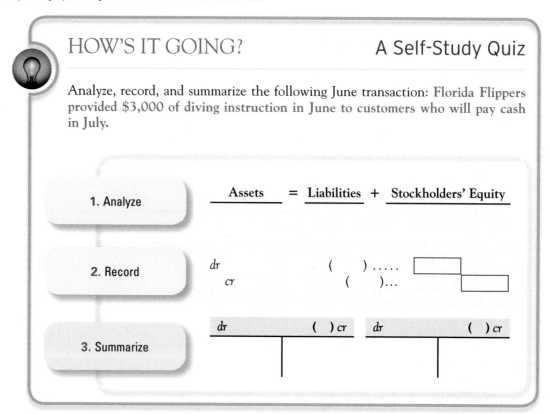

HOW'S IT GOING? A Self-Study Quiz

Analyze, record, and summarize the following June transaction: Florida Flippers provided $3,000 of diving instruction in June to customers who will pay cash in July.

1. Analyze

Assets	=	Liabilities	+	Stockholders' Equity

2. Record

dr ( ) .....
cr ( )...

3. Summarize

dr ( ) cr   dr ( ) cr

(d) Receive Payment on Account

Supercuts received a $300 payment from the TV station. This transaction does not involve additional haircut services, so no additional revenue is generated. Instead, the receipt of cash reduces the amount that Supercuts can collect from this customer in the future, so it causes a decrease in Accounts Receivable.

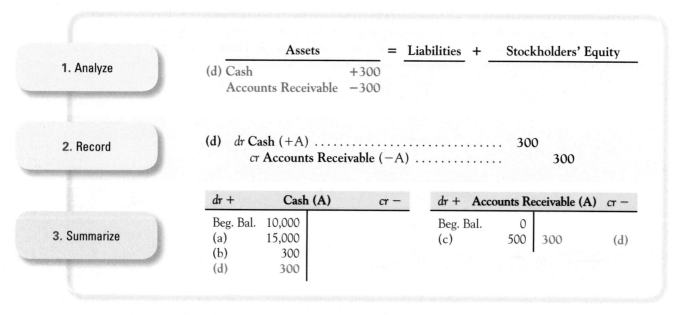

1. Analyze

	Assets		=	Liabilities	+	Stockholders' Equity
(d) Cash		+300				
Accounts Receivable		−300				

2. Record

(d) dr **Cash** (+A) 300
cr **Accounts Receivable** (−A) 300

dr +	Cash (A)	cr −		dr +	Accounts Receivable (A)	cr −
Beg. Bal.	10,000			Beg. Bal.	0	
(a)	15,000			(c)	500	300	(d)
(b)	300					
(d)	300					

3. Summarize

(e) Pay Cash to Employees

Supercuts paid stylists $8,100 for wages related to services they provided in September. The matching concept requires that all expenses related to revenues earned in the current period be recorded in the current period. Increases in expenses are shown as a negative change in stockholders' equity (+E, −SE) because expenses reduce net income, which decreases stockholders' equity.

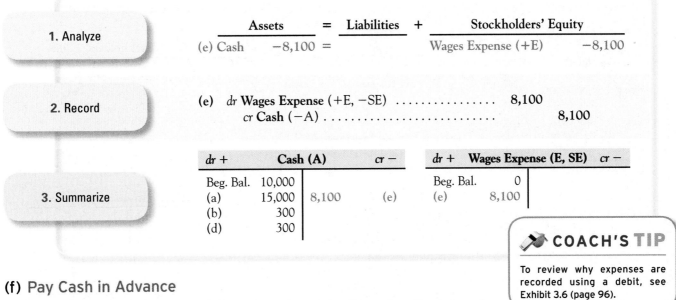

1. Analyze

	Assets	=	Liabilities	+	Stockholders' Equity
(e) Cash	−8,100 =				Wages Expense (+E) −8,100

2. Record

(e) *dr* Wages Expense (+E, −SE) 8,100
    cr Cash (−A) 8,100

3. Summarize

dr +	Cash (A)		*cr* −		*dr* +	Wages Expense (E, SE)	*cr* −
Beg. Bal.	10,000				Beg. Bal.	0	
(a)	15,000	8,100	(e)		(e)	8,100	
(b)	300						
(d)	300						

> **COACH'S TIP**
>
> To review why expenses are recorded using a debit, see Exhibit 3.6 (page 96).

(f) Pay Cash in Advance

On September 1, Supercuts paid $7,200 in advance for September, October, and November rent. This transaction involves paying for the right to use the rented mall space for three months following the payment. At the time the payment is made, this cost provides a future economic benefit to Supercuts (mall space for three months), so it will be initially reported as an asset called *Prepaid rent.* Each month, after the rented space has been used, your salon will reduce the prepaid rent asset and show the amount used up as Rent expense. The adjustment needed to report September's share of the total rent expense (1/3 × $7,200 = $2,400) will be covered in Chapter 4.

1. Analyze

	Assets	=	Liabilities	+	Stockholders' Equity
(f) Cash	−7,200				
Prepaid Rent	+7,200				

2. Record

(f) *dr* Prepaid Rent (+A) 7,200
    cr Cash (−A) 7,200

3. Summarize

dr +	Cash (A)		*cr* −		*dr* +	Prepaid Rent (A)	*cr* −
Beg. Bal.	10,000				Beg. Bal.	0	
(a)	15,000	8,100	(e)		(f)	7,200	
(b)	300	7,200	(f)				
(d)	300						

(g) Pay Cash in Advance

On September 1, Supercuts paid $3,600 for an insurance policy that covers the period from September 1 until August 31 of next year. This transaction provides another example of a prepayment that is initially recorded as an asset. This time, the asset costs $3,600. The adjustment that will be made at the end of September to record the month's insurance expense ($300) will be covered in Chapter 4.

1. Analyze

Assets		= Liabilities +	Stockholders' Equity
(g) Cash	−3,600		
Prepaid Insurance	+3,600		

2. Record

(g)   *dr* **Prepaid Insurance (+A)** 3,600
       cr **Cash (−A)** 3,600

3. Summarize

dr +	Cash (A)		*cr* −
Beg. Bal.	10,000		
(a)	15,000	8,100	(e)
(b)	300	7,200	(f)
(d)	300	3,600	(g)

dr +	Prepaid Insurance (A)	*cr* −
Beg. Bal.	0	
(g)	3,600	

(h) Incur Cost to Be Paid Later

Supercuts received a bill for $400 for running a newspaper ad about special back-to-school prices. The bill will be paid in October. This cost was incurred to generate revenues in September, so according to the matching principle it should be recorded as an expense in September. When costs are incurred before they are paid, a liability is created called *Accounts payable*.

1. Analyze

Assets =	Liabilities	+	Stockholders' Equity
(h)	Accounts Payable +400		Advertising Expense (+E) −400

2. Record

(h)   *dr* **Advertising Expense (+E, −SE)** 400
      cr **Accounts Payable (+L)** 400

3. Summarize

dr −	Accounts Payable (L)		*cr* +
		630	Beg. Bal.
		400	(h)

dr +	Advertising Exp. (E, SE)	*cr* −
Beg. Bal.	0	
(h)	400	

(i) Pay Cash to Supplier

Supercuts paid utility bills totaling $600 for services received and billed in September. Just like transaction (e), the cash payment and expense occurred during the same period.

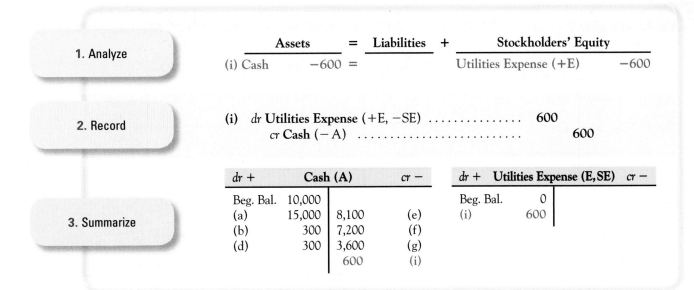

1. Analyze

	Assets	=	Liabilities	+	Stockholders' Equity	
(i) Cash	−600 =				Utilities Expense (+E)	−600

2. Record

(i) *dr* Utilities Expense (+E, −SE) 600
         cr Cash (−A) 600

3. Summarize

dr +	Cash (A)		*cr* −
Beg. Bal.	10,000		
(a)	15,000	8,100	(e)
(b)	300	7,200	(f)
(d)	300	3,600	(g)
		600	(i)

dr +	Utilities Expense (E, SE)	*cr* −
Beg. Bal.	0	
(i)	600	

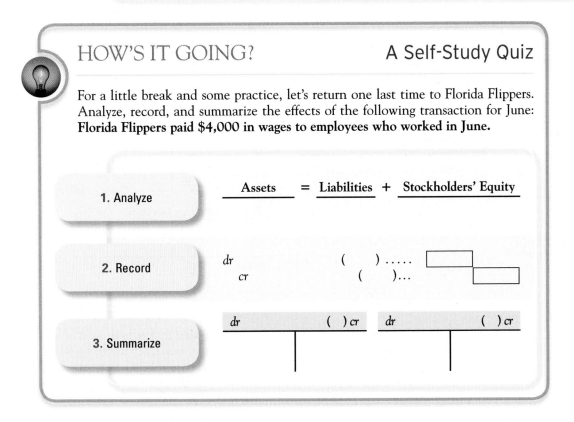

HOW'S IT GOING? A Self-Study Quiz

For a little break and some practice, let's return one last time to Florida Flippers. Analyze, record, and summarize the effects of the following transaction for June: **Florida Flippers paid $4,000 in wages to employees who worked in June.**

1. Analyze

Assets	=	Liabilities	+	Stockholders' Equity

2. Record

dr   (   ) .....
   cr   (   )...

3. Summarize

dr	( ) *cr*	*dr*	( ) *cr*

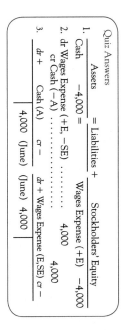

Calculating Account Balances Having entered ("posted") the effects of each journal entry into the T-accounts, we can now calculate the ending balances. In Exhibit 3.7, we have included all the T-accounts for your Supercuts salon (from this chapter as well as Chapter 2). You've heard it before, but we'll just remind you that the ending balance in each account is determined by adding the amounts on the + side and subtracting the amounts on the − side.

UNADJUSTED TRIAL BALANCE

After summarizing journal entries in the various accounts and then calculating ending balances for each account, you should check that the total recorded debits equal the total recorded credits. It's easy to make mistakes when you're doing the recording and

Learning Objective 4
Prepare an unadjusted trial balance.

EXHIBIT 3.7   Supercuts T-Accounts

dr + Cash (A) cr −			
Beg. bal.	10,000		
(a)	15,000	8,100	(e)
(b)	300	7,200	(f)
(d)	300	3,600	(g)
		600	(i)
End. bal.	6,100		

dr + Supplies (A) cr −	
Beg. bal.	630

dr + Accounts Receivable (A) cr −			
Beg. bal.	0		
(c)	500	300	(d)
End. bal.	200		

dr + Prepaid Rent (A) cr −	
Beg. bal.	0
(f)	7,200
End. bal.	7,200

dr + Prepaid Insurance (A) cr −	
Beg. bal.	0
(g)	3,600
End. bal.	3,600

dr + Equipment (A) cr −	
Beg. bal.	60,000

dr − Accounts Payable (L) cr +			
		630	Beg. bal.
		400	(h)
		1,030	End. bal.

dr − Unearned Revenue (L) cr +			
		0	Beg. bal.
		300	(b)
		300	End. bal.

dr − Note Payable (L) cr +			
		20,000	Beg. bal.

dr − Contributed Capital (SE) cr +			
		50,000	Beg. bal.

Beginning balances in this exhibit (September 1) are the ending balances in Exhibit 2.9 (August 31).

dr − Haircut Revenue (R, SE) cr +			
		0	Beg. bal.
		15,000	(a)
		500	(c)
		15,500	End. bal.

dr + Wages Expense (E, SE) cr −	
Beg. bal.	0
(e)	8,100
End. bal.	8,100

dr + Utilities Expense (E, SE) cr −	
Beg. bal.	0
(i)	600
End. bal.	600

dr + Advertising Exp. (E, SE) cr −	
Beg. bal.	0
(h)	400
End. bal.	400

YOU SHOULD KNOW

A **trial balance** is a list of all accounts and their balances, which is used to check on the equality of recorded debits and credits.

summarizing steps by hand. Typical mistakes involve (a) forgetting to post both sides of a journal entry, (b) posting a debit in the credit column (or vice versa), (c) recording the wrong amount, or (d) miscalculating the ending account balance. The best way to ensure your accounts are "in balance" is to prepare a **trial balance,** like the one in Exhibit 3.8. A trial balance is an internal report used to determine whether total debits equal total credits. Also, as you will see in Chapter 4, it's a great tool to use when preparing the financial statements. Typically, a trial balance lists every account name in one column (usually in the order they appear on the balance sheet and income statement) and the ending balances in the appropriate debit or credit column. Ending balances are obtained from the ledgers (T-accounts).

If your trial balance indicates that total debits don't equal total credits, you will experience a sickening feeling in your stomach because this means you've made an error somewhere in preparing or posting the journal entries to the T-accounts. Don't panic or start randomly changing numbers. The first thing to do when you find yourself in a hole is stop digging. Calmly look at the difference between total debits and credits. If it is

- The same as one of your T-account balances, you probably forgot to include the account in your trial balance.

EXHIBIT 3.8 Sample Unadjusted Trial Balance

SUPERCUTS
Unadjusted Trial Balance
As of September 30

Account Name	Debits	Credits
Cash	$ 6,100	
Supplies	630	
Accounts receivable	200	
Prepaid rent	7,200	
Prepaid insurance	3,600	
Equipment	60,000	
Accounts payable		$ 1,030
Unearned revenue		300
Note payable		20,000
Contributed capital		50,000
Retained earnings		0
Haircut revenue		15,500
Wages expense	8,100	
Utilities expense	600	
Advertising expense	400	
Totals	$86,830	$86,830

- ~~Twice the amount of an account balance~~, you may have included it in the wrong column of the trial balance.
- ~~Twice the amount of a transaction~~, you may have posted a debit as a credit or a credit as a debit in your T-accounts.
- ~~Evenly divisible by 9~~, you may have reversed the order of two digits in a number or left a zero off the end of a number. (This is called a transposition error.)
- ~~Evenly divisible by 3~~, you may have hit the key above or below the one you intended to hit (like a 9 instead of a 6) on your numeric keypad.

We don't want to depress you, but even if total debits equal total credits, it's still possible that you've made an error. For example, if you accidentally debit an asset rather than an expense or credit accounts payable instead of unearned revenue, total debits would still equal total credits. So if the trial balance doesn't balance, you know you've made an error for sure. If the trial balance does balance, it's still possible that you've made a mistake.

If you haven't already scanned the trial balance in Exhibit 3.8, take a moment to do it now. Notice that the title says unadjusted trial balance. It is called this because several adjustments will have to be made at the end of the accounting period to update the accounts. For example, some of the benefits of prepaid rent and prepaid insurance were used up in September, but this wasn't recorded yet. If you're really sharp, you'll also have noticed that income taxes haven't been calculated and recorded yet. Although it's possible to prepare preliminary financial statements using the numbers on the unadjusted trial balance, most companies don't. They wait until after the final adjustments are made. These adjustments will ensure the revenues and expenses are up to date and complete so that the (adjusted) net income number will provide a good indication about whether the company was profitable during the period. Don't worry about how to make the end-of-period adjustments yet. We'll spend most of Chapter 4 on that. For now, just realize that the accounts still have to be adjusted before we can prepare financial statements that follow generally accepted accounting principles.

REVIEW OF REVENUES AND EXPENSES

Up to this point of the chapter, you've analyzed some transactions—nine actually—that involve operating activities. While this is a good introduction, it doesn't quite prepare you for the variety of operating activities that most companies engage in. What you really need is a general summary of everything you've learned about revenues, expenses, and journal entries, and then lots of practice applying it to a broad range of activities. Let's start with revenues.

Remember that revenues are recorded when the business fulfills its promise to provide goods or services to customers, which is not necessarily the same time that cash is received. Because of this, we look at three cases, where cash is received (1) at the same time as the promised acts are performed, (2) before the promised acts are performed, and (3) after the promised acts are performed. The journal entries for these situations are shown in middle, left, and right panels below (in that order).

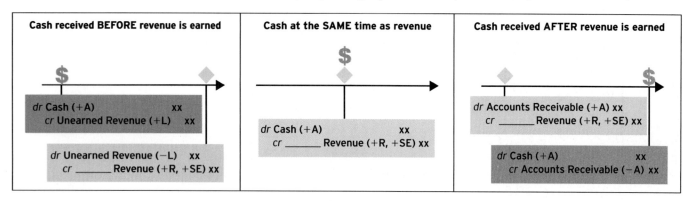

These three panels correspond to the revenue transactions for Supercuts analyzed earlier in this chapter. We use a generic label "_____ Revenue" with the expectation that you will fill in the blank with whatever type of revenue you are recording. That is, when accounting for revenue from cutting hair, you should use an account name like Haircut Revenue. If it's revenue generated from sales of iPods, you could call it Sales Revenue.

Let's look at a similar summary for expenses now. Under accrual accounting, expenses are recorded when incurred (either by acquiring items that do not have future economic benefits or by using up the economic benefits of assets that were acquired in previous periods). Expenses are not necessarily incurred at the same time that cash is paid. Because of this, we look at three cases, where cash is paid (1) at the same time the expense is incurred, (2) before the expense is incurred, and (3) after the expense is incurred. The corresponding journal entries are summarized in the middle, left, and right panels (in that order).

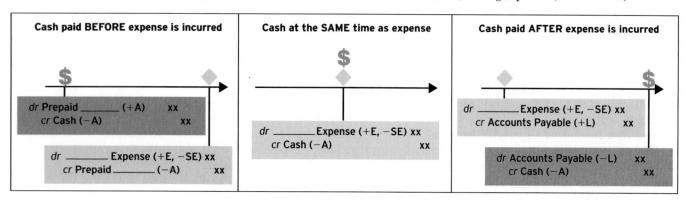

Again, we use generic labels like "Prepaid _____" and "_____ Expense" with the expectation that you will fill in the blank with whatever type of item you are recording (e.g., prepaid rent, rent expense, prepaid insurance, insurance expense).

Evaluate the Results

The income statement provides the main measure of a company's operating performance. The key thing to look for is whether net income is positive (revenues exceed expenses). Beyond that, it's useful to consider whether revenues are growing faster than expenses. If so, the company's net income will be increasing. To be successful, a company's net income should be stable or growing from period to period.

INCOME STATEMENT LIMITATIONS

> **Learning Objective 5**
> Describe limitations of the income statement.

Although an income statement is useful for assessing a company's performance, it does have some limitations that lead to common misconceptions. One of the most common is that some people think net income equals the amount of cash generated by the business during the period. While this is how many of us think about our own income, it's not the way companies recognize revenues and expenses on the income statement. Following the rules of accrual accounting, revenues are recorded when earned and expenses are recorded when incurred, regardless of when cash is received or paid. This distinction between net income and cash receipts/payments means that net income shows whether the company's operating activities are profitable, but it does not indicate whether the company is bringing in more cash than it is spending.

A second limitation is that net income does not measure the change in the value of a company during a period. While net income is something that analysts consider when valuing a company, it's not a measure of it. Many other factors can cause the value of a company to change without affecting net income. A good example is the increase in the value of your Supercuts store that occurs as its reputation for great hairstyling grows. Because the enhanced reputation does not arise from an identifiable transaction, it is not accounted for. So, while net income measures many of the most important events that affect a business's value, it does not include all events that potentially affect a company's value.

A third common misconception is that measuring income just involves counting. (Bean counting, some people call it!) While it's true that accounting involves some counting and precision, estimation also plays a key role when measuring income. For example, Supercuts' equipment will not last forever. Instead, it will be used up over time to generate revenue for the company. The matching principle says equipment should be expensed over the period it is used. This will require estimating how many years the equipment will be used. We will discuss this particular example in Chapter 4 and discuss many other examples involving estimation of revenues and expenses in later chapters. For now, just note that net income is not always a precise measure.

Ethical Insights

Why All the Scandals?

You may have heard about accounting scandals such as Enron and WorldCom (now called Verizon) where managers were accused of cooking the books, and wondered why they did it. In many cases, the simple answer is greed. A drop in net income often causes a decline in stock price, which usually leads to pay reductions or job loss for the senior executives running the company. If the company is actually performing poorly, greed may lead some managers to falsify revenues and hide expenses to make it look like the company is still doing well. While this sometimes fools people for a short time, it rarely works in the long run and often leads to very bad consequences. A few cases involving faulty revenue and expense accounting are shown on page 106. As you look at these, imagine what it must have been like to be Bernie Ebbers—the person who received a 25-year prison sentence at the age of 65. It is probably just as bad as being Barry Minkow, who was sentenced to 25 years in jail at the age of 21.

The CEO	The Fraud	Conviction/Plea	The Outcome
Bernie Ebbers, 65 WorldCom	Recorded operating expenses as if they were assets; resulted in the largest fraud in U.S. history.	Convicted, July 2005.	Sentenced to 25 years.
Sanjay Kumar, 44 Computer Associates	Recorded sales in the wrong accounting period.	Pleaded guilty, April 2006.	Sentenced to 12 years.
Martin Grass, 49 Rite Aid Corp.	Recorded rebates from drug companies before they were earned.	Pleaded guilty, June 2003.	Sentenced to 8 years.
Barry Minkow, 21 ZZZZ Best	Made up customers and sales to show profits when, in reality, the company was a sham.	Convicted, December 1988.	Sentenced to 25 years.

SUPPLEMENT: ACCOUNT NAMES

Exhibit 3S.1 provides a more complete list of revenues and expenses than was presented in the income statement for the Supercuts salon in Exhibit 3.1. As we said in Chapter 2, every company is different, so even these examples will differ from the accounts used by other companies. Exhibit 3S.1 isn't intended to be all-inclusive. It's just supposed to give you ideas about possible account names for companies that aren't in the hair business.

EXHIBIT 3S.1   Sample Chart of Income Statement Accounts

Account Name	Description
Revenues	
Sales Revenues	Sales of products in the ordinary course of business
Service Revenues	Sales of services in the ordinary course of business
Rental Revenues	Amounts earned by renting out company property
Interest Revenues	Amounts earned on savings accounts and certificates of deposit
Dividend Revenues	Dividends earned from investing in other companies
Expenses	
Cost of Goods Sold	Cost of products sold in the ordinary course of business
Repairs & Maintenance	Cost of routine maintenance and upkeep of buildings/equipment
Advertising Expense	Cost of advertising services obtained during the period
Depreciation Expense	Cost of plant and equipment used up during the period
Insurance Expense	Cost of insurance coverage for the current period
Salaries and Wages Expense	Cost of employees' salaries and wages for the period
Rent Expense	Cost of rent for the period
Supplies Expense	Cost of supplies used up during the period
Transportation Expense	Cost of freight to transport goods out to customers
Utilities Expense	Cost of power, light, heat, Internet, and telephone for the period
Amortization Expense	Cost of intangible assets used up or expired during the period
Interest Expense	Interest charged on outstanding debts owed during the period
Income Tax Expense	Taxes charged on net income reported for the period

REVIEW THE CHAPTER

DEMONSTRATION CASE A

Carnival Corporation

1. From the following list of balance sheet and income statement account balances for Carnival Corporation, prepare an income statement for the quarter ended February 28, 2006. (Amounts are reported in millions of US dollars.)

2. Explain what the results suggest about the cruise ship company's operating performance. Net income for the same period last year was $345 (in millions of US dollars).

Transportation Expenses	$ 412	Wage Expenses	$276	Selling Expenses	$ 365
Passenger Ticket Revenue	1,908	Fuel Expenses	215	Prepaid Expenses	210
Onboard Revenue	553	Accounts Payable	656	Ship Expenses	746
Food Expenses	153	Income Tax Expense	14	Unearned Revenue	2,221

Suggested Solution

1. Income Statement

> **COACH'S TIP**
>
> Prepaid expenses of $210 is excluded from the income statement because it is an asset on the balance sheet. Accounts payable of $656 and Unearned revenue of $2,221 are excluded from the income statement because they are liabilities on the balance sheet.

CARNIVAL CORPORATION Income Statement For the quarter ended February 28, 2006 (amounts in millions of US dollars)	
Revenues	
Passenger ticket revenue	$1,908
Onboard revenue	553
Total revenues	2,461
Expenses	
Ship expenses	746
Transportation expenses	412
Selling expenses	365
Wage expenses	276
Fuel expenses	215
Food expenses	153
Income tax expense	14
Total expenses	2,181
Net Income	$ 280

2. The net income of $280 (million) indicates that Carnival Corporation was profitable, meaning that the revenues it earned were greater than the expenses it incurred. Generally, this is a positive sign. However, the decline from the net income of $345 (million) reported for the same quarter in the prior year suggests the company is not doing as well as it once did.

DEMONSTRATION CASE B

This case is a continuation of the Goodbye Grass Corporation case introduced in Chapter 2. The company was established and property and equipment were purchased. The balance sheet at April 30, 2008, based on only the investing and financing activities (from Chapter 2) is as follows:

GOODBYE GRASS CORPORATION
Balance Sheet
At April 30, 2008

Assets		Liabilities	
Current assets		Current liabilities	
Cash	$ 3,800	Accounts payable	$ 400
Note receivable	1,250	Note payable	4,000
Total current assets	5,050	Total current liabilities	4,400
Equipment	4,600		
Land	3,750	**Stockholders' Equity**	
		Contributed capital	9,000
		Retained earnings	0
Total assets	$13,400	Total liabilities and stockholders' equity	$13,400

The following activities also occurred during April 2008:

a. Purchased and used gasoline for mowers and edgers, paying $90 in cash at a local gas station.

b. In early April, received $1,600 cash from the city in advance for lawn maintenance service for April through July ($400 each month). The entire amount is to be recorded as Unearned Revenue.

c. In early April, purchased $300 of insurance covering six months, April through September. The entire payment is to be recorded as Prepaid Insurance.

d. Mowed lawns for residential customers who are billed every two weeks. A total of $5,200 of service was billed and is to be recorded in April.

e. Residential customers paid $3,500 on their accounts.

f. Paid wages every two weeks. Total cash paid in April was $3,900.

g. Received a bill for $320 from the local gas station for additional gasoline purchased on account and used in April.

h. Paid $100 on accounts payable.

Required:

1. Analyze activities (a)–(h) with the goal of indicating their effects on the basic accounting equation (Assets = Liabilities + Stockholders' Equity), using the format shown in the chapter.

2. Prepare journal entries to record the transactions identified among activities (a)–(h).

3. Summarize the effects of each transaction in the appropriate T-accounts. Before entering these effects, set up T-accounts for Cash, Accounts Receivable, Note Receivable, Prepaid Insurance, Equipment, Land, Accounts Payable, Unearned Revenue, Note Payable, Contributed Capital, Retained Earnings, Mowing Revenue, Wages Expense, and Fuel Expense. The beginning balance in each T-account should be the amount shown on the balance sheet above or $0 if the account does not appear on the above balance sheet. After posting the journal entries to the T-accounts, compute ending balances for each of the T-accounts.

4. Use the amounts in the T-accounts to prepare an unadjusted trial balance for Goodbye Grass Corporation at April 30, 2008.

After completing the above requirements, check your answers with the following suggested solution.

Suggested Solution

1. Transaction analysis:

	Assets		=	Liabilities		+	Stockholders' Equity	
a.	Cash	−90					Fuel Expense (+E)	−90

	Assets		=	Liabilities		+	Stockholders' Equity	
b.	Cash	+1,600		Unearned Revenue	+1,600			

	Assets		=	Liabilities		+	Stockholders' Equity	
c.	Cash	−300						
	Prepaid Insurance	+300						

	Assets		=	Liabilities		+	Stockholders' Equity	
d.	Accounts Receivable	+5,200					Mowing Revenue (+R)	+5,200

	Assets		=	Liabilities		+	Stockholders' Equity	
e.	Cash	+3,500						
	Accounts Receivable	−3,500						

	Assets		=	Liabilities		+	Stockholders' Equity	
f.	Cash	−3,900					Wages Expense (+E)	−3,900

	Assets		=	Liabilities		+	Stockholders' Equity	
g.				Accounts Payable	+320		Fuel Expense (+E)	−320

	Assets		=	Liabilities		+	Stockholders' Equity	
h.	Cash	−100		Accounts Payable	−100			

2. Journal entries:

    a. dr Fuel Expense (+E, −SE)............................. 90
          cr Cash (−A)   90

    b. dr Cash (+A)... 1,600
          cr Unearned Revenue (+L)   1,600

    c. dr Prepaid Insurance (+A) 300
          cr Cash (−A)   300

    d. dr Accounts Receivable (+A)........................... 5,200
          cr Mowing Revenue (+R, +SE)   5,200

    e. dr Cash (+A)... 3,500
          cr Accounts Receivable (−A)   3,500

    f. dr Wages Expense (+E, −SE) 3,900
          cr Cash (−A)   3,900

    g. dr Fuel Expense (+E, −SE)............................. 320
          cr Accounts Payable (+L)   320

    h. dr Accounts Payable (−L)............................. 100
          cr Cash (−A)   100

3. T-Accounts:

dr +	Cash (A)	cr −
Bal. fwd. 3,800		
(b) 1,600	90	(a)
(e) 3,500	300	(c)
	3,900	(f)
	100	(h)
End. bal. 4,510		

dr +	Accounts Receivable (A)	cr −
Beg. bal. 0		
(d) 5,200	3,500	(e)
End. bal. 1,700		

dr +	Note Receivable (A)	cr −
Bal. fwd. 1,250		
End. bal. 1,250		

dr +	Prepaid Insurance (A)	cr −
Beg. bal. 0		
(c) 300		
End. Bal. 300		

dr +	Equipment (A)	cr −
Bal. fwd. 4,600		
End. bal. 4,600		

dr +	Land (A)	cr −
Bal. fwd. 3,750		
End. bal. 3,750		

dr −	Accounts Payable (L)	cr +
	400	Beg. bal.
(h) 100	320	(g)
	620	End. bal.

dr −	Unearned Revenue (L)	cr +
	0	Beg. bal.
	1,600	(b)
	1,600	End. bal.

dr −	Note Payable (L)	cr +
	4,000	Bal. fwd.
	4,000	End. bal.

dr −	Contributed Capital (SE)	cr +
	9,000	Bal. fwd.
	9,000	End. bal.

dr −	Retained Earnings (SE)	cr +
	0	Beg. bal.
	0	End. bal.

dr −	Mowing Revenue (R)	cr +
	0	Beg. bal.
	5,200	(d)
	5,200	End. bal.

dr +	Wages Expense (E)	cr −
Beg. bal. 0		
(f) 3,900		
End. Bal. 3,900		

dr +	Fuel Expense (E)	cr −
Beg. bal. 0		
(a) 90		
(g) 320		
End. bal. 410		

4. Unadjusted trial balance:

GOODBYE GRASS CORPORATION
Unadjusted Trial Balance
As of April 30, 2008

Account Name	Debits	Credits
Cash	$ 4,510	
Accounts receivable	1,700	
Note receivable	1,250	
Prepaid insurance	300	
Equipment	4,600	
Land	3,750	
Accounts payable		$ 620
Unearned revenues		1,600
Note payable		4,000
Contributed capital		9,000
Retained earnings		0
Mowing revenue		5,200
Wages expense	3,900	
Fuel expense	410	
Totals	$20,420	$20,420

CHAPTER SUMMARY

Describe common operating transactions and select appropriate income statement account titles. p. 88 LO1

- The income statement reports net income, which is calculated by combining

  Revenues—amounts charged to customers for sales of goods or services provided.

  Expenses—costs of business activities undertaken to earn revenues.

- See Exhibit 3.1 on page 89 for basic income statement format and Exhibit 3S.1 for an expanded list of account titles.

Explain and apply the revenue and matching principles. p. 91 LO2

- The two key concepts underlying accrual basis accounting and the income statement are

  Revenue principle—recognize revenues when they are earned.

  Matching principle—recognize expenses when they are incurred in generating revenue.

Analyze, record, and summarize the effects of operating transactions, using the accounting equation, journal entries, and T-accounts. p. 95 LO3

- The expanded transaction analysis model includes revenues and expenses as subcategories of retained earnings:

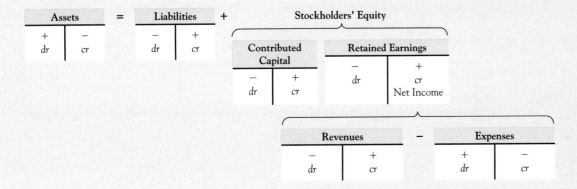

- In journal entry format, increases in revenues are recorded with credits and increases in expenses are recorded with debits.

Prepare an unadjusted trial balance. p. 101 LO4

- The unadjusted trial balance is a list of all accounts and their unadjusted balances, and is used to check on the equality of recorded debits and credits.

Describe limitations of the income statement. p. 105 LO5

- Does not indicate whether the company is bringing in more cash than it is spending.
- Does not directly measure the change in value of a company during the period.
- Estimation plays a key role when measuring income.

KEY TERMS

Accrual Basis Accounting p. 91
Cash Basis Accounting p. 90
Expenses p. 88
Matching Principle p. 93

Net Income p. 89
Revenue Principle p. 92
Revenues p. 88
Time Period Assumption p. 89

Trial Balance p. 102
Unearned Revenue p. 92

PRACTICE MATERIAL

QUESTIONS

1. Indicate the income statement equation and define each element.

2. When accounting was developed in the 14th and 15th centuries, businesses had very short lives. For instance, a business might have been created for a single shipment of goods from Europe to North America. After the goods were delivered and profits were distributed among those who financed the shipment, the business ceased to exist. In more recent centuries, businesses began to experience longer lives. Identify the accounting concept that is needed when accounting for businesses with long lives. Explain what this concept means and why it is necessary for modern-day accounting.

3. Define *accrual basis accounting* and contrast it with *cash basis accounting*.

4. Why is it appropriate to use a cash basis of accounting in your personal life but not in the business world?

5. What does it mean to *recognize* an accounting transaction?

6. When is revenue typically recognized under accrual basis accounting?

7. Explain the matching principle.

8. Explain why stockholders' equity is increased by revenues and decreased by expenses.

9. Explain why revenues are recorded as credits and expenses as debits.

10. Complete the following table by entering either *debit* or *credit* in each cell:

Item	Increase	Decrease
Revenues		
Expenses		

11. Complete the following table by entering either *increase* or *decrease* in each cell:

Item	Debit	Credit
Revenues		
Expenses		

12. What basic characteristic distinguishes items reported on the income statement from items reported on the balance sheet?

13. Which of the four basic accounting reports indicates that it is appropriate to consider revenues and expenses as subcategories of retained earnings? Explain.

14. What is the difference between accounts receivable and revenue?

15. What is the difference between wages payable and wages expense?

16. For each of the following situations, indicate whether it represents an accounting error and explain why it is or is not an error. Also state whether a trial balance would indicate that an error exists for each situation.

    a. Cash received from a customer was debited to accounts receivable and credited to cash.

    b. Revenue was recognized when a customer purchased a gift card for future use.

    c. An expense was recorded as an asset.

    d. The debit side of a journal entry was recorded in the accounts, but the credit side was not.

    e. A company shareholder purchased a new car, but this was not recorded by the company.

17. What are three limitations of the income statement that often lead to misconceptions?

MULTIPLE CHOICE

1. Which of the following items is not a specific account in a company's chart of accounts?
   a. Accounts Receivable
   b. Net Income
   c. Sales Revenue
   d. Unearned Revenue

2. Which of the following accounts normally has a debit balance?
   a. Unearned Revenue
   b. Rent Expense
   c. Retained Earnings
   d. Sales Revenue

3. The matching principle controls
   a. Where on the income statement expenses should be presented.
   b. When revenues are recognized on the income statement.
   c. The ordering of current assets and current liabilities on the balance sheet.
   d. When costs are recognized as expenses on the income statement.

4. When should companies that sell gift cards to customers report revenue?
   a. When the gift card is sold and cash is received.
   b. When the gift card is used by the customer.
   c. At the end of the year in which the gift card is sold.
   d. None of the above.

5. If a company incorrectly records a payment as an asset, rather than as an expense, how will this error affect net income in the current period?
   a. Net income will be too high.
   b. Net income will be too low.
   c. Net income will not be affected by this error.
   d. It's a mystery; nobody really knows.

6. When should a company report the cost of an insurance policy as an expense?
   a. When the company first signs the policy.
   b. When the company pays for the policy.
   c. When the company receives the benefits from the policy over its period of coverage.
   d. When the company receives payments from the insurance company for its insurance claims.

7. When expenses exceed revenues in a given period (and there are no gains or losses),
   a. Stockholders' equity will not be impacted.
   b. Stockholders' equity will be increased.
   c. Stockholders' equity will be decreased.
   d. One cannot determine the impact on stockholders' equity without information about the specific revenues and expenses.

8. Which account is *least* likely to be debited when revenue is recorded?
   a. Accounts Payable
   b. Accounts Receivable
   c. Cash
   d. Unearned Revenue

9. Webby Corporation reported the following amounts on its income statement: service revenues, $32,500; utilities expense, $300; net income, $1,600; and income tax expense, $900. If the only other amount reported on the income statement was for selling expenses, what amount would it be?
   a. $2,200
   b. $29,700
   c. $30,000
   d. $30,900

10. Which of the following is the entry to be recorded by a law firm when it receives a payment from a new client that will be earned when services are provided in the future?
    a. *Debit* Accounts Receivable; *credit* Legal Services Revenue.
    b. *Debit* Unearned Revenue; *credit* Legal Services Revenue.
    c. *Debit* Cash; *credit* Unearned Revenue.
    d. *Debit* Unearned Revenue; *credit* Cash.

MINI-EXERCISES

Available with McGraw-Hill's
Homework Manager

HOMEWORK MANAGER **PLUS**

LO2   **M3-1 Reporting Cash Basis versus Accrual Basis Income**

Mostert Music Company had the following transactions in March:

a. Sold music lessons to customers for $10,000; received $6,000 in cash and the rest on account.
b. Paid $600 in wages for the month.
c. Received a $200 bill for utilities that will be paid in April.
d. Received $1,000 from customers as deposits on music lessons to be given in April.
    Complete the following statements:

Cash Basis Income Statement		Accrual Basis Income Statement	
Revenues		Revenues	
Cash sales	$	Sales to customers	$
Customer deposits			
Expenses		Expenses	
Wages paid		Wages expense	
		Utilities expense	
Cash income	$	Net income	$

LO2   **M3-2 Identifying Revenues**

The following transactions are July 2009 activities of Bill's Extreme Bowling Inc., which operates several bowling centers. If revenue is to be recognized in July, indicate the amount. If revenue is not to be recognized in July, explain why.

Activity	Amount or Explanation
a. Bill's collected $12,000 from customers for games played in July.	
b. Bill's billed a customer for $250 for a party held at the center on the last day of July. The bill is to be paid in August.	
c. Bill's received $1,000 from credit sales made to customers last month (in June).	
d. The men's and women's bowling leagues gave Bill's advance payments totaling $1,500 for the fall season that starts in September.	

LO2   **M3-3 Identifying Expenses**

The following transactions are July 2009 activities of Bill's Extreme Bowling, Inc., which operates several bowling centers. If an expense is to be recognized in July, indicate the amount. If an expense is not to be recognized in July, explain why.

Activity	Amount or Explanation
e. Bill's paid $1,500 to plumbers for repairing a broken pipe in the restrooms.	
f. Bill's paid $2,000 for the June electricity bill and received the July bill for $2,500, which will be paid in August.	
g. Bill's paid $5,475 to employees for work in July.	

M3-4 Recording Revenues

LO3

For each of the transactions in M3-2, write the journal entry using the format shown in the chapter.

M3-5 Recording Expenses

LO3

For each of the transactions in M3-3, write the journal entry using the format shown in the chapter.

M3-6 Determining the Financial Statement Effects of Operating Activities Involving Revenues

LO2

The following transactions are July 2009 activities of Bill's Extreme Bowling, Inc., which operates several bowling centers. For each of the following transactions, complete the spreadsheet, indicating the amount and effect (+ for increase and − for decrease) of each transaction. Write NE if there is no effect. Include revenues as a subcategory of stockholders' equity, as shown for the first transaction, which is provided as an example.

Transaction	Assets	Liabilities	Stockholders' Equity
a. Bill's collected $12,000 from customers for games played in July.	+12,000	NE	Games fees revenue (+R) +12,000
b. Bill's billed a customer for $250 for a party held at the center on the last day of July. The bill is to be paid in August.			
c. Bill's received $1,000 from credit sales made to customers last month (in June).			
d. The men's and women's bowling leagues gave Bill's advance payments totaling $1,500 for the fall season that starts in September.			

M3-7 Determining the Financial Statement Effects of Operating Activities Involving Expenses

LO2

The following transactions are July 2009 activities of Bill's Extreme Bowling, Inc., which operates several bowling centers. For each of the following transactions, complete the spreadsheet, indicating the amount and effect (+ for increase and − for decrease) of each transaction. Write NE if there is no effect. Include expenses as a subcategory of stockholders' equity, as shown for the first transaction, which is provided as an example.

Transaction	Assets	Liabilities	Stockholders' Equity
e. Bill's paid $1,500 to plumbers for repairing a broken pipe in the restrooms.	−1,500	NE	Repairs expense (+E) −1,500
f. Bill's paid $2,000 for the June electricity bill and received the July bill for $2,500, which will be paid in August.			
g. Bill's paid $5,475 to employees for work in July.			

M3-8 Preparing an Income Statement

LO4

Given the transactions in M3-6 and M3-7 (including the examples), prepare an income statement for Bill's Extreme Bowling, Inc. for the month ended July 31, 2009. (This income statement would be considered "preliminary" because it uses unadjusted balances.)

M3-9 Identifying Revenues

LO2

The following transactions are February 2008 activities of Swing Hard Incorporated, which offers indoor golfing lessons in the northeastern United States. If revenue is to be recognized in February, indicate the amount. If revenue is not to be recognized in February, explain why.

Activity	Amount or Explanation
a. Swing Hard collected $15,000 from customers for lessons given in February.	
b. Swing Hard sold a gift card for golf lessons for $150 cash in February.	
c. Swing Hard received $4,000 from credit sales made to customers in January.	
d. Swing Hard collects $2,250 in advance payments for golf lessons to start in June.	
e. Swing Hard bills a customer $125 for golf lessons given between February 25 and February 28. The bill is to be paid in March.	

LO2 **M3-10 Identifying Expenses**

The following transactions are February 2008 activities of Swing Hard Incorporated, which offers indoor golfing lessons in the northeastern United States. If an expense is to be recognized in February, indicate the amount. If an expense is not to be recognized in February, explain why.

Activity	Amount or Explanation
f. Swing Hard paid $4,750 to its golf instructors for the month of February.	
g. Swing Hard paid $1,750 for electricity used in the month of January.	
h. Swing Hard received an electricity bill for $800 for the month of February, to be paid in March.	

LO3 **M3-11 Recording Revenues**

For each of the transactions in M3-9, write the journal entry using the format shown in the chapter.

LO3 **M3-12 Recording Expenses**

For each of the transactions in M3-10, write the journal entry using the format shown in the chapter.

LO2 **M3-13 Determining the Financial Statement Effects of Operating Activities Involving Revenues**

The following transactions are February 2008 activities of Swing Hard Incorporated, which offers golfing lessons in the northeastern United States. For each of the following transactions, complete the spreadsheet, indicating the amount and effect (+ for increase and − for decrease) of each transaction. Write NE if there is no effect. Include revenues as a subcategory of stockholders' equity, as shown for the first transaction, which is provided as an example.

Transaction	Assets	Liabilities	Stockholders' Equity
a. Swing Hard collected $15,000 from customers for lessons given in February.	+15,000	NE	Revenue from lessons (+R) +15,000
b. Swing Hard sold a gift card for golf lessons for $150 cash in February.			
c. Swing Hard received $4,000 from credit sales made to customers in January.			
d. Swing Hard collects $2,250 in advance payments for golf lessons to start in June.			
e. Swing Hard bills a customer $125 for golf lessons given between February 25 thru February 28. The bill is to be paid in March.			

M3-14 Determining the Financial Statement Effects of Operating Activities Involving Expenses

LO2

The following transactions are February 2008 activities of Swing Hard Incorporated, which offers golfing lessons in the northeastern United States. For each of the following transactions, complete the spreadsheet, indicating the amount and effect (+ for increase and − for decrease) of each transaction. Write NE if there is no effect. Include expenses as a subcategory of stockholders' equity, as shown for the first transaction, which is provided as an example.

Transaction	Assets	Liabilities	Stockholders' Equity
f. Swing Hard paid $4,750 for wages to its golf instructors for the month of February.	−4,750	NE	Wages expense (+E) −4,750
g. Swing Hard paid $1,750 for electricity used in the month of January.			
h. Swing Hard received an electricity bill for $800 for the month of February, to be paid in March.			

M3-15 Preparing an Income Statement

LO4

Given the transactions in M3-13 and M3-14 (including the examples), prepare an income statement for Swing Hard Incorporated for the month ended February 29, 2008. (This income statement would be considered "preliminary" because it uses unadjusted balances.)

M3-16 Preparing Financial Statements from a Trial Balance (Dividends Included)

LO4

The following accounts are taken from Buck Up!, Inc., a company that specializes in horse-breaking services and rodeo lessons, as of December 31, 2008.

Buck Up!, Inc.
Unadjusted Trial Balance
As of December 31, 2008

Account Name	Debits	Credits
Cash	$ 59,750	
Accounts receivable	3,300	
Prepaid insurance	1,200	
Equipment	64,600	
Land	23,000	
Accounts payable		$ 29,230
Unearned revenues		1,500
Long-term notes payable		74,000
Contributed capital		5,000
Retained earnings (at December 31, 2007)		14,500
Dividends	3,500	
Horse-breaking revenue		25,200
Rodeo lesson revenue		10,500
Wages expense	3,900	
Maintenance expense	410	
Other expenses	270	
Totals	$159,930	$159,930

Required:

Using the unadjusted trial balance provided, create a classified balance sheet, statement of retained earnings, and income statement for Buck Up!, Inc., for the year ended December 31, 2008. (These financial statements would be considered "preliminary" because they use unadjusted balances.)

TIP: Create the income statement first, followed by the statement of retained earnings, and finally the classified balance sheet. Follow the formats presented in Exhibits 1.3, 1.4, and 2.10.

LO4

Time Warner, Inc.

M3-17 Preparing an Income Statement

The following accounts are taken from the December 31, 2005, financial statements of Time Warner, Inc.

Subscription revenue	$22,222,000,000
Other revenues	13,818,000,000
Salaries expense	10,478,000,000
Cash	4,220,000,000
Accounts receivable	6,411,000,000
Interest expense	1,266,000,000
Accounts payable	1,380,000,000
Advertising revenue	7,612,000,000
Long-term debt	20,238,000,000
Other expenses	27,816,000,000
Unearned revenue	1,473,000,000
Equipment	13,676,000,000
Income tax expense	1,187,000,000

Required:

Prepare an income statement for the year ended December 31, 2005.

TIP: Some of the above accounts are not reported on the income statement.

TIP: Round amounts to an appropriate unit of measure.

LO4

H&R Block, Inc.

M3-18 Preparing an Income Statement

H&R Block, Inc. was founded by Henry and Richard Bloch in 1955. Henry, who served as a navigator on a B-17 bomber in World War II, and Richard, who founded his first business in the 4th grade and attended Wharton at age 16, built H&R Block into the world's largest tax services company, serving over 20 million people in 11 countries around the globe. The following accounts are taken from the financial statements of H&R Block, Inc. at the fiscal year ended April 30, 2006.

Cost of services	$2,383,299,000
Salaries payable	330,946,000
Salaries expense	1,112,585,000
Accounts payable	768,505,000
Service revenue	3,463,111,000
Income tax expense	336,985,000
Cash	1,008,427,000
Accounts receivable	999,765,000
Software revenue	492,502,000
Other revenues	917,188,000
Interest expense	49,059,000
Other expenses	500,465,000
Long-term note payable	417,539,000
Retained earnings (as of April 30, 2005)	3,492,059,000

Required:

Prepare an income statement for the year ended April 30, 2006.

TIP: Some of the above accounts are not reported on the income statement.

TIP: Round the reported amounts to an appropriate unit of measure.

EXERCISES

E3-1 Matching Definitions with Terms

LO1, LO5

Match each definition with its related term by entering the appropriate letter in the space provided.

Term	Definition

_____ 1. Expenses

_____ 2. Matching principle

_____ 3. Revenue principle

_____ 4. Cash basis accounting

_____ 5. Unearned revenue

_____ 6. Accrual basis accounting

_____ 7. Prepaid expenses

A. Record expenses when incurred in earning revenue.

B. A liability account used to record the obligation to provide future services or return cash that has been received before revenues have been earned.

C. Costs that result when a company sacrifices resources to generate revenues.

D. Record revenues when earned, not necessarily when cash is received.

E. Record revenues when received and expenses when paid.

F. A type of asset account used to record the benefits obtained when cash is paid before expenses are incurred.

G. Record revenues when earned and expenses when incurred.

E3-2 Identifying Revenues

LO1, LO2

Apple
Home Depot
AT&T

According to the revenue principle, revenues should be recognized when they are earned, which happens when the company performs acts promised to the customer. For most businesses, this condition is met at the point of delivery of goods or services. The following transactions occurred in September 2009:

a. A customer pays $10 cash for 10 MP3 song files from Apple's iTunes store. Answer from Apple's standpoint.

b. Home Depot provides a carpet installation for $2,000 cash. A comparable installation from other companies costs $3,000.

c. AT&T is scheduled to install digital cable at 1,000 Austin area homes next week. The installation charge is $100 per home. The terms require payment within 30 days of installation. Answer from AT&T's standpoint.

d. AT&T completes the installations described in (c). Answer from AT&T's standpoint.

e. AT&T receives payment from customers for the installations described in (c). Answer from AT&T's standpoint.

f. A customer purchases a ticket from American Airlines in September for $500 cash to travel in December. Answer from American Airlines' standpoint.

Required:

For each of the transactions, if revenue is to be recognized in September, indicate the amount. If revenue is not to be recognized in September, explain why.

E3-3 Identifying Revenues

LO1, LO2

General Motors

According to the revenue principle, revenues should be recognized when they are earned, which happens when the company performs acts promised to the customer. For most businesses, this condition is met at the point of delivery of goods or services. The following transactions occurred in September 2009:

a. General Motors issues $26 million in new common stock.

b. Cal State University receives $20,000,000 cash for 80,000 five-game season football tickets. None of the games have been played.

c. Cal State plays the first football game referred to in (b).

d. Hall Construction Company signs a contract with a customer for the construction of a new $500,000 warehouse. At the signing, Hall receives a check for $50,000 as a deposit to be applied against amounts earned during the first phase of construction. Answer from Hall's standpoint.

e. A popular snowboarding magazine company receives a total of $1,800 today from subscribers. The subscriptions begin in the next fiscal year. Answer from the magazine company's standpoint.

T-Mobile

f. T-Mobile sells a $100 cell phone plan for service in September to a customer who charges the sale on his credit card. Answer from the standpoint of T-Mobile.

Required:

For each of the transactions, if revenue is to be recognized in September, indicate the amount. If revenue is not to be recognized in September, explain why.

LO1, LO2   **E3-4 Identifying Expenses**

Under accrual basis accounting, expenses are recognized when incurred, which means the activity giving rise to the expense has occurred. Assume the following transactions occurred in January 2008:

a. Gateway pays its computer service technicians $90,000 in salary, one half of which was for work done in December 2007 and the other half in January 2008. Answer from Gateway's standpoint.

b. At the beginning of January, Turner Construction Company pays $4,500 in worker's compensation insurance for the first three months of the year.

c. The McGraw-Hill Companies—publisher of this textbook and *BusinessWeek*—uses $1,000 worth of electricity and natural gas in January for which it has not yet been billed.

d. Pooler Company receives and pays in January a $1,500 invoice from a consulting firm for services received in January.

e. The campus bookstore receives consulting services at a cost of $5,000. The terms indicate that payment is due within 30 days of the consultation.

f. Schergevitch Incorporated has its delivery van repaired in January for $280 and charges the amount on account.

Required:

For each of the transactions, if an expense is to be recognized in January, indicate the amount. If an expense is not to be recognized in January, indicate why.

LO1, LO2   **E3-5 Identifying Expenses**

American Express
Waste Management, Inc.

Under accrual basis accounting, expenses are recognized when incurred, which means the activity giving rise to the expense has occurred. The following transactions occurred in January 2008:

a. American Express pays its salespersons $3,500 in commissions related to December financial advisory services sales. Answer from American Express's standpoint.

b. On January 31, American Express determines that it will pay its salespersons $4,200 in commissions related to January sales. The payment will be made in early February. Answer from American Express's standpoint.

c. The city of Omaha hires Waste Management, Inc. to provide trash collection services beginning in January. The city pays $7.2 million for the entire year. Answer from the city's standpoint.

d. The University of Florida pays $10,000 in advance for refundable airline tickets to fly the baseball team to a tournament in California. The first game will be played in March. Answer from the university's standpoint.

e. A Houston Community College employee works eight hours, at $15 per hour, on January 31; payday is not until February 3. Answer from the college's point of view.

f. Wang Company paid $3,600 for a fire insurance policy on January 1. The policy covers 12 months beginning on January 1. Answer from Wang's point of view.

g. Ziegler Company, a farm equipment company, receives a phone bill for $230 of January calls. The bill has not been paid to date.

Required:

For each of the transactions, if an expense is to be recognized in January, indicate the amount. If an expense is not to be recognized in January, indicate why.

LO2   **E3-6 Determining Financial Statement Effects of Various Transactions**

The following transactions occurred during a recent year:

a. Paid wages expense for the period (example).
b. Borrowed cash from local bank.

c. Purchased equipment on credit.
d. Earned sales revenue, collected cash.

e. Incurred utilities expenses, on credit.
f. Earned sales revenue, on credit.
g. Paid cash on account.
h. Incurred delivery expenses, paid cash.
i. Earned service revenue, collected half in cash, balance on credit.

j. Collected cash from customers on account.
k. Incurred advertising expenses, paid half in cash, balance on credit.

Required:

For each of the transactions, complete the table below, indicating the effect (+ for increase and − for decrease) of each transaction. Write NE if there is no effect. Include revenues and expenses as subcategories of stockholders' equity, as shown for the first transaction, which is provided as an example.

Transaction	Assets	Liabilities	Stockholders' Equity
(a) (example)	−	NE	Wages expense (+E)−

E3-7 Determining Financial Statement Effects of Various Transactions

LO2
Wolverine World Wide, Inc.

Wolverine World Wide, Inc., manufactures military, work, sport, and casual footwear and leather accessories under a variety of brand names, such as Caterpillar, Hush Puppies, Wolverine, and Steve Madden. The following transactions occurred during a recent year. Dollars are in thousands.

a. Made cash sales of $49,000 (example).
b. Purchased $300,000 of additional supplies on account.
c. Borrowed $58,000 on long-term notes.
d. Purchased $18,600 in additional property, plant, and equipment.
e. Incurred $87,000 in selling expenses, paying two-thirds in cash and owing the rest on account.
f. Paid $4,700 in interest expense.

Required:

For each of the transactions, complete the table below, indicating the effect (+ for increase and − for decrease) and amount of each transaction. Write NE if there is no effect. Include revenues and expenses as subcategories of stockholders' equity, as shown for the first transaction, which is provided as an example.

Transaction	Assets	Liabilities	Stockholders' Equity
(a) (example)	+49,000	NE	Sales revenue (+R)+49,000

E3-8 Recording Journal Entries

LO2, LO3
Sysco

Sysco, formed in 1969, is America's largest marketer and distributor of food service products, serving nearly 250,000 restaurants, hotels, schools, hospitals, and other institutions. The following transactions are typical of those that occurred in a recent year. (All amounts are rounded to the nearest thousand.)

a. Borrowed $80,000 from a bank, signing a short-term note payable.
b. Provided $10,000 in service to customers, with $9,500 on account and the rest received in cash.
c. Purchased plant and equipment for $130,000 in cash.
d. Paid employee wages of $1,000.
e. Received $410 on account from a customer.
f. Purchased and used fuel of $400,000 in delivery vehicles during the year (paid for in cash).
g. Paid $8,200 cash on accounts payable.
h. Incurred $20,000 in utility expenses during the year, of which $15,000 was paid in cash and the rest owed on account.

Required:

For each of the transactions, prepare journal entries. Determine whether the accounting equation remains in balance and debits equal credits after each entry.

LO2, LO3   **E3-9 Recording Journal Entries**

Greek Peak

Greek Peak is a ski resort in upstate New York. The company sells lift tickets, ski lessons, and ski equipment. It operates several restaurants and rents townhouses to vacationing skiers. The following hypothetical December 2008 transactions are typical of those that occur at the resort.

a.   Borrowed $500,000 from the bank on December 1, signing a note payable, due in six months.
b.   Purchased a new snowplow for $20,000 cash on December 31.
c.   Purchased ski supplies for $10,000 on account.
d.   Incurred $22,000 in routine maintenance expenses for the chairlifts; paid cash.
e.   Received $72,000 for partial season passes (beginning in the new year).
f.   Daily lift passes were sold this month for a total of $76,000 cash.
g.   Received a $320 deposit on a townhouse to be rented for five days in January.
h.   Paid half the charges incurred on account in (c).
i.   Paid $18,000 in wages to employees for the month of December.

Required:

Prepare journal entries for each transaction. Be sure to categorize each account as an asset (A), liability (L), stockholders' equity (SE), revenue (R), or expense (E), and check that debits equal credits for each journal entry.

LO2, LO3   **E3-10 Recording Journal Entries**

Rowland & Sons Air Transport Service, Inc., has been in operation for three years. The following transactions occurred in February 2009:

Feb. 1	Paid $200 for rent of hangar space in February.
Feb. 2	Purchased fuel supplies costing $450 on account for the next flight to Dallas.
Feb. 4	Received customer payment of $800 to ship several items to Philadelphia next month.
Feb. 7	Flew cargo from Denver to Dallas; the customer paid $900 for the air transport.
Feb. 10	Paid pilot $1,200 in wages for flying in February.
Feb. 14	Paid $60 for an advertisement run in the local paper on February 14.
Feb. 18	Flew cargo for two customers from Dallas to Albuquerque for $1,700; one customer paid $500 cash and the other asked to be billed.
Feb. 25	Purchased on account $1,350 in spare parts for the planes.

Required:

Prepare journal entries for each transaction. Be sure to categorize each account as an asset (A), liability (L), stockholders' equity (SE), revenue (R), or expense (E).

LO2, LO3   **E3-11 Recording Journal Entries and Posting to T-Accounts**

Ricky's Piano Rebuilding Company has been operating for one year (2008). At the start of 2009, its income statement accounts had zero balances and its balance sheet account balances were as follows:

Cash	$ 6,000	Accounts Payable	$ 8,000
Accounts Receivable	25,000	Unearned Revenue (deposits)	3,200
Supplies	1,200	Notes Payable	40,000
Equipment	8,000	Contributed Capital	8,000
Land	6,000	Retained Earnings	9,000
Building	22,000		

Required:

1.   Create T-accounts for the balance sheet accounts and for these additional accounts: Piano Rebuilding Revenue, Rent Revenue, Wages Expense, and Utilities Expense. Enter the beginning balances.

2. Prepare journal entries for the following January 2009 transactions, using the letter of each transaction as a reference:

   a. Received a $500 deposit from a customer who wanted her piano rebuilt in February.

   b. Rented a part of the building to a bicycle repair shop for $300 rent received in January.

   c. Delivered five rebuilt pianos to customers who paid $14,500 in cash.

   d. Delivered two rebuilt pianos to customers for $7,000 charged on account.

   e. Received $6,000 from customers as payment on their accounts.

   f. Received an electric and gas utility bill for $350 for January services to be paid in February.

   g. Ordered $800 in supplies.

   h. Paid $1,700 on account in January.

   i. Paid $10,000 in wages to employees in January for work done this month.

   j. Received and paid cash for the supplies in (g).

3. Post the journal entries to the T-accounts. Show the unadjusted ending balances in the T-accounts.

E3-12 Preparing an Unadjusted Trial Balance   LO4

Refer to E3-11.

Required:

Use the balances in the completed T-accounts in E3-11 to prepare an unadjusted trial balance at the end of January 2009.

E3-13 Inferring Operating Transactions and Preparing an Unadjusted   LO2, LO3, LO4
Trial Balance

Virtual Golf Corporation operates indoor golf simulators that allow individual customers and golf club members to experience courses like Pebble Beach and Augusta without leaving their own neighborhood. Its stores are located in rented space in malls and shopping centers. During its first month of business ended April 30, 2008, Virtual Golf Corporation completed eight transactions with the dollar effects indicated in the following schedule:

	Assets				=	Liabilities	+	Stockholders' Equity	
Accounts	Cash	Accounts receivable	Supplies	Equipment	Accounts payable	Unearned revenue	Contributed capital	Retained Earnings	
Beginning balance	$ 0	$ 0	$ 0	$ 0	$ 0	$ 0	$ 0		$ 0
a	+100,000						+100,000		
b	−30,000			+30,000					
c	−200		+1,000		+800				
d	+9,000	+1,000						Sales revenue	+10,000
e	−1,000							Wages expense	−1,000
f					+1,200			Utilities expense	−1,200
g	+2,000					+2,000			
Ending balance	$ 79,800	$ 1,000	$ 1,000	$ 30,000	$2,000	$ 2,000	$ 100,000		$ 7,800

Required:

1. Write a brief explanation of transactions (a) through (h). Include any assumptions that you made.

2. Using the ending balance in each account, prepare an unadjusted trial balance for Virtual Golf Corporation on April 30, 2008.

E3-14 Inferring Transactions and Computing Effects Using T-Accounts   LO1, LO2, LO3

Dow Jones & Company

A recent annual report of Dow Jones & Company, the world leader in business and financial news and information (and publisher of *The Wall Street Journal*), included the following accounts. Dollars are in millions.

dr + Accounts Receivable (A) *cr* −			*dr* + Prepaid Expenses (A) *cr* −			*dr* − Unearned Revenue (L) *cr* +		
1/1	313		1/1	25			240	1/1
	2,573	?		43	?	?	328	
12/31	295		12/31	26			253	12/31

Required:

1. For each T-account, describe the typical transactions that cause it to increase and decrease.
2. Express each T-account in equation format (Beginning + Increase Side − Decrease Side = Ending) and then solve for the missing amounts (in millions). For example, the Accounts Receivable T-account can be expressed as: 313 + 2,573 − ? = 295. By rearranging the equation, you can solve for 313 + 2,573 − 295 = ?.

LO1, LO2   **E3-15 Finding Financial Information as an Investor**

You are evaluating your current portfolio of investments to determine those that are not performing to your expectations. You have all of the companies' most recent annual reports.

Required:

For each of the following, indicate where you would locate the information in a company's financial statements.

1. The total cost incurred for repairs and maintenance during the year.
2. Accounts receivable.
3. Description of a company's revenue recognition policy.
4. The cost of wages incurred during the year.

LO2   **E3-16 Determining Financial Statement Effects of Several Transactions**

In January 2009, Tongo, Inc., a branding consultant, posted the following transactions. Indicate the accounts, amounts, and direction of the effects on the accounting equation. A sample is provided.

a. (*Sample*) Received $9,500 cash for consulting services rendered in January.
b. Issued stock to investors for $10,000 cash.
c. Purchased $12,000 of equipment, paying 25% in cash and owing the rest on a note due in 2 years.
d. Received $7,500 cash for consulting services to be performed in February.
e. Bought $1,000 of supplies on account.
f. Received utility bill for January for $1,250, due February 15.
g. Consulted for customers in January for fees totaling $15,900, due in February.
h. Received $12,000 cash for consulting services rendered in December.
i. Paid $500 toward supplies purchased in e.

	Assets		=	Liabilities	+	Stockholders' Equity	
a.	Cash	+9,500	=			Service revenue (+R)	+9,500

LO3   **E3-17 Preparing Journal Entries**

For each of the transactions in E3-16 (including the sample), write the journal entry using the format shown in this chapter.

LO3   **E3-18 Posting to T-Accounts**

For each of the transactions in E3-16 (including the sample), post the effects to the appropriate T-accounts and determine ending account balances. Beginning account balances have been given. A sample is provided.

dr + Cash (A) *cr* −	
1/1/09 10,000	
a. 9,500	

dr + Accounts Receivable (A) *cr* −	
1/1/09 9,500	

dr + Supplies (A) *cr* −	
1/1/09 800	

dr + Equipment (A) *cr* −	
1/1/09 8,000	

dr − Accounts Payable (L) *cr* +	
	5,000 1/1/09

dr − Note Payable (L) *cr* +	
	0 1/1/09

dr − Unearned Revenue (L) *cr* +	
	2,500 1/1/09

dr − Contributed Capital (SE) *cr* +	
	12,000 1/1/09

dr − Retained Earnings (SE) *cr* +	
	40,000 1/1/09

dr − Service Revenues (R) *cr* +	
	0 1/1/09
	9,500 *a*

dr + Utilities Expense (E) *cr* −	
1/1/09 0	

E3-19 Creating an Unadjusted Trial Balance

LO4

Based on the transactions posted to T-accounts in E3-18, create an unadjusted trial balance for Tongo, Inc. for the month ended January 31, 2009.

E3-20 Inferring Income Statement Transactions and Creating Financial Statements

LO3

An analysis of transactions made during July 2008 by NepCo, an Internet service provider, during its first month of operations is shown below. Increases and decreases in retained earnings are explained.

	Assets				=	Liabilities	+	Stockholders' Equity	
	Cash	Accounts receivable	Supplies	Equipment		Accounts payable	Contributed capital	Retained earnings	
(a)						+710		−710	Utilities expense
(b)		+5,000						+5,000	Service revenue
(c)	+11,000						+11,000		
(d)	−6,000			+10,000		+4,000			
(e)	+1,000							+1,000	Service revenue
(f)			+550			+550			
(g)	−3,000					−3,000			
(h)	−2,000							−2,000	Wage expense
(i)	−750							−750	Rent expense
(j)	+1,500	−1,500							
(k)	−1,000							−1,000	Dividends

Required:

1. Describe the business activities that led to the accounting equation effects for each transaction shown above.
2. Prepare an income statement and a statement of retained earnings for July, and a classified balance sheet as of July 31, 2008. (These financial statements would be considered "preliminary" because they use unadjusted balances.)

LO3 | **E3-21 Determining Financial Statement Effects of Various Transactions**

EZ Reader was founded by John "Bum" Andrews in January 2009 to provide text reading and recording services. Selected transactions for EZ Reader's first month of business are as follows:

a. Issued stock to investors for $50,000 cash.
b. Billed customers $10,500 for services performed in January.
c. Purchased car for $24,500 for use in the business. Paid in cash.
d. Purchased $2,400 of supplies on account.
e. Received $7,500 cash from customers billed in transaction (b).
f. Used $1,500 in utilities, which will be paid in February.
g. Paid employees $3,500 cash for work done in January.
h. Paid $1,200 cash toward supplies purchased in transaction (d).

Required:

For each transaction, give (a) the name of the account being debited or credited, (b) the basic account type (A, L, SE, R, E), (c) whether the account is increased (+) or decreased (−) due to the transaction, and (d) whether the account normally holds a debit or credit balance. Transaction (a) has been given as an example.

	Debit Side of Journal Entry			
	Account Name	Account Type	Direction of Change	Normal Balance
(a)	Cash	A	+	Debit

Credit Side of Journal Entry			
Account Name	Account Type	Direction of Change	Normal Balance
Contributed capital	SE	+	Credit

LO2, LO3, LO4

Sigil Games Online, Inc.

E3-22 Comprehensive Exercise

Sigil Games Online, Inc. was founded in 2002 by Brad McQuaid and Jeff Butler with the mission of creating massively multiplayer online (MMO) games. Thus far, its "vanguard" (and only) product has been the game *Vanguard: Saga of Heroes*, slated for release in winter of 2007. The company intends to sell subscriptions to its game online. For the sake of this exercise, assume that Sigil has been selling subscriptions for *Vanguard* for one full year (2008) at $15 per month. At the start of 2009, its income statement accounts had zero balances and its balance sheet account balances were as follows:

Cash	$1,500,000	Accounts payable	$ 108,000
Accounts receivable	150,000	Unearned revenue	73,500
Supplies	14,700	Long-term notes payable	60,000
Equipment	874,500	Contributed capital	2,500,000
Land	1,200,000	Retained earnings	1,419,700
Building	422,000		

In addition to the above accounts, Sigil's chart of accounts includes the following: Subscription revenue, Licensing revenue, Wages expense, Advertising expense, and Utilities expense.

Required:

1. Analyze the effect of the January 2009 transactions (shown below) on the accounting equation, using the format shown in the demonstration case on page 107.
   a. Received $50,000 cash from customers for subscriptions earned in 2008.
   b. Received $25,000 cash from Electronic Arts, Inc., for licensing revenue earned in the month of January 2009.
   c. Purchased 10 new computer servers for $33,500; paid $10,000 cash and signed a note for the remainder owed.
   d. Paid $10,000 for an Internet advertisement run on Yahoo! in January 2009.
   e. Sold 15,000 monthly subscriptions at $15 each for services provided during the month of January 2009. Half was collected in cash and half was sold on account.
   f. Received an electric and gas utility bill for $5,350 for January 2009 utility services. The bill will be paid in February.

g. Paid $378,000 in wages to employees for work done in January 2009.

h. Purchased $3,000 of supplies on account.

i. Paid $3,000 cash to the supplier in (h).

2. Prepare journal entries for the January 2009 transactions listed in requirement 1, using the letter of each transaction as a reference.

3. Create T-accounts, enter the beginning balances shown above, post the journal entries to the T-accounts, and show the unadjusted ending balances in the T-accounts.

4. Prepare an unadjusted trial balance as of January 31, 2009.

5. Prepare an income statement for the month ended January 31, 2009, using unadjusted balances from requirement 4.

6. Prepare a statement of retained earnings for the month ended January 31, 2009, using the beginning balance given above and the net income from requirement 5. Assume Sigil has no dividends.

7. Prepare a classified balance sheet at January 31, 2009, using your response to requirement 6.

COACHED PROBLEMS

CP3-1 Recording Nonquantitative Journal Entries   LO3

The following list includes a series of accounts for B-ball Corporation, which has been operating for three years. These accounts are listed alphabetically and numbered for identification. Following the accounts is a series of transactions. For each transaction, indicate the account(s) that should be debited and credited by entering the appropriate account number(s) to the right of each transaction. If no journal entry is needed, write *none* after the transaction. The first transaction is used as an example.

TIP: In transaction (h), remember what the matching principle says.

TIP: Think of transaction (j) as two transactions: (1) incur expenses and liability and (2) pay part of the liability.

Account No.	Account Title	Account No.	Account Title
1	Accounts payable	8	Note payable
2	Accounts receivable	9	Prepaid insurance
3	Cash	10	Rent expense
4	Contributed capital	11	Service revenue
5	Equipment	12	Supplies expense
6	Income tax expense	13	Supplies
7	Income taxes payable		

Transactions	Debit	Credit
a. Example: Purchased equipment for use in the business; paid one-third cash and signed a note payable for the balance.	5	3, 8
b. Issued stock to new investors.	____	____
c. Paid cash for rent this period.	____	____
d. Collected cash for services performed this period.	____	____
e. Collected cash on accounts receivable for services performed last period.	____	____
f. Performed services this period on credit.	____	____
g. Paid cash on accounts payable for expenses incurred last period.	____	____
h. Purchased supplies to be used later; paid cash.	____	____
i. Used some of the supplies for operations.	____	____
j. Paid three-fourths of the income tax expense for the year; the balance will be paid next year.	____	____
k. On the last day of the current period, paid cash for an insurance policy covering the next two years.	____	____

LO2, LO3 **CP3-2 Recording Journal Entries**

Ryan Olson organized a new company, MeToo, Inc. The company provides online networking management services on MySpace, Facebook, Friendster, and other electronic social networks. Ryan believes that his target market is college and high school students. You have been hired to record the transactions occurring in the first two weeks of operations, beginning May 1, 2009.

  a. May 1: Issued 1,000 shares of stock to investors for $30 per share.
  b. May 1: Borrowed $50,000 from the bank to provide additional funding to begin operations; the note is due in two years.
  c. May 1: Paid $2,400 for a one-year fire insurance policy (recorded as prepaid insurance).
    TIP: For convenience, simply record the full amount of the payment as an asset (called Prepaid Insurance). At the end of the month, this account will be adjusted to its proper balance. We will study this adjustment process in Chapter 4, so just leave it as prepaid insurance for now.
  d. May 3: Purchased furniture and fixtures for the store for $15,000 on account. The amount is due within 30 days.
  e. May 5: Placed advertisements in local college newspapers for a total of $250 cash.
  f. May 9: Sold services for $400 cash.
  g. May 14: Made full payment for the furniture and fixtures purchased on account on May 3.

Required:

For each of the transactions, prepare journal entries. Be sure to categorize each account as an asset (A), liability (L), stockholders' equity (SE), revenue (R), or expense (E).

LO1, LO2, LO3, LO4 **CP3-3 Analyzing the Effects of Transactions Using T-Accounts and Preparing an Unadjusted Trial Balance**

www.mhhe.com/phillips2e

Barbara Jones, a textbook editor, opened Barb's Book Fixing on February 1, 2008. The company specializes in editing accounting textbooks. You have been hired as manager. Your duties include maintaining the company's financial records. The following transactions occurred in February 2008, the first month of operations.

  a. Received four shareholders' contributions totaling $16,000 cash to form the corporation; issued stock.
  b. Paid three months' rent for the store at $800 per month (recorded as prepaid rent).
    TIP: For convenience, simply record the full amount of the payment as an asset (called prepaid rent). At the end of the month, this account will be adjusted to its proper balance. We will study this adjustment process in Chapter 4, so just leave it as prepaid rent for now.
  c. Purchased supplies for $300 cash.
  d. Negotiated a two-year loan at the bank, depositing $10,000 in the company's bank account.
  e. Used all of the money from *d* to purchase a computer for $2,500 and the balance for furniture and fixtures for the store.
  f. Placed an advertisement in the local paper for $425 cash.
  g. Made sales totaling $1,800; $1,525 was in cash and the rest on accounts receivable.
  h. Incurred and paid employee wages of $420.
  i. Collected accounts receivable of $50 from customers.
  j. Made a repair to one of the computers for $120 cash.
    TIP: Most repairs involve costs that do *not* provide extra future economic benefits. Repairs merely maintain an asset's existing benefits.

Required:

1. Set up appropriate T-accounts for Cash, Accounts receivable, Supplies, Prepaid rent, Equipment, Furniture and fixtures, Notes payable, Contributed capital, Service revenue, Advertising expense, Wages expense, and Repair expense. All accounts begin with zero balances.
   TIP: When preparing the T-accounts, you might find it useful to group them by type: assets, liabilities, stockholders' equity, revenues, and expenses.
2. Record in the T-accounts the effects of each transaction for Barb's Book Fixing in February, referencing each transaction in the accounts with the transaction letter. Show the unadjusted ending balances in the T-accounts.
3. Prepare an unadjusted trial balance at the end of February.

4. Refer to the revenues and expenses shown on the unadjusted trial balance. Based on this information, write a short memo to Barbara offering your opinion on the results of operations during the first month of business.

GROUP A PROBLEMS

PA3-1 Recording Nonquantitative Journal Entries

LO3

The following is a series of accounts for Dewan & Allard, Incorporated, which has been operating for two years. The accounts are listed alphabetically and numbered for identification. Following the accounts is a series of transactions. For each transaction, indicate the account(s) that should be debited and credited by entering the appropriate account number(s) to the right of each transaction. If no journal entry is needed, write *none* after the transaction. The first transaction is given as an example.

Account No.	Account Title	Account No.	Account Title
1	Accounts payable	9	Land
2	Accounts receivable	10	Note payable
3	Advertising expense	11	Prepaid insurance
4	Buildings	12	Service revenue
5	Cash	13	Supplies expense
6	Contributed capital	14	Supplies
7	Income tax expense	15	Wages expense
8	Income taxes payable		

Transactions	Debit	Credit
a. Example: Issued stock to new investors.	5	6
b. Performed services for customers this period on credit.	___	___
c. Purchased on credit but did not use supplies this period.	___	___
d. Prepaid a fire insurance policy this period to cover the next 12 months.	___	___
e. Purchased a building this period by making a 20 percent cash downpayment and signing a note payable for the balance.	___	___
f. Collected cash this year for services that had been provided and recorded in the prior year.	___	___
g. Paid cash this period for wages that had been earned this period.	___	___
h. Paid cash for supplies that had been purchased on accounts payable in the prior period.	___	___
i. Paid cash for advertising expense incurred in the current period.	___	___
j. Incurred advertising expenses on credit to be paid next period, but recorded this period.	___	___
k. Collected cash for services rendered this period.	___	___
l. Used supplies on hand to clean the offices.	___	___
m. Recorded income taxes for this period to be paid at the beginning of the next period.	___	___
n. This period a shareholder sold some shares of her stock to another person for an amount above the original issuance price.	___	___

PA3-2 Recording Journal Entries

LO2, LO3

Diana Mark is the president of ServicePro, Inc., a company that provides temporary employees for not-for-profit companies. ServicePro has been operating for five years; its revenues are increasing with each passing year. You have been hired to help Diana in analyzing the following transactions for the first two weeks of April 2009:

April 2   Purchased office supplies for $500 on account.

April 5   Billed the local United Way office $1,950 for temporary services provided.

April 8	Paid $250 for supplies purchased and recorded on account last period.
April 8	Placed an advertisement in the local paper for $400 cash.
April 9	Purchased a new computer for the office costing $2,300 cash.
April 10	Paid employee wages of $1,200, which were earned by employees in April.
April 11	Received $1,000 on account from the local United Way office billed on April 5.
April 12	Purchased land as the site of a future office for $10,000. Paid $2,000 down and signed a note payable for the balance.
April 13	Issued 2,000 additional shares of stock for $40 per share in anticipation of building a new office.
April 14	Billed Family & Children's Service $2,000 for services rendered this month.
April 15	Received the April telephone bill for $245 to be paid next month.

Required:

For each of the transactions, prepare journal entries. Be sure to categorize each account as an asset (A), liability (L), stockholders' equity (SE), revenue (R), or expense (E).

LO1, LO2, LO3, LO4

www.mhhe.com/phillips2e

PA3-3 Analyzing the Effects of Transactions Using T-Accounts and Preparing an Unadjusted Trial Balance

Spicewood Stables, Inc., was established in Dripping Springs, Texas, on April 1, 2008. The company provides stables, care for animals, and grounds for riding and showing horses. You have been hired as the new Assistant Controller. The following transactions for April 2008 are provided for your review.

a.   Received contributions from five investors of $200,000 in cash ($40,000 each).
b.   Built a barn for $142,000. The company paid half the amount in cash on April 1 and signed a three-year note payable for the balance.
c.   Provided $15,260 in animal care services for customers, all on credit.
d.   Rented stables to customers who cared for their own animals; received cash of $13,200.
e.   Received from a customer $1,500 to board her horse in May, June, and July (record as unearned revenue).
f.   Purchased hay and feed supplies on account for $3,210.
g.   Paid $840 in cash for water utilities incurred in the month.
h.   Paid $1,700 on accounts payable for previous purchases.
i.   Received $1,000 from customers on accounts receivable.
j.   Paid $4,000 in wages to employees who worked during the month.
k.   At the end of the month, prepaid a two-year insurance policy for $3,600.
l.   Received an electric utility bill for $1,200 for usage in April; the bill will be paid next month.

Required:

1.   Set up appropriate T-accounts. All accounts begin with zero balances.
2.   Record in the T-accounts the effects of each transaction for Spicewood Stables in April, referencing each transaction in the accounts with the transaction letter. Show the unadjusted ending balances in the T-accounts.
3.   Prepare an unadjusted trial balance as of April 30, 2008.
4.   Refer to the revenues and expenses shown on the unadjusted trial balance. Based on this information, write a short memo to the five owners offering your opinion on the results of operations during the first month of business.

GROUP B PROBLEMS

LO3

Abercrombie & Fitch

PB3-1 Recording Nonquantitative Journal Entries

Abercrombie & Fitch Co. is a specialty retailer of casual apparel. The company's brand was established in 1892. It was first publicly traded in 1996 and was spun off from The Limited in 1998. The following is a series of accounts for Abercrombie. The accounts are listed alphabetically and numbered for identification. Following the accounts is a series of transactions. For each transaction, indicate the account(s) that should be debited and credited by entering the appropriate account number(s) to the right of each transaction. If no journal entry is needed, write *none* after the transaction. The first transaction is given as an example.

Account No.	Account Title	Account No.	Account Title
1	Accounts payable	7	Prepaid rent
2	Accounts receivable	8	Rent expense
3	Cash	9	Supplies expense
4	Contributed capital	10	Supplies
5	Equipment	11	Unearned revenue
6	Interest revenue	12	Wages expense

Transactions	Debit	Credit
a. Example: Incurred wages expense; paid cash.	12	3
b. Collected cash on account.	___	___
c. Used up supplies (cash register tapes, etc.) this period.	___	___
d. Sold gift certificates to customers; none redeemed this period.	___	___
e. Purchased equipment, paying in part cash and charging the balance on account.	___	___
f. Paid cash to suppliers on account.	___	___
g. Issued additional stock for cash.	___	___
h. Paid rent to landlords for next month's use of mall space.	___	___
i. Earned and received cash for interest on investments.	___	___

PB3-2 Recording Journal Entries

LO2, LO3

Robin Harrington established Time Definite Delivery on January 1, 2009. The following transactions occurred during the company's most recent quarter.

a. Issued stock for $80,000.
b. Provided delivery service to customers, receiving $72,000 in accounts receivable and $16,000 in cash.
c. Purchased equipment costing $82,000 and signed a long-term note for the full amount.
d. Incurred repair costs of $3,000 on account.
e. Collected $65,000 from customers on account.
f. Borrowed $90,000 by signing a long-term note.
g. Prepaid $74,400 cash to rent equipment and aircraft next quarter.
h. Paid employees $38,000 for work done during the quarter.
i. Purchased (with cash) and used $49,000 in fuel for delivery equipment.
j. Paid $2,000 on accounts payable.
k. Ordered, but haven't yet received, $700 in supplies.

Required:

For each of the transactions, prepare journal entries. Be sure to categorize each account as an asset (A), liability (L), stockholders' equity (SE), revenue (R), or expense (E).

PB3-3 Analyzing the Effects of Transactions Using T-Accounts and Preparing an Unadjusted Trial Balance

LO1, LO2, LO3, LO4

Jessica Pothier opened FunFlatables on June 1, 2008. The company rents out moon walks and inflatable slides for parties and corporate events. The company also has obtained the use of an abandoned ice rink located in a local shopping mall, where its rental products are displayed and available for casual hourly rental by mall patrons. The following transactions occurred during the first month of operations.

a. Jessica contributed $50,000 cash to the company in exchange for its stock.
b. Purchased inflatable rides and inflation equipment, paying $20,000 cash.
c. Received $5,000 cash from casual hourly rentals at the mall.

d. Rented rides and equipment to customers for $10,000. Received cash of $2,000 and the rest is due from customers.

e. Received $2,500 from a large corporate customer as a deposit on a party booking for July 4.

f. Began to prepare for the July 4 party by purchasing various party supplies on account for $600.

g. Paid $6,000 in cash for renting the mall space this month.

h. Prepaid next month's mall space rental charge of $6,000.

i. Received $1,000 from customers on accounts receivable.

j. Paid $4,000 in wages to employees for work done during the month.

k. Paid $1,000 for running a television ad this month.

Required:

1. Set up appropriate T-accounts. All accounts begin with zero balances.

2. Record in the T-accounts the effects of each transaction for FunFlatables in June, referencing each transaction in the accounts with the transaction letter. Show the unadjusted ending balances in the T-accounts.

3. Prepare an unadjusted trial balance for the end of June 2008.

4. Jessica has become alarmed at how quickly the company's cash balance has fallen. Refer to the revenues and expenses shown on the unadjusted trial balance and write a short memo to Jessica offering your opinion on the results of operations during the first month of business.

SKILLS DEVELOPMENT CASES

RESTAURANTS, INC.

LO1

S3-1 Finding Financial Information

Refer to the financial statements of Landry's Restaurants in Appendix A at the end of this book, or download the annual report from the *Cases* section of the text's Web site at www.mhhe.com/phillips2e.

Required:

1. Have Landry's total revenues increased, or decreased, in the most recent year? By how much? Calculate this change as a percentage of the previous year's total revenues by dividing the amount of the change by the previous year's revenues and multiplying by 100.

2. State the amount of the largest expense on the most recent income statement and describe the transaction represented by the expense. Did this expense increase, or decrease, from the previous year and by what percentage?

LO1

S3-2 Comparing Financial Information

Refer to the financial statements of Outback Steakhouse, Inc. in Appendix B at the end of this book, or download them from the *Cases* section of the text's Web site at www.mhhe.com/phillips2e.

Required:

1. Has Outback's total revenues increased, or decreased, in the most recent year? By how much? Calculate this change as a percentage of the previous year's total revenues. Is the trend in Outback's revenues more or less favorable than Landry's?

2. State the amount of the largest expense on Outback's income statement and describe the transaction represented by the expense. Did this expense increase, or decrease, and by what percentage, as compared to the previous year? Is the trend in Outback's largest expense more favorable, or less favorable, than the trend for Landry's largest expense?

LO1, LO5

S3-3 Internet-Based Team Research: Examining the Income Statement

As a team, select an industry to analyze. Using your Web browser, each team member should access the annual report or 10-K for one publicly traded company in the industry, with each member selecting a different company. (See S1-3 in Chapter 1 for a description of possible resources for these tasks.)

Required:

1. On an individual basis, each team member should write a short report that lists the following information:

    a. The major revenue and expense accounts on the most recent income statement.

    b. Description of how the company has followed the conditions of the revenue principle.

    c. The percentage of revenues that go to covering expenses, and that are in excess of expenses (in other words, the percentage that remains as net income).

2. Then, as a team, write a short report comparing and contrasting your companies using these attributes. Discuss any patterns across the companies that you as a team observe. Provide potential explanations for any differences discovered.

S3-4 Ethical Decision Making: A Real-Life Example

LO1, LO2, LO3, LO5

Read the following excerpt from a September 2, 2002, article in *Fortune* magazine and answer the questions that appear below.

> Forget about fraud. Companies don't need to lie, cheat, and steal to fool investors. Clever managers have always had, and continue to have, access to perfectly legal tricks to help make their balance sheets and income statements look better than they really are—tricks that *even today* won't jeopardize their ability to swear to the SEC that their books are on the up and up . . . One of the most controversial of all number games—the one that got WorldCom in trouble—is to capitalize expenses. That can have a tremendous impact on the bottom line.

1. In this chapter, you learned that when a company incurs a cost, its accountants have to decide whether to record the cost as an asset or expense. When costs are recorded as an asset, they are said to be *capitalized*. This builds on ideas first presented in Chapter 2, where you learned that it was appropriate to record costs as assets, provided that they possess certain characteristics. What are those characteristics?

2. The author of the article argues that even with clear rules like those referenced in question 1 above, accounting still allows managers to use "tricks" like *capitalizing expenses*. What do you suppose the author means by the expression *capitalizing expenses*?

3. Suppose that, in the current year, a company inappropriately records a cost as an asset when it should be recorded as an expense. What is the effect of this accounting decision on the current year's net income? What is the effect of this accounting decision on the following year's net income?

4. Later in the article (not shown) the author says that the videogame industry is one where companies frequently capitalize software development costs as assets. These costs include wages paid to programmers, fees paid to graphic designers, and amounts paid to game testers. Evaluate whether software development costs are likely to possess the main characteristics possessed by all assets. Can you think of a situation where software development costs might not possess these main characteristics?

5. Do you think it is always easy and straightforward to determine whether costs should be capitalized or expensed? Do you think it is always easy and straightforward to determine whether a manager is acting ethically or unethically? Give examples to illustrate your views.

S3-5 Ethical Decision Making: A Mini-Case

LO1, LO2, LO5

Mike Lynch is the manager of an upstate New York regional office for an insurance company. As the regional manager, his pay package includes a base salary, commissions, and a bonus when the region sells new policies in excess of its quota. Mike has been under enormous pressure lately, stemming largely from two factors. First, he is experiencing mounting personal debt due to a family member's illness. Second, compounding his worries, the region's sales of new insurance policies have dipped below the normal quota for the first time in years.

You have been working for Mike for two years, and like everyone else in the office, you consider yourself lucky to work for such a supportive boss. You also feel great sympathy for his personal problems over the last few months. In your position as accountant for the regional office, you are only too aware of the drop in new policy sales and the impact this will have on the manager's bonus. While you are working on the year-end financial statements, Mike stops by your office.

Mike asks you to change the manner in which you have accounted for a new property insurance policy for a large local business. A check for the premium, substantial in amount, came in the mail on

December 31, the last day of the reporting year. The premium covers a period beginning on January 5. You deposited the check and correctly debited cash and credited an *unearned revenue* account. Mike says, "Hey, we have the money this year, so why not count the revenue this year? I never did understand why you accountants are so picky about these things anyway. I'd like you to change the way you've recorded the transaction. I want you to credit a *revenue* account. And anyway, I've done favors for you in the past, and I am asking for such a small thing in return." With that, he leaves your office.

Required:

How should you handle this situation? What are the ethical implications of Mike's request? Who are the parties who would be helped or harmed if you went along with the request? If you fail to comply with his request, how will you explain your position to him? Justify your answers in writing.

LO1, LO2, LO4   **S3-6 Critical Thinking: Analyzing Changes in Accounts and Preparing a Trial Balance**

Hordichuk Painting Service Company was organized on January 20, 2008, by three individuals, each receiving 5,000 shares of stock from the new company. The following is a schedule of the cumulative account balances immediately after each of the first 9 transactions ending on January 31, 2008.

Accounts	Cumulative Balances								
	a	b	c	d	e	f	g	h	I
Cash	$75,000	$70,000	$85,000	$71,000	$61,000	$61,000	$46,000	$44,000	$60,000
Accounts receivable			12,000	12,000	12,000	26,000	26,000	26,000	10,000
Supplies					5,000	5,000	4,000	4,000	4,000
Office fixtures		20,000	20,000	20,000	20,000	20,000	20,000	20,000	20,000
Land				18,000	18,000	18,000	18,000	18,000	18,000
Accounts payable					3,000	3,000	3,000	1,000	1,000
Notes payable		15,000	15,000	19,000	19,000	19,000	19,000	19,000	19,000
Contributed capital	75,000	75,000	75,000	75,000	75,000	75,000	75,000	75,000	75,000
Paint revenue			27,000	27,000	27,000	41,000	41,000	41,000	41,000
Supplies expense							1,000	1,000	1,000
Wages expense					8,000	8,000	23,000	23,000	23,000

Required:

1. Analyze the changes in this schedule for each transaction; then explain the transaction. Transactions (*a*) and (*b*) are examples:
   a. Cash increased $75,000, and Contributed Capital (stockholders' equity) increased $75,000. Therefore, transaction *a* was an issuance of the capital stock of the corporation for $75,000 cash.
   b. Cash decreased $5,000, office fixtures (an asset) increased $20,000, and notes payable (a liability) increased $15,000. Therefore, transaction *b* was a purchase of office fixtures that cost $20,000. Payment was made as follows: cash, $5,000; notes payable, $15,000.

2. Based only on the preceding schedule, prepare an unadjusted trial balance.

LO2, LO3, LO4   **S3-7 Analyzing Transactions and Preparing an Unadjusted Trial Balance**

www.mhhe.com/phillips2e

Assume you recently started up a new company that rents machines for making frozen drinks like smoothies, frozen juices, tea slush, and iced cappuccinos. For $100, your business will deliver a machine, provide supplies (straws, paper cups), set up the machine, and pick up the machine the next morning. Drink mix and other supplies are sold by other businesses in your city. Being a one-person operation, you are responsible for everything from purchasing to marketing to operations to accounting.

You've decided that you'll just write notes about what happens during the month and then do the accounting at the end of the month. You figure this will be more efficient. Plus, by waiting until the end of the month to do the accounting, you'll be less likely to make a mistake because by that time you'll be way past the accounting cycle chapters. Your notes said the following about your first month of operations:

Oct. 2	Incorporated Slusher Gusher Inc. and contributed $10,000 for stock in the company.
Oct. 12	Paid cash to buy three frozen drink machines on eBay at a total cost of $1,500. What a deal!
Oct. 13	Paid cash to buy $70 of supplies. Wal-Mart was packed.
Oct. 16	Received $500 cash for this past week's rentals. I'm rich!
Oct. 17	Determined that $45 of supplies had been used up. Hmm, looks like I'll need some more.
Oct. 20	Bought $100 of supplies on account. I can't believe the party store gave me credit like that.
Oct. 23	Feeling tired after a busy week (6 rentals this time). Received $400 cash and expect to receive $200 more sometime this week.
Oct. 25	Received $100 cash from one of the customers who hadn't paid up yet. Called the other customer to remind him I'm waiting.
Oct. 26	Ran an ad in the local paper today for $25 cash. Maybe that'll drum up some business.
Oct. 27	Received $150 cash for a two-machine All Saints Day party to be held on November 1. It's a good thing I got this money because no other bookings are in sight for the rest of the month.

Required:

Create a spreadsheet in which to record the effects of the October transactions and calculate end-of-month totals. Using the spreadsheet, prepare a trial balance that checks whether debits = credits. Because you're dealing with your own business this time, you want to be extra sure that you do this just right, so you e-mail your friend Owen for advice. Here's his reply:

From: Owentheaccountant@yahoo.com
To: Helpme@hotmail.com
Cc:
Subject: Excel Help

Wow, you're a CEO already? I always thought you were a mover and a shaker! So you want my advice on how to set up your spreadsheet? My advice is *read the last email I sent.* The main thing that's new here is you'll need to include some columns for revenue and expenses under the stockholders' equity heading. Here's a screenshot of how the right-hand side of your worksheet might look just before you enter the October transactions. Notice that because stockholders' equity is decreased by expenses, the debit side is used to record expenses.

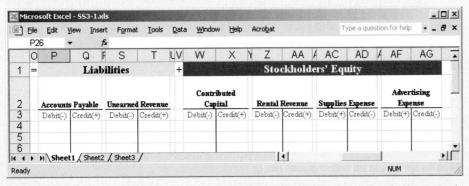

To prepare the trial balance, create three columns. In the first, copy and paste the account names (one per row). In the second column, link in each debit balance by entering = in a cell and then clicking on the debit total from the T-account. Repeat this with all the accounts. Then do the same with the credit balances. At the bottom of the trial balance, use the SUM function to compute totals.

Don't forget to save the file using a name that uniquely identifies you (as my true hero).

4

Adjustments, Financial Statements, and the Quality of Financial Reporting

THAT WAS
THEN

In the previous chapter, you learned how to analyze, record, and summarize the effects of operating transactions on balance sheet and income statement accounts.

LP4

If you've ever used an online course management system, like Blackboard, you'll know how great it is to be able to check your course standing at any given time. Even if you haven't used a system like this, just imagine what it would be like to be able to find out your course grade whenever you want. The key for making this kind of system work effectively is ensuring that it uses grade information that is up to date and complete. To be up to date, it needs to be adjusted for any test-score changes that your instructor has approved. To be complete, it needs to include the results of all assignments and tests that have been graded. With up-to-date and complete information like this, you can know exactly where you stand in the course and you can make better-informed decisions about where to devote your limited study time during the upcoming week.

The same needs exist in business. For investors and creditors to decide where to devote their limited resources, they need financial reports that contain up-to-date and complete information. To ensure this kind of information is available, accountants adjust their company's accounting records before financial statements are prepared and released to users. These adjustments are used to update amounts already recorded in the accounting records and to include events that have occurred but haven't yet been recorded as transactions. For Supercuts, this includes updating the supplies account for shampoo used during the month and including the interest that mounted on debt owed by the company. These kinds of adjustments are required by generally accepted accounting principles to ensure the financial statements include the financial results of *all* the company's activities for the period.

THIS IS
NOW

This chapter concludes the accounting cycle by focusing on adjustments, financial statment preparation, and the closing processes.

In the first section of this chapter, we'll help you to understand why adjustments are a necessary part of accrual basis accounting. Once you understand the purpose of adjustments, you'll be in a better position to learn how to determine what adjustments are needed and how they are recorded and summarized in the accounting system. The second section concludes with the final steps involved in the accounting cycle. In the third part of this chapter, you will learn the importance of adjustments for external financial statement users and, as always, the final section provides lots of opportunities for you to review and work with the material presented in this chapter. Here's an overview of these topics.

ORGANIZATION OF THE CHAPTER

Understand the business	Study the accounting methods	Evaluate the results	Review the chapter
• Why adjustments are needed	• Making required adjustments • Preparing an adjusted trial balance and financial statements • Closing temporary accounts	• The quality of adjusted financial statements	• Demonstration case • Chapter summary • Key terms • Practice material

Understand the Business

WHY ADJUSTMENTS ARE NEEDED

Accounting systems are designed to record most recurring daily transactions, particularly any involving cash. As cash is received or paid, it is recorded in the accounting system. This focus on cash is okay, particularly if cash receipts and payments occur in the same period as the activities that lead to revenues and expenses. As the top timeline in Exhibit 4.1 shows, if cash receipts and payments occur in the same accounting period as the related activities, then **adjustments** are not needed to report revenues and expenses in the proper period. In contrast, the bottom timeline in Exhibit 4.1 shows a situation where the activities that lead to revenues and expenses occur in the current accounting period but their related cash receipts and payments occur in other periods. To record the revenues and expenses from transactions like these in the proper period, adjustments will have to be made to the accounting records in the current accounting period.

Adjustments involve both income statement and balance sheet accounts. They are needed to ensure

- **Revenues** are recorded when earned (the revenue principle),
- **Expenses** are recorded in the same period as the revenues to which they relate (the matching principle),
- **Assets** are reported at amounts representing the economic benefits that remain at the end of the current period, and

Video 4.1

EXHIBIT 4.1	When Adjustments Are Needed

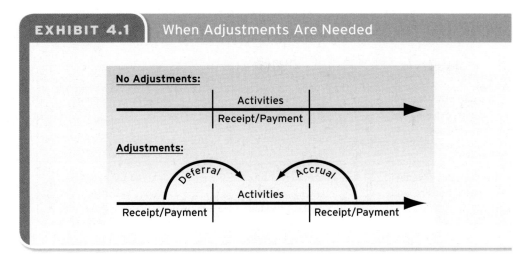

- **Liabilities** are reported at amounts owed at the end of the current period that will require a future sacrifice of resources.

Almost every financial statement account could require adjustment, so rather than try to memorize an endless list of examples, you should instead focus on learning what types of adjustments are needed in general. Later, we'll apply these general concepts to specific examples and give you lots of material to practice working with. In general, adjustments can be grouped into two categories: (1) deferrals, and (2) accruals.

1. Deferral Adjustments

The word *defer* means to postpone until later. In accounting, we say an expense or revenue has been deferred if we have postponed reporting it on the income statement until a later period. As you saw in Chapter 3, when Supercuts pays its rent in advance, the expense is initially deferred as an asset on the balance sheet (in an account called Prepaid rent). The adjustment part comes later, at the end of the month, when one month of the prepaid rent benefits have been used up. The deferral adjustment involves reducing the prepaid rent asset and increasing the rent expense on the income statement.

Deferral adjustments also can involve revenues. For example, when GQ receives cash for subscriptions before it has delivered magazines to subscribers, this revenue is initially deferred as a liability on the balance sheet (in an account called Unearned subscriptions revenue). The liability indicates the company's obligation to deliver magazines in the future. Later, when the company delivers the magazines, thereby meeting its obligation and earning the revenue, a deferral adjustment is made to reduce the liability on the balance sheet and increase subscriptions revenue on the income statement.

You should note two key ideas here.

1. Deferral adjustments are used to reduce amounts previously deferred on the balance sheet and to increase corresponding accounts on the income statement. Previously deferred amounts exist on the balance sheet because the company received cash before earning revenue or paid cash before incurring the expense. When revenues are earned (as defined by the revenue principle) or expenses incurred (as defined by the matching principle), the previously deferred amounts are transferred to the income statement using a deferral adjustment.

2. Each deferral adjustment involves a pair of asset and expense accounts, or liability and revenue accounts. The left side of Exhibit 4.2 shows a partial list of accounts that require deferral adjustments.

2. Accrual Adjustments

Accrual adjustments are needed when a transaction has occurred but has not yet been recorded in the accounting system. This most commonly happens when a company has

Topic Tackler

PLUS

Check out www.mhhe.com/phillips2e for audio, visual, and PowerPoint presentations on this topic.

EXHIBIT 4.2   Examples of Accounts Affected by Adjustments

	Deferral Adjustments				**Accrual Adjustments**		
Assets	Balance Sheet	Income Statement	**Expenses**	**Assets**	Balance Sheet	Income Statement	**Revenues**
	Supplies ————————	Supplies expense			Interest receivable ————	Interest revenue	
	Prepaid rent —————————	Rent expense			Rent receivable ————	Rent revenue	
	Prepaid insurance ————	Insurance expense					
Liabilities	Unearned ticket revenue ———	Ticket sales revenue	**Revenues**	**Liabilities**	Income tax payable —————	Income tax expense	**Expenses**
	Unearned subscriptions——— revenue	Subscriptions revenue			Wages payable —————	Wages expense	
					Interest payable —————	Interest expense	

earned revenue or incurred an expense in the current period but has not yet recorded it because the related cash will not be received or paid until a later period. For example, if Supercuts owes taxes on the income it earned this period, an accrual adjustment will be needed at the end of the month to record increases in its Income tax expense and Income tax payable accounts. Likewise, if interest has been earned on investments but will not be received in cash until later, an accrual adjustment will be needed at the end of the month to record increases in the company's Interest revenue and Interest receivable accounts.

You should note two key ideas here.

1. Accrual adjustments are used to recognize revenue or expenses when they occur, prior to receipt or payment of cash and to adjust corresponding balance sheet accounts.

2. Each accrual adjustment involves a pair of asset and revenue accounts, or liability and expense accounts. Notice that this differs from deferral adjustments, which pair assets with expenses and liabilities with revenues. The right side of Exhibit 4.2 shows a partial list of accounts that require accrual adjustments.

Take a moment right now and glance back at the bottom timeline in Exhibit 4.1 on page 139. The arrow on the left shows when a deferral adjustment is needed and the arrow on the right shows when an accrual adjustment is needed.

HOW'S IT GOING?   A Self-Study Quiz

For each of the following, indicate whether a deferral (D) or accrual (A) adjustment is required on October 31, and what pair of accounts will be affected by it.

			Accounts Affected	
		Type of Adjustment	Balance Sheet	Income Statement
1.	In September, Six Flags received $6,000 from customers for tickets that allow park admission in October.			
2.	The Trump Organization rented office space to tenants in October, but is not expecting payment until November.			
3.	On July 1, Fortune Magazine obtained a two-year bank loan that charges 6% interest each year.			
4.	On October 1, Apple Computer, Inc. paid $24,000 for insurance for October, November, and December.			

Quiz Answers

Type / Balance Sheet & Income Statement Accounts

1. D / Unearned Revenue & Park Admission Revenue
2. A / Rent Receivable & Rent Revenue
3. A / Interest Payable & Interest Expense
4. D / Prepaid Insurance & Insurance Expense

Study the Accounting Methods

MAKING REQUIRED ADJUSTMENTS

The process of making adjustments is similar to what you learned in Chapters 2 and 3. As shown in Exhibit 4.3, the main difference is that adjustments are made at the end of each accounting period immediately prior to preparing financial statements. Adjustments are not made on a daily basis because it's more efficient to do them all at once at the end of each period. After determining the necessary adjustments (in Step 1), they are recorded using **adjusting journal entries** (in Step 2) and then summarized in the accounts (in Step 3). An adjusted trial balance is prepared to ensure total debits still equal total credits after having posted the adjusting journal entries to the accounts. If the accounts are in balance, the financial statements can be prepared and then distributed to interested users.

> **Learning Objective 2**
> Prepare adjustments needed at the end of the period.

> **YOU SHOULD KNOW**
> **Adjusting journal entries (AJEs)** indicate the effects of each period's adjustments in a debits-equal-credits format.

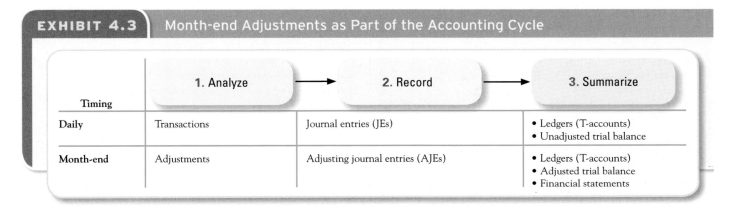

EXHIBIT 4.3	Month-end Adjustments as Part of the Accounting Cycle

Timing	1. Analyze	2. Record	3. Summarize
Daily	Transactions	Journal entries (JEs)	• Ledgers (T-accounts) • Unadjusted trial balance
Month-end	Adjustments	Adjusting journal entries (AJEs)	• Ledgers (T-accounts) • Adjusted trial balance • Financial statements

Adjustment Analysis, Recording, and Summarizing

The unadjusted trial balance is a key starting point for the adjustment process because it presents the unadjusted balances for every account, which will help you identify accounts that require adjustment. Exhibit 4.4 shows the Supercuts unadjusted trial balance at the end of September. This trial balance is identical to Exhibit 3.8 on page 103, except we've included balances for all accounts in Supercuts' chart of accounts, including those that currently have zero balances. Alongside the unadjusted trial balance, we've identified accounts requiring adjustment at the end of September.

In this section, we show how to go about analyzing, recording, and summarizing the required adjustments. Read these pages carefully. They contain the topics that people typically find the most challenging in this chapter.

Deferral Adjustments   Let's begin by looking at deferral adjustments, which are used to update amounts that have been previously deferred on the balance sheet.

(a) Supplies Used during the Period

Of the $630 in supplies received in August, $400 remain on hand at September 30.

The supplies were initially recorded as an asset in August, but some of them have now been used up as of September 30. The matching principle requires an adjustment be made to report the cost of supplies used up this month as an expense (to match against revenues). To determine the cost of supplies used up, you have to do a little calculating. If you had $630 of supplies available for use and only $400 are left at the end of the month, then the $230 difference must be the cost of supplies used this month. In accounting terms, you should reduce the asset (Supplies) by $230 and show this amount as an expense (Supplies expense). The effects of this adjustment on the accounting equation are shown on page 142, along with the required adjusting journal entry and the accounts affected by it.

EXHIBIT 4.4	Unadjusted Trial Balance

SUPERCUTS
Unadjusted Trial Balance
As of September 30, 2008

Account Name	Debits	Credits	Explanation of Adjustments Needed
Cash	$ 6,100		
Supplies	630		Reduce for supplies used up during September.
Accounts receivable	200		Increase for right to collect revenues earned by cutting manager's hair.
Prepaid rent	7,200		Reduce for prepaid September rent benefits now used up.
Prepaid insurance	3,600		Reduce for prepaid September insurance benefits now used up.
Equipment	60,000		
Accumulated depreciation		$ 0	Adjust for equipment benefits used up in September.
Accounts payable		1,030	
Unearned revenue		300	Reduce for gift card obligations met in September.
Wages payable		0	Increase for September wages not yet paid.
Income tax payable		0	Increase for taxes owed on income generated in September.
Interest payable		0	Increase for interest owed on unpaid note in September.
Note payable		20,000	
Contributed capital		50,000	
Retained earnings		0	
Dividends declared	0		
Haircut revenue		15,500	Increase for revenues earned by cutting manager's hair.
Wages expense	8,100		Increase for wages for work done in September.
Rent expense	0		Increase for expense incurred for September rent.
Depreciation expense	0		Increase for expense of using equipment in September.
Utilities expense	600		
Advertising expense	400		
Insurance expense	0		Increase for September insurance benefits used up.
Supplies expense	0		Increase for supplies used up in September.
Interest expense	0		Increase for September interest on unpaid note.
Income tax expense	0		Increase for taxes on income generated in September.
Totals	$86,830	$86,830	

1. Analyze

Assets	= Liabilities +	Stockholders' Equity
(a) Supplies −230 =		Supplies Expense (+E) −230

2. Record

(a)   *dr* Supplies Expense (+E, −SE)   230
         cr Supplies (−A)   230

3. Summarize

dr +	Supplies (A)	*cr* −		*dr* +	Supplies Expense (E, SE)	*cr* −
Unadj. Bal. 630				Unadj. Bal. 0		
	230	AJE (a)		AJE (a) 230		
Adj. Bal. 400				Adj. Bal. 230		

One way to think about adjusting journal entries is that they take you from what was (unadjusted balances, as listed on the unadjusted trial balance) to what should be (the desired adjusted balances that will be reported on the financial statements). In example (a), the unadjusted balances in Supplies and Supplies expense were $630 and $0, respectively, but you wanted to show balances at the end of the month of $400 and $230. To go from what was, to what should be, you needed to reduce Supplies by $230 (by crediting the account) and increase Supplies Expense by $230 (by debiting the account). This was achieved by recording AJE (a). The financial statement effects of this adjustment are pictured in Exhibit 4.5.

COACH'S TIP

The notation "Supplies Expense (+E) −230" implies that the increase in an expense causes a decrease in stockholders' equity (through its negative impact on net income and retained earnings). To review see Exhibit 3.6 on page 96.

EXHIBIT 4.5   Transferring the Cost of an Asset to an Expense Account

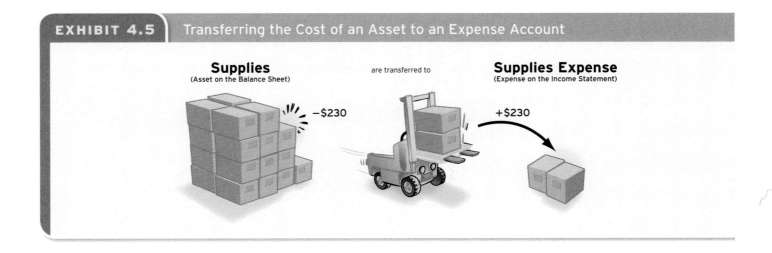

Supplies
(Asset on the Balance Sheet)

are transferred to

Supplies Expense
(Expense on the Income Statement)

−$230

+$230

(b) Rent Benefits Expire during the Period

Three months of rent were prepaid on September 1 for $7,200, but one month has now expired, leaving only two months prepaid at September 30.

To picture how costs relate to various time periods, it's useful to draw a timeline like the one shown in Exhibit 4.6. This timeline shows that the September prepayment of $7,200 represented three equal pieces of $2,400. The benefits of the first piece (pictured in red) have now expired, so they should be reported as an expense on the income statement. Only two of the three months (2/3) remain prepaid on September 30. Thus, the $7,200 that was prepaid on September 1 needs to be adjusted on September 30 to

EXHIBIT 4.6   Using a Timeline to Calculate Adjustments

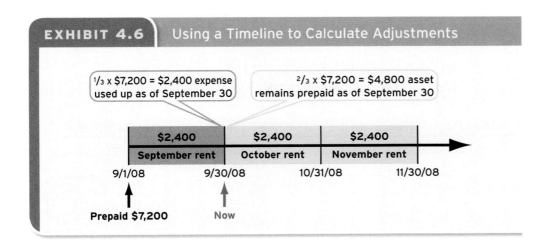

$1/3 \times \$7,200 = \$2,400$ expense used up as of September 30

$2/3 \times \$7,200 = \$4,800$ asset remains prepaid as of September 30

| $2,400 | $2,400 | $2,400 |
| September rent | October rent | November rent |

9/1/08   9/30/08   10/31/08   11/30/08

↑ Prepaid $7,200   ↑ Now

$4,800 (2/3 × $7,200), which is the cost of the two remaining months of prepaid rent to be reported on the September 30 balance sheet (pictured in blue).

The above analysis has determined that an adjustment is needed to reduce Prepaid rent by $2,400, from $7,200 to $4,800. Likewise, the adjustment needs to increase Rent expense by $2,400. These effects are shown as follows:

1. Analyze

	Assets	= Liabilities +	Stockholders' Equity	
(b) Prepaid Rent	−2,400 =		Rent Expense (+E)	−2,400

2. Record

(b)	dr Rent Expense (+E, −SE)	2,400	
	cr Prepaid Rent (−A)		2,400

3. Summarize

dr +	Prepaid Rent (A)	cr −		dr +	Rent Expense (E, SE)	cr −
Unadj. Bal. 7,200				Unadj. Bal. 0		
	2,400	AJE (b)		AJE (b) 2,400		
Adj. Bal. 4,800				Adj. Bal. 2,400		

(c) Insurance Benefits Expire during the Period

Twelve months of insurance were prepaid on September 1 for $3,600, but one month has now expired, leaving only eleven months prepaid at September 30.

On a scrap piece of paper, try drawing a timeline (similar to Exhibit 4.6) as we walk you through the required adjustment. Insurance costing $3,600 was prepaid and recorded as an asset on September 1. One month of insurance coverage has now expired ($300 = 1/12 × $3,600) and only 11 months' coverage remains ($3,300 = 11/12 × $3,600) on September 30. Thus, an adjustment is needed to increase Insurance expense by $300 and reduce Prepaid insurance by $300, from $3,600 to $3,300.

1. Analyze

	Assets	= Liabilities +	Stockholders' Equity	
(c) Prepaid Insurance	−300 =		Insurance Expense (+E)	−300

2. Record

(c)	dr Insurance Expense (+E, −SE)	300	
	cr Prepaid Insurance (−A)		300

3. Summarize

dr +	Prepaid Insurance (A)	cr −		dr +	Insurance Expense (E, SE)	cr −
Unadj. Bal. 3,600				Unadj. Bal. 0		
	300	AJE (c)		AJE (c) 300		
Adj. Bal. 3,300				Adj. Bal. 300		

HOW'S IT GOING?   A Self-Study Quiz

Take a minute to try this quiz to see how well the material has been sinking in. On October 1, Apple, Inc. paid $24,000 for insurance for October, November, and December. On October 31, unadjusted balances for Prepaid Insurance and Insurance Expense were $24,000 and $0, respectively. Based on this information, (1) analyze the accounting equation effects of the adjustment required on October 31, (2) record the adjusting journal entry, and (3) summarize the effects of the adjusting journal entry in the T-accounts shown below.

1. Analyze

$$\underline{\text{Assets}} \quad = \quad \underline{\text{Liabilities}} \quad + \quad \underline{\text{Stockholders' Equity}}$$

2. Record

dr
  cr

. . . .
. . . .

3. Summarize

dr +		cr −		dr +		cr −
Unadj. Bal.				Unadj. Bal.		
Adj. Bal.				Adj. Bal.		

Quiz Answers

	Assets	=	Liabilities	+	Stockholders' Equity
1.	Prepaid Insurance −8,000	=			Insurance Expense (+E) −8,000

2. dr Insurance Expense (+E, −SE) 8,000
    cr Prepaid Insurance (−A) 8,000

3. dr + **Prepaid Insurance (A)** cr −   dr + **Insurance Expense (E)** cr −

Unadj. 24,000	8,000 AJE		Unadj.	0	
			AJE	8,000	
Adj. 16,000			Adj.	8,000	

Notice that for events (a), (b), and (c), the deferral adjustments have two effects: (1) they reduce the **carrying value** of assets on the balance sheet, and (2) they transfer the amount of the reductions to related expense accounts. This happens whether we're adjusting supplies, prepaid rent, or even long-term assets like buildings, vehicles, and equipment. When accounting for the use of long-term assets like buildings, vehicles, and equipment, there is one slight difference in how the carrying value is reduced, as we'll explain next.

> **YOU SHOULD KNOW**
>
> **Carrying value** means the amount an asset or liability is reported at ("carried at") in the financial statements. It is also known as "net book value" or simply "book value."

(d) Depreciation Is Recorded for Use of Equipment

The salon equipment, which was estimated to last five years, has now been used for one month, representing an estimated expense of $1,000.

The matching principle indicates that when equipment is used to generate revenues in the current period, part of its cost should be transferred to an expense account in that period. This process is referred to as **depreciation**, so an account named Depreciation expense reports the equipment cost that relates to the current period. Use of an expense account to report the part of an asset used up is not new to you. What is new, however, is that rather than take the amount of depreciation directly out of the Equipment account, a **contra-account** is created to keep track of all the depreciation recorded against the equipment. This contra-account, named Accumulated depreciation, is like a

> **YOU SHOULD KNOW**
>
> **Depreciation** is the process of allocating the cost of buildings, vehicles, and equipment to the accounting periods in which they are used. A **contra-account** is an account that is an offset to, or reduction of, another account.

negative asset account that is subtracted from the Equipment account in the assets section of the balance sheet, as shown below.

Equipment	$60,000	← Original cost of equipment
Less: Accumulated depreciation	(1,000)	← Running total of depreciation recorded
Equipment, net of accumulated depreciation	59,000	← Carrying value (or net book value)

In our analyses below, we use a small "x" to indicate a contra-account, so the notation for a contra-account for an asset is "xA." An increase in a contra-asset account (+xA) decreases the carrying value of the underlying asset (−A).

1. Analyze

Assets	= Liabilities +	Stockholders' Equity
(d) Accum. Depn. (+xA) −1,000 =		Depreciation Exp. (+E) −1,000

2. Record

(d)   *dr* Depreciation Expense (+E, −SE)   1,000
        cr Accumulated Depreciation (+xA, −A)   1,000

3. Summarize

dr + Equipment (A) *cr* −		*dr* − Accumulated Depreciation (xA) *cr* +		*dr* + Depreciation Expense (E, SE) *cr* −	
Unadj. Bal. 60,000		0 Unadj. Bal.		Unadj. Bal. 0	
		1,000 AJE (d)		AJE (d) 1,000	
Adj. Bal 60,000		1,000 Adj. Bal.		Adj. Bal. 1,000	

There are four aspects of this example that you should note:

1. Accumulated depreciation is a balance sheet account and Depreciation expense is an income statement account.

2. By recording depreciation in Accumulated depreciation separate from the Equipment account, you can report both the original cost of equipment and a running total of the amount that has been depreciated. This gives financial statement users a rough idea of how much of the asset's original cost (representing its original usefulness) has been used up as of the balance sheet date. In our example, approximately 1/60 ($1,000/$60,000) of the equipment's total usefulness has been used up as of September 30.

3. A contra-account always is recorded in a way that opposes the account it offsets. For example, the increase in Accumulated depreciation was recorded with a credit because the account that it offsets, Equipment, was previously recorded with a debit.

4. The amount of depreciation depends on the method used for calculating it. Depreciation methods (and their formulas) will be discussed in Chapter 9.

Just as deferral adjustments are used to record expenses incurred when assets are used up, they also are used to record the revenues earned when a company meets its obligation to provide goods or services to customers. For example, when American Airlines, Dow Jones, and T-Mobile receive cash in advance of providing flights, newspapers, and cell phone service, they initially increase (debit) cash and increase (credit) a liability account called Unearned revenue. Later, when they meet their obligations, a deferral adjustment is recorded, reducing the liability (with a debit) and reporting the revenue earned from these services (with a credit). Let's apply this idea to Supercuts.

(e) Gift Cards Redeemed for Service

Supercuts redeemed $175 of gift cards that customers used to pay for haircuts.

The unadjusted trial balance reports $300 of Unearned revenue, which represents Supercuts' obligation to honor gift cards previously issued to customers. By accepting $175 of gift cards in exchange for haircut services this month, Supercuts has fulfilled a portion of its obligation and has earned additional revenue. Thus, a deferral adjustment is needed to reduce Unearned revenue and increase Haircut revenue.

COACH'S TIP

The word "unearned" in the Unearned revenue account means that the company hasn't done everything it promised to do. In other words, the company has an obligation (liability) to provide something in the future.

1. Analyze

Assets	=	Liabilities	+	Stockholders' Equity
(e)		Unearned Revenue −175		Haircut Revenue (+R) +175

2. Record

(e) dr Unearned Revenue (−L)   175
   cr Haircut Revenue (+R, +SE)   175

3. Summarize

dr − Unearned Revenue (L) cr +		dr − Haircut Revenue (R, SE) cr +	
	300 Unadj. Bal.		15,500 Unadj. Bal.
AJE (e) 175			175 AJE (e)
	125 Adj. Bal.		15,675 Adj. Bal.

Accrual Adjustments   Let's now look at common examples of accrual adjustments, which are adjustments that make the accounting records complete by including transactions that occurred but have not been recorded.

(f) Revenues Earned but Not Yet Recorded

Supercuts provided $40 of haircut services to the salon manager on the last day of September, with payment to be received in October.

Companies that regularly provide services on credit will design their accounting systems to record transactions like this on a daily basis. However, for a business that does not typically extend credit to its customers, like your Supercuts salon, these kinds of events may require an accrual adjustment at month-end. Because these revenues and the right to collect them (Accounts receivable) are earned in September, the revenue principle indicates they should be recorded in September. The accrual adjustment will increase Accounts receivable and increase Haircut revenue.

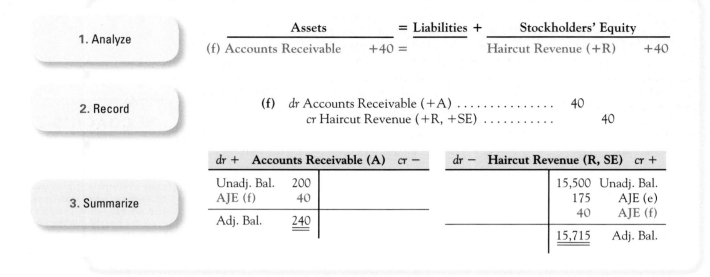

1. Analyze

Assets	= Liabilities +	Stockholders' Equity
(f) Accounts Receivable +40 =		Haircut Revenue (+R) +40

2. Record

(f)   *dr* Accounts Receivable (+A) 40

      cr Haircut Revenue (+R, +SE)   40

3. Summarize

dr + **Accounts Receivable (A)** *cr* −		*dr* − **Haircut Revenue (R, SE)** *cr* +	
Unadj. Bal.	200	15,500	Unadj. Bal.
AJE (f)	40	175	AJE (e)
		40	AJE (f)
Adj. Bal.	240	15,715	Adj. Bal.

Other situations require accrual adjustments for revenue earned but not yet recorded. For example, interest on investments is earned daily but typically is received in cash on a yearly basis, so each month an accrual adjustment is made to increase Interest receivable and Interest revenue for amounts earned but not yet recorded. Also, if a company provides services over two or more accounting periods, such as the Spy vs. Spy advertising campaign that BBDO created for Mountain Dew, it typically will not receive cash or bill its customer until the services have been provided in full. Consequently, an adjustment is needed to record the portion of the total revenue that has been earned as of the end of the month.

(g) Wage Expense Incurred but Not Yet Recorded

Supercuts owes $900 of wages to stylists for work done in the last three days of September.

Back in Chapter 3, Supercuts paid employees $8,100 for work done through September 27 ($300 per day). As of September 30, three additional days of work have been completed at a cost of $900. Although this amount will not be paid until October, the expense relates to work done (and revenues generated) in September, so the matching principle requires an adjustment be made to accrue the $900 of additional wages incurred and owed by Supercuts, as shown here.

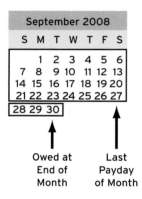

September 2008

S	M	T	W	T	F	S
	1	2	3	4	5	6
7	8	9	10	11	12	13
14	15	16	17	18	19	20
21	22	23	24	25	26	27
28	29	30				

Owed at   Last
End of   Payday
Month   of Month

1. Analyze

Assets	=	Liabilities	+	Stockholders' Equity
(g)		Wages Payable +900		Wages Expense (+E) −900

2. Record

(g)   *dr* **Wages Expense** (+E, −SE)............. 900

      cr **Wages Payable** (+L)...............   900

3. Summarize

dr − **Wages Payable (L)** *cr* +		*dr* + **Wages Expense (E,SE)** *cr* −	
	0 Unadj. Bal.	Unadj. Bal. 8,100	
	900 AJE (g)	AJE (g) 900	
	900 Adj. Bal.	Adj. Bal. 9,000	

(h) Interest Incurred but Not Yet Recorded

Supercuts has not paid or recorded the $100 interest that it owes for this month on its note payable to the bank.

Because the interest relates to September, an adjustment is needed to record Interest expense and, because the interest remains unpaid, the adjustment also is needed to record a liability called Interest payable. Currently, the unadjusted trial balance shows $0 of Interest payable and $0 of Interest expense.

1. Analyze

Assets	=	Liabilities	+	Stockholders' Equity
(h)		Interest Payable +100		Interest Expense (+E) −100

2. Record

(h) *dr* Interest Expense (+E, −SE)   100
     cr Interest Payable (+L)   100

3. Summarize

dr −	Interest Payable (L)	*cr* +
	0	Unadj. Bal.
	100	AJE (h)
	100	Adj. Bal.

dr +	Interest Expense (E,SE)	*cr* −
Unadj. Bal.	0	
AJE (h)	100	
Adj. Bal.	100	

Accrual adjustments also may be required for other expenses, like property taxes and utilities, if incurred and owed during the current period (but not yet recorded). The adjusting journal entry required for each of these items would be identical to the one shown in (h), except that the word *interest* would be replaced with the particular type of cost incurred and the applicable amounts would be used. For purposes of our Supercuts example, we'll assume the only remaining expense to record is the accrual of income taxes that are incurred this month but won't be paid until a later period.

(i) Income Taxes Incurred but Not Yet Recorded

Supercuts pays income tax at an average rate equal to 40 percent of the salon's income before taxes.

Just like you, a corporation is responsible for income tax when it generates more revenue than expenses in the current period. Income tax is calculated by multiplying (1) the company's adjusted income (before income taxes) by (2) the company's tax

	Revenues	Expenses		
Unadjusted totals	$15,500	$ 9,100	←	Calculated from Exhibit 4.4 ($9,100 = $8,100 + 600 + 400)
Adjustments: (a)		+ 230		
(b)		+ 2,400		
(c)		+ 300		
(d)		+ 1,000		
(e)	+ 175			
(f)	+ 40			
(g)		+ 900		
(h)		+ 100		
Adjusted totals	$ 15,715	− $14,030	= $1,685 ←	Adjusted income before income tax

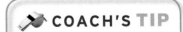

COACH'S TIP

Always calculate income tax expense **after** taking into account all revenue and expense adjustments.

rate. The table on page 149 calculates adjusted income (before income tax) by starting with the unadjusted revenue and expense numbers from the unadjusted trial balance (Exhibit 4.4) and then adding the effects of adjustments to revenues and expenses. Multiply the adjusted income before income tax ($1,685) by the tax rate (40%) to get the amount of income tax ($674).

The unadjusted trial balance shows that no income tax has been recorded (both Income tax payable and Income tax expense are $0). Because income was reported in September, the **matching principle** requires that we record the $674 tax expense in September. Because the tax hasn't been paid yet, a liability also must be recorded.

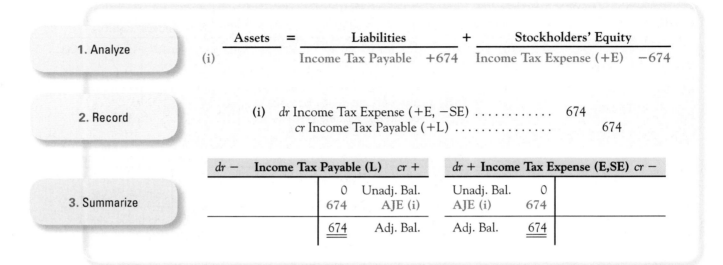

1. Analyze

Assets	=	Liabilities	+	Stockholders' Equity
(i)		Income Tax Payable +674		Income Tax Expense (+E) −674

2. Record

(i) *dr* Income Tax Expense (+E, −SE) 674
      cr Income Tax Payable (+L)   674

3. Summarize

dr −	Income Tax Payable (L)	*cr* +		*dr* +	Income Tax Expense (E,SE)	*cr* −
	0	Unadj. Bal.		Unadj. Bal.	0	
	674	AJE (i)		AJE (i)	674	
	674	Adj. Bal.		Adj. Bal.	674	

HOW'S IT GOING? A Self-Study Quiz

Prior to accruing marketing expenses of $5 million, Pixar's adjusted income before income taxes was $245 million. Assuming the company's average tax rate was 40%, (1) analyze the effect of the required income tax adjustment on the accounting equation, and (2) prepare the adjusting journal entry, assuming that no amounts have been recorded for income taxes.

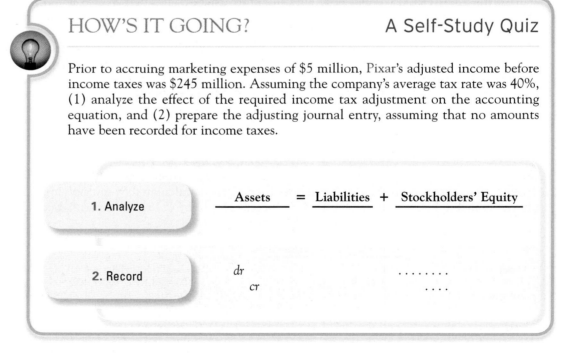

1. Analyze

Assets	=	Liabilities	+	Stockholders' Equity

2. Record

dr . . . .
  cr . . . .

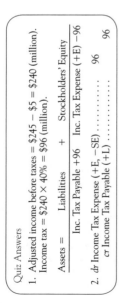

Quiz Answers

1. Adjusted income before taxes = $245 − $5 = $240 (million).
   Income tax = $240 × 40% = $96 (million).

Assets	=	Liabilities	+	Stockholders' Equity
		Inc. Tax Payable +96		Inc. Tax Expense (+E) −96

2. *dr* Income Tax Expense (+E, −SE) 96
    cr Income Tax Payable (+L)   96

Additional Comments

There are two final points to learn before finishing this section. The first point is short. Notice that none of the adjusting journal entries affected the Cash account. **Adjusting journal entries never involve cash.**

The second point relates to dividends, which a corporation uses to distribute profits to stockholders as a return on their investment in the corporation. The decision to pay a dividend is made by the company's board of directors after profits have been generated, so **dividends are not expenses of the business.** Instead, they are a reduction of the stockholders' claim on retained earnings. Consequently, dividends are not reported on the income statement, but instead are subtracted on the statement of retained earnings (as shown in Chapter 1). Dividends are recorded in their own special account called Dividends declared. Because dividends reduce stockholders' equity, they are recorded with a debit just like all reductions in stockholders' equity. Now that we know Supercuts has generated a profit for the month, we'll assume the company pays a dividend to stockholders. (Technically speaking, a dividend can occur any time during the year so it is typically recorded as a daily transaction when declared, rather than at the end of the period as an adjusting journal entry. But, we'll show it here for convenience.)

(j) Dividend Declared and Paid

Supercuts declares and pays a $500 cash dividend.

The dividend is recorded as a reduction in stockholders' equity in a special account called Dividends declared. Because it reduces stockholders' equity, it is recorded as a debit. The corresponding reduction in cash is recorded as a credit.

1. Analyze

	Assets	= Liabilities +	Stockholders' Equity	
(j) Cash	−500 =		Dividends Declared (+D)	−500

2. Record

(j) *dr* Dividends Declared (+D, −SE) 500
      cr Cash (−A)   500

3. Summarize

dr +	Cash (A)	*cr* −		*dr* + Dividends Declared (D,SE) *cr* −	
Unadj. Bal. 6,100				Unadj. Bal. 0	
	500	(j)		(j) 500	
Adj. Bal. 5,600				Adj. Bal. 500	

PREPARING AN ADJUSTED TRIAL BALANCE AND THE FINANCIAL STATEMENTS

Adjusted Trial Balance

Learning Objective 3
Prepare an adjusted trial balance.

Just like the unadjusted trial balance in Chapter 3, an **adjusted trial balance** is prepared to check that the accounts are still in balance. The only difference is that it is prepared after all adjustments have been posted. To prepare the adjusted trial balance for Supercuts, we've first gathered all of the company's T-accounts in Exhibit 4.7. We have calculated adjusted balances by updating the unadjusted balances (from Exhibit 4.4) with entries for items (a)–(j) on pages 141–151. The accounts and ending balances in Exhibit 4.7 are then listed in the adjusted trial balance in Exhibit 4.8, and total debits and credits are calculated. The trial balance proves the accounts are in balance (total debits = $89,544 = total credits), so the financial statements can be prepared.

The balance for each account in the trial balance will be reported only once on either the income statement, statement of retained earnings, or balance sheet. Typically, the income statement is prepared first because the net income number from it flows into the statement of retained earnings, and then the retained earnings number from the

YOU SHOULD KNOW

An **adjusted trial balance** is a list of all accounts and their adjusted balances to check on the equality of recorded debits and credits.

EXHIBIT 4.7 Supercuts' Adjusted Accounts

dr +	Cash (A)		cr −
Unadj. bal.	6,100		
		500	(j)
Adj. bal.	5,600		

dr +	Supplies (A)		cr −
Unadj. bal.	630		
		230	AJE (a)
Adj. bal.	400		

dr +	Accounts Receivable (A)		cr −
Unadj. bal.	200		
AJE (f)	40		
Adj. bal.	240		

dr +	Prepaid Rent (A)		cr −
Unadj. bal.	7,200		
		2,400	AJE (b)
Adj. bal.	4,800		

dr +	Prepaid Insurance (A)		cr −
Unadj. bal.	3,600		
		300	AJE (c)
Adj. bal.	3,300		

dr +	Equipment (A)		cr −
Unadj. bal.	60,000		

dr −	Accumulated Depreciation (xA)		cr +
		0	Unadj. bal.
	1,000		AJE (d)
		1,000	Adj. bal.

dr −	Accounts Payable (L)		cr +
		1,030	Unadj. bal.

dr −	Unearned Revenue (L)		cr +
		300	Unadj. bal.
AJE (e)	175		
		125	Adj. bal.

dr −	Wages Payable (L)		cr +
		0	Unadj. bal.
		900	AJE (g)
		900	Adj. bal.

dr −	Income Tax Payable (L)		cr +
		0	Unadj. bal.
		674	AJE (i)
		674	Adj. bal.

dr −	Interest Payable (L)		cr +
		0	Unadj. bal.
		100	AJE (h)
		100	Adj. bal.

dr −	Note Payable (L)		cr +
		20,000	Unadj. bal.

dr −	Contributed Capital (SE)		cr +
		50,000	Unadj. bal.

dr −	Retained Earnings (SE)		cr +
		0	Unadj. bal.

dr +	Dividends Declared (D, SE)		cr −
Unadj. bal.	0		
AJE (j)	500		
Adj. bal.	500		

dr −	Haircut Revenue (R, SE)		cr +
		15,500	Unadj. bal.
		175	AJE (e)
		40	AJE (f)
		15,715	Adj. bal.

dr +	Wages Expense (E, SE)		cr −
Unadj. bal.	8,100		
AJE (g)	900		
Adj. bal.	9,000		

dr +	Rent Expense (E, SE)		cr −
Unadj. bal.	0		
AJE (b)	2,400		
Adj. bal.	2,400		

dr +	Depreciation Expense (E, SE)		cr −
Unadj. bal.	0		
AJE (d)	1,000		
Adj. bal.	1,000		

dr +	Utilities Expense (E, SE)		cr −
Unadj. bal.	600		

dr +	Advertising Expense (E, SE)		cr −
Unadj. bal.	400		

dr +	Insurance Expense (E, SE)		cr −
Unadj. bal.	0		
AJE (c)	300		
Adj. bal.	300		

dr +	Supplies Expense (E, SE)		cr −
Unadj. bal.	0		
AJE (a)	230		
Adj. bal.	230		

dr +	Interest Expense (E, SE)		cr −
Unadj. bal.	0		
AJE (h)	100		
Adj. bal.	100		

dr +	Income Tax Expense (E, SE)		cr −
Unadj. bal.	0		
AJE (i)	674		
Adj. bal.	674		

| EXHIBIT 4.8 | Supercuts' Adjusted Trial Balance | **SUPER**CUTS |

SUPERCUTS
Adjusted Trial Balance
As of September 30, 2008

Account Name	Debits	Credits
Cash	$ 5,600	
Supplies	400	
Accounts receivable	240	
Prepaid rent	4,800	
Prepaid insurance	3,300	
Equipment	60,000	
Accumulated depreciation		$ 1,000
Accounts payable		1,030
Unearned revenue		125
Wages payable		900
Income tax payable		674
Interest payable		100
Note payable		20,000
Contributed capital		50,000
Retained earnings		0
Dividends declared	500	
Haircut revenue		15,715
Wages expense	9,000	
Rent expense	2,400	
Depreciation expense	1,000	
Utilities expense	600	
Advertising expense	400	
Insurance expense	300	
Supplies expense	230	
Interest expense	100	
Income tax expense	674	
Totals	$89,544	$89,544

> **COACH'S TIP**
>
> In the trial balance, list accounts in the order they will appear in the balance sheet, statement of retained earnings, and income statement.

statement of retained earnings flows into the balance sheet. As you will see in later chapters of this book, the statement of cash flows and notes to the financial statements are prepared last because they include information obtained from the income statement, statement of retained earnings, and balance sheet (plus other sources).

Income Statement and Statement of Retained Earnings

Prepare the income statement by creating the usual heading (who, what, when) and listing the names and amounts for each revenue and expense account from the adjusted trial balance, as shown in Exhibit 4.9.[1] Notice that each major category of items on the income statement is subtotaled prior to computing net income for the period.

Account balances from the adjusted trial balance are also used in the statement of retained earnings, as shown in Exhibit 4.9. Notice that the amount coming from the adjusted trial balance is the beginning-of-year balance for Retained earnings. This

> **Learning Objective 4**
> Prepare financial statements.

[1] Thanks to Philip Fink for suggesting this format.

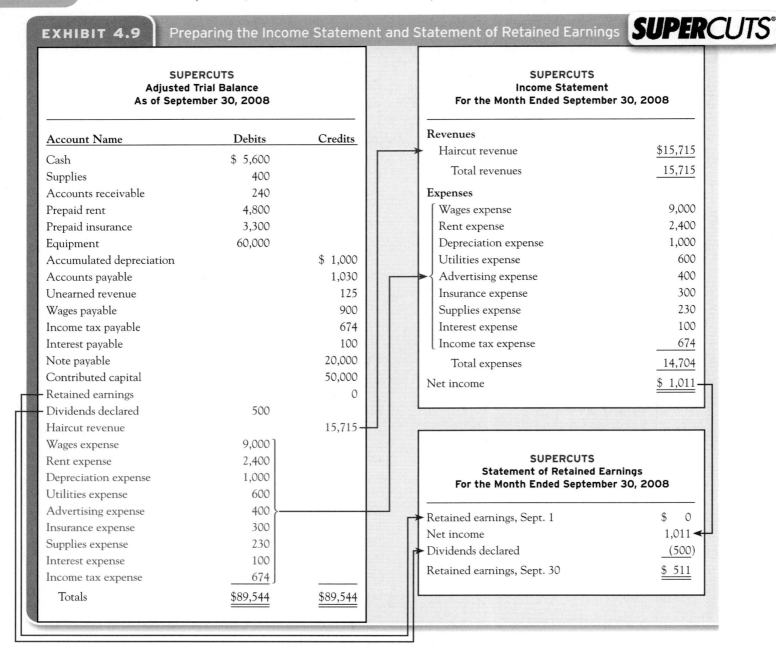

EXHIBIT 4.9 | Preparing the Income Statement and Statement of Retained Earnings **SUPERCUTS**

SUPERCUTS
Adjusted Trial Balance
As of September 30, 2008

Account Name	Debits	Credits
Cash	$ 5,600	
Supplies	400	
Accounts receivable	240	
Prepaid rent	4,800	
Prepaid insurance	3,300	
Equipment	60,000	
Accumulated depreciation		$ 1,000
Accounts payable		1,030
Unearned revenue		125
Wages payable		900
Income tax payable		674
Interest payable		100
Note payable		20,000
Contributed capital		50,000
Retained earnings		0
Dividends declared	500	
Haircut revenue		15,715
Wages expense	9,000	
Rent expense	2,400	
Depreciation expense	1,000	
Utilities expense	600	
Advertising expense	400	
Insurance expense	300	
Supplies expense	230	
Interest expense	100	
Income tax expense	674	
Totals	$89,544	$89,544

SUPERCUTS
Income Statement
For the Month Ended September 30, 2008

Revenues	
Haircut revenue	$15,715
Total revenues	15,715
Expenses	
Wages expense	9,000
Rent expense	2,400
Depreciation expense	1,000
Utilities expense	600
Advertising expense	400
Insurance expense	300
Supplies expense	230
Interest expense	100
Income tax expense	674
Total expenses	14,704
Net income	$ 1,011

SUPERCUTS
Statement of Retained Earnings
For the Month Ended September 30, 2008

Retained earnings, Sept. 1	$ 0
Net income	1,011
Dividends declared	(500)
Retained earnings, Sept. 30	$ 511

 **COACH'S TIP**

Dividends declared is reported only on the statement of retained earnings.

account balance doesn't yet include revenues, expenses, and dividends for the current period because they've been recorded in their own separate accounts. Eventually we will transfer ("close") those accounts into Retained earnings, but that's only done at the end of the year. For now, the Retained earnings account on the adjusted trial balance provides the opening amount on the statement of retained earnings. The amount for net income on the next line of the statement of retained earnings comes from the income statement and the Dividends declared number comes from the adjusted trial balance.

Balance Sheet

Like the other statements, the balance sheet is prepared from the adjusted trial balance, as shown in Exhibit 4.10. When preparing the balance sheet, watch out for three things. First, remember to classify assets and liabilities as current if they will be used up, turned into cash, or fulfilled within 12 months. Second, note that Accumulated depreciation is subtracted from Equipment in the assets section. Third, get the retained earnings balance from the statement of retained earnings, not from the

EXHIBIT 4.10 | Preparing the Balance Sheet   **SUPERCUTS®**

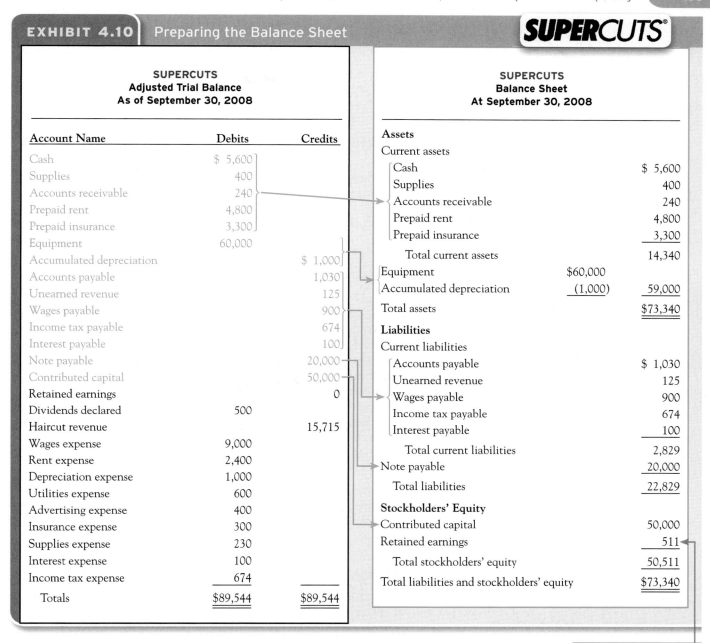

SUPERCUTS
Adjusted Trial Balance
As of September 30, 2008

Account Name	Debits	Credits
Cash	$ 5,600	
Supplies	400	
Accounts receivable	240	
Prepaid rent	4,800	
Prepaid insurance	3,300	
Equipment	60,000	
Accumulated depreciation		$ 1,000
Accounts payable		1,030
Unearned revenue		125
Wages payable		900
Income tax payable		674
Interest payable		100
Note payable		20,000
Contributed capital		50,000
Retained earnings		0
Dividends declared	500	
Haircut revenue		15,715
Wages expense	9,000	
Rent expense	2,400	
Depreciation expense	1,000	
Utilities expense	600	
Advertising expense	400	
Insurance expense	300	
Supplies expense	230	
Interest expense	100	
Income tax expense	674	
Totals	$89,544	$89,544

SUPERCUTS
Balance Sheet
At September 30, 2008

Assets
Current assets

Cash		$ 5,600
Supplies		400
Accounts receivable		240
Prepaid rent		4,800
Prepaid insurance		3,300
Total current assets		14,340
Equipment	$60,000	
Accumulated depreciation	(1,000)	59,000
Total assets		$73,340

Liabilities
Current liabilities

Accounts payable		$ 1,030
Unearned revenue		125
Wages payable		900
Income tax payable		674
Interest payable		100
Total current liabilities		2,829
Note payable		20,000
Total liabilities		22,829

Stockholders' Equity

Contributed capital		50,000
Retained earnings		511
Total stockholders' equity		50,511
Total liabilities and stockholders' equity		$73,340

From the Statement of Retained Earnings.

adjusted trial balance. (The adjusted trial balance still only reports the period's opening retained earnings balance.)

Statement of Cash Flows and Notes

If you didn't look so tired, we'd spend another hour here talking about how the statement of cash flows (SCF) and notes to the financial statements are prepared. But it looks like you'll be ready for a break soon, so we'll leave the SCF for Chapter 12 and we'll slide information about financial statement notes into each of the remaining chapters.

CLOSING TEMPORARY ACCOUNTS

The last step of the accounting cycle is referred to as the *closing process*. As shown in the first column in Exhibit 4.11, this step is performed only at the end of the year, after the financial statements have been prepared. The closing process cleans up the accounting records to get them ready to begin tracking the results in the following year. It's kind of like hitting the trip odometer on your car or the reset button on your X-box.

Learning Objective 5
Explain the closing process.

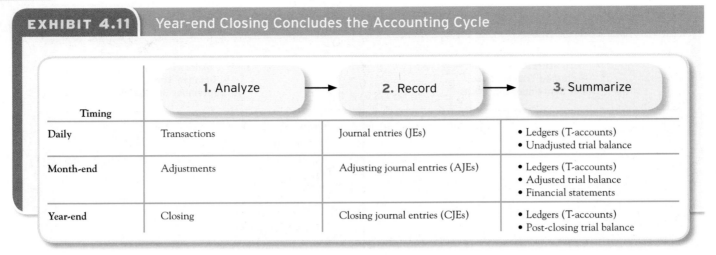

EXHIBIT 4.11 Year-end Closing Concludes the Accounting Cycle

Timing	1. Analyze	2. Record	3. Summarize
Daily	Transactions	Journal entries (JEs)	• Ledgers (T-accounts) • Unadjusted trial balance
Month-end	Adjustments	Adjusting journal entries (AJEs)	• Ledgers (T-accounts) • Adjusted trial balance • Financial statements
Year-end	Closing	Closing journal entries (CJEs)	• Ledgers (T-accounts) • Post-closing trial balance

Topic Tackler

PLUS

Check out www.mhhe.com/phillips2e for audio, visual, and PowerPoint presentations on this topic.

Video 4.2

Closing Income Statement and Dividend Accounts

In Chapter 3, you learned to think of revenue and expense accounts as subcategories of Retained earnings, which are used to track earnings-related transactions of the current year. Earlier in this chapter, you saw that the Dividends declared account is similarly used to track dividends declared during the current year. All revenue, expense, and dividends declared accounts are known as **temporary accounts** because they are used to track only the current year's results. At the end of each year, after all the year's transactions and adjustments are recorded, these temporary accounts are analyzed and closing journal entries are recorded to move the balances from the temporary accounts to where they belong—in Retained earnings. The Retained earnings account, like all other balance sheet accounts, is a **permanent account** because its ending balance from one year becomes its beginning balance for the following year.

The closing process serves two purposes:

1. Transfer net income (or loss) and dividends to Retained earnings. After the closing journal entries are prepared and posted, the balance in the Retained earnings account will agree with the statement of retained earnings and the balance sheet.

2. Establish zero balances in all income statement and dividend accounts. After the closing journal entries are prepared and posted, the balances in the temporary accounts are reset to zero to start accumulating next year's results.

Closing journal entries follow the usual debits-equal-credits format used for the transaction journal entries (in Chapters 2 and 3) and adjusting journal entries (shown earlier in this chapter). Because they're the last thing done during the year, they're posted immediately to the accounts. (Some computerized systems record and post closing journal entries automatically.) Two closing journal entries are needed: [2]

1. Debit each revenue account for the amount of its credit balance, credit each expense account for the amount of its debit balance, and record the difference in Retained earnings. If you've done it right, the amount credited to Retained earnings should equal net income on the income statement. (If the company has a net loss, Retained earnings will be debited.)

2. Credit the Dividends declared account for the amount of its debit balance and debit Retained earnings for the same amount.

Exhibit 4.12 shows the closing process for your Supercuts salon (assuming, for sake of illustration, that it closes its books on the last day of September).

---

[2] Some companies use a four-step process, by closing (1) revenue and (2) expense accounts to a special summary account, called Income summary, (3) which then is closed to Retained earnings, (4) along with Dividends declared.

EXHIBIT 4.12 Analyzing, Preparing, and Summarizing the Closing Journal Entries

1. Analyze

The analysis step for closing the temporary accounts only requires that you identify, from the adjusted trial balance, the temporary accounts with debit balances (to be credited below) and credit balances (to be debited below).

2. Record

CJE 1. Close revenue and expense accounts:

dr Haircut Revenue (−R)	15,715	
cr Wages Expense (−E)		9,000
cr Rent Expense (−E)		2,400
cr Depreciation Expense (−E)		1,000
cr Utilities Expense (−E)		600
cr Advertising Expense (−E)		400
cr Insurance Expense (−E)		300
cr Supplies Expense (−E)		230
cr Interest Expense (−E)		100
cr Income Tax Expense (−E)		674
cr Retained Earnings (+SE)		1,011

CJE 2. Close the dividends declared account:

dr Retained Earnings (−SE)	500	
cr Dividends Declared (−D)		500

3. Summarize

dr −	Haircut Revenue (R, SE)	cr +
	Adj. bal.	15,715
CJE (1) 15,715		
	Closed bal.	0

dr +	Insurance Expense (E, SE)	cr −
Adj. bal.	300	
	300	CJE (1)
Closed bal.	0	

dr +	Wages Expense (E, SE)	cr −
Adj. bal.	9,000	
	9,000	CJE (1)
Closed bal.	0	

dr +	Supplies Expense (E, SE)	cr −
Adj. bal.	230	
	230	CJE (1)
Closed bal.	0	

dr +	Rent Expense (E, SE)	cr −
Adj. bal.	2,400	
	2,400	CJE (1)
Closed bal.	0	

dr +	Interest Expense (E, SE)	cr −
Adj. bal.	100	
	100	CJE (1)
Closed bal.	0	

dr +	Depreciation Expense (E, SE)	cr −
Adj. bal.	1,000	
	1,000	CJE (1)
Closed bal.	0	

dr +	Income Tax Expense (E, SE)	cr −
Adj. bal.	674	
	674	CJE (1)
Closed bal.	0	

dr +	Utilities Expense (E, SE)	cr −
Adj. bal.	600	
	600	CJE (1)
Closed bal.	0	

dr +	Dividends Declared (D, SE)	cr −
Adj. bal.	500	
	500	CJE (2)
Closed bal.	0	

dr +	Advertising Expense (E, SE)	cr −
Adj. bal.	400	
	400	CJE (1)
Closed bal.	0	

dr −	Retained Earnings (SE)	cr +
	Adj. bal.	0
CJE (2) 500	CJE (1)	1,011
	Closed bal.	511

Post-Closing Trial Balance

After the closing journal entries are posted, all temporary accounts should have zero balances. These accounts will be ready for recording transactions next year. The ending balance in Retained earnings is now up to date (it matches the year-end amount on the statement of retained earnings and balance sheet) and is carried forward as the beginning balance for the next year. As the last step of the accounting cycle, you should prepare a **post-closing trial balance** (as shown in Exhibit 4.13). In this context, post means "after," so a post-closing trial balance is an "after-closing" trial balance that is prepared as a final check that total debits still equal total credits and that all temporary accounts have been closed.

Now that we've completed the accounting cycle, it seems appropriate to summarize it one more time. Exhibit 4.11 (on page 156) showed one way to organize the various steps of the accounting cycle. Exhibit 4.14 presents the same ideas in a slightly different format. The steps in the coral, blue, and gold boxes are done daily, monthly, and yearly, respectively.

> **YOU SHOULD KNOW**
>
> A **post-closing trial balance** is prepared as the last step in the accounting cycle to check that debits equal credits and all temporary accounts have been closed.

> **COACH'S TIP**
>
> Total debits on the post-closing trial balance don't equal the total assets on the balance sheet because accumulated depreciation (a credit balance on the trial balance) is subtracted from assets on the balance sheet.

EXHIBIT 4.13 Supercuts' Post-Closing Trial Balance **SUPERCUTS®**

SUPERCUTS
Post-Closing Trial Balance
As of September 30, 2008

Account Name	Debits	Credits
Cash	$ 5,600	
Supplies	400	
Accounts receivable	240	
Prepaid rent	4,800	
Prepaid insurance	3,300	
Equipment	60,000	
Accumulated depreciation		$ 1,000
Accounts payable		1,030
Unearned revenue		125
Wages payable		900
Income tax payable		674
Interest payable		100
Note payable		20,000
Contributed capital		50,000
Retained earnings		511
Dividends declared	0	
Haircut revenue		0
Wages expense	0	
Rent expense	0	
Depreciation expense	0	
Utilities expense	0	
Advertising expense	0	
Insurance expense	0	
Supplies expense	0	
Interest expense	0	
Income tax expense	0	
Totals	$74,340	$74,340

EXHIBIT 4.14	**The Accounting Process**

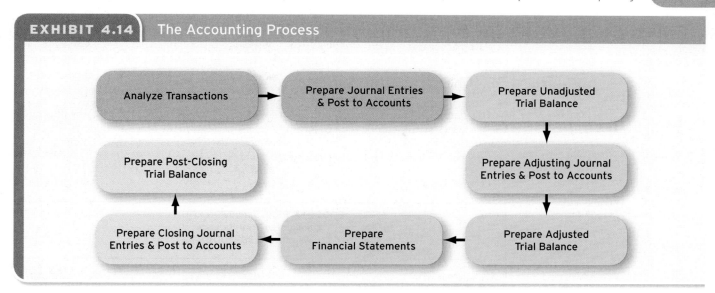

Evaluate the Results

THE QUALITY OF ADJUSTED FINANCIAL STATEMENTS

Learning Objective 6
Explain how adjustments affect information quality.

No doubt you've heard stories about how managers have encouraged their accountants to use adjusting journal entries to defer expenses or accrue revenues that didn't exist. (For an example, see case S4-4 at the end of this chapter.) There's something about accounting fraud that fascinates people, so it's often in the news. The problem with all this attention is that it gives the impression that managers and accountants frequently report assets and revenues that don't exist or they fail to report liabilities and expenses that do exist. And while you hear lots about the damage done by a few high-profile cases of fraud each year, you don't hear about all the other instances where deferral and accrual adjustments have helped financial statement users to better judge how well a company is performing. For the real scoop on the overall effects of adjustments, read the ethical insights box below.

Ethical Insights

Do Adjustments Improve Information Quality?

Many accounting research studies have looked into the question of whether accrual and deferral adjustments make financial statements more or less informative. They've found that while some managers may have used adjustments to mislead, overall, adjustments significantly improve the quality of financial statements. By ensuring that revenues are recognized when they are earned and expenses are recorded when incurred to generate those revenues, these adjustments help financial statement users better evaluate past decisions and predict future financial results.*

*P. Healy and J. Whalen, "A Review of the Earnings Management Literature and Its Implications for Standard Setting," *Accounting Horizons* 13, no. 4 (December 1999).

REVIEW THE CHAPTER

www.mhhe.com/phillips2e

DEMONSTRATION CASE

We take our final look at the accounting activities of Goodbye Grass Corporation by illustrating the activities at the end of the accounting cycle: the adjustment process, financial statement preparation, and the closing process. No adjustments have been made to the accounts yet. Your starting point will be the following unadjusted trial balance as of April 30, 2008:

GOODBYE GRASS CORPORATION
Unadjusted Trial Balance
As of April 30, 2008

Account Name	Debits	Credits
Cash	$ 4,510	
Accounts receivable	1,700	
Note receivable	1,250	
Prepaid insurance	300	
Equipment	4,600	
Accumulated depreciation		$ 0
Land	3,750	
Accounts payable		620
Unearned revenue		1,600
Wages payable		0
Interest payable		0
Income tax payable		0
Note payable		4,000
Contributed capital		9,000
Retained earnings		0
Mowing revenue		5,200
Wages expense	3,900	
Fuel expense	410	
Insurance expense	0	
Depreciation expense	0	
Interest expense	0	
Income tax expense	0	
Totals	$20,420	$20,420

By reviewing the unadjusted trial balance, you identify three deferral accounts (Prepaid insurance, Equipment, and Unearned revenue) that may need to be adjusted in addition to accruals that may be necessary relating to wages, income taxes, and interest incurred on the Note payable. The following information is determined at the end of the accounting cycle:

Deferral Adjustments

a. One-fourth of the $1,600 cash received from the city at the beginning of April for future mowing service has been earned in April. The $1,600 in Unearned revenue represents four months of service (April through July).

b. Insurance purchased at the beginning of April for $300 provides coverage for six months (April through September). The insurance coverage for April has now been used.
c. Mowers, edgers, rakes, and hand tools (equipment) have been used in April to generate revenues. The company estimates $300 in depreciation each year.

Accrual Adjustments

d. Wages have been paid through April 28. Employees worked the last two days of April and will be paid in May. Wages amount to $200 per day.
e. Interest incurred and payable on the note payable is $35 for the month of April.
f. The estimated income tax rate for Goodbye Grass Corporation is 35 percent.

Required:

1. Analyze items (a)–(f) with the goal of identifying the effects of required adjustments on the basic accounting equation (Assets = Liabilities + Stockholders' Equity), using the format shown in the chapter.
2. Record the adjusting journal entries required at the end of April.
3. Summarize the effects of each adjusting journal entry in T-accounts for each account affected. Obtain beginning balances from the unadjusted trial balance, then post the adjusting journal entries from requirement 2, and calculate adjusted April 30 balances.
4. Prepare an adjusted trial balance to ensure debit and credit balances are equal, remembering to include all accounts in the trial balance (and not just the ones affected by the adjusting journal entries).
5. Prepare an income statement, statement of retained earnings, and classified balance sheet from the amounts in the adjusted trial balance.
6. Prepare the closing journal entries that would be required if Goodbye Grass Corporation's fiscal year ended April 30, 2008.

After completing requirements 1–6, check your answers with the following solution.

Suggested Solution

1. Adjustment analysis:

  a. The unadjusted balances are $1,600 for Unearned revenue and $5,200 for Mowing revenue. One-fourth of the $1,600 has been earned in April ($400 = ¼ × $1,600) bringing total mowing revenues for the month to $5,600 ($5,200 + $400). Three-fourths of the $1,600 remain unearned at the end of April ($1,200 = ¾ × $1,600). To reach these desired balances, we need an adjustment that decreases Unearned revenue by $400 and increases Mowing revenue by $400.

Assets	=	Liabilities	+	Stockholders' Equity
		Unearned Revenue −400		Mowing Revenue (+R) +400

  b. The unadjusted balances are $300 for Prepaid insurance and $0 for Insurance expense. One-sixth of the $300 has expired in April resulting in an insurance expense for the month of $50 (= ⅙ × $300). Five of the six months of insurance coverage remain unused at the end of April ($250 = ⅚ × $300). To reach these desired balances, we need an adjustment that decreases Prepaid insurance by $50 and increases Insurance expense by $50.

Assets	=	Liabilities	+	Stockholders' Equity
Prepaid Insurance −50				Insurance Expense (+E) −50

  c. The unadjusted balances are $0 for Accumulated depreciation and $0 for Depreciation expense. Yearly depreciation of $300 equals $25 for just one month ($300 × 1/12). To go from the unadjusted balances of $0 to the desired adjusted balances of $25, we increase the expense and contra-account balances by $25.

Assets	= Liabilities +	Stockholders' Equity
Accumulated Depreciation (+xA) −25		Depreciation Expense (+E) −25

d. The unadjusted balances are $0 for Wages payable and $3,900 for Wages expense. Because the final two days of work done in April are unpaid, we need to record a liability for $400 (2 × $200). Total wages expense for the month should include the $3,900 paid for work from April 1–28 plus the $400 not yet paid for work on April 29 and 30. To reach these desired balances, we need an adjustment increasing Wages payable by $400 and increasing Wages expense by $400.

Assets	=	Liabilities	+	Stockholders' Equity	
		Wages Payable +400		Wages Expense (+E)	−400

e. The unadjusted balances are $0 for Interest payable and $0 for Interest expense. Interest of $35 was incurred in April, so the adjustment needs to increase both accounts by $35.

Assets	=	Liabilities	+	Stockholders' Equity	
		Interest Payable +35		Interest Expense (+E)	−35

f. The unadjusted balances are $0 for Income tax payable and $0 for Income tax expense. The amount of calculated income taxes will increase both of these accounts. Income taxes are calculated as 35 percent of adjusted income before tax for the month, as follows:

	Revenues	Expenses	
Unadjusted totals	$5,200	$4,310	← Calculated from unadjusted trial balance
Adjustments: (a)	+400		($4,310 = $3,900 + 410)
(b)		+ 50	
(c)		+ 25	
(d)		+400	
(e)		+ 35	
Adjusted totals	$5,600 −	$4,820	= $780 Adjusted income before income tax
			× 35% Tax rate
			$ 273 Income tax

Assets	=	Liabilities	+	Stockholders' Equity	
		Income Tax Payable +273		Income Tax Expense (+E)	−273

2.   Adjusting journal entries:

a. dr Unearned Revenue (−L)............................ 400
  cr Mowing Revenue (+R, +SE) 400

b. dr Insurance Expense (+E, −SE) 50
  cr Prepaid Insurance (−A)............................ 50

c. dr Depreciation Expense (+E, −SE)...................... 25
  cr Accumulated Depreciation (+xA, −A) 25

d. dr Wages Expense (+E, −SE)........................... 400
  cr Wages Payable (+L)............................... 400

e. dr Interest Expense (+E, −SE)......................... 35
  cr Interest Payable (+L).............................. 35

f. dr Income Tax Expense (+E, −SE)...................... 273
  cr Income Tax Payable (+L)......................... 273

3. T-accounts:

dr + Prepaid Insurance (A) cr −		dr − Interest Payable (L) cr +		dr + Insurance Expense (E) cr −	
Bal. fwd. 300			0 Beg. bal.	Beg. bal. 0	
	50 (b)		35 (e)	(b) 50	
End. bal. 250			35 End. bal.	End. bal. 50	

dr − Accumulated Depreciation (xA) cr +		dr − Income Tax Payable (L) cr +		dr + Depreciation Expense (E) cr −	
	0 Beg. bal.		0 Beg. bal.	Beg. bal. 0	
	25 (c)		273 (f)	(c) 25	
	25 End. bal.		273 End. bal.	End. bal. 25	

dr − Unearned Revenue (L) cr +		dr − Mowing Revenue (R) cr +		dr + Interest Expense (E) cr −	
	1,600 Bal. fwd.		5,200 Bal. fwd.	Beg. bal. 0	
(a) 400			400 (a)	(e) 35	
	1,200 End. bal.		5,600 End. bal.	End. bal. 35	

dr − Wages Payable (L) cr +		dr + Wages Expense (E) cr −		dr + Income Tax Expense (E) cr −	
	0 Beg. bal.	Bal. fwd. 3,900		Beg. bal. 0	
	400 (d)	(d) 400		(f) 273	
	400 End. bal.	End. bal. 4,300		Eng. bal. 273	

4. Adjusted trial balance:

GOODBYE GRASS CORPORATION
Adjusted Trial Balance
As of April 30, 2008

Account Name	Debits	Credits
Cash	$ 4,510	
Accounts Receivable	1,700	
Notes Receivable	1,250	
Prepaid Insurance	250	
Equipment	4,600	
Accumulated Depreciation		$ 25
Land	3,750	
Accounts Payable		620
Unearned Revenue		1,200
Wages Payable		400
Interest Payable		35
Income Tax Payable		273
Note Payable		4,000
Contributed Capital		9,000
Retained Earnings		0
Mowing Revenue		5,600
Wages Expense	4,300	
Fuel Expense	410	
Insurance Expense	50	
Depreciation Expense	25	
Interest Expense	35	
Income Tax Expense	273	
Totals	$21,153	$21,153

5. Income statement, statement of retained earnings, and balance sheet

---

GOODBYE GRASS CORPORATION
Income Statement
For the Month Ended April 30, 2008

Revenues:	
Mowing revenue	$5,600
Total revenues	5,600
Expenses:	
Wages expense	4,300
Fuel expense	410
Insurance expense	50
Depreciation expense	25
Interest expense	35
Income tax expense	273
Total expenses	5,093
Net Income	**$ 507**

GOODBYE GRASS CORPORATION
Statement of Retained Earnings
For the Month Ended April 30, 2008

Balance, April 1, 2008	$ 0
Net income	507
Dividends	0
Balance, April 30, 2008	**$507**

GOODBYE GRASS CORPORATION
Balance Sheet
As of April 30, 2008

Assets		**Liabilities**	
Current assets:		Current liabilities:	
Cash	$ 4,510	Accounts payable	$ 620
Accounts receivable	1,700	Unearned revenue	1,200
Note receivable	1,250	Wages payable	400
Prepaid insurance	250	Interest payable	35
Total current assets	7,710	Income tax payable	273
Equipment	4,600	Note payable	4,000
Less: Accumulated depreciation	(25)	Total current liabilities	6,528
Land	3,750	**Stockholders' Equity**	
Total assets	$16,035	Contributed Capital	9,000
		Retained Earnings	507
		Total Liabilities and Stockholders' Equity	$16,035

---

6. Closing journal entry:
    If Goodbye Grass Corporation had adopted an April 30 year-end, the company would require a journal entry to close its revenue and expense accounts into Retained earnings. Because the company has not declared a dividend, a Dividends declared account does not exist to be closed into Retained earnings. The closing journal entry needed to close revenues and expenses into Retained earnings is

dr Mowing Revenue (−R)	5,600	
cr Wages Expense (−E)		4,300
cr Fuel Expense (−E)		410
cr Insurance Expense (−E)		50
cr Depreciation Expense (−E)		25
cr Interest Expense (−E)		35
cr Income Tax Expense (−E)		273
cr Retained Earnings (+SE)		507

CHAPTER SUMMARY

Explain why adjustments are needed. p. 138 LO1

Adjustments are needed to ensure:

- Revenues are recorded when earned (the revenue principle),
- Expenses are recorded when incurred to generate revenues (the matching principle),
- Assets are reported at amounts representing the economic benefits that remain at the end of the current period, and
- Liabilities are reported at amounts owed at the end of the current period that will require a future sacrifice of resources.

Prepare adjustments needed at the end of the period. p. 141 LO2

- The process for preparing adjustments includes
  1. Analyzing the unadjusted balances in the pair of balance sheet and income statement accounts to be adjusted, and calculating the amount of the adjustment needed, using a timeline where appropriate.
  2. Preparing an adjusting journal entry to make the adjustment.
  3. Summarizing the adjusting journal entry in the applicable ledger (T-accounts).
- Adjusting journal entries never affect the Cash account.

Prepare an adjusted trial balance. p. 151 LO3

An adjusted trial balance is a list of all accounts with their adjusted debit or credit balances indicated in the appropriate column to provide a check on the equality of the debits and credits.

Prepare financial statements. p. 153 LO4

Adjusted account balances are used in preparing the following financial statements:

- Income Statement: Revenues − Expenses = Net Income.
- Statement of Retained Earnings: Beginning Retained Earnings + Net Income − Dividends Declared = Ending Retained Earnings.
- Balance Sheet: Assets = Liabilities + Stockholders' Equity.
- The statement of cash flows and notes to the financial statements are important components of adjusted financial statements, but they will be studied in later chapters.

Explain the closing process. p. 155 LO5

- Closing journal entries are required to (a) transfer net income (or loss) and dividends declared into retained earnings, and (b) prepare all temporary accounts (revenues, expenses, dividends declared) for the following year by establishing zero balances in these accounts.
- Two closing journal entries are needed:
  1. Debit each revenue account, credit each expense account, and record the difference (equal to net income) in retained earnings.
  2. Credit the dividends declared account for the amount of its balance and debit retained earnings for the same amount.

Explain how adjustments affect information quality. p. 159 LO6

Research shows that, overall, adjustments significantly improve the quality of financial statements, allowing financial statement users to better evaluate past decisions and predict future financial results.

KEY TERMS

PRACTICE MATERIAL

QUESTIONS

1. Briefly explain the purposes of adjustments.
2. Explain the relationships between adjustments and the following Chapter 3 comcepts: (a) the time period assumption, (b) the revenue principle, and (c) the matching principle.
3. List the two types of adjustments and give an example of an adjustment affecting revenues and expenses for each type.
4. Explain the effect of adjusting journal entries on cash.
5. What is a contra-asset? Give an example of one.
6. Explain the differences between depreciation expense and accumulated depreciation.
7. What is an adjusted trial balance? What is its purpose?
8. On December 31, a company makes a $9,000 payment for renting a warehouse in January, February, and March of the following year. Show the accounting equation effects of the transaction on December 31, as well as the adjustments required on January 31, February 28, and March 31.
9. Using the information in question 8, determine the amounts and accounts that will be reported on the January 31 balance sheet and the income statement for the month ended January 31.
10. Using the information in question 8, prepare the journal entry and adjusting journal entries to be made on December 31, January 31, February 28, and March 31.
11. What is the equation for each of the following statements: (a) income statement, (b) balance sheet, and (c) statement of retained earnings?
12. Explain how the financial statements in question 11 relate to each other.
13. What is the purpose of closing journal entries?
14. How do permanent accounts differ from temporary accounts?
15. Why are the income statement accounts closed but the balance sheet accounts are not?
16. Is Dividends declared considered an asset, liability, or stockholders' equity account? Is it a permanent or temporary account? Does it normally have a debit or credit balance?
17. What is a post-closing trial balance? Is it a useful part of the accounting cycle? Explain.

MULTIPLE CHOICE

Topic Tackler

PLUS

Check out www.mhhe.com/phillips2e to practice more multiple choice questions.

Quiz 4

1. Which of the following accounts would not appear in a closing journal entry?
   a. Interest Revenue
   b. Accumulated Depreciation
   c. Retained Earnings
   d. Salary Expense
2. Which account is least likely to appear in an adjusting journal entry?
   a. Cash
   b. Interest Receivable
   c. Income Tax Expense
   d. Salaries Payable
3. When a concert promotions company collects cash for ticket sales two months in advance of the show date, which of the following accounts is recorded?
   a. Accrued Liability
   b. Accounts Receivable
   c. Prepaid Expense
   d. Unearned Revenue

4. On December 31, an adjustment is made to reduce unearned revenue and report (earned) revenue. How many accounts will be included in this adjusting journal entry?

 a. None   c. Two

 b. One   d. Three

5. An adjusting journal entry to recognize accrued salaries payable would cause which of the following?

 a. A decrease in assets and stockholders' equity.

 b. A decrease in assets and liabilities.

 c. An increase in expenses, liabilities, and stockholders' equity.

 d. An increase in expenses and liabilities and a decrease in stockholders' equity.

6. An adjusted trial balance

 a. Shows the ending balances in a debit and credit format before posting the adjusting journal entries.

 b. Is prepared after closing entries have been posted.

 c. Is a tool used by financial analysts to review the performance of publicly traded companies.

 d. Shows the ending balances resulting from the adjusting journal entries in a debit-and-credit format.

7. Company A has owned a building for several years. Which of the following statements regarding depreciation is false from an accounting perspective?

 a. Depreciation expense for the year will equal Accumulated depreciation.

 b. Depreciation is an estimated expense to be recorded each period during the building's life.

 c. As depreciation is recorded, stockholders' equity is reduced.

 d. As depreciation is recorded, total assets are reduced.

8. Which of the following trial balances is used as a source for preparing the income statement?

 a. Unadjusted trial balance   c. Adjusted trial balance

 b. Pre-adjusted trial balance   d. Post-closing trial balance

9. Assume the balance in Prepaid insurance is $2,500 but it should be $1,500. The adjusting journal entry should include which of the following?

 a. Debit to Prepaid insurance for $1,000.   c. Debit to Insurance expense for $1,000.

 b. Credit to Insurance expense for $1,000.   d. Debit to Insurance expense for $1,500.

10. Assume a company receives a bill for $10,000 for advertising done during the current year. If this bill is not yet recorded at the end of the year, what will the adjusting journal entry include?

 a. Debit to Advertising expense of $10,000.   c. Debit to Accrued liabilities of $10,000.

 b. Credit to Advertising expense of $10,000.   d. Need more information to determine.

Solutions to Multiple Choice Questions
1.b   2.a   3.d   4.c   5.d   6.d   7.a   8.c   9.c   10.a

MINI-EXERCISES

Available with McGraw-Hill's Homework Manager   HOMEWORK MANAGER **PLUS**

M4-1 Understanding Concepts Related to Adjustments

Match each situation below to two applicable reasons that require an adjustment to be made.

_____ 1. Northwest Airlines provided flights this month for customers who paid cash last month for tickets.

_____ 2. Abercrombie received a telephone bill for services this month, which must be paid next month.

_____ 3. GSD+M completed work on an advertising campaign that will be collected next month.

_____ 4. The Tiger Woods Foundation used up some of the benefits of its 35,000 square foot building (when teaching students about forensic science, aerospace, and video production).

A. Revenue has been earned.

B. Expense has been incurred.

C. Liability has been incurred.

D. Liability has been fulfilled.

E. Asset has been acquired.

F. Asset has been used up.

LO1
Northwest Airlines
Abercrombie
GSD+M
Tiger Woods Foundation

LO3   M4-2 Preparing an Adjusted Trial Balance

Macro Company has the following adjusted accounts and balances at year-end (June 30, 2009):

Accounts payable	$ 300	Cash	$1,020	Prepaid expenses	$ 40
Accounts receivable	550	Contributed capital	300	Salaries expense	660
Accrued liabilities	150	Depreciation expense	110	Sales revenue	3,600
Accumulated		Income tax expense	110	Supplies	710
depreciation	250	Income tax payable	30	Rent expense	400
Administrative		Interest expense	180	Retained earnings	120
expense	820	Interest revenue	50	Unearned revenue	100
Buildings and		Land	200		
equipment	1,400	Long-term debt	1,300		

Required:

Prepare an adjusted trial balance for Macro Company at June 30, 2009.

LO1, LO2   M4-3 Matching Transactions with Type of Adjustment

Match each transaction with the type of adjustment that will be required, by entering the appropriate letter in the space provided.

Transaction	Type of Adjustment
____ 1. An expense has not yet been incurred, but has been paid in advance.	A. Accrual adjustment
	B. Deferral adjustment
____ 2. Rent has not yet been collected, but is already earned.	
____ 3. Office supplies on hand will be used next accounting period.	
____ 4. An expense has been incurred, but not yet paid or recorded.	
____ 5. Revenue has been collected in advance and will be earned later.	

LO1, LO2   M4-4 Matching Transactions with Type of Adjustment

Match each transaction with the type of adjustment that will be required, by entering the appropriate letter in the space provided.

Transaction	Type of Adjustment
____ 1. Supplies for office use were purchased during the year for $500, and $100 of the office supplies remained on hand (unused) at year-end.	A. Accrual adjustment
	B. Deferral adjustment
____ 2. Interest of $250 on a note receivable was earned at year-end, although collection of the interest is not due until the following year.	
____ 3. At year-end, wages payable of $3,600 had not been recorded or paid.	
____ 4. At year-end, service revenue of $2,000 was collected in cash but was only partly earned.	

LO2   M4-5 Determine Accounting Equation Effects of Adjustments

For each of the following transactions for the Sky Blue Corporation, give the accounting equation effects of the adjustments required at the end of the month on December 31, 2008:

a. Collected $1,200 rent for the period December 1, 2008, to February 28, 2009, which was credited to Unearned rent revenue on December 1, 2008.
b. Paid $2,400 for a two-year insurance premium on December 1, 2008; debited Prepaid insurance for that amount.
c. Used a machine purchased on December 1, 2008 for $48,000. The company estimates *annual* depreciation of $4,800.

M4-6 Recording Adjusting Journal Entries   LO2

Using the information in M4-5, prepare the adjusting journal entries required on December 31, 2008.

M4-7 Determining Accounting Equation Effects of Adjustments   LO2

For each of the following transactions for the Sky Blue Corporation, give the accounting equation effects of the adjustments required at the end of the month on December 31, 2008:

a. Received a $600 utility bill for electricity usage in December to be paid in January 2009.
b. Owed wages to 10 employees who worked three days at $100 each per day at the end of December. The company will pay employees at the end of the first week of January 2009.
c. On December 1, 2008, loaned money to an employee who agreed to repay the loan in one year along with $1,200 for one full year of interest.

M4-8 Recording Adjusting Journal Entries   LO2

Using the information in M4-7, prepare the adjusting journal entries required on December 31, 2008.

M4-9 Reporting an Income Statement   LO4

The Sky Blue Corporation has the following adjusted trial balance at December 31, 2008.

	Debit	Credit
Cash	$ 1,230	
Accounts receivable	2,000	
Prepaid insurance	2,300	
Notes receivable	3,000	
Equipment	12,000	
Accumulated depreciation		$ 300
Accounts payable		1,600
Accrued liabilities payable		3,820
Income taxes payable		2,900
Unearned rent revenue		600
Contributed capital		2,400
Retained earnings		1,000
Dividends declared	300	
Sales revenue		42,030
Rent revenue		300
Wages expense	21,600	
Depreciation expense	300	
Utilities expense	220	
Insurance expense	100	
Rent expense	9,000	
Income tax expense	2,900	
Total	$54,950	$54,950

Prepare an income statement for 2008. How much net income did the Sky Blue Corporation generate during 2008?

M4-10 Reporting a Statement of Retained Earnings   LO4

Refer to M4-9. Prepare a statement of retained earnings for 2008.

M4-11 Reporting a Balance Sheet   LO4

Refer to M4-9. Prepare a classified balance sheet at December 31, 2008. Are the Sky Blue Corporation's assets financed primarily by debt or equity?

M4-12 Recording Closing Journal Entries   LO5

Refer to the adjusted trial balance in M4-9. Prepare closing journal entries on December 31, 2008.

LO2   **M4-13 Preparing and Posting Adjusting Journal Entries**

At December 31, the unadjusted trial balance of H&R Tacks reports Supplies Inventory of $9,000 and Supplies Expense of $0. On December 31, supplies costing $1,300 are on hand. Prepare the adjusting journal entry on December 31. In separate T-accounts for each account, enter the unadjusted balances, post the adjusting journal entry, and report the adjusted balance.

LO2   **M4-14 Preparing and Posting Adjusting Journal Entries**

At December 31, the unadjusted trial balance of H&R Tacks reports Equipment of $30,000 and zero balances in Accumulated Depreciation and Depreciation Expense. Depreciation for the period is estimated to be $6,000. Prepare the adjusting journal entry on December 31. In separate T-accounts for each account, enter the unadjusted balances, post the adjusting journal entry, and report the adjusted balance.

LO2   **M4-15 Preparing and Posting Adjusting Journal Entries**

At December 31, the unadjusted trial balance of H&R Tacks reports Prepaid Insurance of $7,200 and Insurance Expense of $0. The insurance was purchased on July 1 and provides coverage for 12 months. Prepare the adjusting journal entry on December 31. In separate T-accounts for each account, enter the unadjusted balances, post the adjusting journal entry, and report the adjusted balance.

LO2   **M4-16 Preparing and Posting Adjusting Journal Entries**

At December 31, the unadjusted trial balance of H&R Tacks reports Unearned Revenue of $5,000 and Sales and Service Revenues of $33,800. One-half of the unearned revenues have been earned as of December 31. Prepare the adjusting journal entry on December 31. In separate T-accounts for each account, enter the unadjusted balances, post the adjusting journal entry, and report the adjusted balance.

LO2   **M4-17 Preparing and Posting Adjusting Journal Entries**

At December 31, the unadjusted trial balance of H&R Tacks reports Wages Payable of $0 and Wages Expense of $20,000. Employees have been paid for work done up to December 27, but the $1,200 they have earned for December 28–31 has not yet been paid or recorded. Prepare the adjusting journal entry on December 31. In separate T-accounts for each account, enter the unadjusted balances, post the adjusting journal entry, and report the adjusted balance.

LO2   **M4-18 Preparing and Posting Adjusting Journal Entries**

At December 31, the unadjusted trial balance of H&R Tacks reports Interest Payable of $0 and Interest Expense of $0. Interest incurred and owed in December totals $500. Prepare the adjusting journal entry on December 31. In separate T-accounts for each account, enter the unadjusted balances, post the adjusting journal entry, and report the adjusted balance.

LO2   **M4-19 Preparing and Posting Journal Entries for Dividends**

At December 31, the unadjusted trial balance of H&R Tacks reports Dividends Declared of $0 and Dividends Payable of $0. A $200 dividend was declared on December 27, with payment in cash to occur three weeks later. Prepare the required journal entry. In separate T-accounts for each account, enter the unadjusted balances, post the journal entry, and report the adjusted balance.

LO3   **M4-20 Preparing an Adjusted Trial Balance**

The unadjusted trial balance for H&R Tacks reported the following account balances: Cash $5,000; Accounts Receivable $500; Supplies Inventory $9,000; Prepaid Insurance $7,200; Equipment $28,000; Accounts Payable $200; Unearned Revenue $5,000; Notes Payable $3,000; Contributed Capital $22,000; Retained Earnings $5,700; Sales and Service Revenue $33,800; and Wages Expense $20,000. Prepare an adjusted trial balance as of December 31 that includes the entries required in M4-13 through M4-19.

M4-21 Progression of Prepaid Expenses over Several Periods

LO2, LO4, LO5

Midwest Manufacturing purchased a three-year insurance policy for $30,000 on January 2, 2008. Prepare any journal entries, adjusting journal entries, and closing journal entries required on January 2, 2008, December 31, 2008, and December 31, 2009. Summarize these entries in T-accounts for Prepaid insurance, Insurance expense, Cash, and Retained earnings. Assume the January 2, 2008, balances in these accounts were $0, $0, $90,000, and $80,000, respectively. Given only the entries for insurance, indicate what amounts would be reported for each of these accounts on the balance sheet and income statement prepared on December 31, 2008, and December 31, 2009.

EXERCISES

Available with McGraw-Hill's Homework Manager

HOMEWORK MANAGER PLUS

E4-1 Preparing an Adjusted Trial Balance from Adjusted Account Balances

LO3

Gibson Consultants, Inc., provides marketing research for clients in the retail industry. The company had the following adjusted balances at December 31, 2008:

Notes Payable		Accumulated Depreciation		Accrued Liabilities	
	160,000		18,100		25,650

Cash		General and Administrative Expense		Supplies	
173,000		320,050		12,200	

Wages and Benefits Expense		Prepaid Expenses		Interest Expense	
1,590,000		10,200		17,200	

Accounts Receivable		Consulting Fees Earned		Retained Earnings	
225,400			2,564,200		?

Income Taxes Payable		Travel Expense		Building and Equipment	
	2,030	23,990		323,040	

Utilities Expense		Dividends Declared		Unearned Consulting Fees	
25,230		5,000			32,500

Other Revenue		Accounts Payable		Land	
	20,800		86,830	60,000	

Other Operating Expenses		Contributed Capital		Training Expenses	
188,000			233,370	18,600	

Rent Expense		Other Assets	
152,080		145,000	

Required:

1. Prepare an adjusted trial balance for Gibson Consultants, Inc., at December 31, 2008. Solve for the "?" in retained earnings.
2. Does the Retained Earnings balance determined in requirement 1 represent the balance at December 31, 2008, or December 31, 2007? Explain.

LO1   **E4-2 Identifying Adjustments by Scanning a Trial Balance**

Coach, Inc.—the maker of handbags and other women's and men's accessories—was previously owned by Sara Lee Corporation until April 2001, when Coach was spun off as a separate company. Assume the following were reported in Coach's adjusted trial balance and were used to prepare its June 30, 2007, year-end financial statements.

COACH INCORPORATED Adjusted Trial Balance At June 30, 2007 (millions of dollars)		
	Debit	**Credit**
Cash	$ 143	
Accounts receivable	84	
Inventories	233	
Prepaid expenses	41	
Property and equipment	399	
Accumulated depreciation		$ 100
Other assets	726	
Accounts payable		80
Wages payable		250
Income taxes payable		12
Notes payable		35
Other liabilities		60
Contributed capital		585
Retained earnings		10
Sales revenue		2,111
Cost of sales	473	
Selling, general and administrative expenses	874	
Interest revenue		33
Income tax expense	303	
	$3,276	$3,276

Required:

1. Based on the information in the trial balance, list two pairs of balance sheet and income statement accounts that likely required *deferral adjustments* as of June 30 (no computations are necessary).

2. Based on the information in the trial balance, list two pairs of balance sheet and income statement accounts that likely required *accrual adjustments* as of June 30 (no computations are necessary).

LO1, LO2   **E4-3 Recording Adjusting Journal Entries**

Mobo, a wireless phone carrier, completed its first year of operations on December 31, 2008. All of the 2008 entries have been recorded, except for the following:

a.   At year-end, employees earned wages of $6,000, which will be paid on the next payroll date, January 6, 2009.

b.   At year-end, the company had earned interest revenue of $3,000. It will be collected March 1, 2009.

Required:

1. What is the annual reporting period for this company?
2. Identify whether each required adjustment is a deferral or an accrual.
3. Show the accounting equation effects of each required adjustment, using the format shown in the demonstration case.
4. Why are these adjustments needed?

E4-4 Recording Adjusting Journal Entries   LO1, LO2

Refer to E4-3.

Required:

Record the required adjusting journal entry for transactions (a) and (b).

E4-5 Determining Adjustments and Accounting Equation Effects   LO1, LO2

Fes Company is making adjusting journal entries for the year ended December 31, 2008. In developing information for the adjusting journal entries, you learned the following:

a. A two-year insurance premium of $7,200 was paid on January 1, 2008, for coverage beginning on that date. As of December 31, 2008, the unadjusted balances were $7,200 for Prepaid insurance and $0 for Insurance expense.
b. At December 31, 2008, you obtained the following data relating to shipping supplies.

Unadjusted balance in Shipping supplies on December 31, 2008	$15,000
Unadjusted balance in Shipping supplies expense on December 31, 2008	72,000
Shipping supplies on hand, counted on December 31, 2008	10,000

Required:

1. Of the $7,200 paid for insurance, what amount should be reported on the 2008 income statement as Insurance expense? What amount should be reported on the December 31, 2008, balance sheet as Prepaid insurance?
2. What amount should be reported on the 2008 income statement as Shipping supplies expense? What amount should be reported on the December 31, 2008, balance sheet as Shipping supplies?
3. Using the format shown in the demonstration case, indicate the accounting equation effects of the adjustment required for (a) insurance and (b) shipping supplies.

E4-6 Recording Adjusting Journal Entries   LO1, LO2

Refer to E4-5.

Required:

Prepare adjusting journal entries at December 31, 2008, for (a) insurance, and (b) shipping supplies.

E4-7 Recording Typical Adjusting Journal Entries   LO1, LO2

Jaworski's Ski Store is completing the accounting process for its first year ended December 31, 2008. The transactions during 2008 have been journalized and posted. The following data are available to determine adjusting journal entries:

a. The unadjusted balance in Office supplies was $850 at December 31, 2008. The unadjusted balance in Supplies expense was $0 at December 31, 2008. A year-end count showed $100 of supplies on hand.
b. Wages earned by employees during December 2008, unpaid and unrecorded at December 31, 2008, amounted to $3,700. The last paychecks were issued December 28; the next payments will be made on January 6, 2009. The unadjusted balance in Wages expense was $40,000 at December 31, 2008.

c. A portion of the store's basement is now being rented for $1,100 per month to K. Frey. On November 1, 2008, the store collected six months' rent in advance from Frey in the amount of $6,600. It was credited in full to Unearned rent revenue when collected. The unadjusted balance in Rent revenue was $0 at December 31, 2008.

d. The store purchased delivery equipment at the beginning of the year. The estimated depreciation for 2008 is $3,000, although none has been recorded yet.

e. On December 31, 2008, the unadjusted balance in Prepaid insurance was $4,800. This was the amount paid in the middle of the year for a two-year insurance policy with coverage beginning on July 1, 2008. The unadjusted balance in Insurance expense was $800, which was the cost of insurance from January 1 to June 30, 2008.

f. Jaworski's store did some ski repair work for Frey. At the end of December 31, 2008, Frey had not paid for work completed amounting to $750. This amount has not yet been recorded as Repair shop revenue. Collection is expected during January 2009.

Required:

1. For each of the items listed above, indicate the account names and adjusted balances that should be reported on Jaworski's year-end balance sheet and income statement.

2. For each situation, prepare the adjusting journal entry that should be recorded for Jaworski's at December 31, 2008.

LO2, LO4 **E4-8 Determining Financial Statement Effects of Seven Typical Adjusting Journal Entries**

Refer to E4-7.

Required:

For each of the transactions in E4-7, indicate the amount and direction of effects of the adjusting journal entry on the elements of the accounting equation. Using the following format, indicate + for increase, − for decrease, and NE for no effect. Include account names using the format shown in the chapter.

Transaction	Assets	Liabilities	Stockholders' Equity
a			
b			
c			
etc.			

LO2, LO5 **E4-9 Recording Transactions Including Adjusting and Closing Journal Entries**

The following accounts are used by Mouse Potato, Inc., a computer game maker.

Codes	Accounts	Codes	Accounts
A	Accounts Receivable	K	Note Payable
B	Accumulated Depreciation	L	Office Equipment
C	Cash	M	Office Supplies
D	Contributed Capital	N	Retained Earnings
E	Depreciation Expense	O	Service Revenue
F	Dividends Declared	P	Supplies Expense
G	Dividends Payable	Q	Unearned Service Revenue
H	Interest Expense	R	Wage Expense
I	Interest Payable	S	Wages Payable
J	Interest Revenue	T	None of the above

Required:

For each of the following independent situations, give the journal entry by entering the appropriate code(s) and amount(s). We've done the first one for you as an example.

	Independent Situations	Debit		Credit	
		Code	Amount	Code	Amount
a.	Accrued wages, unrecorded and unpaid at year-end, $400 (example).	R	400	S	400
b.	Service revenue collected in advance, $600.				
c.	Dividends declared and paid during year, $900.				
d.	Depreciation expense for year, $1,000.				
e.	Service revenue earned but not yet collected at year-end, $1,000.				
f.	Balance in office supplies account, $400; supplies on hand at year-end, $150.				
g.	At year-end, interest on note payable not yet recorded or paid, $220.				
h.	Adjusted balance at year-end in Service revenue account, $75,000. Give the journal entry to close this one account at year-end.				
i.	Adjusted balance at year-end in Interest Expense account, $420. Give the journal entry to close this one account at year-end.				

E4-10 Inferring Transactions from Accrual Accounts

LO1, LO2

Deere & Company

Deere & Company was incorporated in 1868 and today is the world's leading producer of agricultural equipment. Oddly enough the company also provides credit, managed health care plans, and insurance products for businesses and the general public. The following information is taken from a recent annual report (in millions of dollars):

Income Tax Payable

		Beg. bal.	87
	84	(a)	?
		End. bal.	227

Utilities Payable

		Beg. bal.	53
(b)	?		211
		End. bal.	53

Interest Payable

		Beg. bal.	65
	544	(c)	?
		End. bal.	79

Required:

1. For each accrued liability account, describe the typical transactions that cause it to increase and decrease.

2. Express each T-account in equation format and then solve for the missing amounts for (a), (b), and (c) (in millions). For example, the Interest Payable T-account can be expressed as: Beg. bal. (65) + increases (?) − decreases (544) = End. bal. (79). By rearranging the equation, you can solve for ? = 79 + 544 − 65.

E4-11 Analyzing the Effects of Adjusting Journal Entries on the Income Statement and Balance Sheet

LO2, LO4

On December 31, 2008, Alan and Company prepared an income statement and balance sheet but the boneheads failed to take into account four adjusting journal entries. The income statement, prepared on this incorrect basis, reported income before income taxes of $30,000. The balance sheet (before the effect of income taxes) reflected total assets, $90,000; total liabilities, $40,000; and stockholders' equity, $50,000. The data for the four adjusting journal entries follow:

a. Depreciation of $8,000 for the year on equipment was not recorded.
b. Wages amounting to $17,000 for the last three days of December 2008 were not paid and not recorded (the next payroll will be on January 10, 2009).
c. Rent revenue of $4,800 was collected on December 1, 2008, for office space for the three-month period December 1, 2008, to February 28, 2009. The $4,800 was credited in full to Unearned rent revenue when collected.
d. Income taxes were not recorded. The income tax rate for the company is 30 percent.

Required:

Complete the following table to show the effects of the four adjusting journal entries (indicate deductions with parentheses):

Items	Net Income	Total Assets	Total Liabilities	Stockholders' Equity
Amounts reported	$30,000	$90,000	$40,000	$50,000
Effect of depreciation	____	____	____	____
Effect of wages	____	____	____	____
Effect of rent revenue	____	____	____	____
Adjusted balances	6,600	82,000	55,400	26,600
Effect of income taxes	____	____	____	____
Correct amounts	════	════	════	════

LO2, LO4   **E4-12** **Reporting an Adjusted Income Statement**

Dyer, Inc., completed its first year of operations on December 31, 2008. Because this is the end of the annual accounting period, the company bookkeeper prepared the following preliminary income statement:

Income Statement, 2008		
Rental revenue		$114,000
Expenses:		
Salaries and wages expense	$28,500	
Maintenance expense	12,000	
Rent expense	9,000	
Utilities expense	4,000	
Gas and oil expense	3,000	
Other expenses	1,000	
Total expenses		57,500
Income		$ 56,500

You are an independent CPA hired by the company to audit the firm's accounting systems and financial statements. In your audit, you developed additional data as follows:

a. Wages for the last three days of December amounting to $310 were not recorded or paid.
b. The $400 telephone bill for December 2008 has not been recorded or paid.
c. Depreciation on rental autos, amounting to $23,000 for 2008, was not recorded.
d. Interest of $500 was not recorded on the note payable by Dyer, Inc.
e. The Rental revenue account includes $4,000 revenue to be earned in January 2009.
f. Maintenance supplies costing $600 were used during 2008, but this has not yet been recorded.
g. The income tax expense for 2008 is $7,000, but it won't actually be paid until 2009.

Required:

1. What adjusting journal entry for each item *a* through *g* should be recorded at December 31, 2008? If none is required, explain why.
2. Prepare, in proper form, an adjusted income statement for 2008.

E4-13 Recording Adjusting Entries and Preparing an Adjusted Trial Balance   LO2, LO3

Ninja Sockeye Star prepared the following unadjusted trial balance at the end of its second year of operations ending December 31, 2008.

Account Titles	Debit	Credit
Cash	$12,000	
Accounts receivable	6,000	
Prepaid rent	2,400	
Machinery	21,000	
Accumulated depreciation		$ 1,000
Accounts payable		1,000
Utilities payable		0
Income tax payable		0
Contributed capital		29,800
Retained earnings		2,100
Sales revenue		45,000
Cost of goods sold expense	25,000	
Utilities expense	12,500	
Rent expense	0	
Depreciation expense	0	
Income tax expense	0	
Totals	$78,900	$78,900

Other data not yet recorded at December 31, 2008:

a. Rent incurred during 2008, $1,200.
b. Depreciation expense for 2008, $1,000.
c. Utilities payable, $9,000.
d. Income tax expense, $800.

Required:

1. Using the format shown in the demonstration case, indicate the accounting equation effects of each required adjustment.
2. Prepare the adjusting journal entries required at December 31, 2008.
3. Summarize the adjusting journal entries in T-accounts. After entering the beginning balances and computing the adjusted ending balances, prepare an adjusted trial balance as of December 31, 2008.

E4-14 Recording Four Adjusting Journal Entries and Preparing an   LO2, LO3
     Adjusted Trial Balance

Mint Cleaning Inc. prepared the following unadjusted trial balance at the end of its second year of operations ending December 31, 2008. To simplify this exercise, the amounts given are in thousands of dollars.

Account Titles	Debit	Credit
Cash	$ 38	
Accounts receivable	9	
Prepaid insurance	6	
Machinery	80	
Accumulated depreciation		
Accounts payable		$ 9
Contributed capital		76
Retained earnings		4
Sales revenue		80
Cost of goods sold expense	26	
Wages expense	10	
Totals	$169	$169

Other data not yet recorded at December 31, 2008:

a.   Insurance expired during 2008, $5.   c.   Wages payable, $7.
b.   Depreciation expense for 2008, $4.   d.   Income tax expense, $9.

Required:

1.   Prepare the adjusting journal entries for 2008.
2.   Using T-accounts, determine the adjusted balances in each account and prepare an adjusted trial balance as of December 31, 2008.

LO4   **E4-15 Reporting an Income Statement, Statement of Retained Earnings, and Balance Sheet**

Refer to E4-14.

Required:

Using the adjusted balances in E4-14, prepare an income statement, statement of retained earnings, and balance sheet for 2008.

LO5   **E4-16 Recording Closing Entries**

Refer to E4-14.

Required:

Using the adjusted balances in E4-14, give the closing journal entry for 2008. What is the purpose of "closing the books" at the end of the accounting period?

LO2   **E4-17 Recording Initial Transactions and Subsequent Adjustments**

During the month of September, the Texas Go-Kart Company had the following business activities:

a.   On September 1, paid rent on the track facility for six months at a total cost of $12,000.
b.   On September 1, received $60,000 for season tickets for 12-month admission to the race track.
c.   On September 1, booked the race track for a private organization that will use the track one day per month for $2,000 each time, to be paid in the following month. The organization uses the track on September 30.
d.   On September 1, hired a new manager at a monthly salary of $3,000, to be paid the first Monday following the end of the month.

Required:

Using the following table, first prepare the journal entry, if any, required to record each of the initial business activities on September 1. Then, prepare the adjusting journal entries, if any, required on September 30.

Ref / Date	Journal Entries and Adjusting Journal Entries
(a) Sept 1	
Sept 30	
(b) Sept 1	
Sept 30	
(c) Sept 1	
Sept 30	
(d) Sept 1	
Sept 30	

COACHED PROBLEMS

CP4-1 Preparing an Adjusted Trial Balance, Closing Journal Entry, and Post-Closing Trial Balance

LO3, LO5
Dell Inc.

Dell Inc., which originally was named PC's Limited, is the world's largest computer systems company selling directly to customers. The following is a list of accounts and amounts reported for the fiscal year ended February 3, 2006. The accounts have normal debit or credit balances and the dollars are rounded to the nearest million.

Accounts payable	$ 9,840	Long-term debt	$ 504
Accounts receivable	5,452	Other assets	14,635
Accrued liabilities	6,087	Other liabilities	2,549
Accumulated depreciation	749	Property, plant, and equipment	2,005
Cash	9,807	Research and	
Contributed capital	4,129	development expense	463
Cost of goods sold	45,958	Retained earnings	5,045
Income tax expense	1,002	Sales revenue	55,908
Interest revenue	227	Selling, general, and	
Inventories	576	administrative expenses	5,140

Required:

1. Prepare an adjusted trial balance at February 3, 2006. Is the Retained earnings balance of $5,045 the amount that would be reported on the balance sheet as of February 3, 2006?

   TIP: Dell Inc. did not declare a dividend during 2006 but it did earn net income.

2. Prepare the closing entry required at February 3, 2006.
3. Prepare a post-closing trial balance at February 3, 2006.

CP4-2 Analyzing and Recording Adjusting Journal Entries

LO1, LO2

Jordan Company's annual accounting year ends on December 31. It is now December 31, 2008, and all of the 2008 entries have been made except for the following:

a. The company owes interest of $400 on a bank loan taken out on October 1, 2008. The interest will be paid when the loan is repaid on September 30, 2009.
b. On September 1, 2008, Jordan collected six months' rent of $4,800 on storage space. At that date, Jordan debited Cash and credited Unearned rent revenue for $4,800.
c. The company earned service revenue of $3,000 on a special job that was completed December 29, 2008. Collection will be made during January 2009. No entry has been recorded.
d. On November 1, 2008, Jordan paid a one-year premium for property insurance of $4,200, for coverage starting on that date. Cash was credited and Prepaid insurance was debited for this amount.
e. At December 31, 2008, wages earned by employees but not yet paid totaled $1,100. The employees will be paid on the next payroll date, January 15, 2009.
f. Depreciation of $1,000 must be recognized on a service truck purchased this year.
g. On December 27, 2008, the company received a tax bill of $400 from the city for 2008 property taxes on land. The tax bill is payable during January 2009.
h. The income before any of the adjustments or income taxes was $27,400. The company's federal income tax rate is 30 percent. Compute adjusted income based on a. through g. to determine and record income tax expense.

Required:

1. Determine the accounting equation effects of each required adjustment.

   TIP: In transaction b, Jordan Company has met its obligation for four of the six months, thereby earning 4/6 of the rent collected.

   TIP: In transaction d, two months of insurance coverage has now expired.

   TIP: Adjusted income based on a. through g. should be $30,000.

2. Give the adjusting journal entry required for each transaction at December 31, 2008.

LO2, LO4

www.mhhe.com/phillips2e

CP4-3 Determining Financial Statement Effects of Adjusting Journal Entries

Refer to CP4-2.

Required:

Indicate the financial statement effects (amount and direction) of each adjusting journal entry. Use + for increase, − for decrease, and NE for no effect. Provide an appropriate account name for any revenue and expense effects.

TIP: The first transaction is done for you as an example.

Transaction	Assets	Liabilities	Stockholders' Equity
a	NE	+400	Interest expense (+E) −400
b			
c			
etc.			

LO4

CP4-4 Analyzing a Student's Business and Preparing an Adjusted Income Statement

During the summer between her junior and senior years, Susan Irwin needed to earn enough money for the coming academic year. Unable to obtain a job with a reasonable salary, she decided to try the lawn care business for three months. Susan incorporated "Susan's Lawn Service," and then bought a used pickup truck on June 1 for $1,500. On each door she painted "Susan's Lawn Service, Phone 555-4487." She also spent $900 for mowers, trimmers, and tools. To acquire these items, she borrowed $2,500 cash by signing a note payable promising to pay the $2,500 plus interest of $75 at the end of the three months (ending August 31).

At the end of the summer, Susan realized that she had done a lot of work, and her bank account looked good. This fact made her think about how much profit the business had earned.

A review of the check stubs showed the following: Bank deposits of collections from customers totaled $12,600. The following checks had been written: gas, oil, and lubrication, $920; pickup repairs, $210; mower repair, $75; miscellaneous supplies used, $80; helpers, $4,500; payroll taxes, $175; payment for assistance in preparing payroll tax forms, $25; insurance, $125; telephone, $110; and $2,575 to pay off the note including interest (on August 31). A notebook kept in the pickup, plus some unpaid bills, reflected that customers still owed her $800 for lawn services provided and that she owed $200 for gas and oil (credit card charges). She estimated that the depreciation on the truck and the other equipment amounted to $500 for three months.

Required:

1. Prepare an accrual basis income statement for Susan's Lawn Service covering the quarter from June 1–August 31, 2008. Assume the business is not subject to income tax.
   TIP: Remember that when using accrual basis accounting, revenues will include amounts received in cash as well as amounts charged on credit.
   TIP: Interest on the note payable is an expense, but the repayment of the note's original amount is not (it is a reduction in a liability).
2. Assuming Susan's Lawn Service remains in business, do you see a need for one or more additional financial reports for this company for 2008 and thereafter? Explain.

LO1, LO2, LO3, LO4, LO5

CP4-5 Comprehensive Review Problem: From Recording Transactions (Including Adjusting Journal Entries) to Preparing Financial Statements and Closing Journal Entries (Chapters 2, 3, and 4)

Brothers Harry and Herman Hausyerday began operations of their machine shop (H & H Tool, Inc.) on January 1, 2007. The annual reporting period ends December 31. The trial balance on January 1, 2009, follows (the amounts are rounded to thousands of dollars to simplify):

Account No.	Account Titles	Debit	Credit
01	Cash	$ 3	
02	Accounts receivable	5	
03	Supplies	12	
04	Land		
05	Equipment	60	
06	Accumulated depreciation (on equipment)		$ 6
07	Other assets	4	
11	Accounts payable		5
12	Notes payable		
13	Wages payable		
14	Interest payable		
15	Income tax payable		
21	Contributed capital		65
31	Retained earnings		8
32	Dividends declared		
35	Service revenue		
40	Depreciation expense		
41	Income tax expense		
42	Interest expense		
43	Supplies and other operating expenses		
Totals		**$84**	**$84**

Transactions during 2009 (summarized in thousands of dollars) follow:

a. Borrowed $12 cash on a short-term note payable dated March 1, 2009.
b. Purchased land for future building site, paid cash, $9.
c. Earned revenues for 2009, $160, including $40 on credit and $120 collected in cash.
d. Issued additional shares of stock for $3.
e. Recognized operating expenses for 2006, $85, including $15 on credit and $70 paid in cash.
f. Collected accounts receivable, $24.
g. Purchased other assets, $10 cash.
h. Paid accounts payable, $13.
i. Purchased supplies on account for future use, $18.
j. Signed a $25 service contract to start February 1, 2010.
k. Declared and paid a cash dividend, $17.

Data for adjusting journal entries:

l. Supplies counted on December 31, 2009, $10.
m. Depreciation for the year on the equipment, $6.
n. Accrued interest on notes payable of $1.
o. Wages earned since the December 24 payroll not yet paid, $12.
p. Income tax for the year was $8. It will be paid in 2010.

Required:

1. Set up T-accounts for the accounts on the trial balance and enter beginning balances.
2. Record journal entries for transactions a. through k., and post them to the T-accounts.
   TIP: In transaction e, when credit is used for operating costs, Accounts payable typically is used rather than accrued liabilities. The account Accrued Liabilities typically is used only for accrual adjustments made at the end of the period.
3. Prepare an unadjusted trial balance.
4. Record and post the adjusting journal entries l. through p.
   TIP: To determine the adjustment in l, consider the beginning account balance shown in the trial balance and the information in i. and l.
5. Prepare an adjusted trial balance.
6. Prepare an income statement, statement of retained earnings, and balance sheet.

7. Prepare and post the closing journal entries.
8. Prepare a post-closing trial balance.
9. How much net income did H & H Tool, Inc. generate during 2009? Is the company financed primarily by liabilities or stockholders' equity?

GROUP A PROBLEMS

LO3, LO5

Starbucks Corporation

PA4-1 Preparing a Trial Balance, Closing Journal Entry, and Post-Closing Trial Balance

Starbucks Corporation purchases and roasts high-quality whole bean coffees and sells them along with fresh-brewed coffees, its exclusive line of Frappucino® blended beverages, Italian-style espresso beverages, and premium teas, all in a variety of pompously named sizes. In addition to sales through its company-operated retail stores, Starbucks also sells coffee and tea products through other channels of distribution. The following is a simplified list of accounts and amounts reported in its accounting records. The accounts have normal debit or credit balances and the dollars are rounded to the nearest million. Assume the year ended on September 30, 2005.

Accounts payable	$ 221	Other current assets	$ 71
Accounts receivable	191	Other long-lived assets	461
Accrued liabilities	354	Other operating expenses	197
Accumulated depreciation	300	Prepaid expenses	94
Cash	307	Property, plant and equipment	2,142
Contributed capital	151	Retained earnings	1,445
Depreciation expense	340	Selling expenses	2,605
General and administrative		Service revenues	6,369
expenses	357	Short-term bank debt	476
Income tax expense	302	Store operating expenses	2,166
Interest revenue	92	Supplies	546
Long-term debt	196	Unearned revenue	175

Required:

1. Prepare an adjusted trial balance at September 30, 2005. Is the Retained earnings balance of $1,445 the amount that would be reported on the balance sheet as of September 30, 2005?
2. Prepare the closing entry required at September 30, 2005.
3. Prepare a post-closing trial balance at September 30, 2005.

LO1, LO2

PA4-2 Analyzing and Recording Adjusting Journal Entries

Brokeback Towing Company is at the end of its accounting year, December 31, 2008. The following data that must be considered were developed from the company's records and related documents:

a. On July 1, 2008, a three-year insurance premium on equipment in the amount of $600 was paid and debited in full to Prepaid insurance on that date. Coverage began on July 1.

b. At the end of 2008, the unadjusted balance in the Office supplies account was $1,000. A physical count of supplies on December 31, 2008, indicated supplies costing $300 were still on hand.

c. On December 31, 2008, YY's Garage completed repairs on one of Brokeback's trucks at a cost of $800. The amount is not yet recorded. It will be paid during January 2009.

d. In December the 2008 property tax bill for $1,600 was received from the city. The taxes, which have not been recorded, will be paid on February 15, 2009.

e. On December 31, 2008, the company completed a contract for an out-of-state company for $7,900 payable by the customer within 30 days. No cash has been collected and no journal entry has been made for this transaction.

f. On July 1, 2008, the company purchased a new hauling van. Depreciation for July–December 2008, estimated to total $2,750 has not been recorded.

g. As of December 31, the company owes interest of $500 on a bank loan taken out on October 1, 2008. The interest will be paid when the loan is repaid on September 30, 2009. No interest has been recorded yet.

h. The income before any of the adjustments or income taxes was $30,000. The company's federal income tax rate is 30 percent. Compute adjusted income based on all of the preceding information, and then determine and record income tax expense.

Required:

1. Determine the accounting equation effects of each required adjustment.
2. Give the adjusting journal entry required for each transaction at December 31, 2008.

PA4-3 Determining Financial Statement Effects of Adjusting Journal Entries

Refer to PA4-2.

LO2, LO4

eXcel

www.mhhe.com/phillips2e

Required:

Indicate the financial statement effects (amount and direction) of each adjusting journal entry. Use + for increase, − for decrease, and NE for no effect. Provide an appropriate account name for any revenue and expense effects.

Transaction	Assets	Liabilities	Stockholders' Equity
a			
b			
c			
etc.			

PA4-4 Analyzing a Student's Business and Preparing an Adjusted Income Statement

LO4

Upon graduation from high school, John Abel immediately accepted a job as an electrician's assistant for a large local electrical repair company. After three years of hard work, John received an electrician's license and decided to start his own business. He had saved $12,000, which he invested in the business. First, he transferred this amount from his savings account to a business bank account for Abel Electric Repair Company, Incorporated. His lawyer had advised him to start as a corporation. He then purchased a used panel truck for $9,000 cash and secondhand tools for $1,500; rented space in a small building; inserted an ad in the local paper; and opened the doors on October 1, 2008. Immediately, John was very busy; after one month, he employed an assistant.

Although John knew practically nothing about the financial side of the business, he realized that a number of reports were required and that costs and collections had to be controlled carefully. At the end of the year, prompted in part by concern about his income tax situation (previously he had to report only salary), John recognized the need for financial statements. His wife Jane developed some financial statements for the business. On December 31, 2008, with the help of a friend, she gathered the following data for the three months just ended. Bank account deposits of collections for electric repair services totaled $32,000. The following checks had been written: electrician's assistant, $8,500; payroll taxes, $175; supplies purchased and used on jobs, $9,500; oil, gas, and maintenance on truck, $1,200; insurance, $700; rent, $500; utilities and telephone, $825; and miscellaneous expenses (including advertising), $600. Also, uncollected bills to customers for electric repair services amounted to $3,000. The $200 rent for December had not been paid. John estimated that the depreciation on the truck and tools during the three months was $1,200. Income taxes for the three-month period were $3,480 and will be paid next month.

Required:

1. John knows that you're good with numbers, so he has asked you to prepare a quarterly income statement for Abel Electric Repair for the three months October through December 31, 2008. Do it.
2. Do you think that John may have a need for one or more additional financial reports for 2008 and thereafter? Explain.

LO1, LO2, LO3, LO4, LO5

www.mhhe.com/phillips2e

PA4-5 Comprehensive Review Problem: From Recording Transactions (Including Adjusting Journal Entries) to Preparing Financial Statements and Closing Journal Entries (Chapters 2, 3, and 4)

Drs. Glenn Feltham and Gary Entwistle began operations of their physical therapy clinic called Northland Physical Therapy on January 1, 2008. The annual reporting period ends December 31. The trial balance on January 1, 2009, was as follows (the amounts are rounded to thousands of dollars to simplify):

Account No.	Account Titles	Debit	Credit
01	Cash	$ 7	
02	Accounts receivable	3	
03	Supplies	3	
04	Equipment	6	
05	Accumulated depreciation (equipment)		$ 1
06	Other assets	6	
11	Accounts payable		5
12	Notes payable		
13	Wages payable		
14	Interest payable		
15	Income taxes payable		
16	Unearned revenue		
21	Contributed capital		15
31	Retained earnings		4
32	Dividends declared		
35	Service revenue		
40	Depreciation expense		
41	Income tax expense		
42	Interest expense		
43	Supplies and other operating expenses		
Totals		$25	$25

Transactions during 2009 (summarized in thousands of dollars) follow:

a. Borrowed $22 cash on July 1, 2009, signing a short-term note payable.
b. Purchased equipment for $25 cash on July 1, 2009.
c. Issued additional shares of stock for $5.
d. Earned revenues for 2009 of $55, including $8 on credit and $47 received in cash.
e. Recognized operating expenses for 2009 of $30, including $5 on credit and $25 in cash.
f. Purchased other assets, $3 cash.
g. Collected accounts receivable, $9.
h. Paid accounts payable, $10.
i. Purchased supplies on account for future use, $7.
j. Received a $3 deposit from a hospital for a contract to start January 5, 2010.
k. Declared and paid a cash dividend, $4.

Data for adjusting journal entries:

l. Supplies of $3 were counted on December 31, 2009.
m. Depreciation for 2009, $4.
n. Accrued interest on notes payable of $1.
o. Wages earned since the December 27 payroll not yet paid, $3.
p. Income tax for 2009 was $4, and will be paid in 2010.

Required:

1. Set up T-accounts for the accounts on the trial balance and enter beginning balances.
2. Record journal entries for transactions a. through k., and post them to the T-accounts.
3. Prepare an unadjusted trial balance.
4. Record and post the adjusting journal entries l. through p.
5. Prepare an adjusted trial balance.

6. Prepare an income statement, statement of retained earnings, and balance sheet.
7. Prepare and post the closing journal entries.
8. Prepare a post-closing trial balance.
9. How much net income did the physical therapy clinic generate during 2009? Is the business financed primarily by liabilities or stockholders' equity?

GROUP B PROBLEMS

PB4-1 Preparing a Trial Balance, Closing Journal Entry, and Post-Closing Trial Balance

LO3, LO5

Pacific Sunwear of California, Inc. operates three chains of retail stores under the names "Pacific Sunwear" (also known as "PacSun"), "Pacific Sunwear (PacSun) Outlet," and "d.e.m.o." The following is a simplified list of accounts and amounts (in thousands) reported in the company's accounts for the year ended January 28, 2006.

Accounts payable	$ 47,550	Interest expense	$ 5,673
Accounts receivable	12,679	Inventories	215,140
Accrued liabilities	33,649	Long-term liabilities	138,300
Accumulated depreciation	247,140	Net sales	1,391,473
Cash	95,185	Other current assets	81,357
Contributed capital	24,603	Other long-lived assets	332,893
Depreciation expense	74,617	Prepaid expenses	22,360
General and		Property, plant, and	
administrative expenses	309,218	equipment	295,087
Income tax expense	76,734	Retained earnings	508,314
Income tax payable	14,896	Selling expenses	884,982

Required:

1. Prepare an adjusted trial balance at January 28, 2006. Is the Retained earnings balance of $508,314 the amount that would be reported on the balance sheet as of January 28, 2006?
2. Prepare the closing entry required at January 28, 2006.
3. Prepare a post-closing trial balance at January 28, 2006.

PB4-2 Recording Adjusting Journal Entries

LO1, LO2

Fugly Company's annual accounting year ends on June 30. It is June 30, 2008, and all of the 2008 entries except the following adjusting journal entries have been made:

a. The company earned service revenue of $2,000 on a special job that was completed June 29, 2008. Collection will be made during July 2008; no entry has been recorded.

b. On March 31, 2008, Fugly paid a six-month premium for property insurance in the amount of $3,200 for coverage starting on that date. Cash was credited and Prepaid insurance was debited for this amount.

c. At June 30, 2008, wages of $900 were earned by employees but not yet paid. The employees will be paid on the next payroll date, which is July 15, 2008.

d. On June 1, 2008, Fugly collected two months' maintenance revenue of $450. At that date, Fugly debited Cash and credited Unearned maintenance revenue for $450.

e. Depreciation of $1,500 must be recognized on a service truck purchased on July 1, 2007.

f. Cash of $4,200 was collected on May 1, 2008, for services to be rendered evenly over the next year beginning on May 1. Unearned service revenue was credited when the cash was received.

g. The company owes interest of $600 on a bank loan taken out on February 1, 2008. The interest will be paid when the loan is repaid on January 31, 2009.

h. The income before any of the adjustments or income taxes was $31,675. The company's federal income tax rate is 30 percent. Compute adjusted income based on all of the preceding information, and then determine and record income tax expense.

Required:

1. Determine the accounting equation effects of each required adjustment.
2. Give the adjusting journal entry required for each transaction at June 30, 2008.

LO2, LO4   **PB4-3 Determining Financial Statement Effects of Adjusting Journal Entries**

Refer to PB4-2.

Required:

Indicate the financial statement effects (amount and direction) of each adjusting journal entry. Use + for increase, − for decrease, and NE for no effect. Provide an appropriate account name for any revenue and expense effects.

Transaction	Assets	Liabilities	Stockholders' Equity
a			
b			
c			
etc.			

LO4   **PB4-4 Analyzing a Student's Business and Preparing an Adjusted Income Statement**

Before she could start college in the spring, Kelly Gordon needed to make some money. She was a pro at using presentation software and had a good handle of other cutting-edge graphics software, so she thought the best way to make some money would be to develop some fun applications that her high-school teachers could use in their classes. Based on the advice from a friend of her family, she created a corporation called Gordon's Flash. On July 1, 2008, Kelly began her business by investing $1,000 of her own money in the company and by having her mother invest an additional $3,000 in it. She immediately used some of this money to buy some computer hardware and software, at a total cost of $3,000. She then rented space in a small building, sent a flyer to her former teachers, and got to work creating a Web site and some sample applications. In no time, several of her teachers contacted her and agreed to purchase her services.

After a couple of months of working like mad, Kelly's business teacher asked her how things were going. She told him that she had enough work to keep busy every single minute of her life, but her company's bank account didn't seem to be reflecting that. Her teacher suggested that she prepare an income statement to get a better idea of whether her business was profitable. With his help, she gathered the following data for the three months ended September 30, 2008. The company's bank account showed deposits totaling $3,000 that Kelly had collected for preparing computer-based presentations. The following checks had been written: assistant's pay, $1,800; payroll taxes, $60; computer supplies purchased and used on jobs, $200; insurance, $165; rent, $400; utilities, telephone, and cable modem, $325; and miscellaneous expenses (including advertising), $300. Also, uncollected bills to customers for software programming services amounted to $1,400. The $200 rent for September had not been paid. Kelly estimated that depreciation on the computer hardware and software during the three months was $450. Income taxes for the three-month period were $500.

Required:

1. Prepare a quarterly income statement for Gordon's Flash for the three months July through September 2008.
2. Do you think that Kelly may have a need for one or more additional financial reports for 2008 and thereafter? Explain.

LO1, LO2, LO3, LO4, LO5   **PB4-5 Comprehensive Review Problem: From Recording Transactions (Including Adjusting Journal Entries) to Preparing Financial Statements and Closing Journal Entries (Chapters 2, 3, and 4)**

Alison and Chuck Renny began operations of their furniture repair shop (Lazy Sofa Furniture, Inc.) on January 1, 2008. The annual reporting period ends December 31. The trial balance on January 1, 2009, was as follows (the amounts are rounded to thousands of dollars to simplify):

Account No.	Account Titles	Debit	Credit
01	Cash	$ 5	
02	Accounts receivable	4	
03	Supplies	2	
04	Small tools	6	
05	Equipment		
06	Accumulated depreciation (equipment)		
07	Other assets	9	
11	Accounts payable		$ 7
12	Notes payable		
13	Wages payable		
14	Interest payable		
15	Income tax payable		
16	Unearned revenue		
17	Dividends payable		
21	Contributed capital		15
31	Retained earnings		4
32	Dividends declared		
35	Service revenue		
40	Depreciation expense		
41	Income tax expense		
42	Interest expense		
43	Supplies and other operating expenses		
Totals		$26	$26

Transactions during 2009 (summarized in thousands of dollars) follow:

a. Borrowed $21 cash on July 1, 2009, signing a short-term note payable.
b. Purchased equipment for $18 cash on July 1, 2009.
c. Issued additional shares of stock for $5.
d. Earned revenues for 2009 in the amount of $65, including $9 on credit and $56 received in cash.
e. Recognized operating expenses for 2009, $35, including $7 on credit and $28 in cash.
f. Purchased additional small tools, $3 cash.
g. Collected accounts receivable, $8.
h. Paid accounts payable, $11.
i. Purchased on account supplies for future use, $10.
j. Received a $3 deposit on work to start January 15, 2010.
k. Declared and paid a cash dividend, $10.

Data for adjusting journal entries:

l. Supplies of $4 were counted on December 31, 2009.
m. Depreciation for 2009, $2.
n. Accrued interest on notes payable of $1.
o. Wages earned since the December 24 payroll not yet paid, $3.
p. Income tax for 2009 was $4, and will be paid in 2010.

Required:

1. Set up T-accounts for the accounts on the trial balance and enter beginning balances.
2. Record journal entries for transactions a. through k., and post them to the T-accounts.
3. Prepare an unadjusted trial balance.
4. Record and post the adjusting journal entries l. through p.
5. Prepare an adjusted trial balance.
6. Prepare an income statement, statement of retained earnings, and balance sheet.
7. Prepare and post the closing journal entries.

8. Prepare a post-closing trial balance.
9. How much net income did Lazy Sofa Furniture, Inc., generate during 2009? Is the company financed primarily by liabilities or stockholders' equity?

SKILLS DEVELOPMENT CASES

LO1, LO4

RESTAURANTS, INC.

S4-1 Finding Financial Information

Refer to the financial statements of Landry's Restaurants in Appendix A at the end of this book, or download the annual report from the *Cases* section of the text's Web site at www.mhhe.com/phillips2e.

Required:

1. The company's Prepaid expenses are included in the balance sheet line-item called Other current assets. Refer to the notes to the financial statements to determine the amount of Prepaid expenses as of December 31, 2005.
2. Refer to the notes to the financial statements to determine what is included in the balance sheet line-item called Accrued liabilities. For two of these specific liabilities, explain why Landry's would make an adjustment.
3. How much did Landry's owe for salaries, wages, and other payroll costs at its year-end? Was this an increase or decrease from the previous year?
4. In which line of the income statement does Landry's include the expense for renting restaurant buildings?

LO1, LO4

STEAKHOUSE®

S4-2 Comparing Financial Information

Refer to the financial statements of Outback Steakhouse, Inc. in Appendix B at the end of this book, or download them from the *Cases* section of the text's Web site at www.mhhe.com/phillips2e.

Required:

1. Does Outback report more or less for "Prepaid expenses" (see financial statement note 2) than Landry's?
2. Identify two accrued liabilities included in Outback's balance sheet (see financial statement note 6) and explain why the company would have made an accrual adjustment for these items.
3. How much did Outback owe for accrued payroll and other compensation (note 6). Are these accrued payroll liabilities more or less than Landry's accrued payroll liabilities? Provide one reason that would explain the difference between the two companies' accrued payroll liabilities.

LO1, LO4

S4-3 Internet-Based Team Research: Examining Deferrals and Accruals

As a team, select an industry to analyze. Using your Web browser, each team member should access the annual report or 10-K for one publicly traded company in the industry, with each member selecting a different company. (See S1-3 in Chapter 1 for a description of possible resources for these tasks.)

Required:

1. On an individual basis, each team member should write a short report listing the following:
    a. The company's total assets and total liabilities at the end of each year.
    b. The company's prepaid expenses and accrued liabilities at the end of each year.
    c. The percentage of prepaid expenses to total assets and the percentage of accrued liabilities to total liabilities.
    d. Describe and explain the types of accrued liabilities reported in the notes to the financial statements.
2. Discuss any patterns that you as a team observe. Then, as a team, write a short report comparing and contrasting your companies according to the preceding attributes. Provide potential explanations for any differences discovered.

S4-4 Ethical Decision Making: A Real-Life Example

LO1, LO2, LO4
Safety-Kleen Corp.

On December 12, 2002, the SEC filed a lawsuit against four executives of Safety-Kleen Corp., one of the country's leading providers of industrial waste collection and disposal services. The primary issue was that the executives had directed others in the company to record improper adjustments in 1999 and 2000, which had the effect of overstating net income during those periods. The following table was included in the SEC's court documents to demonstrate the (combined) effect of proper and improper adjustments on net income. (All amounts are in millions.)

	Year (Quarter)				
	1999(Q1)	1999(Q2)	1999(Q3)	1999(Q4)	2000(Q1)
Net income before adjustments	$ 90.9	$ 76.7	$ 47.9	$ 57.3	$ 47.0
Effect of adjustments	36.6	30.9	75.5	53.1	69.8
Net income after adjustments	$127.5	$107.6	$123.4	$110.4	$116.8

The following excerpts from the SEC's complaint describe two of the allegedly improper adjustments:

Improper Capitalization of Operating Expenses

26. As part of the fraudulent accounting scheme, [three top executives] improperly recorded several adjusting entries to capitalize certain operating expenses. These adjustments caused the company to materially overstate both its assets and its earnings. For example, at the end of the third quarter of fiscal 1999, they improperly capitalized approximately $4.6 million of payroll expenses relating to certain marketing and start-up activities.

Improper Treatment of Accruals

33. During the fourth quarter of fiscal 1999, Humphreys [the CFO] created additional fictitious income by directing [other accounting executives] to eliminate a $7.6 million accrual that had been established to provide for management bonuses that had been earned in fiscal 1999, but were to be paid the following quarter. Humphreys' action suggested that no bonuses were going to be paid for that year. In fact, the bonuses for 1999 were paid as scheduled.

Required:

1. Discuss whether large adjustments, such as those included by Safety-Kleen in 1999 and 2000, necessarily indicate improper accounting procedures.
2. What does the SEC's document mean in paragraph 26 when it says three top executives "improperly recorded several adjusting entries to *capitalize* certain operating expenses." Drawing on concepts presented in Chapters 2 and 3, explain why it is improper to record payroll expenses for marketing personnel as assets.
3. Assume the $7.6 million in bonuses referred to in paragraph 33 were recorded in the third quarter of 1999. What journal entry would have been used to record this accrual? Assume this accrual was eliminated in the fourth quarter of 1999. What adjusting journal entry would have been recorded to eliminate (remove) the previous accrual? What journal entry would have been used to record the $7.6 million in bonuses paid in the first quarter of 2000 (assuming the accrual had been removed in the fourth quarter of 1999)? What accounting concept is violated by recording an expense for management bonuses when they are paid rather than when they are earned by managers?

Epilogue:
In April 2005, a federal judge found the company's former CEO and CFO liable for $200 million for their role in the fraud.

S4-5 Ethical Decision Making: A Mini-Case

LO1, LO4
Blockbuster Inc.

Assume you work as an assistant accountant in the head office of a national movie rental business, a la Blockbuster Inc. With the increasing popularity of online movie rental operations, your company has struggled to meet its earnings targets for the year. It is important for the company to meet its earnings targets this year because the company is renegotiating a bank loan next month, and the terms of that loan are likely to depend on the company's reported financial success. Also, the company plans to issue more stock to the public in the upcoming year, to obtain funds for establishing its own presence in the online movie rental business. The chief financial officer (CFO) has approached you with a solution to the earnings dilemma. She proposes that the depreciation period for the stock of reusable DVDs be extended from 3 months to 15 months. She explains that by lengthening the depreciation period, a smaller amount of depreciation expense will be recorded in the current year, resulting in a higher net income. She claims that generally accepted accounting principles require estimates like this, so it wouldn't involve doing anything wrong.

Required:

Discuss the CFO's proposed solution. In your discussion, consider the following questions. Will the change in depreciation affect net income in the current year in the way that the CFO described? How will it affect net income in the following year? Is the CFO correct when she claims that the change in estimated depreciation is allowed by GAAP? Who relies on the video company's financial statements when making decisions? Why might their decisions be affected by the CFO's proposed solution? Is it possible that their decisions would not be affected? What should you do?

LO1, LO2, LO4

S4-6 Critical Thinking: Adjusting an Income Statement and Balance Sheet for Deferrals and Accruals

Pirate Pete Moving Corporation has been in operation since January 1, 2008. It is now December 31, 2008, the end of the annual accounting period. The company has not done well financially during the first year, although revenue has been fairly good. Three stockholders manage the company, but they have not given much attention to recordkeeping. In view of a serious cash shortage, they have applied to your bank for a $20,000 loan. As a loan officer, you requested a complete set of financial statements. The following 2008 annual financial statements were prepared by the company's office staff.

PIRATE PETE MOVING CORPORATION Income Statement For the Period Ended December 31, 2008	
Transportation revenue	$85,000
Expenses:	
Salaries expense	17,000
Supplies expense	12,000
Other expenses	18,000
Total expenses	47,000
Net income	$38,000

PIRATE PETE MOVING CORPORATION Balance Sheet At December 31, 2008	
Assets	
Cash	$ 2,000
Receivables	3,000
Supplies	6,000
Equipment	40,000
Prepaid insurance	4,000
Remaining assets	27,000
Total assets	$82,000
Liabilities	
Accounts payable	$ 9,000
Stockholders' Equity	
Contributed capital	35,000
Retained earnings	38,000
Total liabilities and stockholders' equity	$82,000

After briefly reviewing the statements and "looking into the situation," you requested that the statements be redone (with some expert help) to "incorporate depreciation, accruals, supply counts, income taxes, and so on." As a result of a review of the records and supporting documents, the following additional information was developed:

a. Supplies of $6,000 shown on the balance sheet has not been adjusted for supplies used during 2008. A count of the supplies on hand on December 31, 2008 showed $1,800.

b. The insurance premium paid in 2008 was for years 2008 and 2009. The total insurance premium was debited in full to Prepaid insurance when paid in 2008 and no adjustment has been made.

c. The equipment cost $40,000 when purchased January 1, 2008. It had an estimated annual depreciation of $8,000. No depreciation has been recorded for 2008.

d. Unpaid (and unrecorded) salaries at December 31, 2008, amounted to $2,200.

e. At December 31, 2008, transportation revenue collected in advance amounted to $7,000. This amount was credited in full to Transportation revenue when the cash was collected earlier during 2008.

f. Income taxes for the year are calculated as 25 percent of income before tax.

Required:

1. Prepare the adjusting journal entries required on December 31, 2008, based on the preceding additional information. You may need to create new accounts not yet included in the income statement or balance sheet.

2. Redo the preceding statements after taking into account the adjusting journal entries. One way to organize your response follows:

		Changes		
Items	Amounts Reported	Plus	Minus	Corrected Amounts
(List here each item from the two statements)				

3. The effects of recording the adjusting journal entries were to
   a. *Increase* or *decrease* (select one) Net income by $_____.
   b. *Increase* or *decrease* (select one) Total assets by $_____.

4. Write a letter to the company explaining the results of the adjustments and your preliminary analysis.

S4-7 Aggregating Accounts on an Adjusted Trial Balance to Prepare an Income Statement, Statement of Retained Earnings, and Balance Sheet

LO3, LO4

Escalade, Inc.

www.mhhe.com/phillips2e

Assume you recently were hired for a job in Evansville, Indiana, at the head office of Escalade, Inc.—the company that makes Goalrilla™ and Goaliath® basketball systems, and is the exclusive supplier of Ping Pong® and Stiga® equipment for table tennis. Your first assignment is to review the company's lengthy adjusted trial balance to determine the accounts that can be combined ("aggregated") into single line-items that will be reported on the financial statements. By querying the accounting system, you were able to obtain the following alphabetical list of accounts and their adjusted balances (in thousands) for the year ended December 31.

Accounts payable	$ 2,792	Inventory of finished goods	$10,263	Prepaid insurance	$ 108
Accounts receivable	34,141	Inventory of goods being made	4,536	Prepaid rent	434
Accrued interest payable	42	Inventory of supplies and materials	5,750	Rent expense	7,350
Accrued wages payable	5,856	Long-term bank loan	14,000	Retained earnings	27,571
Accrued warranties payable	1,324	Long-term contract payable	1,837	Salaries expense	3,582
Accumulated depreciation	26,198	Long-term note payable	2,700	Sales commissions expense	3,349
Cash	3,370	Manufacturing equipment	12,962	Sales of basketball systems	98,998
Contributed capital	7,165	Notes payable (current)	11,390	Sales of other products	28,710
Cost of goods sold	111,164	Notes receivable	400	Sales of ping pong tables	27,747
Depreciation expense	862	Office building	2,301	Shipping expenses	1,448
Factory buildings	7,070	Office equipment	2,363	Transport equipment	7,560
Income tax expense	5,804	Office supplies expense	69	Unearned revenue	8,144
Income tax payable	1,189	Other accrued liabilities	1,638	Utilities expense	2,111
Insurance expense	2,368	Other long-term assets	28,310	Wages expense	3,024
Interest expense	950	Packaging expenses	1,010	Warranties expense	1,226
Interest receivable	415			Warehouse buildings	3,001

Required:

With the above account names and balances, prepare an adjusted trial balance using a spreadsheet. Also prepare an income statement, statement of retained earnings, and balance sheet that import their numbers from the adjusted trial balance or from the other statements where appropriate. If similar accounts can be aggregated into a single line-item for each financial statement, use a formula to compute the aggregated amount. To be sure that you understand how to import numbers from other parts of a spreadsheet, you e-mail your friend Owen for advice. Here's his reply.

From:	Owentheaccountant@yahoo.com
To:	Helpme@hotmail.com
Cc:	
Subject:	Excel Help

Hey pal. You're bouncing from job to job like one of those ping-pong balls that your company sells. Okay, to import a number from another spreadsheet, you first click on the cell where you want the number to appear. For example, if you want to enter the Cash balance in the balance sheet, click on the cell in the balance sheet where the cash number is supposed to appear. Enter the equals sign (=) and then click on the tab that takes you to the worksheet containing the adjusted trial balance. In that worksheet, click on the cell that contains the amount you want to import into the balance sheet and then press enter. This will create a link from the adjusted trial balance cell to the balance sheet cell. At the end of this message, I've pasted a screen shot showing the formula I would enter on the balance sheet to import the total of three related inventory accounts from the adjusted trial balance. Don't forget to save the file using a name that indicates who you are.

Microsoft Excel - S4-7

File Edit View Insert Format Tools Data Window Help

C7   =SUM('Trial Balance'!C8:C10)

	A	B	C	D	E	F	G
1		Escalade, Inc.					
2		Balance Sheet					
3		As of December 31 (in thousands)					
4		ASSETS					
5		Cash	$ 3,370				
6		Receivables	34,956				
7		Inventories	20,549				
8		Prepaids	542				

Trial Balance / Income Statement / Statement of Retained Earnings \ Balance Sheet

Ready   NUM

5

Corporate Financial Reporting and Analysis

THAT WAS
THEN

In the previous chapters, you learned about the accounting system that produces the basic financial statements.

LP5

A friend asks you to advise him on whether his favorite basketball team is likely to win the championship this season. While it's tempting to just look at how many tall players they have, you know you'll have to drill down deeper than that. Some teams make more out of their talents than others.

You'll face the same issues when predicting the financial performance of your friend's favorite company. If you're evaluating Activision—a leading maker of videogames for Sony, Nintendo, and Microsoft—you might be tempted to just look at how many different games it produces, but you really should analyze its published financial statements. Start by looking at the sales levels and then drill down further, considering such things as the income generated from those sales and the investment in assets needed to generate those sales. In this chapter, we'll guide you through this with a simple framework for financial statement analysis. Game on.

THIS IS

NOW

This chapter describes the environment in which financial statements are used, and introduces common ratio analyses.

Now that you've seen the basic steps in accounting for business activities, it's time to take a step back and look at financial reporting as it exists in the real world. The first section of this chapter focuses on the financial reporting environment. Because many people rely on financial statements to make decisions, financial reporting has become a high-pressure environment, complete with fraud investigations and legal enforcement. The second section of this chapter focuses on the financial statements themselves, explaining how enhancements in their format and process of distribution make them more useful to financial statement users. The third section shows you how to analyze financial statements to understand how well a company is performing and, as always, the final section provides lots of opportunities for you to review and work with the material presented in this chapter.

ORGANIZATION OF THE CHAPTER

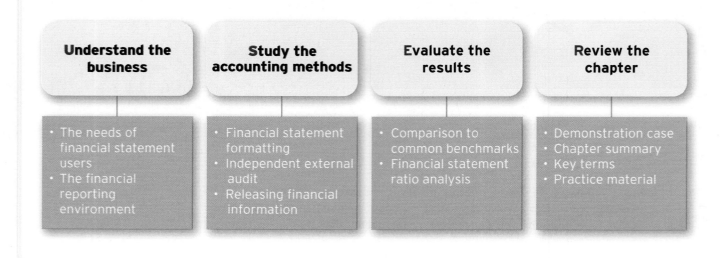

Understand the business	Study the accounting methods	Evaluate the results	Review the chapter
• The needs of financial statement users • The financial reporting environment	• Financial statement formatting • Independent external audit • Releasing financial information	• Comparison to common benchmarks • Financial statement ratio analysis	• Demonstration case • Chapter summary • Key terms • Practice material

Understand the Business

Learning Objective 1
Explain the needs of financial statement users.

THE NEEDS OF FINANCIAL STATEMENT USERS

Chapter 1 provided an overview of the many people who use financial statements to make decisions. A more detailed look at four main user groups is presented in Exhibit 5.1 and explained below.

Managers

Managers at all levels within a company use accounting information to run the business. To make good decisions at Activision, managers need to know detailed information such as sales by game (e.g., Tony Hawk) and game platform (PlayStation, X-box, Wii, PC), profits by genre (e.g., action, role-playing, etc.), and costs by game developer. When accounting information is used to manage the business, it is being used to fulfill a *management* function.

Directors

Directors is the short title used to describe members of the board of directors, who are elected by the company's stockholders to serve as their representatives. Directors oversee the managers of the company, with the primary goal of ensuring that management and financial decisions aim to benefit stockholders. Directors will use the financial statements to evaluate whether the Chief Executive Officer (CEO), Chief Financial Officer (CFO), and other top managers have made wise decisions about the amount to invest in assets and have managed to generate sufficient sales and net income from those assets. When accounting information is used to oversee the business, it is being used in a *governance* role.

Directors

↓ oversee

Officers and Top Managers

Creditors

Creditors use accounting information in several ways. Suppliers, for example, use it to decide whether to enter into contracts with another company, based in part on whether the company has sufficient assets to pay its liabilities. Bankers frequently use financial statement information to limit a company's activities by requiring the company to satisfy certain financial targets such as maintaining specific levels of assets or stockholders' equity. These **loan covenants** help to ensure the company will be able to repay loans owed to the bank when they come due. When accounting information is used to administer contracts, it is being used in a *contracting* role.

Investors

Investors (and their advisers) look to accounting information to help assess the financial strength of a business and, ultimately, to estimate its value. Part of this analysis involves forecasting the company's future revenues, expenses, and net income. Ultimately, the goal is to determine whether to buy, hold, or sell shares of the company's stock. When this text was written, investment advisers had mixed opinions about Activision's stock. Many recommended buying it, but some said to "hold," which meant investors should hit the pause button—the price was not attractive enough to recommend buying the company's stock nor bad enough to recommend selling. When accounting information is used to assess stock prices, it is being used in a *valuation* role.

As Exhibit 5.1 indicates, many different groups use accounting information to make decisions. These decisions can be wide-ranging, affecting employee bonuses, stock prices, and the interest paid on loans. All this attention to a company's financial results creates a high-pressure and potentially explosive environment, as discussed in the next section.

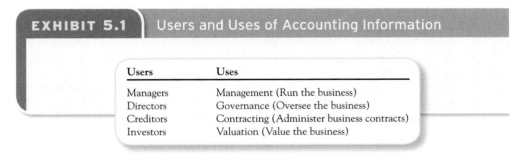

EXHIBIT 5.1	Users and Uses of Accounting Information

Users	Uses
Managers	Management (Run the business)
Directors	Governance (Oversee the business)
Creditors	Contracting (Administer business contracts)
Investors	Valuation (Value the business)

THE FINANCIAL REPORTING ENVIRONMENT

The accounting world was rocked in the early part of this decade with scandal and fraud, leading to significant changes in the financial reporting environment. In this section, we describe what appears to have fueled the fraud and how accounting regulators have responded with changes that are likely to affect your future career.

Accounting Fraud

Three things have to exist for accounting fraud to occur. First, there must be an incentive for someone to commit the fraud. Second, an opportunity must exist to commit the

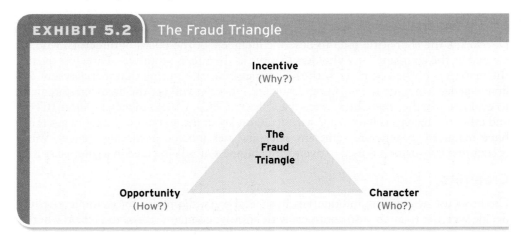

EXHIBIT 5.2 | The Fraud Triangle

fraud. Third, the person committing the fraud must possess personal characteristics that allow the fraud to be rationalized and concealed. Fraud investigators refer to these three elements as the *fraud triangle*, which is shown in Exhibit 5.2.

Incentive to Commit Fraud   Financial misreporting is both unethical and illegal, so there must be enormous incentives driving some accountants and business managers to commit fraud. As shown in Exhibit 5.3 below, incentives can be divided into two categories: (1) creating business opportunities and (2) satisfying personal greed.

1. Creating business opportunities. Management is under constant pressure to produce pleasing financial results for at least three business reasons:
   - *Satisfy loan covenants.* As you learned earlier in this chapter, lenders rely on financial statements to determine whether a company has violated its loan covenants by failing to meet specific financial targets. By overstating their company's financial condition, managers can avoid violating loan covenants which otherwise could require the company to pay a higher interest rate, repay its loan balance right away, or be forced to put up extra collateral to secure its loan.
   - *Increase equity financing.* The amount of money obtained from issuing stock depends, in part, on the price of the stock when it is issued. An issuance of 100,000 shares will yield double the money if the stock price is $20 per share rather than $10 per share. Managers can lead investors to pay more for the company's stock if they overstate the company's financial performance.
   - *Attract business partners.* By making the business appear more stable than it actually is, management can mislead suppliers and other companies into wanting to pursue a business relationship with the company.

EXHIBIT 5.3 | Possible Incentives for Committing Accounting Fraud

Creating Business Opportunities
- Satisfy loan covenants
- Increase equity financing
- Attract business partners

Satisfying Personal Greed
- Enhance job security
- Increase personal wealth
- Obtain bigger paycheck

2. Satisfying personal greed. By producing pleasing financial results, members of top management can benefit personally in three ways:
- *Enhance job security.* The financial statements are a report card on both the company and the company's management. If top management reports strong financial results, they'll likely get to keep their high-paying jobs.
- *Increase personal wealth.* Members of top management often own shares of their company's stock, so their personal shareholdings will be worth more (and their personal wealth will increase) if their company reports financial results that increase its stock price.
- *Obtain a bigger paycheck.* Managers often receive cash bonuses based on the strength of their company's reported financial performance. Better reported results can mean larger bonuses. One of Activision's competitors (Take-Two Interactive) paid a $3 million bonus to its (former) CEO in 2003. At about the same time, the SEC charged the company with overstating its profits.

Opportunity to Commit Fraud   As you saw in Chapters 2–4, financial statements are produced by an accounting system that involves analyzing, recording, and summarizing the results of business activities. Weaknesses in this system create an opportunity for fraudulent information to be entered into it, which increases the risk that the financial statements will be fraudulently misreported. To reduce this risk, certain procedures and policies can be put in place to help ensure that information entered into the accounting system and reported in the financial statements is accurate and complete. These internal controls, as they are called, can't completely eliminate the opportunity for fraud, but they can limit it if they operate effectively. You will learn more about specific internal controls in Chapter 6.

Character to Rationalize and Conceal Fraud   For people to commit fraud and keep it secret, they have to feel "okay" with their actions. Most fraudsters achieve this through a sense of personal entitlement, which outweighs other moral principles, such as fairness, honesty, and concern for others. Many are said to be egotistical and possess an ability to lie or pressure others to look the other way.[1] It's not easy to counteract these undesirable traits, but recent changes in the financial reporting environment begin to do so, as we discuss in the next section.

The Sarbanes-Oxley Act of 2002

The **Sarbanes-Oxley (SOX) Act of 2002** is the most significant change to the financial reporting environment in the United States since the Securities Acts were introduced in the 1930s. All companies that trade on U.S. stock exchanges must comply with the new requirements of SOX. The impact of SOX has been felt by nearly everyone in the business world. Whether you're an accounting major or not, you will likely be affected by SOX.

SOX was created in response to the many financial frauds and scandals occurring in the late 1990s and early 2000s. Confidence in the stock markets had been shaken by frauds involving Enron (now bankrupt) and WorldCom (now called Verizon), so the U.S. Congress passed the act in an attempt to improve the financial reporting environment and restore investor confidence. SOX introduced many new requirements. Some of the key changes are explained below and summarized in Exhibit 5.4.

Counteract Incentives for Committing Fraud.   Those who willfully misrepresent financial results face significantly stiffer penalties, including fines of up to $5 million. Also, maximum jail sentences have been increased to 20 years, which can really add up

> **YOU SHOULD KNOW**
> The Sarbanes-Oxley (SOX) Act is a set of regulations passed by Congress in 2002 in an attempt to improve financial reporting and restore investor confidence.

---

[1]David T. Wolfe and Dana R. Hermanson, "The Fraud Diamond: Considering the Four Elements of Fraud," December 2004, *The CPA Journal*, pp. 38–41.

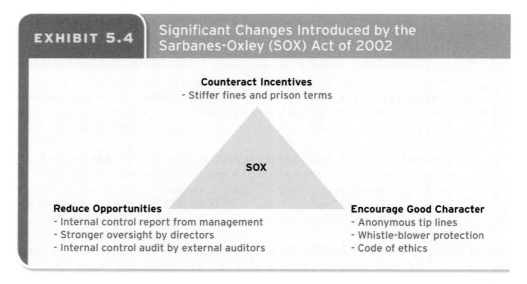

EXHIBIT 5.4   Significant Changes Introduced by the Sarbanes-Oxley (SOX) Act of 2002

Counteract Incentives
- Stiffer fines and prison terms

SOX

Reduce Opportunities
- Internal control report from management
- Stronger oversight by directors
- Internal control audit by external auditors

Encourage Good Character
- Anonymous tip lines
- Whistle-blower protection
- Code of ethics

because federal sentencing guidelines allow judges to declare consecutive jail terms for each violation.

Reduce Opportunities for Fraud.   Of the three parts of the fraud triangle, this is the area that business owners, managers, and accountants can do the most about. Not surprisingly, then, it's also the area affected most by SOX. The main thrust of SOX, as it applies to this area, is to improve internal control over companies' financial reporting. SOX aims to achieve this in three ways:

1. Managers must review how well their company's internal controls worked during the year and issue a report that indicates whether the controls over financial reporting operated effectively. This new requirement means that most marketing managers, for example, now have some accounting responsibilities such as determining whether their staff submit accurate sales and expense reports.

2. The company's board of directors is required to establish an audit committee made up of independent directors to oversee financial matters of the company. One of the primary functions of this committee is to hire external auditors and ensure they are able to effectively perform the work described below in 3.

3. The company's external auditors are now required to test the effectiveness of the company's internal controls and issue a report that indicates whether they agree with the conclusions of the internal control report issued by management (described in 1). As was the case before SOX, the external auditors also must examine the company's financial statements and report whether they were prepared using GAAP.

Encourage Good Character in Employees.   Admittedly, it's difficult for any law to achieve this, but some provisions of SOX should help employees of good character confront those of poor character. For example, audit committees are now required to create tip lines that allow employees to secretly submit concerns about questionable accounting or auditing practices being committed by others. Further, SOX grants legal protection to these whistle-blowers so they aren't retaliated against by those charged with fraud. If you tattle on your boss for submitting a fraudulent expense claim, you can't be fired for it. Finally, to reinforce the importance of good character, companies are required to adopt a code of ethics for their senior financial officers. Google begins its code with "Don't be evil" and then explains what this means in plain English (see investor.google.com/conduct).

HOW'S IT GOING? A Self-Study Quiz

Identify whether each of the following increases (+) or decreases (−) the risk of fraud, arising from incentives (I), opportunities (O), or individuals' character (C).

	+/−	I/O/C
1. Enron implemented a "rank and yank" practice that involved ranking the financial performance of each business unit and then firing managers in the lowest 20%.		
2. Microsoft Corporation invites anonymous or confidential submission of questionable accounting or auditing matters to msft.buscond@alertline.com.		
3. The H. J. Heinz Company board of directors is one of the strongest boards in America, according to Institutional Shareholder Services.		

Ethical Insights

You Can't Count That!

Most of the big accounting frauds involve uncertain judgments or complex accounting decisions that later are found to be inappropriate. However, some frauds have involved blatantly unethical acts. In one famous case, managers at Bausch & Lomb shipped as much as two years' worth of contact lenses to opticians who hadn't even ordered them. These shipments were counted as sales revenue, which led to overstated financial results and unwarranted bonuses. An investigation later found that an environment of extreme pressure created incentives, weak internal controls provided opportunities, and unscrupulous managers possessed the character to commit the fraud.

Study the Accounting Methods

In the previous section, we discussed some of the legal steps taken to combat financial fraud and improve the quality of publicly reported financial statements. In this section, we describe three significant aspects of the accounting process that improve the quality of financial statements and make them more informative for users. These aspects include: (1) enhancing the format of financial statements, (2) obtaining an independent external audit, and (3) releasing additional financial information. Exhibit 5.5 presents a timeline showing the order in which these events typically occur, using Activision as an example.

FINANCIAL STATEMENT FORMATTING

The financial statements shown in previous chapters provided a good introduction to their basic structure and content. However, in comparison to what you'll see in the corporate world, they were somewhat simplified. In this section, we show three alternative formats that are intended to provide additional information for financial statement users.

Learning Objective 3
Prepare a comparative balance sheet, multistep income statement, and statement of stockholders' equity.

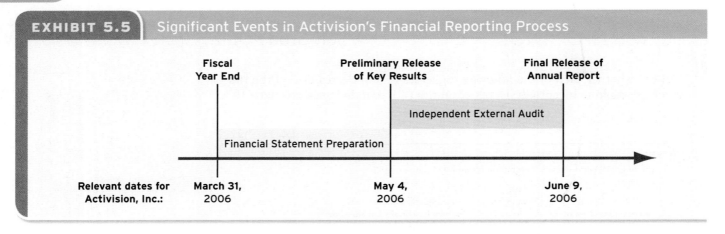

EXHIBIT 5.5 | Significant Events in Activision's Financial Reporting Process

Comparative Financial Statements

To make it easy for financial statement users to compare account balances from one period to the next, most companies report **comparative financial statements.** Comparative financial statements contain two or more columns of numbers, with each column representing the financial results for different time periods. For example, Activision's comparative balance sheets in Exhibit 5.6 show one column with account

EXHIBIT 5.6 | Sample Comparative Balance Sheet   **ACTIVISION.**

ACTIVISION, INC.
Balance Sheet
(in thousands of U.S. dollars)

	March 31, 2006	March 31, 2005
Assets		
Current assets:		
Cash and short-term investments	$ 944,960	$ 840,864
Accounts receivable	28,782	109,144
Inventories	61,483	48,018
Other current assets	80,830	124,438
Total current assets	1,116,055	1,122,464
Software development and intellectual property licenses	102,432	32,672
Property and equipment, net	45,368	30,490
Goodwill	100,446	91,661
Other noncurrent assets	55,222	29,676
Total assets	$1,419,523	$1,306,963
Liabilities and Stockholders' Equity		
Current liabilities		
Accounts payable	$ 88,994	$ 108,984
Accrued liabilities	103,169	98,067
Total current liabilities	192,163	207,051
Other noncurrent liabilities	1,776	—
Total liabilities	193,939	207,051
Stockholders' equity		
Contributed capital	837,071	753,298
Retained earnings	388,513	346,614
Total stockholders' equity	1,225,584	1,099,912
Total liabilities and stockholders' equity	$1,419,523	$1,306,963

EXHIBIT 5.7 | Sample Multistep Income Statement

ACTIVISION.

ACTIVISION, INC.
Income Statement
(in thousands of U.S. dollars)

| | Year ended March 31, | | |
	2006	2005	2004
Total sales revenues	$1,468,000	$1,405,857	$947,656
Expenses			
Cost of sales	940,362	844,946	567,147
Product development	131,782	86,543	97,859
Sales and marketing	283,220	230,058	128,221
General and administrative	94,679	59,739	44,612
Total operating expenses	1,450,043	1,221,286	837,839
Income from operations	17,957	184,571	109,817
Revenue from investments	30,630	13,092	6,175
Income before income tax expense	48,587	197,663	115,992
Income tax expense	6,688	59,328	38,277
Net income	$ 41,899	$ 138,335	$ 77,715

} Core results

} Peripheral results

balances at the end of the most recent year (March 31, 2006) and another column with balances at the end of the previous year (March 31, 2005). This allows you to quickly see that Accounts receivable dropped dramatically (from $109 million to $28.8 million). Note that the balance sheet is still classified, as introduced in Chapter 2. The only difference in a comparative balance sheet is that it uses separate columns to report different points in time.

Income statements also can be presented in a comparative format, often reporting three periods of results as shown in Exhibit 5.7. By including three columns, managers and accountants help reveal trends that persist over longer periods of time. For example, Exhibit 5.7 indicates that Activision has grown its revenues each year since 2004.

Multistep Income Statements   If you look carefully at Exhibit 5.7, you'll notice the income statement format differs in another way from that used in earlier chapters. Earlier chapters used a format that contained a single grouping of revenues and a single grouping of expenses in what is typically called a **single-step income statement** format. Exhibit 5.7 presents an alternative format called the **multistep income statement**. Both formats end up with the same net income at the bottom. However, they differ in how they get there. The purpose of a multistep income statement is to display important measures of profit in addition to net income. It does this, as shown in Exhibit 5.7, by including new subtotals:

1. Income from operations—As an investor or creditor interested in Activision's long-term success, you probably care most about the company's ability to generate income from its core business activities like developing, making, and selling video games. Peripheral activities, like earning revenue from investments, aren't as important in the long-run because they're not the key reason Activision is in business (and they're not as likely to recur in the future). To make it easy for you to distinguish core and peripheral results, the top portion of the income

Topic Tackler

PLUS

Check out www.mhhe.com/phillips2e for audio, visual, and PowerPoint presentations on this topic.

> **YOU SHOULD KNOW**
>
> A **single-step income statement** reports net income by subtracting a single group of expenses from a single group of revenues. A **multistep income statement** reports alternative measures of income by calculating subtotals for core and peripheral business activities.

statement reports revenues and expenses relating only to core activities and presents a subtotal called Income from operations, as shown in Exhibit 5.7. This is a useful measure, because in Activision's case, it reveals that income from operations fell in the most recent year, indicating some difficulties in the company's core business. Revenue from investments did contribute to net income so it is included in the income statement, but since it's not a core business activity for Activision it is shown after income from operations. Other companies, particularly financial institutions like Capital One and Bank of America, would consider revenue from investments a core business activity. But Activision is in business to generate profit from videogame sales, not from interest on investments.

2. Income before income tax expense—This other new subtotal in Exhibit 5.7 indicates how much profit the company would have reported had there been no income taxes. This subtotal is useful because not all companies pay the same rate of tax. So, if you're trying to decide whether to invest in Pfizer or Google, which had effective tax rates in 2006 ranging from 15 to 39 percent, you might be interested in comparing their pretax levels of income. Of course, you will also care about net income, which is obtained by subtracting income tax expense from income before income tax expense. Net income is the same whether a single-step or multistep income statement is presented.

Topic Tackler

PLUS

Check out www.mhhe.com/phillips2e for audio, visual, and PowerPoint presentations on this topic.

Statement of Stockholders' Equity   Previous chapters indicated that companies report a statement of retained earnings to show how net income increased and dividends decreased the retained earnings balance during the period. While this information is useful, it doesn't tell the full story because Retained Earnings is only one of the stockholders' equity accounts. Contributed Capital is another important stockholders' equity account whose balance increases and decreases during the accounting period. To show all the changes, many companies report a more comprehensive version of the statement of retained earnings called the statement of stockholders' equity. The statement of stockholders' equity has a column for each stockholders' equity account and shows the factors that increased and decreased these account balances during the period. Exhibit 5.8 shows a modified version of Activision's statement. Notice how the beginning and ending balances for each account correspond to the balance sheet (in Exhibit 5.6).

EXHIBIT 5.8	Sample Statement of Stockholders' Equity	**ACTIVISION.**

ACTIVISION, INC.
Statement of Stockholders' Equity
For the Year Ended March 31, 2006
(in thousands of U.S. dollars)

	Contributed Capital	Retained Earnings
Balances at March 31, 2005	$753,298	$346,614
Net income		41,899
Dividends declared		-0-
Issuance of shares of stock	90,055	
Buyback of shares of stock	(6,282)	
Balances at March 31, 2006	$837,071	$388,513

HOW'S IT GOING?   A Self-Study Quiz

Best Buy's comparative balance sheets report $3,315 of retained earnings on February 26, 2005, and $4,304 on February 25, 2006. Assume the only other stockholders' equity account was Contributed capital, which had a February 26, 2005, balance of $1,134. The multistep income statement shows income before income taxes of $1,721 and income tax expense of $581. Assume that during the year ended February 25, 2006, $591 was contributed to the company for new shares of stock, dividends of $151 were declared, and $772 of stock was bought back by the company. Complete the statement of stockholders' equity shown below by solving for missing amounts.

	Contributed Capital	Retained Earnings
Beginning balances at February 26, 2005	$1,134	$3,315
Net Income		
Dividends declared		(151)
Issuance of shares of stock	591	
Buyback of shares of stock	(772)	
Ending balances at February 25, 2006		$4,304

INDEPENDENT EXTERNAL AUDIT

To ensure that the financial statements, shown in the previous section, are prepared properly, the SEC requires all publicly traded companies to have their internal controls and financial statements audited by external auditors. Many privately owned companies have their financial statements audited, too, often at the request of lenders or private investors. External audits are conducted by Certified Public Accountants (CPAs) who are independent of the company. These trained professionals examine the company's financial statements (and its accounting system) with the goal of detecting **material** misstatements. It is not practical for auditors to check every single business transaction to ensure it was accurately reported, so they can't be 100 percent sure they have caught *every* error. Instead, their audits provide *reasonable* assurance to financial statement users. After completing the audit, external auditors will attach a report to the financial statements that gives a pass/fail type of opinion. An **unqualified audit opinion** represents a passing grade. For an example of an unqualified audit report, see the one on page A19 for Landry's Restaurants. If the financial statements fail to follow GAAP or if the auditors were not able to complete the tests needed to determine whether GAAP was followed, the audit opinion will be **qualified** (like a bad movie review).

RELEASING FINANCIAL INFORMATION

Preliminary Releases

To provide timely information for all external users, public companies announce annual (and quarterly) results through a press release sent to news agencies. This press release is issued three to five weeks after the accounting period ends. The press release typically includes key figures, management's discussion of the results, and attachments containing a condensed income statement and balance sheet. Exhibit 5.9 shows an excerpt from a typical press release for Activision. Notice that five weeks elapsed between the end of the company's year (March 31) and the date of the press release (May 4). During this time, Activision's accountants were busy determining adjusting journal entries and preparing the financial statements, and its managers were preparing an analysis and discussion of the results.

Learning Objective 4
Describe other significant aspects of the financial reporting process, including external audits and the distribution of financial information.

YOU SHOULD KNOW

Misstatements are **material** if they are large enough to influence the decisions of financial statement users.
An **unqualified audit opinion** indicates that the financial statements are presented in accordance with GAAP. A **qualified audit opinion** indicates that either the financial statements do not follow GAAP or the auditors were not able to complete the tests needed to determine whether the financial statements follow GAAP.

EXHIBIT 5.9	Preliminary Release of Key Results

ACTIVISION REPORTS FISCAL 2006 YEAR END RESULTS

SANTA MONICA, CA—May 4, 2006—Activision, Inc. (Nasdaq: ATVI) today announced record net revenues for the fiscal year ended March 31, 2006.

Net revenues for the fiscal year ended March 31, 2006 were $1,468 million, as compared to $1,406 million for the fiscal year ended March 31, 2005. Net income for the fiscal year was $41.9 million, or $0.14 per diluted share, as compared to net income of $138.3 million, or $0.50 per diluted share reported for the last fiscal year.

Robert Kotick, Chairman and CEO of Activision, Inc. commented, "Activision's fiscal year 2006 net revenues totaled $1,468 million, marking 14 consecutive years of revenue growth. We delivered better than expected results for the fourth quarter. Out balance sheet remains one of the strongest in the industry with nearly $1 billion in cash and short-term investments and $1.2 billion in shareholder's equity."

Many companies, including Activision, follow-up the press release with a conference call broadcast on the Internet that allows analysts to grill the company's senior executives with questions about the financial results. By listening to these calls, you can learn a lot about a company's business strategy, its expectations for the future, and the key factors that analysts consider when they evaluate a company. You can check out this useful source of information by visiting each company's own Web site or the archive of conference calls at biz.yahoo.com/cc.

Financial Statement Release

Several weeks after the preliminary press release, public companies release their complete financial statements as part of an annual (or quarterly) report. The annual report is organized into two main sections. The first half of the report usually begins with a friendly letter to investors from the company's CEO. This is followed by glossy pictures of the company's products and glowing commentaries about the company's brilliant positioning to take over its industry. Having developed the right mood with these jazzy marketing tactics in the first half of the report, the annual report then presents the meat and potatoes: the financial section. The typical elements of the financial section are listed and explained in Exhibit 5.10, along with the pages in Appendix A (at the end of this book) where you should look to see an example of each.

A company's quarterly report is like a supercondensed version of its annual report. Following a short letter to stockholders and abbreviated discussion of the financial results, a quarterly report presents a condensed income statement for the quarter, a condensed balance sheet dated at the end of the quarter, and a condensed statement of cash flows. These condensed financial statements typically show less detail than the annual statements, often omitting the statement of retained earnings and many notes to the financial statements that repeat those in the company's annual report. Also, items 4, 7, 8, and 9 in Exhibit 5.10 are typically omitted. Quarterly financial statements are not audited, so they are labeled as unaudited. Obviously, with all these limitations, the quarterly reports aren't quite as informative as the annual reports, but they have the benefit of being released on a timelier basis (every three months rather than every year).

Securities and Exchange Commission (SEC) Filings   To ensure sufficient, relevant information is available to investors, the SEC requires public companies to electronically file certain reports with the SEC, including an annual report on Form 10-K, quarterly reports on Form 10-Q, and current event reports on Form 8-K. (We wouldn't

---

🏈 COACH'S TIP

Companies require several weeks after the preliminary press release to gather information reported in the financial statement notes or in other parts of the annual report. External auditors also complete their work during this time.

EXHIBIT 5.10 | Typical Elements of an Annual Report's Financial Section

Name of Financial Section	Information Presented	Example in Appendix A
1. Summarized financial data	• key figures covering a period of 5 or 10 years.	p. A11
2. Management's discussion and analysis (MD&A)	• an honest and detailed analysis of the company's financial condition and operating results; a must-read for any serious financial statement user.	p. A12
3. Management's report on internal control	• statements that describe management's responsibility for ensuring adequate internal control over financial reporting and that report on the effectiveness of these controls during the year.	p. A17
4. Auditor's report	• the auditor's conclusion about whether GAAP was followed (and, for public companies, whether internal controls were effective).	p. A18
5. Comparative financial statements	• a multi-year presentation of the four basic statements.	p. A20
6. Financial statement notes	• further information about the financial statements; crucial to understanding the financial statement data.	p. A24
7. Recent stock price data	• brief summary of highs and lows during the year.	p. A30
8. Unaudited quarterly data	• condensed summary of each quarter's results.	p. A41
9. Directors and officers	• a list of who's overseeing and running the company.	

burden you with the details of the form numbers except that most people refer to them by number.) Several of these reports require release of additional information beyond that reported in quarterly or annual reports. This additional information can help you learn lots about a company. For example, Activision's 2006 10-K describes 30 significant business risks that the company faces and outlines the business strategies for addressing those risks. The 8-K reports significant business events that occur between financial statement dates, such as the acquisition of another company, a change in year-end, or a change in auditor.

These filings are available to the public as soon as they are received by the SEC's Electronic Data Gathering and Retrieval Service (EDGAR). As a result, most users can get all the details about a company's financial results in the SEC filings several weeks before the company's glossy reports reach them in the mail or are posted on the company's Web site. To find a company's SEC filings, click on "Search for Company Filings" at www.sec.gov or go to edgarscan.pwcglobal.com.

Investor Information Web Sites   In addition to the above Web sites, Hoovers.com, TheStreet.com, Fool.com, and Yahoo!Finance are four of the thousands of investor information Web sites that contain information about public companies. Some sections of investor information Web sites provide useful information for evaluating and predicting a company's financial performance, whereas others do not. For example, at Yahoo!Finance, you can obtain valuable financial information about Activision and its industry sector, including financial ratios similar to those you'll read about later in this chapter. However, at messages.yahoo.com, you also can chat it up with someone using the alias crazydaytrada.

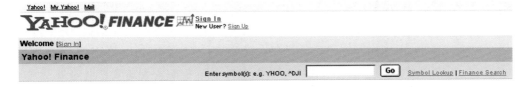

The obvious problem with many of these sites is that it's difficult to sort out what's good versus bad information. For example, in the case of financial ratios, you're rarely told whether the underlying information is audited or unaudited. As a consequence, it's tough to know whether the analyses are as reliable as they might seem. Also, many Web sites do not show the formulas used to calculate ratios. That can be a big deal because ratios with similar sounding names might be calculated differently. In many cases, you'd be better off conducting your own analyses, using the tools we present in the next section.

Evaluate the Results

COMPARISON TO COMMON BENCHMARKS

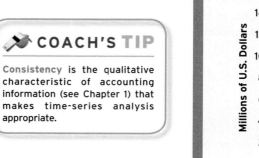

Learning Objective 5
Compare results to common benchmarks.

Now that you've seen how financial statements are typically reported in the corporate world and where to obtain them, you are ready to learn how to evaluate them. If you're like most people, you probably find it hard to know whether Activision's $42 million in net income is a decent level of performance. To interpret financial statement amounts, it's useful to have points of comparison, or benchmarks. Two commonly used benchmarks are

YOU SHOULD KNOW

A **time-series analysis** compares a company's results for one period to its own results over a series of time periods.
A **cross-sectional analysis** compares the results of one company with those of others in the same section of the industry.

1. Prior periods. By comparing Activision's current period results to its own results in prior periods, we can gain a sense of how the company's performance is changing over time. The trend is your friend. In Wall Street language, this comparison of the same company over a series of prior time periods is called **time-series analysis.**

2. Competitors. Although an analysis focused on one company is useful, it doesn't show what's happening in the industry. It's possible that Activision is improving (good), but still hasn't caught up to others in the same industry (not so good). Or it could be that Activision's performance is declining (bad), but it has avoided the severe financial problems others experienced (not so bad). To get this industrywide perspective, most analysts will compare competitors within a particular industry. The name for comparing across companies that compete in the same section of an industry is **cross-sectional analysis.**

In Exhibit 5.11, we present a time-series chart that compares Activision to itself on several key totals from the balance sheet and income statement. From the chart, we can see that Activision's financial profile changed between 2005 and 2006. In comparison to Activision's 2005 year-end balance, less debt was outstanding at the end of 2006. This reduction in liabilities was accompanied by an increase in stockholders' equity, suggesting

COACH'S TIP

Consistency is the qualitative characteristic of accounting information (see Chapter 1) that makes time-series analysis appropriate.

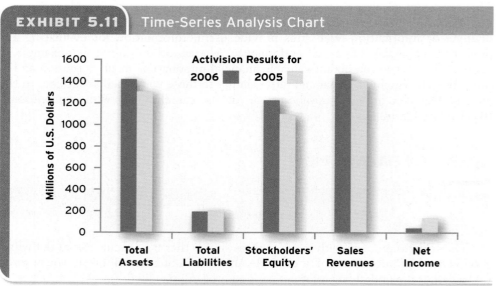

EXHIBIT 5.11   Time-Series Analysis Chart

that Activision's financing strategy shifted away from debt and toward equity. We also see from Exhibit 5.11 that Activision grew modestly, with total assets and sales revenues reaching higher in 2006 than in 2005. Curiously, though, net income in 2006 was down from 2005. That's something analysts would want to learn more about.

In Exhibit 5.12, we present a cross-sectional chart that compares Activision to two of its main competitors—THQ Inc. (THQI) and Electronic Arts (ERTS)—based on financial statement data for the fiscal year ended March 31, 2006.

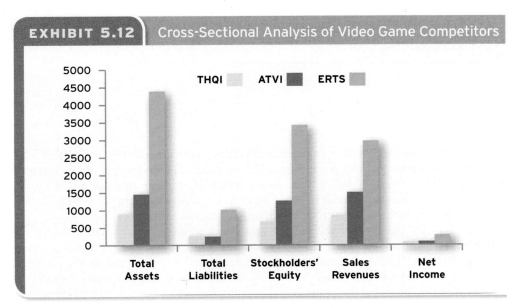

EXHIBIT 5.12 Cross-Sectional Analysis of Video Game Competitors

COACH'S TIP

Comparability is the qualitative characteristic of accounting information that makes cross-sectional analysis appropriate.

The bar chart in Exhibit 5.12 shows that Activision is in the middle between THQ and Electronic Arts across most of the financial measures. It's hard to overlook the towering bars of Electronic Arts, which suggest that this company dominates play in the industry. In fact, Electronic Arts is bigger than both Activision and THQ combined in every category. Given these mammoth differences in size, do analysts simply conclude that Electronic Arts is the winner and give them a pocketful of investment tokens? In a word, no. All that this means is that Electronic Arts is a bigger company. It says nothing about whether it's best at using the resources provided to it. This kind of conclusion usually requires some fraction action, which business professionals refer to more formally as *financial statement ratio analysis*.

COACH'S TIP

Average measures for each industry also can be used in cross-sectional analysis. Obtain these measures from the *Annual Statement Studies* published by the Risk Management Association.

FINANCIAL STATEMENT RATIO ANALYSIS

The goal of ratio analysis is to get to the heart of how well a company performed given the resources it had available. By using ratios, you can control for differences in company size and uncover results that aren't easily detected by looking at total dollar amounts. For example, as you will see below, ratios allow you to discover that although Activision generated $42 million of net income and THQ generated only $34 million, Activision didn't control its expenses as well as THQ.

Learning Objective 6
Calculate and interpret the debt-to-assets, asset turnover, and net profit margin ratios.

A Basic Business Model

Before evaluating Activision's financial performance, it is useful to first consider what's involved in running a business. Most businesses can be broken down into four elements:

1. Obtain financing from lenders and investors, which is used to invest in assets.
2. Invest in assets, which are used to generate revenues.
3. Generate revenues, which lead to producing net income.
4. Produce net income, which is needed to comfort lenders, satisfy investors, and provide resources for future expansion.

EXHIBIT 5.13 | A Basic Business Model

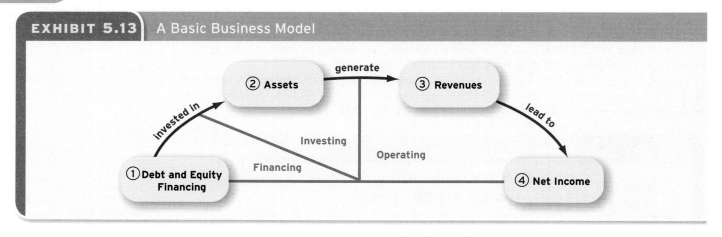

From this description, a business model can be created, as shown in Exhibit 5.13. This business model includes the key financial measures analyzed earlier, including total liabilities (debt), stockholders' equity, assets, revenues, and net income. What's really useful about this business model is that it links one business element to another, so you aren't limited to looking at just total dollar amounts, as we did before.

The business model in Exhibit 5.13 provides a framework for understanding the ratios that we introduce in the next section. Ratios provide measures of key business results, often examining relationships between one element of the business and the next. This is a useful way to think about ratios because it's the same way businesses operate—as a series of interconnected decisions. The last thing we want is for you to view ratios just as a list of individual formulas to memorize without understanding what they mean. Rather, we want you to think of ratios as ways to measure key relationships within a business. It's like using your speedometer to gauge how fast you're going in the car, and then using miles per gallon to understand how it's affecting your fuel efficiency.

Financial Statement Ratios

The business model in Exhibit 5.13 contains three links: (1) debt and equity financing is invested in assets, (2) assets are used to generate revenues, and (3) revenues lead to net income. Using these links, three key financial ratios can be created, as shown below.

FINANCIAL ANALYSIS TOOLS		
Name of Measure	**Formula**	**What It Tells You**
1. Debt-to-assets ratio	$\dfrac{\text{Total Liabilities}}{\text{Total Assets}}$	• The percentage of assets financed by debt • A higher ratio means greater financing risk
2. Asset turnover ratio	$\dfrac{\text{Total Sales Revenue}}{\text{Average Total Assets}}$	• How well assets are used to generate revenues • A higher ratio means greater efficiency
3. Net profit margin ratio	$\dfrac{\text{Net Income}}{\text{Total Sales Revenue}}$	• How well expenses are controlled • A higher ratio means better performance

These three ratios are calculated in the top panel of Exhibit 5.14, using relevant amounts from the three video game companies' financial statements (in the bottom panel). Note that, to calculate average total assets in the bottom of the asset turnover ratio, you need amounts from two balance sheets. An average is needed in the asset

EXHIBIT 5.14 Analysis of Video Game Companies

		THQ Inc.		Activision Inc.		Electronic Arts Inc.	
Debt-to-Assets Ratio	Total Liabilities / Total Assets	$\dfrac{\$220}{\$851}$ = 0.259		$\dfrac{\$194}{\$1,420}$ = 0.137		$\dfrac{\$978}{\$4,386}$ = 0.223	
Asset Turnover Ratio	Total Sales Revenue / Average Total Assets	$\dfrac{\$807}{(\$851 + \$747)/2}$ = 1.01		$\dfrac{\$1,468}{(\$1,420 + \$1,307)/2}$ = 1.08		$\dfrac{\$2,951}{(\$4,386 + \$4,370)/2}$ = 0.67	
Net Profit Margin Ratio	Net Income / Total Sales Revenue	$\dfrac{\$34}{\$807}$ = 0.042		$\dfrac{\$42}{\$1,468}$ = 0.029		$\dfrac{\$236}{\$2,951}$ = 0.080	

Financial Statement Information	THQ		Activision		Electronic Arts	
	2006	2005	2006	2005	2006	2005
Total assets	$851	$747	$1,420	$1,307	$4,386	$4,370
Total liabilities	220	199	194	207	978	872
Total stockholders' equity	631	548	1,226	1,100	3,408	3,498
Total sales revenue	807	757	1,468	1,406	2,951	3,129
Net income	34	63	42	138	236	504

turnover ratio so that the bottom part spans the entire year, just like the top part. In the following discussion, we explain the significance of each of the three ratios and provide examples of how you could conduct similar analyses with other companies.

1. Debt-to-Assets Ratio   The **debt-to-assets ratio** compares total liabilities to total assets. It is usually calculated to three decimal places, and can be expressed as a percentage by multiplying by 100. This ratio indicates the proportion of total assets that are financed by debt. It's important to know how much debt is used to finance assets because debt has to be repaid whether or not a company is doing well financially. If assets are financed mainly by debt, rather than equity, then this ratio will be high, which would suggest the company has adopted a risky financing strategy. Ultimately, a company could be forced into bankruptcy if it took on more debt than it ever could repay. Exhibit 5.14 shows that, for all three companies, debt plays a fairly small role in financing the companies' assets. Activision is the lowest with a debt-to-assets ratio (0.137 or 13.7%) that is lower than either THQ (0.259 or 25.9%) or Electronic Arts (0.223 or 22.3%). This means that the likelihood of Activision being able to repay its existing liabilities is very high, so the company has little financing risk.

2. Asset Turnover Ratio   The **asset turnover ratio** compares total sales revenue to average total assets. It is usually calculated to two decimal places and not expressed as a percentage. This ratio indicates the sales revenue per dollar invested in the assets of the business. The higher the ratio, the more efficiently the company is utilizing its assets. Inefficiently run businesses will have lower ratios because their assets will be more likely to sit around idle and not generate revenue. Exhibit 5.14 shows that Activision and THQ are generating more than one dollar in sales revenue per dollar invested in assets (1.08 and 1.01, respectively). In contrast, Electronic Arts appears rather sluggish, with an asset turnover ratio of 0.67. This indicates that Electronic Arts generated $0.67 dollars of sales revenue (67 cents) per dollar of assets, which is quite a bit less than Activision or THQ.

3. Net Profit Margin Ratio   The **net profit margin ratio** measures the amount of net income (profit) generated from each dollar of sales revenue. It is usually calculated to

YOU SHOULD KNOW

The **debt-to-assets ratio** indicates financing risk by computing the proportion of total assets financed by debt.

COACH'S TIP

The basic accounting equation (A = L + SE) implies that as the ratio of debt-to-assets gets smaller, the ratio of equity-to-assets gets larger (and the ratio of debt-to-equity gets smaller).

YOU SHOULD KNOW

The **asset turnover ratio** indicates how well assets are being used to generate revenues by dividing total assets into total revenue.

YOU SHOULD KNOW

The **net profit margin ratio** indicates how well expenses are controlled by dividing net income by revenue.

three decimal places and can be expressed as a percentage by multiplying by 100. Net profit margin is a key ratio because it indicates how well a company has controlled its expenses. Although it's important for companies to generate lots of revenue, it's equally important to control expenses. A company generating tons of revenue will go bankrupt if its expenses are out of control. Exhibit 5.14 shows that each dollar of sales made by Electronic Arts led to more profit (0.080 or 8.0%) than did the sales made by THQ (0.042 or 4.2%) or Activision (0.029 or 2.9%). By reading the MD&A section of the three companies' annual reports, we found out the cause of these differences. Both THQ and Activision incurred significant selling expenses to keep their game sales up in 2006. Electronic Arts, in contrast, was willing to let its sales fall, expecting that they would rebound in 2007 with the release of the new generation game consoles (Microsoft's X-box 360, Sony's PS3, Nintendo's Wii).

Let's take this analysis one step further by relating the ratios to one another. This might allow us to discover differences in how the companies were managed in 2006. The net profit margin ratio suggests Activision generated less profit on each dollar of sales than Electronic Arts and THQ (0.029 vs. 0.080 and 0.042). But, as the asset turnover ratio shows, Activision generated greater sales per dollar of assets. In a way, Activision adopted a strategy similar to what Wal-Mart does. Wal-Mart generates less profit on each dollar of sales than its competitors, but makes up for it by generating more sales per dollar of assets. This is called a low-margin, high-volume strategy.

Many other financial statement ratios exist to assess profitability (the ability to generate income in the current period), solvency (the ability to use current assets to pay liabilities), and liquidity (the ability to repay lenders when debt matures). Rather than load you up with them all at once, we will introduce them gradually in Chapters 6–12, and then we'll summarize and apply them in a comprehensive analysis in Chapter 13.

HOW'S IT GOING?　　　　　A Self-Study Quiz

Konami Corporation is a Japanese company that makes and sells video games, such as Metal Gear Solid. Financial statement information for 2006 and 2005 is given below. Calculate ratios to indicate whether, relative to Activision, Konami has higher or lower levels of (a) financing risk, (b) asset efficiency, and (c) profitability.

	2006	2005
Total assets	$302,637	$304,321
Total liabilities	138,822	198,464
Total stockholders' equity	163,815	105,857
Total sales revenue	262,137	260,691
Net income	23,008	10,486

Quiz Answers

(a) Debt-to-assets ratio = 138,822/302,637 = 0.459.
This indicates higher financing risk than Activision's 0.137.

(b) Asset turnover ratio = $\dfrac{262,137}{(302,637 + 304,321)/2}$ = 0.86.
This indicates lower asset efficiency than Activision's 1.08.

(c) Net profit margin ratio = 23,008 / 262,137 = 0.088.
This indicates higher profitability than Activision's 0.029.

REVIEW THE CHAPTER

DEMONSTRATION CASE

Some analysts claim the video game business is similar to the book business. In this demonstration case, we'll take a look at just how similar they are in terms of financial results. While we're tempted to analyze the financial statements of the company that published this textbook, it wouldn't provide a clean comparison because McGraw-Hill doesn't just publish books—it also runs Standard & Poor's (a financial services company). So, instead, we'll analyze the financial statements of one of our publisher's main competitors, John Wiley & Sons—a company that operates only in the book business. Shortened versions of that company's financial statements are shown below:

John Wiley & Sons

JOHN WILEY & SONS, INC. Income Statement (modified) (U.S. dollars in thousands) For the Years Ended April 30		
	2006	2005
Total sales revenue	$1,044,185	$974,048
Cost of sales	342,314	325,061
Operating and administrative expenses	535,694	496,726
Other expenses	12,373	9,375
Income from operations	153,804	142,886
Interest expense	9,960	7,223
Income before taxes	143,844	135,663
Income tax expense	33,516	51,822
Net income	$ 110,328	$ 83,841

JOHN WILEY & SONS, INC. Balance Sheet (modified) (U.S. dollars in thousands) April 30		
	2006	2005
Assets		
Current assets	$ 326,308	$ 338,918
Other assets	699,701	693,651
Total assets	$1,026,009	$1,032,569
Liabilities and Shareholders' Equity		
Current liabilities	$ 362,109	$ 341,311
Other liabilities	262,060	294,684
Total liabilities	624,169	635,995
Stockholders' equity	401,840	396,574
Total liabilities and stockholders' equity	$1,026,009	$1,032,569

Required:

1. Compute Wiley's debt-to-assets ratio at the end of the 2006 and 2005 fiscal years. How has Wiley changed its financing strategy from 2005 to 2006? Is this likely to be considered a riskier or safer strategy? How similar is the proportion of debt financing used by the book publisher to that used by the video game companies analyzed in Exhibit 5.14?

2.   Compute Wiley's asset turnover ratio for 2006 and 2005. (In thousands, Wiley's total assets at April 30, 2004, were $1,014,582.) Between 2005 and 2006, was there a change in Wiley's efficiency in using its assets to generate revenues? Does the book publisher generate more or less sales from each dollar invested in assets than the video game companies analyzed in Exhibit 5.14?

3.   Compute Wiley's net profit margin ratio for the 2006 and 2005 fiscal years. How has this aspect of Wiley's financial performance changed? Does the book publisher make more or less profit from each dollar of sales than the video game companies analyzed in Exhibit 5.14?

4.   In the aftermath of the 2001 Enron financial scandal, one of the biggest auditing firms in the world (Arthur Andersen) shut down. On April 15, 2002, John Wiley & Sons announced that KPMG would replace Arthur Andersen as the company's auditor. How would Wiley report this news to the SEC?

After completing requirements 1–4, check your answers with the following solution.

Suggested Solution

1.   Debt-to-Assets Ratio = Total Liabilities ÷ Total Assets

	2006		2005	
$\dfrac{\text{Total Liabilities}}{\text{Total Assets}}$	$\dfrac{\$624,169}{\$1,026,009}$	= 0.608 or 60.8%	$\dfrac{\$635,995}{\$1,032,569}$	= 0.616 or 61.6%

Wiley has moved toward a slightly safer financing strategy in 2006, by relying less on debt (down from 61.6 percent in 2005 to 60.8 percent in 2006). Despite this change, Wiley still relies much more on debt than the video game companies in Exhibit 5.14, which financed less than 25 percent of their total assets using debt.

2.   Asset Turnover Ratio = Total Sales Revenue ÷ Average Total Assets

	2006		2005	
$\dfrac{\text{Total Sales Revenue}}{\text{Average Total Assets}}$	$\dfrac{\$1,044,185}{(\$1,026,009 + \$1,032,569)/2}$	= 1.01	$\dfrac{\$974,048}{(\$1,032,569 + \$1,014,582)/2}$	= 0.95

Wiley generated more sales per dollar invested in assets in 2006 (1.01) than in 2005 (0.95). In comparison to the video game companies in Exhibit 5.14, it appears Wiley's assets are generating sales with nearly the same efficiency.

3.   Net Profit Margin Ratio = Net Income ÷ Total Sales Revenue

	2006		2005	
$\dfrac{\text{Net Income}}{\text{Total Sales Revenue}}$	$\dfrac{\$110,328}{\$1,044,185}$	= 0.106 or 10.6%	$\dfrac{\$83,841}{\$974,048}$	= 0.086 or 8.6%

Wiley has improved its net profit margin from 8.6 percent in 2005 to 10.6 percent in 2006. This means that, in 2006, Wiley made about 10.6 cents of profit for each dollar of sales. These ratios are better than those for the video game companies.

4.   Form 8-K is used to report significant events such as this change in auditor.

CHAPTER SUMMARY

Explain the needs of financial statement users. p. 196   LO1

- The four main financial statement users are:

  Managers, who use accounting information to run the business.

  Directors, who use accounting information to oversee the business.

  Creditors, who use accounting information to administer business contracts.

  Investors, who use accounting information to value the business.

Describe the environment for financial reporting, including the Sarbanes-Oxley   LO2
Act of 2002. p. 197

- For someone to commit fraud, three things must exist: the incentive, opportunity, and character to rationalize and conceal.

- Incentives that motivate managers to misreport financial results include creating business opportunities (by satisfying loan covenants, increasing equity financing, and attracting business partners) and satisfying personal greed (enhancing job security, increasing personal wealth, and obtaining a bigger paycheck).

- The Sarbanes-Oxley (SOX) Act of 2002 reduced the incentive to commit fraud by introducing stiffer penalties. It also limited opportunities by improving internal controls through management reporting, audit committee functioning, and external audit reporting. Finally, it attempted to support employees of good character confronting those of poor character.

Prepare a comparative balance sheet, multistep income statement, and statement   LO3
of stockholders' equity. p. 201

- Comparative financial statements include separate columns for each period's results. See Exhibit 5.6 (p. 202) for an example.

- A multistep income statement includes subtotals to separate core and peripheral results, and to highlight the effect of income taxes. See Exhibit 5.7 (p. 203) for an example.

- The statement of stockholders' equity, which replaces the statement of retained earnings, has columns for each stockholders' equity account and shows the factors that increased and decreased these account balances during the period. See Exhibit 5.8 for an example.

Describe other significant aspects of the financial reporting process, including   LO4
external audits and the distribution of financial information. p. 205

- Financial information can be distributed through press releases, SEC filings, investor information Web sites, and quarterly and annual reports.

- Press releases typically include key figures (sales revenues, net income), management's discussion of the results, and attachments containing a condensed income statement and balance sheet.

- Form 10-K is the SEC's version of the annual report, which includes the annual financial statements, auditor's report, management's discussion and analysis, stock price data, and other financial schedules. Form 10-Q is the SEC's version of the quarterly report, which includes the quarterly financial statements and management's discussion and analysis. Form 8-K is the SEC's form that companies use to report significant current events, such as changes in auditors, press releases issued, and acquisitions of other companies.

Compare results to common benchmarks. p. 208   LO5

- Common benchmarks include: prior periods (used in time-series analysis) and competitors (used in cross-sectional analysis).

Calculate and interpret the debt-to-assets, asset turnover, and net profit margin   LO6
ratios. p. 209

- The debt-to-assets ratio is calculated by dividing total liabilities by total assets. It indicates the percentage of assets financed by debt, with a higher ratio indicating a riskier financing strategy.

- The asset turnover ratio is calculated by dividing total sales revenue for the period by average total assets held during the period. Average total assets usually is calculated by adding the beginning and ending total assets together and dividing by 2. The asset turnover ratio indicates how well assets are used to generate sales, with a higher ratio indicating greater efficiency.

- The net profit margin ratio is calculated by dividing net income by total sales revenue. It indicates the ability to control expenses, with a higher ratio indicating better performance.

Financial Analysis Tools

Name of Measure	Formula	What It Tells You
1. Debt-to-assets ratio	$\dfrac{\text{Total Liabilities}}{\text{Total Assets}}$	• The percentage of assets financed by debt • A higher ratio means greater financing risk
2. Asset turnover ratio	$\dfrac{\text{Total Sales Revenue}}{\text{Average Total Assets}}$	• How well assets are used to generate sales • A higher ratio means greater efficiency
3. Net profit margin ratio	$\dfrac{\text{Net Income}}{\text{Total Sales Revenue}}$	• How well expenses are controlled • A higher ratio means better performance

KEY TERMS

Asset Turnover Ratio p. 211
Comparative Financial Statements p. 202
Cross-sectional Analysis p. 208
Debt-to-assets Ratio p. 211
Loan Covenants p. 197

Material p. 205
Multistep Income Statement p. 203
Net Profit Margin Ratio p. 211
Qualified Audit Opinion p. 205
Sarbanes-Oxley Act p. 199

Single-step Income Statement p. 203
Time-series Analysis p. 208
Unqualified Audit Opinion p. 205

PRACTICE MATERIAL

QUESTIONS

1. Describe one way that each of the four main financial statement user groups uses financial statement information.

2. What are the three points of the fraud triangle? Is fraud more or less likely to occur if one of these elements is missing?

3. Why would managers misrepresent the financial results of their companies? What are the incentives for doing this?

4. What aspect(s) of the Sarbanes-Oxley Act of 2002 might counteract the incentive to commit fraud?

5. What aspect(s) of the Sarbanes-Oxley Act of 2002 might reduce opportunities for fraud?

6. What aspect(s) of the Sarbanes-Oxley Act of 2002 might allow the good character of employees to prevail?

7. What roles do auditors play in the financial reporting process?

8. In what ways are fraudulent financial reporting and academic dishonesty (e.g., cheating on exams) similar? Consider the three points of the fraud triangle.

9. What are two potential problems with relying on investor information Web sites for financial statement ratio analyses?

10. In what three ways might corporate financial statements differ from the examples shown in Chapters 1–4?

11. What two benchmarks are commonly used to interpret and evaluate amounts reported for specific financial statement items?

12. What is the goal of ratio analysis?

13. Explain the simple business model that starts with obtaining financing and then proceeds through other investing and operating decisions.

14. Why do some ratios use just the ending balance sheet amounts whereas others use averages of the beginning and ending balances?

15. What are the key business activities that the debt-to-assets, asset turnover, and net profit margin ratios assess?

MULTIPLE CHOICE

1. If total assets increase but total liabilities remain the same, what is the impact on the debt-to-assets ratio?
   - a. Increases.
   - c. Remains the same.
   - b. Decreases.
   - d. Cannot be determined without additional information.

Topic Tackler

PLUS

Check out www.mhhe.com/phillips2e for more multiple choice questions.

2. Costco and Sam's Club are two companies that offer low prices for items packaged in bulk. This strategy increases total sales volume but generates less profit for each dollar of sales. Which of the following ratios is improved by this strategy?
   - a. Net profit margin.
   - c. Debt-to-assets.
   - b. Asset turnover.
   - d. All of the above.

Quiz 5

3. Which of the following would increase the net profit margin ratio in the current year?
   - a. Increase the amount of research and development in the last month of the year.
   - b. Decrease the amount of sales in the last month of the year.
   - c. Postpone routine maintenance work that was to be done this year.
   - d. All of the above.

4. The asset turnover ratio is directly affected by which of the following categories of business decisions?
   - a. Operating and investing decisions.
   - b. Operating and financing decisions.
   - c. Investing and financing decisions.
   - d. Operating, investing, and financing decisions.

5. Which of the following reports is filed annually with the SEC?
   - a. Form 10-Q
   - c. Form 8-K
   - b. Form 10-K
   - d. Press release

6. Which of the following describes a cross-sectional analysis of your academic performance?
   - a. Counting the number of A's on your transcript.
   - b. Comparing the number of A's you received this year to the number you received last year.
   - c. Comparing the number of A's you received this year to the number your friend received.
   - d. Counting the total number of A's given out to your class as a whole.

7. Which of the following describes a time-series analysis of your academic performance?
   - a. Counting the number of A's on your transcript.
   - b. Comparing the number of A's you received this year to the number you received last year.
   - c. Comparing the number of A's you received this year to the number your friend received.
   - d. Counting the total number of A's given out to your class as a whole.

8. Which of the following is always included in an annual report but never in a quarterly report?
   - a. Balance sheet.
   - c. Management's discussion and analysis.
   - b. Income statement.
   - d. Auditor's report.

9. Which of the following transactions will increase the debt-to-assets ratio?
   - a. The company issues stock to investors.
   - b. The company uses cash to buy land.
   - c. The company issues a note payable to buy machinery.
   - d. None of the above.

Solutions to Multiple Choice Questions

1. b   2. b   3. c   4. a   5. b   6. c   7. b   8. d   9. c   10. d

10. What type of audit report does a company hope to include with its annual report?
   a. Conservative report
   b. Qualified report
   c. Comparable report
   d. Unqualified report

MINI-EXERCISES

LO1

M5-1 Matching Players in the Financial Reporting Process with Their Definitions

Match each player with the related definition by entering the appropriate letter in the space provided.

Players	Definitions
____ 1. Independent auditors	A. Investors and creditors (among others).
____ 2. External users	B. People who are elected by stockholders to oversee a company's management.
____ 3. Directors	C. CPAs who examine financial statements and attest to their fairness.

LO2

M5-2 Matching Sarbanes-Oxley (SOX) Requirements to the Fraud Triangle

Match each of the following SOX requirements to the corresponding element of the fraud triangle by entering the appropriate letter in the space provided.

____ 1. Establish a tip line for employees to report questionable acts.	A. Incentive
____ 2. Increase maximum fines to $5 million.	B. Opportunity
____ 3. Require management to report on effectiveness of internal controls.	C. Character
____ 4. Legislate whistle-blower protections.	
____ 5. Require external auditors' report on internal control effectiveness.	

LO4

M5-3 Identifying the Sequence of Financial Reports and Disclosures

Indicate the order in which the following reports and disclosures are normally issued by public companies in any given year.

No.	Title
____	Form 10-K
____	Annual Report
____	Press release announcing annual earnings

LO3

M5-4 Preparing and Interpreting a Multistep Income Statement

Nutboy Theater Company reported the following single-step income statement. Prepare a multistep income statement for the local theater company. Also, calculate the net profit margin and compare it to the 8% earned in 2007. In which year did the company generate more profit from each dollar of sales?

NUTBOY THEATER COMPANY
Income Statement
For the year ended December 31, 2008

Revenues	
Ticket sales	$50,000
Concession sales	2,500
Interest revenue	200
Other revenue	50
Total revenues	52,750
Expenses	
Salaries and wage expense	30,000
Advertising expense	8,000
Utilities expense	7,000
Income tax expense	2,500
Total expenses	47,500
Net income	$ 5,250

M5-5 Preparing a Statement of Stockholders' Equity   LO3

WER Productions began 2007 with $100,000 of contributed capital and $20,000 of retained earnings. During the year, the company had the following transactions. Prepare a statement of stockholders' equity for the year ended December 31, 2007.

a. Issued stock for $50,000.
b. Declared and paid a cash dividend of $5,000.
c. Reported total revenue of $120,000 and total expenses of $87,000.
d. Repurchased shares of WER stock for $10,000 (the shares had been previously issued for $10,000 and were cancelled upon repurchase).

M5-6 Determining the Accounting Equation Effects of Transactions   LO3

Complete the following table, indicating the sign and amount of the effect (+ for increase, − for decrease, and NE for no effect) of each transaction. Provide an account name for any revenue or expense transactions included in stockholders' equity. Consider each item independently.

a. Recorded services provided on account for $500.
b. Recorded $50 purchase of supplies on account.
c. Recorded advertising expense of $1,000 incurred but not paid for.

Transaction	Assets	Liabilities	Stockholders' Equity
a			
b			
c			

M5-7 Determining the Effects of Transactions on Debt-to-Assets, Asset Turnover, and Net Profit Margin   LO6

Using the transactions in M5-6, complete the following table by indicating the sign of the effect (+ for increase, − for decrease, NE for no effect, and CD for cannot determine) of each transaction. Consider each item independently.

Transaction	Debt-to-Assets	Asset Turnover	Net Profit Margin
a			
b			
c			

LO3   **M5-8 Determining the Accounting Equation Effects of Transactions**

Complete the following table, indicating the sign and amount of the effect (+ for increase, − for decrease, and NE for no effect) of each transaction. Provide an account name for any revenue or expense transactions included in stockholders' equity. Consider each item independently.

a. Issued 10,000 shares of stock for $90,000 cash.
b. Equipment costing $4,000 was purchased by issuing a note payable.
c. Recorded depreciation of $1,000 on the equipment.

Transaction	Assets	Liabilities	Stockholders' Equity
a			
b			
c			

LO6   **M5-9 Determining the Effects of Transactions on Debt-to-Assets, Asset Turnover, and Net Profit Margin**

Using the transactions in M5-8, complete the following table by indicating the sign of the effect (+ for increase, − for decrease, NE for no effect, and CD for cannot determine) of each transaction. Consider each item independently.

Transaction	Debt-to-Assets	Asset Turnover	Net Profit Margin
a			
b			
c			

LO6   **M5-10 Computing and Interpreting the Net Profit Margin Ratio**

Happy's Golf Corporation recently reported the following December 31 amounts in its financial statements (in thousands):

	Prior Year	Current Year
Income from operations	$ 1,700	$1,400
Net income	850	700
Total assets	10,000	9,000
Total stockholders' equity	8,000	7,500
Sales revenue	9,000	7,000

Compute the net profit margin ratio for the current and prior years. What do these analyses indicate?

LO6   **M5-11 Computing and Interpreting the Debt-to-Assets Ratio**

Using the data in M5-10, compute the debt-to-assets ratio for the current and prior years. What do these analyses indicate?

LO6   **M5-12 Computing and Interpreting the Asset Turnover Ratio**

Using the data in M5-10, compute the asset turnover ratio for the current year. Assuming the asset turnover ratio in the prior year was 85.2 percent (0.852), what does your analysis indicate?

LO5, LO6   **M5-13 Computing and Interpreting Financial Ratios**

Columbia Sportswear
Levi Strauss

Key financial data for Columbia Sportswear and Levi Strauss follow. Using two ratios included in this chapter, compare their relative abilities to generate (a) sales from assets and (b) net income from sales. Which company appears more successful on each of the measures?

	Columbia Sportswear (OOO's)	Levi Strauss and Co. (OOO's)
Sales	$1,156	$4,125
Net income	131	156
Total assets, 2005	971	2,814
Total assets, 2004	949	2,886

EXERCISES

Available with McGraw-Hill's
Homework Manager   PLUS

E5-1 Matching Components of the Financial Reporting Process with Their Definitions

LO1, LO4

Match each component with the related definition by entering the appropriate letter in the space provided.

Components	Definitions
____ 1. Investor information Web site	A. Individual who purchases stock in companies for personal ownership or for pension funds or mutual funds.
____ 2. External auditor	
____ 3. Investor	B. Financial institution or supplier that lends money to the company.
____ 4. Creditor	
____ 5. SEC	C. Independent CPA who examines financial statements and attests to their fairness.
	D. Securities and Exchange Commission, which regulates financial disclosure requirements.
	E. Gathers, combines, and transmits financial and related information from various sources.

E5-2 Matching Definitions with Information Releases Made by Public Companies

LO4

Following are the titles of various information releases. Match each definition with the related release by entering the appropriate letter in the space provided.

Information Release	Definitions
____ 1. Annual report	A. Comprehensive report containing the four basic financial statements and related notes, statements by management and auditors, and other descriptions of the company's activities.
____ 2. Form 8-K	
____ 3. Press release	
____ 4. Form 10-Q	B. Annual report filed by public companies with the SEC that contains detailed financial information.
____ 5. Quarterly report	
____ 6. Form 10-K	C. Quarterly report filed by public companies with the SEC that contains unaudited financial information.
	D. A company-prepared news announcement that is normally distributed to major news agencies.
	E. Brief unaudited report for the quarter, normally containing condensed income statement and balance sheet (unaudited).
	F. Report of special events (e.g., auditor changes, mergers and acquisitions) filed by public companies with the SEC.

LO4

E5-3 Finding Financial Information: Matching Information Items to Financial Reports

Following are information items included in various financial reports. Match each information item with the report(s) where it would most likely be found by entering the appropriate letter(s) in the space provided.

Information Item	Report
____ 1. Initial announcement of hiring of new vice president for sales.	A. Annual report
____ 2. Initial announcement of quarterly earnings.	B. Form 8-K
____ 3. Initial announcement of a change in auditors.	C. Press release
____ 4. Complete quarterly income statement, balance sheet, and cash flow statement.	D. Form 10-Q
____ 5. The four basic financial statements for the year.	E. Quarterly report
____ 6. Summarized income statement information for the quarter.	F. Form 10-K
____ 7. Detailed discussion of the company's business risks and strategies.	G. None of the above
____ 8. Detailed notes to financial statements.	
____ 9. Recent stock price data.	
____ 10. Summarized financial data for 5- or 10-year period.	

LO4

E5-4 Understanding the Financial Reporting Process

During the first half of 2006, Mad Catz Interactive, Inc. completed its fiscal year, filed reports with the SEC, and issued various reports to the public. Match each date in the table below with the related activity by entering the appropriate letter in the space provided.

Date Filed/Issued	Activity
____ 1. March 31, 2006	A. Issued annual earnings press release
____ 2. June 8, 2006	B. Filed form 8-K announcing press release
____ 3. June 8, 2006	C. Filed form 10-K
____ 4. June 28, 2006	D. Completed fiscal year

LO1

E5-5 Matching Events with Concepts

Following are accounting concepts covered in Chapters 1 through 5. Match each event (A–K) with its related concept (1–10) by entering the appropriate letter in the space provided. Use one letter for each blank.

Concepts	Events
____ 1. Users of financial statements	A. Counted unused supplies at the end of the period and valued them in U.S. dollars.
____ 2. Objective of financial statements	
____ 3. Consistency	B. Valued an asset at the amount paid to acquire it, even though its market value has increased considerably.
____ 4. Comparability	
____ 5. Separate entity	C. Analyzed the financial statements to assess the company's performance.
____ 6. Unit of measure	
____ 7. Cost principle	D. Established an accounting policy that sales revenue shall be recognized only when services have been provided to the customer.
____ 8. Revenue principle	
____ 9. Matching principle	E. Prepared and distributed financial statements that provide useful economic information.
____ 10. Conservatism	
	F. Established a policy not to include in the financial statements the personal financial affairs of the owners of the business.

G. Changed the company's year-end to correspond to that used by others in the industry.

H. Disclosed all relevant financial information about the business in the financial statements (including the notes to the financial statements).

I. Established a policy to report the company's recurring business activities in the same way from year to year.

J. Adjusted the rent accounts to show the cost of rent relating to the current period.

K. Acquired a vehicle for use in the business, reporting it at the agreed-upon purchase price rather than its higher sticker price.

E5-6 Understanding the Characteristics of Useful Financial Information and the Financial Reporting Process

LO1, LO4, LO6
Atari Incorporated

Atari Incorporated began with $250 and an idea for a video game named Pong, eventually becoming a $28 million enterprise. Over the years, Atari has been owned by a variety of companies, including Time-Warner, Hasbro, and most recently Infogrames (a public company in France). Infogrames made the following announcement in 2003:

> On March 28, 2003, the Company announced that it has changed its fiscal year-end from June 30 to March 31. As a result of this change, the Company's fiscal year 2003 was a nine-month period. The Company believes that the March 31 year-end is consistent with more of its peers in the video game industry, allowing for more meaningful analysis and comparisons within the sector.

Required:

1. To which of the four characteristics of useful information, introduced in Chapter 1, is the company referring?
   TIP: Rather than look for key words in the announcement, read it for meaning.
2. On what SEC form would the change in year-end be reported?
3. Since the 2003 fiscal period includes only nine months, will the debt-to-assets, asset turnover, and net profit margin ratios be meaningful in 2003? Explain your reasoning.

E5-7 Understanding the Characteristics of Useful Financial Information and the Financial Reporting Process

LO1, LO4, LO6
THQ, Inc.

THQ, Inc., is among the five biggest video game makers in the world. On February 13, 2003, THQ made the following announcement:

> On February 13, 2003, we announced a fiscal year-end change from December 31 of each year to March 31 of each year, effective March 31, 2003. We believe that the change in fiscal year will better reflect our natural business year and allow us to provide financial guidance after the holiday selling season.

Required:

1. Does the reason given for the change in year-end indicate that this change will make THQ's financial statements more useful to users? Can you think of a reason that the change in year-end ultimately will result in more useful information for users?
2. On what SEC form would the change in year-end be reported?
3. Since the March 31, 2003 fiscal period includes only three months, will the debt-to-assets, asset turnover, and net profit margin ratios be meaningful in this period? Explain your reasoning.

E5-8 Computing and Interpreting the Net Profit Margin Ratio

LO6
Cendant Corporation

Before spinning off its businesses in 2006, Cendant Corporation owned and operated Super 8 Motels, Ramada, Howard Johnson, Century 21, Orbitz.com, Avis, and Budget. Cendant also was notorious for committing a $3.3 billion accounting fraud in the late 1990s, which sent its former vice chairman to prison for 10 years. On February 13, 2006, the company issued a press release that reported the following amounts (in millions) for the year just ended on December 31, 2005:

	2005	2004
Fee revenue	$18,236	$16,689
Income from operations	869	1,365
Net income	1,341	2,082

Required:

Compute the net profit margin ratio for the current and prior years. What do these analyses indicate?

LO4

Cendant Corporation

E5-9 Understanding the Financial Reporting Process

1.   The information in E5-8 indicated that the Cendant Corporation press release was issued on February 13, yet the company's year-end was six weeks earlier on December 31. Why did the company wait so long to issue the press release? Why weren't the financial results announced on January 1?
2.   The 10-K was filed on March 1, 2006. Why would the company wait so long to file the 10-K? Why wouldn't it be filed at the same time the press release was issued?
3.   Is the company's glossy annual report likely to be issued before or after the 10-K?

LO1, LO6

Better Ingredients.
Better Pizza.

E5-10 Analyzing and Interpreting Asset Turnover and Net Profit Margin

Papa John's is one of the fastest-growing pizza delivery and carry-out restaurant chains in the country. Presented here are selected income statement and balance sheet amounts (in millions).

	Current Year	Prior Year
Total revenues	$969	$925
Net income	46	23
Average total assets	363	361

Required:

1.   Compute the asset turnover and net profit margin ratios for the current and prior years.
2.   Would analysts more likely increase or decrease their estimates of stock value on the basis of these changes? Explain by interpreting what the changes in these two ratios mean.

LO1, LO6

RadioShack Corporation

E5-11 Analyzing and Interpreting Asset Turnover and Net Profit Margin

RadioShack Corporation has populated the world with stores from Greece to Canada, and in the United States, an estimated 94 percent of all Americans live or work within five minutes of the electronics retailer—not bad for a company that originally started business as American Hide & Leather Company. The following amounts (in millions) were reported in RadioShack's income statement and balance sheet.

	2005	2004	2003
Net sales	$5,081	$4,841	$4,649
Net income	267	337	298
Total assets	2,205	2,517	2,244
Total liabilities	1,616	1,595	1,475

Required:

1.   Compute the asset turnover and net profit margin ratios for 2005 and 2004.
2.   Would analysts be more likely to increase or decrease their estimates of stock value on the basis of these changes? Explain what the changes in these two ratios mean.
3.   Compute the debt-to-assets ratio for 2005 and 2004.

4. Would analysts be more likely to increase or decrease their estimates of RadioShack's ability to repay lenders on the basis of this change? Explain by interpreting what the change in this ratio means.

E5-12 Determining the Accounting Equation Effects of Transactions

La-Z-Boy Incorporated is a furniture manufacturer. Listed here are typical aggregate transactions from the first quarter of a recent year (in millions). Complete the following table, indicating the sign (+ for increase, − for decrease, and NE for no effect) and amount of the effect of each transaction. Provide an account name for any revenue or expense transactions included in stockholders' equity. Consider each item independently.

a. Repaid $10 on a note payable to a bank.
b. Recorded collections of cash from customers who owed $32.

Transaction	Assets	Liabilities	Stockholders' Equity
a			
b			

E5-13 Determining the Effects of Transactions on Debt-to-Assets, Asset Turnover, and Net Profit Margin

Using the transactions in E5-12, complete the following table by indicating the sign of the effect (+ for increase, − for decrease, NE for no effect, and CD for cannot determine) of each transaction. Consider each item independently.

Transaction	Debt-to-Assets	Asset Turnover	Net Profit Margin
a			
b			

E5-14 Preparing and Interpreting Financial Statements

The December 31, 2008 and 2007 adjusted trial balances for Sportlife Gym Corporation are shown below.

	2008		2007	
	Debit	Credit	Debit	Credit
Cash	$ 31,500		$ 30,000	
Accounts receivable	2,500		2,000	
Supplies	13,000		13,000	
Prepaid rent	3,000		3,000	
Equipment	350,000		350,000	
Accumulated depreciation		$ 20,000		$ 10,000
Other long-term assets	20,000		12,000	
Accounts payable		5,000		6,000
Unearned revenue		72,000		80,000
Income taxes payable		13,000		14,000
Long-term debt		10,000		200,000
Contributed capital		214,000		50,000
Retained earnings		50,000		19,400
Dividends declared	5,000		0	
Membership revenue		399,000		398,000
Coaching revenue		11,000		10,000
Salaries and wages expense	321,000		319,400	
Rent expense	12,000		12,000	
Depreciation expense	10,000		10,000	
Other operating expenses	6,150		7,700	
Interest revenue		750		700
Interest expense	600		15,000	
Income tax expense	20,000		14,000	
	$794,750	$794,750	$788,100	$788,100

Required:

1. Prepare a comparative classified balance sheet and comparative multistep income statement for 2008 and 2007, and a statement of stockholders' equity for 2008. The change in contributed capital was caused by the issuance of new stock in 2008.
2. Identify two balance sheet and two income statement accounts that changed significantly in 2008. What might be the cause of these changes?
3. Calculate and interpret the debt-to-assets, asset turnover, and net profit margin ratios in 2008 and 2007. Total assets were $400,000 on December 31, 2006.

LO3   E5-15 **Finding Financial Statement Information**

Indicate whether each of the following would be reported on the balance sheet (B/S), income statement (I/S), or statement of stockholders' equity (SSE).

1. Insurance costs paid this year, to expire next year.
2. Insurance costs expired this year.
3. Insurance costs still owed.
4. Cost of equipment used up this accounting year.
5. Equipment book value (carrying value).
6. Amounts contributed by stockholders during the year.
7. Cost of supplies unused at the end of the year.
8. Cost of supplies used during the accounting year.
9. Amount of unpaid loans at end of year.
10. Dividends declared and paid during this year.

COACHED PROBLEMS

LO3   CP5-1 **Determining the Accounting Equation Effects of Transactions**

Yahoo! Inc. is a leading provider of Internet products and services. Listed here are selected aggregate transactions from 2005 (in millions). Complete the following table, indicating the sign (+ for increase, − for decrease, and NE for no effect) and amount of the effect of each transaction. Provide an account name for any revenue or expense transactions included in stockholders' equity. Consider each item independently.

a. Recorded marketing revenues on account of $4,594.
b. Obtained $747 cash by issuing stock.
c. Incurred product development expense of $547, which was paid in cash.

Transaction	Assets	Liabilities	Stockholders' Equity
a			
b			
c			

LO6   CP5-2 **Determining the Effects of Transactions on Debt-to-Assets, Asset Turnover, and Net Profit Margin**

Using the transactions in CP5-1, complete the following table by indicating the sign of the effect (+ for increase, − for decrease, NE for no effect, and CD for cannot determine) of each transaction. Consider each item independently.

TIP: To determine the impact of a transaction on a ratio, try an example with numbers. For example, assume asset turnover ratios of 9/10 or 10/9 and see how an increase of 1 in the top and bottom numbers affects the ratios.

TIP: A = L + SE implies that total assets are almost always greater than total liabilities. This means that if assets and liabilities change by the same dollar amount, the impact on liabilities will be proportionally bigger than the impact on assets.

Transaction	Debt-to-Assets	Asset Turnover	Net Profit Margin
a			
b			
c			

CP5-3 Interpreting Debt-to-Assets, Asset Turnover, and Net Profit Margin Ratios

L06
Best Buy Co. Inc.
Circuit City Stores, Inc.

The following ratios for Best Buy Co. Inc. and its competitor Circuit City Stores, Inc. were obtained using the benchmarking assistant at edgarscan.pwcglobal.com. Compare the two companies based on the following ratios:

Ratio	Best Buy	Circuit City
Debt-to-assets	0.57	0.45
Asset turnover ratio	2.8	2.8
Net profit margin	3.6 %	0.6 %

Required:

1. Which company appears to rely more on debt than stockholders' equity for financing? Describe the ratio that you used to reach this decision, and explain what the ratio means.

2. Which company appears to use its assets more efficiently? Describe the ratio that you used to reach this decision, and explain what the ratio means.

3. Which company appears to better control its expenses? Describe the ratio that you used to reach this decision, and explain what the ratio means.

GROUP A PROBLEMS

Available with McGraw-Hill's Homework Manager

HOMEWORK MANAGER **PLUS**

PA5-1 Determining the Accounting Equation Effects of Transactions

L03

Papa John's International began in the back of a tavern in Jefferson, Indiana, and has since become the third-largest pizza company in America. Listed here are transactions that typically occur each year (in millions). Complete the following table, indicating the sign (+ for increase, − for decrease, and NE for no effect) and amount of the effect of each transaction. Provide an account name for any revenue or expense transactions included in stockholders' equity. Consider each item independently.

a. Repaid bank loan payable of $7.
b. Paid cash to purchase property and equipment costing $6.
c. Purchased additional property and equipment costing $2 by issuing a note payable.
d. Recorded franchise royalty revenues on account of $20.

www.mhhe.com/phillips2e

Transaction	Assets	Liabilities	Stockholders' Equity
a			
b			
c			
d			

PA5-2 Determining the Effects of Transactions on Debt-to-Assets, Asset Turnover, and Net Profit Margin

L06

www.mhhe.com/phillips2e

Using the transactions in PA5-1, complete the following table by indicating the sign of the effect (+ for increase, − for decrease, NE for no effect, and CD for cannot determine) of each transaction. Consider each item independently.

Transaction	Debt-to-Assets	Asset Turnover	Net Profit Margin
a			
b			
c			
d			

L06

Kohl's Corporation
Dillards, Inc.

www.mhhe.com/phillips2e

PA5-3 Interpreting Debt-to-Assets, Asset Turnover, and Net Profit Margin Ratios

The following ratios for Kohl's Corporation and its competitor Dillards, Inc. were obtained using the benchmarking assistant at edgarscan.pwcglobal.com. Compare the two companies based on the following ratios:

Ratio	Kohl's	Dillards
Debt-to-assets	0.35	0.58
Asset turnover ratio	1.68	1.35
Net profit margin	6.3 %	1.6 %

Required:

1. Which company appears to rely more on debt than stockholders' equity for financing? Describe the ratio that you used to reach this decision, and explain what the ratio means.
2. Which company appears to use its assets more efficiently? Describe the ratio that you used to reach this decision, and explain what the ratio means.
3. Which company appears to better control its expenses? Describe the ratio that you used to reach this decision, and explain what the ratio means.

GROUP B PROBLEMS

L03

Regal Entertainment Group

PB5-1 Determining the Accounting Equation Effects of Transactions

Regal Entertainment Group is the largest movie company in the world, taking in over 20 percent of the box office receipts in the United States. Listed here are transactions that typically occur each quarter (in millions). Complete the following table, indicating the sign (+ for increase, − for decrease, and NE for no effect) and amount of the effect of each transaction. Provide an account name for any revenue or expense transactions included in stockholders' equity. Consider each item independently.

a. Paid cash to purchase property and equipment costing $30.
b. Declared and paid cash dividend totaling $40.
c. Recorded depreciation on property and equipment totaling $78.
d. Recorded cash admissions revenues of $450.

Transaction	Assets	Liabilities	Stockholders' Equity
a			
b			
c			
d			

L06

PB5-2 Determining the Effects of Transactions on Debt-to-Assets, Asset Turnover, and Net Profit Margin

Using the transactions in PB5-1, complete the following table by indicating the sign of the effect (+ for increase, − for decrease, NE for no effect, and CD for cannot determine) of each transaction. Consider each item independently.

Transaction	Debt-to-Assets	Asset Turnover	Net Profit Margin
a			
b			
c			
d			

PB5-3 Interpreting Debt-to-Assets, Asset Turnover, and Net Profit Margin Ratios

L06

The following ratios for McDonald's Corporation and its competitor YUM Brands, Inc. (the owner of KFC, Pizza Hut, and Taco Bell) were obtained using the benchmarking assistant at edgarscan.pwcglobal.com. Compare the two companies based on the following ratios:

Ratio	McDonald's	YUM
Debt-to-assets	0.49	0.75
Asset turnover ratio	0.73	1.60
Net profit margin	12.7 %	8.2 %

i'm lovin' it™
YUM Brands, Inc.

Required:

1. Which company appears to rely more on debt than stockholders' equity for financing? Describe the ratio that you used to reach this decision, and explain what the ratio means.

2. Which company appears to use its assets more efficiently? Describe the ratio that you used to reach this decision, and explain what the ratio means.

3. Which company appears to better control its expenses? Describe the ratio that you used to reach this decision, and explain what the ratio means.

SKILLS DEVELOPMENT CASES

S5-1 Finding Financial Information

L06

Refer to the financial statements of Landry's Restaurants in Appendix A at the end of this book, or download the annual report from the *Cases* section of the text's Web site at www.mhhe.com/phillips2e.

RESTAURANTS, INC.

Required:

1. Calculate the debt-to-assets ratio for 2005 and 2004. Based on these calculations, has Landry's financing become more or less risky in 2005 than in 2004?

2. Calculate the asset turnover ratio for 2005 and 2004 (total assets at December 31, 2003, were $1,104,883,000). Based on these calculations, has Landry's used its assets more or less efficiently in 2005 than in 2004?

3. Calculate the net profit margin ratio for 2005 and 2004. Based on these calculations, has Landry's generated more or less profit per dollar of sales in 2005 than in 2004?

S5-2 Comparing Financial Information

L05, L06

Refer to the financial statements of Outback Steakhouse in Appendix B at the end of this book, or download them from the *Cases* section of the text's Web site at www.mhhe.com/phillips2e.

Required:

1. Calculate the debt-to-assets ratio at December 31, 2005. (For purposes of this question, treat the "minority interests in consolidated entities" reported by Outback as an additional liability.) Based on this calculation, was Outback's financing more or less risky than Landry's in 2005?

2. Calculate the asset turnover ratio for the year ended December 31, 2005. Based on this calculation, did Outback use its assets more or less efficiently than Landry's in 2005?

3. Calculate the net profit margin ratio for the year ended December 31, 2005. Based on this calculation, did Outback generate more or less profit per dollar of sales than Landry's in 2005?

LO5, LO6 | **S5-3 Internet-Based Team Research: Examining an Annual Report**

As a team, select an industry to analyze. Using your Web browser, each team member should access the annual report or 10-K for one publicly traded company in the industry, with each member selecting a different company (see S1-3 in Chapter 1 for a description of possible resources for these tasks).

Required:

1. On an individual basis, each team member should write a short report that incorporates the following:

   a. Calculate the debt-to-assets ratio at the end of the current and prior year, and explain any change between the two years.

   b. Calculate the asset turnover ratio at the end of the current and prior year and explain any change between the two years. (To calculate average assets for the prior year, you will need the total assets number for the beginning of the prior year. If this isn't reported in the summarized financial data section in the current annual report, you will need to get it from the prior year's annual report or 10-K.)

   c. Calculate the net profit margin ratio at the end of the current and prior year and explain any change between the two years.

2. Then, as a team, write a short report comparing and contrasting your companies using these attributes. Discuss any patterns across the companies that you observe as a team. Provide potential explanations for any differences discovered.

LO1, LO2, LO6 | **S5-4 Ethical Decision Making: A Real-Life Example**

Aurora Foods Inc.

On February 18, 2000, the board of directors of Aurora Foods Inc.—the maker of Duncan Hines® and Mrs. Butterworth's® products—issued a press release announcing that a special committee had been formed to conduct an investigation into the company's accounting practices. During the financial statement audit for the year ended December 31, 1999, Aurora's auditors had discovered documents that raised questions about how the company accounted for marketing costs incurred to entice grocery stores to promote Aurora's products. The company's stock price fell by 50 percent in the week following this announcement.

After nearly a year of investigation, Aurora filed revised quarterly reports with the SEC, showing that the company had not accrued adequately for liabilities and expenses that had been incurred during the third and fourth quarter of 1998 and during the first three quarters of 1999. Key financial figures for these quarters as initially reported and as later restated are shown below.

(in millions of U.S. dollars)	1998 Q3 (September 30) Initial Report	1998 Q3 (September 30) Restated Report	1998 Q4 (December 31) Initial Report	1998 Q4 (December 31) Restated Report	1999 Q1 (March 31) Initial Report	1999 Q1 (March 31) Restated Report	1999 Q2 (June 30) Initial Report	1999 Q2 (June 30) Restated Report	1999 Q3 (September 30) Initial Report	1999 Q3 (September 30) Restated Report
Assets	$1,457	$1,455	$1,434	$1,448	$1,474	$1,463	$1,558	$1,521	$1,614	$1,553
Liabilities	869	879	830	868	862	882	937	944	983	972
Revenues	220	219	280	277	261	254	222	214	238	231
Net income (loss)	1	(12)	16	5	8	0	8	(4)	11	4

The SEC also investigated and filed a legal claim alleging that Aurora's 36-year-old chief financial officer (CFO) had violated federal securities laws by instructing accounting staff to make false journal entries and prepare two sets of records—one for the company's internal use and another to be provided to the auditors. The SEC alleged that her actions allowed Aurora to meet the net income targets set by Wall Street analysts and the expectations of Aurora investors and to obtain loans from Chase Manhattan Bank and other lenders. The CFO pled guilty to the charges, was sentenced to 57 months in prison, was barred for life from ever serving as an executive of a public company, and had to return to the company the stock and bonuses that had been awarded to her on the basis of Aurora's false and substantially inflated financial results.

Epilogue: On December 8, 2003, Aurora Foods filed for bankruptcy protection after violating several of its lenders' loan covenants. On March 19, 2004, Aurora emerged from bankruptcy and has since merged with Pinnacle Foods, the maker of Vlasic pickles and Swanson TV dinners.

Required:

1. Using the initially reported numbers, calculate the debt-to-assets ratio (reported as a percentage to one decimal place) at the end of each quarter.

2. Using the restated numbers, calculate the debt-to-assets ratio (reported as a percentage to one decimal place) at the end of each quarter.

3. On an overall basis, did the initially reported numbers suggest more or less financing risk than the restated numbers? Of the financial statement users mentioned earlier in this chapter in Exhibit 5.1, which would be most influenced by this impact on the debt-to-assets ratio?

4. Using the initially reported numbers, calculate the asset turnover ratio (to three decimal places) for the last quarter of 1998 and the first three quarters of 1999. (Note that the asset turnover ratio will be substantially less than the examples shown earlier in this chapter because they use only three months of revenues. Do not attempt to convert them to annual amounts.)

5. Using the restated numbers, calculate the asset turnover ratio (to three decimal places) for the last quarter of 1998 and the first three quarters of 1999.

6. On an overall basis, did the initially reported numbers or the restated numbers present Aurora in a better light? Of the financial statement users mentioned earlier in this chapter in Exhibit 5.1, which would be most influenced by this impact on the asset turnover ratio?

7. Using the initially reported numbers, calculate the net profit margin ratio (reported as a percentage to one decimal place) at the end of each quarter.

8. Using the restated numbers, calculate the net profit margin ratio (reported as a percentage to one decimal place) at the end of each quarter.

9. On an overall basis, did the initially reported numbers or the restated numbers present Aurora in a better light? Of the financial statement users mentioned earlier in this chapter in Exhibit 5.1, which would be most influenced by this impact on the net profit margin ratio?

10. What important role(s) did Aurora's auditors play in this case?

11. Based on specific information in the case, identify the incentives or goals that might have led the CFO to misreport Aurora's financial results. Looking back at the consequences of her dishonest actions, did she fulfill those goals in the short run and long run? Speculate about how the requirements of the Sarbanes-Oxley Act of 2002 might have affected the CFO, had this legislation existed prior to 1998.

S5-5 Ethical Decision Making: A Mini-Case

LO2, LO4, LO5, LO6

Assume you've been hired to replace an accounting clerk for a small public company. After your second month on the job, the chief financial officer (CFO) approached you directly with a "special project." The company had just finished installing a new production line earlier in the year, and the CFO wanted you to go through all of the company's expense accounts with the goal of finding any costs that might be related to the machinery's installation or to "tinkering with it" to get the line working just right. He said that the previous accounting clerk, whom you had replaced, didn't understand that these costs should have been recorded as part of the production line (an asset) rather than as expenses of the period. The CFO indicated that there was some urgency, as the company had to finalize its quarterly financial statements so that they could be filed with the SEC. Also, the company was close to violating its loan covenants and it needed a few extra dollars of profit this quarter to ensure the bank didn't demand immediate repayment of the loan. As you thought about this situation, you tried to remember what Chapter 2 in your accounting textbook said regarding the key characteristics of assets.

Required:

1. Which of the three ratios discussed in this chapter (debt-to-assets, asset turnover, and net profit margin) are affected by the decision to record costs as an asset rather than an expense? Indicate whether each ratio will be higher or lower if costs are recorded as an asset rather than an expense.

2. Is there anything in the case that makes you uncomfortable with the work that you've been asked to do?

3. What should you do? Explain and justify your position in a written memo addressed to the CFO.

LO2, LO6
Callaway Golf

S5-6 Critical Thinking: Analyzing Income Statement-Based Executive Bonuses

Callaway Golf believes in tying executives' compensation to the company's performance as measured by accounting numbers. Suppose, in a recent year, Callaway had agreed to pay its executive officers bonuses of up to 60 percent of base salary provided that (a) *asset turnover* meets or exceeds 0.8, and (b) *net profit margin* meets or exceeds 5.0%. Callaway's income statement for 2005 is presented here.

CALLAWAY GOLF COMPANY Income Statement Year Ended December 31, 2005 (in thousands of U.S. dollars)	
Sales revenues	$998,093
Cost of sales	583,679
Selling expenses	290,074
General and administrative	80,145
Research and development expenses	26,989
Total operating expenses	980,887
Income from operations	17,206
Interest expense	2,279
Other expenses	390
Income before income tax expense	14,537
Income tax expense	1,253
Net income	$ 13,284

Callaway executives receive bonuses if *asset turnover* meets (or exceeds) 0.8 and *net profit margin* meets (or exceeds) 5.0 percent. Their bonuses are even larger if asset turnover meets (or exceeds) 1.6 and net profit margin meets (or exceeds) 7.0 percent. Total assets were $735,737 (thousand) and $764,498 (thousand) at December 31, 2004 and 2005, respectively.

Required:

1. Use the preceding information to determine whether Callaway executives met the two bonus targets in 2005.

2. Explain why the bonus arrangement might be based on both *asset turnover* and *net profit margin* ratios, rather than just one of these two ratios.

LO5, LO6
Hershey Foods Corporation

Wm. Wrigley Jr. Company

www.mhhe.com/phillips2e

S5-7 Computing, Charting, and Interpreting Time-Series and Cross-Sectional Analyses

Assume that *Candy Industry Magazine* has contracted you to write an article discussing the financial status of Hershey Foods Corporation over the last few years. The editor suggests that your article should also compare Hershey's recent financial performance to competitors like Tootsie Roll Industries and gum-maker Wm. Wrigley Jr. You gather the following information from the three companies' 10-Ks (all have December 31 year-ends).

(in millions of U.S. dollars)	Hershey Foods Corporation			Tootsie Roll Industries	Wm. Wrigley Jr. Company
	Year 1	Year 2	Year 3	Year 3	Year 3
Total liabilities	$2,100	$2,109	$2,302	$128	$ 700
Total assets	3,247	3,481	3,583	665	2,520
Sales revenues	4,137	4,120	4,172	393	3,069
Net income	207	403	458	65	446

Required:

Enter the above information into a spreadsheet and perform the following analyses:

1. *Time-series analysis:* Demonstrate the changes in Hershey's size over the three years by charting its total liabilities, total assets, sales revenues, and net income.

2. *Cross-sectional analysis:* Demonstrate the size of Hershey relative to Tootsie Roll and Wm. Wrigley Jr. by charting the three companies' total liabilities, total assets, sales revenues, and net income for Year 3.

3. *Ratio analysis:* Compare the performance of Hershey relative to Tootsie Roll and Wm. Wrigley Jr. by computing the debt-to-assets and net profit margin ratios for Year 3.

Although you're confident you can use a spreadsheet to complete the ratio analyses, you realize you'll need Owen's help with the charting to be done in the time-series and cross-sectional analyses. Here's his reply.

From:	Owentheaccountant@yahoo.com
To:	Helpme@hotmail.com
Cc:	
Subject:	Excel Help

I can imagine that the readers of Candy Industry Magazine are on a constant sugar rush, so that's a great idea to present the time-series and cross-sectional analyses in easily digested charts. Using the charting function in Excel isn't too difficult. The first thing to do is enter the data into a spreadsheet exactly as it appears in the table. Next, display the chart toolbar by clicking on View/Toolbar/Chart.

To produce the time-series chart, click on the cell containing Hershey's Year 3 total liabilities and drag to the cell containing Hershey's Year 1 net income. With these cells selected, click on the 3D column chart icon to chart the data. You can change the layout by clicking on the chart and then Chart/Source Data in the pull-down menu. Click on the Data Range tab to indicate whether the data are presented as columns or rows in your spreadsheet (select Columns). To add labels, click on the Series tab, select each series one at a time, and enter a name for each (Series1 should be named Year 3). Before you close the box, click on the icon beside the "Category (X) axis labels:" which will take you back to your spreadsheet. Once there, select the financial statement category names by clicking on the name "total liabilities" and dragging to "net income." After selecting these cells, hit enter on the keyboard. If you followed these directions exactly, you should have a decent looking time-series chart. Play around with the appearance by selecting 3-D View from the Chart pull-down menu. Follow these same basic steps to produce the cross-sectional chart.

6

Internal Control and Financial Reporting for Cash and Merchandising Operations

**THAT WAS
THEN**

Earlier chapters have focused on companies whose operating activities relate to providing services to customers, rather than selling goods.

LP6

During a long night of studying, there's nothing like a revitalizing snack to perk you up, right? Imagine your disappointment if you went to snack on a stack of Pringles™ chips but discovered the container was empty. How could this have happened? Did you forget that you already ate them, or did someone pilfer them? Oh well, there's always the yogurt you've got in the fridge. Oh wait, it's moldy. Looks like you'll have to go to the ATM so you can buy more goodies at a nearby convenience store. But what if you found that someone had emptied almost all of your bank account last month? What an unpleasant surprise that would be! All of these problems could have been avoided had you exercised tighter control over your day-to-day activities.

Good controls also are needed by every business, ranging from small 7-Eleven stores to massive Wal-Mart supercenters. At a very basic level, these businesses face many of the same potential problems as you did in our opening example. They need to ensure they have inventory on hand to meet their customers' needs, but they don't want too much inventory hanging around because it can become spoiled, stale, damaged, obsolete, or stolen before it is sold to customers. To combat these potential problems, most businesses use special accounting systems to track and control inventory purchases and sales. These companies also implement strict controls to monitor their cash levels because, like many inventory items, cash is easy to carry and ready to use—two features that make it attractive to thieves. We'll discuss some common controls in this chapter, which will help you to gain a better understanding of how business operations are managed. It also should give you some useful ideas on how to ensure that your own snacks and cash don't unknowingly disappear.

THIS IS
NOW

This chapter focuses on companies that sell merchandise to customers, and the way they control and report their operating results.

Seventeen years after the company was founded, Wal-Mart rang up yearly sales of one billion dollars. Fourteen years later, it sold that much in a week. Eight years after that, Wal-Mart's sales reached a billion in one day.[1] With its trucks transporting 50 million pallets of goods and its greeters welcoming over 100 million customers every week,[2] Wal-Mart needs state-of-the-art accounting systems to track its inventory purchases and sales and to ensure the cash related to these activities is properly recorded in its accounts. In this chapter, you will learn about unique aspects of operating a merchandising company like Wal-Mart and systems that control operating activities. You'll also learn what to look for in a merchandiser's financial statements. Here's your chapter outline.

ORGANIZATION OF THE CHAPTER

Understand the business	Study the accounting methods	Evaluate the results	Review the chapter
• Operating cycles • Internal control	• Controlling and reporting cash • Controlling and reporting inventory purchases and sales transactions	• Gross profit analysis	• Demonstration case • Chapter summary • Key terms • Practice material

Understand the Business

Learning Objective 1
Distinguish service, merchandising, and manufacturing operations.

OPERATING ACTIVITIES AND CYCLES

Based on their operating activities, businesses can be classified into three types: **(1) service companies, (2) merchandising companies,** and **(3) manufacturing companies.** As Exhibit 6.1 shows, these businesses involve slightly different operating cycles. An operating cycle is the series of activities that a company undertakes to generate sales and, ultimately, cash. The operating cycle for service companies, like Supercuts hair salons and WorldGym fitness clubs, is simple: use cash to provide services that are sold to customers and then collect cash from those customers. The operating cycle for merchandising companies has an additional step: use cash to buy inventory, then sell the inventory to customers and collect cash from those customers. Manufacturing companies, like Ford and Mattel, sell physical products, too. But rather than acquire these in a ready-to-sell format, like a merchandiser, manufacturing companies make their own products from raw materials.

This chapter focuses on merchandising companies. When talking about merchandising companies, most businesspeople refer to two specific subcategories: retail merchandising companies that sell directly to consumers, as Wal-Mart and Old Navy do, and wholesale merchandising companies, like The Pampered Chef, that sell to retail

YOU SHOULD KNOW

A **service company** sells services rather than physical goods. A **merchandising company** sells goods that have been obtained from a supplier. A **manufacturing company** sells goods that it has made itself.

Video 6.1

---

[1] "The 2002 Fortune 500," *Fortune.com*, March 31, 2002.

[2] "Lord of the Things," *Business 2.0* magazine, March 1, 2002.

EXHIBIT 6.1 Operating Cycles for Service, Merchandising, and Manufacturing Companies

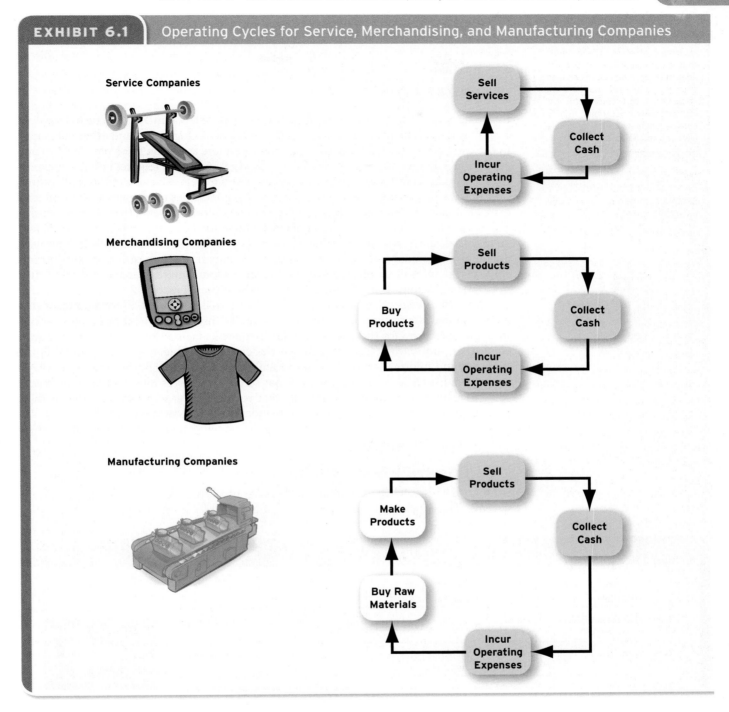

Service Companies

Sell Services → Collect Cash → Incur Operating Expenses →

Merchandising Companies

Buy Products → Sell Products → Collect Cash → Incur Operating Expenses →

Manufacturing Companies

Buy Raw Materials → Make Products → Sell Products → Collect Cash → Incur Operating Expenses →

businesses who in turn sell to end consumers. The discussion in this chapter applies equally to retail and wholesale merchandisers.

As Exhibit 6.1 suggests, the accounting processes that you learned in earlier chapters for service companies continue to apply to merchandising companies. The big difference is that you'll now be learning about how companies account for purchases and sales of products. Unlike services, which can't really be "stored up" for future sale, products can be acquired for future sale. These stored products, called *inventory*, create many of the new accounting issues that you'll learn about in this chapter.

Despite the differences in operating activities shown in Exhibit 6.1, all types of companies share one thing in common: to be successful, they have to be in control of

Learning Objective 2
Explain common principles of internal control.

Video 6.2

their operations. In other words, they must be able to achieve what they set out to do and avoid problems and surprises along the way. To achieve this state of control, companies include as part of their operating activities a variety of procedures and policies that are referred to as **internal controls.**

INTERNAL CONTROLS

Internal control has always been an important part of companies of all sizes. However, with the business failures and accounting scandals involving Enron and other companies in the early 2000s, internal control is gaining a lot more attention these days. As you may recall from Chapter 5, the Sarbanes-Oxley (SOX) Act of 2002 requires public companies to report on and have an independent auditor assess the effectiveness of internal controls over financial reporting. These new rules have led companies to strengthen their internal controls and better inform financial statement users about how effective their accounting systems are in producing accurate financial statements. Effective internal controls play an essential role in creating an ethical business environment and ultimately in improving financial performance. One study found that companies emphasizing strong internal control and an ethical culture grew their revenues four times faster and increased their stock prices 12 times as much as companies without these practices.[3]

From the perspective of a CEO or CFO, internal control is a broad concept that includes much more than accounting. It includes instilling ethical principles, setting strategic objectives for the company, identifying risks facing the company, hiring good employees, motivating them to achieve the company's objectives, and providing the resources and information they need to fulfill those objectives. Rather than overwhelm you with a list of 20 control principles that senior executives must think about,[4] we're going to focus on just five basic principles that you're likely to see as an employee working deeper within a company. We want you to understand why certain types of controls exist so that when you encounter them during your career, you are able to appreciate them and ensure others respect them.

Principles of Internal Control

Exhibit 6.2 presents five principles of internal control that are used to design accounting systems. These principles are applied to all aspects of a company's business activities,

EXHIBIT 6.2	Common Principles of Internal Control

Principle	Explanation	Examples
1. Establish responsibility	Assign each task to only one employee.	Each Wal-Mart cashier uses a different cash drawer.
2. Segregate duties	Do not make one employee responsible for all parts of a transaction.	Wal-Mart cashiers, who ring up sales, do not also approve price changes.
3. Restrict access	Do not provide access to assets or information unless it is needed to fulfill assigned responsibilities.	Wal-Mart secures videogames, cash, and its own computer systems (passwords, firewalls).
4. Document procedures	Prepare documents to show activities that have occurred.	Wal-Mart pays suppliers using pre-numbered checks.
5. Independently verify	Check others' work.	Wal-Mart compares cash balances in its accounting records to the cash balances reported by its bank, and accounts for any differences.

---

[3] "Corporate Culture and Performance," by J.P. Kotter and J.L. Heskett, New York: Maxwell MacMillan International.

[4] These 20 principles are outlined in "Internal Control for Financial Reporting—Guidance for Smaller Public Companies," published June 2006 at www.coso.org by The Committee of Sponsoring Organizations (COSO).

such as human resource management, finance, and marketing, but our focus here is on those that relate to merchandising operations. We should mention that other control principles and many, many examples exist. We can't possibly cover them all, so in this chapter, we give a few examples to show how merchandisers apply the basic principles to activities involving cash, purchases, and sales of inventory. Other internal controls will be discussed in later chapters and in advanced courses in accounting and management.

1. Establish Responsibility   Assign each task to only one employee because it allows you to determine who caused any errors or thefts that occur. That's the reason Wal-Mart assigns a separate cash register drawer to each employee at the beginning of a shift. If two cashiers were to use the same drawer, it would be impossible to know which cashier caused the drawer to be short on cash. With only one person responsible for putting money in and taking money out of the drawer, there's no doubt about who is responsible for a cash shortage.

2. Segregate Duties   **Segregation of duties** involves assigning responsibilities so that one employee can't make a mistake or commit a dishonest act without someone else knowing it. That's why cashiers at Wal-Mart need a manager to approve price changes at the checkout. Without this control, cashiers could ring up a sale, collect cash from the customer, and later reduce the amount of the sale and pocket the excess cash without anyone knowing. Segregation of duties is most effective when responsibilities for related activities are assigned to two or more people and when responsibilities for recordkeeping are assigned to people who do not also handle the assets that they are accounting for. One employee should not initiate, approve, record, and have access to the items involved in a transaction.

> **YOU SHOULD KNOW**
>
> **Segregation of duties** is an internal control that is designed into the accounting system. It involves separating employees' duties so that the work of one person can be used to check the work of another person.

To segregate duties in an effective way, a company should:

1. Never have one individual responsible for initiating, approving, and recording any given transaction, and
2. Separate the responsibility of physically handling assets from the process of recording transactions related to those assets.

3. Restrict Access   Some controls involve rather obvious steps like physically locking up valuable assets (such as Wal-Mart's inventory of video games) and electronically securing access to other assets and information (such as requiring a password to open a cash register or installing a firewall on the computer system). Access should be provided on an as-needed basis. If it's not needed to fulfill your assigned responsibilities, you should be denied access to it.

4. Document Procedures   Documents are such a common part of business that you might not realize they actually represent an internal control. By documenting each business activity, a company creates a record of whether goods have been shipped, customers billed, cash received, and so on. Without documents, a company wouldn't know what transactions have already been or still need to be entered into its accounting system. To enhance this control further, most companies assign a sequential number to each document and then check at the end of every accounting period that each document number corresponds to one, and only one, entry in the accounting system. So the next time you get a movie ticket from your local AMC Theater, a bill for cable services from Time Warner, or an electronic receipt from PayPal, you should realize that these represent important internal controls.

5. Independently Verify   Independent verification can occur in various ways. The most obvious is to hire someone (an internal auditor) to check that the work done by others within the company is appropriate and supported by documentation. Independent verification also can be made part of a person's job. For example, before Wal-Mart issues a check to pay the bill for a truckload of merchandise, a clerk first verifies that the bill relates to goods actually received and is calculated correctly. A final form of independent verification involves comparing the company's accounting information to information kept by an independent third party. This commonly occurs when the company's cash records are compared to a statement of account issued by a bank. This procedure, called a *bank reconciliation,* is demonstrated in the next section.

Limitations of Internal Control

One thing to be aware of is that it's impossible for internal controls to prevent and detect all errors and fraud. People can make mistakes when performing control procedures, work together (collude) to get around particular controls, or even disarm (override) controls.

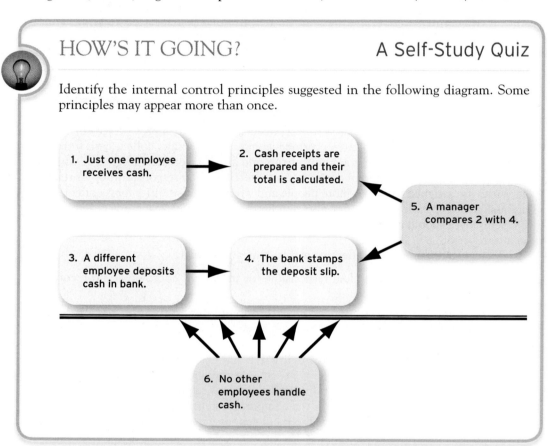

HOW'S IT GOING?   A Self-Study Quiz

Identify the internal control principles suggested in the following diagram. Some principles may appear more than once.

1. Just one employee receives cash.

2. Cash receipts are prepared and their total is calculated.

5. A manager compares 2 with 4.

3. A different employee deposits cash in bank.

4. The bank stamps the deposit slip.

6. No other employees handle cash.

Quiz Answers
1. Establish responsibility
2. Document procedures
3. Segregation of duties
4. Document procedures
5. Independent verification
6. Restrict access

Study the Accounting Methods

CONTROLLING AND REPORTING CASH

Every type of company—service, merchandising, and manufacturing—keeps tight control over its cash. You probably use some of the same cash controls that many companies use, without even knowing it. Go ahead, fill in the following checklist, and we'll tell you how you're doing.

Do You . . .	Yes	No
Keep a limited supply of cash on hand?	☐	☐
Prevent others from writing checks against your bank account?	☐	☐
Regularly account for differences between the balance in your checkbook and the balance on your bank statement?	☐	☐

If you're like most people, you probably answered yes to the first two questions, and no to the third. Unfortunately, this is one instance where two out of three is bad. The process of accounting for differences between your cash records and your bank's records is called "reconciling," and it is one of the most important of all cash controls. By preparing a **bank reconciliation,** you can identify differences that exist between your records and those kept by someone independent of you, which essentially means it's a way to double-check the accuracy of what you've recorded. Businesses consider bank reconciliations so important that they prepare a new one every month. You should, too. In the remainder of this section, we'll show you how.

Need for Reconciliation

A bank reconciliation involves comparing your own cash records to your bank's statement of account to see whether the records are in agreement. If your records agree with the bank's, you're done. You're concerned only with looking into differences. Your records can differ from your bank's records for two basic reasons: (1) you've recorded some items in your records that the bank doesn't know about at the time it prepares your statement of account, or (2) the bank recorded some items in its records that you don't know about until you read your bank statement. Examples of these differences are summarized in Exhibit 6.3 and are discussed below.

1. Bank errors. Bank errors happen in real life just like they do in Monopoly®. If you discover a bank error, you'll need to ask the bank to correct its records, but you needn't change yours.

2. Time lags. Time lags are very common. A time lag occurs, for example, when you make a deposit after the bank's normal business hours. *You* know you've made the deposit, but your bank doesn't know until it processes the deposit the next day. Time lags involving deposits are called *deposits in transit*. Another common time lag is an outstanding check. This occurs when you write and mail a check to a company, but your bank doesn't find out about it until that company deposits the check in its own bank, which then notifies your bank. As you will see later, deposits in transit and outstanding checks are a significant part of a bank reconciliation but they do not require any further action on your part.

3. Interest deposited. You may know that your bank pays interest to you, but you probably don't know exactly how much interest you'll get because it varies depending on the average balance in your account during that month. When you read your bank statement, you'll learn how much interest to add to your records.

4. Electronic funds transfer (EFT). It doesn't happen every day, but occasionally funds may be transferred into or out of your account without you knowing about it. If you discover these electronic transfers on your bank statement, you'll need to adjust your records.

5. Service charges. These are amounts the bank charges you for processing your transactions. Rather than send a bill to you and wait for you to pay it, the bank just takes the amount directly out of your account. You'll need to reduce your records for these charges.

YOU SHOULD KNOW

A **bank reconciliation** is an internal report prepared to verify the accuracy of both the bank statement and the cash accounts of a business or individual.

Learning Objective 3
Perform the key control of reconciling cash to bank statements.

Topic Tackler

PLUS

Check out www.mhhe.com/phillips2e for audio, visual, and PowerPoint presentations on this topic.

EXHIBIT 6.3 Reconciling Differences

Your Bank May Not Know About	You May Not Know About
1. Errors made by the bank	3. Interest the bank has put into your account
2. Time lags	4. Electronic funds transfer (EFT)
a. Deposits that you made recently	5. Service charges taken out of your account
b. Checks that you wrote recently	6. Customer checks you deposited but that bounced
	7. Errors made by you

 **COACH'S TIP**

You'll only need to adjust your cash records for items that appear on the right-hand side of this table.

6. Bounced checks. These are checks that you have previously deposited in your bank account but are later rejected by your bank because the check writer did **not** have **sufficient funds** to cover the check. Because the bank increased your account when you first deposited the check, the bank will decrease your account when it discovers it was not a valid deposit. You will need to reduce the cash balance in your records for these bounced checks, and you'll have to try once again to collect the amount still owed to you by the check writer.

7. Your errors. These are mistakes that you've made or amounts that you haven't yet recorded in your checkbook, such as those ATM slips that you didn't get around to recording before they went through the wash. You'll now have to adjust your records for these items.

The Bank Statement

Before we get into the nitty gritty of how you can prepare a bank reconciliation, let's look at what a typical bank statement reports. Exhibit 6.4 presents a typical bank statement for Wonderful Merchandise and Things (WMT).

Bank Reconciliation

Usually, the ending cash balance as shown on the bank statement does not agree with the ending cash balance shown by the related Cash account on the books of the company.

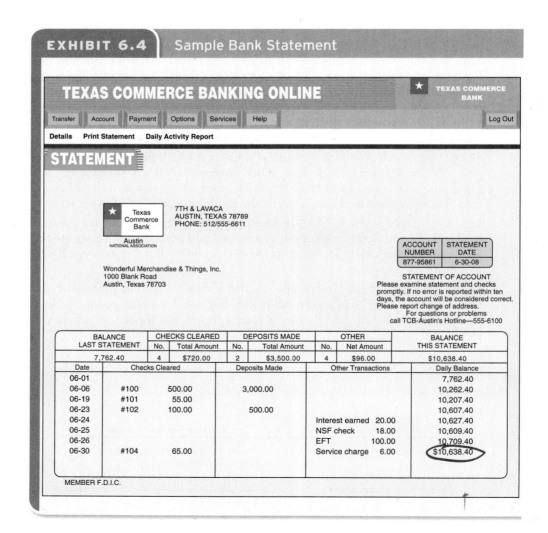

EXHIBIT 6.4   Sample Bank Statement

For example, the Cash account of WMT at the end of June might contain the information shown in the T-account.

dr +	Cash (A)			cr −
June 1 balance	7,762.40			
June 6 deposit	3,000.00	500.00	Check #100 written June 4	
June 23 deposit	500.00	55.00	Check #101 written June 17	
June 30 deposit	1,800.00	100.00	Check #102 written June 20	
		145.00	Check #103 written June 24	
		56.00	Check #104 written June 30	
		815.00	Check #105 written June 30	
Ending balance	11,391.40			

The $10,638.40 ending cash balance shown on the bank statement (Exhibit 6.4) differs from WMT's ending cash balance of $11,391.40. To determine the appropriate cash balance, these balances need to be reconciled. Exhibit 6.5 shows the bank reconciliation prepared by WMT for the month of June. The completed reconciliation finds that the up-to-date cash balance is $11,478.40, an amount that differs from both the bank's statement and WMT's accounting records. This balance is the amount that WMT will report as Cash on its balance sheet after adjusting its records with the journal entries that we present later.

To prepare the bank reconciliation in Exhibit 6.5, WMT compared the entries in its Cash account to the bank statement (Exhibit 6.4) with the following goals:

1. Identify the deposits in transit. A comparison of WMT's recorded deposits with those listed on the bank statement revealed that WMT made a deposit of $1,800 on June 30 that was not listed on the bank statement. More than likely, the bank will process this deposit the next business day (July 1). WMT doesn't have to change its records for this item because it already was in WMT's books on June 30. It is simply a timing difference so the amount is entered on the reconciliation as an addition to update the bank's records.

EXHIBIT 6.5 Sample Bank Reconciliation

June 30, 2008 Bank Reconciliation

Updates to Bank Statement			Updates to Company's Books	
Ending cash balance per bank statement		$10,638.40	Ending cash balance per books	$11,391.40
Additions			Additions	
(1) Deposit in transit		1,800.00	(3a) Interest received from the bank	20.00
		12,438.40	(3b) EFT received from customer	100.00
				11,511.40
Deductions				
(2) Outstanding checks:			Deductions	
# 103	145.00		(3c) NSF check of R. Smith	18.00
# 105	815.00	960.00	(3d) Bank service charges	6.00
Up-to-date ending cash balance		$11,478.40	(4) Error in recording check no. 104	9.00
			Up-to-date ending cash balance	$11,478.40

2. **Identify the outstanding checks.** A comparison of the checks listed on the bank statement with the company's record of written checks showed checks numbered 103 and 105 were still outstanding (had not been processed by the bank) at the end of June. They were entered on the reconciliation (in Exhibit 6.5) as a deduction from the bank account because the bank will eventually reduce the account balance when these checks clear the bank. (They've already been deducted from the company's cash records.) Similar to deposits in transit, outstanding checks arise only from timing differences. Neither the bank nor the company is wrong, but we do need to include these items in the bank reconciliation to compute an up-to-date ending cash balance.

3. **Record other transactions on the bank statement.**
   a. **Interest received** from the bank, $20—entered on the bank reconciliation in Exhibit 6.5 as an addition to the book balance because it's included in the bank balance but not yet in the company's books.
   b. **Electronic funds transfer** received from customer, $100—entered on the bank reconciliation as an addition to the book balance because it's included in the bank balance but not yet in the company's books.
   c. **NSF check** rejected, $18—entered on the bank reconciliation as a deduction from the book balance because it was deducted from the bank statement balance but not yet deducted from the company's cash records.
   d. **Service charges**, $6—entered on the bank reconciliation as a deduction from the book balance because it has been deducted from the bank balance but not yet removed from the Cash account in the company's books.

4. **Determine the impact of errors.** After performing the three steps listed above, WMT found that the reconciliation was out of balance by $9. Upon checking the journal entries made during the month, WMT found that check no. 104 was recorded in the company's accounts as $56 when, in fact, the check had been filled out for $65 (in payment of an account payable). As Exhibit 6.4 shows on page 242, the bank correctly processed the check (on June 30) as $65. To correct its own error, WMT must deduct $9 ($65 − $56) from the company's books side of the bank reconciliation.

COACH'S TIP

This example involves the company's error in recording the amount of the check. In other cases, the bank errs if it processes the check at the wrong amount. In all instances, the amount written on the check is the correct amount at which the transaction should be recorded.

Now that we know the up-to-date cash balance is $11,478.40, we need to prepare and record journal entries that will bring the Cash account to that balance. Remember that the entries on the Bank Statement side of the bank reconciliation do not need to be adjusted by WMT because they will work out automatically when the bank processes them next month. Only the items on the Company's Books side of the bank reconciliation need to be recorded in the company's records, using the following journal entries:

Interest Received:
(a)   dr Cash (+A).   20
          cr Interest Revenue (+R, +SE)   20
      To record interest received from the bank.

EFT Received:
(b)   dr Cash (+A).   100
          cr Accounts Receivable (−A)   100
      To record electronic funds transfer received from customer.

NSF Check Rejected:
(c)   dr Accounts Receivable (+A)   18
          cr Cash (−A).   18
      To record amount rejected by bank and still owed by customer.

Service Charges:
    (d)   *dr* Other Expenses (+E, −SE)   6
           cr Cash (−A)   6
        To record service charge deducted by bank.

Company Error:
    (e)   *dr* Accounts Payable (−L)   9
           cr Cash (−A)   9
        To correct error made in recording a check paid to a creditor.

HOW'S IT GOING?   A Self-Study Quiz

Indicate which of the following items discovered when preparing a bank reconciliation for Nordstrom will need to be recorded in the Cash account on the company's books.

1. Outstanding checks.
2. Deposits in transit.
3. Bank service charges.
4. NSF checks that were deposited.

Reporting Cash and Cash Equivalents   For financial statement reporting, "cash" includes **cash** deposited with banks as well as cash on hand (also called petty cash) and cash equivalents. **Cash equivalents** are short-term, highly liquid investments purchased within three months of maturity. They are considered equivalent to cash because they are both readily convertible to known amounts of cash and so near to maturity that there is little risk their value will change. In your personal life, cash equivalents could include checks you've received but not yet deposited into your bank account, or certificates of deposit (CDs) purchased within three months of maturity.

Ethical Insights

Granny Does Time

Grandmothers seem so trustworthy. But in one well-known case, a granny stole nearly half a million dollars from the small company where she worked as a bookkeeper. How did she do it? It was easy because the owner knew little accounting, so he gave her responsibility for all of the company's accounting work but never independently verified her work. Granny realized this lack of internal control gave her unlimited opportunity, so she wrote checks to herself and recorded them as inventory purchases. Then, when she did the bank reconciliation, she destroyed the checks to cover her tracks. Granny kept this fraud going for eight years, but then confessed after becoming overwhelmed with guilt. If you're wondering why no one ever became suspicious about the recorded inventory purchases that didn't actually occur, keep reading. The next section will tell you why.

CONTROLLING AND REPORTING INVENTORY TRANSACTIONS

Learning Objective 4
Explain the use of a perpetual inventory system as a control.

Merchandising companies spend a great deal of time and money tracking their inventory transactions because, after all, inventory management is vital in their business. A strong accounting system plays three roles in the inventory management process. First, it must provide up-to-date information on inventory quantities and costs, so that managers can make informed decisions. Second, it has to provide accurate information for preparing financial statements. Inventory is reported as an asset on the balance sheet until it is sold, at which time it is removed from the balance sheet and reported on the income statement as an expense called *cost of goods sold*. The third role for an inventory system is to provide information that controls inventory and helps protect it from theft. Companies use one of two types of inventory accounting systems: perpetual or periodic.

Perpetual Inventory System

YOU SHOULD KNOW

In a **perpetual inventory system**, the inventory records are updated "perpetually," that is, every time inventory is bought, sold, or returned. Perpetual systems often are combined with bar codes and optical scanners, as shown here.

In a **perpetual inventory system,** the inventory records are updated every time an item is bought, sold, or returned. You may not realize it, but the bar-code readers at Wal-Mart's checkouts serve two purposes: (1) they calculate and record the sales revenue for each product you're buying, and (2) they remove the product and its cost from Wal-Mart's inventory records. Similar scanners are used back in the "employees only" part of the store where products are unloaded from the trucks or returned to suppliers. As a result of this continual, or perpetual, updating on a transaction-by-transaction basis, the Inventory and Cost of goods sold accounts always contain updated balances.

Periodic Inventory System

YOU SHOULD KNOW

In a **periodic inventory system**, the inventory records are updated "periodically," that is, at the end of the accounting period. To determine how much merchandise has been sold, periodic systems require that inventory be physically counted at the end of the period, as shown here.

A **periodic inventory system** differs from a perpetual system in several ways, many of which we describe in detail later in this chapter. For now, however, the most important difference for you to understand is that, rather than update the inventory records immediately after each purchase and sale (as is done in a perpetual system), a periodic system updates the inventory records only at the end of the accounting period. Consequently, an accurate record of inventory on hand and inventory sold is not available during the period. To determine these amounts, the inventory has to be physically counted. This is what's going on at stores when they are "closed for inventory." This inventory count is then used to compute the correct balances for Inventory and Cost of goods sold, which are adjusted at the end of the period.

Inventory Control

The documentation of inventory transactions in a perpetual inventory system allows companies to keep just the right quantity of products on the shelves for the right amount of time. One study found that efficiencies related to Wal-Mart's perpetual inventory system accounted for over 50 percent of the productivity gains in general merchandise sales in the U.S. economy during 1995–99.[5] This unbelievable performance is likely to continue into the future, as the company adopts new microchip technologies that use radio waves to transmit data automatically from every inventory item that enters, moves within, exits, and later re-enters its stores.

---

[5] "Retail: The Wal-Mart Effect," *The McKinsey Quarterly*, no. 1 (2002).

Another benefit of a perpetual inventory system is that it allows managers to estimate *shrinkage,* which is the politically correct term for loss of inventory from theft, fraud, and error. This independent verification is important because a recent study suggests that over $37 billion of inventory went missing from U.S. retailers in 2005.[6]

You might wonder how companies can estimate how much of their inventory has gone missing, because isn't it, by definition, *missing*? Here's how they do it and how you can use a similar process to figure out if someone is swiping your stuff. It relies on knowing the kinds of transactions that are recorded in the inventory account.

1. Determine what's on hand at the beginning of the period.
2. Monitor every piece of inventory entering and exiting your stock during the period.
   a. Add purchases.
   b. Subtract goods sold.

   By perpetually tracking every movement, your inventory records should match exactly the amount of inventory on hand—unless items have been wrongfully removed.

3. Count the inventory to determine what's actually there. If your records say you have more on hand than what you counted, the difference is the amount of inventory shrinkage—items that have been removed without your permission.

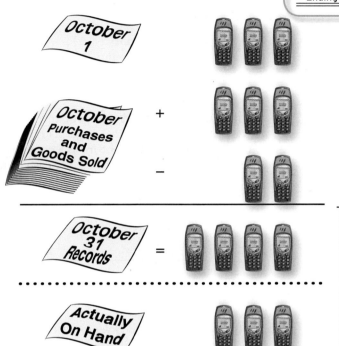

Notice that you can't do this kind of detective work with a periodic inventory system because it doesn't provide an up-to-date record of the inventory that should be on hand when you count it. Also note that, even if you're using a perpetual inventory system, you still need to count the inventory occasionally (at least yearly) to ensure the accounting records are accurate and that any shrinkage is detected. If you don't do this physical count, you could end up like the company in the Ethical Insights story on page 245. The grandmother was able to falsely record payments to herself as if they were inventory purchases because no one checked to see whether the recorded inventory actually existed.

Until recently, periodic inventory systems were commonly used because perpetual systems were too costly to implement. But now this technology has become so inexpensive and common that it's difficult for a merchandiser to survive in business today without using a perpetual system. To ensure you learn the latest in inventory accounting, the next section of this chapter focuses on the accounting process used in perpetual systems. It's possible that you could encounter a periodic system, particularly in smaller companies or large ones that have been slow to switch, so we do discuss the accounting process for periodic systems in the supplement at the end of this chapter.

Inventory Purchase and Sale Transactions

Purchases   In a perpetual system, all purchases of merchandise inventory are recorded directly into the Inventory account. As you learned in earlier chapters, most companies

> **COACH'S TIP**
>
> The process for determining shrinkage is based on the following relationship:
>
> Beginning Inventory
> + Purchases
> − Goods sold
> = Ending inventory

> **Learning Objective 5**
> Analyze purchase and sales transactions under a perpetual inventory system.

> **COACH'S TIP**
>
> Inventory includes only merchandise purchased for sale. Other purchases, such as supplies for internal use, are recorded in different accounts.

Shrinkage =

---

[6] "2005 National Retail Security Survey," Professor Richard Hollinger, University of Florida.

use credit rather than cash to purchase goods, so Accounts Payable usually is the other account affected. If Wal-Mart purchased $5,000 of DVDs on account, this transaction would be analyzed and recorded as follows.

1. Analyze

Assets	=	Liabilities		+ Stockholders' Equity
Inventory +5,000	=	Accounts Payable	+5,000	

2. Record

(b) dr Inventory (+A)   5,000
        cr Accounts Payable (+L)   5,000

COACH'S TIP

Any costs incurred after inventory is ready for sale (such as freight-out to deliver goods to customers) are considered selling expenses.

Transportation Cost A general principle is that a purchaser should include in Inventory any costs needed to get its inventory into a condition and location ready for sale. Transportation (freight-in) is a common example of additional costs to be included in inventory. If Wal-Mart pays $300 cash to a trucker who delivers goods to Wal-Mart, the additional cost of transporting the goods to Wal-Mart would be included in inventory, as shown below:[7]

1. Analyze

Assets	=	Liabilities	+ Stockholders' Equity
Cash −300	=		
Inventory +300			

2. Record

(b) dr Inventory (+A)   300
        cr Cash (−A)   300

YOU SHOULD KNOW

Purchase returns and allowances are a reduction in the cost of inventory purchases associated with unsatisfactory goods.

Purchase Returns and Allowances When goods purchased from a supplier arrive in damaged condition or do not meet specifications, the buyer can either return them for a full refund or keep them and ask for a cost reduction (called an *allowance*). These **purchase returns and allowances** are accounted for by reducing the cost of the inventory and recording the cash refund or the reduction in the liability owed to the supplier. For example, assume that Wal-Mart returned merchandise to its supplier and received a $400 reduction in the balance it owed. The transaction analysis and recording would be

1. Analyze

Assets	=	Liabilities		+ Stockholders' Equity
Inventory −400	=	Accounts Payable	−400	

2. Record

(b) dr Accounts Payable (−L)   400
        cr Inventory (−A)   400

---

[7] Although transportation costs are appropriately included in inventory, some companies record them in a separate account so that this information is readily available for decision-making purposes. For simplicity, we record all inventory-related costs (and credits) directly in the Inventory account.

Purchase Discounts When merchandise is bought on credit, terms such as 2/10, n/30 are sometimes specified. The 2/10 part means that if the purchaser pays within 10 days of the date of purchase, a 2 percent **purchase discount** is given off the purchaser's cost. Although 2 percent might seem small, if taken consistently on all purchases made throughout the year, it can add up to substantial savings. The n/30 part implies that if payment is not made within the 10-day discount period, the full amount is due 30 days after the purchase. If a purchaser fails to pay by the end of this credit period, interest will be charged, further credit can be denied, and "nice people" from a collection agency may contact the purchaser to collect the amount owed. Exhibit 6.6 illustrates a 2/10, n/30 purchase occurring on November 1.

YOU SHOULD KNOW

A **purchase discount** is a cash discount received for prompt payment of a purchase on account.

Topic Tackler

PLUS

Check out www.mhhe.com/phillips2e for audio, visual, and PowerPoint presentations on this topic.

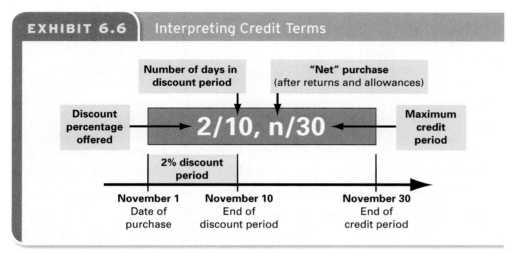

EXHIBIT 6.6	Interpreting Credit Terms

Number of days in discount period

"Net" purchase (after returns and allowances)

Discount percentage offered →

2/10, n/30

← Maximum credit period

2% discount period

November 1	November 10	November 30
Date of purchase	End of discount period	End of credit period

When a purchase discount is offered at the time of purchase, the purchaser accounts for it in two stages. Initially, the inventory purchase is accounted for at its full cost because at the time a company purchases goods, it's not clear whether it will take advantage of the purchase discount. Later, if payment is made within the discount period, the purchaser will reduce Inventory for the purchase discount because this discount, in effect, reduces the cost of the inventory. Let's work through an example of this together. You do the first part involving the initial purchase of $100,000 of inventory (in the Self-Study Quiz). If you need help, review how we accounted for the DVDs purchased at the beginning of this section, on page 248. We'll do the second part involving the analysis and recording of the purchase discount, assuming the purchaser pays within the discount period.

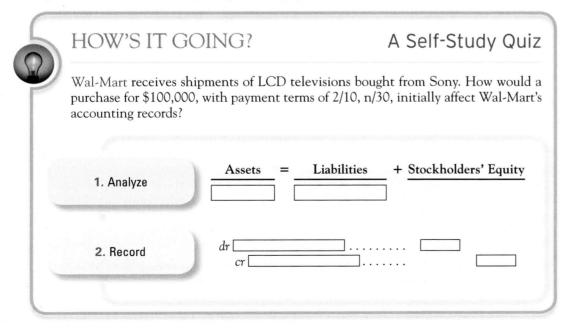

HOW'S IT GOING? A Self-Study Quiz

Wal-Mart receives shipments of LCD televisions bought from Sony. How would a purchase for $100,000, with payment terms of 2/10, n/30, initially affect Wal-Mart's accounting records?

1. Analyze

Assets	=	Liabilities	+ Stockholders' Equity

2. Record

dr [   ] . . . . [   ]
cr [   ] . . . . [   ]

Quiz Answers

Assets	=	Liabilities	+	Stockholders' Equity
Inventory +100,000		Accts. Payable +100,000		

dr Inventory (+A) 100,000
    cr Accounts Payable (+L) 100,000

If Wal-Mart takes advantage of the 2/10, n/30 purchase discount on the $100,000 purchase by paying within the 10-day discount period, the discount would effectively reduce the cost of the inventory purchased by $2,000 (= 2% × $100,000). This transaction would affect Wal-Mart's accounting records as follows:

1. Analyze

Assets	=	Liabilities	+ Stockholders' Equity
Cash −98,000	=	Accounts Payable −100,000	
Inventory −2,000			

2. Record

(b)   dr Accounts Payable (−L)   100,000
          cr Cash (−A)   98,000
          cr Inventory (−A)   2,000

If Wal-Mart paid after the 10-day discount period, it would not be eligible for the 2 percent discount, so it would pay the full $100,000 owed. This payment would be recorded as a decrease in Accounts Payable (debit) and a decrease in Cash (credit) for $100,000.[8]

Summary of Purchase-Related Transactions   You've now seen several types of purchase-related transactions. Before you learn how to account for sales of this merchandise, make sure you understand how these purchase-related transactions affect Inventory, as summarized in the T-account in Exhibit 6.7.

EXHIBIT 6.7	Effects of Purchase-Related Transactions

dr +	Inventory (A)			cr −
Bal. Fwd.	1,290,000			
Purchases	5,000			
Transportation	300	400	Purchase Returns and Allowances	
Purchases	100,000	2,000	Purchase Discounts	
Cost of Goods Available for Sale	1,392,900			

Sales   For all merchandisers, inventory is considered sold when ownership of the goods transfers to the customer. For a retail merchandiser like Wal-Mart, this transfer occurs when a customer buys the goods at the checkout. For a wholesale merchandiser, this transfer of ownership occurs at a time stated in a written sales agreement between the seller and the customer. Most sales agreements use one of two methods: (1) FOB shipping point—when the goods leave the *shipping* department at the seller's premises, or (2) FOB destination—when the goods reach their *destination* at the customer's premises.[9] For the

---

[8] An alternative approach to accounting for purchase discounts (called the net method) exists, but we leave that topic for discussion in intermediate accounting textbooks.

[9] FOB is a shipping acronym for "Free on Board."

examples in this textbook, we assume that ownership transfers when the goods leave the seller's premises (FOB shipping point).

In a perpetual system, two effects are recorded when inventory is sold:

1. Record the increase in Sales Revenue and corresponding increase in either Cash (if it is a cash sale) or Accounts Receivable (if the sale is made on credit).

2. Record a decrease in Inventory and corresponding increase in Cost of Goods Sold.

For example, assume Wal-Mart sells a Schwinn mountain bike for $225 cash when the cost of the bike to Wal-Mart was $175. This transaction is illustrated, analyzed, and recorded in Exhibit 6.8.

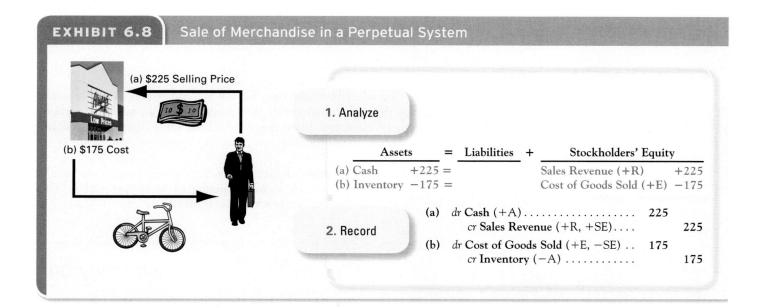

EXHIBIT 6.8   Sale of Merchandise in a Perpetual System

(a) $225 Selling Price

(b) $175 Cost

1. Analyze

Assets	=	Liabilities	+	Stockholders' Equity	
(a) Cash +225 =				Sales Revenue (+R)	+225
(b) Inventory −175 =				Cost of Goods Sold (+E)	−175

2. Record

(a) *dr* **Cash** (+A)................... 225
        cr **Sales Revenue** (+R, +SE)....   225

(b) *dr* **Cost of Goods Sold** (+E, −SE) .. 175
        cr **Inventory** (−A)   175

Notice in Exhibit 6.8 that the first part of Wal-Mart's journal entry involving Cash and Sales Revenue is recorded at the selling price ($225). The second part involving Cost of Goods Sold and Inventory uses Wal-Mart's cost ($175). The $50 difference between selling price and cost ($225 − 175) is called the *gross profit*. Gross profit is not directly recorded in an account by itself, but instead is a subtotal produced by subtracting the cost of goods sold from the selling price.

Sales Returns and Allowances   Sales returns and allowances are the same thing as purchase returns and allowances except that instead of looking at them from the purchaser's perspective, we're now seeing them from the seller's side. For example, suppose that after Wal-Mart sold the Schwinn mountain bike, it was returned to Wal-Mart. Assuming that the bike is still like new, Wal-Mart would refund $225 to the customer, take back the bike, and pretend the sale had never been made in the first place.

To allow its accounting records to reflect this, Wal-Mart would make two entries that basically reverse what this stellar seller recorded above when the bike was initially sold. We say "basically" because there is one catch: Wal-Mart will not directly reduce its Sales Revenue account. Instead, Wal-Mart will track sales returns and allowances in a contra-revenue account, which is deducted from total sales revenue. By using a contra-revenue account, rather than directly reducing the Sales account, Wal-Mart can track the amount of goods returned, which provides clues about whether customers are happy

YOU SHOULD KNOW

Sales returns and allowances are reductions given to customers after goods have been sold and found unsatisfactory.

 **COACH'S TIP**

Just as a contra-asset account (like Accumulated Depreciation in Chapter 4) reduces the total in an asset account (Equipment), a contra-revenue account (like Sales Returns and Allowances) is subtracted from the total in a revenue account (Sales Revenues).

with the quality and price of Wal-Mart's products.[10] To indicate that an increase in a contra-revenue account reduces revenues, which reduces stockholders' equity, use (+xR, −SE) as follows:

	Assets	= Liabilities +	Stockholders' Equity	
1. Analyze				
Cash	−225 =		Sales Returns & Allowances (+xR)	−225
Inventory	+175 =		Cost of Goods Sold (−E)	+175

2. Record

dr Sales Returns & Allowances (+xR, −SE)............	225	
cr Cash (−A)		225
dr Inventory (+A)	175	
cr Cost of Goods Sold (−E, +SE)...................		175

Sales Discounts

You already know that buyers are sometimes given purchase discounts to encourage them to pay promptly for purchases they've made on account. From the seller's point of view, these discounts are called **sales discounts.** Just like purchase discounts, sales discounts involve two parts: (1) the initial sale, and (2) the discount given for prompt payment.

Let's split up and use this as another chance for you to practice the part that you've already seen—accounting for the initial sale using a perpetual inventory system. We'll then show you how to account for the discount when it is taken.

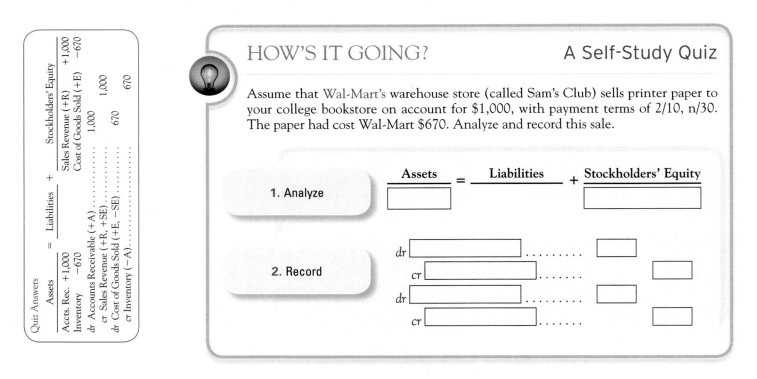

HOW'S IT GOING?   A Self-Study Quiz

Assume that Wal-Mart's warehouse store (called Sam's Club) sells printer paper to your college bookstore on account for $1,000, with payment terms of 2/10, n/30. The paper had cost Wal-Mart $670. Analyze and record this sale.

Quiz Answers

Assets	= Liabilities +	Stockholders' Equity	
Accts. Rec. +1,000		Sales Revenue (+R)	+1,000
Inventory −670		Cost of Goods Sold (+E)	−670

dr Accounts Receivable (+A)	1,000	
cr Sales Revenue (+R, +SE)		1,000
dr Cost of Goods Sold (+E, −SE)	670	
cr Inventory (−A).....................		670

---

[10] We have assumed that the return occurs in the same period as the sale. When significant returns are likely to occur after the period of sale, the seller records an estimate of those expected returns, using methods described in Chapter 8. We also have assumed the returned bike was as good as new. Chapter 7 describes how to account for damaged inventory.

If Wal-Mart receives the customer's $980 payment within the 10-day discount period ($980 = $1,000 − $20 discount), it would be accounted for as follows:

	Assets	=	Liabilities	+	Stockholders' Equity	
1. Analyze	Cash	+980			Sales Discounts (+xR)	−20
	Accounts Receivable	−1,000				

2. Record

dr Cash (−A) 980
dr Sales Discounts (+xR, −SE) 20
    cr Accounts Receivable (−A)   1,000

If the customer doesn't pay by the end of the discount period, Wal-Mart would not allow the customer to take a discount for early payment. Instead, the customer would have to pay the full $1,000, which Wal-Mart would record as an increase in Cash (debit) and a decrease in Accounts Receivable (credit). What if a customer doesn't pay at all? We discuss that important issue in detail in Chapter 8.

Before leaving the topic of sales discounts, we need to clear up a common misconception. Sales discounts differ from the discount that you get as a consumer buying clearance items at a reduced selling price. The sales discounts discussed in this chapter are given in business-to-business (B2B) transactions for prompt payment. We're sorry to say that, as a consumer, you're not likely to be offered this kind of discount.

COACH'S TIP

Sales discounts are calculated after taking into account any sales returns and allowances.

Summary of Sales-Related Transactions   The various sales-related transactions introduced in this section were recorded using contra-revenue accounts. Their effects on sales reporting are summarized in Exhibit 6.9.

As we discussed, the documentation procedure involving contra-revenue accounts acts as an internal control that allows managers to monitor and control how sales discounts, returns, and allowances affect the company's revenues. For example, if customers are frequently returning a product for being defective, it would show up as an increase in the Sales returns and allowances account. Upon seeing the increase, Wal-Mart's managers could decide to discontinue selling the product or find a new supplier for it.

LP6

Detailed information relating to sales discounts and returns is a key part of a merchandiser's business operations, so to avoid revealing these secrets to competitors, most companies report these contra-accounts only on internal financial statements, as shown in Exhibit 6.9. Externally reported income statements almost never report contra-revenue accounts. Instead, they just begin with Net sales. Despite this secrecy, external financial statement users can still conduct useful financial statement analyses, as we'll see in the next section.

EXHIBIT 6.9 | **Effects of Sales-Related Transactions**

Sales revenue.	$4,225
Less: Sales returns and allowances.	225
Sales discounts.	20
Net sales	3,980

Evaluate the Results

GROSS PROFIT ANALYSIS

One of the basic facts of merchandising is that goods have to be sold at a profit for a merchandiser to survive. Sure, cash has to be controlled, but the fact remains that there won't be much cash to control unless goods are sold at a profit. That's the only way companies like Wal-Mart can generate enough money to cover their operating expenses. To make it easy for financial statement users to see how much is earned from product sales, without being clouded by other operating costs, merchandise companies often present their income statement using a multistep format.

Chapter 5 introduced the idea of a multistep income statement, but in case you missed it or forgot what it is, we'll tell you now. A multistep income statement is similar to what you saw in the first few chapters, with expenses being subtracted from revenues to arrive at net income. The big difference is that a multistep format separates the revenues and expenses that relate to core operations from all the other (peripheral) items that affect net income. For merchandisers, a key measure is the amount of profit earned over the cost of goods sold, so their multistep income statements separate cost of goods sold from other expenses. As shown in Exhibit 6.10, this extra step produces a subtotal called **gross profit,** which is the amount the company earned from selling goods, over and above the cost of the goods. If you buy something for $70 and sell it for $100, you'll have a gross profit of $30.

Notice in Exhibit 6.10 that after the gross profit line, the multistep income statement presents other items in a similar format to what you saw for a service company in Chapter 3 (Exhibit 3.1). The category called *Selling, general, and administrative expenses* includes a variety of operating expenses including wages, utilities, advertising, and rent. These expenses are subtracted from gross profit to yield income from operations, which is a measure of the company's income from regular operating activities, before considering the effects of interest, income taxes, and any nonrecurring items.

EXHIBIT 6.10 Sample Multistep Income Statement

WAL★MART
ALWAYS LOW PRICES.
Always

WAL-MART STORES, INC.
Income Statements
Fiscal Years Ended January 31
(amounts in millions)

	2006	2005	2004
Net sales	$312,427	$285,222	$256,329
Cost of goods sold	240,391	219,793	198,747
Gross profit	72,036	65,429	57,582
Selling, general, and administrative expenses	53,506	48,338	42,557
Income from operations	18,530	17,091	15,025
Other expenses	1,172	986	832
Income before income taxes	17,358	16,105	14,193
Income tax expense	6,127	5,838	5,139
Net income	$ 11,231	$ 10,267	$ 9,054

Gross Profit Percentage

Let's focus again on the gross profit line on the income statement in Exhibit 6.10. Although the dollar amount of gross profit can be impressive—yes, Wal-Mart really did generate over $72 billion of gross profit in 2006—this number is difficult to interpret by itself. In Exhibit 6.10, we see that Wal-Mart's gross profit increased from 2004 to 2005 to 2006. The problem is that Wal-Mart also increased its sales over these three years, so we don't know whether the increase in gross profit dollars arises because Wal-Mart increased its sales volume or whether it is generating more profit per sale. To determine the amount of gross profit included in each dollar of sales, analysts typically evaluate the gross profit percentage.

	FINANCIAL ANALYSIS TOOLS	
Name of Measure	Formula	What It Tells You
Gross profit percentage	$\dfrac{(\text{Net Sales} - \text{COGS})}{\text{Net Sales}} \times 100$	• The percentage of profit earned on each dollar of sales, after considering the cost of products sold • A higher ratio means that greater profit is available to cover operating and other expenses

The **gross profit percentage** measures how much above cost a company sells its products. As discussed below, this ratio is used to (1) analyze changes in the company's operations over time, (2) compare one company to another, and (3) determine whether a company is earning enough on each sale to cover its operating expenses. A higher gross profit percentage means that the company is selling products for a greater markup over their cost.

As we can see in the graphic in the margin, Wal-Mart's gross profit percentage increased ever so slightly from 2004 through 2006. Each dollar of sales in 2006 included 23.1 cents of gross profit whereas in the prior two years, an average dollar of sales included 22.9 or 22.5 cents of gross profit. So not only did Wal-Mart sell more in 2006 than in the prior years, it also generated more profit per sale. How was this possible? To find out, you could read the Management's Discussion and Analysis section of Wal-Mart's annual report. You'd find out that Wal-Mart has been able to reduce inventory shrinkage and markdowns, which means more profit from each dollar of sales. You might wonder whether it's even worth talking about a gross profit percentage increase of only 0.6 from 2004 (22.5) to 2006 (23.1). Just remember that a small change in the gross profit percentage can lead to a big change in net income. In Wal-Mart's case, because the company has such a huge sales volume ($312 billion), even just one-tenth of a percentage point increase in gross profit translates into almost half a billion dollars. Yes, that's billion with a "b" ($312 billion × 0.001 = $0.3 billion).

YOU SHOULD KNOW

Gross profit percentage is a ratio indicating the percentage of profit earned on each dollar of sales, after considering the cost of products sold.

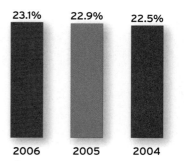

Gross Profit Percentage

Comparing Operating Results across Companies and Industries   Be aware that gross profit percentages can vary greatly between companies. Wal-Mart's gross profit percentage of 23.1 percent is characteristic of its slogan of selling at "Low Prices, Always." In contrast, Saks' high-end department stores carry fashions with high-end prices, ultimately producing a 37.5 percent gross profit percentage. These two companies represent the extremes, with the typical department store earning an average gross profit percentage of 28.1 percent. As Exhibit 6.11 shows, gross profit percentages can vary across industries too. Pharmaceutical companies recently reported an average gross profit percentage of 74.2 percent compared to the 15.2 percent reported by automakers. Of course, these across-industry differences are expected because drug companies need a higher gross profit percentage than carmakers because they have more research and development expenses to cover.

EXHIBIT 6.11 | Average Gross Profit Percentages

Merchandising Sector

Wal-Mart   22.1%

Other department stores   28.1%

Saks   37.5%

Manufacturing Sector

Automotive manufacturing 15.2%

Pharmaceutical and medicine manufacturing   74.2%

Source: Retrieved October 17, 2006, from Industry Center at http://www.investor.reuters.com/.

SUPPLEMENT: PERIODIC INVENTORY SYSTEM

As described in the main body of this chapter, a periodic inventory system updates the inventory records only at the end of the accounting period. Unlike the perpetual inventory system, a periodic system does not track the cost of goods sold during the accounting period. Instead, this information is determined by following a four-step process:

1. Determine beginning inventory. You get this simply by looking in the accounting records for last period's ending inventory balance.

2. Track this period's purchases. The cost of all transactions related to inventory is recorded in separate accounts called Purchases, Purchase Discounts, and Purchase Returns and Allowances.

3. Determine ending inventory. The number of units of inventory on hand at the end of the period is determined through an inventory count. These quantities are then multiplied by the cost of each unit to determine the cost of ending inventory.

4. Calculate the cost of goods sold. This step combines data from the first three steps to "force out" the cost of goods sold. You start with the cost of beginning inventory and add the cost of every piece of inventory that you bought during the period (net of any purchase discounts or purchase returns and allowances). The result is the cost of all of the goods that *could* have been sold during the period. If you sold everything, this would be the cost of goods sold. But you know that some of the goods weren't sold because you counted a bunch of items during the inventory count. So the cost of what you did sell is equal to the difference between what you could have sold and what you didn't sell. To illustrate, let's plug some hypothetical numbers into the cost of goods sold equation:

Beginning inventory		$ 2,000
+ Net purchases		
Purchases	$5,000	
− Purchase discounts	(10)	
− Purchase returns and allowance	(15)	4,985
Cost of goods available for sale		6,985
− Ending inventory		(1,000)
= Cost of goods sold		$ 5,985

The typical journal entries recorded in a periodic inventory system are presented below and contrasted with the entries that would be recorded in a perpetual inventory system. The effects of these journal entries on the accounting equation then are summarized. Note that the total effects are identical, and only the timing and nature of recording differs.

Assume, for this illustration only, that Wal-Mart stocks and sells only one item, the Iowna Clone Phone, and that only the following events occurred in 2007:

Jan. 1	Beginning inventory: 800 units, at unit cost of $50.
Apr. 14	Purchased: 1,100 additional units on account, at unit cost of $50.
Nov. 30	Sold: 1,300 units on account, at unit sales price of $83.
Dec. 31	Counted: 600 units, at unit cost of $50.

PERIODIC RECORDS	PERPETUAL RECORDS
A. Record purchases	**A. Record purchases**
April 14, 2007:	April 14, 2007:

dr Purchases (+A) (1,100 units at $50) 55,000
    cr Accounts Payable (+L) 55,000
	dr Inventory (+A) (1,100 units at $50) 55,000
	    cr Accounts Payable (+L) 55,000

B. Record sales (but not cost of goods sold)	**B. Record sales and cost of goods sold**
November 30, 2007:	November 30, 2007:

dr Accounts Receivable (+A) 107,900
    cr Sales Revenue (+R, +SE) (1,300 units at $83) .. 107,900
	dr Accounts Receivable (+A) 107,900
	    cr Sales Revenue (+R, +SE) (1,300 units at $83) .. 107,900

No cost of goods sold entry	dr Cost of Goods Sold (+E, −SE) .... 65,000 cr Inventory (−A) (1,300 units at $50) 65,000
C. Record end-of-period adjustments	**C. Record end-of-period adjustments**
At the end of the period, compute cost of goods sold using the four-step process and adjust the inventory accounts.	At the end of the accounting period, the balance in the Cost of goods sold account is reported on the income statement. It is not necessary to compute cost of goods sold because the Cost of goods sold account is up to date. Also, the Inventory account shows the ending inventory amount reported on the balance sheet. A physical inventory count is still necessary to assess the accuracy of the perpetual records and identify theft and other forms of shrinkage. Any shrinkage would be recorded by reducing the Inventory account and increasing an expense account (such as Inventory shrinkage or Cost of goods sold). This illustration assumes no shrinkage is detected.
1. Beginning inventory (last period's ending) $40,000	
2. Add net purchases 55,000	
Cost of goods available for sale 95,000	
3. Deduct ending inventory (physical count—600 units at $50) 30,000	
4. Cost of goods sold $65,000	No entry
December 31, 2007:	
Transfer beginning inventory and net purchases to cost of goods sold: (act *as if* all goods were sold)	

dr Cost of Goods Sold (+E, −SE) 95,000
    cr Inventory (−A) (beginning) 40,000
    cr Purchases (−A) 55,000	

Adjust the cost of goods sold by subtracting the amount of ending inventory still on hand: (recognize that not all goods were sold)	
dr Inventory (+A) (ending) .... 30,000 cr Cost of Goods Sold (−E, +SE) 30,000	

Assets	=	Liabilities	+	Stockholders' Equity		Assets	=	Liabilities	+	Stockholders' Equity
Purchases +55,000		Accounts Payable +55,000				Inventory +55,000		Accounts Payable +55,000		
Accts. Rec. +107,900				Sales Revenue +107,900		Accts. Rec. +107,900				Sales Revenue +107,900
Inventory −40,000				Cost of Goods Sold (+E) −95,000		Inventory −65,000				Cost of Goods Sold (+E) −65,000
Purchases −55,000										
Inventory +30,000				Cost of Goods Sold (+E) +30,000						
Totals +97,900		+55,000		+42,900		**Totals** +97,900		+55,000		+42,900

REVIEW THE CHAPTER

DEMONSTRATION CASE A

Kat Bardash, a student at a small state college, has just received her first checking account statement for the month ended September 30. This was her first chance to attempt a bank reconciliation. The bank's statement of account showed the following:

Bank balance, September 1	$1,150
Deposits during September	650
Checks cleared during September	900
Bank service charge	25
Interest earned	5
Bank balance, September 30	880

Kat was surprised that her bank had not yet reported the deposit of $50 she made on September 29 and was pleased that her rent check of $200 had not cleared her account. Her September 30 checkbook balance was $750.

Required:

1. Complete Kat's bank reconciliation. What adjustments, if any, does she need to make in her checkbook?
2. Why is it important for individuals and businesses to do a bank reconciliation each month?

Suggested Solution

1. Kat's bank reconciliation:

Updates to Bank Statement		Updates to Kat's Books	
September 30 cash balance	$880	September 30 cash balance	$750
Additions		Additions	
Deposit in transit	50	Interest earned	5
Deductions		Deductions	
Outstanding check	(200)	Bank service charge	(25)
Up-to-date cash balance	$730	Up-to-date cash balance	$730

Kat should increase her checkbook balance by $5 for the cash given by the bank for interest and reduce her checkbook balance by $25 for the cash given to the bank for service charges. In journal entry format, this would involve:

dr Cash (+A) 5
   cr Interest revenue (+R, +SE) 5

dr Other expenses (+E, −SE) 25
   cr Cash (−A) 25

2. Bank statements, whether personal or business, should be reconciled each month to help ensure that a correct balance is reflected in the depositor's books. Failure to reconcile a bank statement increases the chance that an error will not be discovered and may result in bad checks being written. Businesses reconcile their bank statements for an additional reason: The up-to-date balance that is calculated during reconciliation is reported on the balance sheet.

DEMONSTRATION CASE B

Assume Oakley, Inc.—the maker of sunglasses, goggles, and other products—made merchandise costing $137,200 and sold it on credit to Sunglass Hut for $405,000 with terms 2/10, n/30. Some of the merchandise differed from what Sunglass Hut had ordered, so Oakley agreed to give an allowance of $5,000. Sunglass Hut satisfied the remaining balance (of $400,000) by paying within the discount period.

Sunglass Hut

Required:

1. Assuming that both companies use perpetual inventory systems, prepare the journal entries that both Oakley and Sunglass Hut would use to record the following transactions:
   a. Sale from Oakley to Sunglass Hut.
   b. Allowance granted by Oakley.
   c. Payment made by Sunglass Hut to Oakley.
2. Compute Oakley's net sales, assuming that sales returns and allowances and sales discounts are treated as contra-revenues.
3. Compute Oakley's gross profit and gross profit percentage on the sale. Compare this ratio to the 68.4 percent gross profit percentage recently reported by the Luxottica Group—the Italian company that makes Killer Loop® and Ray-Ban® sunglasses, which are sold through its Sunglass Hut stores. What does it imply about the two companies?

> **COACH'S TIP**
>
> Transaction b depicts an allowance but no return of goods. Had goods been returned, Oakley also would increase its inventory and decrease its cost of goods sold.

Suggested Solution

1. Journal entries:
   a. Sale from Oakley to Sunglass Hut

Oakley		
dr Accounts Receivable (+A)......	405,000	
cr Sales Revenue (+R, +SE)....		405,000
dr Cost of Goods Sold (+E, −SE)...	137,200	
cr Inventory (−A)		137,200

Sunglass Hut		
dr Inventory (+A)...............	405,000	
cr Accounts Payable (+L)......		405,000

b. Allowance granted by Oakley

Oakley		
dr Sales Returns and Allowances (+xR, −SE)	5,000	
cr Accounts Receivable (−A) ...		5,000

Sunglass Hut		
dr Accounts Payable (−L)	5,000	
cr Inventory (−A)............		5,000

c. Payment made by Sunglass Hut to Oakley

Oakley		
dr Cash (+A)....................	392,000	
dr Sales Discounts (+xR, −SE)....	8,000	
cr Accounts Receivable (−A)....		400,000
($8,000 = $400,000 × 2%)		

Sunglass Hut		
dr Accounts Payable (−L)	400,000	
cr Cash (−A)................		392,000
cr Inventory (−A)............		8,000

2. Sales returns and allowances and sales discounts should be subtracted from sales revenue to compute net sales:

Sales revenue	$405,000
Less: Sales returns and allowances	5,000
Sales discounts [0.02 × (405,000 − 5,000)]	8,000
Net sales	392,000

3.   Gross profit and gross profit percentage are calculated as follows:

	In Dollars	Percent of Net Sales
Net sales (calculated in 2.)	$392,000	100.0 %
Less: Cost of goods sold	137,200	35.0 %
Gross profit	254,800	65.0 %

The 65% gross profit percentage indicates that Oakley generates 3.4 cents less gross profit on each dollar of sales than Luxottica (3.4 = 68.4 − 65.0). This difference implies that Luxottica is including a higher markup in its selling prices.

CHAPTER SUMMARY

LO1   Distinguish service, merchandising, and manufacturing operations. p. 236

- Service companies sell services rather than physical goods; consequently, their income statements show costs of services rather than cost of goods sold.

- Merchandise companies sell goods that have been obtained from a supplier. Retail merchandise companies sell directly to consumers whereas wholesale merchandise companies sell to retail companies.

- Manufacturing companies sell goods that they have made themselves.

LO2   Explain common principles of internal control. p. 238

- The concept of internal control is broad. Most employees working within a company will encounter five basic principles: (1) establish responsibility for each task; (2) segregate duties so that one employee cannot initiate, record, approve, and handle a single transaction; (3) restrict access to those employees who have been assigned responsibility; (4) document procedures performed; and (5) independently verify work done by others inside and outside the business.

LO3   Perform the key control of reconciling cash to bank statements. p. 241

- The bank reconciliation requires determining two categories of items: (1) those that have been recorded in the company's books but not in the bank's statement of account, and (2) those that have been reported in the bank's statement of account but not in the company's books. The second category of items provides the data needed to adjust the Cash records to the balance that will be reported on the balance sheet.

LO4   Explain the use of a perpetual inventory system as a control. p. 246

- Perpetual inventory systems protect against undetected theft because they provide an up-to-date record of inventory that should be on hand at any given time, which can be compared to a count of the physical quantity that actually is on hand.

- Perpetual inventory systems serve to promote efficient and effective operations because they are updated every time inventory is purchased, sold, or returned.

LO5   Analyze purchase and sales transactions under a perpetual inventory system. p. 247

- In a perpetual inventory system, the Inventory account is increased every time inventory is purchased. Inventory should include all costs, such as transportation-in, that are needed to get the inventory into a condition and location ready for sale.

- In a perpetual inventory system, the purchaser's Inventory account is decreased whenever the purchaser returns goods to the supplier or is given a discount for prompt payment.

- In a perpetual inventory system, two entries are made every time inventory is sold: one entry records the sale (and corresponding debit to cash or accounts receivable) and the other entry records the cost of the goods sold (and corresponding credit to inventory).
- Sales discounts and sales returns and allowances are reported as contra-revenues, reducing net sales.

Analyze a merchandiser's multistep income statement. p. 254   LO6

- One of the key items in a merchandiser's multistep income statement is gross profit, which is a subtotal calculated by subtracting cost of goods sold from net sales. The gross profit percentage is calculated and interpreted as follows.

Financial Analysis Tools		
Name of Measure	Formula	What It Tells You
Gross profit percentage	$\dfrac{(\text{Net Sales} - \text{COGS})}{\text{Net Sales}} \times 100$	• The percentage of profit earned on each dollar of sales, after considering the cost of products sold • A higher ratio means that greater profit is available to cover operating and other expenses

KEY TERMS

Bank Reconciliation p. 241
Cash p. 245
Cash Equivalents p. 245
Gross Profit (or Gross Margin) p. 254
Gross Profit Percentage p. 255
Internal Control p. 238

Manufacturing Company p. 236
Merchandising Company p. 236
NSF (Not Sufficient Funds) Check p. 242
Periodic Inventory System p. 246
Perpetual Inventory System p. 246

Purchase Discounts p. 249
Purchase Returns and Allowances p. 248
Sales Discounts p. 252
Sales Returns and Allowances p. 251
Segregation of Duties p. 239
Service Company p. 236

PRACTICE MATERIAL

QUESTIONS

1. What is the distinction between service and merchandising companies? What is the distinction between merchandising and manufacturing companies? What is the distinction between retail and wholesale merchandising companies?
2. From the perspective of a CEO or CFO, what does internal control mean?
3. What are five common internal control principles?
4. Why is it a good idea to assign each task to only one employee?
5. Why should responsibilities for certain duties, like cash handling and cash recording, be separated? What types of responsibilities should be separated?
6. What are some of the methods for restricting access?
7. In what ways does documentation act as a control?
8. In what ways can independent verification occur?
9. What are the three limitations of internal control?
10. What are the purposes of a bank reconciliation? What balances are reconciled?
11. Define *cash and cash equivalents*, and indicate the types of items that should be reported as cash and cash equivalents.

12. What is the main distinction between perpetual and periodic inventory systems? Which type of system provides better internal control over inventory? Explain why.

13. Why is a physical count of inventory necessary in a periodic inventory system? Why is it still necessary in a perpetual inventory system?

14. Describe how transportation costs to obtain inventory (freight-in) are accounted for by a merchandising company using a perpetual inventory system. Explain the reasoning behind this accounting treatment.

15. What is the distinction between *purchase returns and allowances* and *purchase discounts?*

16. What is a purchase discount? Use 1/10, n/30 in your explanation.

17. Describe in words the journal entries that are made in a perpetual inventory system when inventory is sold on credit.

18. Explain the difference between sales revenue and net sales.

19. Why are contra-revenue accounts used rather than directly deducting from the sales account (using a debit to sales)?

20. What is gross profit? How is the gross profit percentage computed? Illustrate its calculation and interpretation assuming net sales revenue is $100,000 and cost of goods sold is $60,000.

MULTIPLE CHOICE

Topic Tackler

PLUS

Quiz 6

Check out www.mhhe.com/phillips2e for more multiple choice questions.

1. Mountain Gear, Inc. buys bikes, tents, and climbing supplies from Rugged Rock Corporation for sale to consumers. What type of company is Mountain Gear, Inc.?
   a. Service
   b. Retail merchandiser
   c. Wholesale merchandiser
   d. Manufacturer

2. Which of the following does not enhance internal control?
   a. Assigning different duties to different employees.
   b. Ensuring adequate documentation is maintained.
   c. Allowing access only when required to complete assigned duties.
   d. None of the above—all enhance internal control.

3. Upon review of your company's bank statement, you discover that you recently deposited a check from a customer that was rejected by your bank as NSF. Which of the following describes the actions to be taken when preparing your company's bank reconciliation?

	Balance per Bank	Balance per Book
a.	Decrease	No change
b.	Increase	Decrease
c.	No change	Decrease
d.	Decrease	Increase

4. Upon review of the most recent bank statement, you discover that a check was made out to your supplier for $76 but was recorded in your Cash and Accounts payable accounts as $67. Which of the following describes the actions to be taken when preparing your bank reconciliation?

	Balance per Bank	Balance per Book
a.	Decrease	No change
b.	Increase	Decrease
c.	No change	Decrease
d.	Decrease	Increase

5. Which of the following is false regarding a perpetual inventory system?
   a. Physical counts are never needed since records are maintained on a transaction-by-transaction basis.
   b. The balance in the inventory account is updated with each inventory purchase and sale transaction.
   c. Cost of goods sold is increased as sales are recorded.
   d. The account Purchases is not used as inventory is acquired.

6. Purchase discounts with terms 2/10, n/30 mean
   a. 10 percent discount for payment within 30 days.
   b. 2 percent discount for payment within 10 days or the full amount (less returns) is due within 30 days.
   c. Two-tenths of a percent discount for payment within 30 days.
   d. None of the above.

7. Which of the following describes how payments to suppliers made within the purchase discount period are recorded in a perpetual inventory system (using the method shown in the chapter)?
   a. Reduce Cash, reduce Accounts Payable.
   b. Reduce Cash, reduce Accounts Payable, reduce Inventory.
   c. Reduce Cash, reduce Accounts Payable, increase Purchase Discounts.
   d. Reduce Cash, reduce Accounts Payable, decrease Purchase Discounts.

8. Which of the following is not a component of net sales?
   a. Sales returns and allowances.   c. Cost of goods sold.
   b. Sales discounts.   d. Sales revenue.

9. A $1,000 sale is made on May 1 with terms 2/10, n/30. Items with a $100 selling price are returned on May 3. What amount, if received on May 9, will be considered payment in full?
   a. $700   c. $882
   b. $800   d. $900

10. Earlier this year, your company negotiated larger purchase discounts when paying for its merchandise inventory, which it has consistently taken throughout the year. What effect will this factor have on the company's gross profit percentage this year, in comparison to last year?
    a. The ratio will not change.   c. The ratio will decrease.
    b. The ratio will increase.   d. Either b or c.

MINI-EXERCISES

Available with McGraw-Hill's Homework Manager — MANAGER PLUS

M6-1 Distinguishing among Operating Cycles   LO1

Identify the type of business as service (S), retail merchandiser (RM), wholesale merchandiser (WM), or manufacturer (M) for each of the following.

____ 1. The company reports no inventory on its balance sheet.

____ 2. The company's customers have been slow in paying their accounts because their own customers have been slow in paying.

____ 3. Approximately one-third of the company's inventory requires further work before it will be ready for sale.

____ 4. The company rarely extends credit to its customers when selling goods.

M6-2 Identifying Internal Controls over Financial Reporting   LO2

Fox Erasing has a system of internal control with the following procedures. Match the procedure to the corresponding internal control principle.

Procedure	Internal Control Principle
____ 1. The treasurer signs checks.	A. Establish responsibility.
____ 2. The treasurer is not allowed to make bank deposits.	B. Segregate duties.
____ 3. The company's checks are prenumbered.	C. Restrict access.
____ 4. Unused checks are stored in the vault.	D. Document procedures.
____ 5. A bank reconciliation is prepared each month.	E. Independently verify.

LO2   **M6-3 Identifying Internal Control Principles Applied by a Merchandiser**

Identify the internal control principle represented by each point in the following diagram.

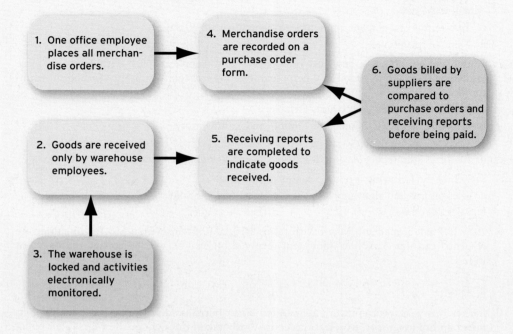

1. One office employee places all merchandise orders.

4. Merchandise orders are recorded on a purchase order form.

6. Goods billed by suppliers are compared to purchase orders and receiving reports before being paid.

2. Goods are received only by warehouse employees.

5. Receiving reports are completed to indicate goods received.

3. The warehouse is locked and activities electronically monitored.

LO3   **M6-4 Organizing Items on the Bank Reconciliation**

Indicate whether the following items would be added (+) or subtracted (−) from the company's books or the bank statement side of a bank reconciliation.

Reconciling Item	Bank Statement	Company's Books
a. Outstanding checks of $12,000		
b. Bank service charge of $15		
c. Deposit in transit of $2,300		
d. Interest earned of $5		

LO3   **M6-5 Preparing Journal Entries after a Bank Reconciliation**

Using the information in M6-4, prepare any journal entries needed to adjust the company's books.

LO4   **M6-6 Choosing between a Perpetual and Periodic Inventory System**

Nordstrom, Inc.   Nordstrom, Inc., started in business in 1901. It only took 100 years, but eventually the company changed from a periodic inventory system to a perpetual inventory system (in 2002). Write a brief report describing how this change is likely to improve the company's inventory control.

LO4   **M6-7 Calculating Shrinkage in a Perpetual Inventory System**

Corey's Campus Store has $50,000 of inventory on hand at the beginning of the month. During the month, the company buys $8,000 of merchandise and sells merchandise that had cost $30,000. At the end of the month, $25,000 of inventory is on hand. How much shrinkage occurred during the month?

LO5   **M6-8 Determining Inventory Cost in a Perpetual System**

Assume Anderson's General Store bought, on credit, a truckload of merchandise from American Wholesaling costing $23,000. If the company was charged $650 in transportation cost by National Trucking, immediately returned goods to American Wholesaling costing $1,200, and then took advantage of AmericanWholesaling's 2/10, n/30 purchase discount, how much should Anderson's report as the cost of inventory?

M6-9 Preparing Journal Entries for Purchases, Purchase Discounts, and Purchase Returns Using a Perpetual System

LO5

Using the information in M6-8, prepare journal entries to record the inventory transactions, assuming Anderson's uses a perpetual inventory system.

M6-10 Recording Journal Entries for Purchases and Sales Using a Perpetual Inventory System

LO4, LO5

Inventory at the beginning of the year cost $13,400. During the year, the company purchased (on account) inventory costing $54,000. Inventory that had cost $60,000 was sold on account for $75,000. At the end of the year, inventory was counted and its cost was determined to be $7,400. (a) Was there any shrinkage? (b) What was the gross profit? (c) Prepare journal entries to record these transactions, assuming a perpetual inventory system is used.

M6-11 Reporting Net Sales and Gross Profit with Sales Discounts

LO5

Merchandise costing $1,500 is sold for $2,000 on terms 2/10, n/30. If the buyer pays within the discount period, what amount will be reported on the income statement as net sales and as gross profit?

M6-12 Recording Journal Entries for Sales and Sales Discounts

LO5

Using the information in M6-11, prepare the journal entries needed at the time of sale and collection, assuming the company uses a perpetual inventory system.

M6-13 Journal Entries to Record Sales Discounts

LO5

Inventory that cost $500 is sold for $700, with terms of 2/10, n/30. Give the journal entries to record (a) the sale of merchandise and (b) collection of the accounts receivable assuming that it occurs during the discount period. (Use the method shown in the chapter for recording sales discounts.)

M6-14 Preparing a Multistep Income Statement

LO6

Sellall Department Stores reported the following amounts in its adjusted trial balance prepared as of its December 31, 2008, fiscal year-end: administrative expenses, $2,400; cost of goods sold, $22,728; income tax expense, $3,000; interest expense, $1,600; interest revenue, $200; general expenses, $2,600; sales revenue, $42,000; sales discounts, $2,200; sales returns and allowances, $1,920; and delivery (freight-out) expense, $300. Prepare a multistep income statement for distribution to external financial statement users, using a format similar to Exhibit 6.10.

M6-15 Computing and Interpreting the Gross Profit Percentage

LO6

Using the information in M6-14, calculate the gross profit percentage for 2008. Evaluate the company's performance using Exhibit 6.11 as a benchmark.

M6-16 Computing and Interpreting the Gross Profit Percentage

LO6

Ziehart Pharmaceuticals reported net sales of $178,000 and cost of goods sold of $58,000. Candy Electronics Corp. reported net sales of $36,000 and cost of goods sold of $26,200. Calculate the gross profit percentage for both companies. From these calculations, can you determine which company is more successful? Explain.

M6-17 Evaluating the Effect of Discounts and Returns on Gross Profit

LO6

One of the few companies to report the extent of sales discounts and returns is sunglass maker Oakley, Inc. In the Management Discussion and Analysis section of its 2005 annual report, Oakley reports the following information about its sales discounts and returns.

	Year Ended December 31,		
	2005	2004	2003
	(in thousands)		
Gross sales	$693,342	$ 621,652	$ 567,077
Discounts and returns	(45,211)	(36,184)	(39,043)
Net sales	648,131	585,468	528,034
Cost of goods sold	277,230	262,483	245,578
Gross profit	370,901	322,985	282,456

Required:

1. For each year, calculate the percentage of sales discounts and returns by dividing Discounts and returns by Gross sales and multiplying by 100. Based on these percentages, explain whether sales discounts and returns have a greater impact in 2005 or 2004.

2. For each year, calculate the gross profit percentage using the formula shown in this chapter (i.e., using net sales).

3. For each year, recalculate the gross profit percentage by replacing net sales with gross sales.

4. Based on a comparison of your calculations in requirements 2 and 3, how important is it to know whether gross profit percentage is calculated using net sales or gross sales?

EXERCISES

Available with McGraw-Hill's
Homework Manager

LO2   **E6-1 Identifying Internal Control Principle and Financial Reporting Control Objective**

At most movie theaters, one employee sells tickets and another employee collects them. One night, when you're at the movies, your friend comments that this is a waste of the theater's money.

Required:

1. Identify the name of the control principle to which this situation relates.
2. Explain to your friend what could happen if the same person did both jobs.

LO2   **E6-2 Identifying Financial Reporting Control Objectives**

Your student club recently volunteered to go door-to-door collecting cash donations on behalf of a local charity. The charity's accountant went berserk when you said you wrote receipts only for donors who asked for one.

Required:

Identify the control principle that you violated, and explain why the accountant reacted so strongly. What controls might be appropriate to use in the future?

LO3   **E6-3 Preparing a Bank Reconciliation and Journal Entries, and Reporting Cash**

Hills Company's June 30, 2008, bank statement and the June ledger account for cash are summarized here:

Bank Statement				
	Checks	Deposits	Other	Balance
Balance, June 1, 2008				$ 7,200
Deposits during June		$18,000		25,200
Checks cleared during June	$19,100			6,100
Bank service charges			$30	6,070
Balance, June 30, 2008				6,070

	+ Cash (A) −			
June 1 Balance	6,800			
June Deposits	19,000	June	Checks written	19,400
June 30 Balance	6,400			

Required:

1. Prepare a bank reconciliation. A comparison of the checks written with the checks that have cleared the bank shows outstanding checks of $700. Some of the checks that cleared in June

were written prior to June. No deposits in transit were noted in May, but a deposit is in transit at the end of June.

2. Give any journal entries that should be made as a result of the bank reconciliation.

3. What is the balance in the Cash account after the reconciliation entries?

4. In addition to the balance in its bank account, Hills Company also has $300 cash on hand. This amount is recorded in a separate T-account called Cash on Hand. What is the total amount of cash that should be reported on the balance sheet at June 30?

E6-4 Preparing a Bank Reconciliation and Journal Entries, and Reporting Cash   LO3

The September 30, 2009, bank statement for Cadieux Company and the September ledger account for cash are summarized here:

Bank Statement				
	Checks	**Deposits**	**Other**	**Balance**
Balance, September 1, 2009				$ 2,000
September 7			NSF $100	1,900
September 11		$3,000		4,900
September 12	#101 $800			4,100
September 17	#102 1,700			2,400
September 26	#103 2,300			100
September 29			EFT 150	250
September 30			Service 20	230

	+ Cash (A) −			
Sept 1 Balance	2,000			
Sept 10	3,000	800	Sept 10	#101
Sept 30	2,500	1,700	Sept 15	#102
		2,300	Sept 22	#103
		50	Sept 28	#104
Sept 30 Balance	2,650			

No outstanding checks and no deposits in transit were noted in August. However, there are deposits in transit and checks outstanding at the end of September. The NSF check and electronic funds transfer (EFT) involved transactions with Cadieux Company's customers.

Required:

1. Prepare a bank reconciliation.

2. Give any journal entries that should be made as the result of the bank reconciliation.

3. What should the balance in the Cash account be after recording the journal entries in requirement 2?

4. If the company also has $400 of cash on hand (recorded in a separate account), what total amount of cash should the company report on the September 30 balance sheet?

E6-5 Inferring Shrinkage Using a Perpetual Inventory System   LO4

Calculate the amount of shrinkage for each of the following independent cases:

Cases	Beginning Inventory	Purchases	Cost of Goods Sold	Ending Inventory (as counted)	Shrinkage
A	$100	$700	$300	$420	$?
B	200	800	850	150	?
C	150	500	200	440	?
D	260	600	650	200	?

LO4

JCPenney Company, Inc.

E6-6 Inferring Shrinkage Using a Perpetual Inventory System

JCPenney Company, Inc., is a major retailer with department stores in all 50 states. The main part of the company's business consists of providing merchandise and services to consumers through department stores. In 2006 JCPenney reported cost of goods sold of $11,405 million, ending inventory for the current year of $3,234 million, and ending inventory for the previous year (2005) of $3,167 million.

Required:

If you knew that the cost of inventory purchases was $11,474 million, could you estimate the cost of shrinkage during the year? If so, prepare the estimate and, if not, explain why.

LO5

E6-7 Recording the Cost of Purchases for a Merchandiser

Apparel.com purchased 80 new shirts and recorded a total cost of $3,015 determined as follows:

Invoice cost	$2,600
Transportation cost (freight-in)	165
Estimated cost of shipping to customers	250
	$ 3,015

Required:

Calculate the correct inventory cost.

LO5

E6-8 Reporting Purchases and Purchase Discounts Using a Perpetual Inventory System

During the months of January and February, Axe Corporation purchased goods from three suppliers. The sequence of events was as follows:

Jan.	6	Purchased goods for $1,200 from Green with terms 2/10, n/30.
	6	Purchased goods from Munoz for $900 with terms 2/10, n/30.
	14	Paid Green in full.
Feb.	2	Paid Munoz in full.
	28	Purchased goods for $350 from Reynolds with terms 2/10, n/45.

Required:

Assume that Axe uses a perpetual inventory system, the company had no inventory on hand at the beginning of January, and no sales were made during January and February. Calculate the cost of inventory as of February 28.

LO5

E6-9 Recording Journal Entries for Purchases and Purchase Discounts Using a Perpetual Inventory System

Using the information in E6-8, prepare journal entries to record the transactions, assuming Axe uses a perpetual inventory system.

LO5

E6-10 Reporting Purchases, Purchase Discounts, and Purchase Returns Using a Perpetual Inventory System

During the month of June, Ace Incorporated purchased goods from two suppliers. The sequence of events was as follows:

June	3	Purchased goods for $3,200 from Diamond Inc. with terms 2/10, n/30.
	5	Returned goods costing $1,100 to Diamond Inc. for full credit.
	6	Purchased goods from Club Corp. for $1,000 with terms 2/10, n/30.
	11	Paid the balance owed to Diamond Inc.
	22	Paid Club Corp. in full.

Required:

Assume that Ace uses a perpetual inventory system and that the company had no inventory on hand at the beginning of the month. Calculate the cost of inventory as of June 30.

E6-11 Recording Journal Entries for Purchases, Purchase Discounts, and Purchase Returns Using a Perpetual Inventory System   LO5

Using the information in E6-10, prepare journal entries to record the transactions, assuming Ace uses a perpetual inventory system.

E6-12 Reporting Net Sales with Credit Sales and Sales Discounts   LO5

During the months of January and February, Solitare Corporation sold goods to three customers. The sequence of events was as follows:

Jan.	6	Sold goods for $100 to Wizard Inc. with terms 2/10, n/30. The goods cost Solitare $70.
	6	Sold goods to SpyderCorp for $80 with terms 2/10, n/30. The goods cost Solitare $60.
	14	Collected cash due from Wizard Inc.
Feb.	2	Collected cash due from SpyderCorp.
	28	Sold goods for $50 to Bridges with terms 2/10, n/45. The goods cost Solitare $30.

Required:

Assuming that sales discounts are reported as contra-revenue, compute net sales for the two months ended February 28.

E6-13 Recording Journal Entries for Net Sales with Credit Sales and Sales Discounts   LO5

Using the information in E6-12, prepare journal entries to record the transactions, assuming Solitare uses a perpetual inventory system.

E6-14 Reporting Net Sales with Credit Sales and Sales Discounts   LO5

The following transactions were selected from the records of Evergreen Company:

July	12	Sold merchandise to Wally Butler, who paid the $1,000 purchase with cash. The goods cost Evergreen Company $600.
	15	Sold merchandise to Claudio's Chair Company at a selling price of $5,000 on terms 3/10, n/30. The goods cost Evergreen Company $3,500.
	20	Sold merchandise to Otto's Ottomans at a selling price of $3,000 on terms 3/10, n/30. The goods cost Evergreen Company $1,900.
	23	Collected payment from Claudio's Chair Company from the July 15 sale.
Aug.	25	Collected payment from Otto's Ottomans from the July 20 sale.

Required:

Assuming that sales discounts are reported as contra-revenue, compute net sales for the two months ended August 31.

E6-15 Recording Journal Entries for Net Sales with Credit Sales and Sales Discounts   LO5

Using the information in E6-14, prepare journal entries to record the transactions, assuming Evergreen Company uses a perpetual inventory system.

E6-16 Reporting Net Sales with Credit Sales, Sales Discounts, and Sales Returns   LO5

The following transactions were selected from among those completed by Bear's Retail Store in 2008:

Nov.	20	Sold two items of merchandise to Cheryl Jahn, who paid the $400 sales price in cash. The goods cost Bear's $300.
	25	Sold 20 items of merchandise to Vasko Athletics at a selling price of $4,000 (total); terms 3/10, n/30. The goods cost Bear's $2,500.
	28	Sold 10 identical items of merchandise to Nancy's Gym at a selling price of $6,000 (total); terms 3/10, n/30. The goods cost Bear's $4,000.
	29	Nancy's Gym returned one of the items purchased on the 28th. The item was in perfect condition, and credit was given to the customer.

Dec. 6   Nancy's Gym paid the account balance in full.

     30   Vasko Athletics paid in full for the invoice of November 25, 2008.

Required:

Assuming that sales returns and sales discounts are reported as contra-revenues, compute net sales for the two months ended December 31, 2008.

LO5   **E6-17 Recording Journal Entries for Net Sales with Credit Sales, Sales Discounts, and Sales Returns**

Using the information in E6-16, prepare journal entries to record the transactions, assuming Bear's Retail Store uses a perpetual inventory system.

LO5   **E6-18 Determining the Effects of Credit Sales, Sales Discounts, and Sales Returns and Allowances on Income Statement Categories**

Rockland Shoe Company records sales returns and allowances and sales discounts as contra-revenues. Complete the following table, indicating the amount and direction of effect (+ for increase, − for decrease, and NE for no effect) of each transaction on each item reported in Rockland's income statement prepared for internal use. Be sure to total the effects.

July 12   Rockland sold merchandise to Kristina Zee at its factory store. Kristina paid for the $300 purchase in cash. The goods cost Rockland $160.

     15   Sold merchandise to Shoe Express at a selling price of $5,000, with terms 3/10, n/30. Rockland's cost was $3,000.

     20   Collected cash due from Shoe Express.

     21   Sold merchandise to Fleet Foot Co. at a selling price of $2,000, with terms 2/10, n/30. Rockland's cost was $1,200.

     23   Fleet Foot Co. returned $1,000 of shoes and promised to pay for the remaining goods in August. The returned shoes were in perfect condition and had cost Rockland $600.

Transaction Date:	July 12	July 15	July 20	July 21	July 23	Totals
Sales Revenues						
Sales Returns and Allowances						
Sales Discounts						
Net Sales						
Cost of Goods Sold						
Gross Profit						

LO5, LO6   **E6-19 Analyzing Sales and Purchases with Discounts**

Cycle Wholesaling sells merchandise on credit terms of 2/10, n/30. A sale for $800 (cost of goods sold of $500) was made to Sarah's Cycles on February 1, 2008. On March 4, 2008, Cycle Wholesaling purchased bicycles from a supplier on credit, invoiced at $8,000 with terms 1/15, n/30. Assume Cycle Wholesaling uses a perpetual inventory system.

Required:

1. Calculate the gross profit percentage for the sale to Sarah's Cycles, assuming the account was collected in full on February 9, 2008.

2. At what cost will the bicycles purchased on March 4 be reported, assuming they are paid for on March 12, 2008?

LO5   **E6-20 Recording Sales and Purchases with Discounts**

Refer to the information in E6-19.

Required:

1. Sales transactions
   a. Give the journal entry Cycle Wholesaling would make to record the sale to Sarah's Cycles.
   b. Give the journal entry to record the collection of the account, assuming it was collected in full on February 9, 2008.
   c. Give the journal entry, assuming, instead, that the account was collected in full on March 2, 2008.
2. Purchase transactions
   a. Give the journal entry to record the purchase on credit.
   b. Give the journal entry to record the payment of Cycle Wholesaling's account, assuming it was paid in full on March 12, 2008.
   c. Give the journal entry, assuming, instead, that the account was paid in full on March 28, 2008.

E6-21 Inferring Missing Amounts Based on Income Statement Relationships   LO6

Supply the missing dollar amounts for the 2008 income statement of Williamson Company for each of the following independent cases:

	Case A	Case B	Case C
Sales revenue	$8,000	$6,000	$?
Sales returns and allowances	150	?	275
Net sales revenue	?	?	5,920
Cost of goods sold	5,750	4,050	5,400
Gross profit	?	1,450	?

E6-22 Inferring Missing Amounts Based on Income Statement Relationships   LO6

Supply the missing dollar amounts for the 2008 income statement of Lewis Retailers for each of the following independent cases:

Cases	Sales Revenue	Beginning Inventory	Purchases	Cost of Goods Sold	Cost of Ending Inventory	Gross Profit
A	$ 650	$100	$700	$300	$?	$?
B	900	200	800	?	150	?
C	?	150	?	200	300	400
D	800	?	600	650	250	?
E	1,000	50	900	?	?	500

E6-23 Analyzing Gross Profit Percentage on the Basis of a Multistep Income Statement   LO6

The following summarized data were provided by the records of Mystery Incorporated for the year ended December 31, 2008:

Sales of merchandise for cash	$240,000
Sales of merchandise on credit	42,000
Cost of goods sold	165,000
Selling expense	40,200
Administrative expense	19,000
Sales returns and allowances	7,000
Income tax expense	17,600

Required:

1. Based on these data, prepare a multistep income statement for internal reporting purposes (showing gross sales, net sales, gross profit, and all other appropriate subtotals).
2. What was the amount of gross profit? What was the gross profit percentage (calculated using the formula shown in this chapter)? Explain what these two amounts mean.
3. Evaluate the 2008 results in light of the 38% gross profit percentage in 2007.

LO6

Wolverine World Wide Inc.

E6-24 Analyzing Gross Profit Percentage on the Basis of an Income Statement

Wolverine World Wide Inc. prides itself as being the "world's leading marketer of U.S. branded non-athletic footwear." The following data (in thousands) were taken from its annual report for the year ended 2005:

Sales of merchandise	$1,060,999
Income taxes	36,780
Cash dividends paid	14,814
Selling and administrative expense	291,891
Cost of products sold	655,800
Interest expense	3,647
Other revenues	1,736

Required:

1. Based on these data, prepare a multistep income statement.
2. How much was the gross profit? What was the gross profit percentage (rounded to the nearest tenth of a percent)? Explain what these two amounts mean.
3. Evaluate the 2005 results in light of the 37.7% gross profit percentage in 2004.
4. Compare Wolverine's gross profit percentage to Wal-Mart's average gross profit percentage of 23.1%. From this information, can you determine which company is more successful? Why or why not?

LO6

Best Buy
Circuit City

E6-25 Comparing Multistep Income Statements

Abbreviated income statements for Best Buy and Circuit City are shown below for the year ended February 28, 2006.

	Best Buy	Circuit City
Net sales	$30,848	$11,598
Cost of goods sold	23,122	8,767
Gross profit	7,726	2,831
Operating expenses	6,082	2,611
Income from operations	1,644	220
Other income	77	19
Income before income taxes	1,721	239
Income tax expense	581	88
Net income	$ 1,140	$ 151

Required:

1. Which company generated more net income and gross profit?
2. Which company generated a greater gross profit percentage? Show calculations.
3. Interpret your findings from 1 and 2.

LO5

E6-26 (Supplement) Recording Purchases and Sales Using Perpetual and Periodic Inventory Systems

Kangaroo Jim Company reported beginning inventory of 100 units at a per unit cost of $25. It had the following purchase and sales transactions during 2006:

Jan. 14   Sold 25 units at unit sales price of $45 on account.

Apr. 9   Purchased 15 additional units at a per unit cost of $25 on account.

Sep. 2   Sold 50 units at a sales price of $50 on account.

Dec. 31   Counted inventory and determined 40 units were still on hand.

Required:

Record each transaction, assuming that Kangaroo Jim Company uses (a) a perpetual inventory system and (b) a periodic inventory system.

COACHED PROBLEMS

CP6-1 Preparing a Bank Reconciliation and Journal Entries, and Reporting Cash

LO3

The April 30, 2008, bank statement for KMaxx Company and the April ledger account for cash are summarized here:

eXcel

Bank Statement				
	Checks	Deposits	Other	Balance
Balance, April 1, 2008				$6,000
April 5	#101 $700			5,300
April 9		$2,500		7,800
April 12	#102 200			7,600
April 19	#103 500			7,100
April 22	#104 1,000			6,100
April 27			EFT $200	5,900
April 30			Service charge 25	5,875

+	Cash (A)	−		
Apr 1 Balance	6,000			
Apr 8	2,500	700	Apr 2 #101	
Apr 28	500	200	Apr 10 #102	
		500	Apr 15 #103	
		1,100	Apr 20 #104	
		300	Apr 29 #105	
Apr 30 Balance	6,200			

No outstanding checks and no deposits in transit were noted in March. However, there are deposits in transit and checks outstanding at the end of April. The electronic funds transfer (EFT) involved an automatic monthly payment to one of KMaxx's creditors. Check #104 was written for $1,100.

Required:

1. Prepare a bank reconciliation for April.
   TIP: Put a check mark beside each item that appears on both the bank statement and what's already been recorded in the accounting records (shown in the T-account). Items left unchecked will be used in the bank reconciliation.
2. Give any journal entries that should be made as a result of the bank reconciliation.
   TIP: Remember to make entries only for items that affect the company's books, not the bank.
3. What should the balance in the Cash account be after recording the journal entries in requirement 2?
4. If the company also has $1,000 of cash on hand (recorded in a separate account), what total amount should the company report as Cash and cash equivalents on the April 30 balance sheet?

LO3 **CP6-2 Identifying Outstanding Checks and Deposits in Transit and Preparing a Bank Reconciliation and Journal Entries**

The August 2008 bank statement and cash T-account for Martha Company follow:

Bank Statement

Date	Checks	Deposits	Other	Balance
Aug. 1				$17,470
2	$300			17,170
3		$12,000		29,170
4	400			28,770
5	250			28,520
9	890			27,630
10	310			27,320
15		4,000		31,320
21	400			30,920
24	21,000			9,920
25		7,000		16,920
30	800			16,120
30			Interest earned $20	16,140
31			Service charge 10	16,130

+ Cash (A) −				
Aug. 1 Balance	17,470	Checks written		
Deposits				
Aug. 2	12,000	300	Aug. 1	
12	4,000	400	2	
24	7,000	250	3	
31	5,000	310	4	
		890	5	
		290	15	
		550	17	
		800	18	
		400	19	
		21,000	23	
Aug. 31 Balance	20,280			

No deposits were in transit and no checks were outstanding at the end of July.

Required:

1. Identify and list the deposits in transit at the end of August.
   TIP: Put a check mark beside each item that appears on both the bank statement and what's already been recorded in the accounting records (shown in the T-account).
2. Identify and list the outstanding checks at the end of August.
3. Prepare a bank reconciliation for August.
   TIP: Any item in the accounting records without check marks should appear on the bank statement side of the bank reconciliation. Any items in the bank statement without check marks should appear on the company's books side of the bank reconciliation.
4. Give any journal entries that the company should make as a result of the bank reconciliation. Why are they necessary?
5. After the reconciliation journal entries are posted, what balance will be reflected in the Cash account in the ledger?
6. If the company also has $100 on hand, which is recorded in a different account called Cash on Hand, what total amount of Cash and cash equivalents should be reported on the August 31, 2008, balance sheet?

CP6-3 Preparing a Multistep Income Statement with Sales Discounts and Sales Returns and Allowances and Computing the Gross Profit Percentage LO6

Psymon Company, Inc., sells heavy construction equipment. The annual fiscal period ends on December 31. The following adjusted trial balance was created from the general ledger accounts on December 31, 2008:

Account Titles	Debit	Credit
Cash	$ 42,000	
Accounts receivable	18,000	
Inventory	65,000	
Property and equipment	50,000	
Accumulated depreciation		$ 21,000
Liabilities		30,000
Contributed capital		90,000
Retained earnings, January 1, 2008		11,600
Sales revenue		182,000
Sales returns and allowances	7,000	
Sales discounts	8,000	
Cost of goods sold	98,000	
Selling expense	17,000	
Administrative expense	18,000	
General expenses	2,000	
Income tax expense	9,600	
Totals	$334,600	$334,600

Required:

1. Prepare a multistep income statement that would be used for internal reporting purposes. Treat sales discounts and sales returns and allowances as contra-revenue accounts.

    TIP: Some of the accounts listed will appear on the balance sheet rather than the income statement.

2. Prepare a multistep income statement that would be used for external reporting purposes, beginning with the amount for *net sales*.

    TIP: Calculate net sales by subtracting sales discounts and sales returns and allowances from sales revenue.

3. Compute and interpret the gross profit percentage (using the formula shown in this chapter).

CP6-4 Recording Sales and Purchases with Discounts and Returns LO5, LO6

Campus Stop, Incorporated, is a student co-op. Campus Stop uses a perpetual inventory system. The following transactions (summarized) have been selected from 2008:

a.	Sold merchandise for cash (cost of merchandise $137,500).	$275,000
b.	Received merchandise returned by customers as unsatisfactory (but in perfect condition), for cash refund (original cost of merchandise $800).	1,600

Purchased items from suppliers on credit:

c.	Purchased merchandise from Super Supply Company with terms 3/10, n/30.	5,000
d.	Purchased merchandise from other suppliers with terms 3/10, n/30.	120,000
e.	Purchased equipment for use in store; paid cash.	2,200
f.	Purchased office supplies for future use in the store; paid cash.	700
g.	Freight on merchandise purchased; paid cash.	400

Paid accounts payable in full during the period as follows:

h.	Paid Super Supply Company after the discount period.	5,000
i.	Paid other suppliers within the 3 percent discount period.	116,400

Required:

1. Assume that Campus Stop had inventory on hand at the beginning of the period at a cost of $200,000. At what amount should inventory be reported at the end of the period?

    TIP: Inventory includes all costs of getting inventory into a condition and location for sale.

2. Compute gross profit and gross profit percentage for sales this period.
3. Prepare journal entries for transactions *a–i*.
   TIP: Inventory includes only merchandise purchased for sale. Other purchases, such as supplies for internal use, are recorded in separate accounts.

LO5, LO6   **CP6-5   Reporting Sales and Purchase Transactions between Wholesale and Retail Merchandisers, with Sales/Purchase Allowances and Sales/Purchase Discounts Using Perpetual Inventory Systems**

The transactions listed below are typical of those involving Amalgamated Textiles and American Fashions. Amalgamated is a wholesale merchandiser and American Fashions is a retail merchandiser. Assume the following transactions between the two companies occurred in the order listed during the year ended December 31, 2008. Assume all sales of merchandise from Amalgamated to American Fashions are made with terms 2/10, n/30, and that the two companies use perpetual inventory systems.

Transactions during 2008:

a. Amalgamated sold merchandise to American Fashions at a selling price of $230,000. The merchandise had cost Amalgamated $175,000.
b. Two days later, American Fashions complained to Amalgamated that some of the merchandise differed from what American Fashions had ordered. Amalgamated agreed to give an allowance of $5,000 to American Fashions.
c. Just three days later, American Fashions paid Amalgamated, which settled all amounts owed.

Required:

1. For each of the events (*a*) through (*c*), indicate the amount and direction of the effect (+ for increase, − for decrease, and NE for no effect) on Amalgamated Textiles in terms of the following items.

Sales Revenues	Sales Returns and Allowances	Sales Discounts	Net Sales	Cost of Goods Sold	Gross Profit

2. Which of the above items are likely to be reported on Amalgamated's external financial statements, and which items will be combined "behind the scenes"?
3. Indicate the effect (direction and amount) of each transaction on the balance in American Fashions' inventory account.
   TIP: When an allowance is granted and no inventory is returned, the seller records the reduction in accounts receivable but no adjustment to its inventory.

LO5   **CP6-6   Journalizing Sales and Purchase Transactions between Wholesale and Retail Merchandisers, with Sales/Purchase Allowances and Sales/Purchase Discounts Using Perpetual Inventory Systems**

Use the information presented in CP6–5 to complete the following requirements.

Required:

1. Prepare the journal entries that Amalgamated Textiles would record, and show any computations.
   TIP: When using a perpetual inventory system, the seller always makes two journal entries when goods are sold.
2. Prepare the journal entries that American Fashions would record, and show any computations.

LO5   **CP6-7   (Supplement) Journalizing Sales and Purchase Transactions between Wholesale and Retail Merchandisers, with Sales/Purchase Allowances and Sales/Purchase Discounts Using Periodic Inventory Systems**

Use the information presented in CP6-5 and transaction (*a*) (only) to complete the following requirements, except assume that both companies use periodic inventory systems.

Required:

1. Prepare the journal entry (or entries) that Amalgamated Textiles would record for transaction (*a*) only.
   TIP: When using a periodic inventory system, the seller only makes one journal entry when goods are sold.

2. Prepare the journal entry (or entries) that American Fashions would record for transaction (*a*) only.

3. Assume that, during the year, American Fashions sold merchandise on credit for $160,000. Prepare the journal entry (or entries) that American Fashions would record.

4. Assume that, at the end of the year, American Fashions counted the inventory on hand that had been purchased from Amalgamated Textiles and determined that its cost was $80,000. Prepare any journal entries that American Fashions would record, and show any computations.

GROUP A PROBLEMS

Available with McGraw-Hill's
Homework Manager

HOMEWORK MANAGER **PLUS**

PA6-1 Preparing a Bank Reconciliation and Journal Entries, and Reporting Cash

LO3

www.mhhe.com/phillips2e

The bookkeeper at Martin Company has asked you to prepare a bank reconciliation as of May 31, 2008. The May 31, 2008, bank statement and the May T-account for cash showed the following (summarized):

Martin Company's bank reconciliation at the end of April 2008 showed a cash balance of $18,800. No deposits were in transit at the end of April, but a deposit was in transit at the end of May.

Bank Statement						
		Checks	Deposits	Other		Balance
Balance, May 1, 2008						$18,800
May 2			$8,000			26,800
May 5	#301	$11,000				15,800
May 7	#302	6,000				9,800
May 8			10,000			19,800
May 14	#303	500				19,300
May 17				Interest	$120	19,420
May 22				NSF	280	19,140
May 27	#304	4,600				14,540
May 31				Service charge	60	14,480
Balance, May 31, 2008						14,480

+ Cash (A) −			
May 1 Balance	18,800		
May 1	8,000	11,000	#301 May 2
May 7	10,000	6,000	#302 May 4
May 29	4,000	500	#303 May 11
		4,600	#304 May 23
		1,300	#305 May 29
May 31 Balance	17,400		

Required:

1. Prepare a bank reconciliation for May.

2. Prepare any journal entries required as a result of the bank reconciliation. Why are they necessary?

3. After the reconciliation journal entries are posted, what balance will be reflected in the *Cash* account in the ledger?

4. If the company also has $50 on hand, which is recorded in a different account called *Cash on Hand*, what total amount of Cash and cash equivalents should be reported on the balance sheet at the end of May?

LO3   **PA6-2 Identifying Outstanding Checks and Deposits in Transit and Preparing a Bank Reconciliation and Journal Entries**

www.mhhe.com/phillips2e

The December 2008 bank statement and cash T-account for Stewart Company follow:

			Bank Statement		
Date	Checks	Deposits	Other		Balance
Dec. 1					$48,000
2	$500				47,500
4	7,000				40,500
6	120				40,380
11	550	$28,000			67,830
13	1,900				65,930
17	12,000				53,930
23	60	36,000			89,870
26	900				88,970
28	2,200				86,770
30	17,000	19,000	NSF*	$300	88,470
31	1,650		Interest earned	50	86,870
31			Service charge	150	86,720

*NSF check from J. Left, a customer.

	+ Cash (A) −		
Dec. 1 Balance	48,000	Checks written during December:	
Deposits			
Dec. 11	28,000	500	60
23	36,000	7,000	900
30	19,000	120	150
31	13,000	550	17,000
		1,900	3,500
		12,000	1,650
		2,200	
Dec. 31 Balance	96,470		

There were no deposits in transit or outstanding checks at November 30.

Required:

1. Identify and list the deposits in transit at the end of December.
2. Identify and list the outstanding checks at the end of December.
3. Prepare a bank reconciliation for December.
4. Give any journal entries that the company should make as a result of the bank reconciliation. Why are they necessary?
5. After the reconciliation journal entries are posted, what balance will be reflected in the *Cash* account in the ledger?
6. If the company also has $300 on hand, which is recorded in a different account called *Cash on Hand*, what total amount of Cash and cash equivalents should be reported on the December 31, 2008, balance sheet?

PA6-3 Preparing a Multistep Income Statement with Sales Discounts and Sales Returns and Allowances and Computing the Gross Profit Percentage LO6

Big Tommy Corporation is a local grocery store organized seven years ago as a corporation. The store is in an excellent location, and sales have increased each year. At the end of 2008, the bookkeeper prepared the following statement (assume that all amounts are correct, but note the incorrect terminology and format):

BIG TOMMY CORPORATION Profit and Loss December 31, 2008	Debit	Credit
Sales		$420,000
Cost of goods sold	$279,000	
Sales returns and allowances	10,000	
Sales discounts	6,000	
Selling expense	58,000	
Administrative expense	16,000	
General expenses	1,000	
Income tax expense	15,000	
Net profit	35,000	
Totals	$420,000	$420,000

Required:

1. Prepare a multistep income statement that would be used for internal reporting purposes. Treat sales returns and allowances and sales discounts as contra-revenue accounts.
2. Prepare a multistep income statement that would be used for external reporting purposes, beginning with the amount for net sales.
3. Compute and interpret the gross profit percentage (using the formula shown in this chapter).

PA6-4 Recording Sales and Purchases with Discounts and Returns LO5, LO6

Hair World Inc. is a wholesaler of hair supplies. Hair World uses a perpetual inventory system. The following transactions (summarized) have been selected from 2008:

a.	Sold merchandise for cash (cost of merchandise $30,600).	$51,200
b.	Received merchandise returned by customers as unsatisfactory (but in perfect condition), for cash refund (original cost of merchandise $360).	600
	Purchased items from suppliers on credit:	
c.	Purchased merchandise from Cari's Comb Company with terms 3/10, n/30	1,000
d.	Purchased merchandise from other suppliers with terms 3/10, n/30.	24,000
e.	Purchased equipment for use in store; paid cash.	400
f.	Purchased office supplies for future use in the store; paid cash.	140
g.	Freight on merchandise purchased; paid cash.	100
	Paid accounts payable in full during the period as follows:	
h.	Paid Cari's Comb Company after the discount period.	1,000
i.	Paid other suppliers within the 3 percent discount period.	23,280

Required:

1. Assume that Hair World had inventory on hand at the beginning of the period at a cost of $100,000. At what amount should inventory be reported at the end of the period?
2. Compute gross profit and gross profit percentage for sales this period.
3. Prepare journal entries for transactions a–i.

LO5, LO6   **PA6-5** **Reporting Sales and Purchase Transactions between Wholesale and Retail Merchandisers, with Sales/Purchase Allowances and Sales/Purchase Discounts Using Perpetual Inventory Systems**

www.mhhe.com/phillips2e

The transactions listed below are typical of those involving New Books Inc. and Readers' Corner. New Books is a wholesale merchandiser and Readers' Corner is a retail merchandiser. Assume the following transactions between the two companies occurred in the order listed during the year ended August 31, 2008. Assume all sales of merchandise from New Books to Readers' Corner are made with terms 2/10, n/30, and that the two companies use perpetual inventory systems.

Transactions during the year ended August 31, 2008 are as follows:

a.   New Books sold merchandise to Readers' Corner at a selling price of $550,000. The merchandise had cost New Books $415,000.

b.   Two days later, Readers' Corner complained to New Books that some of the merchandise differed from what Readers' Corner had ordered. New Books agreed to give an allowance of $10,000 to Readers' Corner.

c.   Just three days later, Readers' Corner paid New Books, which settled all amounts owed.

Required:

1.   For each of the events (a) through (c), indicate the amount and direction of the effect (+ for increase, − for decrease, and NE for no effect) on New Books in terms of the following items.

Sales Revenues	Sales Returns and Allowances	Sales Discounts	Net Sales	Cost of Goods Sold	Gross Profit

2.   Which of the above items are likely to be reported on New Books' external financial statements, and which items will be combined "behind the scenes"?

3.   Indicate the effect (direction and amount) of each transaction on the balance in Readers' Corner's inventory account.

LO5   **PA6-6** **Journalizing Sales and Purchase Transactions between Wholesale and Retail Merchandisers, with Sales/Purchase Allowances and Sales/Purchase Discounts Using Perpetual Inventory Systems**

Use the information presented in PA6-5 to complete the following requirements.

Required:

1.   Prepare the journal entries that New Books would record, and show any computations.

2.   Prepare the journal entries that Readers' Corner would record, and show any computations.

LO5   **PA6-7** **(Supplement) Journalizing Sales and Purchase Transactions between Wholesale and Retail Merchandisers, with Sales/Purchase Allowances and Sales/Purchase Discounts Using Periodic Inventory Systems**

Use the information presented in PA6-5 and transaction (a) (only) to complete the following requirements, except assume that both companies use periodic inventory systems.

Required:

1.   Prepare the journal entries that New Books would record for transaction a only.

2.   Prepare the journal entries that Readers' Corner would record for transaction a only.

3.   Assume that, during the year, Readers' Corner sold merchandise on credit for $250,000. Prepare the journal entries that Readers' Corner would record.

4.   Assume that, at the end of the year, Readers' Corner counted the inventory it had purchased from New Books and determined that its cost was $135,000. Prepare any journal entries that Readers' Corner would record, and show any computations.

GROUP B PROBLEMS

**PB6-1 Preparing a Bank Reconciliation and Journal Entries and
Reporting Cash**

LO3

The bookkeeper at Tony Company has asked you to prepare a bank reconciliation as of February 29, 2008. The February 29, 2008, bank statement and the February T-account for cash showed the following (summarized):

Bank Statement					
	Checks		Deposits	Other	Balance
Balance, February 1, 2008					$49,400
February 2	#101	$15,000			34,400
February 4			$7,000		41,400
February 5				NSF $320	41,080
February 9	#102	11,000			30,080
February 12	#103	7,500			22,580
February 14			9,500		32,080
February 19	#104	9,000			23,080
February 23			14,150		37,230
February 26	#105	6,700			30,530
February 28				Interest 150	30,680
February 29				Service charge 40	30,640

+ Cash (A) −				
Feb 1 Balance	49,400			
Feb 2	7,000	15,000		Feb 1 #101
Feb 13	9,500	11,000		Feb 7 #102
Feb 21	14,150	7,500		Feb 11 #103
Feb 28	7,800	9,000		Feb 17 #104
		6,700		Feb 25 #105
		1,200		Feb 29 #106
Feb 29 Balance	37,450			

Tony Company's bank reconciliation at the end of January 2008 showed no outstanding checks. No deposits were in transit at the end of January, but a deposit was in transit at the end of February.

Required:

1. Prepare a bank reconciliation for February.
2. Prepare any journal entries required as a result of the bank reconciliation. Why are they necessary?
3. After the reconciliation journal entries are posted, what balance will be reflected in the Cash account in the ledger?
4. If the company also has $50 on hand, which is recorded in a different account called Cash on Hand, what total amount of Cash and cash equivalents should be reported on the balance sheet at the end of February?

LO3   **PB6-2 Identifying Outstanding Checks and Deposits in Transit and Preparing a Bank Reconciliation and Journal Entries**

The September 2008 bank statement and cash T-account for Terrick Company follow:

Bank Statement				
Date	Checks	Deposits	Other	Balance
Sept. 1				$75,900
2	$620			75,280
4	2,000			73,280
6	1,500			71,780
11	300	14,000		85,480
13	650			84,830
17	10,000			74,830
23	90	27,000		101,740
26	700			101,040
28	8,000			93,040
29	730	17,000	NSF* $500	108,810
30	400		Interest earned 60	108,470
30			Service charge 40	108,430

*NSF check from B. Frank, a customer.

+ Cash (A) −				
Sept. 1 Balance	75,900	Checks written during September:		
Deposits		620	8,000	
Sept. 11	14,000	2,000	730	
23	27,000	1,500	400	
29	17,000	300	500	
30	21,000	650	6,000	
		10,000	90	
		700		
Sept. 30 Balance	123,410			

There were no deposits in transit or outstanding checks at August 31.

Required:

1. Identify and list the deposits in transit at the end of September.
2. Identify and list the outstanding checks at the end of September.
3. Prepare a bank reconciliation for September.
4. Give any journal entries that the company should make as a result of the bank reconciliation. Why are they necessary?
5. After the reconciliation journal entries are posted, what balance will be reflected in the Cash account in the ledger?
6. If the company also has $200 on hand, which is recorded in a different account called Cash on Hand, what total amount of Cash and cash equivalents should be reported on the September 30, 2008, balance sheet?

LO6   **PB6-3 Preparing a Multistep Income Statement with Sales Discounts and Sales Returns and Allowances and Computing the Gross Profit Percentage**

Emily's Greenhouse Corporation is a local greenhouse organized 10 years ago as a corporation. The greenhouse is in an excellent location, and sales have increased each year. At the end of

2008, the bookkeeper prepared the following statement (assume that all amounts are correct, but note the incorrect terminology and format):

EMILY'S GREENHOUSE CORPORATION
Profit and Loss
December 31, 2008

	Debit	Credit
Sales		$504,000
Cost of goods sold	$311,000	
Sales returns and allowances	11,000	
Sales discounts	8,000	
Selling expense	61,000	
Administrative expense	13,000	
General expenses	3,000	
Income tax expense	18,000	
Net profit	79,000	
Totals	$504,000	$504,000

Required:

1. Prepare a multistep income statement that would be used for internal reporting purposes. Treat sales returns and allowances and sales discounts as contra-revenue accounts.

2. Prepare a multistep income statement that would be used for external reporting purposes, beginning with the amount for *net sales*.

3. Compute and interpret the gross profit percentage (using the formula shown in this chapter).

PB6-4 Recording Sales and Purchases with Discounts and Returns   LO5, LO6

Larry's Hardware, Incorporated, is a locally owned and operated hardware store. Larry's Hardware uses a perpetual inventory system.

The following transactions (summarized) have been selected from 2008:

a.	Sold merchandise for cash (cost of merchandise $325,000).	$500,000
b.	Received merchandise returned by customers as unsatisfactory (but in perfect condition), for cash refund (original cost of merchandise $1,900).	3,000

Purchased items from suppliers on credit:

c.	Purchased merchandise from Do It Yourself Company with terms 3/10, n/30.	27,000
d.	Purchased merchandise from other suppliers with terms 3/10, n/30.	237,000
e.	Purchased equipment for use in store; paid cash.	5,000
f.	Purchased office supplies for future use in the store; paid cash.	400
g.	Freight on merchandise purchased; paid cash.	350

Paid accounts payable in full during the period as follows:

h.	Paid Do It Yourself Company after the discount period.	27,000
i.	Paid other suppliers within the 3 percent discount period.	229,890

Required:

1. Assume that Larry's Hardware had inventory on hand at the beginning of the period at a cost of $350,000. At what amount should inventory be reported at the end of the period?

2. Compute gross profit and gross profit percentage for sales this period.

3. Prepare journal entries for transactions *a–i*.

LO4–LO6   **PB6-5 Reporting Sales and Purchase Transactions between Wholesale and Retail Merchandisers, with Sales/Purchase Allowances and Sales/Purchase Discounts Using Perpetual Inventory Systems**

The transactions listed below are typical of those involving Southern Sporting Goods and Sports R Us. Southern Sporting Goods is a wholesale merchandiser and Sports R Us is a retail merchandiser. Assume the following transactions between the two companies occurred in the order listed during the year ended December 31, 2008. Assume all sales of merchandise from Southern Sporting Goods to Sports R Us are made with terms 2/10, n/30, and that the two companies use perpetual inventory systems.

Transactions during 2008:

a. Southern Sporting Goods sold merchandise to Sports R Us at a selling price of $125,000. The merchandise had cost Southern Sporting Goods $94,000.
b. Two days later, Sports R Us complained to Southern Sporting Goods that some of the merchandise differed from what Sports R Us had ordered. Southern Sporting Goods agreed to give an allowance of $3,000 to Sports R Us.
c. Just three days later Sports R Us paid Southern Sporting Goods, which settled all amounts owed.

Required:

1. For each of the events (a) through (c), indicate the amount and direction of the effect (+ for increase, − for decrease, and NE for no effect) on Southern Sporting Goods in terms of the following items.

Sales Revenues	Sales Returns and Allowances	Sales Discounts	Net Sales	Cost of Goods Sold	Gross Profit

2. Which of the above items are likely to be reported on Southern Sporting Goods' external financial statements, and which items will be combined "behind the scenes?"
3. Indicate the effect (direction and amount) of each transaction on the balance in Sports R Us' inventory account.

LO5   **PB6-6 Journalizing Sales and Purchase Transactions between Wholesale and Retail Merchandisers, with Sales/Purchase Allowances and Sales/Purchase Discounts Using Perpetual Inventory Systems**

Use the information presented in PB6-5 to complete the following requirements.

Required:

1. Prepare the journal entries that Southern Sporting Goods would record and show any computations.
2. Prepare the journal entries that Sports R Us would record and show any computations.

LO5   **PB6-7 (Supplement) Journalizing Sales and Purchase Transactions between Wholesale and Retail Merchandisers, with Sales/Purchase Allowances and Sales/Purchase Discounts Using Periodic Inventory Systems**

Use the information presented in PB6-5 and transaction (a) (only) to complete the following requirements, except assume that both companies use periodic inventory systems.

Required:

1. Prepare the journal entries that Southern Sporting Goods would record for transaction (a) only.
2. Prepare the journal entries that Sports R Us would record for transaction (a) only.
3. Assume that, during the year, Sports R Us sold merchandise on credit for $97,000. Prepare the journal entries that Sports R Us would record.
4. Assume that, at the end of the year, Sports R Us counted the inventory it had purchased from Southern Sporting Goods and determined that its cost was $43,000. Prepare any journal entries that Sports R Us would record, and show any computations.

SKILLS DEVELOPMENT CASES

S6-1 Finding Financial Information

Refer to the financial statements of Landry's Restaurants in Appendix A at the end of this book, or download the annual report from the *Cases* section of the text's Web site at www.mhhe.com/phillips2e.

Required:

1. How much Cash and cash equivalents does the company report at the end of the current year?
2. Assuming that *cost of revenues* is the same thing as cost of goods sold, compute the company's gross profit percentage for the most recent two years. Has it risen or fallen? Explain the meaning of the change.
3. Assume that Landry's experienced no shrinkage in the most current year. Using the balance sheet and income statement, estimate the amount of purchases in the most recent year.

LO3, LO4, LO6

S6-2 Comparing Financial Information

Refer to the financial statements of Outback Steakhouse in Appendix B at the end of this book, or download them from the *Cases* section of the text's Web site at www.mhhe.com/phillips2e.

1. Does Outback report more or less Cash and cash equivalents than Landry's at the end of the year?
2. Assuming that *cost of sales* is the same thing as cost of goods sold, compute the company's gross profit percentage for the most recent two years. Is it greater or less than Landry's? Explain the meaning of the comparison.
3. Assume that Outback experienced no shrinkage in the most recent year. Using the balance sheet and income statement, estimate the amount of purchases in the most recent year. How much greater (or less) were Outback's purchases than Landry's for 2005?

LO3, LO4, LO6

S6-3 Internet-Based Team Research: Examining an Annual Report

As a team, select an industry to analyze. Using your Web browser, each team member should access the annual report or 10-K for one publicly traded company in the industry, with each member selecting a different company. (See S1-3 in Chapter 1 for a description of possible resources for these tasks.)

LO1, LO6

Required:

1. On an individual basis, each team member should write a short report that incorporates the following:
   a. Describe the company's business in sufficient detail to be able to classify it as a service, merchandising, or manufacturing company. What products or services does the company provide?
   b. Calculate the gross profit percentage at the end of the current and prior year, and explain any change between the two years.
2. Then, as a team, write a short report comparing and contrasting your companies using these attributes. Discuss any patterns across the companies that you as a team observe. Provide potential explanations for any differences discovered.

S6-4 Ethical Decision Making: A Real-Life Example

When some people think about inventory theft, they imagine a shoplifter running out of a store with goods stuffed inside a jacket or bag. But that's not what the managers thought at the Famous Footwear store on Chicago's Madison Street. No, they suspected their own employees were the main cause of their unusually high shrinkage. One scam involved dishonest cashiers who would let their friends take a pair of Skechers without paying for them. To make it look like the shoes had been bought, cashiers would ring up a sale, but instead of charging $50 for shoes, they would charge only $2 for a bottle of shoe polish. That's when the company's managers decided to put its

LO2, LO4
Famous Footwear

accounting system to work. In just two years, the company cut its Madison Street inventory losses in half. Here's how a newspaper described the store's improvements:

> **Retailers Crack Down on Employee Theft**
> *SouthCoast Today,* September 10, 2000, Chicago
> By Calmetta Coleman, *Wall Street Journal* Staff Writer
>
> . . . Famous Footwear installed a chainwide register-monitoring system to sniff out suspicious transactions, such as unusually large numbers of refunds or voids, or repeated sales of cheap goods.
>
> . . . [B]efore an employee can issue a cash refund, a second worker must be present to see the customer and inspect the merchandise.
>
> . . . [T]he chain has set up a toll-free hotline for employees to use to report suspicions about co-workers.

These improvements in inventory control came as welcome news for investors and creditors of Brown Shoe Company, the company that owns Famous Footwear. Despite these improvements at the Chicago store, Brown Shoe has been forced to shut down operations in other cities.

Required:

1. Explain how the register-monitoring system would allow Famous Footwear to cut down on employee theft.
2. What is the name of the control and the financial reporting control objective that is addressed by Famous Footwear's new cash refund procedure?
3. If Famous Footwear used a periodic inventory system, rather than a perpetual inventory system, how would the company detect shrinkage?
4. Think of and describe at least four different parties that are harmed by the type of inventory theft described in this case.

L05, L06   **S6-5 Ethical Decision Making: A Mini-Case**

Assume you work as an accountant in the merchandising division of a large public company that makes and sells athletic clothing. To encourage the merchandising division to earn as much profit on each individual sale as possible, the division manager's pay is based, in part, on the division's gross profit percentage. To encourage control over the division's operating expenses, the manager's pay also is based on the division's net income.

You are currently preparing the division's financial statements. The division had a good year, with sales of $100,000, cost of goods sold of $50,000, sales returns and allowances of $6,000, sales discounts of $4,000, and other selling expenses of $30,000. (Assume the division does not report income taxes.) The division manager stresses that "*it would be in your personal interest*" to classify sales returns and allowances, credit card discounts, and sales discounts as selling expenses rather than as contra-revenues on the division's income statement. He justifies this "friendly advice" by saying that he's not asking you to fake the numbers—he just believes that those items are more accurately reported as expenses. Plus, he claims, being a division of a larger company, you don't have to follow GAAP.

Required:

1. Prepare an income statement for the division using the classifications shown in this chapter. Using this income statement, calculate the division's gross profit percentage.
2. Prepare an income statement for the division using the classifications advised by the manager. Using this income statement, calculate the division's gross profit percentage.
3. What reason (other than reporting "more accurately") do you think is motivating the manager's advice to you?
4. Do you agree with the manager's statement that "he's not asking you to fake the numbers"?
5. Do you agree with the manager's statement about not having to follow GAAP?
6. How should you respond to the division manager's "friendly advice"?

S6-6 Critical Thinking: Analyzing Internal Control Weaknesses

LO2

Snake Creek Company has one trusted employee who, as the owner said, "handles all of the book-keeping and paperwork for the company." This employee is responsible for counting, verifying, and recording cash receipts and payments, making the weekly bank deposit, preparing checks for major expenditures (signed by the owner), making small expenditures from the cash register for daily expenses, and collecting accounts receivable. The owners asked the local bank for a $20,000 loan. The bank asked that an audit be performed covering the year just ended. The independent auditor (a local CPA), in a private conference with the owner, presented some evidence of the following activities of the trusted employee during the past year:

a.   Cash sales sometimes were not entered in the cash register, and the trusted employee pock-eted approximately $50 per month.

b.   Cash taken from the cash register (and pocketed by the trusted employee) was replaced with expense memos with fictitious signatures (approximately $12 per day).

c. $300 collected on an account receivable from a valued out-of-town customer was pocketed by the trusted employee and was covered by making a $300 entry as a debit to Sales Returns and a credit to Accounts Receivable.

d. $800 collected on an account receivable from a local customer was pocketed by the trusted employee and was covered by making an $800 entry as a debit to Sales Discounts and a credit to Accounts Receivable.

Required:

1.   What was the approximate amount stolen during the past year?
    TIP: Assume employees work 5 days a week, 52 weeks a year.
2.   What would be your recommendations to the owner?

LO5, LO6

S6-7 Preparing Multistep Income Statements and Calculating Gross Profit Percentage

www.mhhe.com/phillips2e

Assume that you have been hired by Big Sky Corporation as a summer student. The company is in the process of preparing its annual financial statements. To help in the process, you are asked to prepare an income statement for internal reporting purposes and an income statement for external reporting purposes. Your boss has also requested that you determine the company's gross profit percentage based on the statements that you are to prepare. The following adjusted trial balance was created from the general ledger accounts on May 31, 2008.

Account Titles	Debit	Credit
Cash	$ 57,000	
Accounts receivable	67,000	
Inventory	103,000	
Property and equipment	252,000	
Accumulated depreciation		$103,000
Liabilities		75,000
Contributed capital		120,000
Retained earnings, June 1, 2007		145,900
Sales revenue		369,000
Sales returns and allowances	9,500	
Sales discounts	14,000	
Cost of goods sold	248,000	
Selling expense	19,000	
Administrative expense	23,000	
General expenses	5,000	
Income tax expense	15,400	
Totals	$812,900	$812,900

Your boss wants you to create the spreadsheet in a way that automatically recalculates net sales and any other related amounts whenever changes are made to the contra-revenue accounts. To do this, you know that you'll have to use formulas throughout the worksheets and even import or link cells from one worksheet to another. Once again, your friend Owen is willing to help.

From:	Owentheaccountant@yahoo.com
To:	Helpme@hotmail.com
Cc:	
Subject:	Excel Help

Sounds like you are going to get some great experience this summer. Okay, to import a number from another spreadsheet, you first click on the cell where you want the number to appear. For example, if you want to enter the Net sales balance in the external income statement, click on the cell in the external income statement where the net sales number is supposed to appear. Enter the equals sign (=) and then click on the tab that takes you to the worksheet containing the internal income statement. In that worksheet, click on the cell that contains the amount you want to import into the external income statement and then press enter. This will create a link from the internal income statement cell to the external income statement cell. Here's a screen shot showing the formula that will appear after you import the number.

```
Microsoft Excel - SS6-1.xls
File  Edit  View  Insert  Format  Tools  Data  Window  Help  Acrobat
G5        fx  ='Internal Income Statement'!G9
            Big Sky Corporation
            Income Statement
        For the Year Ended May 31, 2008
5  Net sales                         345,500
6  Cost of goods sold                248,000
7  Gross profit                       97,500
Data  Internal Income Statement  External Income Statement  Gross Profit
Ready                                        NUM
```

Don't forget to save the file using a name that indicates who you are.

Required:

Enter the trial balance information into a spreadsheet and complete the following:

1. Prepare a multistep income statement that would be used for internal reporting purposes. Classify sales returns and allowances and sales discounts as contra-revenue accounts.
2. Prepare a multistep income statement that would be used for external reporting purposes, beginning with the amount for net sales.
3. Compute the gross profit percentage.

7 Reporting and Interpreting Inventories and Cost of Goods Sold

YOUR LEARNING OBJECTIVES

Understand the business

LO1 Describe inventory management goals.

LO2 Describe the different types of inventory.

Study the accounting methods

LO3 Compute costs using four inventory costing methods.

LO4 Explain why inventory is reported at the lower of cost or market.

Evaluate the results

LO5 Compute and interpret the inventory turnover ratio.

LO6 Explain how accounting methods affect evaluations of inventory management.

Review the chapter

THAT WAS
THEN

In the previous chapter, we assumed all goods were purchased at the same cost per unit.

LP7

You are near the middle of the term, so it's time to ask yourself how you're doing. If you've taken three tests and scored 40 percent on the first, 70 percent on the second, and 100 percent on the third, are you doing terrible, great, or average? It could be any of these three interpretations, depending on whether you focus on the first test, the last test, or the average of all three. Wouldn't this be a lot easier to figure out if there were rules describing how to interpret your test scores?

The same issue exists when companies report the cost of their inventories. Inflation can cause these costs to increase over time, while technological innovation can cause them to decrease. Either way, inventory is likely to be made up of some items acquired at lower unit costs and others at higher costs. Suppose Oakley, the sunglass maker, produces three pairs of its Straight Jacket sunglasses, at costs of $40, $70, and $100 each. Do these numbers suggest that their cost is low, moderate, or high? As with your test scores, it could mean any of the three, depending on how you look at it. Generally accepted accounting principles allow accountants to use one of several possible methods when determining the costs of inventories and goods sold, with each method leading to a different number. This flexibility of choice can be a good thing because it allows managers to use the method that best fits their business environment. This flexibility also makes it essential, however, that you know which methods are being used and how they work. That's what we'll look at in this chapter.

THIS IS NOW

This chapter demonstrates how to account for similar goods purchased at different unit costs.

Do you know what managers worry about when making inventory decisions, how the results of their decisions are reported, and how you can use the reported results to evaluate the quality of their inventory decisions? If any of your answers are no, then you're doing exactly what you should be doing—reading this chapter. In it, we address these questions, which cover the specific topics shown below.

ORGANIZATION OF THE CHAPTER

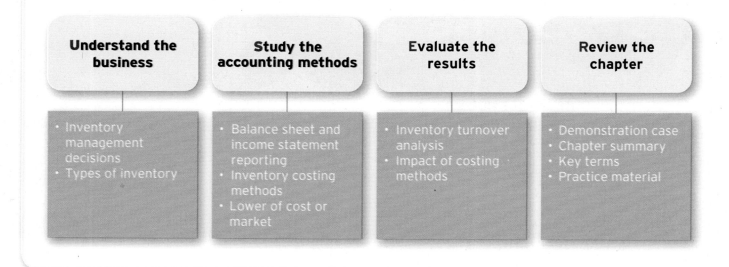

Understand the business	Study the accounting methods	Evaluate the results	Review the chapter
• Inventory management decisions • Types of inventory	• Balance sheet and income statement reporting • Inventory costing methods • Lower of cost or market	• Inventory turnover analysis • Impact of costing methods	• Demonstration case • Chapter summary • Key terms • Practice material

Understand the Business

INVENTORY MANAGEMENT DECISIONS

Learning Objective 1
Describe inventory management goals.

You may not make or sell inventory, but you buy it all the time. The things that concern you as a consumer also concern managers who make inventory decisions. The primary goals of inventory managers are to (1) maintain a sufficient **quantity** of inventory to meet customers' needs and (2) ensure inventory **quality** meets customers' expectations and company standards. At the same time, they try to (3) minimize the **cost** of acquiring and carrying inventory (including costs related to purchasing, production, storage, spoilage, theft, obsolescence, and financing). For many managers, there's a fourth factor that drives their inventory decisions: product **innovation**. In fact, Oakley believes so strongly in product innovation that it once described itself as "a technology company, in business to seek out problems with existing consumer products and solve them in ways that redefine product categories."[1] These four factors are tricky to manage because as one of them changes (e.g., quality) so, too, do the others (e.g., cost). Ultimately, inventory management often comes down to purchasing goods that can be sold soon after they are acquired.

TYPES OF INVENTORY

Learning Objective 2
Describe the different types of inventory.

The generic term *inventory* means goods that are held for sale in the normal course of business or are used to produce other goods for sale. Merchandisers hold **merchandise inventory**, which consists of products acquired in a finished condition, ready for sale without further processing. Manufacturers often hold three types of inventory, with each

[1] Oakley, Inc. 2002 Form 10-K.

representing a different stage in the manufacturing process. They start with **raw materials inventory** such as plastic, steel, or fabrics. When these raw materials enter the production process, they become part of **work in process inventory**, which includes goods that are in the process of being manufactured. When completed, work in process inventory becomes **finished goods inventory**, which is ready for sale just like merchandise inventory. For purposes of this chapter, we'll focus on merchandise inventory, but be aware that the concepts we cover apply equally to manufacturers' inventory.

Two other terms may be used in accounting to describe inventory. **Consignment inventory** refers to goods a company is holding on behalf of the goods' owner. Typically, this arises when a company is willing to sell the goods for the owner (for a fee) but does not want to take ownership of the goods in the event the goods are difficult to sell. Consignment inventory is reported on the balance sheet of the owner, not the company holding the inventory. **Goods in transit** are inventory items being transported. This type of inventory is reported on the balance sheet of the owner, not the company transporting it. As you may remember from Chapter 6, ownership of inventory is determined by the terms of the inventory sales agreement. If a sale is made **FOB destination,** the goods belong to the seller until they are delivered to the customer. If a sale is made **FOB shipping point,** inventory belongs to the customer at the moment it leaves the seller's premises.

> **YOU SHOULD KNOW**
>
> **FOB destination** is a term of sale indicating that goods are owned by the seller until they are delivered to the customer. **FOB shipping point** is a term of sale indicating that goods are owned by the customer the moment they leave the seller's premises.

Study the Accounting Methods

BALANCE SHEET AND INCOME STATEMENT REPORTING

Inventory is reported on the balance sheet as a current asset, as shown in Exhibit 7.1. It is classified as current because the goods included in inventory are expected to be used up or sold and converted into cash within one year. Goods are recorded in inventory at cost, which is the amount given up to acquire them and bring them into a condition and location ready for sale. As discussed in Chapter 6, inventory cost includes the purchase price, as well as any additional costs to prepare the goods for sale. The cost of transporting inventory to the seller's premises (freight-in) are included in inventory. If any purchase discounts have been taken, they are recorded as reductions in the cost of inventory.

EXHIBIT 7.1	Reporting Inventory on the Balance Sheet	**OAKLEY**

OAKLEY, INC.
Consolidated Balance Sheets
At December 31, 2005, 2004, and 2003

	2005	2004	2003
(in thousands)			
Assets			
Current assets			
Cash and cash equivalents	$ 82,157	$ 51,738	$ 49,211
Accounts receivable, net	99,430	102,817	77,989
Inventories	119,035	115,061	98,691
Prepaid income taxes and other	33,554	27,274	21,395
Total current assets	334,176	296,890	247,286

EXHIBIT 7.2 Reporting Cost of Goods Sold on the Income Statement

OAKLEY

OAKLEY, INC.
Consolidated Income Statements
For the Years Ended December 31, 2005, 2004, and 2003

	2005	2004	2003
(in thousands)			
Net sales revenue	$648,131	$585,468	$528,034
Cost of goods sold	277,230	262,483	245,578
Gross profit	370,901	322,985	282,456

When goods are sold, their cost is removed from the inventory account and reported on the income statement as an expense called Cost of goods sold. As highlighted in the income statement excerpt in Exhibit 7.2, Cost of goods sold (CGS) follows directly after sales. Sales revenue is calculated by multiplying the sales price by the number of units sold during the accounting period. Cost of goods sold is calculated by multiplying the same number of units sold by the company's cost per unit. The difference between these two line-items is a subtotal called Gross profit.

Although the cost of inventory and cost of goods sold are reported on different financial statements, they are related to one another. A company starts each accounting period with a stock of inventory called beginning inventory (BI). During the accounting period, new purchases (P) are added to inventory. As shown in Exhibit 7.3, the sum of these two amounts is the cost of **goods available for sale,** which represents the cost of all inventory that was available to be sold during the current period. Some of this inventory will be sold during the period and some will remain unsold at the end of the period. The

YOU SHOULD KNOW

Goods available for sale refers to the sum of beginning inventory and purchases for the period.

EXHIBIT 7.3 Relationship between Inventory and Cost of Goods Sold

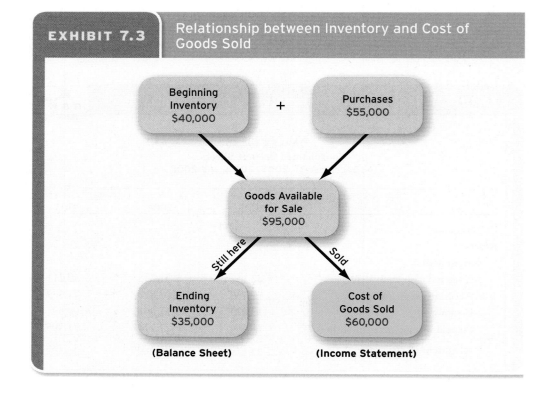

portion of goods available for sale that is sold is reported as Cost of goods sold on the income statement. What remains unsold at the end of the period is reported as ending inventory (EI) on the balance sheet. The ending inventory for one accounting period then becomes the beginning inventory for the next period. The relationships between these various inventory amounts are brought together in the **cost of goods sold (CGS) equation (BI + P − EI = CGS).**

To illustrate the CGS equation, assume that Oakley began the period with $40,000 of Detonator™ watches in beginning inventory, purchased more of these watches during the period for $55,000, and had $35,000 left in inventory at the end of the period. These amounts can be combined as follows to compute cost of goods sold of $60,000:

> **YOU SHOULD KNOW**
>
> The **cost of goods sold (CGS)** equation is: BI + P − EI = CGS.

Beginning inventory	$40,000
+ Purchases of merchandise during the year	+ 55,000
= Goods available for sale	= 95,000
− Ending inventory	− 35,000
= Cost of goods sold	= $60,000

These same relationships can be represented in a T-account as follows:

+	Merchandise Inventory (A)	−
Beginning inventory 40,000		
Purchases of inventory 55,000	60,000	Cost of goods sold
Ending inventory 35,000		

If one of these values is unknown, either the cost of goods sold equation or the inventory T-account can be used to solve for the missing value. See for yourself in the following Self-Study Quiz.

HOW'S IT GOING?   Self-Study Quiz

Assume the following facts for Oakley's Overdrive golf shoe product line for the year 2008:

> Beginning inventory 500 units at unit cost of $100.
> Purchases of inventory 1,200 units at unit cost of $100.
> Sales of 1,100 units at a sales price of $120 (cost per unit $100).

1. Using the cost of goods sold equation or the T-account, compute the dollar amount of Overdrive™ golf shoes in inventory at the end of the period.

			+	Merchandise Inventory (A)	−
Beginning inventory	$ 50,000		BI [ ]		
+ Purchases of merchandise during the year	[ ]		P [ ]	[ ] CGS	
− Ending inventory	[ ]		EI [ ]		
= Cost of goods sold	$[ ]				

2. Prepare the first three lines of the income statement body (showing computation of gross profit) for the Overdrive golf shoe line for the year 2008.

Learning Objective 3
Compute costs using four
inventory costing methods.

Topic Tackler

PLUS

Check out www.mhhe.com/phillips2e for
audio, visual, and PowerPoint presentations
on this topic.

Video 7.1

INVENTORY COSTING METHODS

In the Overdrive golf shoes example presented in the Self-Study Quiz, the cost of all units of the shoes was the same—$100. If inventory costs normally stayed constant like this, we'd be done right now. But just as you don't always get 100 percent on every test, the cost of goods doesn't stay constant forever. In recent years, the costs of many items have risen moderately. In other cases, like LCD TVs, costs have dropped dramatically.

When the costs of inventory change over time, it's not obvious what should be used to determine the cost of goods sold (and the cost of remaining inventory). To see what we mean, think about the following simple example for Oakley:

January	1	Beginning inventory consists of **two** units of snow goggles costing **$70 each.**
March	12	Purchased **five** units of snow goggles costing **$80 each.**
June	9	Purchased **one** unit of snow goggles costing **$100.**
November	5	Sold five units for $120 each.

The sale on November 5 of five units for $120 each would generate sales revenue of $600 ($120 × 5), but what amount would be considered the cost of goods sold? Because the cost of goggles increased from January through June, the answer depends on which goggles are assumed to be sold. Was it five that were bought March 12 for $80 each, or a combination of goggles costing $70, $80, and $100? The effects of this seemingly simple accounting decision can be dramatic. By one study's estimates, the combined effect of this decision on the profits of large U.S. corporations exceeds $60 billion.[2]

Four generally accepted inventory costing methods are available for determining the cost of goods sold (and the cost of goods remaining in ending inventory):

1. Specific identification.
2. First-in, first-out (FIFO).
3. Last-in, first-out (LIFO).
4. Weighted average.

These four methods are alternative ways for splitting the total dollar amount of goods available for sale between ending inventory and cost of goods sold. Any one of these four methods is considered GAAP in the United States. The first method specifically identifies which items remain in inventory and which are sold. The remaining three methods assume that inventory costs flow a particular way out of Inventory on the balance sheet into Cost of goods sold on the income statement.

1. Specific Identification Method

YOU SHOULD KNOW

Specific identification is the
inventory costing method that
identifies the cost of the specific
item that was sold.

When the **specific identification method** is used, the cost of each item sold is individually identified and recorded as Cost of goods sold. This method requires keeping track of the purchase cost of each item. This is usually done by labeling each unit with an inventory number and keeping a separate record of the cost for each inventory number. In our earlier example, if the five goggles sold included one that cost $70, three that cost $80, and one that cost $100, the cost of those items ($70 + 80 + 80 + 80 + 100 = $410) would be reported as cost of goods sold. The cost of the remaining items ($70 + 80 + 80 = $230) would be reported as Inventory on the balance sheet at the end of the period.

Oakley doesn't actually use the specific identification method because each inventory unit in a product line is identical and relatively inexpensive. **The specific identification method tends to be used only when dealing with individually expensive and unique items**—when it's important to know the cost of each particular unit of inventory. CarMax, for example, uses the specific identification method for tracking the cost of used cars in its inventory. Toll Brothers—the country's leading builder of

---

[2] "Big Oil's Accounting Methods Fuel Criticism," *The Wall Street Journal,* August 8, 2006, C1.

luxury homes—reports the cost of its home construction using the specific identification method.

For companies that have large quantities of similar items, a more realistic approach is to assume a particular flow of costs from inventory to cost of goods sold. Under these cost flow assumptions, inventory costs are not based on the actual physical flow of goods on and off the shelves. Rather, they are based on an assumed flow of costs from the balance sheet to the income statement. This is why they are called cost flow **assumptions**. To help you picture these cost flows in your mind's eye, we'll use illustrations that resemble product flows. Remember, though, generally accepted accounting principles do not require that a company use a cost flow assumption that mirrors its actual physical flow of goods. We will apply the methods as if all purchases during the period take place before any sales and cost of goods sold are recorded.[3]

Control Spotlight

Mad Cows, RFID, and Inventory Costing

In response to growing concerns about mad cow disease, the U.S. Department of Agriculture approved the use of radio frequency identification (RFID) systems as part of its national animal identification system. RFID tags make it possible to constantly monitor and electronically accumulate information about each individual animal. Following this lead, Ford and Wal-Mart are now embedding RFID tags in selected items of inventory. In light of these developments, some accountants are predicting a shift to greater use of the specific identification method of inventory costing.

2. First-In, First-Out (FIFO) Method

No, it's not the name of a dog. The **first-in, first-out** method, usually called **FIFO,** is one of the generally accepted cost flow assumptions for computing inventory costs. It assumes that the costs for the oldest goods (the first ones in) are used first to calculate Cost of goods sold and the newer costs are left to calculate ending inventory cost. It's as if costs flow in and out of inventory in the same way as milk cartons slide down the shelf in a grocery store (see Exhibit 7.4). FIFO corresponds to the following two-step process.

Step 1: Each purchase is treated as if it were deposited on the shelf in sequence and slid to the bottom. In our example, the costs for the oldest units (two units in beginning inventory at $70) were first in followed by the next oldest (five units at $80), and finally the most recent purchase (one unit at $100). In total, these costs result in goods available for sale that cost $640.

Step 2: The cost of each unit sold is then removed in sequence, as if the *first* costs *in* are the *first* costs *out.* In our example, five units are sold, so the cost of goods sold is calculated as the cost of the first two units in at $70 and three more units from the next batch of purchases at $80 each. These costs totaling $380 are reported as the Cost of goods sold (CGS).

The costs of any remaining units (two units at $80 and one at $100 = $260) are reported as ending inventory. FIFO allocates the oldest (first-in) unit costs to cost of goods sold and the newest (most recent) unit costs to ending inventory.

---

[3] By assuming all purchases take place before any sales and cost of goods sold are recorded, we are using a periodic inventory system. You might think it's odd that we use a periodic system when we said in Chapter 6 that most modern companies use perpetual inventory systems. We actually have several good reasons for doing this, which we explain in Supplement A at the end of this chapter. For those who would like to learn how cost flow assumptions are applied in perpetual inventory systems, see Supplement A. For purposes of examples shown in the chapter and for problem materials at the end of this chapter, we assume no shrinkage (a topic discussed in Chapter 6).

EXHIBIT 7.4 Inventory Cost Flows Using FIFO (First-in, first-out)

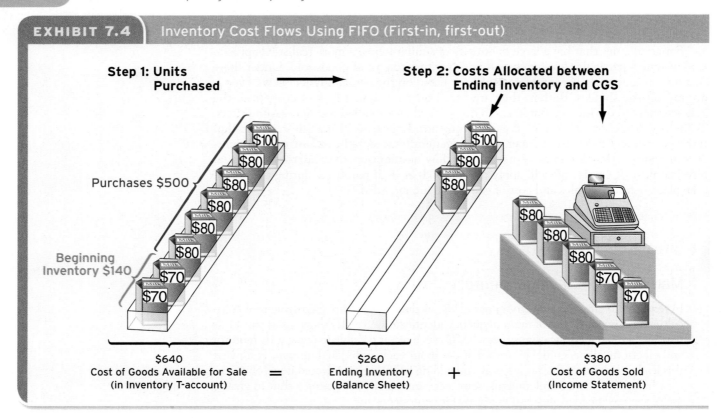

3. Last-In, First-Out (LIFO) Method

The **last-in, first-out** method, usually called **LIFO,** assumes that the costs for the newest goods (the last ones in) are used first and the oldest costs are left in ending inventory. Picture this kind of cost flow as picking paving stones from the top of a stack. Go ahead, take a look at Exhibit 7.5, and then come right back here.

Step 1: As in FIFO, each purchase is treated as if it were deposited from the top (two units at $70 followed by five units at $80, and one unit at $100) resulting in the goods available for sale of $640.

Step 2: Unlike FIFO, where costs are removed from the bottom of a shelf, in LIFO each item sold is treated as if its cost were removed in sequence from the top of a stack (beginning with the most recent purchases). In our example, this would mean we assume the five units sold consist of one unit at $100 followed by four units at $80. The total cost of these five *last-in* goods ($420) is *first-out* when reported as cost of goods sold (CGS).

The costs of the remaining units (one at $80 and two at $70) are reported as ending inventory. LIFO allocates the newest (last-in) unit costs to cost of goods sold and the oldest unit costs to ending inventory.

Notice that the cost flows assumed for LIFO are the exact opposite of FIFO. Here's a summary of whether the oldest or newest unit costs are used to calculate amounts on the balance sheet or income statement.

	FIFO	LIFO
Inventory (balance sheet)	Newest	Oldest
Cost of goods sold (income statement)	Oldest (first-in)	Newest (last-in)

EXHIBIT 7.5 | Inventory Cost Flows Using LIFO (Last-in, first-out)

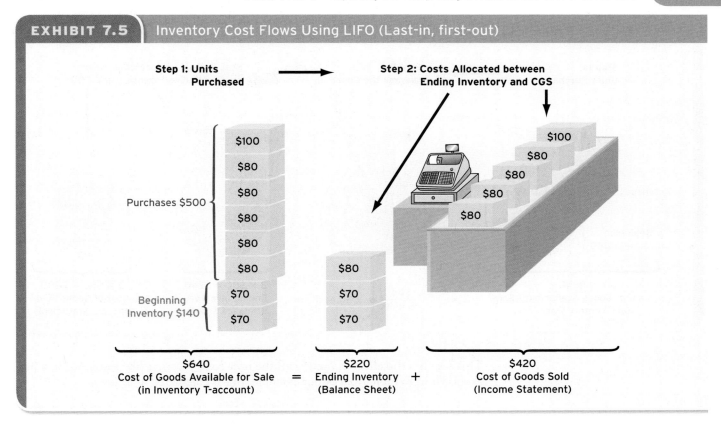

Step 1: Units Purchased

Step 2: Costs Allocated between Ending Inventory and CGS

Purchases $500
- $100
- $80
- $80
- $80
- $80
- $80

Beginning Inventory $140
- $70
- $70

Ending Inventory:
- $80
- $70
- $70

Cost of Goods Sold:
- $100
- $80
- $80
- $80
- $80

$640
Cost of Goods Available for Sale
(in Inventory T-account)

=

$220
Ending Inventory
(Balance Sheet)

+

$420
Cost of Goods Sold
(Income Statement)

Also notice that although they're called "inventory" costing methods, their names actually describe how to calculate the cost of goods sold. That is, the "first-out" part of FIFO and LIFO refers to the goods that are sold (i.e., first out) not the goods that are still here in ending inventory.

4. Weighted Average Cost Method

The **weighted average cost method** applies a methodology similar to how your grade point average is calculated. First, a weighted average unit cost of goods available for sale is calculated, taking into account the number of units purchased at different unit costs (Steps 1a and 1b below). This weighted average unit cost is then used to assign a dollar amount to cost of goods sold and to ending inventory (in Step 2).

> **YOU SHOULD KNOW**
>
> The **weighted average cost method** uses the weighted average unit cost of the goods available for sale for both cost of goods sold and ending inventory.

Step 1a. Determine the number of units and cost of goods available for sale. Using our example, these would be calculated as follows:

Number of Units	×	Unit Cost	=	Total Cost
2	×	$70	=	$140
5	×	$80	=	400
1	×	$100	=	100
8		Available for sale		$640

Step 1b. Calculate the weighted average cost per unit, as follows:

$$\text{Weighted Average Cost} = \frac{\$ \;\; \text{Cost of Goods Available for Sale}}{\# \;\; \text{Number of Units Available for Sale}}$$

>  **COACH'S TIP**
>
> When calculating the weighted average cost, be sure to *weight* the costs by the number of units at each cost. Don't just average the unit costs ($100, $80, $70) without considering the number of units purchased at each cost.

EXHIBIT 7.6 | Inventory Cost Flows Using Weighted Average Cost

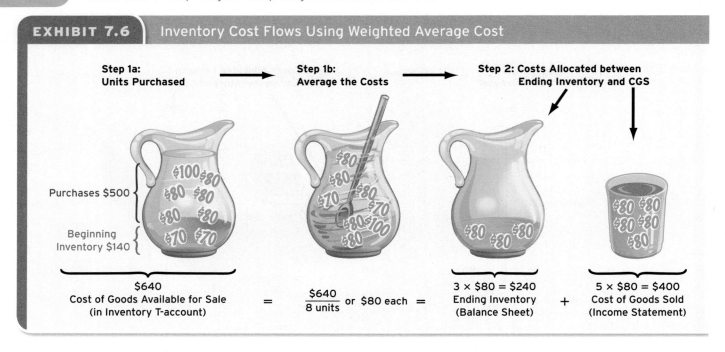

This step has the effect of mixing all the unit costs together like Kool-Aid in a jug, as shown in Exhibit 7.6. For our example, this is calculated as follows:

$$\text{Weighted Average Cost} = \frac{\$640}{8\ \text{Units}} = \$80\ \text{per unit}$$

Step 2. Assign the same weighted average unit cost to cost of goods sold and ending inventory. In our example, this would be calculated as follows

$$\text{Cost of Goods Sold} = 5\ \text{units} \times \$80 = \$400$$

$$\text{Ending Inventory} = 3\ \text{units} \times \$80 = \$240$$

Financial Statement Effects of Costing Methods

The preceding calculations indicate the dollar amount to enter into the accounting system as a reduction in inventory and increase in cost of goods sold. For example, a company using the Weighted Average Cost method (as shown in Exhibit 7.6) would report the following, using journal entries that add up to the amount shown below:

1. Analyze

Assets	=	Liabilities	+	Stockholders' Equity
Inventory −400 =				Cost of Goods Sold (+E) −400

2. Record

(b)   *dr* Cost of Goods Sold (+E, −SE)   400
          cr Inventory (−A)   400

Exhibit 7.7 summarizes the financial statement effects of the FIFO, LIFO, and weighted average methods in our example. Remember that the methods differ only in how they split the cost of goods available for sale between ending inventory and cost of goods sold. If a cost goes into ending inventory, it doesn't go into cost of goods sold. For that reason, the method that gives the highest dollar amount of ending inventory also gives the lowest cost of goods sold. **When costs are rising,** as they are in our example in Exhibit 7.7, FIFO leads to a higher inventory value (making the balance sheet *appear* stronger) and a lower cost of goods sold (resulting in a higher gross profit, making the company *look* more profitable). **When costs are falling,** the effects are reversed, with FIFO giving the lowest ending inventory amount as well as the highest cost of goods sold—a double whammy. Remember that these are not "real" economic effects because the same number of units is either sold or still on hand in ending inventory regardless of the inventory costing method used.

EXHIBIT 7.7	Financial Statement Effects of Inventory Costing Methods		
	FIFO	**LIFO**	**Weighted Average**
Income Statement (I/S) Effects			
Sales	$480	$480	$480
Cost of goods sold	380	420	400
Gross profit	100	60	80
Selling, general, and administrative expenses	40	40	40
Income from operations	60	20	40
Other revenue (expenses)	20	20	20
Income before income taxes	80	40	60
Income tax expense (assume 25%)	20	10	15
Net income	$ 60	$ 30	$ 45
Balance Sheet (B/S) Effects			
Inventory	$260	$220	$240
CGS Equation (Relating the B/S to the I/S)			
Beginning inventory	$140	$140	$140
Plus: Purchases	500	500	500
Cost of goods available for sale	640	640	640
Minus: Ending inventory (on the balance sheet)	260	220	240
Cost of good sold (on the income statement)	$380	$420	$400

Given these effects, you might wonder why a company would ever use a method that produces a lower inventory amount and a higher cost of goods sold. The answer is suggested in Exhibit 7.7, in the line called Income tax expense. **When faced with increasing costs per unit,** as in our example, **a company that uses FIFO will have a higher income tax expense.** This income tax effect is a real cost, in the sense that the company will actually have to pay more income taxes in the current year, thereby reducing the company's cash.

A common question people ask is whether managers are free to choose LIFO one period, FIFO the next, and then back to LIFO, depending on whether unit costs are rising or declining during the period. Because this constant switching would make it difficult to compare financial results across periods, accounting rules prevent it. A change in method is allowed only if it will improve the accuracy with which financial results and financial position are measured. Companies can, however, use different inventory methods for different product lines of inventory, as long as the methods are used consistently over time. Tax rules also limit the methods that can be used. In the United States, the LIFO Conformity Rule requires that if LIFO is used on the income tax return, it also must be used in financial statement reporting. In Canada and Europe, LIFO is not allowed for tax purposes, so it's rarely used in financial statements. International accounting rules do not allow LIFO at all.

Ethical Insights

Just Whom Are You Working For?

Given a choice between FIFO and LIFO, most stockholders would want managers to use the method that results in the lowest income taxes because this saves the company money. Managers, on the other hand, might prefer the method that produces the highest net income, particularly if they are paid a bonus based on reported profits. Clearly, a manager who selects an accounting method that is not optimal for the company solely to increase his or her own pay is engaging in questionable ethical behavior.

Additional Inventory Cost Flow Computations

Now that you've seen how these cost flow assumptions work and that they actually make a difference in the reported results, you could probably use some practice with a more complex example. In the following problem, we will show you how to calculate the cost of ending inventory and cost of goods sold using FIFO.

Assume Oakley started buying and selling a new line of products during the year and had the following transactions, which resulted in a total cost of goods available for sale of $5,850. Based on a year-end inventory count, Oakley determined that 200 units were still on hand. Calculate the cost of ending inventory and cost of goods sold using the FIFO method.

Date	Description	Units	Unit Cost	Total Cost	
January 1	Beginning Inventory	60	$10		$ 600
March 13	Purchase	40	10	$ 400	
April 27	Purchase	100	11	1,100	
June 15	Purchase	150	12	1,800	
August 11	Purchase	150	13	1,950	5,250
	Goods Available for Sale	500			$5,850

Still here   or   Sold

FIFO Ending Inventory	Units	Unit Cost	Total Cost
Last units in (August 11)	150	$13	$1,950
Next units in (June 15)	50	12	600
Total	200		$2,550

FIFO Cost of Goods Sold	Units	Unit Cost	Total Cost
First units in (January 1)	60	$10	$ 600
Next units in (March 13)	40	10	400
Next units in (April 27)	100	11	1,100
Next units in (June 15)	100	12	1,200
Total	300		$3,300

In this example, we directly calculated both the cost of ending inventory and the cost of goods sold. To double check your calculations, you can plug them into the CGS equation or a T-account to make sure they work out, as we do here:

Beginning inventory	$ 600
+ Purchases of merchandise during the year	+ 5,250
= Goods available for sale	= 5,850
− Ending inventory	− 2,550
= Cost of goods sold	= $3,300

dr +	Merchandise Inventory		cr −
Beginning	600		
Purchases	5,250	3,300	Cost of Goods Sold
Ending	2,550		

Now, using this same example, let's review how to use LIFO to calculate the cost of ending inventory and cost of goods sold. Notice that the total cost of goods available for sale ($5,850) does not differ from before. The only difference between LIFO and FIFO is that they assume different units have been sold, so they assign different costs to ending inventory and cost of goods sold.

Date	Description	Units	Unit Cost		Total Cost	
January 1	Beginning Inventory	60	$10		$ 600	
March 13	Purchase	40	10	$ 400		
April 27	Purchase	100	11	1,100		
June 15	Purchase	150	12	1,800		
August 11	Purchase	150	13	1,950	5,250	
	Goods Available for Sale	500			$5,850	

Still here   or   Sold

LIFO Ending Inventory	Units	Unit Cost	Total Cost		LIFO Cost of Goods Sold	Units	Unit Cost	Total Cost
First units in (January 1)	60	$10	$ 600		Last units in (August 11)	150	$13	$1,950
Next units in (March 13)	40	10	400		Next units in (June 15)	150	12	1,800
Next units in (April 27)	100	11	1,100		Total	300		$3,750
Total	200		$2,100					

HOW'S IT GOING?   Self-Study Quiz

Use the CGS equation and a T-account to prove the accuracy of the LIFO calculations shown above.

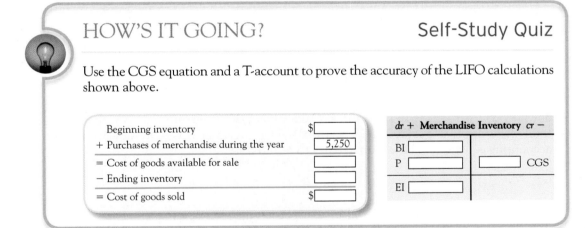

Beginning inventory	$ ☐
+ Purchases of merchandise during the year	5,250
= Cost of goods available for sale	☐
− Ending inventory	☐
= Cost of goods sold	$ ☐

dr + **Merchandise Inventory** *cr* −

BI ☐
P ☐   ☐ CGS
EI ☐

If we used the weighted average cost method in the previous example, the cost of ending inventory and cost of goods sold would be calculated as follows:

Date	Description	Units	Unit Cost	Total Cost
December 31	Goods Available for Sale	500		$5,850

$$\text{Weighted Average Unit Cost} = \frac{\$5,850}{500} = \$11.70$$

Still here   or   Sold

Weighted Average Ending Inventory	Units	Unit Cost	Total Cost	Weighted Average Cost of Goods Sold	Units	Unit Cost	Total Cost
Total	200	$11.70	$2,340	Total	300	$11.70	$3,510

LOWER OF COST OR MARKET

LP7

You've spent a lot of time learning how to calculate inventory costs using different methods. And it's been time well spent because most of the time inventories are reported at cost, just like the cost principle says. However, you're not quite done yet because you need to know what happens when inventory value falls below its recorded cost. The value of inventory can fall below its recorded cost for two reasons: (1) it's easily replaced by identical goods at a lower cost, or (2) it's become outdated or damaged. The first case typically involves high-tech goods like cell phones or Oakley's Plutonite® lenses, which become cheaper to make when companies become more efficient at making them. The second case commonly occurs with fad or seasonal goods, like Oakley's board shorts, when their value drops at the end of the season. In either instance, when the value of inventory falls below its recorded cost, the amount recorded for Inventory is written down to its lower market value. This rule is known as reporting inventories at the **lower of cost or market (LCM),** which ensures inventory assets are not reported at more than they're worth. Let's look at how the inventory write-down is determined and recorded.

Assume Oakley's ending inventory includes two items whose replacement costs have recently fallen as a result of significant improvements in production technology. Each item's replacement cost is used as an estimate of market value, which is then compared to the recorded cost per unit. The lower of these two amounts is called the lower of cost or market, and it is multiplied by the number of units on hand to calculate the amount that this inventory should be reported at after all adjustments have been made.

Item	Quantity	Cost per Item	Replacement Cost (Market) per Item	LCM per Item	Total Lower of Cost or Market
Plutonite lenses	1,000	$165	$150	$150	1,000 × $150 = $150,000
Unobtainium inlays	400	20	25	20	400 × $ 20 = 8,000

Because the market value of the 1,000 Plutonite lenses ($150) is *lower* than the recorded cost ($165), the amount recorded for ending inventory needs to be written down by $15 per lens ($165 − 150). If Oakley has 1,000 units in inventory, then the total write-down is $15,000 ($15 × 1,000). The effects of this write-down on the accounting equation and the journal entry to record it is:

1. Analyze

Assets	=	Liabilities	+	Stockholders' Equity
Inventory −15,000 =				Inventory Write-down (+E) −15,000

2. Record

(a) *dr* Inventory Write-down (+E, −SE)   15,000
       cr Inventory (−A)   15,000

Because the original cost of the other product ($20) is already lower than the market value ($25), no write-down is necessary. The inlays remain on the books at their cost of $20 per unit ($8,000 in total). They are not increased in value to the higher replacement cost because GAAP requires that they be reported at the *lower* of cost or market.

Most companies report any inventory write-downs as an ordinary operating expense and explain the use of the LCM rule for inventory in Note 1 in their financial statement footnotes. Oakley's is shown in Exhibit 7.8.

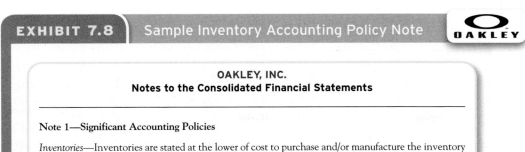

EXHIBIT 7.8 Sample Inventory Accounting Policy Note

OAKLEY

OAKLEY, INC.
Notes to the Consolidated Financial Statements

Note 1—Significant Accounting Policies

Inventories—Inventories are stated at the lower of cost to purchase and/or manufacture the inventory or the current estimated market value of the inventory, using the first-in, first-out method. The Company regularly reviews its inventory quantities on hand and records a provision for excess and obsolete inventory to appropriately reflect net realizable value for all slow-moving and discontinued inventory based upon the Company's estimated forecast of product demand and production requirements.

The failure to estimate the market value of inventory appropriately is one of the most common types of financial statement errors. To learn more about how these and other inventory errors can affect the financial statements, see Supplement B at the end of this chapter.

Evaluate the Results

INVENTORY TURNOVER ANALYSIS

If you see a company's inventory balance increase from $100,000 in one period to $130,000 in the next, is it good news or bad news? It could be good news, if it occurs because management is building up stock in anticipation of increasing sales in the near future. On the other hand, it could be bad news if the buildup is a result of having bought or made a bunch of crusty old inventory that nobody wants. If you work inside the company, it's easy to determine whether the reason for a change in inventory levels is good or bad news: you just talk to the sales managers. But if you're a typical financial statement user on the outside, how can you tell? The method used by most analysts is called an **inventory turnover** analysis.

The idea behind an inventory turnover analysis is shown in Exhibit 7.9. As a company buys goods, its inventory balance goes up, and as it sells goods, the inventory balance goes down. This process of buying and selling is called inventory turnover, and it is repeated over and over during each accounting period, for each line of products.

Analysts assess how many times average inventory has been bought (or made) and sold during the period by calculating the inventory turnover ratio. A higher ratio indicates that inventory moves more quickly from purchase (or production) to the ultimate customer, reducing storage and obsolescence costs. Because less money is tied up in inventory, the excess can be invested to earn interest income or reduce borrowing, which reduces interest expense. More efficient purchasing and production techniques as well as high product demand will boost this ratio. Analysts and creditors compare the

Learning Objective 5
Compute and interpret the inventory turnover ratio.

YOU SHOULD KNOW
Inventory turnover is the process of buying and selling inventory.

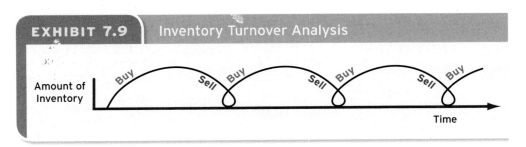

EXHIBIT 7.9 Inventory Turnover Analysis

inventory turnover ratio from period to period because a sudden decline may mean that a company is facing an unexpected drop in demand for its products or is becoming sloppy in its inventory management.

Rather than evaluate the **number** of times inventory turns over during a year, some people find it easier to think in terms of the **length** of time (in days) it takes to sell inventory. It's easy to convert the inventory turnover ratio into the average days to sell. Simply calculate 365 ÷ inventory turnover ratio and you'll have the average **days to sell.** This measure doesn't say anything different about the company's ability to buy and sell inventory—it's just a little easier to interpret. In terms of Exhibit 7.9, the inventory turnover ratio counts the number of loops in a given period of time, whereas the days to sell tells you the average number of days between loops.

FINANCIAL ANALYSIS TOOLS		
Name of Measure	Formula	What It Tells You
Inventory turnover ratio	$\dfrac{\text{Cost of Goods Sold}}{\text{Average Inventory}}$	• The number of times inventory turns over during the period • A higher ratio means faster turnover
Days to sell	$\dfrac{365}{\text{Inventory Turnover Ratio}}$	• Average number of days from purchase to sale • A higher number means a longer time to sell

Comparison to Benchmarks

Inventory turnover ratios and the number of days to sell can be a useful way to compare the inventory management practices of different companies. But use them cautiously because these measures can vary significantly between industries. For merchandisers, inventory turnover refers to buying and selling goods, whereas for manufacturers, it refers to producing and delivering inventory to customers. These differences are reflected in Exhibit 7.10, which shows that McDonald's has a turnover ratio of 35.4, which means it takes about 10 days to sell its entire food inventory (including the stuff in its freezers). The motorcycles at Harley-Davidson hog more time, as indicated by its inventory turnover ratio of 14.7, which equates to about 25 days to produce and sell. Oakley's inventory turned over only 2.4 times during the year, which is just once every 152 days.

EXHIBIT 7.10	Summary of Inventory Turnover Ratio Analyses

Company	Relevant Information (in millions)			2005 Inventory Turnover Calculation		2005 Days to Sell Calculation	
OAKLEY		2005	2004	$\dfrac{\$277.2}{\$(119.0 + 115.1)/2}$	= 2.4 times	$\dfrac{365 \text{ days}}{2.4 \text{ times}}$	= 152.1 days
	CoGS	$277.2	$262.5				
	Inventory	$119.0	$115.1				
HARLEY-DAVIDSON MOTORCYCLES		2005	2004	$\dfrac{\$3,301.7}{\$(221.4 + 226.9)/2}$	= 14.7 times	$\dfrac{365 \text{ days}}{14.7 \text{ times}}$	= 24.8 days
	CoGS	$3,301.7	$3,115.6				
	Inventory	$221.4	$226.9				
i'm lovin' it		2005	2004	$\dfrac{\$5,207.2}{\$(147.0 + 147.5)/2}$	= 35.4 times	$\dfrac{365 \text{ days}}{35.4 \text{ times}}$	= 10.3 days
	CoGS	$5,207.2	$4,852.7				
	Inventory	$147.0	$147.5				

Inventory turnover also can vary significantly between companies within the same industry, particularly if they take different approaches to pricing their inventories. In Chapter 6, we saw that Wal-Mart follows a low-cost pricing policy, which means setting its sales prices only slightly above cost. This policy led Wal-Mart to earn about 23 cents of gross profit on each dollar of sales whereas Saks earned 37 cents of gross profit. But when you consider the inventory turnover measures, you can see the full implications of this pricing policy. Wal-Mart turns its inventory over about 7.8 times a year (47 days), whereas Saks turns inventory over 3.2 times a year (114 days). Often, the company with a lower gross profit percentage has a faster inventory turnover.

With inventory turnover ratios varying between industries and companies, it's most useful to compare a company's turnover with its own results from prior periods. For practice at computing and comparing to prior periods, try the following Self-Study Quiz, which asks you to calculate Oakley's inventory turnover ratio and days to sell in 2004.

HOW'S IT GOING? Self-Study Quiz

Oakley's balance sheet and income statement information for prior years are presented in Exhibit 7.1 and 7.2 (pages 293 and 294). Round the millions shown there to one decimal place to simplify your work.

(a) Calculate Oakley's inventory turnover and days to sell in 2004.

(b) Did Oakley's inventory turnover improve or decline from 2004 (calculated in a) to 2005 (shown in Exhibit 7.10)?

2004 Inventory Turnover:

$$\frac{\boxed{}}{(\boxed{} + \boxed{})/2} = \boxed{} \text{ times}$$

2004 Days to Sell:

$$\frac{365 \text{ days}}{\boxed{} \text{ times}} = \boxed{} \text{ days}$$

Quiz Answers

a. $\dfrac{262.5}{(115.1 + 98.7)/2} = 2.5$ times

$365 \div 2.5 = 146.0$ days

b. Oakley's inventory turnover declined in 2005 (6 more days to sell).

THE IMPACT OF INVENTORY COSTING METHODS

As you saw earlier in Exhibit 7.7 (page 301), different inventory cost flow assumptions can yield different amounts reported for Inventory and Cost of goods sold, even when the underlying business transactions are identical. Because inventory and cost of goods sold numbers are the main inputs into the inventory turnover ratio and days to sell calculations, these two measures of turnover will be affected by the cost flow assumption used. This is a bit of a problem for you, as a financial statement user, because as shown in the graphic in the margin to the right, not all companies use the same cost flow assumption.

Fortunately, U.S. public companies using LIFO also report in the financial statement notes what their inventory balance would have been had they used FIFO. This isn't a big burden on accountants because most LIFO companies actually keep track of the costs of inventory and goods sold during the year using FIFO and then adjust the accounts to LIFO at the end of the year, using what is called a LIFO Reserve. Exhibit 7.11 shows an example of how this adjustment is presented in the notes to the financial statements of Deere & Company, the manufacturer of John Deere farm, lawn, and construction equipment. Until John Deere made its LIFO adjustment at the end of 2005, its inventory was reported in its books at a FIFO cost of $3,267 million. After the adjustment to LIFO, John Deere reported only $2,135 million of inventories on its balance sheet.

Learning Objective 6
Explain how accounting methods affect evaluations of inventory management.

Inventory Costing Methods Used by U.S. Firms

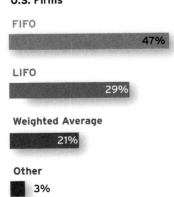

FIFO — 47%

LIFO — 29%

Weighted Average — 21%

Other — 3%

EXHIBIT 7.11 | LIFO Inventory Reporting

DEERE & COMPANY
Notes to the Consolidated Financial Statements

Note 13—Inventories

Most inventories owned by Deere & Company and its United States equipment subsidiaries are valued at cost, on the "last-in, first-out" (LIFO) basis. If all inventories had been valued on a FIFO basis, estimated inventories at October 31 in millions of dollars would have been as follows:

	2005	2004
Total FIFO value	$3,267	$3,001
Adjustment to LIFO basis	1,132	1,002
Inventories	$2,135	$1,999

Notice how huge the difference between FIFO and LIFO can be for an old business like John Deere, which was incorporated in 1868. The cost of inventory using the FIFO assumption ($3,267 in 2005) was over 1.5 times bigger than the cost calculated with the LIFO assumption ($2,135 in 2005). These kinds of differences can have similarly large effects when inventory numbers are used in analyses such as the inventory turnover ratio. The lesson here for now is that, when analyzing a company's inventory or cost of goods sold numbers, you should compare that company only to its own results in prior periods or to another company that uses the same cost flow assumption.[4]

SUPPLEMENT A: APPLYING FIFO AND LIFO IN A PERPETUAL INVENTORY SYSTEM

There were several good reasons for showing, in the previous sections of this chapter, how cost flow assumptions are applied in a periodic inventory system, even though most modern companies use perpetual inventory systems. First, only the LIFO and weighted average calculations differ between periodic and perpetual inventory systems. FIFO calculations don't differ between periodic and perpetual systems. Nearly half of all U.S. companies use FIFO, so even if they calculate costs under a perpetual system, it is identical to calculating costs under a periodic system. Second, most LIFO companies actually use FIFO during the period and then adjust to LIFO at the end of the period. By waiting to the end of the period to calculate this LIFO adjustment, it's *as if* all purchases during the period were recorded before the cost of goods sold is calculated and recorded. In other words, it's *as if* these companies use a periodic inventory system to determine their LIFO inventory numbers, even though they actually track the number of units bought and sold on a perpetual basis. Third, companies typically adjust their records at year-end to match a physical count of the inventory on hand, so as a practical matter, all companies are in substance on a periodic costing system. Fourth, the periodic inventory system is much easier to visualize, so for pedagogical reasons, it's an appropriate way to be introduced to cost flow assumptions.

Despite these reasons, it can be useful to know how to apply cost flow assumptions in a perpetual inventory system. In this supplement, we show how to use the LIFO cost flow assumption to calculate the cost of goods sold and cost of ending inventory on a perpetual basis.[5] In a perpetual inventory system, LIFO numbers are calculated using the cost of goods last in as of the date of sale. This differs from a periodic system, where the cost of

---

[4] LIFO cost of goods sold numbers can be converted to FIFO equivalents using information in the financial statement notes, but we leave that calculation for intermediate accounting textbooks.

[5] Use of the weighted average cost flow assumption in perpetual inventory systems is discussed in intermediate financial accounting textbooks.

goods sold is calculated as if all sales occurred at the end of the period. To illustrate the difference, assume the following:

January   1   Beginning inventory consists of **two** units of snow goggles costing **$70 each.**

March   12   Purchased **five** units of snow goggles costing **$80 each.**

April   27   Sold five units for $120 each.

June   9   Purchased **one** unit of snow goggles costing **$100.**

Note that this example is identical to the one presented earlier in this chapter, except for one important difference. A periodic system assumes that the five units are sold after all purchases have been made. In the current example, the units are sold (and must be recorded under the perpetual system) on April 27 before the June 9 purchase is made and recorded. This small difference changes the LIFO cost of goods sold and ending inventory calculations because at the time of the sale, the goggles last in were acquired on March 12 at $80 each, which excludes the unit purchased on June 9 at $100. Because the June 9 purchase occurs after the cost of goods sold is recorded in the perpetual system, it is included in the cost of inventory still on hand at the end of the period. These perpetual LIFO cost flow calculations are illustrated in Exhibit 7S.1.

EXHIBIT 7S.1	Inventory Cost Flow Calculations Using Perpetual LIFO (Last-in, first-out)

		GOODS IN INVENTORY			GOODS SOLD		
Date	Description	Units	Unit Cost	Total Cost	Units	Unit Cost	Total Cost
January 1	Beginning inventory	2	$70	$140			
March 12	Purchase	5	80	400			
	Goods available for sale	7		540			
April 27	Sale	(5)	80	(400)	5	$80	$400
	Goods available for sale	2		140			
June 9	Purchase	1	100	100			
	Total	3		$240	5		$400

Notice that, in this example of rising costs, the perpetual LIFO cost of goods sold of $400 shown in Exhibit 7S.1 is lower than the periodic LIFO cost of goods sold of $420 calculated earlier in the chapter. Because perpetual LIFO cost of goods sold is lower, income before income taxes is higher, which means that income tax expense is higher under perpetual LIFO than under periodic LIFO. The potential tax savings that can be gained from using periodic LIFO is yet another reason that explains why many LIFO companies calculate and adjust their cost of goods sold and ending inventory at the end of the accounting period *as if* they were using a periodic LIFO inventory system.

SUPPLEMENT B: THE EFFECTS OF ERRORS IN ENDING INVENTORY

As mentioned earlier in the chapter, the failure to apply the LCM rule correctly to ending inventory is considered an error. Other errors can occur when inappropriate quantities or unit costs are used in calculating inventory cost. Regardless of the reason, errors in inventory can significantly affect both the balance sheet and the income statement. As the cost of goods sold equation indicates, a direct relationship exists between ending inventory and cost of goods sold because items not in the ending inventory are assumed to have been sold. Thus, any errors in ending inventory will affect the balance sheet (current assets) and the income statement (cost of goods sold, gross profit, and net

Topic Tackler

PLUS

Check out www.mhhe.com/phillips2e for audio, visual, and PowerPoint presentations on this topic.

income). The effects of inventory errors are felt in more than one year because the ending inventory for one year becomes the beginning inventory for the next year.

To determine the effects of inventory errors on the financial statements in both the current year and the following year, use the cost of goods sold equation. For example, let's assume that ending inventory was overstated in 2007 by $10,000 due to an error that was not discovered until 2008. This would have the following effects in 2007:

2007	
Beginning inventory	Accurate
+ Purchases of merchandise during the year	Accurate
− Ending inventory	Overstated $10,000
= Cost of goods sold	Understated $10,000

Because cost of goods sold was understated, gross profit and income before income taxes would be overstated by $10,000 in 2007. (Net income would be overstated as well, although the effects would be offset somewhat by overstated income tax expense.)

The 2007 ending inventory becomes the 2008 beginning inventory, so even if 2008 ending inventory is calculated correctly, the error in 2007 creates an error in 2008 as shown in the following table:

2008	
Beginning inventory	Overstated $10,000
+ Purchases of merchandise during the year	Accurate
− Ending inventory	Accurate
= Cost of goods sold	Overstated $10,000

Because cost of goods sold is overstated, gross profit and income before income taxes would be understated by the same amount in 2008. (Net income would be understated as well, although the effects would be offset somewhat by understated income tax expense.)

Ignoring income taxes, the effects of these errors on net income in each of the two years is shown in Exhibit 7S.2. Notice that the cost of goods sold is understated in the first year and overstated in the second year. Over the two years, these errors offset one another. Inventory errors will "self-correct" like this only if ending inventory is accurately calculated at the end of the following year and adjusted to that correct balance.

EXHIBIT 7S.2   Two-Year Income Effects of Inventory Error

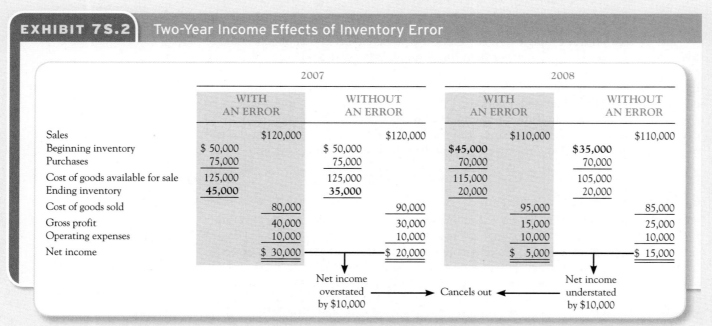

	2007		2008	
	WITH AN ERROR	WITHOUT AN ERROR	WITH AN ERROR	WITHOUT AN ERROR
Sales	$120,000	$120,000	$110,000	$110,000
Beginning inventory	$ 50,000	$ 50,000	$45,000	$35,000
Purchases	75,000	75,000	70,000	70,000
Cost of goods available for sale	125,000	125,000	115,000	105,000
Ending inventory	45,000	35,000	20,000	20,000
Cost of goods sold	80,000	90,000	95,000	85,000
Gross profit	40,000	30,000	15,000	25,000
Operating expenses	10,000	10,000	10,000	10,000
Net income	$ 30,000	$ 20,000	$ 5,000	$ 15,000

Net income overstated by $10,000 ⟶ Cancels out ⟵ Net income understated by $10,000

REVIEW THE CHAPTER

DEMONSTRATION CASE

Ebert Electronics distributes a number of consumer electronics goods. One product has been selected for use in this case. Assume that the following summarized transactions were completed during the year ended December 31, 2008, in the order given (assume that all transactions are cash):

	Units	Unit Cost
a. Beginning inventory (January 1)	11	$200
b. New inventory purchases (March 15)	5	209
c. New inventory purchases (July 21)	9	220
d. Sales (selling price, $420)	12	

Required:

1. Compute the following amounts, assuming the application of the FIFO, LIFO, and weighted average inventory costing methods on a periodic basis:

	Ending Inventory		Cost of Goods Sold	
	Units	Dollars	Units	Dollars
FIFO				
LIFO				
Weighted average				

2. Assuming that inventory cost was expected to follow the trend observed for this particular product and that Ebert Electronics wants to minimize its income taxes, which method would you recommend the company select to account for these inventory items? Explain your answer.

3. Assuming that operating expenses were $500 and the income tax rate is 25 percent, prepare the income statement for the period using the method selected in requirement 2.

4. Compute and interpret the inventory turnover ratio for the current period using the selected method.

Suggested Solution

1. (Calculations are shown on the next page.)

	Ending Inventory		Cost of Goods Sold	
	Units	Dollars	Units	Dollars
FIFO	13	$2,816	12	$2,409
LIFO	13	2,618	12	2,607
Weighted average	13	2,717	12	2,508

Date	Description	Units	Unit Cost	Total Cost
January 1	Beginning Inventory	11	$200	$2,200
March 15	Purchase	5	209	1,045
July 21	Purchase	9	220	1,980
	Goods Available for Sale	25		$5,225

Still here or *Sold*

FIFO

Ending Inventory	Units	Unit Cost	Total Cost
Last units in (July 21)	9	$220	$1,980
Next units in (March 15)	4	209	836
Total	13		$2,816

FIFO

Cost of Goods Sold	Units	Unit Cost	Total Cost
First units in (January 1)	11	$200	$2,200
Next units in (March 15)	1	209	209
Cost of Goods Sold	12		$2,409

LIFO

Ending Inventory	Units	Unit Cost	Total Cost
First units in (January 1)	11	$200	$2,200
Next units in (March 15)	2	209	418
Total	13		$2,618

LIFO

Cost of Goods Sold	Units	Unit Cost	Total Cost
Last units in (July 21)	9	$220	$1,980
Next units in (March 15)	3	209	627
Cost of Goods Sold	12		$2,607

Weighted Average

Weighted Average Cost $= \dfrac{\$5,225}{25 \text{ Units}} = \$209$ per unit

Ending Inventory	Units	Unit Cost	Total Cost
Total	13	$209	$2,717

Weighted Average

Cost of Goods Sold	Units	Unit Cost	Total Cost
Total	12	$209	$2,508

2. LIFO should be selected. Because costs are rising, LIFO produces higher cost of goods sold, lower income before income taxes, and lower income taxes.

3.

EBERT ELECTRONICS
Statement of Income
Year Ended December 31, 2008

Sales (12 × $420)	$5,040
Cost of goods sold	2,607
Gross profit	2,433
Other expenses	500
Income before income taxes	1,933
Income tax expense (25%)	483
Net income	$1,450

4. Inventory turnover ratio = Cost of Goods Sold ÷ Average Inventory
= $2,607 ÷ [($2,200 + $2,618) ÷ 2]
= 1.08

The inventory turnover ratio reflects how many times average inventory was bought and sold during the period. Based on our calculations, Ebert Electronics bought and sold its average inventory a little more than just once during the year, meaning its days to sell was 338 days (365 ÷ 1.08). This seems pitiful when you think Best Buy turns over its inventory of electronics, on average, in just 46 days.

CHAPTER SUMMARY

Describe inventory management goals. p. 292   LO1

- Make or buy a sufficient *quantity*, of *quality* and *innovative* products, at the lowest possible *cost*, so that they can be sold to earn the desired amount of gross profit.

Describe the different types of inventory. p. 292   LO2

- *Merchandise inventory* is bought by merchandisers in a ready to sell format. When *raw materials* enter a manufacturer's production process, they become *work in process* inventory, which is further transformed into *finished goods* that are ultimately sold to customers.

Compute costs using four inventory costing methods. p. 296   LO3

- Any of four generally accepted methods can be used to allocate the cost of inventory available for sale between goods that are sold and goods that remain on hand at the end of the accounting period.
- Specific identification assigns costs to ending inventory and cost of goods sold by tracking and identifying each specific item of inventory.
- Under FIFO, the costs first in are assigned to cost of goods sold, and the costs last in (most recent) are assigned to the inventory that is still on hand in ending inventory.
- Under LIFO, the costs last in are assigned to cost of goods sold, and the costs first in (oldest) are assigned to the inventory that is still on hand in ending inventory.
- Under weighted average cost, the weighted average cost per unit of inventory is assigned equally to goods sold and those still on hand in ending inventory.

Explain why inventory is reported at the lower of cost or market. p. 304   LO4

- The LCM rule ensures inventory assets are not reported at more than they are worth.

Compute and interpret the inventory turnover ratio. p. 304   LO5

- The inventory turnover ratio measures the efficiency of inventory management. It reflects how many times average inventory was acquired and sold during the period. The inventory turnover ratio is calculated by dividing Cost of Goods Sold by Average Inventory.

Explain how accounting methods affect evaluations of inventory management. p. 307   LO6

- To help financial statement users compare the inventory levels and ratios of companies that use different inventory cost flow assumptions, LIFO companies report FIFO numbers in their financial statement notes. Most companies use a LIFO reserve to show how FIFO numbers are converted into LIFO numbers.

Financial Analysis Tools		
Name of Measure	Formula	What It Tells You
Inventory turnover ratio	$\dfrac{\text{Cost of Goods Sold}}{\text{Average Inventory}}$	• The number of times inventory turns over during the period • A higher ratio means faster turnover
Days to sell	$\dfrac{365}{\text{Inventory Turnover Ratio}}$	• Average number of days from purchase to sale • A higher number means a longer time to sell

KEY TERMS

Cost of Goods Sold Equation p. 295
Days to Sell p. 306
First-In, First-Out (FIFO) p. 297
FOB Destination p. 293

FOB Shipping Point p. 293
Goods Available for Sale p. 294
Inventory Turnover p. 305
Last-In, First-Out (LIFO) p. 298

Lower of Cost or Market (LCM) p. 304
Specific Identification p. 296
Weighted Average Cost Method p. 299

PRACTICE MATERIAL

QUESTIONS

1. What are four goals of inventory management?
2. Describe the specific types of inventory reported by merchandisers and manufacturers.
3. If a Chicago-based company ships goods on September 30 to a customer in Hawaii with sales terms FOB destination, does the Chicago-based company include the inventory or the sale in its September financial statements?
4. Define *goods available for sale*. How does it differ from cost of goods sold?
5. Define *beginning inventory* and *ending inventory*.
6. The chapter discussed four inventory costing methods. List the four methods and briefly explain each.
7. Which inventory cost flow method is most similar to the flow of (*a*) a gumball machine, (*b*) bricks off a stack, and (*c*) gasoline out of a tank?
8. "Where possible, the inventory costing method should mimic actual product flows." Do you agree? Explain.
9. Contrast the effects of LIFO versus FIFO on ending inventory when (*a*) costs are rising and (*b*) costs are falling.
10. Contrast the income statement effect of LIFO versus FIFO (on cost of goods sold and gross profit) when (*a*) costs are rising and (*b*) costs are falling.
11. Explain briefly the application of the LCM rule to ending inventory. Describe its effect on the balance sheet and income statement when market is lower than cost.
12. (Supplement A) Distinguish perpetual inventory systems from periodic inventory systems by describing when and how cost of goods sold is calculated.
13. (Supplement B) Explain why an error in ending inventory in one period affects the following period.

Topic Tackler

PLUS

Check out www.mhhe.com/phillips2e for more multiple choice questions.

Quiz 7

MULTIPLE CHOICE

1. Which of the following statements are true regarding cost of goods sold?
   (i) Cost of goods sold represents the costs that a company incurred to purchase or produce inventory in the current period.
   (ii) Cost of goods sold is an expense on the income statement.
   (iii) Cost of goods sold is affected by the inventory method selected by a company (FIFO, LIFO, etc.).
   a. (i) only   **c.** (ii) and (iii)
   b. (ii) only   **d.** All of the above.

2. The inventory costing method selected by a company can affect
   a. The balance sheet.   **c.** The statement of retained earnings.
   b. The income statement.   **d.** All of the above.

3. Which of the following is not a name for a specific type of inventory?
   a. Finished goods.
   c. Raw materials.
   b. Merchandise inventory.
   d. Goods available for sale.

4. Each period, the cost of goods available for sale is allocated between
   a. Assets and liabilities.
   c. Assets and revenues.
   b. Assets and expenses.
   d. Expenses and liabilities.

5. A New York bridal dress designer that makes high-end custom wedding dresses and needs to know the exact cost of each dress most likely uses which inventory costing method?
   a. FIFO
   c. Weighted average
   b. LIFO
   d. Specific identification

6. If costs are rising, which of the following will be true?
   a. The cost of goods sold will be greater if LIFO is used rather than weighted average.
   b. The cost of ending inventory will be greater if FIFO is used rather than LIFO.
   c. The gross profit will be greater if FIFO is used rather than LIFO.
   d. All of the above are true.

7. Which inventory method provides a better matching of current costs with sales revenue on the income statement but also results in older values being reported for inventory on the balance sheet?
   a. FIFO
   c. LIFO
   b. Weighted average
   d. Specific identification

8. Which of the following regarding the *lower of cost or market* rule for inventory are true?
   (i) The lower of cost or market rule is an example of the historical cost principle.
   (ii) When the replacement cost of inventory drops below the original cost of inventory shown in the financial records, net income is reduced.
   (iii) When the replacement cost of inventory drops below the original cost of inventory shown in the financial records, total assets are reduced.
   a. (i) only
   c. (ii) and (iii)
   b. (ii) only
   d. All of the above.

9. An increasing inventory turnover ratio
   a. Indicates a longer time span between the ordering and receiving of inventory.
   b. Indicates a shorter time span between the ordering and receiving of inventory.
   c. Indicates a shorter time span between the purchase and sale of inventory.
   d. Indicates a longer time span between the purchase and sale of inventory.

10. Which of the following is true regarding companies that report their inventories on a LIFO basis?
    a. They will always have a higher income tax expense.
    b. They will always have a higher inventory balance.
    c. Both of the above.
    d. None of the above.

Solutions to Multiple Choice Questions
1.c 2.d 3.d 4.b 5.d 6.d 7.c 8.c 9.c 10.d

MINI-EXERCISES

Available with McGraw-Hill's
Homework Manager

HOMEWORK MANAGER **PLUS**

M7-1 **Items Included in Inventory**

Explain whether the following items should be included in the inventory of The Knot, Inc., a company that arranges and supplies wedding services for couples and other wedding consultants.

a. Goods are being held by The Knot on consignment from Emerald Bridal.
b. Goods in transit to Winston Wedding Consultants, sold by The Knot FOB shipping point.
c. Goods in transit to The Knot, purchased by The Knot FOB shipping point.

LO2
The Knot, Inc.

LO2   **M7-2 Matching Inventory Items to Type of Business**

Match the type of inventory with the type of business by placing checkmarks in the applicable columns:

	Type of Business	
Type of Inventory	Merchandising	Manufacturing
Merchandise		
Finished goods		
Work in process		
Raw materials		

LO3

Dillard's, Inc.

M7-3 Inferring Purchases Using the Cost of Goods Sold Equation

Dillard's, Inc., operates 330 department stores located in 29 states primarily in the Southwest, Southeast, and Midwest. In its annual report for the year ended January 28, 2006, the company reported cost of goods sold of $5,014 million, ending inventory for the current year of $1,803 million, and ending inventory for the previous year of $1,733 million. Is it possible to develop a reasonable estimate of the merchandise purchases for the year? If so, prepare the estimate. If not, explain why.

LO3   **M7-4 Matching Financial Statement Effects to Inventory Costing Methods**

Complete the following table by indicating which inventory costing method (FIFO or LIFO) would lead to the effects noted in the rows, for each of the circumstances described in the columns.

	1. Rising Costs	2. Declining Costs
a. Lowest net income		
b. Lowest ending inventory		

LO3   **M7-5 Matching Inventory Costing Method Choices to Company Circumstances**

Indicate whether a company interested in minimizing its income taxes should choose the FIFO or LIFO inventory costing method under each of the following circumstances.

a. Declining costs   _____
b. Rising costs   _____

LO3   **M7-6 Calculating Sales, Cost of Goods Sold, and Gross Profit under Periodic FIFO, LIFO, and Weighted Average Cost**

Given the following information, calculate sales, cost of goods sold, and gross profit, under (a) FIFO, (b) LIFO, and (c) weighted average. Assume a periodic inventory system is used.

		Units	Unit Cost	Unit Selling Price
July 1	Beginning inventory	100	$10	
July 13	Purchase	500	13	
July 25	Sold	(200)		$15
July 31	Ending inventory	400		

LO3   **M7-7 Calculating Cost of Goods Sold and Ending Inventory under FIFO, LIFO, and Weighted Average Cost (Periodic Inventory)**

Given the following information, calculate the cost of ending inventory and cost of goods sold, assuming a periodic inventory system is used in combination with (a) FIFO, (b) LIFO, and (c) Weighted Average Cost.

		Units	Unit Cost
July 1	Beginning Inventory	2,000	$20
July 5	Sold	1,000	
July 13	Purchased	6,000	22
July 17	Sold	3,000	
July 25	Purchased	8,000	25
July 27	Sold	5,000	

M7-8 Calculating Cost of Goods Sold and Ending Inventory under Periodic FIFO, LIFO, and Weighted Average   LO3

In its first month of operations, Literacy for the Illiterate opened a new bookstore and bought merchandise in the following order: (1) 300 units at $7 on January 1, (2) 450 units at $8 on January 8, and (3) 750 units at $9 on January 29. Assuming 900 units are on hand at the end of the month, calculate the cost of goods sold and ending inventory on January 31 under the (a) FIFO, (b) LIFO, and (c) weighted average cost flow assumptions. Assume a periodic inventory system is used.

M7-9 Reporting Inventory under Lower of Cost or Market   LO4

The Jewel Fool had the following inventory items on hand at the end of the year.

	Quantity	Cost per Item	Replacement Cost per Item
Necklaces	50	$75	$70
Bracelets	25	60	50

Determine the lower of cost or market per unit and the total amount that should be reported on the balance sheet for each item of inventory.

M7-10 Determining the Effects of Inventory Management Changes on the Inventory Turnover Ratio   LO5

Indicate the most likely effect of the following changes in inventory management on the inventory turnover ratio (+ for increase, − for decrease, and NE for no effect).

_____ a. Inventory delivered by suppliers daily (small amounts) instead of weekly (larger amounts).

_____ b. Shorten production process from 10 days to 8 days.

_____ c. Extend payments for inventory purchases from 15 days to 30 days.

M7-11 Calculating the Inventory Turnover Ratio and Days to Sell   LO5
Dillard's
Macy's

Using the data in M7-3, calculate to one decimal place the inventory turnover ratio and days to sell for Dillard's. In a recent year, Macy's reported an inventory turnover retio of 2.6. Which company's inventory turnover is faster?

M7-12 Reporting FIFO Ending Inventory in the Financial Statement Notes   LO6
Koss Corporation

Koss Corporation is a public company with 95 employees involved exclusively in making and selling stereo headphones. Koss reported ending inventory at June 30, 2005 of $7,595,803 under the LIFO costing method. In Note 1 to its financial statements, Koss reported that its FIFO inventory cost was $873,393 higher than LIFO at June 30, 2005. Using Exhibit 7.11 as a guide, show how Koss would report this in its financial statement notes.

M7-13 (Supplement A) Calculating Cost of Goods Sold and Ending Inventory under FIFO, LIFO, Average Cost (Perpetual Inventory)   LO3

Refer to M7-7. Complete the requirements (a) and (b) assuming a perpetual inventory system is used.

M7-14 (Supplement A) Calculating Cost of Goods Sold and Ending Inventory under Perpetual FIFO and LIFO

Repeat M7-8 (parts *a* and *b* only), except assume Literacy for the Illiterate uses a perpetual inventory system and it sold 600 units between January 9 and January 28.

M7-15 (Supplement B) Determining the Financial Statement Effects of Inventory Errors

Assume the 2007 ending inventory of Shea's Shrimp Shack was understated by $10,000. Explain how this error would affect the amounts reported for cost of goods sold and gross profit for 2007 and 2008.

M7-16 (Supplement B) Determining the Financial Statement Effects of Inventory Errors

Repeat M7-15, except assume the 2007 ending inventory was *overstated* by $100,000.

EXERCISES

Available with McGraw-Hill's Homework Manager

LO2

PC Mall, Inc.

E7-1 Items Incuded in Inventory

PC Mall, Inc. is a direct marketer of computer hardware, software, peripherals, and electronics. In its 2005 annual report, the company reported that its revenue is "recognized upon receipt of the product by the customer" and that its "inventories include goods-in-transit to customers at December 31, 2005."

Required:

1. Indicate whether PC Mall's sales terms are FOB shipping point or FOB destination.
2. Assume PC Mall sold inventory on account to eCOST.com on December 28, 2005, which was to be delivered January 3, 2006. The inventory cost PC Mall $25,000 and the selling price was $30,000. What amounts, if any, related to this transaction would be reported on PC Mall's balance sheet and income statement in 2005? In 2006?
3. For a four-month period in 2005, PC Mall placed inventory on consignment with one of its customers. During this period, would the inventory be reported on the balance sheet of PC Mall or its customer?
4. Assume PC Mall purchased electronics on December 29, 2005, which were received on January 2, 2006. Under what terms would these goods be included in PC Mall's inventory on December 31, 2005?

LO3

E7-2 Inferring Missing Amounts Based on Income Statement Relationships

Supply the missing dollar amounts for the 2008 income statement of Lewis Retailers for each of the following independent cases:

Cases	Sales Revenue	Beginning Inventory	Purchases	Total Available	Ending Inventory	Cost of Goods Sold	Gross Profit	Selling and General Expenses	Income from Operations
A	$800	$100	$700	$?	$500	$ 750	$?	$200	$?
B	900	200	700	?	?	?	?	150	0
C	?	150	?	?	250	200	400	100	?
D	800	?	600	?	250	?	?	250	$100

LO3

The Gap, Inc.

E7-3 Inferring Merchandise Purchases

The Gap, Inc., is a specialty retailer that operates stores selling clothes under the trade names Gap, Fourth and Towne, Banana Republic, and Old Navy. Assume that you are employed as a stock analyst and your boss has just completed a review of the Gap annual report for the year ended January 28, 2006. She provided you with her notes, but they are missing some information that you need. Her notes show that the ending inventory for Gap in the current year was $1,696,000,000 and in the previous year was $1,814,000,000. Net sales for the current year were $16,023,000,000. Gross profit was $5,869,000,000 and net income was $1,113,000,000. For your analysis, you determine that you need to know the amount of purchases and cost of goods sold for the year.

Required:

Do you need to ask your boss for her copy of the annual report, or can you develop the information from her notes? Explain and show calculations.

E7-4 Calculating Cost of Ending Inventory and Cost of Goods Sold under   LO3
       Periodic FIFO, LIFO, and Weighted Average

Assume Oahu Kiki's uses a periodic inventory system, which shows the following for the month of January. Sales totaled 240 units.

	Date	Units	Unit Cost	Total Cost
Beginning Inventory	January 1	120	$ 8	$ 960
Purchase	January 15	380	9	3,420
Purchase	January 24	200	11	2,200
Total available				$6,580

Required:

1. Calculate the cost of the 240 units sold under the (a) FIFO, (b) LIFO, and (c) weighted average cost methods.
2. Calculate the cost of ending inventory using the (a) FIFO, (b) LIFO, and (c) weighted average cost methods.
3. Double-check your answer to requirements 1 and 2 by using the cost of goods sold equation.

E7-5 Analyzing and Interpreting the Financial Statement Effects of Periodic   LO3
       FIFO, LIFO, and Weighted Average

Orion Iron Corp. uses a periodic inventory system. At the end of the annual accounting period, December 31, 2009, the accounting records provided the following information:

	Transactions	Units	Unit Cost
a.	Inventory, December 31, 2008	3,000	$12
	For the year 2009:		
b.	Purchase, April 11	9,000	10
c.	Purchase, June 1	8,000	13
d.	Sale, May 1 (sold for $40 per unit)	3,000	
e.	Sale, July 3 (sold for $40 per unit)	6,000	
f.	Operating expenses (excluding income tax expense), $195,000		

Required:

1. Compute the cost of goods sold under (a) FIFO, (b) LIFO, and (c) weighted average.
2. Prepare an income statement that shows 2009 amounts for the FIFO method in one column, the LIFO method in another column, and the weighted average method in a final column. Include the following line items in the income statement: sales, cost of goods sold, gross profit, operating expenses, and income from operations.
3. Compare the income from operations and the ending inventory amounts that would be reported under the three methods. Explain the similarities and differences.
4. Which inventory costing method may be preferred by Orion Iron Corp. for income tax purposes? Explain.

LO3   E7-6 Analyzing and Interpreting the Financial Statement Effects of FIFO, LIFO, and Weighted Average

Scoresby Inc. uses a periodic inventory system. At the end of the annual accounting period, December 31, 2008, the accounting records provided the following information:

Transactions	Units	Unit Cost
a. Inventory, December 31, 2007	3,000	$ 8
For the year 2008:		
b. Purchase, March 5	9,500	9
c. Purchase, September 19	5,000	11
d. Sale, April 15 (sold for $29 per unit)	4,000	
e. Sale, October 31 (sold for $31 per unit)	8,000	
f. Operating expenses (excluding income tax expense), $250,000		

Required:

1. Compute the cost of goods sold under (a) FIFO, (b) LIFO, and (c) weighted average.
2. Prepare an income statement that shows 2008 amounts for the FIFO method in one column, the LIFO method in another column, and the weighted average method in a final column. Include the following line items in the income statement: sales, cost of goods sold, gross profit, operating expenses, and income from operations.
3. Compare the income from operations and the ending inventory amounts that would be reported under the two methods. Explain the similarities and differences.
4. Which inventory costing method may be preferred by Scoresby for income tax purposes? Explain.

LO3   E7-7 Evaluating the Effects of Inventory Methods on Income from Operations, Income Taxes, and Net Income (Periodic)

Courtney Company uses a periodic inventory system. Data for 2007: beginning merchandise inventory (December 31, 2006), 1,000 units at $35; purchases, 4,000 units at $38; operating expenses (excluding income taxes), $71,000; ending inventory per physical count at December 31, 2007, 900 units; sales price per unit, $70; and average income tax rate, 30 percent.

Required:

1. Prepare income statements under the FIFO, LIFO, and weighted average costing methods. Use a format similar to the following:

		Inventory Costing Method		
Income Statement	Units	FIFO	LIFO	Weighted Average
Sales revenue	_____	$ _____	$ _____	$ _____
Cost of goods sold*	_____	_____	_____	_____
Gross profit		_____	_____	_____
Operating expenses		_____	_____	_____
Income from operations		_____	_____	_____
Income tax expense		_____	_____	_____
Net income		══════	══════	══════

Cost of goods sold equation:				
Beginning inventory	_____	$ _____	$ _____	$ _____
Purchases	_____	_____	_____	_____
Goods available for sale	_____	_____	_____	_____
Ending inventory	_____	_____	_____	_____
Cost of goods sold	══════	══════	══════	══════

2. Between FIFO and LIFO, which method is preferable in terms of (a) maximizing income from operations or (b) minimizing income taxes? Explain.
3. What would be your answer to requirement 2 if costs were falling? Explain.

E7-8 Evaluating the Effects of Inventory Methods on Operating Income, Income Taxes, and Net Income   LO3

Following is partial information for the income statement of Timber Company under three different inventory costing methods, assuming the use of a periodic inventory system:

	FIFO	LIFO	Weighted Average
Sales ($50 per unit)			
Cost of goods sold			
Selling and general expenses	$ 1,600	$ 1,600	$ 1,600
Income before income taxes			
Cost of goods sold equation			
Beginning inventory (330 units)	11,220	11,220	11,220
Purchases (475 units)	17,100	17,100	17,100
Goods available for sale			
Ending inventory (510 units)			
Cost of goods sold			

Required:

1. Compute cost of goods sold under the FIFO, LIFO, and weighted average inventory costing methods, and complete the cost of goods sold equation. Assume that each of the 475 units was purchased at the same cost per unit.
2. Prepare an income statement (up to income before income taxes) that compares each method.
3. Rank the three methods in order of highest income before income taxes.
4. Calculate income tax expense under each of the three methods, assuming an income tax rate equal to 30 percent of income before income taxes.
5. Rank the three methods in order of lowest income taxes.

E7-9 Choosing LIFO versus FIFO When Costs Are Rising and Falling   LO3

Use the following information to complete this exercise: sales, 550 units for $12,500; beginning inventory, 300 units; purchases, 400 units; ending inventory, 150 units; and operating expenses, $4,000. Begin by setting up the following table and then complete the requirements that follow.

		Costs Rising		Costs Falling	
		Situation A	Situation B	Situation C	Situation D
		FIFO	LIFO	FIFO	LIFO
Sales revenue		$12,500	$12,500	$12,500	$12,500
Beginning inventory	$3,600				
Purchases	5,200		_____	_____	_____
Goods available for sale	8,800				
Ending inventory	1,950		_____	_____	_____
Cost of goods sold		6,850	_____	_____	_____
Gross profit		5,650			
Operating expenses		4,000	4,000	4,000	4,000
Income from operations		1,650			
Income tax expense (30%)		495	_____	_____	_____
Net income		$ 1,155			

Required:

1. Complete the table for each situation. In Situations A and B (costs rising), assume the following: beginning inventory, 300 units at $12 = $3,600; purchases, 400 units at $13 = $5,200. In Situations C and D (costs falling), assume the opposite; that is, beginning inventory, 300 units at $13 = $3,900; purchases, 400 units at $12 = $4,800. Use periodic inventory procedures.

2. Describe the relative effects on income from operations as demonstrated by requirement 1 when costs are rising and when costs are falling.

3. Describe the relative effects on income taxes for each situation.

4. Would you recommend FIFO or LIFO? Explain.

LO4   **E7-10 Reporting Inventory at Lower of Cost or Market**

Peterson Furniture Designs is preparing the annual financial statements dated December 31, 2007. Ending inventory information about the five major items stocked for regular sale follows:

| | | Ending Inventory, 2007 | | | |
Item	Quantity on Hand	Unit Cost When Acquired (FIFO)	Replacement Cost (Market) at Year-End	LCM Per Item	Total LCM
Alligator Armoires	50	$15	$12		
Bear Bureaus	75	40	40		
Cougar Beds	10	50	52		
Dingo Cribs	30	30	30		
Elephant Dressers	400	10	6		

Required:

Complete the final two columns of the table and then compute the amount that should be reported for the 2007 ending inventory using the LCM rule applied to each item.

LO4   **E7-11 Reporting Inventory at Lower of Cost or Market**

Sandals Company was formed on January 1, 2008, and is preparing the annual financial statements dated December 31, 2008. Ending inventory information about the four major items stocked for regular sale follows:

| | | Ending Inventory, 2008 | |
Product Line	Quantity on Hand	Unit Cost When Acquired (FIFO)	Replacement Cost (Market) at Year-End
Air Flow	20	$12	$14
Blister Buster	75	40	38
Coolonite	35	55	50
Dudesly	10	30	35

Required:

1. Compute the amount that should be reported for the 2008 ending inventory using the LCM rule applied to each item.

2. How will the write-down of inventory to lower of cost or market affect the company's expenses reported for the year ended December 31, 2008?

LO4
RadioShack Corporation

E7-12 Preparing the Journal Entry to Record Lower of Cost or Market (LCM) Adjustments

RadioShack Corporation (RadioShack) sells consumer electronic goods and services through its 4,972 stores and 777 kiosks. In its annual report filed with the SEC for the year ended December 31, 2005, the company reported that it wrote down inventory by approximately $62,000,000 because its cost exceeded its market value. Show the effects of this adjustment on the accounting equation as well as the journal entry that the company would have made to record it.

E7-13 Analyzing and Interpreting the Inventory Turnover Ratio

LO5
Polaris Industries Inc.

Polaris Industries Inc. is the biggest snowmobile manufacturer in the world. It reported the following amounts in its financial statements (in millions):

	2005	2004	2003
Net sales revenue	$1,870	$1,773	$1,552
Cost of sales	1,452	1,349	1,189
Average inventory	188	179	169

Required:

1. Calculate to one decimal place the inventory turnover ratio and average days to sell inventory for 2005, 2004, and 2003.
2. Comment on any trends, and compare the effectiveness of inventory managers at Polaris to inventory managers at its main competitor, Arctic Cat, where inventory turns over 7.5 times per year (48.7 days to sell). Both companies use the same inventory costing method (FIFO).

E7-14 Analyzing and Interpreting the Effects of the LIFO/FIFO Choice on Inventory Turnover Ratio

LO3, LO5

Simple Plan Enterprises uses a periodic inventory system. Its records showed the following:

> Inventory, December 31, 2007, using FIFO → 38 Units @ $14 = $532
>
> Inventory, December 31, 2007, using LIFO → 38 Units @ $10 = $380

Transactions	Units	Unit Cost	Total Cost
Purchase, January 9, 2008	50	15	$ 750
Purchase, January 20, 2008	100	16	1,600
Sale, January 11, 2008 (at $38 per unit)	80		
Sale, January 27, 2008 (at $39 per unit)	56		

Required:

1. Compute cost of goods sold and cost of ending inventory under FIFO and LIFO.
2. Compute the inventory turnover ratio under the FIFO and LIFO inventory costing methods (show computations).
3. Based on your answer to 2, explain whether analysts should consider the inventory costing method when comparing companies' inventory turnover ratios.

E7-15 Comprehensive Financial Statement Exercise

LO3, LO5

College Coasters is a San Antonio based merchandiser specializing in logo-adorned drink coasters. The company reported the following balances in its unadjusted trial balance at December 1, 2007.

Cash	$10,005	Accounts payable	$ 1,500	Cost of goods sold	$8,900
Accounts receivable	2,000	Wages payable	300	Rent expense	1,100
Inventory	500	Taxes payable	0	Wages expense	2,000
Prepaid rent	600	Contributed capital	6,500	Depreciation expense	110
Equipment	810	Retained earnings	3,030	Income tax expense	0
Accumulated depreciation	110	Sales revenue	15,985	Other expenses	1,400

The company buys coasters from one supplier. All amounts in Accounts payable on December 1 are owed to that supplier. The inventory on December 1, 2007, consisted of 1,000 coasters, all of which were purchased in a batch on July 10 at a unit cost of $0.50. College Coasters uses the FIFO cost flow method.

During December 2007, the company entered into the following transactions. Some of these transactions are explained in greater detail below.

Dec.	1	Purchased 500 coasters on account from the regular supplier at a unit cost of $0.52, with terms of 2/10, n/30.
Dec.	2	Purchased 1,000 coasters on account from the regular supplier at a unit cost of $0.55, with terms of 2/10, n/30.
Dec.	15	Paid the supplier $1,600 cash on account.
Dec.	17	Sold 2,000 coasters on account at a unit price of $0.90.
Dec.	23	Paid employees $500, $300 of which related to work done in November and $200 for wages up to December 22.
Dec.	24	Collected $1,000 from customers on account.
Dec.	31	Loaded 1,000 coasters on a cargo ship to be delivered to a customer in Hawaii. The sale was made FOB destination with terms of 2/10, n/30.

Other relevant information includes the following:

a. "Other expenses" includes general, selling, and administrative expenses. College Coasters has not yet recorded $200 of advertising expenses incurred in December and purchased on account.

b. The company estimates that the equipment depreciates at a rate of $10 per month. One month of depreciation needs to be recorded.

c. Wages for the period from December 23–31 are $100 and will be paid on January 15, 2008.

d. The $600 of Prepaid rent relates to a six-month period ending on May 31, 2008.

e. No shrinkage or damage was discovered when the inventory was counted on December 31, 2007.

f. The company did not declare dividends and there were no transactions involving contributed capital.

g. The company has a 30 percent tax rate and has made no tax payments this year.

Required:

1. Analyze the accounting equation effects of each transaction and any adjustments required at month-end.

2. Prepare journal entries to record each transaction and any adjustments required at month-end.

3. Summarize the journal entries in T-accounts. Be sure to include the balances on December 1, 2007, as beginning account balances.

4. Prepare an income statement, statement of stockholders' equity, and classified balance sheet, using the formats presented in Exhibits 6.10, 5.8, and 5.6.

5. Calculate to one decimal place the inventory turnover ratio and days-to-sell in 2007, assuming that inventory was $500 on January 1, 2007. Evaluate these measures in comparison to an inventory turnover ratio of 12.0 during the year ended December 31, 2006.

LO6
Ford Motor Company

E7-16 Analyzing Notes to Adjust Inventory from LIFO to FIFO and Calculating the Effects on the Inventory Turnover Ratio and Days to Sell

The Ford Motor Company uses the LIFO method to determine the cost of most of its inventories, which were reported at a recent year-end as follows:

	Inventory (in $ millions)	
	2005	2004
Finished products	$ 7,224	$ 7,799
Raw material and work in process, supplies	4,056	3,968
Total inventories at FIFO	11,280	11,767
Less: LIFO adjustment	(1,009)	(1,001)
Total inventories	$10,271	$10,766

Required:

1. Given the amount of Ford's LIFO reserve at the end of 2005, are costs rising or falling in this industry?

2. The cost of goods sold reported by Ford for 2005 was $144,944 million. Using the CGS equation and the LIFO balances reported above, determine the cost of inventory acquired (purchases) during 2005.

3. If Ford had used FIFO, its cost of goods sold would have been $144,952 for 2005 (under LIFO it was $144,944 million). Calculate the inventory turnover ratio and days to sell under LIFO and FIFO, and comment on the significance of the inventory costing methods to these analyses of Ford's inventory.

E7-17 (Supplement A) Calculating Cost of Ending Inventory and Cost of Goods Sold under Perpetual FIFO and LIFO LO3

Refer to the information in E7-4. Assume Oahu Kiki uses a perpetual inventory system and that its 240 units were sold between January 16 and 23. Calculate the cost of ending inventory and the cost of goods sold using the FIFO and LIFO methods.

E7-18 (Supplement A) Calculating Cost of Ending Inventory and Cost of Goods Sold under Perpetual FIFO and LIFO LO3

Refer to the information in E7-5. Assume Orion Iron uses a perpetual inventory system. Calculate the cost of ending inventory and the cost of goods sold using the FIFO and LIFO methods.

E7-19 (Supplement B) Analyzing and Interpreting the Impact of an Inventory Error LO3

Dallas Corporation prepared the following two income statements:

	First Quarter 2007		Second Quarter 2007	
Sales revenue		$15,000		$18,000
Cost of goods sold				
Beginning inventory	$ 3,000		$ 4,000	
Purchases	7,000		12,000	
Goods available for sale	10,000		16,000	
Ending inventory	4,000		9,000	
Cost of goods sold		6,000		7,000
Gross profit		9,000		11,000
Operating expenses		5,000		6,000
Income from operations		$4,000		$ 5,000

During the third quarter, the company's internal auditors discovered that the ending inventory for the first quarter should have been $4,400. The ending inventory for the second quarter was correct.

Required:

1. What effect would the error have on total income from operations for the two quarters combined? Explain.

2. What effect would the error have on income from operations for each of the two quarters? Explain.

3. Prepare corrected income statements for each quarter. Ignore income taxes.

COACHED PROBLEMS

LO3   **CP7-1 Analyzing the Effects of Four Alternative Inventory Methods in a Periodic Inventory System**

Scrappers Supplies uses a periodic inventory system. At the end of the annual accounting period, December 31, 2008, the inventory records showed the following:

Transactions	Units	Unit Cost
Beginning inventory, January 1, 2008	200	$30
Transactions during 2008:		
a. Purchase, March 2	300	32
b. Sale, April 1 ($46 each)	(350)	
c. Purchase, June 30	250	36
d. Sale, August 1 ($46 each)	(50)	

TIP: Although the purchases and sales are listed in chronological order, in a periodic inventory system the cost of goods sold is determined *after* all of the purchases have occurred.

Required:

1. Compute the cost of goods available for sale, cost of ending inventory, and cost of goods sold at December 31, 2008, under each of the following inventory costing methods:
    a. Last-in, first-out.
    b. Weighted average cost.
    c. First-in, first-out.
    d. Specific identification, assuming that the April 1, 2008, sale was selected one-fifth from the beginning inventory and four-fifths from the purchase of March 2, 2008. Assume that the sale of August 1, 2008, was selected from the purchase of June 30, 2008.
2. Of the four methods, which will result in the highest gross profit? Which will result in the lowest income taxes?

LO4   **CP7-2 Evaluating the Income Statement and Income Tax Effects of Lower of Cost or Market**

Smart Company prepared its annual financial statements dated December 31, 2008. The company used the FIFO inventory costing method, but it failed to apply LCM to the ending inventory. The preliminary 2008 income statement follows:

Sales revenue		$280,000
Cost of goods sold		
Beginning inventory	$ 30,000	
Purchases	182,000	
Goods available for sale	212,000	
Ending inventory (FIFO cost)	44,000	
Cost of goods sold		168,000
Gross profit		112,000
Operating expenses		61,000
Income from operations		51,000
Income tax expense (30%)		15,300
Net income		$ 35,700

TIP: Inventory write-downs do not affect the cost of goods available for sale. Instead, the effect of the write-down is to reduce ending inventory, which increases cost of goods sold and then affects other amounts reported lower in the income statement.

Assume that you have been asked to restate the 2008 financial statements to incorporate LCM. You have developed the following data relating to the 2008 ending inventory:

Item	Quantity	Acquisition Cost Per Unit	Acquisition Cost Total	Current Replacement Unit Cost (Market)
A	3,000	$3	$ 9,000	$4
B	1,500	4	6,000	2
C	7,000	2	14,000	4
D	3,000	5	15,000	2
			$44,000	

Required:

1. Restate the income statement to reflect LCM valuation of the 2008 ending inventory. Apply LCM on an item-by-item basis and show computations.
2. Compare and explain the LCM effect on each amount that was changed in requirement 1.
3. What is the conceptual basis for applying LCM to merchandise inventories?

CP7-3 Calculating and Interpreting the Inventory Turnover Ratio and Days to Sell

LO5
Circuit City

Circuit City is a leading national retailer of brand-name consumer electronics, personal computers, and entertainment software. The company reported the following amounts in its financial statements (in millions).

	2006	2005
Net sales revenue	$11,598	$10,470
Cost of sales	8,767	7,901
Beginning inventory	1,455	1,517
Ending inventory	1,698	1,455

Required:

1. Determine the inventory turnover ratio and average days to sell inventory for 2006 and 2005. Round your answers to one decimal place.
   TIP: Remember to use costs in both the numerator (CGS) and denominator (average inventory).
2. Comment on any changes in these measures, and compare the effectiveness of inventory managers at Circuit City to inventory managers at Best Buy, where inventory turns over 7.9 times per year (46 days to sell).
3. Circuit City uses the weighted average cost method to determine the cost of goods sold and ending inventory. In contrast, Best Buy uses the FIFO method. If the cost of electronics merchandise is falling, which of these two costing methods will produce the higher cost of goods sold? Will this method produce a higher or lower ending inventory cost than the other method? Taken together, which method will suggest a faster inventory turnover?
   TIP: To answer this requirement, set up a table like this:

	FIFO	WA
CGS	H L	H L
Avg. Inv.	H L	H L

For each part of the ratio, circle whether it will be higher (H) or lower (L) in amount under that method. The larger ratio will be the one with H on top and L on the bottom.

LO3   **CP7-4 (Supplement A) Analyzing the Effects of the LIFO Inventory Method in a Perpetual Inventory System**

Using the information in CP7-1, calculate the cost of goods sold and ending inventory for Scrappers Supplies assuming it uses the LIFO cost method in combination with a perpetual inventory system. Compare these amounts to the periodic LIFO calculations in requirement 1*a* of CP7-1. Does the use of a perpetual inventory system result in a higher or lower cost of goods sold when costs are rising?

TIP: In CP7-4, the sale of 350 units on April 1 is assumed, under LIFO, to consist of the 300 units purchased March 2 and 50 units from beginning inventory.

LO3   **CP7-5 (Supplement B) Analyzing and Interpreting the Effects of Inventory Errors**

www.mhhe.com/phillips2e

Partial income statements for Murphy & Murphy (M & M) reported the following summarized amounts:

	2005	2006	2007	2008
Sales revenue	$50,000	$49,000	$ 71,000	$58,000
Cost of goods sold	32,500	35,000	43,000	37,000
Gross profit	17,500	14,000	28,000	21,000

After these amounts were reported, M & M's accountant determined that the inventory on December 31, 2006, was understated by $3,000. The inventory balance on December 31, 2007, was accurately stated.

Required:

1. Restate the partial income statements to reflect the correct amounts, after fixing the inventory error.

2. Compute the gross profit percentage for all four years both (*a*) before the correction and (*b*) after the correction. Does the pattern of gross profit percentages lend confidence to your corrected amounts? Explain. Round your answer to the nearest percentage.

    TIP: Gross profit percentage is calculated as (Gross profit ÷ Sales revenue) × 100.

GROUP A PROBLEMS

Available with McGraw-Hill's
Homework Manager

MANAGER **PLUS**™

LO3   **PA7-1 Analyzing the Effects of Four Alternative Inventory Methods in a Periodic Inventory System**

Gladstone Company uses a periodic inventory system. At the end of the annual accounting period, December 31, 2007, the accounting records for the most popular item in inventory showed the following:

Transactions	Units	Unit Cost
Beginning inventory, January 1, 2007	1,800	$5.00
Transactions during 2007:		
a. Purchase, January 30	2,500	6.20
b. Sale, March 14 ($5 each)	(1,450)	
c. Purchase, May 1	1,200	8.00
d. Sale, August 31 ($5 each)	(1,900)	

Required:

1. Compute the amount of goods available for sale, ending inventory, and cost of goods sold at December 31, 2007, under each of the following inventory costing methods:

    a. Last-in, first-out.

    b. Weighted average cost.

    c. First-in, first-out.

    d. Specific identification, assuming that the March 14, 2007, sale was selected two-fifths from the beginning inventory and three-fifths from the purchase of January 30, 2007. Assume that the sale of August 31, 2007, was selected from the remainder of the beginning inventory, with the balance from the purchase of May 1, 2007.

2. Of the four methods, which will result in the highest gross profit? Which will result in the lowest income taxes?

PA7-2 Evaluating the Income Statement and Income Tax Effects of Lower of Cost or Market

LO4

Springer Anderson Gymnastics prepared its annual financial statements dated December 31, 2007. The company used the FIFO inventory costing method, but it failed to apply LCM to the ending inventory. The preliminary 2007 income statement follows:

Sales revenue		$140,000
Cost of goods sold		
Beginning inventory	$ 15,000	
Purchases	91,000	
Goods available for sale	106,000	
Ending inventory (FIFO cost)	22,000	
Cost of goods sold		84,000
Gross profit		56,000
Operating expenses		31,000
Income from operations		25,000
Income tax expense (30%)		7,500
Net income		$ 17,500

Assume that you have been asked to restate the 2007 financial statements to incorporate LCM. You have developed the following data relating to the 2007 ending inventory:

		Acquisition Cost		Current Replacement Unit Cost
Item	Quantity	Per Unit	Total	(Market)
A	1,500	$3	$ 4,500	$4
B	750	4	3,000	2
C	3,500	2	7,000	1
D	1,500	5	7,500	3
			$22,000	

Required:

1. Restate the income statement to reflect LCM valuation of the 2007 ending inventory. Apply LCM on an item-by-item basis and show computations.

2. Compare and explain the LCM effect on each amount that was changed in requirement 1.

3. What is the conceptual basis for applying LCM to merchandise inventories?

PA7-3 Calculating and Interpreting the Inventory Turnover Ratio and Days to Sell

Harman International Industries is a world leading producer of loudspeakers and other electronics products, which are sold under brand names like JBL, Infinity, and Harman/Kardon. The company reported the following amounts in its financial statements (in millions):

	2006	2005
Net sales revenue	$3,248	$3,031
Cost of sales	2,095	1,999
Beginning inventory	312	292
Ending inventory	345	312

Required:

1. Determine the inventory turnover ratio and average days to sell inventory for 2006 and 2005. Round to one decimal place.
2. Comment on any changes in these measures, and compare the effectiveness of inventory managers at Harman to inventory managers at Boston Acoustics, where inventory turns over 3.7 times per year (99 days to sell). Both companies use the same inventory costing method (FIFO).

LO3

PA7-4 (Supplement A) Analyzing the Effects of the LIFO Inventory Method in a Perpetual Inventory System

Using the information in PA7-1, calculate the cost of goods sold and ending inventory for Gladstone Company assuming it uses the LIFO cost method in combination with a perpetual inventory system. Compare these amounts to the periodic LIFO calculations in requirement 1a of PA7-1. Does the use of a perpetual inventory system result in a higher or lower cost of goods sold when costs are rising?

LO3

www.mhhe.com/phillips2e

PA7-5 (Supplement B) Analyzing and Interpreting the Effects of Inventory Errors

The income statement for Sherwood Company summarized for a four-year period shows the following:

	2005	2006	2007	2008
Sales revenue	$2,000,000	$2,400,000	$2,500,000	$3,000,000
Cost of goods sold	1,400,000	1,660,000	1,770,000	2,100,000
Gross profit	600,000	740,000	730,000	900,000

An audit revealed that in determining these amounts, the ending inventory for 2006 was overstated by $20,000. The inventory balance on December 31, 2007, was accurately stated. The company uses a periodic inventory system.

Required:

1. Restate the partial income statements to reflect the correct amounts, after fixing the inventory error.
2. Compute the gross profit percentage for each year (a) before the correction and (b) after the correction, rounding to the nearest percentage. Do the results lend confidence to your corrected amounts? Explain.

GROUP B PROBLEMS

Available with McGraw-Hill's Homework Manager

HOMEWORK MANAGER **PLUS**

LO3

PB7-1 Analyzing the Effects of Four Alternative Inventory Methods in a Periodic Inventory System

Mojo Industries uses a periodic inventory system. At the end of the accounting period, January 31, 2009, the inventory records showed the following for an item that sold at $9 per unit:

Transactions	Unit Cost	Units	Total Cost
Inventory, January 1, 2009	$2.50	250	$625
Sale, January 10		(200)	
Purchase, January 12	3.00	300	900
Sale, January 17		(150)	
Purchase, January 26	4.00	80	320

Required:

1. Compute the amount of goods available for sale, ending inventory, and cost of goods sold at January 31, 2009, under each of the following inventory costing methods:

    a. Weighted average cost.

    b. First-in, first-out.

    c. Last-in, first-out.

    d. Specific identification, assuming that the January 10 sale was from the beginning inventory and the January 17 sale was from the January 12 purchase.

2. Of the four methods, which will result in the highest gross profit? Which will result in the lowest income taxes?

PB7-2 Evaluating the Income Statement and Income Tax Effects of Lower of Cost or Market   LO4

Mondetta Clothing prepared its annual financial statements dated December 31, 2008. The company used the FIFO inventory costing method, but it failed to apply LCM to the ending inventory. The preliminary 2008 income statement follows:

Sales revenue		$420,000
Cost of goods sold		
Beginning inventory	$ 45,000	
Purchases	273,000	
Goods available for sale	318,000	
Ending inventory (FIFO cost)	66,000	
Cost of goods sold		252,000
Gross profit		168,000
Operating expenses		93,000
Income from operations		75,000
Income tax expense (30%)		22,500
Net income		$ 52,500

Assume that you have been asked to restate the 2008 financial statements to incorporate LCM. You have developed the following data relating to the 2008 ending inventory:

Item	Quantity	Acquisition Cost Per Unit	Acquisition Cost Total	Current Replacement Unit Cost (Market)
A	3,000	$4.50	$ 13,500	$6.00
B	1,500	6.00	9,000	3.00
C	7,000	3.00	21,000	6.00
D	3,000	7.50	22,500	4.50
			$66,000	

Required

1. Restate the income statement to reflect LCM valuation of the 2008 ending inventory. Apply LCM on an item-by-item basis and show computations.
2. Compare and explain the LCM effect on each amount that was changed in requirement 1.
3. What is the conceptual basis for applying LCM to merchandise inventories?

LO5

Amazon.com

PB7-3 Calculating and Interpreting the Inventory Turnover Ratio and Days to Sell

Amazon.com reported the following amounts in its financial statements (in millions):

	2005	2004
Net sales revenue	$8,490	$6,921
Cost of sales	6,451	5,319
Beginning inventory	480	294
Ending inventory	566	480

Required:

1. Determine the inventory turnover ratio and average days to sell inventory for 2005 and 2004. Round to one decimal place.
2. Comment on any changes in these measures and compare the inventory turnover at Amazon.com to inventory turnover at Borders, where inventory turned over 2.2 times during 2005 (166 days to sell). Based on your own experience, what's the key difference between Amazon.com and Borders that leads one company's results to be the picture of über-efficiency and the other to seem like a library?

LO3

PB7-4 (Supplement A) Analyzing the Effects of the LIFO Inventory Method in a Perpetual Inventory System

Using the information in PB7-1, calculate the cost of goods sold and ending inventory for Mojo Industries assuming it uses the LIFO cost method in combination with a perpetual inventory system. Compare these amounts to the periodic LIFO calculations in requirement 1(c) of PB7-1. Does the use of a perpetual inventory system result in a higher or lower cost of goods sold when costs are rising?

LO3

PB7-5 (Supplement B) Analyzing and Interpreting the Effects of Inventory Errors

"Oops, I Did It Again" was the song being sung by the accountants at Spears & Cantrell when they announced inventory had been overstated by $30 (million) at the end of the second quarter. The error wasn't discovered and corrected in the company's periodic inventory system until after the end of the third quarter. The following table shows the amounts (in millions) that were originally reported by the company.

	Q1	Q2	Q3
Sales revenue	$3,000	$3,600	$3,750
Cost of goods sold	2,100	2,490	2,655
Gross profit	900	1,110	1,095

Required:

1. Restate the income statements to reflect the correct amounts, after fixing the inventory error.
2. Compute the gross profit percentage for each quarter (a) before the correction and (b) after the correction, rounding to the nearest percentage. Do the results lend confidence to your corrected amounts? Explain.

SKILLS DEVELOPMENT CASES

S7-1 Finding Financial Information

LO2, LO3, LO5, LO6

Refer to the financial statements of Landry's Restaurants in Appendix A at the end of this book, or download the annual report from the *Cases* section of the text's Web site at www.mhhe.com/phillips2e.

1. How much inventory does the company hold at the end of the most recent year? Does this represent an increase or decrease in comparison to the prior year?
2. What method(s) does the company use to determine the cost of its inventory? Describe where you found this information.
3. Assuming "Cost of revenues" is equivalent to CGS, compute to one decimal place the company's inventory turnover ratio and days to sell for the most recent year. Are these amounts similar to McDonald's numbers shown in Exhibit 7.10? What does this analysis suggest to you?

S7-2 Comparing Financial Information

LO2, LO3, LO4, LO5, LO6

Refer to the financial statements of Outback Steakhouse in Appendix B at the end of this book, or download them from the *Cases* section of the text's Web site at www.mhhe.com/phillips2e.

1. Does Outback hold more or less inventory than Landry's at the end of the most recent year?
2. What method does Outback use to determine the cost of its inventory? Comment on how this affects comparisons of inventory and cost of goods sold amounts reported by Outback and Landry's.
3. Assuming "Cost of sales" is equivalent to CGS, compute to one decimal place Outback's inventory turnover ratio and days to sell for the most recent year and compare to Landry's. What does this analysis suggest to you?

S7-3 Internet-Based Team Research: Examining an Annual Report

LO1, LO2, LO3, LO5, LO6

As a team, select an industry to analyze. Using your Web browser, each team member should access the annual report or 10-K for one publicly traded company in the industry, with each member selecting a different company. (See S1-3 in Chapter 1 for a description of possible resources for these tasks.)

Required:

1. On an individual basis, each team member should write a short report that incorporates the following:
    a. Describe the types of inventory held by the company. Does the company indicate its inventory management goals anywhere in its annual report?
    b. Describe the inventory costing method that is used. Why do you think the company chose this method rather than the other acceptable methods? Do you think its inventory costs are rising or falling?
    c. Calculate the inventory turnover ratio for the current and prior year, and explain any change between the two years. (To obtain the beginning inventory number for the prior year, you will need the prior year's annual report.)
    d. Search the 10-K for information about the company's approach for applying the LCM rule to inventory. Did the company report the amount of inventory written down during the year?
2. Then, as a team, write a short report comparing and contrasting your companies using these attributes. Discuss any patterns across the companies that you as a team observe. Provide potential explanations for any differences discovered.

S7-4 Ethical Decision Making: A Real-Life Example

LO3, LO4

Assume you are on a jury hearing a trial involving a large national drugstore company. Your immediate task is to identify suspicious events in the following evidence that suggest financial fraud may have occurred.

In just seven years, the company grew from 15 to 310 stores, reporting sales of more than $3 billion. Some retail experts believed the company was going to be the next Wal-Mart. The apparent secret to the company's success was its ability to attract customers to its stores by selling items below cost. Then the company would make it easy for customers to buy other items, particularly pharmaceuticals, which earned a high gross profit. This strategy appeared to be working, so the company's top executives built up massive pharmaceutical inventories at its stores, causing total inventory to increase from $11 million to $36 million to $153 million in the last three years. The company hadn't installed a perpetual inventory system, so inventory had to be physically counted at each store to determine the cost of goods sold. To help its auditors verify the accuracy of these inventory counts, top management agreed to close selected stores on the day inventory was counted. All they asked was that they be given advance notice of which stores' inventory counts the auditors were planning to attend, so that the temporary closures could be conveyed to employees and customers at those stores. The external auditors selected four stores to test each year and informed the company several weeks in advance. To further assist the auditors with counting the inventory, top management reduced the inventory levels at the selected stores by shipping some of their goods to other stores that the auditors weren't attending.

After the inventory was counted and its cost was calculated, the company applied the LCM test. On a store-by-store basis, top management compared the unit cost and market value of inventory items and then prepared journal entries to write down the inventory. Some of the journal entries were large in amount and involved debiting an account called "Cookies" and crediting the inventory account. Management reported that the Cookies account was used to accumulate the required write-downs for all the company's stores. Just before the financial statements were finalized, the cookies account was emptied by allocating it back to each of the stores. In one instance, $9,999,999.99 was allocated from Cookies to a store's account called "Accrued inventory."

Required:

Prepare a list that summarizes the pieces of evidence that indicate that fraud might have occurred and, for each item on the list, explain why it contributes to your suspicion.

Epilogue:

Phar Mor

This case is based on a fraud involving Phar Mor, as described by David Cottrell and Steven Glover in the July 1997 issue of the *CPA Journal*. Phar Mor's management was collectively fined over $1 million and two top managers received prison sentences ranging from 33 months to five years. The company's auditors paid over $300 million in civil judgments for failing to uncover the fraud.

LO3 **S7-5 Ethical Decision Making: A Mini-Case**

David Exler is the CEO of AquaGear Enterprises, a seven-year-old manufacturer of boats. After many long months of debate with the company's board of directors, David obtained the board's approval to expand into water ski sales. David firmly believed that AquaGear could generate significant profits in this market, despite recent increases in the cost of skis. A board meeting will be held later this month for David to present the financial results for the first quarter of ski sales. As AquaGear's corporate controller, you reported to David that the results weren't great. Although sales were better than expected at $165,000 (3,000 units at $55 per unit), the cost of goods sold was $147,500. This left a gross profit of $17,500. David knew this amount wouldn't please the board. Desperate to save the ski division, David asks you to "take another look at the cost calculations to see if there's any way to reduce the cost of goods sold. I know you accountants have different methods for figuring things out, so maybe you can do your magic now when I need it most." You dig out your summary of inventory purchases for the quarter to recheck your calculations, using the LIFO method that has always been used for the company's inventory of boats.

	Date	Units	Unit Cost	Total Cost
Beginning inventory of water skis	January 1	0	–	–
Purchases	January 15	1,500	$30	$ 45,000
Purchases	February 18	2,000	45	90,000
Purchases	March 29	2,500	50	125,000

Required:

1. Calculate cost of goods sold using the LIFO method. Does this confirm the statement you made to David about the gross profit earned on water ski sales in the first quarter?
2. Without doing any calculations, is it likely that any alternative inventory costing method will produce a lower cost of goods sold?

3. Calculate cost of goods sold using the FIFO method. Would use of this method solve David's current dilemma?

4. Is it acceptable within GAAP to report the water skis using one inventory costing method and the boats using a different method?

5. Do you see any problems with using the FIFO numbers for purposes of David's meeting with the board?

S7-6 Critical Thinking: Income Manipulation under the LIFO Inventory Method   LO3

Mandalay Industries sells electronic test equipment. During the year 2008, the inventory records reflected the following:

	Units	Unit Cost	Total Cost
Beginning inventory	15	$12,000	$180,000
Purchases	40	10,000	400,000
Sales (45 units at $25,000 each)			

Inventory is valued at cost using the LIFO inventory method. On December 28, 2008, the unit cost of the test equipment declined to $9,000. The cost is expected to fall again during the first quarter of next year but then increase later in the year.

Required:

1. Complete the following income statement summary assuming LIFO is applied with a periodic inventory system (show computations):

Sales revenue	$_____
Cost of goods sold	_____
Gross profit	_____
Operating expenses	300,000
Income from operations	$_____
Ending inventory	$_____

2. Although costs are likely to fall again early next year, Mandalay's management is considering buying 20 additional units on December 31, 2008, at $9,000 each. Redo the income statement (and ending inventory), assuming that this purchase is made on December 31, 2008.

3. How much did income from operations change because of the decision to purchase additional units on December 31, 2008? Is there any evidence of deliberate income manipulation? Explain.

S7-7 Calculating and Recording the Effects of Lower of Cost or Market (LCM) on Ending Inventory   LO4

Perfumania

www.mhhe.com/phillips2e

Assume you recently obtained a job in the Miami head office of Perfumania, the largest specialty retailer of discounted fragrances in the United States. Your job is to estimate the amount of write-down required to value inventory at the lower of cost or market. The cost of inventory is calculated using the weighted average cost method and, at approximately $70 million, it represents the company's biggest and most important asset. Assume the corporate controller asked you to prepare a spreadsheet that can be used to determine the amount of LCM write-down for the current year. The controller provides the following hypothetical numbers for you to use in the spreadsheet.

Product Line	Quantity on Hand	Weighted Average Unit Cost	Replacement Cost (Market) at Year-End
Alfred Sung Shi	80	$22	$20
Animale	75	15	16
Azzaro	50	10	10
Mambo	30	16	17
OP Juice	400	8	7

You realize that you'll need to multiply the quantity of each item by the lower of cost or market per unit, but you can't figure out how to get the spreadsheet to choose the *lower* number. You e-mailed your friend Owen for help, and here's his reply.

From:	Owentheaccountant@yahoo.com
To:	Helpme@hotmail.com
Cc:	
Subject:	Excel Help

So you don't have a sniff about how to pick the lower of cost or market? You can do this several different ways, but the easiest is to use the MIN command. Set up your spreadsheet similar to the table you sent me, and then add two new columns. In the first new column, enter the command "= MIN(costcell, marketcell)" where costcell is the cell containing the cost per unit and marketcell is the cell containing the market value per unit. Next, in the second new column, multiply the quantity by the LCM per unit. Here's a screenshot of what this will probably look like in your spreadsheet.

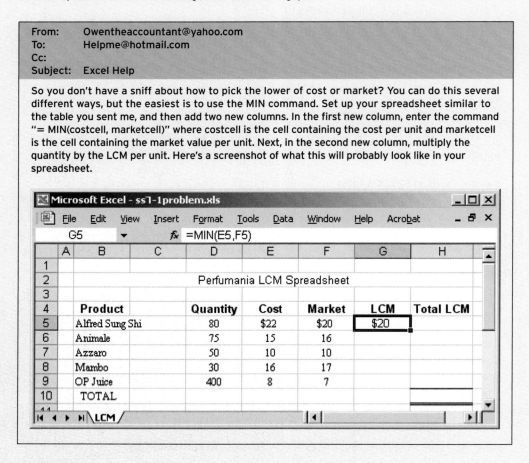

Be sure to enter a formula to sum down the Total LCM column for all the products so that this grand total can be subtracted from the cost presently recorded in the inventory accounting records to determine the write-down.

Required:

1. Prepare a spreadsheet that calculates total LCM for inventory, applied on an item-by-item basis.

2. Prepare a journal entry to record the write-down needed for the five products in this problem.

8

Reporting and Interpreting Receivables, Bad Debt Expense, and Interest Revenue

---

LP8

THAT WAS
THEN

In previous chapters, we quietly assumed that all sales on account ultimately are collected as cash.

One of the most challenging parts of your academic and professional careers will involve managing things that you can't completely control. For example, think about a group project that you have to complete this term. You might believe that, in theory, the work should take only six days from start to finish. But you know from experience that someone in your group is likely to be late with the assigned work or will not complete his or her task at all. The problem is you don't know who it will be, nor do you know how late that person will be—these matters are largely beyond your control. To allow for the possibility that someone will be late, you might set a shorter time period (say four days) for group members to finish their work. By subtracting this two-day allowance, you'll have a realistic basis for planning and successfully completing the group project.

This situation is similar to a problem faced by many companies, including Skechers, a shoe company that sells to Foot Locker and about 3,000 other companies. When Skechers sells to a company on account, it's not clear whether that company will pay what it owes. Skechers' managers know from experience that some customers don't pay. The problem is that, at the time a sale is made, it's not possible to identify who these "bad" customers are. In the rest of this chapter you'll learn about a method of accounting for these uncertainties that is similar to the allowance approach described above for your group project. This method allows Skechers' managers to report in a timely manner how much money their company is likely to collect from customers, which gives financial statement users a realistic basis for making decisions.

THIS IS
NOW

In this chapter, you'll learn how companies handle the situation where customers don't pay all that they owe.

In this chapter, you'll learn about accounting for receivables, which arise either from selling merchandise or services to customers on account (accounts receivable) or lending to others under contract (notes receivable). We'll start by discussing some of the key trade-offs managers consider when deciding whether to extend credit to others. Next, you'll learn about the methods of accounting for accounts receivable and notes receivable. The chapter closes with analyses you can use to evaluate how well a company manages its receivables, followed by lots of practice material. Here's a sketch of the chapter outline.

ORGANIZATION OF THE CHAPTER

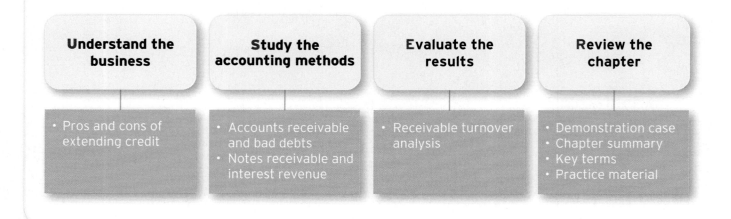

Understand the business	Study the accounting methods	Evaluate the results	Review the chapter
• Pros and cons of extending credit	• Accounts receivable and bad debts • Notes receivable and interest revenue	• Receivable turnover analysis	• Demonstration case • Chapter summary • Key terms • Practice material

Understand the Business

At December 31, 2006, accounts receivable and notes receivable accounted for 25 percent of Skechers' total assets. If the company is to be successful, these assets have to be effectively managed. But what factors do managers consider when selling to customers on account (accounts receivable) or lending to individuals and businesses under contract (notes receivable)?

PROS AND CONS OF EXTENDING CREDIT

Learning Objective 1
Describe the trade-offs of extending credit.

Skechers allows business customers (like DSW and Foot Locker) to open an account and buy shoes on credit, yet it does not extend this option to you—the individual consumer. The reason Skechers is willing to create an account receivable from business customers but not individual consumers is that they carry different advantages and disadvantages. The advantage of extending credit is that it allows Skechers to remain competitive with Reebok, Timberland, and Kenneth Cole who also extend credit to business customers. The disadvantages of extending credit are the following additional costs introduced:

1. **Increased wage costs.** If credit is extended, Skechers will have to hire people to (*a*) evaluate whether each customer is creditworthy, (*b*) track how much each customer owes, and (*c*) follow up to collect the receivable from each customer.

2. **Bad debt costs.** Inevitably, some customers dispute what they owe and pay only a portion of the total amount that they've been charged. In extreme circumstances (such as a customer's bankruptcy), Skechers may never collect the amount that is receivable from the customer. These "bad debts," as they are called, can be a significant additional cost of extending credit.

3. **Delayed receipt of cash.** Even if Skechers were to collect in full from customers, it will likely have to wait 30–60 days before receiving the cash. During this period of time, it's possible Skechers would have to take out a short-term bank loan to obtain cash for other business activities. The interest on such a loan would be another cost of extending credit to customers.

Most managers find that the sales revenue (or, more accurately, the gross profit) to be gained from selling on account to business customers is greater than the additional costs mentioned above. However, when it comes to individual consumers, the additional gross profit doesn't cover all the additional costs that Skechers would incur.

Similar advantages and disadvantages are considered when deciding whether to create notes receivable. A **note receivable** is created when a formal written contract ("note") is established outlining the terms by which a company will receive amounts it is owed. Notes receivable differ from accounts receivable in that notes generally charge interest on outstanding balances. Notes receivable are viewed as a stronger legal claim than accounts receivable, but a new note needs to be created for every transaction, so they are used less frequently—typically when a company sells large dollar-value items (e.g., cars) or lends money to individuals or businesses that do not have an established credit history.

> **YOU SHOULD KNOW**
>
> A **note receivable** is a promise that requires another party to pay the business according to a written agreement.

Study the Accounting Methods

ACCOUNTS RECEIVABLE AND BAD DEBTS

You already know from earlier chapters that **accounts receivable** arise when goods or services are sold on credit. What you may not know is that some accounts receivable are never collected, with a recent study estimating the cost of these bad debts as high as five percent of the net incomes of all U.S. corporations.[1] It's like that "friend" of yours who *says* he'll pay you later, but for one reason or another, never gets around to it.

Two key accounting principles are relevant to accounting for accounts receivable and bad debts. The conservatism principle requires that accounts receivable be reported on the balance sheet at the amount that is expected to actually be collected ("net realizable value") rather than the total that could be collected if customers were to pay in full. At the same time, the matching principle requires that the income statement include all expenses, including bad debts, in the accounting period in which the related credit sales are made. These two principles point to the same solution: reduce both accounts receivable and net income by the amount of credit sales included in receivables and net income this period, but which will never be collected as cash.

The only problem with this solution is that, just as it takes you a while to find out which friends you can't trust, some time will pass before Skechers discovers which particular credit sales and customer balances aren't going to be collected. More than likely, these bad debts will be discovered in an accounting period following the sale, rather than in the same period as the sale. As Exhibit 8.1 shows, if you record sales in one period when they occur and bad debts in a different period when they are discovered, you will violate the matching principle. This failure to match bad debt expense with sales revenue in the same period will lead to distorted views of net income in the period of the sale as well as in the period the bad debt is discovered. To see how this could be a problem, take a moment to read Exhibit 8.1 right now.

Clearly, we need to record bad debts in the same period as the sale. The only way to do this is to estimate the amount of bad debts when the sale is recorded. Later, the

> **Learning Objective 2**
> Estimate and report the effects of uncollectible accounts.

> **YOU SHOULD KNOW**
>
> **Accounts receivable** (also called trade receivables) are amounts owed to a business by its customers.

Topic Tackler

Video 8.1

Check out www.mhhe.com/phillips2e for audio, visual, and PowerPoint presentations on this topic.

---

[1] *Value of Third-Party Debt Collection to the U.S. Economy: Survey and Analysis*, prepared June 27, 2006, for the Association of Credit and Collection Professionals by PricewaterhouseCoopers National Economic Consulting.

EXHIBIT 8.1	Distortion Occurs If Bad Debts Not Matched to Sales

YEAR 1 (CREDIT SALE OCCURS)		YEAR 2 (BAD DEBT DISCOVERED)	
Sales revenues	$10,000	Sales revenues	$ 0
Cost of goods sold	6,000	Cost of goods sold	0
Bad debt expense	0	Bad debt expense	1,000
Net income	$ 4,000	Net income (loss)	$(1,000)

accounting records can be adjusted when uncollectible amounts become known with certainty. This approach is called the **allowance method** and it follows a two-step process, which we'll walk you through below:

1. Record an estimated bad debt expense in the period in which the sale takes place by making an adjusting journal entry at the end of that period.
2. Remove ("write off") specific customer balances in the period they are determined to be uncollectible.

1. Record Estimated Bad Debt Expense

Bad debt expense is an estimate of the credit sales made this period that won't ever be collected from customers. For the year ended December 31, 2006, Skechers estimated its bad debt expense to be $4,591,000.[2] This represented about one-quarter percent of the company's total sales and 6 percent of its net income. The first step of accounting for bad debts is to record this estimate in the accounting system, as discussed below.

Credit sales, when first recorded, affect both the balance sheet (an increase in accounts receivable) and the income statement (an increase in sales revenue). Most of the time, these credit sales will be fully collected. However, on occasion, the company will not succeed in collecting receivables that arise from credit sales. To account for these bad sales on account that have been recorded in Sales Revenue and Accounts Receivable, we should record offsetting amounts in both the balance sheet and income statement. And that's exactly what happens with the allowance method. An adjustment is made at the end of each accounting period to reduce accounts receivable (using a contra-asset account called Allowance for Doubtful Accounts) and reduce net income (using an expense account called Bad Debt Expense). These effects (in thousands) and the adjustment to enter them into the accounting system are:

1. Analyze

Assets	=	Liabilities	+	Stockholders' Equity
Allowance for Doubtful Accounts (+xA) −4,591	=			Bad Debt Expense (+E) −4,591

2. Record

dr Bad Debt Expense (+E, −SE)   4,591
    cr Allowance for Doubtful Accounts (+xA, −A)   4,591

---

[2] In this estimate, Skechers also includes estimated future sales returns and allowances. For ease of understanding, we refer to only the estimated bad debts. Skechers records estimated future sales returns and allowances in the same manner as estimated bad debts.

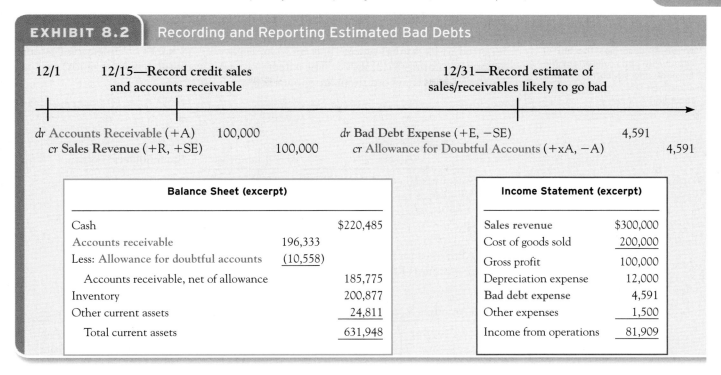

| EXHIBIT 8.2 | Recording and Reporting Estimated Bad Debts |

12/1   12/15—Record credit sales and accounts receivable   12/31—Record estimate of sales/receivables likely to go bad

| dr Accounts Receivable (+A) | 100,000 | |
| cr Sales Revenue (+R, +SE) | | 100,000 |

| dr Bad Debt Expense (+E, −SE) | 4,591 | |
| cr Allowance for Doubtful Accounts (+xA, −A) | | 4,591 |

Balance Sheet (excerpt)		
Cash		$220,485
Accounts receivable	196,333	
Less: Allowance for doubtful accounts	(10,558)	
Accounts receivable, net of allowance		185,775
Inventory		200,877
Other current assets		24,811
Total current assets		631,948

Income Statement (excerpt)	
Sales revenue	$300,000
Cost of goods sold	200,000
Gross profit	100,000
Depreciation expense	12,000
Bad debt expense	4,591
Other expenses	1,500
Income from operations	81,909

Exhibit 8.2 illustrates how the journal entry to record estimated bad debts acts as a partial offset to the original credit sale, in the period in which the sale occurred. It also shows where the accounts appear in the balance sheet and income statement.

Of course, like all contra-asset accounts, the Allowance for doubtful accounts is a permanent account, so its balance carries forward from one accounting period to the next. Bad debt expense, which is a temporary account, will have its balance zeroed out at the end of each accounting period. Consequently, the balance in the Allowance for doubtful accounts will equal the balance in Bad debt expense only during the first year that the Allowance for doubtful accounts is used. This explains why the Allowance for doubtful accounts in the balance sheet in Exhibit 8.2 does not equal the Bad debt expense in the income statement.

You might wonder why the estimated uncollectible accounts aren't simply taken right out of Accounts receivable rather than creating the allowance account that is subtracted from Accounts receivable. The reason for this is that, at the time the estimate is made, there is no way to know which particular customers' accounts receivable are uncollectible. If Skechers were to remove the customer accounts believed to be uncollectible, it would lose track of which customers still owed money. If this were to happen, Skechers would no longer know which customers it should continue pursuing for payment. Instead, it creates the Allowance for doubtful accounts. Because this account is subtracted from Accounts receivable, Skechers complies with the conservatism principle that says companies should report what is likely to be collected. But because the estimated uncollectible portion is not taken directly out of Accounts receivable, Skechers can still track all the customers that owe money—even those that are believed to be unlikely to pay what they owe.

 **COACH'S TIP**

Accounts receivable, net of allowance (shown in Exhibit 8.2) is not a separate account. It is a subtotal that is computed by subtracting the contra-asset account *Allowance for doubtful accounts* from the asset account *Accounts receivable.*

2. Remove (Write Off) Specific Customer Balances

When it becomes clear that a particular customer will not pay its balance, Skechers will remove that customer's account from its accounts receivable records. With the receivable removed, there's no longer a need to include an allowance for it, so the corresponding amount also is removed from the Allowance for doubtful accounts. This act of removing the uncollectible account and its corresponding allowance is called a **write-off.** Skechers reported in its annual report that, in 2006, it gave up all hopes of collecting customer accounts totaling $1,229,000. The effects of these write-offs (in thousands) and the journal entries to record them are shown below:

1. Analyze

Assets	=	Liabilities	+ Stockholders' Equity
Accounts Receivable −1,229			
Allowance for Doubtful			
Accounts (−xA) +1,229			

2. Record

dr Allowance for Doubtful Accounts (−xA, +A) 1,229
   cr Accounts Receivable (−A). 1,229

3. Summarize

dr + Accounts Receivable (A) cr −			dr − Allow, for Doubtful Accts (xA) cr +		
Beg.	197,562			7,196	Beg. Bal.
		1,229 Write-off	Write-off 1,229	4,591	Estimate
End.	196,333			10,558	End. Bal

Notice that a write-off does not affect income statement accounts. The estimated bad debt expense relating to these uncollectible accounts was already recorded with an adjusting journal entry in the period the sale was recorded, so there is no additional expense when the account is written off. Also, notice that the decrease in Accounts receivable offsets the decrease in the Allowance for doubtful accounts, so a write-off does not affect the "Accounts receivable, net of allowance" subtotal on the balance sheet.

Summary of the Allowance Method

To make it easy for you to review the two main steps of the allowance method, here's a quick summary:

Step	Timing	Journal Entry	Financial Statement Effects		
1. Record adjustment for estimated bad debts	End of the period in which sales are made	dr Bad Debt Expense (+E, −SE) cr Allowance for Doubtful Accounts (+xA, −A)	**Balance Sheet** Accounts receivable — no effect; Less: Allowance — increase; Accounts receivable, net — decrease	**Income Statement** Revenues — no effect; Expenses Bad debt expense — increase; Net income — decrease	
2. Identify and write off actual bad debts	As accounts are determined uncollectible	dr Allowance for Doubtful Accounts (−xA, +A) cr Accounts Receivable (−A)	**Balance Sheet** Accounts receivable — decrease; Less: Allowance — decrease; Accounts receivable, net — no effect	**Income Statement** Revenues — no effect; Expenses Bad debt expense — no effect; Net income — no effect	

HOW'S IT GOING?   Self-Study Quiz

Indicate the effect (+ / − / No Effect) of each of the following on net income and total assets.

	Net Income	Total Assets
1. Polaris Industries recorded an increase in estimated bad debts on December 31, 2007.		
2. Kellogg's wrote-off twelve customer account balances during 2008.		

Estimating Bad Debts

In our earlier examples, we simply gave you the estimated amount of uncollectibles to record. In the real world, these bad debts have to be estimated. They can be estimated using one of two methods: the aging of accounts receivable method or the percentage of credit sales method. The most commonly used method is the aging of accounts receivable method (shown below).[3] The **aging of accounts receivable method** is sometimes called the balance sheet approach because it uses one balance sheet account (Accounts receivable) to estimate the appropriate amount for another balance sheet account (Allowance for doubtful accounts). An equally acceptable alternative is the **percentage of credit sales method,** sometimes called the income statement approach. This method uses one income statement account (Sales revenue) to estimate the appropriate amount for another income statement account (Bad debt expense). This method is demonstrated in Chapter Supplement A.

The aging of accounts receivable method gets its name because it bases the estimate of bad debts on the "age" of each amount in accounts receivable. The method follows three steps, as Exhibit 8.3 shows.

> **YOU SHOULD KNOW**
>
> The **aging of accounts receivable method** (also called the balance sheet approach) estimates uncollectible accounts based on the age of each account receivable. The **percentage of credit sales method** (also called the income statement approach) estimates bad debts based on the historical percentage of sales that lead to bad debt losses.

EXHIBIT 8.3 | Estimating Uncollectible Amounts with an Aging of Accounts Receivable

Customer	Total	NUMBER OF DAYS UNPAID				
		0–30	31–60	61–90	Over 90	
Adam's Sports Stores	$ 648	$ 405	$ 198	$ 45	—	
Backyard Shoe Company	2,345	—	—	—	$2,345	← Step 1—Age
Other customers	193,340	99,628	52,822	37,935	2,955	
Total receivable	$196,333	$100,033	$53,020	$37,980	$5,300	
× Estimated bad debt percentages		1%	4%	14%	40%	← Step 2—Estimate
= Estimated uncollectible	$ 10,558	$ 1,000	$ 2,121	$ 5,317	$2,120	← Step 3—Compute

---

[3] In a survey of Credit Research Foundation members, 59 percent of respondents indicated that their Allowance for doubtful accounts estimates were based on analyses of their customers' accounts receivable balances.

1. Prepare an aged listing of accounts receivable, with totals for each aging category. Most computerized accounting systems can produce this report automatically by counting back the number of days to when each receivable was first recorded.

2. Estimate bad debt loss percentages for each category. The percentage used by each company varies according to its circumstances. Generally, the longer an amount remains unpaid, the less likely it is to be collected. Therefore, a higher percentage is applied to amounts uncollected after 120 days than those uncollected after 30 days.

3. Compute the total estimate by multiplying the totals in step 1 by the percentages in step 2, and then summing across all aging categories. The total across all aging categories ($1,000 + 2,121 + 5,317 + 2,120 = $10,558) represents the balance that the Allowance for Doubtful Accounts will need to be adjusted to at the end of the period.

dr – **Allowance for Doubtful Accounts** cr +	
	5,967 Unadj. Bal.
	? AJE
	10,558 Desired Bal.

The Allowance for Doubtful Accounts is a permanent account, which is not closed at the end of the year, so it typically has an existing balance that you need to consider when determining the amount of the adjustment. That is, the amount computed in Step 3 is the desired balance for Allowance for Doubtful Accounts, not the amount of the adjustment. To compute the amount of the adjustment, subtract the existing unadjusted balance from the desired adjusted balance computed in Step 3. For example, if Skechers had an unadjusted credit balance of $5,967 in its Allowance for doubtful accounts and determined it should be a credit balance of $10,558, an adjustment of $4,591 (= $10,558 − 5,967) would need to be recorded (as a credit) to the account, with a corresponding amount added to Bad Debt Expense (with a debit). The impact on the accounting equation and the adjusting journal entry were shown earlier on page 342, but we'll repeat them here to save you the trouble of flipping back.

1. Analyze

Assets	=	Liabilities	+	Stockholders' Equity
Allowance for Doubtful =				Bad Debt
Accounts (+xA) −4,591				Expense (+E) −4,591

2. Record

dr Bad Debt Expense (+E, −SE). 4,591
    cr Allowance for Doubtful Accounts (+xA, −A)   4,591

3. Summarize

dr + **Bad Debt Expense (E, SE)** cr −		dr − **Allow. for Doubtful Accts (xA)** cr +	
Unadj. 0			5,967 Unadj. Bal.
AJE 4,591			4,591 AJE
Adj. 4,591			10,558 Adj. Bal.

Although the Allowance for doubtful accounts normally has a credit balance, you may encounter a situation where it has a debit balance prior to adjusting for uncollectible accounts. This happens when a company has recorded write-offs that exceed its previous estimates of uncollectible accounts. If this happens, you still figure out the amount of the adjustment needed to reach the desired balance calculated under the aging of accounts receivable method. The only difference is that to reach the desired balance, you will have to record an amount equal to the desired balance plus the existing debit balance. After the adjustment is recorded, the Allowance for doubtful accounts will once again return to a credit balance.

HOW'S IT GOING? Self-Study Quiz

In a previous year, Mad Catz reported beginning and ending balances in the Allowance for Doubtful Accounts of $5,971 and $6,329, respectively. It also reported that write-offs of bad accounts amounted to $3,979 (all numbers in thousands of dollars). Assuming no other changes in the account, what amount did Mad Catz record as bad debt expense for the period? Use the following T-accounts to solve for the missing value.

dr + **Bad Debt Expense (E, SE)** cr –		dr – **Allow. for Doubtful Accts (xA)** cr +	
Beg. Bal. 0			5,971 Beg. Bal.
Adj. Bal. ___			___ Adj. Bal.

Other Issues

Revising Estimates   Unless you can see into the future, bad debt estimates will always differ from the amount that is later written off as uncollectible. Rather than go back and revise initial estimates, we simply revise bad debt estimates for the current period. That is, overestimates in prior periods are reduced through lower estimates in the current period, and underestimates in prior periods are adjusted through higher estimates in the current period.

Account Recoveries   In the same way that someone you've written off as a friend might do something to win you back, a customer might pay an account balance that was previously written off. Collection of a previously written off account is called a *recovery* and it is accounted for in two parts. First, put the receivable back on the books by recording the opposite of the write-off. Second, record the collection of the account. To illustrate, let's assume that Skechers collects $50 on an account that had been previously written off. This recovery would be recorded with the following journal entries:

COACH'S TIP

Like the initial write-off, a recovery does not affect Net income.

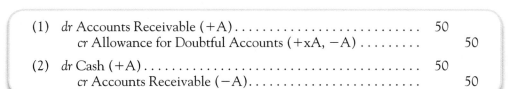

(1)	dr Accounts Receivable (+A)	50		} Reverse the write-off
	cr Allowance for Doubtful Accounts (+xA, –A)		50	
(2)	dr Cash (+A)	50		} Record the collection
	cr Accounts Receivable (–A)		50	

Look closely at the journal entries used for a recovery and you'll see that Accounts receivable is debited and then credited for $50. It's tempting to cancel these two out, but don't do it because it would create an inaccurate credit history for the customer. After all is said and done, the customer's balance was removed because it was actually collected, not written off, so the accounting records should reflect that.

Alternative Methods   Our focus in this section of the chapter has been on the allowance method of accounting for bad debts. You should be aware that some small companies don't use the allowance method. Instead, they use an alternative approach called the *direct write-off method*. Although easier to use, this alternative method violates the conservatism and matching principles, so it is not considered a generally accepted accounting method. However, the Internal Revenue Service (IRS) does use this method for tax purposes. Because of this potential use, we demonstrate it in Chapter Supplement B at the end of this chapter.

NOTES RECEIVABLE AND INTEREST REVENUE

The accounting issues for notes receivable are similar to those for accounts receivable, with one exception. Unlike accounts receivable, which do not charge interest until they've become overdue, notes receivable start charging interest the day they are created. Let's look at how interest is calculated.

Calculating Interest

YOU SHOULD KNOW

The **interest formula** is:
$I = P \times R \times T$
where I = interest calculated, P = principal, R = annual interest rate, and T = time period covered in the interest calculation (number of months out of 12).

To calculate interest, three variables must be considered: (1) the principal, which is simply the amount of the note receivable, (2) the interest rate charged on the note, and (3) the time period covered in the interest calculation. Interest rates are always stated as an annual percentage, even if the note is for less than a year, so the "time" variable represents the portion of a year for which interest is calculated. If a note states 10 percent annual interest, but you are calculating interest for only 7 months, the time variable is 7/12 (7 months out of 12). The **interest formula** in Exhibit 8.4 shows that, to calculate interest, all three variables are multiplied together:

COACH'S TIP

The "time" variable refers to the portion of a year for which interest is calculated, not the portion of the note's entire life. A 2-month interest calculation on a 3-year note has a time variable of 2/12 not 2/36.

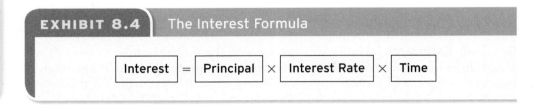

EXHIBIT 8.4   The Interest Formula

$$\text{Interest} = \text{Principal} \times \text{Interest Rate} \times \text{Time}$$

Reporting Interest on Notes Receivable

Although interest on a note receivable is earned each day, interest payments typically are received only once or twice a year. This means that a company with a note receivable needs to accrue interest revenue and an interest receivable at the end of each accounting period (unless an interest payment happens to be received on the last day of the period).

To keep the difference between interest accrual and interest payment dates straight in your mind, you'll find it helpful to use a timeline like the one shown in Exhibit 8.5. This timeline will help you focus on what needs to be accounted for and when. Once you understand this, it will be a lot easier to learn details involving interest calculations and journal entries. As you read each sentence in the following paragraph, see what it relates to in Exhibit 8.5.

Exhibit 8.5 depicts a situation where Skechers creates a one-year note receivable on November 1, 2007. Rather than record the interest earned as each day passes, Skechers waits until either an interest payment is received or the end of its accounting period is reached. On December 31, 2007, Skechers reaches its year-end. Because no interest has been recorded as of that date, Skechers will make an adjusting journal entry on December 31, 2007, to accrue the interest earned but not yet received. The

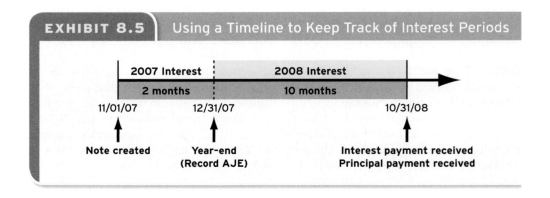

EXHIBIT 8.5   Using a Timeline to Keep Track of Interest Periods

period covered by this accrual is shaded yellow in Exhibit 8.5. If Skechers doesn't prepare monthly or quarterly financial statements, no interest will be recorded again until October 31, 2008, when an interest payment is received. The green shading in Exhibit 8.5 indicates that this payment includes the interest earned and accrued as receivable at December 31, 2007 (shaded in yellow), plus additional interest earned in 2008 (shaded in blue). Finally, on October 31, 2008, Skechers also receives payment for the note's original principal. This simple example demonstrates the four key events that occur with any note: (1) establishing the note, (2) accruing interest earned but not received, (3) recording interest payments received, and (4) recording principal payments received. Before learning more about these events, check on your understanding with this quiz.

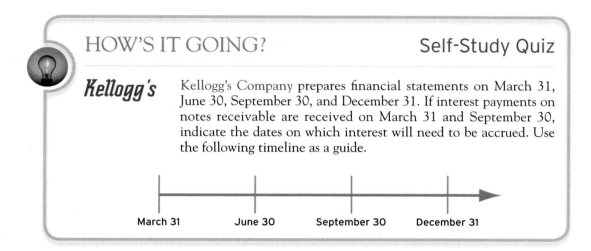

HOW'S IT GOING?   Self-Study Quiz

Kellogg's   Kellogg's Company prepares financial statements on March 31, June 30, September 30, and December 31. If interest payments on notes receivable are received on March 31 and September 30, indicate the dates on which interest will need to be accrued. Use the following timeline as a guide.

March 31 — June 30 — September 30 — December 31

Recording Notes Receivable and Interest Revenue

Let's now add some numbers to the Skechers example, so we can review how to calculate interest and demonstrate how the four events would be reported in the accounting system. On November 1, 2007, Skechers loans $100,000 to an employee and creates a note that requires Skechers be paid 6 percent interest on October 31, 2008. Skechers also is to receive repayment of the $100,000 principal on October 31, 2008. Skechers prepares year-end financial statements as of December 31, 2007, but makes no other adjustments for interest during the year. The following illustrates how to account for (1) establishing the note, (2) accruing interest earned but not received, (3) recording interest payments received, and (4) recording principal payments received.

Establishing a Note Receivable   The exchange of $100,000 cash for a promissory note creates a note receivable that has the following accounting equation effects, which would be recorded using the following journal entry:

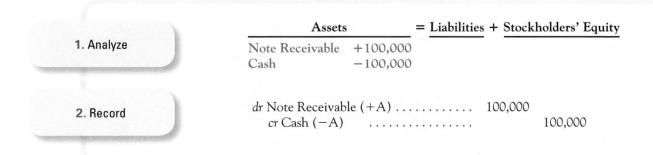

	Assets	= Liabilities + Stockholders' Equity
1. Analyze	Note Receivable +100,000	
	Cash −100,000	

| **2. Record** | *dr* Note Receivable (+A) . . . . 100,000 | |
| | *cr* Cash (−A) . . . . | 100,000 |

Accruing Interest Earned

Under accrual basis accounting, interest revenue is recorded when it is earned rather than when an interest payment is received in cash. Skechers earned two months of interest revenue in the year ended December 31, 2007, because its note receivable was outstanding for all of November and December 2007. When interest is earned in the current period but has not yet been recorded, an adjusting journal entry is used at the end of the current period to accrue the interest earned. The amount of interest to be recorded for the two months of 2007 is computed as follows:

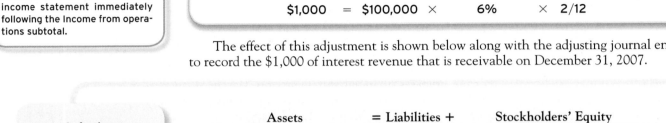

Interest	=	Principal	×	Interest Rate	×	Time
$1,000	=	$100,000	×	6%	×	2/12

> **COACH'S TIP**
>
> Except for banks, interest is considered a peripheral source of revenue, so it is reported on the income statement immediately following the Income from operations subtotal.

The effect of this adjustment is shown below along with the adjusting journal entry to record the $1,000 of interest revenue that is receivable on December 31, 2007.

1. Analyze

Assets	= Liabilities +	Stockholders' Equity
Interest Receivable +1,000		Interest Revenue (+R) +1,000

2. Record

```
dr Interest Receivable (+A) ................  1,000
    cr Interest Revenue (+R, +SE) ...........        1,000
```

Recording Interest Received   On October 31, 2008, Skechers receives $6,000 cash for interest, calculated as $100,000 × 6% × 12/12. As shown on the following timeline, this $6,000 of interest includes the $1,000 that was accrued as interest receivable at December 31, 2007, plus $5,000 earned during the ten-month period from January 1 to October 31, 2008.

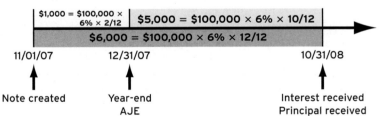

When Skechers receives the $6,000 of interest, it will reduce the $1,000 interest receivable that was previously recorded and the remaining $5,000 will be reported as interest revenue in 2008. These effects and the journal entry to record them follow:

1. Analyze

Assets	= Liabilities +	Stockholders' Equity
Cash +6,000		
Interest Receivable −1,000		Interest Revenue (+R) +5,000

2. Record

```
dr Cash (+A). ...........................  6,000
    cr Interest Receivable (−A) ..............        1,000
    cr Interest Revenue (+R, +SE) ...........        5,000
```

Recording Principal Received   The collection of a note receivable is accounted for just like the collection of an account receivable. Assuming that Skechers receives the $100,000 principal that is due, the accounting equation effects and journal entry for this transaction would be:

1. Analyze

Assets	= Liabilities + Stockholders' Equity
Cash +100, 000	
Note Receivable −100, 000	

2. Record

dr Cash (+A)...................... 100,000
    cr Note Receivable (−A)............   100,000

Accounting for Uncollectible Notes

Just as a customer might fail to pay its accounts receivable balance, some companies also might fail to pay the principal (and interest) that they owe on a note receivable. When the collection of notes receivable is in doubt, a company should record an allowance for doubtful accounts against the notes receivable, just as it records an allowance for doubtful accounts against accounts receivable.

Ethical Insights

Resetting the Clock

Earlier in this chapter, you saw that as customer balances get older, the Allowance for doubtful accounts should be increased. Increases in the Allowance for doubtful accounts require increases in Bad debt expense, so the result of older customer accounts should be a decrease in net income. Managers at MCI knew about these accounting effects, so to avoid reducing net income, they "reset the clock" on amounts owed by customers. The way they did this was by providing loans to customers who used the money to pay off their account balances. By replacing old accounts receivable with new notes receivable, they avoided recording approximately $70 million in bad debts. That didn't last long, though. After the fraud was revealed, the managers involved spent several years in prison and are working to pay off over $10 million in fines. To learn more about how this fraud worked, see skills development case S8-4 at the end of this chapter.

Evaluate the Results

RECEIVABLES TURNOVER ANALYSIS

Learning Objective 4
Compute and interpret the receivables turnover ratio.

Managers, directors, investors, and creditors evaluate the effectiveness of a company's credit-granting and collection activities by conducting a receivables turnover analysis. The idea behind a receivables turnover analysis is shown in Exhibit 8.6. When a company sells goods or services on credit, its receivables balance goes up, and when it collects from customers, the receivables balance goes down. This process of selling and collecting

EXHIBIT 8.6	Receivables Turnover Analysis

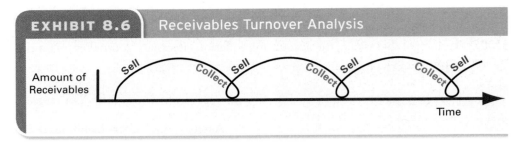

is called **receivables turnover** and it is repeated over and over during each accounting period, for each customer.

To assess how many times, on average, this process of selling and collecting is repeated over and over during the period, financial statement users calculate the receivables turnover ratio. The higher the ratio, the faster the collection of receivables. And, the faster the collection of receivables, the shorter your company's operating cycle, which means more cash available for running the business. A low turnover ratio can be a warning sign, suggesting that the company is allowing a longer time for customers to pay. As you learned earlier in this chapter, the longer an account goes without being collected, the bigger the risk that it will never be collected. Analysts watch for changes in the receivables turnover ratio, because a sudden decline may mean that a company is recording sales that customers are likely to return later or is lengthening credit periods to entice customers to buy as much as possible—a practice known in business as *channel stuffing*.

Rather than evaluate the number of times accounts receivable turn over during a year, some people find it easier to think in terms of the length of time (in days) it takes to collect accounts receivable. It's easy to convert a year's receivables turnover ratio into the average **days to collect:** simply calculate $365 \div$ receivables turnover ratio. This measure doesn't say anything different about the company's ability to collect receivables— it's just a little easier to interpret. In terms of Exhibit 8.6, the receivables turnover ratio counts the number of loops in a given period of time, whereas days to collect tells you the average number of days between loops.

FINANCIAL ANALYSIS TOOLS

Name of Measure	Formula	What It Tells You
Receivables turnover ratio	$\dfrac{\text{Net Sales Revenue}}{\text{Average Net Receivables}}$	• The number of times receivables turn over during the period • A higher ratio means faster turnover
Days to collect	$\dfrac{365}{\text{Receivables Turnover Ratio}}$	• Average number of days from sale on account to collection • A higher number means a longer time to collect

Comparison to Benchmarks

Credit Terms   By calculating days to collect you can compare a company's collection performance to its stated collections policy. You might remember from Chapter 6 that when companies sell on account, they specify the length of credit period (as well as any discounts for prompt payment). By comparing the number of days to collect to the length of credit period, you can gain a sense of whether customers are complying with the stated policy. Managers inside a company watch this closely, but so do investors and creditors on the outside. If customers appear to be disregarding the stated credit period, it may be a sign that they are dissatisfied with the product or service that they have bought.

Companies rarely indicate their normal credit policies as part of their financial statements, but there are some exceptions. For example, Exhibit 8.7 shows an excerpt from Kellogg's 2005 financial statement notes. As the note indicates, this cereal maker's stated policy is to require payment from customers 11–16 days after a sale is made. Its collection period of 18–19 days suggests that customers are generally willing to comply with this period.

EXHIBIT 8.7	Comparing Days to Collect with Stated Credit Terms

Kellogg's "In the United States, the Company generally has required payment for goods sold eleven or sixteen days subsequent to the date of invoice as 2%, 10/net 11 or 1%, 15/net 16, and days sales outstanding (DSO) averages 18–19 days."

COACH'S TIP

Days to collect also is called *days' sales outstanding.*

Other Companies Receivables turnover ratios and the number of days to collect often vary across industries. To illustrate, we have calculated these measures in Exhibit 8.8 for Skechers, Boeing (an airplane manufacturer) and Deere & Co. (a farm implements company). As Exhibit 8.8 shows, Skechers turned over its receivables 7.9 times, which is once every 46 days. Boeing had a turnover ratio of 11.1 times, which means a jet-fast collection period of about 33 days. Deere & Co. limped behind, with a receivables turnover ratio of 6.1, which is about 60 days to collect. With such a big range in ratios between industries, you should compare a company's turnover only with other companies in the same industry or with its figures from prior periods. For practice at computing and comparing to prior periods, try the Self-Study Quiz that follows, which asks you to calculate and interpret Skechers' receivables turnover ratio and days to collect in 2004.

EXHIBIT 8.8	Summary of Receivables Turnover Ratio Analyses

Company	Relevant Information (in millions)		2005 Accounts Receivable Turnover Calculation	2005 Days to Collect Calculation
SKECHERS		2005	2004	$\dfrac{\$1,006}{\$(134.6 + 120.4)/2} = 7.9$ times	$\dfrac{365 \text{ days}}{7.9 \text{ times}} = 46.2$ days
	Net sales	$1,006	$920		
	Net accounts receivable	$134.6	$120.4		
BOEING		2005	2004	$\dfrac{\$54,845}{\$(5,246 + 4,653)/2} = 11.1$ times	$\dfrac{365 \text{ days}}{11.1 \text{ times}} = 32.9$ days
	Net sales	$54,845	$52,457		
	Net accounts receivable	$5,246	$4,653		
JOHN DEERE		2005	2004	$\dfrac{\$19,401}{\$(3,118 + 3,207)/2} = 6.1$ times	$\dfrac{365 \text{ days}}{6.1 \text{ times}} = 59.8$ days
	Net sales	$19,401	$17,673		
	Net accounts receivable	$3,118	$3,207		

HOW'S IT GOING? Self-Study Quiz

Skechers reported net accounts receivable of $98.8 (million) at December 31, 2003.

a. Use this information, along with that in Exhibit 8.8, to calculate Skechers' receivables turnover and days to collect in 2004.

2004 Receivables Turnover:	2004 Days to Collect:
$$\frac{\boxed{}}{(\boxed{} + \boxed{})/2} = \boxed{} \text{ times}$$	$$\frac{365 \text{ days}}{\boxed{} \text{ times}} = \boxed{} \text{ days}$$

b. Did Skechers' receivables turnover improve or decline from 2004 (calculated in *a*) to 2005 (shown in Exhibit 8.8)?

Speeding Up Collections

Factoring Receivables   To generate the cash needed to pay for a company's business activities, managers must ensure that receivables are collected on a timely basis. You might wonder what managers can do to speed up sluggish receivables collections. One obvious tactic is to start hounding customers for payment. This forceful approach has at least two drawbacks: (1) it is time-consuming and costly, and (2) it can annoy customers and cause them to take their business elsewhere. An alternative approach is to sell outstanding accounts receivable to another company (called a *factor*). The way this **factoring** arrangement works is that your company receives cash for the receivables it sells to the factor (minus a factoring fee) and the factor then has the right to collect the outstanding amounts owed by your customers. In the same way that you can get cash immediately at a local Checks Cashed store for any check, factoring is a fast and easy way for your company to get cash for its receivables. However, this does come with costs. First, factoring could send a potentially negative message because it might be seen as a last resort for collecting accounts. Second, the factoring fee can be as much as 3 percent of the receivables sold. If Skechers sold $100,000 of receivables to a factor under such an arrangement, Skechers would receive only $97,000 cash but would give up the potential to collect the full $100,000, resulting in an expense of $3,000. For a company that regularly sells its receivables, this cost of factoring is reported on the income statement as a selling expense. If a company factors infrequently, the fee is considered a peripheral "other" expense.

Credit Card Sales   Another way to avoid lengthy collection periods is to allow customers to pay for goods using national credit cards like Visa, MasterCard, American Express, and Discover Card. Credit card receipts can be deposited directly into a company's bank account as if they're actually cash. This not only speeds up cash collection, but also reduces losses from customers writing bad checks. But, just like factoring, these benefits come at a cost. Credit card companies charge a fee for their services, often around 3 percent of the total sales price. If credit card sales amounted to $100,000, a credit card fee of $3,000 would be deducted, leaving the equivalent of $97,000 cash. These credit card fees are included with selling expenses on the income statement.

Control Spotlight

Segregating Collections and Write-Offs

Chapter 6 explained that a proper segregation of duties helps to prevent errors and fraud from occurring. One way this applies to accounts receivable is in ensuring that the same person does not receive collections from customers and also write off account balances. Without adequate segregation between these duties, a dishonest employee could divert customer payments to his or her own bank account and then cover it up by writing off the customer's balance.

SUPPLEMENT A: PERCENTAGE OF CREDIT SALES METHOD

The percentage of credit sales method is an alternative approach to estimating bad debts. It estimates bad debt expense by multiplying the current year's credit sales times the historical percentage of bad debt losses. For example, if Skechers has credit sales in the current year of $1,836,400 and had experienced bad debt losses of ¼ of 1 percent of credit sales in prior years, Skechers could estimate the current year's bad debt expense as:

Credit sales this year	$1,836,400
× Bad debt loss rate (0.25%)	× .0025
Bad debt expense this year	$ 4,591

The accounts debited and credited when recording this adjustment are identical under both the aging of accounts receivable and percentage of credit sales methods, although the amount of the estimated adjustment may differ. Under the percentage of credit sales method, the amount calculated for the period is directly entered as Bad debt expense. You don't need to worry about the existing balance in the Allowance for doubtful accounts or Bad debt expense accounts. Just enter the calculated amount into the accounting system. The impact on the accounting equation and the required journal entry are just as we showed earlier in this chapter:

	Assets	=	Liabilities	+	Stockholders' Equity
1. Analyze	Allowance for Doubtful Accounts (+xA) −4,591	=			Bad Debt Expense (+E) −4,591

2. Record

dr Bad Debt Expense (+E, −SE)   4,591
    cr Allowance for Doubtful Accounts (+xA, −A)   4,591

SUPPLEMENT B: DIRECT WRITE-OFF METHOD

As described earlier in this chapter, an alternative method exists to account for uncollectible accounts. This alternative approach, called the **direct write-off method,** does not estimate bad debts and does not use an allowance for doubtful accounts. Instead,

> **YOU SHOULD KNOW**
> The **direct write-off method** is a non-GAAP alternative to the allowance method of accounting for uncollectible accounts.

it reports sales when they occur and bad debt expense when it is discovered. This is appropriate for tax purposes but it is not acceptable under generally accepted accounting principles. Consequently, it isn't used very often for external financial reporting.

The reason the direct write-off method isn't considered a GAAP method is that it ignores the conservatism concept and the matching principle. It breaks the conservatism concept by reporting Accounts receivable at the total amount owed by customers (an overly optimistic point of view) rather than what is estimated to actually be collectible (a more realistic viewpoint). The direct write-off method breaks the matching principle by recording Bad debt expense in the period that customer accounts are determined to be bad rather than matching the expense to the revenues reported in the period when the credit sales are actually made. As illustrated in Exhibit 8.1 on page 342, the failure to match Bad debt expense to Sales has a distorting effect on net income in the period of the sale as well as in later periods when bad debts are discovered.

Under the direct write-off method, no journal entries are made until a bad debt is discovered. The journal entry used by the direct write-off method to record $1,000 of bad debt expense when a customer account is determined to be uncollectible is:

dr Bad Debt Expense (+E, −SE)	1,000
cr Accounts Receivable (−A)	1,000

REVIEW THE CHAPTER

DEMONSTRATION CASE A

www.mhhe.com/phillips2e

Shooby Dooby Shoe (SDS) sold $950,000 in merchandise on credit during 2008. Also during 2008, SDS determined that it would not be able to collect a $500 account balance that was owed by a deceased customer (Captain Cutler).

Required:

1. Show how the write-off of the account receivable from Captain Cutler would affect the accounting equation, and prepare the journal entry to record these effects.

2. Assume that SDS uses the aging of accounts receivable method and that, as shown below, it estimates that $11,000 of its year-end accounts receivable is uncollectible. As of December 31, 2008, the Allowance for doubtful accounts had an unadjusted credit balance of $3,000. Show the accounting equation effects of recording the bad debt estimate, and prepare a journal entry to record these effects.

		Number of Days Unpaid			
	Total	0–30	31–60	61–90	>90
Total receivable	$171,000	$50,000	$80,000	$40,000	$1,000
× Estimated bad debt percentages		× 1%	× 5%	× 15%	× 50%
= Estimated uncollectible	$ 11,000	$ 500	$ 4,000	$ 6,000	$ 500

3. Assume that SDS reported net accounts receivable of $160,000 at December 31, 2008, and $167,586 at December 31, 2007. Calculate the receivables turnover ratio for 2008.

4. If the receivables turnover ratio was 6.4 in 2007, what was the number of days to collect in 2007? Given your calculations in 3, conclude whether SDS collections are faster or slower in 2008 than in 2007.

5. (Supplement A) Assume that SDS uses the percentage of credit sales method for estimating bad debt expense rather than the aging of accounts receivable method. If SDS estimates that 1 percent of credit sales will result in bad debts, what will be the effects on the accounting equation? Prepare the journal entry to record these effects.

Suggested Solution

1.

Assets		= Liabilities + Stockholders' Equity
Accounts Receivable	−500	
Allowance for Doubtful Accounts (−xA)	+500	

dr Allowance for Doubtful Accounts (−xA, +A) 500
    cr Accounts Receivable (−A)   500

2. Under the aging of accounts receivable method, we determine the estimated balance for the Allowance for doubtful accounts ($11,000) and then subtract its unadjusted balance ($3,000) to determine the amount of the adjustment ($8,000 = $11,000 − $3,000).

Assets		= Liabilities +	Stockholders' Equity	
Allowance for Doubtful Accounts (+xA)	−8,000		Bad Debt Expense (+E)	−8,000

dr Bad Debt Expense (+E, −SE). 8,000
    cr Allowance for Doubtful Accounts (+xA, −A).   8,000

3. Receivables turnover ratio is calculated as Net sales ÷ Average accounts receivable. The average accounts receivable in 2008 was $163,793 (= ($160,000 + 167,586)/2), so the receivables turnover ratio for 2008 was 5.8 (= $950,000 ÷ 163,793).

4. Days to collect is calculated as 365 ÷ receivables turnover ratio. The 6.4 turnover in 2007 equates to 57 days (and the 5.8 turnover in 2008 equates to 63 days). Collections are slower in 2008 than in 2007.

5. The percentage of credit sales method multiplies historical bad debt losses (1%) by this period's credit sales ($950,000) to directly estimate the amount of Bad debt expense to record ($9,500 = 1% × $950,000).

Assets		= Liabilities +	Stockholders' Equity	
Allowance for Doubtful Accounts (+xA)	−9,500		Bad Debt Expense (+E)	−9,500

dr Bad Debt Expense (+E, −SE) (0.01 × $950,000) 9,500
    cr Allowance for Doubtful Accounts (+xA, −A).   9,500

DEMONSTRATION CASE B

On March 1, 2006, Rocky Mountain Chocolate Factory, Inc. (RMCF) reported it had issued $120,000 of notes receivable, with an annual interest rate of 10 percent. As a public company, RMCF prepares financial statements for external reporting every quarter, ending on May 31, August 31, November 30, and February 28. Assume that the notes were created on March 1 when money was loaned to another company, and that RMCF receives interest payments semi-annually, on July 31 and January 31.

Required:

1. Calculate the amount of interest that RMCF will earn each month after the notes are issued on March 1.
2. Calculate the amount of each interest payment that RMCF receives on July 31, 2006 and on January 31, 2007.
3. Prepare a timeline showing the amount of interest earned each quarter and received on each payment date.
4. Prepare journal entries to record the note's issuance, interest earned, and interest payments received for each quarter and on each payment date.

Suggested Solution

1. Interest earned   = Principal × Interest Rate × Time
   = $120,000 × 10% × 1/12 = $1,000 per month.

2. The period from March 1 to July 31 is five months whereas the period from August 1 to January 31 is six months.

   Interest payment   = Principal × Interest Rate × Time
   = $120,000 × 10% × 5/12 = $5,000 on July 31.

   Interest payment   = Principal × Interest Rate × Time
   = $120,000 × 10% × 6/12 = $6,000 on January 31.

3. Timeline

March 1	May 31	July 31	August 31	November 30	January 31	February 28
$3,000	$2,000	$1,000	$3,000	$2,000	$1,000	
$5,000			$6,000			

4. Journal Entries

   March 1, 2006 (Notes Issued)

   dr Notes Receivable (+A) 120,000
       cr Cash (−A)   120,000

   May 31, 2006 (Interest Accrued)

   dr Interest Receivable (+A) 3,000
       cr Interest Revenue (+R, +SE)   3,000

   July 31, 2006 (Interest Payment Received)

   dr Cash (+A) 5,000
       cr Interest Receivable (−A)   3,000
       cr Interest Revenue (+R, +SE)   2,000

   August 31, 2006 (Interest Accrued)

   dr Interest Receivable (+A) 1,000
       cr Interest Revenue (+R, +SE)   1,000

   November 30, 2006 (Interest Accrued)

   dr Interest Receivable (+A) 3,000
       cr Interest Revenue (+R, +SE)   3,000

   January 31, 2007 (Interest Payment Received)

   dr Cash (+A) 6,000
       cr Interest Receivable (−A)   4,000
       cr Interest Revenue (+R, +SE)   2,000

   February 28, 2007 (Interest Accrued)

   dr Interest Receivable (+A) 1,000
       cr Interest Revenue (+R, +SE)   1,000

CHAPTER SUMMARY

LO1   Describe the trade-offs of extending credit. p. 340

- By extending credit to customers, a company is likely to attract a greater number of customers willing to buy from it.
- The additional costs of extending credit include increased wage costs, bad debt costs, and delayed receipt of cash.

Estimate and report the effects of uncollectible accounts. p. 341 LO2

- Under generally accepted accounting principles, companies must use the allowance method to account for uncollectibles. This method involves the following steps:

  1. Estimate and record uncollectibles with an end-of-period adjusting journal entry that increases Bad debt expense (debit) and increases the Allowance for doubtful accounts (credit).

  2. Identify and write off specific customer balances in the period that they are determined to be uncollectible.

- The adjusting entry (in 1) reduces net income as well as net accounts receivable. The write-off (in 2) has offsetting effects on Accounts receivable and the Allowance for doubtful accounts, ultimately yielding no net effect on "Accounts receivable, net" or on net income.

Compute and report interest on notes receivable. p. 348 LO3

- Interest is calculated by multiplying the principal, interest rate, and time period (number of months out of 12). As time passes and interest is earned on the note, accountants must record an adjusting journal entry that accrues the interest revenue that is receivable on the note.

Compute and interpret the receivables turnover ratio. p. 351 LO4

- The receivables turnover ratio measures the effectiveness of credit-granting and collection activities. It reflects how many times average trade receivables were recorded and collected during the period.

- Analysts and creditors watch this ratio because a sudden decline in it may mean that a company is extending payment deadlines in an attempt to prop up lagging sales or even is recording sales that later will be returned by customers.

Financial Analysis Tools

Name of Measure	Formula	What It Tells You
Receivables turnover ratio	$\dfrac{\text{Net Sales Revenue}}{\text{Average Net Receivables}}$	• The number of times receivables turn over during the period • A higher ratio means faster turnover
Days to collect	$\dfrac{365}{\text{Receivables Turnover Ratio}}$	• Average number of days from sale on account to collection • A higher number means a longer time to collect

KEY TERMS

Accounts Receivable p. 341
Aging of Accounts Receivable Method p. 345
Allowance Method p. 342
Bad Debt Expense p. 342

Days to Collect p. 352
Direct Write-Off Method p. 355 (Supplement B)
Factoring p. 354
Interest Formula p. 348

Notes Receivable p. 341
Percentage of Credit Sales Method p. 345 (Supplement A)
Receivables Turnover p. 352
Write-Off p. 344

PRACTICE MATERIAL

QUESTIONS

1. What are the advantages and disadvantages of extending credit to customers?
2. What are the advantages of notes receivable relative to accounts receivable? Why don't companies use notes receivable for all credit transactions?

3. Which basic accounting principles does the allowance method of accounting for bad debts satisfy?

4. Using the allowance method, is bad debt expense recognized in the period in which (*a*) sales related to the uncollectible account were made or (*b*) the seller learns that the customer is unable to pay?

5. What is the effect of the write-off of uncollectible accounts (using the allowance method) on (*a*) net income and (*b*) net accounts receivable?

6. What is the primary difference between accounts receivable and notes receivable?

7. What are the three components of the interest formula? Explain how this formula adjusts for interest periods that are less than a full year.

8. Are interest revenues most appropriately recognized in the period in which (*a*) a note receivable has remained unpaid or (*b*) the company receives a cash payment for the interest?

9. Does an increase in the receivables turnover ratio generally indicate faster or slower collection of receivables? Explain.

10. What two approaches can managers take to speed up sluggish collections of receivables? List one advantage and disadvantage for each approach.

11. (Supplement A) How does the use of calculated estimates differ between the aging of accounts receivable method and the percentage of credit sales method?

12. (Supplement B) Describe how (and when) the direct write-off method accounts for uncollectible accounts. What are the disadvantages of this method?

13. (Supplement B) A local phone company had a customer who rang up $300 in charges during September, but did not pay. Despite reminding the customer of this balance, the company was unable to collect in October, November, or December. In March, the company finally gave up and wrote off the account balance. What amount of sales, bad debt expense, and net income would the phone company report from these events in September and March if it used the allowance method of accounting for uncollectible accounts? What amounts would be reported if the direct write-off method were used? Which method more accurately reports the financial results?

MULTIPLE CHOICE

Topic Tackler

PLUS

Check out www.mhhe.com/phillips2e for more multiple choice questions.

1. When a company using the allowance method writes off a specific customer's account receivable from the accounting system, how many of the following are true?
   • Total stockholders' equity remains the same.
   • Total assets remain the same.
   • Total expenses remain the same.
   a. None   c. Two
   b. One   d. Three

2. When using the allowance method, as Bad debt expense is recorded,
   a. Total assets remain the same and stockholders' equity remains the same.
   b. Total assets decrease and stockholders' equity decreases.
   c. Total assets increase and stockholders' equity decreases.
   d. Total liabilities increase and stockholders' equity decreases.

3. You have determined that Carefree Company estimates Bad debt expense using the aging of accounts receivable method. Assuming Carefree has no write-offs or recoveries, its estimate of uncollectible receivables resulting from the aging analysis equals
   a. Bad debt expense for the current period.
   b. The ending balance in the Allowance for doubtful accounts for the period.
   c. The change in the Allowance for doubtful accounts for the period.
   d. Both (*a*) and (*c*).

4. Which of the following best describes the proper presentation of accounts receivable in the financial statements?
   a. Accounts receivable plus the Allowance for doubtful accounts in the asset section of the balance sheet.

Quiz 8

b. Accounts receivable in the asset section of the balance sheet and the Allowance for doubtful accounts in the expense section of the income statement.

c. Accounts receivable less Bad debt expense in the asset section of the balance sheet.

d. Accounts receivable less the Allowance for doubtful accounts in the asset section of the balance sheet.

5. If the Allowance for doubtful accounts opened with a $10,000 balance, ended with an adjusted balance of $20,000, and included write-offs of $5,000 (with no recoveries) during the period, what was the amount of Bad debt expense?

   a. $5,000   b. $10,000   c. $15,000

   d. Cannot determine without knowing whether percentage of credit sales or aging of accounts receivable method was used.

6. When an account receivable is "recovered"

   a. Total assets increase.   c. Stockholders' equity increases.

   b. Total assets decrease.   d. None of the above.

7. If a 10 percent note receivable for $10,000 is created on January 1, 2006, and it has a maturity date of December 31, 2010,

   a. No interest revenue will be recorded in 2006.

   b. The note receivable will be classified as a current asset.

   c. Interest revenue of $1,000 will be recorded in 2006.

   d. None of the above.

8. If the receivables turnover ratio decreased during the year,

   a. The days to collect also decreased.

   b. Receivables collections slowed down.

   c. Sales revenues increased at a faster rate than receivables increased.

   d. None of the above.

9. In 2006, Coca-Cola Company had a receivables turnover ratio of 9.9. Which of the following could Coca-Cola do to cause the ratio to increase?

   a. Write off additional customer balances.

   b. Increase the percentages used to estimate bad debts.

   c. Factor its receivables.

   d. All of the above.

10. All else equal, if Skechers incurs a 3 percent fee to factor $10,000 of its accounts receivable, its net income will

   a. Increase by $10,000.   c. Increase by $300.

   b. Increase by $9,700.   d. Decrease by $300.

MINI-EXERCISES

M8-1 Evaluating the Decision to Extend Credit   LO1

Nutware Productions Inc. generated sales of $30,000 and gross profit of $10,000 last year. The company estimates that it would have generated sales of $60,000 had it extended credit, but there would be additional costs for associated wages and bad debts totaling $25,000. Should the company extend credit?

M8-2 Evaluating the Decision to Extend Credit   LO1
                                                                     Bally Total Fitness
On December 22, 2003, Bally Total Fitness issued a press release announcing that it had sold a significant portion of its accounts receivable. The CEO justified the decision by stating that "we focused on simplifying the business." Explain how Bally's decision will simplify its business.

M8-3 Reporting Accounts Receivable and Recording Write-Offs Using the   LO2
           Allowance Method

At the end of 2008, Extreme Fitness has adjusted balances of $800,000 in accounts receivable and $55,000 in allowance for doubtful accounts. On January 2, 2009, the company learns that certain customer accounts are not collectible, so management authorizes a write-off of these accounts totaling $5,000.

a. Show how the company would have reported its receivable accounts on December 31, 2008. As of that date, what amount did Extreme Fitness expect to collect?
b. Prepare the journal entry to write off the accounts on January 2, 2009.
c. Assuming no other transactions occurred between December 31, 2008, and January 3, 2009, show how Extreme Fitness would have reported its receivable accounts on January 3, 2009. As of that date, what amount did Extreme Fitness expect to collect? Has this changed from December 31, 2008? Explain why or why not.

LO2   M8-4 Recording Recoveries Using the Allowance Method

Let's go a bit further with the example from M8-3. Assume that on February 2, 2009, Extreme Fitness received a payment of $500 from one of the customers whose balance had been written off. Prepare the journal entries to record this transaction.

LO2   M8-5 Recording Write-Offs and Bad Debt Expense Using the Allowance Method

Prepare journal entries for each transaction listed.

a. During the period, customer balances are written off in the amount of $17,000.
b. At the end of the period, bad debt expense is estimated to be $14,000.

LO2   M8-6 Determining Financial Statement Effects of Write-Offs and Bad Debt Expense Using the Allowance Method

Using the following categories, indicate the effects of the following transactions. Use + for increase and − for decrease and indicate the accounts affected and the amounts.

a. During the period, customer balances are written off in the amount of $8,000.
b. At the end of the period, bad debt expense is estimated to be $10,000.

Assets	=	Liabilities	+	Stockholders' Equity

LO3   M8-7 Using the Interest Formula to Compute Interest

Complete the following table by computing the missing amounts (?) for the following independent cases.

Principal Amount on Note Receivable	Annual Interest Rate	Time Period	Interest Earned
a. $100,000	10%	6 months	?
b. ?	10%	12 months	$4,000
c. $50,000	?	9 months	$3,000

LO3   M8-8 Recording Note Receivable Transactions

Scotia Corporation hired a new product manager and agreed to provide her a $20,000 relocation loan on a six-month, 7 percent note. Prepare journal entries to record the following transactions for Scotia Corporation. Rather than use letters to reference each transaction, use the date of the transaction.

a. The company loans the money on January 1, 2008.
b. The new employee pays Scotia the full principal and interest on its maturity date.

LO3   M8-9 Recording Note Receivable Transactions

RecRoom Equipment Company received an $8,000, six-month, 6 percent note to settle an $8,000 unpaid balance owed by a customer. Prepare journal entries to record the following transactions for RecRoom. Rather than use letters to reference each transaction, use the date of the transaction.

a. The note is accepted by RecRoom on November 1, 2008, causing the company to increase its Notes receivable and decrease its Accounts receivable.
b. RecRoom adjusts its records for interest earned to December 31, 2008.
c. RecRoom receives the principal and interest on the note's maturity date.

M8-10 Determining the Effects of Credit Policy Changes on Receivables Turnover Ratio and Days to Collect

LO4

Indicate the most likely effect of the following changes in credit policy on the receivables turnover ratio and days to collect (+ for increase, − for decrease, and NE for no effect).

a. Granted credit to less creditworthy customers.
b. Granted credit with shorter payment deadlines.
c. Increased effectiveness of collection methods.

M8-11 Evaluating the Effect of Factoring on the Receivables Turnover Ratio and Computing the Cost of Factoring

LO4

After noting that its receivables turnover ratio had declined, Imperative Company decided for the first time in the company's history to sell $500,000 of receivables to a factoring company. The factor charges a factoring fee of 3 percent of the receivables sold. All else equal, how will this affect Imperative's receivables turnover ratio in the future? How much cash does Imperative receive on the sale? Calculate the factoring fee and describe how it is reported by Imperative Company.

M8-12 Preparing Financial Statements

LO2, LO3
Caterpillar, Inc.

Caterpillar, Inc. reported the following accounts and amounts in its December 31, 2005, year-end financial statements. Show how they would be presented in a classified balance sheet, income statement, and statement of retained earnings. Assume that the Allowance for doubtful accounts relates to Accounts receivable rather than Notes receivable.

TIP: Report amounts using an appropriate unit of measure, as first introduced in Chapter 1.

Accounts payable	$3,471,000,000	Long-term debt	$19,545,000,000
Accounts receivable	7,828,000,000	Long-term notes receivable	10,301,000,000
Allowance for doubtful accounts	302,000,000	Notes receivable–current	6,442,000,000
Cash and cash equivalents	1,108,000,000	Other current assets	2,490,000,000
Contributed capital	1,859,000,000	Other current liabilities	9,952,000,000
Cost of goods sold	26,558,000,000	Other noncurrent assets	5,990,000,000
Dividends declared	645,000,000	Other operating expenses	2,807,000,000
Income tax expense	1,047,000,000	Property, plant and equipment, net	7,888,000,000
Interest expense	260,000,000	Retained earnings, December 31	6,573,000,000
Interest revenue	377,000,000	Retained earnings, January 1	4,364,000,000
Inventories	5,224,000,000	Sales revenue	36,339,000,000
Notes payable–current	5,569,000,000	Selling, general, and administrative expenses	3,190,000,000

M8-13 (Supplement B) Recording Write-Offs and Reporting Accounts Receivable Using the Direct Write-off Method

Complete all the requirements of M8-3, except assume that Extreme Fitness uses the direct write-off method. Note that this means Extreme does not have an Allowance for doubtful accounts balance.

EXERCISES

Available with McGraw-Hill's Homework Manager

HOMEWORK MANAGER PLUS

E8-1 Recording Bad Debt Expense Estimates and Write-Offs Using the Aging of Receivables Method

LO2

At the end of 2008, Blackhorse Productions, Inc., used the aging of accounts receivable method to estimate that its Allowance for Doubtful Accounts should be $19,750. The account had an unadjusted credit balance of $10,000 at December 31, 2008.

Required:

Prepare journal entries for each transaction.

a. The appropriate bad debt adjustment was recorded for the year 2008.
b. On January 31, 2009, an account receivable for $1,000 from March 2008 was determined to be uncollectible and was written off.

LO2   **E8-2 Determining Financial Statement Effects of Bad Debt Expense Estimates and Write-Offs**

Using the following categories, indicate the effects of the transactions listed in E8-1. Use + for increase and − for decrease and indicate the accounts affected and the amounts.

Assets   =   Liabilities   +   Stockholders' Equity

LO2   **E8-3 Recording Write-Offs, Recoveries, and Bad Debt Expense Estimates Using the Aging of Receivables Method**

Prior to recording the following, Elite Electronics, Incorporated had a credit balance of $2,000 in its Allowance for doubtful accounts.

Required:

Prepare journal entries for each transaction.

a. On August 31, 2008, a customer balance for $300 from a prior year was determined to be uncollectible and was written off.
b. On December 15, 2008, the customer balance for $300 written off on August 31, 2008, was collected in full.
c. Based on an aging of accounts receivable, the company determined that the December 31 balance in the allowance for doubtful accounts should be $5,600. On December 31, 2008, the appropriate bad debt adjustment was recorded.

LO2   **E8-4 Determining Financial Statement Effects of Write-Offs, Recoveries, and Bad Debt Expense Estimates**

Using the following categories, indicate the effects of the transactions listed in E8-3. Use + for increase and − for decrease and indicate the accounts affected and the amounts.

Assets   =   Liabilities   +   Stockholders' Equity

LO2   **E8-5 Computing Bad Debt Expense Using Aging of Accounts Receivable Method**

Young and Old Corporation (YOC) uses two aging categories to estimate uncollectible accounts. Accounts less than 60 days are considered young and have a 5% uncollectible rate. Accounts more than 60 days are considered old and have a 35% uncollectible rate.

Required:

1. If YOC has $10,000 of young accounts and $40,000 of old accounts, how much should be reported in the Allowance for doubtful accounts?
2. If YOC's Allowance for doubtful accounts currently has an unadjusted credit balance of $4,000, how much should be credited to the account?
3. If YOC's Allowance for doubtful accounts has an unadjusted debit balance of $500, how much should be credited to the account?
4. Explain how YOC's Allowance for doubtful accounts could have a debit balance.

E8-6 Computing Bad Debt Expense Using Aging of Accounts Receivable Method

Brown Cow Dairy uses the aging approach to estimate bad debt expense. The balance of each account receivable is aged on the basis of three time periods as follows: (1) 1–30 days old, $12,000; (2) 31–90 days old, $5,000; and (3) more than 90 days old, $3,000. Experience has shown that for each age group, the average loss rate on the amount of the receivable due to uncollectibility is (1) 3 percent, (2) 15 percent, and (3) 30 percent, respectively. At December 31, 2008 (end of the current year), the Allowance for doubtful accounts balance was $800 (credit) before the end-of-period adjusting entry is made.

Required:

1. Prepare a schedule to estimate an appropriate year-end balance for the Allowance for doubtful accounts.
2. What amount should be recorded as Bad debt expense for the current year?
3. If the unadjusted balance in the Allowance for doubtful accounts was a $600 debit balance, what would be the amount of Bad debt expense in 2008?

E8-7 Recording and Reporting Allowance for Doubtful Accounts Using Aging of Accounts Receivable Method
LO2

InnovativeTech, Inc. uses the aging approach to estimate bad debt expense. The balance of each account receivable is aged on the basis of three time periods as follows: (1) 1–30 days old, $75,000; (2) 31–90 days old, $10,000; and (3) more than 90 days old, $4,000. Experience has shown that for each age group, the average loss rate on the amount of the receivable due to uncollectibility is (1) 1 percent, (2) 15 percent, and (3) 40 percent, respectively. At December 31, 2009 (end of the current year), the Allowance for doubtful accounts balance was $100 (credit) before the end-of-period adjusting entry is made.

Required:

1. Prepare a schedule to estimate an appropriate year-end balance for the Allowance for doubtful accounts.
2. Prepare the appropriate Bad debt expense adjusting entry for the year 2009.
3. Show how the various accounts related to accounts receivable should be shown on the December 31, 2009, balance sheet.

E8-8 Comprehensive Exercise for Recording and Reporting Credit Sales and Bad Debts Using the Aging of Accounts Receivable Method
LO2
Walgreen's

Okay Optical, Inc. (OOI) began operations in January 2008 selling inexpensive sunglasses to large retailers like Walgreen's and other smaller stores. Assume the following transactions occurred during its first six months of operations.

January	1	Sold merchandise to Walgreen's for $20,000; the cost of these goods to OOI was $12,000.
February	12	Received payment in full from Walgreen's.
March	1	Sold merchandise to Tony's Pharmacy on account for $3,000; the cost of these goods to OOI was $1,400.
April	1	Sold merchandise to Travis Pharmaco on account for $8,000. The cost to OOI was $4,400.
May	1	Sold merchandise to Anjuli Stores on account for $2,000; the cost to OOI was $1,200.
June	17	Received $6,500 on account from Travis Pharmaco.

Required:

1. Complete the following aged listing of customer accounts at June 30.

		UNPAID SINCE			
Customer	Total Balance	June (one month)	May (two months)	April (three months)	March (>three months)
Anjuli Stores	$2,000		$2,000		
Tony's Pharmacy	3,000				$3,000
Travis Pharmaco					
Walgreen's					

2. Estimate the Allowance for doubtful accounts required at June 30, 2008, assuming the following uncollectible rates: one month, 1 percent; two months, 5 percent; three months, 20 percent; more than three months, 40 percent.
3. Show how OOI would report its accounts receivable on its June 30 balance sheet. What amounts would be reported on an income statement prepared for the six-month period ended June 30, 2008?
4. Bonus Question: In July 2008, OOI collected the balance due from Tony's Pharmacy but discovered that the balance due from Travis Pharmaco needed to be written off. Using this information, determine how accurate OOI was in estimating the Allowance for doubtful accounts needed for each of these two customers and in total.

LO3   **E8-9** **Recording Note Receivable Transactions, Including Accrual Adjustment for Interest**

The following transactions took place for Smart Solutions Ltd.

<u>2007</u>

July 1	Loaned $70,000 to an employee of the company and received back a one-year, 10 percent note.
Dec. 31	Accrued interest on the note.

<u>2008</u>

July 1	Received interest and principal on the note. (No interest has been accrued since December 31.)

Required:

Prepare the journal entries that Smart Solutions Ltd. would record for the above transactions.

LO3   **E8-10** **Recording Note Receivable Transactions, Including Accrual Adjustment for Interest**

The following transactions took place for Parker's Grocery.

Jan. 1	Loaned $50,000 to a cashier of the company and received back a one-year, 7 percent note.
June 30	Accrued interest on the note.
Dec. 31	Received interest and principal on the note. (No interest has been accrued since June 30.)

Required:

Prepare the journal entries that Parker's Grocery would record for the above transactions.

LO3   **E8-11** **Recording Note Receivable Transactions, Including Accrual Adjustment for Interest**

To attract retailers to its shopping center, the Marketplace Mall will lend money to tenants under formal contracts, provided that they use it to renovate their store space. On November 1, 2008, the company loaned $100,000 to a new tenant on a one-year note with a stated annual interest rate of 6 percent. Interest is to be received by Marketplace Mall on April 30, 2009, and at maturity on October 31, 2009.

Required:

Prepare journal entries that Marketplace Mall would record related to this note on the following dates: (*a*) November 1, 2008; (*b*) December 31, 2008 (Marketplace Mall's fiscal year-end); (*c*) April 30, 2009; and (*d*) October 31, 2009.

LO2, LO4   **E8-12** **Using Financial Statement Disclosures to Infer Write-Offs and Bad Debt Expense and to Calculate the Receivables Turnover Ratio**

Microsoft Corporation

Microsoft Corporation develops, produces, and markets a wide range of computer software including the Windows operating system. Microsoft reported the following information about net sales revenue and accounts receivable (all amounts in millions).

	June 30, 2006	June 30, 2005
Accounts receivable, net of allowances of $142 and $171	$ 9,316	$ 7,180
Net revenues	44,282	39,788

According to its Form 10-K, Microsoft recorded bad debt expense of $40 and did not recover any previously written off accounts during the year ended June 30, 2006.

Required:

1. What amount of accounts receivable was written off during the year ended June 30, 2006?
2. What was Microsoft's receivables turnover ratio (to one decimal place) in the current year?

E8-13 Using Financial Statement Disclosures to Infer Bad Debt Expense   LO2

The 2006 annual report for Sears Holding Corporation contained the following information (in millions):

SEARS

	2005	2006
Accounts receivable	$686	$846
Allowance for doubtful accounts	(40)	(35)
Accounts receivable, net	$646	$ 811

A footnote to the financial statements disclosed that accounts receivable write-offs amounted to $102 during 2005 and $92 during 2006. Assume that Sears did not record any recoveries.

Required:

Determine the Bad debt expense for 2006 based on the above facts.

E8-14 Determining the Effects of Uncollectible Accounts on the Receivables Turnover Ratio   LO2, LO4

Refer to the information about Sears given in E8-13.

Required:

Complete the following table indicating the direction of the effect (+ for increase, − for decrease, and NE for no effect) of each transaction during 2006:

Transaction	Net Credit Sales	Average Net Accounts Receivable	Receivables Turnover Ratio
a. Writing off $92,000,000 in uncollectible accounts.			
b. Recording bad debt expense.			

E8-15 Analyzing and Interpreting Receivables Turnover Ratio and Days to Collect   LO4

FedEx Corporation

A recent annual report for FedEx Corporation contained the following data (in millions):

	May 31	
	2006	2005
Accounts receivable	$ 3,660	$3,422
Less: Allowance for doubtful accounts	144	125
Accounts receivable, net of allowance	$ 3,516	$3,297
Net sales (assume all on credit)	$32,294	

Required:

1. Determine the accounts receivable turnover ratio and days to collect for the current year. Round your answers to one decimal place.

2. Explain the meaning of each number.

LO2, LO4   **E8-16 Determining the Effects of Bad Debt Write-Offs on the Receivables Turnover Ratio**

During 2008, Jesse Enterprises Corporation recorded credit sales of $650,000. At the beginning of the year, Accounts receivable, net of allowance was $50,000. At the end of the year, *after* the Bad debt expense adjustment was recorded but *before* any bad debts had been written off, Accounts receivable, net of allowance was $49,000.

Required:

1. Assume that on December 31, 2008, accounts receivable totaling $6,000 for the year were determined to be uncollectible and written off. What was the receivables turnover ratio for 2008? Round to one decimal place.

2. Assume instead that on December 31, 2008, $7,000 of accounts receivable was determined to be uncollectible and written off. What was the receivables turnover ratio for 2008? Round to one decimal place.

3. Explain why the answers to requirements 1 and 2 differ or do not differ.

LO2   **E8-17 Recording and Determining the Effects of Write-Offs, Recoveries, and Bad Debt Expense Estimates on the Balance Sheet and Income Statement**

Academic Dishonesty Investigations Ltd. operates a plagiarism detection service for universities and community colleges.

Required:

1. Prepare journal entries for each transaction below.

    a. On March 31, 2008, 10 customers were billed for detection services totaling $25,000.

    b. On October 31, 2008, a customer balance of $1,500 from a prior year was determined to be uncollectible and was written off.

    c. On December 15, 2008, a customer paid an old balance of $900, which had been written off in a prior year.

    d. On December 31, 2008, $500 of bad debts were estimated and recorded for the year 2008.

2. Complete the following table, indicating the amount and effect (+ for increase, − for decrease, and NE for no effect) of each transaction. Ignore income taxes.

Transaction	Accounts receivable, net of allowance	Net sales	Net income
a			
b			
c			
d			

LO2   **E8-18 (Supplement A) Recording, Reporting, and Evaluating a Bad Debt Estimate Using the Percentage of Credit Sales Method**

During the year ended December 31, 2007, Kelly's Camera Shop had sales revenue of $170,000, of which $85,000 was on credit. At the start of 2007, Accounts receivable showed a $10,000 debit balance, and the Allowance for doubtful accounts showed an $800 credit balance. Collections of accounts receivable during 2007 amounted to $68,000.

Data during 2007 follow:

a. On December 10, 2007, a customer balance of $1,500 from a prior year was determined to be uncollectible, so it was written off.

b. On December 31, 2007, a decision was made to continue the accounting policy of basing estimated bad debt losses on 2 percent of credit sales for the year.

Required:

1. Give the required journal entries for the two events in December 2007.
2. Show how the amounts related to Accounts receivable and Bad debt expense would be reported on the balance sheet and income statement for 2007.
3. On the basis of the data available, does the 2 percent rate appear to be reasonable? Explain.

E8-19 (Supplement B) Recording Write-Offs and Reporting Accounts Receivable Using the Direct Write-Off Method

Trevorson Electronics is a small company privately owned by Jon Trevorson, an electrician who installs wiring in new homes. Because the company's financial statements are prepared only for tax purposes, Jon uses the direct write-off method. During 2007, its first year of operations, Trevorson Electronics sold $30,000 of services on account. The company collected $26,000 of these receivables during the year, and Jon believed that the remaining $4,000 was fully collectible. In 2008, Jon discovered that none of the $4,000 would be collected, so he wrote off the entire amount. To make matters worse, Jon sold only $5,000 of services during the year.

Required:

1. Prepare journal entries to record the transactions in 2007 and 2008.
2. Using only the information provided (ignore other operating expenses), prepare comparative income statements for 2007 and 2008. Was 2007 really as profitable as indicated by its income statement? Was 2008 quite as bad as indicated by its income statement? What should Jon do if he wants better information for assessing his company's ability to generate profit?

COACHED PROBLEMS

CP8-1 Recording Accounts Receivable Transactions Using the Aging of Accounts Receivable Method

LO2

A.T. Cross Company

The A.T. Cross Company is well known for its Cross pens. The company recently reported the following amounts in its unadjusted trial balance as of December 31, 2005:

	Debits	Credits
Accounts receivable	$32,850,941	
Allowance for doubtful accounts		$ 907,050
Sales		112,114,878

Required:

1. Assume Cross uses the aging of accounts receivable method and estimates that $1,007,000 of accounts receivable will be uncollectible. Prepare the adjusting journal entry required at December 31, 2005, for recording bad debt expense.
   TIP: The aging of accounts receivable method focuses on calculating what the adjusted Allowance for doubtful accounts balance should be. You need to consider the existing balance when determining the adjustment.
2. Repeat requirement 1, except this time assume the unadjusted balance in Cross's allowance for doubtful accounts at December 31, 2005, was a debit balance of $10,050.
   TIP: See page 346 for advice on how to handle debit balances.
3. If one of Cross's main customers declared bankruptcy in 2006, what journal entry would be used to write off its $10,000 balance?

CP8-2 (Supplement A) Recording Bad Debts Using the Percentage of Credit Sales Method

LO2

Complete requirement 1 of CP8-1, except assume Cross uses ¼ of 1 percent of sales to estimate its bad debt expense for the year.
   TIP: The percentage of credit sales method directly calculates bad debt expense.

LO2

Sonic Corp.

CP8-3 Interpreting Disclosure of Allowance for Doubtful Accounts

Sonic Corp. runs the largest chain of drive-in restaurants in the United States. It has an allowance for doubtful accounts that relates to its accounts and notes receivable. In its 2005 10-K, Sonic reported the following changes in the allowance for doubtful accounts (in thousands):

Balance at Beginning of Period	Charged to Bad Debt Expenses	Amounts Written Off	Recoveries	Balance at End of Period
$526	$414	$542	$109	$507

Required:

1. Create a T-account for the Allowance for doubtful accounts and enter into it the amounts from the above schedule. Then write the T-account in equation format to prove that the above items account for the changes in the account.

   TIP: The allowance increases when estimates are charged to Bad debt expense and when recoveries are reported. The allowance decreases when accounts are written off.

2. Record summary journal entries related to (a) estimating bad debt expense, (b) write-offs of specific balances during the year, and (c) recovering previous write-offs.

   TIP: Use the generic account name "receivables" to refer to the combined accounts receivable and notes receivable.

3. If Sonic had written off an additional $20,000 of accounts receivable during the period, how would net accounts and notes receivable have been affected? How would net income have been affected? Explain why.

LO3

CP8-4 Recording Notes Receivable Transactions

Jung & Newbicalm Advertising (JNA) recently hired a new creative director, Howard Rachell, for its Madison Avenue office in New York. To persuade Howard to move from San Francisco, JNA agreed to advance him $100,000 on April 30, 2007 on a one-year, 10 percent note, with interest payments required on October 31, 2007, and April 30, 2008. JNA issues quarterly financial statements on March 31, June 30, September 30, and December 31.

Required:

1. Prepare the journal entry that JNA will make to record the promissory note created on April 30, 2007.

   TIP: See demonstration case B for a similar problem.

2. Prepare the journal entries that JNA will make to record the interest accruals at each quarter end and interest payments at each payment date.

   TIP: Interest receivable will be accrued at the end of each quarter, and then will be reduced when the interest payment is received.

3. Prepare the journal entry that JNA will make to record the principal payment at the maturity date.

LO2, LO3

CP8-5 Recording and Reporting Accounts Receivable and Notes Receivable Transactions

Sports USA, Inc., distributes athletic gear to sporting goods stores throughout the country. Most of its sales are made on account, but some particularly large items (such as sport court systems) are sold in exchange for notes receivable. Sports USA reported the following balances in its December 31, 2007, unadjusted trial balance:

	Debit	Credit
Accounts receivable	$1,110,000	
Allowance for doubtful accounts		$6,000
Bad debt expense	0	
Interest receivable	0	
Interest revenue		0
Notes receivable	30,000	

Notes receivable consists of principal owed by a customer on a two-year, 5 percent note accepted on November 1, 2007. The note requires the customer to make annual interest payments on October 31, 2008, and 2009. Sports USA has no concerns about the collectibility of this note. Sports USA does estimate that $56,000 of its accounts receivable will be uncollectible.

Required:

1. Prepare the December 31, 2007, adjusting journal entries related to accounts receivable and notes receivable.
   TIP: The note receivable has been outstanding for two months in 2007, so the company has earned two months of interest.
2. Show how the adjusted balances for the above balance sheet accounts will be reported on Sports USA's classified balance sheet as of December 31, 2007.
   TIP: Current assets include assets that will be used up or converted to cash during 2008.

CP8-6 Analyzing Allowance for Doubtful Accounts, Receivables Turnover Ratio, and Days to Collect

LO4
Mattel, Inc.

Mattel and Hasbro are two of the largest and most successful toymakers in the world, in terms of the products they sell and their receivables management practices. To evaluate their ability to collect on credit sales, consider the following information reported in their 2005, 2004 and 2003 annual reports (amounts in millions).

	Mattel			Hasbro		
Fiscal Year Ended:	2005	2004	2003	2005	2004	2003
Net sales	$5,179	$5,103	$4,960	$3,088	$2,998	$3,139
Accounts receivable	785	792	571	553	616	647
Allowance for doubtful accounts	25	33	28	30	37	39
Accounts receivable, net of allowance	760	759	543	523	579	608

Required:

1. Calculate the receivables turnover ratios and days to collect for Mattel and Hasbro for 2005 and 2004. (Round to one decimal place.) Which of the companies is quicker to convert its receivables into cash?
   TIP: In your calculations, use average accounts receivable, net of allowance.
2. In its annual report filed with the SEC, Mattel's management discusses and analyzes its financial results. As part of this discussion, Mattel admits that it factored $443 million of receivables in 2005 and $446 in 2004. Given this additional information, recalculate what the receivables turnover ratio and days to collect would have been in 2005 if Mattel had not factored its receivables. (Round to one decimal place.) Does this help to explain the apparent differences determined in requirement 1 above?
   TIP: To remove the effect of factoring, add the amount factored to "Accounts receivable, net of allowance" for each of the two years and recalculate the average net receivable balance to use in your computations.

GROUP A PROBLEMS

Available with McGraw-Hill's Homework Manager　HOMEWORK MANAGER **PLUS**

PA8-1 Recording Accounts Receivable Transactions Using the Aging Method

LO2
Kraft Foods Inc.

Kraft Foods Inc. is the second-largest food and beverage company in the world. Assume the company recently reported the following amounts in its unadjusted trial balance as of December 31, 2007 (all amounts in millions):

	Debits	Credits
Accounts receivable	$3,900	
Allowance for doubtful accounts		$　110
Sales		32,010

www.mhhe.com/phillips2e

Required:

1. Assume Kraft uses the aging of accounts receivable method and estimates that $233 of accounts receivable will be uncollectible. Prepare the adjusting journal entry required at December 31, 2007, for recording bad debt expense.

2. Repeat requirement 2, except this time assume the unadjusted balance in Kraft's allowance for doubtful accounts at December 31, 2007, was a debit balance of $20.

3. If one of Kraft's main customers declared bankruptcy in 2008, what journal entry would be used to write off its $15 balance?

LO2

PA8-2 (Supplement A) Recording Accounts Receivable Transactions Using the Percentage of Credit Sales Method

Complete the requirements of PA8-1, except assume Kraft uses ½ of 1 percent of sales to estimate its bad debt expense for the year.

LO2

Stride Rite, Corp.

eXcel

www.mhhe.com/phillips2e

PA8-3 Interpreting Disclosure of Allowance for Doubtful Accounts

Stride Rite, Corp., designs, develops, and markets performance-oriented athletic footwear, athletic apparel, and casual leather footwear. It recently disclosed the following information concerning the allowance for doubtful accounts on its Form 10-K annual report.

SCHEDULE II				
Valuation and Qualifying Accounts				
(dollars in thousands)				
Allowance for Doubtful Accounts	Balance at Beginning of Year	Additions Charged to Bad Debt Expense	Deductions from Allowance	Balance at End of Year
2005	$1,547	$1,400	$ 1,638	$1,309
2004	3,216	?	2,280	1,547
2003	3,773	1,343	?	3,216

Required:

1. Create a T-account for the Allowance for doubtful accounts and enter into it the 2005 amounts from the above schedule. Then write the T-account in equation format to prove that the above items account for the changes in the account.

2. Record summary journal entries for 2005 related to (a) estimating bad debt expense and (b) writing off specific balances.

3. Supply the missing dollar amounts noted by ? for 2004 and 2003.

4. If Stride Rite had written off an additional $200 of accounts receivable during 2005, how would net receivables have been affected? How would net income have been affected? Explain why.

LO3

PA8-4 Recording Notes Receivable Transactions

C&S Marketing (CSM) recently hired a new marketing director, Jeff Otos, for its downtown Minneapolis office. As part of the arrangement, CSM agreed on February 28, 2007, to advance Jeff $50,000 on a one-year, 8 percent note, with interest to be paid at maturity on February 28, 2008. CSM prepares financial statements on June 30 and December 31.

Required:

1. Prepare the journal entry that CSM will make to record the execution of the note.
2. Prepare the journal entries that CSM will make to accrue interest on June 30 and December 31.
3. Prepare the journal entry that CSM will make to record the interest and principal payments on February 28, 2008.

LO2, LO3

eXcel

www.mhhe.com/phillips2e

PA8-5 Recording and Reporting Accounts Receivable and Notes Receivable Transactions

Merle Adventures, Inc., is a distributor of kayaking equipment. Most of its sales are made on account, but some particularly large orders are sold in exchange for notes receivable. Merle Adventures reported the following balances in its December 31, 2008, unadjusted trial balance:

	Debit	Credit
Accounts receivable	$2,700,000	
Allowance for doubtful accounts		$11,000
Bad debt expense	0	
Interest receivable	0	
Interest revenue		0
Notes receivable	20,000	

Notes receivable consists of principal owed by a customer on a two-year, 6 percent note accepted on November 1, 2008. The note requires the customer to make annual interest payments on October 31, 2009 and 2008. Merle Adventures has no concerns about the collectibility of this note. Merle Adventures estimates that $25,000 of its accounts receivable will be uncollectible.

Required:

1. Prepare the December 31, 2008, adjusting journal entries related to accounts receivable and notes receivable.
2. Show how the adjusted balances for the above balance sheet accounts will be reported on Merle Adventures' classified balance sheet as of December 31, 2008.

PA8-6 Analyzing Allowance for Doubtful Accounts, Receivables Turnover Ratio, and Days to Collect

LO4
Coca-Cola
PepsiCo

Coca-Cola and PepsiCo are two of the largest and most successful beverage companies in the world in terms of the products that they sell and in terms of their receivables management practices. To evaluate their ability to collect on credit sales, consider the following information reported in their 2005, 2004 and 2003 annual reports (amounts in millions).

	Coca-Cola			PepsiCo		
Fiscal Year Ended:	2005	2004	2003	2005	2004	2003
Net sales	$23,104	$21,742	$20,857	$32,562	$29,261	$26,971
Accounts receivable	2,353	2,313	2,152	3,261	2,999	2,830
Allowance for doubtful accounts	72	69	61	105	116	121
Accounts receivable, net of allowance	2,281	2,244	2,091	3,156	2,883	2,709

Required:

Calculate the receivables turnover ratios and days to collect for Coca-Cola and PepsiCo for 2005 and 2004. (Round to one decimal place.) Which of the companies is quicker to convert its receivables into cash?

www.mhhe.com/phillips2e

GROUP B PROBLEMS

PB8-1 Recording Accounts Receivable Transactions Using the Allowance Method

LO2
Intel Corporation

Intel Corporation is a well-known supplier of computer chips, boards, systems, and software building blocks. Assume the company recently reported the following amounts in its unadjusted trial balance as December 31, 2008 (all amounts in millions):

	Debits	Credits
Accounts receivable	$3,300	
Allowance for doubtful accounts		$ 65
Sales		32,404

Required:

1. Assume Intel uses the aging of accounts receivable method and estimates that $200 of accounts receivable will be uncollectible. Prepare the adjusting journal entry required at December 31, 2008, for recording bad debt expense.

2. Repeat requirement 1, except this time assume the unadjusted balance in Intel's allowance for doubtful accounts at December 31, 2008, was a debit balance of $20.

3. If one of Intel's main customers declared bankruptcy in 2009, what journal entry would be used to write off its $15 balance?

LO2

PB8-2 (Supplement A) Recording Accounts Receivable Transactions Using the Percentage of Credit Sales Method

Complete the requirements of PB8-1, except assume Intel uses ¼ of 1 percent of sales to estimate its Bad debt expense for the year.

LO2

Xerox Corporation

PB8-3 Interpreting Disclosure of Allowance for Doubtful Accounts

Xerox Corporation is the company that made the photocopier popular, although it now describes itself as a technology and services enterprise that helps businesses deploy document management strategies and improve productivity. It recently disclosed the following information concerning the allowance for doubtful accounts on its Form 10-K annual report.

SCHEDULE II Valuation and Qualifying Accounts (dollars in millions)				
Allowance for Doubtful Accounts	Balance at Beginning of Year	Additions Charged to Bad Debt Expense	Deductions from Allowance	Balance End of Year
2005	$459	$ 72	$166	$365
2004	533	?	184	459
2003	606	224	?	533

Required:

1. Create a T-account for the allowance for doubtful accounts and enter into it the 2005 amounts from the above schedule. Then, write the T-account in equation format to prove that the above items account for the changes in the account.

2. Record summary journal entries for 2005 related to (*a*) estimating bad debt expense and (*b*) writing off specific balances.

3. Supply the missing dollar amounts noted by ? for 2004 and 2003.

4. If Xerox had written off an additional $20 of accounts receivable during 2005, how would net accounts receivable have been affected? How would net income have been affected? Explain why.

LO3

PB8-4 Recording Notes Receivable Transactions

Stinson Company recently agreed to loan an employee $100,000 for the purchase of a new house. The loan was executed on May 31, 2007, and is a one-year, 6 percent note, with interest payments required on November 30, 2007, and May 31, 2008. Stinson Co. issues quarterly financial statements on March 31, June 30, September 30, and December 31.

Required:

1. Prepare the journal entry that Stinson Co. will make to record the execution of the note.

2. Prepare the journal entries that Stinson Co. will make to record the interest accruals at each quarter end and interest payments at each payment date.

3. Prepare the journal entry that Stinson Co. will make to record the principal payment at the maturity date.

LO2, LO3

PB8-5 Recording and Reporting Accounts Receivable and Notes Receivable Transactions

Tractors-R-Us is a supplier of garden tractors. Most of its sales are made on account, but some particularly large orders are sold in exchange for notes receivable. Tractors-R-Us reported the following balances in its December 31, 2007, unadjusted trial balance:

	Debit	Credit
Accounts receivable	$1,650,000	
Allowance for doubtful accounts		$16,000
Bad debt expense	0	
Interest receivable	0	
Interest revenue		0
Notes receivable	115,000	

Notes receivable consists of principal owed by a customer on a two-year, 5 percent note accepted on July 1, 2007. The note requires the customer to make annual interest payments on June 30, 2008, and 2009. Tractors-R-Us has no concerns about the collectibility of this note. Tractors-R-Us does estimate, however, that $25,000 of its accounts receivable will be uncollectible.

Required:

1. Prepare the December 31, 2007, adjusting journal entries related to accounts receivable and notes receivable.
2. Show how the adjusted balances for the above balance sheet accounts will be reported on Tractors-R-Us' classified balance sheet as of December 31, 2007.

PB8-6 Analyzing Allowance for Doubtful Accounts, Receivables Turnover Ratio, and Days to Collect

LO4

Wal-Mart and Target are two of the largest and most successful retail chains in the world. To evaluate their ability to collect on credit sales, consider the following information reported in their 2005 and 2004 annual reports (amounts in millions).

Fiscal Year Ended:	Wal-Mart			Target		
	2005	2004	2003	2005	2004	2003
Net sales	$312,427	$285,222	$256,329	$52,620	$46,839	$42,025
Accounts receivable	2,662	1,715	1,254	6,117	5,456	4,973
Allowance for doubtful accounts	186	129	90	451	387	352
Accounts receivable, net of allowance	2,476	1,586	1,164	5,666	5,069	4,621

Required:

Calculate the receivables turnover ratios and days to collect for Wal-Mart and Target for 2005 and 2004. (Round to one decimal place.) Which of the companies is quicker to convert its receivables into cash?

SKILLS DEVELOPMENT CASES

S8-1 Finding Financial Information

LO2, LO4

Refer to the financial statements of Landry's Restaurants in Appendix A at the end of this book, or download the annual report from the *Cases* section of the text's Web site at www.mhhe.com/phillips2e.

1. Does the company report an allowance for doubtful accounts on the balance sheet or in the notes? Explain why it does or does not. (*Hint:* Consider the nature of its receivables.)
2. Compute the company's receivables turnover ratio and days to collect for the most recent year. Are these comparable to the examples shown in Exhibit 8.8? Explain any unusual differences.

S8-2 Comparing Financial Information

LO2, LO4

Refer to the financial statements of Outback Steakhouse in Appendix B at the end of this book, or download them from the *Cases* section of the text's Web site at www.mhhe.com/phillips2e.

1. How much does Outback report (in note 2 of the financial statements) for Accounts receivable at December 31, 2005? Explain whether accounts receivable is a significant asset to Outback. Does Outback report an Allowance for doubtful accounts? Explain why it does or does not. (*Hint:* Consider the nature of the company's business operations.)

2. Based on your observations for requirement 1, describe the usefulness of the receivables turnover ratio and days to collect analyses for companies that are only involved in operating restaurants. Can you think of any other businesses for which this description might apply?

LO1, LO2, LO4   **S8-3 Internet-Based Team Research: Examining an Annual Report**

As a team, select an industry to analyze. Using your Web browser, each team member should access the annual report or 10-K for one publicly traded company in the industry, with each member selecting a different company. (See S1-3 in Chapter 1 for a description of possible resources for these tasks.)

Required:

1. On an individual basis, each team member should write a short report that incorporates the following:

   a. Calculate the receivables turnover ratio for the current and prior year, and explain any change between the two years. (To obtain the beginning accounts receivable number for the prior year, you will need the prior year's annual report.)

   b. Look in the 10-K for the Schedule II analysis of "Valuation and Qualifying Accounts," which provides additional disclosures concerning the allowance for doubtful accounts. From this schedule, determine the level of bad debt expense, as a percentage of sales, for the current and prior year.

2. Then, as a team, write a short report comparing and contrasting your companies using these attributes. Discuss any patterns across the companies that you as a team observe. Provide potential explanations for any differences discovered.

LO2, LO3   **S8-4 Ethical Decision Making: A Real-Life Example**

MCI

You work for a company named MCI and you have been assigned the job of adjusting the company's Allowance for doubtful accounts balance. You obtained the following aged listing of customer account balances for December.

Accounts Receivable Aged Listing—December 31						
Customer	Total	0–30 days	31–60 days	61–90 days	91–120 days	>120 days
AfriTel	40,000	20,000	10,000	5,000	5,000	0
CT&T	0	0	0	0	0	0
GlobeCom	28,000	0	18,000	8,000	1,000	1,000
Hi-Rim	35,000	0	0	0	0	35,000
Level 8	162,000	63,000	44,000	29,000	13,000	13,000
NewTel	0	0	0	0	0	0
Telemedia	0	0	0	0	0	0
Others	485,000	257,000	188,000	28,000	11,000	1,000
TOTAL	750,000	340,000	260,000	70,000	30,000	50,000

Historically, bad debt loss rates for each aging category have been 1% (0–30 days), 5% (31–60 days), 8% (61–90 days), 10% (91–120 days), and 50% (>120 days). Using these rates, you calculate a desired balance for the allowance. No entries have been made to the account since the end of November when the account had a credit balance of $46,820.

To check the reasonableness of the calculated balance, you obtain the aged listings for prior months (shown on page 377). As you scan the listings, you notice something odd. Several account balances, which had grown quite large by the end of November, had disappeared in the final month of the year. You ask the accounts receivable manager, Walter Pavlo, what happened. He said the customers "obtained some financing . . . I guess out of nowhere" and they must have used it to pay off their account balances. As strange as this seemed, you decided that these accounts receivable balances no longer existed, so an allowance for doubtful accounts was not needed for them.

	Total Accounts Receivable as of ...					
	Q1	Q2	Q3		Q4	
Customer	(March 31)	(June 30)	(September 30)	(October 31)	(November 30)	(December 31)
AfriTel	19,000	19,000	21,000	16,000	20,000	40,000
CT&T	0	30,000	100,000	100,000	100,000	0
GlobeCom	29,000	28,000	31,000	27,000	28,000	28,000
Hi-Rim	0	0	25,000	35,000	35,000	35,000
Level 8	229,000	229,000	198,000	174,000	190,000	162,000
NewTel	0	0	25,000	25,000	25,000	0
Telemedia	0	0	2,000	2,000	2,000	0
Others	524,000	489,000	375,000	503,000	463,000	485,000
TOTAL	801,000	795,000	777,000	882,000	863,000	750,000

Required:

1. Calculate the balance that should be reported in Allowance for doubtful accounts as of December 31.
2. Prepare the adjusting journal entry that is required on December 31.
3. Show how accounts receivable would be reported on the balance sheet at December 31.
4. If the balances for CT&T, NewTel, and Telemedia at the end of November continued to exist at the end of December (in the over 120 days category), what balance would you have estimated for the Allowance for doubtful accounts on December 31? Would this have changed MCI's net income in the current year? Explain.
5. A few days later, you overhear Mr. Pavlo talking about the account receivable from Hi-Rim. Apparently, MCI will soon loan Hi-Rim some money, creating a note receivable. Hi-Rim will use the money to pay off the accounts receivable balance it owes to MCI. You are aware that Mr. Pavlo receives a bonus based on MCI's net income. Should you investigate this matter further? Explain why or why not.

Epilogue: The events described above are based on an article in the June 10, 2002, issue of *Forbes* magazine that describes how, in the mid-1990s, Walter Pavlo was pressured to commit accounting fraud at MCI. Ironically, MCI was later taken over by WorldCom—the company that went on to commit the world's largest accounting fraud at the time.

S8-5 Ethical Decision Making: A Mini-Case   LO2

Having just graduated with a business degree, you're excited to begin working as a junior accountant at Clear Optics, Inc. The company supplies lenses, frames, and sunglasses to opticians and retailers throughout the country. Clear Optics is currently in the process of finalizing its third quarter (Q3) operating results. All Q3 adjusting entries have been made, except for bad debt expense. The preliminary income statement for Q3 is shown below, along with reported results for Q2 and Q1.

CLEAR OPTICS, INC.
Quarterly Income Statements
(amounts in thousands of U.S. dollars)

	Q3 (preliminary)	Q2 (as reported)	Q1 (as reported)
Net sales	$135,800	$135,460	$130,100
Cost of goods sold	58,400	58,250	55,990
Gross profit	77,400	77,210	74,110
Selling, general, and administrative expenses	56,560	53,975	53,690
Bad debt expense	—	6,050	4,200
Income before income taxes	20,840	17,185	16,220
Income tax expense	5,620	5,155	5,020
Net income	$ 15,220	$ 12,030	$ 11,200

The corporate controller has asked you to examine the Allowance for doubtful accounts and use the aged listing of accounts receivable to determine the adjustment needed to record estimated bad debts for the quarter. The controller states that, "Although our customers are somewhat slower in paying this quarter, we can't afford to increase the allowance for doubtful accounts. If anything, we need to decrease it—an adjusted balance of about $8,000 is what I'd like to see. Play around with our estimated bad debt loss rates until you get it to work."

You were somewhat confused by what the controller had told you, but you chalked it up to your lack of experience and decided to analyze the Allowance for doubtful accounts. You summarized the transactions recorded in the Allowance for doubtful accounts using the T-account below:

Allowance for Doubtful Accounts			
		7,900	January 1 bal. fwd.
Q1 Write-offs	4,110	4,200	Q1 Bad debts estimate
		7,990	March 31 adjusted
Q2 Write-offs	4,120	6,050	Q2 Bad debts estimate
		9,920	June 30 adjusted
Q3 Write-offs	4,030	—	
		5,890	September 30 unadjusted

Required:

1. What bad debts estimate for Q3 will produce the $8,000 balance that the controller would like to see?
2. Prepare the adjusting journal entry that would be required to record this estimate.
3. If the entry in requirement 2 is made, what does it do to the Q3 income and the trend in earnings? (Assume that income tax expense does not change.)
4. Reconsider the statement the controller made to you. Is his suggestion a logical way to use the aging method to estimate bad debts?
5. What would be the Q3 net income if the bad debt expense estimate was the average of bad debt expense in Q2 and Q1? What would this do to the trend in net income across the three quarters? (Assume that income tax expense does not change.)
6. Is there any evidence of unethical behavior in this case? Explain your answer.

LO1, LO4   S8-6 Critical Thinking: Analyzing

Problem Solved Company has been operating for five years as a software consulting firm. During this period, it has experienced rapid growth in sales revenue and in accounts receivable. To solve its growing receivables problem, the company hired you as its first corporate controller. You have put into place more stringent credit-granting and collection procedures that you expect will reduce receivables by approximately one-third by year-end. You have gathered the following data related to the changes (in thousands):

	(in thousands)	
	Beginning of Year	End of Year (projected)
Accounts receivable	$1,000,608	$660,495
Less: Allowance for doubtful accounts	36,800	10,225
Accounts receivable, net	$ 963,808	$650,270
	Prior Year	Current Year (projected)
Net sales (assume all on credit)	$ 7,515,444	$7,015,069

Required:

1. Compute, to one decimal place, the accounts receivable turnover ratio based on three different assumptions:

   a. The stringent credit policies reduce Accounts receivable, net and decrease Net sales as projected in the table.

   b. The stringent credit policies reduce Accounts receivable, net as projected in the table but do not decrease Net sales from the prior year.

   c. The stringent credit policies are not implemented, resulting in no change from the beginning of the year Accounts receivable balance and no change in Net sales from the prior year.

2. On the basis of your findings in requirement 1, write a brief memo explaining the potential benefits and drawbacks of more stringent credit policies and how they are likely to affect the accounts receivable turnover ratio.

S8-7 Using an Aging Schedule to Estimate Bad Debts and Improve Collections from Customers

LO2

www.mhhe.com/phillips2e

Assume you were recently hired by Caffe D'Amore, the company that formulated the world's first flavored instant cappuccino and now manufactures several lines of coffee flavored cappuccino mixes. Given the company's tremendous sales growth, Caffe D'Amore's receivables also have grown. Your job is to evaluate and improve collections of the company's receivables.

By analyzing collections of accounts receivable over the past five years, you were able to estimate bad debt loss rates for balances of varying ages. To estimate this year's uncollectible accounts, you jotted down the historical loss rates on the last page of a recent aged listing of outstanding customer balances (see below).

Customer	Total	Number of Days Unpaid				
		1-30	31-60	61-90	91-120	Over 120
Subtotal from previous page	$280,000	$150,000	$60,000	$40,000	$20,000	$10,000
Jumpy Jim's Coffee	1,000					1,000
Pasadena Coffee Company	24,500	14,500	8,000	2,000		
Phillips Blender House	17,000	12,000	4,000		1,000	
Pugsly's Trading Post	26,600	19,600	7,000			
Q-Coffee	12,400	8,400	3,000	1,000		
Special Sips	10,000	6,000	4,000			
Uneasy Isaac's	3,500	500				3,000
Total accounts receivable	375,000	211,000	86,000	43,000	21,000	14,000
Bad debt loss rates		1%	5%	10%	15%	30%

Required:

1. Enter the above totals in a spreadsheet and then insert formulas to calculate the total estimated uncollectible balance.

2. Prepare the year-end adjusting journal entry to adjust the allowance for doubtful accounts to the balance you calculated above. Assume the allowance account has an unadjusted credit balance of $8,000.

3. Of the customer account balances shown above on the last page of the aged listing, which should be your highest priority for contacting and pursuing collection?

4. Assume Jumpy Jim's Coffee account is determined to be uncollectible. Prepare the journal entry to write off the entire account balance.

9

Reporting and Interpreting Long-Lived Tangible and Intangible Assets

THAT WAS
THEN

In the past few chapters, you learned about the sale of goods and services to customers.

Cedar Fair. L.P.

If you're an average American, you gobble about three pounds of peanut butter per year, which equals 1,500 peanut butter sandwiches eaten before your high school graduation.[1] That makes you an expert at knowing how much peanut butter to spread on sandwiches. It also prepares you for learning how to report depreciation on long-lived assets. Really. Reporting depreciation is a lot like spreading peanut butter on sandwiches. The amount of peanut butter to spread on each sandwich is just like the amount of depreciation to spread over each accounting period. It depends on three factors: (1) the amount that you begin with in the jar (or the cost you begin with in the account), (2) the amount you need to leave in the jar (or account), and (3) the number of sandwiches (or accounting periods) that you'll be spreading it over. Just like peanut butter on a sandwich, there'll be a little depreciation if it's spread over many years or lots if it's spread over fewer years.

For the rest of this chapter, we're going to focus on the amusement park business at Cedar Fair. We're not leaving peanuts completely behind, because just as Mickey is Disney's mascot and Bugs Bunny gives character to Six Flags, Snoopy and the whole Charlie Brown gang from the PEANUTS® comic strip are featured at Cedar Fair. With seven amusement parks and six waterparks throughout the United States, Cedar Fair is one of the biggest and best amusement park businesses in the world.[2] As of December 31, 2005, its rides, hotels, and other long-lived assets accounted for over 96 percent of its total assets, so it's the perfect setting for you to learn how these assets are reported and the analyses you can conduct to determine how well they're managed.

[1] Retrieved September 8, 2006, from www.peanutbutter.com/funfacts.asp.
[2] "Cedar Fair, L.P.'s Flagship Park, Cedar Point, again Voted Best Amusement Park in the World," company press release, August 28, 2006.

THIS IS
NOW

This chapter focuses on the assets that enable companies to produce and sell goods and services.

The main topics of this chapter are shown below. When you begin the first section, focus on understanding what long-lived assets are and why they're important to many business decisions. In the second section, you'll study the accounting methods and procedures used inside the business to track these assets from the time they are first acquired, to when they are used, to when they are discarded. In the last parts of the chapter, you'll see how analysts outside the organization evaluate how effectively these assets have been used, taking into account the effects that different accounting methods have on analyses of reported financial results.

ORGANIZATION OF THE CHAPTER

Understand the business	Study the accounting methods	Evaluate the results	Review the chapter
• Definition and classification of long-lived assets	• Tangible assets • Intangible assets	• Management decisions • Turnover analysis • Impact of depreciation differences	• Demonstration case • Chapter summary • Key terms • Practice material

Understand the Business

DEFINITION AND CLASSIFICATION OF LONG-LIVED ASSETS

Learning Objective 1
Define, classify, and explain the nature of long-lived assets.

YOU SHOULD KNOW

Long-lived assets are the resources owned by a business that enable it to produce the goods or services that are sold to customers.

Long-lived assets are business assets acquired for use over one or more years. These assets are not intended for resale. Instead, they are considered "productive" assets in the sense that they enable the business to produce the goods or services that are sold to customers. Examples include Pizza Aroma's ovens that bake the pizza it sells, the salons Supercuts uses for providing haircare services, the stores in which Wal-Mart sells its products, and the legal rights Oakley relies on to protect its sunglasses from counterfeiting and piracy. So when you hear the label "long-lived assets," don't just think of rusty old equipment, because this class of assets is much broader than that. Long-lived assets include the following:

1. Tangible assets. These are long-lived assets that have physical substance, which simply means that you can see, touch, or kick them. The most prominent examples of tangible assets are land, buildings, machinery, vehicles, office equipment, and furniture and fixtures which are typically grouped into a single line item on the balance sheet called Property, plant, and equipment. Because many long-lived tangible assets are fixed in place, they are also known as *fixed assets*. For Cedar Fair, tangible assets include the 50 roller coasters that race through its parks in California, the Midwest, and Northeastern United States.

2. Intangible assets. These long-lived assets have special rights, but no physical substance. The existence of most intangible assets is indicated only by legal documents that describe certain legal rights. Unlike tangible assets like store

buildings and cash registers that you see in your daily life, you probably have less familiarity with intangible assets. For this reason, we'll describe the various types of intangibles in detail later in this chapter. For now you can think of this category as including things like brand names, trademarks, and licensing rights that allow Cedar Fair to use PEANUTS® characters throughout its parks.

A third category of long-lived assets that are depleted over time, like an oil well or gold mine, is common in natural resource industries. Chapter Supplement A describes how these natural resource assets are accounted for.

Exhibit 9.1 shows how Cedar Fair reports long-lived assets on its balance sheet. From this exhibit, you can see how important tangible and intangible assets are to Cedar Fair. Of the $1 billion in assets owned by Cedar Fair, over $967 million are long-lived assets.

EXHIBIT 9.1 Cedar Fair's Assets — **CedarfaiR.L.P.**		
December 31	2005	2004
(in thousands)		
Assets		
Current assets		
Cash	$ 4,421	$ 3,353
Receivables	7,259	4,766
Inventories	17,678	17,632
Prepaids	11,252	7,209
Total current assets	40,610	32,960
Property and equipment		
Land	174,081	174,143
Land improvements	163,952	153,498
Buildings	308,748	298,037
Rides and equipment	714,862	671,830
Construction in progress	23,434	20,470
	1,385,077	1,317,978
Less accumulated depreciation	(417,821)	(371,007)
	967,256	946,971
Intangible assets	16,928	13,277
	$1,024,794	$ 993,208

Study the Accounting Methods

In this section, you will study the accounting decisions that relate to long-lived assets. We'll start with tangible long-lived assets and consider key accounting decisions related to their (1) acquisition, (2) use, and (3) disposal. Accounting for intangible assets will be the focus of the last part of this section.

TANGIBLE ASSETS

Exhibit 9.1 reports several types of property and equipment, including a few that were introduced in earlier chapters (land, buildings, equipment). Also included are two other accounts that we haven't discussed before: land improvements and construction in progress. Land improvements differ from land in that land improvements deteriorate over time, whereas land is assumed to last forever. Land improvements include, for example, sidewalks, pavement, and landscaping. Construction in progress includes the costs of constructing new buildings and equipment. These costs are moved from this account into the applicable building or equipment account when the construction is completed.

Learning Objective 2
Apply the cost principle to the acquisition of long-lived assets.

Video 9.1

Acquisition of Tangible Assets

The general rule for tangible assets, under the cost principle, is that all reasonable and necessary costs of acquiring and preparing an asset for use should be recorded as a cost of the asset. The act of recording costs as assets (rather than as expenses) is what accountants and analysts call **capitalizing** the costs.

For tangible assets, it's not always obvious whether a cost is reasonable and necessary for acquiring or preparing them for use, so the decision to capitalize versus expense a cost is one that requires judgment. It is also one that has been exploited in recent years, as discussed in the following Ethical Insights box. As you read this box and the next couple of pages, focus on learning what kinds of costs should be capitalized and what kinds should be expensed.

> **YOU SHOULD KNOW**
>
> To **capitalize** a cost is to record it as an asset, rather than an expense.

Ethical Insights

The Biggest and Simplest Accounting Fraud

In the early 2000s, an $11 billion accounting fraud was committed at WorldCom (now called Verizon) in part by capitalizing rather than expensing costs that had the characteristics of rent. This accounting decision led WorldCom to report huge increases in assets (rather than expenses) in the periods in which the costs were incurred. The result was a balance sheet that appeared stronger (larger assets) and an income statement that appeared more profitable (lower expenses) than they would have had these costs been expensed. Learn more about this fraud in case S9-4 at the end of this chapter.

To help you understand the types of costs that should be capitalized when a tangible asset is acquired, we list several costs below that are considered necessary for acquiring and preparing tangible assets for use. Notice that the costs to be capitalized are not just the amounts paid to purchase or construct the assets themselves. For example, the land account at Cedar Fair would include legal fees incurred to purchase the arm of land that you can see crossing Sandusky Bay in the picture below. Fees for land surveyors and title searches on other pieces of land also would be capitalized in the Land account. Take a moment right now to read the lists of other similar types of costs that are capitalized when acquiring buildings and equipment.

Land

Purchase cost
Legal fees
Survey fees
Title search fees

Equipment

Purchase/construction cost
Sales taxes
Transportation costs
Installation and start-up costs

Buildings

Purchase/construction cost
Legal fees
Appraisal fees
Architect fees

LP9

If a company buys land, a building, or a piece of used equipment and incurs demolition, renovation, or repair costs before it can be used, these additional costs would be capitalized as a cost of the land, building, or equipment. These costs are capitalized because they are needed to prepare the asset for use.

In some instances, land, buildings, and equipment will be purchased as a group, as they were when Cedar Fair bought Six Flags Worlds of Adventure amusement park on April 8, 2004, for $145 million. When this kind of "basket purchase" occurs, the total cost is split between each asset in proportion to the market value of the assets as a whole. For example, if Cedar Fair were to pay $10 million for a hotel and the land surrounding it, based on an appraisal that estimates the land contributes 40 percent of the property's value and the building makes up the remaining 60 percent, Cedar Fair would record 40 percent of the total cost as land ($4 million) and the other 60 percent as buildings ($6 million). Splitting the total purchase price among individual assets is necessary because, later, the cost of each different type of asset will be depreciated over different periods of time. Land, for example, is not depreciated so any costs assigned to Land will remain in that account until the land is sold.

To illustrate how the costs of tangible assets are recorded, let's consider the Top Thrill Dragster that Cedar Fair purchased in 2002 from Intamin, a Swiss roller-coaster manufacturing company. At the time it was purchased, the Top Thrill Dragster was the biggest and fastest roller coaster in the world. Some of its specs are presented in the following graphic.

Top Thrill Dragster

Ride Height:	42 stories
Vertical Drop:	400 ft.
Track Length:	2,800 ft.
Ride Time:	17 seconds
Angle of Descent:	90 degrees
Angle of Twist:	270 degrees
Launch Speed:	120 mph in 4 seconds
Ride Capacity:	1,500 riders per hour

We'll assume that the list price for the roller coaster (including sales taxes) was $26 million, but Cedar Fair received a discount of $1 million from this. This means that the net purchase price of the roller coaster to Cedar Fair was actually $25 million. In addition, we'll assume Cedar Fair paid $125,000 to have the roller coaster delivered and $625,000 to have it assembled and prepared for use. Cedar Fair would calculate the costs to be capitalized as follows:

Invoice price	$26,000,000
Less: Discount	1,000,000
Net cash invoice price	25,000,000
Add: Transportation costs paid by Cedar Fair	125,000
Installation costs paid by Cedar Fair	625,000
Total cost of the roller coaster	$25,750,000

The total cost of $25,750,000 would be the amount recorded in the Rides and equipment account, regardless of how it is paid for or financed. As we show in the following examples, the method of payment or financing affects only whether the purchase causes a reduction in cash, an increase in liabilities, or both.

Cash Purchase Assuming that Cedar Fair paid cash for the roller coaster and related transportation and installation costs, the transaction would have the following effects, which would be recorded as follows:

1. Analyze

Assets		= Liabilities	+ Stockholders' Equity
Cash	−25,750,000		
Rides and Equipment	+25,750,000		

2. Record

dr Rides and Equipment (+A)	25,750,000	
cr Cash (−A)		25,750,000

You might find it hard to believe that Cedar Fair would pay cash for assets that cost over $25 million, but this really isn't unusual. Companies often use cash that has been generated from operations or that has been borrowed from a bank for this purpose. It's also possible for the seller to extend credit to the buyer, a situation that we examine next.

Credit Purchase   If we assume that Cedar Fair signed a note payable for the new roller coaster and paid cash for the transportation and installation costs, the accounting equation effects and journal entry would be:

1. Analyze

Assets		=	Liabilities	+ Stockholders' Equity
Cash	−750,000		Note Payable +25,000,000	
Rides and Equipment	+25,750,000			

2. Record

dr Rides and Equipment (+A)	25,750,000	
cr Cash (−A)		750,000
cr Note Payable (+L)		25,000,000

HOW'S IT GOING?   A Self-Study Quiz

In a recent year, the New Bakery Company of Ohio opened a new computer-integrated baking plant priced at $21 million. The plant can make 3,420 buns per minute, which are enough buns for 1.2 billion Wendy's sandwiches a year. Assume that the company paid $800,000 for sales taxes on the plant; $70,000 for transportation costs; and $50,000 for installation and preparation of the assets before use.

1. Compute the acquisition cost to be recorded as Property, plant, and equipment (PPE).

2. Under the following assumptions, indicate the effects of the acquisition on the accounting equation. Use + for increase and − for decrease, and indicate the accounts and amounts.

	Assets	=	Liabilities	+	Stockholders' Equity
a. Paid all in cash.					
b. Paid $1,000,000 in cash and the rest by signing a promissory note.					

Source: *American Way,* February 1, 2003, p. 53.

Quiz Answers
1. $21,000,000 + 800,000 + 70,000 + 50,000 = $21,920,000
2.
Assets	=	Liabilities	+ Equity
a. PPE +21,920,000			
Cash −21,920,000			
b. PPE +21,920,000		Note Payable +20,920,000	
Cash −1,000,000			

Before we leave this section, we should mention that not all fixed asset costs are capitalized. The cost of some fixed assets, like staplers or hole punches, is such a small dollar amount that it's not worth the trouble of recording them as fixed assets. Outback Steakhouse, for example, reports in its financial statement notes that all expenditures less than $1,000 are expensed when incurred. Such policies are acceptable because immaterial (relatively small dollar) amounts will not affect users' decisions when analyzing financial statements. Other costs that are expensed when incurred include insurance, interest on loans to purchase fixed assets, and (as discussed in the next section) ordinary repairs and maintenance.

Use of Tangible Assets

Maintenance Costs Incurred during Time of Use   Most tangible assets require substantial expenditures over the course of their lives to maintain or enhance their ability to operate. Maintenance is a big deal in the roller-coaster industry where it's important to have safe rides. Despite the tremendous stress created by frequent use and wicked-fast speeds, surprisingly few accidents occur, with a recent estimate reporting the odds of a serious amusement park injury at 1 in 23 million. You're 38 times more likely to get hit by lightning.[3] This level of safety comes from spending a lot of money on two types of maintenance during a ride's period of use:

1. **Ordinary repairs and maintenance.** Ordinary repairs and maintenance are expenditures for routine maintenance and upkeep of long-lived assets. Just like an oil change for your car, these expenditures are recurring in nature, involve relatively small amounts at each occurrence, and do not directly lengthen the useful life of the asset. Because these expenditures occur frequently to maintain the productive capacity of the asset for a short time, they are recorded as expenses in the current period.

    In the case of Cedar Fair, examples of ordinary repairs and maintenance include greasing the tracks on the Steel Venom roller coaster at Valleyfair in Minnesota, replacing the lights on the eight-story tall Ferris wheel at Michigan's Adventure, and tightening the seams on a water slide at Knott's Soak City in California.

2. **Extraordinary repairs, replacements, and additions.** These expenditures occur infrequently, involve large amounts, and increase an asset's economic usefulness in the future through increased efficiency, increased capacity, or longer life. Examples include additions, major overhauls, complete reconditioning, and major replacements and improvements, such as the complete replacement of the passenger train on a roller coaster. Because these costs increase the usefulness of tangible assets beyond their original condition, they are added to the appropriate long-lived asset accounts.

    Exhibit 9.2 presents a brief excerpt from the Management's Discussion and Analysis (MD&A) section of Cedar Fair's 2005 annual report, which describes the policies used to account for expenditures made when buildings, rides, and equipment are being used. After reading how Cedar Fair explains its accounting policy, take a minute to try the self-study quiz that follows it.

> **YOU SHOULD KNOW**
>
> **Ordinary repairs and maintenance** are expenditures for routine operating upkeep of long-lived assets and are recorded as expenses.

> **YOU SHOULD KNOW**
>
> **Extraordinary repairs** are expenditures that increase a tangible asset's economic usefulness in the future and are recorded as increases in asset accounts, not as expenses. In contrast to ordinary repairs, extraordinary repairs are done less frequently and yield longer-lasting benefits.

---

[3] "Newtonian Nightmare Rack-and-Pinion Inversions and Pneumatic Accelerators. This Is Fun?" *Forbes*, July 23, 2001, p. 112.

EXHIBIT 9.2	Accounting Policy for Tangible Asset Repairs

Cedar Fair
Notes to the Financial Statements
Key Accounting Policies

Expenditures made to maintain (tangible) assets in their original operating condition are expensed as incurred, and improvements and upgrades are capitalized.

HOW'S IT GOING?   A Self-Study Quiz

As you know from living in an apartment, dorm, or house, buildings require continuous maintenance and repair. For each of the following expenditures, indicate whether it should be expensed in the current period or capitalized as part of the cost of the building.

Expense or Capitalize?

1. Replacing electrical wiring throughout the building.
2. Repairing the hinge on the front door of the building.
3. Yearly cleaning of the building's air conditioning filters.
4. Making major structural improvements to a clubhouse.

Quiz Answers
1. Capitalize—extends life.
2. Expense
3. Expense
4. Capitalize—extends life.

YOU SHOULD KNOW

Depreciation is the allocation of the cost of long-lived tangible assets over their productive lives using a systematic and rational method.

YOU SHOULD KNOW

Book (or carrying) value is the acquisition cost of an asset less accumulated depreciation.

Depreciation Expense   In addition to repairs and maintenance, another expense is reported every period that a tangible asset is used. This expense, called **depreciation,** does not involve new payments for using the asset. Instead, depreciation expense is the allocation of existing costs that have been previously recorded as a long-lived tangible asset. The idea is that the cost of a long-lived tangible asset is essentially a prepaid cost representing future benefits. These benefits are used up when the asset is used, so following the matching principle, a portion of the asset's cost is moved from the balance sheet to the income statement as an expense in the period the asset is used to generate revenue. For Cedar Fair, revenues are earned when its rides are open to customers, so depreciation expense also is recorded at that time to show the allocated cost of the tangible assets that are used to generate those revenues.

The amount of depreciation recorded during each period is reported on the income statement as Depreciation expense. The amount of depreciation accumulated since the asset's acquisition date is reported on the balance sheet as a contra-account, Accumulated depreciation, and is deducted from the related asset's cost. The net amounts on the balance sheet are called *book values* or *carrying values*. The **book (or carrying) value** of a long-lived asset is its acquisition cost less the accumulated depreciation from acquisition date to the balance sheet date.

If you're not crystal clear on how these things are reported, take a quick look at Exhibit 9.1 on page 383. You should see that, at the end of 2005, Cedar Fair's total cost of property and equipment (in thousands) was $1,385,077, accumulated depreciation was $417,821, and the book (or carrying) value was $967,256 ($1,385,077 − 417,821). Depreciation expense for the year (of $55,765) is included in Cedar Fair's 2005 income statement. Although some companies report depreciation expense as a separate type of operating expense, many (including Cedar Fair) include it in Selling, general, and administrative expenses for external reporting purposes.

To calculate depreciation expense, you need three amounts:

1. Asset cost. This includes all the costs capitalized for the asset, which as you saw earlier in this chapter, can include purchase cost, sales tax, legal fees, and other costs needed to acquire and prepare the asset for use.

2. Residual value. **Residual value** is an estimate of the amount that the company will get when it disposes of the asset. Cedar Fair will recover some of the initial cost of its roller coasters when it disposes of them by either selling them "as is" to local amusement companies or by dismantling them and selling their parts to other roller coaster or scrap metal companies.

3. Useful life. **Useful life** is an estimate of the asset's useful economic life to the company (rather than its economic life to all potential users). Economic life may be expressed in terms of years or units of asset capacity, such as the number of units it can produce or the number of miles it will travel. Land is the only tangible asset that's assumed to have an unlimited (indefinite) useful life. Because of this, land is not depreciated.

The basic idea of depreciation is to match the dollar amount of the asset that will be used up (asset cost minus residual value) to the periods it will be used to generate revenue (useful life). Notice that residual value is taken into account when calculating depreciation because we want to leave a little of the asset's cost in the accounts when we're done depreciating it. We do this because, when we dispose of the asset, we're likely to get back some of what we initially paid for it. So, the amount to be depreciated over the asset's life is the difference between its cost and residual value, an amount called the **depreciable cost.** Depreciation will be recorded each year of an asset's useful life until its total accumulated depreciation equals its depreciable cost. After that point, no additional depreciation is reported, even if the company continues to use the asset.

The effects of depreciation and the journal entry to record it were introduced in Chapter 4. As a quick reminder, $20,000 of depreciation would lead to the following:

1. Analyze

Assets	=	Liabilities	+	Stockholders' Equity
Accumulated				Depreciation
Depreciation (+xA) −20,000				Expense (+E) −20,000

2. Record

dr Depreciation Expense (+E, −SE)   20,000
   cr Accumulated Depreciation (+xA, −A)   20,000

If every company used the same techniques for calculating depreciation, we'd stop right here. However, because companies own different assets and use them differently, accountants and managers are allowed to choose from several different acceptable depreciation methods. These alternative depreciation methods produce different depreciation numbers, so you need to understand how the alternative methods work to understand how to interpret differences in depreciation.

Depreciation Methods We will discuss the three most common depreciation methods:

1. Straight-line
2. Units-of-production
3. Declining-balance

To show how each method works, let's assume that Cedar Fair acquired a new go-cart ride on January 1, 2007. The relevant information is shown in Exhibit 9.3.

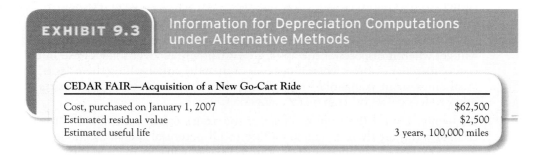

EXHIBIT 9.3	Information for Depreciation Computations under Alternative Methods

CEDAR FAIR—Acquisition of a New Go-Cart Ride	
Cost, purchased on January 1, 2007	$62,500
Estimated residual value	$2,500
Estimated useful life	3 years, 100,000 miles

Straight-Line Method. Under the **straight-line depreciation method,** an equal amount of depreciation is reported in each period of the asset's estimated useful life. The straight-line formula to estimate annual depreciation expense is

$$(\text{Cost} - \text{Residual Value}) \times \frac{1}{\text{Useful Life}} = \text{Depreciation Expense}$$

In the straight-line formula, Cost − Residual Value is the total amount to be depreciated (the depreciable cost). The straight-line depreciation rate equals 1 ÷ Useful Life. Using the information in Exhibit 9.3, the depreciation expense for Cedar Fair's new ride would be $20,000 per year, calculated as shown in the depreciation schedule below:

		INCOME STATEMENT	BALANCE SHEET		
(Cost − Residual Value) × 1/Useful Life					
Year	Yearly Computation	Depreciation Expense	Cost	Accumulated Depreciation	Book Value
At acquisition			$62,500	$ 0	$62,500
2007	($62,500 − $2,500) × 1/3	$20,000	62,500	20,000	42,500
2008	($62,500 − $2,500) × 1/3	20,000	62,500	40,000	22,500
2009	($62,500 − $2,500) × 1/3	20,000	62,500	60,000	2,500
	Total	$60,000			

Annual Depreciation

Straight-line

Year

Notice that, as the name *straight-line* suggests,

- Depreciation expense is a constant amount each year.
- Accumulated depreciation increases by an equal amount each year.
- Book value decreases by the same equal amount each year.

Notice also that, at the end of the asset's life, accumulated depreciation ($60,000) equals the asset's depreciable cost ($62,500 − $2,500), and book value ($2,500) equals residual value.

As you will see with other depreciation methods, the straight-line method relies on estimates of an asset's useful life and its residual value at the end of that life. A question people often ask is how do accountants estimate useful lives and residual values? While some of this information can be obtained from the fixed asset supplier or other sources (e.g., reseller databases, insurance companies), the simple answer is that it is based on their professional judgment. Useful lives and residual values are difficult things to estimate with precision, so accountants are encouraged to update depreciation calculations regularly for new estimates, as discussed in Supplement B at the end of the chapter.

Units-of-Production Method. Like the straight-line method, the **units-of-production depreciation method** assigns an asset's depreciable cost to each period of its useful life— only there's one key difference. Whereas straight-line bases depreciation on the amount of time passed, units-of-production bases it on the amount of asset production. An asset's production can be defined in terms of miles, products, or machine hours operated. The formula to estimate depreciation expense under the units-of-production method is

$$(\text{Cost} - \text{Residual Value}) \times \frac{\text{Actual Production This Period}}{\text{Estimated Total Production}} = \text{Depreciation Expense}$$

If we assume the go-cart in Exhibit 9.3 was driven 30,000 miles in 2007, 50,000 miles in 2008, and 20,000 miles in 2009, units-of-production depreciation in each year of the asset's life would be calculated as follows:

(Cost − Residual Value) × Actual/Estimated Total Production		INCOME STATEMENT	BALANCE SHEET		
Year	Yearly Computation	Depreciation Expense	Cost	Accumulated Depreciation	Book Value
At acquisition			$62,500	$ 0	$62,500
2007	$(62,500 − 2,500) × (30,000/100,000 miles)	$18,000	62,500	18,000	44,500
2008	$(62,500 − 2,500) × (50,000/100,000 miles)	30,000	62,500	48,000	14,500
2009	$(62,500 − 2,500) × (20,000/100,000 miles)	12,000	62,500	60,000	2,500
	Total	$60,000			

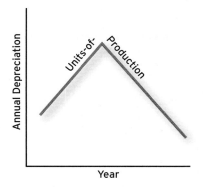

Notice that under the units-of-production method, the depreciation expense, accumulated depreciation, and book value vary from period to period, depending on the number of units produced.

Declining-Balance Method. Under the **declining-balance depreciation method,** depreciation expense is higher in the early years of an asset's life and lower in the later years. This is why it is sometimes called an *accelerated depreciation method.* Although accelerated methods aren't often used for financial reporting purposes in the United States, they are commonly used in financial reporting in other countries like Japan and Canada and in tax reporting in the United States (a point we discuss in greater detail below).

Declining-balance depreciation is based on applying a depreciation rate to the book value of the asset at the beginning of the accounting period. Notice in the formula below that book value (cost − accumulated depreciation) is used rather than depreciable cost (cost − residual value). This slight difference in the formula produces declining amounts of depreciation as the asset ages. The 2 ÷ Useful Life rate used in the formula is double the straight-line rate and, therefore, this particular version of declining-balance depreciation is called the *double-declining-balance method:*

$$(\text{Cost} - \text{Accumulated Depreciation}) \times \frac{2}{\text{Useful Life}} = \text{Depreciation Expense}$$

Be aware that the formula uses the accumulated depreciation balance at the beginning of each year. In the first year of an asset's life, the beginning balance in accumulated depreciation will be zero. However, as depreciation is recorded with each passing year, the accumulated depreciation balance will increase, which causes the amount of depreciation to decline over time. Also be aware that residual value is not included in the formula for computing depreciation expense under the declining-balance method, so you have to take extra care to ensure an asset's book value is not being depreciated below its residual value. If the normal depreciation calculated for the year reduces book value below residual value, a smaller amount of depreciation must be recorded, so that book value equals residual value. Let's show you what we mean by computing depreciation for each of the three years of our example:

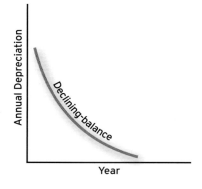

(Cost − Accumulated Depreciation) × 2/Useful Life		INCOME STATEMENT	BALANCE SHEET		
Year	Yearly Computation	Depreciation Expense	Cost	Accumulated Depreciation	Book Value
At acquisition			$62,500	$ 0	$62,500
2007	($62,500 − $ 0) × 2/3	$41,667	62,500	41,667	20,833
2008	($62,500 − $41,667) × 2/3	$13,889	62,500	55,556	6,944
2009	($62,500 − $55,556) × 2/3	~~4,629~~	62,500	~~60,185~~	~~2,315~~
		4,444	62,500	60,000	2,500
	Total	$60,000			

Computed amount is too large

Notice that the calculated depreciation expense for 2009 ($4,629) is not recorded because that would cause the asset's book value to fall below its residual value. Instead, just enough depreciation is recorded ($4,444) to make the book value of the asset equal to its residual value of $2,500.

Summary.   Exhibit 9.4 summarizes the depreciation expense that would be reported in each year of our example under the three alternative depreciation methods. Notice that the amount of depreciation expense in each year of an asset's life depends on the method used, which also means that the amount of net income reported can vary depending on the depreciation method used. At the end of an asset's life, after it has been fully depreciated, the total amount of depreciation will equal the asset's depreciable cost, regardless of the depreciation method used.

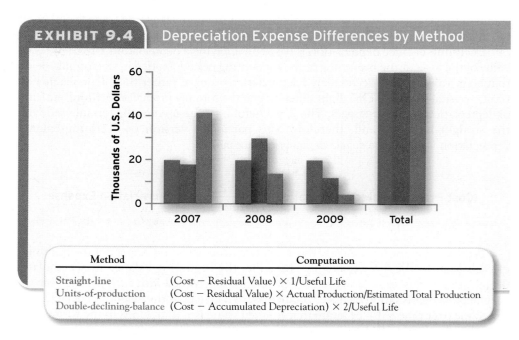

EXHIBIT 9.4   Depreciation Expense Differences by Method

Method	Computation
Straight-line	(Cost − Residual Value) × 1/Useful Life
Units-of-production	(Cost − Residual Value) × Actual Production/Estimated Total Production
Double-declining-balance	(Cost − Accumulated Depreciation) × 2/Useful Life

Managers and accountants are allowed to choose any rational and systematic depreciation methods, provided that they describe them in their financial statement notes. Also, because not every tangible asset is identical, different depreciation methods can be used for different classes of assets, provided the methods are used consistently over time so that financial statement users can easily compare across periods. So what methods do companies use? In a recent survey, straight-line was used most frequently (89 percent), followed by accelerated methods such as double-declining-balance (7 percent), then units-of-production (3 percent), and others (1 percent).[4] Straight-line is the preferred choice because it's the easiest to use and understand, plus it does a good job of matching depreciation expense to revenues when assets are used evenly over their useful lives. Units-of-production typically is used when asset use fluctuates significantly from period to period. Declining-balance methods apply best to assets that are most productive when they are new and quickly lose their usefulness as they get older.

HOW'S IT GOING?   A Self-Study Quiz

Assume that Cedar Fair has acquired new equipment at a cost of $24,000. The equipment has an estimated life of six years, an estimated operating life of 5,000 hours, and an estimated residual value of $3,000. Determine depreciation expense for the second year under each of the following methods:

1. Straight-line method.

    $\boxed{\$(24{,}000 -)} \times \boxed{/6} = \boxed{\$}$

2. Double-declining-balance method.

    Year 1: $\boxed{\$(24{,}000 -)} \times \boxed{/} = \boxed{\$}$

    Year 2: $\boxed{\$(24{,}000 -)} \times \boxed{/} = \boxed{\$}$

3. Unit-of-production method (assume the equipment ran for 800 hours in Year 2).

    $\boxed{\$(-)} \times \boxed{/5{,}000} = \boxed{\$}$

Tax Depreciation. Before we leave the topic of depreciation methods, we should note that most public companies use one method of depreciation for reporting to stockholders and a different method for determining income taxes. Keeping two sets of accounting records like this is both ethical and legal because the objective of GAAP differs from that of the Internal Revenue Code.

Financial Reporting (GAAP)	**Tax Reporting (Internal Revenue Code)**
The objective of financial reporting is to provide economic information about a business that is useful in projecting future cash flows of the business.	The objective of the Internal Revenue Code is to raise sufficient revenues to pay for the expenditures of the federal government and to encourage certain social and economic behaviors.

---

[4] AICPA 2005 *Accounting Trends & Techniques.* Other methods, such as sum-of-years digits depreciation, are covered in intermediate accounting textbooks.

One of the government's objectives is to encourage economic renewal and growth. To achieve this, the IRS allows companies to deduct larger amounts of tax depreciation in early years of an asset's life than what is allowed by GAAP.[5] The deduction reduces the company's income taxes significantly in the years immediately following the purchase of a long-lived asset. Although the IRS allows supersized deductions in an asset's early years, it doesn't allow a company to depreciate more than an asset's depreciable cost over its life. So, the tax savings enjoyed in the early years of an asset's life will eventually be paid back in later years of the asset's life. The amount of tax put off (deferred) as a result of taking large tax depreciation deductions is reported as a long-term liability called *deferred income taxes*. Although the deferral only temporarily delays having to pay taxes, it can be worth the effort of keeping two sets of records. The following companies report that they deferred significant tax obligations in 2005 by choosing different depreciation methods for tax and financial reporting purposes.

Company	Deferred Tax Liabilities	Percentage Due to Applying Different Depreciation Methods
AT&T Corp.	$15,713 million	89%
Southwest Airlines	2,905 million	77
Revlon, Inc.	26 million	94

This table shows that, like most individuals, companies follow an economic rule called the least and the latest rule. All taxpayers want to pay the least tax that is legally permitted, and at the latest possible date. If you had the choice of paying $10,000 to the federal government at the end of this year or at the end of next year, you would choose the end of next year. By doing so, you could invest the money for an extra year and earn a significant return on the investment. Companies similarly take large tax depreciation deductions to defer their taxes to later years.

Asset Impairment Losses

The book value of tangible assets declines as they age, as a result of recording depreciation. However, since depreciation is not intended to report assets at their current value, it's possible that the declining book value of long-lived tangible assets could exceed their current value—particularly if they become impaired. **Impairment** occurs when events or changed circumstances cause the estimated future cash flows from using these assets to fall below their book value. If the estimated future cash flows are less than the asset's book value, the asset's book value should be written down to what it's worth (called *fair value*), with the amount of the write-down reported as an impairment loss. Impairment losses typically are included with Other expenses, reported below the income from operations line in the bottom part of the income statement.

Cedar Fair recorded a write-down in 2002 after a rare engineering phenomenon called "vortex shedding" reportedly caused a steel support tower in one of its VertiGo slingshot rides to snap during the off-season. Even though only one of the rides was affected, Cedar Fair dismantled and removed its two VertiGo rides.[6] To see how this bizarre event would be accounted for, let's assume that the book value of Cedar Fair's VertiGo rides was $8 million. We'll also assume that the future cash flows from the rides were only $4.8 million, because let's face it, few people are willing to go on a ride that

---

[5] Most corporations use the IRS-approved Modified Accelerated Cost Recovery System (MACRS) to calculate depreciation expense for their tax returns. MACRS is similar to the declining-balance method and is applied over relatively short asset lives set by the IRS to yield high tax deductions for depreciation expense in the early years.

[6] "Insurer Refuses Damage Payment to Sandusky, Ohio-Based Amusement Park Company," *Knight Ridder/Tribune Business News*, February 11, 2003.

snapped apart, even if it is fixable. If the fair value of the rides is estimated to be $4.8 million, which represents what other amusement park companies and scrap dealers might be expected to pay for the rides' parts, the impairment loss is calculated as $8 million minus $4.8 million. The effects of this impairment loss are shown below, along with the journal entry that would be used to record the $3.2 million write-down.

	Assets	= Liabilities +	Stockholders' Equity
1. Analyze	Rides and Equipment −3,200,000		Loss Due to Impairment (+E) −3,200,000

2. Record		
dr Loss Due to Impairment of Assets (+E, −SE)	3,200,000	
cr Rides and Equipment (−A)		3,200,000

When Cedar Fair reported this loss on the income statement, it caused a huge reduction in net income. Because the loss was so large and unusual in nature, it was reported as a separate line-item called "non-recurring loss." Cedar Fair also described the impairment loss and asset write-down in the financial statement notes, as shown in Exhibit 9.5.

COACH'S TIP

If long-lived tangible assets increase in value, the accounting records are not adjusted to write up their value.

EXHIBIT 9.5 | Financial Statement Note Describing Impairment

Impairment of Long-Lived Assets   During the first quarter of 2002, we removed certain fixed assets from service at our parks, and recorded a provision of $3.2 million for the estimated portion of the net book value of these assets that may not be recoverable.

Disposal of Tangible Assets

In some cases, a business may voluntarily decide not to hold a long-term asset for its entire life. For example, your local gym might decide to replace its treadmills with elliptical trainers, or a company may drop a product from its line and no longer need the equipment that was used to produce its product. To get rid of used assets, companies do just what you do. They trade them in on a new asset, sell them on eBay, or "retire" them to a junkyard. Sometimes, assets are damaged or destroyed in storms, fires, or accidents, creating what are politely called involuntary disposals.

The disposal of a depreciable asset usually requires two accounting adjustments:

1. Update the depreciation expense and accumulated depreciation accounts. If a long-lived asset is disposed of halfway into the year, record half of the annual depreciation. Chapter Supplement B presents additional information on calculating depreciation for partial years.

2. Record the disposal. The cost of the asset and any accumulated depreciation at the date of disposal must be removed from the accounts. The difference between any resources received on disposal of an asset and its book value at the date of disposal is treated as a gain or loss on the disposal of the asset, which is reported on the income statement. It's not really related to operations because it arises from peripheral or incidental activities, so it's usually shown below the income from operations line, in the bottom half of the income statement. For example, in the income statement in Exhibit 6.10 on page 254, gains (or losses) on asset disposals would be combined with Other revenues (expenses).

Learning Objective 5
Analyze the disposal of long-lived tangible assets.

Topic Tackler

PLUS

Check out www.mhhe.com/phillips2e for audio, visual, and PowerPoint presentations on this topic.

Earlier in this chapter, you saw how to compute and record depreciation expense on a long-lived asset, so let's look instead at an example where we only have to account for the disposal. Assume that, at the end of year 16, Cedar Fair sold one of its hotels for $3 million cash. The original $20 million cost of the hotel was depreciated using the straight-line method over 20 years with no residual value ($1 million depreciation expense per year). The gain or loss on disposal is calculated as the difference between the asset's selling price and its net book value (NBV). For our example, the net book value is

Original cost of hotel	$20,000,000
Less: Accumulated depreciation ($1,000,000 × 16 years)	16,000,000
Net book value (NBV) at date of sale	$ 4,000,000

The selling price ($3,000,000) is less than the NBV ($4,000,000), so the difference ($1,000,000) is reported as a loss on sale. The effects of the loss and the hotel sale on Cedar Fair are shown below, along with the journal entry to record them.

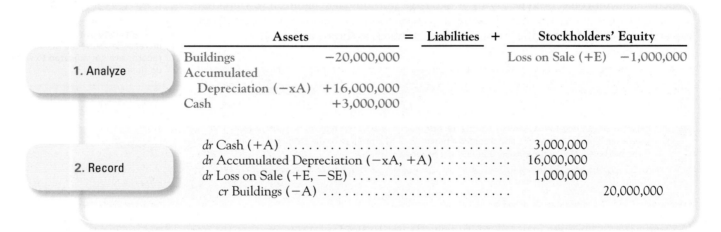

1. Analyze

	Assets		=	Liabilities	+	Stockholders' Equity	
Buildings		−20,000,000				Loss on Sale (+E)	−1,000,000
Accumulated							
Depreciation (−xA)	+16,000,000						
Cash	+3,000,000						

2. Record

dr Cash (+A)	3,000,000
dr Accumulated Depreciation (−xA, +A)	16,000,000
dr Loss on Sale (+E, −SE)	1,000,000
cr Buildings (−A)	20,000,000

A common error is to remove only the NBV from the asset account. Be sure you don't do this—instead, reduce both the asset and accumulated depreciation accounts for their full cost and accumulated depreciation (updated to the time of disposal).

HOW'S IT GOING?   A Self-Study Quiz

Assume that Cedar Fair sold the hotel described above at the end of year 16 for $5,000,000 cash. Also assume that depreciation had been updated to that point in time, resulting in Accumulated depreciation of $16,000,000 at the time of sale. Complete the accounting equation effects of the disposal below.

	Assets	=	Liabilities	+	Stockholders' Equity
Buildings	−20,000,000				[ ]
Accumulated					
Depreciation (−xA)	[ ]				
Cash	+5,000,000				

INTANGIBLE ASSETS

Intangible assets are long-lived assets that lack physical substance. Their existence is indicated by legal documents of the types described below.

- Trademarks. A **trademark** is a special name, image, or slogan identified with a product or a company, like the name Kleenex or the image of McDonald's golden arches. The symbol ® signifies a trademark registered with the U.S. Patent and Trademark Office and ™ indicates unregistered trademarks—both of which are considered intangible assets.

- Copyrights. A **copyright** gives the owner the exclusive right to publish, use, and sell a literary, musical, artistic, or dramatic work for a period not exceeding 70 years after the author's death. The book you are reading is copyrighted, which makes it illegal, for example, for an instructor to copy several chapters from this book and hand them out in class without first obtaining permission from the copyright owner.

- Patents. A **patent** is an exclusive right granted by the federal government for a period of 20 years, typically to whoever invents a new product or discovers a new process. The patent enables the owner to be the only one who can use, manufacture, or sell the patented item. This protection is intended to encourage people to be inventive because it prevents others from simply copying innovations until after the inventor has had time to earn some money from the new product or process. One of the first roller-coaster patents was granted in 1884 for what was then called a "gravity pleasure road."

- Licensing rights. **Licensing rights** are limited permissions to use something according to specific terms and conditions. Your university or college likely has obtained the licensing right to make computer programs available for use on your campus network. A licensing right also is what allows Cedar Fair to showcase Snoopy at its parks.

- Franchises. A **franchise** is a contractual right to sell certain products or services, use certain trademarks, or perform activities in a geographical region. Krispy Kreme, for example, granted the Icon Doughnut Development Co. the franchise rights to operate stores using the Krispy Kreme name, store format, recipes, and ingredients in the Pacific Northwest. Krispy Kreme typically grants these rights in exchange for an up-front fee ranging from $20,000 to $40,000 per store plus ongoing fees of 4.5–5.5 percent of store sales.[7]

- Goodwill. **Goodwill** tops the charts as the most frequently reported intangible asset. It encompasses lots of good stuff like a favorable location, an established customer base, a great reputation, and successful business operations. Although many companies have probably built up their own goodwill, GAAP doesn't allow it to be reported as an intangible asset on the balance sheet unless it has been purchased from another company. To understand the reasons behind this, keep reading. We explain them in the next section.

Acquisition, Use, and Disposal

Acquisition   The costs of intangible assets are recorded as assets only if they have been purchased. If an intangible asset is being self-constructed or internally developed, its costs are reported as **research and development** expenses. The primary reason that the cost of self-developed intangibles is reported as an expense rather than an asset is that it's easy for people to claim that they've developed a valuable (but invisible) intangible asset. But to believe what they are saying, you really need to see some evidence that it's actually worth what they say it's worth. And that only happens when someone gives up their hard-earned cash to buy it. At that time, the purchaser records the

---

Learning Objective 6
Analyze the acquisition, use, and disposal of long-lived intangible assets.

YOU SHOULD KNOW

A **trademark** is a special name, image, or slogan identified with a product or company.
A **copyright** is a form of protection provided to the original authors of literary, musical, artistic, dramatic, and other works of authorship.
A **patent** is a right to exclude others from making, using, selling, or importing an invention.
A **licensing right** is the limited permission to use property according to specific terms and conditions set out in a contract.
A **franchise** is a contractual right to sell certain products or services, use certain trademarks, or perform activities in a certain geographical region.
Goodwill is the premium a company pays to obtain the favorable reputation associated with another company.

YOU SHOULD KNOW

Research and development costs are expenditures that may someday lead to patents, copyrights, or other intangible assets, but the uncertainty about their future benefits requires that they be expensed.

---

[7] Krispy Kreme 2003 Annual Report, and May 1, 2001 press release, "Krispy Kreme Continues Expansion through New Area Developer Agreements and New Store Openings."

intangible asset at its acquisition cost. This general rule applies to trademarks, copyrights, patents, licensing rights, franchises, and goodwill.

Goodwill is a particularly interesting type of intangible asset because it represents the value paid for the unidentifiable assets of another business. You might wonder how you can put a value on something you can't identify, but it is possible. When one company buys another business, the purchase price often is greater than the value of all of the **net assets** of the business. Why would a company pay more for a business as a whole than it would pay if it bought the assets individually? The answer is to obtain its goodwill. You could easily buy equipment to produce and sell a bunch of generic chocolate-wafer cookies, but this strategy likely wouldn't be as successful as acquiring the goodwill associated with the Oreo business. That's part of the reason Kraft Foods paid $40 billion more than the value of Nabisco's net assets—to acquire the goodwill associated with Nabisco's Oreo and Ritz snacks business.

For accounting purposes, goodwill (also called *cost in excess of net assets acquired*) is defined as the difference between the purchase price of a company as a whole and the fair market value of its net assets:

> Purchase price
> − Fair market value of identifiable assets, net of liabilities
> = Goodwill to be reported

Both parties to the sale estimate an acceptable amount for the goodwill of the business and add it to the appraised value of the business's net assets. Then the sales price of the business is negotiated. As per the cost principle, the resulting goodwill is recorded as an intangible asset (but only when it has been purchased at a measurable cost).

Use The rules of accounting for intangible assets after they have been purchased depend on whether the intangible asset has a limited or unlimited life.

- Limited life. The cost of intangible assets with a limited life (copyrights, patents, licensing rights, and franchises) is spread on a straight-line basis over each period of useful life in a process called **amortization**, which is similar to depreciation. Most companies do not estimate a residual value for their intangible assets because, unlike tangible assets that can be sold as scrap, intangibles usually have no value at the end of their useful lives. Amortization is reported as an expense each period on the income statement and also is subtracted directly from the applicable intangible asset accounts on the balance sheet.[8]

  Let's assume Cedar Fair purchases a patent for an uphill water-coaster for $800,000 and intends to use it for 20 years. Each year, the company would record $40,000 in patent amortization expense ($800,000 ÷ 20 years). The effect of this amortization and the journal entry to record it are shown below.

YOU SHOULD KNOW

Net assets is the shorthand term used to refer to assets minus liabilities.

YOU SHOULD KNOW

Amortization is the name given to allocating the cost of intangible assets over their limited useful lives.

1. Analyze

Assets		=	Liabilities	+	Stockholders' Equity	
Patents	−40,000				Amortization Expense (+E)	−40,000

2. Record

dr Amortization Expense (+E, −SE) 40,000
    cr Patents (−A) 40,000

---

[8] Consistent with the procedure for recording accumulated depreciation, an accumulated amortization account may be used. In practice, however, most companies directly reduce the intangible asset account.

- **Unlimited life.** Intangibles with unlimited or indefinite lives (trademarks and goodwill) are not amortized. However, they are tested for possible impairment, just like long-lived tangible assets. If an intangible asset is impaired, its book value is written down (decreased) to its fair value.

Disposal Just like long-lived tangible assets, disposals of intangible assets result in gains (or losses) if the amounts received on disposal are greater than (less than) their book values.

The accounting rules for long-lived tangible and intangible assets are summarized and compared in Exhibit 9.6.

EXHIBIT 9.6 Accounting Rules for Long-Lived Tangible and Intangible Assets

Stage	Subject	Tangible Assets	Intangible Assets
Acquire	**Purchased asset**	Capitalize all related costs	Capitalize all related costs
Use	**Repairs and maintenance**		
	Ordinary	Expense related costs	Not applicable
	Extraordinary	Capitalize related costs	Not applicable
	Depreciation/amortization		
	Limited life	One of several methods: • Straight-line • Units-of-production • Declining-balance	Straight-line method
	Unlimited life	Do not depreciate (e.g., land)	Do not amortize (e.g., goodwill)
	Impairment test	Write down if necessary	Write down if necessary
Dispose	**Report gain (loss) when . . .**	Receive more (less) on disposal than book value	Receive more (less) on disposal than book value

Evaluate the Results

MANAGEMENT DECISIONS

> **Learning Objective 7**
> Interpret the fixed asset turnover ratio.

One of the major challenges business managers face is forecasting the right amount to invest in long-lived assets. If they underestimate the amount needed to produce goods or provide services for customers, they will miss an opportunity to earn revenue. On the other hand, if they overestimate the amount needed, their companies will incur excessive costs that will reduce profitability.

If you've ever played RollerCoaster Tycoon®, you know the amusement park business provides an outstanding example of the difficulties involved in these long-lived asset decisions. If an amusement park builds more rides than it needs to satisfy park-goers, the rides will run with empty seats. The company will still incur all of the costs to run the rides, but it will generate only a fraction of the possible revenue. Unlike merchandise companies, an amusement park cannot build up an "inventory" of unused seats to be sold in the future. On the other hand, an amusement park also can run into trouble if it doesn't have enough rides to satisfy park-goers. Just think how you felt the last time you had to wait an hour or more in line. To keep its customers on rides rather than in lines, Cedar Fair is always adding new rides. This is one of the reasons its main park is voted no. 1 in the amusement industry for best ride capacity, year after year.[9]

---

[9] See footnote 2.

In addition to accurately forecasting the right number of rides, a business like Cedar Fair also has to pick the right type of ride. This is a key feature that distinguishes Cedar Fair from competitors like Disney, Six Flags, and Universal Studios. Cedar Fair prides itself on having the tallest and fastest roller coasters in the world. Cedar Fair's business strategy is to continually introduce the latest ride technologies into its parks, which enables it to compete head-on with the other big-name companies that instead emphasize other aspects of their parks.

TURNOVER ANALYSIS

Just as managers carefully plan what to invest in long-lived assets, financial analysts closely evaluate how well management uses these assets to generate revenues. The fixed asset turnover ratio provides a good measure of this.

FINANCIAL ANALYSIS TOOLS		
Name of Measure	**Formula**	**What It Tells You**
Fixed asset turnover ratio	$\dfrac{\text{Net Sales Revenue}}{\text{Average Net Fixed Assets}}$	• Dollars of sales generated for each dollar invested in (tangible) fixed assets • A higher ratio implies greater efficiency

The fixed asset turnover ratio measures the sales dollars generated by each dollar invested in (tangible) fixed assets. Just as miles-per-gallon provides a measure of a car's fuel efficiency, the fixed asset turnover ratio provides a measure of fixed asset operating efficiency. Generally speaking, a high or increasing turnover ratio relative to the industry's average or the company's prior periods suggests better use of fixed assets, in the sense that each dollar of fixed assets is generating more dollars of sales.

Be aware that fixed asset turnover ratios can vary between industries because capital intensity—the need for tangible assets—varies widely. A company like Yahoo!, for example, needs fewer fixed assets to generate revenues, so it is likely to have a high turnover ratio in comparison to companies like Cedar Fair and Six Flags, which need to invest lots of money in fixed assets to attract customers. In Exhibit 9.7, we've shown the fixed asset turnover ratios for these three companies in 2005. For practice at computing and comparing to prior periods, try the Self-Study Quiz that follows.

EXHIBIT 9.7	Summary of Fixed Asset Turnover Ratio Analyses

Company	Relevant Information (in millions)				2005 Fixed Asset Turnover Calculation	
Cedar Fair		2005	2004		$\dfrac{\$568.7}{\$(967.3 + 947.0)/2}$	= 0.59
	Sales	$568.7	$542.0			
	Net Fixed					
	Assets	$967.3	$947.0			
Six Flags		2005	2004		$\dfrac{\$1,089.7}{\$(1,927.6 + 1,946.2)/2}$	= 0.56
	Sales	$1,089.7	$998.6			
	Net Fixed					
	Assets	$1,927.6	$1,946.2			
YAHOO!		2005	2004		$\dfrac{\$5,257.7}{\$(697.5 + 531.7)/2}$	= 8.55
	Sales	$5,257.7	$3,574.5			
	Net Fixed					
	Assets	$697.5	$531.7			

HOW'S IT GOING?   Self-Study Quiz

Cedar Fair reported net fixed assets of $777.0 (million) at December 31, 2003.

a. Use this information, along with that in Exhibit 9.7, to calculate Cedar Fair's fixed asset turnover ratio in 2004.

2004 Fixed Asset Turnover

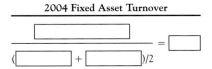

b. Did Cedar Fair's fixed asset turnover improve or decline from 2004 (calculated in *a*) to 2005 (shown in Exhibit 9.7)?

THE IMPACT OF DEPRECIATION DIFFERENCES

Learning Objective 8
Describe factors to consider when comparing across companies.

Just as differences in the nature of business operations affect financial analyses and the conclusions that you draw from them, so too do differences in depreciation. Depreciation can vary from one company to the next as a result of using different depreciation methods, different estimated useful lives, or different estimated residual values. In this section, we present a simple example to show how different depreciation methods can affect analyses throughout the life of a long-lived asset. Don't let the simplicity of this example fool you. The differences in this example are identical to what often happens in the real world.

Assume that Cedar Fair and Six Flags each acquire a new roller coaster at the beginning of the year for $15.5 million, and estimate that the roller coasters will have residual values of $1.5 million at the end of their seven-year useful lives. Everything about the roller coasters is identical, except we'll assume Cedar Fair uses the straight-line depreciation method and Six Flags uses the double-declining-balance method. Exhibit 9.8 shows the yearly depreciation to be reported by the two companies. Notice that early in the asset life, prior to year 4, the straight-line depreciation expense reported by Cedar Fair is less than the declining-balance depreciation expense reported by Six Flags. This means that even if the two companies attract exactly the same number of customers, which lead to exactly the same total revenues, the reported net income will differ each year just because the two companies use different (but equally acceptable) methods of depreciation. This example

EXHIBIT 9.8 | Straight-Line and Double-Declining-Balance Depreciation Schedules

CEDAR FAIR (STRAIGHT-LINE)				SIX FLAGS (DOUBLE-DECLINING-BALANCE)		
Depreciation Expense	Accumulated Depreciation	Book Value	Year	Depreciation Expense	Accumulated Depreciation	Book Value
$2,000,000	$ 2,000,000	$13,500,000	1	$4,429,000	$ 4,429,000	$11,071,000
2,000,000	4,000,000	11,500,000	2	3,163,000	7,592,000	7,908,000
2,000,000	6,000,000	9,500,000	3	2,259,000	9,851,000	5,649,000
2,000,000	8,000,000	7,500,000	4	1,614,000	11,465,000	4,035,000
2,000,000	10,000,000	5,500,000	5	1,153,000	12,618,000	2,882,000
2,000,000	12,000,000	3,500,000	6	823,000	13,441,000	2,059,000
2,000,000	14,000,000	1,500,000	7	559,000	14,000,000	1,500,000

COACH'S TIP

For tips and practice involving the calculations in Exhibit 9.8, try S9-7 at the end of this chapter.

shows why, as a user of financial statements, you need to understand what accounting methods are used by companies that you may be comparing.

The differences don't stop at depreciation expense, however. Let's take the example one step further and assume that the two companies sell the roller coasters at the end of year 4 for $6,000,000. Since we've assumed the disposal occurs on the last day of the year, a full year of depreciation will be recorded prior to the disposal. Thus, at the time of disposal, Cedar Fair's asset will have a book value of $7,500,000 whereas Six Flags will have a book value of $4,035,000, as shown in the highlighted line in Exhibit 9.8. To account for the disposal at the end of year 4, the companies will record what they receive, remove what they give up (the book value of the asset), and recognize a gain or loss for the difference between what is received and given up. Exhibit 9.9 shows these calculations for the two companies.

EXHIBIT 9.9 | Calculation of Gain/Loss on Disposal

	Cedar Fair	Six Flags
Selling price	$ 6,000,000	$ 6,000,000
Net book value (NBV)	(7,500,000)	(4,035,000)
Gain (loss) on disposal	$(1,500,000)	$ 1,965,000

Based on the information in Exhibit 9.9, which company appears better managed? Someone who doesn't understand accounting is likely to say Six Flags is better managed because it reports a gain on disposal whereas Cedar Fair reports a loss. You know that this can't be right because both companies have experienced exactly the same business events. They bought the same asset at the same cost ($15.5 million) and sold it for the same amount of money ($6 million). The only difference between them is that Cedar Fair reported less depreciation over the years leading up to the disposal, so its roller coaster has a larger book value at the time of disposal. Six Flags reported more depreciation in years 1 through 4, so it has a smaller book value at the time of disposal. As a financial statement user, you should realize that any disposal gain or loss reported on the income statement tells you as much (and, in many cases, more) about the method previously used to depreciate assets than about the apparent "wisdom" or management ability to negotiate the sale of long-lived assets.

Although our example used different depreciation methods, the same effects can exist between two companies that use the same depreciation methods but estimate different useful lives or different residual values for their long-lived assets. Useful lives vary for several reasons, including differences in: (a) the type of equipment used by each company, (b) the frequency of repairs and maintenance, (c) the frequency and duration of use, and (d) the degree of conservatism in management's estimates. How big can these differences get? Well, even within the same industry, sizable differences can exist. The financial statement notes of various companies in the airline industry, for example, reveal the following differences in estimated useful lives of their airplanes and other flight equipment:

Company	Estimated Life (in years)
US Airways	Up to 30
Southwest	Up to 25
Alaska Airlines	Up to 20
Singapore Airlines	Up to 15

Some analysts try to sidestep possible differences in depreciation calculations by focusing on financial measures that exclude the effects of depreciation. One popular measure is called **EBITDA** (pronounced something like *'e bit, duh*). This might seem like a goofy name, but it's actually the first letters of "earnings before interest, taxes, depreciation, and amortization." Analysts calculate EBITDA by starting with net income and adding back depreciation and amortization expense (as well as nonoperating expenses like interest and taxes). The idea is that this measure allows analysts to conduct financial analyses without having to deal with possible differences in depreciation and amortization.

> **YOU SHOULD KNOW**
>
> **EBITDA** is an abbreviation for "earnings before interest, taxes, depreciation, and amortization," which is a measure of operating performance that some managers and analysts use in place of net income.

SUPPLEMENT A: NATURAL RESOURCES

Industries such as oil and gas, mining, and timber harvesting, rely significantly on a third category of long-lived assets called *natural resources*. These natural resources, whether in the form of oil wells, mineral deposits, or timber tracts, provide the raw materials for products that are sold by companies like ExxonMobil and International Paper. When a company first acquires or develops a natural resource, the cost of the natural resource is recorded in conformity with the cost principle. As the natural resource is used up, its acquisition cost must be split among the periods in which revenues are earned in conformity with the matching principle. The term **depletion** describes the process of allocating a natural resource's cost over the period of its extraction or harvesting. The units-of-production method is often used to compute depletion.

Depletion is similar to the concepts of depreciation and amortization discussed earlier in the chapter for tangible and intangible assets, with one important exception. When a natural resource such as timberland is depleted, the company obtains inventory (logs). Because depletion of the natural resource is necessary to obtain the inventory, the depletion computed during a period is added to the cost of the inventory, not expensed in the period. For example, if a timber tract costing $530,000 is depleted over its estimated cutting period based on a "cutting" rate of approximately 20 percent per year, it would be depleted by $106,000 each year. Recording this depletion would have the following effects on the company's accounting equation, which would be recorded with the journal entry shown below.

> **YOU SHOULD KNOW**
>
> **Depletion** is the process of allocating a natural resource's cost over the period of its extraction or harvesting.

1. Analyze

Assets		= Liabilities +	Stockholders' Equity
Timber Inventory	+106,000		
Timber Tract	−106,000		

2. Record

Timber Inventory (+A)..................................... 106,000
  Timber Tract (−A) (or Accumulated Depletion +xA, −A) 106,000

SUPPLEMENT B: CHANGES IN DEPRECIATION

CHANGES IN ESTIMATES

Depreciation is based on two estimates, useful life and residual value. These estimates are made at the time a depreciable asset is acquired. As you gain experience with the asset, one or both of these initial estimates may need to be revised. In addition, extraordinary repairs and additions may be added to the original acquisition cost at some time during the asset's use. When it is clear that either estimate should be revised to a significant degree or that the asset's cost has changed, the undepreciated asset balance (less any residual value estimated at that date) should be assigned to each of the remaining years of estimated life using a new amount of depreciation. This is called a *prospective change in estimate*.

To compute the new depreciation expense due to the changes described above, substitute the book value for the original acquisition cost, the new residual value for the original residual value, and the estimated remaining life for the original useful life. As an illustration, the formula using the straight-line method follows:

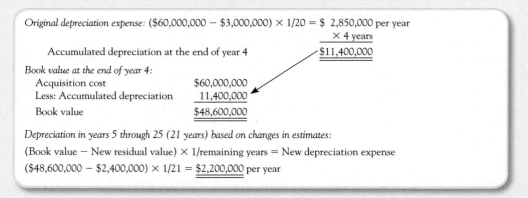

$$(\text{Cost} - \text{Residual Value}) \times \frac{1}{\text{Useful Life}} = \text{Depreciation Expense}$$

$$(\text{Book Value} - \text{New Residual Value}) \times \frac{1}{\text{Remaining Life}} = \text{Depreciation Expense}$$

Assume Cedar Fair purchased the largest and fastest roller coaster in the universe for $60,000,000 with an estimated useful life of 20 years and estimated residual value of $3,000,000. Shortly after the start of year 5, Cedar Fair changed the initial estimated life to 25 years and lowered the estimated residual value to $2,400,000. At the end of year 5, the computation of the new amount for depreciation expense is as follows:

Original depreciation expense: ($60,000,000 − $3,000,000) × 1/20 = $ 2,850,000 per year
                                                                    × 4 years

Accumulated depreciation at the end of year 4 $11,400,000

Book value at the end of year 4:
Acquisition cost $60,000,000
Less: Accumulated depreciation   11,400,000
Book value $48,600,000

Depreciation in years 5 through 25 (21 years) based on changes in estimates:
(Book value − New residual value) × 1/remaining years = New depreciation expense
($48,600,000 − $2,400,000) × 1/21 = $2,200,000 per year

Companies may also change depreciation methods (for example, from declining-balance to straight-line), although such a change requires significantly more disclosure, as described in intermediate accounting textbooks. Under GAAP, changes in accounting estimates and depreciation methods should be made only when a new estimate or accounting method "better measures" the periodic income of the business.

PARTIAL YEAR CALCULATIONS

Purchases and disposals of long-lived assets seldom occur on the first or last day of the accounting period. Consequently, the need often arises to calculate depreciation for periods shorter than a full year. When using the straight-line or declining-balance methods, the annual depreciation is multiplied by the fraction of the year for which depreciation is being calculated. For example, if Cedar Fair owns a roller coaster for only two months of the year, its regular annual depreciation would be multiplied by 2/12, representing the two months out of 12 that it is owned. The units-of-production method does not require this kind of modification because it is based on actual production for the period. If the length of the accounting period is shorter than a year, then the level of actual production will already reflect that shorter period.

REVIEW THE CHAPTER

DEMONSTRATION CASE

Diversified Industries (DI) started as a house construction company. In recent years, it has expanded into heavy construction, ready-mix concrete, sand and gravel, construction supplies, and earth-moving services. The company completed the following transactions during 2008. Amounts have been simplified.

www.mhhe.com/phillips2e

2008

Jan. 1   The management decided to buy a 10-year-old building for $175,000 and the land on which it was situated for $130,000. DI paid $100,000 in cash and signed a note payable for the rest.

Jan. 3   DI paid $38,000 in cash for renovations to the building prior to its use.

July 10   DI paid $1,200 cash for ordinary repairs on the building.

Dec. 31   DI considered the following information to determine year-end adjustments:

a. The building will be depreciated on a straight-line basis over an estimated useful life of 30 years. The estimated residual value is $33,000.
b. DI purchased another company two years ago at $100,000 more than the fair values of the net assets acquired. The goodwill has an unlimited life.
c. At the beginning of the year, DI owned equipment with a cost of $650,000 and accumulated depreciation of $150,000. The equipment is being depreciated using the double-declining-balance method, with a useful life of 20 years and no residual value.
d. At year-end, DI tested its long-lived assets for possible impairment of their value. Included in its equipment was a piece of old excavation equipment with a cost of $156,000 and book value of $120,000, after making the adjustment for (c). Due to its smaller size and lack of safety features, the old equipment has limited use. The future cash flows and fair value are expected to be $35,000. Goodwill was found to be not impaired.

December 31, 2008, is the end of the annual accounting period.

Required:

1. Indicate the accounts affected and the amount and direction (+ for increase and − for decrease) of the effect of each of the preceding events and required adjustments on the financial statement categories at the end of the year. Use the following headings:

Date	Assets	=	Liabilities	+	Stockholders' Equity

2. Prepare the journal entries to record each event that occurred during the year and the adjusting journal entries required at December 31.
3. Show the December 31, 2008, balance sheet classification and amount for each of the following items:
   Fixed assets—land, building, and equipment.
   Intangible asset—goodwill.
4. Assuming that the company had sales of $1,000,000 for the year and a book value of $500,000 for fixed assets at the beginning of the year, compute the fixed asset turnover ratio. Explain its meaning.

Suggested Solution

1. Effects of events (with computations in notes below the table):

Date	Assets		=	Liabilities	+	Stockholders' Equity	
Jan. 1	Cash Land Building	−100,000 +130,000 +175,000		Note Payable +205,000			
Jan. 3 (1)	Cash Building	−38,000 +38,000					
July 10 (2)	Cash	−1,200				Repairs Expense (+E)	−1,200
Dec. 31 (a) (3)	Accumulated Depreciation (+xA)	−6,000				Depreciation Expense (+E)	−6,000
Dec. 31 (b) (4)	No entry						
Dec. 31 (c) (5)	Accumulated Depreciation (+xA)	−50,000				Depreciation Expense (+E)	−50,000
Dec. 31 (d) (6)	Equipment	−85,000				Loss Due to Asset Impairment (+E)	−85,000

(1) Capitalize the $38,000 expenditure because it is necessary to prepare the asset for use.

(2) This is an ordinary repair and should be expensed.

(3)
Cost of building		Straight-line depreciation
Initial payment	$175,000	($213,000 cost − $33,000 residual value) ×
Renovations prior to use	38,000	1/30 years = $6,000 annual depreciation
Acquisition cost	$213,000	

(4) Goodwill has indefinite life and is therefore not amortized. Goodwill is tested for impairment but as described later in the case, was found to be not impaired.

(5) Double-declining-balance depreciation
($650,000 cost − $150,000 accumulated depreciation) × 2/20 years = $50,000 depreciation for the year.

(6) Asset impairment test
The book value of old equipment ($120,000) exceeds expected future cash flows ($35,000). The asset has become impaired, so it needs to be written down to its fair value.

Impairment loss:	
Book value	$120,000
Less: Fair value	(35,000)
Loss due to impairment	$ 85,000

2. Journal entries for events during the year:

January 1, 2008
dr Land (+A)	130,000	
dr Building (+A)	175,000	
cr Cash (−A)		100,000
cr Note Payable (+L)		205,000

January 3, 2008
dr Building (+A)	38,000	
cr Cash (−A)		38,000

July 10, 2008
dr Repairs Expense (+E, −SE)	1,200	
cr Cash (−A)		1,200

Adjusting journal entries at December 31, 2008:

a. dr Depreciation Expense (+E, −SE)......................... 6,000
      cr Accumulated Depreciation (+xA, −A) 6,000

b. No adjusting journal entry required because goodwill is assumed to have an unlimited (or indefinite) life.

c. dr Depreciation Expense (+E, −SE).......................... 50,000
      cr Accumulated Depreciation (+xA, −A) 50,000

d. dr Loss Due to Asset Impairment (+E, −SE)................... 85,000
      cr Equipment (−A) 85,000

3. Partial balance sheet, December 31, 2008:

Assets		
Fixed assets		
Land		$130,000
Building	$213,000	
Less: Accumulated depreciation	6,000	207,000
Equipment ($650,000 − 85,000)	565,000	
Less: Accumulated depreciation ($150,000 + 50,000)	200,000	365,000
Total fixed assets		702,000
Intangible asset		
Goodwill		100,000

4. Fixed asset turnover ratio:

$$\frac{\text{Sales}}{(\text{Beginning Net Fixed Asset Balance} + \text{Ending Net Fixed Asset Balance}) \div 2} = \frac{\$1,000,000}{(\$500,000 + \$702,000) \div 2} = 1.66$$

This construction company is capital intensive. The fixed asset turnover ratio measures the company's efficiency at using its investment in property, plant, and equipment to generate sales. Approximately $1.66 of sales were generated for each dollar of fixed assets.

CHAPTER SUMMARY

Define, classify, and explain the nature of long-lived assets. p. 382   LO1

- Long-lived assets are those that a business retains for long periods of time for use in the course of normal operations rather than for sale. They may be divided into tangible assets (land, buildings, equipment) and intangible assets (including goodwill, patents, and franchises).

Apply the cost principle to the acquisition of long-lived assets. p. 383   LO2

- Acquisition cost of property, plant, and equipment is the cash-equivalent purchase price plus all reasonable and necessary expenditures made to acquire and prepare the asset for its intended use. Expenditures made after the asset is in use are either expensed or capitalized as a cost of the asset:
  a. Expenditures are expensed if they recur frequently, involve relatively small amounts, and do not directly lengthen the asset's useful life. These are considered ordinary repairs and maintenance expense.
  b. Expenditures are capitalized as a cost of the asset if they provide benefits for one or more accounting periods beyond the current period. This category includes extraordinary repairs, replacements, and additions.

LO3 **Apply various depreciation methods as future economic benefits are used up over time. p. 389**

- In conformity with the matching principle, the cost of long-lived tangible assets (less any estimated residual value) is allocated to depreciation expense over each period benefited by the assets.
- Because of depreciation, the book value of an asset declines over time and net income is reduced by the amount of the expense.
- Common depreciation methods include straight-line (a constant amount over time), units-of-production (a variable amount over time), and double-declining-balance (a decreasing amount over time).

LO4 **Explain the effect of asset impairment on the financial statements. p. 394**

- When events or changes in circumstances reduce the estimated future cash flows of a long-lived asset below its book value, the book value of the asset should be written down, with the amount of the write-down reported as an impairment loss.

LO5 **Analyze the disposal of long-lived tangible assets. p. 395**

When assets are disposed of through sale or abandonment,
- Record additional depreciation arising since the last adjustment was made.
- Remove the cost of the old asset and its related accumulated depreciation.
- Recognize the cash proceeds (if any).
- Recognize any gains or losses when the asset's book value is not equal to the cash received.

LO6 **Analyze the acquisition, use, and disposal of long-lived intangible assets. p. 397**

- Intangible assets are recorded at cost, but only when purchased. The costs of most internally developed intangible assets are expensed as research and development when incurred.
- Intangibles are reported at book value on the balance sheet.
- Amortization is calculated for intangibles with limited useful lives, using the straight-line method.
- Intangibles with unlimited useful lives, including goodwill, are not amortized, but are reviewed for impairment.

LO7 **Interpret the fixed asset turnover ratio. p. 399**

- The fixed asset turnover ratio measures the company's efficiency at using its investment in property, plant, and equipment to generate sales. Higher turnover ratios imply greater efficiency.

LO8 **Describe factors to consider when comparing across companies. p. 401**

- Companies in different industries require different levels of investment in long-lived assets. Beyond that, you should consider whether differences exist in depreciation methods, estimated useful lives, and estimated residual values, which can affect the book value of long-lived assets as well as ratios calculated using these book values and any gains or losses reported at the time of asset disposal.

	Financial Analysis Tools	
Name of Measure	Formula	What It Tells You
Fixed asset turnover ratio	$\dfrac{\text{Net Sales Revenue}}{\text{Average Net Fixed Assets}}$	• Dollars of sales generated for each dollar invested in (tangible) fixed assets • A higher ratio implies greater efficiency

KEY TERMS

Amortization p. 398
Book (or Carrying) Value p. 388
Capitalize p. 384
Copyright p. 397
Declining-Balance Depreciation
  Method p. 391
Depletion p. 403
Depreciable Cost p. 389
Depreciation p. 388

EBITDA p. 403
Extraordinary Repairs p. 387
Franchise p. 397
Goodwill p. 397
Impairment p. 394
Licensing Right p. 397
Long-Lived Assets p. 382
Net Assets p. 398
Ordinary Repairs and Maintenance p. 387

Patent p. 397
Research and Development p. 397
Residual (or Salvage) Value p. 389
Straight-Line Depreciation Method p. 390
Trademark p. 397
Units-of-Production Depreciation
  Method p. 391
Useful Life p. 389

PRACTICE MATERIAL

QUESTIONS

1. Define long-lived assets. What are the two common categories of long-lived assets? Describe each.
2. Under the cost principle, what amounts should be recorded as a cost of a long-lived asset?
3. What is the term for recording costs as assets rather than as expenses? Describe how the decision to record costs as assets, rather than expenses, affects the balance sheet and income statement.
4. Distinguish between ordinary repairs and extraordinary repairs. How is each accounted for?
5. Describe the relationship between the matching principle and accounting for long-lived assets.
6. Why are different depreciation methods allowed?
7. In computing depreciation, three values must be known or estimated. Identify and describe each.
8. What type of depreciation expense pattern is used under each of the following methods and when is its use appropriate?
   a. The straight-line method.
   b. The units-of-production method.
   c. The double-declining-balance method.
9. What is an *asset impairment*? How is it accounted for?
10. What is book value? When equipment is sold for more than book value, how is the transaction recorded? How is it recorded when the selling price is less than book value?
11. Distinguish between depreciation and amortization.
12. Define *goodwill*. When is it appropriate to record goodwill as an intangible asset?
13. How is the fixed asset turnover ratio computed? Explain its meaning.
14. (Supplement A) How does depletion affect the balance sheet and income statement? Why is depletion accounted for in a manner that differs from depreciation and amortization?
15. (Supplement B) Over what period should an addition to an existing long-lived asset be depreciated? Explain.

MULTIPLE CHOICE

1. Which of the following should be capitalized when a piece of production equipment is acquired for a factory?
   a. Sales taxes.   c. Installation costs.
   b. Transportation costs. d. All of the above.
2. When recording depreciation, which of the following statements is true?
   a. Total assets increase and stockholders' equity increases.
   b. Total assets decrease and total liabilities increase.

Topic Tackler

PLUS

Quiz 9

Check out www.mhhe.com/phillips2e for more multiple choice questions.

    c. Total assets decrease and stockholders' equity increases.

    d. None of the above are true.

3. Under what depreciation method(s) is an asset's book value used to calculate depreciation each year?

    a. Straight-line method.   **c.** Declining-balance method.

    b. Units-of-production method.   **d.** All of the above.

4. A company wishes to report the highest earnings possible according to GAAP. Therefore, when calculating depreciation for financial reporting purposes,

    a. It will follow the MACRS depreciation rates prescribed by the IRS.

    b. It will select the shortest lives possible for its assets according to GAAP.

    c. It will select the longest lives possible for its assets according to GAAP.

    d. It will estimate lower residual values for its assets.

5. Barber, Inc., followed the practice of depreciating its building on a straight-line basis. A building was purchased on January 1, 2007, and it had an estimated useful life of 20 years and a residual value of $20,000. The company's depreciation expense for 2007 was $20,000 on the building. What was the original cost of the building?

    a. $360,000   **c.** $400,000

    b. $380,000   **d.** $420,000

6. ACME, Inc., uses straight-line depreciation for all of its depreciable assets. ACME sold a used piece of machinery on December 31, 2007, that it purchased on January 1, 2006, for $10,000. The asset had a five-year life, zero residual value, and accumulated depreciation as of December 31, 2006, of $2,000. If the sales price of the used machine was $7,500, the resulting gain or loss on disposal was which of the following amounts?

    a. Loss of $3,500.   **c.** Loss of $1,500.

    b. Gain of $3,500.   **d.** Gain of $1,500.

7. What assets should be amortized using the straight-line method?

    a. Land.   **c.** Intangible assets with unlimited lives.

    b. Intangible assets with limited lives.   **d.** All of the above.

8. How many of the following statements regarding goodwill are true?

    • Goodwill is not reported unless purchased in an exchange.

    • Goodwill must be reviewed annually for possible impairment.

    • Impairment of goodwill results in a decrease in net income.

    a. None   **c.** Two

    b. One   **d.** Three

9. The Simon Company and the Allen Company each bought a new delivery truck on January 1, 2006. Both companies paid exactly the same cost, $30,000 for their respective vehicles. As of December 31, 2007, the book value of Simon's truck was less than the Allen Company's book value for the same vehicle. Which of the following are acceptable explanations for the difference in book value?

    a. Both companies elected straight-line depreciation, but the Simon Company used a longer estimated life.

    b. The Simon Company estimated a lower residual value, but both estimated the same useful life and both elected straight-line depreciation.

    c. Because GAAP specifies rigid guidelines regarding the calculation of depreciation, this situation is not possible.

    d. None of the above explain the difference in book value.

10. (Supplement B) Thornton Industries purchased a machine for $45,000 and is depreciating it with the straight-line method over a life of 10 years, using a residual value of $3,000. At the beginning of the sixth year, a major overhaul was made costing $5,000, and the estimated useful life was extended to 13 years, and no change was made to the estimated residual value. Depreciation expense for year 6 is

    a. $1,885   **c.** $3,250

    b. $2,000   **d.** $3,625

Solutions to Multiple Choice Questions
1. d 2. d 3. c 4. c 5. d 6. d 7. b 8. d 9. b 10. c

MINI-EXERCISES

Available with McGraw-Hill's
Homework Manager

MANAGER **PLUS**

M9-1 Classifying Long-Lived Assets and Related Cost Allocation Concepts

LO1, LO3, LO6

For each of the following long-lived assets, indicate its nature and related cost allocation concept. Use the abbreviations shown on the right:

Asset	Nature	Cost Allocation		Nature
1. Operating license	_____	_____	L	Land
2. Property	_____	_____	B	Building
3. New engine for old machine	_____	_____	E	Equipment
4. Delivery vans	_____	_____	I	Intangible
5. Production plant	_____	_____		
6. Warehouse	_____	_____		Cost Allocation
7. Copyright	_____	_____	D	Depreciation
8. Trademark	_____	_____	A	Amortization
9. Computers	_____	_____	NO	No cost allocation

M9-2 Deciding Whether to Capitalize or Expense

LO2, LO6

American Golf Corporation

American Golf Corporation operates over 170 golf courses throughout the country. For each of the following items, enter the correct letter to show whether the cost should be capitalized (C) or expensed (E).

Transactions

_____ 1. Purchased a golf course in Orange County, California.

_____ 2. Paid a landscaping company to clear one hundred acres of land on which to build a new course.

_____ 3. Paid a landscaping company to apply fertilizer to the fairways on its Coyote Hills Golf Course.

_____ 4. Hired a building maintenance company to build a 2,000 square foot addition on a clubhouse.

_____ 5. Hired a building maintenance company to replace the locks on a clubhouse and equipment shed.

_____ 6. Paid an advertising company to create a campaign to build goodwill.

M9-3 Deciding Whether to Capitalize an Expense

LO2, LO6

For each of the following items, enter the correct letter to the left to show whether the expenditure should be capitalized (C) or expensed (E).

Transactions

_____ 1. Paid $600 for ordinary repairs.

_____ 2. Paid $16,000 for extraordinary repairs.

_____ 3. Paid cash, $200,000, for addition to old building.

_____ 4. Paid $250 for routine maintenance.

_____ 5. Purchased a machine, $70,000; gave long-term note.

_____ 6. Purchased a patent, $45,300 cash.

_____ 7. Paid $20,000 for monthly salaries.

LO3   **M9-4 Computing Book Value (Straight-Line Depreciation)**

Calculate the book value of a two-year-old machine that cost $200,000, has an estimated residual value of $40,000, and has an estimated useful life of four years. The company uses straight-line depreciation.

LO3   **M9-5 Computing Book Value (Units-of-Production Depreciation)**

Calculate the book value of a two-year-old machine that cost $200,000, has an estimated residual value of $40,000, and has an estimated useful life of 20,000 machine hours. The company uses units-of-production depreciation and ran the machine 3,000 hours in year 1 and 8,000 hours in year 2.

LO3   **M9-6 Computing Book Value (Double-Declining-Balance Depreciation)**

Calculate the book value of a two-year-old machine that cost $200,000, has an estimated residual value of $40,000, and has an estimated useful life of four years. The company uses double-declining-balance depreciation. Round to the nearest dollar.

LO4   **M9-7 Identifying Asset Impairment**

For each of the following impaired assets, indicate the amount of impairment loss to report.

	Book Value	Fair Value	Amount of Loss?
a. Machine	$ 17,000	$ 9,000	
b. Copyright	41,000	39,000	
c. Factory building	60,000	30,000	
d. Building	250,000	210,000	

LO5   **M9-8 Recording the Disposal of a Long-Lived Asset**

Prepare journal entries to record these transactions: (*a*) Morrell Corporation disposed of two computers at the end of their useful lives. The computers had cost $4,800 and their Accumulated depreciation was $4,800. No residual value was received. (*b*) Assume the same information as (*a*), except that Accumulated depreciation, updated to the date of disposal, was $3,600.

LO5   **M9-9 Reporting and Recording the Disposal of a Long-Lived Asset (Straight-Line Depreciation)**

As part of a major renovation at the beginning of the year, Hauser Pharmaceuticals, Inc., sold shelving units (store fixtures) that were 10 years old for $1,000 cash. The shelves originally cost $6,400 and had been depreciated on a straight-line basis over an estimated useful life of 10 years with an estimated residual value of $400. Assuming that depreciation has been recorded to the date of sale, show the effect of the disposal on the accounting equation. Prepare the journal entry to record the sale of the shelving units.

LO6   **M9-10 Capitalizing versus Expensing Intangible Asset Costs**

Most highly visible companies spend significant amounts of money to protect their intellectual property, ensuring that no one uses this property without direct permission. For example, to include logos throughout this book, we had to obtain written permission from each company—a process that stretched over nearly a year and often resulted in requests being denied. Discuss whether companies should capitalize or expense the money paid to employees who evaluate requests for use of their logos and who search for instances where the companies' intellectual property has been used without permission. Draw an analogy to similar costs incurred for employees responsible for the use and upkeep of tangible assets.

LO6   **M9-11 Computing Goodwill and Patents**

Taste-T Company has been in business for 30 years and has developed a large group of loyal restaurant customers. Down Home Foods made an offer to buy Taste-T Company for $6,000,000.

The market value of Taste-T's recorded assets, net of liabilities, on the date of the offer is $5,600,000. Taste-T also holds a patent for a fluting machine that the company invented (the patent with a market value of $200,000 was never recorded by Taste-T because it was developed internally). How much has Down Home Foods included for intangibles in its offer of $6,000,000? Assuming Taste-T accepts this offer, which company will report goodwill on its balance sheet?

M9-12 Computing and Evaluating the Fixed Asset Turnover Ratio

LO7

The following information was reported by Amuse Yourself Parks (AYP) for 2005:

Net fixed assets (beginning of year)	$8,450,000
Net fixed assets (end of year)	8,250,000
Net sales for the year	4,175,000
Net income for the year	1,700,000

Compute the company's fixed asset turnover ratio for the year. What can you say about AYP's fixed asset turnover ratio when compared to Cedar Fair's 2005 ratio in Exhibit 9.7?

EXERCISES

Available with McGraw-Hill's
Homework Manager

HOMEWORK
MANAGER **PLUS**

E9-1 Preparing a Classified Balance Sheet

LO1

The following is a list of account titles and amounts (in millions) reported at December 25, 2005, by Hasbro, Inc., a leading manufacturer of games, toys, and interactive entertainment software for children and families:

Buildings and improvements	$ 174	Goodwill	$467
Prepaids and other current assets	185	Machinery and equipment	332
Allowance for doubtful accounts	30	Accumulated depreciation	227
Other noncurrent assets	226	Inventories	179
Cash and cash equivalents	942	Other intangibles, net	613
Accounts receivable	553	Land and improvements	7

Required:

Prepare the asset section of a classified balance sheet for Hasbro, Inc.

E9-2 Computing and Recording a Basket Purchase and Straight-Line Depreciation

LO2, LO3

Bridge City Consulting bought a building and the land on which it is located for $182,000 cash. The land is estimated to represent 70 percent of the purchase price. The company also paid renovation costs on the building of $22,000.

Required:

1. Explain how the renovation costs should be accounted for.
2. Give the journal entry to record all expenditures. Assume that all transactions were for cash and they occurred at the start of the year.
3. Compute straight-line depreciation on the building at the end of one year, assuming an estimated 12-year useful life and a $4,600 estimated residual value.
4. What should be the book value of the land and building at the end of year 2?

E9-3 Determining Financial Statement Effects of an Asset Acquisition and Straight-Line Depreciation

LO2, LO3

Conover Company ordered a machine on January 1, 2007, at a purchase price of $30,000. On date of delivery, January 2, 2007, the company paid $8,000 on the machine and signed a note payable for the balance. On January 3, 2007, it paid $250 for freight on the machine. On January 5, Conover paid installation costs relating to the machine amounting to $1,500. On December 31, 2007 (the end of the accounting period), Conover recorded depreciation on the machine using the straight-line method with an estimated useful life of 10 years and an estimated residual value of $2,750.

Required:

1. Indicate the effects (accounts, amounts, and + or −) of each transaction (on January 1, 2, 3, and 5) on the accounting equation. Use the following schedule:

Date	Assets	=	Liabilities	+	Stockholders' Equity

2. Compute the acquisition cost of the machine.
3. Compute the depreciation expense to be reported for 2007.
4. What should be the book value of the machine at the end of 2008?

LO2, LO3　**E9-4 Recording Straight-Line Depreciation and Repairs**

Wiater Company operates a small manufacturing facility. At the beginning of 2008, an asset account for the company showed the following balances:

Manufacturing equipment	$160,000
Accumulated depreciation through 2007	110,000

During 2008, the following expenditures were incurred for repairs and maintenance:

Routine maintenance and repairs on the equipment	$ 1,850
Major overhaul of the equipment that improved efficiency	21,000

The equipment is being depreciated on a straight-line basis over an estimated life of 15 years with a $10,000 estimated residual value. The annual accounting period ends on December 31.

Required:

Indicate the effects (accounts, amounts, and + or −) of the following two items on the accounting equation, using the headings shown below.

1. The adjustment for depreciation made at the end of 2007.
2. The two expenditures for repairs and maintenance during 2008.

Item	Assets	=	Liabilities	+	Stockholders' Equity

LO2, LO3　**E9-5 Determining Financial Statement Effects of Straight-Line Depreciation and Repairs**

Refer to the information in E9-4.

Required:

1. Give the adjusting journal entry that would have been made at the end of 2007 for depreciation on the manufacturing equipment.
2. Starting at the beginning of 2008, what is the remaining estimated life?
3. Give the journal entries to record the two expenditures for repairs and maintenance during 2008.

LO3　**E9-6 Computing Depreciation under Alternative Methods**

PlasticWorks Corporation bought a machine at the beginning of the year at a cost of $12,000. The estimated useful life was five years, and the residual value was $2,000. Assume that the estimated productive life of the machine is 10,000 units. Expected annual production was: year 1, 3,000 units; year 2, 3,000 units; year 3, 2,000 units; year 4, 1,000 units; and year 5, 1,000 units.

Required:

1. Complete a depreciation schedule for each of the alternative methods.
   a. Straight-line.
   b. Units-of-production.
   c. Double-declining-balance.

		Income Statement	Balance Sheet		
		Depreciation		Accumulated	
Year	Computation	Expense	Cost	Depreciation	Book Value
At acquisition					
1					

2. Which method will result in the highest net income in year 2? Does this higher net income mean the machine was used more efficiently under this depreciation method?

E9-7 Computing Depreciation under Alternative Methods

LO3

Sonic Corporation

Sonic Corporation purchased and installed electronic payment equipment at its drive-inn restaurants in San Marcos, TX, at a cost of $27,000. The equipment has an estimated residual value of $1,500. The equipment is expected to process 255,000 payments over its three-year useful life. Per year, expected payment transactions are 61,200, year 1; 140,250, year 2; and 53,550, year 3.

Required:

Complete a depreciation schedule for each of the alternative methods.
1. Straight-line.
2. Units-of-production.
3. Double-declining-balance.

		Income Statement	Balance Sheet		
		Depreciation		Accumulated	
Year	Computation	Expense	Cost	Depreciation	Book Value
At acquisition					
1					

E9-8 Interpreting Management's Choice of Different Depreciation Methods for Tax and Financial Reporting

LO3

FedEx Corporation

The annual report for FedEx Corporation includes the following information:

> For financial reporting purposes, depreciation and amortization of property and equipment is provided on a straight-line basis over the asset's service life. For income tax purposes, depreciation is generally computed using accelerated methods.

Required:

Explain why FedEx uses different methods of depreciation for financial reporting and tax purposes.

LO3 **E9-9 Inferring Asset Age from Straight-Line Depreciation**

On January 1, 2007, the records of Tuff Turf Corporation (TTC) showed the following regarding production equipment:

Equipment (estimated residual value, $2,000)	$14,000
Accumulated depreciation (straight-line, one year)	2,000

Required:

Based on the data given, compute the estimated useful life of the truck.

LO4 **E9-10 Exploring Financial Statement Effects of Asset Impairment**

Refer to E9-9.

Required:

If TTC's management estimated that the equipment had future cash flows and a fair value of only $6,800 at December 31, 2007, how would this affect TTC's balance sheet and income statement? Explain.

LO5

FedEx Corporation

E9-11 Demonstrating the Effect of Book Value on Reporting an Asset Disposal

FedEx Corporation is the world's leading express-distribution company. In addition to the world's largest fleet of all-cargo aircraft, the company has more than 53,700 ground vehicles that pick up and deliver packages. Assume that FedEx sold a delivery truck for $16,000. FedEx had originally purchased the truck for $28,000, and had recorded depreciation for three years.

Required:

1. Calculate the amount of gain or loss on disposal, assuming that
   a. The accumulated depreciation was $12,000.
   b. The accumulated depreciation was $10,000.
   c. The accumulated depreciation was $15,000.

2. Using the following structure, indicate the effects (accounts, amounts, and + or −) for the disposal of the truck in each of the three preceding situations.

Part	Assets	=	Liabilities	+	Stockholders' Equity

3. Based on the three preceding situations, explain how the amount of depreciation recorded up to the time of disposal affects the amount of gain or loss on disposal.

LO5 **E9-12 Demonstrating the Effect of Book Value on Recording Asset Disposal Journal Entries**

Refer to the information in E9-11.

Required:

1. Give the journal entry for the disposal of the truck, assuming that
   a. The accumulated depreciation was $12,000.
   b. The accumulated depreciation was $10,000.
   c. The accumulated depreciation was $15,000.
2. Based on the three preceding situations, explain how the amount of depreciation recorded up to the time of disposal affects the amount of gain or loss on disposal.

E9-13 Computing and Reporting the Acquisition and Amortization of Three Different Intangible Assets

LO6

Kreiser Company had three intangible assets at the end of 2007 (end of the accounting year):

a.   A patent purchased from J. Miller on January 1, 2007, for a cash cost of $5,640. When purchased, the patent had an estimated life of fifteen years.

b.   A trademark was registered with the federal government for $10,000. Management estimated that the trademark could be worth as much as $200,000 because it has an indefinite life.

c.   Computer licensing rights were purchased on January 1, 2006, for $60,000. The rights are expected to have a four-year useful life to the company.

Required:

1.   Compute the acquisition cost of each intangible asset.

2.   Compute the amortization of each intangible for the year ended December 31, 2007.

3.   Show how these assets and any related expenses should be reported on the balance sheet and income statement for 2007.

E9-14 Recording the Purchase, Amortization, and Impairment of a Patent

LO4, LO6
Nutek, Inc.

Nutek, Inc., holds a patent for the Full Service™ handi-plate, which the company's 2003 10-K described as "a patented plastic buffet plate that allows the user to hold both a plate and cup in one hand" and that "has a multitude of uses including social gatherings such as backyard barbecues, buffets, picnics, tailgate and parties of any kind." (No, we're not making this up.) Nutek also purchased a patent for $1,000,000 for "a specialty line of patented switch plate covers and outlet plate covers specifically designed to light up automatically when the power fails." Assume the switch plate patent was purchased January 1, 2007, and it is being amortized over a period of 10 years. Assume Nutek does not use an accumulated amortization account but instead charges amortization directly against the intangible asset account.

Required:

1.   Describe the effects of the purchase and amortization of the switch plate patent on the 2007 balance sheet and income statement.

2.   Give the journal entries to record the purchase and amortization of the switch plate patent in 2007.

3.   After many months of unsuccessful attempts to manufacture the switch plate covers, Nutek determined the patent was significantly impaired and its book value on January 1, 2008, was written off. Describe the financial statement effects of accounting for the asset impairment and give the journal entry to record the impairment.

E9-15 Computing and Interpreting the Fixed Asset Turnover Ratio from a Financial Analyst's Perspective

The following data were included in a recent Apple Inc. annual report (in millions):

LO7
Apple Inc.

	2005	2004	2003	2002	2001	2000	1999
Net sales	$13,931	$8,279	$6,207	$5,742	$5,363	$7,983	$6,134
Net property, plant, and equipment	817	707	669	669	564	419	318

Required:

1.   Compute Apple's fixed asset turnover ratio for 2000, 2002, and 2004 (the even years). Round your answer to one decimal place.

2.   If you were a financial analyst, what would you say about the results of your analyses?

LO3, LO7   **E9-16 Computing Depreciation and Book Value for Two Years Using Alternative Depreciation Methods and Interpreting the Impact on the Fixed Asset Turnover Ratio**

Torge Company bought a machine for $65,000 cash. The estimated useful life was five years, and the estimated residual value was $5,000. Assume that the estimated useful life in productive units is 150,000. Units actually produced were 40,000 in year 1 and 45,000 in year 2.

Required:

1. Determine the appropriate amounts to complete the following schedule. Show computations.

	Depreciation Expense for		Book Value at the End of	
Method of Depreciation	Year 1	Year 2	Year 1	Year 2
Straight-line				
Units-of-production				
Double-declining-balance				

2. Which method would result in the lowest net income for year 1? For year 2?
3. Which method would result in the lowest fixed asset turnover ratio for year 1? Why?

LO1–LO6   **E9-17 Finding Financial Information as a Potential Investor**

You are considering investing in various stocks. You have received several annual reports of major companies.

Required:

For each of the following, indicate where you would locate the information in an annual report.
TIP: The information might be available in more than one location of the annual report.

1. The detail on major classifications of long-lived assets.
2. The accounting method(s) used for financial reporting purposes.
3. The amount of assets written off as impaired during the year.
4. Net amount of property, plant, and equipment.
5. Policies on amortizing intangibles.
6. Depreciation expense.
7. Any significant gains or losses on disposals of fixed assets.
8. Prior year's accumulated depreciation.

LO2, LO3   **E9-18 Comprehensive Exercise in Accounting for Operating Activities (Including Depreciation) and Preparing Financial Statements**

Grid Iron Prep Inc. (GIPI) is a service business incorporated in January 2007 to provide personal training for athletes aspiring to play college football. The following transactions occurred during the year ended December 31, 2007.

a. GIPI issued stock in exchange for $90,000 cash.
b. GIPI purchased a gymnasium building and gym equipment at the beginning of the year for $50,000, 80% of which related to the gymnasium and 20% to the equipment.
c. GIPI paid $250 cash to have the gym equipment refurbished before it could be used.
d. GIPI collected $36,000 cash in training fees during the year, of which $2,000 were customer deposits to be earned in 2008.
e. GIPI paid $23,000 of wages and $7,000 in utilities.
f. GIPI provided $3,000 in training during the final month of the year and expected collection in 2008.
g. GIPI will depreciate the gymnasium building using the double-declining-balance method over 20 years. Gym equipment will be depreciated using the straight-line method, with an estimated residual value of $2,250 at the end of its four-year useful life.
h. GIPI received a bill for $350 of advertising done during December. The bill has not been paid or recorded.

i. GIPI will record an estimated five percent of its accounts receivable as not collectible.
j. GIPI's income tax rate is 30%. Assume depreciation for tax is the same amount as depreciation for financial reporting purposes.

Required:

1. Prepare journal entries to record the transactions and adjustments listed in *a–j*.
2. Prepare GIPI's annual income statement, statement of retained earnings, and classified balance sheet.

E9-19 (Supplement A) Calculating and Reporting Depletion

LO3

Louisiana Oil Company (LOC) paid $3,000,000 for an oil reserve estimated to hold 50,000 barrels of oil. Oil production is expected to be 10,000 barrels in year 1, 30,000 barrels in year 2, and 10,000 barrels in year 3. LOC expects to begin selling barrels from its oil inventory in year 2.

Required:

Assuming these estimates are accurate, describe the amounts, financial statements, and classifications that would be used for the oil reserves and oil inventory at the end of year 1.

E9-20 (Supplement B) Determining Financial Statement Effects of a Change in Estimate

LO3

Refer to E9-4.

Required:

Using the following format, indicate the effects (accounts, amounts, and + or −) of the 2008 adjustment for depreciation of the manufacturing equipment, assuming no change in the estimated life or residual value. Show computations.

Date	Assets	=	Liabilities	+	Stockholders' Equity

E9-21 (Supplement B) Recording a Change in Estimate

LO3

Refer to E9-4.

Required:

Give the adjusting entry that should be made at the end of 2008 for depreciation of the manufacturing equipment, assuming no change in the original estimated total life or residual value. Show computations.

COACHED PROBLEMS

CP9-1 Computing Acquisition Cost and Recording Depreciation under Three Alternative Methods

LO2, LO3

www.mhhe.com/phillips2e

At the beginning of the year, McCoy Company bought three used machines from Colt, Inc. The machines immediately were overhauled, installed, and started operating. Because the machines were different, each was recorded separately in the accounts.

	Machine A	Machine B	Machine C
Amount paid for asset	$6,600	$25,600	$6,400
Installation costs	300	600	200
Renovation costs prior to use	1,500	400	1,000
Repairs after production began	400	350	325

By the end of the first year, each machine had been operating 8,000 hours.

Required:

1. Compute the cost of each machine. Explain the rationale for capitalizing or expensing the various costs.

2. Give the journal entry to record depreciation expense at the end of year 1, assuming the following:

| Machine | Estimates | | Depreciation Method |
	Life	Residual Value	
A	5 years	$ 500	Straight-line
B	40,000 hours	1,000	Units-of-production
C	5 years	2,000	Double-declining-balance

TIP: Remember that the formula for double-declining-balance uses cost minus accumulated depreciation (not residual value).

LO5   **CP9-2 Recording and Interpreting the Disposal of Long-Lived Assets**

During 2008, Bhumika Company disposed of two different assets. On January 1, 2008, prior to their disposal, the accounts reflected the following:

Asset	Original Cost	Residual Value	Estimated Life	Accumulated Depreciation (straight line)
Machine A	$76,200	$4,200	15 years	$57,600 (12 years)
Machine B	20,000	3,000	8 years	12,750 (6 years)

The machines were disposed of in the following ways:

a. Machine A: Sold on January 2, 2008, for $8,200 cash.
b. Machine B: On January 2, 2008, this machine suffered irreparable damage from an accident and was removed immediately by a salvage company at no cost.

Required:

1. Give the journal entries related to the disposal of each machine at the beginning of 2008.
   TIP: When no cash is received on disposal, the loss on disposal will equal the book value of the asset at the time of disposal.

2. Explain the accounting rationale for the way that you recorded each disposal.

LO6   **CP9-3 Determining Financial Statement Effects of Activities Related to Intangible Assets**

During the 2008 annual accounting period, Chu Corporation completed the following transactions:

a. On January 1, 2008, purchased a license for $4,200 cash (estimated useful life, three years).
b. On July 1, 2008, purchased another business for cash. The $130,000 purchase price included $115,000 for tangible assets of the business and $24,000 for its liabilities, which were assumed by Chu. The remainder was goodwill with an indefinite life.
c. Expenditures during 2008 for research and development totaled $8,700.

Required:

1. For each of these transactions, indicate the accounts, amounts, and effects (+ for increase and − for decrease) on the accounting equation. Use the following structure:

Date	Assets	=	Liabilities	+	Stockholders' Equity

TIP: Goodwill is the amount paid over and above the value of net assets. Net assets are calculated as assets minus liabilities.

2. For each of the intangible assets, compute amortization for the year ended December 31, 2008.

CP9-4 (Supplement B) Analyzing and Recording Entries Related to a Change in Estimated Life and Residual Value

LO3

Reader's Digest is a global publisher of magazines, books, and music and video collections and is one of the world's leading direct-mail marketers. Many direct-mail marketers use high-speed Didde press equipment to print their advertisements. These presses can cost more than $1 million. Assume that Reader's Digest owns a Didde press acquired at an original cost of $600,000. It is being depreciated on a straight-line basis over a 20-year estimated useful life and has a $75,000 estimated residual value. At the end of 2007, the press had been depreciated for a full eight years. In January 2008, a decision was made, on the basis of improved maintenance procedures, that a total estimated useful life of 25 years and a residual value of $109,500 would be more realistic. The accounting period ends December 31.

Required:

1. Compute (a) the amount of depreciation expense recorded in 2007, and (b) the book value of the printing press at the end of 2007.

2. Compute the amount of depreciation that should be recorded in 2008. Show computations.
   TIP: At the time of an estimate change, the updated book value on that date is used as if it is the cost of the asset from that date on, to be spread over the remaining useful life.

3. Give the adjusting entry for depreciation at December 31, 2008.

GROUP A PROBLEMS

Available with McGraw-Hill's
Homework Manager

HOMEWORK MANAGER **PLUS** HM

PA9-1 Computing Acquisition Cost and Recording Depreciation under Three Alternative Methods

LO2, LO3

www.mhhe.com/phillips2e

At the beginning of the year, Chemical Control Corporation bought three used machines from Radial Compression Incorporated. The machines immediately were overhauled, installed, and started operating. Because the machines were different, each was recorded separately in the accounts.

	Machine A	Machine B	Machine C
Cost of the asset	$10,000	$31,500	$22,000
Installation costs	1,600	2,100	800
Renovation costs prior to use	600	1,400	1,600
Repairs after production began	500	400	700

By the end of the first year, each machine had been operating 7,000 hours.

Required:

1. Compute the cost of each machine. Explain the rationale for capitalizing or expensing the various costs.

2. Give the journal entry to record depreciation expense at the end of year 1, assuming the following:

	Estimates		
Machine	Life	Residual Value	Depreciation Method
A	4 years	$ 1,000	Straight-line
B	33,000 hours	2,000	Units-of-production
C	5 years	1,400	Double-declining-balance

LO5   **PA9-2 Recording and Interpreting the Disposal of Long-Lived Assets**

During 2007, Ly Company disposed of two different assets. On January 1, 2007, prior to their disposal, the accounts reflected the following:

Asset	Original Cost	Residual Value	Estimated Life	Accumulated Depreciation (straight-line)
Machine A	$24,000	$2,000	5 years	$ 17,600 (4 years)
Machine B	59,200	3,200	14 years	48,000 (12 years)

The machines were disposed of in the following ways:

a. Machine A: Sold on January 1, 2007, for $5,750 cash.
b. Machine B: On January 1, 2007, this machine suffered irreparable damage from an accident and was removed immediately by a salvage company at no cost.

Required:

1. Give the journal entries related to the disposal of each machine at the beginning of 2007.
2. Explain the accounting rationale for the way that you recorded each disposal.

LO6   **PA9-3 Determining Financial Statement Effects of Activities Related to Intangible Assets**

www.mhhe.com/phillips2e

Norton Pharmaceuticals entered into the following transactions that potentially affect intangible assets:

a. On January 1, 2007, the company spent $18,600 cash to buy a patent that expires in 15 years.
b. During 2007, the company spent $25,480 working on a new drug that will be submitted for FDA testing in 2008.
c. Norton Pharmaceuticals purchased another business in 2007 for a cash lump-sum payment of $650,000. Included in the purchase price was "Goodwill, $75,000."

Required:

1. For each of these transactions, indicate the accounts, amounts, and effects (+ for increase and − for decrease) on the accounting equation. Use the following structure:

Item	Assets	=	Liabilities	+	Stockholders' Equity

2. For each of the intangible assets, compute amortization for the year ended December 31, 2007.

GROUP B PROBLEMS

LO2, LO3   **PB9-1 Computing Acquisition Cost and Recording Depreciation under Three Alternative Methods**

At the beginning of the year, Oakmont Company bought three used machines from American Manufacturing, Inc. The machines immediately were overhauled, installed, and started operating. Because the machines were different, each was recorded separately in the accounts.

	Machine A	Machine B	Machine C
Amount paid for asset	$19,600	$10,100	$9,800
Installation costs	300	500	200
Renovation costs prior to use	100	300	600
Repairs after production began	220	900	480

By the end of the first year, each machine had been operating 4,000 hours.

Required:

1. Compute the cost of each machine. Explain the rationale for capitalizing or expensing the various costs.
2. Give the journal entry to record depreciation expense at the end of year 1, assuming the following:

Machine	Estimates Life	Residual Value	Depreciation Method
A	7 years	$ 1,100	Straight-line
B	40,000 hours	900	Units-of-production
C	4 years	2,000	Double-declining-balance

PB9-2 Recording and Interpreting the Disposal of Long-Lived Assets

LO5

During 2007, Rayon Corporation disposed of two different assets. On January 1, 2007, prior to their disposal, the accounts reflected the following:

Asset	Original Cost	Residual Value	Estimated Life	Accumulated Depreciation (straight-line)
Machine A	$60,000	$11,000	7 years	$28,000 (4 years)
Machine B	14,200	1,925	5 years	7,365 (3 years)

The machines were disposed of in the following ways:

a. Machine A: Sold on January 2, 2007, for $33,500 cash.
b. Machine B: On January 2, 2007, this machine suffered irreparable damage from an accident and was removed immediately by a salvage company at no cost.

Required:

1. Give the journal entries related to the disposal of each machine at the beginning of 2007.
2. Explain the accounting rationale for the way that you recorded each disposal.

PB9-3 Determining Financial Statement Effects of Activities Related to Intangible Assets

LO6

Pandey Company entered into the following transactions that potentially affect intangible assets:

a. Soon after Pandey Company started business, in January 2006, it purchased another business for a cash lump-sum payment of $400,000. Included in the purchase price was "Goodwill, $60,000." The account balance hasn't changed in two years.
b. The company purchased a patent at a cash cost of $54,600 on January 1, 2007. The patent has an estimated useful life of 13 years.
c. In 2007, Pandey hired a director of brand development to create a marketable identity for the company's products. The director devoted the entire year to this work, at a cost to the company of $125,000.

Required:

1. For each of these transactions, indicate the accounts, amounts, and effects (+ for increase and − for decrease) on the accounting equation in 2007. Use the following structure:

Item	Assets	=	Liabilities	+	Stockholders' Equity

2. For each of the intangible assets, compute amortization for the year ended December 31, 2007.

SKILLS DEVELOPMENT CASES

LO2, LO3, LO6, LO7

RESTAURANTS, INC.

S9-1 Finding Financial Information

Refer to the financial statements of Landry's Restaurants in Appendix A at the end of this book, or download the annual report from the *Cases* section of the text's Web site at www.mhhe.com/phillips2e.

Required:

1. What method of depreciation does the company use?
2. What is the amount of accumulated depreciation at the end of the current year? What percentage, rounded to one decimal place, is this of the total cost of property and equipment?
3. For depreciation purposes, what is the estimated useful life of buildings?
4. What amount of depreciation and amortization expense was reported for the current year? What percentage of total revenues, rounded to one decimal place, is it?
5. What amount did the company report for intangible assets in the current year?
6. What is the fixed asset turnover ratio for the current year (rounded to two decimal places)?
7. For each of the preceding questions, where did you locate the information?

LO2, LO3, LO6, LO7

S9-2 Comparing Financial Information

Refer to the financial statements of Outback Steakhouse in Appendix B at the end of this book, or download them from the *Cases* section of the text's Web site at www.mhhe.com/phillips2e.

Required:

1. What method(s) of depreciation does the company use?
2. What is the amount of accumulated depreciation at December 31, 2005? What percentage, rounded to one decimal place, is this of the total cost of property and equipment? Is this a larger (or smaller) percentage of the total cost of property and equipment than Landry's? What does it suggest to you about the length of time the assets have been depreciated?
3. Outback's estimated useful life of buildings differs from that estimated by Landry's. How will this affect the fixed asset turnover ratios of the two companies?
4. What amount of depreciation and amortization expense was reported for the current year? What percentage of total revenues, rounded to one decimal place, is it? Compare this percentage to that of Landry's and describe what this implies about the two companies' operations.
5. What amount, if any, did the company report for intangible assets and goodwill in the current year?
6. What is the fixed asset turnover ratio for the current year (rounded to two decimal places)? Compare this ratio to that of Landry's and describe what it implies about the operations of the two companies.

LO1, LO3, LO6, LO7

S9-3 Internet-Based Team Research: Examining an Annual Report

As a team, select an industry to analyze. Using your Web browser, each team member should access the annual report or 10-K for one publicly traded company in the industry, with each member selecting a different company. (See S1-3 in Chapter 1 for a description of possible resources for these tasks.)

Required:

1. On an individual basis, each team member should write a short report that incorporates the following:
   a. Describe the depreciation methods used.
   b. Compute the percentage of fixed asset cost that has been depreciated. What does this imply about the length of time the assets have been depreciated?
   c. Compute the fixed asset turnover ratios for the current and prior years. What does this tell you about the efficiency of the company's asset use?
   d. Describe the kinds of intangible assets, if any, that the company reports on the balance sheet.

2. Then, as a team, write a short report comparing and contrasting your companies using these attributes. Discuss any patterns across the companies that you as a team observe. Provide potential explanations for any differences discovered.

S9-4 Ethical Decision Making: A Real-Life Example   LO2, LO7

Assume you work as a staff member in a large accounting department for a multinational public company. Your job requires you to review documents relating to the company's equipment purchases. Upon verifying that purchases are properly approved, you prepare journal entries to record the equipment purchases in the accounting system. Typically, you handle equipment purchases costing $100,000 or less.

This morning, you were contacted by the executive assistant to the chief financial officer (CFO). She says that the CFO has asked to see you immediately in his office. Although your boss's boss has attended a few meetings where the CFO was present, you have never met the CFO during your three years with the company. Needless to say, you are anxious about the meeting.

Upon entering the CFO's office, you are warmly greeted with a smile and friendly hand-shake. The CFO compliments you on the great work that you've been doing for the company. You soon feel a little more comfortable, particularly when the CFO mentions that he has a special project for you. He states that he and the CEO have negotiated significant new arrangements with the company's equipment suppliers, which require the company to make advance payments for equipment to be purchased in the future. The CFO says that, for various reasons that he didn't want to discuss, he will be processing the payments through the operating division of the company rather than the equipment accounting group. Given that the payments will be made through the operating division, they will initially be classified as operating expenses of the company. He indicates that clearly these advance payments for property and equipment should be recorded as assets, so he will be contacting you at the end of every quarter to make an adjusting journal entry to capitalize the amounts inappropriately classified as operating expenses. He advises you that a new account, called Prepaid Equipment, has been established for this purpose. He quickly wraps up the meeting by telling you that it is important that you not talk about the special project with anyone. You assume he doesn't want others to become jealous of your new important responsibility.

A few weeks later, at the end of the first quarter, you receive a voicemail from the CFO stating "The adjustment that we discussed is $771,000,000 for this quarter." Before deleting the message, you replay it to make sure you heard it right. Your company generates over $8 billion in revenues and incurs $6 billion in operating expenses every quarter, but you've never made a journal entry for that much money. So, just to be sure there's not a mistake, you send an e-mail to the CFO confirming the amount. He phones you back immediately to abruptly inform you, "There's no mistake. That's the number." Feeling embarrassed that you may have annoyed the CFO, you quietly make the adjusting journal entry.

For each of the remaining three quarters in that year and for the first quarter in the following year, you continue to make these end-of-quarter adjustments. The "magic number" as the CFO liked to call it was $560,000,000 for Q2, $742,745,000 for Q3, $941,000,000 for Q4, and $818,204,000 for Q1 of the following year. During this time, you've had several meetings and lunches with the CFO where he provides you the magic number, sometimes supported with nothing more than a Post-it note with the number written on it. He frequently compliments you on your good work and promises that you'll soon be in line for a big promotion.

Despite the CFO's compliments and promises, you are growing increasingly uncomfortable with the journal entries that you've been making. Typically, whenever an ordinary equipment purchase involves an advance payment, the purchase is completed a few weeks later. At that time, the amount of the advance is removed from an Equipment Deposit account and transferred to the appropriate equipment account. This hasn't been the case with the CFO's special project. Instead, the Prepaid Equipment account has continued to grow, now standing at over $3.8 billion. There's been no discussion about how or when this balance will be reduced, and no depreciation has been recorded for it.

Just as you begin to reflect on the effect the adjustments have had on your company's fixed assets, operating expenses, and operating income, you receive a call from the vice president for internal audit. She needs to talk with you this afternoon about "a peculiar trend in the company's fixed asset turnover ratio and some suspicious journal entries that you've been making."

Required:

1. Complete the following table to determine what the company's accounting records would have looked like had you not made the journal entries as part of the CFO's special project. Comment on how the decision to capitalize amounts, which were initially recorded as operating expenses, has affected the level of income from operations in each quarter.

(amounts in millions of U.S. dollars)	Q1 Year 1 (March 31) With the Entries	Q1 Year 1 (March 31) Without the Entries	Q2 Year 1 (June 30) With the Entries	Q2 Year 1 (June 30) Without the Entries	Q3 Year 1 (September 30) With the Entries	Q3 Year 1 (September 30) Without the Entries	Q4 Year 1 (December 31) With the Entries	Q4 Year 1 (December 31) Without the Entries	Q1 Year 2 (March 31) With the Entries	Q1 Year 2 (March 31) Without the Entries
Property and equipment, net	$38,614	$	$35,982	$	$38,151	$	$38,809	$	$39,155	$
Sales revenues	8,825	8,825	8,910	8,910	8,966	8,966	8,478	8,478	8,120	8,120
Operating expenses	7,628		8,526		7,786		7,725		7,277	
Income from operations	1,197		384		1,180		753		843	

2. Using the publicly reported numbers (which include the special journal entries that you recorded), compute the fixed asset turnover ratio (rounded to two decimal places) for the periods ended Q2–Q4 of year 1 and Q1 of year 2. What does the trend in this ratio suggest to you? Is this consistent with the changes in operating income reported by the company?

3. Before your meeting with the vice president for internal audit, you think about the above computations and the variety of peculiar circumstances surrounding the "special project" for the CFO. What in particular might have raised your suspicion about the real nature of your work?

4. Your meeting with internal audit was short and unpleasant. The vice president indicated that she had discussed her findings with the CFO before meeting with you. The CFO claimed that he too had noticed the peculiar trend in the fixed assets turnover ratio, but that he hadn't had a chance to investigate it further. He urged internal audit to get to the bottom of things, suggesting that perhaps someone might be making unapproved journal entries. Internal audit had identified you as the source of the journal entries and had been unable to find any documents that approved or substantiated the entries. She ended the meeting by advising you to find a good lawyer. Given your current circumstances, describe how you would have acted earlier had you been able to foresee where it might lead you.

5. In the real case on which this one is based, the internal auditors agonized over the question of whether they had actually uncovered a fraud or whether they were jumping to the wrong conclusion. *The Wall Street Journal* mentioned this on October 30, 2002, by stating, "it was clear . . . that their findings would be devastating for the company. They worried about whether their revelations would result in layoffs. Plus, they feared that they would somehow end up being blamed for the mess." Beyond the personal consequences mentioned in this quote, describe other potential ways in which the findings of the internal auditors would likely be devastating for the publicly traded company and those associated with it.

WorldCom
Verizon

Epilogue: This case is based on a fraud committed at WorldCom (now called Verizon). The case draws its numbers, the nature of the unsupported journal entries, and the CFO's role in carrying out the fraud from a report issued by WorldCom's bankruptcy examiner. Year 1 in this case was actually 2001 and year 2 was 2002. This case excludes other fraudulent activities that contributed to WorldCom's $11 billion fraud. The 63-year-old CEO was sentenced to 25 years in prison for planning and executing the biggest fraud in the history of American business. The CFO, who cooperated in the investigation of the CEO, was sentenced to five years in prison.

S9-5 Ethical Decision Making: A Mini-Case

Assume you are one of three members of the accounting staff working for a small, private company. At the beginning of this year, the company expanded into a new industry by acquiring equipment that will be used to make several new lines of products. The owner and general manager of the company has indicated that, as one of the conditions for providing financing for the new equipment, the company's bank will receive a copy of the company's annual financial statements. Another condition of the loan is that the company's total assets cannot fall below $250,000. Violation of this condition gives the bank the option to demand immediate repayment of the loan. Before making the adjustment for this year's depreciation, the company's total assets are reported at $255,000. The owner has asked you to take a look at the facts regarding the new equipment and "work with the numbers to make sure everything stays onside with the bank."

A depreciation method has yet not been adopted for the new equipment. Equipment used in other parts of the company is depreciated using the double-declining-balance method. The cost of the new equipment was $35,000 and the manager estimates it will be worth "at least $7,000" at the end of its four-year useful life. Because the products made with the new equipment are only beginning to catch on with consumers, the company used the equipment to produce just 4,000 units this year. It is expected that, over all four years of its useful life, the new equipment will make a total of 28,000 units.

Required:

1. Calculate the depreciation that would be reported this year under each of the three methods shown in this chapter. Which of the methods would meet the owner's objective?

2. Evaluate whether it is ethical to recommend that the company use the method identified in requirement 1. What two parties are most directly affected by this recommendation? How would each party be benefited or harmed by the recommendation? Does the recommendation violate any laws or applicable rules? Are there any other factors that you would consider before making a recommendation?

S9-6 Critical Thinking: Analyzing the Effects of Depreciation Policies on Income

As an aspiring financial analyst, you have applied to a major Wall Street firm for a summer job. To screen potential applicants, the firm provides you a short case study and asks you to evaluate the financial success of two hypothetical companies that started operations on January 1, 2006. Both companies operate in the same industry, use very similar assets, and have very similar customer bases. Among the additional information provided about the companies are the following comparative income statements.

	Fast Corporation		Slow Corporation	
	2007	2006	2007	2006
Net sales	$60,000	$60,000	$60,000	$60,000
Cost of goods sold	20,000	20,000	20,000	20,000
Gross profit	40,000	40,000	40,000	40,000
Selling, general, and administrative expenses	19,000	19,000	19,000	19,000
Depreciation expense	3,555	10,667	5,000	5,000
Income from operations	17,445	10,333	16,000	16,000
Other gains (losses)	2,222	–	(1,000)	–
Income before income taxes	$ 19,667	$ 10,333	$ 15,000	$ 16,000

Required:

Prepare an analysis of the two companies with the goal of determining which company is better managed. If you could request two additional pieces of information from these companies' financial statements, describe specifically what they would be and explain how they would help you to make a decision.

LO3

www.mhhe.com/phillips2e

S9-7 Preparing Depreciation Schedules for Straight-Line and Double-Declining-Balance

To make some extra money, you've started preparing templates of business forms and schedules for others to download from the Internet (for a small fee). After relevant information is entered into each template, it automatically performs calculations using formulas you have entered into the template. For the depreciation template, you decide to produce two worksheets—one that calculates depreciation and book value under the straight-line method and another that calculates these amounts using the double-declining-balance method. The templates perform straightforward calculations of depreciation and book value, when given the cost of an asset, its estimated useful life, and its estimated residual value. These particular templates won't handle disposals or changes in estimates—you plan to create a deluxe version for those functions. To illustrate that your templates actually work, you enter the information used to produce the depreciation schedules shown in Exhibit 9.8, with Cedar Fair and Six Flags as examples.

Although you're confident you can use appropriate formulas in the spreadsheet to create a template for the straight-line method, you're a little uncertain about how to make the double-declining-balance method work. As usual, you e-mail your friend Owen for advice. Here's what he said:

From:	Owentheaccountant@yahoo.com
To:	Helpme@hotmail.com
Cc:	
Subject:	Excel Help

I wish I'd thought of charging money for showing how to do ordinary accounting activities. You'd have made me rich by now. ☺ Here's how to set up your worksheets. Begin by creating an "input values" section. This section will allow someone to enter the asset cost, residual value, and estimated life in an area removed from the actual depreciation schedule. You don't want someone accidentally entering amounts over formulas that you've entered into the schedule.

The cells from the input values section will be referenced by other cells in the depreciation schedule. You will want to enter formulas in the cells for the first year row, and then copy and paste them to rows for the other years. When doing this, you will need to use what is called an "absolute reference," which means that the cell reference does not change when one row is copied and pasted to a different row. Unlike an ordinary cell reference that has a format of A1, an absolute reference has the format of $A$1, which prevents the spreadsheet from changing either the column (A) or row (1) when copying the cell to other cells. You may find this useful when preparing both the straight-line and double-declining-balance schedules.

To create the depreciation schedules, use five columns labeled: (1) year, (2) beginning of year accumulated depreciation, (3) depreciation, (4) end of year accumulated depreciation, and (5) end of year book value.

Microsoft Excel - ss9-1.xls

File Edit View Insert Format Tools Data Window Help Acrobat

D8   =IF((C8+(($C$3-C8)*2/$C$5))>$C$3-$C$4,F7-$C$4,($C$3-C8)*2/$C$5)

	B	C	D	E	F
2	**Input Values**				
3	Cost	$ 15,500			
4	RV	$ 1,500			
5	Life	$ 7			
6					
7	Year	BOY-AD	**Depn**	EOY-AD	EOY-BV
8	1	0	$4,429	$4,429	$11,071
9	2	4,429	$3,163	$7,592	$7,908
10	3	7,592	$2,259	$9,851	$5,649
11	4	9,851	$1,614	$11,465	$4,035
12	5	11,465	$1,153	$12,618	$2,882
13	6	12,618	$823	$13,441	$2,059
14	7	13,441	$559	$14,000	$1,500

straight-line double-declining

> The double-declining-balance template will be the trickiest to create because you need to be
> concerned that the book value is not depreciated below the residual value in the last year of
> the asset's life. To force the template to automatically watch for this, you will need to use
> the IF function. I have included a screenshot of a template I created, using the IF function to
> properly calculate depreciation for all years of the asset's life. Notice the formula shown in
> the formula bar at the top.

Required:

Create the spreadsheet templates to calculate depreciation and book value using the straight-line
and double-declining-balance methods. Demonstrate that the template works by reproducing the
schedules in Exhibit 9.8.

TIP: To switch between displaying cell formulas and their values, press CTRL and ~ (tilde) at the
same time. Also, use Excel's help feature to obtain further information about the IF
function.

10

Reporting and Interpreting Liabilities

THAT WAS
THEN

Previous chapters focused on items related to the assets section of the balance sheet.

LP10

GENERAL MILLS

They've turned in the reports, and they're just waiting to hear their letter grade. They're expecting an A and would be devastated if it's a B. Sounds like some high-achieving students, right? It could be. But it's actually the Jolly Green Giant, Lucky the Leprechaun, Poppin' Fresh, and their corporate bosses at General Mills. That's right. This magically delicious company and all its characters receive a letter grade just like you and your friends. Their grading process differs a bit from yours, because their grade is assigned by credit rating agencies like Standard & Poor's, Fitch, and Moody's, indicating the company's ability to pay its liabilities on a timely basis. Another difference is that their grades can range from AAA to D. The AAA rating is given to companies in rock-solid financial condition, and the D goes to those likely to pay less than half of what they owe. In general, anything above BB is considered a good to high-quality credit rating, which is what General Mills typically earns.

In this chapter, you will learn about the accounting procedures and financial ratios used to report and interpret liabilities, and how they influence credit ratings. Although we focus on corporate reporting and analyses, this chapter also can help you to understand the kind of information others use to evaluate your own personal credit rating.

THIS IS
NOW

This chapter focuses on items related to the liabilities section of the balance sheet.

As you might suspect, liabilities are a key ingredient in credit ratings. So that's where we'll start: helping you to understand what liabilities are and how they're accounted for. You'll use this knowledge later in the chapter when learning about the financial analyses and other information used to evaluate whether a company is likely to meet its financial obligations. The organization of this chapter is shown below.

ORGANIZATION OF THE CHAPTER

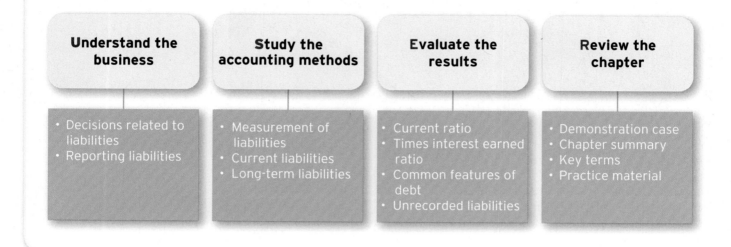

Understand the business	Study the accounting methods	Evaluate the results	Review the chapter
• Decisions related to liabilities • Reporting liabilities	• Measurement of liabilities • Current liabilities • Long-term liabilities	• Current ratio • Times interest earned ratio • Common features of debt • Unrecorded liabilities	• Demonstration case • Chapter summary • Key terms • Practice material

Understand the Business

Learning Objective 1
Explain how the reporting of liabilities assists decision makers.

DECISIONS RELATED TO LIABILITIES

When a friend asks to borrow something and promises to pay you back later, you get to experience what it's like to be a credit manager for a company. Before lending something to a friend or extending credit to another company, two questions should quickly come to mind:

1. How much does the person or company owe to others? For what?
2. Can you expect the person or company to repay each of its debts? When?

If you're a credit manager, you can usually find answers to these questions in a company's financial statements. Let's assume we are credit managers at Seneca Foods, a canned veggies supplier to Big G (that's the Wall Street nickname for General Mills). Let's see if we can answer these questions by looking at the liabilities section of the General Mills balance sheet at the end of its 2006 fiscal year, which is shown in Exhibit 10.1.

Starting with the first question, does General Mills owe anything to others? You bet! The liabilities section of the balance sheet, shown in Exhibit 10.1, indicates that General Mills owed about $11.3 billion at the end of 2006. If you knew nothing else about General Mills, you might feel uneasy about its creditworthiness because the company owes so much to others. Let's see if this feeling changes as we now move to the second question.

REPORTING LIABILITIES

When can you expect General Mills to repay its debts? The balance sheet responds to this question by classifying some liabilities as current. **Current liabilities** are short-term obligations that will be paid with current assets within the current operating cycle of the

YOU SHOULD KNOW

Current liabilities are short-term obligations that will be paid with current assets within the current operating cycle or one year, whichever is longer.

EXHIBIT 10.1 | General Mills' Liabilities

Liabilities (in millions)	2006	2005
Current liabilities		
Accounts payable	$ 1,151	$ 1,136
Accrued liabilities	1,353	1,111
Notes payable	1,503	299
Current portion of long-term debt	2,131	1,638
Total current liabilities	6,138	4,184
Long-term debt	2,415	4,255
Other liabilities	2,746	2,818
Total liabilities	11,299	11,257

business or within one year of the balance sheet date, whichever is longer. Because most companies have an operating cycle that is shorter than a year, the definition of current liabilities can be simplified as liabilities that are due within one year. This means that $6.1 billion of the $11.3 billion of total liabilities shown in Exhibit 10.1 will be paid within one year. This should make you feel a little more comfortable, particularly if you require General Mills to pay your company in one year or less. The remaining $5.2 billion of liabilities are due more than a year from the balance sheet date. Although these longer-term obligations rarely get a separate subheading of their own, people often refer to them as noncurrent or long-term liabilities.

Study the Accounting Methods

MEASUREMENT OF LIABILITIES

A company must record a liability when a transaction or event obligates the company to give up assets or services in the future. The dollar amount reported for liabilities is the result of three things:

> **Learning Objective 2**
> Explain how to account for common types of current liabilities.

1. The initial amount of the liability. A liability is initially recorded at its cash equivalent, which is the amount of cash that a creditor would accept to settle the liability immediately after the transaction or event occurred. This cash-equivalent amount excludes interest which makes sense because if you borrowed $10 from a friend and paid it back a split-second later, you wouldn't have to pay interest.

2. Additional amounts owed to the creditor. Liabilities are increased whenever a company acquires additional goods or services on credit, or interest is charged on its unpaid balances.

3. Payments or services provided to the creditor. Liabilities are reduced whenever the company makes payments or provides services to the creditor.

CURRENT LIABILITIES

Let's look more closely at each current liability listed in Exhibit 10.1.

Accounts Payable

Most companies purchase goods and services from other companies on credit. Typically, these transactions involve three stages: (1) order the goods/services, (2) receive the goods/services, and (3) pay for the goods/services. Accountants record liabilities at the stage that "obligates the company to give up assets or services." When do *you* think Big G becomes obligated to pay for the grain it buys to make Wheaties® or Cheerios®?

Video 10.1

If the grain order is never filled, General Mills wouldn't be expected to pay for it. So the receipt of goods/services is the point at which a liability is created and recorded. Like Big G, most companies call this liability "accounts payable." According to Exhibit 10.1, General Mills owes about $1.1 billion in accounts payable at the end of 2006. The great thing about using accounts payable to buy goods/services is that suppliers don't charge interest on unpaid balances unless they are overdue.

Accrued Liabilities

Often, a business incurs an expense in one accounting period and makes a cash payment in a later period. To account for these situations, an adjusting entry typically is made at the end of the first of these periods to record the expense and a liability. Chapter 4 called this an accrual adjustment, so it seems appropriate that most companies combine these types of liabilities in a single line on the balance sheet called **accrued liabilities.** Companies record accrued liabilities for various expenses, including electricity, salaries, taxes, and interest. General Mills explains in a note to its financial statements, similar to Exhibit 10.2, that its accrued liabilities include accrued salaries, taxes, and interest.

EXHIBIT 10.2	General Mills' Other Current Liabilities	GENERAL MILLS

(in millions)	2006
Accrued liabilities:	
Accrued salaries	$ 308
Accrued taxes	743
Accrued interest	152
Miscellaneous	150
Total accrued liabilities	$1,353

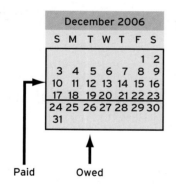

December 2006

S	M	T	W	T	F	S
					1	2
3	4	5	6	7	8	9
10	11	12	13	14	15	16
17	18	19	20	21	22	23
24	25	26	27	28	29	30
31						

Paid   Owed

Accrued Salaries   At the end of each accounting period, employees usually will have earned salaries that have not yet been paid. For example, assume General Mills paid its employees on December 23 but hadn't paid the $1,000,000 owed to them for work done during the last week of the month. To match the cost of these salaries to the period in which employees performed the work, General Mills would record an expense of $1 million on December 31. Since this amount had not been paid at December 31, the expense would be accompanied by a liability for $1 million, as shown below.

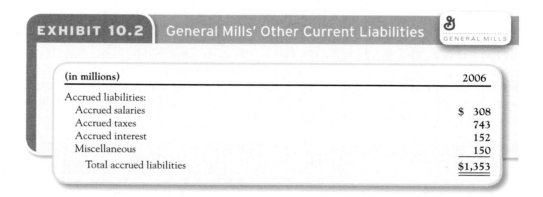

1. Analyze

Assets	=	Liabilities	+	Stockholders' Equity
		Salaries Payable +1,000,000		Salaries Expense (+E) −1,000,000

2. Record

dr Salaries Expense (+E, −SE) 1,000,000
    cr Salaries Payable (+L)   1,000,000

Along with unpaid salaries, most companies also include the cost of employment benefits promised to and earned by employees but not yet paid. These benefits include retirement programs, vacation time, and health insurance.

Accrued Payroll Taxes   A company's employment responsibilities include more than just paying employees and providing vacations and other benefits. All businesses must also account for a variety of payroll taxes including federal, state, and local income taxes, Social Security taxes, and federal and state unemployment taxes. If you've ever been an employee, you probably already know that the government requires your employer to deduct payroll taxes from your gross pay. Let's look at the two largest components of payroll taxes: employee income taxes and FICA taxes.

1. Employee income taxes withheld. The government requires employers to withhold income taxes for each employee, essentially turning employers into collection agencies for the government. The amount of income tax withheld is recorded by the employer as a current liability on the day it is deducted from employees' pay. It remains as a current liability until the company forwards that amount to the government.

2. FICA taxes withheld. FICA taxes are amounts paid for Medicare and Social Security as required by the Federal Insurance Contributions Act. In 2007, employers were required to withhold 1.45 percent from each employee's earnings for Medicare as well as 6.2 percent on earnings up to $97,500 for Social Security, and then forward these amounts to the government.

To illustrate the effects of these items, let's assume General Mills had the following information in its payroll records for the first two weeks of January:

Gross salaries and wages earned by employees	$1,800,000	
Less: Income taxes withheld from employees	275,000	} Owed to government
Less: FICA taxes withheld from employees	105,000	
Net pay to employees	$1,420,000 →	Cash paid to employees

The total salary and wages is $1,800,000, which is recorded as an expense. The biggest chunk of this cost is paid to employees ($1,420,000), with the remainder owed to the government for income taxes withheld ($275,000) or FICA withheld ($105,000). These items affect the accounting equation as shown below, and would be recorded with the journal entry that follows.

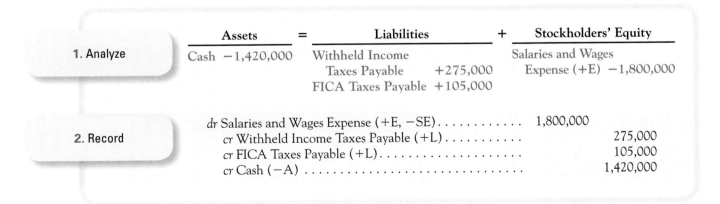

1. Analyze	Assets	=	Liabilities	+	Stockholders' Equity
	Cash −1,420,000		Withheld Income Taxes Payable +275,000		Salaries and Wages Expense (+E) −1,800,000
			FICA Taxes Payable +105,000		

2. Record

```
dr Salaries and Wages Expense (+E, −SE). . . . . . . . . . . .   1,800,000
     cr Withheld Income Taxes Payable (+L). . . . . . . . . . .                275,000
     cr FICA Taxes Payable (+L). . . . . . . . . . . . . . . . . .                105,000
     cr Cash (−A) . . . . . . . . . . . . . . . . . . . . . . . . . . .            1,420,000
```

Payroll taxes don't affect just the employees. Employers also are charged payroll taxes based on what employees are paid. For example, the FICA rate for employers is equal to that for employees. For our earlier example, this means that General Mills would be liable for $105,000 in employer FICA taxes. This represents an additional cost that would have the following financial effects, to be recorded with the journal entry shown next.

1. Analyze	Assets	=	Liabilities	+	Stockholders' Equity
			FICA Taxes Payable +105,000		Payroll Tax Expense (+E) −105,000

2. Record

dr Payroll Tax Expense (+E, −SE). 105,000
   cr FICA Taxes Payable (+L)   105,000

Notice that after the employer contribution for FICA is considered, the total payroll cost ($1,800,000 salaries and wages + $105,000 payroll tax) will be greater than the gross pay promised to employees. In reality, payroll costs are even greater than we have shown here because employers also may be required to make contributions for workers' compensation benefits and unemployment insurance.

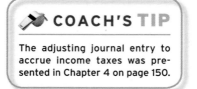

COACH'S TIP

The adjusting journal entry to accrue income taxes was presented in Chapter 4 on page 150.

Accrued Income Taxes   Corporations pay taxes not only on payroll but also on income they earn, just like you. The corporate tax return, which the IRS calls a Form 1120, is similar to the company's income statement, except that it calculates *taxable* income by subtracting tax-allowed expenses from revenues. This taxable income is then multiplied by a tax rate, which for most large corporations is about 35 percent. Corporate income taxes are due two and a half months after year-end, although most corporations are required to pay advance installments during the year.

Notes Payable

In Chapter 8, we described how a company accounts for promissory notes as Notes Receivable when it lends money to someone. In this section, you'll see things from the other side of the transaction—when a company borrows money by issuing promissory notes (Notes Payable).

To illustrate, assume that on November 1, 2007, General Mills negotiates with Citigroup to borrow $100,000 cash on a one-year note. Citigroup charges 6 percent interest, which is the normal rate at the time. Interest is to be paid by General Mills one year later, on October 31, 2008. The principal also is to be repaid on the note's October 31, 2008, maturity date. We will assume General Mills adjusts its accounting records on December 31, 2007. These events can be summarized graphically as shown in Exhibit 10.3:

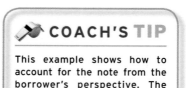

COACH'S TIP

This example shows how to account for the note from the borrower's perspective. The same example is presented on page 438 from the lender's perspective.

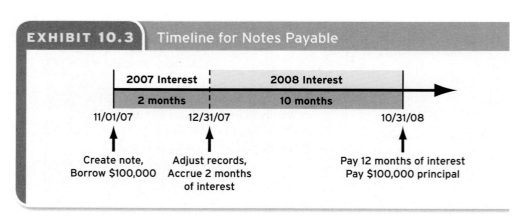

EXHIBIT 10.3   Timeline for Notes Payable

2007 Interest   2008 Interest
2 months   10 months
11/01/07   12/31/07   10/31/08

Create note,   Adjust records,   Pay 12 months of interest
Borrow $100,000   Accrue 2 months   Pay $100,000 principal
               of interest

When accounting for this note, General Mills will need to record an increase in cash when the note is created, as well as reductions in cash when interest and principal are paid to Citigroup. In addition, under the matching principle, General Mills will need to adjust its records to account for the interest incurred each accounting period. In reality, this kind of adjustment would be made by General Mills every month or quarter but, for simplicity, we've assumed it only occurs once (on December 31, 2007). Our discussion below addresses these three elements, which exist for any promissory note.

1. **The note is issued and cash is received.** When General Mills receives $100,000 cash from Citigroup on November 1, 2007, it becomes obligated to repay that amount. The financial effects are analyzed below and would be recorded with the journal entry that follows:

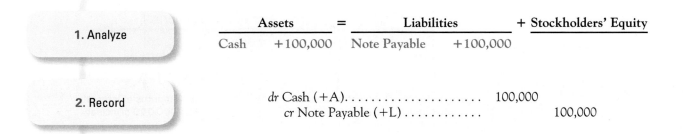

1. Analyze

	Assets	=	Liabilities	+ Stockholders' Equity
Cash	+100,000	Note Payable	+100,000	

2. Record

dr Cash (+A).   100,000
  cr Note Payable (+L)   100,000

2. **Interest is owed at the end of the accounting period.** Interest is kind of like "rent" for using someone else's money over time. Although interest accumulates continuously, it is paid periodically. Typically, interest is paid monthly or, in some cases, only once or twice per year. Rather than record the unpaid interest on each passing day, most companies record it at the end of the accounting period. These interest obligations are recorded as a current liability in an account called Interest payable or Accrued interest payable.

   When General Mills adjusts its records on December 31, 2007, it records the amount of interest incurred during the period but not yet paid. This time period is represented by the yellow shading in Exhibit 10.3. As you may recall from Chapter 8, interest is calculated using the formula:

$$\boxed{\text{Interest}} = \boxed{\text{Principal}} \times \boxed{\text{Interest Rate}} \times \boxed{\text{Time}}$$

   As of December 31, the note has been outstanding for only two months and no interest payments have been made, so the unpaid interest is $1,000 = $100,000 \times 6\% \times 2/12. Notice in these calculations that the principal is the amount owed at the beginning of the interest period, which is equal to the amount of the liability recorded in the Note payable account on November 1. The interest rate is the annual rate stated on the note, and time is the fraction of the year for which interest is being calculated (2 months out of 12).

   The financial effects of this adjustment are analzyed below and would be recorded with the adjusting journal entry that follows.

1. Analyze

Assets	=	Liabilities	+	Stockholders' Equity
		Interest Payable +1,000		Interest Expense (+E) −1,000

2. Record

dr Interest Expense (+E, −SE)   1,000
  cr Interest Payable (+L)   1,000

3. **Payments are made to the lender.** General Mills makes its interest payment on October 31, 2008, which is twelve months after the note was signed. This payment totals $6,000 (= $100,000 × 6% × 12/12). As shown on the timeline below, the $6,000 interest payment includes two months of interest ($1,000) recorded in 2007 as an expense and liability plus ten additional months of interest relating to the period from January 1 to October 31, 2008 ($5,000 = $100,000 × 6% × 10/12).

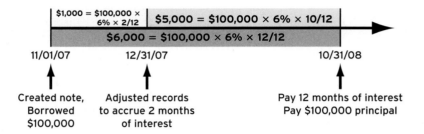

The financial effects of the $6,000 interest payment are to reduce the $1,000 interest liability recorded in 2007 and to report the $5,000 of interest relating to 2008 as an expense of 2008. These effects are analyzed below and would be recorded using the journal entry that follows:

1. Analyze

Assets	=	Liabilities	+	Stockholders' Equity	
Cash −6,000		Interest Payable −1,000		Interest Expense (+E) −5,000	

2. Record

dr Interest Payable (−L)   1,000
dr Interest Expense (+E, −SE)   5,000
    cr Cash (−A)   6,000

The principal payment of $100,000, also made on October 31, 2008, would eliminate the note payable as shown below:

1. Analyze

Assets	=	Liabilities	+ Stockholders' Equity
Cash −100,000		Note Payable −100,000	

2. Record

dr Note Payable (−L)   100,000
    cr Cash (−A)   100,000

HOW'S IT GOING? A Self-Study Quiz

Assume Starbucks issues a 5 percent, $12,000 note on December 1. How would this transaction and the month-end interest adjustment affect the accounting equation?

1. Analyze

	Assets	=	Liabilities	+	Stockholders' Equity
12/1					
12/31					

Current Portion of Long-Term Debt

Remember when you were in grade 9 and it seemed like it would be forever before you'd graduate from high school? At that time, graduation was something that would happen in the long term. Later, however, when you made it to your senior year, high school graduation had become a current event—something that was less than a year away. We remind you of this to help you understand what happens with long-term debt.

If a company borrows money with the promise to repay it in two years, the amount of the loan is classified as long-term debt. Only the accrued interest on the loan is reported as a current liability in that year's balance sheet. After a year passes, however, the loan becomes a current liability, just as your graduation became a current event. When that happens, the loan needs to be reported in the current liabilities section of the balance sheet. Accountants don't actually create a different account for this—they just take the amount of principal to be repaid in the upcoming year out of total long-term debt and report it as a current liability called Current portion of long-term debt. An example of this is given in the final line item that General Mills reports in the current liabilities section of the balance sheet in Exhibit 10.1 on page 433. Notice how, in 2006, General Mills reports a current liability for the $2.1 billion of long-term debt that was expected to be paid in 2007. Similarly, in 2005, current liabilities included $1.6 billion of long-term debt expected to be paid in 2006. This reclassification of long-term debt into current liabilities is needed so that the balance sheet accurately reports the dollar amount of existing liabilities that will be paid in the upcoming year.

HOW'S IT GOING? A Self-Study Quiz

Assume that on December 31, 2007, Blockbuster borrowed $10,000, a portion of which is to be repaid each year on November 30. Specifically, Blockbuster will make the following principal payments: 2008, $1,000; 2009, $2,000; 2010, $3,000; and 2011, $4,000. Show how this loan will be reported in the December 31, 2008 and 2007 balance sheets, assuming that principal payments will be made when required.

	As of December 31	
	2008	2007
Current liabilities:		
Current portion of long-term debt	$	$
Long-term debt		
Total liabilities	$ 9,000	$10,000

Additional Current Liabilities

Because of the nature of Big G's business, it does not report certain current liabilities that are common to other companies. In this section, we will look at two of them.

Sales Tax Payable   Retail companies are required to charge a sales tax in all but five states (Alaska, Delaware, Montana, New Hampshire, and Oregon). Retailers collect sales tax from consumers at the time of sale and forward it to the state government. Just like payroll taxes, the tax collected by the company is reported as a current liability until it is forwarded to the government. It is not an expense to the retailer because the tax is simply collected and passed on to the government. So if Best Buy sold a TV for $1,000 cash plus 5 percent sales tax, the company would earn $1,000 in sales and have a $50 liability (5% × $1,000) for the sales tax collected. The financial effects of this sale are analyzed below and would be recorded with the journal entry that follows.

1. Analyze

Assets	=	Liabilities	+	Stockholders' Equity
Cash +1,050		Sales Tax Payable +50		Sales Revenue (+R) +1,000

2. Record

dr Cash (+A).   1,050
    cr Sales Tax Payable (+L) ($1,000 × 5%)   50
    cr Sales Revenue (+R, +SE)   1,000

When Best Buy pays the sales tax to the state government, Sales tax payable would be reduced (with a debit) and Cash would be reduced (with a credit) for the amount remitted.

Unearned Revenue   Back in Chapter 4, you learned that some companies receive cash before they provide goods or services to customers. Airlines are paid in advance of providing flights, retailers receive cash for gift cards that can be used for future purchases of goods and services, and other companies receive money for subscriptions before the subscriptions begin. InterActiveCorp (IAC)—the owner of Ticketmaster and Match.com—provides an example of this. Consider what happens, for example, when IAC receives cash for subscription services to Match.com. Because IAC receives cash before providing subscription services, it initially records a liability (called Unearned revenue). This is a liability because IAC has an obligation to provide what the subscriber paid for. Therefore, as the subscription services are provided, IAC reduces this liability and reports the earned subscription fees as revenue. For example, assume that on October 1, InterActiveCorp receives cash for a three-month subscription paid in advance at a rate of $10 per month (or $30 in total). The financial effects and related journal entries occur in two stages:

1. **Receive cash and create a liability** (on October 1):

1. Analyze

Assets	=	Liabilities	+ Stockholders' Equity
Cash +30		Unearned Revenue +30	

2. Record

dr Cash (+A).   30
    cr Unearned Revenue (+L)   30

2. Fulfill part of the liability and earn revenue (on October 31):

1. Analyze	Assets	=	Liabilities	+	Stockholders' Equity
			Unearned Revenue −10		Subscription Revenue (+R) +10

2. Record	
dr Unearned Revenue (−L) 10	
cr Subscription Revenue (+R, +SE)	10

As each month passes, InterActiveCorp will make an adjustment (like the one above in step 2) to show that it has continued to fulfill its obligation and earn its subscription revenues. Don't let the tiny amounts in our examples fool you. Unearned revenues can be huge. For InterActiveCorp, they total over $120 million. That's more than the company's Accounts payable.

LONG-TERM LIABILITIES

When a company like General Mills requires significant amounts of financing to expand its business, it will either borrow money through long-term loans (debt financing) or issue more shares of stock (equity financing). We explain long-term debt financing in this section and equity financing in Chapter 11. We also discuss the pros and cons of these two types of financing in Chapter 11, after you've become a little more familiar with them.

> **Learning Objective 3**
> Analyze and record bond liability transactions.

Long-term debt financing typically is obtained in one of two ways: a private loan agreement or publicly issued debt certificates. In a private loan agreement, the borrower identifies a potential lender, such as a bank, and negotiates the terms of the loan with that lender. This is just like the notes payable that you studied in the previous section, except that this time it extends more than one year. Publicly issued debt certificates, on the other hand, are used when a company needs more money than any single lender can provide. Because several hundred (or thousand) lenders might be involved in this type of financing, the company can't possibly negotiate different loan terms with each potential lender. Instead, the borrowing process begins with the company setting standard terms that will apply to each lender. Next, the company finds interested lenders. Notice how the order of steps differs between a private loan agreement and publicly issued debt certificates. This seemingly minor difference, shown in Exhibit 10.4, will become important later when we explain how publicly issued debt works.

EXHIBIT 10.4 Two Ways to Obtain Corporate Debt Financing

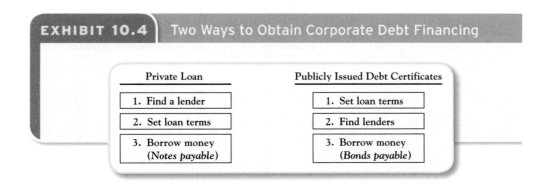

Private Loan	Publicly Issued Debt Certificates
1. Find a lender	1. Set loan terms
2. Set loan terms	2. Find lenders
3. Borrow money (Notes payable)	3. Borrow money (Bonds payable)

Since you've already learned how to account for private loans (Notes payable) and the interest that accrues on them, we'll focus this section on accounting for loans obtained through publicly issued debt. The terms of these loans, such as the interest rate and the date on which the debt is to be repaid in full (maturity date), are detailed in a document called a *bond certificate*. An example of a bond certificate is shown on page 444. Interested lenders "buy" a company's bond certificates on a bond market similar to a stock exchange. From the company's point of view, the "sale" of its bond certificates is actually the creation of a loan called Bonds payable. The company receives cash in exchange for its promise to repay the lenders according to the terms stated on the bond certificates.

Bonds Payable

Topic Tackler

PLUS

Check out www.mhhe.com/phillips2e for audio, visual, and PowerPoint presentations on this topic.

On the surface, a bond is a lot like your typical bank loan or long-term promissory note. It states the interest payments, a maturity date, and the amount that is to be paid at maturity. Interest payments typically are made once (annually) or twice a year (semiannually), but to keep things manageable, we cover only annual interest payments in this book. The amount paid at maturity, which is called the *face value*, is often $1,000 per bond certificate. To understand what the borrower will be required to pay in cash to the lender, from the day a bond is issued to the day it matures, you need to know only the interest rate, maturity date, and face value—all of which are stated on the bond certificate.

Let's look at an example. Assume that on January 1, 2007, General Mills receives $100,000 for bonds issued with a maturity date of January 1, 2011. The bonds pay $100,000 at maturity and also state an interest rate of 6 percent, which is paid each year on January 1. These bond payments can be summarized on a timeline as follows:

1/1/2007	1/1/2008	1/1/2009	1/1/2010	1/1/2011
Issue 100 bonds, $1,000 face value each	Pay 12 months of interest	Pay 12 months of interest	Pay 12 months of interest	Pay 12 months of interest
Borrow $100,000				Pay $100,000 principal

This looks a lot like the notes payable timeline in Exhibit 10.3, doesn't it? When lenders pay face value for the bonds, the accounting also is very similar.

Accounting for Bonds Issued at Face Value   Financial effects arise when (1) bonds are first issued, (2) additional amounts are owed to lenders for interest, (3) payments are made to lenders, and (4) the bond liability is paid off. In this section, we illustrate these financial effects using the General Mills bond described above as an example.

1. **Issue the bonds and receive cash.** The financial effects of the bond issuance on the borrower, General Mills, are analyzed below and would be recorded on January 1, 2007, with the journal entry that follows.

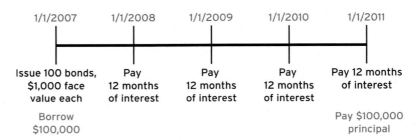

1. Analyze

Assets	=	Liabilities	+ Stockholders' Equity
Cash +100,000		Bonds Payable +100,000	

2. Record

dr Cash (+A)   100,000
  cr Bonds Payable (+L)   100,000

2. **Owe interest at the end of the accounting period.** The matching principle requires that interest expense be recorded in the period that the Bonds payable liability is outstanding. If General Mills hasn't made any entries for the bonds since January 1, 12 months of interest expense will need to be recorded for the period ended December 31, 2007. In our example, this interest isn't actually paid until January 1 of the following year, so a liability also is recorded on December 31, 2007. Interest is calculated the same way as it was for notes payable, as explained earlier in this chapter, as Principal × Rate × Time ($100,000 × 6% × 12/12 = $6,000). This interest has the following financial effects, which are recorded with the journal entry shown below.

> **COACH'S TIP**
>
> If the interest payment occurs on the same day that interest expense is recorded, journal entries 2 and 3 could be combined into one. We show them separately to remind you that interest expense is recorded even if the interest payment hasn't yet been made.

1. Analyze

Assets	=	Liabilities	+	Stockholders' Equity
		Interest Payable +6,000		Interest Expense (+E) −6,000

2. Record

dr Interest Expense (+E, −SE) 6,000
   cr Interest Payable (+L) 6,000

3. **Pay the lenders.** When General Mills pays the interest on January 1, 2008, the financial effects and related journal entry are:

1. Analyze

Assets	=	Liabilities	+ Stockholders' Equity
Cash −6,000		Interest Payable −6,000	

2. Record

dr Interest Payable (−L) 6,000
   cr Cash (−A) 6,000

The accrual of interest expense (in step 2) and recording of interest payments (in step 3) will continue until the maturity date. At maturity, the bonds will be fully repaid, with the following effects on the accounting equation that are recorded with the journal entry that follows.

1. Analyze

Assets	=	Liabilities	+ Stockholders' Equity
Cash −100,000		Bonds Payable −100,000	

2. Record

dr Bonds Payable (−L) 100,000
   cr Cash (−A) 100,000

Bonds Issued below or above Face Value   If lenders always paid **face value** to acquire a bond, you'd have this topic aced already. However, sometimes the amount of money that lenders are willing to pay up-front differs from what the borrower promises to repay at maturity. Before getting into the mechanics of accounting for this, it's useful to understand why this might occur.

The key to understanding this is to remember that the borrower sets the terms of a bond before finding interested lenders. Consequently, it is possible that the interest rate promised by the borrower (as stated on the bond certificate) differs from what lenders want to earn when lending to the company. If the borrower sets a **stated interest rate** (say 6 percent) that pays less than what lenders desire (say 8 percent), lenders won't be attracted to the bond. It's just like asking you to give up $1,000 for an entertainment system that doesn't have all the features you want. You aren't going to buy it unless (*a*) the necessary features are added, or (*b*) you're given a discount off the initial price. In the case of a bond, it's not practical to add or change its features because they've gone through a lengthy regulatory approval process and they're actually printed on the face of the bond certificate. Instead, what happens is lenders pay less money up-front to acquire the bond— they get a discount! This discount allows them to pay less up-front and still receive the full face value at maturity, which has the effect of increasing the amount they earn on the bond. From the borrowing company's point of view, this discount has the effect of increasing the interest costs incurred on the bond.

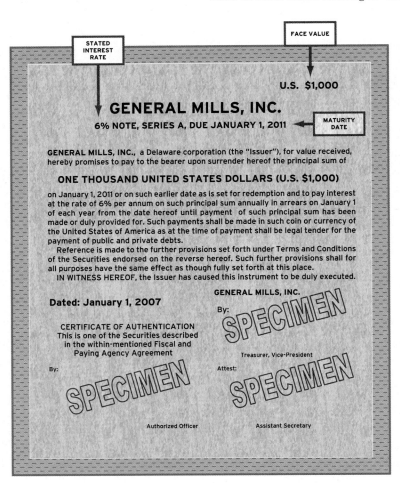

The opposite happens if bonds have features that make them *attractive* to lenders. Just as you might have to pay a premium to get tickets to popular concerts or sporting events, lenders will give up more money to acquire a bond if its interest rate (6 percent) is higher than what similar bonds in the market pay (say 4 percent). Lenders are willing to pay a premium provided that they don't have to pay so much that they'd earn less than what they expect to earn from other similarly attractive bonds. The main point here is that bonds will issue at amounts other than face value if their stated interest rate differs from the rate desired by lenders.

Before we discuss how to account for bonds issued at amounts other than face value, let's summarize some important terms. First, let's start with the things you can see on a bond certificate. The value stated on the bond is called the *face value*. For clarity, we will always use this term when referring to it, but you probably should be aware that other people use alternative terms (such as *par value*). The interest rate stated on the bond is called the *stated interest rate*. Again, we will always use this term, but alternatives exist (such as *coupon rate* or *contract rate*).

Now, instead of talking about what's written on the face of the bond, let's turn to the terms that describe its true substance. The amount that the borrower actually receives when a bond is issued is called the **issue price.** The exact amount of the issue price is determined by the lenders who decide how much they're willing to give up to acquire the bond. Theoretically, this amount is based on a mathematical calculation called a **present value,** which is discussed in Appendix C at the end of this book. Bond dealers and news reports typically quote the bond issue price as a percentage of the face value of the bond (although they don't include the percentage symbol). So a $1,000 bond issued at a price of 95 means the bond issued for 95 percent of $1,000, or $950. The interest rate that lenders in the bond market demand from a bond (and use in their present value calculations to determine the bond issue price) is called the **market interest rate.** Some people also refer to this as the *yield, discount rate,* or *effective-interest rate.* Okay, now you're ready to pull together all these terms by considering how they relate to premiums and discounts, as shown here.

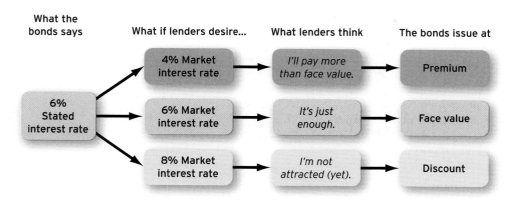

Two common questions at this point are "why would the borrower allow lenders to take a discount?" and "why would lenders be willing to pay a premium?" The answer to both of these questions is the same. The discount or premium merely is an adjustment that ensures the bond issues at an amount that is fair to both the borrower and the lenders. As a result of allowing a discount (or paying a premium), the bond will, in effect, yield the best interest rate available to both the borrower and the lenders—the rate that would emerge if the borrower and lenders were to directly negotiate the terms of the bond. Quite simply, the market interest rate is the rate the lenders would earn if they invested in bonds of other similar companies and it is the interest rate the company would incur if it were to borrow from other lenders. From the borrower's point of view, the market interest rate represents the borrower's "true" cost of borrowing.

Topic Tackler

PLUS

Check out www.mhhe.com/phillips2e for audio, visual, and PowerPoint presentations on this topic.

HOW'S IT GOING?   A Self-Study Quiz

For each of the following independent situations, indicate whether the bonds issued at a premium (P), a discount (D), or face value (FV).

1. Stated interest rate = 7% and market interest rate = 7% [ ]
2. Stated interest rate = 5% and market interest rate = 6% [ ]
3. Bond issue price = $10,100 and bond face value = $10,000. [ ]

Quiz Answers
1. FV
2. D
3. P

Accounting for Bonds Issued at a Discount   The main difference between bonds issued at a discount and bonds issued at face value is that the borrower receives less money up-front from lenders when bonds issue at a discount. The borrower still makes interest and face value payments according to the terms stated on the face of the bond. Let's look at the case where $100,000 in four-year General Mills bonds are issued, promising to pay a stated interest rate of only 6 percent when lenders expect to earn the market interest rate of 8 percent. To get the 8 percent that they expect, the lenders are willing to pay an issue price of only $93,376. That is, they've determined (by using present value calculations shown in Appendix C) that if they pay $93,376 and receive back $6,000 interest every year plus $100,000 at maturity, in effect they will earn 8 percent on the amount they've lent. The issuance of $100,000 of bonds for $93,376 cash implies a discount of $6,624 ($100,000 − $93,376). Because the borrower receives $93,376 on the date of issuance, this is the amount that in effect is owed on that day. Ultimately on the maturity date, however, the $100,000 face value will be paid. Both of these facts are taken into account when determining the accounting equation effects and the journal entry to record:

	Assets	=	Liabilities		+ Stockholders' Equity
1. Analyze	Cash +93,376		Bonds Payable	+100,000	
			Discount on Bonds Payable (+xL)	−6,624	

2. Record	dr Cash (+A).....................................	93,376
	dr Discount on Bonds Payable (+xL, −L)	6,624
	cr Bonds Payable (+L)	100,000

COACH'S TIP

Although the Discount on bonds payable is recorded with a debit, it is not an asset—it is a contra-liability, which we designate with "xL".

Notice that Bonds payable are recorded at their face value ($100,000), which is the principal amount to be paid at maturity. To show the amount effectively owed on the date the bond is first issued ($93,376), a contra-liability account called Discount on bonds payable is used. This account is deducted from the Bonds payable account on the balance sheet, as shown in Exhibit 10.5. The Bonds payable account reports the amount that General Mills will owe on the bond at maturity ($100,000), whereas the line entitled Bonds payable, net of discount (often called the *carrying value*) reports the liability based on what General Mills owed when the bond was issued. General Mills received only $93,376 when the bond issued on January 1, so that net amount is shown as a liability on that date.

EXHIBIT 10.5   Sample Balance Sheet Reporting of Bond Discount

GENERAL MILLS, INC.
Balance Sheet (excerpt)
January 1, 2007

Long-term liabilities	
Bonds payable	$100,000
Less: Discount on bonds payable	6,624
Bonds payable, net of discount	93,376

In our example, General Mills received only $93,376 when the bond was issued, but must pay back $100,000 when the bond matures. Big G will pay back more than it initially received as a way of adjusting the interest that lenders will earn. Remember that the terms of the bond were already set when the bond was issued, so the only way to adjust the lenders' interest was to discount the issue price for the bond. In effect, the discount represents additional (prepaid) interest. From the perspective of General Mills, this discount lowers the issue price, which means the borrower receives less money than it repays at maturity, thereby increasing the total cost of borrowing. In effect, General Mills incurs interest equal to 8 percent on the amount effectively borrowed ($93,376), rather than the 6 percent stated on the face of the bond.

To comply with the matching concept, this extra cost of borrowing must be matched to the periods in which the bond liability is owed. This is done each accounting period by taking an amount out of Discount on bonds payable and adding it to Interest expense of that period. This process (called *amortizing* the discount) causes the Discount on bonds payable account to slowly decline to zero over the life of the bond, which causes the carrying value of the bond to increase until it reaches face value when the bond matures. This is shown in Exhibit 10.6.

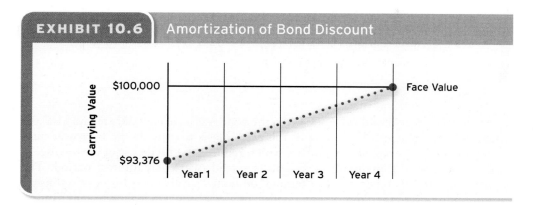

EXHIBIT 10.6 | Amortization of Bond Discount

Two different amortization methods can be used to compute and record the amount to be taken out of Discount on bonds payable and added to Interest expense: (1) straight-line, and (2) effective-interest. Generally accepted accounting principles require that the effective-interest method be used, unless the straight-line method results in numbers that are not significantly (materially) different. Some people believe that straight-line is the easier method to understand, so we present it first in Supplement A at the end of this chapter. Effective-interest (a conceptually superior method) is detailed in Supplement B. An approach that blends the simplicity of the straight-line method with the conceptual strengths of the effective-interest method is presented in Supplement C. If you've been assigned any of these supplements, don't jump to them yet. We'll tell you later when it's best to read them.

Accounting for Bonds Issued at a Premium   When a bond issues at a premium, the borrower receives the face value of the bond plus the amount of the premium. This means that, on the day of issue, the company owes more than just the face value of the bond. Let's look at the case where the market interest rate is 4 percent yet the General Mills bond states an interest rate of 6 percent. In this situation, lenders are willing to pay an issue price of $107,260 (which they've determined using present value calculations shown in Appendix C). The accounting equation effects and journal entry to record the issuance of the bond on January 1, 2007, for $107,260 are:

	Assets	=	Liabilities		+ Stockholders' Equity
1. Analyze	Cash +107,260		Bonds Payable	+100,000	
			Premium on Bonds Payable	+7,260	

2. Record	*dr* Cash (+A)	107,260	
	cr Bonds Payable (+L)		100,000
	cr Premium on Bonds Payable (+L)		7,260

The carrying value of the bond is the total of the two accounts, Bonds payable and Premium on bonds payable, as shown in Exhibit 10.7.

EXHIBIT 10.7   Sample Balance Sheet Reporting of Bond Premium

GENERAL MILLS, INC.
Balance Sheet (excerpt)
January 1, 2007

GENERAL MILLS

Long-term liabilities	
Bonds payable	$100,000
Add: Premium on bonds payable	7,260
Bonds payable, including premium	107,260

General Mills received $107,260 when the bond was issued but only repays $100,000 when the bond matures. The effect of the premium is to provide the borrower more money than what is repaid at maturity, which reduces the total cost of borrowing. As with a discount, the premium of $7,260 is spread over each interest period. This amortization process reduces both Premium on bonds payable and Interest expense in each period, causing the Premium on bonds payable account to decline to zero over the life of the bond. This also causes the carrying value of the bond to decrease until it reaches face value when the bond matures, as shown in Exhibit 10.8. Procedures that accomplish this are explained in chapter Supplements A, B, and C. At this point, read any of the chapter supplements that you have been assigned, then come back here and continue with the remainder of this section. The supplements begin on page 453.

EXHIBIT 10.8   Amortization of Bond Premium

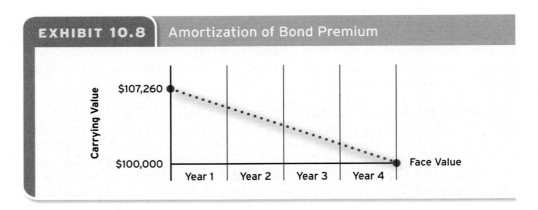

Early Retirement of Debt

Most bonds are retired (paid off) at maturity. There are some instances, however, where a company may decide to retire bonds before their maturity date. A company with lots of cash can retire debt early to reduce future interest expense, thereby increasing net income in the future. Even companies that don't have extra cash might retire bonds early, particularly if interest rates have fallen since the original bonds were issued. By issuing new bonds at the lower interest rate and using the money received from this new bond issuance to retire the old bonds before their maturity date, companies can reduce their future interest expense (which increases future earnings).

An early retirement of bonds has three financial effects: (1) cash is paid by the borrower, (2) the borrower's bond liability is eliminated, and (3) either a gain arises or a loss is incurred. Whether a gain arises or a loss is incurred depends on what the bonds are worth in the marketplace at the time of the retirement. A gain arises if the cash that must be paid to retire the bonds is less than the carrying value of the bonds. A loss is incurred if the company has to pay more than the carrying value of the bonds at the time of retirement.

To illustrate these effects, assume that in 1999, General Mills issued $1 million of bonds at face value. Nine years later, in 2008, the headlines of *The Wall Street Journal* report that the bonds are retired early at 103, requiring a payment of $1,030,000 ($1 million × 103%). The debt retirement causes the following financial effects, which would be recorded with the journal entry shown below:

	Assets	=	Liabilities	+	Stockholders' Equity
1. Analyze	Cash −1,030,000		Bonds Payable −1,000,000		Loss on Bonds Retired (+E) −30,000

2. Record

dr Bonds Payable (−L) 1,000,000
dr Loss on Bonds Retired (+E, −SE) 30,000
    cr Cash (−A) 1,030,000

There are two things to note about the example above. First, the loss on bond retirement would be reported on the income statement with other gains and losses, somewhere between Income from operations and Income before income taxes. Second, our example doesn't involve removing a bond discount or bond premium account because we have assumed the bonds were issued at face value. For bonds that are issued below or above face value, any premium or discount balance existing at the time of retirement would be removed as well.

Now that you have seen how liabilities are accounted for inside a company, let's consider them again from the outside. How do users judge whether liabilities are likely to be repaid in full?

Evaluate the Results

When evaluating the ability of another person or company to pay you, a great place to start is with credit reports issued by credit rating agencies. However, credit raters don't report on everyone (particularly smaller companies). Even if they did, their reports might be too general and not address your specific concerns. So you really need to understand how to analyze a set of financial statements yourself in the same way a credit rater would. Essentially, you're going to assess whether the company has the assets available to pay what it currently owes, and whether the company is likely to generate the resources needed to pay future amounts owed. Two financial ratios commonly used to make these assessments are the current ratio and the times interest earned ratio.

Learning Objective 4
Interpret the current ratio and the times interest earned ratio.

FINANCIAL ANALYSIS TOOLS		
Name of Measure	**Formula**	**What It Tells You**
Current ratio	$\dfrac{\text{Current Assets}}{\text{Current Liabilities}}$	• Whether current assets are sufficient to pay current liabilities • A higher ratio means greater ability to pay
Times interest earned ratio	$\dfrac{(\text{Net Income} + \text{Interest Expense} + \text{Income Tax Expense})}{\text{Interest Expense}}$	• Whether sufficient resources are generated to cover interest costs • A higher number means greater coverage

CURRENT RATIO

You might recall from Chapter 5 that one measure, called the Debt-to-Assets ratio, indicates the proportion of total assets that are financed by total liabilities. This provided a measure of a company's *solvency,* which is the ability to pay amounts in the long run. The **current ratio** is a complementary measure that is commonly used to evaluate **liquidity,** which is the ability to pay liabilities as they come due in the short run. Specifically, the current ratio measures whether the company has enough current assets to pay its current liabilities. Generally speaking, a high ratio suggests good liquidity. An old rule of thumb was that companies should have a current ratio between 1 and 2. Today, many successful companies use sophisticated management techniques to minimize the funds invested in current assets and, as a result, have current ratios below 1.

General Mills is a company that minimizes what it holds in current assets. As shown in Exhibit 10.9, its total current assets are less than its total current liabilities, which makes its ratio less than one ($3,176 ÷ 6,138 = 0.52). For many companies, a ratio less than one can be a significant concern. It's not a big deal for General Mills because as explained in its financial statement notes, the company's operating activities generate nearly $5 million in cash each day. Plus, the company has arranged a **line of credit** with banks that provides cash on an as-needed basis. Rather than hold extra cash to enhance its liquidity, General Mills can use its line of credit to borrow only when money is actually needed.

EXHIBIT 10.9	General Mills' Current Assets and Current Liabilities

(in millions)	2006	2005
Assets		
Current assets		
Cash	$ 647	$ 573
Receivables, less allowance for doubtful accounts	1,076	1,034
Inventories	1,055	1,037
Prepaid expenses and other current assets	398	411
Total current assets	3,176	3,055
Liabilities		
Current liabilities		
Accounts payable	$1,151	$1,136
Other current liabilities	1,353	1,111
Notes payable	1,503	299
Current portion of long-term debt	2,131	1,638
Total current liabilities	6,138	4,184

Ethical Insights

Doctoring the Current Ratio

Although the current ratio can be a useful measure of a company's ability to pay liabilities, analysts need to be aware that it can be influenced by entering into seemingly normal transactions just before the end of an accounting period. For example, if the current ratio is less than one, it can be improved by purchasing inventory on account just prior to the financial statement date. If the ratio is greater than one, it can be improved by paying down accounts payable just prior to the date of the financial statements. Whether these actions are considered ethical depends on whether they are done for legitimate business reasons or solely to manipulate the perceptions of external users.

TIMES INTEREST EARNED RATIO

By studying how (and when) accountants report interest owed on debt, you now know that liabilities do not include all of the future interest payments that will be made on existing liabilities. Liabilities include only the unpaid interest for periods leading up to the balance sheet date. This means that the current ratio and any other ratios based on recorded liabilities don't tell you much about whether the company will be able to make future interest payments. One way to judge a company's future ability to pay interest is to analyze whether, in the past, it has generated enough income to cover its interest expense. Barring huge changes, the past can be a fair predictor of the future. The measure that most analysts use for this is the **times interest earned ratio.**

Look back to the formula for the times interest earned ratio in the Financial Analysis Box on page 449. Notice that the ratio adds interest and income tax expenses back into net income. The reason for this is fairly simple. We want to know whether the company generates enough income before the costs of financing and taxes to cover its interest expense. The way to determine this is to add these expenses back into net income. In general, a high times interest earned ratio is viewed more favorably than a low ratio. A high ratio indicates an extra margin of protection in the event that future profitability declines.

To illustrate the calculation of the times interest earned ratio, we provide a condensed version of the General Mills income statement to the right. For 2006, the top number in the ratio is calculated by adding interest expense ($399) and income tax expense ($541) back into net income ($1,090) and dividing the result ($2,030 = $1,090 + 399 + 541) by interest expense ($399). The result is a times interest earned ratio of 5.09 ($2,030 ÷ $399), which means that Big G generates more than enough income to cover its interest expense—over $5 of income (before the costs of financing and taxes) for each dollar of interest expense.

Every now and then you'll see a times interest earned ratio that is less than one or it might even be a negative number. When the times interest earned ratio is less than one, the company is not generating enough income to cover its interest expense. This is a big problem. Most companies survive only a couple of years like this before declaring bankruptcy.

GENERAL MILLS
Income Statement
For the years 2006 and 2005

GENERAL MILLS

(in millions)	2006	2005
Net sales	$11,640	$11,244
Expenses:		
Cost of sales	6,966	6,834
Selling, general, and administrative	2,644	2,051
Interest, net	399	455
Total expenses	10,039	9,340
Income before income taxes	1,631	1,904
Income tax expense	541	664
Net income	$ 1,090	$ 1,240

2006 Times Interest Earned Ratio:

(Net income + interest expense + income tax expense) ÷ Interest expense = ($1,090 + $399 + $541) ÷ $399 = 5.09

HOW'S IT GOING?　　　　　　A Self-Study Quiz

Balance sheet and income statement information for General Mills is reported in Exhibit 10.9 on page 450 and above.

1. Calculate the current ratio and times interest earned (TIE) ratios for General Mills in 2005. Round to two decimal places.

2005 Current Ratio:

$$\frac{\boxed{}}{\boxed{}} = \boxed{}$$

2005 Times Interest Earned Ratio:

$$\frac{\boxed{} + \boxed{} + \boxed{}}{\boxed{}} = \boxed{} \text{ times}$$

2. If you were a credit analyst evaluating the company's 2006 financial situation, would you say General Mills is more or less likely to pay its liabilities than in the prior year (2005)?

Quiz Answers
1. Current ratio: 0.73 = $3,055 ÷ $4,184
   TIE ratio: 5.18 = ($1,240 + 455 + 664) ÷ 455
2. Both the current ratio and the times interest earned ratio declined in 2006, suggesting that the company is less likely to pay its liabilities than in 2005.

COMMON FEATURES OF DEBT

Salty, sweet, crunchy, and chewy are adjectives that describe snacks that Big G sells (at a rate of four products every second from vending machines in the United States).[2] These adjectives are useful because they describe differences among the products, which help us to choose the products we want. In the same way, various adjectives are used to describe key terms in a debt agreement (e.g., secured, callable, convertible), which help creditors and borrowers choose the loan terms they want. We explain some of the more important ones below.

To reduce the risk of a loan, a lender can require a borrower to offer specific assets as security to the lender. This simply means that if the borrower does not satisfy its liability, the lender may take ownership of the assets used as security. A liability supported by this type of agreement is called a *secured debt*. Most car loans and house loans require you to offer your car or house as security for the loan. Some lenders are willing to loan money without security (called *unsecured debt*), but they typically demand a higher interest rate in return for taking on this extra risk. Another tactic that reduces risk is to allow lenders to revise loan terms (e.g., demand immediate repayment of the loan) if certain ratios, calculated using the borrower's financial statements, get out of whack. Escape hatches like these, which are common in many lending agreements, are called *loan covenants*. Borrowers report significant loan covenants in their financial statement notes. Exhibit 10.10 lists these and other common loan terms along with explanations of them.

EXHIBIT 10.10 | **Explanations of Important Loan Terms**

Loan Terms	What They Mean	Effects
Security	Security guarantees that the borrower's assets will be given to the lender if the borrower doesn't pay.	Reduces risk to lenders, making them willing to accept a lower interest rate.
Loan covenants	Conditions that, if violated, allow the lender to renegotiate loan terms.	Reduces risk to lenders, making them willing to accept a lower interest rate.
Seniority	Debt designated as "senior" is paid first in the event of bankruptcy, followed by "subordinated" debt.	Reduces risk to senior lenders, making them willing to accept a lower interest rate.
Convertibility	Gives the lender an option to accept the borrower's stock as payment for the outstanding loan.	Gives greater control to lenders, reducing their risk and making them willing to accept a lower interest rate.
Callability	Gives the borrower control over the decision to fully repay the lender before the loan's maturity date.	Gives greater control to borrowers, causing lenders to demand a higher interest rate.

Ethical Insights

Hide and Seek Isn't a Game

Hide and seek was fun to play as a kid. But when the executives at Enron used it as their guide to financial reporting, the fun ended. Investors, creditors, auditors, and practically everyone else in the business world has been affected by the Enron scandal that erupted in 2001. What exactly did Enron executives do wrong? Well, a lot of things. To understand precisely what they did, you'll need to take advanced courses in financial accounting. At a very simple level, however, one of their biggest offenses was to "hide" debt owed by the company. In essence, the company didn't report all of its true liabilities.

---

[1] General Mills, Inc., *2001 Annual Report*

UNRECORDED LIABILITIES

As a result of Enron, everyone in the business world has become much more sensitive to financial commitments that aren't reported on the balance sheet. As you will learn in this section, fraud isn't the only reason a company has unrecorded liabilities. In some cases, the accounting rules themselves actually require that certain liabilities *not* be reported on the balance sheet. We'll briefly introduce one topic (contingent liabilities) where accounting rules can lead to unrecorded liabilities. You will learn about other instances of these off-balance-sheet liabilities in intermediate accounting textbooks.

A **contingent liability** is a potential liability (and loss) that arises as a result of past transactions or events, but the company is unable to determine whether it actually will be liable (or for what amount) until a future event occurs or fails to occur. The most common example of this is a lawsuit. Until it becomes clear that the company is liable and at what amount, the contingent liability and potential loss are reported only in the company's notes to the financial statements. As you might expect, the actual accounting rules don't use loosey-goosey language like "until it becomes clear." Instead, they refer to the likelihood that the company will be found liable and whether the amount of liability and loss is estimable (let's just pretend that's a real word). Exhibit 10.11 tells you all you need to know for now about accounting for contingent liabilities.

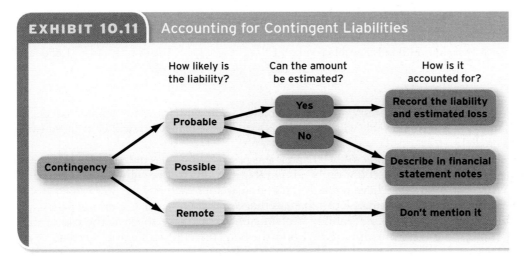

EXHIBIT 10.11 | Accounting for Contingent Liabilities

In closing, we'll remind you that these unrecorded liabilities aren't illegal or unethical. In fact, good accounting requires that they remain unrecorded, at least until there's a reliable basis for recording them. Some companies are so up-front about potentially significant unrecorded liabilities that they even direct you to them by including a line item in the balance sheet (following the liabilities section) called "commitments and contingencies," which often references an explanatory note to the financial statements. Because these potential liabilities haven't been recorded in the accounting records, the line item consists only of the name, without corresponding dollar amounts. It may look odd at first, but just think of it as a friendly reminder to consider potentially significant (but currently unrecorded) liabilities. The balance sheet of Landry's Restaurants provides a good example of this (in Appendix A at the end of the book).

SUPPLEMENT A: STRAIGHT-LINE AMORTIZATION

STRAIGHT-LINE AMORTIZATION OF A BOND DISCOUNT

Earlier in the chapter, we described how, when a bond is issued at a discount, lenders provide the borrower less money than what is repaid at maturity, which increases the cost of borrowing above the interest rate stated on the bond. For example, if $100,000 in bonds were issued for $93,376, the discount of $6,624 ($100,000 − $93,376) is an additional cost of borrowing, over and above the 6 percent annual interest stated on the face of the bond. To comply with the matching concept, this extra cost of borrowing must be matched to the periods in which the bond liability is owed. This is done each accounting period by taking an amount out of Discount on bonds payable and adding it to Interest expense of that period.

The **straight-line method of amortization** spreads this additional cost equally over the life of the bond. In our example, the bond matures in four years. Thus, the amount amortized in each period would be $6,624 ÷ 4 = $1,656. We add this amount to the promised interest payment ($6,000) to compute interest expense for the period ($7,656). The accounting equation effects and journal entry for recording interest on the bond on December 31, using the straight-line method of amortization, are

	Assets	=	Liabilities		+	Stockholders' Equity	
1. Analyze			Interest Payable	+6,000		Interest Expense (+E)	−7,656
			Discount on Bonds Payable (−xL)	+1,656			

2. Record

dr Interest Expense (+E, −SE) ($6,000 + $1,656) 7,656
    cr Interest Payable (+L) ($100,000 × 6% × 12/12) 6,000
    cr Discount on Bonds Payable (−xL, +L) 1,656

When the $6,000 interest payment is actually made, which in our example occurs on January 1, Interest Payable will be reduced (with a debit) and Cash will be reduced (with a credit).

As shown graphically in the chapter, this process continues until the bond matures, at which point the Discount on bonds payable account will be fully amortized to zero. While you probably believe us on this, it's often useful to actually see how it happens. In Exhibit 10A.1, we summarize the changes that occur *during* each accounting period and how they affect the bond liability accounts on the balance sheet at the *end* of each period. You can see in Exhibit 10A.1 how the bond discount (column E) decreases each period by $1,656 after recording the amount of amortization (column B).

EXHIBIT 10A.1 | Bond Discount Amortization Schedule (Straight-Line)

	CHANGES DURING THE PERIOD			ENDING BOND LIABILITY BALANCES		
Period Ended	(A) Interest Payable	(B) Amortization of Discount	(C) (= A + B) Interest Expense	(D) Bonds Payable	(E) Discount on Bonds Payable	(F) (= D + E) Bonds Payable, Net of Discount
01/01/07	—	—	—	100,000	6,624	93,376
12/31/07	6,000	1,656	7,656	100,000	4,968	95,032
12/31/08	6,000	1,656	7,656	100,000	3,312	96,688
12/31/09	6,000	1,656	7,656	100,000	1,656	98,344
12/31/10	6,000	1,656	7,656	100,000	0	100,000

Recorded each period with the following entry:

dr Interest Expense (+E, −SE). . . . . (C)
    cr Interest Payable (+L) . . . . (A)
    cr Discount on Bonds Payable
      (−xL, +L) . . . . (B)

Reported at the end of each period on the balance sheet:

Liabilities:
Bonds payable (D)
Less: Discount on bonds payable (E)
Bonds payable, net of discount (F)

STRAIGHT-LINE AMORTIZATION OF A BOND PREMIUM

As with a discount, whenever a premium exists ($7,260 in our earlier example), it must be spread over each interest period. Using the straight-line method, the amortization of premium each year is $7,260 ÷ 4 periods = $1,815. This amount is subtracted from the interest that will be paid ($6,000) to calculate the amount of interest expense to report each period ($4,185). Notice that by amortizing the premium in this way, the company's interest expense is less than its interest payment each period, which is consistent with our earlier comment that a premium has the effect of reducing the cost of borrowing below the stated interest rate that appears on the bond certificate.

For this bond premium example, the accounting equation effects and journal entry for recording interest on December 31 is:

1. Analyze

Assets	=	Liabilities		+	Stockholders' Equity	
		Premium on Bonds Payable	−1,815		Interest Expense (+E)	−4,185
		Interest Payable	+6,000			

2. Record

dr Interest Expense (+E, −SE) 4,185
dr Premium on Bonds Payable (−L) 1,815
    cr Interest Payable (+L) 6,000

When the $6,000 interest payment is made on January 1, Interest payable will be reduced (with a debit) and Cash will be reduced (with a credit). Notice that the $6,000 interest payment each period is made up of $4,185 interest expense and $1,815 premium amortization. In other words, the payment includes interest expense for the current period plus a return of part of the premium that lenders paid when they first bought the bonds.

In Exhibit 10A.2, we present a bond amortization schedule that summarizes the changes that occur *during* each interest period and how they affect the bond liability accounts on the balance sheet at the *end* of each period. Notice that the Premium on bonds payable (column E) decreases each period by $1,815 after recording the amount of amortization (column B), ultimately reaching zero at the end of the bond's four-year life.

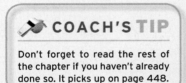

COACH'S TIP

Don't forget to read the rest of the chapter if you haven't already done so. It picks up on page 448.

EXHIBIT 10A.2 Bond Premium Amortization Schedule (Straight-Line)

	CHANGES DURING THE PERIOD			ENDING BOND LIABILITY BALANCES		
Period Ended	(A) Interest Payable	(B) Amortization of Premium	(C) (= A − B) Interest Expense	(D) Bonds Payable	(E) Premium on Bonds Payable	(F) (= D + E) Bonds Payable, Including Premium
01/01/07	—	—	—	100,000	7,260	107,260
12/31/07	6,000	1,815	4,185	100,000	5,445	105,445
12/31/08	6,000	1,815	4,185	100,000	3,630	103,630
12/31/09	6,000	1,815	4,185	100,000	1,815	101,815
12/31/10	6,000	1,815	4,185	100,000	0	100,000

Recorded each period with the following entry:

dr Interest Expense (+E, −SE) . . . . (C)
dr Premium on Bonds Payable (−L) . . . . (B)
    cr Interest Payable (+L) . . . . (A)

Reported at the end of each period on the balance sheet:

Liabilities:
Bonds payable   (D)
Add: Premium on bonds payable   (E)
Bonds payable, including premium   (F)

SUPPLEMENT B: EFFECTIVE-INTEREST AMORTIZATION

The **effective-interest method** is considered a conceptually superior method of accounting for bonds because it correctly calculates interest expense by multiplying the true cost of borrowing times the amount of money actually owed to lenders. The true cost of borrowing is the market interest rate that lenders used to determine the bond issue price. The actual amount owed to lenders is the carrying value of the bond, which equals the cash received when the bond was issued plus any interest costs that haven't been paid.

To clearly understand the effective-interest method, it helps to see how a bond's issue price depends on the market interest rate. As we mentioned in the chapter, lenders decide how much to pay for a bond by using a mathematical calculation called a *present value*. You can read instructions about how to calculate present values in Appendix C at the end of this book, but for now just focus on understanding what a present value is. Present value is the idea that something is worth more if you get it today than if you get it some time in the future. For example, if someone offered to pay you $100,000 today or $100,000 five years from now, you'd be better off taking it today. You could invest the money and earn interest for five years, making it worth way more than $100,000. The same idea explains why you could be equally happy with receiving $100,000 in five years or some smaller amount today. To figure out how much this smaller amount is, you just calculate the present value of $100,000. The only pieces of information you need for this calculation are (1) the amounts to be received in the future, (2) the number of months between now and then, and (3) the interest rate you expect to earn during that time.

In the bond context, lenders get some of this information from the face of the bond and then they determine how much to pay for the bond by calculating the present value of the amounts paid periodically (as interest) and at maturity (as face value), using the interest rate that they want to earn. We have summarized this calculation in Exhibit 10B.1 for General Mills' 6 percent, four-year bond described in the chapter. We show three different scenarios, with each one involving different market interest rates but the same 6 percent stated interest rate. The first column calculates the amount of money that lenders would be willing to give up if they needed to earn 4 percent on the amount they pay for the bond. The second column calculates the amount lenders would pay if they wanted to earn an interest rate of 6 percent. The third column calculates the amount that lenders would be willing to pay if they wanted to earn 8 percent on the amount they pay for the bond. (For detailed calculations underlying the amounts in Exhibit 10B.1, see Appendix C at the end of the book.)

EXHIBIT 10B.1 | Computing the Present Value of Bond Payments

	MARKET INTEREST RATES		
	4%	6%	8%
Present value of $100,000 face value (principal) paid four years from now	$ 85,480	$ 79,210	$73,500
Present value of $6,000 (interest) paid once a year for four years	21,780	20,790	19,876
Amount to pay	$107,260	$100,000	$93,376

Notice that when the bond pays interest at a rate that exactly matches the rate expected by lenders in the market (6 percent), they are willing to pay face value for it. If the 6 percent interest rate stated on the bond is more than lenders expect (4 percent), they pay a premium for the bond (as shown in the first column). If the 6 percent interest promised is less than the market interest rate (8 percent), lenders pay less than face value for the bond, resulting in a discount as suggested in the third column. Let's now look at what happens to a bond discount and premium under the effective-interest amortization method.

EFFECTIVE-INTEREST AMORTIZATION OF A BOND DISCOUNT

When a company issues a bond at a discount, it receives less money up-front than it repays at maturity. This creates a true cost of borrowing that is greater than the interest rate stated on the face of the bond. In other words, the true interest expense is greater than the interest paid. Under the effective-interest method, this extra (unpaid) interest is added to the bond liability each period—a process known as amortizing the bond discount.

Let's continue the bond discount example presented earlier in the chapter. We had already recorded the issuance of bonds that stated a face value of $100,000 along with an annual interest rate of 6 percent paid on January 1 each year. The bonds were issued for $93,376, which implied a discount of $6,624 and a market interest rate of 8 percent.

Although the actual interest payment isn't made until January 1, the company has to record interest expense at the end of each year on December 31. Interest expense for the year is calculated by multiplying the amount actually borrowed by the market interest rate for the year ($93,376 × 8% × 12/12 = $7,470). The promised interest payment was indicated on the face of the bond as the face value times the stated interest rate for a full year ($100,000 × 6% × 12/12 = $6,000). The difference between the interest expense and the promised interest payment is the amount of discount that is amortized ($7,470 − $6,000 = $1,470). The accounting equation effects and journal entry for recording them on December 31, 2007, are:

> **COACH'S TIP**
>
> Because the promised interest payment is less than the interest expense, the bond liability will increase (by reducing the contra-liability).

1. Analyze

Assets =	Liabilities		+	Stockholders' Equity	
	Discount on Bonds Payable (−xL)	+1,470		Interest Expense (+E)	−7,470
	Interest Payable	+6,000			

2. Record

dr Interest Expense (+E, −SE)	7,470	
cr Discount on Bonds Payable (−xL,+L)		1,470
cr Interest Payable (+L)		6,000

When the $6,000 interest payment is made on January 1, 2008, Interest payable will be reduced (with a debit) and Cash will be reduced (with a credit).

The T-account presented in the margin shows how the above journal entry reduces the balance of the Discount on bonds payable account. A reduction of this contra-liability account increases the carrying value of the long-term liability, as you can see by moving from left to right in Exhibit 10B.2.

Discount on Bonds Payable (xL)

1/1/07	6,624		
		1,470	12/31/07
12/31/07	5,154		

EXHIBIT 10B.2 Sample Balance Sheet Reporting of Bond Discount

GENERAL MILLS, INC.
Balance Sheet (excerpt)

	January 1, 2007	December 31, 2007
Long-term liabilities		
Bonds payable	$100,000	$100,000
Less: Discount on bonds payable	6,624	5,154
Bonds payable, net of discount	93,376	94,846

Let's now consider the interest expense for 2008. As in 2007, the 2008 interest expense is calculated using the market interest rate. However, the amount of bonds payable actually owed at the end of 2007 increased, as shown in Exhibit 10B.2. Thus, interest expense also will increase, calculated as the unpaid balance on December 31, 2007, of $94,846 (see Exhibit 10B.2) times the market interest rate for the full year ($94,846 × 8% × 12/12 = $7,587 rounded). The difference between the 2008 interest expense ($7,587) and the promised cash payment ($6,000) is the amount of discount that is amortized ($1,587 = $7,587 − $6,000) in 2008. That is, because the true interest expense ($7,587) is greater than the promised payment ($6,000), the bond liability is increased (by reducing the contra-liability). This is reflected in the accounting equation and recorded with the journal entry on December 31 as follows:

COACH'S TIP

The interest expense for 2008 is greater than that for 2007 because the carrying value of Bonds payable was greater in 2008 than in 2007.

1. Analyze

Assets	=	Liabilities	+	Stockholders' Equity
		Discount on Bonds (−xL) +1,587		Interest Expense (+E) −7,587
		Interest Payable +6,000		

2. Record

dr Interest Expense (+E, −SE)...................... 7,587
  cr Discount on Bonds Payable (−xL, +L)............   1,587
  cr Interest Payable (+L)........................   6,000

Again, when the $6,000 interest payment is made on January 1, Interest payable will be reduced (with a debit) and Cash will be reduced (with a credit).

Some companies use a bond amortization schedule to summarize the detailed computations required under the effective-interest amortization method. A typical schedule is presented in Exhibit 10B.3. The paragraph following the exhibit describes how to read the schedule.

EXHIBIT 10B.3   Bond Discount Amortization Schedule (Effective-Interest)

	CHANGES DURING THE PERIOD			ENDING BOND LIABILITY BALANCES		
Period Ended	(A) Interest Expense	(B) Interest Payable	(C) (= A − B) Amortization of Discount	(D) Bonds Payable	(E) Discount on Bonds Payable	(F) (= D − E) Bonds Payable, Net of Discount
01/01/07	—	—	—	100,000	6,624	93,376
12/31/07	7,470	6,000	1,470	100,000	5,154	94,846
12/31/08	7,587	6,000	1,587	100,000	3,567	96,433
12/31/09	7,715	6,000	1,715	100,000	1,852	98,148
12/31/10	7,852	6,000	1,852	100,000	0	100,000

Recorded each period with the following entry:

dr Interest Expense (+E, −SE)................. (A)
  cr Interest Payable (+L) ....   (B)
  cr Discount on Bonds Payable
    (−xL, +L)............................   (C)

Reported at the end of each period on the balance sheet:

Liabilities:
Bonds payable   (D)
 Less: Discount on bonds payable   (E)
Bonds payable, net of discount   (F)

The amortization schedule begins, in the first row, with the balance in Bonds payable (column D, $100,000) and Discount on bonds payable (column E, $6,624) on the date of the bond issuance. The carrying value reported on the balance sheet as Bonds payable, net of discount (column F, $93,376) is computed by subtracting the $6,624 discount from the $100,000 face value. This carrying value is then multiplied by the market interest rate for the full year ($93,376 × 8% × 12/12) to calculate interest expense for the first year (column A, $7,470). The interest to be paid (column B, $6,000) is computed by multiplying the face value of the bond by its stated interest rate for 12 months ($100,000 × 6% × 12/12). The amount of discount amortization (column C, $1,470) is computed by subtracting the promised interest payment of $6,000 (column B) from the interest expense of $7,470 (column A). The amount of discount amortization ($1,470) is subtracted from the previous balance in the Discount on bonds payable (column E; $6,624) to arrive at a new balance ($5,154), which is subtracted from the face value (column D, $100,000) to compute a new carrying value for the bonds (column F, $94,846). This new carrying value at the end of the first year (12/31/07) becomes the starting point for calculating interest expense in the following year. Take a moment right now to ensure you can calculate the amounts in Exhibit 10B.3 for the period ended 12/31/08. If you need help getting started, see the coach's tip.

COACH'S TIP

The interest expense for 12/31/08 is calculated as the carrying value at the beginning of the year (which is the $94,846 at 12/31/07) times the market interest rate (8%) for the full year (12/12). That is, $94,846 × 8% × 12/12 = $7,587 rounded.

EFFECTIVE-INTEREST AMORTIZATION OF A BOND PREMIUM

The effective-interest method is applied in the same way for a premium as it was for a discount. Interest expense is computed by multiplying the current unpaid balance times the market interest rate for the length of the interest period. The amount of the bond premium to amortize is then calculated as the difference between interest expense and the cash interest payment promised on the bond. Let's use our earlier example of a bond premium to illustrate. The example involved 6 percent bonds with a face value of $100,000 issued when the market interest rate was 4 percent. The issue price of the bonds was $107,260, so the bond premium was $7,260.

The interest expense at the end of the year is calculated by multiplying the amount actually owed times the market interest rate for the full year ($107,260 × 4% × 12/12 = $4,290). The promised interest payment is calculated by multiplying the face value by the stated interest rate for the full year ($100,000 × 6% × 12/12 = $6,000). The difference between the interest expense and the promised interest payment is the amount of premium that is amortized ($6,000 − $4,290 = $1,710). The accounting equation effects and required journal entry are shown below.

COACH'S TIP

Notice that, for each interest period, the borrower will pay more than its true cost of borrowing. The extra amount included in each payment goes to reducing the total bond liability (by reducing the premium).

	Assets	=	Liabilities		+	Stockholders' Equity	
1. Analyze			Premium on Bonds Payable	−1,710		Interest Expense (+E)	−4,290
			Interest Payable	+6,000			

2. Record

dr Interest Expense (+E, −SE)	4,290	
dr Premium on Bonds Payable (−L)	1,710	
cr Interest Payable (+L)		6,000

When the $6,000 interest payment is made on January 1, Interest payable will be reduced (with a debit) and Cash will be reduced (with a credit). Notice in the example above that the promised interest payment ($6,000) is greater than the interest expense ($4,290), so the bond premium decreases. This illustrates the basic difference between effective-interest amortization of a bond premium versus a bond discount. Amortization of a premium reduces the carrying value of the liability whereas the amortization of a discount increases it. An amortization schedule for our premium example is provided in Exhibit 10B.4. We completed the first two annual interest periods and left the last two for you to complete as part of the Self-Study Quiz that follows.

COACH'S TIP

Don't forget to read the rest of the chapter if you haven't already done so. It picks up on page 448.

EXHIBIT 10B.4 | Bond Premium Amortization Schedule (Effective-Interest)

	CHANGES DURING THE PERIOD			ENDING BOND LIABILITY BALANCES		
Period Ended	(A) Interest Expense	(B) Interest Payable	(C) (= B − A) Amortization of Premium	(D) Bonds Payable	(E) Premium on Bonds Payable	(F) (= D + E) Bonds Payable, Including Premium
01/01/07	—	—	—	100,000	7,260	107,260
12/31/07	4,290	6,000	1,710	100,000	5,550	105,550
12/31/08	4,222	6,000	1,778	100,000	3,772	103,772
12/31/09	☐	☐	☐	☐	☐	☐
12/31/10	☐	☐	☐	☐	☐	☐

Recorded each period with the following entry:

dr Interest Expense (+E, −SE).................	(A)	
dr Premium on Bonds Payable (−L).............	(C)	
cr Interest Payable (+L)		(B)

Reported at the end of each period on the balance sheet:

Liabilities:
Bonds payable   (D)
Add: Premium on bonds payable   (E)
Bonds payable, including premium   (F)

HOW'S IT GOING?   A Self-Study Quiz

Complete the bond premium amortization schedule in Exhibit 10B.4 for the periods ended 12/31/09 and 12/31/10.

SUPPLEMENT C: SIMPLIFIED EFFECTIVE-INTEREST AMORTIZATION

The approach shown in this supplement presents a simplified explanation of how to account for bond liabilities and interest expense. You should be aware that this approach involves taking a shortcut. While the shortcut will help you to focus on the line items that ultimately are reported on the financial statements, it requires that we ignore a few accounts that are typically used behind the scenes in real-world accounting systems. Be sure to check with your instructor (or course outline) to see whether you are expected to read this supplement.

If you're like most people, you probably have to concentrate really hard when reading about how a *reduction* in a contra-liability account causes an *increase* in the carrying value of a bond. You may even whisper this thought quietly to yourself a few times before it starts making sense. In this section, we present a shortcut when accounting for bonds that will allow you to avoid thinking in "double-negatives" like this. Hopefully it will also help you to stop whispering to yourself when you read.

The shortcut involves simplifying only one aspect of what you studied earlier in this chapter. Rather than record a discount or premium in a separate account, we will combine it with the bonds payable in an account that we will call *Bonds payable, net.* This name is used to remind you that we are focusing on what is ultimately reported in the financial statements rather than what is actually used behind the scenes. This shortcut greatly simplifies how we account for the initial bond issuance, interest owed and paid to the lenders, and removal of the bond liability at maturity.

ACCOUNTING FOR BONDS ISSUED BELOW FACE VALUE

Initial Bond Issuance

Let's illustrate with the example from the chapter in which General Mills issued bonds on January 1, 2007, for $93,376 cash. The accounting equation effects and journal entry relating to this transaction are:

1. Analyze

Assets	=	Liabilities	+ Stockholders' Equity
Cash +93,376		Bonds Payable, Net +93,376	

2. Record

dr Cash (+A)   93,376
    cr Bonds Payable, Net (+L)   93,376

Rather than record the Bonds payable at face value ($100,000), with an offsetting Discount on bonds payable account (of $6,624), we have combined them together in an account called Bonds payable, net (resulting in $93,376).

With this simplified approach, we still describe bonds as being issued at a discount or premium because the recorded liability is either less or greater than the face value. What has changed, though, is that we no longer need a separate discount or premium account to adjust from the face value to the true liability. Instead, the liability is reported directly in Bonds payable, net.

> **COACH'S TIP**
>
> If this example were to involve bonds issued at a premium, the same journal entry would be used, just with a different amount ($107,260 for the bond premium example described in the chapter).

Interest Owed and Paid

Interest Owed   One of the advantages of this simplified approach is that we no longer choose between the straight-line or effective-interest method of amortization because there is no discount or premium account to amortize. An additional advantage is that interest expense is calculated directly, using an interest formula similar to what you learned earlier:

| Interest | = | Amount Owed | × | Interest Rate | × | Time |

The amount owed is the cash that was received when the bond was issued plus any unpaid interest cost. With the simplified approach, the amount owed is the balance in the Bonds payable, net, account at the beginning of the interest period. The rate of interest is the market interest rate that was used to determine the present value of the bond when it was issued.

Let's illustrate by recording interest owed for the first annual interest period ended December 31, 2007. The amount owed at the beginning of this period is the $93,376 reported in the Bonds payable, net, account on January 1, 2007. From this, we calculate the interest expense as:

$93,376 (amount owed) × 8% (market interest rate) × 12/12 (time)
    = $7,470 (Interest expense)

This interest expense differs from what General Mills actually promised to pay. From the face of the bond we can calculate the amount of interest to be paid for this period as

> $100,000 (face value) × 6% (stated interest rate) × 12/12 (time)
> = $6,000 (interest payment)

COACH'S TIP

Recording the $1,470 in Bonds Payable, Net, is appropriate because General Mills will pay this amount at maturity, as part of the face value of the bond.

Notice that General Mills is going to pay only $6,000 when its interest expense is $7,470. Because the company pays less than the cost of interest, its Bonds payable, net, liability will increase by the amount of interest expense that won't be paid this interest period ($1,470 = $7,470 − $6,000). The accounting equation effects and required journal entry on December 31, 2007, are shown below.

1. Analyze

Assets	=	Liabilities		+	Stockholders' Equity	
		Interest Payable	+6,000		Interest Expense (+E)	−7,470
		Bonds Payable, Net	+1,470			

2. Record

dr Interest Expense (+E, −SE)   7,470
    cr Interest Payable (+L)   6,000
    cr Bonds Payable, Net (+L)   1,470

Interest Paid   The interest payment on January 1, 2008, would have the following accounting equation effects, which would be recorded with the journal entry shown below.

1. Analyze

Assets		=	Liabilities		+	Stockholders' Equity
Cash	−6,000		Interest Payable	−6,000		

2. Record

dr Interest Payable (−L)   6,000
    cr Cash (−A)   6,000

Let's continue to look at the financial effects of the bond in the following year.

Bonds Payable, Net (L)		
	93,376	1/1/07
	1,470	12/31/07
	94,846	1/1/08

Interest Owed   Once again, Interest expense is calculated by multiplying the amount owed at the beginning of the interest period times the market interest rate for the year. The amount owed at the beginning of 2008 is shown in the T-account in the margin. After the $1,470 was added to the Bonds payable, net account on December 31, 2007, the amount owed increased to $94,846. From this, we can calculate the Interest expense for 2008 as

> $94,846 (amount owed) × 8% (market interest rate) × 12/12 (time) = $7,587

The amount of interest payable is based on what General Mills actually promised to pay ($6,000). Notice that General Mills is going to pay only $6,000 when its Interest expense is $7,587. Because the interest payment is less than the cost of interest, the company increases Bonds payable, net, liability by the difference ($1,587 = $7,587 − $6,000).

The accounting equation effects and required journal entry on December 31, 2008, are shown below.

	Assets	=	Liabilities		+	Stockholders' Equity	
1. Analyze			Interest Payable	+6,000		Interest Expense (+E)	−7,587
			Bonds Payable, Net	+1,587			

2. Record

dr Interest Expense (+E, −SE) 7,587
   cr Interest Payable (+L)   6,000
   cr Bonds Payable, Net (+L)   1,587

Interest Paid   As before, when Big G pays interest on January 1, 2009, the accounting equation effects and required journal entry are:

	Assets		=	Liabilities		+	Stockholders' Equity
1. Analyze	Cash	−6,000		Interest Payable	−6,000		

2. Record

dr Interest Payable (−L) 6,000
   cr Cash (−A)   6,000

Interest expense and interest payments will continue as long as the bonds remain outstanding, although the amount of Interest expense will change as the Bonds payable, net, balance changes.

In Exhibit 10C.1, we present a bond amortization schedule that summarizes the balance in Bonds payable, net, at the beginning of each interest period (column A), the

COACH'S TIP

The interest expense for 2008 is greater than that for 2007 because the balance in Bonds payable, net was greater in 2008 than 2007.

EXHIBIT 10C.1   Bond Amortization Schedule (Simplified Effective-Interest)

BEGINNING OF PERIOD		CHANGES DURING THE PERIOD			END OF PERIOD	
Period	(A) Bonds Payable, Net	(B) = (A) × 8% × 12/12 Interest Expense	(C) Interest Payable	(D) = (B) − (C) Interest Added to Bonds Payable	(E) = (A) + (D) Bonds Payable, Net	
1/1/07-12/31/07	93,376	7,470	6,000	1,470	94,846	Reported on
1/1/08-12/31/08	94,846	7,587	6,000	1,587	96,433	the balance
1/1/09-12/31/09	96,433	7,715	6,000	1,715	98,148	sheet at the
1/1/10-12/31/10	98,148	7,852	6,000	1,852	100,000	end of each period.

Recorded during each period with the following entry:

dr Interest Expense (+E, −SE) . . . .   (B)
   cr Interest Payable (+L) . . . .   (C)
   cr Bonds Payable, Net (+L) . . . .   (D)

changes that occur during each interest period (columns B, C, and D), and the Bonds payable, net, balance at the *end* of each period (column E). Notice in column E that as the bonds approach maturity, the Bonds payable, net, account approaches the face value of the bonds.

The amortization schedule begins, in the first row, with the balance in Bonds payable, net, immediately after the bond issuance. Interest expense (column B) is calculated by multiplying the amount owed at the beginning of the interest period (column A) times the market interest rate times the length of period. Interest payable (column C) is calculated as the face value times the stated interest rate times the length of period. Unpaid interest (column D) is the difference between the interest expense (column B) and the interest payment that will be made (column C). The ending balance in Bonds payable, net (column E) is the beginning balance (column A) plus the unpaid interest (column D). The ending balance for one year (column E) then becomes the beginning balance for the next year (column A), which is the starting point for calculating interest expense in that year.

ACCOUNTING FOR BONDS ISSUED ABOVE FACE VALUE

When a bond issues at a premium, interest expense and interest payments are accounted for in a manner similar to that shown in the previous section for a bond issued at a discount. The only difference is that because a premium reduces the cost of borrowing, interest expense is less than the promised cash payment for each interest period. The extra amount included in each payment goes to paying down Bonds payable, net. To illustrate, we extend the bond premium example introduced earlier in the chapter, which involved a four-year bond (with a face value of $100,000 and stated interest rate of 6%) that was issued at a price of $107,260. This price implies a market interest rate of 4%, so the Interest expense for the first year is $4,290 ($107,260 × 4% × 12/12). The stated interest payment for the year is $6,000 ($100,000 × 6% × 12/12), which is greater than the Interest expense of $4,290. The extra $1,710 included in the payment represents a repayment of the bond liability, which has the following accounting equation effects that would be recorded with the journal entry shown below.

Assets	=	Liabilities		+	Stockholders' Equity	
1. Analyze		Interest Payable	+6,000		Interest Expense (+E)	−4,290
		Bonds Payable, Net	−1,710			

2. Record

dr Interest Expense (+E, −SE) 4,290
dr Bonds Payable, Net (−L) 1,710
    cr Interest Payable (+L) 6,000

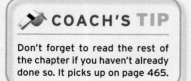

COACH'S TIP

Don't forget to read the rest of the chapter if you haven't already done so. It picks up on page 465.

When the $6,000 interest payment is made on January 1, Interest payable will be reduced (with a debit) and Cash will be reduced (with a credit). And as we saw before, these entries to record interest expense and interest payments will continue each period until the bond matures or is retired early.

REVIEW THE CHAPTER

DEMONSTRATION CASE A: ACCRUED LIABILITIES AND UNEARNED REVENUE

Online Games, Inc. reported the following information in its accounting records on December 31, 2007.

Annual subscription payments received in December 2007 for 2008 services	$12,000
Gross salaries earned by employees (12/26–12/31)	3,600
Income taxes withheld from employees (12/26–12/31)	550
FICA taxes withheld from employees (12/26–12/31)	210
Net payment to employees	2,840

The 2008 subscription payments will be earned equally throughout each month of 2008. The employees were paid $2,840 on December 31, 2007, but the withholdings have not yet been remitted nor have the matching employer FICA contributions.

Required:

1. Describe how the 2008 subscription payments should be reported in the balance sheet and income statement on (a) December 31, 2007, and (b) January 31, 2008.
2. Show the accounting equation effects and give the journal entries for (a) the receipt of annual subscription payments in December 2007, and (b) any required adjustments for the subscription payments on January 31, 2008.
3. Compute the total payroll costs relating to the period from December 26–31, 2007.
4. Show the accounting equation effects and give the journal entry on December 31, 2007, to adjust for payroll costs relating to December 26–31, 2007.

Suggested Solution

1. a. On December 31, 2007, the $12,000 of advanced subscription payments would be reported on the balance sheet as a current liability called Unearned revenue. No amounts relating to payments for 2008 subscriptions would be reported in the 2007 income statement.
   b. On January 31, 2008, one month of subscription services would be earned, so the Unearned revenue account on the balance sheet would be reduced by $1,000 (= $12,000 × 1/12) and the Subscription revenue account on the income statement would be increased by $1,000.

2. a. December 2007 (receipt of 2008 subscription payments):

Assets	=	Liabilities	+	Stockholders' Equity
Cash +12,000		Unearned revenue +12,000		

dr Cash (+A) 12,000
  cr Unearned revenue (+L) 12,000

   b. January 31, 2008 (earned one month of 2008 subscriptions):

Assets	=	Liabilities	+	Stockholders' Equity
		Unearned revenue −1,000		Subscription revenue (+R) +1,000

dr Unearned revenue (−L) 1,000
  cr Subscription revenue (+R, +SE) 1,000

3. Computation of total payroll costs:

Employee:	Net pay to employees	$2,840
	Income taxes withheld from employees	550
	FICA taxes withheld from employees	210
	Total cost of salaries and wages	3,600
Employer:	FICA taxes (matching contribution)	210
	Total employee and employer costs	$ 3,810

4. <u>Employee-related payroll costs:</u>

Assets	=	Liabilities	+	Stockholders' Equity
Cash −2,840		Withheld income taxes payable +550 FICA taxes payable +210		Salaries and wages expense (+E) −3,600

```
dr Salaries and wages expense (+E, −SE). . . . . . . . . . . . . .   3,600
    cr Withheld income taxes payable (+L). . . . . . . . . . . .           550
    cr FICA taxes payable (+L) . . . . . . . . . . . . . . . . . . . . .           210
    cr Cash (−A) . . . . . . . . . . . . . . . . . . . . . . . . . . . . .         2,840
```

<u>Employer-related payroll costs:</u>

Assets	=	Liabilities	+	Stockholders' Equity
		FICA taxes payable +210		Payroll tax expense (+E) −210

```
dr Payroll tax expense (+E, −SE) . . . . . . . . . . .   210
    cr FICA taxes payable (+L). . . . . . . . . . . . . .         210
```

DEMONSTRATION CASE B: NOTES PAYABLE AND ACCRUED INTEREST

On June 30, 2006, Caterpillar Inc. had $24.3 billion in current assets and $21.1 billion in current liabilities. On August 3, 2006, Caterpillar received $500 million when it issued promissory notes that will mature in 2016. The notes pay interest on February 15 at the annual rate of 6.05 percent, which was comparable to other interest rates available in the market. Caterpillar's fiscal year ends on December 31.

Required:

1. Describe which sections of Caterpillar's classified balance sheet are affected by its issuance of promissory notes.
2. Give the journal entry on August 3, 2006, to record the issuance of the notes.
3. Give the journal entry on December 31, 2006, to record interest expense, assuming none had been accrued prior to that date.
4. Give the journal entry on February 15, 2007, to record the first interest payment.
5. Compute Caterpillar's current ratio at June 30, 2006.
6. Assume that, as of December 31, 2006, Caterpillar had not yet used the cash from the issuance of notes on August 3, 2006. What is the effect, if any, of the note issuance on the company's current ratio at the end of its fiscal year?

Suggested Solution

1. The issuance of notes increases Caterpillar's cash (a current asset) and its notes payable (a long-term liability) by $500 million.
2. August 3, 2006 (issuance date):

```
dr Cash (+A). . . . . . . . . . . . . . . . . . . . . . . . . . . . . . . . . . . .   500,000,000
    cr Notes Payable (+L) . . . . . . . . . . . . . . . . . . . . . . . . . . . . .         500,000,000
```

3. December 31, 2006 (accrual of interest expense for 5 months):

```
dr Interest Expense (+E, −SE) ($500,000,000 × 6.05% × 5/12). .   12,604,167
    cr Interest Payable (+L) . . . . . . . . . . . . . . . . . . . . . . . . . . . . .         12,604,167
```

4. February 15, 2007 (first interest payment date):

```
dr Interest Expense (+E, −SE) ($500,000,000 × 6.05% × 1.5/12)    3,781,250
dr Interest Payable (−L) . . . . . . . . . . . . . . . . . . . . . . . . . . . . .   12,604,167
    cr Cash (−A) ($500,000,000 × 6.05% × 6.5/12). . . . . . . . . .         16,385,417
```

5.   June 30, 2006 current ratio = Current assets ÷ Current Liabilities

$$= 24{,}300{,}000{,}000 \div 21{,}100{,}000{,}000 = 1.15$$

6.   December 31, 2006 current ratio = Current assets ÷ Current Liabilities

$$= (24{,}300{,}000{,}000 + 500{,}000{,}000)$$
$$\div (21{,}100{,}000{,}000 + 12{,}604{,}167) = 1.17$$

The issuance of the notes increases the current ratio, because the cash from the notes increased current assets by $500 million, but the only increase in current liabilities was a relatively small amount of interest payable. The $500 million in notes payable increased long-term liabilities.

DEMONSTRATION CASE C: BONDS PAYABLE

To raise funds to build a new plant, Reed Company issued bonds with the following terms:

Face value of the bonds: $100,000.
Dates: Issued January 1, 2007; due in 5 years on January 1, 2012.
Interest rate: 6 percent per year, payable on January 1 each year.

The bonds were issued on January 1, 2007, at 104.3, implying a 5 percent market rate of interest. The annual accounting period for Reed Company ends on December 31.

Required:

1.   How much cash did Reed Company receive from the issuance of the bonds? Show computations.
2.   What was the amount of premium on the bonds payable? Over how many months should it be amortized?
3.   Show the accounting equation effects and give the journal entry on January 1, 2007, for recording the issuance of the bonds.
4.   (Supplement A) Show the accounting equation effects and give the journal entry required on December 31, 2007, relating to interest on the bond. Use the straight-line amortization method.
5.   (Supplement B) Show the accounting equation effects and give the journal entry required on December 31, 2007, relating to interest on the bond. Use the effective-interest amortization method.
6.   (Supplement C) Show the accounting equation effects and give the journal entries required on January 1, 2007, relating to the bond issuance and on December 31, 2007, relating to interest on the bond. Use the simplified effective-interest amortization method.

Suggested Solution

1.   Sale price of the bonds: $100,000 × 104.3% = $104,300.
2.   Premium on the bonds payable: $104,300 − $100,000 = $4,300.

Months amortized: From date of issue, January 1, 2007, to maturity date, January 1, 2012
= 5 years × 12 months per year = 60 months.

3.   January 1, 2007 (issuance date):

Assets		=	Liabilities		+	Stockholders' Equity
Cash	+104,300		Bonds Payable	+100,000		
			Premium on			
			Bonds Payable	+4,300		

dr Cash (+A).   104,300
    cr Premium on Bonds Payable (+L).   4,300
    cr Bonds Payable (+L)   100,000

4. December 31, 2007 (interest accrual):

Assets	=	Liabilities		+	Stockholders' Equity	
		Interest Payable	+6,000		Interest Expense (+E)	−5,140
		Premium on				
		Bonds Payable	−860			

dr Premium on Bonds Payable (−L) ($4,300 × 12/60 months)   860
dr Interest Expense (+E, −SE) ($6,000 − $860).   5,140
   cr Interest Payable (+L) ($100,000 × 6% × 12/12)   6,000

5. December 31, 2007 (interest accrual):

Assets	=	Liabilities		+	Stockholders' Equity	
		Interest Payable	+6,000		Interest Expense (+E)	−5,215
		Premium on				
		Bonds Payable	−785			

dr Interest Expense (+E, −SE) ($104,300 × 5% × 12/12)   5,215
dr Premium on Bonds Payable (−L) ($6,000 − $5,215)   785
   cr Interest Payable (+L) ($100,000 × 6% × 12/12)   6,000

6. January 1, 2007 (issuance date):

Assets		=	Liabilities		+	Stockholders' Equity
Cash	+104,300		Bonds Payable, Net	+104,300		

dr Cash (+A)   104,300
   cr Bonds Payable, Net (+L)   104,300

December 31, 2007 (interest accrual):

Assets	=	Liabilities		+	Stockholders' Equity	
		Interest Payable	+6,000		Interest Expense (+E)	−5,215
		Bonds Payable, Net	−785			

dr Interest Expense (+E, −SE) ($104,300 × 5% × 12/12)   5,215
dr Bonds Payable, Net (−L) ($6,000 − $5,215)   785
   cr Interest Payable (+L) ($100,000 × 6% × 12/12)   6,000

CHAPTER SUMMARY

LO1   **Explain how the reporting of liabilities assists decision makers. p. 432**

- Liabilities report any probable future sacrifices of economic benefits that arise from past transactions. Examples include accounts payable, accrued liabilities, notes payable, and bonds payable.

- Liabilities are classified as current if due to be paid with current assets within the current operating cycle of the business or within one year of the balance sheet date (whichever is longer). All other liabilities are considered long term.

LO2   **Explain how to account for common types of current liabilities. p. 433**

- Liabilities are initially reported at their cash equivalent value, which is the amount of cash that a creditor would accept to settle the liability immediately after the transaction or event occurred.

- Liabilities are increased whenever additional obligations arise (including interest) and are reduced whenever the company makes payments or provides services to the creditor.

LO3   **Analyze and record bond liability transactions. p. 441**

- For most public issuances of debt (bonds), the amount borrowed by the company does not equal the amount repaid at maturity. The effect of a bond discount is to provide the borrower less money than the value stated on the face of the bond, which increases the cost of borrowing above the interest rate stated on the bond. The effect of a bond premium is to provide the borrower more money than repaid at maturity, which decreases the cost of borrowing below the stated interest rate.

- Interest expense reports the cost of borrowing, which equals the periodic interest payments plus (or minus) the amount of the bond discount (or premium) amortized in that interest period.

Interpret the current ratio and times interest earned ratio. p. 449   LO4

- The current ratio measures liquidity, which is the company's ability to pay its current liabilities using its current assets.
- The times interest earned ratio measures a company's ability to meet its interest obligations with resources generated from its profit-making activities.

Describe the additional liabilities information reported in the notes to the financial statements. p. 452   LO5

- The notes to the financial statements describe specific features of debt as well as significant financial commitments, such as contingent liabilities.
- A contingent liability is a potential liability (and loss) that has arisen as a result of a past transaction or event. Its ultimate outcome will not be known until a future event occurs or fails to occur.

Financial Analysis Tools		
Name of Measure	Formula	What It Tells You
Current ratio	$\dfrac{\text{Current Assets}}{\text{Current Liabilities}}$	• Whether current assets are sufficient to pay current liabilities • A higher ratio means greater ability to pay
Times interest earned ratio	$\dfrac{\text{(Net Income + Interest Expense + Income Tax Expense)}}{\text{Interest Expense}}$	• Whether sufficient resources are generated to cover interest costs • A higher number means greater coverage

KEY TERMS

Accrued Liabilities p. 434
Contingent Liability p. 453
Current Liabilities p. 432
Current Ratio p. 450
Discount p. 445
Effective-Interest Method
  (Supplement B) p. 456

Face Value p. 444
Issue Price p. 444
Line of Credit p. 450
Liquidity p. 450
Market Interest Rate p. 445
Premium p. 445
Present Value p. 444

Stated Interest Rate p. 444
Straight-Line Method
  (Supplement A) p. 454
Times Interest Earned Ratio p. 451

PRACTICE MATERIAL

QUESTIONS

1. Define *liability*. What's the difference between a current liability and a long-term liability?
2. What three factors influence the dollar amount reported for liabilities?
3. Define *accrued liability*. Give an example of a typical accrued liability.

4. Why is unearned revenue considered a liability?

5. Why are payroll taxes and sales taxes considered liabilities?

6. If a company has a long-term loan that has only two years remaining until it matures, how is it reported on the balance sheet (*a*) this year, and (*b*) next year?

7. What are the reasons that some bonds are issued at a discount and others are issued at a premium?

8. Why are publicly issued debt certificates more likely to involve a discount or premium than a private debt agreement?

9. What is the difference between the stated interest rate and the market interest rate on a bond?

10. Will the stated interest rate be higher than the market interest rate or will the market interest rate be higher than the stated interest rate when a bond is issued at (*a*) face value, (*b*) a discount, and (*c*) a premium?

11. What is the carrying value of a bond payable?

12. What is the current ratio? How is it related to the classification of liabilities?

13. What is the difference between a secured and an unsecured loan? Which type carries more risk for the lender?

14. What is a contingent liability? How is a contingent liability reported?

15. (Supplement A) How is interest expense calculated using the straight-line method of amortization for a bond issued at (*a*) a discount and (*b*) a premium?

16. (Supplement B) How is interest expense calculated using the effective-interest method of amortization for a bond issued at (*a*) a discount and (*b*) a premium?

17. (Supplement C) How is interest expense calculated using the simplified approach to the effective-interest method for a bond issued at (*a*) a discount and (*b*) a premium?

MULTIPLE CHOICE

Topic Tackler

PLUS

Quiz 10

Check out www.mhhe.com/phillips2e for more multiple choice questions.

1. Which of the following best describes *accrued liabilities?*

   a. Long-term liabilities.

   b. Current amounts owed to suppliers of inventory.

   c. Expenses incurred, but not paid at the end of the accounting period.

   d. Revenues that have been collected, but not earned.

American Greetings Corporation

2. As of February 28, 2006, American Greetings Corporation had 9,700 full-time and 19,800 part-time employees. Assume that in the last pay period of the year, the company paid $8,000,000 to employees after deducting $2,000,000 for employee income taxes, $612,000 for FICA taxes, and $700,000 for other payroll taxes. No payments have been made to the government relating to these taxes. Which of the following statements is true regarding this pay period?

   a. FICA taxes payable is $612,000.

   b. FICA taxes payable is $1,224,000.

   c. Salaries and wages expense is $6,000,000.

   d. None of the above is true.

Warnaco Group Inc.

3. Assume that Warnaco Group Inc., the makers of Calvin Klein underwear, borrowed $100,000 from the bank to be repaid over the next five years, with principal payments beginning next month. Which of the following best describes the presentation of this debt in the balance sheet as of today (the date of borrowing)?

   a. $100,000 in the long-term liability section.

   b. $100,000 *plus* the interest to be paid over the five-year period in the long-term liability section.

   c. A portion of the $100,000 in the current liability section, and the remainder of the principal in the long-term liability section.

   d. A portion of the $100,000 plus interest in the current liability section, and the remainder of the principal plus interest in the long-term liability section.

4. Assume that Speedo International received $400,000 for long-term promissory notes that were issued on November 1. The notes pay interest on April 30 and October 31 at the annual rate of 6 percent, which was comparable to other interest rates in the market at that time. Which of the following journal entries would be required at December 31?

   a. *dr* Interest Expense 4,000
       cr Interest Payable   4,000

   b. *dr* Interest Expense 4,000
       cr Cash   4,000

   c. *dr* Interest Expense 4,000
       dr Interest Payable 8,000
       cr Cash   12,000

   d. *dr* Interest Expense 8,000
       dr Interest Payable 4,000
       cr Cash   12,000

Speedo International

5. Which of the following does not impact the calculation of the cash interest payments to be made to bondholders?
   a. Face value of the bond.
   b. Stated interest rate.
   c. Market interest rate.
   d. The length of time between payments.

6. Which of the following is false when a bond is issued at a premium?
   a. The bond will issue for an amount above its face value.
   b. Interest expense will exceed the cash interest payments.
   c. The market interest rate is lower than the stated interest rate.
   d. The issue price will be quoted at a number greater than 100.

7. When the company that borrows money by issuing a bond has the right to terminate a relationship with a lender early and repay the amount borrowed ahead of schedule, we say that the loan is
   a. Convertible
   b. Secured
   c. Amortizable
   d. Callable

8. To determine if a bond will be issued at a premium, discount, or at face value, one must know which of the following pairs of information?
   a. The face value and the stated interest rate on the date the bonds were issued.
   b. The face value and the market interest rate on the date the bonds were issued.
   c. The stated interest rate and the market interest rate on the date the bonds were issued.
   d. You can't tell without having more information.

9. For the year ended December 31, 2005, Land O' Lakes, Inc., reported income from operations of $83,665, net income of $128,943, interest expense of $79,873, and income tax expense of $5,505. What was this dairy company's times interest earned ratio (rounded) for the year?
   a. 0.62
   b. 1.61
   c. 2.04
   d. 2.68

Land O' Lakes, Inc.

10. Big Hitter Corp. is facing a class-action lawsuit in the upcoming year. It is possible, but not probable, that the company will have to pay a settlement of approximately $2,000,000 in the upcoming year. How would this fact be reported, if at all, in the financial statements to be issued at the end of the current month?
    a. Report $2,000,000 as a current liability.
    b. Report $2,000,000 as a long-term liability.
    c. Describe the potential liability in the notes to the financial statements.
    d. Reporting is not required in this case.

Solutions to Multiple Choice Questions
1. c 2. b 3. c 4. a 5. c 6. b 7. d 8. c 9. d 10. c

MINI-EXERCISES

LO2

M10-1 Recording Unearned Revenues

A local theater company sells 1,500 season ticket packages at a price of $250 per package. The first show in the five-show season starts this week. Show the accounting equation effects and prepare the journal entries related to (a) the sale of the season tickets before the first show and (b) the revenue earned after putting on the first show.

LO2

Ahlers Clocks

M10-2 Recording Sales and State Tax

Ahlers Clocks is a retailer of wall, mantle, and grandfather clocks and is located in the Empire Mall in Sioux Falls, South Dakota. Assume that a grandfather clock was sold for $5,000 cash plus 4 percent sales tax. The clock had originally cost Ahlers $3,000. Show the accounting equation effects and prepare the journal entry related to this transaction. Assume Ahlers uses a perpetual inventory system, as explained in Chapter 6.

LO2

M10-3 Calculating Payroll Tax Liabilities

Lightning Electronics is a midsize manufacturer of lithium batteries. The company's payroll records for the November 1–14 pay period show that employees earned wages totaling $100,000 but that employee income taxes totaling $14,000 and FICA taxes totaling $5,250 were withheld from this amount. The net pay was directly deposited into the employees' bank accounts. What was the amount of net pay? What amount would be reported as the total payroll costs for this pay period? Consider both employee and employer payroll taxes.

LO2

M10-4 Reporting Payroll Tax Liabilities

Refer to M10-3. Prepare the journal entry or entries that Lightning would use to record the payroll. Include both employee and employer taxes.

LO2

M10-5 Reporting Current and Noncurrent Portions of Long-Term Debt

Assume that on December 1, 2008, your company borrowed $14,000, a portion of which is to be repaid each year on November 30. Specifically, your company will make the following principal payments: 2009, $2,000; 2010, $3,000; 2011, $4,000; and 2012, $5,000. Show how this loan will be reported in the December 31, 2009 and 2008 balance sheets, assuming that principal payments will be made when required.

LO2

M10-6 Recording a Note Payable

Greener Pastures Corporation borrowed $1,000,000 on November 1, 2007. The note carried a 6 percent interest rate with the principal and interest payable on June 1, 2008. Show the accounting equation effects and prepare the journal entries for (a) the note issued on November 1 and (b) the interest accrual on December 31.

LO2

M10-7 Reporting Interest and Long-Term Debt, Including Current Portion

Barton Chocolates used a promissory note to borrow $1,000,000 on July 1, 2007, at an annual interest rate of 6 percent. The note is to be repaid in yearly installments of $200,000, plus accrued interest, on June 30 of every year until the note is paid in full (on June 30, 2012). Show how the results of this transaction would be reported in a classified balance sheet prepared as of December 31, 2007.

LO3

Ford Motor Company

M10-8 Determining Bond Discount or Premium from Quoted Price

On October 1, 2006, biz.yahoo.com quoted a bond price of 102.1 for Ford Motor Company's 6.5 percent bonds maturing on January 25, 2007. Were the bonds selling at a discount or premium? Does this mean the market interest rate for comparable bonds was higher or lower than 6.5 percent?

LO3

M10-9 Computing and Reporting a Bond Liability at an Issuance Price of 98

E-Tech Initiatives Limited plans to issue $500,000, 10-year, 4 percent bonds. Interest is payable annually on December 31. All of the bonds will be issued on January 1, 2007. Show how the bonds would be reported on the January 2, 2007, balance sheet if they are issued at 98.

M10-10 **Computing and Reporting a Bond Liability at an Issuance Price of 103** LO3

Repeat M10-9 assuming the bonds are issued at 103.

M10-11 **Recording Bonds Issued at Face Value** LO3

Schlitterbahn Waterslide Company issued 25,000, 10-year, 6 percent, $100 bonds on January 1, 2008, at face value. Interest is payable each January 1. Show the accounting equation effects and prepare journal entries for (*a*) the issuance of these bonds on January 1, 2008, (*b*) accrual of interest on December 31, 2008, and (*c*) the interest payment on January 1, 2009.

M10-12 **Determining Financial Statement Effects of an Early Retirement of Debt** LO3

If the market price of a bond increased after it was issued and the company decided to retire its debt early, would you expect the company to report a gain or loss on debt retirement? Describe the financial statement effects of a debt retirement under these circumstances.

M10-13 **Computing the Current Ratio and the Times Interest Earned Ratio** LO4

The balance sheet for Shaver Corporation reported the following: total assets, $250,000; noncurrent assets, $150,000; current liabilities, $40,000; total stockholders' equity, $90,000; net income, $3,320; interest expense, $4,400; income before income taxes, $5,280. Compute Shaver's current ratio and times interest earned ratio. Based on these ratios, does it appear Shaver will be able to meet its obligations to pay current liabilities and future interest obligations as they become payable?

M10-14 **Analyzing the Impact of Transactions on the Current Ratio** LO4

BSO, Inc., has current assets of $1,000,000 and current liabilities of $500,000, resulting in a current ratio of 2.0. For each of the following transactions, determine whether the current ratio will increase, decrease, or remain the same.

a. Purchased $20,000 of new inventory on credit.
b. Paid accounts payable in the amount of $50,000.
c. Recorded accrued salaries in the amount of $100,000.
d. Borrowed $250,000 from a local bank, to be repaid in 90 days.

M10-15 **Reporting a Contingent Liability** LO5

Buzz Coffee Shops is famous for its large servings of hot coffee. After a famous case involving McDonald's, the lawyer for Buzz warned management (during 2005) that it could be sued if someone were to spill hot coffee and be burned. "With the temperature of your coffee, I can guarantee it's just a matter of time before you're sued for $1,000,000." Unfortunately, in 2006, the prediction came true when a customer filed suit. The case went to trial in 2007, and the jury awarded the customer $400,000 in damages, which the company immediately appealed. During 2008, the customer and the company settled their dispute for $150,000. What is the proper reporting of this liability each year?

M10-16 **(Supplement A) Recording Bond Issuance and Interest Payment** LO3
  (Straight-Line Amortization)

Simko Company issued $600,000, 10-year, 5 percent bonds on January 1, 2007. The bonds were issued for $580,000. Interest is payable annually on January 1. Using straight-line amortization, prepare journal entries to record (*a*) the bond issuance on January 1, 2007, (*b*) the accrual of interest on December 31, 2007, and (*c*) the payment of interest on January 1, 2008.

M10-17 **(Supplement B) Recording Bond Issuance and Interest Payment** LO3
  (Effective-Interest Amortization)

Clem Company issued $800,000, 10-year, 5 percent bonds on January 1, 2007. The bonds sold for $741,000. Interest is payable annually on January 1. Using effective-interest amortization, prepare journal entries to record (*a*) the bond issuance on January 1, 2007, (*b*) the accrual of interest on December 31, 2007, and (*c*) the payment of interest on January 1, 2008. The market interest rate on the bonds is 6 percent.

M10-18 **(Supplement C) Recording Interest Accrual and Interest Payment** LO3
  (Simplified Approach to Effective-Interest Amortization)

On December 31, 2007, the balance sheet of Buchheit Enterprises reported $95,000 in a liability called "Bonds payable, net." This liability related to a $100,000 bond with a stated interest rate of

5 percent that was issued when the market interest rate was 6 percent. Assuming that interest is paid each January 1, prepare separate journal entries to record (a) accrual of interest on December 31, 2008, and (b) payment of the interest on January 1, 2009, using the simplified approach shown in chapter supplement C.

EXERCISES

Available with McGraw-Hill's Homework Manager

LO2

Target Corporation

E10-1 Determining Financial Statement Effects of Transactions Involving Notes Payable

Many businesses borrow money during periods of increased business activity to finance inventory and accounts receivable. Target Corporation is one of America's largest general merchandise retailers. Each Christmas, Target builds up its inventory to meet the needs of Christmas shoppers. A large portion of Christmas sales are on credit. As a result, Target often collects cash from the sales several months after Christmas. Assume that on November 1, 2007, Target borrowed $6 million cash from Metropolitan Bank and signed a promissory note that matures in six months. The interest rate was 7.5 percent payable at maturity. The accounting period ends December 31.

Required:

1. Indicate the accounts, amounts, and effects (+ for increase, − for decrease, and NE for no effect) of the (a) issuance of the note on November 1, (b) impact of the adjusting entry on December 31, 2007, and (c) the payment of the note and interest on April 30, 2008, on the accounting equation. Use the following structure for your answer:

Date	Assets	=	Liabilities	+	Stockholders' Equity

2. If Target needs extra cash every Christmas season, should management borrow money on a long-term basis to avoid negotiating a new short-term loan each year? Explain your answer.

LO2

E10-2 Recording a Note Payable through Its Time to Maturity with Discussion of Management Strategy

Use the information in E10-1 to complete the following requirements.

Required:

1. Give the journal entry to record the note on November 1, 2007.
2. Give any adjusting entry required on December 31, 2007.
3. Give the journal entry to record payment of the note and interest on the maturity date, April 30, 2008, assuming that interest has not been recorded since December 31, 2007.
4. If Target needs extra cash every Christmas season, should management borrow money on a long-term basis to avoid the necessity of negotiating a new short-term loan each year? Explain your answer.

LO2

E10-3 Recording Payroll Costs with Discussion

McLoyd Company completed the salary and wage payroll for March 2007. The payroll provided the following details:

Salaries and wages earned	$230,000
Employee income taxes withheld	50,200
FICA taxes withheld	16,445

Required:

1. Considering both employee and employer payroll taxes, calculate the total labor cost for the company.
2. Prepare the journal entry to record the payroll for March, including employee deductions (but excluding employer FICA taxes).
3. Prepare the journal entry to record the employer's FICA taxes.

E10-4 Recording Payroll Costs with and without Withholdings   LO2

Assume an employee of Rocco Rock Company earns $1,000 of gross wages during the current pay period, and is required to remit to the government $100 for income tax and $50 for FICA. Consider the following two procedures for paying the employee:

Procedure 1 (Withholdings)	Procedure 2 (No Withholdings)
Rocco Rock Company pays the employee net wages of $850 and will remit income taxes and FICA on behalf of the employee.	Rocco Rock Company pays the employee gross wages of $1,000 and the employee is responsible for remitting income taxes and FICA himself.

Required:

1. Ignoring employer payroll taxes, under each procedure calculate (a) the total labor cost for the company, and (b) the amount of cash the employee will have after satisfying all responsibilities to the government.
2. Explain why procedure 1 (withholdings) is the approach required by the government.
3. Considering that employers are responsible for matching employees' FICA contributions, explain why employers might also prefer procedure 1 over procedure 2.
4. Prepare the journal entries required by the employer under procedure 1, assuming that the employee is paid in cash, but the withholdings and matching employer FICA contribution have not been paid.

E10-5 Determining the Impact of Current Liability Transactions, Including Analysis of the Current Ratio   LO2, LO4

Bryant Company sells a wide range of inventories, which are initially purchased on account. Occasionally, a short-term note payable is used to obtain cash for current use. The following transactions were selected from those occurring during 2007:

a. On January 10, 2007, purchased merchandise on credit for $18,000. The company uses a perpetual inventory system.
b. On March 1, 2007, borrowed $40,000 cash from City Bank and signed a promissory note with a face amount of $40,000, due at the end of six months, accruing interest at an annual rate of 8 percent, payable at maturity.

Required:

1. For each of the transactions, indicate the accounts, amounts, and effects (+ for increase, − for decrease, and NE for no effect) on the accounting equation. Use the following structure:

Date	Assets	=	Liabilities	+	Stockholders' Equity

2. What amount of cash is paid on the maturity date of the note?
3. Discuss the impact of each transaction on the current ratio. (Assume Bryant Company's current assets have always been greater than its current liabilities.)

E10-6 Determining and Recording the Financial Statement Effects of Unearned Subscription Revenue   LO2

Reader's Digest Association is a publisher of magazines, books, and music collections. The following note is from its June 30, 2006, annual report:

Revenues
Sales of our magazine subscriptions are deferred (as unearned revenue) and recognized as revenues proportionately over the subscription period.

Assume that Reader's Digest collected $394 million in 2007 for magazines that will be delivered in future years. During fiscal 2008, the company delivered $190 million worth of magazines on those subscriptions.

Required:

1. Using the information given, indicate the accounts, amounts, and accounting equation effects (+ for increase, − for decrease, and NE for no effect) of the transactions involving $394 million and $190 million. Use the following structure:

Year	Assets	=	Liabilities	+	Stockholders' Equity

2. Using the information given, prepare the journal entries that would be recorded in each year.

LO3   E10-7 Preparing Journal Entries to Record Issuance of Bonds, Accrual of Interest, and Payment of Interest

On January 1, 2007, Applied Technologies Corporation (ATC) issued $600,000 in bonds that mature in 10 years. The bonds have a stated interest rate of 10 percent. When the bonds were issued, the market interest rate was 10 percent. The bonds pay interest once per year on January 1.

Required:

1. Determine the price at which the bonds were issued and the amount that ATC received at issuance.
2. Prepare the journal entry to record the bond issuance.
3. Prepare the journal entry to accrue interest on December 31, 2007, assuming no interest has been accrued earlier in the year.
4. Prepare the journal entry to record the interest payment on January 1, 2008.

LO3   E10-8 Preparing Journal Entries to Record Issuance of Bonds at Face Value, Accrual of Interest, Payment of Interest, and Early Retirement

On January 1, 2007, Innovative Solutions, Inc., issued $200,000 in bonds at face value. The bonds have a stated interest rate of 6 percent. The bonds mature in 10 years and pay interest once per year on January 1.

Required:

1. Prepare the journal entry to record the bond issuance.
2. Prepare the journal entry to accrue interest on December 31, 2007.
3. Prepare the journal entry to record the interest payment on January 1, 2008.
4. Assume the bonds were retired immediately after the first interest payment on January 1, 2008, at a quoted price of 102. Prepare the journal entry to record the early retirement of the bonds.

LO3, LO4   E10-9 Describing the Effects of a Premium Bond Issue and Interest Payment on the Financial Statements, Current Ratio, and Times Interest Earned Ratio

Grocery Corporation received $300,328 for $250,000, 11 percent bonds issued on January 1, 2008, at a market interest rate of 8 percent. The bonds stated that interest would be paid each January 1 and that they mature on January 1, 2018.

Required:

1. Describe how the bond issuance affects the 2008 balance sheet and income statement, specifically identifying the account names and direction of effects (ignore amounts). Also, describe its impact on the current ratio and times interest earned ratios, if any.
2. Without doing calculations, describe how the balance sheet and income statement are affected by the recording of interest on December 31, 2008. Also, describe the impact, if any, of the December 31 interest accrual and the January 1 interest payment on the current ratio and times interest earned ratio.

E10-10 Calculating the Current Ratio and Times Interest Earned Ratio

LO4
Kraft Foods Inc.

According to its Web site, Kraft Foods Inc. sells enough Kool-Aid® mix to make 1,000 gallons of the drink every minute during the summer and over 560 million gallons each year. At December 31, 2005, the company reported the following amounts (in millions) in its financial statements:

	2005	2004
Total current assets	$8,153	$9,722
Total current liabilities	8,724	9,078
Interest expense	636	666
Income tax expense	1,209	1,274
Net income	2,632	2,665

Required:

1. Compute the current ratio and times interest earned ratio (to two decimal places) for 2005 and 2004.
2. Did Kraft appear to have increased or decreased its ability to pay current liabilities and future interest obligations as they become due?

E10-11 (Supplement A) Recording the Effects of a Premium Bond Issue and First Interest Period (Straight-Line Amortization)

LO3

Refer to the information in E10-9 and assume Grocery Corporation uses the straight-line method to amortize the bond premium.

Required:

1. Prepare the journal entry to record the bond issuance.
2. Prepare the journal entry to record the interest accrual on December 31, 2008.

E10-12 (Supplement B) Recording the Effects of a Premium Bond Issue and First Interest Period (Effective-Interest Amortization)

LO3

Refer to the information in E10-9 and assume Grocery Corporation uses the effective-interest method to amortize the bond premium.

Required:

1. Prepare the journal entry to record the bond issuance.
2. Prepare the journal entry to record the interest accrual on December 31, 2008.

E10-13 (Supplement C) Recording the Effects of a Premium Bond Issue and First Interest Period (Simplified Approach to Effective-Interest Amortization)

LO3

Refer to the information in E10-9 and assume Grocery Corporation accounts for the bond using the shortcut approach shown in chapter supplement C.

Required:

1. Prepare the journal entry to record the bond issuance.
2. Prepare the journal entry to record the interest accrual on December 31, 2008.

E10-14 (Supplement A) Recording the Effects of a Discount Bond Issue and First Interest Payment and Preparing a Discount Amortization Schedule (Straight-Line Amortization)

LO3

On January 1, 2007, when the market interest rate was 9 percent, Seton Corporation completed a $200,000, 8 percent bond issue for $187,163. The bonds were dated January 1, 2007, pay interest each December 31, and mature 10 years from January 1, 2007. Seton amortizes the bond discount using the straight-line method.

Required:

1. Prepare the journal entry to record the bond issuance.
2. Prepare the journal entry to record the interest payment on December 31, 2007.
3. Prepare a bond discount amortization schedule for these bonds, using the format shown in Exhibit 10A.1. Round calculations to the nearest dollar.

LO3   **E10-15 (Supplement B) Recording the Effects of a Discount Bond Issue and First Interest Payment and Preparing a Discount Amortization Schedule (Effective-Interest Amortization)**

Refer to the information in E10-14 and assume Seton Corporation uses the effective-interest method to amortize the bond discount.

Required:

1. Prepare the journal entry to record the bond issuance.
2. Prepare the journal entry to record the interest payment on December 31, 2007.
3. Prepare a bond discount amortization schedule for these bonds, using the format shown in Exhibit 10B.3. Round calculations to the nearest dollar.

LO3   **E10-16 (Supplement C) Recording the Effects of a Discount Bond Issue and First Interest Payment and Preparing a Discount Amortization Schedule (Simplified Approach to Effective-Interest Amortization)**

Refer to the information in E10-14 and assume Seton Corporation accounts for the bond using the shortcut approach shown in chapter supplement C.

Required:

1. Prepare the journal entry to record the bond issuance.
2. Prepare the journal entry to record the interest payment on December 31, 2007.
3. Prepare a bond discount amortization schedule for these bonds, using the format shown in Exhibit 10C.1. Round calculations to the nearest dollar.

COACHED PROBLEMS

LO2, LO4   **CP10-1 Determining Financial Effects of Transactions Affecting Current Liabilities with Evaluation of Effects on the Current Ratio**

EZ Curb Company completed the following transactions during 2007. The annual accounting period ends December 31, 2007.

Jan.	8	Purchased merchandise on account at a cost of $14,000. (Assume a perpetual inventory system.)
	17	Paid for the January 8 purchase.
Apr.	1	Received $40,000 from National Bank after signing a 12-month, 6 percent, promissory note.
June	3	Purchased merchandise on account at a cost of $18,000.
July	5	Paid for the June 3 purchase.
Aug.	1	Rented out a small office in a building owned by EZ Curb Company and collected six months' rent in advance amounting to $6,000. (Use an account called Unearned rent revenue.)
Dec.	20	Received a $100 deposit from a customer as a guarantee to return a large trailer "borrowed" for 30 days. **TIP:** Consider whether EZ Curb Company has an obligation to return the money when the trailer is returned.
Dec.	31	Determined that wages of $6,500 were earned but not yet paid on December 31 (ignore payroll taxes).
Dec.	31	Adjusted the accounts at year-end, relating to interest and rent.

Required:

1. For each listed transaction and related adjusting entry, indicate the accounts, amounts, and effects (+ for increase, − for decrease, and NE for no effect) on the accounting equation, using the following format:

Date	Assets	=	Liabilities	+	Stockholders' Equity

2. For each transaction and related adjusting entry, state whether the current ratio is increased, decreased, or there is no change. (Assume EZ Curb Company's current assets have always been greater than its current liabilities.)

CP10-2 Recording and Reporting Current Liabilities with Evaluation of Effects on the Current Ratio

LO2, LO4

Using data from CP10-1, complete the following requirements.

Required:

1. Prepare journal entries for each of the transactions.
2. Prepare any adjusting entries required on December 31, 2007.
3. Show how all of the liabilities arising from these items are reported on the balance sheet at December 31, 2007.
4. Complete requirement 2 of CP10-1, if you have not already done so.

CP10-3 Recording and Reporting Current Liabilities

LO2

During 2007, Riverside Company completed the following two transactions. The annual accounting period ends December 31.

a. Paid and recorded wages of $130,000 during 2007; however, at the end of December 2007, three days' wages are unpaid and unrecorded because the weekly payroll will not be paid until January 6, 2008. Wages for the three days total $3,800.

b. Collected rent revenue of $3,600 on December 10, 2007, for office space that Riverside rented to another business. The rent collected was for 30 days from December 11, 2007, to January 10, 2008, and was credited in full to Rent revenue.

Required:

1. Give the adjusting entry required on December 31, 2007, for unpaid wages from December 2007.
2. Give (a) the journal entry for the collection of rent on December 10, 2007, and (b) the adjusting journal entry on December 31, 2007.

    TIP: Notice that the revenue recorded on December 10 includes revenue for 10 days (out of 30) that isn't earned until after December 31. This means the Unadjusted rent revenue is too high.

3. Show how any liabilities related to these items should be reported on the company's balance sheet at December 31, 2007.
4. Explain why the accrual basis of accounting provides more relevant information to financial analysts than the cash basis.

CP10-4 Comparing Bonds Issued at Par, Discount, and Premium

LO3

Sikes Corporation, whose annual accounting period ends on December 31, issued the following bonds:

Date of bonds: January 1, 2007.

Maturity amount and date: $200,000 due in 10 years (December 31, 2016).

Interest: 10 percent per year payable each December 31.

Date sold: January 1, 2007.

Required:

1. Provide the following amounts to be reported on the January 1, 2007, financial statements immediately after the bonds are issued:

	Case A (issued at 100)	Case B (at 96)	Case C (at 102)
a. Bonds payable	$	$	$
b. Unamortized premium (or discount)			
c. Bonds payable, net			

TIP: See Exhibit 10.5 for an illustration distinguishing Bonds payable from Bonds payable, net.

2. Assume that a retired person has written to you (an investment adviser) asking, "Why should I buy a bond at a premium when I can find one at a discount? Isn't that stupid? It's like paying list price for a car instead of negotiating a discount." Write a brief message in response to the question.

LO3

Hilton Hotels Corporation

CP10-5 Comparing Carrying Value and Market Value and Recording Early Retirement of Debt

The name Hilton is well known for its hotels and notorious daughters. The Hilton Hotels Corporation annual report contained the following information concerning long-term debt:

Long-Term Debt

The estimated current market value of long-term debt is based on the quoted market price for the same or similar issues. The current carrying value for long-term debt is $1,132.5 (million) and the current market value is $1,173.5 (million).

Required:

1. Explain why there is a difference between the carrying value and the current market value of the long-term debt for Hilton.
   TIP: Think about whether changes in the market interest rate affect the carrying value and/or current market value of bonds.

2. Assume that Hilton retired all of its long-term debt early (a very unlikely event) by buying the bonds in the bond market. This required a cash payment equal to the current market value. Prepare the journal entry to record the transaction.

LO5

Brunswick Corporation

CP10-6 Determining Financial Statement Reporting of Contingent Liabilities

Brunswick Corporation is a multinational company that manufactures and sells marine and recreational products. A prior annual report contained the following information:

Litigation

A jury awarded $44.4 million in damages in a suit brought by Independent Boat Builders, Inc., a buying group of boat manufacturers and its 22 members. Under the antitrust laws, the damage award has been tripled, and the plaintiffs will be entitled to their attorney's fees and interest. The Company has filed an appeal contending the verdict was erroneous as a matter of law, both as to liability and damages.

Required:

What are the alternative ways in which Brunswick could account for this litigation?
TIP: Consider the different possible outcomes that could arise from the appeal.

CP10-7 (Supplement A) Recording Bond Issuance and Interest Payments   **LO3**
(Straight-Line Amortization)

Southwest Corporation issued bonds with the following details:

Face value: $600,000.

Interest: 9 percent per year payable each December 31.

Terms: Bonds dated January 1, 2007, due five years from that date.

The annual accounting period ends December 31. The bonds were issued at 104 on January 1, 2007, when the market interest rate was 8 percent. Assume straight-line amortization.

Required:

1. Compute the issue (sale) price of the bonds (show computations).
   TIP: The issue price typically is quoted at a percentage of face value.
2. Give the journal entry to record the issuance of the bonds.
3. Give the journal entries to record the payment of interest on December 31, 2007 and 2008.
4. How much interest expense would be reported on the income statements for 2007 and 2008? Show how the liability related to the bonds should be reported on the balance sheets at December 31, 2007 and 2008.

CP10-8 (Supplement B) Recording Bond Issuance and Interest Payments   **LO3**
(Effective-Interest Amortization)

Complete the requirements of CP10-7, assuming Southwest Corporation uses effective-interest amortization.

CP10-9 (Supplement C) Recording Bond Issuance and Interest Payments   **LO3**
(Simplified Approach to Effective-Interest Amortization)

Complete the requirements of CP10-7, assuming Southwest Corporation uses the simplified approach shown in chapter supplement C.

CP10-10 (Supplement A) Completing an Amortization Schedule (Straight-Line   **LO3**
Amortization)

The Peg Corporation (TPC) issued bonds and received cash in full for the issue price. The bonds were dated and issued on January 1, 2006. The stated interest rate was payable at the end of each year. The bonds mature at the end of four years. The following schedule has been prepared (amounts in thousands):

Date	Cash	Interest	Amortization	Balance
January 1, 2006				$6,101
End of year 2006	$450	$425	$25	?
End of year 2007	450	?	25	6,051
End of year 2008	450	?	25	6,026
End of year 2009	450	424	26	6,000

Required:

1. Complete the amortization schedule.
   TIP: The switch in amortization from $25 to $26 in 2009 is caused by rounding.
2. What was the maturity amount (face value) of the bonds?
3. How much cash was received at date of issuance (sale) of the bonds?
4. Was there a premium or a discount? If so, which and how much was it?
5. How much cash is paid for interest each period and will be paid in total for the full life of the bond issue?
6. What is the stated interest rate?
7. What is the market interest rate?
8. What amount of interest expense should be reported on the income statement each year?
9. Show how the bonds should be reported on the balance sheet at the end of 2007 and 2008.

LO3   **CP10-11 (Supplements B or C) Completing an Amortization Schedule (Effective-Interest Amortization or Simplified Approach)**

Hondor Corporation issued bonds and received cash in full for the issue price. The bonds were dated and issued on January 1, 2007. The stated interest rate was payable at the end of each year. The bonds mature at the end of four years. The following schedule has been completed (amounts in thousands):

Date	Cash	Interest	Amortization	Balance
January 1, 2007				$6,101
End of year 2007	$450	$427	$23	6,078
End of year 2008	450	426	24	6,054
End of year 2009	450	?	?	?
End of year 2010	450	?	27	6,000

Required:

1. Complete the amortization schedule.
2. What was the maturity amount (face value) of the bonds?
3. How much cash was received at date of issuance (sale) of the bonds?
4. Was there a premium or a discount? If so, which and how much was it?
5. How much cash is paid for interest each period and will be paid in total for the full life of the bond issue?
6. What is the stated interest rate?
   TIP: The stated interest rate can be calculated by comparing the cash payment to the face value of the bond.
7. What is the market interest rate?
8. What amount of interest expense should be reported on the income statement each year?
9. Show how the bonds should be reported on the balance sheet at the end of 2007 and 2008.

GROUP A PROBLEMS

Available with McGraw-Hill's
Homework Manager

LO2, LO4   **PA10-1 Determining Financial Effects of Transactions Affecting Current Liabilities with Evaluation of Effects on the Current Ratio**

Jack Hammer Company completed the following transactions during 2007. The annual accounting period ends December 31, 2007.

Apr. 30	Received $550,000 from Commerce Bank after signing a 12-month, 6 percent, promissory note.
June 6	Purchased merchandise on account at a cost of $75,000.
July 15	Paid for the June 6 purchase.
Aug. 31	Signed a contract to provide security service to a small apartment complex and collected six months' fees in advance amounting to $12,000. (Use an account called Unearned service revenue.)
Dec. 31	Determined salary and wages of $40,000 earned but not yet paid December 31 (ignore payroll taxes).
Dec. 31	Adjusted the accounts at year-end, relating to interest and security service.

Required:

1. For each listed transaction and related adjusting entry, indicate the accounts, amounts, and effects (+ for increase, − for decrease, and NE for no effect) on the accounting equation, using the following format:

Date	Assets	=	Liabilities	+	Stockholders' Equity

2. For each item, state whether the current ratio is increased, decreased, or there is no change. (Assume Jack Hammer's current assets have always been greater than its current liabilities.)

PA10-2 Recording and Reporting Current Liabilities with Evaluation of Effects on the Current Ratio

LO2, LO4

Using data from PA10-1, complete the following requirements.

e**X**cel

www.mhhe.com/phillips2e

Required:

1. Prepare journal entries for each of the transactions.
2. Prepare all adjusting entries required on December 31, 2007.
3. Show how all of the liabilities arising from these items are reported on the balance sheet at December 31, 2007.
4. Complete requirement 2 of PA10-1, if you have not already done so.

PA10-3 Recording and Reporting Current Liabilities

LO2

During 2007, Lakeview Company completed the following two transactions. The annual accounting period ends December 31.

a. Paid and recorded wages of $80,000 during 2007; however, at the end of December 2007, three days' wages are unpaid and unrecorded because the weekly payroll will not be paid until January 6, 2008. Wages for the three days total $1,600.
b. Collected rent revenue of $3,600 on December 10, 2007, for office space that Lakeview rented to another business. The rent collected was for 30 days from December 11, 2007, to January 10, 2008, and was credited in full to Rent revenue.

Required:

1. Give the adjusting entry required on December 31, 2007, for unpaid wages from December 2007.
2. Give (a) the journal entry for the collection of rent on December 10, 2007, and (b) the adjusting journal entry on December 31, 2007.
3. Show how any liabilities related to these items should be reported on the company's balance sheet at December 31, 2007.
4. Explain why the accrual basis of accounting provides more relevant information to financial analysts than the cash basis.

PA10-4 Comparing Bonds Issued at Par, Discount, and Premium

LO3

Net Work Corporation, whose annual accounting period ends on December 31, issued the following bonds:

Date of bonds: January 1, 2007.

Maturity amount and date: $200,000 due in 10 years (December 31, 2016).

Interest: 10 percent per year payable each December 31.

Date issued: January 1, 2007.

Required:

1. Provide the following amounts to be reported on the January 1, 2007, financial statements immediately after the bonds were issued:

	Case A (issued at 100)	Case B (at 97)	Case C (at 101)
a. Bonds payable	$	$	$
b. Unamortized premium or discount			
c. Bonds payable, net			

2. Assume that you are an investment adviser and a retired person has written to you asking, "Why should I buy a bond at a premium when I can find one at a discount? Isn't that stupid? It's like paying list price for a car instead of negotiating a discount." Write a brief message in response to the question.

LO3

Quaker Oats

PepsiCo

PA10-5 Comparing Carrying Value and Market Value and Recording Early Retirement of Debt

Quaker Oats is a well-known name at most breakfast tables. Before it was acquired by PepsiCo, Quaker Oats reported the following information about its long-term debt in its annual report:

Long-Term Debt

The fair value of long-term debt was $779.7 million at the end of the current fiscal year, which was based on market prices for the same or similar issues or on the current rates offered to the Company for similar debt of the same maturities. The carrying value of long-term debt as of the same date was $759.5 million.

Required:

1. Explain what is meant by "fair value." Explain why there is a difference between the carrying value and the fair value of the long-term debt for Quaker Oats.

2. Assume that Quaker Oats retired all of its long-term debt early (a very unlikely event) by buying the bonds in the bond market. This required a cash payment equal to the current market value. Prepare the journal entry to record the transaction.

LO5

Macromedia, Inc.

PA10-6 Determining Financial Statement Reporting of Contingent Liabilities

Macromedia, Inc., is the original maker of shockwave and flash technologies. Its 2002 annual report indicated that a lawsuit had been filed in 2000 against the company and five of its former officers for securities fraud in connection with allegedly making false or misleading statements about its financial results. The lawsuit was settled on January 9, 2002, as described in the following note:

Legal

The settlement amount was $48.0 million, of which approximately $19.5 million was paid by insurance. As a result, the Company recorded a $28.5 million charge as a component of other income (expense) in its consolidated statements of operations during fiscal year 2002.

Required:

Explain why Macromedia didn't record a contingent liability in 2000 when the lawsuit was filed.

GROUP B PROBLEMS

LO2, LO4

PB10-1 Determining Financial Effects of Transactions Affecting Current Liabilities with Evaluation of Effects on the Current Ratio

Tiger Company completed the following transactions during 2007. The annual accounting period ends December 31, 2007.

Jan.	3	Purchased merchandise on account at a cost of $24,000. (Assume a perpetual inventory system.)
	27	Paid for the January 3 purchase.
Apr.	1	Received $80,000 from Atlantic Bank after signing a 12-month, 5 percent, promissory note.
June	13	Purchased merchandise on account at a cost of $8,000.
July	25	Paid for the June 13 purchase.

Aug. 1   Rented out a small office in a building owned by Tiger Company and collected eight months' rent in advance amounting to $8,000. (Use an account called Unearned rent revenue.)

Dec. 31   Determined wages of $12,000 were earned but not yet paid on December 31 (ignore payroll taxes).

Dec. 31   Adjusted the accounts at year-end, relating to interest and rent.

Required:

1. For each listed transaction and related adjusting entry, indicate the accounts, amounts, and effects (+ for increase, − for decrease, and NE for no effect) on the accounting equation, using the following format:

Date	Assets	=	Liabilities	+	Stockholders' Equity

2. For each item, state whether the current ratio is increased, decreased, or there is no change. (Assume Tiger Company's current assets have always been greater than its current liabilities.)

PB10-2 Recording and Reporting Current Liabilities with Evaluation of Effects on the Current Ratio   LO2, LO4

Using data from PB10-1, complete the following requirements.

Required:

1. Prepare journal entries for each of the transactions.
2. Prepare any adjusting entries required on December 31, 2007.
3. Show how all of the liabilities arising from these items are reported on the balance sheet at December 31, 2007.
4. Complete requirement 2 of PB10-1, if you have not already done so.

PB10-3 Recording and Reporting Current Liabilities   LO2

During 2007, Sandler Company completed the following two transactions. The annual accounting period ends December 31.

a. Paid and recorded wages of $240,000 during 2007; however, at the end of December 2007, two days' wages are unpaid and unrecorded because the weekly payroll will not be paid until January 5, 2008. Wages for the two days total $3,000.
b. Collected rent revenue of $1,500 on December 10, 2007, for office space that Sandler rented to another business. The rent collected was for 30 days from December 11, 2007, to January 10, 2008, and was credited in full to Rent revenue.

Required:

1. Give the adjusting entry required on December 31, 2007, for unpaid wages from December 2007.
2. Give (a) the journal entry for the collection of rent on December 10, 2007, and (b) the adjusting journal entry on December 31, 2007.
3. Show how any liabilities related to these items should be reported on the company's balance sheet at December 31, 2007.
4. Explain why the accrual basis of accounting provides more relevant information to financial analysts than the cash basis.

PB10-4 Completing Schedule Comparing Bonds Issued at Par, Discount, and Premium   LO3

Marshalls Corporation sold a $500,000, 7 percent bond issue on January 1, 2007. The bonds pay interest each December 31 and mature 10 years from January 1, 2007.

Required:

1. Provide the following amounts to be reported on the January 1, 2007, financial statements immediately after the bonds were issued:

	Case A (issued at 100)	Case B (at 98)	Case C (at 102)
a. Bonds payable	$	$	$
b. Unamortized premium or discount			
c. Bonds payable, net			

2. Assume that you are an investment adviser and a retired person has written to you asking, "Why should I buy a bond at a premium when I can find one at a discount? Isn't that stupid? It's like paying list price for a car instead of negotiating a discount." Write a brief message in response to the question.

LO3

AMC Entertainment, Inc.

PB10-5 Recording and Explaining the Early Retirement of Debt

AMC Entertainment, Inc., owns and operates 239 movie theaters worldwide, with 3,120 screens in 28 states. On August 12, 1992, the company sold 11 7/8 percent bonds in the amount of $52,720,000 and used the $52,720,000 cash proceeds to retire bonds with a coupon rate of 13.6 percent. At that time, the 13.6 percent bonds had a book value of $50,000,000.

Required:

1. Prepare the journal entries to record the issuance of the new bonds and the early retirement of the old bonds. Assume both the new and old bonds were issued at face value.
2. How should AMC report any gain or loss on this transaction?
3. Why might the company have issued new bonds to retire the old bonds?

SKILLS DEVELOPMENT CASES

LO4

S10-1 Finding Financial Information

Refer to the financial statements of Landry's Restaurants in Appendix A at the end of this book, or download the annual report from the *Cases* section of the text's Web site at www.mhhe.com/phillips2e.

1. Calculate, to two decimal places, the company's current ratio at the most recent year-end. Does this ratio cause you any concern about the company's ability to pay its current liabilities? As part of your answer, consider the available borrowing capacity as of December 31, 2005 (discussed in the second paragraph of Note 5).
2. Calculate, to two decimal places, the company's times interest earned ratio for the most recent year. Does this ratio cause you any concern about the company's ability to meet future interest obligations as they become payable?

LO4

S10-2 Comparing Financial Information

Refer to the financial statements of Outback Steakhouse in Appendix B at the end of this book, or download them from the *Cases* section of the text's Web site at www.mhhe.com/phillips2e.

1. Calculate, to two decimal places, the company's current ratio at the most recent year-end. Does this ratio cause you any concern about the company's ability to pay its current liabilities? As part of your answer, consider the lines of credit that are available under the credit facility (discussed in Note 7).
2. Calculate, to two decimal places, the company's times interest earned ratio for the most recent year. Does it appear that Landry's or Outback will be better able to meet future interest obligations as they become payable?

S10-3 Internet-Based Team Research: Examining an Annual Report

As a team, select an industry to analyze. Using your Web browser, each team member should access the annual report or 10-K for one publicly traded company in the industry, with each member selecting a different company. (See S1-3 in Chapter 1 for a description of possible resources for these tasks.)

Required:

1. On an individual basis, each team member should write a short report that incorporates the following:
    a. What are the most significant types of current liabilities owed by the company?
    b. Read the company's financial statement note regarding long-term debt and commitments and contingencies. Does the company have any significant amounts coming due in the next five years?
    c. Compute and analyze the current ratio and times interest earned ratio.
2. Then, as a team, write a short report comparing and contrasting your companies using these attributes. Discuss any patterns across the companies that you as a team observe. Provide potential explanations for any differences discovered.

S10-4 Ethical Decision Making: A Real-Life Example

Many retired people invest a significant portion of their money in bonds of corporations because of their relatively low level of risk. During the 1980s, significant inflation caused some interest rates to rise to as high as 15 percent. Retired people who bought bonds that paid only 6 percent continued to earn at the lower rate. During the 1990s, inflation subsided and interest rates declined. Many corporations took advantage of the callability feature of these bonds and retired the bonds early. Many of these early retirements of high interest rate bonds were replaced with low interest rate bonds.

Required:

In your judgment, is it ethical for corporations to continue paying low interest rates when rates increase but to call bonds when rates decrease? Why or why not?

S10-5 Ethical Decision Making: A Mini-Case

Assume that you are a portfolio manager for a large insurance company. The majority of the money you manage is from retired school teachers who depend on the income you earn on their investments. You have invested a significant amount of money in the bonds of a large corporation and have just received news released by the company's president explaining that it is unable to meet its current interest obligations because of deteriorating business operations related to increased international competition. The president has a recovery plan that will take at least two years. During that time, the company will not be able to pay interest on the bonds and, she admits, if the plan does not work, bondholders will probably lose more than half of their money. As a creditor, you can force the company into immediate bankruptcy and probably get back at least 90 percent of the bondholders' money. You also know that your decision will cause at least 10,000 people to lose their jobs if the company ceases operations.

Required:

Given only these two options, what should you do? Consider who would be helped or harmed by the two options.

S10-6 Critical Thinking: Evaluating Effects on Current Ratio

Assume you work as an assistant to the chief financial officer (CFO) of Fashions First, Inc. The CFO reminds you that the fiscal year-end is only two weeks away and that he is looking to you to ensure the company stays in compliance with its loan covenant to maintain a current ratio of 1.25 or higher. A review of the general ledger indicates that current assets total $690,000 and current liabilities are $570,000. Your company has an excess of cash ($300,000) and an equally large balance in accounts payable ($270,000), although none of its accounts payable are due until next month.

Required:

1. Determine whether the company is currently in compliance with its loan covenant.
2. Assuming the level of current assets and current liabilities remains unchanged until the last day of the fiscal year, evaluate whether Fashions First should pay down $90,000 of its accounts payable on the last day of the year, before the accounts payable become due.

LO3

www.mhhe.com/phillips2e

S10-7 (Supplement A) Preparing a Bond Amortization Schedule (Straight-Line Amortization)

Assume the authors of a popular introductory accounting text have hired you to create spreadsheets that will calculate bond discount amortization schedules like those shown in Exhibits 10A.1, 10B.3, and 10C.1. As usual, you e-mail your friend Owen for some guidance. Much to your disappointment, you receive an auto-reply message from Owen indicating that he's gone skiing in New Zealand. After a bit of panicking, you realize you can refer to Owen's previous e-mail messages for spreadsheet advice that will help you complete this task. From his advice for Chapter 9, you decide to create a data input section for the stated interest rate, market interest rate, face value, issue price, and years to maturity. The spreadsheet file also will have a separate amortization schedule worksheet that contains only formulas, references to the cells in the data input section, and references to other cells in the amortization schedule. All amounts will be rounded to the nearest dollar (using the Round function in Excel), which means the discount amortization in the final year might be off a few dollars (unless you use the IF function in Excel to eliminate any remaining discount in the final year of the bond's life, in the same way that Owen showed in Chapter 9 for declining-balance depreciation).

Required:

Prepare a worksheet that uses formulas to reproduce the straight-line bond discount amortization schedule shown in Exhibit 10A.1. Display both the completed spreadsheet and a "formulas revealed" (Ctrl ~) version of it.

LO3

www.mhhe.com/phillips2e

S10-8 (Supplement B) Preparing a Bond Amortization Schedule (Effective-Interest Amortization)

Refer to the information in S10-7 and prepare a worksheet that uses formulas to reproduce the effective-interest bond discount amortization schedule shown in Exhibit 10B.3. Display both the completed spreadsheet and a "formulas revealed" (Ctrl ~) version of it.

LO3

www.mhhe.com/phillips2e

S10-9 (Supplement C) Preparing a Bond Amortization Schedule (Simplified Approach to Effective-Interest Amortization)

Refer to the information in S10-7 and prepare a worksheet that uses formulas to reproduce the bond discount amortization schedule, shown in Exhibit 10C.1, for the simplified approach. Display both the completed spreadsheet and a "formulas revealed" (Ctrl ~) version of it.

11

Reporting and Interpreting Stockholders' Equity

THAT WAS
THEN

The last chapter focused
on debt financing, as
reported in the liabilities
section of the balance
sheet.

LP11

SONIC
America's
Drive-In.

News about shares of stock is everywhere. You've probably read it in *The Wall Street Journal,* listened to it on MSNBC, or searched for it at Yahoo!Finance. Behind this fascination with stock is a dream that many people share: taking a small amount of money and turning it into a fortune. That's what Sonic Corp.–America's largest drive-in restaurant chain–has managed to do. When it first started operations about 35 years ago, Sonic was selling 100 shares of stock to its store owners for $100. As the company grew larger and more profitable, the value of its stock increased. By 1995, Sonic was selling 100 shares to investors for $2,125. Since then, Sonic's shares have split five times, which means those 100 shares have multiplied into 760 shares, which Sonic is now buying back for over $22 a share. That's more than $16,700, or an increase of nearly 800% in a little more than a decade!

In this chapter, you will see how companies like Sonic Corp. account for various stock transactions, including issuances, splits, and dividends. Soon you'll understand many of the stock terms used in the news.

Way back in Chapter 1, you learned that several forms of business exist, including sole proprietorships, partnerships, limited liability companies, and corporations. In the body of this chapter, we focus on how corporations report their stockholders' equity.[1] You'll begin with a brief introduction to corporate ownership and then proceed to learn about the types of business transactions that affect stockholders' equity. We should mention right from the outset that all transactions between a company and its stockholders affect only balance sheet accounts. None of the transactions in this chapter affect the income statement. Nonetheless, knowing how these transactions are reported is crucial when evaluating how well a company has performed for its stockholders, as you will see in the third section of the chapter. As always, the final section presents material for review and practice.

ORGANIZATION OF THE CHAPTER

Understand the business	Study the accounting methods	Evaluate the results	Review the chapter
• Corporate ownership • Equity versus debt financing	• Common stock transactions • Stock dividends and stock splits • Preferred stock • Retained earnings	• Earnings per share (EPS) • Return on equity (ROE) • Price/earnings (P/E) ratio	• Demonstration case • Chapter summary • Key terms • Practice material

Understand the Business

Learning Objective 1
Explain the role of stock in financing a corporation.

Video 11.1

CORPORATE OWNERSHIP

If you were to write down the names of 50 familiar businesses, probably all of them would be corporations. This is understandable because, according to Bizstats.com, corporations account for 85% of the total sales reported by U.S. businesses. Many Americans own shares in corporations, either directly or indirectly through a mutual fund or pension program.

You probably recall from Chapter 1 that the act of creating a corporation is costly, so why is the corporate form so popular? One reason is that it limits the legal liability of its owners. Another reason is that corporations can raise large amounts of money because investors can easily participate in a corporation's ownership. This ease of participation is related to several factors.

- *Shares of stock can be purchased in small amounts.* According to Yahoo!Finance, you could have become one of Sonic's owners in 2006 by buying a share of the company's stock for just $22.

- *Ownership interests are transferable.* The shares of public companies are regularly bought and sold on established markets such as the New York Stock Exchange. So if you decide to sell your shares in Sonic, or buy more, it's quick and easy to do. Sonic is traded under the ticker symbol SONC.

---

[1] Chapter Supplement A discusses accounting for owners' equity in proprietorships, partnerships, and other business forms.

- *Stockholders are not liable for the corporation's debts.* Creditors have no legal claim on the personal assets of stockholders like they do on the personal assets belonging to owners of sole proprietorships and partnerships. So if you owned stock in the old Montgomery Ward department store, which went bankrupt and was liquidated in 2000, you would lose what you paid to buy the stock but, unless you personally guaranteed the company's debt, you wouldn't have to pay the hundreds of millions the company owed.

The law recognizes a corporation as a separate legal entity. It may own assets, incur liabilities, expand and contract in size, sue others, be sued, and enter into contracts independently of its owners. A corporation exists separate and apart from its owners, which means it doesn't die when its owners die. Thomas Edison died in 1931, but the company he founded (General Electric) continues in existence today.

To protect everyone's rights, the creation and oversight of corporations are tightly regulated by law. Corporations are created by submitting an application to a state government (not the federal government). Because laws vary from state to state, you might decide to create a corporation in a state other than the one in which it operates. Although Sonic has its headquarters in Oklahoma City, it was actually incorporated in Delaware. More than half of the largest corporations in America are incorporated in Delaware because it has some of the most favorable laws for establishing corporations. If the application to create a corporation is approved, the state issues a charter, also called the articles of incorporation, which spells out information about the corporation such as its name, address, nature of business, and ownership structure.

The ownership structure of a corporation can vary from one company to the next. In the most basic form, a corporation must have one type of stock, appropriately called **common stock.** Owners of common stock usually enjoy a number of benefits:

> **YOU SHOULD KNOW**
>
> **Common stock** is the basic voting stock issued by a corporation to stockholders.

- *Voting rights.* For each share you own, you get a set number of votes on major issues. Some classes of common stock can carry more votes than others, so watch for this if you care about voting on which accounting firm will be appointed as external auditors and who will serve on the board of directors. (In case you don't remember from Chapter 5, the board of directors is the group that appoints the corporation's officers and governs top management, as shown in Exhibit 11.1).

EXHIBIT 11.1 | Typical Organizational Structure of a Corporation

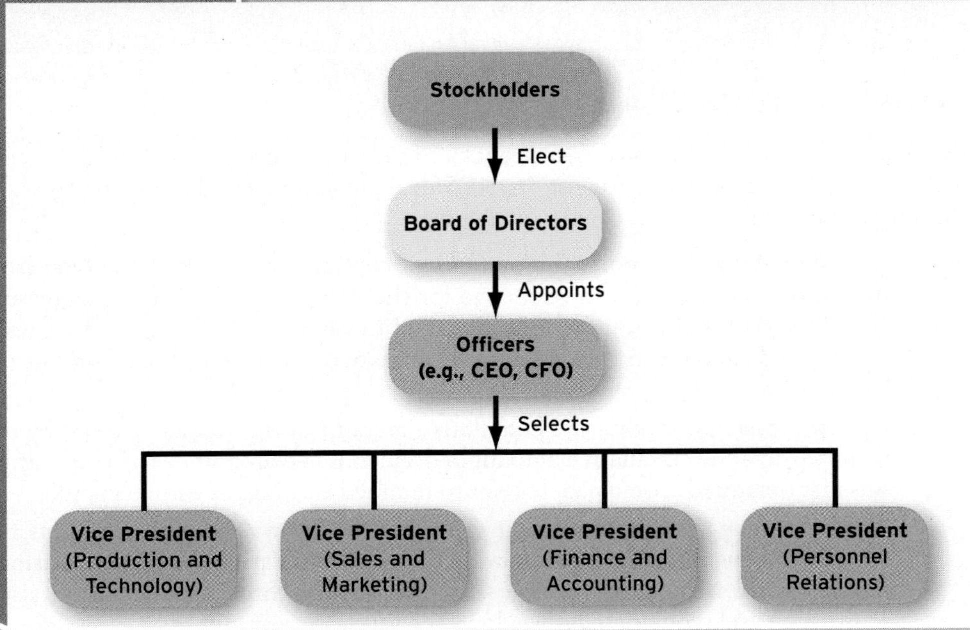

- **Dividends.** Stockholders receive a share of the corporation's profits when distributed as dividends.
- **Residual claim.** If the company ceases operations, stockholders share in any assets remaining after creditors have been paid.
- **Preemptive rights.** Existing stockholders may be given the first chance to buy newly issued stock before it is offered to others.

EQUITY VERSUS DEBT FINANCING

Whenever a company needs a large amount of long-term financing, its executives will have to decide whether to obtain it by issuing new stock to investors (called *equity financing*) or borrowing money from lenders (*debt financing*). Each form of financing has certain advantages over the other, as listed in Exhibit 11.2. These factors play a big role in determining whether equity or debt financing is most appropriate for each particular corporation. One company, for example, might be primarily concerned about the impact of financing on income taxes and decide to rely on debt financing because its interest payments are tax deductible. A different company might be so concerned about being able to pay its existing liabilities that it can't afford to take on additional debt. By using equity financing, which doesn't have to be repaid, the company could obtain the financing it needs. Ultimately, the decision to pursue additional equity or debt financing depends on the circumstances.

EXHIBIT 11.2	**Advantages of Equity and Debt Financing**

Advantages of Equity Financing	Advantages of Debt Financing
1. **Equity does not have to be repaid.** Debt must be repaid or refinanced.	1. **Interest on debt is tax deductible.** Dividends on stock are not tax deductible.
2. **Dividends are optional.** Interest must be paid on debt.	2. **Debt does not change stockholder control.** In contrast, a stock issue gives new stockholders the right to vote and share in the earnings, diluting existing stockholders' control.

Study the Accounting Methods

Learning Objective 2
Explain and analyze common stock transactions.

Topic Tackler

⚡PLUS

Check out www.mhhe.com/phillips2e for audio, visual, and PowerPoint presentations on this topic.

COMMON STOCK TRANSACTIONS

Exhibit 11.3 shows the kinds of items that Sonic reported in the stockholders' equity section of its balance sheet at August 31, 2005. It includes two familiar line items and a third new line item:

1. Contributed capital reports the amount of capital the company received from investors' contributions, in exchange for the company's stock. For this reason, contributed capital is sometimes called paid-in capital. As Exhibit 11.3 suggests, contributed capital can include several components, which we'll explain later in this section.

2. Retained earnings reports the cumulative amount of net income earned by the company less the cumulative amount of dividends declared since the corporation was first organized. Some people refer to retained earnings as earned capital.

3. Treasury stock reports shares that were previously owned by stockholders but have been bought back and are now held by the corporation. To fully understand treasury stock, it's helpful to follow stock transactions through from authorization to issuance and repurchase, as we do in the following section.

EXHIBIT 11.3 | Excerpt from Sonic Corp.'s Balance Sheet

SONIC CORP.
Partial Balance Sheets

(dollars in thousands)	August 31, 2005	August 31, 2004
STOCKHOLDERS' EQUITY		
Contributed Capital		
Common Stock, Par Value $0.01 per share		
Authorized: 100,000,000 Shares		
Issued: 75,800,000 Shares in 2005		
74,600,000 Shares in 2004	$ 758	$ 746
Additional Paid-In Capital	121,982	105,012
Preferred Stock, Par Value $0.01 per share; none outstanding	—	—
	122,740	105,758
Retained Earnings	426,783	351,402
	549,523	457,160
Treasury Stock, at cost; 16,500,000 Common Shares in 2005	(164,984)	(122,398)
Total Stockholders' Equity	384,539	334,762

Authorization, Issuance, and Repurchase of Stock

A corporation's charter indicates the maximum number of shares of stock that the corporation is allowed to issue. Look closely at the Contributed Capital section of Exhibit 11.3 and you will see that Sonic is **authorized** to issue 100 million common shares. The next line in Exhibit 11.3 tells us how many shares have actually been given to stockholders. As of August 31, 2005, 75.8 million common shares have been **issued.** These shares will be owned forever by one investor or another, unless the company buys them back. Shares that have been issued and haven't been bought back by the corporation are called **outstanding** shares. In other words, outstanding shares are those owned by investors. Shares that have been bought back by the corporation are called **treasury stock.** During the time treasury stock is held by the corporation, the shares do not carry voting, dividend, or other stockholder rights.

Sonic reports its treasury stock in the second-last line of Exhibit 11.3. It is shown as a negative amount because it represents shares that are no longer outstanding with investors. As of August 31, 2005, Sonic had bought back 16.5 million of the 75.8 million shares previously issued. From this information, you should be able to compute the number of shares still outstanding, which is important for financial analysts who need to express certain dollar amounts on a per share basis. Earnings per share (EPS)—a key financial ratio that we discuss later in this chapter—is expressed in terms of the number of outstanding shares owned by investors. Be sure you can map the number of shares reported in Exhibit 11.3 into relationships among the number of authorized, issued, outstanding, and treasury stock, as diagrammed in Exhibit 11.4 on page 496.

Stock Authorization   Before stock can be issued, its specific rights and characteristics must be authorized and defined in the corporate charter. This authorization does not affect the accounting records, but it does establish certain characteristics that, later, will affect how the stock is accounted for. One characteristic of importance is the stock's **par value.** Oddly enough, par value has little meaning today. It is an old concept from long ago,

> **YOU SHOULD KNOW**
>
> The **authorized** number of shares is the maximum number of shares of capital stock of a corporation that can be issued, as specified in the charter. **Issued shares** represent the total number of shares of stock that have been sold. **Outstanding shares** consist of issued shares that are currently held by stockholders other than the corporation itself. **Treasury stock** consists of issued shares that have been bought back by the company.

> **YOU SHOULD KNOW**
>
> **Par value** is an insignificant value per share of capital stock specified in the charter.

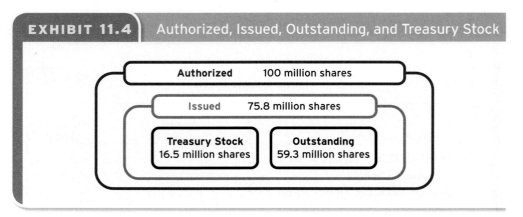

EXHIBIT 11.4   Authorized, Issued, Outstanding, and Treasury Stock

Authorized   100 million shares

Issued   75.8 million shares

Treasury Stock
16.5 million shares

Outstanding
59.3 million shares

originally introduced to prevent stockholders from removing contributed capital of businesses that were about to go bankrupt. Stronger laws and regulations exist today to prevent this from happening, so par value no longer has a business use. Yet, many states still require that corporations specify a par value for stock. Typically, par value is set at a token amount, such as $0.01 per share, as is the case with Sonic's stock described in Exhibit 11.3. Some states have dropped the requirement to specify a par value and instead allow the issuance of no-par value stock. **No-par value stock** is just like stock with par value, except it does not have a specified legal value per share. In any event, par value is a legal concept and is not related in any way to the market value of the company's stock.

Stock Issuance   The sale of stock from the corporation to an investor is called a *stock issuance*. The very first sale of a company's stock to the public is called an *initial public offering*, or *IPO*. This is what most people are referring to when they say a private company is going public. If a company has issued stock previously, additional issuances of new stock by the company are called *seasoned new issues*. Whether stock is issued as part of an IPO or as a seasoned new issue, a company accounts for it in the same way.

Most sales of stock to the public are cash transactions. To illustrate the accounting for an issuance of stock, assume that during the next fiscal year, Sonic sells 100,000 shares of its $0.01 par value stock at the market price existing at the time of issuance of $30 per share. The accounting equation effects of this stock issuance and the journal entry to record them would be:

	Assets	=	Liabilities	+	Stockholders' Equity	
1. Analyze	Cash +3,000,000				Common Stock	+1,000
					Additional Paid-In Capital	+2,999,000

2. Record
dr Cash (+A) (100,000 × $30)   3,000,000
    cr Common Stock (+SE) (100,000 × $0.01)   1,000
    cr Additional Paid-In Capital (+SE) ($3,000,000 − $1,000) . .   2,999,000

Notice that the increase in the Common stock account is the number of shares sold times the par value per share (100,000 × $0.01), and the increase in the Additional paid-in capital account is the amount of cash received in excess of this amount. If the corporate charter does not specify a par value for the stock, the total proceeds from the sale of stock will be entered in the common stock account.

Stock Sold between Investors   When a company sells stock to the public, the transaction is between the issuing corporation and the buyer. After this initial stock sale, investors can sell shares to other investors without directly affecting the corporation. For example, if investor Aaron Cadieux sold 1,000 shares of Sonic stock to Tara Rink, Sonic would not record a journal entry on its books. Mr. Cadieux received cash for the shares he sold, and Mrs. Rink received stock for the cash she paid. Sonic did not receive or pay anything. These transactions involve only the owners of the company and not the corporation itself. It's like an auto dealer who records the initial sale of a car to a customer but doesn't later record another sale when the customer sells the car to someone else.

Stock Used to Compensate Employees To encourage employees to work hard for a corporation, employee pay packages often include a combination of base pay, cash bonuses, and stock options. Stock options allow employees to buy the company's stock at a predetermined price during a specified time period. The idea behind this is that if employees work hard and meet the corporation's goals, the company's stock price is likely to increase. If the stock price increases, employees can exercise their option to buy the company's stock at the lower grant price and then turn around and sell it at the higher stock market price for a profit. If the stock price declines, employees haven't lost anything. Accounting rules require that, at the time the company grants stock options, an expense must be reported for the estimated cost associated with stock options. The specific accounting procedures for this will be discussed in an intermediate accounting course.

> **COACH'S TIP**
>
> Remember the separate entity assumption from Chapter 1, which states that owners' transactions are recorded only if they directly involve the corporation.

Ethical Insights

At Whose Expense?

Some critics claim that stock options, which are intended to give the senior executives of a company the same goals as stockholders, often come at the expense of existing stockholders. When senior executives exercise their stock options to buy new stock, existing stockholders lose voting power because their percentage of ownership in the company is diluted. Furthermore, critics contend that stock options create an incentive for senior executives to overstate financial results in an attempt to increase the company's stock price so they can exercise their options for huge personal gains.

Repurchase of Stock A corporation may want to repurchase its stock from existing stockholders for a variety of reasons, including: (1) to distribute excess cash to stockholders, (2) to send a signal to investors that the company itself believes its own stock is worth purchasing, (3) to obtain shares that can be reissued as payment for purchases of other companies, and (4) to obtain shares to reissue to employees as part of employee stock option plans. Because of Securities and Exchange Commission regulations concerning newly issued shares, it is generally less costly for companies to give employees repurchased shares than to issue new ones.

Most companies record the purchase of treasury stock based on the cost of the shares when they are purchased by the company. This approach is called the cost method. Assume that during the next fiscal year, Sonic bought 50,000 shares of its stock in the market when it was selling for $25 per share (total cost = 50,000 shares × $25 = $1,250,000). Using the cost method, the effects of this repurchase on the accounting equation and the journal entry for it would be:

	Assets	=	**Liabilities**	+	**Stockholders' Equity**	
1. Analyze	Cash −1,250,000				Treasury Stock (+xSE) −1,250,000	

2. Record

dr Treasury Stock (+xSE, −SE) 1,250,000
    cr Cash (−A)   1,250,000

Note that Treasury Stock is not an asset. It is a contra-equity account that is subtracted from total stockholders' equity. This practice makes sense because treasury stock is stock that is not outstanding and therefore should be removed from total stockholders' equity. Look at the second-last line of Exhibit 11.3 on page 495 to see how Sonic reported its $164,984 of treasury stock on August 31, 2005.

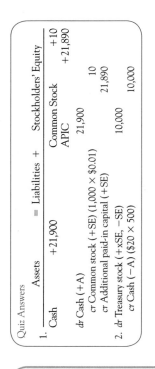

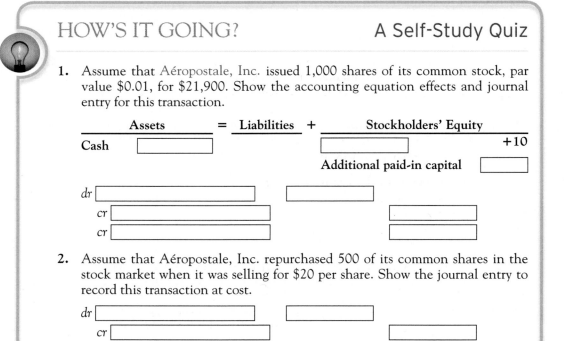

HOW'S IT GOING?   A Self-Study Quiz

1. Assume that Aéropostale, Inc. issued 1,000 shares of its common stock, par value $0.01, for $21,900. Show the accounting equation effects and journal entry for this transaction.

Assets	=	Liabilities	+	Stockholders' Equity
Cash				+10
				Additional paid-in capital

dr

   cr

   cr

2. Assume that Aéropostale, Inc. repurchased 500 of its common shares in the stock market when it was selling for $20 per share. Show the journal entry to record this transaction at cost.

dr

   cr

COACH'S TIP

Notice that the contra-account Treasury Stock is reduced only for the cost of each treasury share. Any amount received for treasury stock in excess of its cost is recorded as an increase in Additional paid-in capital, as shown below.

Reissuance of Treasury Stock When a company resells shares of its treasury stock, it does not report a gain or loss on sale, even if it sells the shares for more or less than they cost when the company reacquired them. GAAP does not permit a corporation to report income or losses from investments in its own stock because transactions with the owners are not considered profit-making activities. Instead, this type of transaction affects only the balance sheet, just like other stock issuances. To illustrate, let's extend our previous example where Sonic had repurchased its stock at a cost of $25 per share. If Sonic resells 5,000 shares of this treasury stock for $26 per share (5,000 × $26 = $130,000), the accounting equation effects and journal entry would be:

1. Analyze

	Assets	=	Liabilities	+	Stockholders' Equity	
Cash	+130,000				Treasury Stock (−xSE)	+125,000
					Additional Paid-In Capital	+5,000

2. Record

dr Cash (+A) (5,000 × $26) 130,000
   cr Treasury Stock (−xSE, +SE) (5,000 × $25)   125,000
   cr Additional Paid-In Capital (+SE) [5,000 × ($26 − $25)]....   5,000

If treasury stock were reissued at a price below its repurchase price, the difference between the repurchase price ($25 per share) and the reissue price (say, $23 per share) is recorded as a reduction in Additional paid-in capital. The accounting equation effects and journal entry for reissuing at an amount less than its cost are:

	Assets	=	Liabilities	+	Stockholders' Equity	
1. Analyze	Cash +115,000				Treasury Stock (−xSE)	+125,000
					Additional Paid-In Capital	−10,000

2. Record

dr Cash (+A) (5,000 × $23) 115,000
dr Additional Paid-In Capital (−SE) [5,000 × ($25 − $23)] 10,000
  cr Treasury Stock (−xSE, +SE) (5,000 × $25)............... 125,000

Dividends on Common Stock

Investors buy common stock because they expect a return on their investment. This return can come in two forms: dividends and increases in stock price. Some investors prefer to buy stocks that pay little or no dividends (called a *growth* investment), because companies that reinvest the majority of their earnings tend to increase their future earnings potential, along with their stock price. Dell Corporation, for example, has never paid a dividend, yet if your parents had bought 100 Dell shares when they were first issued on June 22, 1988, for $850, the investment would be worth about $200,000 at the time this chapter was being written. Rather than wait for growth in stock value, other investors, such as retired people who need a steady income, prefer to receive their return in the form of dividends. These people often seek stocks that consistently pay dividends (called an *income* investment), such as Coca-Cola, which has paid cash dividends each year since 1893.

Topic Tackler

PLUS

Check out www.mhhe.com/phillips2e for audio, visual, and PowerPoint presentations on this topic.

A corporation does not have a legal obligation to pay dividends. It is a decision made by the board of directors, and it is made each time a dividend is to be paid. Once the board of directors formally declares a dividend, a liability is created. If Sonic were to declare a dividend, its press release would contain the following information:

Sonic Corporation Announces Cash Dividend

Oklahoma City, Okla., May 20, 2006—Sonic Corporation (Nasdaq: SONC) announced today that the Company's Board of Directors declared a cash dividend of $.02 per common share, payable on or about July 1, 2006 to stockholders of record as of June 14, 2006.

Notice that this announcement contains three important dates: (1) the declaration date (May 20), (2) the date of record (June 14), and (3) the date of payment (July 1).

1. Declaration date–May 20. The **declaration date** is the date on which the board of directors officially approves the dividend. As soon as the board makes the declaration, the company records an increase in its liabilities and a corresponding increase in the Dividends declared account. Dividends declared temporarily summarizes all dividends declared during the year and later is closed to Retained earnings at year-end, causing a decrease in Retained earnings. Remember, dividends are distributions of a company's accumulated prior earnings, so they are reported on the statement of retained earnings (or the more general statement of stockholders' equity shown in Chapter 5). Dividends declared by a company are not reported on its income statement because they are not expenses of the current period. With 59,300,000 common shares outstanding, the $0.02 dividend

per share would equal $1,186,000 ($0.02 × 59,300,000). The accounting equation effects and journal entry to record them would be:

1. Analyze

Assets	=	Liabilities	+	Stockholders' Equity
		Dividends Payable +1,186,000		Dividends Declared (+D) −1,186,000

2. Record

dr Dividends Declared (+D, −SE).   1,186,000
   cr Dividends Payable (+L)   1,186,000

2. **Date of record–June 14.** After a dividend is declared, the corporation needs some time to identify who will receive the dividend. The **record date** is the date on which the corporation finalizes its list of current stockholders. The dividend is payable only to those names listed on the record date. No journal entry is made on this date.

3. **Date of payment–July 1.** The **payment date** is the date on which the cash is disbursed to pay the dividend liability. It follows the date of record, as described in the dividend announcement. Continuing our example above, when the dividend is paid and the liability satisfied on July 1, the accounting equation effects and journal entry are:

1. Analyze

Assets	=	Liabilities	+	Stockholders' Equity
Cash −1,186,000		Dividends Payable −1,186,000		

2. Record

dr Dividends Payable (−L)   1,186,000
   cr Cash (−A)   1,186,000

These three dates and the corresponding balance sheet effects are summarized in the timeline in Exhibit 11.5.

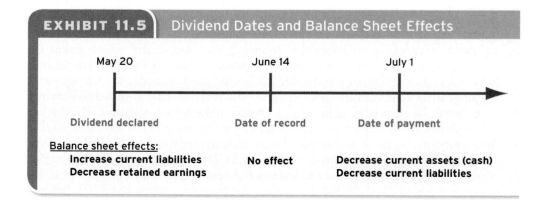

EXHIBIT 11.5   Dividend Dates and Balance Sheet Effects

May 20	June 14	July 1
Dividend declared	Date of record	Date of payment

Balance sheet effects:
| Increase current liabilities
Decrease retained earnings | No effect | Decrease current assets (cash)
Decrease current liabilities |

Notice that the declaration of a cash dividend will reduce Retained earnings when Dividends declared is closed at the end of each fiscal year. Also notice that the payment of a cash dividend reduces Cash by the same amount. These two observations explain two key financial requirements that the board of directors must consider when declaring a cash dividend:

1. **Sufficient retained earnings.** The corporation must have accumulated a sufficient amount of Retained earnings to cover the amount of the dividend. State incorporation laws often restrict cash dividends to the balance in the Retained earnings account. A company might be further restricted if it has a lending agreement with a bank containing loan covenants that require an even larger minimum balance in Retained earnings. If the company were to violate this clause, the bank could require renegotiation of the loan and possibly demand its immediate repayment. Because this particular restriction on Retained earnings can severely limit the ability to pay dividends, accounting rules require that companies disclose it in their financial statement notes.

2. **Sufficient cash.** The corporation must have sufficient cash to pay the dividend and meet the operating needs of the business. The cash generated in the past through profitable operations may already have been spent before the dividend was declared. In the case of Sonic, this money may have been used to install new debit machines at its drive-ins or pay down some of its debt. So, the mere fact that the Retained earnings account has a large credit balance does not mean that there is sufficient cash to pay a dividend. Remember, retained earnings is not cash.

COACH'S TIP

A lender imposes dividend restrictions because it doesn't want to lend money to a corporation and then have the corporation pay it out in dividends to stockholders.

HOW'S IT GOING?   A Self-Study Quiz

Answer the following questions concerning dividends:

1. On which dividend date is a liability created?
2. A cash outflow occurs on which dividend date?
3. What are the two fundamental requirements for the payment of a dividend?

STOCK DIVIDENDS AND STOCK SPLITS

Stock Dividends

The term *dividend,* when used alone with no adjectives, implies a cash dividend. However, there are some dividends that are not paid with cash but instead involve payment with additional shares of stock. These dividends, called **stock dividends,** are distributions of additional shares of a corporation's stock to its stockholders on a pro rata basis at no cost to the stockholder. The phrase *pro rata basis* means that each stockholder receives additional shares equal to the percentage of shares held. A stockholder with 10 percent of the outstanding shares would receive 10 percent of any additional shares issued as a stock dividend.

The value of a stock dividend is the subject of much debate. In reality, a stock dividend by itself has no economic value. All stockholders receive a pro rata distribution of shares, which means that each stockholder owns exactly the same proportion of the company after a stock dividend as he or she did before the dividend. If you get change for a dollar, you do not have more wealth because you hold four quarters instead of only one dollar. Similarly, if you own 10 percent of a company, you are not wealthier simply because the company declares a stock dividend and gives you (and all other stockholders) more shares of stock.

YOU SHOULD KNOW

A **stock dividend** is a distribution of additional shares of a corporation's own stock.

Video 11.2

The stock market reacts immediately when a stock dividend is issued, and the stock price falls proportionally. Theoretically, if the stock price was $60 before a stock dividend and the dividend doubles the number of shares outstanding, the price per share would fall to $30. Thus, an investor would own 100 shares worth $6,000 before the stock dividend (100 × $60) and 200 shares worth $6,000 after the stock dividend (200 × $30). In reality, the fall in price is not exactly proportional to the number of new shares issued. In some cases, the stock dividend makes the stock more attractive to new investors. Many investors prefer to buy stock in round lots, which are multiples of 100 shares. An investor with $10,000 might not buy a stock selling for $150, for instance, because she cannot afford to buy 100 shares. However, she might buy the stock if the price were less than $100 as the result of a stock dividend. Thus, one of the main reasons for issuing a stock dividend is that it reduces the market price per share of stock.

When a stock dividend occurs, the company must decrease the Retained earnings account to show that a dividend was declared and increase the Common stock account to show that additional shares were issued. The amount recorded depends on whether the stock dividend is classified as large or small. Most stock dividends are classified as large. A large stock dividend involves the distribution of additional shares that amount to more than 20–25 percent of currently outstanding shares. A small stock dividend involves the distribution of shares that amount to less than 20–25 percent of the outstanding shares. If the stock dividend is classified as large, the amount recorded is based on the par value of the additional shares issued. If the stock dividend is small (less than 20–25 percent), the amount recorded should be the total market value of the shares issued, with the par value of the stock recorded in the Common stock account and the excess in the Additional paid-in capital account.

If we assume that Sonic issues 50,000,000 of its $0.01 par value common shares as a large stock dividend, the company would move $500,000 (50,000,000 × $0.01) from Retained earnings to the company's Common stock account as shown below, using the journal entry that follows:

1. Analyze

Assets	=	Liabilities	+	Stockholders' Equity	
				Retained Earnings	−500,000
				Common Stock	+500,000

2. Record

dr Retained Earnings (−SE) ($0.01 × 50,000,000)   500,000
    cr Common Stock (+SE)   500,000

Notice that the stock dividend does not change total stockholders' equity. It changes only the balances of some of the accounts that make up stockholders' equity.

Before we leave this section, we must caution you on a potential point of confusion. Most companies refer to the 100 percent stock dividend discussed in this section as a "stock split effected as a stock dividend." Although they *say* stock split, they actually mean a stock dividend as described above. A true stock split is different, both in terms of how it is done and how it is accounted for, as we discuss in the following section.

Stock Splits

Stock splits are not dividends. While they are similar to a stock dividend, they are quite different in terms of how they occur and how they affect the stockholders' equity accounts. In a **stock split**, the total number of authorized shares is increased by a specified amount, such as 2-for-1. In this instance, each share held is called in and two new shares are issued in its place. Cash is not affected when the company splits its stock, so the total resources of the company do not change. It's just like taking a four-piece pizza and cutting each piece into two smaller pieces.

Typically, a stock split involves revising the corporate charter to reduce the per-share par value of all authorized shares, so that the total par value across all shares is unchanged. For instance, if a company with 1 million shares outstanding executes a 2-for-1 stock split, it reduces the per-share par value of its stock from $0.01 to $0.005 and doubles the number of shares outstanding. The decrease in par value per share offsets the increase in the number of shares, so the financial position of the company is not affected and no journal entry is needed.

Stockholders' Equity	Before a 2-for-1 Stock Split	After a 2-for-1 Stock Split
Number of shares outstanding	1,000,000	2,000,000
Par value per share	$ 0.01	$ 0.005
Total par value outstanding	$ 10,000	$ 10,000
Retained earnings	650,000	650,000
Total stockholders' equity	$ 660,000	$ 660,000

Exhibit 11.6 reviews the similarities and differences between stock dividends and stock splits. Notice that although they have similar effects on the number of shares outstanding, they are accounted for differently.

EXHIBIT 11.6   Similarities and Differences between Stock Dividends and Stock Splits

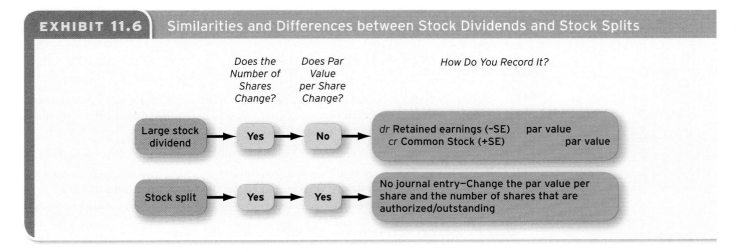

If you're like most new financial managers, you probably wonder how a company's board of directors chooses between a large 100 percent stock dividend and a 2-for-1 stock split when both increase the number of shares outstanding and decrease the per-share market price. The answer, it seems, is closely related to how stock dividends and splits are accounted for. As you can see in Exhibit 11.6, a stock dividend causes a reduction in Retained earnings, whereas a "true" stock split doesn't. By itself, this accounting difference might not mean much, but remember that a company needs to have an adequate balance in Retained earnings to declare cash dividends in the future. So if you're managing a company that expects some financial struggles in the future, you'll want to use a 2-for-1 stock split because this doesn't reduce Retained earnings, which means it doesn't reduce your ability to declare cash dividends in the future. On the other hand, if your company is expecting financial success in the near future, you won't care that Retained earnings is reduced by a stock dividend because future earnings will build up Retained earnings enough to allow cash dividends to be declared. In fact, you'll probably *want* to use a stock dividend just to show how confident you are that your company is expecting to do well in the near future. This reasoning suggests that a company's board may declare stock dividends rather than stock splits to signal to financial statement users that strong financial performance is forecast for the company in the near future.

Exhibit 11.7 shows the typical components of the stockholders' equity section of the balance sheet and highlights amounts (in blue) that are changed by a 2-for-1 stock split, a 100% stock dividend, and an equivalent ($10,000) cash dividend. Notice that the cash dividend is the only distribution that affects total stockholders' equity because it is the only one that distributes the company's resources to stockholders.

EXHIBIT 11.7   Comparison of Distributions to Stockholders

| | | AFTER | | |
Stockholders' Equity	BEFORE	2-for-1 Stock Split	100% Stock Dividend	$10,000 Cash Dividend
Contributed Capital				
Number of common shares outstanding	1,000,000	2,000,000	2,000,000	1,000,000
Par value per common share	$ 0.01	$ 0.005	$ 0.01	$ 0.01
Common stock, at par	$ 10,000	$ 10,000	$ 20,000	$ 10,000
Additional paid-in capital	30,000	30,000	30,000	30,000
Retained Earnings	650,000	650,000	640,000	640,000
Total stockholders' equity	$ 690,000	$ 690,000	$ 690,000	$ 680,000

HOW'S IT GOING?   A Self-Study Quiz

Vandalay Industries wanted to reduce the market price of its stock, so it issued 100,000 new shares of common stock (par value $10) in a 100 percent stock dividend when the market value was $30 per share.

1. Prepare the journal entry that Vandalay would use to record this transaction.
2. What journal entry would be required if the transaction instead involved a 2-for-1 stock split? Theoretically, what would be the new stock price after the split?

Quiz Answers
1. dr Retained Earnings (−SE)   1,000,000
   cr Common Stock (+SE)   1,000,000
2. No journal entry is required in the case of a stock split. Theoretically, the new price would be one-half of what it was before the split ($30 × ½ = $15).

PREFERRED STOCK

In addition to common stock, some corporations issue **preferred stock.** Preferred stock differs from common stock based on a number of rights granted to the stockholders. The most significant differences are:

- **Preferred stock generally does not grant voting rights.** As a result, preferred stock does not appeal to investors who want some control over the operations of a company. It does appeal, though, to existing common stockholders because preferred stock allows a company to raise funds without reducing common stockholders' control.
- **Preferred stock is less risky.** Generally, preferred stock is less risky than common stock because preferred stockholders are paid dividends before common stockholders. Also, if the corporation goes out of business, creditors are paid first,

followed by preferred stockholders. Common stockholders are paid last, using whatever assets remain after having paid preferred stockholders.

- **Preferred stock typically has a fixed dividend rate.** For example, "6 percent preferred stock, par value $10 per share" pays a dividend each year of 6 percent of par, or $0.60 per share. If preferred stock has no par value, the preferred dividend would be specified as $0.60 per share. The fixed dividend is attractive to certain investors who want a stable income from their investments.

Preferred Stock Issuance

Just like an issuance of common stock, a preferred stock issuance will increase a company's cash and its stockholders' equity. To illustrate, assume that during the upcoming fiscal year, Sonic issued 1,000,000 shares of its $.01 par value preferred stock for $5 per share ($5 × 1,000,000 shares = $5,000,000 cash received). As shown below, the Preferred stock account would increase by its par value for each share issued ($0.01 × 1,000,000 = $10,000) and the amount of cash received in excess of par value would be recorded as Additional paid-in capital—preferred:

	Assets	=	Liabilities	+	Stockholders' Equity	
1. Analyze	Cash +5,000,000				Preferred Stock	+10,000
					Additional Paid-In Capital-Preferred	+4,990,000

2. Record		
dr Cash (+A) (1,000,000 × $5)	5,000,000	
cr Preferred Stock (+SE) (1,000,000 × $.01)		10,000
cr Additional Paid-In Capital—Preferred (+SE)		4,990,000

Preferred Stock Dividends

Because investors who purchase preferred stock give up voting rights that are available to investors in common stock, preferred stock offers dividend preferences. The two most common dividend preferences are called current and cumulative.

Current Dividend Preference   A **current dividend preference** requires that preferred dividends be paid before any dividends are paid to holders of common stock. This preference is always a feature of preferred stock. After the current dividend preference has been met and if no other preference exists, dividends can be paid to the common stockholders. To illustrate, consider the following example:

> **YOU SHOULD KNOW**
>
> **Current dividend preference** is the feature of preferred stock that grants priority on preferred dividends over common dividends.

Sophia Company

Preferred stock outstanding, 6%, par $20; 2,000 shares
Common stock outstanding, par $10; 5,000 shares

Assume the preferred stock carries only a current dividend preference and that dividends totaling $8,000 and $10,000 are declared in 2007 and 2008. In each year, a portion of the total dividends would first go to the preferred stockholders, and only the excess would go to the common stockholders.

Year	Total Dividends Declared	Dividends on 6% Preferred Stock*	Dividends on Common Stock**
2007	$ 8,000	$2,400	$5,600
2008	10,000	2,400	7,600

* Dividends on preferred stock = 2,000 shares × $20 par value × 6% dividend = $2,400
** Dividends on common stock = Total dividends declared − Dividends on preferred stock

Had Sophia Company not declared dividends in 2007, preferred stockholders would have had preference to $2,400 of dividends only in 2008. The current dividend preference does not carry over to later years unless the preferred stock is designated as cumulative, as discussed next.

Cumulative Dividend Preference   This preference states that if all or a part of the current dividend is not paid in full, the cumulative unpaid amount, known as **dividends in arrears,** must be paid before any future common dividends can be paid. Of course, if the preferred stock is noncumulative, dividends can never be in arrears; any preferred dividends that are not declared are permanently lost. Because preferred stockholders are unwilling to accept this unfavorable feature, preferred stock is usually cumulative.

To illustrate the cumulative preference, assume that Sophia Company has the same amount of stock outstanding as in the last example. In this case, however, assume that dividends are in arrears for 2005 and 2006. The following table shows that, in 2007, dividends in arrears are satisfied first, followed by the current dividend preference, and the excess goes to common stockholders. In 2008, preferred dividends include only the current preference of that year because dividends in arrears were fulfilled in 2007.

		DIVIDENDS ON 6% PREFERRED STOCK		
Year	Total Dividends Declared	In arrears*	Current**	Dividends on Common Stock***
2007	$ 8,000	$4,800	$2,400	$ 800
2008	10,000	—	2,400	7,600

* Dividends in arrears preference = 2,000 shares × $20 par value × 6% dividend × 2 years = $4,800
** Current dividend preference = 2,000 shares × $20 par value × 6% dividend = $2,400
*** Dividends on common stock = Total dividends declared − Total dividends on preferred stock

Because dividends are not an actual liability until the board of directors declares them, dividends in arrears are not reported on the balance sheet. Instead, they are disclosed in the notes to the financial statements. The following note from American Skiing—the company that operates ski, snowboard, and golf resorts throughout the United States, including Colorado's Steamboat and Vermont's Killington—is typical:

As of July 31, 2005, cumulative dividends in arrears totaled approximately $23.7 million and $109.3 million for the Series C-1 Preferred Stock and Series C-2 Preferred Stock, respectively.

RETAINED EARNINGS

As its name suggests, Retained earnings represents the company's total earnings that have been retained in the business (rather than being distributed to stockholders). The balance in this account increases each year that the company reports net income on the income statement, and it decreases each year that the company reports a net loss (expenses greater than revenues) or declares cash or stock dividends to stockholders. Think of retained earnings as the amount of equity that the company itself has generated for stockholders (through profitable operations) but not yet distributed to them.

Should a company ever accumulate more net losses than net income over its life, it will report a negative (debit) balance in the Retained earnings account. This amount is (a) shown in parentheses in the stockholders' equity section of the balance sheet, (b) deducted when computing total stockholders' equity, and (c) typically called an Accumulated deficit rather than Retained earnings. Exhibit 11.8 provides a recent example courtesy of the digital music pioneer Napster, Inc.

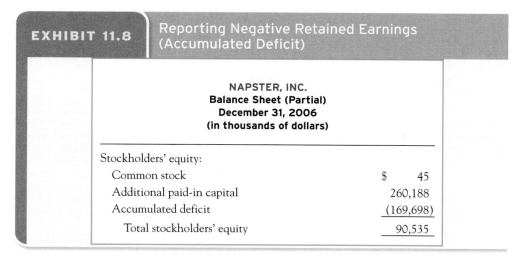

EXHIBIT 11.8 — Reporting Negative Retained Earnings (Accumulated Deficit)

NAPSTER, INC.
Balance Sheet (Partial)
December 31, 2006
(in thousands of dollars)

Stockholders' equity:	
Common stock	$ 45
Additional paid-in capital	260,188
Accumulated deficit	(169,698)
Total stockholders' equity	90,535

Evaluate the Results

Now that you know how dividends and other stockholders' equity transactions are accounted for inside a company, it's time to evaluate things from the outside. In this section, you will learn to use three ratios to evaluate how well a company appears to be using its capital to generate returns for the company and, ultimately, for its stockholders.

EARNINGS PER SHARE (EPS)

The most famous of all ratios, earnings per share (EPS), reports how much profit is earned for each share of common stock outstanding. The calculation of EPS can involve many details and intricacies, but in its basic form, it is computed by dividing "bottom line" net income by the average number of common shares outstanding. Most companies report EPS on the income statement immediately below Net income or in the notes to the financial statements.[2]

> **Learning Objective 5**
> Analyze the earnings per share (EPS), return on equity (ROE), and price/earnings (P/E) ratios.

You might be wondering why *earnings* per share is so popular when dividends and stock prices ultimately determine the return to stockholders. The reason is that current earnings can predict future dividends and stock prices. If a company generates increased earnings in the current year, it will be able to pay higher dividends in future years. In other words, current EPS influences expectations about future dividends, which investors factor into the current stock price. That's why the stock price of Sonic Corporation increased by 6 percent on March 21, 2006, immediately after the company announced that its EPS for the quarter would come in higher than in the previous year.

Another reason that EPS is so popular is that it allows you to easily compare results over time. For example, for the 2005 fiscal year, Sonic earned net income of $75 million, compared to $63 million for the previous year. It's hard to know whether that's a good increase for stockholders, because it's possible that the increase in net income was accompanied by an increase in the number of shares outstanding. By considering earnings on a per-share basis, we adjust for the effect of additional stock issued, resulting in a clearer picture of what increases mean for each investor.

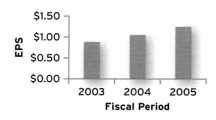

[2] Although companies report their annual EPS numbers only at the end of their fiscal years, most analysts find it useful to update annual EPS as each quarter's results are reported. To do this, analysts will compute their own "trailing 12 months" EPS measure by summing the most recent four quarters of EPS. This way, they can get a timely measure of year-long EPS, without having to wait until the end of the fiscal year.

As you could see from the graph, the increase in net income from $63 million to $75 million actually did translate into EPS growth from $1.06 to $1.26 for each investor.

FINANCIAL ANALYSIS TOOLS		
Name of Measure	**Formula**	**What It Tells You**
Earnings per share (EPS)	$\dfrac{\text{Net Income}}{\text{Average Number of Common Shares Outstanding}}$	• The amount of income generated for each share of common stock owned by stockholders • A higher ratio means greater profitability
Return on equity (ROE)	$\dfrac{\text{Net Income}}{\text{Average Stockholders' Equity}}$	• The amount of income earned for each dollar of stockholders' equity • A higher ratio means stockholders are likely to enjoy greater returns
Price/Earnings (P/E) ratio	$\dfrac{\text{Current Stock Price (per share)}}{\text{Earnings per Share (annual)}}$	• How many times more than the current year's earnings investors are willing to pay for a company's common stock • A higher number means investors anticipate an improvement in the company's future results

Exhibit 11.9 (on page 509) shows how to calculate EPS for Sonic and its most similar competitor Checkers Drive-In. We should caution you against comparing EPS across companies. The number of shares outstanding for one company can differ dramatically from the number outstanding for a different company, simply because one chooses to issue more shares of stock than the other. Also, as you have seen in earlier chapters, net income can be affected by differences in how two companies cost inventory (Chapter 7), estimate bad debts (Chapter 8), depreciate long-lived tangible assets (Chapter 9), and estimate losses from contingent liabilities (Chapter 10). So, while EPS is an effective and widely used measure for comparing a company with itself over time, it is not appropriate for comparing across companies.

RETURN ON EQUITY (ROE)

Like EPS, return on equity (ROE) reports a company's return to investors. However, rather than relate net income to the average *number* of shares outstanding, the return on equity (ROE) ratio relates net income to the average *dollars* of stockholder investment and earnings reinvested in the company.[3] Because ROE uses dollars contributed to and reinvested in the company, this ratio can be appropriately compared across companies.

The results reported in Exhibit 11.9 indicate that Sonic's 2005 return to common stockholders of 21.0% was quite a bit higher than Checkers' return of 11.4%. Sonic's ROE also was higher than the average ROE for the entire restaurant industry, which according to Yahoo!Finance was about 16.5%. These results suggest that Sonic is earning good returns on stockholders' equity. In the next section, we'll see whether this affects the amount that investors were willing to pay for shares in Sonic.

PRICE/EARNINGS (P/E) RATIO

While EPS and ROE are useful for evaluating a company's return to stockholders, they don't help you determine what a reasonable price would be for the company's stock. Sophisticated techniques to value a company are taught in advanced courses in finance, but for this course, let's focus on a simple tool. The price/earnings ratio is the most basic

---

[3] If a company has preferred stock outstanding, the ROE ratio can be adjusted to focus on the common stockholders' perspective. Simply deduct any preferred dividends from net income and exclude any preferred stock accounts from the calculation of average stockholders' equity.

EXHIBIT 11.9 | Summary of EPS, ROE, and P/E Ratio Analyses

Company	Relevant Information (in millions)			2005 EPS	2005 ROE	2005 P/E
		2005	2004			
SONIC America's Drive-In.	Net income	$75.4	$63.0	$\dfrac{\$75.4}{60.0}$ $= \$1.26$	$\dfrac{\$75.4}{\$(384.5 + 334.8)/2}$ $= 0.210$ or 21.0%	$\dfrac{\$29.50}{\$1.26}$ $= 23.4$
	Average number of shares	60.0	59.3			
	Stockholders' equity	$384.5	$334.8			
	Stock price	$29.50	$30.50			
		2005	2004			
Checkers BURGERS. FRIES. COLA	Net income	$9.1	$11.5	$\dfrac{\$9.1}{11.3}$ $= \$0.81$	$\dfrac{\$9.1}{\$(86.3 + 73.0)/2}$ $= 0.114$ or 11.4%	$\dfrac{\$15.16}{\$0.81}$ $= 18.7$
	Average number of shares	11.3	11.6			
	Stockholders' equity	$86.3	$73.0			
	Stock price	$15.16	$13.40			

way to determine the value investors place on a company's common stock. The P/E ratio, as most people call it, measures how many times more than current year's earnings investors are willing to pay for a company's stock. It is calculated as shown in the far right column of Exhibit 11.9, by dividing a company's stock price by its EPS for the year.

Generally, a relatively high P/E ratio means investors expect the company to improve in the future and increase its profits, so they have factored the future earnings into the current stock price. A relatively low P/E ratio typically means that they don't expect strong future performance. P/E ratios can vary significantly across industries, so you'll find them most meaningful when comparing a company over time with itself or with competitors in the same industry. Sonic's P/E ratio of 23.4 in 2005 was higher than both Checkers (18.7) and the industry average (19.5). This suggests that investors were anticipating good things to come from Sonic.

HOW'S IT GOING?   Self-Study Quiz

Sonic reported stockholders' equity of $265.4 (million) at its 2003 fiscal year-end. The price per share of common stock at that time was $30.72.

a. Use this information, along with that in Exhibit 11.9, to calculate Sonic's Earnings per Share (EPS), Return on Equity (ROE), and Price/Earnings (P/E) ratios for 2004.

2004 EPS: 2004 ROE: 2004 P/E:

$$\frac{\Box}{\Box} = \Box \qquad \frac{\Box}{(\Box + \Box)/2} = \Box \qquad \frac{\Box}{\Box} = \Box$$

b. Did Sonic's EPS and ROE improve or decline from 2004 (calculated in a) to 2005 (shown in Exhibit 11.9)? Does the 2004 P/E ratio suggest investors anticipated the changes that occurred in 2005?

SUPPLEMENT: OWNERS' EQUITY FOR OTHER FORMS OF BUSINESS

OWNER'S EQUITY FOR A SOLE PROPRIETORSHIP

A sole proprietorship is an unincorporated business owned by one person. Only two owner's equity accounts are needed: (1) a capital account for the proprietor (H. Simpson, Capital) and (2) a drawing (or withdrawal) account for the proprietor (H. Simpson, Drawings).

The capital account of a sole proprietorship serves two purposes: to record investments by the owner and to accumulate periodic income or loss. The drawing account is used to record the owner's withdrawals of cash or other assets from the business, similar to recording dividends declared by corporations. The drawing account is closed to the capital account at the end of each accounting period. Thus, after the drawing account is closed, the capital account reflects the cumulative total of all investments by the owner and all earnings of the business less all withdrawals from the entity by the owner.

In most respects, the accounting for a sole proprietorship is the same as for a corporation. Exhibit 11A.1 presents the recording of selected transactions of Homer's Dough Store and the owner's equity section of the balance sheet.

Because a sole proprietorship does not pay income taxes, its financial statements do not report Income tax expense or Income taxes payable. Instead, the net income of a sole proprietorship is taxed when it is included on the owner's personal income tax return. Likewise, the owner's salary is not recognized as an expense in a sole proprietorship because an employer/employee contractual relationship cannot exist with only one party involved. The owner's salary is therefore accounted for as a distribution of profits—a withdrawal—instead of salary expense, as it would be in a corporation.

OWNERS' EQUITY FOR A PARTNERSHIP

The Uniform Partnership Act, which most states have adopted, defines a partnership as "an association of two or more persons to carry on as co-owners of a business for profit." Small businesses and professionals such as accountants, doctors, and lawyers often use the partnership form of business.

A partnership is formed by two or more persons reaching mutual agreement about the terms of the relationship. The law does not require an application for a charter as in the case of a corporation. Instead, the agreement between the partners constitutes a partnership contract. This agreement should specify matters such as division of income, management responsibilities, transfer or sale of partnership interests, disposition of assets upon liquidation, and procedures to be followed in case of the death of a partner. If the partnership agreement does not specify these matters, the laws of the resident state are binding.

In comparison to a corporation, the primary advantages of a partnership are (1) ease of formation, (2) complete control by the partners, and (3) lack of income taxes on the business itself. The primary disadvantage is the unlimited liability of each partner for the partnership's debts. If the partnership does not have sufficient assets to satisfy outstanding debt, creditors of the partnership can seize each partner's personal assets. In some cases, this can even result in one partner being held responsible for another partner's share of the partnership's debt.

As with a sole proprietorship, accounting for a partnership follows the same underlying principles as any other form of business organization, except for those entries that directly affect owners' equity. Accounting for partners' equity follows the same pattern as for a sole proprietorship, except that separate capital and drawings accounts must be established for each partner. Investments by each partner are credited to that partner's Capital account and withdrawals are debited to the respective Drawings account. The net income of a partnership is divided among the partners in accordance with the partnership agreement and credited to each account. The respective Drawings accounts are closed to the partner Capital accounts. After the closing process, each partner's Capital

> **COACH'S TIP**
>
> The capital account is like all the stockholders' equity accounts for a corporation combined into a single account. The drawing account is like the dividends declared account for a corporation.

EXHIBIT 11A.1	Accounting for Owner's Equity for a Sole Proprietorship

Selected Entries during 2007

January 1, 2007

H. Simpson started a retail store by investing $150,000 of personal savings. The accounting equation effects and journal entry follow:

Assets	=	Liabilities	+	Owner's Equity	
Cash +150,000				H. Simpson, Capital	+150,000

dr Cash (+A) 150,000
    cr H. Simpson, Capital (+OE)   150,000

During 2007

Each month during the year, Simpson withdrew $1,000 cash from the business for personal living costs. Accordingly, each month the financial effects and required journal entry are:

Assets	=	Liabilities	+	Owner's Equity	
Cash −1,000				H. Simpson, Drawings (+D)	−1,000

dr H. Simpson, Drawings (+D, −OE) 1,000
    cr Cash (−A)   1,000

Note: At December 31, 2007, after the last withdrawal, the drawings account reflected a debit balance of $12,000.

December 31, 2007

The usual journal entries for the year, including adjusting and closing entries for the revenue and expense accounts, resulted in revenue of $48,000 and expenses of $30,000. The net income of $18,000 was closed to the capital account as follows:

Assets	=	Liabilities	+	Owner's Equity	
				Revenues (−R)	−48,000
				Expenses (−E)	+30,000
				H. Simpson, Capital	+18,000

dr Individual Revenue Accounts (−R) 48,000
    cr Individual Expense Accounts (−E)   30,000
    cr H. Simpson, Capital (+OE)   18,000

December 31, 2007

The drawings account was closed as follows:

Assets	=	Liabilities	+	Owner's Equity	
				H. Simpson, Capital	−12,000
				H. Simpson, Drawings (−D)	+12,000

dr H. Simpson, Capital (−OE) 12,000
    cr H. Simpson, Drawings (−D, +OE)   12,000

Balance Sheet, December 31, 2007 (partial)

Owner's Equity

H. Simpson, capital, January 1, 2007	$150,000
Add: Net income for 2007	18,000
Total	168,000
Less: Withdrawals for 2007	(12,000)
H. Simpson, capital, December 31, 2007	$156,000

account reflects the cumulative total of all that partner's investments plus that partner's share of the partnership earnings less all that partner's withdrawals.

Exhibit 11A.2 presents selected journal entries and partial financial statements for AB Partnership to illustrate the accounting for the distribution of income and partners' equity.

EXHIBIT 11A.2 | Accounting for Partners' Equity

Selected Entries during 2007

January 1, 2007

A. Able and B. Baker organized AB Partnership on this date. Able contributed $60,000 and Baker $40,000 cash to the partnership and agreed to divide net income (and net loss) 60 percent and 40 percent, respectively. The financial effects of this investment on the business and the journal entry to record them are

Assets	=	Liabilities	+	Partners' Equity	
Cash +100,000				A. Able, Capital	+60,000
				B. Baker, Capital	+40,000

```
dr Cash (+A)............................    100,000
    cr A. Able, Capital (+OE) ..............            60,000
    cr B. Baker, Capital (+OE) ..............            40,000
```

During 2007

The partners agreed that Able would withdraw $1,000 and Baker $650 per month in cash. Accordingly, each month the following financial effects were recorded with the journal entry that appears below:

Assets	=	Liabilities	+	Partners' Equity	
Cash −1,650				A. Able, Drawings	−1,000
				B. Baker, Drawings	−650

```
dr A. Able, Drawings (−OE) ..............    1,000
dr B. Baker, Drawings (−OE)..............      650
    cr Cash (−A) ........................             1,650
```

Note: At December 31, 2007, after the last withdrawals, the Drawings account for Able had a debit balance of $12,000 and the Drawings account for Baker had a debit balance of $7,800.

December 31, 2007

Assume that the normal closing entries for the revenue and expense accounts resulted in revenue of $78,000, expenses of $48,000, and net income of $30,000. The partnership agreement specified Abel would receive 60 percent of net income ($18,000 = 60% × $30,000) and Baker would get 40 percent ($12,000 = 40% × $30,000). The financial effects and related closing entry follow:

Assets	=	Liabilities	+	Partners' Equity	
				Revenues (−R)	−78,000
				Expenses (−E)	+48,000
				A. Able, Capital	+18,000
				B. Baker, Capital	+12,000

```
dr Individual Revenue Accounts (−R)........................    78,000
    cr Individual Expense Accounts (−E).....................            48,000
    cr A. Able, Capital (+OE) (60% × $30,000) ..............            18,000
    cr B. Baker, Capital (+OE) (40% × $30,000) ..............           12,000
```

December 31, 2007

The financial effects of closing the drawings accounts and the related closing journal entry are

Assets	=	Liabilities	+	Partners' Equity	
				A. Able, Capital	−12,000
				B. Baker, Capital	−7,800
				A. Able, Drawings	+12,000
				B. Baker, Drawings	+7,800

```
dr A. Able, Capital (−OE)....................    12,000
dr B. Baker, Capital (−OE) ..................     7,800
    cr A. Able, Drawings (+OE) ..............             12,000
    cr B. Baker, Drawings (+OE) ..............             7,800
```

A separate statement of partners' capital, similar to a corporation's statement of stockholders' equity, is customarily prepared to supplement the balance sheet, as shown next:

EXHIBIT 11A.2 Accounting for Partners' Equity (*Continued*)

AB PARTNERSHIP
Statement of Partners' Equity
For the Year Ended December 31, 2007

	A. Able	B. Baker	Total
Investment, January 1, 2007	$ 60,000	$40,000	$100,000
Add: Additional investments during the year	0	0	0
Add: Net income for the year	18,000	12,000	30,000
Totals	78,000	52,000	130,000
Less: Drawings during the year	(12,000)	(7,800)	(19,800)
Partners' equity, December 31, 2007	$ 66,000	$44,200	$110,200

OTHER BUSINESS FORMS

In addition to sole proprietorships, partnerships, and corporations, other forms of business exist. These forms blend features of the "pure" organizational forms described earlier in this chapter to create hybrid business forms such as S Corporations, Limited Liability Partnerships (LLPs), and Limited Liability Companies (LLCs). The LLC in particular is an increasingly common form of business that combines legal characteristics of corporations (such as a separate legal identity and limited liability) with the tax treatment of partnerships (where tax is paid by the individual owners rather than by the business entity itself). Accounting for these hybrid entities generally follows the methods shown earlier in this chapter.

The financial statements of an LLC follow the same format as those for a partnership, which differs from a corporation in the following ways: (1) the financial statements include an additional section entitled Distribution of Net Income; (2) the owners' equity section of the balance sheet is detailed for each owner; (3) the income statement does not report income tax expense because these forms of business do not pay income tax (owners must report their share of the entity's profits on their individual tax returns); and (4) unless other contractual arrangements exist, amounts paid to the owners are not recorded as expenses but instead are accounted for as withdrawals of capital.

REVIEW THE CHAPTER

DEMONSTRATION CASE A: STOCK ISSUANCE AND REPURCHASES

This case focuses on selected transactions from the first year of operations of Zoogle Corporation, which became a public company on January 1, 2007, for the purpose of operating a lost-pet search business. The charter authorized the following stock:

> Common stock, $0.10 par value, 20,000 shares.
> Preferred stock, 5 percent noncumulative, $100 par value, 5,000 shares.

The following summarized transactions, selected from 2007, were completed on the dates indicated:

a. Jan. 1   Issued a total of 8,000 shares of $0.10 par value common stock for cash at $50 per share.

b. Feb. 1   Sold 2,000 shares of preferred stock at $102 per share; cash collected in full.

c. July 1   Purchased 400 shares of common stock that had been issued earlier. Zoogle Corporation paid the stockholder $54 per share for the stock, which is currently held in treasury.

d. Aug. 1   Sold 30 shares of the common treasury stock at $56 per share.

e. Dec. 31   The board decided not to declare any dividends for the current year.

Required:

1. Give the appropriate journal entries, and show calculations for each transaction.
2. Prepare the stockholders' equity section of the balance sheet for Zoogle Corporation at December 31, 2007. Assume that Retained earnings is $31,000.

Suggested Solution

1. Journal entries:

a. Jan. 1, 2007   dr Cash (+A) ($50 × 8,000 shares)   400,000
          cr Common Stock (+SE) ($0.10 × 8,000 shares)   800
          cr Additional Paid-In Capital: Common (+SE)   399,200

b. Feb. 1, 2007   dr Cash (+A) ($102 × 2,000 shares)   204,000
          cr Preferred Stock (+SE) ($100 par × 2,000 shares) . .   200,000
          cr Additional Paid-In Capital: Preferred (+SE)   4,000
          (($102 − $100) × 2,000 shares)

c. July 1, 2007   dr Treasury Stock (+xSE, −SE).   21,600
          cr Cash (−A) ($54 × 400 shares)   21,600

d. Aug. 1, 2007   dr Cash (+A) ($56 × 30 shares)   1,680
          cr Treasury Stock (−xSE, +SE) ($54 × 30 shares) . .   1,620
          cr Additional Paid-In Capital: Common (+SE)   60

e. Dec. 31, 2007   No journal entry is required.

2. Stockholders' equity section of the balance sheet:

ZOOGLE CORPORATION
Partial Balance Sheet
At December 31, 2007

Stockholders' Equity		
Contributed capital		
Preferred stock, 5% (par value $100; 5,000 authorized shares, 2,000 issued and outstanding shares)	$200,000	
Additional paid-in capital, preferred stock	4,000	
Common stock ($.10 par value; authorized 20,000 shares, issued 8,000 shares of which 370 shares are held as treasury stock)	800	
Additional paid-in capital, common stock	399,260	
Total contributed capital		$604,060
Retained earnings		31,000
Treasury stock, at cost, 370 common shares		(19,980)
Total stockholders' equity		615,080

PRACTICE MATERIAL

QUESTIONS

1. Identify the primary advantages of the corporate form of business.
2. What are the relative advantages of equity versus debt financing?
3. Explain each of the following terms: (*a*) authorized common stock, (*b*) issued common stock, and (*c*) outstanding common stock.
4. What are the differences between common stock and preferred stock?
5. What is the distinction between par value and no-par value capital stock?
6. What are the usual characteristics of preferred stock?
7. What are the two basic sources of stockholders' equity? Explain each.
8. What is treasury stock? Why do corporations acquire treasury stock?
9. How is treasury stock reported on the balance sheet? How is the "gain or loss" on reissued treasury stock reported on the financial statements?
10. What are the two financial requirements to support the declaration of a cash dividend? What are the effects of a cash dividend on assets and stockholders' equity?
11. What is the difference between cumulative and noncumulative preferred stock?
12. What is a stock dividend? How does a stock dividend differ from a cash dividend?
13. What are the primary reasons for issuing a stock dividend?
14. Identify and explain the three important dates with respect to dividends.
15. Why is the EPS number so popular? What are its limitations?
16. How do stock repurchases affect the EPS and ROE ratios?
17. What is one interpretation of a high P/E ratio?

MULTIPLE CHOICE

1. Which feature is not applicable to common stock ownership?
   a. Right to receive dividends before preferred stock shareholders.
   b. Right to vote on appointment of external auditor.
   c. Right to receive residual assets of the company should it cease operations.
   d. All of the above are applicable to common stock ownership.

2. Which statement regarding treasury stock is false?
   a. Treasury stock is considered to be issued but not outstanding.
   b. Treasury stock has no voting, dividend, or liquidation rights.
   c. Treasury stock reduces total stockholders' equity on the balance sheet.
   d. None of the above are false.

3. Which of the following statements about stock dividends is true?
   a. Stock dividends are reported on the income statement.
   b. Stock dividends increase total stockholders' equity.
   c. Stock dividends decrease total stockholders' equity.
   d. None of the above.

4. Which of the following is ordered from the largest number of shares to the smallest number of shares?
   a. Shares authorized, shares issued, shares outstanding.
   b. Shares issued, shares outstanding, shares authorized.
   c. Shares outstanding, shares issued, shares authorized.
   d. Shares in treasury, shares outstanding, shares issued.

Topic Tackler

PLUS

Quiz 11

Check out www.mhhe.com/phillips2e for more multiple choice questions.

5. Which of the following statements about the relative advantages of equity and debt financing is false?

   a. An advantage of equity financing is that it does not have to be repaid.

   b. An advantage of equity financing is that dividends are optional.

   c. An advantage of equity financing is that new stockholders get to vote and share in the earnings of the company.

   d. An advantage of debt financing is that interest is tax deductible.

6. A journal entry is not recorded on what date?

   a. Date of declaration.

   b. Date of record.

   c. Date of payment.

   d. A journal entry is recorded on all of the above dates.

7. Which of the following transactions will increase the return on equity?

   a. Declare and issue a stock dividend.

   b. Split the stock 2-for-1.

   c. Repurchase the company's stock.

   d. None of the above.

8. Which statement regarding dividends is false?

   a. Dividends represent a sharing of corporate profits with owners.

   b. Both stock and cash dividends reduce retained earnings.

   c. Cash dividends paid to stockholders reduce net income.

   d. None of the above statements are false.

9. When treasury stock is purchased with cash, what is the impact on the balance sheet equation?

   a. No change—the reduction of the asset Cash is offset with the addition of the asset Treasury Stock.

   b. Assets decrease and stockholders' equity increases.

   c. Assets increase and stockholders' equity decreases.

   d. Assets decrease and stockholders' equity decreases.

10. In what situation does an investor's personal wealth increase immediately?

   a. When receiving a cash dividend.

   b. When receiving a stock dividend.

   c. When a stock split is announced.

   d. An investor's personal wealth is increased instantly in all of the above situations.

Solutions to Multiple Choice Questions

1. *a* 2. *d* 3. *d* 4. *a* 5. *c* 6. *b* 7. *c* 8. *c* 9. *d* 10. *a*

MINI-EXERCISES

Available with McGraw-Hill's Homework Manager

LO1 **M11-1 Equity versus Debt Financing**

Indicate whether each of the following relates to equity (E) or debt (D) financing, and whether it makes that form of financing more, or less, favorable.

____ 1. Interest is tax deductible.

____ 2. Dividends are optional.

____ 3. It must be repaid.

____ 4. Additional stock issuances dilute existing stockholders' control.

LO1 **M11-2 Evaluating Stockholders' Rights**

Name four rights of stockholders. Which of these seems most important? Why?

LO1 **M11-3 Computing the Number of Unissued Shares**

The balance sheet for Crutcher Corporation reported 147,000 shares outstanding, 300,000 shares authorized, and 10,000 shares in treasury stock. Compute the maximum number of new shares that Crutcher could issue.

M11-4 Analyzing and Recording the Sale of Common Stock   LO2

To expand operations, Aragon Consulting issued 100,000 shares of previously unissued common stock with a par value of $1. The selling price for the stock was $75 per share. Analyze the accounting equation effects and record the journal entry for the sale of stock. Would your answer be different if the par value were $2 per share? If, so, analyze the accounting equation effects and record the journal entry for the sale of stock with a par value of $2.

M11-5 Analyzing and Recording the Sale of No-Par Value Common Stock   LO2

Refer to M11-4. Assume the issued stock has no par value. Analyze the accounting equation effects and record the journal entry for the sale of the no-par value stock at $75. Do the effects on total assets, total liabilities, and total stockholders' equity differ from those in M11-4?

M11-6 Comparing Common Stock and Preferred Stock   LO2, LO4

Your parents have just retired and have asked you for some financial advice. They have decided to invest $100,000 in a company very similar to Sonic Corp. The company has issued both common and preferred stock. Which type of stock would you recommend? What factors are relevant to this recommendation?

M11-7 Determining the Effects of Treasury Stock Transactions   LO2

Trans Union Corporation sold 5,000 shares for $50 per share in the current year, and it sold 10,000 shares for $37 per share in the following year. The year after that, the company purchased 20,000 shares of its own stock for $45 per share. Determine the impact (increase, decrease, or no change) of each of these transactions on the following classifications:

1. Total assets.
2. Total liabilities.
3. Total stockholders' equity.
4. Net income.

M11-8 Determining the Amount of a Dividend   LO3

Netpass Company has 300,000 shares of common stock authorized, 270,000 shares issued, and 50,000 shares of treasury stock. The company's board of directors declares a dividend of 50 cents per share of common stock. What is the total amount of the dividend that will be paid?

M11-9 Recording Dividends   LO3

On April 15, 2007, the board of directors for Auction.com declared a cash dividend of 40 cents per share payable to stockholders of record on May 20. The dividends will be paid on June 14. The company has 500,000 shares of stock outstanding. Prepare any necessary journal entries for each date.

M11-10 Determining the Impact of a Stock Dividend   LO3

Sturdy Stone Tools, Inc., announced a 100 percent stock dividend. Determine the impact (increase, decrease, no change) of this dividend on the following:

1. Total assets.
2. Total liabilities.
3. Common stock.
4. Total stockholders' equity.
5. Market value per share of common stock.

M11-11 Determining the Impact of a Stock Split   LO3

Complete the requirements of M11-10 assuming that the company announced a 2-for-1 stock split.

M11-12 Recording a Stock Dividend   LO3

To reduce its stock price, Shriver Food Systems, Inc., declared and issued a 50 percent stock dividend. The company has 800,000 shares authorized and 200,000 shares outstanding. The par value of the stock is $1 per share and the market value is $100 per share. Prepare the journal entry to record this large stock dividend.

LO4   **M11-13 Determining the Amount of a Preferred Dividend**

Colliers, Inc., has 100,000 shares of cumulative preferred stock outstanding. The preferred stock pays dividends in the amount of $2 per share but because of cash flow problems, the company did not pay any dividends last year. The board of directors plans to pay dividends in the amount of $1 million this year. What amount will go to preferred stockholders? How much will be available for common stock dividends?

LO5   **M11-14 Calculating and Interpreting Earnings per Share (EPS) and Return on Equity (ROE)**

Academy Driving School reported the following amount in its financial statements:

	2008	2007
Number of common shares	11,500	11,500
Net income	$23,000	$18,000
Cash dividends paid on common stock	$3,000	$3,000
Total stockholders' equity	$240,000	$220,000

Calculate 2008 EPS and ROE. Another driving school in the same city reported a higher net income ($45,000) in 2008, yet its EPS and ROE ratios were lower than those for the Academy Driving School. Explain how this apparent inconsistency could occur.

LO5   **M11-15 Determining the Impact of Transactions on Components of Earnings per Share (EPS) and Return on Equity (ROE)**

Indicate the direction of effect (+ for increase, − for decrease, or NE for no effect) of each of the following transactions on the accounting equation in the table below. The first transaction is shown as an example.

	Assets	=	Liabilities	+	Stockholders' Equity
a. (example) Purchased 50 shares into treasury for $5,000.	Cash −5,000				Treasury stock (+xSE) −5,000
b. Declared and paid a cash dividend of $600.					
c. Declared and issued a stock dividend valued at $10,000 on no-par preferred stock.					
d. Sold inventory for $80 cash, when it had cost $55.					
e. Sold and issued common stock at par for $60,000 cash.					

LO5   **M11-16 Determining the Impact of Transactions on Earnings per Share (EPS) and Return on Equity (ROE)**

Indicate the direction of effect (+ for increase, − for decrease, or NE for no effect) of each of the transactions listed in M11-15 on EPS and ROE.

LO5   **M11-17 Inferring Financial Information Using the P/E Ratio**

In 2006, Rec Room Sports reported earnings per share of $8.50 when its stock was selling for $212.50. In 2007, its earnings increased by 20 percent. If all other relationships remain constant, what is the price of the stock? Explain.

M11-18 (Supplement) Comparing Stockholder's Equity to Owner's Equity

Daniel Harrison contributed $20,000 to start his business. At the end of the year, the business had generated $30,000 in sales revenues, incurred $18,000 in operating expenses, and distributed $5,000 for Daniel to use to pay some personal expenses. Prepare the section of the balance sheet showing (*a*) his stockholder's equity, assuming this is a corporation with no-par value stock, or (*b*) his owner's equity, assuming this is a sole proprietorship.

EXERCISES

Available with McGraw-Hill's
Homework Manager

HOMEWORK MANAGER **PLUS**™

E11-1 Computing Shares Outstanding

LO1

Big Dog Sportswear

The 2005 annual report for Big Dog Sportswear disclosed that 30 million shares of common stock have been authorized. At the end of 2004, 10,709,030 shares had been issued and the number of shares in treasury stock was 1,529,998. During 2005, 75,250 additional common shares were issued, and 180,600 additional shares were purchased for treasury stock.

Required:

Determine the number of shares outstanding at the end of 2005.

E11-2 Reporting Stockholders' Equity and Determining Dividend Policy

LO2, LO3

Incentive Corporation was organized in 2007 to operate a financial consulting business. The charter authorized the following capital stock: common stock, par value $4 per share, 12,000 shares. During the first year, the following selected transactions were completed:

a. Sold and issued 6,000 shares of common stock for cash at $20 per share.
b. Sold and issued 2,000 shares of common stock for cash at $23 per share.

Required:

1. Show the effects of each transaction on the accounting equation.
2. Give the journal entry required for each of these transactions.
3. Prepare the stockholders' equity section as it should be reported on the 2007 year-end balance sheet. At year-end, the accounts reflected a profit of $100.
4. Incentive Corporation has $30,000 in the company's bank account. Should the company declare cash dividends at this time? Explain.

E11-3 Preparing the Stockholders' Equity Section of the Balance Sheet

LO2, LO4

North Wind Aviation received its charter during January 2007. The charter authorized the following capital stock:

> Preferred stock: 8 percent, par $10, authorized 20,000 shares.
> Common stock: par $7, authorized 50,000 shares.

During 2007, the following transactions occurred in the order given:

a. Issued a total of 40,000 shares of the common stock to the company's founders for $11 per share.
b. Sold 5,000 shares of the preferred stock at $18 per share.
c. Sold 3,000 shares of the common stock at $14 per share and 1,000 shares of the preferred stock at $28.
d. Net income for the first year was $48,000.

Required:

Prepare the stockholders' equity section of the balance sheet at December 31, 2007.

LO2, LO3, LO4   **E11-4 Reporting the Stockholders' Equity Section of the Balance Sheet**

Shelby Corporation was organized in January 2008 by 10 stockholders to operate an air conditioning sales and service business. The charter issued by the state authorized the following capital stock:

> Common stock, $1 par value, 200,000 shares.
> Preferred stock, $8 par value, 6 percent, 50,000 shares.

During January and February 2008, the following stock transactions were completed:

a. Collected $40,000 cash from each of the 10 organizers and issued 2,000 shares of common stock to each of them.
b. Sold 15,000 shares of preferred stock at $25 per share; collected the cash and immediately issued the stock.

Net income for 2008 was $40,000; cash dividends declared and paid at year-end were $10,000.

Required:

Prepare the stockholders' equity section of the balance sheet at December 31, 2008.

LO2, LO4   **E11-5 Determining the Effects of the Issuance of Common and Preferred Stock**

Inside Incorporated, was issued a charter on January 15, 2007, that authorized the following capital stock:

> Common stock, $6 par, 100,000 shares, one vote per share.
> Preferred stock, 7 percent, par value $10 per share, 5,000 shares, nonvoting.

During 2007, the following selected transactions were completed in the order given:

a. Sold and issued 20,000 shares of the $6 par common stock at $18 cash per share.
b. Sold and issued 3,000 shares of preferred stock at $22 cash per share.
c. At the end of 2007, the accounts showed net income of $38,000.

Required:

1. Prepare the stockholders' equity section of the balance sheet at December 31, 2007.
2. Assume that you are a common stockholder. If Inside Incorporated needed additional capital, would you prefer to have it issue additional common stock or additional preferred stock? Explain.

LO2, LO4   **E11-6 Recording and Reporting Stockholders' Equity Transactions**

AvA School of Learning obtained a charter at the start of 2008 that authorized 50,000 shares of no-par common stock and 20,000 shares of preferred stock, par value $10. During 2008, the following selected transactions occurred:

a. Collected $40 cash per share from four individuals and issued 5,000 shares of common stock to each.
b. Sold and issued 6,000 shares of common stock to an outside investor at $40 cash per share.
c. Sold and issued 8,000 shares of preferred stock at $20 cash per share.

Required:

1. Give the journal entries indicated for each of these transactions.
2. Prepare the stockholders' equity section of the balance sheet at December 31, 2008. At the end of 2008, the accounts reflected net income of $36,000.

E11-7 Finding Amounts Missing from the Stockholders' Equity Section   LO2, LO4

The stockholders' equity section on the December 31, 2006, balance sheet of Chemfast Corporation reported the following amounts:

Contributed capital	
Preferred stock (par $20; authorized 10,000 shares, ? issued, of which 500 shares are held as treasury stock)	$104,000
Additional paid-in capital, preferred	14,300
Common stock (no-par; authorized 20,000 shares, issued and outstanding 8,000 shares)	600,000
Retained earnings	30,000
Cost of 500 shares of preferred treasury stock	9,500
Assume that no shares of treasury stock have been sold in the past.	

Required:

Complete the following statements and show your computations.

1. The number of shares of preferred stock issued was _____.
2. The number of shares of preferred stock outstanding was _____.
3. The average sale price of the preferred stock when issued was $ _____ per share.
4. The average issue price of the common stock was $_____.
5. The treasury stock transaction increased (decreased) stockholders' equity by _____.
6. How much did the treasury stock cost per share? $_____.
7. Total stockholders' equity is $_____.

E11-8 Recording Treasury Stock Transactions and Analyzing Their Impact   LO2, LO3

During 2007, the following selected transactions affecting stockholders' equity occurred for Corner Corporation:

Feb.	1	Purchased 400 shares of the company's own common stock at $22 cash per share.
Jul.	15	Sold 100 of the shares purchased on February 1, 2007, for $24 cash per share.
Sept.	1	Sold 60 more of the shares purchased on February 1, 2007, for $20 cash per share.

Required:

1. Show the effects of each transaction on the accounting equation.
2. Give the indicated journal entries for each of the transactions.
3. What impact does the purchase of treasury stock have on dividends paid?
4. What impact does the sale of treasury stock for an amount higher than the purchase price have on net income?

E11-9 Recording Stockholders' Equity Transactions   LO2, LO3

The annual report for Malibu Beachwear reported the following transactions affecting stockholders' equity:

a. Purchased $3.5 million in treasury stock.
b. Declared and paid cash dividends in the amount of $254.2 million.
c. Issued 100 percent common stock dividend involving 222.5 million additional shares with a total par value of $556.3 million.

Required:

1. Indicate the effect (increase, decrease, or no effect) of each of these transactions on total assets, liabilities, and stockholders' equity.
2. Prepare journal entries to record each of these transactions.

LO3, LO4   **E11-10 Computing Dividends on Preferred Stock and Analyzing Differences**

The records of Hoffman Company reflected the following balances in the stockholders' equity accounts at December 31, 2007:

> Common stock, par $12 per share, 40,000 shares outstanding.
> Preferred stock, 8 percent, par $10 per share, 6,000 shares outstanding.
> Retained earnings, $220,000.

On January 1, 2008, the board of directors was considering the distribution of a $62,000 cash dividend. No dividends were paid during 2006 and 2007.

Required:

1. Determine the total and per-share amounts that would be paid to the common stockholders and to the preferred stockholders under two independent assumptions:
   a. The preferred stock is noncumulative.
   b. The preferred stock is cumulative.
2. Briefly explain why the dividends per share of common stock were less for the second assumption.
3. What factors would cause a more favorable dividend for the common stockholders?

LO3   **E11-11 Recording the Payment of Dividends and Preparing a Statement of Retained Earnings**

The 2006 annual report for Sneers Corporation disclosed that the company declared and paid preferred dividends in the amount of $119.9 million in 2006. It also declared and paid dividends on common stock in the amount of $2 per share. During 2006, Sneers had 1,000,000,000 shares of common authorized; 387,570,300 shares had been issued; 41,670,300 shares were in treasury stock. The balance in Retained earnings was $1,554 million on December 31, 2005, and 2006 Net income was $858 million.

Required:

1. Prepare journal entries to record the declaration, and payment, of dividends on (a) preferred and (b) common stock.
2. Using the information given above, prepare a Statement of Retained Earnings for the year ended December 31, 2006.

LO3   **E11-12 Analyzing Stock Dividends**

On December 31, 2007, the stockholders' equity section of the balance sheet of R & B Corporation reflected the following:

Common stock (par $10; authorized 60,000 shares, outstanding 25,000 shares)	$250,000
Additional paid-in capital	12,000
Retained earnings	75,000

On February 1, 2008, the board of directors declared a 12 percent stock dividend to be issued April 30, 2008. The market value of the stock on February 1, 2008, was $18 per share.

Required:

1. For comparative purposes, prepare the stockholders' equity section of the balance sheet (a) immediately before the stock dividend and (b) immediately after the stock dividend.
   TIP: Use two columns for the amounts in this requirement.
2. Explain the effects of this stock dividend on the assets, liabilities, and stockholders' equity.
3. How would your answers to requirements 1 and 2 change if the stock dividend were 100%?

E11-13 **Recording Dividends**

Black & Decker is a leading global manufacturer and marketer of power tools, hardware, and home improvement products. A press release on April 27, 2006, contained the following announcement:

> The Corporation also announced that its Board of Directors declared a quarterly cash dividend of $0.38 per share of the company's outstanding common stock payable June 30, 2006, to stockholders of record at the close of business on June 16, 2006.

At the time of the press release, Black & Decker had 150,000,000 shares authorized and 75,750,000 outstanding. The par value for the company's stock is $.50 per share.

Required:

Prepare journal entries as appropriate for each of the three dates mentioned above.

E11-14 **Comparing Stock Dividends and Splits**

On July 1, 2007, Jones Corporation had the following capital structure:

Common stock, par $1,200,000 authorized shares, 150,000 issued and outstanding	$150,000
Additional paid-in capital	88,000
Retained earnings	172,000
Treasury stock	None

Required:

Complete the following table based on three independent cases involving stock transactions:

Case 1: The board of directors declared and issued a 10 percent stock dividend when the stock was selling at $8 per share.

Case 2: The board of directors declared and issued a 100 percent stock dividend when the stock was selling at $8 per share.

Case 3: The board of directors voted a 2-for-1 stock split. The market price prior to the split was $8 per share.

		Case 1	Case 2	Case 3
Items	Before Stock Transactions	After 10% Stock Dividend	After 100% Stock Dividend	After Stock Split
Number of shares outstanding				
Par per share	$ 1	$	$	$
Common stock account	$	$	$	$
Additional paid-in capital	88,000			
Retained earnings	172,000			
Total stockholders' equity	$	$	$	$

E11-15 **Analyzing Dividends in Arrears**

Mission Critical Software, Inc., was a leading provider of systems management software for Windows NT network and Internet infrastructure. Like many start-up companies, Mission Critical struggled with cash flows as it developed new business opportunities. A student found a financial statement for Mission Critical that stated that the increase in dividends in arrears on preferred stock this year was $264,000.

The student who read the note suggested that the Mission Critical preferred stock would be a good investment because of the large amount of dividend income that would be earned when the company started paying dividends again: "As the owner of the stock, I'll get dividends for the period I hold the stock plus some previous periods when I didn't even own the stock." Do you agree? Explain.

LO3, LO4   **E11-16 Determining the Impact of Cash and Stock Dividends**

Superior Corporation has the following capital stock outstanding at the end of 2007:

> Preferred stock, 6 percent, par $15, outstanding shares, 8,000.
> Common stock, par $8, outstanding shares, 30,000.

On October 1, 2007, the board of directors declared dividends as follows:

> Preferred stock: Full cash preference amount, payable December 20, 2007.
> Common stock: 10 percent common stock dividend (i.e., one additional share for each 10 held), to be issued on December 20, 2007.

On December 20, 2007, the market prices were preferred stock, $40, and common stock, $32.

Required:

At each date indicated above, describe the overall effect of the cash and stock dividends on the assets, liabilities, and stockholders' equity of the company.

LO3, LO4   **E11-17 Determining the Financial Statement Effects of Cash and Stock Dividends**

Lynn Company has outstanding 60,000 shares of $10 par value common stock and 25,000 shares of $20 par value preferred stock (8 percent). On December 1, 2007, the board of directors voted an 8 percent cash dividend on the preferred stock and a 10 percent stock dividend on the common stock. At the date of declaration, the common stock was selling at $35 and the preferred at $20 per share. The dividends are to be paid, or issued, on February 15, 2008. The annual accounting period ends December 31.

Required:

Explain the comparative effects of the two dividends on the assets, liabilities, and stockholders' equity (*a*) through December 31, 2007, (*b*) on February 15, 2008, and (*c*) the overall effects from December 1, 2007, through February 15, 2008. A schedule using the following structure might be helpful:

	Comparative Effects Explained	
Item	Cash Dividend on Preferred	Stock Dividend on Common
(*a*) Through December 31, 2007:		
Effect on Assets		
Effect on Liabilities		
Effect on Stockholders' Equity		

LO3, LO5   **E11-18 Preparing a Statement of Retained Earnings and Partial Balance Sheet and Evaluating Dividend Policy**

The following account balances were selected from the records of fast-food restaurant Blake Corporation at December 31, 2007, after all adjusting entries were completed:

Common stock (par $15; authorized 100,000 shares, issued 35,000 shares, of which 1,000 shares are held as treasury stock)	$525,000
Additional paid-in capital	180,000
Dividends declared and paid in 2007	28,000
Retained earnings, January 1, 2007	76,000
Treasury stock at cost (1,000 shares)	20,000
Net income for the year was $48,000.	

Required:

1. Prepare the statement of retained earnings for the year ended December 31, 2007, and the stockholders' equity section of the balance sheet at December 31, 2007.
2. Determine the number of shares of stock that received dividends.
3. Compute the ROE ratio, assuming total stockholders' equity was $629,000 on December 31, 2006. How does it compare to the ratios shown in Exhibit 11.9?

E11-19 Analyzing Stock Repurchases and Stock Dividends

LO3, LO5
Winnebago Industries

Winnebago is a familiar name on vehicles traveling U.S. highways. The company manufactures and sells large motor homes for vacation travel. These motor homes can be quickly recognized because of the company's "flying W" trademark. An April 12, 2006, press release contained the following information:

> Winnebago Industries, Inc., (NYSE: WGO) today announced a new $50 million stock repurchase authorization. Since 1997, Winnebago Industries has repurchased approximately 22.8 million shares for an aggregate price of approximately $308.5 million.

Required:

1. Determine the impact of this stock buyback on the financial statements.
2. Why might the board have decided to repurchase the stock?
3. What impact will this purchase have on Winnebago's future dividend obligations?
4. On January 14, 2004, the company's board of directors declared a 2-for-1 stock split effected in the form of a 100 percent stock dividend distributed on March 5, 2004. Why would Winnebago choose a stock dividend rather than an actual stock split?
5. What impact would this stock dividend have had on Winnebago's financial statements? What impact would it have had on the EPS and ROE ratios?

E11-20 (Supplement A) Comparing Stockholders' Equity Sections for Alternative Forms of Organization

Assume for each of the following independent cases that the annual accounting period ends on December 31, 2007, and that the total of all revenue accounts was $150,000 and the total of all expense accounts was $130,000.

Case A: Assume that the company is a *sole proprietorship* owned by Proprietor A. Prior to the closing entries, the Capital account reflected a credit balance of $50,000 and the Drawings account a balance of $8,000.

Case B: Assume that the company is a *partnership* owned by Partner A and Partner B. Prior to the closing entries, the owners' equity accounts reflected the following balances: A, Capital, $40,000; B, Capital, $38,000; A, Drawings, $5,000; and B, Drawings, $9,000. Profits and losses are divided equally.

Case C: Assume that the company is a *corporation*. Prior to the closing entries, the stockholders' equity accounts showed the following: Capital Stock, par $10, authorized 30,000 shares, outstanding 15,000 shares; Additional paid-in capital, $5,000; Retained Earnings, $65,000.

Required:

1. Give all the closing entries required at December 31, 2007, for each of the separate cases.
2. Show how the equity section of the balance sheet would appear at December 31, 2007, for each case. Show computations.

E11-21 Comprehensive Exercise Involving Common Stock Issuance, Purchase, Reissuance, and Cash Dividends

LO2, LO3

American Laser, Inc. reported the following stockholders' equity account balances on January 1, 2008.

Common stock, 10,000 shares of $1 par	$10,000	Retained earnings	$120,000
Additional paid-in capital-common	90,000	Treasury stock	0

The company entered into the following transactions during 2008.

Jan. 15	Issued 5,000 shares of $1 par common stock for $50,000 cash.
Feb. 15	Purchased 3,000 shares of $1 par common stock into treasury for $33,000 cash.
Mar. 15	Reissued 2,000 shares of treasury stock for $24,000 cash.
Aug. 15	Reissued 600 shares of treasury stock for $4,600 cash.
Sept. 15	Declared (but did not pay) a $1 cash dividend on each outstanding share of common stock.

Required:

1. Analyze the effects of each transaction on total assets, liabilities, and stockholders' equity.
2. Prepare journal entries to record each transaction.
3. Prepare the stockholders' equity section of the balance sheet at December 31, 2008. At the end of 2008, the accounts reflected net income of $20,000.

COACHED PROBLEMS

LO2

CP11-1 Analyzing Accounting Equation Effects, Recording Journal Entries, and Preparing a Partial Balance Sheet Involving Stock Issuance, Purchase, and Reissuance Transactions

Worldwide Company obtained a charter from the state in January 2007, which authorized 200,000 shares of common stock, $10 par value. The stockholders were 30 local citizens. During the first year, the company earned $38,200 and the following selected transactions occurred in the order given:

a. Sold 60,000 shares of the common stock at $12 per share.
b. Purchased 2,000 shares at $15 cash per share from one of the 30 stockholders who needed cash and wanted to sell the stock back to the company.
c. Resold 1,000 of the shares of the treasury stock purchased in transaction *b* two months later to another individual at $18 cash per share.

Required:

1. Indicate the effects of each transaction on the accounting equation.
2. Prepare journal entries to record each transaction.
3. Prepare the stockholders' equity section of the balance sheet at December 31, 2007.
   TIP: Because this is the first year of operations, Retained earnings has a zero balance at the beginning of the year.

LO3

Federated Department Stores

CP11-2 Recording Dividends

Federated Department Stores operates two well-known national department stores: Macy's and Bloomingdale's. A recent press release contained the following information:

CINCINNATI—May 19, 2006—The Board of Directors of Federated Department Stores, Inc. (NYSE:FD) today approved a split of the company's common stock on a two-for-one basis. Additional shares issued as a result of the stock dividend will be distributed after close of trading on June 9, 2006, to shareholders of record on May 26, 2006. At the company's Annual Meeting this morning, Federated shareholders approved an increase in the number of authorized shares of Federated common stock from 500 million to 1 billion. With the stock split, Federated's quarterly dividend will be 12.75 cents per outstanding common share, payable July 3, 2006, to Federated shareholders of record at the close of business on June 16, 2006.

Required:

1. Prepare any journal entries that Federated Department Stores should make as the result of the stock dividend. Assume that, at the time of the stock dividend, the company had

175 million shares outstanding, the par value was $0.01 per share, and the market value is $73 per share.

> **TIP:** Although the press release refers to a stock split, the transaction actually involved a 100% stock dividend. Large stock dividends, such as a 100% dividend, are recorded at par value.

2. What two requirements would the board of directors have considered before making the dividend decision?

CP11-3 Finding Missing Amounts

LO2, LO3, LO5

At December 31, 2007, the records of Nortech Corporation provided the following selected and incomplete data:

> Common stock (par $10; no changes during 2007).
> Shares authorized, 200,000.
> Shares issued, ____?____; issue price $17 per share.
> Common stock account $1,250,000.
> Shares held as treasury stock, 3,000 shares, cost $20 per share.
> Net income for 2007, $118,000.
> Dividends declared and paid during 2007, $73,200.
> Retained earnings balance, January 1, 2007, $155,000.

Required:

1. Complete the following:
   Shares authorized _____.
   Shares issued _____.
   Shares outstanding _____.
   > **TIP:** To determine the number of shares issued, divide the balance in the Common stock account by the par value per share.
2. The balance in the Additional paid-in capital account would be $_____.
3. Earnings per share is $_____.
4. Dividends paid per share of common stock is $_____.
5. Treasury stock should be reported in the stockholders' equity section of the balance sheet in the amount of $_____.
6. Assume that the board of directors approved a 2-for-1 stock split. After the stock split, the par value per share will be $_____.
7. Disregard the stock split (assumed above). Assume instead that a 100 percent stock dividend was declared and issued after the treasury stock had been acquired, when the market price of the common stock was $21. Give any journal entry that should be made.

CP11-4 Comparing Stock and Cash Dividends

LO2, LO3, LO4

eXcel

www.mhhe.com/phillips2e

Water Tower Company had the following stock outstanding and Retained earnings at December 31, 2007:

Common stock (par $8; outstanding, 30,000 shares)	$240,000
Preferred stock, 7% (par $10; outstanding, 6,000 shares)	60,000
Retained earnings	280,000

The board of directors is considering the distribution of a cash dividend to the common and preferred stockholders. No dividends were declared during 2005 or 2006. Three independent cases are assumed:

Case A: The preferred stock is noncumulative; the total amount of dividends is $30,000.

Case B: The preferred stock is cumulative; the total amount of dividends is $12,600. Dividends were not in arrears prior to 2005.

Case C: Same as Case B, except the amount is $66,000.

Required:

1. Compute the amount of dividends, in total and per share, that would be payable to each class of stockholders for each case. Show computations.

   TIP: Preferred stockholders with cumulative dividends are paid dividends for any prior years (in arrears) *and* for the current year before common stockholders are paid.

2. On case C, assume that a 100 percent common stock dividend was issued when the market value per share was $24. Complete the following schedule.

| | Amount of Dollar Increase (Decrease) | |
Item	Case C (Cash Dividend)	Stock Dividend
Assets	$	$
Liabilities	$	$
Stockholders' equity	$	$

LO5

Aaron Rents, Inc.

Rent-A-Center, Inc.

CP11-5 Computing and Interpreting Return on Equity (ROE) and Price/Earnings (P/E) Ratios

Aaron Rents, Inc. and Rent-A-Center, Inc., are two publicly traded rental companies. They reported the following in their 2005 financial statements (in thousands of dollars, except per share amounts and stock prices):

| | Aaron Rents, Inc. | | Rent-A-Center, Inc. | |
	2005	2004	2005	2004
Net income	$ 57,993	$ 52,616	$ 135,738	$155,855
Total stockholders' equity	434,471	375,178	823,432	794,271
Earnings per share	1.16	1.06	1.86	1.99
Stock price when annual results reported	23.10	19.50	20.80	25.50

Required:

1. Compute the 2005 ROE for each company. Express ROE as a percentage rounded to one decimal place. Which company appears to generate greater returns on stockholders' equity in 2005?

   TIP: Remember that the bottom of the ROE ratio uses the *average* stockholders' equity.

2. Compute the 2005 P/E ratio for each company (rounded to one decimal place). Do investors appear to value one company more than the other? Explain.

3. Rent-A-Center repurchased 5,901 (thousand) shares of common stock in 2005 at $20 per share. Recalculate the company's ROE for 2005 assuming that this stock repurchase did not occur. Does this change your interpretation of the ROE ratios calculated in requirement 1?

GROUP A PROBLEMS

Available with McGraw-Hill's
Homework Manager

LO2

PA11-1 Analyzing Accounting Equation Effects, Recording Journal Entries, and Preparing a Partial Balance Sheet Involving Stock Issuance and Purchase Transactions

Global Marine obtained a charter from the state in January 2007, which authorized 1,000,000 shares of common stock, $5 par value. During the first year, the company earned $429,000 and the following selected transactions occurred in the order given:

  a. Sold 700,000 shares of the common stock at $54 per share. Collected the cash and issued the stock.

  b. Purchased 25,000 shares at $50 cash per share to use as stock incentives for senior management.

Required:

1. Indicate the effects of each transaction on the accounting equation.
2. Prepare journal entries to record each transaction.
3. Prepare the stockholders' equity section of the balance sheet at December 31, 2007.

PA11-2 Recording Dividends

National Beverage Corp. produces soft drinks, bottled waters, and juices sold under the brand names Shasta®, Faygo®, and Everfresh®. A press release contained the following information:

L03
National Beverage Corp.

> March 5—National Beverage Corp. today announced that its Board of Directors has declared a special "one-time" cash dividend of $1.00 per share on approximately 36.6 million outstanding shares (subsequent to the Company's payment of a 100% stock dividend on March 22). The dividend will be paid on or before April 30 to shareholders of record at the close of business on March 26.

Required:

1. Prepare any journal entries that National Beverage Corp. should make as the result of information in the preceding report. Assume that the company has 18.3 million shares outstanding on March 5, the par value is $0.01 per share, and the market value is $10 per share.
2. What two requirements would the board of directors have considered before making the dividend decisions?

PA11-3 Finding Missing Amounts

At December 31, 2007, the records of Kozmetsky Corporation provided the following selected and incomplete data:

L02, L03, L04, L05

> Common stock (par $1; no changes during 2007).
> Shares authorized, 5,000,000.
> Shares issued, _____?_____; issue price $80 per share.
> Shares held as treasury stock, 100,000 shares, cost $60 per share.
> Net income for 2007, $4,800,000.
> Common stock account $1,500,000.
> Dividends declared and paid during 2007, $2 per share.
> Retained earnings balance, January 1, 2007, $82,900,000.

Required:

1. Complete the following:
    Shares issued _____.
    Shares outstanding _____.
2. The balance in the Additional paid-in capital account would be $_____.
3. Earnings per share is $_____. Round your answer to two decimal places.
4. Total dividends paid on common stock during 2007 is $_____.
5. Treasury stock should be reported in the stockholders' equity section of the balance sheet in the amount of $_____.
6. Assume that the board of directors voted a 2-for-1 stock split. After the stock split, the par value per share will be $_____.
7. Disregard the stock split (assumed above). Assume instead that a 100 percent stock dividend was declared and issued after the treasury stock had been acquired, when the market price of the common stock was $21. Explain how stockholders' equity will change.

LO2, LO3, LO4   **PA11-4 Comparing Stock and Cash Dividends**

Ritz Company had the following stock outstanding and Retained earnings at December 31, 2007:

Common stock (par $1; outstanding, 500,000 shares)	$500,000
Preferred stock, 8% (par $10; outstanding, 21,000 shares)	210,000
Retained earnings	900,000

The board of directors is considering the distribution of a cash dividend to the common and preferred stockholders. No dividends were declared during 2005 or 2006. Three independent cases are assumed:

Case A: The preferred stock is noncumulative; the total amount of dividends is $30,000.

Case B: The preferred stock is cumulative; the total amount of dividends is $30,000. Dividends were not in arrears prior to 2005.

Case C: Same as Case B, except the amount is $75,000.

Required:

1. Compute the amount of dividends, in total and per share, payable to each class of stockholders for each case. Show computations. Round per-share amounts to two decimal places.

2. On case C, assume that the company issued a 100 percent stock dividend on the outstanding common shares when the market value per share was $50. Complete the following comparative schedule, including explanation of the comparative differences.

	Amount of Dollar Increase (Decrease)	
Item	Case C (Cash Dividend)	Stock Dividend
Assets	$	$
Liabilities	$	$
Stockholders' equity	$	$

LO5   **PA11-5 Computing and Interpreting Return on Equity (ROE) and Price/Earnings (P/E) Ratios**

Two magazine companies reported the following in their 2006 financial statements (in thousands of dollars, except per-share amounts and stock prices):

	BusinessWorld		Fun and Games	
	2006	2005	2006	2005
Net income	$55,000	$54,302	$ 91,420	$ 172,173
Total stockholders' equity	587,186	512,814	894,302	934,098
Earnings per share	3.20	3.19	2.10	3.98
Stock price when annual results reported	54.40	51.04	32.55	59.70

Required:

1. Compute the 2006 ROE for each company (express ROE as a percentage rounded to one decimal place). Which company appears to generate greater returns on stockholders' equity in 2006?

2. Compute the 2006 P/E ratio for each company. Do investors appear to value one company more than the other? Explain.

3. Fun and Games repurchased 32,804 (thousand) shares of common stock in 2006 at $4 per share. Recalculate the company's ROE for 2006 assuming that this stock repurchase did not occur. Does this new ROE change your interpretation of the ROE ratios calculated in requirement 1?

GROUP B PROBLEMS

PB11-1 Analyzing Accounting Equation Effects, Recording Journal Entries, and Preparing a Partial Balance Sheet Involving Stock Issuance and Purchase Transactions   LO2

Whyville Corporation obtained its charter from the state in January 2007, which authorized 500,000 shares of common stock, $1 par value. During the first year, the company earned $58,000 and the following selected transactions occurred in the order given:

a. Sold 200,000 shares of the common stock at $23 per share. Collected the cash and issued the stock.
b. Purchased 5,000 shares at $24 cash per share to use as stock incentives for senior management.

Required:

1. Indicate the effects of each transaction on the accounting equation.
2. Prepare journal entries to record each transaction.
3. Prepare the stockholders' equity section of the balance sheet at December 31, 2007.

PB11-2 Recording Dividends   LO3

Yougi Corp. is an animation studio operating in South Florida. A recent press release contained the following information:

> April 1, 2006–Yougi Corp. today announced that its Board of Directors has declared a cash dividend of $0.50 per share on 605,000 outstanding preferred shares. The dividend will be paid on or before May 31, 2006, to preferred shareholders of record at the close of business on May 26, 2006. The Board of Directors also announced a 100% common stock dividend will occur on May 31, 2006, on its 1,900,000 outstanding $0.01 par common stock for stockholders of record on May 26, 2006.

Required:

1. Prepare any journal entries that Yougi Corp. should make as the result of information in the preceding report.
2. What two requirements would the board of directors have considered before making the dividend decision?

PB11-3 Finding Missing Amounts   LO2, LO3, LO4, LO5

At December 31, 2007, the records of Seacrest Enterprises provided the following selected and incomplete data:

> Common stock (par $0.50; no changes during 2007).
> Shares authorized, 10,000,000.
> Shares issued, ___?___; issue price $10 per share.
> Shares held as treasury stock, 50,000 shares, cost $11 per share.
> Net income for 2007, $2,400,000.
> Common stock account $750,000.
> Dividends declared and paid during 2007, $1 per share.
> Retained earnings balance, January 1, 2007, $36,400,000.

Required:

1. Complete the following:
   Shares issued _____.
   Shares outstanding _____.
2. The balance in the Additional paid-in capital account would be $_____.
3. Earnings per share is $_____. Round your answer to two decimal places.
4. Total dividends paid on common stock during 2007 is $_____.

5. Treasury stock should be reported in the stockholders' equity section of the balance sheet in the amount of $_____.

6. Assume that the board of directors voted a 2-for-1 stock split. After the stock split, the par value per share will be $_____.

7. Disregard the stock split (assumed above). Assume instead that a 100 percent stock dividend was declared and issued after the treasury stock had been acquired, when the market price of the common stock was $21. Explain how stockholders' equity will change.

LO2, LO3, LO4   **PB11-4 Comparing Stock and Cash Dividends**

Carlos Company had the following stock outstanding and Retained earnings at December 31, 2008:

Common stock (par $1; outstanding, 490,000 shares)	$490,000
Preferred stock, 8% (par $10; outstanding, 19,000 shares)	190,000
Retained earnings	966,000

The board of directors is considering the distribution of a cash dividend to the common and preferred stockholders. No dividends were declared during 2006 or 2007. Three independent cases are assumed:

Case A: The preferred stock is noncumulative; the total amount of dividends is $24,000.

Case B: The preferred stock is cumulative; the total amount of dividends is $24,000. Dividends were not in arrears prior to 2006.

Case C: Same as Case B, except the amount is $67,000.

Required:

1. Compute the amount of dividends, in total and per share, payable to each class of stockholders for each case. Show computations. Round per-share amounts to two decimal places.

2. On case C, assume that the company issued a 100 percent stock dividend on the outstanding common shares when the market value per share was $45. Complete the following comparative schedule, including explanation of the comparative differences.

	Amount of Dollar Increase (Decrease)	
Item	Case C (Cash Dividend)	Stock Dividend
Assets	$	$
Liabilities	$	$
Stockholders' equity	$	$

LO5   **PB11-5 Computing and Interpreting Return on Equity (ROE)**

Two music companies reported the following in their 2006 financial statements (in thousands of dollars, except per-share amounts and stock prices):

	Urban Youth		Sound Jonx	
	2006	2005	2006	2005
Net income	$27,500	$ 24,302	$ 41,500	$36,739
Total stockholders' equity	387,101	300,399	516,302	521,198
Earnings per share	1.10	1.00	0.95	0.85
Stock price when annual results reported	20.35	18.50	16.15	14.45

Required:

1. Compute the 2006 ROE for each company (express ROE as a percentage rounded to one decimal place). Which company appears to generate greater returns on stockholders' equity in 2006?

2. Compute the 2006 P/E ratio for each company. Do investors appear to value one company more than the other? Explain.

3. Sound Jonx repurchased 5,000 (thousand) shares of common stock in 2006 at $13 per share. Recalculate the company's ROE for 2006 assuming that this stock repurchase did not occur. Does this new ROE change your interpretation of the ROE ratios calculated in requirement 1?

SKILLS DEVELOPMENT CASES

S11-1 Finding Financial Information

Refer to the financial statements of Landry's Restaurants in Appendix A at the end of this book, or download the annual report from the *Cases* section of the text's Web site at www.mhhe.com/phillips2e.

LO1, LO2, LO3, LO5

Required:

1. How many shares of common stock are authorized? How many shares are issued? How many shares are outstanding? What does this suggest to you about the number of shares held in treasury?
2. According to the statement of stockholders' equity, how much did the company declare in dividends during the current year? Using your answer to requirement 1, calculate approximately how much this was per share. Does this correspond to what is reported in Note 6 of the financial statements?
3. Note 6 to the financial statements indicates that Landry's purchased treasury stock for approximately $133.8 million. According to the statement of stockholders' equity, how much was it exactly? (You might find it odd that Landry's purchased treasury stock during the year but reported none at year-end. The explanation for this is that Landry's cancelled the treasury stock during the year. Cancellation of treasury stock is typically taught in intermediate accounting.)
4. How has Landry's basic earnings per share changed over the past three years? Based on these prior results, can you predict whether EPS is likely to increase or decrease in the following year?
5. Calculate the ROE ratio for Landry's in the current and prior year (express ROE as a percentage rounded to one decimal place). Has it improved or declined?
    TIP: The total stockholders' equity at the beginning of the prior year is reported in the statement of stockholders' equity.

S11-2 Comparing Financial Information

Refer to the financial statements of Outback Steakhouse in Appendix B at the end of this book, or download them from the *Cases* section of the text's Web site at www.mhhe.com/phillips2e.

LO1, LO2, LO3, LO5

Required:

1. Did Outback have more or fewer authorized shares of common stock than Landry's?
2. From the statement of stockholders' equity, what total amount of cash dividends did Outback declare during the current year? What was this on a per-share basis? Compared to Landry's, is Darden's policy on dividends better, worse, or just different?
3. How many shares of common stock had Outback issued as of December 31, 2005? How many shares were held in treasury at that time? Using this information, determine the number of shares outstanding at the end of the current year.
4. How has Outback's basic EPS changed over the past three years? Based on this trend, what do you predict will happen in the following year? Were the changes in EPS caused primarily by changes in Outback's Net income or average number of shares outstanding?
5. Calculate the ROE ratio for Outback in the current and prior year (express ROE as a percentage rounded to one decimal place). (Total stockholders' equity at the beginning of the prior year is reported in the statement of stockholders' equity.) How does Outback compare to Landry's on this ratio?

S11-3 Internet-Based Team Research: Examining an Annual Report

LO3, LO5

As a team, select an industry to analyze. Using your Web browser, each team member should access the annual report or 10-K for one publicly traded company in the industry, with each member selecting a different company. (See S1-3 in Chapter 1 for a description of possible resources for these tasks.)

Required:

1. On an individual basis, each team member should write a short report that incorporates the following:
    a. Has the company declared cash or stock dividends during the past three years?
    b. What is the trend in the company's EPS over the past three years?
    c. Compute and analyze the return on equity ratio over the past two years.
2. Then, as a team, write a short report comparing and contrasting your companies using these attributes. Discuss any patterns across the companies that you as a team observe. Provide potential explanations for any differences discovered.

LO1, LO2   **S11-4 Ethical Decision Making: A Real-Life Example**

Activision became a public company with an initial public offering of stock on June 9, 1983, at $12 per share. In June 2002, Activision issued 7.5 million additional shares to the public at approximately $33 per share in a seasoned new issue. In October 2002, when its stock was trading at about $22 per share, Activision executives announced that the company would spend up to $150 million to buy back stock from investors. On January 8, 2003, *The Wall Street Journal* reported that several analysts were criticizing Activision's executives because the company had sold the shares to the public at a high price ($33) and then were offering to buy them back at the going market price, which was considerably lower than the issue price in 2002.

Required:

1. Do you think it was inappropriate for Activision to offer to buy back the stock at a lower price in October 2002?
2. Would your answer to question 1 be different if Activision had not issued additional stock in June 2002?
3. The above *Wall Street Journal* article also reported that, in December 2002, Activision executives had purchased over 530,000 shares of stock in the company at the then-current price of $13.32 per share. If you were an investor, how would you feel about executives buying stock in their own company?
4. Would your answer to question 3 be different if you also learned that the executives had sold nearly 2.5 million shares of Activision stock earlier in the year, when the price was at least $26.08 per share?

LO3   **S11-5 Ethical Decision Making: A Mini-Case**

You are the president of a very successful Internet company that has had a remarkably profitable year. You have determined that the company has more than $10 million in cash generated by operating activities not needed in the business. You are thinking about paying it out to stockholders as a special dividend. You discuss the idea with your vice president, who reacts angrily to your suggestion:

> Our stock price has gone up by 200 percent in the last year alone. What more do we have to do for the owners? The people who really earned that money are the employees who have been working 12 hours a day, six or seven days a week to make the company successful. Most of them didn't even take vacations last year. I say we have to pay out bonuses and nothing extra for the stockholders.

As president, you know that you are hired by the board of directors, which is elected by the stockholders.

Required:

What is your responsibility to both groups? To which group would you give the $10 million? Why?

LO3   **S11-6 Critical Thinking: Making a Decision as an Investor**

You have retired after a long and successful career as a business executive and now spend a good portion of your time managing your retirement portfolio. You are considering three basic investment alternatives. You can invest in (1) corporate bonds currently paying 7 percent interest, (2) conservative stocks that pay substantial dividends (typically 5 percent of the stock price every year), and (3) growth-oriented technology stocks that pay no dividends.

Required:

Analyze each of these alternatives and select one. Justify your selection.

S11-7 Charting Stock Price Movement around Important Announcement Dates LO1

Using a Web search engine like Google, find either an earnings or dividend announcement for two different companies. Using a source such as bigcharts.com, determine the closing stock price for each company for each day during the five business days before and after the announcement. Using a separate worksheet for each company, prepare a line chart of its stock price movement.

Required:

Examine the charts for each company. Does the stock price appear to change as a consequence of their announcements? Explain why or why not.

12

Reporting and Interpreting the Statement of Cash Flows

THAT WAS
THEN

In the previous chapters, you learned about the income statement, statement of retained earnings, and balance sheet.

LP12

Have you ever closely analyzed your bank statements to see how much money you bring in and pay out during a typical month? According to one recent survey, an average college student earns $645 and spends about $1,080 each month.[1] You don't have to be a financial genius to figure out that this means a net outflow of $435 cash each month. At this rate, your savings will quickly disappear and you'll need to obtain a loan or other source of financing to see you through to graduation.

Most businesses face the same issues as you. For example, Nautilus Inc.—the maker of Stairmaster® and Bowflex® fitness equipment—reported a net outflow of cash for its day-to-day operating activities in 2005. Fortunately, the company had saved up lots of cash in prior years and was able to take out new loans in 2005, so it didn't run out of cash. But to ensure its long-term survival, the company needs to be on top of changes in its cash situation. Investors and creditors also will be closely monitoring its cash inflows and outflows to decide whether the company is likely to pay dividends and other amounts owed. Information for making these kinds of decisions is reported in the statement of cash flows. The statement of cash flows reports changes in the company's cash situation, similar to your personal bank statement.

THIS IS NOW

This chapter focuses on the fourth main financial statement— the statement of cash flows.

[1] Harris Interactive, "College Students Tote $122 Billion in Spending Power Back to Campus This Year," August 18, 2004, Retrieved October 27, 2006 from http://www.harrisinteractive.com/news/allnewsbydate.asp?NewsID=835.

We begin this chapter by explaining how a statement of cash flows presents information about business activities in a way not shown in a balance sheet or income statement. An important part of this is the classification of cash flows as relating to operating, investing, or financing activities. In the second section, you'll study how these different types of cash flows are reported in the statement of cash flows. The third section will introduce some of the tools that investors and creditors use to evaluate the statement of cash flows. As always, the final section reviews the main points of the chapter and provides lots of practice material for these topics. The chapter outline is:

ORGANIZATION OF THE CHAPTER

Understand the business	**Study the accounting methods**	**Evaluate the results**	**Review the chapter**
• Business activities and cash flows • Classifying cash flows	• Relationship with other financial statements • Preparing the statement of cash flows	• Quality of income ratio • Capital acquisitions ratio • Cash coverage ratio	• Demonstration case • Chapter summary • Key terms • Practice material

Understand the Business

BUSINESS ACTIVITIES AND CASH FLOWS

Learning Objective 1
Identify cash flows arising from operating, investing, and financing activities.

Video 12.1

To this point in the course, we've analyzed business activities to identify their financial effects on assets, liabilities, stockholders' equity, revenues, and expenses. We've emphasized that business activities have financial effects even when they don't involve cash. That's why accrual accounting exists. When accurately reported, accrual-based net income is the best measure of whether a company has been profitable during the period.

Despite the importance of net income, companies can't use net income to pay wages, dividends, or loans. These activities require cash, so financial statement users need information about the company's cash situation. The balance sheet shows a company's cash balance at a point in time, but it doesn't indicate where the cash came from. It might have been generated by the company's day-to-day operations, or it might have come from selling the company's buildings or from obtaining new loans. What users really need is a report that explains the activities that lead to the amount of cash on the balance sheet. The income statement doesn't provide this because it focuses on just the operating results of the business, excluding cash that is received or paid when taking out or paying down loans, issuing or buying the company's own stock, and selling or investing in long-lived assets. Also, the accrual-based income statement reports revenues when earned and expenses when incurred, which may differ from the timing of cash receipts and payments. Nautilus, for example, reported a hefty amount of net income in each quarter of 2005, yet its related cash flows were negative in three of those four quarters.

Differences like these between net income and cash flows are said to be the reason that GAAP requires every company to report a statement of cash flows. The purpose of the statement of cash flows is to show how each major type of business activity caused a company's cash to increase or decrease during the accounting period.

For purposes of the statement of cash flows, cash is defined to include cash and cash equivalents. As explained in Chapter 6, cash equivalents are short-term, highly liquid investments purchased within three months of maturity. They are considered equivalent to cash because they are both

1. Readily convertible to known amounts of cash, and
2. So near to maturity that there is little risk their value will change.

Ethical Insights

Cash Isn't Estimated

Critics of accrual-based net income claim it can be manipulated because it relies on many estimates (of bad debts, inventory market values, assets' useful lives), but cash flows do not involve estimates so they are not easily manipulated. A cash balance changes only when cash has been received or paid. One particularly dramatic illustration of the subjectivity of net income, but not cash, involved the bankruptcy of a department store chain operated by the W. T. Grant Company. Through biased estimates, the company reported net income for nine consecutive years but then shocked everyone when it declared bankruptcy and shut down the following year. At the time, a statement of cash flows wasn't required. Had it been, it would have shown that the company's operations led to net cash outflows in seven of the ten years.

James A. Largay, III, and Clyde P. Stickney, "Cash Flows, Ratio Analysis and the W.T. Grant Company Bankruptcy," *Financial Analysts Journal* 36, no. 4: 51–54, July/August 1980.

CLASSIFYING CASH FLOWS

The statement of cash flows requires that all cash inflows and outflows be classified as relating to the company's operating, investing, or financing activities. This classification of cash flows is useful because most companies experience different cash flow patterns as they develop and mature. Think back to Chapter 1 when Pizza Aroma had just started. The first thing the owner needed to get his idea off the ground was financing, which he could then use to invest in assets that later would be needed to operate his business. At this early stage, financing and investing cash flows were crucial for Pizza Aroma. For an established business, like Activision in Chapter 5, operating activities often are the focus. Financial statement users are interested in a company's ability to generate operating cash flows that will allow it to continue investing in additional assets and repay the financing it originally obtained. Creditors and investors will tolerate poor operating cash flows for only so long before they stop lending to or investing in the company. For any company to survive in the long run, the amount of cash generated through daily operating activities has to exceed the amount spent on them.

A condensed (and colorful) version of Nautilus Inc.'s statement of cash flows is presented in Exhibit 12.1. We've condensed the statement to show only the subtotals that report the net cash inflows (or outflows) relating to the company's operating, investing, and financing activities. We use different colors to highlight the sections so that you can easily match them to their specific components discussed later in the chapter. A complete version of Nautilus's statement of cash flows is presented later in the chapter (Exhibit 12.10 on page 558). For now, just focus on Exhibit 12.1 so that you can see that the net cash flows from each category combine to explain the total net increase (or decrease) in cash during the period.

Topic Tackler

PLUS

Check out www.mhhe.com/phillips2e for audio, visual, and PowerPoint presentations on this topic.

EXHIBIT 12.1   Condensed Statement of Cash Flows (in thousands)

Net cash provided by (used for) operating activities	$(38,091)
+ (−) Net cash provided by (used for) investing activities	(2,087)
+ (−) Net cash provided by (used for) financing activities	28,896
Net increase (decrease) in cash	(11,282)
Cash and cash equivalents at beginning of period	19,266
Cash and cash equivalents at end of period	$ 7,984

As Exhibit 12.1 shows, the negative cash flows used for operating and investing activities (shown in parentheses) are offset somewhat by the positive cash flows provided by financing activities to result in a net decrease in cash of $11,282 (thousand). When added to the beginning cash position of $19,266 (thousand), this decrease explains how Nautilus reached its ending cash position of $7,984 (thousand), shown in Exhibit 12.1 (and also reported on its December 31 balance sheet). In short, by looking only at the subtotals, users can determine that although Nautilus obtained additional financing during the year, the company spent even more on operating and investing activities, which caused its cash balance to decrease. Analysts are likely to be concerned that this well-established company has negative operating cash flows, so they would look further into this situation to determine whether it is a sign of future problems for the company. Later in this chapter, we'll show you how to dig deeper into each of these categories when evaluating a company's cash flows. Right now, though, let's see what activities are classified as operating, investing, and financing.

Operating Activities

Cash flows from operating activities (or simply called *cash flows from operations*) are the cash inflows and outflows that relate directly to revenues and expenses reported on the income statement. Operating activities involve day-to-day business activities with customers, suppliers, employees, landlords, and others. Typical operating inflows and outflows of cash are listed below.

Inflows	Outflows
Cash provided by	*Cash used for*
Customers	Purchase of services (electricity, etc.) and goods for resale
Dividends and interest on investments	Salaries and wages
	Income taxes
	Interest on liabilities

The difference between these cash inflows and outflows is reported on the statement of cash flows as a subtotal called *Net cash provided by (used for) operating activities*.

Investing Activities

Cash flows from investing activities are cash inflows and outflows related to the purchase and disposal of investments and long-lived assets. Typical investing inflows and outflows of cash include:

Inflows	Outflows
Cash provided by	*Cash used for*
Sale or disposal of property, plant, and equipment	Purchase of property, plant, and equipment
Sale or maturity of investments (including securities and notes receivable)	Purchase of investments in securities
	Notes receivable when lending to others

The difference between these cash inflows and outflows is reported on the statement of cash flows as a subtotal called *Net cash provided by (used for) investing activities*.

Financing Activities

Cash flows from financing activities include exchanges of cash with stockholders and cash exchanges with lenders (for principal on loans). Common financing inflows and outflows of cash include:

Inflows	Outflows
Cash provided by	*Cash used for*
Borrowing from lenders through formal debt contracts	Repaying principal to lenders
Issuing stock to owners	Repurchasing stock from owners
	Paying dividends to owners

The difference between these cash inflows and outflows is reported on the statement of cash flows as a subtotal called *Net cash provided by (used for) financing activities*.

One way to classify cash flows into the operating, investing, and financing categories is to think about the balance sheet accounts to which the cash flows relate. Although exceptions exist, a general rule is that operating cash flows cause changes in current assets and current liabilities, investing cash flows affect noncurrent assets, and financing cash flows affect noncurrent liabilities or stockholders' equity accounts.[2] Exhibit 12.2 shows how this general rule relates the three sections of the statement of cash flows (SCF) to each of the main sections of a classified balance sheet.

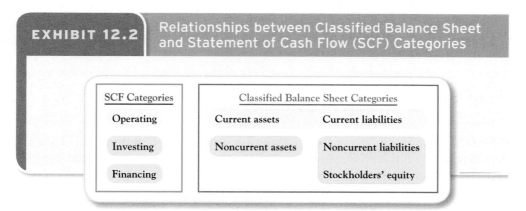

EXHIBIT 12.2 Relationships between Classified Balance Sheet and Statement of Cash Flow (SCF) Categories

SCF Categories	Classified Balance Sheet Categories	
Operating	Current assets	Current liabilities
Investing	Noncurrent assets	Noncurrent liabilities
Financing		Stockholders' equity

HOW'S IT GOING? A Self-Study Quiz

Brunswick Corporation produces the Life Fitness line of gym equipment, which competes head-on with Nautilus Inc. A listing of some of its cash flows follows. Indicate whether each item is disclosed in the operating activities (O), investing activities (I), or financing activities (F) section of the statement of cash flows.

- [ ] *a.* Stock issued to stockholders.
- [ ] *b.* Collections from customers.
- [ ] *c.* Interest paid on debt.
- [ ] *d.* Purchase of plant and equipment.
- [ ] *e.* Acquisition of investment securities.
- [ ] *f.* Cash dividends paid.

Quiz Answers
a. F, *b.* O, *c.* O, *d.* I, *e.* I, *f.* F

---

[2] Exceptions to this general rule are discussed in detail in intermediate accounting. They include investing activities that affect current assets (e.g., short-term investments) and financing activities that affect current liabilities (e.g., dividends payable, short-term notes payable).

Study the Accounting Methods

RELATIONSHIP WITH OTHER FINANCIAL STATEMENTS

The statement of cash flows is intended to provide a cash-based view of a company's business activities during the accounting period. It uses the same transactions that have been reported in the income statement and balance sheet but converts them from the accrual basis to a cash basis. This conversion is done by analyzing the income statement and the changes in balance sheet accounts, and relating these changes to the three sections of the cash flow statement. To prepare a statement of cash flows, you need the following:

1. Comparative balance sheets, showing beginning and ending balances, used in calculating the cash flows from all activities (operating, investing, and financing).
2. A complete income statement, used primarily in calculating cash flows from operating activities.
3. Additional details concerning selected accounts that increase and decrease as a result of investing and/or financing activities.

Our approach to preparing the cash flow statement focuses on the changes in the balance sheet accounts. It relies on a simple manipulation of the balance sheet equation:

$$\text{Assets} = \text{Liabilities} + \text{Stockholders' Equity}$$

First, assets can be split into cash and all the other assets (that we'll call *noncash assets*):

$$\text{Cash} + \text{Noncash Assets} = \text{Liabilities} + \text{Stockholders' Equity}$$

If we pick up the noncash assets and move them to the right side of the equation, we get

$$\text{Cash} = \text{Liabilities} + \text{Stockholders' Equity} - \text{Noncash Assets}$$

Given this relationship, the changes (Δ) in cash between the beginning and end of the period must equal the changes (Δ) in the amounts on the right side of the equation between the beginning and end of the period:

$$\Delta\,\text{Cash} = \Delta\,\text{Liabilities} + \Delta\,\text{Stockholders' Equity} - \Delta\,\text{Noncash Assets}$$

In words, this equation says that changes in cash must be accompanied by and can be explained by changes in liabilities, stockholders' equity, and noncash assets. Exhibit 12.3 illustrates this basic idea for selected cash transactions.

EXHIBIT 12.3 | Effects of Cash Transactions on Other Balance Sheet Accounts

Category	Transaction	Cash Effect	Other Account Affected
Operating	Collect accounts receivable	+Cash	−Accounts Receivable (A)
	Pay accounts payable	−Cash	−Accounts Payable (L)
	Prepay rent	−Cash	+Prepaid Rent (A)
	Pay interest	−Cash	−Retained Earnings (SE)
	Sell goods/services for cash	+Cash	+Retained Earnings (SE)
Investing	Purchase equipment for cash	−Cash	+Equipment (A)
	Sell investment securities for cash	+Cash	−Investments (A)
Financing	Pay back debt to bank	−Cash	−Note Payable (L)
	Issue stock for cash	+Cash	+Contributed Capital (SE)

REPORTING OPERATING CASH FLOWS

As defined earlier, operating cash flows are cash inflows and outflows that relate directly to revenues and expenses reported on the income statement, and include transactions with customers, suppliers, employees, landlords and others. Two alternative methods may be used when presenting the operating activities section of the statement:

1. The **direct method** reports the total cash inflow or outflow from each main type of transaction with the various parties listed earlier. The difference between these cash inflows and outflows is the Net cash provided by (used for) operating activities.

2. The **indirect method** starts with net income from the income statement and then adjusts it by removing items that do not involve cash but were included in net income and adding items that involved cash but were not yet included in net income. By adjusting net income for these items, we calculate Net cash provided by (used for) operating activities.

> Net income
> +/− Adjustments
> _____
> Net cash provided by (used for) operating activities

YOU SHOULD KNOW

The **direct method** of presenting the operating activities section of the cash flow statement reports the components of cash flows from operating activities as gross receipts and gross payments. The **indirect method** of presenting the operating activities section of the cash flow statement adjusts net income to compute cash flows from operating activities.

The most important thing to remember about these two methods is that they are simply different ways to arrive at the same number. Net cash flows provided by (used for) operating activities is the same under the direct and indirect methods. (For a quick check of this, compare the bottom line amounts in Exhibits 12.6 and 12.7 on pages 549 and 553). Also, note that the choice between the direct and indirect methods affects only the operating activities section of the statement of cash flows, not the investing and financing sections. The FASB states that it prefers the direct method and has even considered requiring that it be the only method used, but for now each company's management is allowed to choose the method used. As it turns out, nearly 99% of large U.S. companies, including Nautilus, use the indirect method.[3] We will begin by presenting the commonly used indirect method in Part A. The direct method will be shown in Part B. Check with your course outline (or instructor) to determine whether you are responsible for both or only one of these parts. After you have completed the assigned part(s), move on to the section called "Reporting Cash Flows from Investing Activities" on page 554.

Learning Objective 2a
Report cash flows from operating activities, using the indirect method.

PART A: INDIRECT METHOD

To prepare the operating section using the indirect method, we will follow the three steps shown in Exhibit 12.4. These steps draw extensively on the comparative balance sheet and the income statement for Nautilus, which are shown together in Exhibit 12.5. To get a glimpse of what we're trying to accomplish, take a peek at the schedule of operating cash flows in Exhibit 12.6 on page 549. That's what we will end up with when we complete the three steps in Exhibit 12.4. It will become the basis for the operating activities section of a complete statement of cash flows, which is shown later in Exhibit 12.10.

EXHIBIT 12.4	Steps to Determine Operating Cash Flows—Indirect Method

Step 1: Identify balance sheet accounts related to operating activities.
Step 2: Create a schedule of operating activities (like the one shown in Exhibit 12.6), which begins by assuming net income is a cash inflow.
Step 3: Remove the effects of accrual accounting adjustments included in net income (Step 2), using changes in balance sheet accounts that relate to operations (Step 1).

---

[3] AICPA 2005, *Accounting Trends & Techniques*. Some people have speculated that the indirect method is so common because the FASB requires companies using the direct method to also report a reconciliation of net income to cash flow. This reconciliation is similar, if not identical, to the indirect method.

EXHIBIT 12.5   Comparative Balance Sheet and Current Income Statement

NAUTILUS, INC.
Balance Sheet*

NAUTILUS

Related Cash Flow Section	(unaudited) In Thousands	December 31, 2005*	December 31, 2004*	
	Assets			
	Current assets:			Change
Δ in Cash	Cash and cash equivalents	$ 7,984	$ 19,266	−11,282
O	Accounts receivable	116,908	95,593	+21,315
O	Inventories	96,084	49,104	+46,980
O	Prepaid expenses	24,215	16,591	+7,624
	Total current assets	245,191	180,554	
I	Equipment	215,130	127,724	+87,406
O	Less: Accumulated depreciation	(47,035)	(33,956)	−13,079
I	Investments	—	85,319	−85,319
	Total assets	$413,286	$359,641	
	Liabilities and Stockholders' Equity			
	Current liabilities:			
O	Accounts payable	$ 61,132	$ 57,861	+3,271
O	Accrued liabilities	36,941	38,463	−1,522
	Total current liabilities	98,073	96,324	
F	Long-term debt	62,747	11,281	+51,466
	Total liabilities	160,820	107,605	
	Stockholders' equity:			
F	Contributed capital	4,343	13,562	−9,219
O, F†	Retained earnings	248,123	238,474	+9,649
	Total stockholders' equity	252,466	252,036	
	Total liabilities and stockholders' equity	$413,286	$359,641	

NAUTILUS, INC.
Income Statement*
For the Year Ended December 31, 2005

NAUTILUS

(unaudited) In Thousands	
Net sales	$631,310
Cost of goods sold	352,496
Gross profit	278,814
Operating expenses:	
Selling, general, and administrative expenses	231,931
Depreciation	13,079
Total operating expenses	245,010
Income from operations	33,804
Interest revenue	1,489
Net income before taxes	35,293
Income tax expense	12,293
Net income	$ 23,000

* Certain balances have been adjusted to simplify the presentation.
† This line item includes transactions related to both operating and financing activities.

Step 1

For each balance sheet account, subtract the prior year balance from the current year balance and mark an "O" beside the account if it relates to operating activities. Operating activities typically affect

- **Current assets** Current assets are used up or converted to cash through the company's regular operating activities. For example, when inventories are sold, they create accounts receivable, which are turned into cash when collected. When marking an "O" beside the current assets that relate to operating activities, exclude cash because the change in cash is what we're trying to explain.
- **Current liabilities** Current liabilities, such as accounts payable and accrued liabilities, arise from buying goods or services that are used in a company's operations. Mark these items with an O.
- **Accumulated depreciation** This contra-asset account increases each period by the amount of depreciation expense. Because depreciation expense affects net income, this account is related to operating activities.[4]
- **Retained earnings** This line item increases each period by the amount of net income, which is the starting point for the Operating section. It decreases when dividends are declared and paid (a financing activity). To show that the account relates to both operating and financing activities, mark it with O and F.

While you're at it, also mark whether other balance sheet accounts relate to investing (I) or financing (F) activities. This will make it easier later when preparing the investing and financing sections of the statement of cash flows. The left column in Exhibit 12.5 shows how we have classified the balance sheet accounts for Nautilus, and the right column shows the changes in account balances, which we will use in the following steps.

Step 2

Start a schedule of cash flows from operating activities with the net income reported on the income statement. Our Nautilus example (in Exhibit 12.6) begins with the $23,000 net income reported on the income statement in Exhibit 12.5. By starting with net income, we assume all revenues resulted in cash inflows and all expenses resulted in cash outflows. There are lots of places where that isn't true, so Step 3 is needed to adjust for this.

Step 3

Adjust net income for the effects of items marked "O" that reflect differences in the timing of accrual basis net income and cash flows. The following adjustments are the ones most frequently encountered:

Income Statement Amounts and Balance Sheet Changes	Impact on the Cash Flow Calculation
Net income	Starting point
Depreciation expense included in accumulated depreciation	Added
Decreases in current assets	Added
Increases in current liabilities	Added
Increases in current assets	Subtracted
Decreases in current liabilities	Subtracted

Step 3 is completed in two parts:

Step 3a Adjust net income for depreciation expense. Depreciation is subtracted on the income statement to determine net income, but depreciation does not affect cash. By adding depreciation expense to our starting point on the statement of cash flows, we

---

[4] The balance in Accumulated depreciation also changes when fixed assets, like buildings and equipment, are sold. See chapter Supplement A for further information on these events.

COACH'S TIP

Use this table to remember how to adjust for changes in current assets and liabilities. The + and − indicate whether balance sheet changes are added or subtracted in the statement of cash flows.

	Current Assets	Current Liabilities
Increase	−	+
Decrease	+	−

COACH'S TIP

The depreciation addback is not intended to suggest that depreciation creates an increase in cash. Rather, it's just showing that depreciation does not cause a decrease in cash. This is a subtle, but very important, difference in interpretation.

eliminate the effect of having deducted it in the income statement. It's like depreciation expense digs a hole in the income statement and you need to fill that hole back in on the statement of cash flows by adding back the amount of depreciation expense. In the Nautilus case, we remove the effect of depreciation expense by adding back $13,079 to net income (see Exhibit 12.6).[5]

Step 3b   Adjust net income for changes in current assets and current liabilities. Each *change* in current assets (other than cash) and current liabilities causes a difference between net income and cash flow from operating activities. When converting net income to cash flow from operating activities, apply the following general rules:

- Add the change when a current asset decreases or current liability increases.
- Subtract the change when a current asset increases or current liability decreases.

Understanding what makes these current assets and current liabilities increase and decrease is the key to understanding the logic of these additions and subtractions, so take your time when reading the following explanations.

Change in Accounts Receivable   We illustrate the logic behind Step 3b with the first operating item (O) listed on the Nautilus balance sheet in Exhibit 12.5, accounts receivable. Accounts receivable is related to both sales and cash collected from customers. We want the statement of cash flows to include cash collected from customers, but the indirect method started with net income. With this starting point, it's as if we've included all sales as a cash inflow. Yet, not all sales have been collected because some are still in accounts receivable at year-end. To adjust for this, we must consider the *change* in accounts receivable. If accounts receivable increased, it means credit sales were greater than the amount of cash collected (as shown in the T-account below). Had accounts receivable decreased, it would have meant credit sales were less than cash collections from customers.

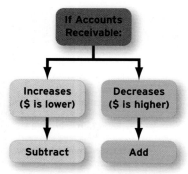

Accounts Receivable (A)			
Beginning balance	95,593		
Sales revenue (on account)	631,310	Cash collected from customers	609,995
Ending balance	116,908		

Change +$21,315

In the Nautilus case, accounts receivable increased, which means sales revenue was greater than the cash collected from customers. To convert from the higher sales number included in net income to the lower cash collected from customers, we subtract the difference ($631,310 − $609,995 = $21,315).

Notice that the adjustment on the statement of cash flows is not the cash collections of $609,995. Because we started with net income, which already included sales of $631,310, the amount of the adjustment is the difference between $631,310 and $609,995, which is the same amount as the change in accounts receivable:

Ending balance	$116,908
− Beginning balance	95,593
= Change	$ 21,315

This actually provides a shortcut for determining adjustments on the statement of cash flows: simply adjust for the changes in current asset and current liability accounts that relate to operating activities. One way to remember whether to add or subtract the amount is to think about whether the change in the current asset or current liability

---

[5] Amortization expense for intangible assets (discussed in Chapter 9) is handled in exactly the same way as depreciation expense. Gains and losses on sales of equipment also are dealt with in a similar manner and are discussed in chapter Supplement A. Other additions and subtractions for long-lived assets are discussed in more advanced accounting courses.

account is explained by a debit or credit. If the change in the account is explained by a debit, the adjustment is reported like a corresponding credit to cash (subtracted). In the accounts receivable example, shown below, the net increase is explained by a debit to accounts receivable, so the appropriate adjustment in the statement of cash flows is treated like a credit to cash (i.e., the net change is subtracted).

Accounts Receivable (A)		
Beg.	95,593	
Increase	21,315	
End.	116,908	

Cash Flows from Operating Activities	
Net income	23,000
Accounts receivable increase	(21,315)
. . .	. . .
Net cash inflow	

EXHIBIT 12.6 Schedule for Net Cash Flow from Operating Activities–Indirect Method

CONVERSION OF NET INCOME TO NET CASH FLOW FROM OPERATING ACTIVITIES

Items	Amount	Explanation
	(in thousands)	
Net income, accrual basis	$23,000	From the income statement.
Add (subtract) to convert to cash basis:		
Depreciation	+13,079	Add because depreciation expense does not affect cash but was subtracted when computing net income.
Accounts receivable increase	−21,315	Subtract because the cash collected from customers is less than accrual basis revenues.
Inventory increase	−46,980	Subtract because purchases are more than the cost of goods sold expense.
Prepaid expense increase	−7,624	Subtract because cash prepayments for expenses are more than accrual basis expenses.
Accounts payable increase	+3,271	Add because amounts purchased on account are more than cash payments to suppliers.
Accrued liabilities decrease	−1,522	Subtract because accrual basis expenses are less than the cash payments for expenses.
Net cash inflow (outflow)	(38,091)	Subtotal for the operating cash flows section.

Change in Inventory The income statement reports merchandise sold for the period, whereas cash flow from operating activities must reflect Nautilus's cash purchases. As shown in the T-account on the left, purchases of goods increase the balance in inventory, and recording merchandise sold decreases the balance in inventory.

Inventories (A)		
Beg. bal.		
Purchases		Cost of goods sold
End. bal.		

Inventories (A)		
Beg.	49,104	
Increase	46,980	
End.	96,084	

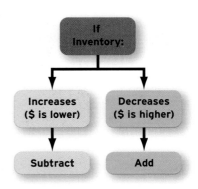

The Nautilus balance sheet (Exhibit 12.5) indicates that inventory increased by $46,980, which means that the amount of purchases is more than the amount of merchandise sold. The increase (the extra purchases) must be subtracted from net income to convert to cash flow from operating activities in Exhibit 12.6. (A decrease would be added.)

Change in Prepaids The income statement reports expenses of the period, but cash flow from operating activities must reflect the cash payments. Cash prepayments increase the balance in prepaids, and recording of expenses decreases the balance in prepaids.

Prepaids (A)		
Beg. bal.		
Cash prepayments		Used-up / expensed
End. bal.		

Prepaids (A)		
Beg.	16,591	
Increase	7,624	
End.	24,215	

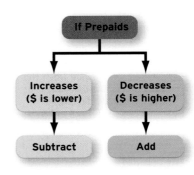

The Nautilus balance sheet (Exhibit 12.5) indicates a $7,624 increase in Prepaids which means that new cash prepayments were more than expenses. These extra cash prepayments must be subtracted in Exhibit 12.6. (A decrease would be added.)

Change in Accounts Payable Cash flow from operations must reflect cash purchases, but not all purchases are for cash. Purchases on account increase accounts payable and cash paid to suppliers decreases accounts payable.

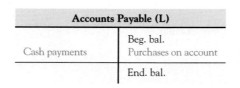

Accounts Payable (L)	
	Beg. bal.
Cash payments	Purchases on account
	End. bal.

Accounts Payable (L)	
	Beg. 57,861
	Increase 3,271
	End. 61,132

Accounts payable increased by $3,271 this period, which means that cash payments to suppliers were less than purchases on account. This increase in accounts payable (cash payments lower than purchases) must be added in Exhibit 12.6. (A decrease would be subtracted.)

Change in Accrued Liabilities The income statement reports all accrued expenses, but the cash flow statement must reflect actual payments for those expenses. Recording accrued expenses increases the balance in accrued liabilities and cash payments for the expenses decreases accrued liabilities.

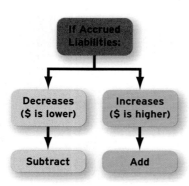

Accrued Liabilities (L)	
	Beg. bal.
Cash payments	Accrue expenses
	End. bal.

Accrued Liabilities (L)		
		Beg. 38,463
Decrease	1,522	
		End. 36,941

Accrued liabilities for Nautilus (Exhibit 12.5) decreased by $1,522, which indicates that cash payments were more than the new accrued expenses. The decrease in accrued liabilities (extra cash paid) must be subtracted in Exhibit 12.6. (An increase would be added.)

Summary We can summarize the typical additions and subtractions that are required to reconcile net income with cash flow from operating activities as follows:[6]

	ADDITIONS AND SUBTRACTIONS TO RECONCILE NET INCOME TO CASH FLOW FROM OPERATING ACTIVITIES	
Item	**When Item Increases**	**When Item Decreases**
Depreciation	+	n/a
Accounts receivable	−	+
Inventory	−	+
Prepaids	−	+
Accounts payable	+	−
Accrued liabilities	+	−

[6] This summary excludes additions and subtractions for losses and gains arising on disposal of certain assets, which are discussed in chapter Supplement A.

HOW'S IT GOING? A Self-Study Quiz

Indicate whether the following items taken from Brunswick Corporation's cash flow statement would be added (+), subtracted (−), or not included (0) in the reconciliation of net income to cash flow from operations.

☐	a.	Decrease in inventories.
☐	b.	Increase in accounts payable.
☐	c.	Depreciation expense.

☐	d.	Increase in accounts receivable.
☐	e.	Increase in accrued liabilities.
☐	f.	Increase in prepaid expenses.

If your instructor has assigned only the indirect method, you should skip the next section and move on to the discussion of Reporting Cash Flows from Investing Activities (page 554).

PART B: DIRECT METHOD

Learning Objective 2b
Report cash flows from operating activities, using the direct method.

The direct method presents a summary of all operating transactions that result in either a debit or a credit to cash. It is prepared by adjusting each revenue and expense on the income statement from the accrual basis to the cash basis. We will complete this process for all of the revenues and expenses reported in the Nautilus income statement in Exhibit 12.5 and accumulate them in a new schedule in Exhibit 12.7. Notice that, with the direct method, we work directly with each revenue and expense listed on the income statement and ignore any totals or subtotals (such as net income).

Converting Sales Revenues to Cash Inflows

When sales are recorded, accounts receivable increases, and when cash is collected, accounts receivable decreases. This means that if accounts receivable increase by $21,315, then sales on account were $21,315 more than the cash collected. To convert sales revenue to the cash collected, we need to subtract $21,315 from sales revenue. The following flowchart shows this visually:

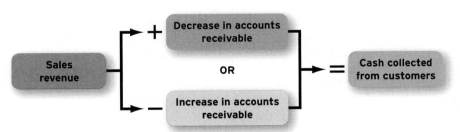

Using information from the Nautilus income statement and balance sheet presented in Exhibit 12.5, we compute cash collected from customers as follows:

Net sales	$631,310
− Increase in Accounts Receivable	21,315
Cash collected from customers	$609,995

Accounts Receivable (A)	
Beg.	95,593
Increase	21,315
End.	116,908

Converting Cost of Goods Sold to Cash Paid to Suppliers

Cost of goods sold represents the cost of merchandise sold during the accounting period. It may be more or less than the amount of cash paid to suppliers during the period. In the case of Nautilus, Inventory increased during the year, because the company bought more merchandise than it sold. If the company paid cash to suppliers of inventory, it would have paid more cash to suppliers than the amount of Cost of goods sold. So, the increase in Inventory must be added to Cost of goods sold to compute cash paid to suppliers.

Typically, companies buy inventory on account from suppliers (as indicated by an Accounts payable balance on the balance sheet). Consequently, we need to consider more than just the change in Inventory to convert Cost of goods sold to cash paid to suppliers. The credit purchases and payments that are recorded in Accounts payable must also be considered. Credit purchases increase Accounts payable, and cash payments decrease it. The overall increase in Accounts payable reported by Nautilus in Exhibit 12.5 indicates that cash payments were less than credit purchases, so the difference must be subtracted in the computation of total cash payments to suppliers. In other words, to fully convert Cost of goods sold to a cash basis, you must consider changes in both Inventory and Accounts payable in the following manner:

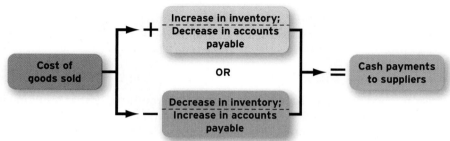

Inventories (A)

Beg.	49,104
Increase	46,980
End.	96,084

Using information from Exhibit 12.5, we compute cash paid to suppliers as follows:

Cost of goods sold	$352,496
+ Increase in Inventory	46,980
− Increase in Accounts Payable	3,271
Cash payments to suppliers	$396,205

Accounts Payable (L)

Beg.	57,861
Increase	3,271
End.	61,132

Converting Operating Expenses to a Cash Outflow

The total amount of an expense on the income statement may differ from the cash outflow associated with that activity. Some amounts, like prepaid rent, are paid before they are recognized as expenses. When prepayments are made, the balance in the asset Prepaids increases. When expenses are recorded, Prepaids decreases. When we see Nautilus's prepaids increase by $7,624 during the year, it means the company paid more cash than it recorded as operating expenses. The increase must be added in computing cash paid for operating expenses.

Some other expenses, like accrued wages, are paid for after they are recorded. In this case, when expenses are recorded, the balance in Accrued liabilities increases. When payments are made, Accrued liabilities decreases. When Nautilus's Accrued liabilities decrease by $1,522, it means the company paid that much more cash than it recorded as operating expenses. This amount must be added in computing cash paid for expenses.

Generally, other operating expenses can be converted from the accrual basis to the cash basis in the following manner:

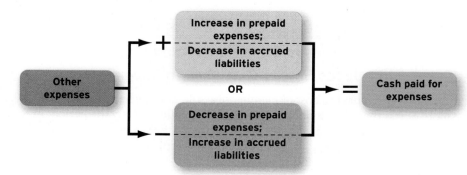

Using information from Exhibit 12.5, we can compute cash paid for expenses as follows:

Prepaid Expenses (A)		
Beg.	16,591	
Increase	7,624	
End.	24,215	

Selling, general, and administrative expenses	$231,931
+ Increase in Prepaid Expenses	7,624
+ Decrease in Accrued Liabilities	1,522
Cash payments for expenses	$241,077

Accrued Liabilities (L)		
	Beg.	38,463
Decrease 1,522		
	End.	36,941

You don't have to convert depreciation expense on the income statement to the cash basis for the statement of cash flows because depreciation doesn't involve cash. It is merely reporting previously incurred costs as an expense in the current period. Noncash expenses like depreciation (or, similarly, revenues that don't affect cash) are omitted when the statement of cash flows is prepared using the direct method. Because of this, be sure to exclude any Depreciation expense that might have been included in Selling, general, and administrative expenses.

The next account listed on the income statement in Exhibit 12.5 is interest revenue of $1,489. Because there is no balance in Interest receivable, all of the interest revenue must have been received in cash. Thus, interest revenue equals interest received.

Interest revenue	$1,489
No change in Interest Receivable	0
Cash receipts for interest	$1,489

The same logic can be applied to income taxes. Nautilus presents Income tax expense of $12,293. Because there is no balance in Income taxes payable (or any other tax account) on the balance sheet in Exhibit 12.5, income tax paid must be equal to income tax expense.

Income tax expense	$12,293
No change in Taxes Payable	0
Cash payments for income taxes	$12,293

Now that we've considered all the line items shown in the income statement in Exhibit 12.5, it's time to gather all the operating cash inflows and outflows that we calculated above. This information is shown in Exhibit 12.7. If Nautilus were to report its statement of cash flows using the direct method, the information in Exhibit 12.7 would replace the operating activities section shown in Exhibit 12.10 on page 558.

EXHIBIT 12.7	Nautilus Inc.: Schedule for Net Cash Flow from Operating Activities–Direct Method

(in thousands)	
Cash flows from operating activities:	
Cash collected from customers	$ 609,995
Cash payments to suppliers	(396,205)
Cash payments for operating expenses	(241,077)
Cash received for interest	1,489
Cash payments for income taxes	(12,293)
Net cash provided by (used in) operating activities	(38,091)

To summarize, the following adjustments must commonly be made to convert income statement items to the related operating cash flow amounts:

Income Statement Account	+/− Change in Balance Sheet Account(s)	= Operating Cash Flow
Sales Revenue	+ Decrease in Accounts Receivable (A) − Increase in Accounts Receivable (A)	= Collections from customers
Cost of Goods Sold	+ Increase in Inventory (A) − Decrease in Inventory (A) − Increase in Accounts Payable (L) + Decrease in Accounts Payable (L)	= Payments to suppliers of inventory
Other Expenses	+ Increase in Prepaid Expenses (A) − Decrease in Prepaid Expenses (A) − Increase in Accrued Expenses (L) + Decrease in Accrued Expenses (L)	= Payments to suppliers of services (e.g., rent, utilities, wages, interest)
Interest Expense	− Increase in Interest Payable (L) + Decrease in Interest Payable (L)	= Payments of interest
Income Tax Expense	+ Increase in Prepaid Income Taxes (Deferred Taxes) (A) − Decrease in Prepaid Income Taxes (Deferred Taxes) (A) − Increase in Income Taxes Payable (Deferred Taxes) (L) + Decrease in Income Taxes Payable (Deferred Taxes) (L)	= Payments of income taxes

HOW'S IT GOING?   A Self-Study Quiz

Indicate whether the following items taken from a cash flow statement would be added (+), subtracted (−), or not included (0) when calculating cash flow from operations using the direct method.

- [ ] *a.* Increase in inventories.
- [ ] *b.* Payment of dividends to stockholders.
- [ ] *c.* Cash collections from customers.
- [ ] *d.* Purchase of plant and equipment for cash.
- [ ] *e.* Payments of interest to lenders.
- [ ] *f.* Payment of taxes to the government.

Quiz Answers
a. −, *b.* 0, *c.* +, *d.* 0, *e.* −, *f.* −

Learning Objective 3
Report cash flows from investing activities.

REPORTING CASH FLOWS FROM INVESTING ACTIVITIES

To prepare this section of the statement of cash flows, you must analyze accounts related to Investments and Property, plant, and equipment.[7] Unlike the analysis of operating activities, where you were concerned only with the *net* change in selected balance sheet accounts, an analysis of investing (and financing) activities requires that you identify the

---

[7] Investing activities also include other long-term assets described in Chapter 9 (intangible assets) and Appendix D (long-term investments in other companies). Although not shown here, the cash flows for intangible assets are similar to those shown in this section for property, plant, and equipment, and the cash flows for long-term investments are similar to the investments shown in this section.

causes of *both* increases and decreases in account balances. The following relationships are the ones that you will encounter most frequently:

Related Balance Sheet Accounts	Investing Activity	Cash Flow Effect
Investments	Purchase of investment securities for cash	Outflow
	Sale (maturity) of investment securities for cash	Inflow
Property, plant, and equipment	Purchase of property, plant, and equipment for cash	Outflow
	Sale of property, plant, and equipment for cash	Inflow

In the case of Nautilus, the balance sheet (Exhibit 12.5) shows two investing assets (noted with an I) that changed during the year: Investments and Equipment.

Investments

To figure out the cause(s) for the changes in this account, accountants would examine the detailed accounting records for investments. It's possible that Nautilus purchased and sold investments during the year, which creates both outflows and inflows of cash to be reported in the statement of cash flows. We'll assume the records show that Nautilus did not buy any investments but rather just sold its entire portfolio, which had cost $85,319. The amount of cash received when investments are sold will be reported as an investing cash inflow. To simplify matters, we'll assume the investments are sold for their cost of $85,319, as shown in the schedule of investing activities in Exhibit 12.8.[8]

Short-Term Investments (A)			
Beg. bal.	85,319		
		Sold	85,319
End. bal.	0		

Equipment

To figure out the cause(s) for the change in the equipment account, accountants would examine the detailed accounting records for equipment. Purchases of equipment increase the account, and disposals of equipment decrease it. For purposes of our example, we have assumed that Nautilus purchased equipment for $87,406 cash. This purchase is a cash outflow, which we subtract in the schedule of investing activities in Exhibit 12.8. In our example, this purchase fully explains the change in the Equipment balance, as shown in the Equipment T-account. For simplicity, we have assumed that Nautilus did not sell any equipment during the year. Chapter Supplement A explains how sales of property, plant, and equipment affect the statement of cash flows.

Equipment (A)		
Beg. bal.	127,724	
Purchases	87,406	
End. bal.	215,130	

---

[8] The amount of cash received is reported in the investing activities section as an inflow regardless of whether that amount is more or less than the cost of the investments. If the cash received on sale of investments differs from their cost, a gain or loss on sale will have been included in net income and will be adjusted for in an indirect method statement of cash flows, as discussed in chapter Supplement A.

EXHIBIT 12.8	Nautilus Inc.: Schedule for Net Cash Flow from Investing Activities

Items	Amount	Explanations
	(in thousands)	
Proceeds from sale of investments	$ 85,319	Receipt of cash from sale of investments
Purchases of equipment	(87,406)	Payment of cash for equipment
Net cash inflow (outflow)	(2,087)	Subtotal for the statement of cash flows

REPORTING CASH FLOWS FROM FINANCING ACTIVITIES

Learning Objective 4
Report cash flows from financing activities.

This section of the cash flow statement includes changes in liabilities owed to owners (dividends payable) and financial institutions (notes payable and other types of debt), as well as changes in stockholders' equity accounts. Interest is considered an operating activity so it is excluded from financing cash flows. The following relationships are the ones that you will encounter most often:

COACH'S TIP

Remember that dividends received from investing in other companies, interest received, and interest paid all affect net income, so they are reported as operating (not financing) cash flows.

Related Balance Sheet Accounts	Financing Activity	Cash Flow Effect
Notes payable	Borrowing cash from bank or other financial institutions	Inflow
	Repayment of loan principal	Outflow
Bonds payable	Issuance of bonds for cash	Inflow
	Repayment of bond principal	Outflow
Contributed capital	Issuance of stock for cash	Inflow
	Repurchase of stock with cash	Outflow
Retained earnings	Payment of cash dividends	Outflow

To compute cash flows from financing activities, you should review changes in all debt and stockholders' equity accounts. In the case of the Nautilus, when we look at changes in the balance sheet (Exhibit 12.5), we find that Long-term debt, Contributed capital, and Retained earnings changed during the period (noted with an F).

Long-Term Debt

We'll assume the change in Long-term debt resulted from using notes to borrow $51,466 during the period, as shown in the T-account below. We include this cash inflow in the schedule of financing activities, shown in Exhibit 12.9.

Long-Term Debt (L)		
	Beg. bal.	11,281
	Borrowings	51,466
	End. bal.	62,747

Contributed Capital

The change in Contributed capital resulted from the repurchase of company stock for $9,219 in cash, which is a cash outflow. This accounts for the $9,219 decrease in Contributed capital, and is listed in the schedule of financing activities in Exhibit 12.9.

Contributed Capital (SE)		
	Beg. bal.	13,562
Repurchase stock 9,219		
	End. bal.	4,343

Retained Earnings

Net income increases Retained earnings and Dividends decrease Retained earnings. The cash effects related to net income have been included in the operating activities section of the statement of cash flows, so the only change in Retained earnings that remains to be accounted for is the cash outflow for any dividends paid. From the income statement, we know that Nautilus reported net income of $23,000. From the statement of retained earnings (or statement of stockholders' equity), we know that Nautilus declared dividends of $13,351. The balance sheet does not report any Dividends payable, so it appears the full amount of dividends was paid in cash. We include this in the schedule of financing activities in Exhibit 12.9. Together, net income and dividends account for the increase in Retained earnings, as shown in the following T-account.

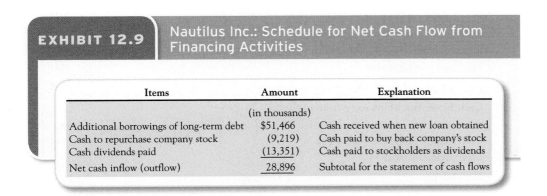

Retained Earnings (SE)			
		Beg. bal.	238,474
Dividends	13,351	Net Income	23,000
		End. bal.	248,123

EXHIBIT 12.9 | **Nautilus Inc.: Schedule for Net Cash Flow from Financing Activities**

Items	Amount	Explanation
	(in thousands)	
Additional borrowings of long-term debt	$51,466	Cash received when new loan obtained
Cash to repurchase company stock	(9,219)	Cash paid to buy back company's stock
Cash dividends paid	(13,351)	Cash paid to stockholders as dividends
Net cash inflow (outflow)	28,896	Subtotal for the statement of cash flows

FORMAT FOR THE STATEMENT OF CASH FLOWS

Now that you have determined the cash flows for the three main types of business activities in Exhibits 12.9, 12.8, and either 12.7 or 12.6, you can prepare the statement of cash flows in a proper format. Exhibit 12.10 shows the statement of cash flows for Nautilus using the indirect method. The direct method would be identical except the operating activities section would list the items in Exhibit 12.7. Under either method, the statement of cash flows combines cash flows from operating, investing, and financing activities to produce an overall net increase (or decrease) in cash. This net change is added to the beginning cash balance to arrive at the ending cash balance, which is the same cash balance as reported on the balance sheet.

NONCASH INVESTING AND FINANCING ACTIVITIES

In addition to their cash flows, all companies are required to report material investing and financing transactions that did not have cash flow effects (called *noncash investing and financing activities*). For example, the purchase of a $10,000 piece of equipment with a $10,000 note payable to the supplier does not cause either an inflow or an outflow of cash. As a result, these activities are not listed in the three main sections of the statement of cash flows. This important information is normally presented for users in a supplementary schedule to the statement of cash flows or in the financial statement notes. Supplementary information must also report (for companies using the indirect method) the amount of cash paid for interest and for income taxes.

COACH'S TIP

When doing homework problems, assume that all changes in noncurrent account balances are caused by cash transactions (unless the problem also describes changes caused by noncash investing and financing activities).

NAUTILUS, INC.
Statement of Cash Flows*
For the Year Ended December 31, 2005

NAUTILUS

Cash Flows from Operating Activities:	
Net income	$23,000
Adjustments to reconcile net income to net cash provided by operating activities:	
Depreciation	13,079
Changes in current assets and current liabilities	
Accounts receivable	(21,315)
Inventories	(46,980)
Prepaids	(7,624)
Accounts payable	3,271
Accrued liabilities	(1,522)
Net cash provided by (used in) operating activities	(38,091)
Cash Flows from Investing Activities:	
Proceeds from sale of investments	85,319
Purchases of equipment	(87,406)
Net cash provided by (used in) investing activities	(2,087)
Cash Flows from Financing Activities:	
Additional borrowings of long-term debt	51,466
Cash to repurchase company stock	(9,219)
Cash dividends paid	(13,351)
Net cash provided by (used in) financing activities	28,896
Net increase (decrease) in cash and cash equivalents	(11,282)
Cash and cash equivalents at beginning of period	19,266
Cash and cash equivalents at end of period	$ 7,984

*Certain amounts have been adjusted to simplify the presentation.

> **COACH'S TIP**
>
> If you have difficulty remembering the order in which to report operating (O), investing (I), and financing (F) cash flows, say to yourself, "OIF, why can't I remember?"

Evaluate the Results

Learning Objective 5
Interpret cash flows from operating, investing, and financing activities.

When evaluating the statement of cash flows, a good place to start is with the subtotals of each of the three main sections. As we discussed at the beginning of this chapter, expect different patterns of cash flows from operating, investing, and financing activities depending on how well established a company is. An established, healthy company will show positive cash flows from operations, which are sufficiently large to pay for replacing current property, plant, and equipment and to pay dividends to stockholders. Any additional cash (called free cash flow) can (a) be used to expand the business through additional investing activities, (b) be used for other financing activities, or (c) simply build up the company's cash balance. After considering where the company stands in relation to this big picture, you're ready to look at the details within each of the three sections.

INTERPRETING OPERATING CASH FLOWS

The operating activities section indicates how well a company is able to generate cash internally through its operations and management of current assets and current liabilities.

Most analysts believe this is the most important section of the statement because, in the long run, operations are the only continuing source of cash. Investors will not invest in a company if they do not believe that cash generated from operations will be available to pay dividends or expand the company. Similarly, creditors will not lend money or extend credit if they believe that cash generated from operations will be insufficient to repay them.

When evaluating the operating activities section of the statement of cash flows, consider the absolute amount of cash flow (is it positive or negative?), keeping in mind that operating cash flows have to be positive over the long run for a company to be successful. Also, look at the relationship between operating cash flows and net income, using a ratio called the Quality of Income Ratio.

FINANCIAL ANALYSIS TOOLS

Name of Measure	Formula	What It Tells You
Quality of income ratio	$\dfrac{\text{Net Cash Flow from Operating Activities}}{\text{Net Income}}$	• Whether operating cash flows and net income are in sync • A ratio near 1.0 means operating cash flows and net income are in sync

The quality of income ratio measures the portion of income that was generated in cash. All other things equal, a quality of income ratio near 1.0 indicates a high likelihood that revenues are realized in cash and that expenses are associated with cash outflows. This ratio is most useful when compared to industry competitors or to prior periods. Any major deviations (say below 0.5 or above 1.5) should be investigated. In some cases, a deviation may be nothing to worry about, but in others, it could be the first sign of big problems to come. Four potential causes of deviations to consider include:

1. Seasonality. As in the Nautilus case, seasonal variations in sales and inventory levels can cause the ratio to fluctuate from one quarter to the next. Usually, this isn't a cause for alarm.

2. The corporate life cycle (growth in sales). New companies often experience rapid sales growth. When sales are increasing, accounts receivable and inventory normally increase faster than the cash flows being collected from sales. This often reduces operating cash flows below net income, which, in turn, reduces the ratio. This isn't a big deal, provided that the company can get cash from financing activities until operating activities begin to generate positive cash flows.

3. Changes in management of operating activities. If a company's operating assets (like accounts receivable and inventories) are allowed to grow out of control, its operating cash flows and quality of income ratio will decrease. More efficient management will have the opposite effect. To investigate this potential cause more closely, use the inventory and accounts receivable turnover ratios covered in Chapters 7 and 8.

4. Changes in revenue and expense recognition. Most cases of fraudulent financial reporting involve aggressive revenue recognition (recording revenues before they are earned) or delayed expense recognition (failing to report expenses when they are incurred). Both of these tactics cause net income to increase in the current period, making it seem as though the company has improved its performance. Neither of these tactics, though, affects cash flows from operating activities. As a result, if revenue and expense recognition policies are changed to boost net income, the quality of income ratio will drop, providing one of the first clues that the financial statements might contain errors or fraud.

INTERPRETING INVESTING CASH FLOWS

To maintain its ability to efficiently produce sales and services, a company must replace existing equipment as it wears down. A good measure for determining whether the company is generating enough cash internally to purchase new long-term assets (such as equipment) is the capital acquisitions ratio. The capital acquisitions ratio reflects the extent to which purchases of Property, plant, and equipment (PPE) are financed from operating activities (without the need for outside debt or equity financing or the sale of investments or other long-term assets). A ratio greater than 1.0 indicates that, all else equal, outside financing was not needed to replace equipment in the current period. Assuming this continues in the future, the higher a company's capital acquisitions ratio, the less likely that external financing will be needed to fund future expansion.

	FINANCIAL ANALYSIS TOOLS	
Name of Measure	Formula	What It Tells You
Capital acquisitions ratio	$\dfrac{\text{Net Cash from Operations}}{\text{Cash Paid for PPE}}$	• Whether operating cash flows are sufficient to pay for PPE purchases • A higher ratio means less need for external financing

The cash paid for property, plant, and equipment (used in the bottom part of the ratio) is reported in the investing activities section of the statement of cash flows in a line item called "Purchases of property, plant and equipment." These expenditures can vary greatly from year to year, so the ratio typically is calculated as an average over a longer period, for instance, three years. Also, when using these cash flows in the ratio, there's no need to include the parentheses that are used in the statement of cash flows. In Exhibit 12.11, we present the three-year average capital acquisitions ratio for Nautilus and its most similar competitor (Cybex International). These ratios show that Nautilus has financed about 52% of its purchases of property, plant, and equipment with cash generated from operating activities. In contrast, Cybex generated almost twice as much cash from operating activities as it used to buy new property, plant, and equipment.

EXHIBIT 12.11 | Capital Acquisition Ratios

Company	Relevant Information (in millions)					Average 2003–05 Ratio Calculation
		2005	2004	2003	Average	
NAUTILUS	Net operating cash	$(38.1)	$47.0	$44.7	$17.9	$\dfrac{\$17.9}{\$34.5} = 0.52$ or 52%
	Cash for PPE	$ 87.4	$ 9.0	$ 7.0	$34.5	
		2005	2004	2003	Average	
CYBEX	Net operating cash	$7.2	$4.5	$0.8	$4.2	$\dfrac{\$4.2}{\$2.3} = 1.83$ or 183%
	Cash for PPE	$4.2	$2.1	$0.6	$2.3	

HOW'S IT GOING? A Self-Study Quiz

The relevant cash flows for Brunswick Corp. are shown below. Calculate the capital acquisitions ratio and indicate whether the relationship between Brunswick's operating cash flows and purchases of property, plant, and equipment is more like Nautilus or Cybex.

(in millions)	2005	2004	2003	Average	Ratio
Cash flow from operating activities	$432	$415	$395	$	
Purchases of property, plant, and equipment	$233	$171	$160	$188	

Quiz Answers

$414 ÷ $188 = 2.20 or 220%

Brunswick's operations generated more than double the amount of cash spent on Property, plant, and equipment, similar to Cybex

Because the needs for investment in plant and equipment differ dramatically across industries (for example, consider Nautilus versus Supercuts), a particular company's ratio should be compared only with its prior years' figures or with other companies in the same industry. Also, while a high ratio can indicate strong cash flows, it also might suggest a failure to update plant and equipment, which can limit a company's ability to compete in the future. The main point is that you have to interpret the ratio in relation to the company's other activities and business strategy.

INTERPRETING FINANCING CASH FLOWS

The long-term growth of a company can be financed from internally generated funds (cash from operating activities), the issuance of stock (equity financing), and money borrowed on a long-term basis (debt financing). Debt financing is the riskiest source of financing because: (1) interest must be paid on debt (dividends do not have to be paid), and (2) debt must be repaid (stock does not). To determine possible changes in the risk related to a company's financing strategy, examine each line item in the financing activities section. All else equal, a company that borrows additional money will be taking on greater risk than a company that pays down its debt.

In addition to considering changes in financing strategy, it also is useful to consider whether a company is generating sufficient cash flow to pay the interest it owes on debt. The times interest earned ratio (introduced in Chapter 10) is one way of assessing a company's ability to pay interest (by comparing net income before interest and taxes to the amount of interest expense). The problem with that ratio is that interest is paid with cash (not the net income used in that ratio). A different way to see whether a company has been able to pay its interest is to use the cash coverage ratio, which compares the cash flows generated from the company's operations to the cash paid for interest.

	FINANCIAL ANALYSIS TOOLS	
Name of Measure	**Formula**	**What It Tells You**
Cash coverage ratio	$$\frac{\text{Net Cash Flow from Operating Activities} + \text{Interest Paid} + \text{Income Taxes Paid}}{\text{Interest Paid}}$$	• Whether operating cash flows (before financing and tax payments) are sufficient to cover interest payments • A ratio greater than 1.0 means operating cash flows are sufficient

In a statement of cash flows prepared using the indirect method, you'll find interest and income taxes paid reported as supplementary cash flow information either at the bottom of the statement of cash flows or in the notes to the financial statements.

SUPPLEMENT A: REPORTING SALES OF PROPERTY, PLANT, AND EQUIPMENT (INDIRECT METHOD)

Whenever a company sells Property, plant, and equipment (PPE), it records three things: (1) decreases in the PPE accounts for the assets sold, (2) an increase in the Cash account for the cash received on disposal, and (3) a gain if the cash received is more than the book value of the assets sold (or a loss if the cash received is less than the book value of the assets sold). The only part of this transaction that qualifies for the statement of cash flows is the cash received on disposal. This is classified as an investing activity, just like the original equipment purchase.

Okay, that seems straightforward, so why do we have a separate chapter supplement for this kind of transaction? Well, there is one complicating factor. Gains and losses on

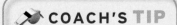

COACH'S TIP

If you're a little rusty on the journal entry to record this disposal, it would be worth your time to review the material on page 396 of Chapter 9.

disposal are included in the computation of net income, which is the starting point for the operating activities section when prepared using the indirect method. So, just as we had to fill in the hole that depreciation created on the income statement, we also have to fill in any holes created by losses reported on disposals of PPE. This means the operating activities section of an indirect method statement of cash flows will add back any losses deducted on the income statement. As the following example shows, the flip side is true for gains on disposal (they are subtracted).

To illustrate, assume that Nautilus sold a piece of its manufacturing equipment for $80,000. The equipment originally cost $100,000 and had $22,000 of accumulated depreciation at the time of disposal. The disposal would have been analyzed and recorded as follows:

	Assets	= Liabilities +	Stockholders' Equity
1. Analyze	Cash	+80,000		Gain on disposal (+R) +2,000
	Accumulated depreciation (−xA) +22,000		
	Property, plant, and equipment −100,000		

2. Record	dr Cash (+A) 80,000	
	dr Accumulated depreciation (−xA, +A)............ 22,000	
	cr Property, plant, and equipment (−A)............	100,000
	cr Gain on disposal (+R, +SE)...................	2,000

The $80,000 inflow of cash is reported as an investing activity. The $22,000 and $100,000 are taken into account when considering changes in PPE account balances. Lastly, the $2,000 gain was included in net income, so we must remove (subtract) it in the operating activities section of the statement. Thus, the disposal would affect two parts of the statement of cash flows:

Cash provided by operating activities	
Net income	$21,998
Adjustments to reconcile net income to net cash from operations:	
Depreciation	3,767
Gain on disposal of property, plant, and equipment	(2,000)
. . .	. . .
Net cash provided by (used for) operating activities	. . .
Cash provided by (used for) investing activities	
Additions to property, plant, and equipment	(6,884)
Cash received from sale of property, plant, and equipment	80,000
. . .	. . .
Net cash provided by (used for) investing activities	. . .

SUPPLEMENT B: SPREADSHEET APPROACH (INDIRECT METHOD)

As situations become more complex, the analytical approach that we used to prepare the statement of cash flows for Nautilus becomes cumbersome and inefficient. In actual practice, many companies use a spreadsheet approach to prepare the statement of cash flows. The spreadsheet is based on the same logic that we used in the main body of the chapter. The spreadsheet's primary advantage is that it offers a more systematic way to keep track of information. You may find it useful even in simple situations.

Exhibit 12B.1 shows the Nautilus spreadsheet, which we created as follows:

1. Make four columns to record dollar amounts. The first column is for the beginning balances for items reported on the balance sheet, the next two columns reflect debit and credit changes to those balances, and the final column contains the ending balances for the balance sheet accounts.

2. Enter each account name from the balance sheet in the far left of the top half of the spreadsheet.

3. As you analyze changes in each balance sheet account, enter the explanation of each item to be reported on the statement of cash flows in the far left of the bottom half of the spreadsheet.

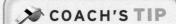

COACH'S TIP

Think of the statement of cash flows (in the bottom half of the spreadsheet) as a big Cash T-account.

Changes in the various balance sheet accounts are analyzed in terms of debits and credits in the top half of the spreadsheet with the offsetting debits and credits being recorded in the bottom half of the spreadsheet in terms of their impact on cash flows. The change in each balance sheet account other than cash contributes to explaining the change in the Cash account.

Let's go through each of the entries on the spreadsheet for Nautilus shown in Exhibit 12B.1, starting with the first one shown in the bottom half of the spreadsheet.

a. Net income of $23,000 is shown as an inflow in the operating activities section, with the corresponding credit going to Retained earnings in the top half of the spreadsheet (to show that net income increased retained earnings).

b. Depreciation expense of $13,079 is added back to net income because this type of expense does not cause a cash outflow when it is recorded. The corresponding credit explains the increase in the Accumulated depreciation account during the period.

c. The increase in Accounts receivable means that cash collections from customers were less than sales on account. Net income includes the sales number, so to adjust down to the actual cash collected, we subtract the extra amount. This appears in our spreadsheet like a credit to cash and a corresponding debit to Accounts receivable.

d. This entry reconciles the purchases of Inventory with Cost of goods sold. It is subtracted from net income because more inventory was purchased than was sold.

e. This entry reconciles the prepayment of expenses with their expiration. It is subtracted from net income because cash payments for new prepayments are more than the amounts that were reported as expenses when they expired.

f. This entry reconciles cash paid to suppliers with purchases on account. It is added because more was purchased on account than was paid in cash.

g. This entry reconciles the accrual of liabilities for operating expenses with payments for these expenses. The decrease in Accrued liabilities is subtracted because the cash paid for accrued liabilities was more than the expenses recorded alongside accrued liabilities. The credit to Cash corresponds to the net debit to Accrued liabilities.

h. This entry records the receipt of cash on sale of investments.

i. This entry records the purchases of new equipment for cash.

j. This entry records cash provided by borrowing additional long-term debt.

k. This entry records cash paid to repurchase the company's stock.

l. This entry records the payment of dividends in cash.

m. This entry shows that the change in cash (in the top part of the spreadsheet) is accounted for by the net cash flows listed in the bottom part of the spreadsheet.

Check to see that Debits = Credits in your spreadsheet, because if they don't, you've missed something along the way. The bottom part of the spreadsheet can be used to prepare the formal statement of cash flows shown in Exhibit 12.10.

EXHIBIT 12B.1 Spreadsheet to Prepare Statement of Cash Flows, Indirect Method

NAUTILUS, INC.
For the Year Ended December 31, 2005

NAUTILUS

| | Beginning Balances, | Analysis of Changes | | Ending Balances, |
(in thousands)	December 31, 2004	Debit	Credit	December 31, 2005
Items from Balance Sheet				
Cash and cash equivalents (A)	19,266		(m) 11,282	7,984
Accounts receivable (A)	95,593	(c) 21,315		116,908
Inventories (A)	49,104	(d) 46,980		96,084
Prepaid expenses (A)	16,591	(e) 7,624		24,215
Equipment (A)	127,724	(i) 87,406		215,130
Accumulated depreciation (xA)	33,956		(b) 13,079	47,035
Investments (A)	85,319		(h) 85,319	—
Accounts payable (L)	57,861		(f) 3,271	61,132
Accrued liabilities (L)	38,463	(g) 1,522		36,941
Long-term debt (L)	11,281		(j) 51,466	62,747
Contributed capital (SE)	13,562	(k) 9,219		4,343
Retained earnings (SE)	238,474	(l) 13,351	(a) 23,000	248,123

| | | Cash | | |
		Inflows	Outflows	Subtotals
Statement of Cash Flows				
Cash flows from operating activities:				
Net income		(a) 23,000		
Adjustments to reconcile net income to cash provided by operating activities				
Depreciation		(b) 13,079		
Changes in assets and liabilities:				
Accounts receivable			(c) 21,315	
Inventories			(d) 46,980	
Prepaid expenses			(e) 7,624	
Accounts payable		(f) 3,271		
Accrued liabilities			(g) 1,522	
				(38,091)
Cash flows from investing activities:				
Proceeds on sale of investments		(h) 85,319		
Purchases of equipment			(i) 87,406	
				(2,087)
Cash flows from financing activities:				
Additional long-term debt borrowed		(j) 51,466		
Stock repurchases			(k) 9,219	
Cash dividends paid			(l) 13,351	
				28,896
Net increase in cash and cash equivalents		(m) 11,282		
		374,834	374,834	(11,282)

REVIEW THE CHAPTER

DEMONSTRATION CASE A: INDIRECT METHOD

During a recent quarter (ended March 31), Brunswick Corporation reported net income of $3,800 (all numbers in thousands). The balance in cash and cash equivalents at the beginning of the quarter (on January 1) was $351,400, and at the end of the quarter on March 31 was $280,000. The company also reported the following activities:

Brunswick Corporation

a. Borrowed $2,200 of debt.
b. Accounts receivable increased by $40,300.
c. Paid $31,800 in cash for purchase of property, plant, and equipment.
d. Recorded depreciation of $35,600.
e. Salaries payable increased by $10,210.
f. Other accrued liabilities decreased by $35,000.
g. Prepaid expenses decreased by $14,500.
h. Inventories increased by $20,810.
i. Accounts payable decreased by $10,200.
j. Issued stock to employees for $400 in cash.

Required:

Based on this information, prepare the cash flow statement using the indirect method. Evaluate the cash flows reported in the statement.

Suggested Solution:

<table>
<tr><td colspan="2" align="center">**BRUNSWICK CORPORATION**
Statement of Cash Flows
For the Quarter Ended March 31</td></tr>
<tr><td>**(in thousands)**</td><td></td></tr>
<tr><td>**Cash flows from operating activities**</td><td></td></tr>
<tr><td>Net income</td><td>$ 3,800</td></tr>
<tr><td>Adjustments</td><td></td></tr>
<tr><td>Depreciation</td><td>35,600</td></tr>
<tr><td>Change in accounts receivable</td><td>(40,300)</td></tr>
<tr><td>Change in inventories</td><td>(20,810)</td></tr>
<tr><td>Change in prepaid expenses</td><td>14,500</td></tr>
<tr><td>Change in accounts payable</td><td>(10,200)</td></tr>
<tr><td>Change in salaries payable</td><td>10,210</td></tr>
<tr><td>Change in other accrued liabilities</td><td>(35,000)</td></tr>
<tr><td>Net cash provided by (used for) operating activities</td><td>(42,200)</td></tr>
<tr><td>**Cash flows from investing activities**</td><td></td></tr>
<tr><td>Additions to property, plant, and equipment</td><td>(31,800)</td></tr>
<tr><td>Net cash provided by (used for) investing activities</td><td>(31,800)</td></tr>
<tr><td>**Cash flows from financing activities**</td><td></td></tr>
<tr><td>Proceeds from debt borrowings</td><td>2,200</td></tr>
<tr><td>Proceeds from issuance of stock to employees</td><td>400</td></tr>
<tr><td>Net cash provided by (used for) financing activities</td><td>2,600</td></tr>
<tr><td>**Increase (decrease) in cash and cash equivalents**</td><td>(71,400)</td></tr>
<tr><td>Cash and cash equivalents, December 31</td><td>351,400</td></tr>
<tr><td>Cash and cash equivalents, March 31</td><td>$280,000</td></tr>
</table>

Despite reporting profits this quarter, the company has negative cash flows from operations. This is caused primarily by build-ups of accounts receivable and inventories, with no corresponding reduction in spending for accounts payable and other accrued liabilities. This is potentially troublesome because it suggests the company may be encountering difficulties in selling its products and when collecting on past sales. In addition to the drain on cash for operating activities, the company also spent over $30 million for additional property, plant, and equipment. Financing activities had relatively little effect on cash flows during the period. The company entered this quarter with lots of cash (over $350 million) and, despite the shortfall in cash flow, still has lots remaining to finance future activities.

DEMONSTRATION CASE B: DIRECT METHOD

During a recent quarter (ended March 29), Cybex International reported that its cash and cash equivalents had increased from $216 on December 31 to $469 on March 29 (all amounts in thousands). The company also indicated the following:

a.　Paid $13,229 to suppliers for inventory purchases.
b.　Borrowed $2,400 from one of the company's main stockholders.
c.　Paid $554 in cash for purchase of property, plant, and equipment.
d.　Reported sales on account of $20,608. The company reported accounts receivable of $13,628 at the beginning of the quarter and $12,386 at the end of the quarter.
e.　Paid operating expenses totaling $6,188.
f.　Cash payments for interest totaled $1,060.
g.　Made payments of $2,625 for principal owed on long-term debt.
h.　Paid $284 cash for other financing activities.
i.　Paid $57 cash for income taxes.

Required:

Based on this information, prepare the cash flow statement using the direct method. Evaluate the cash flows reported in the statement.

Suggested Solution:

CYBEX INTERNATIONAL Statement of Cash Flows For the Quarter Ended March 29	CYBEX
(in thousands)	
Operating activities	
Cash collected from customers ($13,628 + 20,608 − 12,386)	$ 21,850
Cash paid to suppliers	(13,229)
Cash paid for operating expenses	(6,188)
Cash paid for interest	(1,060)
Cash paid for income taxes	(57)
Net cash flow provided by operating activities	1,316
Investing activities	
Additions to property, plant, and equipment	(554)
Net cash flow provided by (used for) investing activities	(554)
Financing activities	
Proceeds from borrowing from a related party (stockholder)	2,400
Repayment of long-term debt principal	(2,625)
Payments for other financing activities	(284)
Net cash flow provided by (used for) financing activities	(509)
Increase (decrease) in cash and cash equivalents	253
Cash and cash equivalents, December 31	216
Cash and cash equivalents, March 29	$ 469

Cybex reported a net inflow of $1,316 cash from operating activities during the quarter. These cash flows were more than enough to pay for the property, plant, and equipment purchased this quarter, as indicated by its capital acquisitions ratio of 2.38 ($1,316 ÷ $554). Some of the extra cash from operations that was not used to purchase property, plant, and equipment (also called *free cash flow*) could be used to pay down debt or to increase the company's cash balance. The financing activities section suggests that the company paid down a significant amount of long-term debt ($2,625), in part by borrowing funds from a related party ($2,400). Borrowing from a related party (particularly a major stockholder) is unusual, which would prompt analysts to investigate further. The company's quarterly report explains that its lenders had demanded immediate repayment of their loans because the company had violated its debt covenants. A major stockholder loaned money to the company so that it could make this repayment.

CHAPTER SUMMARY

Identify cash flows arising from operating, investing, and financing activities. p. 540
    LO1

- The statement has three main sections: Cash flows from operating activities, which are related to earning income from normal operations; Cash flows from investing activities, which are related to the acquisition and sale of productive assets; and Cash flows from financing activities, which are related to external financing of the enterprise.

- The net cash inflow or outflow for the period is the same amount as the increase or decrease in cash and cash equivalents for the period on the balance sheet. Cash equivalents are highly liquid investments purchased within three months of maturity.

Report cash flows from operating activities, using the indirect method. p. 545
    LO2a

- The indirect method for reporting cash flows from operating activities reports a conversion of net income to net cash flow from operating activities.

- The conversion involves additions and subtractions for (1) noncash expenses (such as depreciation expense) and revenues that do not affect current assets or current liabilities, and (2) changes in each of the individual current assets (other than cash) and current liabilities (other than debt to financial institutions, which relates to financing).

Report cash flows from operating activities, using the direct method. p. 551
    LO2b

- The direct method for reporting cash flows from operating activities accumulates all of the operating transactions that result in either a debit or a credit to cash into categories. The most common inflows are cash received from customers and dividends and interest on investments. The most common outflows are cash paid for purchase of services and goods for resale, salaries and wages, income taxes, and interest on liabilities. It is prepared by adjusting each item on the income statement from an accrual basis to a cash basis.

Report cash flows from investing activities. p. 554
    LO3

- Investing activities reported on the cash flow statement include cash payments to acquire fixed assets and investments and cash proceeds from the sale of fixed assets and investments.

Report cash flows from financing activities. p. 556
    LO4

- Cash inflows from financing activities include cash proceeds from issuance of debt and common stock. Cash outflows include cash principal payments on debt, cash paid for the repurchase of the company's stock, and cash dividend payments. Cash payments associated with interest are a cash flow from operating activities.

Interpret cash flows from operating, investing, and financing activities. p. 558
    LO5

- A healthy company will generate positive cash flows from operations, some of which will be used to pay for purchases of property, plant, and equipment. Any additional cash (called *free cash flow*) can be used to further expand the business, be used to pay down some of the company's debt, or returned to stockholders. A company is in trouble if it is unable to generate positive cash flows from operations in the long-run because eventually creditors will stop lending to the company and stockholders will stop investing in it.

- Three common ratios for assessing operating, investing, and financing cash flows are the quality of income ratio, the capital acquisitions ratio, and the cash coverage ratio.

Financial Analysis Tools		
Name of Measure	Formula	What It Tells You
Quality of income ratio	Net Cash Flow from Operating Activities / Net Income	• Whether operating cash flows and net income are in sync • A ratio near 1.0 means operating cash flows and net income are in sync
Capital acquisitions ratio	Net Cash Flow from Operating Activities / Cash Paid for PPE	• Whether operating cash flows are sufficient to pay for PPE purchases • A higher ratio means less need for external financing
Cash coverage ratio	Net Cash Flow from Operating Activities + Interest Paid + Income Taxes Paid / Interest Paid	• Whether operating cash flows (before financing and tax payments) are sufficient to cover interest payments • A ratio greater than 1.0 means operating cash flows are sufficient

KEY TERMS

Cash Flows from Financing Activities p. 543

Cash Flows from Investing Activities p. 542

Cash Flows from Operating Activities (Cash Flows from Operations) p. 542

Direct Method p. 545

Indirect Method p. 545

PRACTICE MATERIAL

QUESTIONS

1. Compare the purposes of the income statement, the balance sheet, and the statement of cash flows.
2. What information does the statement of cash flows report that is not reported on the other required financial statements?
3. What are cash equivalents? How are they reported on the statement of cash flows?
4. What are the major categories of business activities reported on the statement of cash flows? Define each of these activities.
5. What are the typical cash inflows from operating activities? What are the typical cash outflows from operating activities?
6. Describe the types of items used to compute cash flows from operating activities under the two alternative methods of reporting.
7. Under the indirect method, depreciation expense is added to net income to report cash flows from operating activities. Does depreciation cause an inflow of cash?
8. Explain why cash outflows during the period for purchases and salaries are not specifically reported on a statement of cash flows prepared using the indirect method.
9. Explain why a $50,000 increase in inventory during the year must be included in computing cash flows from operating activities under both the direct and indirect methods.

10. What are the typical cash inflows from investing activities? What are the typical cash out-flows from investing activities?

11. What are the typical cash inflows from financing activities? What are the typical cash out-flows from financing activities?

12. What are noncash investing and financing activities? Give one example. How are noncash investing and financing activities reported on the statement of cash flows?

13. (Supplement A) How is the sale of equipment reported on the statement of cash flows using the indirect method?

MULTIPLE CHOICE

1. Where is the change in cash shown in the statement of cash flows?
   a. In the top part, before the operating activities section.
   b. In one of the operating, investing, or financing activities sections.
   c. In the bottom part, following the financing activities section.
   d. None of the above.

Topic Tackler

PLUS   Quiz 14

Check out www.mhhe.com/phillips2e for more multiple choice questions.

2. In what order do the three sections of the statement of cash flows appear when reading from top to bottom?
   a. Financing, investing, operating.
   b. Investing, operating, financing.
   c. Operating, financing, investing.
   d. Operating, investing, financing.

3. Total cash inflow in the operating section of the statement of cash flows should include which of the following?
   a. Cash received from customers at the point of sale.
   b. Cash collections from customer accounts receivable.
   c. Cash received in advance of revenue recognition (unearned revenue).
   d. All of the above.

4. If the balance in Prepaid expenses increased during the year, what action should be taken on the statement of cash flows when following the indirect method, *and why?*
   a. The change in the account balance should be subtracted from net income, because the net increase in Prepaid expenses did not impact net income but did reduce the cash balance.
   b. The change in the account balance should be added to net income, because the net increase in Prepaid expenses did not impact net income but did increase the cash balance.
   c. The net change in Prepaid expenses should be subtracted from net income, to reverse the income statement effect that had no impact on cash.
   d. The net change in Prepaid expenses should be added to net income, to reverse the income statement effect that had no impact on cash.

5. Which of the following would not appear in the investing section of the statement of cash flows?
   a. Purchase of inventory.
   b. Sale of investments.
   c. Purchase of land.
   d. All of the above would appear in the investing section of the statement of cash flows.

6. Which of the following items would not appear in the financing section of the statement of cash flows?
   a. The issuance of the company's own stock.
   b. The repayment of debt.
   c. The payment of dividends.
   d. All of the above would appear in the financing section of the statement of cash flows.

7. Which of the following is not added when computing cash flows from operations using the indirect method?
   a. The net increase in accounts payable.
   b. The net decrease in accounts receivable.
   c. The net decrease in inventory.
   d. All of the above should be added.

8. If a company engages in a material noncash transaction, which of the following is required?
   a. The company must include an explanatory narrative or schedule accompanying the statement of cash flows.
   b. No disclosure is necessary.
   c. The company must include an explanatory narrative or schedule accompanying the balance sheet.
   d. It must be reported in the investing and financing sections of the statement of cash flows.

9. The *total* change in cash as shown near the bottom of the statement of cash flows for the year should agree to which of the following?
   a. The difference in Retained earnings when reviewing the comparative balance sheet.
   b. Net income or net loss as found on the income statement.
   c. The difference in cash when reviewing the comparative balance sheet.
   d. None of the above.

10. Which of the following is a ratio used to assess the extent to which operating cash flows are sufficient to cover replacement of property, plant, and equipment?
    a. Free cash flow.   c. Cash coverage ratio.
    b. Capital acquisitions ratio. d. Quality of income ratio.

Solutions to Multiple Choice Questions

1. c 2. d 3. d 4. d 5. a 6. d 7. d 8. a 9. c 10. b

MINI-EXERCISES

Available with McGraw-Hill's
Homework Manager

LO1, LO5

M12-1 Identifying Companies from Cash Flow Patterns

Based on the cash flows shown, classify each of the following cases as a growing start-up company (S), a healthy established company (E), or an established company facing financial difficulties (F).

	Case 1	Case 2	Case 3
Cash provided by (used for) operating activities	$(120,000)	$ 3,000	$80,000
Cash provided by (used for) investing activities	10,000	(70,000)	(40,000)
Cash provided by (used for) financing activities	75,000	75,000	(30,000)
Net change in cash	(35,000)	8,000	10,000
Cash position at beginning of year	40,000	2,000	30,000
Cash position at end of year	$ 5,000	$10,000	$40,000

LO1

The Buckle, Inc.

M12-2 Matching Items Reported to Cash Flow Statement Categories (Indirect Method)

The Buckle, Inc., operates over 330 stores in 38 states, selling brand name apparel like Lucky jeans and Fossil belts and watches. Some of the items included in its 2005 statement of cash flows presented using the *indirect method* are listed here. Indicate whether each item is disclosed in the operating activities (O), investing activities (I), or financing activities (F) section of the statement or (NA) if the item does not appear on the statement.

_____ 1. Purchase of investments.

_____ 2. Proceeds from issuance of stock.

_____ 3. Purchase of property and equipment.

_____ 4. Depreciation.

_____ 5. Accounts payable (decrease).

_____ 6. Inventories (increase).

M12-3 Determining the Effects of Account Changes on Cash Flows from Operating Activities (Indirect Method)

LO2A

Indicate whether each item would be added (+) or subtracted (−) in the computation of cash flow from operating activities using the indirect method.

_____ 1. Depreciation.

_____ 2. Inventories decrease.

_____ 3. Accounts payable decrease.

_____ 4. Accounts receivable increase.

_____ 5. Accrued liabilities increase.

M12-4 Matching Items Reported to Cash Flow Statement Categories (Direct Method)

LO1, LO2B

Prestige Manufacturing Corporation reports the following items in its 2007 statement of cash flows presented using the *direct method*. Indicate whether each item is disclosed in the operating activities (O), investing activities (I), or financing activities (F) section of the statement or (NA) if the item does not appear on the statement.

_____ 1. Payment for equipment purchase.

_____ 2. Repayments of bank loan.

_____ 3. Dividends paid.

_____ 4. Proceeds from issuance of stock.

_____ 5. Interest paid.

_____ 6. Receipts from customers.

M12-5 Computing Cash Flows from Operating Activities (Indirect Method)

LO2A

For each of the following independent cases, compute cash flows from operating activities. Assume the list below includes all balance sheet accounts related to operating activities.

	Case A	Case B	Case C
Net income	$200,000	$360,000	$ 20,000
Depreciation expense	40,000	80,000	150,000
Accounts receivable increase (decrease)	100,000	(20,000)	(200,000)
Inventory increase (decrease)	(50,000)	50,000	(100,000)
Accounts payable increase (decrease)	(110,000)	70,000	120,000
Accrued liabilities increase (decrease)	60,000	(80,000)	(220,000)

M12-6 Computing Cash Flows from Operating Activities (Indirect Method)

LO2A

For the following two independent cases, show the cash flows from operating activities section of the 2007 statement of cash flows using the indirect method.

	Case A		Case B	
	2007	2006	2007	2006
Sales revenue	$10,000	$9,000	$21,000	$18,000
Cost of goods sold	6,000	5,500	12,000	11,000
Gross profit	4,000	3,500	9,000	7,000
Depreciation expense	1,000	1,000	2,000	1,500
Salaries expense	2,500	2,000	5,000	5,000
Net income	500	500	2,000	500
Accounts receivable	300	400	750	600
Inventories	600	500	790	800
Accounts payable	800	700	800	850
Salaries payable	1,000	1,200	200	250

LO2B   **M12-7 Computing Cash Flows from Operating Activities (Direct Method)**

For each of the following independent cases, compute cash flows from operating activities using the direct method. Assume the list below includes all items relevant to operating activities.

	Case A	Case B	Case C
Sales revenue	$70,000	$55,000	$95,000
Cost of goods sold	35,000	32,000	65,000
Depreciation expense	10,000	2,000	10,000
Other operating expenses	5,000	13,000	8,000
Net income	25,000	8,000	12,000
Accounts receivable increase (decrease)	(1,000)	4,000	3,000
Inventory increase (decrease)	2,000	0	(4,000)
Accounts payable increase (decrease)	0	3,000	(2,000)
Accrued liabilities increase (decrease)	1,000	(2,000)	1,000

LO2B   **M12-8 Computing Cash Flows from Operating Activities (Direct Method)**

Refer to the two cases presented in M12-6, and show the cash flow from operating activities section of the 2007 statement of cash flows using the direct method.

LO3   **M12-9 Computing Cash Flows from Investing Activities**

Based on the following information, compute cash flows from investing activities.

Cash collections from customers	$800
Purchase of used equipment	850
Depreciation expense	200
Sale of investments	300

LO4   **M12-10 Computing Cash Flows from Financing Activities**

Based on the following information, compute cash flows from financing activities.

Purchase of investments	$ 250
Dividends paid	800
Interest paid	400
Additional borrowing from bank	2,000

LO3, LO4   **M12-11 Reporting Noncash Investing and Financing Activities**

Which of the following transactions would be considered noncash investing and financing activities?

_____ 1. Additional borrowing from bank.

_____ 2. Purchase of equipment with investments.

_____ 3. Dividends paid in cash.

_____ 4. Purchase of a building with a promissory note.

LO5   **M12-12 Interpreting Cash Flows from Operating, Investing, and Financing Activities**

Quantum Dots, Inc., is a nanotechnology company that manufactures "quantum dots," which are tiny pieces of silicon consisting of 100 or more molecules. Quantum dots can be used to illuminate very small objects, enabling scientists to see the blood vessels beneath a mouse's skin ripple with each heartbeat, at the rate of 100 times per second. Evaluate this research intensive company's cash flows, assuming the following was reported in its statement of cash flows.

	Current Year	Previous Year
Cash flows from operating activities		
Net cash provided by (used for) operating activities	$ (50,790)	$(46,730)
Cash flows from investing activities		
Purchases of research equipment	(250,770)	(480,145)
Proceeds from selling all short-term investments	35,000	—
Net cash provided by (used for) investing activities	(215,770)	(480,145)
Cash flows from financing activities		
Additional long-term debt borrowed	100,000	200,000
Proceeds from stock issuance	140,000	200,000
Cash dividends paid	—	(10,000)
Net cash provided by (used for) financing activities	240,000	390,000
Net increase (decrease) in cash	(26,560)	(136,875)
Cash at beginning of period	29,025	165,900
Cash at end of period	$ 2,465	$ 29,025

M12-13 Calculating and Interpreting the Capital Acquisitions Ratio   LO5

Capital Corporation reported the following information in its statement of cash flows:

	2006	2007	2008
Net cash flow from operating activities	$35,000	$32,000	$23,000
Interest paid	2,000	3,000	2,500
Income taxes paid	9,000	8,500	6,500
Purchases of property, plant, and equipment	31,818	22,857	20,325

Calculate, to one decimal place, the average capital acquisitions ratio for the period covering 2006–2008 and the capital acquisitions ratio for *each* year during the period. What does this analysis tell you about the company's need for using external financing to replace property, plant, and equipment?

M12-14 Calculating and Interpreting the Cash Coverage Ratio   LO5

Using the information in M12-13, calculate the cash coverage ratio for Capital Corporation for each of the three years. What do these ratios tell you about the company's ability to pay its interest costs?

M12-15 Calculating and Interpreting the Quality of Income Ratio   LO5

Dan's Products, Inc., reported net income of $80,000, depreciation expense of $2,000, and cash flow from operations of $60,000. Compute the quality of income ratio. What does the ratio tell you about the company's accrual of revenues and/or deferral of expenses?

EXERCISES   Available with McGraw-Hill's Homework Manager   HOMEWORK MANAGER **PLUS**

E12-1 Matching Items Reported to Cash Flow Statement Categories (Indirect Method)   LO1, LO2A
Nike, Inc.

Nike, Inc., is the best-known sports shoe, apparel, and equipment company in the world because of its association with sports stars such as LeBron James. Some of the items included in its recent statement of cash flows presented using the *indirect method* are listed here.

Indicate whether each item is disclosed in the operating activities (O), investing activities (I), or financing activities (F) section of the statement or (NA) if the item does not appear on the statement.

_____ 1. Additions to long-term debt.

_____ 2. Depreciation.

_____ 3. Additions to property, plant, and equipment.

_____ 4. Increase (decrease) in notes payable. (The amount is owed to financial institutions.)

_____ 5. (Increase) decrease in other current assets.

_____ 6. Cash received from disposal of property, plant, and equipment.

_____ 7. Reductions in long-term debt.

_____ 8. Issuance of stock.

_____ 9. (Increase) decrease in inventory.

_____ 10. Net income.

LO2A, LO2B

E12-2 Comparing the Direct and Indirect Methods

To compare statement of cash flows reporting under the direct and indirect methods, enter check marks to indicate which line items are reported on the statement of cash flows with each method.

Cash Flows (and Related Changes)	Statement of Cash Flows Method	
	Direct	Indirect
1. Net income		
2. Receipts from customers		
3. Accounts receivable increase or decrease		
4. Payments to suppliers		
5. Inventory increase or decrease		
6. Accounts payable increase or decrease		
7. Payments to employees		
8. Wages payable, increase or decrease		
9. Depreciation expense		
10. Cash flows from operating activities		
11. Cash flows from investing activities		
12. Cash flows from financing activities		
13. Net increase or decrease in cash during the period		

LO2A

E12-3 Reporting Cash Flows from Operating Activities (Indirect Method)

The following information pertains to Guy's Gear Company:

Sales		$80,000
Expenses:		
Cost of goods sold	$50,000	
Depreciation expense	6,000	
Salaries expense	12,000	68,000
Net income		$ 12,000
Accounts receivable decrease	$ 5,000	
Merchandise inventory increase	8,000	
Salaries payable increase	500	

Required:

Present the operating activities section of the statement of cash flows for Guy's Gear Company using the indirect method.

E12-4 Reporting and Interpreting Cash Flows from Operating Activities from an Analyst's Perspective (Indirect Method)

LO2A, LO5

New Vision Company completed its income statement and balance sheet for 2007 and provided the following information:

Service revenue		$66,000
Expenses:		
Salaries	$42,000	
Depreciation	7,300	
Utilities	7,000	
Other expenses	1,700	58,000
Net income		$ 8,000
Decrease in accounts receivable	$ 12,000	
Bought a small service machine	5,000	
Increase in salaries payable	9,000	
Decrease in other accrued liabilities	4,000	

Required:

1. Present the operating activities section of the statement of cash flows for New Vision Company using the indirect method.
2. Of the potential causes of differences between cash flow from operations and net income, which are the most important to financial analysts?

E12-5 Reporting and Interpreting Cash Flows from Operating Activities from an Analyst's Perspective (Indirect Method)

LO2A, LO5

Sizzler International, Inc.

Sizzler International, Inc., operates 700 family restaurants around the world. The company's annual report contained the following information (in thousands):

Operating Activities	
Net loss	$(9,482)
Depreciation	33,305
Increase in receivables	170
Decrease in inventories	643
Increase in prepaid expenses	664
Decrease in accounts payable	2,282
Decrease in accrued liabilities	719
Increase in income taxes payable	1,861
Reduction of long-term debt	12,691
Additions to equipment	29,073

Required:

1. Based on this information, compute cash flow from operating activities using the indirect method.
2. What were the major reasons that Sizzler was able to report a net loss but positive cash flow from operations?
3. Of the potential causes of differences between cash flow from operations and net income, which are the most important to financial analysts?

LO2A

Colgate-Palmolive

E12-6 Inferring Balance Sheet Changes from the Cash Flow Statement (Indirect Method)

Colgate-Palmolive was founded in 1806. Its statement of cash flows for the first quarter of 2006 reported the following information (in millions):

Operating Activities	
Net income	$ 952.2
Depreciation	243.5
Cash effect of changes in	
Accounts receivable	(122.9)
Inventories	(128.9)
Accounts payable	122.8
Other	303.2
Net cash provided by operations	$1,369.9

Required:

Based on the information reported in the operating activities section of the statement of cash flows for Colgate-Palmolive, determine whether the following accounts increased or decreased during the period: Accounts receivable, Inventories, and Accounts payable.

LO2A

Apple Inc.

E12-7 Inferring Balance Sheet Changes from the Cash Flow Statement (Indirect Method)

The statement of cash flows for Apple Inc. for the six-month period ended April 1, 2006, contained the following information (in millions):

Operating Activities	
Net income	$975
Depreciation	102
Changes in assets and liabilities	
Accounts receivable	34
Inventories	(39)
Other current assets	(892)
Accounts payable	329
Other adjustments	(351)
Net cash provided by operations	$ 158

Required:

For each of the asset and liability accounts listed in the operating activities section of the statement of cash flows, determine whether the account balances increased or decreased during the period.

LO2B, LO5

E12-8 Reporting and Interpreting Cash Flows from Operating Activities from an Analyst's Perspective (Direct Method)

Refer to the information for New Vision Company in E12-4.

Required:

1. Present the operating activities section of the statement of cash flows for New Vision Company using the direct method. Assume that other accrued liabilities relate to other expenses on the income statement.
2. Of the potential causes of differences between cash flow from operations and net income, which are the most important to financial analysts?

E12-9 Reporting and Interpreting Cash Flows from Operating Activities from an Analyst's Perspective (Direct Method)

LO2B, LO5

Sizzler International, Inc.

Refer back to the information given for E12-5, plus the following summarized income statement for Sizzler International, Inc.:

Revenues	$136,500
Cost of sales	45,500
Gross profit	91,000
Salary expense	56,835
Depreciation	33,305
Other expenses	7,781
Net loss before income taxes	(6,921)
Income tax expense	2,561
Net loss	$ (9,482)

Required:

1. Based on this information, compute cash flow from operating activities using the direct method. Assume that prepaid expenses and accrued liabilities relate to other expenses.
2. What were the major reasons that Sizzler was able to report a net loss but positive cash flow from operations?
3. Of the potential causes of differences between cash flow from operations and net income, which are the most important to financial analysts?

E12-10 Analyzing Cash Flows from Operating Activities (Indirect Method) and Calculating and Interpreting the Quality of Income Ratio

LO2A, LO5

PepsiCo

The 2005 annual report for PepsiCo contained the following information for the period (in millions):

Net income	$4,078
Cash dividends paid	1,642
Depreciation	1,308
Increase in accounts receivable	272
Increase in inventory	132
Increase in prepaid expense	56
Increase in accounts payable	188
Increase in taxes payable	609
Decrease in other liabilities related to operations	791

Required:

1. Compute cash flows from operating activities for PepsiCo using the indirect method.
2. Compute the quality of income ratio to one decimal place.
3. What was the main reason that PepsiCo's quality of income ratio did not equal 1.0?

E12-11 Calculating and Understanding Operating Cash Flows Relating to Inventory Purchases (Indirect Method)

LO2A

The following information was reported by three companies. When completing the requirements, assume that any and all purchases on account are for inventory.

	Aztec Corporation	Bikes Unlimited	Campus Cycles
Cost of goods sold	$175	$175	$350
Inventory purchases from suppliers made using cash	200	0	200
Inventory purchases from suppliers made on account	0	200	200
Cash payments to suppliers on account	0	160	160
Beginning inventory	100	100	200
Ending inventory	125	125	250
Beginning accounts payable	0	80	80
Ending accounts payable	0	120	120

Required:

1. What amount did each company deduct on the income statement related to inventory?
2. What total amount did each company pay out in cash during the period related to inventory purchased with cash and on account?
3. By what amount do your answers in 1 and 2 differ for each company?
4. By what amount did each company's inventory increase (decrease)? By what amount did each company's accounts payable increase (decrease)?
5. Using the indirect method of presentation, what amount(s) must each company add (deduct) from net income to convert from accrual to cash basis?
6. Describe any similarities between your answers to requirements 3 and 5. Are these answers the same? Why or why not?

LO3, LO4   E12-12 Reporting Cash Flows from Investing and Financing Activities

Rowe Furniture Corporation is a Virginia-based manufacturer of furniture. In a recent quarter, it reported the following activities:

Net income	$ 4,135
Purchase of property, plant, and equipment	871
Borrowings under line of credit (bank)	1,417
Proceeds from issuance of stock	11
Cash received from customers	29,164
Payments to reduce long-term debt	46
Sale of investments	134
Proceeds from sale of property and equipment	6,594
Dividends paid	277
Interest paid	90

Required:

Based on this information, present the cash flows from investing and financing activities sections of the cash flow statement.

LO3, LO4, LO5   **E12-13 Reporting and Interpreting Cash Flows from Investing and**
Gibraltar Steel Corporation   **Financing Activities with Discussion of Management Strategy**

Gibraltar Steel Corporation is a manufacturer of steel products in Buffalo, New York. In a prior year, it reported the following activities:

Net income	$ 5,213
Purchase of property, plant, and equipment	10,468
Payments of notes payable (bank)	8,598
Net proceeds of stock issuance	26,061
Depreciation	3,399
Long-term debt reduction	17,832
Proceeds from sale of investments	131
Proceeds from sale of property, plant, and equipment	1,817
Proceeds from long-term debt borrowed	10,242
Decrease in accounts receivable	1,137
Proceeds from notes payable (bank)	3,848

Required:

1. Based on this information, present the cash flows from investing and financing activities sections of the cash flow statement.

2. Referring to your response to requirement 1, comment on what you think Gibraltar's management plan was for the use of the cash generated by the stock issuance.

E12-14 Analyzing and Interpreting the Capital Acquisitions Ratio   LO5

Sportsnet Corporation reported the following data for the three most recent years (in thousands):

	(in thousands)		
	2008	2007	2006
Cash flows from operating activities	$ 801	$1,480	$619
Cash flows from investing activities	(1,504)	(1,415)	(662)
Cash flows from financing activities	42,960	775	360

Assume that all investing activities involved acquisition of new plant and equipment.

Required:

1. Compute the capital acquisitions ratio for the three-year period in total.

2. What portion of Sportsnet's investing activities was financed from cash flows from operating activities? What portion was financed from external sources or preexisting cash balances during the three-year period?

3. What do you think is the likely explanation for the dramatic increase in cash flow from financing activities during the period?

E12-15 Calculating and Interpreting the Capital Acquisitions Ratio   LO5

The Walt Disney Company reported the following in its 2005 annual report.   Walt Disney Company

	2005	2004	2003
Net income	$2,533	$2,345	$1,267
Net cash provided by operating activities	4,269	4,370	2,901
Purchase of parks, resorts, and other property	(1,823)	(1,427)	(1,049)
Cash paid for interest	641	624	705
Cash paid for income taxes	1,572	1,349	371

Required:

1. Calculate, to two decimal places, the average capital acquisitions ratio for the period covering 2003–2005.

2. Interpret the results of your calculations in requirement 1. What do they suggest about the company's need for external financing to acquire property and equipment?

LO5   **E12-16 Calculating and Interpreting the Cash Coverage Ratio**

Refer to the information about the Walt Disney Company in E12-15.

Required:

1. Calculate, to one decimal place, the cash coverage ratio for each year.
2. Interpret the results of your calculations in requirement 1. What do they suggest about the company's ability to pay interest on its debt financing?

LO5   **E12-17 Calculating and Interpreting the Quality of Income Ratio**

Refer to the information about the Walt Disney Company in E12-15.

Required:

1. Calculate, to one decimal place, the quality of income ratio for each year.
2. Interpret the results of your calculations in requirement 1. Given what you know about the Walt Disney Company from your own personal observations, provide one reason that could explain the sizable difference between net income and net cash provided by operating activities.

E12-18 (Supplement A) Determining Cash Flows from the Sale of Property

AMC Entertainment

The first company in the theatre industry to introduce a customer loyalty program (like frequent flyer miles for movie watchers) was AMC Entertainment. During 2003, the company sold property for $5,494,000 cash and recorded a gain on sale of $1,385,000. During 2004, the company sold property for $9,289,000 cash and recorded a gain on sale of $2,590,000.

Required:

For the property sold by AMC each year, compute the book value of the property sold and show how the disposals would be reported on the comparative statements of cash flows, using the following format (which assumes the indirect method):

	2003	2004
Cash flows from operating activities		
Gain on sale of property		
Cash flows from investing activities		
Proceeds from disposition of property		

E12-19 (Supplement A) Determining Cash Flows from the Sale of Equipment

During the period, Teen's Trends sold some excess equipment at a loss. The following information was collected from the company's accounting records:

From the income statement	
Depreciation expense	$ 700
Loss on sale of equipment	4,000
From the balance sheet	
Beginning equipment	12,500
Ending equipment	7,000
Beginning accumulated depreciation	2,000
Ending accumulated depreciation	2,200

No new equipment was bought during the period.

Required:

For the equipment that was sold, determine its original cost, its accumulated depreciation, and the cash received from the sale.

E12-20 (Supplement B) Preparing a Statement of Cash Flows, Indirect Method: Complete Spreadsheet

To prepare a statement of cash flows for Golf Champion Store, you examined the company's accounts, noting the following:

> Purchased equipment, $20,000, and issued a promissory note in full payment.
> Purchased a long-term investment for cash, $15,000.
> Paid cash dividend, $12,000.
> Sold equipment for $6,000 cash (cost, $21,000, accumulated depreciation, $15,000).
> Issued shares of stock, 500 shares at $12 per share cash.
> Net income was $20,200.
> Depreciation expense was $3,000.

You also created the following spreadsheet to use when preparing the statement of cash flows.

	Beginning Balances, December 31, 2006	Analysis of Changes Debit	Analysis of Changes Credit	Ending Balances, December 31, 2007
Balance sheet items				
Cash	$ 20,500			$ 19,200
Accounts receivable	22,000			22,000
Merchandise inventory	68,000			75,000
Investments	0			15,000
Equipment	114,500			113,500
Accumulated depreciation	32,000			20,000
Accounts payable	17,000			14,000
Wages payable	2,500			1,500
Income taxes payable	3,000			4,500
Notes payable	54,000			74,000
Contributed capital	100,000			106,000
Retained earnings	16,500			24,700
		Inflows	Outflows	
Statement of cash flows				
Cash flows from operating activities				
Cash flows from investing activities				
Cash flows from financing activities				
Net increase (decrease) in cash				
Totals				

Required:

Complete the spreadsheet to prepare the statement of cash flows using the indirect method.

COACHED PROBLEMS

CP12-1 Determining Cash Flow Statement Effects of Transactions

LO1

Motorola, Inc.

Motorola, Inc., is best known for its cell phones and modems, which have become so small that they are being integrated into new high-tech sunglasses. For each of the following first-quarter transactions, indicate whether operating (O), investing (I), or financing activities (F) are affected and whether the effect is a cash inflow (+) or outflow (−), or (NE) if the transaction has no effect on cash.

TIP: Think about the journal entry recorded for the transaction. The transaction affects net cash flows if and only if the account Cash is affected.

_____ 1. Purchased new equipment by signing a promissory note.

_____ 2. Recorded and paid income taxes to the federal government.

_____ 3. Issued shares of stock for cash.

_____ 4. Prepaid rent for the following period.

_____ 5. Recorded an adjusting entry for expiration of a prepaid expense.

_____ 6. Paid cash to purchase new equipment.

_____ 7. Issued long-term debt for cash.

_____ 8. Collected payments on account from customers.

_____ 9. Recorded and paid salaries to employees.

LO2A   **CP12-2 Computing Cash Flows from Operating Activities (Indirect Method)**

The income statement and selected balance sheet information for Hamburger Heaven for the year ended December 31, 2007, are presented below.

Income Statement	
Sales revenue	$2,060
Expenses:	
Cost of goods sold	900
Depreciation expense	200
Salaries expense	500
Rent expense	250
Insurance expense	80
Interest expense	60
Utilities expense	50
Net income	$ 20

Selected Balance Sheet Accounts		
	2007	2006
Merchandise inventory	$ 82	$ 60
Accounts receivable	380	450
Accounts payable	240	210
Salaries payable	29	20
Utilities payable	20	60
Prepaid rent	2	7
Prepaid insurance	14	5

TIP: Prepaid rent decreased in 2007 because the amount taken out of Prepaid rent (and subtracted from net income as Rent expense) was more than the amount paid for rent in cash during 2007.

Required:

Prepare the cash flows from operating activities section of the 2007 statement of cash flows using the indirect method.

LO2B   **CP12-3 Computing Cash Flows from Operating Activities (Direct Method)**

Refer to the information in CP12-2.

Required:

Prepare the cash flows from operating activities section of the 2007 statement of cash flows using the direct method.

TIP: Convert the cost of goods sold to cash paid to suppliers by adding the increase in inventory and subtracting the increase in accounts payable.

CP12-4 Preparing a Statement of Cash Flows (Indirect Method)

Hunter Company is developing its annual financial statements at December 31, 2008. The statements are complete except for the statement of cash flows. The completed comparative balance sheets and income statement are summarized:

www.mhhe.com/phillips2e

	2008	2007
Balance Sheet at December 31		
Cash	$ 44,000	$ 18,000
Accounts receivable	27,000	29,000
Merchandise inventory	30,000	36,000
Property and equipment	111,000	102,000
Less: Accumulated depreciation	(36,000)	(30,000)
	$176,000	$155,000
Accounts payable	$ 25,000	$ 22,000
Wages payable	800	1,000
Note payable, long-term	38,000	48,000
Contributed capital	80,000	60,000
Retained earnings	32,200	24,000
	$176,000	$155,000
Income Statement for 2008		
Sales	$100,000	
Cost of goods sold	61,000	
Other expenses	27,000	
Net income	$ 12,000	

Additional Data:

a. Bought equipment for cash, $9,000.
b. Paid $10,000 on the long-term note payable.
c. Issued new shares of stock for $20,000 cash.
d. Declared and paid a $3,800 cash dividend.
e. Other expenses included depreciation, $6,000; wages, $10,000; taxes, $3,000; other, $8,000.
f. Accounts payable includes only inventory purchases made on credit. Because there are no liability accounts relating to taxes or other expenses, assume that these expenses were fully paid in cash.

Required:

1. Prepare the statement of cash flows for the year ended December 31, 2008, using the indirect method.
2. Use the statement of cash flows to evaluate Hunter's cash flows.
   TIP: The demonstration cases provide good examples of information to consider when evaluating cash flows.

CP12-5 Preparing and Interpreting a Statement of Cash Flows (Indirect Method)

Soft Touch Company was started several years ago by two golf instructors. The company's comparative balance sheets and income statement are presented below, along with additional information.

	2008	2007
Balance Sheet at December 31		
Cash	$ 12,000	$ 8,000
Accounts receivable	2,000	3,500
Equipment	11,000	10,000
Less: Accumulated depreciation	(3,000)	(2,500)
	$22,000	$19,000
Accounts payable	$ 1,000	$ 2,000
Wages payable	1,000	1,500
Long-term bank loan payable	3,000	1,000
Contributed capital	10,000	10,000
Retained earnings	7,000	4,500
	$22,000	$19,000
Income Statement for 2008		
Lessons revenue	$75,000	
Wages expense	70,000	
Other expenses	2,500	
Net income	$ 2,500	

Additional Data:

a. Bought new clubs for cash, $1,000.
b. Borrowed $2,000 cash from the bank during the year.
c. Other expenses included depreciation, $500; utilities, $1,000; taxes, $1,000.
d. Accounts payable includes only purchases of services made on credit for operating purposes. Because there are no liability accounts relating to utilities or taxes, assume that these expenses were fully paid in cash.

Required:

1. Prepare the statement of cash flows for the year ended December 31, 2008, using the indirect method.
2. Use the statement of cash flows to evaluate the company's cash flows.
    TIP: The demonstration cases provide good examples of information to consider when evaluating cash flows.

LO2B, LO3, LO4, LO5   **CP12-6 Preparing and Interpreting a Statement of Cash Flows (Direct Method)**

Refer to CP12-5.

Required:

Complete requirements 1 and 2 using the direct method.
TIP: Remember to exclude depreciation expense when converting other expenses to the cash basis.

GROUP A PROBLEMS

Available with McGraw-Hill's
Homework Manager

HOMEWORK
MANAGER **PLUS**

LO1   **PA12-1 Determining Cash Flow Statement Effects of Transactions**

Motif Furniture is an Austin-based furniture company. For each of the following first-quarter transactions, indicate whether operating (O), investing (I), or financing activities (F) are affected and whether the effect is a cash inflow (+) or outflow (−), or (NE) if the transaction has no effect on cash.

_____ 1. Bought used equipment for cash.

_____ 2. Paid cash to purchase new equipment.

_____ 3. Declared and paid cash dividends to stockholders.

_____ 4. Collected payments on account from customers.

_____ 5. Recorded an adjusting entry to record accrued salaries expense.

_____ 6. Recorded and paid interest on debt to creditors.

_____ 7. Repaid principal on loan from bank.

_____ 8. Prepaid rent for the following period.

_____ 9. Made payment to suppliers on account.

PA12-2 Computing Cash Flows from Operating Activities (Indirect Method)   LO2A

The income statement and selected balance sheet information for Direct Products Company for the year ended December 31, 2007, is presented below.

Income Statement	
Sales revenue	$48,600
Expenses:	
Cost of goods sold	21,000
Depreciation expense	2,000
Salaries expense	9,000
Rent expense	4,500
Insurance expense	1,900
Interest expense	1,800
Utilities expense	1,400
Net income	$ 7,000

Selected Balance Sheet Accounts		
	2007	2006
Accounts receivable	$560	$580
Merchandise inventory	990	770
Accounts payable	440	460
Salaries payable	100	70
Utilities payable	20	15
Prepaid rent	25	20
Prepaid insurance	25	28

Required:

Prepare the cash flows from operating activities section of the 2007 statement of cash flows using the indirect method.

PA12-3 Computing Cash Flows from Operating Activities (Direct Method)   LO2B

Refer to the information in PA12-2.

Required:

Prepare the cash flows from operating activities section of the 2007 statement of cash flows using the direct method.

PA12-4 Preparing a Statement of Cash Flows (Indirect Method)   LO2A, LO3, LO4, LO5

XS Supply Company is developing its annual financial statements at December 31, 2007. The statements are complete except for the statement of cash flows. The completed comparative balance sheets and income statement are summarized:

	2007	2006
Balance Sheet at December 31		
Cash	$ 34,000	$ 29,000
Accounts receivable	35,000	28,000
Merchandise inventory	41,000	38,000
Property and equipment	121,000	100,000
Less: Accumulated depreciation	(30,000)	(25,000)
	$201,000	$170,000
Accounts payable	$ 36,000	$ 27,000
Wages payable	1,200	1,400
Note payable, long-term	38,000	44,000
Contributed capital	88,600	72,600
Retained earnings	37,200	25,000
	$201,000	$170,000
Income Statement for 2006		
Sales	$120,000	
Cost of goods sold	70,000	
Other expenses	37,800	
Net income	$ 12,200	

Additional Data:

a. Bought equipment for cash, $21,000.
b. Paid $6,000 on the long-term note payable.
c. Issued new shares of stock for $16,000 cash.
d. No dividends were declared or paid.
e. Other expenses included depreciation, $5,000; wages, $20,000; taxes, $6,000; other, $6,800.
f. Accounts payable includes only inventory purchases made on credit. Because there are no liability accounts relating to taxes or other expenses, assume that these expenses were fully paid in cash.

Required:

1. Prepare the statement of cash flows for the year ended December 31, 2007, using the indirect method.
2. Evaluate the statement of cash flows.

LO2A, LO3, LO4, LO5   **PA12-5 Preparing and Interpreting a Statement of Cash Flows (Indirect Method)**

Heads Up Company was started several years ago by two hockey instructors. The company's comparative balance sheets and income statement are presented below, along with additional information.

	2008	2007
Balance Sheet at December 31		
Cash	$ 6,000	$4,000
Accounts receivable	1,000	1,750
Equipment	5,500	5,000
Less: Accumulated depreciation	(1,500)	(1,250)
	$ 11,000	$9,500
Accounts payable	$ 500	$ 1,000
Wages payable	500	750
Long-term bank loan payable	1,500	500
Contributed capital	5,000	5,000
Retained earnings	3,500	2,250
	$ 11,000	$9,500
Income Statement for 2008		
Lessons revenue	$37,500	
Wages expense	35,000	
Other expenses	1,250	
Net income	$ 1,250	

Additional Data:

a. Bought new hockey equipment for cash, $500.

b. Borrowed $1,000 cash from the bank during the year.

c. Other expenses included depreciation, $250; rent, $500; taxes, $500.

d. Accounts payable includes only purchases of services made on credit for operating purposes. Because there are no liability accounts relating to rent or taxes, assume that these expenses were fully paid in cash.

Required:

1. Prepare the statement of cash flows for the year ended December 31, 2008, using the indirect method.

2. Use the statement of cash flows to evaluate the company's cash flows.

PA12-6 Preparing and Interpreting a Statement of Cash Flows (Direct Method) LO2B, LO3, LO4, LO5

Refer to PA12-5.

Required:

Complete requirements 1 and 2 using the direct method.

GROUP B PROBLEMS

PB12-1 Determining Cash Flow Statement Effects of Transactions LO1

Fantatech Inc. designs, develops, and produces high-tech entertainment products, including VirtuaSports, that allow novice players to experience hazardous and difficult real-life sports in virtual reality. The company also produces a 4D theatre system that combines 3D visual effects with special effects such as vibrating chairs, simulated drops, and scented air blasts. For each of the following transactions listed in Fantatech's annual report, indicate whether operating (O), investing (I), or financing activities (F) are affected and whether the effect is a cash inflow (+) or outflow (−), or (NE) if the transaction has no effect on cash.

Fantatech Inc.

_____ 1. Received deposits from customers for products to be delivered the following period.

_____ 2. Principal repayments on loan.

_____ 3. Paid cash to purchase new equipment.

_____ 4. Received proceeds from loan.

_____ 5. Collected payments on account from customers.

_____ 6. Recorded and paid salaries to employees.

_____ 7. Paid cash for building construction.

_____ 8. Recorded and paid interest to debt holders.

PB12-2 Computing Cash Flows from Operating Activities (Indirect Method) LO2A

The income statement and selected balance sheet information for Calendars Incorporated for the year ended December 31, 2007, is presented below.

Income Statement	
Sales revenue	$78,000
Expenses:	
Cost of goods sold	36,000
Depreciation expense	16,000
Salaries expense	10,000
Rent expense	2,500
Insurance expense	1,300
Interest expense	1,200
Utilities expense	1,000
Net income	$10,000

Selected Balance Sheet Accounts		
	2007	2006
Merchandise inventory	$ 430	$ 490
Accounts receivable	1,800	1,500
Accounts payable	1,200	1,300
Salaries payable	450	300
Utilities payable	100	0
Prepaid rent	50	100
Prepaid insurance	70	90

Required:

Prepare the cash flows from operating activities section of the 2007 statement of cash flows using the indirect method.

LO2B   **PB12-3 Computing Cash Flows from Operating Activities (Direct Method)**

Refer to the information in PB12-2.

Required:

Prepare the cash flows from operating activities section of the 2007 statement of cash flows using the direct method.

LO2A, LO3, LO4, LO5   **PB12-4 Preparing a Statement of Cash Flows (Indirect Method)**

Audio City, Inc., is developing its annual financial statements at December 31, 2007. The statements are complete except for the statement of cash flows. The completed comparative balance sheets and income statement are summarized:

	2007	2006
Balance Sheet at December 31		
Cash	$ 63,000	$ 65,000
Accounts receivable	15,000	20,000
Merchandise inventory	22,000	20,000
Property and equipment	210,000	150,000
Less: Accumulated depreciation	(60,000)	(45,000)
	$250,000	$210,000
Accounts payable	$ 8,000	$ 19,000
Wages payable	2,000	1,000
Note payable, long-term	60,000	75,000
Contributed capital	100,000	70,000
Retained earnings	80,000	45,000
	$250,000	$210,000
Income Statement for 2007		
Sales	$ 190,000	
Cost of goods sold	90,000	
Other expenses	60,000	
Net income	$ 40,000	

Additional Data:

a. Bought equipment for cash, $60,000.
b. Paid $15,000 on the long-term note payable.
c. Issued new shares of stock for $30,000 cash.
d. Dividends of $5,000 were paid in cash.
e. Other expenses included depreciation, $15,000; wages, $20,000; taxes, $25,000.
f. Accounts payable includes only inventory purchases made on credit. Because a liability relating to taxes does not exist, assume that they were fully paid in cash.

Required:

1. Prepare the statement of cash flows for the year ended December 31, 2007, using the indirect method.
2. Evaluate the statement of cash flows.

PB12-5 Preparing and Interpreting a Statement of Cash Flows (Indirect Method)   LO2A, LO3, LO4, LO5

Dive In Company was started several years ago by two diving instructors. The company's comparative balance sheets and income statement are presented below, along with additional information.

	2008	2007
Balance Sheet at December 31		
Cash	$ 3,200	$4,000
Accounts receivable	1,000	500
Prepaids	100	50
	$ 4,300	$4,550
Wages payable	$ 350	$ 1,100
Contributed capital	1,200	1,000
Retained earnings	2,750	2,450
	$ 4,300	$4,550
Income Statement for 2008		
Lessons revenue	$33,950	
Wages expense	30,000	
Other operating expenses	3,650	
Net income	$ 300	

Additional Data:

a. Prepaid expenses relate to rent paid in advance.
b. Other operating expenses were paid in cash.
c. An owner contributed capital by paying $200 cash in exchange for the company's stock.

Required:

1. Prepare the statement of cash flows for the year ended December 31, 2008, using the indirect method.
2. Use the statement of cash flows to evaluate the company's cash flows.

PB12-6 Preparing and Interpreting a Statement of Cash Flows (Direct Method)   LO2B, LO3, LO4, LO5

Refer to PB12-5.

Required:

Complete requirements 1 and 2 using the direct method.

SKILLS DEVELOPMENT CASES

S12-1 Finding Financial Information   LO1, LO5

Refer to the financial statements of Landry's Restaurants in Appendix A at the end of this book, or download the annual report from the *Cases* section of the text's Web site at www.mhhe.com/phillips2e.

Required:

1. Which of the two basic reporting approaches for the cash flows from operating activities did Landry's use?

2. What amount of tax payments did Landry's make during the current year? Where did you find this information?

3. Including business acquisitions, what was the capital acquisitions ratio averaged across the three years shown in Landry's statement of cash flows? Ignoring business acquisitions, what was the capital acquisitions ratio averaged across the three years shown in Landry's statement of cash flows? Calculate the capital acquisitions ratio to two decimal places.

4. How much cash did Landry's pay for interest during the current year? Using this information, calculate and interpret the cash coverage ratio for the most recent year. Calculate the cash coverage ratio to one decimal place.

5. In the most recent year reported, Landry's generated $151,056,018 from operating activities. Where did Landry's spend this money? List the two largest cash outflows.

LO1, LO5

S12-2 Comparing Financial Information

Refer to the financial statements of Outback Steakhouse in Appendix B at the end of this book, or download them from the *Cases* section of the text's Web site at www.mhhe.com/phillips2e.

Required:

1. Which of the two basic reporting approaches for the cash flows from operating activities did Outback Steakhouse use? Is this the same as what Landry's used?

2. What amount of tax payments did Outback make during 2005? Where did you find this information? Is this more or less than Landry's paid?

3. Ignoring business acquisitions, what was the capital acquisitions ratio computed to two decimal places and averaged across the three years shown in Outback's statement of cash flows? Do net operating cash flows pay for a greater or lesser proportion of Outback's capital acquisitions than Landry's?

4. How much cash did Outback pay for interest during 2005? Using this information, calculate to one decimal place Outback's cash coverage ratio for the most recent year and interpret it. Compare this to Landry's and draw a conclusion about the companies' relative abilities to pay for interest.

5. In 2005, Outback generated $373 million from operating activities. Where did Outback spend this money? List the two largest cash outflows reported in the investing or financing activities sections. Do Outback's uses differ significantly from Landry's?

LO5

S12-3 Internet-Based Team Research: Examining an Annual Report

As a team, select an industry to analyze. Using your Web browser, each team member should access the annual report or 10-K for one publicly traded company in the industry, with each member selecting a different company. (See S1-3 in Chapter 1 for a description of possible resources for these tasks.)

Required:

1. On an individual basis, each team member should write a short report that incorporates the following:
   a. Has the company generated positive or negative operating cash flows during the past three years?
   b. Has the company been expanding over the period? If so, what appears to have been the source of financing for this expansion (operating cash flow, additional borrowing, issuance of stock)?
   c. Compute and analyze the capital acquisitions ratio averaged over the past three years.
   d. Compute and analyze the cash coverage ratio in each of the past three years.
   e. Compute and analyze the quality of income ratio in each of the past three years.

2. Then, as a team, write a short report comparing and contrasting your companies using these attributes. Discuss any patterns across the companies that you as a team observe. Provide potential explanations for any differences discovered.

LO1, LO5
Enron

S12-4 Ethical Decision Making: A Real-Life Example

In a February 19, 2004, press release, the Securities and Exchange Commission described a number of fraudulent transactions that Enron executives concocted in an effort to meet the company's financial targets. One particularly well-known scheme is called the "Nigerian barge" transaction, which took place in the fourth quarter of 1999. According to court documents, Enron arranged to sell three electricity-generating power barges moored off the coast of Nigeria. The "buyer" was the investment banking firm of Merrill Lynch. Although Enron reported this transaction as a sale in its income statement, it turns out this was no ordinary sale. Merrill Lynch didn't really want the barges and had only agreed to buy them because Enron guaranteed, in a secret side-deal, that it would arrange for the barges to be bought back from Merrill Lynch within six months of the initial transaction. In addition, Enron promised to pay Merrill Lynch a hefty fee for doing the deal. In an interview on National Public Radio on August 17, 2002, Michigan Senator Carl Levin declared, "(t)he case of the Nigerian barge transaction was, by any definition, a loan."

Required:

1. Discuss whether the Nigerian barge transaction should have been considered a loan rather than a sale. As part of your discussion, consider the following questions. Doesn't the Merrill Lynch payment to Enron at the time of the initial transaction automatically make it a sale, not a loan? What aspects of the transaction are similar to a loan? Which aspects suggest revenue has not been earned by Enron?

2. The income statement effect of recording the transaction as a sale rather than a loan is fairly clear: Enron was able to boost its revenues and net income. What is somewhat less obvious, but nearly as important, are the effects on the statement of cash flows. Describe how including the transaction with sales of other Enron products, rather than as a loan, would change the statement of cash flows.

3. How would the difference in the statement of cash flows (described in your response to requirement 2) affect financial statement users?

S12-5 Ethical Decision Making: A Mini-Case

Assume you serve on the board of a local golf and country club. In preparation for renegotiating the club's bank loans, the president indicates that the club needs to increase its operating cash flows before the end of the current year. With a wink and sly smile, the club's treasurer reassures the president and other board members that he knows a couple of ways to boost the club's operating cash flows. First, he says, the club can sell some of its accounts receivable to a collections company that is willing to pay the club $97,000 up front for the right to collect $100,000 of the overdue accounts. That will immediately boost operating cash flows. Second, he indicates that the club paid about $200,000 last month to relocate the 18th fairway and green closer to the clubhouse. The treasurer indicates that although these costs have been reported as expenses in the club's own monthly financial statements, he feels an argument can be made for reporting them as part of land and land improvements (a long-lived asset) in the year-end financial statements that would be provided to the bank. He explains that, by recording these payments as an addition to a long-lived asset, they will not be shown as a reduction in operating cash flows.

Required:

1. Does the sale of accounts receivable to generate immediate cash harm or mislead anyone? Would you consider it an ethical business activity?

2. If cash is spent on long-lived assets, such as land improvements, how is it typically classified in the statement of cash flows? If cash is spent on expenses, such as costs for regular upkeep of the grounds, how is it typically classified in the statement of cash flows?

3. What facts are relevant to deciding whether the costs of the 18th hole relocation should be reported as an asset or as an expense? Is it appropriate to make this decision based on the impact it could have on operating cash flows?

4. As a member of the board, how would you ensure that an ethical decision is made?

S12-6 Critical Thinking: Interpreting Adjustments Reported on the Statement of Cash Flows from a Management Perspective (Indirect Method)

QuickServe, a chain of convenience stores, was experiencing some serious cash flow difficulties because of rapid growth. The company did not generate sufficient cash from operating activities to finance its new stores, and creditors were not willing to lend money because the company had not produced any income for the previous three years. The new controller for QuickServe proposed a reduction in the estimated life of store equipment to increase depreciation expense; thus, "we can improve cash flows from operating activities because depreciation expense is added back on the statement of cash flows." Other executives were not sure that this was a good idea because the increase in depreciation would make it more difficult to have positive earnings: "Without income, the bank will never lend us money."

Required:

What action would you recommend for QuickServe? Why?

LO2A

www.mhhe.com/phillips2e

S12-7 Using a Spreadsheet that Calculates Cash Flows from Operating Activities (Indirect Method)

You've recently been hired by B2B Consultants to provide financial advisory services to small business managers. B2B's clients often need advice on how to improve their operating cash flows and, given your accounting background, you're frequently called upon to show them how operating cash flows would change if they were to speed up their sales of inventory and their collections of accounts receivable or delay their payment of accounts payable. Each time you're asked to show the effects of these business decisions on the cash flows from operating activities, you get the uneasy feeling that you might inadvertently miscalculate their effects. To deal with this once and for all, you e-mail your friend Owen and ask him to prepare a template that automatically calculates the net operating cash flows from a simple comparative balance sheet. You received his reply today.

From:	Owentheaccountant@yahoo.com
To:	Helpme@hotmail.com
Cc:	
Subject:	Excel Help

Hey pal. I like your idea of working smarter, not harder. Too bad it involved me doing the thinking. Anyhow, I've created a spreadsheet file that contains four worksheets. The first two tabs (labeled BS and IS) are the input sheets where you would enter the numbers from each client's comparative balance sheet and income statement. Your clients are small, so this template allows for only the usual accounts. Also, I've assumed that depreciation is the only reason for a change in accumulated depreciation. If your clients' business activities differ from these, you'll need to contact me for more complex templates. The third worksheet calculates the operating cash flows using the indirect method and the fourth does this calculation using the direct method. I'll attach the screenshots of each of the worksheets so you can create your own. To answer "what if" questions, all you'll need to do is change selected amounts in the balance sheet and income statement.

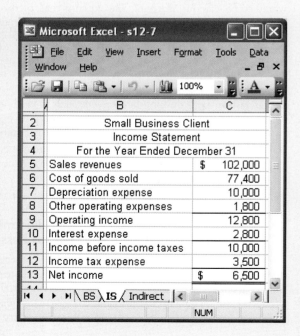

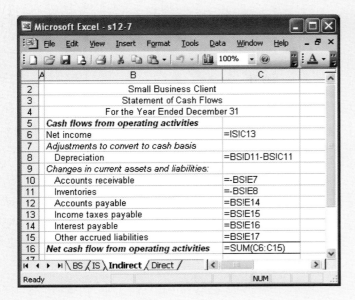

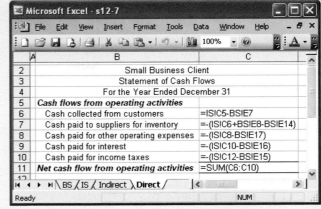

Required:

Copy the information from the worksheets for the balance sheet, income statement, and statement of cash flows (indirect method only) into a spreadsheet file. What was the net cash flow from operating activities?

S12-8 Using a Spreadsheet that Calculates Cash Flows from Operating Activities (Direct Method)

LO2B

www.mhhe.com/phillips2e

Refer to the information presented in S12-7.

Required:

Copy the information from the worksheets for the balance sheet, income statement, and statement of cash flows (direct method only) into a spreadsheet file. What was the net cash flow from operating activities?

S12-9 Using a Spreadsheet to Answer "What If" Management Decisions (Indirect or Direct Method)

LO5

www.mhhe.com/phillips2e

Change the amounts for selected balance sheet accounts in the spreadsheets created for either S12-7 or S12-8 to calculate the cash flows from operating activities if, just before the current year-end, the company's management took the actions listed in the following requirements. Consider each question independently, unless indicated otherwise.

Required:

1. What if the company collected $10,000 of the accounts receivable?
2. What if the company had paid down its interest payable by an extra $2,000?
3. What if the company waited an additional month before paying $6,000 of its accounts payable?
4. What if the company had reported $5,000 more depreciation expense?
5. What if all four of the above events had taken place?

13

Measuring and Evaluating Financial Performance

THAT WAS
THEN

In the previous chapters, you learned how to report and interpret the financial effects of various business activities.

LP13

You made it to Chapter 13. In accounting slang, "Chapter 11" and "Chapter 13" are labels used for different forms of bankruptcy protection that buy time for people rearranging their financial affairs, but that's not what Chapter 13 in this textbook is about. In fact, we focus on a company that's nowhere near that situation. In this chapter, you'll learn how to determine this by analyzing the financial statements of Landry's Restaurants—the company that owns and operates restaurants like Rainforest Café and Saltgrass Steakhouse.

Measuring and evaluating financial performance is like judging gymnastics or figure skating at the Olympics. You have to know three things: (1) the general categories to evaluate for each event, (2) the particular elements to consider within each category, and (3) how performance for each element is measured. You probably use a similar approach when judging your eating experience at Landry's many restaurants. General categories, like value or enjoyment, can be broken down into particular elements like price, service, and serving size, which can be measured in terms of money, time, and ounces of steak. On the financial side, analysts evaluate general categories like profitability, liquidity, and solvency, which are broken down into particular elements like profit margin and asset turnover. For each of these elements, analysts measure performance using financial ratios, which themselves are based on information reported in the financial statements. In the end, you'll use your judgment to combine all these measures into an overall assessment.

THIS IS
NOW

This chapter synthesizes previous chapters, by evaluating the financial statements and accounting decisions of a publicly traded company.

We begin this chapter by describing how to use trend and ratio analyses to understand the financial results of business activities. These analyses typically involve two parts, calculation and interpretation, which we present in the second and third sections of the chapter using the financial statements of Landry's Restaurants. We conclude these analyses by reviewing many of the key accounting decisions and concepts on which you'll depend when evaluating financial statements. As always, the chapter ends with a review of the topics and a plateful of practice material.

ORGANIZATION OF THE CHAPTER

Understand the business	Study the accounting methods	Evaluate the results	Review the chapter
• Trend and ratio analyses	• Calculating trends • Calculating ratios	• Interpreting trends and ratios • Underlying accounting decisions and concepts	• Demonstration case • Chapter summary • Key terms • Practice material

Understand the Business

Learning Objective 1
Describe the purposes and uses of trend and ratio analyses.

As you first learned in Chapter 1, the goal of accounting is to provide information that allows decision makers to understand and evaluate the results of business activities. Throughout this course, you have learned that no single number fully captures the results of all business activities nor does it predict a company's success or failure. Instead, to understand and evaluate the results of business activities, you need to look at a business from many different angles. An understanding of whether a business is successful will emerge only after you have learned to combine all of your evaluations into a complete picture or story that depicts the company's performance. Our goal for this chapter is to demonstrate how you can do this, relying primarily on trend and ratio analyses to develop the "story" of how well a company has performed.

TREND AND RATIO ANALYSES

Topic Tackler

PLUS

Check out www.mhhe.com/phillips2e for audio, visual, and PowerPoint presentations on this topic.

Most good stories have a plot, which the reader comes to understand as it unfolds over time or as one event connects to another. This is the same way that financial trend and ratio analyses work. Trend analyses are conducted to help financial statement users recognize important financial changes that unfold over time. Trend analysis compares individual financial statement line items over time, with the general goal of identifying significant sustained changes (trends). These changes are typically described in terms of dollar amounts and year-over-year percentages. For example, trend analyses could be used to determine the dollar amount and percentage by which cost of goods sold increased this year, relative to prior years. Ratio analyses, on the other hand, are conducted to understand relationships among various items reported in the financial statements.

Ratio analyses involve comparing amounts for one or more financial statement items to amounts for other items for the same year. Ratio analyses are useful because they take into account differences in the size of amounts being compared, which allows you to evaluate how well a company has performed given the level of other company resources. For example, while a trend analysis can reveal that cost of goods sold increased during the year, ratio analyses could indicate whether the increase in cost of goods sold is fully explained by the increase in sales volume or partly explained by other factors (like an increase in the cost of buying each unit of inventory). Knowing whether other factors are involved is important because it could affect your interpretation of trends.

Most analysts classify ratios into three categories of performance:

1. **Profitability**, which relates to performance in the current period. In particular, the focus is on the company's ability to generate income during the period.

2. **Liquidity**, which relates to the company's short-term survival. In particular, the focus is on the company's ability to use current assets to repay liabilities as they become due in the short term.

3. **Solvency**, which relates to the company's long-run survival. In particular, the focus is on the company's ability to repay lenders when debt matures (and to make required interest payments prior to the date of maturity).

These three categories emphasize different aspects of a company's performance that could be important depending on the particular decision an analyst is making.

Before we show you how to calculate trends and ratios (in the next section), we must emphasize that no analysis is complete unless it leads to an interpretation that helps financial statement users understand and evaluate a company's financial results. Without interpretation, trends and ratios can appear as nothing more than a list of disconnected numbers. To make it easier to interpret trends and ratios, and thereby discover the story or events that explain a company's results, it's useful to organize analyses using the categories of profitability, liquidity, and solvency.

> **YOU SHOULD KNOW**
>
> **Profitability** is the extent to which a company generates income. **Liquidity** is the extent to which a company is able to pay its currently maturing obligations. **Solvency** is the ability to survive long enough to repay lenders when debt matures.

Study the Accounting Methods

CALCULATING TRENDS

Trend analyses involve examining changes in each line in the financial statements over time. Trend analyses are also known as **horizontal analyses** (because they compare horizontally across each financial statement line item) and as **time-series analyses** (because they compare over a series of time periods). Regardless of their name, trend analyses are usually calculated in terms of year-over-year dollar and percentage changes. A year-over-year percentage change simply expresses the dollar change of the current year as a percentage of the prior year total, using the following calculation:

> **Learning Objective 2**
> Calculate financial trends and ratios.

> **YOU SHOULD KNOW**
>
> **Horizontal (or time-series) analyses** are trend comparisons across time, often expressing changes in account balances as a percentage of prior year balances.

$$\text{Year-Over-Year Change (\%)} = \frac{\text{Change This Year}}{\text{Prior Year's Total}} \times 100$$
$$= \frac{(\text{Current Year's Total} - \text{Prior Year's Total})}{\text{Prior Year's Total}} \times 100$$

To show you how to calculate trend analyses, we analyze the financial statements of Landry's Restaurants. The annual report for Landry's appears in Appendix A at the end of the book but to save you the trouble of flipping back and forth, we've presented a summary of the balance sheets, income statements, and statements of cash flows

Video 13.1

from the three most recent years in Exhibits 13.1–13.3. To the immediate left of the balance sheet and income statement, we show the dollar and percentage changes from 2004 to 2005. The dollar change is calculated by subtracting the 2004 balance from the 2005 balance. The percentage change is calculated by dividing this difference by the 2004 balance. For example, Exhibit 13.1 shows that Cash decreased by $162,178 ($39,216 − $201,394) in 2005 relative to 2004, which is a decrease of 80.5% ($162,178 ÷ $201,394). Dollar and percentage changes in 2004, relative to 2003, are shown to the right of each statement.

EXHIBIT 13.1 | Horizontal Analysis of Summarized Balance Sheets

LANDRY'S RESTAURANTS, INC.
Balance Sheets
(in thousands)

2005 vs. 2004 Percent	2005 vs. 2004 Amount	December 31	2005	2004	2003	2004 vs. 2003 Amount	2004 vs. 2003 Percent
		Assets					
		Current assets					
−80.5%	−$162,178	Cash	$ 39,216	$ 201,394	$ 35,211	+$166,183	+472.0%
+18.2%	+$ 3,377	Accounts receivable	21,973	18,596	23,272	−$ 4,676	−20.1%
+8.6%	+$ 4,713	Inventories	59,717	55,004	47,772	+$ 7,232	+15.1%
+13.5%	+$ 3,043	Other current assets	25,532	22,489	14,349	+$ 8,140	+56.7%
−50.8%	−$151,045	Total current assets	146,438	297,483	120,604	+$176,879	+146.7%
+37.0%	+$372,962	Property and equipment, net	1,380,259	1,007,297	965,575	+$ 41,722	+4.3%
+113.8%	+$ 45,710	Goodwill and other assets	85,882	40,172	16,606	+$ 23,566	+141.9%
+19.9%	+$267,627	Total assets	$1,612,579	$1,344,952	$1,102,785	+$242,167	+22.0%
		Liabilities and Stockholders' Equity					
+62.2%	+$ 84,532	Current liabilities	$ 220,500	$ 135,968	$ 159,581	−$ 23,613	−14.8%
+43.9%	+$267,221	Long-term debt	875,308	608,087	338,654	+$269,433	+79.6%
+47.3%	+$351,753	Total liabilities	1,095,808	744,055	498,235	+$245,820	+49.3%
−14.0%	−$ 84,126	Stockholders' equity	516,771	600,897	604,550	−$ 3,653	−0.6%
+19.9%	+$267,626	Total liabilities and stockholders' equity	$1,612,579	$1,344,952	$1,102,785	+$242,167	+22.0%

Be aware that because each year-over-year percentage change is calculated relative to the prior year, it can appear more important than it actually is if the prior year balance is small. For example, Landry's income statement in Exhibit 13.2 shows that Income tax expense increased by over 480% in 2005, relative to 2004, which might seem like a super-important change. However, the dollar amount of the change was only $17,063, which was less than the change in almost every other line in the income statement. The percentage was magnified because $17,063 was divided by the small prior year balance of $3,545. To avoid focusing on unimportant changes, use the percentage changes to identify potentially significant changes and then check that the dollar change also is significant.

Notice that, in Exhibit 13.3, we present the summarized statements of cash flows without an accompanying horizontal analysis. A horizontal analysis of the statement of cash flows is not useful because the statement of cash flows already reports changes (in cash) during each year. Calculating the change in these changes, although possible, isn't likely to help you better understand a company's financial performance.

EXHIBIT 13.2 Horizontal Analysis of Summarized Income Statements

LANDRY'S RESTAURANTS, INC.
Income Statements
(in thousands)

2005 vs. 2004		Year Ended December 31	2005	2004	2003	2004 vs. 2003	
Percent	Amount					Amount	Percent
+6.7%	+$78,331	Net sales revenue	$1,245,806	$1,167,475	$1,105,755	+$61,720	+5.6%
+2.1%	+$ 6,920	Cost of revenues	333,028	326,108	321,783	+$ 4,325	+1.3%
+8.5%	+$71,411	Gross profit	912,778	841,367	783,972	+$57,395	+7.3%
+6.6%	+$49,803	Operating and other expenses	805,917	756,114	718,608	+$37,506	+5.2%
+172.9%	+$26,252	Interest expense	41,438	15,186	9,561	+$ 5,625	+58.8%
+481.3%	+$17,063	Income tax expense	20,608	3,545	10,889	−$ 7,344	−67.4%
−32.6%	−$21,707	Net income	$ 44,815	$ 66,522	$ 44,914	+$21,608	+48.1%
−18.3%	−$ 0.45	Earnings per share	$ 2.01	$ 2.46	$ 1.63	+$ .83	+50.9%

EXHIBIT 13.3 Summarized Statements of Cash Flows

LANDRY'S RESTAURANTS, INC.
Statements of Cash Flows
(in thousands)

	Year Ended December 31		
	2005	2004	2003
Cash Flows from Operating Activities			
Net income	$ 44,815	$ 66,522	$ 44,914
Adjustments to reconcile to cash flows from operations	106,241	45,091	79,022
Net cash provided by (used in) operating activities	151,056	111,613	123,936
Cash Flows from Investing Activities			
Net cash paid for property and equipment	(114,438)	(104,574)	(163,377)
Cash paid for business acquisitions	(135,487)	(12,931)	(27,036)
Net cash provided by (used in) investing activities	(249,925)	(117,505)	(190,413)
Cash Flows from Financing Activities			
Net cash from issuing (repurchasing) common stock	(125,652)	(62,781)	(8,417)
Amounts borrowed (paid) in other financing activities	62,343	234,856	96,227
Net cash provided by (used in) financing activities	(63,309)	172,075	87,810
Net Increase (Decrease) in Cash	(162,178)	166,183	21,333
Cash at beginning of year	201,394	35,211	13,878
Cash at end of year	$ 39,216	$ 201,394	$ 35,211
Supplemental Disclosure of Cash Flows			
Cash paid during the period for interest	$ 45,297	$ 15,988	$ 8,675
Cash paid during the period for income taxes	$ 4,838	$ 9,949	$ 5,699

Topic Tackler

PLUS

Check out www.mhhe.com/phillips2e for audio, visual, and PowerPoint presentations on this topic.

CALCULATING RATIOS

Exhibit 13.4 summarizes the ratios introduced in previous chapters and groups them as relating to profitability, liquidity, or solvency. This exhibit also shows the amounts that were taken from Landry's financial statements (in Exhibits 13.1–13.3) to calculate these ratios for 2005. The 2004 and 2003 ratios are presented for comparative purposes.

EXHIBIT 13.4 | Ratios Used for Financial Statement Analyses

LANDRY'S RESTAURANTS, INC.
Summary of Financial Ratios

Chapter/Page	Ratio	Formula	Year Ended December 31 2005	2004	2003
Profitability Ratios					
(a) 5 (p. 210)	Net profit margin = 3.6% = $44,815/$1,245,806 × 100	$\dfrac{\text{Net income}}{\text{Net sales revenue}}$	3.6%	5.7%	4.1%
(b) 6 (p. 255)	Gross profit percentage = 73.3% = $912,778/$1,245,806 × 100	$\dfrac{\text{Net sales revenue} - \text{Cost of goods sold}}{\text{Net sales revenue}}$	73.3%	72.1%	70.9%
(c) 5 (p. 210)	Asset turnover = 0.84 = $1,245,806/[($1,612,579 + $1,344,952)/2]	$\dfrac{\text{Net sales revenue}}{\text{Average total assets}}$	0.84	0.95	1.09
(d) 9 (p. 400)	Fixed asset turnover = 1.04 = $1,245,806/[($1,380,259 + $1,007,297)/2]	$\dfrac{\text{Net sales revenue}}{\text{Average net fixed assets}}$	1.04	1.18	2.41
(e) 11 (p. 508)	Return on equity (ROE) = 8.0% = $44,815/[($516,771 + $600,897)/2] × 100	$\dfrac{\text{Net income}}{\text{Average stockholders' equity}}$	8.0%	11.0%	15.4%
(f) 11 (p. 508)	Earnings per share (EPS) = EPS is reported on the income statement.	$\dfrac{\text{Net income}}{\text{Average number of common shares}}$	$2.01	$2.46	$1.63
(g) 12 (p. 559)	Quality of income = 3.37 = $151,056/$44,815	$\dfrac{\text{Net cash from operations}}{\text{Net income}}$	3.37	1.68	2.76
(h) 11 (p. 508)	Price/earnings (P/E) ratio = 15.4 = $31/$2.01	$\dfrac{\text{Stock price}}{\text{EPS}}$	15.4	12.6	19.0
Liquidity Ratios					
(i) 8 (p. 352)	Receivables turnover = 61.4 = $1,245,806/[($21,973 + $18,596)/2]	$\dfrac{\text{Net sales revenue}}{\text{Average net receivables}}$	61.4	55.8	114.9
8 (p. 352)	Days to collect = 5.9 = 365/61.4	$\dfrac{365}{\text{Receivables turnover ratio}}$	5.9	6.5	3.2
(j) 7 (p. 306)	Inventory turnover = 5.8 = $333,028/[($59,717 + $55,004)/2]	$\dfrac{\text{Cost of sales}}{\text{Average inventory}}$	5.8	6.3	13.4
7 (p. 306)	Days to sell = 62.9 = 365/5.8	$\dfrac{365}{\text{Inventory turnover ratio}}$	62.9	57.9	27.2
(k) 10 (p. 449)	Current ratio = 0.66 = $146,438/$220,500	$\dfrac{\text{Current assets}}{\text{Current liabilities}}$	0.66	2.19	0.76

EXHIBIT 13.4	Ratios Used for Financial Statement Analyses (*Continued*)

Solvency Ratios

(l)	5 (p. 210)	**Debt-to-assets =**	$\dfrac{\text{Total liabilities}}{\text{Total assets}}$	0.68	0.55	0.45
		0.68 = $1,095,808/$1,612,578				
(m)	10 (p. 449)	**Times interest earned =**	$\dfrac{\text{Net income + Interest expense +}}{\text{Income tax expense}}{\text{Interest expense}}$	2.6	5.6	6.8
		2.6 = ($44,815 + $41,438 + $20,608)/$41,438				
(n)	12 (p. 561)	**Cash coverage =**	$\dfrac{\text{Net cash from operations + Interest paid + Income taxes paid}}{\text{Interest paid}}$	4.4	8.6	15.9
		4.4 = ($151,056 + $45,297 + $4,838)/$45,297				
(o)	12 (p. 560)	**Capital acquisitions ratio =**	$\dfrac{\text{Net cash from operations}}{\text{Cash paid for PPE}}$	0.60	0.95	0.65
		0.60 = $151,056/$249,925				

You may notice that a few of the ratios in Exhibit 13.4 compare one amount to another larger amount on the same financial statement. For example, the debt-to-assets ratio compares total liabilities to total assets on the balance sheet. Similarly, the net profit margin and gross profit percentage ratios compare net income and gross profit to net sales revenues on the income statement. These particular comparisons have become "standard" ratios because they frequently reveal important observations about each financial statement. However, other important relationships might exist within a financial statement, which are not revealed through the standard ratios listed in Exhibit 13.4. To identify these other relationships, some analysts conduct vertical analyses. **Vertical analyses** express each financial statement amount as a percentage of another amount on that financial statement. A vertical analysis of the income statement will calculate and report each item as a percentage of sales revenue, as shown in Exhibit 13.5. For example,

> **YOU SHOULD KNOW**
>
> Like some ratios, **vertical analyses** express each financial statement amount as a percentage of another amount on the same financial statement.

EXHIBIT 13.5	Vertical Analysis of Summarized Income Statements

LANDRY'S RESTAURANTS, INC.
Income Statements
(dollars in thousands)

Year Ended December 31	%	2005	%	2004	%	2003
Net sales revenue	100.0%	$1,245,806	100.0%	$1,167,475	100.0%	$1,105,755
Cost of revenues	26.7	333,028	27.9	326,108	29.1	321,783
Gross profit	73.3	912,778	72.1	841,367	70.9	783,972
Operating and other expenses	64.7	805,917	64.8	756,114	65.0	718,608
Interest expense	3.3	41,438	1.3	15,186	0.9	9,561
Income tax expense	1.7	20,608	0.3	3,545	1.0	10,889
Net income	3.6%	$ 44,815	5.7%	$ 66,522	4.0%	$ 44,914

the 2005 percentage for Interest expense of 3.3% was calculated by dividing Interest expense ($41,438) by Net sales revenue ($1,245,806) and multiplying by 100 to express the amount as a percentage.[1]

Quiz Answers
Gross profit percentage = $(3.6 − 1.3)/3.6 × 100
= 63.8%
Net profit margin = $(0.15)/3.6 × 100 = 4.2%
Sales increase (percentage) = $(3.6 − 3.2)/3.2 × 100
= 12.5%

HOW'S IT GOING?   Self-Study Quiz

Outback Steakhouse reported net income of $150 million on sales of $3.6 billion for the year ended December 31, 2005. If the company's cost of sales was $1.3 billion in 2005, what was the company's gross profit percentage and net profit margin? If sales were $3.2 billion in 2004, what was the year-over-year percentage increase in 2005?

$$\text{Gross profit percentage} = \frac{(\$\boxed{} - \boxed{}) \text{ billion}}{\$3.6 \text{ billion}} \times 100 = \boxed{}$$

$$\text{Net profit margin} = \frac{\$0.15 \text{ billion}}{\boxed{}} \times 100 = \boxed{}$$

$$\text{Sales increase (percentage)} = \frac{(\$\boxed{} - \boxed{}) \text{ billion}}{\$\boxed{} \text{ billion}} \times 100 = \boxed{}$$

Evaluate the Results

INTERPRETING TRENDS AND RATIOS

Learning Objective 3
Interpret the results of trend and ratio analyses.

LP13

As noted in the previous section, financial statement analyses are not complete unless they lead to interpretations that help users understand and evaluate a company's financial results. When interpreting trend and ratio analyses, your goals should be to understand what each analysis is telling you and then combine them into a coherent "story" that explains the results of the company's business activities. We demonstrate how to do this, beginning with interpretations of each set of analyses shown in Exhibits 13.1−13.5 and later concluding with an overall summary of Landry's results.

Trends Revealed in Horizontal Analyses

Exhibits 13.1−13.3 indicate that Landry's grew significantly in 2004 and again in 2005. For example, Exhibit 13.1 shows that total assets increased approximately 20 percent in each of these years. Similarly, Exhibit 13.2 shows that net sales revenues, gross profit, and operating expenses increased in 2004 and 2005, with the increases ranging from 5.2 to 8.5 percent over the prior year. You can find what caused these increases by reading the Management Discussion and Analysis (MD&A) section of Landry's 2005 annual report. Two factors contributed to the company's growth. First, Landry's opened 25 new restaurants during 2004 and 2005. Second, Landry's bought the Golden Nugget Hotel and Casino in September 2005.

These two factors affected several line items on Landry's 2005 balance sheet in Exhibit 13.1. Obviously, property and equipment was affected by the restaurant expansion and casino purchase, with this line item increasing by $372 million (37 percent) in 2005. Cash and long-term debt also were affected, as they provided the means for

---
[1] A vertical analysis of the balance sheet expresses each item as a percentage of total assets. Vertical analyses are rarely conducted on the statement of cash flows, statement of retained earnings, and/or statement of stockholders' equity.

financing the expansion and purchase. Exhibit 13.1 shows that cash decreased by $162 million (80 percent) and long-term debt increased by $267 million (43.9 percent) in 2005. These balance sheet changes also were accompanied by changes in the income statement shown in Exhibit 13.2. Of particular concern is the effect that the long-term debt increase had on interest expense in 2005. Exhibit 13.2 shows that interest expense increased by $26 million, which along with increased operating expenses led to a decline in Landry's 2005 net income and earnings per share.

In summary, the story revealed by the trend analyses is that Landry's has grown significantly in the past two years. While this growth has led to increases in sales and gross profit, it also has caused operating expenses to increase. Because Landry's growth was financed using additional debt, the company incurred substantial interest expense. The higher interest expense, combined with higher operating expenses, more than offset the increase in gross profit, causing a decrease in net income in 2005. Cash flows have also been affected by the growth, again indicating greater reliance on debt financing.

Relationships Revealed in Ratio Analyses

As shown throughout other chapters in this book, benchmarks help when interpreting a company's ratios. These benchmarks can include the company's prior year results, as well as the results of close competitors or the average for the industry. In a competitive economy, companies strive to outperform one another, so comparisons against other companies can provide clues about who is likely to survive and thrive in the long run. We focus on two close competitors: Outback Steakhouse (whose annual report is reproduced in Appendix B at the end of this book) and Darden Restaurants (owner of Red Lobster, Olive Garden, and Bahama Breeze).

Profitability Ratios The analyses in this section focus on the level of profits the company generated during the period.

(a) Net profit margin

Net profit margin represents the percentage of sales revenues that ultimately make it into net income, after deducting expenses. As shown in Exhibit 13.4, Landry's net profit margins for each of the last three years are

Year Ended December 31		2005	2004	2003
(a) Net profit margin = $\dfrac{\text{Net income}}{\text{Net sales revenue}}$		3.6%	5.7%	4.1%

Having completed a horizontal analysis that showed a decrease in net income and increase in sales, you shouldn't be surprised to see that Landry's net profit margin was lower in 2005 than in the two prior years. What might come as a surprise, though, is just how close Landry's was to reporting a net loss. The net profit margin ratio of 3.6 percent for 2005 indicates that, for each dollar of sales, Landry's generated only 3.6¢ of net income. That's pretty disappointing compared to the average restaurant company, which according to Yahoo! Finance enjoyed a net profit margin ratio of 6.2 percent. Landry's decrease from 5.7 percent in 2004 to 3.6 percent in 2005 also is a downer because, when considered in light of over $1 billion in sales, this drop of 2.1 percent (5.7 − 3.6) equates to a profit decline of about $21 million.

(b) Gross profit percentage

The horizontal analysis indicated that Landry's 2005 and 2004 gross profits increased in total dollar amount, but it doesn't indicate whether the increase was caused only by greater total sales or also by greater profit per sale. This is where the gross profit percentage is particularly helpful. The gross profit percentage indicates how much

COACH'S TIP

Industry averages are reported in the *Annual Statement Studies*, which are published by the Risk Management Association. You can obtain industry averages also from marketguide.com, edgarscan. pwcglobal.com, or Yahoo! Finance, all of which were available for free at the time this book was written.

profit was made, on average, on each dollar of sales after deducting the cost of goods sold. Landry's gross profit percentages for the last three years are

Year Ended December 31	2005	2004	2003
(b) Gross profit percentage = $\dfrac{\text{Net sales revenue} - \text{Cost of goods sold}}{\text{Net sales revenue}}$	73.3%	72.1%	70.9%

This analysis shows that, in 2005, after paying for the cost of the food and drinks sold during the year, 73.3 percent of each sales dollar was left to cover other costs like employee wages, advertising, utilities, and other expenses. The increase in gross profit percentage in 2005 over 2004 (73.3% − 72.1%) means that Landry's made 1.2¢ more gross profit on each dollar of sales in 2005 than in 2004. Two potential explanations for this increase are that (1) Landry's charged higher selling prices without corresponding increases in the cost of its food and beverages, and (2) Landry's obtained its food and beverages at a lower unit cost. Landry's MD&A explains that the increase in gross profit percentage came from charging slightly higher prices in 2005.

One question remains after analyzing these two ratios. If the amount of gross profit per dollar of sales (gross profit percentage) increased in 2005, why then did the net income earned from each dollar of sales (net profit margin) decrease in 2005? The answer to this question is suggested by the vertical analysis of Landry's 2005 income statement. As shown in Exhibit 13.5, Landry's interest expense was a much bigger percentage of sales in 2005 than in 2004. By taking on additional debt to finance the company's recent growth, Landry's incurred more interest expense than ever before, causing its net income and net profit margin to suffer.

(c) Asset turnover

The asset turnover ratio indicates the amount of sales revenue generated for each dollar invested in assets. The ratios for the three years are

Year Ended December 31	2005	2004	2003
(c) Asset turnover = $\dfrac{\text{Net sales revenue}}{\text{Average total assets}}$	0.84	0.95	1.09

The asset turnover analysis suggests that Landry's assets didn't generate sales as efficiently in 2005 as in prior years. To understand what caused this, it's useful to focus on key assets that are used to generate sales. For a restaurant company like Landry's, the key asset is restaurant property, which can be compared to sales using the fixed asset turnover ratio discussed next.

(d) Fixed asset turnover

The fixed asset turnover ratio indicates how much the company generates in sales for each dollar invested in fixed assets like restaurant buildings. The ratios for the three years are

Year Ended December 31	2005	2004	2003
(d) Fixed asset turnover = $\dfrac{\text{Net sales revenue}}{\text{Average net fixed assets}}$	1.04	1.18	2.41

This analysis shows that Landry's cranked out $1.04 of sales in 2005 for each dollar invested in fixed assets. Is this good? Well, the declining trend isn't great, but it's understandable given that our trend analyses revealed that Landry's added 25 restaurants in the past two years. It's likely that these restaurants will take some time to establish a strong customer base and begin generating sales at full capacity. Plus, the purchase of the Golden Nugget in September 2005 also would have hurt this ratio because the costs of the hotel and casino are included in fixed assets, but Landry's generated only four months of sales from them in 2005. Landry's fixed asset turnover ratios are low compared to its competitors. The 2005 fixed asset turnover ratio was 2.74 for Outback Steakhouse and 2.38 for Darden. Landry's expects these kinds of differences, as it has adopted a strategy of owning about one-third of the buildings and waterfront properties in which its restaurants are located. Many of Landry's competitors rent, rather than own their properties, so they report higher levels of sales relative to their fixed assets. In a presentation to analysts, Landry's CEO justified this strategy by pointing out that Landry's has lower rent costs than its competitors. "In case there are ever tough times, we own all this real estate. We can have a dip in business and never get strangled like a lot of other companies who pay 5–7 percent (of revenue) for rent."

(e) Return on equity (ROE)

The return on equity ratio compares the amount of net income to average stockholders' equity. Like the interest rate on your savings account, ROE reports the net amount earned this period as a percentage of each dollar contributed to and retained in the business. Although Landry's net income declined in 2005, it's not obvious whether the company's ROE also will have fallen. Landry's bought back some of its stock during 2005, which decreased its average stockholders' equity. Whether the drop in net income occurred at a greater rate than the decrease in stockholders' equity will determine whether Landry's ROE decreased or increased in 2005. Landry's ROE ratios for the past three years are

Year Ended December 31	2005	2004	2003
(e) Return on equity (ROE) = $\dfrac{\text{Net income}}{\text{Average stockholders' equity}}$	8.0%	11.0%	15.4%

Landry's ROE of 8.0 percent in 2005 is down significantly from 2004 and 2003. This decline in ROE would be troubling to investors because it suggests the company is generating a smaller return on amounts contributed to and retained in the company. What also would be troubling is that, during this period, much larger ROEs were reported by competitors Outback Steakhouse (13.4 percent) and Darden Restaurants (27.0 percent) and by the restaurant industry as a whole (17.3 percent according to Yahoo! Finance).

(f) Earnings per share (EPS)

Earnings per share (EPS) indicates the amount of earnings generated for each share of outstanding common stock. Consistent with the decline in ROE, the EPS ratio decreased in 2005 as shown below.

Year Ended December 31	2005	2004	2003
(f) Earnings per share (EPS) = $\dfrac{\text{Net income}}{\text{Average number of common shares}}$	$2.01	$2.46	$1.63

(g) Quality of income

The quality of income ratio relates operating cash flows (from the statement of cash flows) to net income, as follows:

Year Ended December 31	2005	2004	2003
(g) Quality of income = $\dfrac{\text{Net cash from operations}}{\text{Net income}}$	3.37	1.68	2.76

The ratio of 3.37 in 2005 indicates that Landry's generated $3.37 of operating cash flow for every dollar of net income. Because this ratio is much greater than 1.0, it is interpreted as "high quality," meaning that operations are producing even more positive results (cash flows from operating activities) than what is suggested by the net income number. Most cash-based businesses, like restaurants, have high quality of income ratios because their sales are collected in cash immediately, and they report substantial noncash expenses like depreciation. Consistent with this expectation, we see high quality of income ratios for competitors Darden (2.12) and Outback Steakhouse (2.54).

(h) Price/earnings (P/E) ratio

The price/earnings (P/E) ratio relates the company's stock price to its EPS, as follows:

Year Ended December 31		2005	2004	2003
(h) Price/earnings ratio = $\dfrac{\text{Stock price}}{\text{EPS}}$		15.4	12.6	19.0

Using the going price for Landry's stock when its 2005 earnings were announced, the P/E ratio was 15.4, which means investors were willing to pay 15.4 times earnings to buy a share of Landry's stock. According to Yahoo! Finance, the average P/E ratio for restaurant companies at that time was around 20, suggesting that investors were less willing to buy stock in Landry's than in other restaurant companies.

Topic Tackler

PLUS

Check out www.mhhe.com/phillips2e for audio, visual, and PowerPoint presentations on this topic.

Let's pause to summarize what we've learned so far. Landry's increased its assets by nearly 20 percent in both 2004 and 2005, by opening new restaurants and buying a casino business. This expansion increased sales revenue by about 6 percent in each year and, thanks also to modest increases in menu prices, increased its gross profits. These gross profit increases were partly eaten up by operating expenses, which grew at a rate of 6 percent (like sales). Unfortunately, the sizable interest expense that Landry's incurred on additional debt taken out to finance its expansion caused the company's net income to fall, leaving a net profit margin of just 3.6 percent. The decline in net income also caused Landry's EPS and ROE ratios to fall from prior years. Its relatively low P/E ratio, compared to the industry as a whole, suggests that investors were unwilling to overlook these declines, despite the strong positive impact that the company's earnings had on its cash flows from operations. The bottom line is that Landry's expansion might later prove to be beneficial, but it had a negative impact on profitability in 2005.

Liquidity Ratios   The analyses in this section focus on the company's ability to survive in the short term, by converting assets to cash that can be used to pay current liabilities as they come due.

(i) Receivables turnover

Most restaurant companies have low levels of accounts receivable relative to sales revenue because the majority of their sales are collected immediately as cash. Although the formula calls for net **credit** sales in the top of the ratio, companies never separate credit sales from cash sales. Consequently, financial statement users end up having to use total sales revenue in the formula, resulting in a receivables turnover ratio that is not terribly meaningful for businesses like restaurants, which make few sales on account. We presented the ratio in Exhibit 13.4 simply to remind you how it's calculated.

(j) Inventory turnover

As you probably know from personal experience, food can go bad quickly if it's left sitting out. The inventory turnover ratio indicates how frequently inventory is bought and sold during the year, and "days to sell" converts this ratio into the number of days between buying and selling.

Year Ended December 31		2005	2004	2003
(j)	Inventory turnover = $\dfrac{\text{Cost of sales}}{\text{Average inventory}}$	5.8	6.3	13.4
	Days to sell = $\dfrac{365}{\text{Inventory turnover ratio}}$	62.9	57.9	27.2

At first glance, you might be alarmed by Landry's inventory turnover ratio. (We were.) A turnover of 5.8 during 2005 suggests the company's inventory was on hand, on average, for almost 63 days. Two months is a long time for steak to sit out. After doing a little digging, though, we found a couple of reasons not to be too worried. First, Landry's financial statement notes reveal that nearly 40 percent of its inventory consists of T-shirts and other retail goods, which take longer to sell. Second, improvements in food preservation technology (such as cryogenic freezing) allow items to be "fresh frozen" and held in inventory for a long time, apparently without harming flavor or freshness. Darden appears to rely on this technology too, to keep about 47 days worth of inventory on hand. Outback Steakhouse, on the other hand, brags about making everything fresh, including its croutons. Is its inventory turnover ratio consistent with this claim? Sort of. Outback's turnover ratio of 19.9 is the biggest in the group, but it still means the average item is in inventory for 18.3 days before being served. Not so fresh.

(k) Current ratio

The current ratio compares current assets to current liabilities, as follows:

Year Ended December 31		2005	2004	2003
(k)	Current ratio = $\dfrac{\text{Current assets}}{\text{Current liabilities}}$	0.66	2.19	0.76

Seeing a drop in the current ratio from 2.19 at the end of 2004 to 0.66 in 2005, you might think that Landry's was in big trouble. The 2005 current ratio indicates that the company's current assets were only 66 percent of its current liabilities. For many companies, this would be a major problem. It's not a concern for Landry's, for four reasons: (1) the company collects the majority of its revenues in cash as soon as its goods are sold, (2) the company sells its complete inventory of goods, on average, within 63 days of purchase, which is about the same number of days of credit that suppliers typically offer, (3) the company consistently generates positive cash flows from operations (see Exhibit 13.3), and (4) Landry's has arranged a line of credit with banks to cover times when it is temporarily short on cash (for more information on this point, see the discussion about General Mills in Chapter 10). Comparing across the restaurant industry, we find that Landry's current ratio is actually stronger than Outback Steakhouse (at 0.50) and Darden (0.37). So rather than be shocked by how low the current ratio is in 2005, you should probably wonder why it was so high in 2004. Our hunch is that Landry's was hoarding cash in anticipation of buying the Golden Nugget Hotel and Casino.

In summary, the liquidity ratios suggest that Landry's has efficiently managed its short-term position. The company doesn't keep a lot of current assets on hand relative to its current liabilities. But then again, nobody really wants a restaurant to stockpile a bunch of food or let cash sit idle in the bank.

Solvency Ratios The analyses in this section focus on how well the company is positioned for long-term survival, in terms of its ability to repay debt when it matures, to pay interest until that time, and to finance the replacement and/or expansion of long-term assets.

(l) Debt-to-assets

The debt-to-assets ratio indicates the proportion of total assets that are financed by creditors. Remember, creditors have to be paid regardless of how tough a year a company might have had, so the higher the ratio, the riskier the financing strategy. Landry's ratio for the three years was

COACH'S TIP

Instead of the debt-to-assets ratio, analysts might use a debt-to-equity ratio which gives the same basic information as debt-to-assets. Debt-to-equity typically is calculated as total liabilities ÷ total stockholders' equity. As with debt-to-assets, the higher the debt-to-equity ratio, the more the company relies on debt (rather than equity) financing.

Year Ended December 31	2005	2004	2003
(l) Debt-to-assets $= \dfrac{\text{Total liabilities}}{\text{Total assets}}$	0.68	0.55	0.45

Landry's ratio of 0.45 back in 2003 indicates that creditors had contributed 45 percent of the financing used by Landry's, implying that stockholders' equity was the main source of financing at 55 percent. You can see that this has changed significantly as of the end of 2005, with creditors now contributing 68 percent of Landry's financing. Landry's now relies on debt financing more than its competitors, with debt-to-assets ratios of 0.43 for Outback Steakhouse and 0.59 for Darden.

(m) Times interest earned

The times interest earned ratio indicates how many times interest is covered by operating results. This ratio is calculated using accrual-based interest expense and net income (before interest and taxes), as follows:

Year Ended December 31	2005	2004	2003
(m) Times interest earned $= \dfrac{\text{Net income} + \text{Interest expense} + \text{Income tax expense}}{\text{Interest expense}}$	2.6	5.6	6.8

COACH'S TIP

If the company reports a net loss, rather than net income, include the loss as a negative number in the formula. A negative ratio indicates that the operating results (before the costs of financing and taxes) are less than the interest costs.

A times interest earned ratio above 1.0 indicates that net income (before the costs of financing and taxes) is sufficient to cover interest expense. Landry's ratio of 2.6 indicates the company is generating enough profit to cover its interest expense, but not with a lot of room to spare. This shouldn't come as a surprise because our earlier profitability analyses pointed to higher interest expenses as a significant hurdle the company would have to overcome.

(n) Cash coverage ratio

Like the times interest earned ratio, the cash coverage ratio indicates how many times interest is covered by operating results. Rather than use accrual-based numbers, however, the cash coverage ratio compares the cash generated from the company's business operations (before interest and taxes) to its interest payments, as follows:

Year Ended December 31	2005	2004	2003
(n) Cash coverage $= \dfrac{\text{Net cash from operations} + \text{Interest paid} + \text{Income taxes paid}}{\text{Interest paid}}$	4.4	8.6	15.9

This analysis shows that if the cash generated from operations wasn't spent on other financing or investing activities, Landry's could cover its interest payments several times over. Clearly, the ratio has taken a slide in 2004 and 2005, but the ratio remains above 1.0, so the company appears able to handle the interest on loans from bankers and other long-term debtholders.

(o) Capital acquisitions ratio

The capital acquisitions ratio compares cash flows from operations to cash paid for property and equipment (including businesses acquired). The ratio for the three years follows

Year Ended December 31		2005	2004	2003
(o) Capital acquisitions ratio = $\dfrac{\text{Net cash from operations}}{\text{Cash paid for PPE}}$		0.60	0.95	0.65

The 0.95 capital acquisitions ratio in 2004 indicates that when Landry's was expanding by opening new restaurants, it nearly generated enough cash flow from operations to buy the new property and equipment that it had acquired. In 2005, when the company bought the Golden Nugget, its operating cash flows were 60 percent of what was spent on expansion. These figures are typical of a company that is growing rather rapidly.

In summary, the story that is suggested by these solvency ratios is that Landry's has grown significantly and has financed this growth through internal operating cash flows and external sources of debt financing. By far, the most significant shift is the increasing reliance on debt financing, resulting in larger interest payments, which the company appears able to cover through positive operating cash flows. Whether this shift to more debt financing will prove to be a good or bad decision is not yet clear, but it certainly has increased the current risk profile of the company.

HOW'S IT GOING?   Self-Study Quiz

In 2004, Applebee's recorded a $2,100,000 inventory write-down for "excess inventories of riblets that no longer met the company's quality standards." Mmm. Complete the following table by showing the impact (+, −, no change) of this inventory write-down on selected measures of profitability, liquidity, and solvency.

Impact of Inventory Write-Down
a. Net profit margin ratio
b. Current ratio
c. Cash coverage ratio

UNDERLYING ACCOUNTING DECISIONS AND CONCEPTS

Accounting Decisions

In the analyses just presented, we've compared Landry's with Darden and Outback Steakhouse. Where appropriate, we've discussed how differences in strategy (e.g., buying versus renting restaurant space) and business operations (e.g., selling food and merchandise versus food only) affect interpretations of the financial ratios. You also should consider whether interpretations of differences between companies' financial ratios might be caused by the companies making different accounting decisions.

Information about a company's accounting decisions is presented in an accounting policies note to the financial statements. Exhibit 13.6 compares the policies used by the three restaurant companies when accounting for food inventory and depreciation—the areas with the greatest potential impact on the results of restaurant companies. As you can see, the three companies use similar, but not identical, policies. The inventory costing method varies, with Landry's and Darden using weighted average cost and

Learning Objective 4
Describe how trend and ratio analyses depend on key accounting decisions and concepts.

EXHIBIT 13.6   Comparison of Accounting Methods

	Landry's Restaurants	Darden Restaurants	Outback Steakhouse
Food inventory	Weighted average cost	Weighted average cost	FIFO
Depreciation	Straight-line Buildings: 5-40 yrs Equipment: 5-15 yrs	Straight-line Buildings: 7-40 yrs Equipment: 2-10 yrs	Straight-line Buildings: 20-30 yrs Equipment: 2-15 yrs

Outback using FIFO to calculate the costs of ending inventory and goods sold. Although these different methods create somewhat different numbers, their overall impact on our ratios is likely to be minor because, at any point in time, inventory is a small part of the companies' total assets (less than 7 percent for each company).

The three companies calculate depreciation using the straight-line method with a similar range of estimated useful lives of buildings and equipment. Because buildings and equipment make up over two-thirds of each company's assets, these similarities go a long way toward making the financial results comparable across the companies. The conclusion from our analysis of Exhibit 13.6 is that although some differences exist among the companies' accounting policies, they are unlikely (in this case) to have a major impact on our comparisons.

Accounting Concepts

Before wrapping up this chapter, it's worth revisiting the accounting concepts that were introduced in previous chapters. At this stage of the course, you should have developed a fairly good understanding of the rules of accounting and can better appreciate why accounting relies on these particular concepts. Exhibit 13.7 presents the conceptual framework for financial accounting and reporting that was first introduced in Chapter 1. The concepts that you have already learned about in prior chapters are highlighted in red in Exhibit 13.7.

As shown in Exhibit 13.7, the primary objective of financial accounting and reporting is to provide useful financial information for people external to a company to use in making decisions about the company. To be useful, this information must be relevant (it matters), reliable (it can be trusted), comparable (everyone follows the same rules), and consistent (the rules don't change from one period to the next). The relevance of accounting information is a key concern when accounting standard setters at the FASB establish new accounting rules. Reliability of financial information has been a recent focus with the implementation of the Sarbanes-Oxley Act of 2002, which as

EXHIBIT 13.7   Conceptual Framework for Financial Accounting and Reporting

Objective:	To provide useful financial information to external users for decision making. (Ch. 1)
Characteristics of Useful Financial Information:	Relevance, Reliability, Comparability, Consistency (Ch. 1)
Elements:	Assets, Liabilities, Stockholders' Equity, Revenues, Expenses (Ch. 1-3)
Assumptions:	Unit of Measure (Ch. 1), Separate Entity (Ch. 1), Going Concern, Time Period (Ch. 3)
Principles:	Cost (Ch. 2), Revenue Recognition (Ch. 3), Matching (Ch. 3), Full Disclosure
Constraints:	Cost-benefit, Materiality (Ch. 5), Industry Practices, Conservatism (Ch. 2)

Chapter 5 described now requires companies to improve their systems of internal control and auditors to expand their testing of and reporting about the effectiveness of those systems. As always, information comparability and consistency continues to be a consideration when standard setters introduce new rules and when auditors test to ensure companies have implemented them properly.

As Exhibit 13.7 indicates, only four accounting concepts have not been introduced in previous chapters, so we will explain them here. The concept of **going concern** (also called *continuity*) is an assumption that quietly underlies accounting rules. It is the belief that any business will be capable of continuing its operations long enough to realize its recorded assets and meet its obligations in the normal course of business. If a company runs into severe financial difficulty (such as bankruptcy), this assumption may no longer be appropriate, leading to what is called a *going-concern problem*. If ever a company encounters a going-concern problem, it may require the company to adjust the amount and classification of items in its financial statements, which would be explained in the financial statement notes and to which the auditor's report would draw attention. Some of the factors that commonly contribute to going-concern problems are listed in Exhibit 13.8. Notice that some of the analyses presented earlier in this chapter are key inputs into determining whether a company has a going-concern problem.

EXHIBIT 13.8 | Factors Contributing to Going-Concern Problems

Revealed by Financial Analyses	Revealed by Other Analyses
• Declining sales	• Overdependence on one customer
• Declining gross profit	• Insufficient product innovation/quality
• Significant one-time expenses	• Significant barriers to expansion
• Fluctuating net income	• Loss of key personnel without replacement
• Insufficient current assets	• Inability to negotiate favorable purchases
• Excessive reliance on debt financing	• Inadequate maintenance of long-lived assets
• Adverse financial commitments	• Loss of a key patent

One of the principles of accounting that was not previously explained is full disclosure. Simply put, the principle of **full disclosure** is that financial reports should present all information that is needed to properly interpret the results of the company's business activities. This doesn't mean that every single transaction needs to be explained in detail, but rather that adequate information needs to be presented to allow financial statement users to fairly interpret reports about the company's income, financial position, and cash flows.

Despite the best efforts to make accounting rules applicable in as many situations as possible, there are limits on how broadly they can be applied. These limits, or constraints, are listed in Exhibit 13.7. Two constraints not introduced in previous chapters relate to industry practices and cost-benefit trade-offs. The **industry practices constraint** is that companies in some industries, such as financial services, oil and gas, and agricultural production, have such special circumstances that they need to use accounting rules that differ somewhat from what companies in most other industries use. The **cost-benefit constraint** recognizes that it is costly for companies to gather all the financial information that could possibly be reported. Accounting rules need to be implemented only to the extent that the benefits outweigh the costs of doing so. This latter constraint explains why Darden Restaurants follows a policy of expensing all building-related costs less than $1,000, even if these costs extend the life of buildings.

Before closing the book on this topic (and possibly this course), take a moment to attempt the following Self-Study Quiz. It'll give you a good idea of whether you should do a detailed review of the concepts introduced in earlier chapters or whether you're ready to move on to review and practice key aspects of this chapter.

HOW'S IT GOING? — A Self-Study Quiz

Match each statement below to the assumption, principle, or constraint to which it most closely relates.

1. Everything comes down to dollars and cents.
2. That's not our issue. It's for somebody else to report.
3. Don't sweat it. It's not big enough to worry about.
4. We'll make an exception, but only because you're special.
5. If it relates to this period, you'd better report it.
6. I've told you everything you could possibly want to know.
7. When in doubt, don't be overly optimistic.
8. I know it's a long time, but let's look at it in stages.
9. You can reach a point where it's just not worth all the trouble.
10. At that rate, you may not survive past the end of the year.

(a) Separate entity
(b) Conservatism
(c) Going concern
(d) Unit of measure
(e) Time period
(f) Cost-benefit
(g) Materiality
(h) Industry practices
(i) Full disclosure
(j) Matching

Quiz Answers
1. (d) 2. (a) 3. (g) 4. (h) 5. (j)
6. (i) 7. (b) 8. (e) 9. (f) 10. (c)

You have now seen enough to interpret most basic financial statements. When analyzing real-world financial statements, you will probably encounter nonrecurring or other special items reported in the income statement. These items are discussed in the following chapter supplement.

SUPPLEMENT: NONRECURRING AND OTHER SPECIAL ITEMS

Nonrecurring Items

Until 2005, three different types of nonrecurring items were reported in income statements: discontinued operations, extraordinary items, and cumulative effects of changes in accounting methods. R. J. Reynolds Tobacco Holdings, Inc., (RJR) reported all three types of nonrecurring items in a single comparative income statement, shown in Exhibit 13A.1. (In case you were wondering, we aren't trying to promote the tobacco industry. RJR is just one of the few real-world cases where all three types of nonrecurring items were reported in a single set of financial statements.) Recently, however, new accounting standards have nearly eliminated income statement reporting of extraordinary items and cumulative effects of changes in accounting methods. The definition of *extraordinary* has become so restricted that few events—not even the losses arising from the 9/11 terrorist attacks—qualify as extraordinary. Cumulative effects of changes in accounting methods are now reported as adjustments to Retained earnings, rather than included in the income statement in the period the change is made. The technical procedures used to make these adjustments are discussed in intermediate accounting courses.

Discontinued operations result from abandoning or selling a major business component. The discontinued operations line on the income statement includes any gain or loss on disposal of the discontinued operation as well as any operating income generated during the current year prior to its disposal. Because gains or losses from discontinued operations appear below the Income tax expense line on the income statement, any additional tax effects related to the gains or losses are included in their

YOU SHOULD KNOW

Discontinued operations result from the disposal of a major component of the business and are reported net of income tax effects.

EXHIBIT 13A.1	Nonrecurring Items Reported Net of Tax on the Income Statement

R.J. REYNOLDS TOBACCO HOLDINGS, INC.
Condensed Income Statements
December 31,
(in millions)

	2003	2002
Net sales	$ 5,267	$6,211
Cost of products sold	3,218	3,732
Selling, general, and administrative expenses	1,327	1,463
Asset impairment expenses	4,563	237
Operating income (loss)	(3,841)	779
Interest and other expenses, net	77	96
Income (loss) before income taxes	(3,918)	683
Income tax expense (benefit)	(229)	265
Net income (loss) from continuing operations	(3,689)	418
Gain on sale of discontinued operations, net of income taxes	122	40
Extraordinary item, net of income taxes	121	—
Cumulative effect of accounting change, net of income taxes	—	(502)
Net loss	$(3,446)	$ (44)

reported amounts. RJR's net gain of $122 million in 2003 relates to the sale of an international business unit. Obviously, the sale of a particular business unit can happen only once, so these results are reported separately to inform users that they will not recur to affect the company's future results.

Other Special Items

In some cases, you may see that companies include additional items on their income statements after the net income line. These items may be added to or subtracted from net income to arrive at something called *Comprehensive income*. As you can learn in detail in intermediate courses in financial accounting, these items represent gains or losses relating to changes in the value of certain balance sheet accounts. While most gains and losses are included in the computation of net income, some (relating to changes in foreign currency exchange rates and the value of certain investments, for example) are excluded from net income and included only when computing comprehensive income. The main reason for excluding these gains and losses from net income is that the changes in value that created them may very well disappear before they are ever realized (when the company gets rid of the assets or liabilities to which they relate). For this reason, most analysts will take a moment to consider the size of these special items in relation to net income but, if they are not large, will exclude them from the profitability ratios presented earlier in this chapter.[2]

---

[2] Rather than show the computation of comprehensive income on the face of the income statement, companies are allowed to show it instead either in a statement of stockholders' equity or in a separate statement of comprehensive income. One survey indicates that about 84 percent of companies show the computation in a statement of stockholders' equity (AICPA 2005 *Accounting Trends & Techniques*).

REVIEW THE CHAPTER

This section provides a chance to solidify your understanding of key points. It's worth your time to work through the following demonstration case, scan the chapter summary, test your understanding of key terms, and then practice, practice, practice.

DEMONSTRATION CASE

www.mhhe.com/phillips2e

The following ratios for Outback Steakhouse were presented as benchmarks for interpreting Landry's 2005 ratios:

Fixed asset turnover = 2.74

Return on equity = 13.4

Quality of income = 2.54

Days to sell = 18.3

Current ratio = 0.50

Debt-to-assets = 0.43

Required:

1. With reference to the annual report for Outback Steakhouse in Appendix B, show how the ratios listed above were calculated.
2. Interpret the meaning of the ratios calculated in requirement 1.

Suggested Solution

1. Calculating ratios (dollar amounts in 000s)

Fixed asset turnover	=	Net sales revenue ÷ Average net fixed assets
	=	$3,590,869 ÷ [($1,387,700 + $1,233,995)/2]
	=	2.74
Return on equity	=	Net income ÷ Average stockholders' equity
	=	$146,746 ÷ [($1,144,420 + $1,047,111)/2]
	=	0.134 or 13.4%
Quality of income	=	Cash flow from operating activities ÷ Net income
	=	$373,117 ÷ $146,746
	=	2.54
Days to sell	=	365 ÷ Inventory turnover ratio
	=	365 ÷ (Cost of goods sold ÷ Average inventory)
	=	365 ÷ [$1,315,340 ÷ ($68,468 + $63,448)/2]
	=	18.3
Current ratio	=	Current assets ÷ Current liabilities
	=	$249,692 ÷ $501,538
	=	0.50
Debt-to-assets	=	Total liabilities ÷ Total assets
	=	($803,743 + $44,259) ÷ $1,992,422
	=	0.43

2. Interpreting ratios

- A fixed asset turnover ratio of 2.74 means that, on average, Outback generated $2.74 of sales for each dollar of fixed assets.
- A return on equity of 13.4 percent means that Outback's net income for the year was 13.4 percent of the amount investors had contributed to and left in the company.
- A quality of income ratio of 2.54 means that for every dollar of net income, Outback actually generated $2.54 of cash from operating activities.

- The days to sell ratio of 18.3 means that, on average, 18 days would elapse between the time inventory was first acquired and later sold.
- A current ratio of 0.50 means that Outback had only 50 cents of current assets for each dollar of current liabilities at year-end.
- A debt-to-assets ratio of 0.43 means that Outback relied on short-term and long-term debt to finance 43 percent of its assets, implying that stockholders' equity provided financing for 57 percent (100 − 43) of its total assets.

CHAPTER SUMMARY

Describe the purposes and uses of trend and ratio analyses. p. 596   LO1

- Trend analyses compare financial statement items to comparable amounts in prior periods, with the goal of identifying sustained changes ("trends").
- Ratio analyses compare one or more financial statement items to an amount for other items for the same year. Ratios take into account differences in the size of amounts to allow for evaluations of performance given existing levels of other company resources.
- When comparing over time and across companies, watch out for possible differences in business strategy, operations, accounting policies, and nonrecurring events that can affect reported financial results.

Calculate financial trends and ratios. p. 597   LO2

- Trend analyses (also called horizontal analyses) involve computing the dollar amount by which each account changes from one period to the next, and expressing that change as a percentage of the balance for the prior period.
- Financial ratios are commonly classified as relating to profitability, liquidity, or solvency. Exhibit 13.4 lists these ratios and shows how to compute them.
  - Profitability ratios focus on measuring the adequacy of income by comparing it to other items reported on the financial statements.
  - Liquidity ratios measure a company's ability to meet its current maturing debt.
  - Solvency ratios measure a company's ability to meet its long-term obligations.
- Financial ratios also include vertical analyses, which express each line of the income statement (or balance sheet) as a percentage of total sales (or total assets).

Interpret the results of trend and ratio analyses. p. 602   LO3

- Trend and ratio analyses are not complete unless they lead to an interpretation that helps financial statement users understand and evaluate a company's financial results.
- An understanding of whether a business is successful emerges only after you have learned to combine trend and ratio analyses into a complete picture or story that depicts the company's performance.
- To assist in developing this picture or story, most analysts compare to benchmarks such as the company's performance in prior years or to competitors' performance in the current year.

Describe how trend and ratio analyses depend on key accounting decisions and concepts. p. 609   LO4

- Before comparing across companies or time periods, users should determine the extent to which differences in accounting decisions (e.g., methods used to account for inventory costing, fixed asset depreciation, contingent liabilities, etc.) might reduce comparability or consistency of the financial information being compared.
- Many accounting concepts were presented throughout earlier chapters, all of which aim to make accounting information more useful for creditors and investors. Four new concepts were explained in this chapter:
  - Going-concern (continuity) assumption—it is assumed that a business will continue to operate into the foreseeable future.

- Full disclosure principle—a company's financial statements should provide all information that is important to users' decisions.
- Industry practices constraint—general purpose accounting rules may not apply equally to all industries, recognizing that some industries may use industry-specific measurements and reporting practices.
- Cost-benefit constraint—accounting rules should be followed to the extent that the benefits to users outweigh the costs of providing the required information.

> ### Financial Analysis Tools
>
> See Exhibit 13.4 on pages 600–601 for a summary

KEY TERMS

Cost-Benefit Constraint p. 611

Discontinued Operations p. 612

Full Disclosure Principle p. 611

Going-Concern Assumption p. 611

Horizontal Analysis p. 597

Industry Practices Constraint p. 611

Liquidity p. 597

Profitability p. 597

Solvency p. 597

Vertical Analysis p. 601

PRACTICE MATERIAL

QUESTIONS

1. What is the general goal of trend analysis?
2. How is a year-over-year percentage calculated?
3. What is ratio analysis? Why is it useful?
4. What benchmarks are commonly used for interpreting ratios?
5. Into what three categories of performance are most financial ratios split? To what in particular do each of these categories relate?
6. Why are some analyses called *horizontal* and others called *vertical*?
7. What are the characteristics of useful financial information? How does each characteristic contribute to making financial information useful?
8. What is the primary objective of financial reporting?
9. What is the full disclosure principle?
10. What is the going-concern assumption? What is a going-concern problem? What factors can contribute to such a problem?
11. How do industry practices and cost-benefit constraints impact financial reporting?
12. (Supplement) Name the most commonly reported nonrecurring item, and explain where and how it is reported on the income statement.

Topic Tackler

PLUS

Check out www.mhhe.com/phillips2e for more multiple choice questions.

Quiz 13

MULTIPLE CHOICE

1. Which of the following ratios is *not* used to analyze profitability?
   a. Quality of income ratio.
   b. Gross profit percentage.
   c. Current ratio.
   d. Return on equity.

2. Which of the following would *not* directly change the receivables turnover ratio for a company?

   a. Increases in the selling prices of your inventory.

   b. A change in your credit policy.

   c. Increases in the cost you incur to purchase inventory.

   d. All of the above would directly change the receivables turnover ratio.

3. Which of the following ratios is used to analyze liquidity?

   a. Earnings per share.

   b. Debt-to-assets.

   c. Current ratio.

   d. Both *b* and *c*.

4. Analysts use ratios to

   a. Compare different companies in the same industry.

   b. Track a company's performance over time.

   c. Compare a company's performance to industry averages.

   d. All of the above describe ways that analysts use ratios.

5. Which of the following ratios incorporates cash flows from operations?

   a. Inventory turnover.

   b. Earnings per share.

   c. Quality of income.

   d. All of the above.

6. Given the following ratios for four companies, which company is least likely to experience problems paying its current liabilities promptly?

	Current Ratio	Receivable Turnover Ratio
a.	1.2	7.0
b.	1.2	6.0
c.	1.0	6.0
d.	0.5	7.0

7. A decrease in Selling and administrative expenses would directly impact what ratio?

   a. Fixed asset turnover ratio.

   b. Times interest earned.

   c. Current ratio.

   d. Gross profit percentage.

8. A bank is least likely to use which of the following ratios when analyzing the likelihood that a borrower will pay interest and principal on its loans?

   a. Cash coverage ratio.

   b. Debt-to-assets ratio.

   c. Times interest earned ratio.

   d. Return on equity ratio.

9. Which of the following accounting concepts do accountants and auditors assess by using financial analyses?

   a. Cost benefit.

   b. Materiality.

   c. Industry practices.

   d. Going-concern assumption.

10. (Supplement) Which of the following items is reported net of related income taxes?

    a. Gain or loss from discontinued operations.

    b. Gain or loss from disposal of property, plant, and equipment.

    c. Interest on long-term debt.

    d. Gain or loss from early extinguishment of debt.

Solutions to Multiple Choice Questions

1. *c*   2. *c*   3. *c*   4. *d*   5. *c*   6. *a*   7. *b*   8. *d*   9. *d*   10. *a*

MINI-EXERCISES

Available with McGraw-Hill's Homework Manager

MANAGER PLUS

LO2 **M13-1 Calculations for Horizontal and Vertical Analyses**

Using the following income statements, perform the calculations needed for horizontal and vertical analyses. Round percentages to one decimal place.

LOCKEY FENCING CORPORATION Income Statements For the Years Ended December 31		
	2006	2005
Net sales	$100,000	$75,000
Cost of goods sold	58,000	45,000
Gross profit	42,000	30,000
Selling, general, and administrative expenses	9,000	4,500
Income from operations	33,000	25,500
Interest expense	3,000	3,750
Income before income taxes	30,000	21,750
Income tax expense	9,000	6,525
Net income	$ 21,000	$15,225

LO3 **M13-2 Interpreting Horizontal Analyses**

Refer to the calculations from M13-1. What are the two most significant year-over-year changes in terms of dollars and in terms of percentages? Give one potential cause of each of these changes.

LO3 **M13-3 Interpreting Vertical Analyses**

Refer to the calculations from M13-1. Which of the ratios from Exhibit 13.4 have been included in these calculations? Have these two ratios improved or deteriorated in 2006 compared to 2005?

LO2 **M13-4 Inferring Financial Information Using Gross Profit Percentage**

Your campus computer store reported revenue of $168,000. The company's gross profit percentage was 60.0 percent. What amount of Cost of goods sold did the company report?

LO2 **M13-5 Inferring Financial Information Using Gross Profit Percentage and Year-over-Year Comparisons**

A consumer products company reported a 25 percent increase in sales from 2007 to 2008. Sales in 2007 were $200,000. In 2008, the company reported Cost of goods sold in the amount of $150,000. What was the gross profit percentage in 2008? Round to one decimal place.

LO2 **M13-6 Computing the Return on Equity Ratio**

Given the following data, compute the 2008 return on equity ratio (expressed as a percentage with one decimal place).

	2008	2007
Net income	$ 1,850,000	$ 1,600,000
Stockholders' equity	10,000,000	13,125,000
Total assets	24,000,000	26,000,000
Interest expense	400,000	300,000

M13-7 Analyzing the Inventory Turnover Ratio

LO3

A manufacturer reported an inventory turnover ratio of 8.6 during 2007. During 2008, management introduced a new inventory control system that was expected to reduce average inventory levels by 25 percent without affecting sales volume. Given these circumstances, would you expect the inventory turnover ratio to increase or decrease during 2008? Explain.

M13-8 Inferring Financial Information Using the Current Ratio

LO2

Mystic Laboratories reported total assets of $11,200,000 and noncurrent assets of $1,480,000. The company also reported a current ratio of 1.5. What amount of current liabilities did the company report?

M13-9 Analyzing the Impact of Accounting Alternatives

LO4

Nevis Corporation operates in an industry where costs are falling. The company is considering changing its inventory method from FIFO to LIFO and wants to determine the impact that the change would have on selected accounting ratios in future years. In general, what impact would you expect on the following ratios: net profit margin, fixed asset turnover, and current ratio?

M13-10 Inferring Financial Information Using the P/E Ratio

LO2

In 2006, Big W Company reported earnings per share of $2.50 when its stock was selling for $50.00. In 2007, its earnings increased by 10 percent. If all other relationships remain constant, what is the price of the stock? Explain.

M13-11 Identifying Relevant Ratios

LO3

Identify the ratio that is relevant to answering each of the following questions.

a. How much net income does the company earn from each dollar of sales?
b. Is the company financed primarily by debt or equity?
c. How many dollars of sales were generated for each dollar invested in fixed assets?
d. How many days, on average, does it take the company to collect on credit sales made to customers?
e. How much net income does the company earn for each dollar owners have invested in it?
f. Does the company's net income convert into more or less cash flow from operating activities?
g. Does the company have sufficient assets to convert into cash for paying liabilities as they come due in the upcoming year?

M13-12 Interpreting Ratios

LO3

Generally speaking, do the following indicate good or bad news?

a. Increase in times interest earned ratio.
b. Decrease in days to sell.
c. Increase in gross profit percentage.
d. Decrease in EPS.
e. Increase in asset turnover ratio.
f. Decrease in cash coverage ratio.

M13-13 (Supplement) Analyzing the Impact of a Nonrecurring Item

Northern Drilling Corporation operates an oil exploration company in Alaska. In March 2007, one of the company's drilling platforms was destroyed by a tornado, resulting in an uninsured equipment loss of $4 million. How would this event, which is highly unusual for Alaska, affect the following ratios: net profit margin, fixed asset turnover, and current ratio?

EXERCISES

Available with McGraw-Hill's
Homework Manager

HOMEWORK MANAGER **PLUS**

E13-1 Preparing and Interpreting a Schedule for Horizontal and Vertical Analyses

LO2, LO3
Chevron Corp.

The average price of a gallon of gas in 2005 jumped $0.43 (24 percent) from $1.81 in 2004 (to $2.24 in 2005). Let's see whether these changes are reflected in the income statement of Chevron Corp. for the year ended December 31, 2005 (amounts in millions).

	2005	2004
Total revenues	$198,200	$155,300
Costs of crude oil and products	140,902	104,948
Other operating costs	32,101	29,801
Income before income tax expense	25,197	20,551
Income tax expense	11,098	7,223
Net income	$ 14,099	$ 13,328

Required:

1. Conduct a horizontal analysis by calculating the year-over-year changes in each line item, expressed in dollars and in percentages (rounded to one decimal place). How did the change in gas prices compare to the changes in Chevron Corp.'s total revenues and costs of crude oil and products?

2. Conduct a vertical analysis by expressing each line as a percentage of total revenues (round to one decimal place). Excluding income tax and other operating costs, did Chevron earn more profit per dollar of revenue in 2005 compared to 2004?

LO2, LO3

Chevron Corp.

E13-2 Computing and Interpreting Profitability Ratios

Use the information for Chevron Corp. in E13-1 to complete the following requirements.

Required:

1. Compute the gross profit percentage for each year (one decimal place). Assuming that the change for 2004 to 2005 is the beginning of a sustained trend, is Chevron likely to earn more or less gross profit from each dollar of sales in 2006?

2. Compute the net profit margin for each year (expressed as a percentage with one decimal place). Given your calculations here and in requirement 1, explain whether Chevron did a better or worse job of controlling expenses other than the costs of crude oil and products in 2005 relative to 2004.

3. Chevron reported average net fixed assets of $54.2 billion in 2005 and $45.1 billion in 2004. Compute the fixed asset turnover ratios for both years (round to two decimal places). Did the company better utilize its investment in fixed assets to generate revenues in 2005 or 2004?

4. Chevron reported average stockholders' equity of $54.0 billion in 2005 and $40.8 billion in 2004. Compute the return on equity ratios for both years (expressed as a percentage with one decimal place). Did the company generate greater returns for stockholders in 2005 or 2004?

LO2, LO3

Chevron Corp.

E13-3 Computing a Commonly Used Solvency Ratio

Use the information for Chevron Corp. in E13-1 to complete the following requirement.

Required:

Interest expense in the amount of $482 million was included with "other operating costs" in 2005 ($406 million in 2004). Compute the times interest earned ratios for each year (round to one decimal place). In your opinion, does Chevron generate sufficient net income (before taxes and interest) to cover the cost of debt financing?

LO2, LO3

E13-4 Preparing and Interpreting a Schedule for Horizontal and Vertical Analyses

The average cost of low-end laptops fell about $200 (25 percent) from $800 in 2005 to $600 in 2006. Let's see whether these changes are reflected in the income statement of Computer Tycoon Inc. for the year ended December 31, 2006.

	2005	2006
Sales revenues	$121,761	$98,913
Cost of goods sold	71,583	59,249
Operating expenses	36,934	36,943
Interest expense	474	565
Income before income tax expense	12,770	2,156
Income tax expense	5,540	1,024
Net income	$ 7,230	$ 1,132

Required:

1. Conduct a horizontal analysis by calculating the year-over-year changes in each line item, expressed in dollars and in percentages (rounded to one decimal place). How did the change in computer prices compare to the changes in Computer Tycoon's sales revenues?

2. Conduct a vertical analysis by expressing each line as a percentage of total revenues (round to one decimal place). Excluding income tax, interest, and operating expenses, did Computer Tycoon earn more profit per dollar of sales in 2006 compared to 2005?

E13-5 Computing Profitability Ratios

LO2, LO3

Use the information in E13-4 to complete the following requirements.

Required:

1. Compute the gross profit percentage for each year (one decimal place). Assuming that the change for 2005 to 2006 is the beginning of a sustained trend, is Computer Tycoon likely to earn more or less gross profit from each dollar of sales in 2007?

2. Compute the net profit margin for each year (expressed as a percentage with one decimal place). Given your calculations here and in requirement 1, explain whether Computer Tycoon did a better or worse job of controlling operating expenses in 2006 relative to 2005.

3. Computer Tycoon reported average net fixed assets of $54,200 in 2006 and $45,100 in 2005. Compute the fixed asset turnover ratios for both years (round to two decimal places). Did the company better utilize its investment in fixed assets to generate revenues in 2006 or 2005?

4. Computer Tycoon reported average stockholders' equity of $54,000 in 2006 and $40,800 in 2005. Compute the return on equity ratios for both years (expressed as a percentage with one decimal place). Did the company generate greater returns for stockholders in 2006 or 2005?

E13-6 Computing a Commonly Used Solvency Ratio

LO2, LO3

Use the information in E13-4 to complete the following requirement.

Required:

Compute the times interest earned ratios for 2006 and 2005. In your opinion, does Computer Tycoon generate sufficient net income (before taxes and interest) to cover the cost of debt financing?

E13-7 Matching Each Ratio with Its Computational Formula

LO2

Match each ratio or percentage with its formula by entering the appropriate letter for each numbered item.

Ratios or Percentages	Formula
____ 1. Current ratio	A. Net income ÷ Net sales revenue
____ 2. Net profit margin	B. (Net sales revenue − Cost of goods sold) ÷ Net sales revenue
____ 3. Inventory turnover ratio	C. Current assets ÷ Current liabilities
____ 4. Cash coverage ratio	D. Cost of goods sold ÷ Average inventory
____ 5. Fixed asset turnover	E. Net credit sales revenue ÷ Average net receivables
	F. Net cash flows from operating activities ÷ Net income
____ 6. Capital acquisitions ratio	G. Net income ÷ Average number of common shares outstanding
____ 7. Return on equity	H. Total liabilities ÷ Total assets
____ 8. Times interest earned	I. (Net income + Interest expense + Income tax expense) ÷ Interest expense
____ 9. Debt-to-assets ratio	J. Net cash flows from operating activities ÷ Cash paid for property, plant, and equipment
____ 10. Price/earnings ratio	K. Current market price per share ÷ Earnings per share
____ 11. Receivables turnover ratio	L. Net income ÷ Average total stockholders' equity
____ 12. Earnings per share	M. Net cash flows from operating activities (before interest and taxes) ÷ Interest paid
____ 13. Quality of income ratio	
____ 14. Gross profit percentage	N. Net sales revenue ÷ Average net fixed assets

LO2, LO3

E13-8 Computing and Interpreting Selected Liquidity Ratios

DuckWing Stores (DWS) reported sales for the year of $600,000, of which one-half was on credit. The average gross profit percentage was 40 percent on sales. Account balances follow:

	Beginning	Ending
Accounts receivable (net)	$45,000	$55,000
Inventory	60,000	40,000

Required:

1. Compute the turnover ratios for accounts receivable and inventory (round to one decimal place).
2. By dividing 365 by your ratios from requirement 1, calculate the average days to collect receivables and the average days to sell inventory (round to one decimal place).
3. Explain what each of these ratios and measures mean.

LO2, LO3

Cintas Corporation

E13-9 Computing and Interpreting Liquidity Ratios

Cintas Corporation is the largest uniform supplier in North America. More than five million people wear Cintas clothing each day. Selected information from a recent balance sheet follows. For Year 2, the company reported sales revenue of $2,686,585,000 and cost of goods sold of $1,567,377,000.

Cintas	Year 2	Year 1
Balance Sheet (amounts in thousands)		
Cash	$ 32,239	$ 52,182
Accounts receivable, less allowance of $7,737 and $9,229	278,147	225,735
Inventories	228,410	164,906
Prepaid expenses	7,607	7,237
Other current assets	25,420	57,640
Accounts payable	53,909	60,393
Wages payable	25,252	29,004
Income taxes payable	69,545	73,163
Accrued liabilities	127,882	131,705
Long-term debt due within one year	28,251	18,369

Required:

Assuming that 60 percent of sales are on credit, compute the current ratio (two decimal places), inventory turnover ratio (one decimal place), and accounts receivable turnover ratio (one decimal place) for Year 2. Explain what each ratio means.

E13-10 Analyzing the Impact of Selected Transactions on the Current Ratio   **LO2, LO3**

In its most recent annual report, Appalachian Beverages reported current assets of $54,000 and a current ratio of 1.80. Assume that the following transactions were completed: (1) purchased merchandise for $6,000 on account, and (2) purchased a delivery truck for $10,000, paying $1,000 cash and signing a two-year promissory note for the balance.

Required:

Compute the updated current ratio, rounded to two decimal places, after each transaction.

E13-11 Analyzing the Impact of Selected Transactions on the Current Ratio   **LO2, LO3**

In its most recent annual report, Sunrise Enterprises reported current assets of $1,090,000 and current liabilities of $602,000.

Required:

Determine for each of the following transactions whether the current ratio, and each of its two components, for Sunrise will increase, decrease, or have no change: (1) sold long-term assets for cash, (2) accrued severance pay for terminated employees, (3) wrote down the carrying value of certain inventory items that were deemed to be obsolete, and (4) acquired new inventory by signing an 18-month promissory note (the supplier was not willing to provide normal credit terms).

E13-12 Analyzing the Impact of Selected Transactions on the Current Ratio   **LO2, LO3**
The Sports Authority, Inc.

The Sports Authority, Inc., is the country's largest private full-line sporting goods retailer. Stores are operated under four brand names: Sports Authority, Gart Sports, Oshman's, and Sportmart. Assume one of the Sports Authority stores reported current assets of $88,000 and its current ratio was 1.75. Assume that the following transactions were completed: (1) paid $6,000 on accounts payable, (2) purchased a delivery truck for $10,000 cash, (3) wrote off a bad account receivable for $2,000, and (4) paid previously declared dividends in the amount of $25,000.

Required:

Compute the updated current ratio, rounded to two decimal places, after each transaction.

E13-13 Analyzing the Impact of Selected Transactions on the Current Ratio   **LO2, LO3**

Current assets totaled $500,000, the current ratio was 2.00, and the company uses the perpetual inventory method. Assume that the following transactions were completed: (1) sold $12,000 in merchandise on short-term credit for $15,000, (2) declared but did not pay dividends of $50,000, (3) paid prepaid rent in the amount of $12,000, (4) paid previously declared dividends in the amount of $50,000, (5) collected an account receivable in the amount of $12,000, and (6) reclassified $40,000 of long-term debt as a current liability.

Required:

Compute the updated current ratio, rounded to two decimal places, after each transaction.

E13-14 Computing the Accounts Receivable and Inventory Turnover Ratios   **LO2, LO3**
P&G

Procter & Gamble is a multinational corporation that manufactures and markets many products that you use every day. In 2006, sales for the company were $68,222 (all amounts in millions). The annual report did not report the amount of credit sales, so we will assume that all sales were on credit. The average gross profit percentage was 51 percent. Account balances follow:

	Beginning	Ending
Accounts receivable (net)	$5,266	$7,336
Inventory	5,006	6,291

Required:

1. Rounded to one decimal place, compute the turnover ratios for accounts receivable and inventory.
2. By dividing 365 by your ratios from requirement 1, calculate the average days to collect receivables and the average days to sell inventory.
3. Interpret what these ratios and measures mean.

LO2, LO3

Dollar General Corporation

E13-15 Inferring Financial Information from Profitability and Liquidity Ratios

Dollar General Corporation operates approximately 8,250 general merchandise stores that feature quality merchandise at low prices to meet the needs of middle-, low-, and fixed-income families in southern, eastern, and midwestern states. For the year ended February 3, 2006, the company reported average inventories of $1,425 (in millions) and an inventory turnover of 4.3. Average total fixed assets were $1,137 (million), and the fixed asset turnover ratio was 7.5.

Required:

1. Calculate Dollar General's gross profit percentage (expressed as a percentage with one decimal place). What does this imply about the amount of gross profit made from each dollar of sales?
   TIP: Work backward from the fixed asset turnover and inventory turnover ratios to compute the amounts needed for the gross profit percentage.
2. Is this an improvement from the gross profit percentage of 29.5 percent earned during the year ended January 31, 2004?

LO2, LO3

E13-16 Using Financial Information to Identify Mystery Companies

The following selected financial data pertain to four unidentified companies (balance sheet amounts reported in millions):

	Companies			
	1	2	3	4
Balance Sheet Data				
Cash	$ 5.1	$ 8.8	$ 6.3	$10.4
Accounts receivable	13.1	41.5	13.8	4.9
Inventory	4.6	3.6	65.1	35.8
Property and equipment	53.1	23.0	8.8	35.7
Selected Ratios				
Gross profit percentage	N/A*	N/A	45.2	22.5
Net profit margin ratio (%)	0.3	16.0	3.9	1.5
Current ratio	0.7	2.2	1.9	1.4
Inventory turnover	N/A	N/A	1.4	15.5
Debt-to-assets	0.7	0.5	0.6	0.7

* N/A = Not applicable.

This financial information pertains to the following companies:

a. Cable TV company.
b. Grocery store.
c. Accounting firm.
d. Retail jewelry store.

Required:

Match each company with its financial information, and explain the basis for your answers.

LO4

E13-17 Analyzing the Impact of Alternative Inventory Methods on Selected Ratios

Company A uses the FIFO method to cost inventory, and Company B uses the LIFO method. The two companies are exactly alike except for the difference in inventory costing methods. Costs of inventory items for both companies have been falling steadily in recent years, and each company has increased its inventory each year. Ignore income tax effects.

Required:

Identify which company will report the higher amount for each of the following ratios. If it is not possible to identify which will report the higher amount, explain why.

1. Current ratio.
2. Debt-to-assets ratio.
3. Earnings per share.

COACHED PROBLEMS

CP13-1 Analyzing Comparative Financial Statements Using Year-over-Year Percentages

LO2, LO3

The comparative financial statements prepared at December 31, 2006, for Golden Corporation showed the following summarized data:

www.mhhe.com/phillips2e

	2006	2005	Increase (Decrease) 2006 over 2005	
			Amount	Percentage
Income Statement				
Sales revenue	$180,000*	$165,000		
Cost of goods sold	110,000	100,000		
Gross profit	70,000	65,000		
Operating expenses	53,300	50,400		
Interest expense	2,700	2,600		
Income before income taxes	14,000	12,000		
Income tax expense	4,000	3,000		
Net income	$ 10,000	$ 9,000		
Balance Sheet				
Cash	$ 4,000	$ 8,000		
Accounts receivable (net)	19,000	23,000		
Inventory	40,000	35,000		
Property and equipment (net)	45,000	38,000		
	$108,000	$104,000		
Current liabilities (no interest)	$ 16,000	$ 19,000		
Long-term liabilities (6% interest)	45,000	45,000		
Common stock (par $5)	30,000	30,000		
Additional paid-in captial	5,000	5,000		
Retained earnings[†]	12,000	5,000		
	$108,000	$104,000		

* One-third of all sales are on account.

[†] During 2006, cash dividends amounting to $3,000 were declared and paid.

Required:

1. Complete the two final columns shown beside each item in Golden Corporation's comparative financial statements. Round the percentages to one decimal place.

   TIP: Calculate the increase (decrease) by subtracting 2005 from 2006. Calculate the percentage by dividing the amount of increase (decrease) by the 2005 balance.

2. Does anything significant jump out at you from the year-over-year analyses?

LO2, LO3

www.mhhe.com/phillips2e

CP13-2 Analyzing Comparative Financial Statements Using Selected Ratios

Use the data given in CP13-1 for Golden Corporation.

Required:

1. Compute the gross profit percentages in 2006 and 2005. Round the percentages to one decimal place. Is the trend going in the right direction?
2. Compute the net profit margin ratios in 2006 and 2005. Round the percentages to one decimal place. Is the trend going in the right direction?
3. Compute the earnings per share for 2006 and 2005. Does the trend look good or bad? Explain.

   TIP: To calculate EPS, use the balance in the Common stock account to determine the number of shares outstanding. The common stock balance includes the par value per share times the number of shares.

4. Stockholders' equity totaled $30,000 at the end of 2004. Compute the return on equity (ROE) ratios for 2005 and 2006. Express the ROE as percentages rounded to one decimal place. Is the trend going in the right direction?
5. Net property and equipment totaled $35,000 at the end of 2004. Compute the fixed asset turnover ratios for 2006 and 2005. Round the ratios to two decimal places. Is the trend going in the right direction?
6. Compute the debt-to-assets ratios for 2006 and 2005. Round the ratios to two decimal places. Is debt providing financing for a larger or smaller proportion of the company's asset growth? Explain.
7. Compute the times interest earned ratios for 2006 and 2005. Round the ratios to one decimal place. Do they look good or bad? Explain.
8. After Golden released its 2006 financial statements, the company's stock was trading at $30. After the release of its 2005 financial statements, the company's stock price was $21 per share. Compute the P/E ratios for both years, rounded to one decimal place. Does it appear that investors have become more (or less) optimistic about Golden's future success?

LO2, LO3

Activision, Inc.

CP13-3 Vertical Analysis of a Balance Sheet

A condensed balance sheet for Activision and a partially completed vertical analysis are presented below.

ACTIVISION INC.
Balance Sheet (summarized)
March 31, 2006
(in millions of U.S. dollars)

Cash and short-term investments	$ 945	67%	Accounts payable	$ 89		7%
Accounts receivable	29	2	Accrued liabilities	103	(d)	
Inventories	61	4	Long-term debt	2		0
Other current assets	81	(a)	Total Liabilities	194	(e)	
Software development	102	(b)	Contributed capital	837		59
Property and equipment	45	(c)	Retained earnings	389		27
Other assets	156	11	Total Stockholders' Equity	1,226		86
Total Assets	$1,420	100%	Total Liabilities & Stockholders' Equity	$1,420		100%

Required:

1. Complete the vertical analysis by computing each line item (a)–(e) as a percentage of total assets. Round to the nearest whole percentage.

   TIP: Cash was 67 percent of total assets, computed as ($945 ÷ $1,420) × 100.

2. What percentages of Activision's assets relate to software development versus property and equipment? What business reasons would explain this relative emphasis?

CP13-4 Vertical Analysis of an Income Statement

LO2, LO3

A condensed income statement for Activision and a partially completed vertical analysis are presented below.

	2006			2005	
Net revenues	$1,468		100%	$1,406	100%
Cost of sales	940	(a)		845	60
Product development expense	132	(b)		87	6
Sales and marketing expense	283	(c)		230	17
General and administrative expense	95		7	60	4
Operating income	18		1	185	13
Revenue from investments	31		2	13	1
Income before income taxes	49		3	198	14
Income tax expense	7		0	59	4
Net income	$ 42	(d)	%	$ 138	10%

ACTIVISION INC.
Income Statement (summarized)
For the Year Ended March 31
(in millions of U.S. dollars)

Required:

1. Complete the vertical analysis by computing each line item (a)–(d) as a percentage of net revenues. Round to the nearest whole percentage.

   TIP: Cost of sales was 60 percent of net revenues in 2005, which was computed as ($845 ÷ $1,406) × 100.

2. Does Activision's 2006 cost of sales, as a percentage of revenues, represent better or worse performance as compared to 2005?

CP13-5 Interpreting Profitability, Liquidity, Solvency, and P/E Ratios

LO2, LO3
Federated Department Stores
Dillard's, Inc.

Macy's is a national retail department store owned by Federated Department Stores (FDS). The company's total revenues in 2006 were $22 billion. Dillard's is a somewhat smaller national department store company with $7.7 billion of revenues for 2006. The following ratios for the two companies were obtained for a recent year from www.marketguide.com:

Ratio	FDS	Dillard's
Gross profit percentage	34.1%	32.6%
Net profit margin	8.1%	0.5%
Return on equity	12.9%	1.7%
EPS	$ 3.76	$ 0.11
Receivables turnover ratio	5.2	6.8
Inventory turnover ratio	2.6	2.7
Current ratio	2.00	2.26
Debt-to-assets	0.40	0.47
P/E ratio	12.1	43.7

Required:

1. Which company appears more profitable? Describe the ratio(s) that you used to reach this decision.
2. Which company appears more liquid? Describe the ratio(s) that you used to reach this decision.
3. Which company appears more solvent? Describe the ratio(s) that you used to reach this decision.

4. Are the conclusions from your analyses in requirements 1–3 consistent with the value of the two companies suggested by the P/E ratios of the two companies? If not, offer one explanation for any apparent inconsistency.

    TIP: Remember that the top number in the P/E ratio represents investors' expectations about future financial performance whereas the bottom number reports past financial performance.

LO2, LO3, LO4   **CP13-6 Using Ratios to Compare Alternative Investment Opportunities**

The 2007 financial statements for Armstrong and Blair companies are summarized here:

	Armstrong Company	Blair Company
Balance Sheet		
Cash	$ 35,000	$ 22,000
Accounts receivable (net)	40,000	30,000
Inventory	100,000	40,000
Property and equipment (net)	180,000	300,000
Other assets	45,000	408,000
Total assets	$400,000	$800,000
Current liabilities	$ 100,000	$ 50,000
Long-term debt	60,000	370,000
Total liabilities	160,000	420,000
Common stock (par $10)	150,000	200,000
Additional paid-in capital	30,000	110,000
Retained earnings	60,000	70,000
Total liabilities and stockholders' equity	$400,000	$800,000
Income Statement		
Sales revenue (1/3 on credit)	$450,000	$ 810,000
Cost of goods sold	(245,000)	(405,000)
Expenses (including interest and income tax)	(160,000)	(315,000)
Net income	$ 45,000	$ 90,000
Selected Data from 2005 Statements		
Accounts receivable (net)	$ 20,000	$ 38,000
Inventory	92,000	45,000
Property and equipment (net)	180,000	300,000
Long-term debt	60,000	70,000
Total stockholders' equity	231,000	440,000
Other Data		
Estimated value of each share at end of 2006	$ 18	$ 27
Average income tax rate	30%	30%
Dividends declared and paid in 2006	$ 36,000	$ 150,000

The companies are in the same line of business and are direct competitors in a large metropolitan area. Both have been in business approximately 10 years, and each has had steady growth. The management of each has a different viewpoint in many respects. Blair is more conservative, and as its president said, "We avoid what we consider to be undue risk." Both companies use straight-line depreciation, but Blair estimates slightly shorter useful lives than Armstrong. Neither company is publicly held. Blair Company has an annual audit by a CPA but Armstrong Company does not.

Required:

1. Calculate the ratios in Exhibit 13.4 for which sufficient information is available. Round all calculations to two decimal places.

    TIP: To calculate EPS, use the balance in the common stock account to determine the number of shares outstanding. The common stock balance includes the par value per share times the number of shares.

2. A client of yours has decided to buy shares in one of the two companies. Based on the data given, prepare a comparative written evaluation of the ratio analyses (and any other available information) and conclude with your recommended choice.

    TIP: Comment on how accounting differences affect your evaluations, if at all.

CP13-7 Analyzing an Investment by Comparing Selected Ratios   LO2, LO3

You have the opportunity to invest $10,000 in one of two companies from a single industry. The only information you have follows. The word *high* refers to the top third of the industry; *average* is the middle third; *low* is the bottom third.

Ratio	Company A	Company B
Current	High	Average
Inventory turnover	Low	Average
Debt-to-assets	High	Average
Times interest earned	Low	Average
Price/earnings	Low	Average

Required:

Which company would you select? Write a brief explanation for your recommendation.

TIP: When interpreting ratios, think about how they are related to one another. For example, the current ratio and the inventory turnover ratio both include the inventory balance. This means that the low inventory turnover ratio can help you to interpret the high current ratio.

GROUP A PROBLEMS

Available with McGraw-Hill's
Homework Manager

HOMEWORK
MANAGER PLUS™

PA13-1 Analyzing Financial Statements Using Ratios and Percentage Changes   LO2, LO3

eXcel

www.mhhe.com/phillips2e

The comparative financial statements prepared at December 31, 2006, for Pinnacle Plus showed the following summarized data:

	2006	2005	Increase (Decrease) 2006 over 2005 Amount	Percentage
Income Statement				
Sales revenue*	$ 110,000	$ 99,000		
Cost of goods sold	52,000	48,000		
Gross profit	58,000	51,000		
Operating expenses	36,000	33,000		
Interest expense	4,000	4,000		
Income before income taxes	18,000	14,000		
Income tax expense (30%)	5,400	4,200		
Net income	$ 12,600	$ 9,800		
Balance Sheet				
Cash	$ 49,500	$ 18,000		
Accounts receivable (net)	37,000	32,000		
Inventory	25,000	38,000		
Property and equipment (net)	95,000	105,000		
Total assets	$206,500	$193,000		
Accounts payable	$ 42,000	$ 35,000		
Income taxes payable	1,000	500		
Note payable, long-term	40,000	40,000		
Total liabilities	83,000	75,500		
Common stock (par $10)	90,000	90,000		
Retained earnings†	33,500	27,500		
Total liabilities and stockholders' equity	$206,500	$193,000		

* One-half of all sales are on credit.
† During 2006, cash dividends amounting to $6,600 were declared and paid.

Required:

1. Complete the two final columns shown beside each item in Pinnacle Plus's comparative financial statements. Round the percentages to one decimal place.
2. Does anything significant jump out at you from the year-over-year analyses?

LO2, LO3   **PA13-2 Analyzing Comparative Financial Statements Using Selected Ratios**

Use the data given in PA13-1 for Pinnacle Plus.

Required:

1. Compute the gross profit percentages in 2006 and 2005. Round the percentages to one decimal place. Is the trend going in the right direction?
2. Compute the net profit margin ratios in 2006 and 2005. Round the percentages to one decimal place. Is the trend going in the right direction?
3. Compute the earnings per share for 2006 and 2005. Does the trend look good or bad? Explain.
4. Stockholders' equity totaled $100,000 at the end of 2004. Compute the return on equity (ROE) ratios for 2005 and 2006. Express the ROE as percentages rounded to one decimal place. Is the trend going in the right direction?
5. Net property and equipment totaled $110,000 at the end of 2004. Compute the fixed asset turnover ratios for 2006 and 2005. Round the ratios to two decimal places. Is the trend going in the right direction?
6. Compute the debt-to-assets ratios for 2006 and 2005. Round the ratios to two decimal places. Is debt providing financing for a larger or smaller proportion of the company's asset growth? Explain.
7. Compute the times interest earned ratios for 2006 and 2005. Round the ratios to one decimal place. Do they look good or bad? Explain.
8. After Pinnacle Plus released its 2006 financial statements, the company's stock was trading at $18. After the release of its 2005 financial statements, the company's stock price was $15 per share. Compute the P/E ratios for both years, rounded to one decimal place. Does it appear that investors have become more (or less) optimistic about Pinnacle's future success?

LO2, LO3   **PA13-3 Vertical Analysis of a Balance Sheet**
Kellwood Company

A condensed balance sheet for Kellwood Company and a partially completed vertical analysis are presented below.

KELLWOOD COMPANY
Balance Sheet (summarized)
January 31, 2004
(in millions of U.S. dollars)

Cash and short-term investments	$ 433	29%		Current liabilities	$ 409	27%
Accounts receivable	294	19		Long-term liabilities	495	33
Inventories	206	14		Total Liabilities	904	(b)
Other current assets	109	(a)		Contributed capital	118	(c)
Property and equipment	27	2		Retained earnings	492	32
Other assets	445	29		Total Stockholders' Equity	610	(d)
Total Assets	$1,514	100%		Total Liabilities & Stockholders' Equity	$1,514	100%

Required:

1. Complete the vertical analysis by computing each line item (a)–(d) as a percentage of total assets. Round to the nearest whole percentage.
2. What percentages of Kellwood's assets relate to inventories versus property and equipment? What does this tell you about the relative significance of these two assets to Kellwood's business?
3. What percentage of Kellwood's assets is financed by total stockholder's equity? By total liabilities?

PA13-4 Vertical Analysis of an Income Statement

LO2, LO3
Kellwood Company

A condensed income statement for Kellwood Company and a partially completed vertical analysis are presented below.

KELLWOOD COMPANY Income Statement (summarized) For the Year Ended (in millions of U.S. dollars)					
	January 31, 2006		February 1, 2005		
Sales revenues	$2,062	100%	$2,200		100%
Cost of products sold	1,637	79	1,721	(d)	
Selling, general, and administrative expenses	333	(a)	346		16
Other operating expenses	53	3	12		1
Interest expense	22	(b)	26		1
Income before income taxes	17	1	95	(e)	
Income tax expense	6	0	33		1
Net income	$ 11	(c) %	$ 62	(f)	%

Required:

1. Complete the vertical analysis by computing each line item (a)–(f) as a percentage of sales revenues. Round to the nearest whole percentage.
2. Does Kellwood's cost of products sold for the year ended January 31, 2006, as a percentage of revenues, represent better or worse performance as compared to that for the year ended February 1, 2005?
3. Do the percentages that you calculated in 1 (c) and (f) indicate whether Kellwood's net profit margin has changed over the two years?

PA13-5 Interpreting Profitability, Liquidity, Solvency, and P/E Ratios

LO2, LO3
Coca-Cola Company
PepsiCo.

Coke and Pepsi are well-known international brands. Coca-Cola sells more than $23 billion worth of beverages each year while annual sales of Pepsi products exceed $32 billion. Compare the two companies as a potential investment based on the following ratios:

Ratio	Coca-Cola	PepsiCo
Gross profit percentage	48.5%	49.0%
Net profit margin	2.6%	4.1%
Return on equity	66.2%	23.3%
EPS	$ 3.40	$ 1.54
Receivables turnover ratio	11.5	9.8
Inventory turnover ratio	15.1	12.8
Current ratio	1.47	1.40
Debt-to-assets	0.94	0.72
P/E ratio	16.4	18.7

Required:

1. Which company appears more profitable? Describe the ratio(s) that you used to reach this decision.
2. Which company appears more liquid? Describe the ratio(s) that you used to reach this decision.
3. Which company appears more solvent? Describe the ratio(s) that you used to reach this decision.
4. Are the conclusions from your analyses in requirements 1–3 consistent with the value of the two companies suggested by the P/E ratios of the two companies? If not, offer one explanation for any apparent inconsistency.

LO2, LO3, LO4   **PA13-6 Using Ratios to Compare Loan Requests from Two Companies**

The 2008 financial statements for Royale and Cavalier companies are summarized here:

	Royale Company	Cavalier Company
Balance Sheet		
Cash	$ 25,000	$ 45,000
Accounts receivable (net)	55,000	5,000
Inventory	110,000	25,000
Property and equipment (net)	550,000	160,000
Other assets	140,000	57,000
Total assets	$880,000	$292,000
Current liabilities	$ 120,000	$ 15,000
Long-term debt	190,000	55,000
Capital stock (par $20)	480,000	210,000
Additional paid-in capital	50,000	4,000
Retained earnings	40,000	8,000
Total liabilities and stockholders' equity	$880,000	$292,000
Income Statement		
Sales revenue	$800,000	$280,000
Cost of goods sold	(480,000)	(150,000)
Expenses (including interest and income tax)	(240,000)	(95,000)
Net income	$ 80,000	$ 35,000
Selected Data from 2007 Statements		
Accounts receivable, net	$ 47,000	$ 11,000
Long-term debt	190,000	55,000
Property and equipment, net	550,000	160,000
Inventory	95,000	38,000
Total stockholders' equity	570,000	202,000
Other Data		
Per share price at end of 2008	$ 14.00	$ 11.00
Average income tax rate	30%	30%

These two companies are in the same line of business and in the same state but in different cities. One-half of Royale's sales are on credit, whereas one-quarter of Cavalier's sales are on credit. Each company has been in operation for about 10 years. Both companies received an unqualified audit opinion on the financial statements, which means the independent auditors found nothing wrong. Royale Company wants to borrow $75,000 cash, and Cavalier Company is asking for $30,000. The loans will be for a two-year period. Both companies estimate bad debts based on an aging analysis, but Cavalier has estimated slightly higher uncollectible rates than Royale.

Required:

1. Calculate the ratios in Exhibit 13.4 for which sufficient information is available. Round all calculations to two decimal places.
2. Assume that you work in the loan department of a local bank. You have been asked to analyze the situation and recommend which loan is preferable. Based on the data given, your analysis prepared in requirement 1, and any other information, give your choice and the supporting explanation.

LO2, LO3   **PA13-7 Analyzing an Investment by Comparing Selected Ratios**

You have the opportunity to invest $10,000 in one of two companies from a single industry. The only information you have is shown here. The word *high* refers to the top third of the industry; *average* is the middle third; *low* is the bottom third.

Ratio	Company A	Company B
Current	Low	High
Inventory turnover	High	Low
Debt-to-assets	Low	Average
Times interest earned	High	Average
Price/earnings	High	Average

Required:

Which company would you select? Write a brief explanation for your recommendation.

GROUP B PROBLEMS

PB13-1 Analyzing Financial Statements Using Ratios and Percentage Changes   LO2, LO3

The comparative financial statements prepared at December 31, 2007, for Tiger Audio showed the following summarized data:

	2007	2006	Increase (Decrease) 2007 over 2006 Amount	Increase (Decrease) 2007 over 2006 Percentage
Income Statement				
Sales revenue*	$222,000	$185,000		
Cost of goods sold	127,650	111,000		
Gross profit	94,350	74,000		
Operating expenses	39,600	33,730		
Interest expense	4,000	3,270		
Income before income taxes	50,750	37,000		
Income tax expense (30%)	15,225	11,100		
Net income	$ 35,525	$ 25,900		
Balance Sheet				
Cash	$ 40,000	$ 38,000		
Accounts receivable (net)	18,500	16,000		
Inventory	25,000	22,000		
Property and equipment (net)	127,000	119,000		
Total assets	$ 210,500	$195,000		
Accounts payable	$ 27,000	$ 25,000		
Income taxes payable	3,000	2,800		
Note payable, long-term	75,500	92,200		
Total liabilities	105,500	120,000		
Capital stock (par $1)	25,000	25,000		
Retained earnings†	80,000	50,000		
Total liabilities and stockholders' equity	$ 210,500	$195,000		

* One-half of all sales are on credit.
† During 2007, cash dividends amounting to $5,525 were declared and paid.

Required:

1. Complete the two final columns shown beside each item in Tiger Audio's comparative financial statements. Round the percentages to one decimal place.
2. Does anything significant jump out at you from the year-over-year analyses?

LO2, LO3   **PB13-2 Analyzing Comparative Financial Statements Using Selected Ratios**

Use the data given in PB13-1 for Tiger Audio.

Required:

1. Compute the gross profit percentages in 2007 and 2006. Is the trend going in the right direction?
2. Compute the net profit margin ratios in 2007 and 2006. Is the trend going in the right direction?
3. Compute the earnings per share for 2007 and 2006. Does the trend look good or bad? Explain.
4. Stockholders' equity totaled $65,000 at the end of 2005. Compute the return on equity ratios for 2007 and 2006. Is the trend going in the right direction?
5. Net property and equipment totaled $115,000 at the end of 2005. Compute the fixed asset turnover ratios for 2007 and 2006. Is the trend going in the right direction?
6. Compute the debt-to-assets ratios for 2007 and 2006. Is debt providing financing for a larger or smaller proportion of the company's asset growth? Explain.
7. Compute the times interest earned ratios for 2007 and 2006. Do they look good or bad? Explain.
8. After Tiger released its 2007 financial statements, the company's stock was trading at $17. After the release of its 2006 financial statements, the company's stock price was $12 per share. Compute the P/E ratios for both years. Does it appear that investors have become more (or less) optimistic about Tiger's future success?

LO2, LO3   **PB13-3 Vertical Analysis of a Balance Sheet**

Southwest Airlines

A condensed balance sheet for Southwest Airlines and a partially completed vertical analysis are presented below.

SOUTHWEST AIRLINES
Balance Sheet (summarized)
December 31, 2005
(in millions of U.S. dollars)

Cash	$ 2,531	18%		Current liabilities	$ 6,149	43%
Accounts receivable	258	2		Long-term liabilities	1,394 *(b)*	
Inventory of parts and supplies	150	1		Total Liabilities	7,543	53
Other current assets	681	4		Contributed capital	1,226	9
Property and equipment	8,767 *(a)*			Retained earnings	5,449	38
Other assets	1,831	13		Total Stockholder's Equity	6,675 *(c)*	
Total Assets	$14,218	100%		Total Liabilities & Stockholders' Equity	$14,218	100%

Required:

1. Complete the vertical analysis by computing each line item (a)–(c) as a percentage of total assets. Round to the nearest whole percentage.
2. What percentages of Southwest's assets relate to inventory of parts and supplies versus property and equipment? What does this tell you about the relative significance of these two assets to Southwest's business?
3. What percentage of Southwest's assets is financed by total stockholders' equity? By total liabilities?

PB13-4 Vertical Analysis of an Income Statement

LO2, LO3

Southwest Airlines

A condensed income statement for Southwest Airlines and a partially completed vertical analysis are presented below.

SOUTHWEST AIRLINES
Income Statement (summarized)
For the Year Ended December 31
(in millions of U.S. dollars)

	2005			2004		
Sales revenues	$7,584		100%	$6,530		100%
Salaries, wages, and benefits	2,702		36	2,443	(d)	
Fuel, oil, repairs, and maintenance	1,772	(a)		1,458		22
Other operating expenses	2,290	(b)		2,075		32
Other expenses (revenues and gains)	(54)		0	65		1
Income before income taxes	874		11	489	(e)	
Income tax expense	326		4	176		2
Net income	$ 548	(c)	%	$ 313	(f)	%

Required:

1. Complete the vertical analysis by computing each line item (a)–(f) as a percentage of sales revenues. Round to the nearest whole percentage.
2. Does the percentage that you calculated in 1(a) suggest that Southwest tried to increase its profit by cutting repairs and maintenance costs in 2005 compared to 2004?
3. Do the percentages that you calculated in 1(c) and (f) indicate whether Southwest's net profit margin is continuing to improve or decline?

PB13-5 Interpreting Profitability, Liquidity, Solvency, and P/E Ratios

LO2, LO3

Mattel, Inc..

Mattel and Hasbro are the two biggest makers of games and toys in the world. Mattel sells over $5 billion of products each year while annual sales of Hasbro products exceed $3 billion. Compare the two companies as a potential investment based on the following ratios:

Ratio	Mattel	Hasbro
Gross profit percentage	48.3%	58.7%
Net profit margin	10.3%	5.7%
Return on equity	23.6%	13.6%
EPS	$ 1.23	$ 0.91
Receivables turnover ratio	7.2	6.4
Inventory turnover ratio	5.5	5.7
Current ratio	1.86	1.89
Debt-to-assets	0.24	0.33
P/E ratio	15.2	18.9

Required:

1. Which company appears more profitable? Describe the ratio(s) that you used to reach this decision.
2. Which company appears more liquid? Describe the ratio(s) that you used to reach this decision.
3. Which company appears more solvent? Describe the ratio(s) that you used to reach this decision.
4. Are the conclusions from your analyses in requirements 1–3 consistent with the value of the two companies suggested by the P/E ratios of the two companies? If not, offer one explanation for any apparent inconsistency.

LO2, LO3, LO4   **PB13-6 Using Ratios to Compare Loan Requests from Two Companies**

The 2007 financial statements for Thor and Gunnar Companies are summarized here:

	Thor Company	Gunnar Company
Balance Sheet		
Cash	$ 35,000	$ 54,000
Accounts receivable (net)	77,000	6,000
Inventory	154,000	30,000
Property and equipment (net)	770,000	192,000
Other assets	196,000	68,400
Total assets	$1,232,000	$350,400
Current liabilities	$ 168,000	$ 18,000
Long-term debt (12% interest rate)	266,000	66,000
Capital stock (par $20)	672,000	252,000
Additional paid-in capital	70,000	4,800
Retained earnings	56,000	9,600
Total liabilities and stockholders' equity	$1,232,000	$350,400
Income Statement		
Sales revenue	$ 1,120,000	$336,000
Cost of goods sold	(672,000)	(180,000)
Expenses (including interest and income tax)	(336,000)	(114,000)
Net income	$ 112,000	$ 42,000
Selected Data from 2006 Statements		
Accounts receivable, net	$ 65,800	$ 13,200
Inventory	133,000	45,600
Property and equipment, net	770,000	192,000
Long-term debt (12% interest rate)	266,000	66,000
Total stockholders' equity	798,000	266,400
Other Data		
Per share price at end of 2007	$ 13.20	$ 19.60
Average income tax rate	30%	30%

These two companies are in the same line of business and in the same state but in different cities. One-half of Thor's sales are on credit, whereas one-quarter of Gunnar's sales are on credit. Each company has been in operation for about 10 years. Both companies received an unqualified audit opinion on the financial statements, which means the independent auditors found nothing wrong. Thor Company wants to borrow $105,000 cash, and Gunnar Company is asking for $36,000. The loans will be for a two-year period.

Required:

1. Calculate the ratios in Exhibit 13.4 for which sufficient information is available. Round all calculations to two decimal places.

2. Assume that you work in the loan department of a local bank. You have been asked to analyze the situation and recommend which loan is preferable. Based on the data given, your analysis prepared in requirement 1, and any other information, give your choice and the supporting explanation.

LO2, LO3   **PB13-7 Analyzing an Investment by Comparing Selected Ratios**

You have the opportunity to invest $10,000 in one of two companies from a single industry. The only information you have is shown here. The word *high* refers to the top third of the industry; *average* is the middle third; *low* is the bottom third.

Ratio	Company A	Company B
EPS	High	High
Return on equity	High	Average
Debt-to-assets	High	Low
Current	Low	Average
Price/earnings	Low	High

Required:

Which company would you select? Write a brief explanation for your recommendation.

SKILLS DEVELOPMENT CASES

S13-1 Comparing Financial Information

Refer to the financial statements of Outback Steakhouse in Appendix B at the end of this book, or download them from the *Cases* section of the text's Web site at www.mhhe.com/phillips2e. From the list of ratios that were discussed in this chapter, select and compute the ratios that help you evaluate the company. Calculate ratios for at least two years. Remember that 2003 stockholders' equity balances are reported on the statement of stockholders' equity. For ratios that require other balance sheet information prior to 2004, use the 2004 year-end balances as if they are representative of the balances in 2003. Assume a stock price of $31 for each year, and treat the "minority interests in consolidated entities" as an additional liability. Provide a written analysis that interprets your ratio computations.

LO2, LO3

S13-2 Finding Financial Information

Download the financial statements of Darden Restaurants, Inc. for the years ended May 28, 2006 and 2005 from the company's Web site or the sources listed in S1-3. From the list of ratios that were discussed in this chapter, select, compute, and interpret the ratios that help you compare Darden Restaurants to the 2005 and 2004 results for Landry's reported in the chapter. Assume a stock price of $36, $33, and $21 for Darden in 2006, 2005, and 2004, respectively.

LO2, LO3
Darden Restaurants, Inc.

S13-3 Internet-Based Team Research: Examining an Annual Report

As a team, select an industry to analyze. Using your Web browser, each team member should access the annual report or 10-K for one publicly traded company in the industry, with each member selecting a different company. (See S1-3 in Chapter 1 for a description of possible resources for these tasks.)

LO1, LO2, LO3

Required:

1. On an individual basis, each team member should write a short report that incorporates horizontal and vertical analyses and as many of the ratios from the chapter as are applicable given the nature of the selected company.

2. Then, as a team, write a short report comparing and contrasting your companies using these attributes. Discuss any patterns across the companies that you as a team observe. Provide potential explanations for any differences discovered.

S13-4 Ethical Decision Making: A Real-Life Example

During its deliberations on the Sarbanes-Oxley Act, the U.S. Senate considered numerous reports evaluating the quality of work done by external auditors. One study by Weiss Ratings, Inc., focused on auditors' ability to predict bankruptcy. The study criticized auditors for failing to identify and report going-concern problems for audit clients that later went bankrupt. Based on a sample of 45 bankrupt companies, the Weiss study concluded that had auditors noted unusual levels for just two of seven typical financial ratios, they would have identified 89 percent of the sample companies that later went bankrupt. A follow-up to the Weiss study found that had the criteria in the Weiss study been applied to a larger sample of nonbankrupt companies, 46.9 percent of nonbankrupt companies would have been predicted to go bankrupt.* In other words, the Weiss criteria would have incorrectly predicted bankruptcy for nearly half of the companies in the follow-up study and would have led the auditors to report that these clients had substantial going-concern problems when, in fact, they did not. Discuss the negative consequences that arise when auditors fail to identify and report going-concern problems. Who is harmed by these failures? Discuss the negative consequences that arise when auditors incorrectly report going-concern problems when

LO4

---

* Michael D. Akers, Meredith A. Maher, and Don E. Giacomino, "Going-Concern Opinions: Broadening the Expectations Gap," *CPA Journal*, October 2003. Retrieved November 20, 2006 from www.nysscpa.org/cpajournal/2003/1003/features/f103803.htm.

they do not exist. Who is harmed by these errors? In your opinion, which of the potential consequences is worse?

LO3 **S13-5 Ethical Decision Making: A Mini-Case**

Capital Investments Corporation (CIC) requested a sizable loan from First Federal Bank to acquire a large piece of land for future expansion. CIC reported current assets of $1,900,000 (including $430,000 in cash) and current liabilities of $1,075,000. First Federal denied the loan request for a number of reasons, including the fact that the current ratio was below 2:1. When CIC was informed of the loan denial, the controller of the company immediately paid $420,000 that was owed to several trade creditors. The controller then asked First Federal to reconsider the loan application. Based on these abbreviated facts, would you recommend that First Federal approve the loan request? Why? Are the controller's actions ethical?

LO4 **S13-6 Critical Thinking: Analyzing the Impact of Alternative Depreciation Methods on Ratio Analysis**

Speedy Company uses the double-declining-balance method to depreciate its property, plant, and equipment, and Turtle Company uses the straight-line method. The two companies are exactly alike except for the difference in depreciation methods.

Required:

1. Identify the financial ratios discussed in this chapter that are likely to be affected by the difference in depreciation methods.
2. Which company will report the higher amount for each ratio that you have identified in response to requirement 1? If you cannot be certain, explain why.

LO2 **S13-7 Using a Spreadsheet to Calculate Financial Statement Ratios**

www.mhhe.com/phillips2e

Enter the financial statement information from Exhibits 13.1, 13.2, and 13.3 into three separate worksheets in one spreadsheet file. Using the cell referencing instructions given in S6-1 for "importing" information from different worksheets, create a fourth worksheet that uses the formulas in Exhibit 13.4 to recalculate all the ratios for Landry's for 2004 and 2005. (For the EPS ratio, simply import the amount reported on the face of the income statement.)

Appendix A

Landry's Restaurants, Inc.
2005 Annual Report

Landry's Redefining
ENTERTAINMENT
Golden Ticket to Food and Fun!
Landry's Restaurants, Inc. | 2005 Annual Report

Landry's Restaurants, Inc. – more than 26,000 employees in 35 states and 7 international locations

Landry's around the U.S.

Great dining from coast to coast. Over 300 full-service units in 35 states.

LANDRY'S LOCATIONS

Alabama	Jacksonville *(2 locations)*	Lafayette	**New York**	Nashville *(3 locations)*
Birmingham	Melbourne	New Orleans *(2 locations)*	Dobbs Ferry	**Texas**
Hoover	Miami Area *(3 locations)*	Bossier City	**North Carolina**	Amarillo
Huntsville	Naples	**Maryland**	Asheville	Austin Area *(5 locations)*
Arizona	Orlando Area *(8 locations)*	Annapolis	Charlotte	Beaumont
Phoenix Area *(4 locations)*	Palm Beach Area	Baltimore	Fayetteville	Corpus Christi
Tucson	*(3 locations)*	Gaithersburg	**Ohio**	*(3 locations)*
California	Pensacola	Towson	Akron	Dallas/Ft. Worth
Los Angeles Area	Tampa Area	**Massachusetts**	Canton	*(28 locations)*
(11 locations)	*(3 locations)*	Boston Area *(2 locations)*	Cincinnati	El Paso
Malibu	**Georgia**	**Michigan**	Cleveland Area	Galveston
Mammoth Lakes	Atlanta *(7 locations)*	Ann Arbor *(2 locations)*	*(3 locations)*	Houston Area
Monterey	Savannah	Detroit Area	Columbus *(2 locations)*	*(51 locations)*
Sacramento *(2 locations)*	**Idaho**	*(10 locations)*	Dayton	Kemah
San Diego Area	Boise	**Minnesota**	Toledo	*(7 locations)*
(11 locations)	**Illinois**	Bloomington	**Oklahoma**	Lubbock
San Francisco Area	Chicago Area *(8 locations)*	Maple Grove	Norman	McAllen
(3 locations)	Fairview Heights	Roseville	Oklahoma City	San Antonio
Ventura	Peoria	**Missouri**	*(2 locations)*	*(7 locations)*
Colorado	**Indiana**	Branson	Tulsa	**Utah**
Denver Area *(8 locations)*	Hobart	Independence	**Oregon**	Salt Lake City
Connecticut	Indianapolis	St. Louis *(3 locations)*	Portland	*(3 locations)*
West Hartford	*(3 locations)*	St. Peters	**Pennsylvania**	**Virginia**
Delaware	**Kansas**	**Nevada**	Philadelphia	Alexandria
Wilmington	Olathe	Lake Tahoe	Pittsburgh *(2 locations)*	Chesapeake
Florida	Overland Park	Las Vegas *(6 locations)*	**South Carolina**	Fairfax *(2 locations)*
Daytona Beach	**Kentucky**	**New Jersey**	Charleston	Fredericksburg
Deerfield Beach	Bellevue	Edison	Greenville	Norfolk
Destin Beach *(2 locations)*	Lexington	Trenton Area *(3 locations)*	Hilton Head	Sterling
Fort Lauderdale Area	Louisville	Weehawken	Myrtle Beach *(5 locations)*	**Washington**
(3 locations)	**Louisiana**	**New Mexico**	**Tennessee**	Seattle
Fort Myers	Baton Rouge	Albuquerque	Memphis *(3 locations)*	Vancouver

Landry's Restaurants, Inc. ventures into the gaming

industry with a bang, adding to its portfolio of strong brands

We hit the jackpot in 2005 with our purchase of The Golden Nugget. The Golden Nugget is one of the most storied names in the gaming industry, having been in business nearly 60 years. The Golden Nugget acquisition adds to our strong brands and allowed us to enter the gaming industry with locations in Las Vegas and Laughlin, Nevada. While gaming is a new business venture, operating hotels and restaurants comes second nature to us. With our purchase of The Golden Nugget Casinos and Hotels, we acquired over 2,200 guest rooms and 12 food service outlets, not to mention room service and catering. Entertaining our guests is what we do best. With the tenured management at The Golden Nugget properties overseeing the gaming and our experience in food service and hospitality, we believe we can provide our guests with the entertainment experience that they are seeking. In addition, with our over 300 properties coast to coast, we have a tremendous customer base that we can cross market to like no other gaming operator.

As we expand into gaming, we are redirecting our resources because we believe that we will receive better long-term value for our shareholders. Gaming companies tend to trade at a higher stock multiple than restaurant companies, and the life cycle of a well-maintained casino is usually a lot longer than a restaurant. Besides, the cash flow generated from a single casino can be equivalent to up to 50 or more restaurants, and so it becomes easier to manage and operate one casino than 50 restaurants spread across the country. Like a fine wine, The Golden Nugget in Las Vegas has aged and requires capital so it can be renovated to enable us to better compete with our Las Vegas strip competitors. We have already directed some of our capital by opening our upscale Vic & Anthony's Steakhouse in The Golden Nugget – Las Vegas and our family-friendly Joe's Crab Shack in the Golden Nugget – Laughlin. More is to come in 2006.

In December 2004, we changed the Company's capital structure in order to take advantage of historically low interest rates. The capital we borrowed enabled us to repurchase $133.8 million of the Company's common stock during 2005 and also allowed us to acquire The Golden Nugget. Naturally, the borrowed funds significantly increased our interest expense in 2005, which directly impacted our net income. Our interest expense in 2005 was $41.4 million compared with $15.2 million in 2004. As a result, our net income decreased to $44.8 million in 2005. We incurred interest expense on the borrowed funds for the entire year and had only the fourth-quarter earnings from The Golden Nugget to offset the added interest expense as the transaction did not close until very late in the third quarter of 2005. Meanwhile, our revenues continued to grow with a record $1.25 billion in 2005.

Although 2005 commenced a new beginning for Landry's, our restaurants continued to provide enjoyable dining experiences for our guests and financial performance for our shareholders. Our brands remain some of the most well-known in the restaurant industry. Nevertheless, we are in a very competitive industry with virtually no barrier of entry. Therefore, it is incumbent upon us to reinvest and, at times, reinvent our brands to remain a top of mind consumer choice. I can assure you, we are up to the challenge.

Looking ahead, we will continue to allocate fewer resources to opening new restaurants and look to generate better returns from our existing asset base. We have some exciting projects in the works, including the Tower of the Americas in San Antonio, Texas, T-Rex and the remodeling of The Golden Nugget – Las Vegas. We also will continue to focus on gaming opportunities when it makes sense for us to do so. Landry's employees remain hard working and dedicated to the success of the Company. We remain committed to delivering solid growth in shareholder value over the long-term.

Tilman J. Fertitta
Chairman of the Board, President & Chief Executive Officer

Highlights in 2005
Diversification, $46 million in revenue from retail sales, new properties.

2005MILESTONES

Along with great food, there's a heap of fun on Landry's plates. Shareholders should enjoy our results just as much

International growth:
Landry's international profile is growing. In 2005, the Company had operations in Mexico, Canada, Great Britain, Japan and France. In 2006, Egypt will be added to the menu.

Restaurant level profits:
61 Landry's units had more than $1 million in restaurant level profits in 2005, and 96 units had more than $750,000 in restaurant level profits.

Big catch:
Seafood brands including Joe's Crab Shack, Landry's Seafood House, Charley's Crab and Chart House accounted for 63% of Landry's restaurant sales in 2005.

Locations:
Landry's owns almost 28% of the properties where its restaurants are located.

Stable culture:
Most of Landry's core management team has grown along with the Company, which also boasts lower general management turnover as compared with industry averages. In 2005, the company saw only 12.6% general manager turnover.

Retail:
Landry's retail sales totaled more than $46 million in 2005. More than 10 million items are sold annually in Landry's retail shops.

Restaurant level profits
rose 5% in 2005.

Revenue increase
Landry's saw a 7.5% increase in revenue in fiscal 2005, to about $1.3 billion.

Stock price
In the past five years, Landry's stock price has risen more than 216%, while the Standard & Poor's 500 index lost 14.2%.

Landry's added 13 units
in fiscal 2005, ending the year with 318 units in a total of 35 states and 7 international locations.

Landry's at a glance

Strong leadership and diversified assets marked one more successful year for the Company.

FINANCIAL FEATURES

Financial Features: Landry's at a Glance

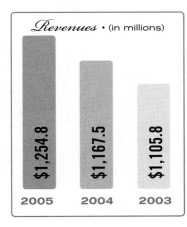

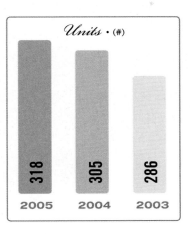

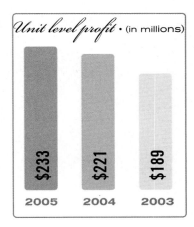

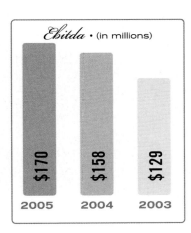

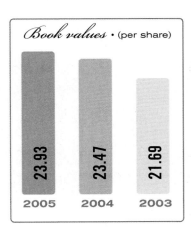

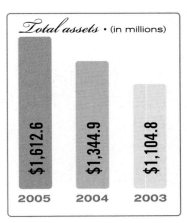

Year Ended December 31		2005		2004		2003
Revenues	$	1,254,805,671	$	1,167,475,165	$	1,105,755,057
Operating income	$	106,956,166	$	98,795,737	$	66,826,302
Income before taxes*	$	65,423,180	$	70,066,506	$	55,802,370
Net income*	$	44,815,036	$	66,521,728	$	44,913,853
Earnings per share (diluted)*	$	1.95	$	2.39	$	1.59

Year Ended December 31		2005		2004		2003
Total assets	$	1,612,578,813	$	1,344,952,271	$	1,104,883,485
Short-term debt	$	1,851,741	$	1,700,496	$	1,963,189
Long-term debt	$	816,043,799	$	559,545,092	$	299,735,906
Stockholders' equity	$	516,770,461	$	600,896,966	$	599,893,913

*Income before taxes, net income and earnings per share decreased in 2005 as a result of increased interest expense associated with the Company's December 2004 refinancing in preparation for the Golden Nugget acquisition which closed September 2005.

With its newest major acquisition, Landry's is entertaining a big audience

Golden Nugget, Las Vegas

GGET GOLDEN NUGGET GOLD

Landry's scored a 24-karat purchase in 2005, acquiring one of the most legendary brands in gaming. With the Golden Nugget – including the landmark Las Vegas casino and its sister property in Laughlin, Nevada – the Company sees excellent opportunities for growth and exciting synergy with its other hotel, restaurant and entertainment divisions.

The lavish, 7-acre flagship property offers 1,907 guestrooms and some of Las Vegas' most dynamic suites. It's the city's only hotel to have earned AAA's Four Diamond Award for 29 consecutive years. Landry's is quickly building upon $35 million in enhancements made by the previous owners in 2003. One of Landry's signature concepts, the upscale Vic & Anthony's Steakhouse, opened here in December 2005. Coming in 2006 are Grotto, the Company's authentic Italian eatery; and a new concept, Lillie's Noodle House, offering Cantonese, Szechwan and Pan Asian dishes in a casual, contemporary setting.

An Aquarium Restaurant is on the drawing board for 2007.

Renovation of the nearly 40,000-square-foot casino area is ongoing, with a new high-limit slot salon and a VIP lounge already open. Among more amenities coming as we reposition the Golden Nugget as a one-of-a-kind entertainment venue are: a magnificent pool with cascading waterfalls, a thrilling waterslide that tunnels through a shark tank. New cabanas atop the poolside "mountain." A remodeled spa and salon. A revamped fitness center. A lively nightclub overlooking downtown's popular Fremont Street Experience and a new hotel tower in 2007. With a history of successful revitalization projects – as seen with its aquarium, hospitality and restaurant concepts in downtown Denver, downtown Houston and the Kemah Boardwalk on Galveston Bay – Landry's is betting that the timing is right for downtown Las Vegas' rebirth.

Selected Financial Data

Year Ended December 31,	2005	2004	2003	2002	2001
Income statement data					
Revenues	$ 1,254,806	$ 1,167,475	$1,105,755	$ 894,795	$746,642
Operating costs and expenses:					
Cost of revenues	333,028	326,108	321,783	257,945	219,684
Labor	377,215	337,633	323,284	259,198	215,662
Other operating expenses	311,648	282,412	271,271	224,122	186,529
General and administrative expenses	57,694	58,320	51,704	43,384	38,004
Depreciation and amortization	63,493	57,294	49,092	40,729	34,975
Asset impairment expense (1)	–	1,709	13,144	2,200	2,394
Pre-opening expenses	4,772	5,203	8,650	4,591	2,598
Total operating costs and expenses	1,147,850	1,068,679	1,038,928	832,169	699,846
Operating income	106,956	98,796	66,827	62,626	46,796
Other (income) expense:					
Interest (income) expense, net	41,438	15,185	9,561	4,997	9,402
Other, net	95	13,544	1,463	(887)	(56)
Total other (income) expense (2)	41,533	28,729	11,024	4,110	9,346
Income before taxes	65,423	70,067	55,803	58,516	37,450
Provision for income taxes (3)	20,608	3,545	10,889	18,025	11,502
Net income	$ 44,815	$ 66,522	$ 44,914	$ 40,491	$ 25,948
Earnings per share information:					
Basic					
Net income (loss)	$ 2.01	$ 2.46	$ 1.63	$ 1.56	$ 1.19
Weighted average number of common					
shares outstanding	22,300	27,000	27,600	25,900	21,750
Diluted					
Net income (loss)	$ 1.95	$ 2.39	$ 1.59	$ 1.51	$ 1.15
Weighted average number of common and					
common share equivalents outstanding	23,000	27,800	28,325	26,900	22,535
Other data					
EBITDA (Earnings before interest, taxes,					
depreciation, and amortization):					
Operating Income	$ 106,956	$ 98,796	$ 66,827	$ 62,626	$ 46,796
Add back:					
Depreciation and amortization	63,493	57,294	49,092	40,729	34,975
Asset impairment expense	–	1,709	13,144	2,200	2,394
EBITDA	$ 170,449	$ 157,799	$ 129,063	$ 105,555	$ 84,165
Balance sheet data (at end of period)					
Working capital (deficit)	$ (74,062)	$ 161,515	$ (38,767)	$ (55,475)	$ (6,017)
Total assets	$ 1,612,579	$1,344,952	$ 1,104,883	$ 934,898	$692,105
Short-term notes payable and current portion					
of notes and other obligations	$ 1,852	$ 1,700	$ 1,963	$ 1,783	$ –
Long-term notes and other obligations,					
net of current portion	$ 816,044	$ 559,545	$ 299,736	$ 189,404	$ 175,000
Stockholders' equity	$ 516,770	$ 600,897	$ 599,894	$ 563,406	$ 391,032

(1) In 2004, 2003, 2002, and 2001, we recorded asset impairment charges of $1.7 million ($1.2 million after tax), $13.1 million ($9.1 million after tax), $2.2 million ($1.5 million after tax) and $2.4 million ($1.6 million after tax), respectively, related to the adjustment to estimated fair value of certain restaurant properties and assets. The Company considers the asset impairment expense as additional depreciation and amortization, although shown as a separate line item in the consolidated income statements.

(2) In 2004, we recorded prepayment penalty expense and other costs related to the refinancing of our long-term debt of approximately $16.6 million ($11.3 million after tax).

(3) In 2004 and 2003, we recognized $18.5 million and $6.3 million in income tax benefits for a reduction of the valuation allowance and deferred tax liabilities attributable to tax benefits deemed realizable and reduced accruals.

EBITDA is not a generally accepted accounting principles ("GAAP") measurement and is presented solely as a supplemental disclosure because we believe that it is a widely used measure of operating performance. EBITDA is not intended to be viewed as a source of liquidity or as a cash flow measure as used in the statement of cash flows. EBITDA is simply shown above as it is a commonly used non-GAAP valuation statistic.

(4) Income before taxes, net income and earnings per share decreased in 2005 as a result of increased interest expense associated with the Company's December 2004 refinancing in preparation for the Golden Nugget acquisition which closed September 2005.

Management's Discussions
FORWARD-LOOKING STATEMENTS

This report contains forward-looking statements within the meaning of Section 27A of the Securities Act of 1933 and Section 21E of the Securities Exchange Act of 1934. All statements other than statements of historical fact are "forward-looking statements" for purposes of federal and state securities laws. Forward-looking statements may include the words "may," "will," "plans," "believes," "estimates," "expects," "intends" and other similar expressions. Our forward-looking statements are subject to risks and uncertainty, including, without limitation, our ability to continue our expansion strategy, our ability to make projected capital expenditures, as well as general market conditions, competition, and pricing. Forward-looking statements include statements regarding:

- potential acquisitions of other restaurants, restaurant concepts, gaming operations and lines of businesses in other sectors of the hospitality and entertainment industries;
- future capital expenditures, including the amount and nature thereof;
- business strategy and measures to implement such strategy;
- competitive strengths;
- goals;
- expansion and growth of our business and operations;
- future commodity prices;
- availability of food products, materials and employees;
- consumer perceptions of food safety;
- changes in local, regional and national economic conditions;
- the effectiveness of our marketing efforts;
- changing demographics surrounding our restaurants, hotels and casinos;

- the effect of changes in tax laws;
- actions of regulatory, legislative, executive or judicial decisions at the federal, state or local level with regard to our business and the impact of any such actions;
- our ability to maintain regulatory approvals for our existing businesses and our ability to receive regulatory approval for our new businesses;
- our expectations of the continued availability and cost of capital resources;
- same store sales;
- earnings guidance;
- the seasonality of our business;
- weather and acts of God;
- food, labor, fuel and utilities costs;
- plans;
- references to future success; and
- the risks described in "Risk Factors."

Although we believe that the assumptions underlying our forward-looking statements are reasonable, any of the assumptions could be inaccurate, and, therefore, we cannot assure you that the forward-looking statements included in this report will prove to be accurate. In light of the significant uncertainties inherent in our forward-looking statements, the inclusion of such information should not be regarded as a representation by us or any other person that our objectives and plans will be achieved. Some of these and other risks and uncertainties that could cause actual results to differ materially from such forward-looking statements are more fully described under Item 1A. "Risk Factors" and elsewhere in this report, or in the documents incorporated by reference herein.

Management's Discussions
FINANCIAL CONDITION AND RESULTS OF OPERATIONS

Introduction

We primarily own and operate full-service, casual dining restaurants and two casinos. As of December 31, 2005, we operated 311 full service restaurants. In addition to these units, there were several limited menu restaurants and other properties (as described in Item 1. Business), and the Golden Nugget Hotels and Casinos in Las Vegas and Laughlin, Nevada as more fully described below.

On September 27, 2005, Landry's Gaming, Inc., an unrestricted subsidiary, purchased the Golden Nugget Hotels and Casinos in downtown Las Vegas and Laughlin, Nevada ("GN") for $163.0 million in cash, the assumption of $155.0 million of Senior Secured Notes due 2011 and the assumption of approximately $27.0 million under an existing senior revolving credit facility and the further assumption of certain working capital including $27.5 million in cash.

Under the terms of the purchase agreement, the currently outstanding Senior Secured Notes due 2011 remain outstanding obligations of GN following the closing. The Golden Nugget—Las Vegas occupies approximately eight acres in downtown Las Vegas with approximately 38,000 square feet of gaming area. The property also features three towers containing 1,907 rooms, the largest number of guestrooms in downtown Las Vegas. The Golden Nugget—Laughlin is located on 13 acres on the Colorado River with 32,000 square feet of gaming space and 300 rooms. The results of operations for these properties are included in our financial statements from the date of acquisition.

During 2003, we completed a series of relatively small acquisitions, including: separate acquisitions of several well-known individual upscale Houston restaurants; Ocean Journey (a 12 acre aquarium complex in Denver,

Management's Discussions

FINANCIAL CONDITION AND RESULTS OF OPERATIONS

Colorado): the Holiday Inn on the Beach in Galveston, Texas; and the Galveston Flagship Hotel (subject to an existing lease), for an aggregate cash purchase price of all such acquisitions of approximately $27.0 million, plus the assumption of an $11.4 million non-recourse long-term note payable. These acquisitions included certain future commitments as described in Notes to the Consolidated Financial Statements, Commitments and Contingencies in the paragraph titled "Building Commitments." The estimated cost of such future commitments are included in the Contractual Obligations table amounts under Other Long-Term Obligations, that is included within this Item 7.

The Specialty Growth Division is primarily engaged in operating complementary entertainment and hospitality activities, such as miscellaneous beverage carts and various kiosks, amusement rides and games and some associated limited hotel properties, generally at locations in conjunction with our core restaurant operations. The total assets, revenues, and operating profits of these complementary "specialty" business activities are considered not material to the overall business and below the threshold of a separate reportable business segment under SFAS No. 131.

We are in the business of operating restaurants, two casinos and the above-mentioned complementary activities. We do not engage in real estate operations other than those associated with the ownership and operation of our business. We own a fee interest (own the land and building) in a number of properties underlying our businesses, but do not engage in real estate sales or real estate management in any significant fashion or format. The Chief Executive Officer, who is responsible for our operations, reviews and evaluates both core and non-core business activities and results, and determines financial and management resource allocations and investments for all business activities.

The restaurant and gaming industries are intensely competitive and affected by changes in consumer tastes and by national, regional, and local economic conditions and demographic trends. The performance of individual restaurants or casinos may be affected by factors such as: traffic patterns, demographic considerations, marketing, weather conditions, and the type, number, and location of competing restaurants and casinos.

We have many well established competitors with greater financial resources, larger marketing and advertising budgets, and longer histories of operation than ours, including competitors already established in regions where we are planning to expand, as well as competitors planning to expand in the same regions. We face significant competition from other casinos in the markets in which we operate and from other mid-priced, full-service, casual dining restaurants offering or promoting seafood and other types and varieties of cuisine. Our competitors include national, regional, and local restaurant chains and casinos as well as local owner-operated restaurants and casinos. We also compete with other restaurants, retail establishments and gaming companies for restaurant and casino sites. We intend to pursue an acquisition strategy.

Results of Operations
Profitability

The following table sets forth the percentage relationship to total revenues of certain operating data for the periods indicated:

Year Ended December 31,	2005	2004	2003
Revenues	100.0%	100.0%	100.0%
Cost of revenues	26.5%	27.9%	29.1%
Labor	30.1%	28.9%	29.2%
Other operating expenses	24.8%	24.2%	24.5%
Unit level profit	18.6%	19.0%	17.2%

Year ended December 31, 2005 Compared to the Year ended December 31, 2004

Restaurant and hospitality revenues increased $21,689,779, or 1.9%, from $1,167,475,165 to $1,189,164,944 for the year ended December 31, 2005 compared to the year ended December 31, 2004. The total increase/change in revenue is comprised of the following approximate amounts: 2005 restaurant openings— $30.5 million; restaurant closings decreased 2005 revenues—$8.2 million; locations open 2005 and 2004 including "honeymoon" periods—decreased $4.0 million; day lost due to leap year—decreased $3.4 million; units closed for an extended period as a result of the hurricane—decreased $2.2 million; and the remainder of the difference is attributable to the change in sales for stores not open a full comparable period. The total number of units open as of December 31, 2005 and 2004 were 311 and 297, respectively.

Gaming revenues increased $65,640,727 for the year ended December 31, 2005 as a result of the acquisition of GN. The results of GN are included from the September 27, 2005 acquisition date.

As a primary result of increased revenues, cost of revenues increased $6,919,686, or 2.1%, from $326,108,007 to $333,027,693 in the year ended December 31, 2005, compared to the same period in the prior year. Cost of revenues as a percentage of revenues for the year ended December 31, 2005, decreased to 26.5% from 27.9% in 2004. The decrease in cost of revenues as a percentage of revenues primarily reflects a moderate menu price increase, stable commodities prices, a shift in product mix and the acquisition of the Golden Nugget.

Labor expenses increased $39,581,759, or 11.7%, from $337,633,530 to $377,215,289 in the year ended December 31, 2005, compared to the same period in the prior year, principally as a result of increased revenues. Labor expenses as a percentage of revenues for the year ended December 31, 2005 increased to 30.1% from 28.9% in 2004, principally due to increased hourly wage rates and higher overtime and the acquisition of the Golden Nugget.

Other operating expenses increased $29,235,924, or 10.4%, from $282,411,954 to $311,647,878 in the year ended December 31, 2005, compared to the same period in the prior year, principally as a result of increased revenues. Such expenses increased as a percentage of revenues to 24.8% in 2005 from 24.2% in 2004, as a primary result of higher utilities, increased rent expense and the acquisition of the Golden Nugget.

General and administrative expenses decreased $626,169, or 1.1%, from $58,319,642 to $57,693,473 in the year ended December 31, 2005, compared to the same period in the prior year, and decreased as a percentage of revenues to 4.6% in 2005 from 5.0% in 2004. The decrease is due to lower professional fees related to Sarbanes-Oxley and leverage associated with the acquisition of the Golden Nugget.

Combined depreciation and amortization expense and asset impairment expense increased an aggregate of

$4,489,970, or 7.6%, from an aggregate of $59,002,777 to $63,492,747 in the year ended December 31, 2005, compared to the same period in the prior year. The increase for 2005 was primarily due to an increase in depreciation related to the addition of new restaurants and equipment and the acquisition of the Golden Nugget offset by a decrease in impairment charges.

The $1.7 million impairment charge in fiscal 2004 resulted from sales declines in one particular restaurant, combined with deterioration in the specific restaurant's profitability and management's lowered outlook for improvement in such specific property. Assets that were impaired are primarily leasehold improvements and to a lesser extent equipment.

Restaurant pre-opening expenses were $4,772,425 for the year ended December 31, 2005, compared to $5,203,518 for the same period in the prior year. The decrease for the 2005 period was attributable to a decrease in units opened in 2005 as compared to 2004.

The increase in net interest expense for the year ended December 31, 2005 as compared to the prior year is primarily due to higher borrowings, as well as an increase in our average borrowing rate.

Other expense, net for 2005 was immaterial. Other expense, net for 2004 was comprised primarily of $14.6 million in pre-payment penalties, and related fees associated with the pay down of our $150.0 million senior notes and bank credit facility both of which were entered into in 2003 partially offset by $1.1 million in business interruption insurance recoveries.

Provision for income taxes increased by $17,063,366 to $20,608,144 in the year ended December 31, 2005 from $3,544,778 in 2004 primarily due to a net $18.5 million income tax benefit in 2004 gained from a reversal of the remaining valuation allowance attributable to tax benefits associated with the Rainforest Cafe acquisition deemed realizable. The previously established valuation allowance was reversed at December 31, 2004, due to the strong 2004 and future forecasted profitability of the Rainforest Cafe restaurants, a successful transition from a tax-loss incurring stand-alone public company to a highly profitable and taxable income producing wholly-owned subsidiary, coupled with the approaching end of specific recognition limitations on allowable deductions and tax assets and the 2004 resolution of certain tax issues, which caused management to believe the remaining deferred tax assets previously reserved would more likely than not be realized.

Year ended December 31, 2004 Compared to the Year ended December 31, 2003

Revenues increased $61,720,108 or 5.6%, from $1,105,755,057 to $1,167,475,165 in the year ended December 31, 2004, compared to the year ended December 31, 2003. The total increase/change in revenue is comprised of the following approximate amounts: 2004 restaurant openings–$87 million; restaurant closings decrease to 2004 revenues–$13 million; locations open 2004 and 2003 including "honeymoon" periods– decrease $13 million. The total number of units open as of December 31, 2004 and 2003 were 297 and 286, respectively.

As a primary result of increased revenues, cost of revenues increased $4,324,630, or 1.3%, from $321,783,377 to $326,108,007 in the year ended December 31, 2004, compared to the same period in the prior year. Cost of revenues as a percentage of revenues for the year ended December 31, 2004, decreased to 27.9% from 29.1% in 2003. The decrease in cost of revenues as a percentage of revenues primarily reflects a moderate menu price increase, stable commodities prices and a shift in product mix.

Labor expenses increased $14,349,131, or 4.4%, from $323,284,399 to $337,633,530 in the year ended December 31, 2004, compared to the same period in the prior year, principally as a result of increased revenues. Restaurant labor expenses as a percentage of revenues for the year ended December 31, 2004, decreased to 28.9% from 29.2% in 2003, principally due to efficiencies gained from improved

scheduling and training techniques.

Other operating expenses increased $11,141,084, or 4.1%, from $271,270,870 to $282,411,954 in the year ended December 31, 2004, compared to the same period in the prior year, principally as a result of increased revenues. Such expenses decreased as a percentage of revenues to 24.2% in 2004 from 24.5% in 2003, as a primary result of lower advertising partially offset by increased rent expense.

General and administrative expenses increased $6,615,542, or 12.8%, from $51,704,100 to $58,319,642 in the year ended December 31, 2004, compared to the same period in the prior year, and increased as a percentage of revenues to 5.0% in 2004 from 4.7% in 2003. The increase is due to increased compensation and personnel and higher professional fees related to Sarbanes-Oxley.

Combined depreciation and amortization expense and asset impairment expense decreased an aggregate of $3,233,054, or 5.2%, from an aggregate of $62,235,831 to $59,002,777 in the year ended December 31, 2004, compared to the same period in the prior year. The decrease for 2004 was primarily due to an increase in depreciation related to the addition of new restaurants and equipment offset by a decrease in impairment charges. Asset impairment expense of approximately $1,700,000 relating to underperforming and closed restaurants was recorded for 2004, while approximately $13,100,000 was included in the 2003 amount.

The impairment charge in fiscal 2004 resulted from sales declines in one particular restaurant, combined with deterioration in the specific restaurant's profitability and management's lowered outlook for improvement in such specific property. Assets that were impaired are primarily leasehold improvements and to a lesser extent equipment. A similar evaluation of our units was performed in 2003, resulting in the write down of six underperforming and three closed restaurants. Included in the 2003 amounts were four Landry's division, three Joe's Crab Shack, and two Crab House units. The following is a summary of related charges and expenses:

Years Ended December 31,	2004	2003
Asset Impairment	$1,700,000	$13,100,000
Accrued Estimated Lease Termination Payments	–	1,300,000
	$1,700,000	$14,400,000

Restaurant pre-opening expenses were $5,203,518 for the year ended December 31, 2004, compared to $8,650,178 for the same period in the prior year. The decrease for the 2004 period was attributable to a decrease in units opened in 2004 as compared to 2003.

The increase in net interest expense in the year ended December 31, 2004 as compared to the prior year is primarily due to higher borrowings, as well as an increase in our average borrowing rate.

The increase in other expense, net is comprised primarily of $14.6 million in pre-payment penalties, and related fees associated with the pay down of our $150 million senior notes and bank credit facility both of which were entered into in 2003 partially offset by $1.1 million in business interruption insurance recoveries. Other expense for 2003 is primarily expenses related to abandoned project costs.

Provision for income taxes decreased by $7,343,739 to $3,544,778 in the year ended December 31, 2004 from $10,888,517 in 2003 primarily due to changes in our pre-tax income offset by a net $18.5 million income tax benefit gained from a reversal of the remaining valuation allowance attributable to tax benefits associated with the Rainforest Cafe acquisition deemed realizable. The previously established valuation allowance was reversed at December 31, 2004, due to the strong 2004 and future forecasted profitability of the Rainforest Cafe restaurants,

Management's Discussions
FINANCIAL CONDITION AND RESULTS OF OPERATIONS

a successful transition from a tax-loss incurring stand-alone public company to a highly profitable and taxable income producing wholly-owned subsidiary, coupled with the approaching end of specific recognition limitations on allowable deductions and tax assets and the 2004 resolution of certain tax issues, which caused management to believe the remaining deferred tax assets previously reserved would more likely than not be realized. In 2003, an income tax benefit of $6.3 million was recognized from reversal of the valuation reserve attributable to tax assets deemed realizable and reduced accruals.

Liquidity and Capital Resources

In December 2004, we refinanced our existing revolving credit facility and existing senior notes by entering into a new five year $300.0 million Bank Credit Facility and a six year $150.0 million Term Loan. The Bank Credit Facility matures in December 2009 and the Term Loan matures in December 2010. Interest on the Bank Credit Facility is payable monthly or quarterly at Libor or the bank's base rate plus a financing spread. Interest on the Term Loan is payable quarterly at Libor plus a financing spread. The financing spread under the Bank Credit Facility and the Term Loan is currently 1.50% and 1.75%, respectively, for Libor borrowings and 0.50% and 0.75% for base rate borrowings. As of December 31, 2005, we had approximately $215.9 million available under the existing credit facility for expansion and working capital purposes.

Concurrent with the closing of the Bank Credit Facility and Term Loan in December 2004, we also issued $400.0 million in senior notes through a private placement offering. The senior notes are general unsecured obligations of the Company and mature December 2014. Interest is payable semi-annually at 7.5%. On June 16, 2005, we completed an exchange offering whereby substantially all of the senior notes issued under the private placement were exchanged for senior notes registered under the Securities Act of 1933.

Net proceeds from the Bank Credit Facility and senior notes totaled $536.6 million and were used to repay all outstanding liabilities under the existing credit facility and senior notes. These debt repayments resulted in a pre-tax charge of $16.6 million in the fourth quarter of 2004.

The Bank Credit Facility and Term Loan are secured by substantially all real and personal property of subsidiaries and governed by certain financial covenants, including minimum fixed charge, net worth, and our financial leverage ratios as well as limitations on dividend payments, capital expenditures and other restricted payments as defined in the agreements.

In October 2003, we refinanced a previous bank credit facility by issuing long-term notes totaling $150.0 million through a private placement of debt and amending and extending the existing bank credit facility to a four-year $200.0 million revolving credit facility (the "Former Bank Credit Facility") later increased to $225.0 million. The long-term notes had maturities ranging from October 2009 through October 2013, and the Former Bank Credit Facility matured in October 2007. Interest on the long-term notes was paid quarterly at an average rate of 5.95%. Interest on the Former Bank Credit Facility was payable monthly or quarterly at Libor or the bank's base rate plus a financing spread. The Former Bank Credit Facility, long-term notes, and all future related liabilities were paid down in full with the proceeds from the December 2004 refinancing.

A wholly-owned subsidiary of ours assumed an $11.4 million 9.39% non-recourse, long-term note payable (due May 2010) in connection with an asset purchase in March 2003. Principal and interest payments under this note aggregate $102,000 monthly.

During the year ended December 31, 2005, we repurchased $133.8 million of common stock. In September 2003, we authorized an open market stock repurchase program for $60.0 million. In October 2004, we authorized a $50.0 million stock repurchase program. In 2005, we authorized a $100.0 million stock repurchase program. We expect to make opportunistic repurchases of our common stock.

Working capital decreased from a surplus of $161.5 million as of December 31, 2004 to $74.1 million deficit as of December 31, 2005 primarily due to the purchase of the Golden Nugget Hotels and Casinos and repurchase of our common stock during 2005. Cash flow to fund future operations, new restaurant development, and acquisitions will be generated from operations, available capacity under the current Bank Credit Facility and additional financing, if appropriate.

In 2005, we spent $163.0 million to acquire GN and $118.5 million on capital expenditures including opening 13 new units and acquiring $23.7 million in land for future development. In 2006, we expect to spend approximately $180.0 million, including opening 12 units and spending $85.0 million in 2006 to renovate the Golden Nugget Hotel and Casino in downtown Las Vegas, Nevada followed by a casino expansion and new hotel tower in 2007.

As of December 31, 2005, we had contractual obligations as described below. These obligations are expected to be funded primarily through cash on hand, cash flow from operations, working capital, the Bank Credit Facility and additional financing sources in the normal course of business operations. Our obligations include off balance sheet arrangements whereby the liabilities associated with non cancelable operating leases, unconditional purchase obligations and standby letters of credit are not fully reflected in our balance sheets.

Contractual Obligations (in thousands)	2006	2007–2008	2009–2010	Thereafter
Long-Term Debt	$ 1,851,741	$ 3,645,025	$158,411,035	$555,000,000
Operating Leases	$ 47,758,691	$ 86,987,095	$ 71,510,862	$290,208,754
Unconditional Purchase Obligations	$ 73,222,438	$ 7,030,718	$ 2,231,015	$ 641,982
Other Long-Term Obligations	$ 4,185,413	$ 2,650,000	$ 18,000,000	$ —
Total Cash Obligations	$ 127,018,283	$ 100,312,838	$250,152,912	$845,850,736

Other Commercial Commitments (in thousands)	2006	2007–2008	2009–2010	Thereafter
Line of Credit	$ —	$ —	$ 96,000,000	$ —
Standby Letters of Credit	$ 12,592,451	$ —	$ —	$ —
Total Commercial Commitments	$ 12,592,451	$ —	$ 96,000,000	$ —

In connection with our purchase of an 80% interest in the restaurant concept T-Rex in February 2006, we have committed to spend an estimated $48.0 million during 2006, 2007 and 2008 to complete one T-Rex restaurant in Kansas City, Kansas, construct one T-Rex restaurant as well as an Asian themed restaurant in Walt Disney World's Florida theme parks and construct one additional T-Rex restaurant in the northeast.

From time to time, we review opportunities for restaurant acquisitions and investments in the hospitality, entertainment (including gaming), amusement, food service and facilities management and other industries. Our exercise of any such investment opportunity may impact our development plans and capital expenditures. We believe that adequate sources of capital are available to fund our business activities through December 31, 2006.

As a primary result of establishing long-term borrowings, we will incur higher interest expense in the future. However, we have mitigated a portion of the higher interest expense by entering into fair value hedges with a notional amount of $100.0 million, whereby we swapped higher fixed interest rates of the 7.5% senior notes due 2014 for floating interest rates equal to six month Libor plus a financing spread of 2.34% to 2.38%.

Since April 2000, we have paid an annual $0.10 per share dividend, declared and paid in quarterly amounts. We increased the annual dividend to $0.20 per share in April 2004.

Seasonality and Quarterly Results

Our business is seasonal in nature. Our reduced winter volumes cause revenues and, to a greater degree, operating profits to be lower in the first and fourth quarters than in other quarters. We have and continue to open restaurants in highly seasonal tourist markets. Joe's Crab Shack restaurants tend to experience even greater seasonality and sensitivity to weather than our other restaurant concepts. Periodically, our sales and profitability may be negatively affected by adverse weather. The timing of unit openings can and will affect quarterly results

Critical Accounting Policies

Restaurant and other properties are reviewed on a property by property basis for impairment whenever events or changes in circumstances indicate that the carrying amount of an asset may not be recovered. The recoverability of properties that are to be held and used is measured by comparison of the estimated future undiscounted cash flows associated with the asset to the carrying amount of the asset. Goodwill and other nonamortizing intangible assets are reviewed for impairment at least annually using estimates of future operating results. If such assets are considered to be impaired, an impairment charge is recorded in the amount by which the carrying amount of the assets exceeds their fair value. Properties to be disposed of are reported at the lower of their carrying amount or fair value, reduced for estimated disposal costs, and are included in other current assets.

We operate approximately 311 properties and periodically we expect to experience unanticipated individual unit deterioration in revenues and profitability, on a short-term and occasionally longer-term basis. When such events occur and we determine that the associated assets are impaired, we will record an asset impairment expense in the quarter such determination is made. Due to our average restaurant net investment cost, generally excluding the owned land component, of approximately $2.0 million, such amounts could be significant when and if they occur. However, such asset impairment expense does not affect our financial liquidity, and is usually excluded from many valuation model calculations.

We maintain a large deductible insurance policy related to property, general liability and workers' compensation coverage. Predetermined loss limits have been arranged with insurance companies to limit our per occurrence cash outlay. Accrued expenses and other liabilities include estimated costs to settle unpaid claims and estimated incurred but not reported claims using actuarial methodologies.

We account for income taxes in accordance with SFAS No. 109, "Accounting for Income Taxes". SFAS No. 109 requires the recognition of deferred tax assets, net of applicable reserves, related to net operating loss carryforwards and certain temporary differences. A valuation allowance is recognized if, based on the weight of available evidence, it is more likely than not that some portion or all of the deferred tax asset will not be recognized. We regularly assess the likelihood of realizing the deferred tax assets based on forecasts of future taxable income and available tax planning strategies that could be implemented and adjust the related valuation allowance if necessary.

Our income tax returns are subject to examination by the Internal Revenue Service and other tax authorities. We regularly assess the potential outcomes of these examinations in determining the adequacy of our provision for income taxes and our income tax liabilities. Inherent in our determination of any necessary reserves are assumptions based on past experiences and judgments about potential actions by taxing authorities. Our estimate of the potential outcome for any uncertain tax issue is highly judgmental. We believe that we have adequately provided for any reasonable and foreseeable outcome related to uncertain tax matters.

We follow the intrinsic value method of accounting for stock options, and as such do not record compensation expense related to amounts outstanding. Effective with the quarter ending March 31, 2006, we will expense compensation related to stock options in accordance with SFAS 123(R).

The preparation of financial statements in conformity with accounting principles generally accepted in the United States requires management to make estimates and assumptions that affect the amounts reported in the financial statements and accompanying notes. Estimates are used for, but not limited to, the recognition and measurement of current and deferred income tax assets and liabilities; the assessment of recoverability of long-lived assets; costs to settle unpaid claims and the valuation of inventory. Actual results may differ materially from those estimates and services.

Recent Accounting Pronouncements

In November 2004, the FASB issued Statement of Financial Accounting Standards (SFAS) No. 151, "Inventory Costs" which amended ARB 43. The statement clarifies that abnormal amounts of idle facility expense, freight, handling costs and wasted materials should be recognized as current period charges, effective for fiscal years beginning after June 15, 2005. Adoption of this standard is not expected to have a material impact on the Company's consolidated financial statements.

In December 2004, the FASB issued SFAS No. 153, "Exchange of Non-Monetary Assets." This statement amends APB 29 to require certain non-monetary exchange transactions to be recorded on a carry over cost basis if future cash flows are not expected to change significantly. The statement is effective for fiscal periods beginning after June 15, 2005. Adoption of SFAS No. 153 is not expected to have a material impact on the Company's consolidated financial statements.

In December 2004, the FASB issued SFAS No. 123R, "Share-Based Payments." This statement requires the expensing of stock options in the financial statements for periods no later than annual periods beginning after June 15, 2005. SFAS No. 123R requires companies to use either the modified-prospective or modified-retrospective

Management's Discussions

FINANCIAL CONDITION AND RESULTS OF OPERATIONS

transition method. The Company will implement the statement during the first quarter of 2006 using the modified-prospective transition method and we expect that the recognition requirements under SFAS No. 123 will be reasonably similar to the fair value results included in our pro forma disclosures assuming similar assumptions, stock prices and number of grants. Additional grants would increase compensation expense.

In March 2005, the SEC issued Staff Accounting Bulletin 107 (SAB 107) to simplify some of the implementation challenges of SFAS 123R. In particular, SAB 107 provides supplemental implementation guidance on SFAS 123R including guidance on valuation methods, classification of compensation expense, inventory capitalization of share-based compensation costs, income tax effects, disclosures in Management's Discussion and Analysis and several other issues. We will apply the principles of SAB 107 in conjunction with the adoption of SFAS 123R.

In May 2005, the FASB issued Statement of Financial Accounting Standards (SFAS) No. 154, "Accounting Changes and Error Corrections," which replaces Accounting Principles Board (APB) No. 20, "Accounting Changes," and Statement of Financial Accounting Standards No. 3, "Reporting Accounting Changes in Interim Financial Statements." SFAS 154 applies to all voluntary changes in accounting principle, and changes the requirements for accounting and reporting a change in accounting principles. SFAS 154 requires retroactive application to prior periods'

financial statements of a voluntary change in accounting principle unless it is impracticable to do so. APB 20 previously required that most voluntary changes in accounting principle be recognized with a cumulative effect adjustment in net income of the period of the change. SFAS 154 is effective for accounting changes made in annual periods beginning after December 15, 2005.

In October 2005, the FASB issued FASB Staff Position (FSP) 13-1 "Accounting for Rental Costs Incurred During a Construction Period." The FSP requires rental costs associated with both ground and building operating leases that are incurred during a construction period be expensed on a straight line basis starting from the beginning of the lease term. The statement is effective for periods beginning after December 15, 2005. Adoption of FSP 13-1 is not expected to have a material impact on the Company's consolidated financial statements.

Impact of Inflation

We do not believe that inflation has had a significant effect on our operations during the past several years. We believe we have historically been able to pass on increased costs through menu price increases, but there can be no assurance that we will be able to do so in the future. Future increases in labor costs, including expected future increases in federal minimum wages, energy costs, and land and construction costs could adversely affect our profitability and ability to expand.

Controls and Procedures

Conclusion Regarding the Effectiveness of Disclosure Controls and Procedures

We carried out an evaluation, with the participation of our principal executive officer and principal financial officer, of the effectiveness of our disclosure controls and procedures as of December 31, 2005. Based on this evaluation, our principal executive officer and principal financial officer concluded that, as of December 31, 2005, our disclosure controls and procedures, as defined in Rule 13a-15(e), were effective to ensure that information required to be disclosed by the issuer in the reports that it files or submits under the Securities Exchange Act of 1934 (the "Exchange Act") are recorded, processed, summarized and reported within the time periods specified in the Securities and Exchange Commission's rules and forms.

Management's Report on Internal Control Over Financial Reporting

Our management is responsible for establishing and maintaining adequate internal control over financial reporting, as defined in Exchange Act Rule 13a-15(f). Under the supervision and with the participation of management, including our principal executive officer and principal financial officer, we conducted an evaluation of the effectiveness of our internal control over financial reporting as of December 31, 2005 based on the framework in Internal Control–Integrated Framework issued by the Committee of Sponsoring Organizations of the Treadway Commission ("COSO"). Based on this evaluation, our management

concluded that our internal control over financial reporting was effective as of December 31, 2005.

Our evaluation did not include the internal control over financial reporting relating to Golden Nugget, Inc. (formerly Poster Financial Group, Inc.) which we acquired on September 27, 2005 (see Note 2 to the consolidated financial statements). Total assets and revenues for the acquisition represent approximately $388 million and $65 million, respectively, of the related consolidated financial statement amounts as of and for the year ended December 31, 2005.

Grant Thornton LLP, the independent registered public accounting firm that audited our consolidated financial statements included in this Annual Report on Form 10-K, has audited our management's assessment of the effectiveness of our internal control over financial reporting as of December 31, 2005, as stated in their report which is included herein.

Changes in Internal Control over Financial Reporting

Our management carried out an evaluation, with the participation of our principal executive officer and principal financial officer, of changes in our internal control over financial reporting, as defined in Exchange Act Rule 13a-15(f). Based on this evaluation, our management determined that no change in our internal control over financial reporting occurred during the fourth quarter of fiscal 2005 that has materially affected, or is reasonably likely to materially affect, our internal control over financial reporting.

Report of Independent Registered Public Accounting Firm

To the Board of Directors and Stockholders
Landry's Restaurants, Inc.

We have audited management's assessment, included in the accompanying Management's Report on Internal Control Over Financial Reporting, appearing under Item 9A, that Landry's Restaurants, Inc. and subsidiaries maintained effective internal control over financial reporting as of December 31, 2005, based on criteria established in Internal Control—Integrated Framework issued by the Committee of Sponsoring Organizations of the Treadway Commission (COSO). Landry's Restaurants, Inc. and subsidiaries' management is responsible for maintaining effective internal control over financial reporting and for its assessment of the effectiveness of internal control over financial reporting. Our responsibility is to express an opinion on management's assessment and an opinion on the effectiveness of the company's internal control over financial reporting based on our audit.

We conducted our audit in accordance with the standards of the Public Company Accounting Oversight Board (United States). Those standards require that we plan and perform the audit to obtain reasonable assurance about whether effective internal control over financial reporting was maintained in all material respects. Our audit included obtaining an understanding of internal control over financial reporting, evaluating management's assessment, testing and evaluating the design and operating effectiveness of internal control, and performing such other procedures as we considered necessary in the circumstances. We believe that our audit provides a reasonable basis for our opinions.

A company's internal control over financial reporting is a process designed to provide reasonable assurance regarding the reliability of financial reporting and the preparation of financial statements for external purposes in accordance with generally accepted accounting principles. A company's internal control over financial reporting includes those policies and procedures that (1) pertain to the maintenance of records that, in reasonable detail, accurately and fairly reflect the transactions and dispositions of the assets of the company; (2) provide reasonable assurance that transactions are recorded as necessary to permit preparation of financial statements in accordance with generally accepted accounting principles, and that receipts and expenditures of the company are being made only in accordance with authorizations of management and directors of the company; and (3) provide reasonable assurance regarding prevention or timely detection of unauthorized acquisition, use, or disposition of the company's assets that could have a material effect on the financial statements.

Because of its inherent limitations, internal control over financial reporting may not prevent or detect misstatements. Also, projections of any evaluation of effectiveness to future periods are subject to the risk that controls may become inadequate because of changes in conditions, or that the degree of compliance with the policies or procedures may deteriorate.

As described in Management's Report on Internal Control Over Financial Reporting, management excluded from its assessment of Landry's Restaurants, Inc. and subsidiaries' internal control over financial reporting as of December 31, 2005, the internal control over financial reporting related to Golden Nugget, Inc. (formerly Poster Financial Group, Inc.), which was acquired by the company during September 2005. Our audit of internal control over financial reporting of Landry's Restaurants, Inc. and subsidiaries also excluded Golden Nugget, Inc. Assets of approximately $388 million and total revenues of approximately $65 million of Golden Nugget, Inc. are included in the consolidated financial statements of Landry's Restaurants, Inc. and subsidiaries as of and for the year ended December 31, 2005.

In our opinion, management's assessment that Landry's Restaurants, Inc. and subsidiaries maintained effective internal control over financial reporting as of December 31, 2005, is fairly stated, in all material respects, based on criteria established in Internal Control—Integrated Framework issued by the Committee of Sponsoring Organizations of the Treadway Commission (COSO). Also, in our opinion, Landry's Restaurants, Inc. and subsidiaries maintained, in all material respects, effective internal control over financial reporting as of December 31, 2005, based on criteria established in Internal Control—Integrated Framework issued by the Committee of Sponsoring Organizations of the Treadway Commission (COSO).

We also have audited, in accordance with the standards of the Public Company Accounting Oversight Board (United States), the consolidated balance sheets of Landry's Restaurants, Inc. and subsidiaries as of December 31, 2005 and 2004, and the related consolidated statements of income, stockholders' equity, and cash flows for each of the years then ended, and our report dated March 9, 2006 expressed an unqualified opinion on those consolidated financial statements.

GRANT THORNTON LLP
Houston, Texas
March 9, 2006

Report of Independent Registered Public Accounting Firm

To the Board of Directors and Stockholders of Landry's Restaurants, Inc.

We have audited the accompanying consolidated balance sheets of Landry's Restaurants, Inc. and subsidiaries as of December 31, 2005 and 2004, and the related consolidated statements of income, stockholders' equity, and cash flows for the years then ended. These financial statements are the responsibility of the Company's management. Our responsibility is to express an opinion on these financial statements based on our audits.

We conducted our audits in accordance with the standards of the Public Company Accounting Oversight Board (United States). Those standards require that we plan and perform the audit to obtain reasonable assurance about whether the financial statements are free of material misstatement. An audit includes examining, on a test basis, evidence supporting the amounts and disclosures in the financial statements. An audit also includes assessing the accounting principles used and significant estimates made by management, as well as evaluating the overall financial statement presentation. We believe that our audits provide a reasonable basis for our opinion.

In our opinion, the consolidated financial statements referred to above present fairly, in all material respects, the financial position of Landry's Restaurants, Inc. and subsidiaries as of December 31, 2005 and 2004, and the results of their operations and their cash flows for the years then ended in conformity with accounting principles generally accepted in the United States of America.

We also have audited, in accordance with the standards of the Public Company Accounting Oversight Board (United States), the effectiveness of Landry's Restaurants, Inc. and subsidiaries' internal control over financial reporting as of December 31, 2005, based on criteria established in Internal Control—Integrated Framework issued by the Committee of Sponsoring Organizations of the Treadway Commission (COSO) and our report dated March 9, 2006, expressed an unqualified opinion on management's assessment of the effectiveness of internal control over financial reporting and an unqualified opinion on the effectiveness of internal control over financial reporting.

GRANT THORNTON LLP
Houston, Texas
March 9, 2006

Report of Independent Public Registered Public Accounting Firm

To Landry's Restaurants, Inc.:

We have audited the accompanying consolidated balance sheet of Landry's Restaurants, Inc. and subsidiaries as of December 31, 2003 and the related consolidated statements of income, stockholders' equity and cash flows for the year then ended. These financial statements are the responsibility of the Company's management. Our responsibility is to express an opinion on these financial statements based on our audit.

We conducted our audit in accordance with the standards of the Public Accounting Oversight Board (United States). Those standards require that we plan and perform the audit to obtain reasonable assurance about whether the financial statements are free of material misstatement. We were not engaged to perform an audit of the Company's internal control over financial reporting. Our audit included consideration of internal control over financial reporting as a basis for designing audit procedures that are appropriate in the circumstances, but not for the purpose of expressing an opinion on the effectiveness of the Company's internal control over financial reporting. Accordingly we express no such opinion. An audit includes examining, on a test basis, evidence supporting the amounts and disclosures in the financial statements. An audit also includes assessing the accounting principles used and significant estimates made by management, as well as evaluating the overall financial statement presentation. We believe that our audit provides a reasonable basis for our opinion.

In our opinion, the financial statements referred to above present fairly, in all material respects, the consolidated financial position of Landry's Restaurants, Inc., and subsidiaries at December 31, 2003 and the results of their operations and their cash flows for the year then ended, in conformity with U.S. generally accepted accounting principles.

ERNST & YOUNG LLP
Houston, Texas
February 11, 2004
except for Note 10 as to which the date is March 14, 2005

Landry's Restaurants, Inc.
CONSOLIDATED BALANCE SHEETS

December 31,	2005	2004
Assets		
Current assets:		
Cash and cash equivalents	$ 39,215,562	$ 201,394,032
Accounts receivable—trade and other, net	21,973,228	18,595,531
Inventories	59,716,920	55,004,153
Deferred taxes	12,763,948	10,859,160
Other current assets	12,768,611	11,630,527
Total current assets	146,438,269	297,483,403
Property and equipment, net	1,380,258,684	1,007,296,936
Goodwill and trademarks	46,716,151	20,225,297
Other intangible assets, net	3,459,417	216,806
Other assets, net	35,706,292	19,729,829
Total assets	$1,612,578,813	$1,344,952,271
Liabilities and stockholders' equity		
Current liabilities:		
Accounts payable	$ 90,489,190	$ 48,341,318
Accrued liabilities	123,098,491	84,955,488
Income taxes payable	5,060,885	971,175
Current portion of long-term notes and other obligations	1,851,741	1,700,496
Total current liabilities	220,500,307	135,968,477
Long-term notes, net of current portion	816,043,799	559,545,092
Deferred taxes	21,635,903	13,343,631
Other liabilities	37,628,343	35,198,105
Total liabilities	1,095,808,352	744,055,305
Commitments and contingencies		
Stockholders' equity:		
Common stock, $0.01 par value, 60,000,000 shares authorized,		
21,593,823 and 25,607,573 issued and outstanding, respectively	215,938	256,076
Additional paid-in capital	324,570,406	401,228,736
Deferred stock compensation	(6,392,177)	(4,281,670)
Retained earnings	198,376,294	203,693,824
Total stockholders' equity	516,770,461	600,896,966
Total liabilities and stockholders' equity	$1,612,578,813	$1,344,952,271

The accompanying notes are an integral part of these consolidated financial statements.

Landry's Restaurants, Inc.
CONSOLIDATED STATEMENTS OF INCOME

Year Ended December 31,	2005	2004	2003
Revenues	$1,254,805,671	$ 1,167,475,165	$1,105,755,057
Operating costs and expenses:			
Cost of revenues	333,027,693	326,108,007	321,783,377
Labor	377,215,289	337,633,530	323,284,399
Other operating expenses	311,647,878	282,411,954	271,270,870
General and administrative expenses	57,693,473	58,319,642	51,704,100
Depreciation and amortization	63,492,747	57,294,123	49,091,466
Asset impairment expense	—	1,708,654	13,144,365
Pre-opening expenses	4,772,425	5,203,518	8,650,178
Total operating costs and expenses	1,147,849,505	1,068,679,428	1,038,928,755
Operating income	106,956,166	98,795,737	66,826,302
Other expense (income):			
Interest expense, net	41,437,790	15,185,605	9,561,482
Other, net	95,196	13,543,626	1,462,450
	41,532,986	28,729,231	11,023,932
Income before income taxes	65,423,180	70,066,506	55,802,370
Provision for income taxes	20,608,144	3,544,778	10,888,517
Net income	$ 44,815,036	$ 66,521,728	$ 44,913,853
Earnings per share information:			
Basic			
Net income	$ 2.01	$ 2.46	$ 1.63
Weighted average number of common shares outstanding	22,300,000	27,000,000	27,600,000
Diluted			
Net income	$ 1.95	$ 2.39	$ 1.59
Weighted average number of common and common share equivalents outstanding	23,000,000	27,800,000	28,325,000

The accompanying notes are an integral part of these consolidated financial statements.

Landry's Restaurants, Inc.
CONSOLIDATED STATEMENTS OF STOCKHOLDERS' EQUITY

	Common Stock Shares	Common Stock Amount	Additional Paid-In Capital	Deferred Stock Compensation	Retained Earnings	Total
Balance, December 31, 2002	27,771,479	$ 277,715	$ 441,338,043	$ —	$ 121,790,044	$ 563,405,802
Net income	—	—	—	—	44,913,853	44,913,853
Dividends paid	—	—	—	—	(2,768,997)	(2,768,997)
Purchase of common stock held for treasury	(468,823)	(4,688)	(6,347,881)	—	(2,064,842)	(8,417,411)
Exercise of stock options and tax benefit	251,196	2,512	2,676,904	—	—	2,679,416
Issuance of restricted stock	100,000	1,000	1,949,000	(1,950,000)	—	—
Amortization of deferred compensation	—	—	—	81,250	—	81,250
Balance, December 31, 2003	27,653,852	276,539	439,616,066	(1,868,750)	161,870,058	599,893,913
Net income	—	—	—	—	66,521,728	66,521,728
Dividends paid	—	—	—	—	(4,783,404)	(4,783,404)
Purchase of common stock held for treasury	(2,291,800)	(22,918)	(42,843,341)	—	(19,914,558)	(62,780,817)
Exercise of stock options and tax benefit	145,521	1,455	1,612,011	—	—	1,613,466
Issuance of restricted stock	100,000	1,000	2,844,000	(2,845,000)	—	—
Amortization of deferred compensation	—	—	—	432,080	—	432,080
Balance, December 31, 2004	25,607,573	256,076	401,228,736	(4,281,670)	203,693,824	600,896,966
Net income	—	—	—	—	44,815,036	44,815,036
Dividends paid	—	—	—	—	(4,611,364)	(4,611,364)
Purchase of common stock held for treasury	(4,823,986)	(48,240)	(88,209,338)	—	(45,521,202)	(133,778,780)
Exercise of stock options and tax benefit	710,236	7,102	8,752,008	—	—	8,759,110
Issuance of restricted stock	100,000	1,000	2,799,000	(2,800,000)	—	—
Amortization of deferred compensation	—	—	—	689,493	—	689,493
Balance, December 31, 2005	21,593,823	$215,938	$ 324,570,406	$ (6,392,177)	$ 198,376,294	$ 516,770,461

The accompanying notes are an integral part of these consolidated financial statements.

Landry's Restaurants, Inc.
CONSOLIDATED STATEMENTS OF CASH FLOWS

Year Ended December 31,	2005	2004	2003
Cash flows from operating activities:			
Net income	$ 44,815,036	$ 66,521,728	$ 44,913,853
Adjustments to reconcile net income to net cash provided by operating activities:			
Depreciation and amortization	63,492,747	57,294,123	49,091,466
Asset impairment expense	—	1,708,654	13,144,365
Deferred tax provision (benefit)	9,698,299	(3,937,176)	10,621,027
Deferred rent and other charges (income), net	528,291	3,151,551	987,648
Financing prepayment expenses	—	16,649,009	—
Changes in assets and liabilities, net of acquisitions:			
(Increase) decrease in trade and other receivables	2,136,302	5,834,208	(3,342,672)
(Increase) decrease in inventories	(1,862,207)	(7,231,855)	(6,651,658)
(Increase) decrease in other assets	434,688	(4,377,660)	4,425,932
Increase (decrease) in accounts payable and accrued liabilities	31,812,862	(23,999,700)	10,745,609
Total adjustments	106,240,982	45,091,154	79,021,717
Net cash provided by operating activities	151,056,018	111,612,882	123,935,570
Cash flows from investing activities:			
Property and equipment additions and other	(118,487,055)	(110,670,371)	(163,376,622)
Proceeds from disposition of property and equipment	4,049,764	6,095,733	—
Business acquisitions, net of cash acquired	(135,487,498)	(12,930,565)	(27,035,893)
Net cash used in investing activities	(249,924,789)	(117,505,203)	(190,412,515)
Cash flows from financing activities:			
Purchases of common stock for treasury	(125,651,865)	(62,780,817)	(8,417,411)
Proceeds from exercise of stock options	451,775	1,349,771	1,826,816
(Payments) borrowings of debt and related expenses, net	(19,010,143)	(176,313,705)	(1,906,503)
Proceeds (payments) on credit facility, net	85,511,898	(122,000,000)	(49,000,000)
Financing proceeds, net	—	536,603,189	148,076,160
Dividends paid	(4,611,364)	(4,783,404)	(2,768,997)
Net cash (used in) provided by financing activities	(63,309,699)	172,075,034	87,810,065
Net increase (decrease) in cash and equivalents	(162,178,470)	166,182,713	21,333,120
Cash and cash equivalents at beginning of year	201,394,032	35,211,319	13,878,199
Cash and cash equivalents at end of year	$ 39,215,562	$ 201,394,032	$ 35,211,319
Supplemental disclosures of Cash flow information:			
Cash paid during the year for:			
Interest	$ 45,297,362	$ 15,988,418	$ 8,675,327
Income taxes	$ 4,838,396	$ 9,949,203	$ 5,698,821

The accompanying notes are an integral part of these consolidated financial statements.

Landry's Restaurants, Inc.
NOTES TO CONSOLIDATED FINANCIAL STATEMENTS

1. Nature Of Business and Summary of Significant Accounting Policies

Nature of Business

Landry's Restaurants, Inc. is a national, diversified restaurant, hospitality and entertainment company principally engaged in the ownership and operation of full service, casual dining restaurants, primarily under the names Landry's Seafood House, Joe's Crab Shack, The Crab House, Charley's Crab, The Chart House and Saltgrass Steak House. In addition, we own and operate domestic and license international rainforest themed restaurants under the trade name Rainforest Cafe.

On September 27, 2005, Landry's Gaming Inc., an unrestricted subsidiary of Landry's Restaurants, Inc., completed the acquisition of Golden Nugget, Inc. (GN, formerly Poster Financial Group, Inc.), owner of the Golden Nugget Hotels and Casinos in downtown Las Vegas and Laughlin, Nevada as further described in Note 2.

Principles of Consolidation

The accompanying financial statements include the consolidated accounts of Landry's Restaurants, Inc., a Delaware holding company and its wholly and majority owned subsidiaries and partnership.

Revenue Recognition

Restaurant and hospitality revenues are recognized when the goods and services are delivered. Casino revenue is the aggregate net difference between gaming wins and losses, with liabilities recognized for funds deposited by customers before gaming play occurs ("casino front money") and for chips in the customers possession ("outstanding chip liability"). Revenues are recognized net of certain sales incentives as well as accruals for the cost of points earned in point-loyalty programs. The retail value of accommodations, food and beverage, and other services furnished to hotel-casino guests without charge is deducted from revenue as promotional allowances. Proceeds from the sale of gift cards are deferred and recognized as revenue when redeemed by the holder.

Accounts Receivable

Accounts receivable is comprised primarily of amounts due from our credit card processor, receivables from national storage and distribution companies and at December 31, 2005, casino and hotel receivables. The receivables from national storage and distribution companies arise when certain of our inventory items are conveyed to these companies at cost (including freight and holding charges but without any general overhead costs). These conveyance transactions do not impact the consolidated statements of income as there is no profit recognition and no revenue or expenses are recognized in the financial statements since they are without economic substance other than drayage. We reacquire these items, although not obligated to, when subsequently delivered to the restaurants at cost plus the distribution company's contractual mark-up. Accounts receivable are reduced to reflect estimated fair values by an allowance for doubtful accounts based on historical collection experience and specific review of individual accounts. Receivables are written off when they are deemed to be uncollectible. Also included in accounts receivable is income tax receivables of $1.1 million and $4.6 million in 2005 and 2004, respectively.

Inventories

Inventories consist primarily of food and beverages used in restaurant operations and complementary retail goods and are recorded at the lower of cost or market value as determined by the average cost for food and beverages and by the retail method on the first-in, first-out basis for retail goods.

Inventories consist of the following:

December 31,	2005	2004
Food and beverage	$ 43,004,866	$ 41,676,925
Retail goods	16,712,054	13,327,228
	$ 59,716,920	$ 55,004,153

Property and Equipment

Property and equipment are recorded at cost. Expenditures for major renewals and betterments are capitalized while maintenance and repairs are expensed as incurred.

We compute depreciation using the straight-line method. The estimated lives used in computing depreciation are generally as follows: buildings and improvements—5 to 40 years; furniture, fixtures and equipment—5 to 15 years; and leasehold improvements—shorter of 40 years or lease term, including extensions where such are reasonably assured of renewal.

Leasehold improvements are depreciated over the shorter of the estimated life of the asset or the lease term plus option periods where failure to renew results in economic penalty. Any contributions made by landlords or tenant allowances with economic value are recorded as a long-term liability and amortized as a reduction to rent expense over the life of the lease plus option periods where failure to renew results in economic penalty.

Interest is capitalized in connection with restaurant construction and development activities, and other real estate development projects. The capitalized interest is recorded as part of the asset to which it relates and is amortized over the asset's estimated useful life. During 2005, 2004 and 2003, we capitalized interest expense of approximately $1.6 million, $1.2 million and $2.1 million, respectively.

Our properties are reviewed for impairment on a property by property basis whenever events or changes in circumstances indicate that the carrying amount of an asset may not be recovered. The recoverability of properties that are to be held and used is measured by comparison of the estimated future undiscounted cash flows associated with the asset to the carrying amount of the asset. If such assets are considered to be impaired, an impairment charge is recorded in the amount by which the carrying amount of the assets exceeds their fair value. Properties to be disposed of are reported at the lower of their carrying amount or fair value, reduced for estimated disposal costs, and are included in other current assets.

Pre-Opening Costs

Pre-opening costs are expensed as incurred and include the direct and incremental costs incurred in connection with the commencement of each restaurant's operations, which are substantially comprised of training-related costs.

Development Costs

Certain direct costs are capitalized in conjunction with site selection for planned future restaurants, acquiring restaurant

Landry's Restaurants, Inc.
NOTES TO CONSOLIDATED FINANCIAL STATEMENTS

properties and other real estate development projects. Direct and certain related indirect costs of the construction department, including rent and interest, are capitalized in conjunction with construction and development projects. These costs are included in property and equipment in the accompanying consolidated balance sheets and are amortized over the life of the related building and leasehold interest. Costs related to abandoned site selections, projects, and general site selection costs which cannot be identified with specific restaurants are expensed.

Advertising

Advertising costs are expensed as incurred during such year. Advertising expenses were $33.5 million, $29.6 million and $33.6 million in 2005, 2004 and 2003, respectively.

Goodwill and Other Intangible Assets

Goodwill and trademarks are not amortized, but instead tested for impairment at least annually. Other intangible assets are amortized over their expected useful life or the life of the related agreement.

Insurance

We maintain large deductible insurance policies related to property, general liability and workers' compensation coverage. Predetermined loss limits have been arranged with insurance companies to limit our per occurrence cash outlay. Accrued liabilities include the estimated costs to settle unpaid claims and estimated incurred but not reported claims using actuarial methodologies.

Financial Instruments

The fair values of cash and cash equivalents, accounts receivable, accounts payable and accrued liabilities approximate the carrying amounts due to their short maturities. The fair value of our fixed rate long-term debt instruments are estimated based on quoted market prices, where available, or on the amount of future cash flows associated with each instrument, discounted using our current borrowing rate for comparable debt instruments. The estimated fair values of our long-term debt, including the current portions, are as follows:

December 31,	2005		2004	
	Carrying Value	Fair Value	Carrying Value	Fair Value
7.5% Senior Notes due December 2014	$ 400,000,000	$ 376,000,000	$ 400,000,000	$ 400,000,000
8.75% senior secured notes due December 2011	159,081,197	161,393,750	—	—
7.0% Seller note due November 2010	4,000,000	4,000,000	—	—
9.39% non-recourse note payable due May 2010	11,007,078	11,294,720	11,171,760	11,294,921
	$ 574,088,275	$ 552,688,470	$ 411,171,760	$ 411,294,921

Deferred Rent

Rent expense under operating leases is calculated using the straight-line method whereby an equal amount of rent expense is attributed to each period during the term of the lease, regardless of when actual payments are made. The lease term begins on the date we are obligated under the lease and includes option periods where failure to renew results in economic penalty. Generally, this results in rent expense in excess of cash payments during the early years of a lease and rent expense less than cash payments in the later years. The difference between rent expense recognized and actual rental payments is recorded as deferred rent and included in other long term liabilities.

We utilize interest rate swap agreements to manage our exposure to interest rate risk. Our interest rate swap agreements qualify as fair value hedges and are recorded at fair value. As such, the gains or losses on the swaps are offset by corresponding gains or losses on the related debt.

Earnings Per Share and Stock Option Accounting

Basic earnings per share is computed by dividing net income by the weighted average number of shares of common stock outstanding during the year. Diluted earnings per share reflects the potential dilution that could occur if contracts to issue common stock were exercised or converted into common stock. For purposes of this calculation, outstanding stock options and restricted stock grants are considered common stock equivalents using the treasury stock method, and are the only such equivalents outstanding.

A reconciliation of the amounts used to compute earnings per share is as follows:

Year Ended December 31,	2005	2004	2003
Net Income	$ 44,815,036	$ 66,521,728	$ 44,913,853
Weighted average common shares outstanding—basic	22,300,000	27,000,000	27,600,000
Dilutive common stock equivalents:			
Stock options	685,000	800,000	725,000
Restricted stock	15,000	—	—
Weighted average common and common share equivalents outstanding—diluted	23,000,000	27,800,000	28,325,000
Net income per share—basic	$ 2.01	$ 2.46	$ 1.63
Net income per share—diluted	$ 1.95	$ 2.39	$ 1.59

Landry's Restaurants, Inc.
NOTES TO CONSOLIDATED FINANCIAL STATEMENTS

We follow the intrinsic value method of accounting for stock options, and as such do not record compensation expense related to grants where the exercise price is at or above our share price on the date of grant.

The table below illustrates the effect on net income and earnings per share if compensation costs had been determined using the fair value method prescribed by SFAS No. 123.

Year Ended December 31,	2005	2004	2003
Net income, as reported	$ 44,815,036	$ 66,521,728	$ 44,913,853
Less: stock based compensation expense using			
fair value method, net of related tax effects	(1,625,000)	(1,200,000)	(2,100,000)
Pro forma net income	$ 43,190,036	$ 65,321,728	$ 42,813,853
Earnings per share			
Basic, as reported	$ 2.01	$ 2.46	$ 1.63
Basic, pro forma	$ 1.94	$ 2.42	$ 1.55
Diluted, as reported	$ 1.95	$ 2.39	$ 1.59
Diluted, pro forma	$ 1.88	$ 2.35	$ 1.51

The fair value of each option grant in 2004 was estimated on the date of grant using the Black-Scholes option-pricing model with the following weighted average assumptions: expected lives of 6 years, expected stock price volatility of approximately 40%, dividend yield of 0.7% and a risk-free interest rate of approximately 3.9%. The weighted average fair value per share of options granted during 2004 was $11.83. There were no stock options granted during 2005 and only 16,000 options were granted in 2003 which were not deemed material for the above calculations.

Cash Equivalents

We consider investments with a maturity of three months or less when purchased to be cash equivalents.

Use of Estimates

The preparation of financial statements in conformity with accounting principles generally accepted in the United States requires management to make estimates and assumptions that affect the reported amounts of assets and liabilities and disclosures of contingent assets and liabilities at the date of the financial statements and the reported amounts of revenues and expenses during the reporting period. Actual results may differ from those estimates and services.

Recent Accounting Pronouncements

In November 2004, the FASB issued Statement of Financial Accounting Standards (SFAS) No. 151, "Inventory Costs" which amended ARB 43. The statement clarifies that abnormal amounts of idle facility expense, freight, handling costs and wasted materials should be recognized as current period charges, effective for fiscal years beginning after June 15, 2005. Adoption of this standard is not expected to have a material impact on our consolidated financial statements.

In December 2004, the FASB issued SFAS No. 153, "Exchange of Non-Monetary Assets." This statement amends APB 29 to require certain non-monetary exchange transactions to be recorded on a carry over cost basis if future cash flows are not expected to change significantly. The statement is effective for fiscal periods beginning after June 15, 2005. Adoption of SFAS No. 153 is not expected to have a material impact on the Company's consolidated financial statements.

In December 2004, the FASB issued SFAS No. 123R, "Share-Based Payments." This statement requires the expensing of stock options in the financial statements for periods no later than annual periods beginning after June 15, 2005. SFAS No. 123R requires companies to use either the modified-prospective or modified-retrospective transition method. We will implement the statement during the first quarter of 2006 using the modified-prospective transition method and we expect that the recognition requirements under SFAS No. 123 will be reasonably similar to the fair value results included in our pro forma disclosures assuming similar assumptions, stock prices and number of grants. Additional grants would increase compensation expense.

In March 2005, the SEC issued Staff Accounting Bulletin 107 (SAB 107) to simplify some of the implementation challenges of SFAS 123R. In particular, SAB 107 provides supplemental implementation guidance on SFAS 123R including guidance on valuation methods, classification of compensation expense, inventory capitalization of share-based compensation costs, income tax effects, disclosures in Management's Discussion and Analysis and several other issues. We will apply the principles of SAB 107 in conjunction with the adoption of SFAS 123R.

In May 2005, the FASB issued Statement of Financial Accounting Standards (SFAS) No. 154, "Accounting Changes and Error Corrections," which replaces Accounting Principles Board (APB) No. 20, "Accounting Changes," and Statement of Financial Accounting Standards No. 3, "Reporting Accounting Changes in Interim Financial Statements." SFAS 154 applies to all voluntary changes in accounting principle, and changes the requirements for accounting and reporting a change in accounting principles. FAS 154 requires retroactive application to prior periods' financial statements of a voluntary change in accounting principle unless it is impracticable to do so. APB 20 previously required that most voluntary changes in accounting principle be recognized with a cumulative effect adjustment in net income of the period of the change. FAS 154 is effective for accounting changes made in annual periods beginning after December 15, 2005.

In October 2005, the FASB issued FASB Staff Position (FSP) 13-1 "Accounting for Rental Costs Incurred During a Construction Period." The FSP requires rental costs

Landry's Restaurants, Inc.
NOTES TO CONSOLIDATED FINANCIAL STATEMENTS

associated with both ground and building operating leases that are incurred during a construction period be expensed on a straight line basis starting from the beginning of the lease term. The statement is effective for periods beginning after December 15, 2005. Adoption of FSP 13-1 is not expected to have a material impact on the Company's consolidated financial statements.

2. Acquisitions

On September 27, 2005, we completed the acquisition of 100 percent of the capital stock of GN, owner of the Golden Nugget Hotels and Casinos in downtown Las Vegas and Laughlin, Nevada, for approximately $163.0 million in cash, the assumption of $155.0 million of 8.75% Senior Secured Notes due 2011 and $27.0 million under an existing Senior Revolving Credit facility and the further assumption of certain working capital, including $27.5 million in cash. The results of GN's operations have been included in our consolidated financial statements since the acquisition date. The assets acquired and liabilities assumed are included in the accompanying balance sheet as of December 31, 2005 at estimated fair values as determined by third party appraisals and management estimates based on currently available information and preliminary plans for future operations. The allocation of purchase price is preliminary and is subject to revision based on the final determination of fair values. A summary of the assets acquired and liabilities assumed in the acquisition follows:

Current assets	$ 42,597,414
Property and equipment	319,770,221
Intangible assets	29,620,000
Other long-term assets	11,156,347
Total assets acquired	403,143,982
Current liabilities	(54,239,750)
Long-term debt	(185,904,232)
Total liabilities assumed or created	(240,143,982)
Net assets acquired	163,000,000
Less: Cash acquired	(27,512,502)
Net cash paid	$ 135,487,498

Acquired intangible assets include $26.2 million assigned to the trademark "Golden Nugget," which has been in use for more than 50 years and is one of the most recognizable names in the casino industry. Also included is $3.4 million assigned to customer lists underlying the slot player clubs at each of the casinos. There was no goodwill recorded in connection with the transaction.

As a result of the acquisition, we have recorded direct acquisition costs for the estimated incremental costs to rationalize activities at the two locations and for associated employee contract terminations and severance costs. Accounting principles generally accepted in the United States, provide that these direct acquisition expenses, which are not associated with the generation of future revenues and have no future economic benefit, be reflected as assumed liabilities in the allocation of the purchase price. The acquisition liabilities included in the purchase price allocation aggregate approximately $4.9 million.

The following unaudited pro forma financial information presents the consolidated results of operations as if the acquisition occurred on January 1, 2005, after including certain pro forma adjustments for interest expense, depreciation and amortization, and income taxes.

Year Ended December 31,	2005	2004
Revenue	$1,441,586,485	$1,424,936,787
Net income	$ 43,588,282	$ 62,186,411
Basic earnings per share	$ 1.95	$ 2.30
Diluted earnings per share	$ 1.90	$ 2.24

The pro forma financial information is not necessarily indicative of the combined results of operations had the transaction occurred on January 1, 2005 or the results of operations that may be obtained in the future.

During 2003, we made several individual property acquisitions that aggregated $27.0 million, plus $11.4 million of assumed debt, and included $5.1 million in goodwill.

3. Property and Equipment and Other Assets

Property and equipment is comprised of the following:

December 31,	2005	2004
Land	$ 304,029,054	$ 178,365,122
Buildings and improvements	476,878,646	272,152,965
Furniture, fixtures and equipment	334,459,193	273,446,996
Leasehold improvements	563,172,902	545,402,565
Construction in progress	33,975,852	16,209,718
	1,712,515,647	1,285,577,366
Less—accumulated depreciation	(332,256,963)	(278,280,430)
Property and equipment, net	$1,380,258,684	$1,007,296,936

We continually evaluate unfavorable cash flows, if any, related to underperforming restaurants. Periodically it is concluded that certain properties have become impaired based on the existing and anticipated future economic outlook for such properties in their respective market areas. We recorded asset impairment depreciation charges of approximately $1.7 million and $13.1 million in 2004 and 2003, respectively, representing the difference between the estimated fair value and carrying value for those restaurant properties. The impairment in 2004 related to one under performing unit and the 2003 impairment related to six underperforming and three closed restaurants.

These impairment charges resulted from sales declines, deterioration in the specific restaurant's profitability, perceived continued deterioration of the market area and/or specific location, and management's lowered outlook for further opportunity and/or improvement in forecasted sales and profitability trends for such specific property. Assets that were impaired are primarily leasehold improvements and to a lesser extent equipment. The following is a summary of related charges:

Year Ended December 31,	2005	2004	2003
Asset Impairment	$ —	$1,700,000	$13,100,000
Accrued Estimated Lease Termination Payments	$ —	$ —	$ 1,300,000
	$ —	$1,700,000	$14,400,000

We consider the asset impairment expense as additional depreciation and amortization, although shown as a separate line item in the Consolidated Statements of Income. Estimated fair values of impaired properties are based on comparable valuations, cash flows and management judgement.

Other current assets are comprised of the following:

December 31,	2005	2004
Prepaid expenses	$ 5,847,792	$ 4,673,319
Assets held for sale (expected to be sold within one year)	$ 2,941,507	$ 5,390,648
Deposits	$ 3,979,312	$ 1,566,560
	$12,768,611	$11,630,527

Other expense (income) for 2005 is not material. Other expense (income) for 2004 is primarily make whole payments and related fees aggregating $14.6 million associated with the pre-payment of our $150.0 million in senior notes and Former Bank Credit Facility offset by $1.1 million in business interruption recoveries related to storm damage. Other expense (income) for 2003 is primarily expenses related to abandoned development projects.

4. Accrued Liabilities

Accrued liabilities are comprised of the following:

	2005	2004
Payroll and related costs	$ 27,174,355	$ 16,468,491
Rent and insurance	30,112,058	25,753,353
Taxes, other than payroll and income taxes	22,250,385	19,064,713
Deferred revenue (gift cards and certificates)	15,308,080	12,751,757
Accrued interest	2,805,847	507,532
Casino deposits, outstanding chips and other gaming	9,851,072	–
Other	15,596,694	10,409,642
	$123,098,491	$ 84,955,488

5. Debt

In connection with the acquisition of GN, one of our unrestricted subsidiaries assumed $155.0 million in 8.75% senior secured notes due December 2011 with a fair value of $159.3 million. The notes pay interest on a semi-annual basis in June and December. The notes are guaranteed, jointly and severally, by all of GN's current and future restricted subsidiaries on a senior secured basis. The notes are collateralized by a pledge of capital stock of GN's future restricted subsidiaries and a security interest in substantially all of GN's and the guarantors' current and future assets that is junior to the security interest granted to the lenders under GN's senior revolving credit facility. We are filing the results of operations of GN in a separate report on Form 10-K in order to comply with the reporting requirements set forth in the indenture governing these notes.

Also, as a result of the acquisition of GN, we assumed $27.0 million in debt under a $43.0 million bank senior secured revolving credit facility. The revolving credit facility bears interest at Libor or at bank's base rate plus a financing spread, 2.0% for Libor and 1.0% for base rate borrowings at December 31, 2005 and matures in January 2009. The financing spread and commitment fee increase or decrease based on a financial leverage ratio as defined in the credit agreement. As of December 31, 2005, $2.5 million in letters of credit were outstanding with $18.5 million of available borrowing capacity.

The GN debt agreements contain various restrictive covenants including minimum EBITDA, fixed charge and financial leverage ratios, limitations on capital expenditures, and other restricted payments as defined in the agreements. As of December 31, 2005, GN was in compliance with all such covenants. In December 2004, we entered into a $450.0 million "Bank Credit Facility" and "Term Loan" consisting of a $300.0 million revolving credit facility and a $150.0 million term loan. The revolving credit facility matures in December 2009 and bears interest at Libor or the bank's base rate plus a financing spread, 1.50% for Libor and 0.50% for base rate borrowings at December 31, 2005. In addition, the revolving credit facility requires a commitment fee on the unfunded portion. The financing spread and commitment fee increases or decreases based on a financial leverage ratio as defined in the credit agreement. The term loan matures in December 2010 and, at December 31, 2005, bears interest at Libor plus 1.75% or the bank's base rate plus 0.75%. Quarterly principal payments of $375,000 are due through December 2009 with the remaining balance payable in equal quarterly installments of $35,625,000 in 2010. We and certain of our guarantor subsidiaries granted liens on substantially all real and personal property as security under the Bank Credit Facility and Term Loan. As of December 31, 2005 our average interest rate or floating-rate debt was 6.3%, we had approximately $10.1 million in letters of credit outstanding and available borrowing capacity of $215.9 million.

Concurrently, we issued $400.0 million in 7.5% senior notes through a private placement which are due in December 2014. The notes are general unsecured obligations and require semi-annual interest payments in June and December. On June 16, 2005, we completed an exchange offering whereby substantially all of the senior notes issued under the private placement were exchanged for senior notes registered under the Securities Act of 1933.

Net proceeds from the $450.0 million Bank Credit Facility and Term Loan and $400 million in 7.5% senior notes totaled $536.6 million and were used to repay all outstanding liabilities under the Former Bank Credit Facility and $150 million in senior notes. These debt repayments resulted in a pre-tax charge of $16.6 million in the fourth quarter of 2004.

In connection with the 7.5% senior notes, we entered into two interest swap agreements with the objective of managing our exposure to interest rate risk and lowering interest expense. The first agreement was effective December 28, 2004, maturing in December 2014, for a notional amount of $50.0 million and interest at Libor plus 2.38%. The second agreement was effective March 10, 2005, also maturing December 2014, for a notional amount of $50.0 million and interest at Libor plus 2.34%. Our interest rate swap agreements qualify as fair value hedges and meet the criteria for the "short cut method" under SFAS No. 133, "Accounting for Derivative Instruments and Hedging Activities." The aggregate estimated fair value of these swaps at December 31, 2005 was a liability of $1.1 million, which is included in other liabilities with an offsetting adjustment to the carrying value of the debt on our consolidated balance sheet.

Our debt agreements contain various restrictive covenants including minimum fixed charge, net worth, and financial leverage ratios as well as limitations on dividend payments, capital expenditures and other restricted payments as defined in the agreements. At December 31, 2005, we were in compliance with all such covenants.

We assumed an $11.4 million, 9.39% non-recourse, long-term mortgage note payable, due May 2010, in connection with an asset purchase in March 2003. Principal and interest payments aggregate $102,000 monthly.

Principal payments for all long-term debt aggregate $1,852,000 in 2006, $1,883,000 in 2007, $1,762,000 in 2008, $97,740,000 in 2009, $156,671,000 in 2010 and $555,000,000 thereafter.

Landry's Restaurants, Inc.
NOTES TO CONSOLIDATED FINANCIAL STATEMENTS

Long-term debt is comprised of the following:

December 31,	2005	2004
$300.0 million Bank Syndicate Credit Facility, Libor + 1.50% interest only, due December 2009	$ 74,000,000	$ —
$150.0 million Term loan facility, Libor + 1.75%, interest paid quarterly, $375,000 principal paid quarterly, due December 2010	148,500,000	150,000,000
$400.0 million Senior Notes, 7.5% interest only, due December 2014	400,000,000	400,000,000
Non-recourse long-term note payable, 9.39% interest, principal and interest aggregate $101,762 monthly, due May 2010	11,007,078	11,171,760
Other long-term notes payable with various interest rates, principal and interest paid monthly	399,004	163,057
$155.0 million GN senior secured notes, 8.75% interest only, due December 2011	159,081,197	—
$43.0 million GN senior secured revolving credit facility, Libor + 2.0%, interest only, due January 2009	22,001,719	—
$4.0 million seller note, 7.0%, interest paid monthly, due November 2010	4,000,000	—
Interest rate swap	(1,093,458)	(89,229)
Total debt	817,895,540	561,245,588
Less current portion	(1,851,741)	(1,700,496)
Long-term portion	$ 816,043,799	$ 559,545,092

6. Stockholders' Equity

In connection with our stock buy back programs, we repurchased into treasury approximately 4,824,000, 2,292,000, and 469,000 shares of common stock for approximately $133.8 million, $62.8 million and $8.4 million in 2005, 2004 and 2003, respectively. Cumulative repurchases as of December 31, 2005 were 17.6 million shares at a cost of approximately $290.5 million

Commencing in 2000, we began to pay an annual $0.10 per share dividend, declared and paid in quarterly installments of $0.025 per share. In April 2004, this was increased to $0.20 per share, paid in quarterly installments of $0.05 per share.

We maintain two stock option plans, which were originally adopted in 1993, (the Stock Option Plans), as amended, pursuant to which options may be granted to our eligible employees and non-employee directors for the purchase of an aggregate of 2,750,000 shares of our common stock. The Stock Option Plans are administered by the Compensation Committee of the Board of Directors (the Committee), which determines at its discretion, the number of shares subject to each option granted and the related purchase price, vesting and option periods. The Committee may grant either non-qualified stock options or incentive stock options, as defined by the Internal Revenue Code of 1986, as amended.

We also maintain the 1995 Flexible Incentive Plan, which was adopted in 1995, (Flex Plan), as amended, for our key employees. Under the Flex Plan eligible employees may receive stock options, stock appreciation rights, restricted stock, performance awards, performance stock and other awards, as defined by the Board of Directors or the Compensation Committee. The aggregate number of shares of common stock which may be issued under the Flex Plan (or with respect to which awards may be granted) may not exceed 2,000,000 shares.

In March 2003, we established the 2002 Employee/ Rainforest Conversion Plan pursuant to which stock options may be granted to employees, non-employee directors and consultants for up to an aggregate of 2,162,500 shares of common stock. The Compensation Committee of the Board of Directors determines the number of shares, prices and vesting schedule of individual grants.

In June 2003, we established an Equity Incentive Plan pursuant to which stock options or restricted stock may be granted to eligible employees for an aggregate of 700,000 shares. The Compensation Committee of the Board of Directors determines the number of shares, prices, and vesting schedule of individual grants. In addition, we will issue pursuant to an employment agreement, over its five year term, 500,000 shares of restricted stock, with a 10 year vest from grant date, and a minimum of 800,000 stock options. In August 2004, 100,000 restricted common shares were issued subject to vesting on the tenth anniversary. In February 2005, an additional 100,000 restricted common shares were issued with similar vesting terms. In February 2006, an additional 100,000 restricted common shares were also issued with similar vesting terms. The unamortized balance of non-vested restricted common stock grants is reflected as deferred compensation included in stockholders' equity and the related expense is amortized over the vesting periods.

In connection with the acquisition of Rainforest Cafe, we issued approximately 500,000 vested stock options to employees of Rainforest Cafe as replacement for existing options outstanding at the date of the merger. The fair value of these options was included in the purchase price of Rainforest Cafe.

At December 31, 2005, options for 1,897,252 shares were outstanding at prices ranging from $6.00 to $27.50 per share. As of December 31, 2005, all options have been granted at the stock price on the grant date and are generally exercisable beginning one year from the date of grant with annual vesting periods over three to five years.

The following table provides certain information with respect to stock options outstanding as of December 31:

	2005		2004		2003	
	Shares	Average Exercise Price	Shares	Average Exercise Price	Shares	Average Exercise Price
Options outstanding beginning of year	2,638,323	$ 15.12	2,410,874	$ 11.97	2,694,470	$ 11.57
Granted	–	–	501,500	$ 27.50	16,000	$ 20.26
Exercised	(710,236)	$ 12.11	(169,851)	$ 10.30	(251,196)	$ 7.28
Terminated	(30,835)	$ 16.29	(104,200)	$ 11.69	(48,400)	$ 14.36
Options outstanding end of year	1,897,252	$ 16.22	2,638,323	$ 15.12	2,410,874	$ 11.97
Options exercisable end of year	1,356,852	$ 13.44	1,843,114	$ 12.04	1,902,274	$ 11.82

The following table provides certain information with respect to stock options outstanding as of December 31, 2005:

Range of Exercise Price	Stock Options Outstanding	Weighted Average Exercise Price	Weighted Average Remaining Life Outstanding
< $9.00	688,682	$ 7.73	4.5
$9.00–$13.50	164,996	$ 13.53	1.7
$13.51–$20.25	519,949	$ 17.19	6.6
> $20.25	523,625	$ 27.26	8.3
	1,897,252	$ 16.22	5.9

7. Income Taxes

An analysis of the provision for income taxes for the years ended December 31, 2005, 2004, and 2003 is as follows:

Year Ended December 31,	2005	2004	2003
Tax provision:			
Current income taxes	$10,909,845	$7,481,954	$ 267,490
Deferred income taxes	$ 9,698,299	(3,937,176)	10,621,027
Total provision	$20,608,144	$3,544,778	$10,888,517

Our effective tax rate, for the years ended December 31, 2005, 2004, and 2003, differs from the federal statutory rate as follows:

	2005	2004	2003
Statutory rate	35.0%	35.0%	35.0%
FICA tax credit	(9.8)	(8.2)	(9.3)
State income tax, net of federal tax benefit	4.5	2.5	3.7
Recognition of tax carryforward assets and other tax attributes	(0.8)	(26.4)	(11.3)
Other	2.6	2.2	1.4
	31.5%	5.1%	19.5%

Deferred income tax assets and liabilities as of December 31 are comprised of the following:

	2005	2004
Deferred Income Taxes:		
Current assets– accruals and other	$ 12,764,000	$ 10,859,000
Non-current assets:		
AMT credit, FICA credit carryforwards, and other	$ 32,870,000	$ 32,488,000
Net operating loss carryforwards	27,777,000	28,317,000
Deferred rent and unfavorable leases	8,123,000	8,543,000
Valuation allowance for NOL and credit carryforwards	(8,713,000)	(7,220,000)
Non-current deferred tax asset	60,057,000	62,128,000
Non-current liabilities– property and other	(81,693,000)	(75,471,000)
Net non-current tax asset (liability)	$ (21,636,000)	$(13,343,000)
Total net deferred tax asset (liability)	$ (8,872,000)	$ (2,484,000)

At December 31, 2005 and 2004, we had operating loss carryovers for Federal Income Tax purposes of $75.2 million and $76.3 million, respectively, which expire in 2018 through 2025. These operating loss carryovers, credits, and certain other deductible temporary differences, are related to the acquisitions of Rainforest Cafe and Saltgrass Steak House, and their utilization is subject to Section 382 limits. Because of these limitations, we established a valuation allowance against a portion of these deferred tax assets to the extent it was more likely than not that these tax benefits will not be realized. In 2005 and 2004, there was a reduction of the valuation allowance and deferred tax liabilities aggregating $1.1 million and $18.5 million, respectively. The valuation allowance and certain deferred tax liabilities were reduced for the following reasons: NOL utilizations; the strength of the 2004 earnings; our future forecasted taxable income profitability; the completion of a successful integration of Rainforest Cafe from a stand-alone loss entity to a profitable wholly-owned subsidiary of the Company; the approaching end-specific recognition limitations (i.e. built-in-loss limitations) on allowable deductions; and the closing of audits with favorable results. Management believes that the combination of the above factors indicates that a portion of the deferred tax assets previously reserved will more likely than not be realized.

The 2005 state rate increased over prior year due to certain state income tax filing positions. This increase in the state rate was partially offset by a reduction in our overall state effective tax rate realized primarily due to the acquisition of GN in Nevada, a jurisdiction with no income tax. We are currently being audited by several states with regard to state income and franchise tax for periods prior to 2005.

At December 31, 2005 and 2004, we have general business tax credit carryovers and minimum tax credit carryovers of $28.0 million and $31.0 million, respectively. The general business carryover includes $1.5 million from Saltgrass Steak House, which is fully reserved. The general business credit carryovers expire in 2012 through 2025, while the minimum tax credit carryovers have no expiration date. The use of these credits is limited if we are subject to the alternative minimum tax. We believe it is more likely than not that we will generate sufficient income in future years to utilize the non-reserved credits.

The Internal Revenue Service (IRS) has examined our Federal Income Tax Returns and certain pre-acquisition returns for Rainforest Cafe for years 1997 through 2001. In 2004, these examinations were completed and closed without adjustment. The IRS has examined the Federal Income Tax Return of a 2001 pre-acquisition return

Landry's Restaurants, Inc.
NOTES TO CONSOLIDATED FINANCIAL STATEMENTS

for Saltgrass Steak House. The examination has been completed and closed with no material adjustment.

8. Commitments and Contingencies
Lease Commitments

We have entered into lease commitments for restaurant facilities as well as certain fixtures, equipment and leasehold improvements. Under most of the facility lease agreements, we pays taxes, insurance and maintenance costs in addition to the rent payments. Certain facility leases also provide for additional contingent rentals based on a percentage of sales in excess of a minimum amount. Rental expense under operating leases was approximately $57.5 million, $56.4 million and $55.2 million, during the years ended December 31, 2005, 2004, and 2003, respectively. Percentage rent included in rent expense was $13.8 million, $13.6 million, and $12.3 million, for 2005, 2004 and 2003, respectively.

In 2004, we entered into an aggregate $25.5 million equipment operating lease agreement replacing two existing agreements and including additional equipment. The lease expires in 2014. We guarantee a minimum residual value related to the equipment of approximately 66% of the total amount funded under the agreement. We may purchase the leased equipment throughout the lease term for an amount equal to the unamortized lease balance. We believe that the equipment's fair value is sufficient such that no amounts will be due under the residual value guarantee.

In connection with substantially all of the Rainforest Cafe leases, amounts are provided for unfavorable leases, rent abatements, and scheduled increases in rent. Such amounts are recorded as other long-term liabilities in our consolidated balance sheets, and amortized or accrued as an adjustment to rent expense, included in other restaurant operating expenses, on a straight-line basis over the lease term, including options where failure to exercise such options would result in economic penalty.

The aggregate amounts of minimum operating lease commitments maturing in each of the five years and thereafter subsequent to December 31, 2005 are as follows:

2006	$ 47,758,691
2007	46,172,751
2008	40,814,345
2009	37,320,509
2010	34,190,353
Thereafter	290,208,754
Total minimum rentals	$ 496,465,403

Building Commitments

As of December 31, 2005, we had future development, land purchases and construction commitments expected to be expended within the next twelve months of approximately $21.6 million, including completion of construction of certain new restaurants. In addition, we have committed $4.9 million through 2006 for the renovation of the Tower of the Americas in San Antonio, Texas which we will operate for at least the next 15 years.

In connection with our purchase of an 80% interest in the restaurant concept T-Rex in February 2006, we have committed to spend an estimated $48.0 million during 2006, 2007 and 2008 to complete one T-Rex restaurant in Kansas City, Kansas, construct one T-Rex restaurant as well as an Asian themed restaurant in Walt Disney World Florida theme parks and construct an additional T-Rex restaurant in the northeast.

In 2003, we purchased the Flagship Hotel and Pier from the City of Galveston, Texas, subject to an existing lease. Under this agreement, we have committed to spend an additional $15.0 million to transform the hotel and pier into a 19th century style Inn and entertainment complex complete with rides and carnival type games. The property is currently occupied by a tenant and renovations are not expected to begin until 2009.

During November 2003, we purchased two casual Italian restaurants. Under the purchase agreement, we are committed to building an additional four casual Italian restaurants by the end of 2008, or make certain payments in lieu of development. In conjunction with the agreement to develop additional restaurants, the seller agrees to provide consulting services to ensure the consistency and the quality of the food and service are maintained through this expansion period.

Employee Benefits and Other

We sponsor qualified defined contribution retirement plans (401(k) Plan) covering eligible salaried employees. The 401(k) Plans allow eligible employees to contribute, subject to Internal Revenue Service limitations on total annual contributions, up to 100% of their base compensation as defined in the 401(k) Plans, to various investment funds. We match in cash at a discretionary rate which totalled $.3 million in 2005. Employee contributions vest immediately while our contributions vest 20% annually beginning in the participant's second year of eligibility for restaurant and hospitality employees and in the participant's first year of eligibility for casino employees.

We also initiated non-qualified defined contribution retirement plans (the "Plans") covering certain management employees. The Plans allow eligible employees to defer receipt of their base compensation and of their eligible bonuses, as defined in the Plans. We match in cash at a discretionary rate which totalled $.3 million in 2005. Employee contributions vest immediately while our contributions vest 20% annually. We established a Rabbi Trust to fund the Plan's obligation for the restaurant and hospitality employees. The market value of the trust assets is included in other assets, and the liability to the Plans' participants is included in other liabilities.

Our casino employees at the Golden Nugget in Las Vegas, Nevada that are members of various unions are covered by union-sponsored, collective bargained, multi-employer health and welfare and defined benefit pension plans. We recorded an expense of $2.2 million for our obligation to these plans since the September 27, 2005 acquisition date of GN (Note 2). The plans' sponsors have not provided sufficient information to permit us to determine its share of unfunded vested benefits, if any. However, based on available information, we do not believe that unfunded amounts attributable to our casino operations are material.

We are self-insured for most health care benefits for our non-union casino employees. The liability for claims filed and estimates of claims incurred but not reported is included in "accrued liabilities" in the accompanying consolidated balance sheet as of December 31, 2005.

In connection with the Galveston Convention Center Management Contract, we agreed to fund operating losses, if any, subject to certain rights of reimbursement. Under the agreements, we have the right to one-half of any profits generated by the operation of the Convention Center.

Litigation and Claims

On February 18, 2005, and subsequently amended, a purported class action lawsuit against Rainforest Cafe, Inc. was filed in the Superior Court of California in San Bernardino by Michael D. Harrison, et. al. Subsequently, on September 20, 2005, another purported class action lawsuit against Rainforest Cafe, Inc. was filed in the Superior Court of California in Los Angeles by Dustin Steele, et. al. On January 26, 2006, both lawsuits were consolidated into one action by the state Superior Court in San Bernardino. The lawsuits allege that Rainforest Cafe violated wage and hour laws, including not providing meal and rest breaks, uniform violations and failure to pay overtime. The Plaintiffs seek to recover damages, including unpaid wages, reimbursement for uniform expenses and penalties imposed by state law. The Company denies Plaintiff's claims and intends to vigorously defend this matter.

We are subject to legal proceedings and claims that arise in the ordinary course of business. Management does not believe that the outcome of any of these matters will have a material adverse effect on our financial position, results of operations or cash flows.

9. Segment Information

Our operating segments are aggregated into reportable business segments based primarily on the similarity of their economic characteristics, products, services, and delivery methods. Following the acquisition of the Golden Nugget Hotels and Casinos on September 27, 2005 (Note 2), it was determined that we operate two reportable business segments as follows:

Restaurant and Hospitality

Our restaurants operate primarily under the names of Joe's Crab Shack, Rainforest Cafe, Saltgrass Steak House, Landry's Seafood House, The Crab House, Charley's Crab and The Chart House. As of December 31, 2005, we owned and operated 311 full-service and limited-service restaurants in 35 states and were the second largest full-service seafood restaurant operator in the United States. We are also engaged in the ownership and operation of select hospitality and entertainment businesses that complement our restaurant operations and provide our customers with unique dining, leisure and entertainment experiences.

Gaming

We operate the Golden Nugget Hotels and Casinos in Las Vegas and Laughlin, Nevada. These locations emphasize the creation of the best possible gaming and entertainment experience for their customers by providing a combination of comfortable and attractive surroundings. This is accomplished through luxury rooms and amenities coupled with competitive gaming tables and superior player rewards programs.

The accounting policies of the segments are the same as described in Note 1. We evaluate segment performance based on unit level profit, which excludes general and administrative expense, depreciation expense, net interest expense and other non-operating income or expense. Financial information by reportable business segment is as follows:

	2005	2004	2003
Revenue:			
Restaurant and Hospitality	$ 1,189,164,944	$ 1,167,475,165	$ 1,105,755,057
Gaming	65,640,727	–	–
Consolidated revenue	$ 1,254,805,671	$ 1,167,475,165	$ 1,105,755,057
Unit level profit:			
Restaurant and Hospitality	$ 221,099,886	$ 221,321,674	$ 189,416,411
Gaming	11,814,925	–	–
Total unit level profit	$ 232,914,811	$ 221,321,674	$ 189,416,411
Depreciation, amortization and impairment:			
Restaurant and Hospitality	$ 60,737,897	$ 59,002,777	$ 62,235,831
Gaming	2,754,850	–	–
	$ 63,492,747	$ 59,002,777	$ 62,235,831
Segment assets:			
Restaurant and Hospitality	$ 1,018,786,122	$ 977,299,092	$ 939,427,297
Gaming	399,255,216	–	–
Corporate and other (1)	194,537,475	367,653,179	165,456,188
	$ 1,612,578,813	$1,344,952,271	$1,104,883,485
Capital expenditures:			
Restaurant and Hospitality	85,033,748	105,331,189	140,837,348
Gaming	11,391,309	–	–
Corporate and other	22,061,998	5,339,182	22,539,274
	118,487,055	110,670,371	163,376,622
Income before taxes:			
Unit level profit	$ 232,914,811	$ 221,321,674	$ 189,416,411
Depreciation, amortization and impairment	63,492,747	59,002,777	62,235,831
General and administrative	62,465,898	63,523,160	60,354,278
Interest expense, net	41,437,790	15,185,605	9,561,482
Other expenses (income)	95,196	13,543,626	1,462,450
Consolidated income before taxes	$ 65,423,180	$ 70,066,506	$ 55,802,370

(1) Includes intersegment eliminations

Condensed Consolidating Financial Statements

BALANCE SHEET DECEMBER 31, 2005

10. Supplemental Guarantor Information

In December 2004, we issued, in a private offering, $400.0 million of 7.5% senior notes due in 2014 (see "Debt"). In June 2005, substantially all of these notes were exchanged for substantially identical notes in an exchange offer registered under the Securities Act of 1933. These notes are fully and unconditionally guaranteed by us and certain of our subsidiaries, "Guarantor Subsidiaries."

The following condensed consolidating financial statements present separately the financial position, results of operations and cash flows of our Guarantor Subsidiaries and Non-guarantor Subsidiaries on a combined basis with eliminating entries.

	Parent	Guarantor	Non-guarantor Subsidiaries	Eliminations	Consolidated Equity
Assets					
Current assets:					
Cash and cash equivalents	$ 3,655,367	$ 10,372,914	$ 25,187,281	$ —	$ 39,215,562
Accounts receivable—trade and other, net	7,339,839	9,334,310	5,299,079	—	21,973,228
Inventories	38,668,993	17,346,920	3,701,007	—	59,716,920
Deferred taxes	12,763,948	—	—	—	12,763,948
Other current assets	1,384,892	3,704,169	7,679,550	—	12,768,611
Total current assets	63,813,039	40,758,313	41,866,917	—	146,438,269
Property and equipment, net	74,902,018	902,795,708	402,560,958	—	1,380,258,684
Goodwill and trademarks	1,968,604	18,527,547	26,220,000	—	46,716,151
Investment in and advances to subsidiaries	1,077,872,314	(515,463,662)	(236,587,317)	(325,821,335)	—
Other intangible assets, net	—	148,195	3,311,222	—	3,459,417
Other assets, net	22,274,045	1,963,384	11,468,863	—	35,706,292
Total assets	$ 1,240,830,020	$ 448,729,485	$ 248,840,643	$ (325,821,335)	$ 1,612,578,813
Liabilities and stockholders' equity					
Current liabilities:					
Accounts payable	$ 48,264,012	$ 31,848,310	$ 10,376,868	$ —	$ 90,489,190
Accrued liabilities	15,240,460	74,142,174	33,715,857	—	123,098,491
Income taxes payable	3,294,035	—	1,766,850	—	5,060,885
Current portion of long-term notes and other obligation	1,538,930	—	312,811	—	1,851,741
Total current liabilities	68,337,437	105,990,484	46,172,386	—	220,500,307
Long-term notes, net of current portion	619,994,855	—	196,048,944	—	816,043,799
Deferred taxes	21,635,903	—	—	—	21,635,903
Other liabilities	14,091,364	21,858,169	1,678,810	—	37,628,343
Total liabilities	724,059,559	127,848,653	243,900,140	—	1,095,808,352
Commitments and contingencies:					
Total stockholders' equity	516,770,461	320,880,832	4,940,503	(325,821,335)	516,770,461
Total liabilities and stockholders' equity	$ 1,240,830,020	$ 448,729,485	$ 248,840,643	$ (325,821,335)	$ 1,612,578,813

Condensed Consolidating Financial Statements

BALANCE SHEET DECEMBER 31, 2004

	Parent	Guarantor	Non-guarantor Subsidiaries	Eliminations	Consolidated Equity
Assets					
Current assets:					
Cash and cash equivalents	$ 192,679,301	$ 5,923,478	$ 2,791,253	$ —	$ 201,394,032
Accounts receivable—trade and other, net	10,256,627	8,114,520	224,384	—	18,595,531
Inventories	37,824,160	16,878,980	301,013	—	55,004,153
Deferred taxes	10,859,160	—	—	—	10,859,160
Other current assets	2,855,754	3,329,122	5,445,651	—	11,630,527
Total current assets	254,475,002	34,246,100	8,762,301	—	297,483,403
Property and equipment, net	73,767,370	887,811,651	45,717,915	—	1,007,296,936
Goodwill and trademarks	1,697,750	18,527,547	—	—	20,225,297
Investment in and advances to subsidiaries	864,745,965	(610,127,864)	(40,284,199)	(214,333,902)	—
Other intangible assets, net	—	216,806	—	—	216,806
Other assets, net	17,538,832	2,190,997	—	—	19,729,829
Total assets	$1,212,224,919	$ 332,865,237	$ 14,196,017	$ (214,333,902)	$ 1,344,952,271
Liabilities and stockholders' equity					
Current liabilities:					
Accounts payable	$ 23,160,088	$ 24,544,797	$ 636,433	$ —	$ 48,341,318
Accrued liabilities	12,925,743	70,441,426	1,588,319	—	84,955,488
Income taxes payable	971,175	—	—	—	971,175
Current portion of long-term notes and other obligation	1,535,814	—	164,682	—	1,700,496
Total current liabilities	38,592,820	94,986,223	2,389,434	—	135,968,477
Long-term notes, net of current portion	548,538,015	—	11,007,077	—	559,545,092
Deferred taxes	13,343,631	—	—	—	13,343,631
Other liabilities	10,853,487	24,344,618	—	—	35,198,105
Total liabilities	611,327,953	119,330,841	13,396,511	—	744,055,305
Commitments and contingencies:					
Total stockholders' equity	600,896,966	213,534,396	799,506	(214,333,902)	600,896,966
Total liabilities and stockholders' equity	$1,212,224,919	$ 332,865,237	$ 14,196,017	$(214,333,90 2)	$ 1,344,952,271

Condensed Consolidating Financial Statements

INCOME STATEMENT FOR THE YEAR ENDED DECEMBER 31, 2005

	Parent	Guarantor	Non-guarantor Subsidiaries	Eliminations	Consolidated Equity
Revenues	$ 4,703,194	$ 1,155,158,002	$ 94,944,475	$ —	$ 1,254,805,671
Operating costs and Expenses:					
Cost of revenues	—	322,306,751	10,720,942	—	333,027,693
Labor	—	340,091,882	37,123,407	—	377,215,289
Other operating expenses	2,875,014	277,459,378	31,313,486	—	311,647,878
General and administrative expenses	57,693,473	—	—	—	57,693,473
Depreciation and amortization	3,224,100	56,532,940	3,735,707	—	63,492,747
Asset impairment expense	—	—	—	—	—
Pre-opening expenses	—	4,089,683	682,742	—	4,772,425
Total operating costs and expenses	63,792,587	1,000,480,634	83,576,284	—	1,147,849,505
Operating income	(59,089,393)	154,677,368	11,368,191	—	106,956,166
Other expenses (income):					
Interest expense, net	36,568,825	—	4,868,965	—	41,437,790
Other, net	58,421	124,135	(87,360)	—	95,196
	36,627,246	124,135	4,781,605	—	41,532,986
Income (loss) before income taxes	(95,716,639)	154,553,233	6,586,586	—	65,423,180
Provision (benefit) for income taxes	(29,044,243)	47,880,392	1,771,995	—	20,608,144
Equity in earnings of subsidiaries	111,487,432	—	—	(111,487,432)	—
Net income	$ 44,815,036	$ 106,672,841	$ 4,814,591	$ (111,487,432)	$ 44,815,036

Condensed Consolidating Financial Statements
INCOME STATEMENT FOR THE YEAR ENDED DECEMBER 31, 2004

	Parent	Guarantor	Non-guarantor Subsidiaries	Eliminations	Consolidated Equity
Revenues	$ 3,548,026	$ 1,143,113,243	$ 20,813,896	$ —	$ 1,167,475,165
Operating costs and Expenses:					
Cost of revenues	—	321,120,939	4,987,068	—	326,108,007
Labor	—	331,204,729	6,428,801	—	337,633,530
Other operating expenses	2,218,765	272,634,068	7,559,121	—	282,411,954
General and administrative expenses	58,319,642	—	—	—	58,319,642
Depreciation and amortization	3,162,150	53,635,891	496,082	—	57,294,123
Asset impairment expense	—	1,708,654	—	—	1,708,654
Pre-opening expenses	—	5,203,518	—	—	5,203,518
Total operating costs and expenses	63,700,557	985,507,799	19,471,072	—	1,068,679,428
Operating income	(60,152,531)	157,605,444	1,342,824	—	98,795,737
Other expenses (income):					
Interest expense, net	14,144,556	—	1,041,049	—	15,185,605
Other, net	13,527,432	16,480	(286)	—	13,543,626
	27,671,988	16,480	1,040,763	—	28,729,231
Income (loss) before income taxes	(87,824,519)	157,588,964	302,061	—	70,066,506
Provision (benefit) for income taxes	(4,442,929)	7,972,426	15,281	—	3,544,778
Equity in earnings of subsidiaries	149,903,318	—	—	(149,903,318)	—
Net income	$ 66,521,728	$ 149,616,538	$ 286,780	$ (149,903,318)	$ 66,521,728

Condensed Consolidating Financial Statements

INCOME STATEMENT FOR THE YEAR ENDED DECEMBER 31, 2003

	Parent	Guarantor	Non-guarantor Subsidiaries	Eliminations	Consolidated Equity
Revenues	$ 2,020,909	$1,081,136,281	$ 22,597,867	$ —	$1,105,755,057
Operating costs and Expenses:					
Cost of revenues	—	316,138,033	5,645,344	—	321,783,377
Labor	—	316,564,648	6,719,751	—	323,284,399
Other operating expenses	(132,347)	263,645,309	7,757,908	—	271,270,870
General and administrative expenses	51,704,100	—	—	—	51,704,100
Depreciation and amortization	3,485,665	44,630,494	975,307	—	49,091,466
Asset impairment expense	—	13,144,365	—	—	13,144,365
Pre-opening expenses	—	8,650,178	—	—	8,650,178
Total operating costs and expenses	55,057,418	962,773,027	21,098,310	—	1,038,928,755
Operating income	(53,036,509)	118,363,254	1,499,557	—	66,826,302
Other expenses (income):					
Interest expense, net	8,693,222	(756)	869,016	—	9,561,482
Other, net	1,328,757	128,755	4,938	—	1,462,450
	10,021,979	127,999	873,954	—	11,023,932
Income (loss) before income taxes	(63,058,488)	118,235,255	625,603	—	55,802,370
Provision (benefit) for income taxes	(12,289,351)	23,055,875	121,993	—	10,888,517
Equity in earnings of subsidiaries	95,682,990	—	—	(95,682,990)	—
Net income	$ 44,913,853	$ 95,179,380	$ 503,610	$ (95,682,990)	$ 44,913,853

Condensed Consolidating Financial Statements

STATEMENT OF CASH FLOWS YEAR ENDED DECEMBER 31, 2005

	Parent	Guarantor	Non-guarantor Subsidiaries	Eliminations	Consolidated Equity
Cash flows from operating activities:					
Net income	$ 44,815,036	$ 106,672,841	$ 4,814,591	$ (111,487,432)	$ 44,815,036
Adjustments to reconcile net income to net cash provided by operating activities:					
Depreciation and amortization	3,224,100	56,532,940	3,735,707	—	63,492,747
Asset impairment expense	—	—	—	—	—
Deferred tax provision (benefit)	9,698,299	—	—	—	9,698,299
Deferred rent and other charges (income)	2,935,245	(2,620,941)	213,987	—	528,291
Changes in assets and liabilities, net and other, net of acquisitions	(183,144,942)	(84,699,317)	188,878,472	111,487,432	32,521,645
Total adjustments	(167,287,298)	(30,787,318)	192,828,166	111,487,432	106,240,982
Net cash provided by (used in) operating activities	(122,472,262)	75,885,523	197,642,757	—	151,056,018
Cash flows from Investing activities:					
Property and equipment additions and/or transfers	(8,759,223)	(73,436,087)	(36,291,745)	—	(118,487,055)
Proceeds from disposition of property and equipment	364,466	2,000,000	1,685,298	—	4,049,764
Business acquisitions, net of cash acquired	—	—	(135,487,498)	—	(135,487,498)
Net cash used in investing activities	(8,394,757)	(71,436,087)	(170,093,945)	—	(249,924,789)
Cash flows from financing activities:					
Purchase of common stock	(125,651,865)	—	—	—	(125,651,865)
Proceeds from exercise of stock options	451,775	—	—	—	451,775
Payments on other debt and related expenses, net	(2,345,461)	—	(16,664,682)	—	(19,010,143)
Proceeds from credit facility, net	74,000,000	—	11,511,898	—	85,511,898
Dividends paid	(4,611,364)	—	—	—	(4,611,364)
Net cash used in financing activities	(58,156,915)	—	(5,152,784)	—	(63,309,699)
Net increase (decrease) in cash and cash equivalents	(189,023,934)	4,449,436	22,396,028	—	(162,178,470)
Cash and cash equivalents at beginning of year	192,679,301	5,923,478	2,791,253	—	201,394,032
Cash and cash equivalents at end of year	$ 3,655,367	$ 10,372,914	$ 25,187,281	$ —	$ 39,215,562

Condensed Consolidating Financial Statements
STATEMENT OF CASH FLOWS YEAR ENDED DECEMBER 31, 2004

	Parent	Guarantor	Non-guarantor Subsidiaries	Eliminations	Consolidated Equity
Cash flows from operating activities:					
Net income	$ 66,521,728	$ 149,616,538	$ 286,780	$ (149,903,318)	$ 66,521,728
Adjustments to reconcile net income to net cash provided by operating activities:					
Depreciation and amortization	3,162,151	53,635,890	496,082	–	57,294,123
Asset impairment expense	–	1,708,654	–	–	1,708,654
Deferred tax provision (benefit)	(3,937,176)	–	–	–	(3,937,176)
Deferred rent and other charges (income), net	1,540,225	1,611,326	–	–	3,151,551
Financing prepayment expenses	16,649,009	–	–	–	16,649,009
Change in assets and liabilities, net and other, net of acquisitions	(137,439,971)	(65,754,095)	23,515,741	149,903,318	(29,775,007)
Total adjustments	(120,025,762)	(8,798,225)	24,011,823	149,903,318	45,091,154
Net cash provided by (used in) operating activities	(53,504,034)	140,818,313	24,298,603	–	111,612,882
Cash flows from Investing activities:					
Property and equipment additions and/or transfers	52,291,808	(141,495,080)	(21,467,099)	–	(110,670,371)
Proceeds from disposition of property and equipment	3,925,733	2,170,000	–	–	6,095,733
Business acquisitions, net of cash acquired	(12,930,565)	–	–	–	(12,930,565)
Net cash (used in) investing activities	43,286,976	(139,325,080)	(21,467,099)	–	(117,505,203)
Cash flows from financing activities:					
Purchase of common stock for treasury	(62,780,817)	–	–	–	(62,780,817)
Proceeds from exercise of stock options	1,349,771	–	–	–	1,349,771
Payments of debt and related expenses, net	(176,149,022)	–	(164,683)	–	(176,313,705)
Proceeds from credit facility, net	(122,000,000)	–	–	–	(122,000,000)
Financing proceeds, net	536,603,189	–	–	–	536,603,189
Dividends paid	(4,783,404)	–	–	–	(4,783,404)
Net cash used in financing activities	172,239,717	–	(164,683)	–	172,075,034
Net increase (decrease) in cash and cash equivalents	162,022,659	1,493,233	2,666,821	–	166,182,713
Cash and cash equivalents at beginning of year	30,656,642	4,430,245	124,432	–	35,211,319
Cash and cash equivalents at end of year	$ 192,679,301	$ 5,923,478	$ 2,791,253	$ –	$ 201,394,032

Condensed Consolidating Financial Statements
STATEMENT OF CASH FLOWS YEAR ENDED DECEMBER 31, 2003

	Parent	Guarantor	Non-guarantor Subsidiaries	Eliminations	Consolidated Equity
Cash flows from operating activities:					
Net income	$ 44,913,853	$ 95,179,380	$ 503,610	$ (95,682,990)	$ 44,913,853
Adjustments to reconcile net income to net cash provided by operating activities:					
Depreciation and amortization	3,485,665	44,630,494	975,307	—	49,091,466
Asset impairment expense	—	13,144,365	—	—	13,144,365
Deferred tax provision (benefit)	10,621,027	—	—	—	10,621,027
Deferred rent and other charges (income), net	1,776,991	(789,343)	—	—	987,648
Change in assets and liabilities, net and other, net of acquisitions	(121,070,081)	19,725,523	10,838,779	95,682,990	5,177,211
Total adjustments	(105,186,398)	76,711,039	11,814,086	95,682,990	79,021,717
Net cash provided by (used in) operating activities	(60,272,545)	171,890,419	12,317,696	—	123,935,570
Cash flows from Investing activities:					
Property and equipment additions and/or transfers	15,641,256	(166,818,219)	(12,199,659)	—	(163,376,622)
Proceeds from disposition of property and equipment	—	—	—	—	—
Business acquisitions, net of cash acquired	(27,035,893)	—	—	—	(27,035,893)
Net cash (used) in investing activities	(11,394,637)	(166,818,219)	(12,199,659)	—	(190,412,515)
Cash flows from financing activities:					
Purchase of common stock for treasury	(8,417,411)	—	—	—	(8,417,411)
Proceeds from exercise of stock options	1,826,816	—	—	—	1,826,816
Payments of debt and related expenses, net	(1,806,595)	—	(99,908)	—	(1,906,503)
Payments on credit facility, net	(49,000,000)	—	—	—	(49,000,000)
Financing proceeds, net	148,076,160	—	—	—	148,076,160
Dividends paid	(2,768,997)	—	—	—	(2,768,997)
Net cash used in financing activities	87,909,973	—	(99,908)	—	87,810,065
Net increase (decrease) in cash and cash equivalents	16,242,791	5,072,200	18,129	—	21,333,120
Cash and cash equivalents at beginning of year	14,413,851	(641,955)	106,303	—	13,878,199
Cash and cash equivalents at end of year	$ 30,656,642	$ 4,430,245	$ 124,432	$ —	$ 35,211,319

Landry's Restaurants, Inc.

NOTES TO CONSOLIDATED FINANCIAL STATEMENTS

11. Certain Transactions

In 1996, we entered into a Consulting Service Agreement (the "Agreement") with Fertitta Hospitality, LLC ("Fertitta Hospitality"), which is jointly owned by the Chairman and Chief Executive Officer of the Company and his wife. Pursuant to the Agreement, the Company provided to Fertitta Hospitality management and administrative services. Under the Agreement, the Company received a fee of $2,500 per month plus the reimbursement of all out-of-pocket expenses and such additional compensation as agreed upon. In 2003, a new agreement was signed ("Management Agreement"). Pursuant to the Management Agreement, the Company receives a monthly fee of $7,500, plus reimbursement of expenses. The Management Agreement provides for a renewable three-year term.

In 1999, we entered into a ground lease with 610 Loop Venture, LLC, a company wholly owned by the Chairman and Chief Executive Officer of the Company, on land owned by the Company adjacent to the Company's corporate headquarters. Under the terms of the ground lease, 610 Loop Venture pays the Company base rent of $12,000 per month plus pro-rata real property taxes and insurance. 610 Loop Venture also has the option to purchase certain property based upon a contractual agreement. In 2004, the ground lease was extended for a 5 year term.

In 2002, the Company entered into an $8,000 per month, 20 year, with option renewals, ground lease agreement with Fertitta Hospitality for a new Rainforest Cafe on prime waterfront land in Galveston, Texas. The annual rent is equal to the greater of the base rent or percentage rent up to six percent, plus taxes and insurance. In 2005 and 2004, the Company paid base and percentage rent aggregating $507,000 and $514,000, respectively.

As permitted by the employment contract between the Company and the Chief Executive Officer, charitable contributions were made by the Company to a charitable Foundation that the Chief Executive Officer served as Trustee in the amount of $135,000, $146,000 and $170,000 in 2005, 2004 and 2003, respectively. The contributions were made in addition to the normal salary and bonus permitted under the employment contract.

The Company, on a routine basis, holds or hosts promotional events, training seminars and conferences for its personnel. In connection therewith, the Company incurred in 2005, 2004 and 2003 expenses in the amount of $279,000, $68,000 and $138,000, respectively, at resort hotel properties owned by the Company's Chief Executive Officer and managed by the Company.

The Company and Fertitta Hospitality jointly sponsored events and promotional activities in 2005, 2004 and 2003 which resulted in shared costs and use of Company personnel or Fertitta Hospitality employees and assets.

The foregoing agreements were entered into between related parties and were not the result of arm's-length negotiations. Accordingly, the terms of the transactions may have been more or less favorable to the Company than might have been obtained from unaffiliated third parties.

12. Quarterly Financial Data (Unaudited)

The following is a summary of unaudited quarterly consolidated results of operations (in thousands, except per share data):

	March 31, 2005	June 30, 2005	September 30, 2005	December 31, 2005
Quarter Ended:				
Revenues	$ 281,345	$ 325,152	$ 319,511	$ 328,798
Cost of revenues	$ 78,584	$ 89,915	$ 86,604	$ 77,924
Operating income	$ 19,871	$ 34,414	$ 32,698	$ 19,973
Net income	$ 7,378	$ 17,543	$ 15,978	$ 3,917
Net income per share (basic)	$ 0.30	$ 0.80	$ 0.75	$ 0.18
Net income per share (diluted)	$ 0.29	$ 0.78	$ 0.73	$ 0.18

	March 31, 2004	June 30, 2004	September 30, 2004	December 31, 2004
Quarter Ended:				
Revenues	$ 275,676	$ 317,616	$ 314,378	$ 259,805
Cost of revenues	$ 77,720	$ 89,109	$ 86,747	$ 72,533
Operating income	$ 19,326	$ 34,108	$ 32,686	$ 12,676
Net income	$ 11,102	$ 21,596	$ 20,782	$ 13,042
Net income per share (basic)	$ 0.40	$ 0.78	$ 0.76	$ 0.51
Net income per share (diluted)	$ 0.39	$ 0.76	$ 0.74	$ 0.49

Appendix

B

Outback Steakhouse, Inc. 10-K/A Report

OUTBACK STEAKHOUSE, INC.

Overview

We are one of the largest casual dining restaurant companies in the world, with seven restaurant concepts, nearly 1,300 systemwide restaurants and 2005 annual revenues for Company-owned stores exceeding $3.6 billion. We operate in all 50 states and in 21 countries internationally, predominantly through Company-owned stores, but we also operate under a variety of partnerships and franchises.

The restaurant industry is a highly competitive and fragmented business, which is subject to sensitivity from changes in the economy, trends in lifestyles, seasonality (customer spending patterns at restaurants are generally highest in the first quarter of the year and lowest in the third quarter of the year) and fluctuating costs. Operating margins for restaurants are susceptible to fluctuations in prices of commodities, which include among other things, beef, chicken, seafood, butter, cheese, produce and other necessities to operate a store, such as natural gas or other energy supplies. Additionally, the restaurant industry is characterized by a high initial capital investment, coupled with high labor costs. The combination of these factors underscores our initiatives to drive increased sales at existing stores in order to raise margins and profits, because the incremental sales contribution to profits from every additional dollar of sales above the minimum costs required to open, staff and operate a store is very high.

Source: OSI RESTAURANT PARTN, 10-K/A, January 08, 2007

OUTBACK STEAKHOUSE, INC.
Consolidated Balance Sheets (in thousands)

	December 31	
	2005	2004
Assets		
Current assets		
Cash and cash equivalents	$ 84,876	$ 87,977
Short-term investments	1,828	1,425
Inventories	68,468	63,448
Deferred income tax assets	43,697	36,975
Other current assets	50,823	52,293
Total current assets	249,692	242,118
Property, fixtures, and equipment, net	1,387,700	1,233,995
Investments in and advances to unconsolidated affiliates, net	21,397	15,762
Deferred income tax assets	36,180	9,129
Goodwill	112,627	109,028
Intangible assets	11,562	21,683
Other assets	142,114	71,438
Notes receivable collateral for franchisee guarantee	31,150	30,239
	$1,992,422	$1,733,392
Liabilities and Stockholders' Equity		
Current liabilities		
Accounts payable	98,020	74,162
Sales taxes payable	17,761	26,735
Accrued expenses	135,660	102,458
Current portion of partner deposit and accrued buyout liability	15,175	13,561
Unearned revenue	170,785	156,382
Income taxes payable	695	87
Current portion of long-term debt	63,442	54,626
Total current liabilities	501,538	428,011
Partner deposit and accrued buyout liability	72,900	64,411
Deferred rent	61,509	49,410
Long-term debt	90,623	59,900
Guaranteed debt of franchisee	31,283	30,343
Other long-term liabilities	45,890	6,114
Total liabilities	803,743	638,189
Commitments and contingencies		
Minority interests in consolidated entities	44,259	48,092
Stockholders' equity		
Common stock, $0.01 par value, 200,000 shares authorized; 78,750 and 78,750 shares issued; 74,854 and 73,767 shares outstanding as of December 31, 2005 and 2004, respectively	788	788
Additional paid-in capital	293,368	273,442
Retained earnings	1,057,944	981,823
Accumulated other comprehensive income (loss)	384	(2,118)
Unearned compensation related to outstanding restricted stock	(40,858)	–
	1,311,626	1,253,935
Less treasury stock, 3,896 and 4,983 shares at December 31, 2005 and 2004, respectively, at cost	(167,206)	(206,824)
Total stockholders' equity	1,144,420	1,047,111
	$1,992,422	$1,733,392

The accompanying notes are an integral part of these Consolidated Financial Statements.

OUTBACK STEAKHOUSE, INC.
Consolidated Statements of Income
(in thousands, except per share amounts)

| | Years Ended December 31 | | |
	2005	2004	2003
Revenues			
Restaurant sales	$3,590,869	$ 3,197,536	$2,654,541
Other revenues	21,848	18,453	17,786
Total revenues	3,612,717	3,215,989	2,672,327
Costs and expenses			
Cost of sales	1,315,340	1,203,107	987,866
Labor and other related	930,356	817,214	670,798
Other restaurant operating	783,745	667,797	537,854
Depreciation and amortization	127,773	104,767	85,076
General and administrative	197,135	174,047	138,063
Hurricane property losses	3,101	3,024	–
Provision for impaired assets and restaurant closings	27,170	2,394	5,319
Contribution for "Dine Out for Hurricane Relief"	1,000	1,607	–
Income from operations of unconsolidated affiliates	(1,479)	(1,725)	(6,015)
Total costs and expenses	3,384,141	2,972,232	2,418,961
Income from operations	228,576	243,757	253,366
Other income (expense), net	(2,070)	(2,104)	(1,100)
Interest income	2,087	1,349	1,479
Interest expense	(6,848)	(3,629)	(1,810)
Income before provision for income taxes and elimination of minority interest	221,745	239,373	251,935
Provision for income taxes	73,808	78,622	85,214
Income before elimination of minority interest	147,937	160,751	166,721
Elimination of minority interest	1,191	9,180	2,476
Net income	$ 146,746	$ 151,571	$ 164,245
Basic earnings per common share			
Net income	$ 1.98	$ 2.05	$ 2.18
Basic weighted average number of shares outstanding	73,952	74,117	75,256
Diluted earnings per common share			
Net income	$ 1.92	$ 1.95	$ 2.10
Diluted weighted average number of shares outstanding	76,541	77,549	78,393
Cash dividends per common share	$ 0.52	$ 0.52	$ 0.49

The accompanying notes are an integral part of these Consolidated Financial Statements.

OUTBACK STEAKHOUSE, INC.
Consolidated Statements of Stockholders' Equity
(in thousands)

	Common Stock Shares	Common Stock Amount	Additional Paid-In Capital	Retained Earnings	Accumulated Other Comprehensive Income (Loss)	Unearned Compensation	Treasury Stock	Total
Balance, December 31, 2002	75,880	$788	$ 242,416	$ 766,137	$ –	$ –	$ (86,948)	$ 922,393
Purchase of treasury stock	(3,784)	–	–	–	–	–	(143,191)	(143,191)
Reissuance of treasury stock	2,183	–	–	(19,133)	–	–	68,331	49,198
Dividends ($0.49 per share)	–	–	–	(36,917)	–	–	–	(36,917)
Stock option income tax benefit	–	–	13,189	–	–	–	–	13,189
Stock option compensation expense	–	–	1,580	–	–	–	–	1,580
Net income, as restated	–	–	–	164,245	–	–	–	164,245
Foreign currency translation adjustment	–	–	–	–	(2,078)	–	–	(2,078)
Total comprehensive income	–	–	–	–	–	–	–	162,167
Balance, December 31, 2003	74,279	788	257,185	874,332	$(2,078)	–	(161,808)	968,419
Purchase of treasury stock	(2,155)	–	–	–	–	–	(95,554)	(95,554)
Reissuance of treasury stock	1,643	–	–	(5,556)	–	–	50,538	44,982
Dividends ($0.52 per share)	–	–	–	(38,524)	–	–	–	(38,524)
Stock option income tax benefit	–	–	14,527	–	–	–	–	14,527
Stock option compensation expense	–	–	1,730	–	–	–	–	1,730
Net income, as restated	–	–	–	151,571	–	–	–	151,571
Foreign currency translation adjustment	–	–	–	–	(40)	–	–	(40)
Total comprehensive income	–	–	–	–	–	–	–	151,531
Balance, December 31, 2004	73,767	788	273,442	981,823	(2,118)	–	(206,824)	1,047,111
Purchase of treasury stock	(2,177)	–	–	–	–	–	(92,363)	(92,363)
Reissuance of treasury stock	2,220	–	(3,686)	(28,687)	–	–	88,280	55,907
Dividends ($0.52 per share)	–	–	–	(38,753)	–	–	–	(38,753)
Stock option income tax benefit	–	–	16,514	–	–	–	–	16,514
Stock option compensation expense	–	–	3,412	–	–	–	–	3,412
Issuance of restricted stock	1,044	–	3,686	(3,185)	–	(44,202)	43,701	–
Amortization of restricted stock	–	–	–	–	–	3,344	–	3,344
Net income, as restated	–	–	–	146,746	–	–	–	146,746
Foreign currency translation adjustment	–	–	–	–	2,502	–	–	2,502
Total comprehensive income	–	–	–	–	–	–	–	149,248
Balance, December 31, 2005	74,854	$788	$293,368	$1,057,944	$ 384	$(40,858)	$ (167,206)	$1,144,420

The accompanying notes are an integral part of these Consolidated Financial Statements.

OUTBACK STEAKHOUSE, INC.
Consolidated Statements of Cash Flows (in thousands)

	Years Ended December 31		
	2005	2004	2003
Cash flows from operating activities:			
Net income	$ 146,746	$ 151,571	$ 164,245
Adjustments to reconcile net income to cash provided by operating activities:			
Depreciation and amortization	127,773	104,767	85,076
Provision for impaired assets and restaurant closings and hurricane losses	30,271	5,418	5,319
Stock-based compensation expense	6,756	–	–
Employee partner stock buyout expense	6,718	7,495	4,791
Income tax benefit credited to equity	16,514	14,527	13,189
Minority interest in consolidated entities' income	1,191	9,180	2,476
Income from operations of unconsolidated affiliates	(1,479)	(1,725)	(6,015)
Change in deferred income taxes	(33,773)	(12,844)	(4,152)
Loss on disposal of property, fixtures and equipment	3,605	4,102	3,705
Change in assets and liabilities, net of effects of acquisitions and FIN 46R consolidations:			
Increase in inventories	(5,635)	(2,773)	(24,102)
Increase in other current assets	(288)	(9,348)	(5,619)
(Increase) decrease in other assets	(10,301)	(20,440)	2,610
Increase in accounts payable, sales taxes payable and accrued expenses	48,130	29,025	20,056
Increase in partner deposit and accrued buyout liability	9,003	8,077	2,413
Increase in deferred rent	12,099	8,123	7,622
Increase in unearned revenue	14,403	21,514	17,033
Increase (decrease) in income taxes payable	608	(541)	(13,425)
Increase (decrease) in other long-term liabilities	776	925	(1,000)
Net cash provided by operating activities	373,117	317,053	274,222
Cash flows used in investing activities:			
Purchase of investment securities	(5,568)	(60,125)	(78,557)
Maturities and sales of investment securities	5,165	79,524	78,309
Cash paid for acquisitions of businesses, net of cash acquired	(5,200)	(28,066)	(47,677)
Cash paid for designation rights	–	(42,500)	–
Capital expenditures	(327,862)	(254,871)	(193,828)
Proceeds from the sale of property, fixtures and equipment	11,508	2,583	2,275
Proceeds from the sale of designation rights	–	11,075	–
Increase in cash from adoption of FIN 46R	–	1,080	–
Payments from unconsolidated affiliates	131	1,361	13,518
Distributions to unconsolidated affiliates	–	(121)	(1,830)
Investments in and advances to unconsolidated affiliates	(1,956)	(247)	(1,345)
Net cash used in investing activities	(323,782)	(290,307)	(229,135)
Cash flows used in financing activities:			
Proceeds from issuance of long-term debt	174,373	127,444	29,497
Proceeds from minority interest contributions	8,635	5,100	13,825
Distributions to minority interest	(17,899)	(8,151)	(10,907)
Repayments of long-term debt	(141,084)	(71,369)	(23,663)
Proceeds from sale-leaseback transactions	5,000	–	–
Dividends paid	(38,753)	(38,524)	(36,917)
Payments for purchase of treasury stock	(92,363)	(95,554)	(143,191)
Proceeds from reissuance of treasury stock	49,655	39,393	41,583
Net cash used in financing activities	(52,436)	(41,661)	(129,773)
Net decrease in cash and cash equivalents	(3,101)	(14,915)	(84,686)
Cash and cash equivalents at the beginning of the period	87,977	102,892	187,578
Cash and cash equivalents at the end of the period	$ 84,876	$ 87,977	$ 102,892
Supplemental disclosures of cash flow information:			
Cash paid for interest	$ 6,916	$ 3,683	$ 1,964
Cash paid for income taxes	88,516	79,117	81,944

The accompanying notes are an integral part of these Consolidated Financial Statements.

OUTBACK STEAKHOUSE, INC.
NOTES TO CONSOLIDATED FINANCIAL STATEMENTS

1. Summary of Significant Accounting Policies

Basis of Presentation—Outback Steakhouse, Inc. (the "Company") develops and operates casual dining restaurants primarily in the United States. The Company's restaurants are generally organized as partnerships, with the Company as the general partner.

Principles of Consolidation—The Consolidated Financial Statements include the accounts and operations of the Company and affiliated partnerships in which the Company is a general partner and owns a controlling financial interest. The Consolidated Financial Statements also include the accounts and operations of a consolidated venture in which the Company has a less than majority ownership. The Company consolidates this venture because the Company controls the executive committee (which functions as a board of directors) through representation on the committee by related parties and is able to direct or cause the direction of management and operations on a day-to-day basis. Additionally, the majority of capital contributions made by the Company's partner in the consolidated venture have been funded by loans to the partner from a third party where the Company is required to be a guarantor of the debt, which provides the Company control through its collateral interest in the joint venture partner's membership interest. The portion of income or loss attributable to the minority interests, not to exceed the minority interest's equity in the consolidated entity, is eliminated in the line item in the Company's Consolidated Statements of Income entitled "Elimination of minority interest." All material intercompany balances and transactions have been eliminated.

The unconsolidated affiliates are accounted for using the equity method.

Restatement of Previously Issued Consolidated Financial Statements—In October 2006, the Company identified errors in its accounting for unearned revenue for unredeemed gift cards and certificates. Upon completion of the review of accounting policies for gift cards and certificates as well as a review of certain other balance sheet accounts, the Company has restated its consolidated financial statements for certain prior periods to correct these and other errors.

Reclassification—Certain prior year amounts shown in the accompanying consolidated financial statements have been reclassified to conform with the 2005 presentation. Distribution expense to employee partners has been included in the line item "Labor and other related" expenses for managing partner distributions and in "General and administrative" expenses for area operating partner distributions in the Consolidated Statements of Income. Employee partner stock buyout expense has been included in "General and administrative" expenses in the Consolidated Statements of Income. These reclassifications had no effect on total assets, total liabilities, stockholders' equity, or net income.

Use of Estimates—The preparation of financial statements in conformity with generally accepted accounting principles requires management to make estimates and assumptions that affect the reported amounts of assets and liabilities and disclosure of contingent assets and liabilities at the date of the financial statements and the reported amounts of revenues and expenses during the reporting period. Actual results could differ from those estimated.

Cash and Cash Equivalents—Cash equivalents consist of investments which are readily convertible to cash with an original maturity date of three months or less.

Short-Term Investments—The Company's short-term investments, consisting primarily of high grade debt securities, are classified as held-to-maturity because the

Company has the positive intent and ability to hold the securities to maturity. Held-to-maturity securities are stated at amortized cost, adjusted for amortization of premiums and accretion of discounts to maturity, which approximates fair value at December 31, 2005. The Company owns no investments that are considered to be available-for-sale or trading securities. At December 31, 2005, all held-to-maturity securities had maturities of less than one year and are classified as current assets.

Concentrations of Credit Risk—Financial instruments which potentially subject the Company to concentrations of credit risk are cash and cash equivalents, and short-term investments. The Company attempts to limit its credit risk associated with cash and cash equivalents and short-term investments by utilizing outside investment managers with major financial institutions that, in turn, invest in investment-grade commercial paper and other corporate obligations rated A or higher, certificates of deposit, government obligations and other highly rated investments and marketable securities. At times, cash balances may be in excess of FDIC insurance limits.

Inventories—Inventories consist of food and beverages, and are stated at the lower of cost (first-in, first-out) or market. The Company will periodically make advance purchases of various inventory items to ensure adequate supply or to obtain favorable pricing. At December 31, 2005 and 2004, inventories included advance purchases of approximately $27,185,000 and $23,040,000, respectively.

Goodwill—Goodwill represents the residual purchase price after allocation of the purchase price of a business to the individual fair values of assets acquired. On an annual basis, the Company reviews the recoverability of goodwill based primarily upon an analysis of discounted cash flows of the related reporting unit as compared to the carrying value or whenever events or changes in circumstances indicate that the carrying amounts may not be recoverable. Generally, the Company performs its annual assessment for impairment during the third quarter of its fiscal year, unless facts and circumstances require differently.

Unearned Revenue—Unearned revenue represents the Company's liability for gift cards and certificates that have been sold but not yet redeemed and are recorded at the redemption value. The Company recognizes restaurant sales and reduces the related deferred liability when gift cards and certificates are redeemed or the likelihood of the gift card or certificate being redeemed by the customer is remote (gift card breakage). As of December 31, 2005, the Company has determined that redemption of gift cards and certificates issued by the Outback, Carrabba's, and Bonefish concepts on or before three years prior to the balance sheet date is remote. The Company recognizes breakage income as a component of "Restaurant sales" in the Consolidated Statements of Income.

Property, Fixtures, and Equipment—Property, fixtures, and equipment are stated at cost, net of accumulated depreciation. At the time property, fixtures, and equipment are retired, or otherwise disposed of, the asset and accumulated depreciation are removed from the accounts and any resulting gain or loss is included in earnings. The Company expenses repair and maintenance costs incurred to maintain the appearance and functionality of the restaurant that do not extend the useful life of any restaurant asset or are less than $1,000. Improvements to leased properties are depreciated over the shorter of their useful life or the lease term, which includes cancelable renewal periods where failure to exercise such options would result in an economic penalty. Depreciation is computed on the straight-line method over the following estimated useful lives:

Buildings and building improvements	20 to 30 years
Furniture and fixtures	5 to 7 years
Equipment	2 to 15 years
Leasehold improvements	5 to 20 years

The Company's accounting policies regarding property, fixtures and equipment include certain management judgments and projections regarding the estimated useful lives of these assets and what constitutes increasing the value and useful life of existing assets. These estimates, judgments and projections may produce materially different amounts of depreciation expense than would be reported if different assumptions were used.

Operating Leases—Rent expense for the Company's operating leases, which generally have escalating rentals over the term of the lease, is recorded on a straight-line basis over the lease term and those renewal periods that are reasonably assured. The initial lease term begins when the Company has the right to control the use of the leased property, which is typically before rent payments are due under the terms of the lease. The difference between rent expense and rent paid is recorded as deferred rent and is included in the Consolidated Balance Sheets.

Impairment of Long-Lived Assets—The Company assesses the potential impairment of identifiable intangibles, long-lived assets, and goodwill whenever events or changes in circumstances indicate that the carrying value may not be recoverable. Recoverability of assets is measured by comparing the carrying value of the asset to the future cash flows expected to be generated by the asset. In evaluating long-lived restaurant assets for impairment, the Company considers a number of factors such as:

Restaurant sales trends

Local competition

Changing demographic profiles

Local economic conditions

New laws and government regulations that adversely affect sales and profits

The ability to recruit and train skilled restaurant employees

If the aforementioned factors indicate that the Company should review the carrying value of the restaurant's long-lived assets, it performs an impairment analysis. Identifiable cash flows that are largely independent of other assets and liabilities typically exist for land and buildings, and for combined fixtures, equipment and improvements for each restaurant. If the total future cash flows are less than the carrying amount of the asset, the carrying amount is written down to the estimated fair value, and a loss resulting from value impairment is recognized by a charge to earnings.

Judgments and estimates made by the Company related to the expected useful lives of long-lived assets are affected by factors such as changes in economic conditions and changes in operating performance. As the Company assesses the ongoing expected cash flows and carrying amounts of its long-lived assets, these factors could cause the Company to realize a material impairment charge.

Construction in Progress—The Company capitalizes all direct costs incurred to construct its restaurants. Upon opening, these costs are depreciated and charged to expense based upon their property classification. The amount of interest capitalized in connection with restaurant construction was approximately $378,000, $207,000 and $202,000 in 2005, 2004 and 2003, respectively.

Revenue Recognition—The Company records revenues from normal recurring sales upon the performance of services. Revenue from the sales of franchises is recognized as income when the Company has substantially performed all of its material obligations under the franchise agreement. Continuing royalties, which are a percentage of net sales of franchised restaurants, are accrued as income when earned. These revenues are included in the line "Other revenues" in the Consolidated Statements of Income.

Distribution Expense to Employee Partners—The Company requires its general managers and area operating partners to enter into five- to seven-year employment agreements and purchase an interest in their restaurant's annual cash flows for the duration of the agreement. Payments made to managing partners pursuant to these programs are included in the line item "Labor and other related" expenses, and payments made to area operating partners pursuant to these programs are included in the line item "General and administrative" expenses in the Consolidated Statements of Income.

Employee Partner Stock Buyout Expense–Area operating partners are required to purchase a 4% to 9% interest in the restaurants they develop for an initial investment of $50,000. This interest gives the area operating partner the right to receive a percentage of his or her restaurants' annual cash flows for the duration of the agreement. Under the terms of these partners' employment agreements, the Company has the option to purchase their interest after a five-year period under the conditions of the agreement. The Company estimates future purchases of area operating partners' interests using current information on restaurant performance to calculate and record an accrued buyout liability in the line item "Partner deposit and accrued buyout liability" in the Consolidated Balance Sheets. Expenses associated with recording the buyout liability are included in the line "General and administrative" expenses in the Consolidated Statements of Income. When partner buyouts occur, they are completed primarily through issuance of cash and the Company's common stock to the partner equivalent to the fair value of their interest. In the period the Company completes the buyout, an adjustment is recorded to recognize any remaining expense associated with the purchase and reduce the related accrued buyout liability.

Advertising Costs–The Company's policy is to report advertising costs as expenses in the year in which the costs are incurred or the first time the advertising takes place. The total amounts charged to advertising expense were approximately $159,242,000, $126,404,000 and $102,523,000 in 2005, 2004, and 2003, respectively.

Income Taxes–The Company uses the asset and liability method which recognizes the amount of current and deferred taxes payable or refundable at the date of the financial statements as a result of all events that have been recognized in the consolidated financial statements as measured by the provisions of enacted tax laws.

The minority interest in affiliated partnerships includes no provision or liability for income taxes, as any tax liability related thereto is the responsibility of the individual minority partners. Minority interest in certain foreign affiliated corporations is presented net of any provision or liability for income taxes.

Stock-Based Compensation–The Company accounts for its stock-based employee compensation under the intrinsic value method. No stock-based employee compensation cost is reflected in net income to the extent options granted had an exercise price equal to or exceeding the fair market value of the underlying common stock on the date of grant. SFAS No. 123R "Share-Based Payment" will be adopted January 1, 2006. The following table provides pro forma net income and earnings per-share amounts using the fair value based method of SFAS No. 123, "Accounting for Stock-Based Compensation" (in thousands, except per-share data):

| | Years Ended December 31 | | |
	2005	2004	2003
Net income	$146,746	$151,571	$164,245
Stock-based employee compensation expense included in net income, net of related taxes	7,092	4,576	3,129
Total stock-based employee compensation expense determined under fair value based method, net of related taxes	(23,012)	(20,196)	(20,331)
Pro forma net income	$130,826	$135,951	$147,043
Earnings per common share:			
Basic	$ 1.98	$ 2.05	$ 2.18
Basic–pro forma	$ 1.77	$ 1.83	$ 1.95
Diluted	$ 1.92	$ 1.95	$ 2.10
Diluted–pro forma	$ 1.72	$ 1.77	$ 1.90

Stock-Based Compensation (Continued)—The preceding pro forma results were calculated with the use of the Black-Scholes option pricing model. The following assumptions were used for the years ended December 31, 2005, 2004, and 2003, respectively: (1) risk-free interest rates of 4.22%, 3.63% and 2.80%; (2) dividend yield of 1.24%, 1.25% and 1.45%; (3) expected lives of 7.1, 6.3 and 5.0 years; and (4) volatility of 28.9%, 30.0% and 31.0%. Results may vary depending on the assumptions applied within the model. The effect of applying SFAS No. 123 for providing these pro forma disclosures may not be representative of the effects on net income for future years or under SFAS No. 123R, when adopted. In 2005, we identified certain assumptions surrounding the forfeiture of stock options used in our Black-Scholes model calculation and attribution of expense that were not correctly reflected in our previously reported pro forma expense. For 2005, 2004, and 2003, we are presenting pro forma compensation expense amounts that reflect actual attribution and forfeitures that have occurred in the respective periods.

In 2004, the Board of Directors approved an amendment and restatement (the "Amendment") of the Company's Amended and Restated Stock Option Plan (the "Plan") to allow for the grant of shares of restricted common stock under the Plan and to increase the number of shares for which options and shares of restricted common stock may be granted under the Plan by 1,000,000, or from 22,500,000 to 23,500,000. This amendment was approved by vote of the shareholders of the Company on April 21, 2004.

Restricted stock awards are recognized as unearned compensation, a component of stockholders' equity, based on the fair market value of the Company's common stock on the grant date. This unearned compensation is amortized to compensation expense over the vesting period.

On April 27, 2005, the Company's Board of Directors approved a grant of restricted common stock to the Company's Chief Executive Officer under the Amended and Restated Managing Partner Stock Plan. Under the terms of the grant, 300,000 shares of restricted common stock were issued and will vest as follows: on December 31, 2009, 90,000 shares, plus an additional 30,000 shares if the market capitalization of the Company exceeds $6,060,000,000; on December 31, 2011, 90,000 shares, plus an additional 30,000 shares if the market capitalization of the Company exceeds $8,060,000,000; and on December 31, 2014, the balance of all remaining unvested shares. On December 8, 2005, the Company's Board of Directors approved an additional grant of restricted stock to the Company's Chief Executive Officer under the Amended and Restated Managing Partner Stock Plan. Under the terms of the grant, 150,000 shares of restricted stock were issued effective December 31, 2005 and will vest as follows: on December 31, 2009, 75,000 shares and on December 31, 2011, the remaining 75,000 shares.

On July 27, 2005, the Company's Board of Directors approved a grant of 50,000 shares of its restricted common stock to the Senior Vice President of Real Estate and Development as an inducement grant in connection with his hiring. These shares were not issued under any existing stock plan of the Company. Under the terms of the grant, the 50,000 shares of restricted stock will vest as follows: on June 13, 2008, 10,000 shares; on June 13, 2010, 10,000 shares; on June 13, 2012, 15,000 shares; and on June 13, 2015, the balance of all remaining unvested shares.

On October 26, 2005, the Company's Board of Directors approved a grant of 100,000 shares of its restricted common stock to the Senior Vice President and Chief Financial Officer as an inducement grant in connection with his hiring, effective November 1, 2005. These shares were not issued under any existing stock plan. Under the terms of the grant, the 100,000 shares of restricted stock will vest as follows: on November 1, 2010, 50,000 shares, plus an additional 10,000 shares if the market capitalization of the Company exceeds $6,000,000,000; and on November 1, 2012, the balance of all remaining unvested shares.

Earnings per Common Share—Earnings per common share are computed in accordance with SFAS No. 128, "Earnings Per Share," which requires companies to present basic earnings per share and diluted earnings per share. Basic earnings per share are computed by dividing net income by the weighted average number of shares of common stock outstanding during the year. Diluted earnings per common share are computed by dividing net income by the weighted average number of shares of common stock outstanding and restricted stock and dilutive options outstanding during the year.

Recently Issued Financial Accounting Standards

"Share-Based Payment"

In December 2004, the FASB issued SFAS No. 123 (Revised), "Share-Based Payment," a revision of SFAS No. 123, "Accounting for Stock-Based Compensation." SFAS No. 123R requires the fair value measurement of all stock-based payments to employees, including grants of employee stock options, and recognition of those expenses in the statement of operations. SFAS No. 123R is effective at the beginning of the next fiscal year after June 15, 2005. The Company will continue to account for stock-based compensation using the intrinsic value method until adoption of SFAS No. 123R on January 1, 2006. Historically, the compensation expense recognized related to stock options under this method has been minimal. As a result, adoption of the provisions of SFAS No. 123R is expected to have a material impact to reported net income and earnings per share, particularly as a result of stock options issued and pending changes to the Company's managing partner program, described below. The Company will adopt SFAS No. 123R using the modified prospective method and recognize compensation expense on the unvested portion of previously issued awards over the remaining vesting period.

As part of the Company's managing partner program, the managing partner (and chef partner at Fleming's and Roy's) of each domestic restaurant is required, as a condition of employment, to sign a five-year employment agreement and is required to purchase an interest in the restaurant he or she is employed to manage. This interest gives the managing partner and chef partner the right to receive a percentage of their restaurant's monthly cash flows for the duration of the five-year agreement. For managing partners, the purchase price has been $25,000 for an interest ranging from 6% to 10% and for chef partners has ranged from a purchase price of $10,000 to $15,000 for an interest ranging from 2% to 5%. Upon completion of each five-year term of employment, each managing partner and chef partner has historically been issued stock options with the number of options determined by a formula based on a multiple of the cash flows distributed from their interest. However, all new managing partner and chef partner agreements entered into on and after March 1, 2006, will provide for participation in a new deferred compensation program, which will replace the issuance of stock options upon completion of each term of employment. Managing partners and chef partners will also be given the opportunity to amend their existing agreements to provide for participation in this deferred compensation program in lieu of issuance of stock options during a roll-out period in 2006.

The estimated pretax impact of adopting SFAS No. 123R for 2006, relating to prior years' unvested stock option grants only, will be approximately $12,000,000 to $15,000,000. SFAS No. 123R also requires the benefits of tax deductions in excess of recognized compensation cost to be reported as a financing cash flow, rather than as an operating cash flow as required under current literature. This requirement will reduce net operating cash flows and increase net financing cash flows in the periods after adoption. The Company cannot estimate what those amounts will be in the future because they depend on, among other things, when employees exercise stock options.

"Accounting for Conditional Asset Retirement Obligations"

In March 2005, the FASB issued FASB Interpretation No. 47, "Accounting for Conditional Asset Retirement Obligations" ("FIN 47"), which is an interpretation of SFAS No. 143, "Accounting for Asset Retirement Obligations." The Interpretation clarifies that the term conditional asset retirement obligation refers to the legal obligation to perform an asset retirement activity in which the timing or method of settlement is conditional on a future event that may or may not be within the control of the entity. Adoption of FIN 47 is required by the fiscal year ending after December 15, 2005. The Company adopted FIN 47 on December 31, 2005, with no material impact on its financial statements.

"Accounting Changes and Error Corrections"

In June 2005, the FASB issued SFAS No. 154, "Accounting Changes and Error Corrections," which will require entities that voluntarily make a change in accounting principle to apply that change retrospectively to prior periods' financial statements, unless this would be impracticable. SFAS No. 154 supersedes Accounting Principles Board Opinion No. 20, "Accounting Changes" ("APB 20"), which previously required that most voluntary changes in accounting principle be recognized by including in the current period's net income the cumulative effect of changing to the new accounting principle. SFAS No. 154 also makes a distinction between "retrospective application" of an accounting principle and the "restatement" of financial statements to reflect the correction of an error.

Also under SFAS No. 154, if an entity changes its method of depreciation, amortization, or depletion for long-lived, nonfinancial assets, the change must be accounted for as a change in accounting estimate. Under APB 20, such a change would have been reported as a change in accounting principle. SFAS No. 154 applies to accounting changes and error corrections that are made in fiscal years beginning after December 15, 2005. The Company does not believe the adoption of SFAS No. 154 will have a material impact on its financial statements.

"Accounting for Purchased or Acquired Leasehold Improvements"

In June 2005, the FASB's Emerging Issues Task Force reached a consensus on Issue No. 05-6, "Determining the Amortization Period for Leasehold Improvements Purchased after Lease Inception or Acquired in a Business Combination" ("EITF 05-6"). This guidance requires that leasehold improvements acquired in a business combination or purchased subsequent to the inception of a lease be amortized over the shorter of the useful life of the assets or a term that includes required lease periods and renewals that are reasonably assured at the date of the business combination or purchase. The guidance is applicable only to leasehold improvements that are purchased or acquired in reporting periods beginning after June 29, 2005. The adoption of EITF 05-6 did not have a material impact on the Company's financial statements.

2. Other Current Assets

Other current assets consisted of the following (in thousands):

	DECEMBER 31	
	2005	2004
Prepaid expenses	$16,625	$23,020
Accounts receivable	29,270	19,473
Accounts receivable—franchisees	1,777	1,453
Assets held for sale	—	4,810
Deposits	2,651	2,537
Other current assets	500	1,000
	$50,823	$52,293

3. Property, Fixtures, and Equipment, Net

Property, fixtures, and equipment consisted of the following (in thousands):

	DECEMBER 31	
	2005	2004
Land	$ 200,394	$ 196,137
Buildings and building improvements	689,056	603,125
Furniture and fixtures	231,608	184,949
Equipment	498,018	425,197
Leasehold improvements	345,640	305,618
Construction in progress	68,878	52,373
Accumulated depreciation	(645,894)	(533,404)
	$1,387,700	$1,233,995

The Company expensed repair and maintenance costs of approximately $86,000,000, $76,000,000, and $63,000,000 for the years ended December 31, 2005, 2004, and 2003, respectively. Depreciation expense for the years ended December 31, 2005, 2004, and 2003 was $126,115,000, $104,013,000, and $85,076,000, respectively.

During 2004, the Company recorded a provision for impaired assets and restaurant closings of approximately $2,394,000, which included approximately $415,000 for the impairment of two domestic Outback Steakhouse restaurants, $1,893,000 for one Outback Steakhouse restaurant closing in Japan (which includes $812,000 of goodwill written off for this location), and $86,000 for one Carrabba's Italian Grill restaurant closing. Additionally, during August and September 2004, four hurricanes caused losses from property damage of approximately $3,024,000, which included $1,300,000 from the destruction of the Outback Steakhouse restaurant in the Cayman Islands. The Company has decided not to reopen this location.

During 2005, the Company recorded a provision for impaired assets and restaurant closings of approximately $27,170,000, which included approximately $7,581,000 for an impairment charge against the deferred license fee receivable related to certain nonrestaurant operations, approximately $14,975,000 for an impairment charge for intangible and other asset impairments related to the pending sale of Paul Lee's Chinese Kitchen, approximately $1,992,000 for the impairment of two Bonefish Grill restaurants in Washington, approximately $816,000 for the impairment of two domestic Outback Steakhouse restaurants and approximately $1,806,000 for the closing of five domestic Outback Steakhouse restaurants. Two of these Outback restaurants closed during 2005, and the other three have closed or will close in 2006.

On August 3, 2004, the Company was approved by the United States Bankruptcy Court for the District of Delaware as the successful bidder at an auction of designation rights for 76 properties of Chi-Chi's, Inc. and its affiliates. The Company's objective in acquiring these rights was to have access to restaurant sites for conversion to one of its concepts under its current expansion plans. The original 76 properties included 23 locations with owned land and building, 15 sale-leaseback properties with reversion rights and purchase options, 23 ground leases and 15 leases. The properties included any real property, furniture, fixtures and equipment and liquor licenses. The designation rights allowed the Company to transfer properties to itself, to transfer properties to others or to require Chi-Chi's to retain properties. The purchase price for the designation rights was $42,500,000. The Company was responsible for paying the carrying costs on each of the properties from the closing date until the date the property was designated for transfer.

3. Property, Fixtures, and Equipment, Net (*Continued*)

In October 2004, the Company received $1,100,000 from Chi-Chi's when it exercised the right to exclude one property from the designation rights listing. Additionally, in October 2004, the Company completed an assignment of designation rights to a third party on 25 properties in exchange for $9,975,000. Both transactions reduced the total purchase price of the remaining properties. The Company required Chi-Chi's to retain 18 properties, leaving 32 properties to which the Company had rights as of June 30, 2005. In July 2005, the Company executed its option on the 10 remaining sale-leaseback properties with reversion rights and purchase options for approximately $1,400,000, and in August 2005, the Company sold two of the properties with owned land and building. Thus, the remaining properties include 20 properties with owned land and building, eight ground leases and two leases, all of which were designated by September 30, 2005.

The net purchase price of $31,425,000 for the designation rights and capitalized carrying costs on rejected properties of $844,000 were allocated to properties the Company expected to designate for conversion into one of its concepts as follows (in thousands):

Land	$16,270
Buildings	4,949
Assets held for sale	4,810
Liquor licenses	3,490
Favorable leases	2,750
	$32,269

On October 11, 2005, the Company executed a sale agreement for certain land in Las Vegas, Nevada, where a Company-owned Outback Steakhouse is currently operated. Pursuant to the agreement if the sale is consummated after the inspection and title and survey contingency periods, the Company will receive $8,800,000 on the closing date of the sale, which will be on or before March 31, 2008, and will be provided space in a new development to operate an Outback Steakhouse. The purchaser will pay the Company an additional $5,000,000 if plans for the new restaurant are not agreed upon prior to the closing date.

On October 26, 2005, the Company's Board of Directors approved up to $24,000,000 to be used for the purchase and development of 46 acres in Tampa, Florida. This purchase closed in December 2005.

4. Goodwill and Intangible Assets

The change in the carrying amount of goodwill for the years ended December 31, 2005 and 2004 is as follows (in thousands):

December 31, 2003	$ 88,054
Acquisitions (see Note 13 of Notes to Consolidated Financial Statements)	21,786
Impairment loss (see Note 6 of Notes to Consolidated Financial Statements)	(812)
December 31, 2004	109,028
Acquisitions (see Note 13 of Notes to Consolidated Financial Statements)	4,124
Acquisition adjustment	(525)
December 31, 2005	$112,627

4. Goodwill and Intangible Assets (*Continued*)

Intangible assets consisted of the following (in thousands):

	Weighted Average Amortization Period (Years)	DECEMBER 31 2005	2004
Trademarks (gross)	24	$ 8,344	$12,344
Less: accumulated amortization		(511)	(295)
Net trademarks		7,833	12,049
Trade dress (gross)	15	777	6,777
Less: accumulated amortization		(72)	(320)
Net trade dress		705	6,457
Favorable leases (gross, lives ranging from 2 to 24 years)	20	3,224	3,224
Less: accumulated amortization		(200)	(47)
Net favorable leases		3,024	3,177
Intangible assets, less total accumulated amortization of $783 and $662 at December 31, 2005 and 2004, respectively	22	$11,562	$21,683

The aggregate amortization expense related to these intangible assets was $1,421,000 and $662,000 for the years ended December 31, 2005 and 2004, respectively. The Company did not have these intangible assets in 2003. Thus, there was not any amortization expense recorded. Annual amortization expense related to these intangible assets for the next five years is anticipated to be approximately $600,000.

5. Other Assets

Other assets consisted of the following (in thousands):

	DECEMBER 31 2005	2004
Other assets	$ 59,921	$47,089
Insurance receivable (see Notes 8 and 12)	41,696	—
Liquor licenses, net of accumulated amortization of $5,037 and $4,291 at December 31, 2005 and 2004, respectively	15,728	13,699
Deferred license fee, net of valuation provision of approximately $0 and $3,000 at December 31, 2005 and 2004, respectively	2,136	10,650
Assets held for sale	22,633	—
	$142,114	$71,438

In accordance with SFAS No. 144, "Accounting for the Impairment or Disposal of Long-Lived Assets," the Company has classified certain land and building assets as "held for sale" in its Consolidated Balance Sheets. Assets held for sale as of December 31, 2005 consisted of $21,439,000 of land and $1,194,000 of buildings. Assets held for sale as of December 31, 2004 were classified as other current assets and consisted of $2,584,000 of land, $1,726,000 of buildings and $500,000 of equipment (see Note 2 of Notes to Consolidated Financial Statements). No gain or loss has been recorded as it is anticipated that proceeds from the sale will exceed the net book value of the assets.

In January 2001, the Company entered into a ten-year licensing agreement with an entity owned by minority interest owners of certain nonrestaurant operations. The licensing agreement transferred the right and license to use certain assets of these nonrestaurant operations. As of July 19, 2005, the Company began renegotiating the terms of this licensing agreement, and as a result, the Company assessed the recoverability of the carrying value of the associated deferred license fee and determined that an impairment charge was necessary. Thus, a $7,581,000 pretax charge was recorded against the deferred license fee to reflect management's best estimate of its current net realizable value as of June 30, 2005. The negotiation of the deferred license fee was finalized on September 20, 2005. The $7,000,000 agreed-upon license fees are to be received in $500,000 increments on July 31 of each year from 2006 to 2019 inclusive.

In 1996, the Company entered into key man life insurance policies for three of the Company's founders. During 1999 through 2001, the Company entered into collateral assignment split dollar arrangements with five officers on life insurance policies owned by individual trusts for each officer. The primary purpose of these split dollar policies was to provide liquidity in the officers' estates to pay estate taxes minimizing the need for the estate to liquidate its holdings of the Company's stock. The Company will recover the premiums it has paid either through policy withdrawals or from life insurance benefits in the event of death. Premiums were paid only through 2001 and resumed in 2005 after these collateral assignment arrangements were converted to endorsement split dollar arrangements. The Company is now the owner of the policies and has included the amount of its collateral interest in the cash value of the policies in Other Assets.

6. Accrued Expenses

Accrued expenses consisted of the following (in thousands):

	DECEMBER 31	
	2005	2004
Accrued payroll and other compensation	$ 53,709	$ 38,552
Accrued insurance	29,801	21,818
Other accrued expenses	52,150	42,088
	$135,660	$102,458

Remaining accrued restaurant closing expenses of less than $100,000 were included in other accrued expenses as of December 31, 2005 and 2004, related to restaurant closing provisions.

7. Long-Term Debt

Long-term debt consisted of the following (in thousands):

	DECEMBER 31	
	2005	2004
Revolving lines of credit, uncollateralized, interest rates ranging from 5.00% to 5.21% at December 31, 2005 and 2.89% to 3.05% at December 31, 2004	$ 73,000	$ 55,000
Outback Korea notes payable, interest rates ranging from 4.95% to 6.06% at December 31, 2005 and 5.45% to 7.00% at December 31, 2004	46,670	27,717
Outback Japan notes payable, uncollateralized, interest rates of 0.86% at December 31, 2005 and ranging from 0.95% to 0.96% at December 31, 2004	5,085	5,769
Outback Japan revolving lines of credit, interest rates ranging from 0.69% to 0.77% at December 31, 2005 and 0.68% to 0.77% at December 31, 2004	14,636	18,895
Other notes payable, uncollateralized, interest rates ranging from 2.07% to 7.00% at December 31, 2005 and 2004	8,424	7,145
Sale-leaseback obligation	6,250	—
Guaranteed debt of franchisee	31,283	30,343
	185,348	144,869
Less current portion	63,442	54,626
Less guaranteed debt of franchisee	31,283	30,343
Long-term debt of Outback Steakhouse, Inc.	$ 90,623	$ 59,900

Effective April 27, 2004, the Company replaced a $125,000,000 revolving credit facility that was scheduled to mature in December 2004, with a new uncollateralized three-year $150,000,000 revolving bank credit facility that matures in June 2007. The revolving line of credit permits borrowing at interest rates ranging from 50 to 90 basis points over the 30, 60, 90, or 180 day London Interbank Offered Rate (LIBOR) (ranging from 4.39% to 4.69% at December 31, 2005, and ranging from 2.42% to 2.78% at December 31, 2004). At December 31, 2005, the unused portion of the revolving line of credit was $77,000,000. Subsequent to December 31, 2005, the Company amended this line of credit (see Note 18 of Notes to Consolidated Financial Statements).

The credit agreement contains certain restrictions and conditions as defined in the agreement that require the Company to maintain consolidated net worth equal to or greater than consolidated total debt and to maintain a ratio of total consolidated debt to EBITDAR (earnings before interest, taxes, depreciation, amortization and rent) equal to or less than 3.0 to 1.0. At December 31, 2005, the Company was in compliance with these debt covenants.

The Company also replaced a $15,000,000 line of credit that was scheduled to mature in December 2004, with a new $20,000,000 uncollateralized line of credit. On April 28, 2005, the Company amended this $20,000,000 line of credit to a maximum borrowing of $30,000,000. This line of credit matures in June 2007 and permits borrowing at interest rates ranging from 50 to 90 basis points over LIBOR for loan draws and 65 to 112.5 basis points over LIBOR for letter of credit advances. The credit agreement contains certain restrictions and conditions as defined in the agreement. At December 31, 2005 and 2004, approximately $20,072,000 and $11,782,000, respectively, of the line of credit was committed for the issuance of letters of credit as required by insurance companies that underwrite the Company's workers' compensation insurance and also, where required, for construction of new restaurants. The remaining $9,928,000 at December 31, 2005 was available to the Company. However, subsequent to year-end, approximately $5,000,000 of additional letters of credit was committed against the line, and the Company amended this line of credit (see Note 18 of Notes to Consolidated Financial Statements).

As of December 31, 2005, the Company had approximately $8,424,000 of notes payable at interest rates ranging from 2.07% to 7.00%. These notes have been primarily issued for buyouts of general manager interests in the cash flows of their restaurants and generally are payable over five years.

The Company has notes payable with banks bearing interest at rates ranging from 4.95% to 6.06% and from 5.45% to 7.00% at December 31, 2005 and 2004, respectively, to finance development of the Company's restaurants in South Korea. The notes are denominated and payable in Korean won, with outstanding balances as of December 31, 2005 maturing at dates ranging from January 2006 to January 2007. As of December 31, 2005 and 2004, the outstanding balance was approximately $46,670,000 and $27,717,000, respectively. Certain of the notes payable are collateralized by lease and other deposits. At December 31, 2005 and 2004, collateralized notes totaled approximately $34,326,000 and $25,346,000, respectively. The Company has been pre-approved by these banks for additional borrowings of approximately $4,826,000 and $1,078,000 at December 31, 2005 and 2004, respectively.

The Company has notes payable with banks to finance the development of the Company's restaurants in Japan ("Outback Japan"). The notes are payable to banks, collateralized by letters of credit and lease deposits of approximately $3,100,000 and $3,600,000 at December 31, 2005 and 2004, respectively, and bear interest at 0.86% and at rates ranging from 0.95% to 0.96% at December 31, 2005 and 2004, respectively. The notes are denominated and payable in Japanese yen, with outstanding balances as of December 31, 2005 maturing in September 2006. As of December 31, 2005 and 2004, outstanding balances totaled approximately $5,085,000 and $5,769,000, respectively.

In October 2003, Outback Japan established a revolving line of credit to finance the development of new restaurants in Japan and refinance certain notes payable. The line permits borrowing up to a maximum of $10,000,000 with interest rates ranging from 70.0 to 107.5 basis points over LIBOR. The line originally matured in December 2004, but was amended in April 2004 with a new maturity date in June 2007.

As of December 30, 2005 and 2004, the Company had borrowed approximately $9,043,000 and $10,260,000, respectively, on the line of credit at an average interest rate of 0.69%, with draws as of December 31, 2005 maturing from February 2006 to June 2006. The revolving line of credit contains certain restrictions and conditions as defined in the agreement. As of December 31, 2005, the Company was in compliance with all of the debt covenants. Subsequent to December 31, 2005, Outback Japan amended this line of credit (see Note 18 of Notes to Consolidated Financial Statements).

In February 2004, Outback Japan established an additional revolving line of credit to finance the development of new restaurants in Japan and refinance certain notes payable. The line permits borrowing up to a maximum of $10,000,000 with interest of LIBOR divided by a percentage equal to 1.00 minus the Eurocurrency Reserve Percentage. The line matures in December 2006. As of December 31, 2005 and 2004, the Company had borrowed approximately $5,593,000 and $8,635,000, respectively, on the line of credit at an average interest rate of 0.76%, with draws as of December 31, 2005 maturing from January 2006 to February 2006. The revolving line of credit contains certain restrictions and conditions as defined in the agreement. As of December 31, 2005, the Company was in compliance with all of the debt covenants.

In August 2005, the Company entered into a sale-leaseback arrangement for five of its properties. Pursuant to this arrangement, the Company sold these properties for a total of $6,250,000, including $1,250,000 for tenant improvements. The Company then leased the sites back for a 30-year term and will make lease payments on the first day of each calendar month. Since this transaction does not qualify for sale-leaseback accounting treatment, the Company has included the proceeds in the Company's Consolidated Balance Sheet as long-term debt.

The Company is the guarantor of an uncollateralized line of credit that permits borrowing of up to $35,000,000 for a limited liability company, T-Bird Nevada, LLC (T-Bird"), owned by its California franchisee. This line of credit was scheduled to mature in December 2004 but was replaced in January 2005 by an amended agreement with a new maturity date in December 2008. The line of credit bears interest at rates ranging from 50 to 90 basis points over LIBOR. The Company was required to consolidate T-Bird effective January 1, 2004 upon adoption of FIN 46R (see Note 1 of Notes to Consolidated Financial Statements). At December 31, 2005 and 2004, the outstanding balance on the line of credit was approximately $31,283,000 and $30,343,000, respectively, and is included in the Company's Consolidated Balance Sheets as long-term debt. T-Bird uses proceeds from the line of credit for the purchase of real estate and construction of buildings to be opened as Outback Steakhouse restaurants and leased to the Company's franchisees. According to the terms of the line of credit, T-Bird may borrow, repay, reborrow or prepay advances at any time before the termination date of the agreement.

If a default under the line of credit were to occur requiring the Company to perform under the guarantee obligation, the Company has the right to call into default all of its franchise agreements in California and exercise any rights and remedies under those agreements as well as the right to recourse under loans T-Bird has made to individual corporations in California which own the land and/or building which is leased to those franchise locations. Events of default are defined in the line of credit agreement and include the Company's covenant commitments under existing lines of credit. The Company is not the primary obligor on the line of credit, and it is not aware of any noncompliance with the underlying terms of the line of credit agreement that would result in it having to perform in accordance with the terms of the guarantee. The Company also guarantees additional term loans associated with the owner of T-Bird, which are not consolidated, and which had outstanding balances of approximately $15,209 and $176,000 as of December 31, 2005 and 2004, respectively.

Debt Guarantees   The Company is the guarantor of an uncollateralized line of credit that permits borrowing of up to a maximum of $24,500,000 for its joint venture partner, RY-8, Inc. ("RY-8"), in the development of Roy's restaurants. The line of credit originally expired in December 2004 and was renewed with a new termination date of June 30, 2007.

According to the terms of the credit agreement, RY-8 may borrow, repay, reborrow, or prepay advances at any time before the termination date of the agreement. On the termination date of the agreement, the entire outstanding principal amount of the loan then outstanding and any accrued interest is due. At December 31, 2005 and 2004, the outstanding balance on the line of credit was approximately $22,926,000 and $21,987,000, respectively.

RY-8's obligations under the line of credit are unconditionally guaranteed by the Company and Roy's Holdings, Inc, ("RHI"). If an event of default occurs (as defined in the agreement, and including the Company's covenant commitments under existing lines of credit) then the total outstanding balance, including any accrued interest, is immediately due from the guarantors.

If an event of default occurs and RY-8 is unable to pay the outstanding balance owed, the Company would, as guarantor, be liable for this balance. However, in conjunction with the credit agreement, RY-8 and RHI have entered into an Indemnity Agreement and a Pledge of Interest and Security Agreement in favor of the Company. These agreements provide that if the Company is required to perform its obligation as guarantor pursuant to the credit agreement, then RY-8 and RHI will indemnify OSI against all losses, claims, damages or liabilities which arise out of or are based upon its guarantee of the credit agreement. RY-8's and RHI's obligations under these agreements are collateralized by a first priority lien upon and a continuing security interest in any and all of RY-8's interests in the joint venture.

As a result of the Company's recourse provisions and collateral, the estimated fair value of the guarantee to be recorded is immaterial to its financial condition and financial statements.

The Company is the guarantor of up to $9,445,000 of a $68,000,000 note for an unconsolidated affiliate, Kentucky Speedway, in which the Company has a 22.5% equity interest and for which the Company operates catering and concession facilities. Payments of this note began in December 2003 with final maturity in December 2022. At December 31, 2005 and 2004, the outstanding balance and the Company's guarantee of the note were approximately $63,300,000 and $9,445,000, and $65,000,000 and $9,445,000, respectively. This guarantee has not been modified since the effective date of FIN 45 and is thus not subject to the recognition or measurement requirements of FIN 45.

The aggregate payments of debt outstanding at December 31, 2005, for the next five years, are summarized as follows: 2006—$63,442,000; 2007—$80,979,000; 2008—$33,051,000; 2009—$1,138,000; 2010—$488,000; and thereafter—$6,250,000. The carrying amount of long-term debt approximates fair value.

Debt and Debt Guarantee Summary (in thousands):

	Total	Payable during 2006	Payable during 2007–2010	Payable after 2010
Debt	$185,348	$63,442	$115,656	$6,250
Debt guarantees	33,960	9,460	24,500	—
Amount outstanding under debt guarantees	32,386	9,460	22,926	—

8. Other Long-Term Liabilities

Other long-term liabilities consisted of the following (in thousands):

	DECEMBER 31	
	2005	2004
Litigation (See Notes 5 and 12)	$39,000	$ —
Accrued insurance liability	6,696	4,000
Other deferred liability	194	2,114
	$45,890	$6,114

9. Foreign Currency Translation and Comprehensive Income

For all significant non-U.S. operations, the functional currency is the local currency. Assets and liabilities of those operations are translated into U.S. dollars using the exchange rates in effect at the balance sheet date. Results of operations are translated using the average exchange rates for the reporting period. Translation gains and losses are reported as a separate component of accumulated other comprehensive income (loss) in stockholders' equity.

Comprehensive income includes net income and foreign currency translation adjustments. Total comprehensive income for the years ended December 31, 2005, 2004, and 2003 was approximately $149,248,000, $151,531,000, and $162,167,000, respectively, which included the effect of gains and (losses) from translation adjustments of approximately $2,502,000, ($40,000), and ($2,078,000), respectively.

10. Stockholders' Equity

The Company repurchased shares of its common stock, $.01 par value, as follows (in thousands):

	YEARS ENDED DECEMBER 31		
	2005	2004	2003
Number of shares repurchased	2,177	2,155	3,784
Aggregate purchase price	$92,363	$95,554	$143,191

Repurchased shares are carried as treasury stock on the Consolidated Balance Sheets and are recorded at cost. During 2005, 2004, and 2003, the Company reissued approximately 3,264,000, 1,643,000, and 1,951,000 shares of treasury stock, respectively, that had a cost of approximately $131,981,000, $50,538,000, and $60,606,000, respectively for exercises of stock options and grants of restricted stock.

11. Income Taxes

Provision for income taxes consisted of the following (in thousands):

	YEARS ENDED DECEMBER 31		
	2005	2004	2003
Current provision:			
Federal	$82,058	$76,321	$82,711
State	17,836	11,213	9,322
Foreign	10,072	4,310	—
	109,966	91,844	92,033
Deferred provision:			
Federal	(31,383)	(11,569)	(6,298)
State	(2,966)	(1,653)	(521)
Foreign	(1,809)	—	—
	(36,158)	(13,222)	(6,819)
Income tax provision	$73,808	$78,622	$85,214

The reconciliation of income taxes calculated at the United States federal tax statutory rate to the Company's effective tax rate is as follows:

	YEARS ENDED DECEMBER 31		
	2005	2004	2003
Income taxes at federal statutory rate	35.0%	35.0%	35.0%
State and local income taxes, net of federal benefit	4.1	4.0	3.3
Employment related credits, net	(6.8)	(5.3)	(4.4)
Other, net	1.0	(0.9)	(0.1)
Total	33.3%	32.8%	33.8%

The income tax effects of temporary differences that give rise to significant portions of deferred tax assets and liabilities are as follows (in thousands):

	DECEMBER 31	
	2005	2004
Deferred income tax assets:		
Deferred rent	$22,947	$17,613
Insurance reserves	13,208	8,509
Unearned revenue	25,979	24,006
Depreciation	10,748	—
Deferred compensation	2,425	—
Goodwill and amortization	866	4,696
Foreign net operating loss carryforward	3,439	4,035
Other, net	6,808	8,280
Gross deferred income tax assets	86,420	67,139
Valuation allowance	(6,543)	(7,855)
	79,877	59,284
Deferred income tax liabilities:		
Depreciation	—	(13,180)
Net deferred tax asset (liability)	$79,877	$46,104

The changes in the valuation allowance account for the deferred tax assets are as follows (in thousands):

	YEARS ENDED DECEMBER 31		
	2005	2004	2003
Balance at January 1	$7,855	$6,081	$1,568
Additions charged to costs and expenses	526	1,774	679
Other additions (1)	—	—	3,834
Change in assessments about the realization of deferred tax assets	(1,838)	—	—
Balance at December 31	$6,543	$7,855	$6,081

(1) Increase to valuation allowance upon acquisition of deferred tax assets in the Company's 2003 purchase of Japanese operations (see Note 13 of Notes to Consolidated Financial Statements).

A provision was not made for any United States or additional foreign taxes on undistributed earnings related to the Company's foreign affiliates as these earnings were and are expected to continue to be permanently reinvested. If the Company identifies an exception to its general reinvestment policy of undistributed earnings, additional taxes will be posted.

12. Commitments and Contingencies

Operating Leases—The Company leases restaurant and office facilities and certain equipment under operating leases having initial terms expiring between 2006 and 2021. The restaurant facility leases primarily have renewal clauses from five to 30 years exercisable at the option of the Company. Certain of these leases require the payment of contingent rentals based on a percentage of gross revenues, as defined by the terms of the applicable lease agreement. Total rental expense for the years ended December 31, 2005, 2004, and 2003 was approximately $95,169,000, $79,331,000, and $62,741,000, respectively, and included contingent rent of approximately $5,826,000, $4,695,000, and $3,669,000, respectively.

Future minimum rental payments on operating leases (including leases for restaurants scheduled to open in 2006) are as follows (in thousands):

2006	$ 85,358
2007	81,438
2008	75,685
2009	69,584
2010	63,345
Thereafter	204,289
Total minimum lease payments	$579,699

In January 2005, the Company executed a lease termination agreement whereby it will receive $6,000,000 upon vacating a premises currently occupied by a Company–owned Outback Steakhouse. The termination date will be the later of May 1, 2006 or 30 days following receipt of the payment. The Company will record a gain upon disposal of this restaurant, which will be recorded when the cash is received by the Company, and it has fulfilled its obligations under the agreement.

Development Costs—During September 2003, the Company formed a limited liability company to develop Paul Lee's Chinese Kitchen ("Paul Lee's") restaurants. Under the terms of the agreement, the Company committed to the first $10,000,000 of future development costs to open the first five restaurants, all of which had been expended as of March 31, 2005. In January 2006, the Company committed to a plan to sell its interest in the Paul Lee's Chinese Kitchen joint venture to its partner.

Purchase Obligations—The Company has minimum purchase commitments with various vendors through January 2008. Outstanding commitments as of December 31, 2005, were approximately $777,198,000 and consist primarily of minimum purchase commitments of beef, pork, chicken, and other food products related to normal business operations and contracts for advertising, marketing, sports sponsorships, printing, and technology.

Litigation and Other Matters—The Company is subject to legal proceedings claims and liabilities that arise in the ordinary course of business. In the opinion of management, the amount of the ultimate liability with respect to those actions will not materially affect the Company's financial position or results of operations and cash flows.

In June 2003, in a civil case against the Company in Indiana state court alleging liability under the "dramshop" liquor liability statute, a jury returned a verdict in favor of the two plaintiffs who were injured by a drunk driver. The portion of the verdict against the Company was $39,000,000. The Company appealed the verdict to the Indiana Court of Appeals. On July 25, 2005, the Court of Appeals affirmed the verdict of the trial courts. The Company petitioned the Court of Appeals for rehearing and rehearing was denied. The Company filed a petition for transfer with the Indiana Supreme Court. On February 21, 2006, the Indiana Supreme Court granted transfer. That ruling means the Supreme Court has vacated the Court of Appeals' decision and has accepted the case for review. As of the date of this filing, the Indiana Supreme Court has not rendered any decision on the merits of the case nor indicated when or how it might rule.

The Company has insurance coverage related to this case provided by its primary carrier for $21,000,000 and by an excess insurance carrier for the balance of the verdict of approximately $19,000,000. The excess insurance carrier has filed a declaratory judgment suit claiming it was not notified of the case and is therefore not liable for its portion of the verdict. The Company does not believe the excess carrier's case has any merit and is vigorously defending this case. Activity in this case has been held in abeyance pending resolution of appeals in the "dramshop" case. The Company has filed counterclaims against the excess carrier and crossclaims against the primary carrier and its third-party administrator. The Company's third-party administrator has executed an indemnification agreement indemnifying the Company against any liability resulting from the alleged failure to give notice to the excess insurance carrier.

As a result of the affirmation verdict by the Court of Appeals, the Company has recorded the $39,000,000 verdict as a noncurrent liability in its Consolidated Balance Sheet as well as a noncurrent receivable for the same amount which would be due from insurance carriers should this verdict prevail upon appeal.

In connection with the Company's customary review of the results of international operations, it recently discovered that employees of Aussie Chung Ltd., the Company's 82% owned subsidiary in South Korea, may have made improper payments to government officials. Following that discovery, the Company's Audit Committee engaged outside counsel to investigate the matter, and that investigation is substantially complete. Based on the results of the investigation to date, the payments, which were less than $75,000, may have violated the U.S. Foreign Corrupt Practices Act as well as South Korean law. The chief executive officer, chief operating officer and director of treasury of Aussie Chung have resigned as employees and from all offices they hold with that company and, in the case of the chief executive officer and chief operating officer, from its board of directors. The chief executive officer and the chief operating officer are minority owners of Aussie Chung. No other employees of Aussie Chung and no members of the Company's management outside South Korea were implicated in the improper payments.

The Company has voluntarily reported this matter to the staff of the Securities and Exchange Commission and the U.S. Department of Justice. If the U.S. authorities determine that there has been a violation of the Foreign Corrupt Practices Act, they may seek to impose sanctions on the Company that may include injunctive relief, fines, penalties and modifications to the Company's business practices. The Company could also face sanctions from South Korean authorities.

It is not possible at this time to predict whether the authorities will seek to impose sanctions on the Company, and if they do, what those sanctions might be. It is also not possible to predict how any U.S. or South Korean governmental investigation or resulting sanctions may impact the Company's business in South Korea. Depending upon how these matters are resolved, the Company's results of operations and prospects for growth in South Korea could be significantly impacted. In 2005, Aussie Chung had revenues and net income of $220,291,000 and $11,458,000, respectively, representing approximately 5.8% and 7.8% of the Company's consolidated revenues and net income.

12. Commitments and Contingencies (*Continued*)

Guarantees—The Company guarantees debt owed to banks by some of its franchisees, joint venture partners and unconsolidated affiliates. The maximum amount guaranteed is approximately $33,960,000 with outstanding guaranteed amounts of approximately $32,386,000 at December 31, 2005. The Company would have to perform under the guarantees if the borrowers default under their respective loan agreements. The default would trigger a right for the Company to take over the borrower's franchise or partnership interest.

Long-Term Incentives—On December 8, 2005, the Board approved long-term incentive agreements for certain of its brand presidents. The agreements had not been entered into as of December 31, 2005, but payments will be contingent on employment as brand president for a ten-year term (a reduced payment may be made upon completion of the eighth year). The agreements will provide for minimum payments of $500,000 to $1,000,000 per individual upon completion of the term. In addition, upon completion of the term, the individual will receive 5% of the excess, if any, of cumulative operating profit of the brand over the cumulative cost of capital employed in the brand. The cost of capital is subject to annual adjustment by the Company.

Insurance—The Company purchased insurance for individual claims that exceed the amounts listed in the following table:

	2005	2004	2003
Workers' compensation	$1,000,000	$1,000,000	$1,000,000
General liability (1)	1,500,000	1,500,000	1,000,000
Health (2)	300,000	300,000	230,000
Property coverage	5,000,000	5,000,000	5,000,000

(1) Beginning in 2004, for claims arising from liquor liability, there is an additional $1,000,000 deductible until a $2,000,000 aggregate has been met. At that time, any claims arising from liquor liability revert to the general liability deductible.

(2) The Company is self-insured for all aggregate health benefits claims, limited to $300,000 per covered individual per year.

The Company records a liability for all unresolved claims and for an estimate of incurred but not reported claims at the anticipated cost to the Company based on estimates provided by a third party administrator and insurance company. The Company's accounting policies regarding insurance reserves include certain actuarial assumptions and management judgments regarding economic conditions, the frequency and severity of claims and claim development history and settlement practices. Unanticipated changes in these factors may produce materially different amounts of expense that would be reported under these programs.

13. Business Combinations

In January 2003, the Company acquired two restaurants from Fleming's Prime Steakhouse II, LLC, the operator of three unaffiliated Fleming's Prime Steakhouses. The estimated fair market value of the assets received was deemed to satisfy outstanding principal and accrued interest on amounts owed by FPSH II to the Company of approximately $5,569,000. As a result of this transaction, the Company recorded goodwill of approximately $3,674,000, all of which is deductible for income tax purposes.

In April 2003, the Company obtained a controlling interest in its franchise operating restaurants in Japan. The results of the Japanese operations and the associated minority interest have been reflected in the consolidated financial statements since that date. As part of this realignment, the Company contributed approximately $2,488,000 in capital and became directly liable for approximately $19,741,000 of debt that the Company previously guaranteed for the franchise (see Note 7 of Notes to Consolidated Financial

Statements). As a result of this transaction, the Company recorded goodwill of approximately $10,440,000, none of which is deductible for income tax purposes.

In July 2003, the Company acquired from a franchisee 14 Outback Steakhouse restaurants operating in Alabama and Florida for approximately $29,500,000 in cash and the retirement of approximately $1,200,000 in the franchisee's debt. The results of the Alabama restaurants have been reflected in the consolidated financial statements since that date. As a result of this transaction, the Company recorded goodwill of approximately $19,903,000, all of which is deductible for income tax purposes.

In August 2003, the Company acquired from a franchisee a 68.4% interest in two Bonefish Grill restaurants operating in Indiana and Kentucky. The Company also increased its ownership in one Bonefish Grill restaurant operating in Indiana from 45% to 68.4%. The results of these restaurants and the associated minority interest have been reflected in the consolidated financial statements since that date. The purchase price for these acquisitions was approximately $4,400,000 in cash and the Company recorded goodwill of approximately $2,845,000 associated with this transaction, all of which is deductible for income tax purposes.

In September 2003, the Company acquired from a franchisee five Outback Steakhouse restaurants operating in New York for a total of approximately $13,164,000 of which $12,077,000 was paid in cash and $1,087,000 as settlement of receivables. The results of the New York restaurants have been reflected in the consolidated financial statements since that date. The Company recorded goodwill of approximately $1,440,000 associated with this transaction, all of which is deductible for income tax purposes.

In September 2003, the Company acquired from a franchisee one Roy's restaurant operating in Chicago for approximately $1,800,000 in cash. The results of the Chicago restaurant have been reflected in the consolidated financial statements since that date. The Company recorded goodwill of approximately $288,000 associated with this transaction, all of which is deductible for income tax purposes.

In March 2004, the Company acquired the 36% minority ownership interests of its partners in nine Carrabba's restaurants in Texas for approximately $3,738,000 in cash. The Company completed this acquisition because it believes the additional cash flows provided from 100% ownership of these restaurants will meet its internally required rate of return and provide additional shareholder value. No minority interest for these stores has been reflected in the consolidated financial statements since that date. The Company recorded goodwill of approximately $4,722,000 associated with this transaction, all of which is expected to be deductible for income tax purposes.

In January 2004, one of the cofounders of Bonefish Grill died. Under the terms of the Bonefish agreements, the Company purchased the 25% ownership interest of this founder in a Bonefish partnership that owns and operates Bonefish Grill restaurants in Florida for approximately $9,522,000 in cash. Since the date of acquisition, the Company has reduced the minority partner's remaining interest in this entity to 25% in the consolidated financial statements. The Company recorded goodwill of approximately $3,332,000 associated with this transaction, all of which is expected to be deductible for income tax purposes. Additionally, the Company recorded trademark and trade dress assets with values of approximately $1,000,000 and $75,000, which will be amortized over useful lives of 20 and 15 years, respectively, and favorable lease intangibles of approximately $474,000, which will be amortized over the remaining terms of the associated leases, ranging from 2 to 24 years.

In September 2004, the Company acquired an additional 39% ownership interest in the joint venture that operates Fleming's for approximately $24,300,000 in cash and $14,700,000 paid in satisfaction of amounts outstanding under loans previously made by the Company to the joint venture partners. The Company completed this acquisition because it believes as development of new restaurants continues the additional cash flows provided from 90% ownership of this joint venture will meet its internally required rate of return and provide additional shareholder value. Since the date of acquisition, the Company has reduced the minority partners remaining interest to 10% in the consolidated financial statements. In connection with the allocation of the purchase

13. Business Combinations (*Continued*)

price paid to acquire the additional ownership interest, the Company recorded tax-deductible goodwill of approximately $13,732,000 and trademark and trade dress assets with values of approximately $6,747,000 and $702,000, which will be amortized over 25 and 15 years, respectively (see Note 15 of Notes to Consolidated Financial Statements).

On January 1, 2005, the Company acquired the 50% minority ownership interests of its partner in four Carrabba's restaurants in Ohio for approximately $5,200,000 in cash and the assumption of the employee partner buyout liability for these stores of approximately $590,000. The Company completed this acquisition because it believes the additional cash flows provided from 100% ownership of these restaurants will meet its internally required rate of return and provide additional shareholder value. No minority interest for these stores has been reflected in the Consolidated Financial Statements since that date. The Company recorded goodwill of approximately $4,100,000 associated with this transaction, all of which is expected to be deductible for income tax purposes (see Note 15 of Notes to Consolidated Financial Statements).

On a pro forma basis, the effects of the acquisitions were not significant to the Company's results of operations.

14. Stock-Based Compensation Plans and Other Benefit Plans

The Company's Amended and Restated Stock Option Plan (the "Stock Option Plan") was approved by the shareholders of the Company in April 1999, and has subsequently been amended as deemed appropriate by the Company's Board of Directors or shareholders. There are currently 23,500,000 shares of the Company's common stock which may be issued and sold upon exercise of options under the Stock Option Plan. The term of options granted is determined by the Board of Directors and optionees generally vest in the options over a one to ten year period.

The purpose of the Stock Option Plan is to attract competent personnel, to provide long-term incentives to Directors and key employees, and to discourage employees from competing with the Company.

In 2002, the Company adopted the 2002 Managing Partner Stock Option Plan to provide for the issuance of options to Managing Partners and other key employees of the Company upon commencement of employment and to Managing Partners upon completion of the term of their employment agreements. In 2005, this plan was amended to allow the issuance of restricted stock and was renamed the 2005 Amended and Restated Managing Partner stock Plan ("the MP Stock Plan"). No options or restricted stock may be granted under the MP Stock Plan to Directors or Officers of the Company or any of its subsidiaries or affiliated partnerships. The Managing Partner Stock Plan is administrated by the Board of Directors. There are currently 7,500,000 shares of the Company's common stock that may be issued or sold upon exercise of options under the MP Stock Plan. The term of options and restricted stock granted under the MP Stock Plan is determined by the Board of Directors and generally ranges from ten to fifteen years.

Options under the Stock Option Plan and the MP Stock Plan may be options that qualify under Section 422 of the Internal Revenue Code ("Incentive Stock Options") or options that do not qualify under Section 422 ("Nonqualified Options"). To date, the Company has only issued Nonqualified Options.

The exercise price for options granted under the Stock Option Plan generally cannot be less than fair market value at the date of grant of the shares covered by the option. The exercise price of options granted under the MP Stock Plan was historically determined by using a three-month weighted average stock price to eliminate the daily trading increases and decreases in the stock price. This averaging method resulted in certain option grants under the MP Stock Plan that were above or below the closing price as of the exact grant date. Compensation expense resulted if the exercise price of these options was less than the market price on the date of grant. The Company discontinued use of the average stock price in November 2005.

As of December 31, 2005, the Company had granted to employees of the Company a cumulative total of approximately 23,316,000 options (after forfeitures) under the Stock Option Plan to purchase the Company's common stock at prices ranging from $0.19 to $43.90 per share, which was the estimated fair market value at the time of each grant, and approximately 618,000 shares of restricted stock. As of December 31, 2005, the Company had granted to employees of the Company a cumulative total of approximately 6,806,000 options (after forfeitures) under the MP Stock Plan to purchase the Company's common stock at prices ranging from $29.23 to $46.93 per share and approximately 280,000 shares of restricted stock. As of December 31, 2005, options for approximately 2,377,000 shares and no shares of restricted stock were exercisable in total under both of the plans.

The remaining contractual life for options granted to corporate employees was approximately four to ten years, three to nine years and two to eight years and for options granted to restaurant Managing Partners was approximately nine to fifteen years, eight to fourteen years and seven to thirteen years for the options granted during 2005, 2004, and 2003, respectively.

The following table presents activity in the Company's stock option plans for the years ended December 31, 2005, 2004, and 2003 (in thousands, except option prices and excluding restricted stock):

	Options	Weighted Average Exercise Price
Outstanding at December 31, 2002	15,856	$25.56
Granted	2,824	36.56
Exercised	(1,951)	21.24
Forfeited	(353)	30.76
Outstanding at December 31, 2003	16,376	27.41
Granted	3,514	42.60
Exercised	(1,602)	22.34
Forfeited	(429)	31.66
Outstanding at December 31, 2004	17,859	30.47
Granted	1,427	43.03
Exercised	(2,130)	23.38
Forfeited	(513)	37.24
Outstanding at December 31, 2005	16,643	32.25

The following table summarizes information concerning currently outstanding and exercisable stock options issued at December 31, 2005 (in thousands, except option prices):

Range of Exercise Prices	OPTIONS OUTSTANDING			OPTIONS EXERCISABLE	
	Number Outstanding at December 31, 2005	Weighted Average Remaining Contractual Life (Years)	Weighted Average Exercise Price	Number Exercisable at December 31, 2005	Weighted Average Exercise Price
$14.30–$21.45	1,352	5.4	$17.33	570	$17.64
$21.52–$32.18	7,060	7.8	26.96	1,594	26.23
$32.43–$46.93	8,231	10.5	39.24	213	36.26
	16,643	9.0	32.25	2.377	25.07

14. Stock-Based Compensation Plans and Other Benefit Plans (*Continued*)

The weighted average estimated fair value of stock options granted during 2005, 2004, and 2003 was $14.80, $12.67, and $10.29 per share, respectively. As of December 31, 2005, 2004, and 2003 there were 2,377,000, 2,755,000, and 2,253,000 options exercisable at weighted average exercise prices of $25.07, $23.73, and $22.08, respectively.

Tax benefits resulting from the exercise of nonqualified stock options reduced taxes currently payable by approximately $16,514,000, $14,527,000, and $13,189,000 in 2005, 2004, and 2003, respectively. The tax benefits are credited to additional paid-in capital.

The Company has a qualified defined contribution 401(K) plan covering substantially all full-time employees, except officers and certain highly compensated employees. Assets of this plan are held in trust for the sole benefit of the employees. The Company contributed approximately $1,500,000, $1,350,000, and $1,071,000 to the 401(K) plan during the plan years ended December 31, 2005, 2004, and 2003, respectively.

In 2004, the Board of Directors approved an amendment and restatement (the "Amendment") of the Company's Amended and Restated Stock Option Plan (the "Plan") to allow for the grant of shares of restricted common stock under the plan and to increase the number of shares for which options and shares of restricted common stock may be granted under the Plan by 1,000,000, or from 22,500,000 to 23,500,000. This amendment was approved by vote of the shareholders of the Company on April 21, 2004.

The following table presents restricted stock activity in the Company's plans for the year ended December 31, 2005 (in thousands, except average fair value):

	Number of Restricted Share Awards	Weighted Average Fair Value per Award
Restricted share awards outstanding at December 31, 2004	—	—
Granted	1,061	$41.57
Vested	—	—
Forfeited	(17)	43.28
Restricted share awards outstanding at December 31, 2005	1,044	41.54

Compensation expense recognized in net earnings for awards granted during the year ended December 31, 2005 was approximately $3,344,000. The Company did not grant restricted stock during the years ended December 31, 2004 and 2003. At December 31, 2005, unrecognized compensation expense related to restricted stock awards totaled approximately $40,858,000 and will be recognized over a weighted average period of 5.4 years.

15. Related Party Transactions

During 2001, Mr. Lee Roy Selmon, a member of the Board of Directors invested approximately $101,000 for a 10% interest in the operations of a Company-owned restaurant that bears his name and to which he is making a material image contribution. Mr. Selmon will receive a 1% royalty from all future Lee Roy Selmon's restaurants developed by the Company. In 2005, Mr. Selmon received distributions from the Selmon's partnership in the amount of approximately $65,000 and royalties in the amount of approximately $41,000. Mr. Selmon also serves on the board of directors of Fifth Third Bank, Florida region, which is a division of Fifth Third Bancorp. Some of the

Company's individual restaurant locations have depository relationships with Fifth Third Bancorp.

A member of the Board of Directors, through his wholly owned corporation, has made investments in the aggregate amount of approximately $331,000 in seven limited partnerships that are parties to joint ventures that own and operate certain Carrabba's Italian Grill restaurants. In 2005, this director received distributions of approximately $42,000 from these partnerships.

A member of the Board of Directors and a named executive officer of the Company, through his revocable trust in which he and his wife are the grantors and trustees, and are the sole beneficiaries, owns a 100% interest in AWA III Steakhouse, Inc., which owns 2.5% of Outback/Fleming's, LLC, the joint venture that operates Fleming's Prime Steakhouse and Wine Bars. In 2005, this director and officer did not receive any distributions from these investments and paid in capital of approximately $364,000.

A named executive officer of the Company has made investments in the aggregate amount of approximately $625,000 in 27 limited partnerships that are parties to joint ventures that own and operate either certain Carrabba's Italian Grill restaurants or Bonefish Grill restaurants. In 2005, this officer received distributions from these partnerships of approximately $91,000. On January 1, 2005, the Company acquired four joint venture Carrabba's restaurants from these limited partnerships (see Note 13 of Notes to Consolidated Financial Statements). This officer received approximately $141,000 as a result of his ownership interest in these joint venture restaurants. In addition, on August 1, 2005, this officer assigned to the Company his interests in 17 restaurants operating as either Carrabba's Italian Grills or Bonefish Grills for an aggregate purchase price of approximately $286,000. He had contributed an aggregate amount of approximately $317,000 for these interests.

A named executive officer of the Company has made investments in the aggregate amount of approximately $593,000 in 27 limited partnerships that are parties to joint ventures that own and operate one Outback Steakhouse or certain Carrabba's Italian Grill restaurants or Bonefish Grill restaurants. In 2005, this officer received distributions from these partnerships of approximately $81,000. On January 1, 2005, the Company acquired four joint venture Carrabba's restaurants from these limited partnerships (see Note 13 of Notes to Consolidated Financial Statements). This officer received approximately $202,000 as a result of his ownership interest in these joint venture restaurants. In addition, on August 1, 2005, this officer assigned to the Company his interests in 25 restaurants operating as Outback Steakhouses, Carrabba's Italian Grills or Bonefish Grills to which he had contributed an aggregate amount of approximately $246,000. The officer agreed to assign his interests in the 25 restaurants to the Company for an aggregate purchase price of approximately $268,000.

A named executive officer of the Company has made investments in the aggregate amount of approximately $250,000 in seven limited partnerships that are parties to joint ventures that own and operate either certain Carrabba's Italian Grill restaurants or Outback Steakhouse restaurants. In 2005, this officer received distributions from these partnerships of approximately $36,000. On December 5, 2005, this officer transferred to the Company his limited partnership interests in three Outback Steakhouse restaurants to which he had contributed an aggregate amount of approximately $150,000. He received approximately $162,000 in exchange for these assignments.

A sibling of a named executive officer of the Company has made investments in the aggregate amount of approximately $375,000 in two limited partnerships that each own and operate one Outback Steakhouse restaurant. In 2005, this sibling received distributions from these partnerships in the aggregate amount of approximately $162,000.

The parents and a certain sibling of a member of the Board of Directors made investments in the aggregate amount of approximately $131,000 in three unaffiliated limited partnerships that own and operate three Outback Steakhouse restaurants pursuant to franchise agreements with Outback Steakhouse of Florida, Inc. and received

15. Related Party Transactions (*Continued*)

distributions from the partnerships in the aggregate amount of approximately $29,000 during 2005.

The relatives of a member of the Board of Directors made investments of approximately $66,000 in one unaffiliated limited partnership that owns and operates two Bonefish Grill restaurants as a franchisee of Bonefish. They received distributions from this partnership in the aggregate amount of approximately $15,000 during 2005.

In January 2006, a member of the Company's Board of Directors became a director on the board of Bank of America Corporation. The Company has various corporate banking relationships with Bank of America, and they participate as a lender in the Company's $150,000,000 revolving credit facility. In addition, individual restaurant locations have depository relationships with Bank of America in the ordinary course of business.

16. Segment Reporting

In June 1997, the FASB issued SFAS No. 131, "Disclosures about Segments of an Enterprise and Related Information." The Company operates restaurants under eight brands that have similar investment criteria and economic and operating characteristics and are considered one reportable operating segment. Management does not believe that the Company has any material reporting segments. Approximately 7%, 6%, and 4% of the Company's total revenues for the years ended December 31, 2005, 2004, and 2003, respectively, were attributable to operations in foreign countries, and approximately 7%, 6% and 5% of the Company's total long-lived assets were located in foreign countries where the Company holds assets as of December 31, 2005, 2004, and 2003, respectively.

17. Earnings per Share

The following table represents the computation of basic and diluted earnings per common share as required by SFAS No. 128 "Earnings Per Share" (in thousands, except per-share data):

| | YEARS ENDED DECEMBER 31 | | |
	2005	2004	2003
Net income	$146,746	$151,571	$164,245
Basic weighted average number of common shares outstanding	73,952	74,117	75,256
Basic earnings per common share	$1.98	$2.05	$2.18
Effect of dilutive stock options	2,589	3,432	3,137
Diluted weighted average number of common shares outstanding	76,541	77,549	78,393
Diluted earnings per common share	$1.92	$1.95	$2.10

Diluted earnings per common share excludes antidilutive stock options of approximately 2,393,000, 1,671,000, and 724,000 during 2005, 2004 and 2003, respectively.

18. Subsequent Events

On January 24, 2006, the Company entered into an agreement in principle to sell its 50% interest in the Paul Lee's Chinese Kitchen ("PLCK") joint venture to its partner. Upon closing the sale, the Company will receive a promissory note with a maximum principal amount of $2,000,000 due and payable February 1, 2011, with interest payable annually to the extent that cash flows from PLCK can fund those payments (any unpaid interest will increase the principal balance of the note). If PLCK is sold or liquidated prior to full payment of the note, the Company will receive, in full satisfaction of the note, 50% of the proceeds of sale or liquidation up to the outstanding principal and accrued and unpaid interest amounts under the note. Additionally, the Company will have a "reinvestment option" whereby at any time the note remains outstanding, the Company may acquire a 50% ownership interest in PLCK upon payment of 50% of all capital contributions made to PLCK by the other partner subsequent to the sale and an additional amount equal to the greater of $1,000,000 and 10% of the additional capital invested after the sale. The Company does not expect to incur material costs or future cash expenditures as a result of the sale. In connection with the planned sale of Paul Lee's Chinese Kitchen, the Company recorded intangible and other asset impairments totaling approximately $7,500,000, net of minority interest, in its financial results for the fourth quarter of 2005.

On January 24, 2006, the Company's Board of Directors declared a quarterly dividend of $0.13 per share of the Company's common stock. The dividend was paid March 3, 2006 to shareholders of record as of February 17, 2006.

On February 6, 2006, the Company purchased ten Outback Steakhouses from its franchisee in Eastern Canada for approximately $7,400,000 in cash and the assumption of the employee partner buyout liability for these locations of approximately $743,000 and accrued vacation liability of approximately $24,000. The Company completed this acquisition because it believes the additional cash flows provided from ownership of these restaurants will meet its internally required rate of return and provide additional shareholder value. The Company recorded goodwill of approximately $3,482,000 associated with this transaction, $2,612,000 of which is expected to be deductible for income tax purposes.

On February 13, 2006, the Company's Board of Directors authorized the repurchase of an additional 1,500,000 shares of the Company's common stock. As a result of this authorization, the Company has the ability to repurchase up to 3,000,000 shares under authorized plans in addition to repurchasing shares on a regular basis to offset shares issued as a result of stock option exercises.

In February 2006, the Company entered into a verbal agreement to sell two of its Company-owned Bonefish Grills to a franchisee. This transaction will be effective as of January 1, 2006, and should be finalized in March 2006.

Effective March 10, 2006, the Company amended a $150,000,000 revolving credit facility that was scheduled to mature in June 2007 with a new $225,000,000 maximum borrowing amount and maturity date of June 2011. The amended line of credit permits borrowing at interest rates ranging from 45 to 65 basis points over the 30, 60, 90, or 180 day London Interbank Offered Rate (LIBOR). The credit agreement contains certain restrictions and conditions as defined in the agreement that require the Company to maintain consolidated net worth equal to or greater than consolidated total debt and a maximum total consolidated debt to EBITDAR (earnings before interest, taxes, depreciation, amortization and rent) ratio of 3.0 to 1.0.

The Company also amended a $30,000,000 line of credit that was scheduled to mature in June 2007 with a new $40,000,000 maximum borrowing amount and maturity date of June 2011. The amended line permits borrowing at interest rates ranging from 45 to 65 basis points over LIBOR for loan draws and 55 to 80 basis points over LIBOR for letters of credit. The credit agreement contains certain restrictions and conditions as defined in the agreement.

Effective March 10, 2006, Outback Japan amended its $10,000,000 revolving credit facility that was scheduled to mature in June 2007, with a new maturity date in June 2011. The amended line of credit permits borrowing at interest rates ranging from 45 to 65 basis points over LIBOR. The credit agreement amendment contains certain restrictions and conditions as defined in the agreement.

19. Selected Quarterly Financial Data (Unaudited)

The following table presents selected quarterly financial data for the periods ending as indicated, which has been restated to correct the errors that are discussed in Note 1—Restatement of Previously Issued Consolidated Financial Statements (in thousands, except per-share data):

	2005			
	March 31	June 30	September 30	December 31
Revenues	$898,443	$919,113	$872,871	$922,290
Income from operations	82,633	64,922	47,741	33,280
Income before provision for income taxes and elimination of minority interest	80,909	63,770	46,476	30,590
Net income (1)	50,351	39,534	29,472	27,389
Basic earnings per share	$0.68	$0.53	$0.40	$0.37
Diluted earnings per share	$0.65	$0.51	$0.38	$0.36

	2004			
	March 31	June 30	September 30	December 31
Revenues	$797,289	$808,776	$783,620	$826,304
Income from operations	77,426	68,000	42,281	56,050
Income before provision for income taxes and elimination of minority interest	76,180	67,368	41,239	54,586
Net income (1)	47,676	42,587	26,618	34,690
Basic earnings per share	$0.64	$0.57	$0.36	$0.47
Diluted earnings per share	$0.61	$0.55	$0.35	$0.45

(1)   Net income includes $951,000, $7,679,000, $1,396,000 and $17,144,000 in provisions for impaired assets and restaurant closings in the first, second, third and fourth quarters of 2005, respectively, and $2,394,000 in provisions for impaired assets and restaurant closings in the third quarter of 2004.

Report of Independent Registered Certified Public Accounting Firm

To the Board of Directors and Shareholders of Outback Steakhouse, Inc:

We have completed integrated audits of Outback Steakhouse, Inc.'s 2005 and 2004 consolidated financial statements and of its internal control over financial reporting as of December 31, 2005, and an audit of its 2003 consolidated financial statements in accordance with the standards of the Public Company Accounting Oversight Board (United States). Our opinions, based on our audits, are presented below.

CONSOLIDATED FINANCIAL STATEMENTS

In our opinion, the consolidated financial statements listed in the index appearing under Item 15(a)(1) present fairly, in all material respects, the financial position of Outback Steakhouse, Inc. and its subsidiaries at December 31, 2005 and 2004, and the results of their operations and their cash flows for each of the three years in the period ended December 31, 2005, in conformity with accounting principles generally accepted in the United States of America. These financial statements are the responsibility of the Company's management. Our responsibility is to express an opinion on these financial statements based on our audits. We conducted our audits of these statements in accordance with the standards of the Public Company Accounting Oversight Board (United States). Those standards require that we plan and perform the audit to obtain reasonable assurance about whether the financial statements are free of material misstatement. An audit of financial statements includes examining, on a test basis, evidence supporting the amounts and disclosures in the financial statements, assessing the accounting principles used and significant estimates made by management, and evaluating the overall financial statement presentation. We believe that our audits provide a reasonable basis for our opinion.

As discussed in Note 1 to the consolidated financial statements, the Company has restated its 2005, 2004 and 2003 consolidated financial statements.

INTERNAL CONTROL OVER FINANCIAL REPORTING

Also, we have audited management's assessment, included in "Management's Report on Internal Control Over Financial Reporting" appearing under Item 9A, that Outback Steakhouse, Inc. did not maintain effective internal control over financial reporting as of December 31, 2005, because of the effect of not having effective controls over the completeness and accuracy of unearned revenue, based on criteria established in *Internal Control—Integrated Framework* issued by the Committee of Sponsoring Organizations of the Treadway Commission ("COSO"). The Company's management is responsible for maintaining effective internal control over financial reporting and for its assessment of the effectiveness of internal control over financial reporting. Our responsibility is to express opinions on management's assessment and on the effectiveness of the Company's internal control over financial reporting based on our audit.

We conducted our audit of internal control over financial reporting in accordance with the standards of the Public Company Accounting Oversight Board (United States). Those standards require that we plan and perform the audit to obtain reasonable assurance about whether effective internal control over financial reporting was maintained in all material respects. An audit of internal control over financial reporting includes obtaining an understanding of internal control over financial reporting, evaluating management's assessment, testing and evaluating the design and operating effectiveness of internal control, and performing such other procedures as we consider necessary in the circumstances. We believe that our audit provides a reasonable basis for our opinions.

A company's internal control over financial reporting is a process designed to provide reasonable assurance regarding the reliability of financial reporting and the preparation of financial statements for external purposes in accordance with generally accepted accounting principles. A company's internal control over financial reporting includes those policies and procedures that (i) pertain to the maintenance of records that, in reasonable detail, accurately and fairly reflect the transactions and dispositions of the assets of the company; (ii) provide reasonable assurance that transactions are recorded as necessary to permit preparation of financial statements in accordance with generally accepted accounting principles, and that receipts and expenditures of the company are being made only in accordance with authorizations of management and directors of the company; and (iii) provide reasonable assurance regarding prevention or timely detection of unauthorized acquisition, use, or disposition of the company's assets that could have a material effect on the financial statements.

Because of its inherent limitations, internal control over financial reporting may not prevent or detect misstatements. Also, projections of any evaluation of effectiveness to future periods are subject to the risk that controls may become inadequate because of changes in conditions, or that the degree of compliance with the policies or procedures may deteriorate.

A material weakness is a control deficiency, or combination of control deficiencies, that results in more than a remote likelihood that a material misstatement of the annual or interim financial statements will not be prevented or detected. The following material weakness has been identified and included in management's assessment as of December 31, 2005. The Company did not maintain effective controls over the completeness and accuracy of unearned revenue. Specifically, the Company did not have controls designed and in place to ensure that the Company's obligations related to gift cards and gift certificates as presented in the financial statements were reconciled to the underlying detail of gift cards and gift certificates outstanding and that revenue was recognized in accordance with generally accepted accounting principles. This control deficiency resulted in the restatement of the Company's consolidated financial statements as of December 31, 2005 and 2004 and for the years ended December 31, 2005, 2004 and 2003, all quarters for 2005 and 2004, and the first and second quarters of 2006. In addition, this control deficiency could result in a material misstatement to unearned revenue for gift cards and certificates, revenue and related expenses that would result in a material misstatement to the Company's annual or interim consolidated financial statements that would not be prevented or detected. Accordingly, the Company's management determined that this control deficiency constitutes a material weakness. This material weakness was considered in determining the nature, timing, and extent of audit tests applied in our audit of the 2005 consolidated financial statements, and our opinion regarding the effectiveness of the Company's internal control over financial reporting does not affect our opinion on those consolidated financial statements.

Management and we previously concluded that the Company maintained effective internal control over financial reporting as of December 31, 2005. However, management has subsequently determined that the material weakness described above existed as of December 31, 2005. Accordingly, "Management's Report on Internal Control Over Financial Reporting" has been restated and our present opinion on internal control over financial reporting, as presented herein, is different from that expressed in our previous report.

In our opinion, management's assessment that Outback Steakhouse, Inc. did not maintain effective internal control over financial reporting as of December 31, 2005, is fairly stated, in all material respects, based on criteria established in *Internal Control— Integrated Framework* issued by the COSO. Also, in our opinion, because of the effects of the material weakness described above on the achievement of the objectives of the control criteria, Outback Steakhouse, Inc. has not maintained effective internal control over financial reporting as of December 31, 2005, based on the criteria established in *Internal Control—Integrated Framework* issued by the COSO.

/s/ PricewaterhouseCoopers LLP

Tampa, Florida
March 16, 2006, except for the restatement discussed in Note 1 to the consolidated financial statements and the matter described in the penultimate paragraph of "Management's Report on Internal Control Over Financial Reporting," as to which the date is January 5, 2007.

Appendix C

Present and Future Value Concepts

The concepts of present value (PV) and future value (FV) are based on the time value of money. The **time value of money** is the idea that, quite simply, money received today is worth more than money to be received one year from today (or at any other future date), because it can be used to earn interest. If you invest $1,000 today at 10 percent, you will have $1,100 in one year. So $1,000 in one year is worth $100 less than $1,000 today because you lose the opportunity to earn the $100 in interest.

In some business situations, you will know the dollar amount of a cash flow that occurs in the future and will need to determine its value now. This type of situation is known as a **present value** problem. The opposite situation occurs when you know the dollar amount of a cash flow that occurs today and need to determine its value at some point in the future. These situations are called **future value** problems. The value of money changes over time because money can earn interest. The following table illustrates the basic difference between present value and future value problems:

	Now	Future
Present value	?	$1,000
Future value	$1,000	?

Present and future value problems may involve two types of cash flow: a single payment or an annuity (which is the fancy word for a series of equal cash payments). Thus, you need to learn how to deal with four different situations related to the time value of money:

1. Future value of a single payment
2. Present value of a single payment
3. Future value of an annuity
4. Present value of an annuity

Most inexpensive handheld calculators and any spreadsheet program can perform the detailed arithmetic computations required to solve future value and present value problems. In later courses and in all business situations, you will probably use a calculator or computer to solve these problems. At this stage, we encourage you to solve problems using Tables C.1 through C.4 at the end of this appendix. We believe that using the tables will give you a better understanding of how and why present and future value concepts apply to business problems. The tables give the value of a $1 cash flow (single payment or annuity) for different periods (n) and at different interest rates (i). If a problem involves payments other than $1, it is necessary to multiply the value from the table by the amount of the payment.[1]

Computing Future and Present Values of a Single Amount

FUTURE VALUE OF A SINGLE AMOUNT

In future value of a single amount problems, you will be asked to calculate how much money you will have in the future as the result of investing a certain amount in the present. If you were to receive a gift of $10,000, for instance, you might decide to put it in a savings account and use the money as a down payment on a house after you graduate. The future value computation would tell you how much money will be available when you graduate.

To solve a future value problem, you need to know three items:

1. Amount to be invested.
2. Interest rate (i) the amount will earn.
3. Number of periods (n) in which the amount will earn interest.

The future value concept is based on compound interest, which simply means that interest is calculated on top of interest. Thus, the amount of interest for each period is calculated using the principal plus any interest not paid out in prior periods. Graphically, the calculation of the future value of $1 for three periods at an interest rate of 10 percent may be represented as follows:

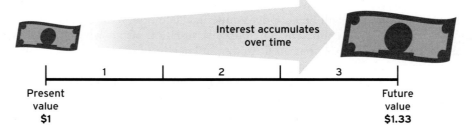

Assume that on January 1, 2007, you deposit $1,000 in a savings account at 10 percent annual interest, compounded annually. At the end of three years, the $1,000 will have increased to $1,331 as follows:

Year	Amount at Start of Year	+	Interest During the Year	=	Amount at End of Year
1	$1,000	+	$1,000 × 10% = $100	=	$1,100
2	1,100	+	1,100 × 10% = 110	=	1,210
3	1,210	+	1,210 × 10% = 121	=	1,331

---

[1] Present value and future value problems involve cash flows. The basic concepts are the same for cash inflows (receipts) and cash outflows (payments). No fundamental differences exist between present value and future value calculations for cash payments versus cash receipts.

We can avoid the detailed arithmetic by referring to Table C.1, Future Value of $1, on page C12. For $i = 10\%$, $n = 3$, we find the value 1.3310. We then compute the balance at the end of year 3 as follows:

$$\$1,000 \times 1.3310 = \$1,331$$

> From Table C.1,
> Interest rate = 10%
> $n = 3$

Note that the increase of $331 is due to the time value of money. It is interest revenue to the owner of the savings account and interest expense to the bank.

PRESENT VALUE OF A SINGLE AMOUNT

The present value of a single amount is the worth to you today of receiving that amount some time in the future. For instance, you might be offered an opportunity to invest in a financial instrument that would pay you $1,000 in 3 years. Before you decided whether to invest, you would want to determine the present value of the instrument.

To compute the present value of an amount to be received in the future, we must discount (a procedure that is the opposite of compounding) at i interest rate for n periods. In discounting, the interest is subtracted rather than added, as it is in compounding. Graphically, the present value of $1 due at the end of the third period with an interest rate of 10 percent can be represented as follows:

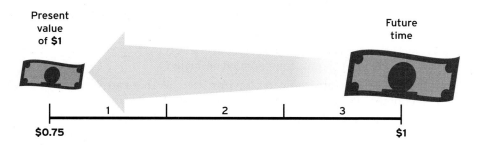

Assume that today is January 1, 2007, and you have the opportunity to receive $1,000 cash on December 31, 2009. At an interest rate of 10 percent per year, how much is the $1,000 payment worth to you on January 1, 2007? You could discount the amount year by year,[2] but it is easier to use Table C.2, Present Value of $1, on page C13. For $i = 10\%$, $n = 3$, we find that the present value of $1 is 0.7513. The present value of $1,000 to be received at the end of three years can be computed as follows:

> From Table C.2
> Interest rate = 10%
> $n = 3$

$$\$1,000 \times 0.7513 = \$751.30$$

It's important to learn not only how to compute a present value but also to understand what it means. The $751.30 is the amount you would pay now to have the right to

---

[2] The detailed discounting is as follows:

Periods	Interest for the Year	Present Value*
1	$1,000 − ($1,000 × 1/1.10) = $90.91	$1,000 − $90.91 = $909.09
2	$909.09 − ($909.09 × 1/1.10) = $82.65	$909.09 − $82.65 = $826.44
3	$826.44 − ($826.44 × 1/1.10) = $75.14[†]	$826.44 − $75.14 = $751.30

*Verifiable in Table C.2.
[†]Adjusted for rounding

receive $1,000 at the end of three years, assuming an interest rate of 10 percent. Conceptually, you should be indifferent between having $751.30 today and receiving $1,000 in three years. If you had $751.30 today but wanted $1,000 in three years, you could simply deposit the money in a savings account that pays 10% interest and it would grow to $1,000 in three years. Alternatively, if you had a contract that promised you $1,000 in three years, you could sell it to an investor for $751.30 in cash today because it would permit the investor to earn the difference in interest.

What if you could only earn 6 percent during the three-year period from January 1, 2007, to December 31, 2009? What would be the present value on January 1, 2007, of receiving $1,000 on December 31, 2009? To answer this we would take the same approach, using Table C.2, except that the interest rate would change to $i = 6\%$. Referring to Table C.2, we see the present value factor for $i = 6\%$, $n = 3$, is 0.8396. Thus, the present value of $1,000 to be received at the end of three years, assuming a 6 percent interest rate, would be computed as $1,000 \times 0.8396 = $839.60. Notice that when we assume a 6 percent interest rate the present value is greater than when we assumed a 10 percent interest rate. The reason for this difference is that, to reach $1,000 three years from now, you'd need to deposit more money in a savings account now if it earns 6 percent interest than if it earns 10 percent interest.

HOW'S IT GOING?   A Self-Study Quiz

1. If the interest rate in a present value problem increases from 8 percent to 10 percent, will the present value increase or decrease?

2. What is the present value of $10,000 to be received 10 years from now if the interest rate is 5 percent, compounded annually?

3. If $10,000 is deposited now in a savings account that earns 5 percent interest compounded annually, how much will it be worth 10 years from now?

Computing Future and Present Values of an Annuity

> **YOU SHOULD KNOW**
>
> An **annuity** is a series of periodic cash receipts or payments that are equal in amount each interest period.

Instead of a single payment, many business problems involve multiple cash payments over a number of periods. An **annuity** is a series of consecutive payments characterized by

1. An equal dollar amount each interest period.
2. Interest periods of equal length (year, half a year, quarter, or month).
3. An equal interest rate each interest period.

Examples of annuities include monthly payments on a car or house, yearly contributions to a savings account, and monthly pension benefits.

FUTURE VALUE OF AN ANNUITY

If you are saving money for some purpose, such as a new car or a trip to Europe, you might decide to deposit a fixed amount of money in a savings account each month. The future value of an annuity computation will tell you how much money will be in your savings account at some point in the future.

The future value of an annuity includes compound interest on each payment from the date of payment to the end of the term of the annuity. Each new payment accumulates less interest than prior payments, only because the number of periods remaining in which to accumulate interest decreases. The future value of an annuity of $1 for three periods at 10 percent may be represented graphically as

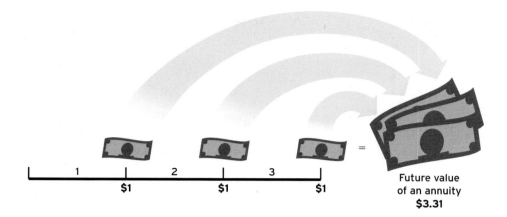

Future value
of an annuity
$3.31

Assume that each year for three years, you deposit $1,000 cash in a savings account at 10 percent interest per year. You make the first $1,000 deposit on December 31, 2007, the second one on December 31, 2008, and the third and last one on December 31, 2009. The first $1,000 deposit earns compound interest for two years (for a total principal and interest of $1,210); the second deposit earns interest for one year (for a total principal and interest of $1,100). The third deposit earns no interest because it was made on the day that the balance is computed. Thus, the total amount in the savings account at the end of three years is $3,310 ($1,210 + $1,100 + $1,000).

To calculate the future value of this annuity, we could compute the interest on each deposit, similar to what's described above. However, a faster way is to refer to Table C.3, Future Value of an Annuity of $1 for $i = 10\%$, $n = 3$ to find the value 3.3100. The future value of your three deposits of $1,000 each can be computed as follows:

> From Table C.3,
> Interest rate = 10%
> $n = 3$

$$\$1,000 \times 3.3100 = \$3,310$$

The Power of Compounding

Compound interest is a remarkably powerful economic force. In fact, the ability to earn interest on interest is the key to building economic wealth. If you save $1,000 per year for the first 10 years of your career, you will have more money when you retire than you would if you had saved $15,000 per year for the last 10 years of your career. This surprising outcome occurs because the money you save early in your career will earn more interest than the money you save at the end of your career. If you start saving money now, the majority of your wealth will not be the money you saved but the interest your money was able to earn.

The chart in the margin illustrates the power of compounding over a brief 10-year period. If you deposit $1 each year in an account earning 10 percent interest, at the end of just 10 years, only 63 percent of your balance will be made up of money you have saved. The rest will be interest you have earned. After 20 years, only 35 percent of your balance will be from saved money. The lesson associated with compound interest is that even though saving money is hard, you should start now.

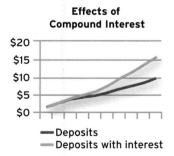

**Effects of
Compound Interest**

— Deposits
— Deposits with interest

PRESENT VALUE OF AN ANNUITY

The present value of an annuity is the value now of a series of equal amounts to be received (or paid out) for some specified number of periods in the future. It is computed by discounting each of the equal periodic amounts. A good example of this type of problem is a retirement program that offers employees a monthly income after retirement.

The present value of an annuity of $1 for three periods at 10 percent may be represented graphically as

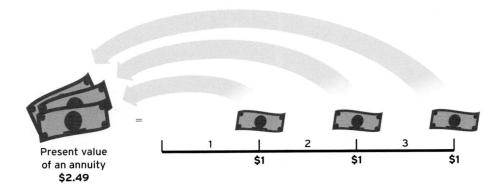

Present value
of an annuity
$2.49

Assume you are to receive $1,000 cash on each December 31, 2007, 2008, and 2009. How much would the sum of these three $1,000 future amounts be worth on January 1, 2007, assuming an interest rate of 10 percent per year? One way to determine this is to use Table C.2 to calculate the present value of each single amount as follows:

		FACTOR FROM TABLE C.2		
Year	**Amount**	**$i = 10\%$**		**Present Value**
1	$1,000	×	0.9091 ($n = 1$)	=	$ 909.10
2	$1,000	×	0.8264 ($n = 2$)	=	826.40
3	$1,000	×	0.7513 ($n = 3$)	=	751.30
			Total present value	=	$2,486.80

Alternatively, we can compute the present value of this annuity more easily by using Table C.4, as follows:

From Table C.4,
Interest rate = 10%
$n = 3$

$$\$1,000 \times 2.4869 = \$2,487 \text{ (rounded)}$$

INTEREST RATES AND INTEREST PERIODS

COACH'S TIP

The help function in Excel describes how to calculate the present value of an annuity using its PV worksheet function.

The preceding illustrations assumed annual periods for compounding and discounting. Although interest rates are almost always quoted on an annual basis, many compounding periods encountered in business are less than one year. When interest periods are less than a year, the values of n and i must be restated to be consistent with the length of the interest compounding period.

To illustrate, 12 percent interest compounded annually for five years requires the use of $n = 5$ and $i = 12\%$. If compounding is quarterly, however, there will be four interest periods per year (20 interest periods in five years), and the quarterly interest rate is one quarter of the annual rate (3 percent per quarter). Therefore, 12 percent interest compounded quarterly for five years requires use of $n = 20$ and $i = 3\%$.

Accounting Applications of Present Values

Many business transactions require the use of future and present value concepts. In finance classes, you will see how to apply future value concepts. In this section, we apply present value concepts to three common accounting cases.

Case A—Present Value of a Single Amount

On January 1, 2007, General Mills bought some new delivery trucks. The company signed a note and agreed to pay $200,000 on December 31, 2008, an amount representing the cash equivalent price of the trucks plus interest for two years. The market interest rate for this note was 12 percent.

> 1. How should the accountant record the purchase?

Answer: This case requires the computation of the present value of a single amount. In conformity with the cost principle, the cost of the trucks is their current cash equivalent price, which is the present value of the future payment. The problem can be shown graphically as follows:

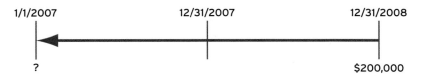

1/1/2007	12/31/2007	12/31/2008
?		$200,000

The present value of the $200,000 is computed as follows:

> From Table C.2,
> Interest rate = 12%
> $n = 2$

$$\$200,000 \times 0.7972 = \$159,440$$

This transaction has the following financial effects, and would be recorded with the journal entry shown below.

Assets	=	Liabilities	+ Stockholders' Equity
Delivery Trucks +159,440		Note Payable +159,440	

dr Delivery Trucks (+A)............................	159,440	
cr Note Payable (+L)............................		159,440

> 2. How should the effects of interest be reported at the end of 2007 and 2008?

Answer: Interest expense would be calculated, reported, and recorded as follows:

<u>December 31, 2007</u>

> Interest = Principal × Rate × Time
> = $159,440 × 12% × 12/12 = $19,132 (rounded)

Assets	=	Liabilities	+	Stockholders' Equity
		Note Payable +19,132		Interest Expense (+E) −19,132

dr Interest Expense (+E, −SE).......................	19,132	
cr Note Payable (+L).............................		19,132

COACH'S TIP

The interest is recorded in the Note payable account because it would be paid as part of the note at Maturity.

December 31, 2008

Interest = Principal × Rate × Time
=($159,440 + $19,132) × 12% × 12/12 = 21,428 (rounded)

Assets	=	Liabilities	+	Stockholders' Equity
		Note Payable +21,428		Interest Expense (+E) −21,428

dr Interest Expense (+E, −SE) 21,428
  cr Note Payable (+L)............................. 21,428

Note Payable (L)

159,440	Jan. 1, 2007
19,132	Interest 2007
21,428	Interest 2008
200,000	Dec. 31, 2008

3. What is the effect of the $200,000 debt payment made on December 31, 2008?

Answer: At this date the amount to be paid is the balance in *Note Payable*, after it has been updated for interest pertaining to 2008, as shown in the T-account in the margin. Notice that, just prior to its repayment, the balance for the note on December 31, 2008 is the same as the maturity amount on the due date.

The debt payment has the following financial effects, and would be recorded with the journal entry shown below.

Assets	=	Liabilities	+	Stockholders' Equity
Cash −200,000		Note Payable −200,000		

dr Note Payable (−L)........................... 200,000
  cr Cash (−A) 200,000

Case B—Present Value of an Annuity

On January 1, 2007, General Mills bought new milling equipment. The company elected to finance the purchase with a note payable to be paid off in three years in annual installments of $163,686. Each installment includes principal plus interest on the unpaid balance at 11 percent per year. The annual installments are due on December 31, 2007, 2008, and 2009. This problem can be shown graphically as follows:

1/1/2007	12/31/2007	12/31/2008	12/31/2009
?	$163,686	$163,686	$163,686

1. What is the amount of the note?

Answer: The note is the present value of each installment payment, $i = 11\%$ and $n = 3$. This is an annuity because the note repayment is made in three equal installments. The amount of the note is computed as follows:

From Table C.4,
Interest rate = 11%
$n = 3$

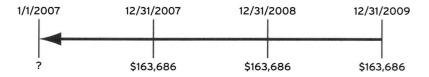

$163,686 × 2.4437 = $400,000

The acquisition on January 1, 2007, would be accounted for as follows:

Assets	=	Liabilities	+ Stockholders' Equity
Milling Equipment +400,000		Note Payable +400,000	

dr Milling Equipment (+A)......................	400,000	
cr Note Payable (+L)...........................		400,000

2. How should the payments made at the end of each year be accounted for?

Answer:

December 31, 2007
Each payment includes both interest and principal. The interest part of the first payment is calculated as:

$$\text{Interest} = \text{Principal} \times \text{Rate} \times \text{Time}$$
$$= \$400,000 \times 11\% \times 12/12 = \$44,000$$

Now that we know the interest component, the principal portion of the first payment of $163,686 can be calculated ($163,686 − $44,000 = $119,686). Thus, the first payment on December 31, 2007, would be accounted for as:

Assets	=	Liabilities	+	Stockholders' Equity
Cash −163,686		Note Payable −119,686		Interest Expense (+E) −44,000

dr Interest Expense (+E, −SE)	44,000	
dr Note Payable (−L) ($163,686 − $44,000)	119,686	
cr Cash (−A).................................		163,686

December 31, 2008
The interest portion of the second and third payments would be calculated in the same way, although notice that the principal balance in the Note Payable account changes after each payment.

$$\text{Interest} = \text{Principal} \times \text{Rate} \times \text{Time}$$
$$= [(\$400,000 − \$119,686) \times 11\% \times 12/12] = \$30,835$$

$$\text{Principal} = \text{Payment} − \text{Interest}$$
$$= \$163,686 − \$30,835 = \$132,851$$

Assets	=	Liabilities	+	Stockholders' Equity
Cash −163,686		Note Payable −132,851		Interest Expense (+E) −30,835

dr Interest Expense (+E, −SE)	30,835	
dr Note Payable (−L)...........................	132,851	
cr Cash (−A).................................		163,686

December 31, 2009

> Interest = Principal × Rate × Time
> = [($400,000 − $119,686 − $132,851) × 11% × 12/12]
> = $16,223 (adjusted to accommodate rounding)
>
> Principal = Payment − Interest
> = $163,686 − $16,223 = $147,463

Note Payable (L)			
		400,000	Jan. 1, 2007
Dec. 31, 2007	119,686		
Dec. 31, 2008	132,851		
Dec. 31, 2009	147,463		
		0	Dec. 31, 2009

Assets	=	Liabilities	+	Stockholders' Equity
Cash −163,686		Note Payable −147,463		Interest Expense (+E) −16,223

> dr Interest Expense (+E, −SE) 16,223
> dr Note Payable (−L) 147,463
>   cr Cash (−A) 163,686

Case C—Present Value of a Single Amount and an Annuity

On January 1, 2007, General Mills issued 100 four-year, $1,000 bonds. The bonds pay interest annually at a rate of 6 percent of face value. What total amount would investors be willing to pay for the bonds if they require an annual return of: (*a*) 4 percent, (*b*) 6 percent, or (*c*) 8 percent?

Answer: This case requires the computation of the present value of a single amount (the $100,000 face value paid at maturity) plus the present value of an annuity (the annual interest payments of $6,000). The problem can be shown graphically as follows:

COACH'S TIP

Each interest payment of $6,000 is calculated as: $100,000 × 6% × 12/12.

(a) 4 Percent Market Interest Rate

The present value of the $100,000 face value is computed as follows:

From Table C.2,
Interest rate = 4%
n = 4

> $100,000 × 0.8548 = $85,480

The present value of the $6,000 annuity is computed as follows:

From Table C.4,
Interest rate = 4%
n = 4

> $6,000 × 3.6299 = $21,780*

*Adjusted to accommodate rounding in the present value factor.

The present value of the total bond payments, computed using the discount rate of 4 percent, is $107,260 (= $85,480 + $21,780).

(b) 6 Percent Market Interest Rate

The present value of the $100,000 face value is computed as follows:

$$\$100,000 \times 0.7921 = \$79,210$$

> From Table C.2,
> Interest rate = 6%
> n = 4

The present value of the $6,000 annuity is computed as follows:

$$\$6,000 \times 3.4651 = \$20,790*$$

> From Table C.4,
> Interest rate = 6%
> n = 4

*Adjusted to accommodate rounding in the present value factor.

The present value of the total bond payments, computed using the discount rate of 6%, is $100,000 (= $79,210 + $20,790).

(c) 8 Percent Market Interest Rate

The present value of the $100,000 face value is computed as follows:

$$\$100,000 \times 0.7350 = \$73,500$$

> From Table C.2,
> Interest rate = 8%
> n = 4

The present value of the $6,000 annuity is computed as follows:

$$\$6,000 \times 3.3121 = \$19,876*$$

> From Table C.4,
> Interest rate = 8%
> n = 4

*Adjusted to accommodate rounding in the present value factor.

COACH'S TIP

> The present values in *a*, *b*, and *c* demonstrate the calculation of the bond issue prices used in Chapter 10.

The present value of the total bond payments, computed using the discount rate of 8%, is $93,376 (= $73,500 + $19,876).

The following table summarizes these calculations:

	MARKET INTEREST RATES		
	4%	6%	8%
Present value of $100,000 face value (principal) paid four years from now	$ 85,480	$ 79,210	$73,500
Present value of $6,000 (interest) paid once a year for four years	21,780	20,790	19,876
Amount to pay	**$107,260**	**$100,000**	**$93,376**

Of course, these calculations are just the starting point for understanding how bond liabilities are determined and reported. You'll need to read Chapter 10 for information about how bond liabilities are accounted for.

TABLE C.1

Future Value of $1

Periods	2%	3%	3.75%	4%	4.25%	5%	6%	7%	8%
0	1.	1.	1.	1.	1.	1.	1.	1.	1.
1	1.02	1.03	1.0375	1.04	1.0425	1.05	1.06	1.07	1.08
2	1.0404	1.0609	1.0764	1.0816	1.0868	1.1025	1.1236	1.1449	1.1664
3	1.0612	1.0927	1.1168	1.1249	1.1330	1.1576	1.1910	1.2250	1.2597
4	1.0824	1.1255	1.1587	1.1699	1.1811	1.2155	1.2625	1.3108	1.3605
5	1.1041	1.1593	1.2021	1.2167	1.2313	1.2763	1.3382	1.4026	1.4693
6	1.1262	1.1941	1.2472	1.2653	1.2837	1.3401	1.4185	1.5007	1.5869
7	1.1487	1.2299	1.2939	1.3159	1.3382	1.4071	1.5036	1.6058	1.7138
8	1.1717	1.2668	1.3425	1.3686	1.3951	1.4775	1.5938	1.7182	1.8509
9	1.1951	1.3048	1.3928	1.4233	1.4544	1.5513	1.6895	1.8385	1.9990
10	1.2190	1.3439	1.4450	1.4802	1.5162	1.6289	1.7908	1.9672	2.1589
20	1.4859	1.8061	2.0882	2.1911	2.2989	2.6533	3.2071	3.8697	4.6610

Periods	9%	10%	11%	12%	13%	14%	15%	20%	25%
0	1.	1.	1.	1.	1.	1.	1.	1.	1.
1	1.09	1.10	1.11	1.12	1.13	1.14	1.15	1.20	1.25
2	1.1881	1.2100	1.2321	1.2544	1.2769	1.2996	1.3225	1.4400	1.5625
3	1.2950	1.3310	1.3676	1.4049	1.4429	1.4815	1.5209	1.7280	1.9531
4	1.4116	1.4641	1.5181	1.5735	1.6305	1.6890	1.7490	2.0736	2.4414
5	1.5386	1.6105	1.6851	1.7623	1.8424	1.9254	2.0114	2.4883	3.0518
6	1.6771	1.7716	1.8704	1.9738	2.0820	2.1950	2.3131	2.9860	3.8147
7	1.8280	1.9487	2.0762	2.2107	2.3526	2.5023	2.6600	3.5832	4.7684
8	1.9926	2.1436	2.3045	2.4760	2.6584	2.8526	3.0590	4.2998	5.9605
9	2.1719	2.3579	2.5580	2.7731	3.0040	3.2519	3.5179	5.1598	7.4506
10	2.3674	2.5937	2.8394	3.1058	3.3946	3.7072	4.0456	6.1917	9.3132
20	5.6044	6.7275	8.0623	9.6463	11.5231	13.7435	16.3665	38.3376	86.7362

TABLE C.2
Present Value of $1

Periods	2%	3%	3.75%	4%	4.25%	5%	6%	7%	8%
1	0.9804	0.9709	0.9639	0.9615	0.9592	0.9524	0.9434	0.9346	0.9259
2	0.9612	0.9426	0.9290	0.9246	0.9201	0.9070	0.8900	0.8734	0.8573
3	0.9423	0.9151	0.8954	0.8890	0.8826	0.8638	0.8396	0.8163	07938
4	0.9238	0.8885	0.8631	0.8548	0.8466	0.8227	0.7921	0.7629	0.7350
5	0.9057	0.8626	0.8319	0.8219	0.8121	0.7835	0.7473	0.7130	0.6806
6	0.8880	0.8375	0.8018	0.7903	0.7790	0.7462	0.7050	0.6663	0.6302
7	0.8706	0.8131	0.7728	0.7599	0.7473	0.7107	0.6651	0.6227	0.5835
8	0.8535	0.7894	0.7449	0.7307	0.7168	0.6768	0.6274	0.5820	0.5403
9	0.8368	0.7664	0.7180	0.7026	0.6876	0.6446	0.5919	0.5439	0.5002
10	0.8203	0.7441	0.6920	0.6756	0.6595	0.6139	0.5584	0.5083	0.4632
20	0.6730	0.5537	0.4789	0.4564	0.4350	0.3769	0.3118	0.2584	0.2145

Periods	9%	10%	11%	12%	13%	14%	15%	20%	25%
1	0.9174	0.9091	0.9009	0.8929	0.8850	0.8772	0.8696	0.8333	0.8000
2	0.8417	0.8264	0.8116	0.7972	0.7831	0.7695	0.7561	0.6944	0.6400
3	0.7722	0.7513	0.7312	0.7118	0.6931	0.6750	0.6575	0.5787	0.5120
4	0.7084	0.6830	0.6587	0.6355	0.6133	0.5921	0.5718	0.4823	0.4096
5	0.6499	0.6209	0.5935	0.5674	0.5428	0.5194	0.4972	0.4019	0.3277
6	0.5963	0.5645	0.5346	0.5066	0.4803	0.4556	0.4323	0.3349	0.2621
7	0.5470	0.5132	0.4817	0.4523	0.4251	0.3996	0.3759	0.2791	0.2097
8	0.5019	0.4665	0.4339	0.4039	0.3762	0.3506	0.3269	0.2326	0.1678
9	0.4604	0.4241	0.3909	0.3606	0.3329	0.3075	0.2843	0.1938	0.1342
10	0.4224	0.3855	0.3522	0.3220	0.2946	0.2697	0.2472	0.1615	0.1074
20	0.1784	0.1486	0.1240	0.1037	0.0868	0.0728	0.0611	0.0261	0.0115

TABLE C.3

Future Value of Annuity of $1

Periods*	2%	3%	3.75%	4%	4.25%	5%	6%	7%	8%
1	1.	1.	1.	1.	1.	1.	1.	1.	1.
2	2.02	2.03	2.0375	2.04	2.0425	2.05	2.06	2.07	2.08
3	3.0604	3.0909	3.1139	3.1216	3.1293	3.1525	3.1836	3.2149	3.2464
4	4.1216	4.1836	4.2307	4.2465	4.2623	4.3101	4.3746	4.4399	4.5061
5	5.2040	5.3091	5.3893	5.4163	5.4434	5.5256	5.6371	5.7507	5.8666
6	6.3081	6.4684	6.5914	6.6330	6.6748	6.8019	6.9753	7.1533	7.3359
7	7.4343	7.6625	7.8386	7.8983	7.9585	8.1420	8.3938	8.6540	8.9228
8	8.5830	8.8923	9.1326	9.2142	9.2967	9.5491	9.8975	10.2598	10.6366
9	9.7546	10.1591	10.4750	10.5828	10.6918	11.0266	11.4913	11.9780	12.4876
10	10.9497	11.4639	11.8678	12.0061	12.1462	12.5779	13.1808	13.8164	14.4866
20	24.2974	26.8704	29.0174	29.7781	30.5625	33.0660	36.7856	40.9955	45.7620

Periods*	9%	10%	11%	12%	13%	14%	15%	20%	25%
1	1.	1.	1.	1.	1.	1.	1.	1.	1.
2	2.09	2.10	2.11	2.12	2.13	2.14	2.15	2.20	2.25
3	3.2781	3.3100	3.3421	3.3744	3.4069	3.4396	3.4725	3.6400	3.8125
4	4.5731	4.6410	4.7097	4.7793	4.8498	4.9211	4.9934	5.3680	5.7656
5	5.9847	6.1051	6.2278	6.3528	6.4803	6.6101	6.7424	7.4416	8.2070
6	7.5233	7.7156	7.9129	8.1152	8.3227	8.5355	8.7537	9.9299	11.2588
7	9.2004	9.4872	9.7833	10.0890	10.4047	10.7305	11.0668	12.9159	15.0735
8	11.0285	11.4359	11.8594	12.2997	12.7573	13.2328	13.7268	16.4991	19.8419
9	13.0210	13.5975	14.1640	14.7757	15.4157	16.0853	16.7858	20.7989	25.8023
10	15.1929	15.9374	16.7220	17.5487	18.4197	19.3373	20.3037	25.9587	33.2529
20	51.1601	57.2750	64.2028	72.0524	80.9468	91.0249	102.4436	186.6880	342.9447

*There is one payment each period.

TABLE C.4

Present Value of Annuity of $1

Periods*	2%	3%	3.75%	4%	4.25%	5%	6%	7%	8%
1	0.9804	0.9709	0.9639	0.9615	0.9592	0.9524	0.9434	0.9346	0.9259
2	1.9416	1.9135	1.8929	1.8861	1.8794	1.8594	1.8334	1.8080	1.7833
3	2.8839	2.8286	2.7883	2.7751	2.7620	2.7232	2.6730	2.6243	2.5771
4	3.8077	3.7171	3.6514	3.6299	3.6086	3.5460	3.4651	3.3872	3.3121
5	4.7135	4.5797	4.4833	4.4518	4.4207	4.3295	4.2124	4.1002	3.9927
6	5.6014	5.4172	5.2851	5.2421	5.1997	5.0757	4.9173	4.7665	4.6229
7	6.4720	6.2303	6.0579	6.0021	5.9470	5.7864	5.5824	5.3893	5.2064
8	7.3255	7.0197	6.8028	6.7327	6.6638	6.4632	6.2098	5.9713	5.7466
9	8.1622	7.7861	7.5208	7.4353	7.3513	7.1078	6.8017	6.5152	6.2469
10	8.9826	8.5302	8.2128	8.1109	8.0109	7.7217	7.3601	7.0236	6.7101
20	16.3514	14.8775	13.8962	13.5903	13.2944	12.4622	11.4699	10.5940	9.8181

Periods*	9%	10%	11%	12%	13%	14%	15%	20%	25%
1	0.9174	0.9091	0.9009	0.8929	0.8550	0.8772	0.8696	0.8333	0.8000
2	1.7591	1.7355	1.7125	1.6901	1.6681	1.6467	1.6257	1.5278	1.4400
3	2.5313	2.4869	2.4437	2.4018	2.3612	2.3216	2.2832	2.1065	1.9520
4	3.2397	3.1699	3.1024	3.0373	2.9745	2.9137	2.8550	2.5887	2.3616
5	3.8897	3.7908	3.6959	3.6048	3.5172	3.4331	3.3522	2.9906	2.6893
6	4.4859	4.3553	4.2305	4.1114	3.9975	3.8887	3.7845	3.3255	2.9514
7	5.0330	4.8684	4.7122	4.5638	4.4226	4.2883	4.1604	3.6046	3.1611
8	5.5348	5.3349	5.1461	4.9676	4.7988	4.6389	4.4873	3.8372	3.3289
9	5.9952	5.7590	5.5370	5.3282	4.1317	4.9464	4.7716	4.0310	3.4631
10	6.4177	6.1446	5.8892	5.6502	5.4262	5.2161	5.0188	4.1925	3.5705
20	9.1285	8.5136	7.9633	7.4694	7.0248	6.6231	6.2593	4.8696	3.9539

*There is one payment each period.

KEY TERMS

Annuity p. C4

Future Value p. C1

Present Value p. C1

Time Value of Money p. C1

PRACTICE MATERIAL

QUESTIONS

1. Explain the concept of the time value of money.
2. Explain the basic difference between future value and present value.
3. If you deposited $10,000 in a savings account that earns 10 percent, how much would you have at the end of 10 years? Use a convenient format to display your computations.
4. If you hold a valid contract that will pay you $8,000 cash 10 years from now and the going rate of interest is 10 percent, what is its present value? Use a convenient format to display your computations.
5. What is an annuity?
6. Use tables C.1 to C.4 to complete the following schedule:

	TABLE VALUES		
	$i = 5\%, n = 4$	$i = 10\%, n = 7$	$i = 14\%, n = 10$
FV of $1			
PV of $1			
FV of annuity of $1			
PV of annuity of $1			

7. If you deposit $1,000 at the end of each period for 10 interest periods and you earn 8 percent interest, how much would you have at the end of period 10? Use a convenient format to display your computations.

MULTIPLE CHOICE

1. You are saving up for a Porsche Carrera Cabriolet, which currently sells for nearly half a million dollars. Your plan is to deposit $15,000 at the end of each year for the next 10 years. You expect to earn 5 percent each year. How much will you have saved after 10 years, rounded to the nearest 10 dollars?
   a. $150,000.
   b. $188,670.
   c. $495,990.
   d. None of the above.

2. Which of the following is a characteristic of an annuity?
   a. An equal dollar amount each interest period.
   b. Interest periods of equal length.
   c. An equal interest rate each interest period.
   d. All of the above are characteristics of an annuity.

3. Which of the following is most likely to be an annuity?
   a. Monthly payments on a credit card bill.
   b. Monthly interest earned on a checking account.
   c. Monthly payments on a home mortgage.
   d. Monthly utility bill payments.

4. Assume you bought a state of the art entertainment system, with no payments to be made until two years from now, when you must pay $6,000. If the going rate of interest on most loans is 5 percent, which table in this appendix would you use to calculate the system's equivalent cost if you were to pay for it today?
   a. Table C.1 (Future Value of $1)
   b. Table C.2 (Present Value of $1)
   c. Table C.3 (Future Value of Annuity of $1)
   d. Table C.4 (Present Value of Annuity of $1)

5. Assuming the facts in question 4, what is the system's equivalent cost if you were to pay for it today?
   a. $5,442   c. $11,100
   b. $6,615   d. $12,300

6. Assume you bought a car using a loan that requires payments of $3,000 to be made at the end of every year for the next three years. The loan agreement indicates the annual interest rate is 6 percent. Which table in this appendix would you use to calculate the car's equivalent cost if you were to pay for it in full today?
   a. Table C.1 (Future Value of $1)
   b. Table C.2 (Present Value of $1)
   c. Table C.3 (Future Value of Annuity of $1)
   d. Table C.4 (Present Value of Annuity of $1)

7. Assuming the facts in question 6, what is the car's equivalent cost if you were to pay for it today? Round to the nearest hundred dollars.
   a. $2,600   c. $8,000
   b. $3,600   d. $9,600

8. Which of the following statements are true?
   a. When the interest rate increases, the present value of a single amount decreases.
   b. When the number of interest periods increase, the present value of a single amount increases.
   c. When the interest rate increases, the present value of an annuity increases.
   d. None of the above are true.

9. Which of the following describes how to calculate a bond's issue price?

	Face Value	Interest Payments
a.	Present value of single amount.	Future value of annuity.
b.	Future value of single amount.	Present value of annuity.
c.	Present value of single amount.	Present value of annuity.
d.	Future value of single amount.	Future value of annuity.

10. If interest is compounded quarterly, rather than yearly, how do you adjust the number of years and annual interest rate when using the present value tables?

	Number of years	Annual interest rate
a.	Divide by 4	Divide by 4
b.	Divide by 4	Multiply by 4
c.	Multiply by 4	Divide by 4
d.	Multiply by 4	Multiply by 4

Answers to Multiple Choice Questions

1. b   2. d   3. c   4. b   5. a   6. d   7. c   8. a   9. c   10. c

MINI-EXERCISES

MC-1 Computing the Present Value of a Single Payment

What is the present value of $500,000 to be paid in 10 years, with an interest rate of 8 percent?

MC-2 Computing the Present Value of an Annuity

What is the present value of 10 equal payments of $15,000, with an interest rate of 10 percent?

MC-3 Computing the Present Value of a Complex Contract

As a result of a slowdown in operations, Mercantile Stores is offering to employees who have been terminated a severance package of $100,000 cash; another $100,000 to be paid in one year; and an annuity of $30,000 to be paid each year for 20 years. What is the present value of the package, assuming an interest rate of 8 percent?

MC-4 Computing the Future Value of an Annuity

You plan to retire in 20 years. Calculate whether it is better for you to save $25,000 a year for the last 10 years before retirement or $15,000 for each of the 20 years. Assume you are able to earn 10 percent interest on your investments.

EXERCISES

EC-1 Computing Growth in a Savings Account: A Single Amount

On January 1, 2007, you deposited $6,000 in a savings account. The account will earn 10 percent annual compound interest, which will be added to the fund balance at the end of each year.

Required (round to the nearest dollar):

1. What will be the balance in the savings account at the end of 10 years?
2. What is the interest for the 10 years?
3. How much interest revenue did the fund earn in 2007? 2008?

EC-2 Computing Deposit Required and Accounting for a Single-Sum Savings Account

On January 1, 2007, Alan King decided to transfer an amount from his checking account into a savings account that later will provide $80,000 to send his son to college (four years from now). The savings account will earn 8 percent, which will be added to the fund each year-end.

Required (show computations and round to the nearest dollar):

1. How much must Alan deposit on January 1, 2007?
2. Give the journal entry that Alan should make on January 1, 2007 to record the transfer.
3. What is the interest for the four years?
4. Give the journal entry that Alan should make on (a) December 31, 2007, and (b) December 31, 2008.

EC-3 Recording Growth in a Savings Account with Equal Periodic Payments

On each December 31, you plan to transfer $2,000 from your checking account into a savings account. The savings account will earn 9 percent annual interest, which will be added to the savings account balance at each year-end. The first deposit will be made December 31, 2007 (at the end of the period).

Required (show computations and round to the nearest dollar):

1. Give the required journal entry on December 31, 2007.
2. What will be the balance in the savings account at the end of the 10th year (i.e., 10 deposits)?
3. What is the total amount of interest earned on the 10 deposits?
4. How much interest revenue did the fund earn in 2008? 2009?
5. Give all required journal entries at the end of 2008 and 2009.

EC-4 Computing Growth for a Savings Fund with Periodic Deposits

On January 1, 2007, you plan to take a trip around the world upon graduation four years from now. Your grandmother wants to deposit sufficient funds for this trip in a savings account for you. On the basis of a budget, you estimate that the trip currently would cost $15,000. Being the generous and sweet lady she is, your grandmother decided to deposit $3,500 in the fund at the end of each of the next four years, starting on December 31, 2007. The savings account will earn 6 percent annual interest, which will be added to the savings account at each year-end.

Required (show computations and round to the nearest dollar):

1. How much money will you have for the trip at the end of year 4 (i.e., after four deposits)?
2. What is the total amount of interest earned over the four years?
3. How much interest revenue did the fund earn in 2007, 2008, 2009, and 2010?

EC-5 Computing Value of an Asset Based on Present Value

You have the chance to purchase an oil well. Your best estimate is that the oil well's net royalty income will average $25,000 per year for five years. There will be no residual value at that time. Assume that the cash inflow occurs at each year-end and that considering the uncertainty in your estimates, you expect to earn 15 percent per year on the investment. What should you be willing to pay for this investment right now?

COACHED PROBLEM

CPC-1 Comparing Options Using Present Value Concepts

After hearing a knock at your front door, you are surprised to see the Prize Patrol from a large, well-known magazine subscription company. It has arrived with the good news that you are the big winner, having won "$20 million." You discover that you have three options: (1) you can receive $1 million per year for the next 20 years, (2) you can have $8 million today, or (3) you can have $2 million today and receive $700,000 for each of the next 20 years. Your financial adviser tells you that it is reasonable to expect to earn 10 percent on investments. Which option do you prefer? What factors influence your decision?

TIP: All three scenarios require you to determine today's value of the various payment options. These are present value problems.

GROUP A PROBLEM

PAC-1 Comparing Options Using Present Value Concepts

After completing a long and successful career as senior vice president for a large bank, you are preparing for retirement. After visiting the human resources office, you have found that you have several retirement options: (1) you can receive an immediate cash payment of $1 million, (2) you can receive $60,000 per year for life (your remaining life expectancy is 20 years), or (3) you can receive $50,000 per year for 10 years and then $70,000 per year for life (this option is intended to give you some protection against inflation). You have determined that you can earn 8 percent on your investments. Which option do you prefer and why?

GROUP B PROBLEM

PBC-1 Comparing Options Using Present Value Concepts

After incurring a serious injury caused by a manufacturing defect, your friend has sued the manufacturer for damages. Your friend received three offers from the manufacturer to settle the lawsuit; (1) receive an immediate cash payment of $100,000, (2) receive $6,000 per year for life (your friend's remaining life expectancy is 20 years), or (3) receive $5,000 per year for 10 years and then $7,000 per year for life (this option is intended to compensate your friend for increased aggravation of the injury over time). Your friend can earn 8 percent interest and has asked you for advice. Which option would you recommend and why?

Appendix

D Reporting and Interpreting Investments in Other Corporations

You're probably already thinking about how you're going to celebrate the end of the term with your friends. Perhaps you'll dine out, go to a nightclub, or just simply relax in front of the TV at somebody's place. While you can't always control what your friends decide to do, by being involved in the decision making you can make sure they hear what you'd like before a decision is made.

The managers at Motorola feel the same way—not about end-of-term celebrations but instead about business decisions that are made by other companies that supply services to or buy products from Motorola. To ensure the impact on Motorola is considered in these decisions, Motorola might buy some of the stock issued by these other companies. As explained in Chapter 11, by becoming a common stockholder, Motorola gets to vote on important decisions being made by these other companies. If Motorola buys enough common stock in other corporations, it could have a significant or possibly controlling influence over their decisions. In this appendix, you'll learn how Motorola accounts for the investments it makes in other corporations.

Understand the Business

WHY A COMPANY INVESTS IN OTHER CORPORATIONS

A company can invest in either stock or bonds issued by another corporation. This appendix focuses on just stock investments. In principle, bond investments are accounted for in a manner similar to what we describe below for certain stock investments, but there are several technical differences that we leave for intermediate accounting courses.

A company might invest in stock issued by other corporations for one of four reasons:

1. Take control. A company might want to expand into other industries or markets, and the fastest way to do this is to take over control of another corporation (typically by buying 50 percent or more of its stock).

2. Exert significant influence. Instead of controlling the decisions of another corporation, the company might be satisfied with just having a significant influence on the decisions made by the other corporation. After buying 20–50 percent of the common stock of a supplier or customer, a company usually will be able to exert this significant influence.

3. Passively invest in securities available for sale. A company might have generated some extra cash from its operating activities, which it invests in another corporation's stock to earn dividends. The company doesn't become actively involved in the decisions made by the other companies. Rather, this is a passive form of investment where the company just plunks down some money and waits for the investment to pay off. Because these investments can be sold whenever the company is short of cash, they are called **securities available for sale.**

4. Profit from buying and selling. A company might actually be in the business of trading securities, which means trying to earn profits by buying securities at one price and selling them in the near future at a higher price. Investments made with this goal in mind are considered **trading securities.**

It's useful to understand these four reasons not only to be a wiser business person, but also because they relate to how investments in other corporations are accounted for. As Exhibit D.1 indicates, the methods used to account for these investments depend on the company's level of involvement in the other corporation and on the investing company's basic reason for investing in other corporations. As a guideline for determining the investor's level of involvement, the percent of stock ownership is considered, using percentages shown in the first column of Exhibit D.1. So, for example, an investor owning 50 percent or more of the stock of another corporation is presumed to control the other corporation. Other factors, like participation in setting operating and financing policies, also are considered. The following sections of this appendix discuss the different accounting methods listed in the third column of Exhibit D.1.

EXHIBIT D.1 | **Accounting for Investments in Other Corporations' Stock**

Level of Involvement in Decision Making (Percent of Ownership)	Reason for the Investment	Method of Accounting	How It Works
Control (more than 50%)	Take over the company → Consolidation		Combine the financial statements of parent and subsidiaries
Significant Influence (20–50%)	Influence the company → Equity Method		Record Investment at cost, add % share of net income, deduct % share of dividends
Passive (less than 20%)	Invest excess cash to earn greater return	→ Market Value for Securities Available for Sale	Record investment at cost but adjust to market value at period-end; report dividends and realized gains/losses as investment income on the income statement; report unrealized gains/losses in stockholders' equity
Passive (less than 20%)	Securities trading	→ Market Value for Trading Securities	Record investment at cost but adjust to market value at period-end; report dividends and all gains/losses (either realized or unrealized) as investment income on the income statement.

Study the Accounting Methods

Consolidation Method for Investments Involving Control

When a company controls the decisions of other companies, it is called the **parent.** The **subsidiary** is the company that the parent controls. Although we haven't made a big deal out of it, in earlier chapters you've studied many companies that were the parent of several subsidiaries. For example, Regis Corporation is the parent of Supercuts and Carlton Hair International, and General Mills is the parent of Pillsbury and Häagen-Dazs International. So, how is it that you didn't know that these parent companies had invested in subsidiary companies until now? Why didn't they report an asset called *investments?* The answer is that the parent companies have accounted for their investments using the consolidation method.

Under the consolidation method, the parent company prepares a set of **consolidated financial statements** that combines the accounts of the parent company with the accounts of all its subsidiary companies. The parent doesn't report a separate investment account on its balance sheet because it includes all of the accounts of the subsidiaries in its own consolidated financial statements. Basically, the consolidation method can be thought of as adding together separate financial statements for two or more companies to make it appear as if a single company exists. So, for example, the $3.77 billion of cash reported in the assets section of Motorola's balance sheet in Exhibit D.2 includes the cash in Motorola's bank accounts as well as the cash in its subsidiary companies' accounts. The same is true of the Inventories account, Notes Payable account, Sales account, and so on.

Motorola, Inc., is the parent of several subsidiaries, including River Delta Networks and General Instrument Corporation. Although these subsidiaries exist as separate legal entities, their financial successes and failures ultimately belong to Motorola, so it makes sense for Motorola to report them as if they were Motorola's own financial results. To inform you that the financial statements include the parent and subsidiary companies, the first financial statement note proudly announces that the financial statements are prepared on a consolidated basis. Also, the heading of each financial statement is marked as consolidated, as shown in Motorola's balance sheet in Exhibit D.2.

You probably will notice that in Exhibit D.2, Motorola reports Investments totaling more than $1.6 billion at December 31, 2005. This particular line item does not represent the amount Motorola has invested in subsidiaries because each account of each subsidiary already has been combined into the consolidated financial statements. Instead, the Investments account shown in Exhibit D.2 relates to investments where Motorola has either significant influence or passive interest in other corporations, as discussed in the following sections.

> **YOU SHOULD KNOW**
>
> **Consolidated financial statements** combine the financial statements of parent and subsidiary companies into a single set of financial statements.

EXHIBIT D.2	Excerpt from Motorola's Consolidated Balance Sheet

MOTOROLA, INC. AND SUBSIDIARIES
Consolidated Balance Sheets (Partial)
(in millions)

	December 31	
	2005	**2004**
Assets		
Current assets		
Cash	$ 3,774	$ 2,846
Accounts receivable, net	5,779	4,525
Inventories, net	2,552	2,546
Other current assets	15,764	11,198
Total current assets	27,869	21,115
Property, plant, and equipment, net	2,271	2,332
Investments	1,654	3,241
Other assets	3,885	4,235
Total assets	$35,679	$30,923

Equity Method for Investments Involving Significant Influence

The equity method is used when an investor can exert significant influence over an investee, which is presumed if the investor owns between 20 and 50 percent of the investee's outstanding voting stock. Because the investor does not actually control the investee's assets or its operating decisions, the accounts of the investee are not consolidated within each account of the investor. Instead, the investor records its investment in a single account called Investments. It's just like how you'd account for a building. Rather than record the stairs, doors, floors, and roofing in separate accounts, they're all included in a single account. Under the equity method, the investor initially records its investment at cost and then, every year after that, records its share of the investee's net income and its share of dividends distributed by the investee for that year. These items affect the Investments account as follows:

- **Net income of investee.** When the investee reports net income for the year, the investor increases (debits) its Investments account for its percentage share of the investee's net income. The investee's earnings represent a future benefit to the investor because they imply the investor can expect to enjoy greater dividends or increased investment value in the future. The credit portion of the journal entry is recorded as Investment Income, which is reported on the income statement along with other nonoperating items like Interest expense and other gains and losses. (If the investee reports a net loss for the year, the investor records a debit to Investment Loss for its share of the net loss along with a credit that reduces its Investments account.)

- **Dividends received from investee.** If the investee pays dividends during the year, the investor increases Cash and reduces its Investments account when it receives its share of the dividends.

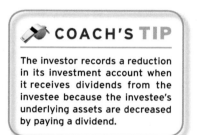

COACH'S TIP

The investor records a reduction in its investment account when it receives dividends from the investee because the investee's underlying assets are decreased by paying a dividend.

Investments (A)	
Beginning balance	
Cost of investments purchased (also credit to Cash)	
Company's % share of investee's net income (also credit to Investment Income)	Company's % share of investee's dividends declared for the period (also debit to Cash)
Ending balance	

Purchase of Stock   To illustrate the equity method of accounting, let's assume that at the end of 2006, Motorola had no significant influence investments. On January 1, 2007, Motorola bought 40,000 common shares of Personal Communications Corporation (PCC) for $300,000 cash. PCC had 100,000 shares of common stock outstanding, so Motorola's purchase represented 40 percent and, therefore, Motorola was presumed to have significant influence over the investee (PCC). As a consequence, Motorola must use the equity method to account for this investment. The initial purchase of this investment is accounted for as follows.

1. Analyze

Assets		=	Liabilities	+	Stockholders' Equity
Investments	+300,000				
Cash	−300,000				

2. Record

dr Investments (+A)	300,000	
cr Cash (−A)		300,000

Share of Net Income Earned   Because Motorola can influence PCC's processes for earning income, Motorola bases its investment income on PCC's earnings. During 2007, PCC reported net income of $250,000 for the year. Motorola's percentage share of PCC's income was $100,000 (40% × $250,000), which is accounted for as follows:

1. Analyze

Assets	= Liabilities +	Stockholders' Equity
Investments +100,000		Investment Income (+R) +100,000

2. Record

dr Investments (+A)......................... 100,000
    cr Investment Income (+R, +SE)   100,000

If PCC were to report a net loss for the period, Motorola would have recorded its percentage share of the loss by decreasing the Investments account and recording an Investment Loss, which would be reported in the nonoperating section of the income statement, with Interest revenue, Interest expense, and gains and losses on sales of assets.

Dividends Received   Because Motorola can exert significant influence over PCC's dividend policies, any dividends it receives from PCC should *not* be recorded as investment income. Instead, any dividends it receives will reduce its Investments account because dividends reduce the underlying assets of PCC. Assume that, at the end of 2007, PCC declared and paid a cash dividend of $2 per share to stockholders. Motorola received $80,000 in cash ($2 × 40,000 shares) from PCC, which the equity method accounts for as follows:

1. Analyze

Assets	= Liabilities +	Stockholders' Equity
Cash +80,000		
Investments −80,000		

2. Record

dr Cash (+A) 80,000
    cr Investments (−A)   80,000

3. Summarize

+ Investments (A) −			− Investment Income (R, SE) +	
Beg. bal. 0				0 Beg. bal.
Purchase 300,000				
Share of PCC's 100,000	80,000	Share of PCC's dividends		100,000 Share of PCC's net income
net income				
End. bal. 320,000				100,000 End. bal.

HOW'S IT GOING?   A Self-Study Quiz

Assume that on January 1, 2007, Nokia bought 30 percent of the common stock of Intellicorp Company (IC) for $120,000. IC reported net income of $100,000 for the year ended December 31, 2007. IC also declared and paid dividends totaling $50,000 for the year.

a.   At what amount should Nokia report its investment in IC at December 31, 2007?

b.   What amount should Nokia report as investment income?

Market Value Methods for Passive Investments

Unlike investments involving control or significant influence, investments in securities available for sale and trading securities are accounted for at their market values. Before we discuss how the market value method is applied, let's consider the rationale for reporting these passive investments at market value. It's actually a rarity in accounting to report assets at market value because it means that, in some instances, they'll be reported at an amount higher than historical cost. Let's take a closer look at this approach, which is dubbed "mark-to-market accounting."

1. Why are passive investments reported at fair market value on the balance sheet? Two primary factors determine the answer to this question:

   • **Relevance.** Analysts who study financial statements often attempt to forecast a company's future cash flows. They want to know how a company can generate cash for purposes such as expansion of the business, payment of dividends, or survival during a prolonged economic downturn. One source of cash is the sale of passive investments. The best estimate of the cash that could be generated by the sale of these securities is their current market value.

   • **Measurability.** Accountants record only those items that can be measured in dollar terms with a high degree of reliability. Determining the fair market value of most assets is very difficult because they are not actively traded. For example, although the Empire State Building is the most important asset owned by the Empire State Company, its balance sheet reports the building in terms of its cost in part because of the difficulty in determining an objective value for it. Contrast the difficulty of determining the value of a building with the ease of determining the value of securities that Motorola owns. A quick look at stockcharts.com is all that is needed to determine the current price of IBM or Microsoft stock because these securities are traded each day on established stock exchanges.

2. When the investment account is adjusted to reflect changes in fair market value, what other account is affected when the asset account is increased or decreased? Under the double-entry method of accounting, every journal entry affects at least two accounts. An asset valuation account is added to or subtracted from the investment account (maintained at cost) to produce the market value that is reported on the balance sheet. The second account affected is **Unrealized Holding Gains or Losses** that are recorded whenever the fair market value of investments changes. These are called *unrealized* because no actual sale has taken place. Simply by holding the security, the value has changed. If the value of the investments increased by $100,000 during the year, an adjusting journal entry records the increase in the asset valuation account and an unrealized holding gain for $100,000. If the value of the investments decreased by $75,000 during the year, an adjusting journal entry records the decrease in the asset valuation account

and an unrealized holding loss of $75,000. The financial statement treatment of the unrealized holding gains or losses depends on whether the investment is classified as securities available for sale or trading securities.

Securities Available for Sale

Exhibit D.3 displays information from Note 3 of Motorola's financial statements, which indicates that most of the investments reported on Motorola's balance sheet are securities available for sale (in millions, securities available for sale comprise $1,222 out of $1,654). The details reported in Exhibit D.3 indicate that Motorola's securities available for sale (or SAS for short) initially cost $1,065 million, but were worth $1,222 million at December 31, 2005.

EXHIBIT D.3	Motorola's Note Describing Securities Available for Sale (in millions)

	December 31, 2005
Securities available for sale (SAS)	
Investment in SAS (at cost)	$1,065
Allowance to value SAS at market	157
Market value of securities available for sale	1,222
Equity method and other investments	432
Total investments	$1,654

To simplify our look at the accounting procedures that ultimately led to the amounts in Exhibit D.3, let's assume that Motorola had no passive investments at the end of 2004. The way in which the market value method is applied to securities available for sale is shown below.

Purchase of Stock   At the beginning of 2005, Motorola purchases 10 million shares of common stock of Wireless Networks Inc. (WNI) for $106.50 per share. There were 100 million outstanding shares, so Motorola owns 10 percent of WNI (10 million ÷ 100 million), which is considered a passive investment in securities available for sale (SAS). Such investments are recorded initially at cost (10 million shares × $106.50 = $1,065 million):

1. Analyze

Assets		=	Liabilities	+	Stockholders' Equity
Investment in SAS	+1,065				
Cash	−1,065				

2. Record

dr Investment in SAS (+A)   1,065
    cr Cash (−A)   1,065

After stock has been purchased, it can earn a return from two sources: (1) dividends, and (2) price increases. We will discuss price increases in a few moments, but for now let's focus on dividends.

Dividends Received   Under the market value method, when dividends are received, the investor reports them as revenue on the income statement in an account called

Investment Income. If Motorola receives a $1 per share cash dividend from WNI, which totals $10 million ($1 × 10 million shares), it would be accounted for as:

1. Analyze

Assets	=	Liabilities	+	Stockholders' Equity	
Cash +10				Investment Income (+R) +10	

2. Record

dr Cash (+A) 10
　　cr Investment Income (+R, +SE) .... 　　10

COACH'S TIP

Unlike the equity method, dividends received are reported under the market value method as investment income. Another difference from the equity method is that the investor's share of the investee's net income is not recorded under the market value method.

Price Increases   At the end of the accounting period, passive investments are reported on the balance sheet at fair market value. Let's assume that WNI had a $122.22 per share market value at the end of the year. That is, Motorola's investment had gained $15.70 per share ($122.20 − $106.50 = $15.70) for the year. Since the investment has not been sold, this is only a holding gain, not a realized gain. The market value method for SAS investments requires that, unlike dividends, all unrealized holding gains or losses should *not* be reported in the investor's net income. Because the investor expects to hold SAS investments into the future, it's likely that the value of the SAS investment will change again before any gain or loss is actually realized. Thus, unrealized gains or losses of this year might be recovered or become even larger next year. Either way, the unrealized gains and losses of this period are not likely to represent the true gains or losses that will be realized when the stock is ultimately sold, so they are not included in net income. Instead, they are recorded in a stockholders' equity account called Unrealized Gains and Losses in Equity. Only when the security is sold do the gains or losses become realized, at which time they are removed from stockholders' equity and included in net income.

In summary, reporting the SAS investment at market value requires adjusting it to market value at the end of each period using the account Allowance to Value SAS at Market along with a corresponding entry to Unrealized Gains and Losses in Equity. If the ending balance in the Allowance to Value SAS at Market account is a debit, it is added to the Investment in SAS account when it is reported on the balance sheet. If it is a credit balance, it is subtracted. The Unrealized Gains and Losses in Equity account is reported in the stockholders' equity section of the balance sheet, either increasing stockholders' equity (if it represents an unrealized holding gain) or decreasing it (if it represents an unrealized holding loss).

The following chart is used to compute any unrealized gain or loss in securities available for sale:

Year	Market Value	−	Cost	=	Balance Needed in Valuation Allowance	−	Unadjusted Balance in Valuation Allowance	=	Amount for Adjusting Entry
2005	$1,222	−	$1,065	=	$157	−	$0	=	$157
	($122.20 × 10)		($106.50 × 10)				(We assumed there were no passive investments at the end of the prior year.)		An unrealized gain for the period

Assets	=	Liabilities	+	Stockholders' Equity	
Allowance to Value SAS at Market +157				Unrealized Gains and Losses in Equity +157	

An adjusting entry at the end of 2005 is recorded as follows:

	Allowance to Value SAS at Market (A)	
Beg. bal.	0	
AJE	157	
End. bal.	157	

dr Allowance to Value SAS at Market (+A) 157

    cr Unrealized Gains and Losses in Equity (+SE)   157

As Exhibit D.3 showed, the ending balance in Allowance to Value SAS at Market account is added to the Investment in SAS account balance when determining the amount to report as Investments on the balance sheet. If management intends to sell these investments within a year, they would be classified as current. Given that all of Motorola's investments appear below the current assets subtotal in Exhibit D.2 (on page D3), we can assume that Motorola's management expects to keep its SAS investments beyond the end of the upcoming year. The account called Unrealized Gains and Losses in Equity is reported in the stockholders' equity section just like Retained earnings. If the balance is a net unrealized loss, it would be reported as a negative amount, just like the Treasury stock discussed in Chapter 11. Assuming that Motorola has a $157 credit balance in its Unrealized Gains and Losses in Equity account at the end of 2005, its stockholders' equity would be reported as shown in Exhibit D.4.

EXHIBIT D.4 Balance Sheet Reporting of Unrealized Gains and Losses in Equity

(in millions)	December 31, 2005
Stockholders' Equity	
Common stock, $3 par value	
Issued shares: 2005—2,502.7	
Outstanding shares: 2005—2,501.1	$ 7,508
Additional paid-in capital	4,691
Retained earnings	5,897
Unrealized gains and losses in equity	157
Total stockholders' equity	$18,253

Sale of Stock When SAS investments are sold, three balance sheet accounts (in addition to Cash) can be affected:

- Investment in SAS.
- Allowance to Value SAS at Market.
- Unrealized Gains and Losses in Equity.

To illustrate, let's assume Motorola sold the WNI stock when the stock market reopened on January 2, 2006, after the New Year's holiday. If the stock price was still $122.20 per share that day, Motorola would receive (in millions) $1,222 cash ($122.20 × 10 million shares) for stock that cost $1,065, resulting in a realized gain of $157, which would be reported as investment income. Two journal entries are needed to record this sale. In entry 1, the cash received, stock given up, and gain realized by the sale are recorded. In entry 2, the valuation allowance and the related

Unrealized Gains and Losses in Equity account would be eliminated because the gain has now been realized.

> 1. *dr* Cash (+A) 1,222
>   *cr* Investment in SAS (−A).   1,065
>   *cr* Investment Income (+R, +SE)   157
> 2. *dr* Unrealized Gains and Losses in Equity (−SE)   157
>   *cr* Allowance to Value SAS at Market (−A)   157

Trading Securities

Trading securities are similar to securities available for sale in many ways. First, trading securities are considered passive investments because the investor does not acquire a sufficient quantity of stock to significantly influence the operating or financing decisions of the investee. Second, investments in trading securities are reported on the balance sheet at market value. Third, stock classified as trading securities also can earn a return from two sources: dividends and price increases.

Trading securities differ from securities available for sale in one small but very important way. Trading securities are purchased with the intent to profit primarily from price increases. "Buy low, sell high" is the motto of investors who invest in securities for trading purposes. This isn't the case with securities available for sale, where the investing company is likely to wait out periods of price changes because its goal is to safely "park" its excess cash in investments that generate a greater return than a bank's savings account.

Because trading securities are purchased with intent to profit from fluctuations in their stock prices, all gains and losses on trading securities are reported in the income statement regardless of whether they are realized or unrealized. In terms of accounting procedures, this means that rather than record unrealized gains and losses in a stockholders' equity account (as they were for securities available for sale), they are recorded in a temporary revenue or expense account, which is closed into Retained earnings at the end of every year. If Motorola's investment in WNI stock had been considered an investment in trading securities (TS), the effects of adjusting the Investment in TS to market value at the end of 2005 would have been:

1. Analyze

Assets	=	Liabilities	+	Stockholders' Equity
Allowance to Value				Investment Income (+R) +157
TS at Market +157				

2. Record

> *dr* Allowance to Value TS at Market (+A)   157
>   *cr* Investment Income (+R, +SE)   157

COACH'S TIP

Notice that unrealized gains on trading securities are reported on the income statement as investment income whereas, on SAS investments, they are reported on the balance sheet as stockholders' equity.

The purchase of stock and dividends received for trading securities are accounted for the same way as they were for securities available for sale (except that references to SAS in the account names are replaced with TS). And, similar to what you saw earlier for securities available for sale, the Allowance to Value TS at Market is combined with the Investment in TS account, with the total being reported on the balance sheet as Investments. Because investments in trading securities are intended to be sold in the near future, they are always classified as current assets.

Now that you've seen all four methods of accounting for investments in the stock of other corporations, return to Exhibit D.1 on page D2. Make sure you understand the final column that summarizes how the methods of accounting work for each type of investment.

DEMONSTRATION CASE A: EQUITY METHOD FOR SIGNIFICANT INFLUENCE INVESTMENTS

On January 1, 2007, Connaught Company purchased 40 percent of the outstanding voting shares of London Company on the open market for $85,000 cash. London declared $10,000 in cash dividends and reported net income of $60,000 for the year.

Required:

1. Prepare the journal entries for 2007.
2. What accounts and amounts were reported on Connaught's balance sheet at the end of 2007? On Connaught's income statement for 2007?

Suggested Solution

1. Jan. 1   *dr* Investments (+A) 85,000
                    cr Cash (−A)   85,000

   Dividends *dr* Cash (+A) (40% × $10,000) 4,000
                    cr Investments (+A)........................   4,000

   Dec. 31   *dr* Investments (+A) (40% × $60,000) 24,000
                    cr Investment Income (+R, +SE)   24,000

2. **On the Balance Sheet**   **On the Income Statement**
   Noncurrent assets: Other items:
     Investments $105,000   Investment income $24,000
      ($85,000 − $4,000 + $24,000)

DEMONSTRATION CASE B: MARKET VALUE METHOD FOR SECURITIES AVAILABLE FOR SALE

Howell Equipment Corporation sells and services a major line of farm equipment. Both sales and service operations have been profitable. The following transactions affected the company during 2007:

a. Jan. 1   Purchased 2,000 shares of common stock of Elk Company at $40 per share. This purchase represented 1 percent of the shares outstanding. Based on management's intent, the Elk Company shares are considered securities available for sale.

b. Dec. 28   Received $4,000 cash dividend on the Elk Company stock.

c. Dec. 31   Determined that the current market price of the Elk stock was $41.

Required:

1. Prepare the journal entry for each of these transactions.
2. What accounts and amounts will be reported on the balance sheet at the end of 2007? On the income statement for 2007?

Suggested Solution

1. *a.* Jan. 1   *dr* Investment in SAS (+A) 80,000
                       cr Cash (−A) (2,000 shares × $40 per share)   80,000

   b. Dec. 28 *dr* Cash (+A)................................ 4,000
                       cr Investment Income (+R, +SE)   4,000

   c. Dec. 31 *dr* Allowance to Value SAS at Market (+A) 2,000
                       cr Unrealized Gains and Losses in Equity (+SE) ...   2,000

Year	Market Value		Cost		Balance Needed in Valuation Allowance		Unadjusted Balance in Valuation Allowance		Adjustment to Valuation Allowance
2007	$82,000	−	$80,000	=	$2,000	−	$0	=	$2,000
	($41 × 2000 shares)								An unrealized gain for the period

2.

On the Balance Sheet		On the Income Statement	
Current or noncurrent assets:		Other items:	
Investment in SAS ($80,000 cost + $2,000 allowance)	$82,000	Investment income	$4,000
Stockholders' equity:			
Unrealized gains and losses in equity	2,000		

DEMONSTRATION CASE C: MARKET VALUE METHOD FOR TRADING SECURITIES

Assume the same facts as in Case B, except that the securities were purchased for the purpose of active trading.

Required:

1. Prepare the journal entry for each of these transactions.
2. What accounts and amounts will be reported on the balance sheet at the end of 2007? On the income statement for 2007?

Suggested Solution

1. a. Jan. 1   dr Investment in TS (+A)   80,000
   cr Cash (−A) (2,000 shares × $40)   80,000

   b. Dec. 28   dr Cash (+A)   4,000
   cr Investment Income (+R, +SE)   4,000

   c. Dec. 31   dr Allowance to Value TS at Market (+A).........   2,000
   cr Investment Income (+R, +SE)   2,000

Year	Market Value		Cost		Balance Needed in Valuation Allowance		Unadjusted Balance in Valuation Allowance		Adjustment to Valuation Allowance
2007	$82,000	−	$80,000	=	$2,000	−	$0	=	$2,000
	($41 × 2000 shares)								An unrealized gain for the period

2.

On the Balance Sheet		On the Income Statement	
Current assets:		Other nonoperating items:	
Investment in TS ($80,000 cost + $2,000 allowance)	$82,000	Investment income ($4,000 dividend + $2,000 unrealized gain)	$6,000

KEY TERMS

Consolidated Financial Statements p. D3   Subsidiary Company p. D2   Unrealized Holding Gains and or
Parent Company p. D2   Trading Securities p. D2   Losses p. D6
Securities Available for Sale p. D2

PRACTICE MATERIAL

QUESTIONS

1. When is it appropriate to use consolidation, equity, or market value methods for an investment in another corporation?
2. How do the accounting methods used for securities available for sale and trading securities differ?
3. How do the accounting methods used for passive investments and investments involving a significant influence differ?
4. How do the accounting methods used for investments involving a significant influence and investments involving control differ?
5. What are consolidated financial statements and what do they attempt to accomplish?
6. Under the equity method, dividends received from the investee company are not recorded as revenue. Recording dividends as revenue would involve double counting. Explain.
7. What are the two sources of return for passive investments?
8. Where are unrealized gains and losses reported for securities available for sale? Where are unrealized gains and losses reported for trading securities? What's the reason for this reporting difference?

MULTIPLE CHOICE

1. Company A owns 40 percent of Company B and exercises significant influence over the management of Company B. Therefore, Company A uses what accounting method for reporting its ownership of stock in Company B?
   a. The consolidation method.
   b. The market value method for securities available for sale.
   c. The equity method.
   d. The market value method for trading securities.

2. Company A purchases 10 percent of Company X and intends to hold the stock for at least five years. At the end of the current year, how would Company A's investment in Company X be reported on Company A's December 31 (year-end) balance sheet?
   a. At original cost, in the current assets section.
   b. At the December 31 market value, in the current assets section.
   c. At original cost, in the noncurrent assets section.
   d. At the December 31 market value, in the noncurrent assets section.

3. Consolidated financial statements are required in which of the following situations?
   a. Only when a company can exert significant influence over another company.
   b. Only when a company has a passive investment in another company.
   c. Only when a parent company can exercise control over its subsidiary.
   d. None of the above.

4. When recording dividends received from a stock investment accounted for using the equity method, which of the following statements is true?
   a. Total assets are increased and net income is increased.
   b. Total assets are increased and total stockholders' equity is increased.
   c. Total assets are decreased and total stockholders' equity is decreased.
   d. Total assets and total stockholders' equity do not change.

5. When using the equity method of accounting, when is revenue recorded on the books of the investor company?

  a. When the market value of the investee stock increases.

  b. When a dividend is received from the investee.

  c. When the investee company reports net income.

  d. Both *b* and *c* above.

6. Dividends received from stock that is reported as *securities available for sale* in the balance sheet are reported as which of the following?

  a. An increase to cash and a decrease to the investment account.

  b. An increase to cash and an unrealized gain on the balance sheet.

  c. An increase to cash and an increase to investment income.

  d. An increase to cash and an unrealized gain on the income statement.

7. Realized gains and losses are recorded on the income statement for which of the following transactions in *trading securities* and *securities available for sale*?

  a. When adjusting *trading securities* to market value.

  b. When adjusting *securities available for sale* to market value.

  c. Only when recording the sale of *trading securities*.

  d. When recording the sale of either *trading securities* or *securities available for sale*.

8. Schlumber Corp. paid $200,000 to purchase 30 percent of the stock of Schleep, Inc., this year. At the end of the year, Schleep reported net income of $50,000 and declared and paid dividends of $20,000. If Schlumber uses the equity method to account for its investment in Schleep, at what amount would the investment be reported at the end of the year?

  a. $200,000   c. $215,000

  b. $209,000   d. $221,000

9. During the current year, Winterpeg Enterprises purchased common shares of Lakeview Development Corp. (LDC) for $200,000, received a $2,000 dividend from LDC, and saw the market value of its investment in LDC increase by $4,000 by year-end. If Winterpeg considers its investment in LDC to be securities available for sale, what amount will Winterpeg report as investment income on its income statement this year?

  a. $2,000   c. $6,000

  b. $4,000   d. None of the above.

10. Assume the same facts as described in 9, except that Winterpeg considers its investment in LDC to be trading securities. What amount will Winterpeg report as investment income on its income statement this year?

  a. $2,000   c. $6,000

  b. $4,000   d. None of the above.

MINI-EXERCISES

MD-1 Recording Equity Method Securities Transactions

On January 2, 2007, Ubuy.com paid $100,000 to acquire 25 percent (10,000 shares) of the common stock of E-Net Corporation. The accounting period for both companies ends December 31. Give the journal entries for the purchase on January 2, and for each of the following transactions that occurred during 2007:

July 2   E-Net declared and paid a cash dividend of $3 per share.

Dec. 31   E-Net reported net income of $200,000.

MD-2 Determining Financial Statement Effects of Equity Method Securities

Using the following categories, indicate the effects (direction and amount) of the transactions listed in MD-1. Use + for increase and − for decrease.

	Balance Sheet			Income Statement		
Transaction	Assets	Liabilities	Stockholders' Equity	Revenues	Expenses	Net Income

MD-3 Recording Trading Securities Transactions

During 2007, Princeton Company acquired some of the 50,000 outstanding shares of the common stock of Cox Corporation as trading securities. The accounting period for both companies ends December 31. Give the journal entries for each of the following transactions that occurred during 2007:

July 2	Purchased 8,000 shares of Cox common stock at $28 per share.
Dec. 15	Cox Corporation declared and paid a cash dividend of $2 per share.
31	Determined the current market price of Cox stock to be $29 per share.

MD-4 Determining Financial Statement Effects of Trading Securities Transactions

Using the following categories, indicate the effects (direction and amount) of the transactions listed in MD-3. Use + for increase and − for decrease.

	Balance Sheet			Income Statement		
Transaction	Assets	Liabilities	Stockholders' Equity	Revenues	Expenses	Net Income

MD-5 Recording Available for Sale Securities Transactions

Using the data in MD-3, assume that Princeton Company purchased the voting stock of Cox Corporation for its portfolio of securities available for sale instead of its trading securities portfolio. Give the journal entries for each of the transactions listed.

MD-6 Determining Financial Statement Effects of Securities Available for Sale Transactions

Using the following categories, indicate the effects (direction and amount) of the transactions referenced in MD-5. Use + for increase and − for decrease.

	Balance Sheet			Income Statement		
Transaction	Assets	Liabilities	Stockholders' Equity	Revenues	Expenses	Net Income

MD-7 Recording the Purchase and Sale of a Passive Investment

Rocktown Corporation bought 600 shares of General Electric stock on March 20, 2007, for its trading securities portfolio at $29 per share. Rocktown sold the stock at $33 per share on June 23, 2007. Prepare the journal entries to record the transactions on each of these dates, assuming that the investment had not yet been adjusted to market value (that is, the investment was still recorded at cost at the time of sale).

EXERCISES

ED-1 Recording and Reporting an Equity Method Security

Felicia Company acquired 21,000 of the 60,000 shares of outstanding common stock of Nueces Corporation during 2007 as a long-term investment. The annual accounting period for both companies ends December 31. The following transactions occurred during 2007:

Jan. 10	Purchased 21,000 shares of Nueces common stock at $12 per share.
Dec. 31	Nueces Corporation reported net income of $90,000.
Dec. 31	Nueces Corporation declared and paid a cash dividend of $0.60 per share.
Dec. 31	Determined the market price of Nueces stock to be $11 per share.

Required:

1. What accounting method should the company use? Why?
2. Give the journal entries for each of these transactions. If no entry is required, explain why.
3. Show how the long-term investment and the related revenue should be reported on the 2007 financial statements of Felicia Company.

ED-2 Recording Holding Gains for Securities Available for Sale

On June 30, 2006, MetroMedia, Inc., purchased 10,000 shares of Mitek stock for $20 per share. The following information pertains to the price per share of Mitek stock:

	Price
12/31/2006	$24
12/31/2007	31

Required:

Assume that management considers the stock to be securities available for sale. Prepare the journal entries required on each date given.

ED-3 Recording Holding Gains for Trading Securities

Refer to the data in ED-2.

Required:

Assume that MetroMedia management purchased the Mitek stock as trading securities. Prepare the journal entries required on each date given.

ED-4 Reporting Holding Gains for Securities Available for Sale and Trading Securities

Refer to the data in ED-2.

Required:

1. Assume that management intends to hold the stock as securities available for sale for three years or more. Show how the stock investment and its holding gains would be reported at the end of 2007 and 2006 on the classified balance sheet and income statement.
2. Assume that management purchased the stock as trading securities. Show how the investment and holding gains would be reported at the end of 2007 and 2006 on the classified balance sheet and income statement.

ED-5 Recording Holding Losses for Securities Available for Sale

On March 10, 2006, Global Solutions, Inc., purchased 5,000 shares of Superior Technologies stock for $50 per share. The following information pertains to the price per share of Superior Technologies stock:

	Price
12/31/2006	$45
12/31/2007	42

Required:

Assume that management considers the stock to be securities available for sale. Prepare the journal entries required on each date given.

ED-6 Recording Holding Losses for Trading Securities

Refer to the data in ED-5.

Required:

Assume that Global Solutions purchased the Superior Technologies stock as trading securities. Prepare the journal entries required on each date given.

ED-7 Reporting Holding Gains for Securities Available for Sale and Trading Securities

Refer to the data in ED-5.

Required:

1. Assume that management intends to hold the stock as securities available for sale for three years or more. Show how the stock investment and its holding gains would be reported at each year-end on the classified balance sheet and income statement.
2. Assume that management purchased the stock as trading securities. Show how the investment and holding gains would be reported at each year-end on the classified balance sheet and income statement.

COACHED PROBLEMS

CPD-1 Recording Passive Investments and Investments for Significant Influence

On August 4, 2006, Cappio Corporation purchased 1,000 shares of Maxwell Company for $45,000. The following information applies to the stock price of Maxwell Company:

	Price
12/31/2006	$52
12/31/2007	47
12/31/2008	38

Maxwell Company declares and pays cash dividends of $2 per share on June 1 of each year.

Required:

1. Prepare journal entries to record the facts in the case, assuming that Cappio considers the shares to be securities available for sale.
   TIP: The Allowance to Value at Market should change from a debit balance at the end of 2006 and 2007 to a credit balance at the end of 2008.

2. Prepare journal entries to record the facts in the case, assuming that Cappio considers the shares to be trading securities.

   TIP: The Allowance to Value at Market should change from a debit balance at the end of 2006 and 2007 to a credit balance at the end of 2008.

3. Prepare journal entries to record the facts in the case, assuming that Cappio uses the equity method to account for the investment. Cappio owns 30 percent of Maxwell, and Maxwell reported $50,000 in income each year.

CPD-2 Comparing Methods to Account for Various Levels of Ownership of Voting Stock

Bart Company had outstanding 30,000 shares of common stock, par value $10 per share. On January 1, 2008, Homer Company purchased some of these shares at $25 per share, with the intent of holding them for a long time. At the end of 2008, Bart Company reported the following: net income, $50,000, and cash dividends declared and paid during the year, $25,500. The market value of Bart Company stock at the end of 2008 was $22 per share.

Required:

1. This problem involves two separate cases. For each case (shown in the table), identify the method of accounting that Homer Company should use. Explain why.

   TIP: Divide the number of shares purchased by the number outstanding to determine the percent of ownership. Then refer to Exhibit D.1.

2. Give the journal entries for Homer Company at the dates indicated for each of the two independent cases. If no entry is required, explain why. Use the following format:

	Case A: 3,600 Shares Purchased	Case B: 10,500 Shares Purchased
1. Accounting method?		
2. Journal entries made by Homer Company:		
a. To record the acquisition of Bart Company at January 1, 2008.		
b. To recognize the income reported by Bart Company for 2008.		
c. To recognize the dividends declared and paid by Bart Company.		
d. Entry to recognize market value effect at end of 2008.		

3. Complete the following schedule to show the separate amounts that should be reported on the 2008 financial statements of Homer Company:

	Dollar Amounts	
	Case A	Case B
Balance sheet		
Investments		
Stockholders' equity		
Income statement		
Investment income		

4. Explain why assets, stockholders' equity, and investment income for the two cases are different.

GROUP A PROBLEMS

PAD-1 Recording Passive Investments and Investments for Significant Influence

On July 12, 2006, Rossow Corporation purchased 1,000 shares of Reimer Company for $30,000. The following information applies to the stock price of Reimer Company:

	Price
12/31/2006	$33
12/31/2007	28
12/31/2008	20

Reimer Company declares and pays cash dividends of $2 per share on May 1 of each year.

Required:

1. Prepare journal entries to record the facts in the case, assuming that Rossow considers the shares to be securities available for sale.
2. Prepare journal entries to record the facts in the case, assuming that Rossow considers the shares to be trading securities.
3. Prepare journal entries to record the facts in the case, assuming that Rossow uses the equity method to account for the investment. Rossow owns 30 percent of Reimer, and Reimer reported $50,000 in income each year.

PAD-2 Comparing the Market Value and Equity Methods

Lisa Corporation had outstanding 100,000 shares of common stock. On January 10, 2008, Marg Company purchased a block of these shares in the open market at $20 per share, with the intent of holding the shares for a long time. At the end of 2008, Lisa reported net income of $300,000 and cash dividends of $0.60 per share. At December 31, 2008, Lisa Corporation stock was selling at $18 per share.

Required:

1. This problem involves two separate cases. For each case (shown in the table), identify the method of accounting that Marg Company should use. Explain why.
2. Give the journal entries for Marg Company at the dates indicated for each of the two independent cases. If no entry is required, explain why. Use the following format:

	Case A: 10,000 Shares Purchased	Case B: 40,000 Shares Purchased
1. Accounting method?		
2. Journal entries made by Marg Company:		
a. To record the acquisition of Lisa Company on January 10, 2008.		
b. To recognize the income reported by Lisa Company for 2008.		
c. To recognize the dividends declared and paid by Lisa Company.		
d. Entry to recognize market value effect at end of 2008.		

3. Complete the following schedule to show the separate amounts that should be reported on the 2008 financial statements of Marg Company:

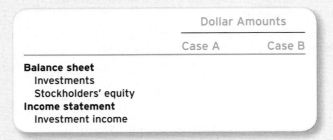

	Dollar Amounts	
	Case A	Case B
Balance sheet		
Investments		
Stockholders' equity		
Income statement		
Investment income		

4. Explain why assets, stockholders' equity, and investment income for the two cases are different.

A

Account A standardized format that organizations use to accumulate the dollar effects of transactions on each financial statement item. (11)

Accounting A system of analyzing, recording, and summarizing the results of a business's operating, investing, and financing activities. (5)

Accounting Period The time period covered by the financial statements.

Accounting Process The process used by businesses to analyze, record, and summarize transactions and adjustments, prepare financial statements, and prepare the records for the next cycle. (159)

Accounts Payable Amounts owed by the business to suppliers for past transactions. (48)

Accounts Receivable (Trade Receivables, Receivables) Amounts owed to the business by customers for past transactions. (341)

Accrual Basis Accounting Recording revenues when earned and expenses when incurred, regardless of the timing of cash receipts or payments. (91)

Accrued Expenses See *Accrued Liabilities*.

Accrued Liabilities Previously unrecorded expenses that need to be adjusted at the end of the accounting period to reflect the amount incurred and its related liability account. (434)

Accrued Revenues Previously unrecorded revenues that need to be adjusted at the end of the accounting period to reflect the amount earned and its related receivable account. (140)

Acquisition Cost Cash equivalent amount paid or to be paid for an asset. (397)

Adjusted Trial Balance A list of all accounts and their adjusted balances to check on the equality of recorded debits and credits. (151)

Adjusting Journal Entries Entries necessary at the end of each accounting period to measure all revenues and expenses of that period. (141)

Adjustments See *Adjusting Journal Entries*. (138)

Aging of Accounts Receivable Method Using the age of each accounts receivable to estimate uncollectible amounts. (345)

Allowance for Doubtful Accounts (Allowance for Bad Debts, Allowance for Uncollectible Accounts, Reserve for Bad Debts) Contra-asset account containing the estimated dollar value of uncollectible accounts receivable. (343)

Allowance Method Bases bad debt expense on an estimate of uncollectible accounts. (342)

Amortization (1) For intangible assets, this is the systematic and rational allocation of the cost of an intangible asset over its useful life. (2) For bonds payable, this involves allocating any premium or discount over the life of the bond. (398)

Annuity A series of periodic cash receipts or payments that are equal in amount each interest period. (C4)

Assets Probable future economic benefits owned by the business as a result of past transactions. (45)

Asset Turnover Ratio Indicates how well assets are being used to generate revenues. (211)

Audit An examination of a company's financial statements (and management's report on internal control effectiveness) with the goal of detecting misstatements.

Audit Report Describes the auditors' opinion of the fairness of the financial statement presentations and management's assessment of internal control effectiveness. (205)

Authorized Number of Shares Maximum number of shares of corporation's capital stock that can be issued. (495)

Average Cost Method See *Weighted Average Cost Method*. (299)

B

Bad Debt Expense (Doubtful Accounts Expenses, Uncollectible Accounts Expense, Provision for Uncollectible Accounts) Expense associated with estimated uncollectible accounts receivable. (342)

Balance When used as a noun, balance is the dollar amount recorded in an account; when used as a verb, balance is the act of ensuring total assets equals total liabilities plus stockholders' equity. (61)

Balance Sheet (Statement of Financial Position) Reports the amount of assets, liabilities, and stockholders' equity of an accounting entity at a point in time. (9)

Bank Reconciliation Process of using both the bank statement and the cash accounts of a business to determine the appropriate amount of cash in a bank account, after taking into consideration delays or errors in processing cash transactions. (241)

Bank Statement Monthly report from a bank that shows deposits recorded, checks cleared, other debits and credits, and a running bank balance. (243)

Basic Accounting Equation (Balance Sheet Equation) Assets = Liabilities + Stockholders' Equity. (8)

Board of Directors A group of people elected by the stockholders of a company to oversee the decisions made by officers and managers of the company. (197)

Bond Certificate The bond document that each bondholder receives. (444)

Bond Discount The difference between issue price and face value when a bond is sold for less than face value. (445)

Bond Premium The difference between issue price and face value when a bond is sold for more than face value. (447)

Bond Principal The amount (1) payable at the maturity of the bond and (2) on which the periodic cash interest payments are computed. (442)

Book Value See *Net Book Value*. (388)

C

Callable Bonds Bonds that may be called for early repayment at the option of the company that issued the bond. (452)

Capitalize To record a cost as an asset rather than an expense. (384)

Carrying Value See *Net Book Value*. (145)

Cash Money or any instrument that banks will accept for deposit and immediate credit to the company's account, such as a check, money order, or bank draft. (245)

Cash Basis Accounting Recording revenues when cash is received and expenses when cash is paid. (90)

Cash Equivalents Short-term, highly liquid investments purchased within three months of maturity. (245)

Cash Flows from Financing Activities Cash inflows and outflows related to external sources of financing (owners and lenders). (543)

Cash Flows from Investing Activities Cash inflows and outflows related to the purchase or sale of long-lived productive assets. (543)

Cash Flows from Operating Activities (Cash Flows from Operations) Cash inflows and outflows directly related to earnings from normal operations. (542)

Certificate of Deposit A savings certificate, generally issued by commercial banks, entitling the holder to receive interest after a specified maturity date.

Chart of Accounts A summary of all account names and corresponding account numbers used to record financial results in the accounting system. (46)

Classified Balance Sheet A balance sheet that classifies assets and liabilities into current and other (long-term) categories. (62)

Closing Entries Made at the end of the accounting period to transfer balances in temporary accounts to *Retained Earnings* and to establish a zero balance in each of the temporary accounts. (157)

Closing Journal Entries See *Closing Entries*. (157)

Common Stock The basic voting stock issued by a corporation. (493)

Comparable Information Information that can be compared across businesses because similar accounting methods have been applied. (16)

Comparative Financial Statements Report numbers for two or more time periods to make it easy for users to compare account balances from one period to the next. (202)

Comprehensive Income Includes net income plus net unrealized gains or losses on securities available for sale and other adjustments (related to pensions and foreign currency translation) which are directly credited or debited to the stockholders' equity accounts. (613)

Conservatism An accounting concept that suggests care should be taken not to overstate assets and revenues or understate liabilities and expenses. (63)

Consistent Information Information that can be compared over time because similar accounting methods have been applied.

Consolidated Financial Statements The financial statements of two or more companies that have been combined into a single set of financial statements as if the companies were one. (D3)

Contingent Liability Potential liability that has arisen as the result of a past event, not a liability until some future event occurs. (453)

Continuity Assumption See *Going-Concern Assumption*. (611)

Contra-Account An account that is an offset to, or reduction of, another account. (145)

Contract Rate See *Stated Interest Rate*. (444)

Contributed Capital The result of owners providing to the business cash (and sometimes other assets). (494)

Convertible Bonds Bonds that may be converted to other securities of the issuer (usually common stock). (452)

Copyright A form of protection provided to the original authors of literary, musical, artistic, dramatic, and other works of authorship. (397)

Corporation A business organized as a legal entity separate and distinct from its owners under state law. (5)

Cost The amount of resources that a company sacrifices to obtain goods or services; often said to be incurred when the company pays cash or uses credit to acquire the item.

Cost-Benefit Constraint Suggests that the benefits of accounting for and reporting information should outweigh the costs. (611)

Cost of Goods Sold (CGS) Equation BI + P − EI = CGS; beginning inventory plus purchases minus ending inventory. (295)

Cost Principle Requires assets to be recorded at the historical cash-equivalent cost, which is the amount paid or payable on the date of the transaction. (49)

Coupon Rate See *Stated Interest Rate*. (444)

Credit When used as a noun, credit is the right side of an account; when used as a verb, credit is the act of recording the credit portion of a journal entry to a particular account. (55)

Creditor Any business or individual to whom the company owes money. (7)

Cross-Sectional Analysis Compares one company's financial results to that of other companies competing in the same industry. (208)

Cumulative Dividend Preference Preferred stock feature that requires specified current dividends not paid in full to accumulate for every year in which they are not paid. These cumulative preferred dividends must be paid before any common dividends can be paid. (506)

Cumulative Effects of Changes in Accounting Methods Amounts reflected on the income statement for adjustments made to balance sheet accounts when applying new accounting principles. (613)

Current Assets Assets that will be used up or turned into cash within 12 months or the next operating cycle, whichever is longer. (62)

Current Dividend Preference The feature of preferred stock that grants priority to preferred dividends over common dividends. (505)

Current Liabilities Short-term obligations that will be paid in cash (or fulfilled with other current assets) within 12 months or the next operating cycle, whichever is longer. (62, 432)

Current Ratio Ratio of current assets to current liabilities, used to evaluate liquidity. (450)

D

Days to Collect Measure of the average number of days from the time a sale is made on account to the time it is collected. (352)

Days to Sell Measure of the average number of days from the time inventory is bought to the time it is sold. (306)

Debit When used as a noun, debit is the left side of an account; when used as a verb, debit is the act of recording the debit portion of a journal entry to a particular account. (55)

Debt Covenants See *Loan Covenants*. (197)

Debt-to-Assets Ratio Measures the proportion of total assets financed by debt, computed as total liabilities divided by total assets. (211)

Declaration Date The date on which the board of directors officially approves a dividend. (499)

Declining-Balance Depreciation The method that allocates the cost of an asset over its useful life based on a multiple of (often two times) the straight-line rate. (391)

Deferred Expenses Previously acquired assets that need to be adjusted at the end of the accounting period to reflect the amount of expense incurred in using the asset to generate revenue.

Deferred Revenues Previously recorded liabilities that need to be adjusted at the end of the period to reflect the amount of revenue earned.

Deferred Tax Items Caused by reporting revenues and expenses according to GAAP on a company's income statement at a time that differs from their reporting on the tax return.

Depletion Process of allocating a natural resource's cost over the periods of its extraction or harvesting. (403)

Depreciable Cost The portion of the asset's cost that will be used up during its life. It is calculated as asset cost minus residual value, and it is allocated to depreciation expense throughout the asset's life. (389)

Depreciation Process of allocating the cost of buildings and equipment over their productive lives using a systematic and rational method of allocation. (145, 388)

Direct Method A method of presenting the operating activities section of the statement of cash flows, in which each line of the income statement is reported in terms of gross cash receipts and payments. (545)

Discontinued Operations Financial results from the disposal of a major component of the business. (612)

Discount For bonds, occurs when the issue price is less than the face value. Alternatively used in the context of sales discounts and purchase discounts. (445)

Discount Rate The interest rate used to compute present values. (445)

Dividends Payments a company periodically makes to its stockholders as a return on their investment. (9)

Dividends in Arrears Dividends on cumulative preferred stock that have not been declared in prior years. (506)

E

Earnings Forecasts Predictions of earnings for future accounting periods.

Earned To have done what is necessary to obtain the right to receive payment. (91)

EBITDA Abbreviation for "earnings before interest, taxes, depreciation, and amortization," which is a measure of operating performance that some managers and analysts use in place of net income. (403)

Effective-Interest Method Amortizes a bond discount or premium on the basis of the market interest rate. (456)

Effective Interest Rate Another name for the market rate of interest on a bond. (456)

Electronic Funds Transfer Funds transferred into or out of your account. (241)

Equity Method Used when an investor can exert significant influence over an investee. It requires the investor to record its share of net income and dividends reported by the investee. (D4)

Estimated Useful Life Expected service life of a long-lived asset to the present owner. (389)

Expenditures Outflows of cash for any purpose.

Expenses Decreases in assets or increases in liabilities from ongoing operations, incurred to generate revenues during the current period. (88)

Extraordinary Items Gains and losses that are both unusual in nature and infrequent in occurrence. (613)

Extraordinary Repairs Infrequent expenditures that increase an asset's economic usefulness in the future, and that are capitalized. (387)

F

Face Value (Par Value) The amount of a bond payable at its maturity; used to compute interest payments. (444)

Factoring An arrangement where receivables are sold to another company (called a *factor*) for immediate cash (minus a factoring fee). (354)

Financial Accounting Standards Board (FASB) The private sector body given the primary responsibility to work out the concepts and detailed rules that become generally accepted accounting principles. (18, 545)

Financial Statements Reports that summarize the financial results of business activities. (7)

Financial Statement Users People who base their decisions, in part, on information reported in a company's financial statements. (196)

Financing Activities Related to exchanging money with lenders or owners. (15)

Finished Goods Inventory Manufactured goods that are completed and ready for sale. (293)

First-In, First-Out (FIFO) Method Assumes that the first goods purchased (the first in) are the first goods sold. (297)

Fiscal Any matters relating to money; typically used to describe a specified period of time used for financial reporting. (10)

Fixed Assets Tangible assets that are fixed in place, such as land, buildings, and production equipment. (400)

FOB Destination Term of sale indicating that goods are owned by the seller until delivered to the customer. (293)

FOB Shipping Point Term of sale indicating that goods are owned by the customer the moment they leave the seller's premises. (293)

Form 10-K The annual report that publicly traded companies must file with the SEC. (206)

Form 10-Q The quarterly report that publicly traded companies must file with the SEC. (206)

Franchise A contractual right to sell certain products or services, use certain trademarks, or perform activities in a certain geographical region. (397)

Free Cash Flow Computed as Cash Flows from Operating Activities − Dividends − Capital Expenditures. (557)

Full Disclosure Principle States that relevant information should be disclosed in either the main financial statements or the notes to the financial statements. (611)

Future Value The sum to which an amount will increase as the result of compound interest. (C1)

G

Generally Accepted Accounting Principles (GAAP) The rules used to calculate and report information in the financial statements. (18)

Going-Concern Assumption States that businesses are assumed to continue to operate into the foreseeable future. (611)

Goods Available for Sale The sum of beginning inventory and purchases for the period. (294)

Goodwill (Cost in Excess of Net Assets Acquired) For accounting purposes, the excess of the purchase price of a business over the market value of the business's assets and liabilities. (397)

Gross Profit (Gross Margin, Margin) Net sales less cost of goods sold. (254)

Gross Profit Percentage Indicates how much above cost a company sells its products; calculated as Gross Profit divided by Net Sales. (255)

H

Historical Cost Principle See *Cost Principle*. (49)

Horizontal Analysis Trend comparisons across time, often expressing changes in account balances as a percentage of prior year balances. (597)

I

Impairment Occurs when the cash to be generated by an asset is estimated to be less than the carrying value of that asset, and requires that the carrying value of the asset be written down. (394)

Income from Operations (Operating Income) Equals net sales less cost of goods sold and other operating expenses. (15)

Income Statement (Statement of Income, Statement of Profit and Loss, Statement of Operations) Reports the revenues less the expenses of the accounting period. (9)

Incur To make oneself subject to; typically refers to expenses, which are incurred by using up the economic benefits of assets or becoming obligated for liabilities, resulting in a decrease in the company's resources in the current period. (90)

Indirect Method A method of presenting the operating activities section of the statement of cash flows, in which net income is adjusted to compute cash flows from operating activities. (545)

Industry Practices A constraint that recognizes that companies in certain industries must follow accounting rules peculiar to that industry. (611)

Intangible Assets Assets that have special rights but not physical substance. (397)

Interest Formula $I = P \times R \times T$, where I = interest calculated; P = principal; R = annual interest rate; and T = time period covered in the interest calculation (number of months out of 12). (348)

Internal Controls Processes by which a company provides reasonable assurance regarding the reliability of the company's financial reporting, the effectiveness and efficiency of its operations, and its compliance with applicable laws and regulations. (238)

Inventory Tangible property held for sale in the normal course of business or used in producing goods or services for sale. (292)

Inventory Turnover The process of buying and selling inventory. (305)

Investing Activities Involve buying or selling long-lived items such as land, buildings, and equipment. (15)

Investments in Associated (or Affiliated) Companies Investments in stock held for the purpose of influencing the operating and financing strategies for the long term. (D4)

Issue Price The amount of money that a lender pays (and the company receives) when a bond is issued. (444)

Issued Shares Total number of shares of stock that have been sold; equals shares outstanding plus treasury shares held. (495)

J

Journal A record of each day's transactions. (54)

Journal Entry An accounting method for expressing the effects of a transaction on accounts in a debits-equal-credits format. (55)

Journalize The process of noting a transaction in the journal in the debits-equal-credits journal entry format.

L

Last-In, First-Out (LIFO) Method Assumes that the most recently purchased units (the last in) are sold first. (298)

Ledger A collection of records that summarize the effects of transactions entered in the journal. (54)

Lenders A creditor that has loaned money to the company. (51)

Liabilities Probable debts or obligations of the entity that result from past transactions, which will be fulfilled by providing assets or services. (45)

Licensing Right The limited permission to use property according to specific terms and conditions set out in a contract. (397)

LIFO Reserve A contra-asset for the excess of FIFO over LIFO inventory. (301)

Line Item An account name or title reported in the body of a financial statement; can represent a single account or the total of several accounts.

Line of Credit A prearranged agreement that allows a company to borrow any amount of money at any time, up to a prearranged limit. (450)

Liquidity The ability to pay current obligations. (450, 597)

Loan Covenants Terms of a loan agreement that, if broken, entitle the lender to renegotiate terms of the loan including its due date. (197)

Long-Lived Assets Tangible and intangible resources owned by a business and used in its operations over several years. (382)

Long-Term Assets Resources that will be used up or turned into cash more than 12 months after the balance sheet date. (62)

Long-Term Liabilities All of the entity's obligations that are not classified as current liabilities. (45)

Lower of Cost or Market (LCM) Valuation method departing from the cost principle; recognizes a loss when asset value drops below cost. (304)

M

Manufacturing Company A company that sells goods that it has made itself. (236)

Market Interest Rate The current rate of interest that exists when a debt is incurred. Also called *yield, discount rate,* or *effective interest rate.* (445)

Market Value Method Reports securities at their current market value. (D6)

Matching Principle Requires that expenses be recorded when incurred in earning revenue. (93)

Material Amounts that are large enough to influence a user's decision. (205)

Merchandise Inventory Goods held for resale in the ordinary course of business. (292)

Merchandising Company A company that sells goods which have been obtained from a supplier. (236)

Multistep Income Statement Reports alternative measures of income by calculating subtotals for core and peripheral business activities. (203)

N

Net To combine by subtracting one or more amounts from another. (8)

Net Assets Shorthand term used to refer to assets minus liabilities. (398)

Net Book Value (Book Value, Carrying Value) The amount at which an asset or liability is reported after deducting any contra-accounts. (145)

Net Income Equal to revenues minus expenses. (89)

Net Income before Income Taxes Revenues and gains minus losses and all expenses except income tax expense.

Net Profit Margin Ratio Indicates how well expenses are controlled, by dividing net income by revenue. (211)

Net Sales Total sales revenue minus Sales Returns and Allowances and Sales Discounts. (253)

Noncash Investing and Financing Activities Transactions that do not have direct cash flow effects; reported as a supplement to the statement of cash flows in narrative or schedule form. (557)

Noncumulative Preferred Stock Preferred stock that does not have cumulative dividend rights, such that dividend rights do not carry over from one year to the next. (505)

Noncurrent (or long-term) assets and liabilities are those that do not meet the definition of current. (62)

No-Par Value Stock Capital stock that has no specified par value. (496)

Notes (Footnotes) Provide supplemental information about the financial condition of a company, without which the financial statements cannot be fully understood. (15)

Notes Receivable Written promises that require another party to pay the business under specified conditions (amount, time, interest). (341)

NSF Checks (Not Sufficient Funds) Checks written for an amount greater than the funds available to cover them. (242)

O

Obsolescence The process of becoming out of date or falling into disuse. (292)

Operating Activities The day-to-day events involved in running a business. (15)

Operating Cycle (Cash-to-Cash Cycle) The time and activities needed for a company to sell goods and services to customers, collect cash from customers, and pay cash to suppliers. (237)

Ordinary Repairs and Maintenance Expenditures for the normal operating upkeep of long-lived assets, recorded as expenses. (387)

Outstanding Shares Total number of shares of stock that are owned by stockholders on any particular date. (495)

P

Paid-In Capital (Additional Paid-In Capital, Contributed Capital in Excess of Par) The amount of contributed capital less the par value of the stock. (495)

Par Value (1) For shares of stock, this is a legal amount per share established by the board of directors; it establishes the minimum amount a stockholder must contribute and has no relationship to the market price of the stock. (2) For bonds, see *Face Value*. (495)

Parent Company The entity that gains a controlling influence over another company (the subsidiary). (D2)

Partnerships Business organizations owned by two or more people. Each partner often is personally liable for debts that the partnership cannot pay. (4)

Patent A right to exclude others from making, using, selling, or importing an invention. (397)

Payment Date The date on which a cash dividend is paid to the stockholders of record. (500)

Percentage of Credit Sales Method Bases bad debt expense on the historical percentage of credit sales that result in bad debts. (345)

Periodic Inventory System A system in which ending inventory and cost of goods sold are determined only at the end of the accounting period based on a physical inventory count. (246)

Permanent Accounts The balance sheet accounts that carry their ending balances into the next accounting period. (156)

Perpetual Inventory System A system in which a detailed inventory record is maintained recording each purchase and sale of inventory during the accounting period. (246)

Post-Closing Trial Balance Prepared as the last step in the accounting cycle to check that debits equal credits and that all temporary accounts have been closed. (158)

Preferred Stock Stock that has specified rights over common stock. (504)

Premium For bonds, occurs when the issue price is greater than the face value. (445)

Prepaid Expenses A general account name used to describe payments made in advance of receiving future services; typically includes prepaid rent, prepaid insurance, and other specific types of prepayments. (99)

Present Value The current value of an amount to be received in the future; a future amount discounted for compound interest. (444, C1)

Press Release A written public news announcement normally distributed to major news services.

Private Company A company that has its stock bought and sold privately. (5)

Profit An alternative term for net income. (8)

Profitability Extent to which a company generates income. (597)

Public Company A company that has its stock bought and sold on public stock exchanges. (5)

Public Company Accounting Oversight Board Makes the rules used by auditors of public companies. (19)

Purchase Discount Cash discount received for prompt payment of an account. (249)

Purchase Returns and Allowances A reduction in the cost of purchases associated with unsatisfactory goods. (248)

Q

Qualified Audit Opinion Indicates that either the financial statements do not follow GAAP or the auditors were not able to complete the tests needed to determine whether the financial statements follow GAAP. (205)

R

Ratio (Percentage) Analysis An analytical tool that measures the proportional relationship between two financial statement amounts. (596)

Raw Materials Inventory Items acquired for the purpose of processing into finished goods. (293)

Receivables Turnover The process of selling and collecting on an account. The receivables turnover ratio determines how many times this process occurs during the period on average. (352)

Record Date The date on which the corporation prepares the list of current stockholders as shown on its records. Dividends are paid only to the stockholders who own stock on that date. (500)

Relevant Information Information that can influence a decision. It is timely and has predictive and/or feedback value.

Reliable Information Information that is accurate, unbiased, and verifiable.

Research and Development Costs Expenditures that may someday lead to patents, copyrights, or other intangible assets, but the uncertainty about their future benefits requires that they be expensed. (397)

Residual (or Salvage) Value Estimated amount to be recovered, less disposal costs, at the end of the company's estimated useful life of an asset. (389)

Retained Earnings Cumulative earnings of a company that are not distributed to the owners; profits from the current year and all prior years that are reinvested ("retained") in the business. (10)

Revenue Principle Revenues are recorded when goods or services are delivered, there is evidence of an arrangement for customer payment, the price is fixed or determinable, and collection is reasonably assured. (92)

Revenue Recognition Policy An accounting policy that describes when a company reports revenue from providing services or goods to customers.

Revenues Increases in assets or settlements of liabilities arising from ongoing operations. (88)

S

Sales (or Cash) Discount Cash discount offered to customers to encourage prompt payment of an account receivable. (252)

Sales Returns and Allowances Reduction of sales revenues for return of or allowances for unsatisfactory goods. (251)

Sarbanes-Oxley Act of 2002 (SOX) A set of laws established to strengthen corporate reporting in the United States. (19, 199)

Securities and Exchange Commission (SEC) The U.S. government agency that determines the financial statements that public companies must provide to stockholders and the rules that they must use in producing those statements. (19)

Securities Available for Sale All passive investments other than trading securities (classified as either short term or long term). (D2)

Segregation of Duties An internal control that involves separating employees' duties so that the work of one person can be used to check the work of another person. (239)

Separate-Entity Assumption States that business transactions are separate from and should exclude the personal transactions of the owners. (8)

Service Company A company that sells services rather than physical goods. (236)

Single-step Income Statement Reports net income by subtracting a single group of expenses from a single group of revenues. (203)

Sole Proprietorship A business organization owned by one person who is liable for debts the business cannot pay. (5)

Solvency Ability to survive long enough to repay lenders when debt matures. (597)

Specific Identification Method A method of assigning costs to inventory, which identifies the cost of each specific item purchased and sold. (296)

Stated Interest Rate The rate of cash interest per period specified in a bond contract. Also called *coupon rate* or *contract rate*. (444)

Statement of Cash Flows Reports inflows and outflows of cash during the accounting period in the categories of operating, investing, and financing. (10)

Statement of Retained Earnings Reports the way that net income and the distribution of dividends affected the financial position of the company during the accounting period. (10)

Stock Dividend Declared by the board of directors to distribute to existing stockholders additional shares of a corporation's own stock. (501)

Stock Split An increase in the total number of authorized shares by a specified ratio; does not decrease retained earnings. (502)

Stockholders' Equity (Owners' Equity or Shareholders' Equity) The financing provided by the owners and the operations of the business. (45)

Straight-Line Amortization Method of amortizing a bond discount or premium that allocates an equal dollar amount to each interest period. (454)

Straight-Line Depreciation Method Method that allocates the cost of an asset in equal periodic amounts over its useful life. (390, 454)

Subsidiary Company A business that is controlled by another company (the parent). (D2)

T

10-K See *Form 10-K*. (206)

10-Q See *Form 10-Q*. (206)

T-Account A simplified version of a ledger account used for summarizing transaction effects and determining balances for each account. (56)

Tangible Assets Assets that have physical substance. (382)

Temporary Accounts Income statement accounts that are closed to *Retained Earnings* at the end of the accounting period. (156)

Tests of Liquidity Ratios that measure a company's ability to meet its currently maturing obligations. (450)

Tests of Profitability Ratios that compare income with one or more primary activities.

Tests of Solvency Ratios that measure a company's ability to meet its long-term obligations.

Ticker Symbol The one- to four-letter abbreviation used to identify a company on a public securities exchange.

Time Period Assumption The assumption that allows the long life of a company to be reported in shorter time periods. (89)

Time-Series Analysis Compares a company's results for one period to its own results over a series of time periods. (208)

Times Interest Earned Ratio Determines the extent to which earnings before taxes and financing costs are sufficient to cover interest expense incurred on debt. (451)

Time Value of Money The idea that money received today is worth more than the same amount received in the future because money received today can be invested to earn interest over time. (C1)

Trademark An exclusive legal right to use a special name, image, or slogan. (397)

Trading Securities All investments in stocks or bonds that are held primarily for the purpose of active trading (buying and selling) in the near future (classified as short term). (D2)

Transaction An exchange or an event that has a direct economic effect on the assets, liabilities, or stockholders' equity of a business. (47)

Transaction Analysis The process of studying a transaction to determine its economic effect on the business in terms of the accounting equation. (47)

Treasury Stock A corporation's own stock that has been issued but was subsequently reacquired by and is still being held by the corporation. (495)

Trial Balance A list of all accounts with their balances to provide a check on the equality of the debits and credits. (102)

U

Unearned Revenue A liability representing a company's obligation to provide goods or services to customers in the future. (92)

Unit-of-Measure Assumption States that accounting information should be measured and reported in the national monetary unit. (10)

Units-of-Production Depreciation Method that allocates the cost of an asset over its useful life based on its periodic output in relation to its total estimated output. (391)

Unqualified Audit Opinion Auditors' statements that the financial statements are fair presentations in all material respects in conformity with GAAP. (205)

Unrealized Holding Gains and Losses Amounts associated with price changes of securities that are currently held. (D6)

Useful Life The expected service life of an asset to the present owner. (389)

V

Vertical Analysis Expresses each financial statement amount as a percentage of another amount on the same financial statement. (601)

W

Weighted Average Cost Method Uses the weighted average unit cost of goods available for sale for calculations of both the cost of goods sold and ending inventory. (299)

Work in Process Inventory Goods in the process of being manufactured. (293)

Write-Off The removal from an uncollectable account and its corresponding allowance from the accounting records. (344)

Y

Yield See *Market Interest Rate*. (445)

PHOTO CREDITS

Helpful Review Tools

EXHIBIT 1.8 — Relationships among the Financial Statements

PIZZA AROMA

PIZZA AROMA INC.
Income Statement
For the Month Ended September 30, 2008

Revenues	
Pizza revenue	$11,000
Total revenues	11,000
Expenses	
Supplies expense	4,000
Wages expense	2,000
Rent expense	2,000
Utilities expense	600
Insurance expense	300
Advertising expense	100
Total expenses	9,000
Net income	$ 2,000

PIZZA AROMA INC.
Statement of Retained Earnings
For the Month Ended September 30, 2008

Retained earnings, Sept. 1, 2008	$ 0
Add: Net income	2,000
Subtract: Dividends	(1,000)
Retained earnings, Sept. 30, 2008	$1,000

PIZZA AROMA INC.
Statement of Cash Flows
For the Month Ended September 30, 2008

Cash flows from operating activities	$ 5,000
Cash flows from investing activities	(40,000)
Cash flows from financing activities	49,000
Change in cash	14,000
Beginning cash balance, Sept. 1, 2008	0
Ending cash balance, Sept. 30, 2008	$14,000

PIZZA AROMA INC.
Balance Sheet
At September 30, 2008

Assets	
Cash	$14,000
Accounts receivable	1,000
Supplies	3,000
Equipment	40,000
Total assets	$58,000
Liabilities and Stockholders' Equity	
Liabilities	
Accounts payable	$ 7,000
Note payable	20,000
Total liabilities	27,000
Stockholders' equity	
Contributed capital	30,000
Retained earnings	1,000
Total stockholders' equity	31,000
Total liabilities and stockholders' equity	$58,000

EXHIBIT 2.8 — Tools Used in the Accounting Cycle

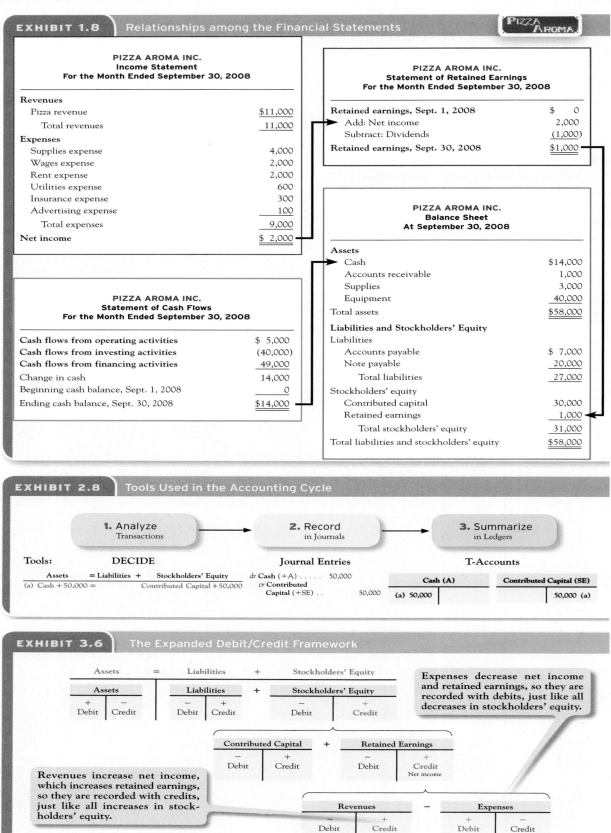

1. Analyze Transactions → **2. Record** in Journals → **3. Summarize** in Ledgers

Tools: DECIDE | Journal Entries | T-Accounts

Assets = Liabilities + Stockholders' Equity
(a) Cash +50,000 = Contributed Capital +50,000

dr Cash (+A) 50,000
cr Contributed Capital (+SE) . . 50,000

Cash (A) — (a) 50,000
Contributed Capital (SE) — 50,000 (a)

EXHIBIT 3.6 — The Expanded Debit/Credit Framework

Assets = Liabilities + Stockholders' Equity

Assets	Liabilities	Stockholders' Equity
+ Debit / − Credit	− Debit / + Credit	− Debit / + Credit

Contributed Capital + Retained Earnings
− Debit / + Credit — − Debit / + Credit (Net income)

Revenues − Expenses
− Debit / + Credit — + Debit / − Credit

Expenses decrease net income and retained earnings, so they are recorded with debits, just like all decreases in stockholders' equity.

Revenues increase net income, which increases retained earnings, so they are recorded with credits, just like all increases in stockholders' equity.

Ratios Used for Financial Analyses

EXHIBIT 13.4 | Ratios Used for Financial Statement Analyses

LANDRY'S RESTAURANTS, INC.
Summary of Financial Ratios

Chapter/Page	Ratio	Formula	Year Ended December 31		
			2005	2004	2003
Profitability Ratios					
(a) 5 (p. 210)	**Net profit margin =** $3.6\% = \$44,815/\$1,245,806 \times 100$	$\dfrac{\text{Net income}}{\text{Net sales revenue}}$	3.6%	5.7%	4.1%
(b) 6 (p. 255)	**Gross profit percentage =** $73.3\% = \$912,778/\$1,245,806 \times 100$	$\dfrac{\text{Net sales revenue} - \text{Cost of goods sold}}{\text{Net sales revenue}}$	73.3%	72.1%	70.9%
(c) 5 (p. 210)	**Asset turnover =** $0.84 = \$1,245,806/[(\$1,612,579 + \$1,344,952)/2]$	$\dfrac{\text{Net sales revenue}}{\text{Average total assets}}$	0.84	0.95	1.09
(d) 9 (p. 400)	**Fixed asset turnover =** $1.04 = \$1,245,806/[(\$1,380,259 + \$1,007,297)/2]$	$\dfrac{\text{Net sales revenue}}{\text{Average net fixed assets}}$	1.04	1.18	2.41
(e) 11 (p. 508)	**Return on equity (ROE) =** $8.0\% = \$44,815/[(\$516,771 + \$600,897)/2] \times 100$	$\dfrac{\text{Net income}}{\text{Average stockholders' equity}}$	8.0%	11.0%	15.4%
(f) 11 (p. 508)	**Earnings per share (EPS) =** EPS is reported on the income statement.	$\dfrac{\text{Net income}}{\text{Average number of common shares}}$	$2.01	$2.46	$1.63
(g) 12 (p. 559)	**Quality of income =** $3.37 = \$151,056/\$44,815$	$\dfrac{\text{Net cash from operations}}{\text{Net income}}$	3.37	1.68	2.76
(h) 11 (p. 508)	**Price/earnings (P/E) ratio =** $15.4 = \$31/\$2.01$	$\dfrac{\text{Stock price}}{\text{EPS}}$	15.4	12.6	19.0
Liquidity Ratios					
(i) 8 (p. 352)	**Receivables turnover =** $61.4 = \$1,245,806/[(\$21,973 + \$18,596)/2]$	$\dfrac{\text{Net sales revenue}}{\text{Average net receivables}}$	61.4	55.8	114.9
8 (p. 352)	**Days to collect =** $5.9 = 365/61.4$	$\dfrac{365}{\text{Receivables turnover ratio}}$	5.9	6.5	3.2
(j) 7 (p. 306)	**Inventory turnover =** $5.8 = \$333,028/[(\$59,717 + \$55,004)/2]$	$\dfrac{\text{Cost of sales}}{\text{Average inventory}}$	5.8	6.3	13.4
7 (p. 306)	**Days to sell =** $62.9 = 365/5.8$	$\dfrac{365}{\text{Inventory turnover ratio}}$	62.9	57.9	27.2
(k) 10 (p. 449)	**Current ratio =** $0.66 = \$146,438/\$220,500$	$\dfrac{\text{Current assets}}{\text{Current liabilities}}$	0.66	2.19	0.76
Solvency Ratios					
(l) 5 (p. 210)	**Debt-to-assets =** $0.68 = \$1,095,808/\$1,612,578$	$\dfrac{\text{Total liabilities}}{\text{Total assets}}$	0.68	0.55	0.45
(m) 10 (p. 449)	**Times interest earned =** $2.6 = (\$44,815 + \$41,438 + \$20,608)/\$41,438$	$\dfrac{\text{Net income} + \text{Interest expense} + \text{Income tax expense}}{\text{Interest expense}}$	2.6	5.6	6.8
(n) 12 (p. 561)	**Cash coverage =** $4.4 = (\$151,056 + \$45,297 + \$4,838)/\$45,297$	$\dfrac{\text{Net cash from operations} + \text{Interest paid} + \text{Income taxes paid}}{\text{Interest paid}}$	4.4	8.6	15.9
(o) 12 (p. 560)	**Capital acquisitions ratio =** $0.60 = \$151,056/\$249,925$	$\dfrac{\text{Net cash from operations}}{\text{Cash paid for PPE}}$	0.6	0.95	0.65

Chapter Title	Chapter Focus Company	Company Logo	Type of Company	Contrast Companies	Key Ratios
1 Business Decisions and Financial Reporting	Pizza Aroma	PIZZA AROMA	Restaurant	Under Armour, Inc. Southwest Airlines Regal Entertainment	
2 Reporting Investing and Financing Results on the Balance Sheet	Supercuts	SUPERCUTS®	Hair salon chain	Hasbro, Inc. Half Price Books, Inc. Starbucks Corporation	Ratios are not introduced until the accounting cycle chapters are completed.
3 Reporting Operating Results on the Income Statement	Supercuts	SUPERCUTS®	Hair salon chain	Time Warner, Inc. Ambercrombie & Fitch H & R Block, Inc. Sigil Games Online	
4 Adjustments, Financial Statements, and the Quality of Financial Reporting	Supercuts	SUPERCUTS®	Hair salon chain	Coach, Inc. Dell Computer, Inc. Pacific Sunwear of California, Inc.	
5 Corporate Financial Reporting and Analysis	Activision, Inc.	ACTIVISION.	Video game developer	Electronic Arts Inc. THQ Inc. John Wiley & Sons	Debt-to-Assets Asset Turnover Net Profit Margin
6 Internal Control and Financial Reporting for Cash and Merchandising Operations	Wal-Mart Stores, Inc.	WAL★MART® ALWAYS LOW PRICES. Always.	Discount retail store	Saks Sunglass Hut JCPenney, Inc. Best Buy Circuit City	Gross Profit Percentage